THE NAVAL INSTITUTE GUIDE TO THE
Ships and Aircraft of the U.S. Fleet

SEVENTEENTH EDITION

THE NAVAL INSTITUTE GUIDE TO THE

Ships and Aircraft of the U.S. Fleet

Norman Polmar

Samuel Loring Morison, Senior Researcher—Ships
Richard R. Burgess, Senior Researcher—Aviation

Naval Institute Press
Annapolis, Maryland

ISBN 1-55750-656-6
ISSN 1530-650X

Printed in the United States of America on acid-free paper ∞
08 07 06 05 04   9 8 7 6 5 4 3 2

Photo on p. viii: U.S. naval forces—especially aircraft carriers—continue to have an important role in supporting U.S. political-military interests throughout the world. Here the island structure of the carrier KITTY HAWK (CV 63) towers over EA-6B Prowler electronic countermeasures aircraft from squadron VAQ-136 supporting a multiservice, multinational exercise in South Korea. (PHAN Alex C. Witte)

To the memory of
Admiral Elmo R. (Bud) Zumwalt, U.S. Navy
Chief of Naval Operations, 1970–1974
and
Admiral J. M. (Mike) Boorda, U.S. Navy
Chief of Naval Operations, 1992–1994

★ ★ ★ ★

Officers, Gentlemen, Seamen, and Friends

Contents

Preface

As this edition of *Ships and Aircraft* appears, the U.S. Navy is undergoing major changes. The end of the Cold War brought a rapid decline in force levels of surface ships, submarines, and aircraft. From a total of some 525 ships—albeit counting methods differ—and 5,000 aircraft at the end of the Cold War, the Navy entering the 21st century is fighting to maintain 300 ships and almost 4,000 aircraft in active service.

At the same time, critical changes are occurring in naval technology and in roles and missions of U.S. military forces. The former includes the advances being made in surface ship design and the adoption of a fleet of Unmanned Aerial Vehicles (UAV), while the latter centers on increasing naval operations in littoral waters and in support of forces ashore.

Further changes are expected to come about in the wake of the quadrennial defense review of 2001.

Men and, increasingly, women must operate these ships and aircraft and must form the Marine Forces that will fight ashore. Continuing the all-volunteer manning that has marked the U.S. armed forces since the early 1970s, today's sailors and Marines are among the most proficient and capable in the nation's history. Still, the excellent U.S. economy and competition for technically skilled and trained personnel have caused a continuing shortage of recruits and of experienced personnel in some categories. This situation and the high cost of taking men and women to sea has led to revolutionary ship manning concepts for the next large U.S. surface combatant, now designated DD 21.

But in other ways, the naval forces continue to be among the most conservative and resistant to change of all U.S. military forces. This has been due in large part to the Navy's leadership of the last decade, as discussed in chapter 1, "State of the Fleet."

This is the fleet described in this edition of *Ships and Aircraft*. Although the fleet is significantly smaller than when the previous edition appeared in 1997, several new ship and aircraft programs have been added or expanded, leading to little change in the length of the book. All ship and aircraft listings—and other entries—have been reviewed and revised, and, of course, updated.

Many individuals and organizations have provided assistance in producing this book. First and foremost, I am in debt to Jack Brostrom, who edited this edition; his sharp red pencil and perceptive questions have made the book more readable and accurate. In the same manner, Samuel Loring Morison and Richard Burgess, managing editor of *Sea Power* (Navy League), have spent many, many hours researching ship and aircraft data for this edition and have replied to my interminable questions.

Several photographers have provided a veritable stream of photographs of U.S. ships and aircraft. Beyond those that appear in the book, their other photos are an invaluable source of intelligence on shipboard weapons and electronics. The views of Leo Van Ginderen abound in these pages. Many views also were provided by Dr. Giorgio Arra, John Bouvia, Jürg E. Kürsener, and my long-time colleague Stefan Terzibaschitsch.

The photos credited to the U.S. Navy came from many sources, most from the Navy's Office of Information, whose still photo section under Christopher Madden has provided outstanding service; his assistants, Lt. Rick Naystatt, JO2 Todd Stevens, PH2 Timothy Altevogt, Diane Mason, and Henrietta Wright have demonstrated both knowledge and patience in their help.

Help with illustrations also has been provided by Kenneth Carter and Patricia Toombs of the public affairs directorate of the Department of Defense.

Others who have provided assistance are:

A. D. Baker III, editor of the invaluable *Combat Fleets of the World*; Ens. Chuck Bell, Mine Warfare Command; Cynthia Brewer, Army missile test facility at Kwajalein, Marshall Islands; David Caskey, Naval Sea Systems Command; Lt. Stephen Canfield, Submarine Development Group 5; Cynthia Curiel, Ryan Aeronautical Center; Steven E. Daskell of Veridian Corp.; Lt. Amy Derrick, Office of Navy Information (CHINFO); Jerri Fuller Dickseski, Newport News Shipbuilding; Larry Donaldson, C-130 floatplane marketing director, Lockheed Martin; Timothy Douglas, Lockheed Martin; Michael Drake, Naval Sea Systems Command at Port Hueneme, Calif.; Jessica Eichenberg, communications, Scripps Institution of Oceanography; the late Susan Fili, Naval Sea Systems Command; Meredith S. Foster, Halter Marine; Tiffeny Francis, Bollinger Shipyard; Johanne Gallant, public relations, Bombardier Aéronautique; Rich Greenleaf, public relations, Naval Test Pilot School; Capt. Daniel N. Hartwell, commanding officer, USS INCHON; Margaret Holtz, public affairs officer, Military Sealift Command, and her most helpful assistants Nancy Breen and Barry Lake; Lt.(jg) Andrea Johnson, public affairs officer, Strategic Communications Wing 1; Cullen Johnson, senior communications coordinator, Newport News Shipbuilding; Lt.(jg) Barbara J. Kelly, public affairs officer, Chief of Naval Air Training; Cdr. Glen King, public affairs officer, Naval Reserve Force; Vice Adm. John B. (Bat) LaPlante, McDermott International; Lt. Steve Mavica, CHINFO; James McIngvale, Litton/Ingalls Shipbuilding; Barbara McMichael, Army Transportation Corps; Janet McMullen, Lockheed Martin; Peter Mersky, former editor of *Approach* (Naval Safety Center); the indefatigable Ted Minter, who has provided invaluable research; Lon Nordeen, author and marketing, Boeing McDonnell Douglas; Ronald O'Rourke, Congressional Research Service; John M. Paul, United Defense; ETC Richard S. Richard, Assault Craft Unit 4; Rusty Robinson, Bath Iron Works; Myia Rogers, JSF Communications, Lockheed Martin; John Romer and Rebecca March, Naval Air Warfare Center, Patuxent River, Md.; Kent Rump, Ryan Aeronautical Center; Sandy Russell, managing editor, *Naval Aviation News*; Jim Saye, Lockheed Martin; Lt. Cdr. Irene Smith, office of the Director of Surface Warfare; Lt. Jensin W. Sommer, CHINFO; Jennifer L. Spears, Raytheon Systems; Peter Swartz, Center for Naval Analyses; Tim Travis, Raytheon/Beech; Ralph Thon, product development, Orange Shipbuilding Co.; William S. Tuttle, public relations manager, United Technologies/Sikorsky Aircraft; Judy Van Benthuysen, CHINFO; Jeff Van Keuren, United Defense LP; Jack Walsh, editor of the most useful *Naval Systems Update*; and Sandra J. Witt, Lockheed Martin.

Capt. Peter J. Mitchell, public affairs, Headquarters, U.S. Marine Corps, provided answers to many questions about the Corps.

Several military personnel and civilians at Coast Guard headquarters have provided extensive assistance, among them PA2 Stephen J. Baker, Lt. Brian Bezio, PA1 Telfair Brown, Capt. Eric Fagerholm, Evelyn Jutte, Patricia Miller, Lt. Cdr. Janis E. Nagy, and Scott Price. Also helpful has been Lt. Cdr. Joseph DiRenzo III, at the time assigned to the USS CONSTELLATION battle group.

The database of the Federation of American Scientists, maintained by John Pike, has been a useful backup reference.

Dr. Scott C. Truver, a vice president of the Anteon Corp. (formerly TECHMATICS), and members of his staff have been most helpful in my research efforts, especially Morgan Einbinder, Edward Feege, Stephen Keller, Rick Lazisky, John Patrick, and Jon Walman, while Deepa Shukla has been invaluable in helping with illustrations.

Several members of the Naval Institute Press made major contributions to making this edition a reality, most especially J. Randall Baldini, Tom Cutler, Rebecca Edwards Hinds, and Karen Doody, while Susan Artigiani and Tom Harnish provided valuable marketing support. Dawn Stitzel, photo archivist of the Naval Institute, and Dave Hofeling were helpful in researching photos, as has been Marcia Smith of *Sea Power* (Navy League).

As with many of my writing projects, I appreciate the guidance and support of Fred Rainbow, editor in chief of the Naval Institute *Proceedings,* and his staff, especially Julie Olver, who edits my regular column in the *Proceedings,* Fred Schultz and Mac Greeley of *Naval History,* and their staff members Liese Carrington, Jaci Day, Maya Krigman, and Beth Tucker.

The compilation of the next edition of *Ships and Aircraft* begins almost immediately, to be published three years after this volume went to press. Comments and photographs should be submitted directly to the author in care of the U.S. Naval Institute or via e-mail to <wordsmh@msn.com>.

NORMAN POLMAR

THE NAVAL INSTITUTE
GUIDE TO THE
Ships and Aircraft
of the U.S. Fleet

CHAPTER 1

State of the Fleet

The ships and aircraft of the U.S. Fleet continue to have a major role in supporting U.S. political-military interests at the start of the 21st century. Aircraft carriers in particular have been employed in conflicts and crises to good effect, even when land bases in the area were available to U.S. forces. Here an F/A-18C Hornet lands aboard the ENTERPRISE (CVN 65) while carrying out carrier qualifications in the Atlantic in early 2000. (U.S. Navy, PH2 Michael W. Pendergrass)

The U.S. Navy is ill-prepared to enter the 21st century. The service is plagued by major personnel problems, too few ships for assigned missions, less-than-optimal aircraft, and, to some degree, a headquarters organization that is unable to develop a unified naval strategy. The Marine Corps, while better off in most respects than the other armed services, is experiencing a decline in amphibious lift and is engaged in several expensive projects that will provide minimal enhancement of its combat capabilities.

Much of this situation is the result of lackluster leadership in the Navy during much of the last decade. In the 1990s the civilian and uniformed leaders of the Navy have produced or adhered to policies that deterred effective fleet development, innovation, and even confidence. The noteworthy exceptions have been the brief tenures of Admiral J. M. ("Mike") Boorda as Chief of Naval Operations (April 1994–May 1996) and Dr. Richard Danzig as Secretary of the Navy (from November 1998).[1]

The leadership problem has been manifested in the lack of articulation of the important and unique role of the Navy in post–Cold War crises, confrontations, and conflicts; the continuation of separate and independent stratagems developed by the Navy's warfare communities or "unions" as they compete for funding; and the significant shortfalls in Navy personnel recruiting and retention.

Significantly, the Navy has been directly involved in *every* U.S. military operation of the past decade. These have included actions in which the Navy has been the principal or a critical participating force, and others where naval participation has been minimal. (The Marine Corps, like the Army and Air Force, has participated in some but not all operations.)

Within the Navy unions—air, surface, and submarine—there continues a spirit of independence and that each "can do it all." This is different than competition among warfare areas, which is a positive condition and should be encouraged.

In 1992 the Chief of Naval Operations (CNO), Admiral Frank Kelso, reorganized the Office of the Chief of Naval Operations (OPNAV) in an effort to reduce the independence of the warfare communities (see chapter 5 of this edition of *Ships and Aircraft*).

---

1. Danzig served as Under Secretary of the Navy from 1993 to 1997.

Kelso changed the heads of the three primary communities from Deputy CNOs at the vice admiral level to warfare "directors" with the rank of rear admiral. This change, ironically, elevated the influence of the submarine community because the Director of Naval Nuclear Propulsion—a full admiral with an eight-year tenure stipulated by law—became the de facto head of the submarine community although he was not in a "line" position. (The heads of the other warfare communities became the senior type commanders, i.e., vice admirals in the Atlantic or Pacific Fleets.)

The continued prominence of the unions has inhibited development of an effective overall Navy strategy and creates a continuing internal Navy debate over resources that is more acrimonious than in the other services. Also, new projects that are not obvious components of a specific warfare area are unlikely to be objectively considered or funded. Mine warfare is a classic example of this situation, as aircraft and submarines lay mines, while surface ships and—to a lesser degree—aircraft (helicopters) are the principal mine countermeasures forces.

Similarly, the proposed arsenal ship of the early 1990s failed to gain warfare sponsors after the death of Admiral Boorda. The surface warfare community saw the arsenal ship as a threat to the new DD 21 destroyer program, while the aviation and submarine communities saw the new ship as a threat to their attack/strike roles (see below).[2]

This situation is perplexing. Solutions, admittedly, are difficult. One option would be to return the warfare directorates to three-star rank so that they again could become the heads of their respective communities and could more effectively deliberate OPNAV issues. They still would report to the three-star Deputy CNO for Resources, Warfare Requirements, and Assessments.

Further, the unions could be better integrated—as are today's fleet operations. One approach would be to assign the deputy director for each warfare area from a *different* warfare community; for example, the Deputy Director of Surface Warfare would be an aviation or submarine officer. This dissimilar deputy concept was used by Admiral Ernest J. King, Commander in Chief U.S. Fleet and CNO during World War II, who, disturbed by squabbling among senior aviators and surface officers, dictated that fleet and task force commanders would have deputies or chiefs of staff from other com-

munities. Thus, Vice Admiral Marc A. Mitscher, commander of the Fast Carrier Task Force (TF 38), was assigned Commodore Arleigh A. Burke, a veteran destroyer officer, as his chief of staff. Such assignments proved to be highly beneficial to the commands as well as to the officers themselves.

In fall 2000 the newly appointed CNO, Admiral Vernon E. Clark, began a reorganization of Navy headquarters in the hope of correcting some of these problems (see Addenda).

A final subject of concern in this regard—in part a result of the diverse communities—is the conservative nature of U.S. ship design. U.S. warship design of the 1980s and 1990s has been characterized by a lack of imagination and innovation. The warfare sponsors tend to propose and develop ships that are improvements of and replacements for existing ships. This is demonstrated, for example, by the decision to make the next aircraft carrier an improved version of the NIMITZ (CVN 68) class, which traces its design directly to the canceled carrier UNITED STATES (CVA 58), which was designed in the mid-1940s. The aviation community has resisted several radical carrier design proposals by Navy agencies, while the Director of Nuclear Propulsion has insured that the carrier will have nuclear propulsion regardless of the potential effectiveness and cost of alternatives (see chapter 13).

Likewise, the new amphibious ships of the SAN ANTONIO (LPD 17) class are highly conservative in design, tracing their lines directly to the ASHLAND (LSD 1) of 1943, the first U.S. Navy ship with a docking well for landing craft. Several innovations have been proposed—but rejected by the surface warfare community—such as providing a full flight deck and a "dry" docking well. The full-deck configuration, as in the larger LHA/LHD-type ships as well as the smaller Japanese LSTs of the OSUMI class, provides for enhanced helicopter and Unmanned Aerial Vehicle (UAV) operation, or simply more deck space for transporting helicopters and ground vehicles. The dry well would cost less than a "wet" docking well, have reduced maintenance requirements, and permit a smaller ship, while still enabling the operation of assault amphibian vehicles (AAVs) and air cushion landing craft (LCACs). Only conventional landing craft (LCU/LCM) would be excluded, but sufficient wet wells for those craft will be available in the fleet in LHA/LHD/LSD-type ships.

In the same regard, the now-building nuclear-propelled attack submarines of the VIRGINIA (SSN 774) class are, in many respects, scaled-down versions of the previous SEAWOLF (SSN 21) design. The

---

2. The U.S. submarine force entered the conventional strike role in 1978 with the introduction of the Tomahawk Land-Attack Missile (TLAM) to attack submarines.

The Japanese landing ship OSUMI shows her carrier-type main deck configuration, a highly innovative approach to landing ship design. The OSUMI displaces 14,700 tons at full load and is almost 584 feet (178 m) long. Although designated an LST, the OSUMI has a docking well and can accommodate 330 troops, or three times that number for short periods. (Courtesy *Ships of the World*)

VIRGINIA design was pursued by the Navy after Congress specifically directed the Navy to instead develop a series of competitive prototypes for the next-generation attack submarine.[3] Thus, the same SSN types that were developed for the open-ocean (and under-ice) operations of the Cold War will be the submarines employed in future littoral operations against Third World nations.

At the same time, the submarine community has consistently rejected any objective discussion or proposals for the U.S. Navy to procure a small number of non-nuclear submarines for use as targets in Anti-Submarine Warfare (ASW) training and for research and development work (see chapter 11).[4]

Two innovative ship programs were proposed in the 1990s. First came the Surface Combatant 21 project, which led to the DD 21 land-attack destroyer. While this ship will be larger than the previous ARLEIGH BURKE (DDG 51) class, the ship is being designed primarily for operations in littoral areas—that is, the land-attack role in support of ground forces, as well as the strike role—and not for traditional blue-water operations. Also significant, the manning goal for the ship is 95 officers and enlisted men and women—just 25 percent the size of the crew of a BURKE-class destroyer.[5] Also, the DD 21 will be the first major U.S. surface warship in some 60 years to have electric drive.[6]

More innovative was the aborted arsenal ship. Developed in the mid-1990s, the arsenal ship was to be a "missile carrier" to complement cruisers and destroyers in a variety of warfare roles. This was the first totally new warship concept since the strategic missile submarine (SSB/SSBN) was developed in the late 1950s. But the arsenal ship died with Admiral Boorda. (See appendix E for a description of the arsenal ship.) Significantly, in the presidential campaign of 2000, the arsenal ship was endorsed by candidates George W. Bush and Bill Bradley.

While the Navy—with the two above exceptions—has sought to develop follow-on designs to existing ship types, the U.S. Coast Guard in sharp contrast is attempting a different approach for its next-generation capabilities in the so-called Deepwater Project. The Coast Guard has asked competing industry teams to propose an integrated force "architecture" or "system of systems" to carry out the Deepwater missions in an effective manner at the lowest cost. This is a quite different approach than simply seeking a follow-on cutter (surface ship), fixed-wing aircraft, and helicopter to replace the existing force.

Systems that could be considered under the Deepwater Project include surface ships, land-based aircraft, ship-based aircraft (helicopters, Vertical/Short Takeoff and Landing [VSTOL], and UAV types), satellites, and even smaller surface craft that could be supported or carried by a larger ship. While the next-generation cutters, aircraft, and C[4]I systems may be direct follow-ons to their predecessors, they may not be type-for-type replacements.[7]

While new ships generally are more capable and easier to maintain than the ships they replace, the size of the U.S. fleet has declined precipitously in the past decade while becoming more expensive to procure. In the first decade of the 21st century, the Navy is scheduled to have just over 300 ships in commission. That represents the smallest U.S. fleet since 1931, although the methods of "counting ships" has changed several times. However, even the current means of tabulating ships is not realistic. For example, while the Navy is authorized and has "on the books" 12 aircraft carriers, one ship is always undergoing a three-year (nuclear) refueling and overhaul, effectively reducing the force to 11 carriers (with only ten air wings).

The shortfall in carriers—coupled with efforts by the Navy leadership not to exceed six-month deployments because of personnel concerns—led to an awkward situation in the spring of 1999 when the air campaign against Serbia began. A few days before the shooting started, the carrier ENTERPRISE (CVN 65), having been forward-deployed for almost six months, departed the Mediterranean en route to her home port of Norfolk, Va. The carrier THEODORE ROOSEVELT (CVN 71) was preparing to depart the East Coast to replace the "Big E" in the Persian Gulf, while the carrier KITTY HAWK (CV 63) was in the Western Pacific.

When the Kosovo campaign, which most U.S. political *and* military leaders expected to take only a few days, erupted into a much larger conflict than envisioned, the ROOSEVELT was rushed to the Mediterranean and into the Aegean Sea to take part in the air strikes. The KITTY HAWK, meanwhile, rushed south, through the Indonesian Straits, and across the Indian Ocean to fill the ROOSEVELT's intended station in the Persian Gulf area. The KITTY HAWK, in conjunction with land-based U.S. air forces in Turkey and Saudi Arabia, thereafter patrolled the "no fly" zones over northern and southern Iraq and periodically joined in strikes against Iraqi air defenses.

Because of this shell game, for 86 days there was no U.S. carrier available in the Western Pacific. (A carrier on the West Coast was essentially ready to deploy, but it was felt that her air wing was not ready, and the ship continued her "work up" for deployment later in the area.) To compensate for the carrier shortfall, it was necessary to deploy U.S. Air Force aircraft from the United States to bases in South Korea.

This situation occurred with a force of 11 operational carriers. Indeed, the Kosovo campaign—considered a "one conflict" situation, while U.S. defense strategy calls for the armed forces being able to simultaneously fight two Major Regional Conflicts (MRC)—showed the inability of the U.S. fleet to effectively carry out the U.S. engagement strategy with just over 300 ships.

According to the currently approved Department of Defense force levels, the active fleet of the early 21st Century is to have:

14	strategic missile submarines
55	attack submarines
12	aircraft carriers
27	cruisers
89	destroyers/frigates
36	amphibious warfare ships
7	mine countermeasures ships
34	combat logistic ships
23	support ships

These ships are (inaccurately) designated "battle force ships." In addition, there are 23 reserve battle force ships that comprise the Naval Reserve Force (NRF):

16	frigates
2	tank landing ships
1	mine countermeasures support ship
21	mine countermeasures ships

As this edition of *Ships and Aircraft* went to press, the actual numbers of ships in the active fleet were slightly higher.

The Navy's current forward-deployment schedule, derived largely from Cold War deployment patterns, provides for a six-month forward deployment period based on the concept of one ship forward with two ships back—in overhaul, local operations, and training, and with their crews being given leave and training—providing approximately one year between deployments. This policy provides for the forward deployment of three carrier battle groups and three amphibious groups, the latter consisting of three or four "amphibs."

Funds are provided in the budget for an Operational Tempo (OPTEMPO) of 50.5 underway days per quarter for ships forward deployed and 28 underway days per quarter for non-deployed ships. This OPTEMPO has been difficult to maintain in view of the response to crises and conflicts, along with the continuing operations in the Persian Gulf area and elsewhere. When trouble appears to be brewing virtually anywhere in the world, the first question still asked in the White House appears to be, "Where are the carriers?"

---

3. See Tom Philpott, "Congressional Watch," U.S. Naval Institute *Proceedings* (May 1997), pp. 132–135, and commentary by N. Polmar, *Proceedings* (June 1997), pp. 14, 16, 18.

4. Paranoia over the non-nuclear submarine issue also led to the U.S. Navy rejecting foreign efforts to construct submarines in U.S. shipyards—even those yards not engaged in nuclear submarine construction. Australia, Israel, and South Korea expressed such interest in the 1980s, and Egypt in the 1990s.

5. The numbers for both ships include an air detachment of about 21 personnel to operate and support two SH-60 LAMPS III helicopters.

6. The last major U.S. warships built with electric drive were the large aircraft carriers LEXINGTON (CV 2) and SARATOGA (CV 3); they were completed in 1927 and served until sunk in 1942 and retired in 1945, respectively. They were the largest aircraft carriers operated by the Navy in World War II.

7. C[4]I = Command, Control, Communications, Computers, and Intelligence.

SHIPS AND SHIPBUILDING

All of the Navy's warfare communities are seeking additional ships. The Navy's shipbuilding situation can only become more difficult, barring a major and prolonged crisis or conflict. Regardless of the political party in the White House, major increases in defense spending and especially in the shipbuilding budget are unlikely. In 1999, Secretary of the Navy Danzig declared that it might be necessary to stretch out the existing, austere shipbuilding program to help pay for fiscal shortfalls. The plan put forward—to pay for rising fuel costs, higher pay for personnel, and less fiscal savings than hoped for—provided for canceling the VIRGINIA-class SSN ($2 *billion*) in Fiscal Year (FY) 2003, one BURKE-class DDG ($1 *billion*) in FY 2005, and one ADC(X) support ship ($700 million).

Under the current shipbuilding plan (see table 1-1), procurement funding has increased from $5.45 *billion* in FY 1999 to $6.47 *billion* in FY 2000, and it will increase to an estimated $10.7 *billion* in FY 2001 with the completion of funding for another nuclear carrier (CVN 77). It is impossible to accelerate the procurement of aircraft carriers, assuming a continuation of construction of NIMITZ-class derivatives, which is the course upon which the Navy is steadfastly embarked at this time.

The carrier force could be increased to 12 operational ships by retaining an older ship after 2003, when the RONALD REAGAN (CVN 76) is placed in commission. Such action is difficult because of the manning requirements and maintenance/modernization costs—but it could be done.

The surface combat force level—cruisers, destroyers, and frigates—currently is set at 116 ships. New destroyers are being constructed at the rate of three ships per year; assuming a 30-year service life, this would eventually sustain a force of only 90 ships. Again, older ships could be retained in service or new ships could be "given" a 40-year service life, which would provide a force of some 120 ships. It should be noted that the seven destroyers of the SPRUANCE (DD 963) class not fitted with Vertical Launching Systems (VLS) were retired after 20 years of service, an indication of the difficulty and cost of retaining and upgrading older ships. It would certainly have been feasible to provide those seven ships with 61-cell VLS for Tomahawk missiles.

A more feasible means of maintaining 116 surface combatants—and increasing the numbers to reflect realistic needs—would be a slight increase in construction rates. For example, going from 3 to 3.5 ships per year with a 35-year service life could provide 122 ships; the annual cost increase would be about $460 million per year, roughly 2 percent of the annual shipbuilding budget.

The submarine issues are more complex. The 1990s were a lean period for submarine construction, with only four SSNs being authorized.[8] The planned construction of VIRGINIA-class SSNs during the next few years will be at the rate of one submarine per year, which is sufficient to support a force of just 30 SSNs. There are proposals to convert four ex-Trident ballistic missile submarines (SSBN) to a cruise missile/special operations configuration (SSGN). The four conversions will be expensive (at least $1 *billion* each) and, at this writing, are considered unlikely.

Retaining older submarines of the highly capable Los ANGELES (SSN 688) class in service would be expensive, as they require (nuclear)

---

8. The submarine authorizations were two SEAWOLF (SSN 21) class (in FY 1991 and FY 1996) and two VIRGINIA (SSN 774) class (in FY 1998 and FY 1999).

The construction of surface combatants—these are destroyers of the ARLEIGH BURKE (DDG 51) class—continues at the rate of three ships per year, to be replaced on the building ways at Litton/Ingalls and Bath Iron Works by the DD 21 land attack destroyers. But these are too few ships to sustain the force goal for surface combatants. The same situation is true for submarine construction. (John Bouvia)

TABLE 1-1. FISCAL YEARS 1998 THROUGH 2006 SHIPBUILDING PROGRAM

Type/Class		FY 1998 Actual	FY 1999 Actual	FY 2000 Actual	FY 2001 Plan	FY 2002 Plan	FY 2003 Plan	FY 2004 Plan	FY 2005 Plan	FY 2006 Plan
SSN 774	Virginia	1	1	—	1	1	1	1	1	1
CVNX	(carrier)	—	—	—	AP*	AP	AP	AP	AP	1
CVN 77	(carrier)	—	—	AP	1	—	—	—	—	—
DD 21	(destroyer)	—	—	—	—	—	—	AP	1	3
DDG 51	Arleigh Burke	4	3	3	3	2	2	2	1	—
JCC**	(command ship)	—	—	—	—	—	—	1	1	—
LHD 1	Wasp	—	AP	AP	AP	1	—	—	—	—
LPD 17	San Antonio	—	1	2	2	2	2	2	—	—
T-AKE	replenishment ship	—	—	1	1	3	3	2	2	2
Total		5	5	6	8	9	8	8	6	7
Conversions										
Submarines***		—	—	2	1	1	2	1	2	1
CVN 68 Modernization		1	AP	AP	AP	1	AP	AP	—	1
CG 47 Modernization		—	—	—	—	1	3	4	4	4
LCAC SLEP		—	—	2	1	2	3	3	4	4

* AP = Advance Procurement (funds).
** JCC = Joint Command Ship.
*** These funds could be applied to either Los Angeles (SSN 688) refuelings or Trident SSGN conversions/refuelings.

refueling. Nevertheless, that action could be more attractive in the *near term* because of the expected cost of building Virginia SSNs—at least $2 *billion* each. (It should be noted that Los Angeles–class SSNs were being retired in the late 1990s after only 17 years of service.)

Increasing the construction rate of the Virginia class to 1.5 SSNs per year would provide 45 SSNs (1.5 × 30); 1.5 SSNs per year with a service life increase to 35 years would provide 52 SSNs (1.5 × 35). More submarines appear to be required. However, must they all be the relatively high-mix Virginias, or can *some* of them be less-capable nuclear or non-nuclear submarines? An increase in SSN force levels—with the submarine community asking for 68 submarines—would require a building rate of at least two Virginias per year at an increase of at least $2 *billion* annually. That would mean an increase of approximately 20 percent or greater in the shipbuilding budget for submarines alone.

In 1987 the Virginia SSN program was called the "single most controversial procurement issue in the last Congress and maybe in this one as well" by Rep. Duncan Hunter (R-Calif.).[9] Following the unprecedented controversy over procurement of the Seawolf-class SSNs, it is apparent that the Navy's submarine program will continue to be one of the most contentious for the foreseeable future.

A further complication of the shipbuilding program is the drive to build "smart ships," using technology to reduce manning costs, as well as Commercial-Off-The-Shelf (COTS) components to reduce construction costs. The Navy has evaluated smart-ship concepts in a guided missile cruiser and an amphibious ship with significant success, although very complex changes must be made in both manning policies and ship hardware. The DD 21's manning goal of 95 is the result of extensive efforts in this area.

Smart ship technologies, however, are relatively expensive, as automated systems, extensive monitoring, and backups must be developed and provided. Nevertheless, considering high personnel costs, a smart ship is the obvious direction in which to go. Unfortunately, this level of crew reduction is not forthcoming in the submarine community, where people are more expensive to recruit, train, and retain than are the crews of surface ships.

Beyond the above arsenal ship, one other new start has been proposed during the next few years—the "streetfighter." This is being touted as a highly capable, corvette-size warship (that is, under 1,000 tons full load displacement), specifically for operations in littoral areas (see chapter 20). Like the arsenal ship, there is considerable controversy over the concept, with proponents pointing out the U.S. Navy's lack of ships for such a role, while opponents fear interference with the DD 21 program if there are two new surface combatant programs in the next few years.

---

9. Hearings before the Military Procurement Subcommittee, House National Security Committee, Washington, D.C., 18 March 1997.

AIRCRAFT AND MISSILES

Naval Aviation—the Navy and Marine Corps air arms—has been reduced in numbers of squadrons, with the Navy now operating only ten active and one reserve carrier air wings, compared to 11 and two at the end of the Cold War. Some experts argue that today's carrier air wings are relatively less capable than they were a decade ago because of the reduction of F-14 Tomcat fighter squadrons from two to one in most air wings and the demise of the A-6E Intruder attack aircraft. Also, the removal of the S-3B Viking from the ASW role marks a reduction in capability in that critical warfare area.

Annual aircraft procurement is increasing, with the Navy and Marine Corps filling their fighter-attack squadrons with the F/A-18E/F Hornet, and with the advanced MV-22 Osprey, a Short Take-Off/Vertical Landing (STOVL) aircraft, entering service to replace the venerable CH-46 Sea Knight helicopter in the Marine vertical-assault role. The air training community, also reduced in size, is being modernized with the new T-6A Texan and T-45 Goshawk trainers, while the shipboard ASW helicopters are being modified to the multirole SH-60R configuration. (U.S. Navy and Marine Corps aircraft procurement plans are shown in chapter 27, table 27-1.)

Still, the portrait of Naval Aviation is mixed.

The F/A-18 has encountered technical difficulties—which the Navy and the manufacturer, Boeing McDonnell Douglas, have assured Congress have been solved. It also lacks stealth characteristics, which are considered vital for some tactical operations. And, while the F/A-18 has the dual-mission capabilities of an attack aircraft and a fighter, its range/payload is far less than the recently retired A-6E Intruder.

Looking at near-term naval aviation, there is a significant reduction in carrier/surface combatant ASW capabilities with the shift in S-3B Viking roles and modification of the SH-60B/F to multimission configurations. Coupled with the shortage of surface combatants and the decline in land-based P-3C Orion maritime patrol squadrons, this situation is of major concern to many observers. The cause of this concern is the proliferation in the Third World of submarines that have limited open-ocean effectiveness but are a significant danger to naval operations in littoral/coastal waters. U.S. Navy exercises with South American navies during the UNITAS operations and with some other navies, especially when against the small but determined Israeli submarine force, demonstrate the continued threat of these undersea craft.

In the longer term, the Navy and Marine Corps (as well as the U.S. Air Force and Royal Navy) are scheduled to fly the Joint Strike Fighter (JSF). In naval aviation, this aircraft is to succeed the F-14 Tomcat and F/A-18 Hornet. The delays and increased costs in procurement of the F/A-18E/F, and the similar problems with the Air Force's F-22 Raptor fighter aircraft, can be expected to slow the procurement of the JSF.

A plane captain wipes down the canopy of an F-14 Tomcat aboard the carrier ENTERPRISE during flight operations in the Persian Gulf. Navy strike aircraft and missile-launching ships and submarines have carried out strikes against Iraq, Afghanistan, Sudan, Kosovo, and Serbia during the past few years. This F-14 had launched 13 laser-guided bombs during the ship's 1999 deployment. (U.S. Navy, PHAN Darryl Wood)

Such delays would be critical for the Marine Corps, which requires the JSF to replace the aging AV-8B Harrier for both amphibious ship (LHA/LHD) and land operations. The Royal Navy will face a similar predicament with the replacement of its Harrier force aboard its STOVL carriers. At the same time, a JSF with an effective STOVL capability could open discussions of employing LHA/LHD-type ships in a greater range of operations, and possibly the consideration of smaller "attack" carriers (CV/CVN).

Also disconcerting is the UAV picture. The Navy pioneered the development of modern remotely piloted aircraft in the U.S. armed forces, first with the Drone Anti-Submarine Helicopter (DASH) in the 1960s and then with the Israeli-developed Pioneer, which became operational in the U.S. Navy and Marine Corps in 1987 (see chapter 27). Finally, on 10 February 2000 selection was announced of a derivative of Schweizer Aircraft's Model 333 turbine helicopter as the next-generation Tactical Unmanned Aerial Vehicle (TUAV) for the Navy and Marine Corps. Given the name Fire Scout, this TUAV is a sensor platform and will not carry weapons. Also, it will have limited, if any, stealth characteristics.

Much more success can be claimed in the area of missiles. The Navy-developed Tomahawk Land-Attack Missile (TLAM) has become a "weapon of choice" in confrontations and conflicts. From its first use in combat in the 1991 war against Iraq (288 being fired) to the "punishment strikes" against Iraq, the counter-terrorist strikes against Sudan and Afghanistan, and the 1999 campaign against Serbia (approximately 200 fired plus a fusillade from a British SSN), the TLAM has demonstrated to be an effective and accurate weapon.[10] These weapons had the advantage of being capable of day or night attack against the most heavily defended targets without putting air crews at risk.

Many other precision-guided munitions were launched by Navy and Marine aircraft, although Naval Aviation contributed a relatively small fraction of the total air-missile strikes against Serbian forces and the Serb infrastructure. Further, the above-discussed withdrawal of the carrier ENTERPRISE from the Mediterranean meant that the Kosovo campaign was under way for 14 days before the first carrier strikes were flown (from the THEODORE ROOSEVELT).

Nevertheless, the Navy did make significant and in some instances unique contributions to the Kosovo campaign; these may portend the future role of naval forces in littoral operations:

Tactical reconnaissance: Navy F-14s fitted with the TARPS reconnaissance package and Marine F/A-18Ds with the ATARS package were the only manned tactical reconnaissance aircraft in the area.[11] Despite the availability of satellites, U-2 aircraft, and UAVs, manned aerial "recce" again was found invaluable, although far from the ideal tactical system. This Navy-Marine capability should be increased, possibly to the extent of providing more TARPS, as well as specialized pilot training, to F-14 squadrons and adding F/A-18D ATARS to carrier air wings as F-14s are retired.

Suppression of Enemy Air Defenses (SEAD): The Navy–Marine Corps EA-6B Prowlers are the only U.S. Electronic Countermeasures (ECM)/electronic attack aircraft. Flying from the ROOSEVELT and from land bases, the Prowler was invaluable in the conflict, providing ECM warning and striking hostile radar sites. The shortfall in these aircraft was evident and, although a new electronic attack (VQ) squadron is being formed, development of the EA-6B replacement must be accelerated. Today a variant of the F/A-18F appears the most likely candidate for Navy-Marine service. This, too, is an area for the exploitation of UAV platforms.

Tomahawk Land-Attack Missiles (TLAM): Although only some 200 were fired in a campaign of almost three months, their use was important. Later blocks of the TLAM and the forthcoming Tactical Tomahawk (TACTOM) will provide increased effectiveness, but Tomahawk is based on technology more than 30 years old and a new VLS strike missile (for surface and submarine use) must be accorded high priority. However, the Allied aircraft and TLAM attacks in Serbia and Kosovo in the spring of 1999 (Operation Allied Force) demonstrated that the effectiveness of current precision guidance can enable warheads much smaller than the 1,000 pounds (453.6 kg) of the Tomahawk to effectively destroy virtually all potential targets in Third World operations. Accordingly, consideration is being given to the development of a new generation of smaller guided weapons for use from surface ships and submarines against land targets. Obviously, such development will require several years and additional

10. Of approximately 200 U.S. TLAMs launched in the Serbian campaign, 98 percent launched successfully and an estimated 84 percent struck their aim points.

11. TARPS = Tactical Air Reconnaissance Pod System; ATARS = Advanced Tactical Air Reconnaissance System.

resources, but the cost of the smaller weapons will be far less than that of the TLAMs, which cost in excess of $1 million per missile.

Naval air responsiveness: Most U.S. tactical air strikes in the campaign flew from Aviano airfield in northern Italy. The field, with takeoffs easily observed by civilians outside the perimeter fence, had significant political limitations on its use. There were no such limitations for the U.S. carrier ROOSEVELT and helicopter carrier NASSAU (LHD 4) and the British and French carriers that participated in the campaign. Further, the carriers were able to respond more rapidly to calls for manned aircraft because of their proximity off the coast and the periodic aircraft congestion at Aviano.

Platform flexibility: The hallmark of warships is their flexibility. In the Kosovo campaign, amphibious ships were able to launch Harrier strikes, as well as Pioneer UAVs, while destroyers and frigates and their helicopters, intended for seeking out Soviet submarines, were able to provide surveillance of Yugoslav naval units and interdict attempts to smuggle arms ashore.

Naval forces were not used to their fullest extent because of other U.S. and NATO forces in the area. However, more imaginative uses of naval forces were certainly possible. For example, considerable delays and controversy followed the decision to deploy 24 U.S. Army AH-64A Apache helicopter gunships for attacking Serbian tanks and other armored vehicles.[12] The Navy's leadership could have offered an LHA/LHD to transport the Apaches to the campaign. It would have taken but a day or two to load the Apaches, their crews, maintenance personnel, and others, plus their support vans, munitions, and equipment. They could then have been transported to the theater in perhaps ten days, with crews rested and well fed and not exhausted by the transatlantic flights, which also consumed several hundred missions by cargo aircraft.

Further, the Apaches could have been kept aboard ship, making some training flights, until facilities could be made ready for them ashore. Instead, even after considerable delays, they were flown into already congested facilities that were not capable of supporting the helicopters or their people. The words of Winston Churchill, written more than 50 years ago, remain true today:

> Strange as it may seem, the Air Force, except in the air, is the least mobile of all the Services. A squadron can reach its destination in a few hours, but its establishment, depots, fuel, spare parts, and workshops take many weeks, and even months, to develop.[13]

THE PEOPLE

"People are our most important asset" is an expression often heard from naval leaders. And yet, according to Secretary of the Navy Danzig, the Navy's leadership "does not act that way" and historically has looked upon its personnel as "cheap labor."[14]

Secretary Danzig, during his relatively brief tenure at the end of the Clinton administration, has attempted to force the Navy's leadership to understand the costs and burdens imposed by current service practices. Some of the more notorious examples of misuse of serving personnel have been exposed in the press,[15] while the author of this volume has observed such situations as a Navy first class cryptologist (CTR1) assigned to the National Security Agency being used at NSA headquarters to stand watch at bathrooms to make certain visitors did not go astray.

Danzig's efforts have included reducing the duty requirements for ships' crews while their ship is in port—cutting down on watchstanding, mess catering, and other requirements, including maintenance and, especially, ship painting. Further, he pointed out the need to increase the quality of life for sailors aboard ship, noting that U.S.

Navy ships have the lowest habitability standards among all NATO ships.

The last time a senior Navy official made a major effort to improve the quality of life in this manner was in the early 1970s by Admiral Elmo R. Zumwalt, then Chief of Naval Operations. But unlike Zumwalt, who was reacting to the personnel turmoil caused by the end of the Vietnam War, shutdown of the draft, and popular unrest in the United States, Danzig is committed to getting the Navy's leadership to support and institutionalize his policies.

This emphasis on improving the lot of naval personnel—officers and enlisted alike—comes at a time when the Navy cannot recruit and retain the needed personnel. Such problems have been continually suffered by the aviation and submarine officer communities but now are essentially Navy-wide. With an authorized force level of 372,000 personnel (see chapter 9), the Navy was short some 22,000 men and women. Many ships go to sea with significantly fewer personnel than authorized, while plans to partially man the carrier JOHN F. KENNEDY (CV 67) with reserve personnel have failed (see chapter 13).[16]

Although 22,000 is only a 6 percent shortage, the situation is worse because the strong and high-technology U.S. economy bleeds off skilled people and, even at fully authorized strength, Navy manning would be tight. Writing in the U.S. Naval Institute *Proceedings*, a master chief petty officer observed:

> To continue sending ships to sea without the required manning means we will never get ahead of the retention problem in the fleet. Every day I hear our young sailors complain of the extended working hours and how they don't have time to work on [qualification] courses, take college courses. . . . Numbers do matter and those numbers need to include personnel and money for base pay and parts. Call it the triad of readiness: Force—Personnel—Money. Skimp on any one and we'll have a readiness problem like we have today.[17]

In response to the personnel shortage, the Navy has undertaken a conscious effort at recruiting and has introduced retention programs such as the Selective Reenlistment Bonus (SRB), Enlistment Bonus (EB), and Navy College Fund (NCF). Indeed, the Navy has even sought to authorize the award of the Navy and Marine Corps Achievement Medal for someone bringing in four recruits.

Some critics contend that the Navy personnel policies cannot attract the kinds of people wanted in the numbers needed for reasons other than money and awards. One officer, writing in *Proceedings*, asked whether the Navy is "sending the right message" in its recruiting. Comparing Navy and Marine Corps recruiting techniques, the officer noted that the Marines portray a "warrior ethos," while the Navy's ads speak of a "career journey" with equal opportunity, advanced education, and "attending" flight school. "Does one 'attend' Parris Island [Marine recruit training]?" he asked. He concluded:

> Could the nation and current service members be proud of the Navy as displayed in the advertisement? With respect to our emphasis on equal opportunity and education, probably so. With respect to the Navy being a challenging organization with a proud heritage and a dedication to remaining a supreme fighting force, however—our recruiting and retention numbers provide the answer.[18]

The Army and Air Force also have fallen short of their recruiting and retention goals. In contrast, the Marine Corps has been able to maintain its authorized strength of 172,000 officers and enlisted personnel.

The future recruiting and retention situation will be more complicated. Recent studies by the Department of Defense indicate that a

---

12. The Apache helicopter battalion, with 12 OH-58D Kiowa Warrior helicopters in addition to the Apaches to spot targets, required the movement of more than 2,500 personnel, all flown from the United States to Albania.

13. Winston S. Churchill, *Their Finest Hour* (Boston: Houghton Mifflin, 1949), p. 434.

14. Secretary Danzig, U.S. Naval Institute symposium, Virginia Beach, Va., 29 September 1999.

15. See, for example, Greg Jaffe and Thomas E. Ricks, "Of Men and Money, And How the Pentagon Often Wastes Both," *Wall Street Journal*, 22 September 1999, pp. A1, A8.

16. For example, in the fall of 1998 the carrier ENTERPRISE deployed to the Mediterranean/Persian Gulf with a shortage of almost 400 crewmen; the carrier HARRY S. TRUMAN (CVN 75) was commissioned with a shortage of some 390.

17. Master Chief Machinist's Mate Mark Butler, USN, Commentary on "Numbers Do Matter," U.S. Naval Institute *Proceedings* (January 2000), p. 24.

18. Lt. Christian Bonat, USN, "Is the Navy Sending the Right Message?" U.S. Naval Institute *Proceedings* (November 1999), p. 96.

The Navy and Marine Corps are manpower-intensive services. Finding quality people in the numbers needed is an increasing problem for the Navy. Secretary of the Navy Richard Danzig has attempted to reduce the more mundane jobs in the Navy, a feeling no doubt shared by these sailors painting the carrier ABRAHAM LINCOLN (CVN 72) during a port visit while in the Persian Gulf. (U.S. Navy, PHAN Matthew Hollowell)

The different recruiting methods of the Marine Corps and Navy are clearly shown in these posters; the Marines *(left)* challenge the individual, while the Navy offers a myriad of opportunities. Few civilian activities can compare to the Marine challenges, but opportunities similar to the Navy's offerings abound in the American society. (U.S. Navy)

significant number—75 percent—of blacks and other minorities in the armed forces say they have experienced discrimination. Less than half of those believed that complaints were thoroughly investigated.[19]

This situation, coupled with the continuing controversy over women in the military, especially at sea, and complaints of gender biases and exploitation, undoubtedly have an unfavorable impact on recruiting and retention. The problem is further exacerbated by the growing controversy about homosexuals serving in the armed forces, especially at sea.

While proponents of full gender and sexual preference integration in the military are quick to point to President Truman's racial integration of the services in the period immediately after World War II, they ignore certain basic "facts of life"—that sex and human reactions to it are very different than skin color example. Also largely ignored is the impact of dealing with the myriad of gender and homosexual issues on commanding officers, executive officers, master chiefs, and others who already are overburdened with operational and administrative burdens, especially in a smaller, "zero defects"–oriented Navy.

Indeed, while diligently working to alleviate some of the people problems, Secretary Danzig exacerbated the personnel disarray by, in June 1999, proposing that women serve in U.S. submarines.[20] The subsequent controversy showed the depths of despair among the officers and enlisted men who are being told to "make it work"; their efforts could better be allocated to making the existing minority and gender integration programs a success, and possibly spending more effort on battle readiness.

Thus the Navy's personnel situation must be considered precarious at the start of the 21st century. That of the Marine Corps is less so, in part because of its leaders having, and imparting to every recruit and officer candidate, the *warrior ethos.*

FUTURE WAR

The Navy and Marine Corps will continue to be called upon for the foreseeable future to support U.S. political, economic, and military interests. The Navy-Marine team has the advantage over the other services in being able to forward deploy and remain at sea, virtually indefinitely if the Personnel Tempo (PERSTEMPO) can be discarded during a crisis or confrontation. Naval forces still do not require

overflight rights nor do they risk political problems by putting troops into foreign territory. Further, sending a forward-deployed ship or submarine, or even one from its home port to a crisis area, generally is far less expensive than deploying troops or tactical aircraft from the United States.

In addition to the traditional naval missions, two new ones for naval forces appeared in the 1990s: land attack with cruise missiles and ballistic missile defense.

Historically, ships have used cannon and, from the early 1930s, aircraft to strike targets ashore.[21] Strike aircraft, however, require large ships to carry, arm, service, launch, and recover them. The small number of carriers in the world's navies reflects the cost and limitations of air strike from the sea. But beginning with the Persian Gulf War in 1991, Tomahawk TLAMs have demonstrated that smaller cruisers, destroyers, and submarines can strike targets far inland. Indeed, the 1999 TLAM strike against suspected terrorist training camps in Afghanistan showed that naval forces could effectively strike targets in countries without a coastline. As discussed above, it is important for the Navy to further develop this weapon. While the accuracy and range of TLAM and the new TACTOM appear adequate, weapon speed and warheads do not appear optimum for certain targets. (TACTOM will be more capable against mobile and rapidly relocatable targets.) The Navy must objectively analyze the potential role of strike missiles as a component of a "system of systems" and evaluate the role of cruise missiles in conjunction with aircraft carriers, and what the optimum launch platforms (given the limited funding available)—whether surface or submarine—are, and what the configurations of these ships should be.

The second new mission area is ballistic missile defense. The threat from tactical ballistic and cruise missiles to U.S. and allied forces overseas, and under some circumstances to allied nations, has sparked a new requirement. The Iraqi use of Scud-type ballistic missiles against targets in Saudi Arabia and Israel during January 1991 awakened U.S. interest in developing a Theater Ballistic Missile Defense (TBMD) capability. In 1995, Secretary of Defense William J. Perry observed: "The capability to protect noncombatants will become increasingly vital to the U.S. leadership role in the world as ballistic missiles proliferate and aggressors attempt to deter the formation of defensive coalitions through the threat of missile attacks."[22]

Ships fitted with the SPY-1 radar and flexible VLS launchers have an inherent capability—albeit limited—against ballistic missiles.

19. See, for example, Robert Suro and Michael A. Fletcher, "Seventy-Five Percent of Military's Minorities See Racism," *Washington Post*, 23 November 1999, pp. A1, A10.
20. Secretary Danzig made the proposal during a speech before a meeting of the Naval Submarine League in Alexandria, Va., on 4 June 1999.

21. In early 1932, the Japanese Navy employed the carriers HOSHO and KAGA to strike targets ashore during the assault on China.
22. Secretary of Defense William J. Perry, *Annual Report to the President and Congress* (Washington, D.C.: GPO, 1995), p. 241.

Increasingly, the Navy and Marine Corps are being cast in the role of peacekeepers. The impact of these operations on readiness and training could be significant, while these activities also consume spare parts and cause wear on equipment. Here Marines in East Timor unload trucks and supplies from the Navy-manned LCU 1651 for the United Nations High Commissioner for Refugees. (U.S. Marine Corps, Sgt. Bryce Piper)

U.S. submarines—whose most important characteristic is stealth—are increasingly being "seen," as the OKLAHOMA CITY (SSN 723) is here during a port visit to Zeebrugge, Belgium, in March–April 2000. (Leo Van Ginderen)

Shipboard radars, fire control systems, and missiles can be upgraded to provide an enhanced tactical/theater ballistic missile defense capability (see chapter 15). Again, ships can provide this function without introducing troops ashore.

The Navy–Marine Corps team has been provided with major responsibilities in the post–Cold War era. Strike and ballistic missile defense are being added to those responsibilities. The Navy and Marine Corps, with some 300 ships, 2,400 aircraft, 350,000 naval personnel, and 172,000 Marines, are today hard pressed to carry out their assigned responsibilities. The Navy and Marine Corps cannot continue to be effective in crises and confrontations—and periodic conflicts—without major increases in their force structure and assets, or a reevaluation of their deployment and employment policies.

CHAPTER 2

Glossary of Abbreviations

The fleet oiler Rappahannock (T-AO 204) carries out an UNREP of the carrier Kitty Hawk (CV 63) off the coast of Japan. The fleet oiler, like most Navy UNREP ships, is operated by MSC. The vast amounts of ship and aviation fuels that are transferred during UNREPs can require the ships to steam a few tens of yards apart for several hours if the carrier is "dry." (U.S. Navy, PHCS Rod Sato)

The following are abbreviations that appear in multiple chapters. The more esoteric abbreviations relevant to only one or two chapters are not provided here, but are addressed within specific chapters, especially those related to aviation, aircraft, weapons, and sensors.

AA	Anti-Aircraft
AAM	Air-to-Air Missile
AAW	Anti-Air Warfare
ABL	Armored Box Launcher
AEW	Airborne Early Warning
AN/	prefix for U.S. military electronic equipment; in this volume, the AN/ is omitted, with only the subsequent three-letter designations being used (e.g., BQS-6 vice AN/BQS-6)
ARG	Amphibious Ready Group
ARM	Anti-Radiation [-Radar] Missile
ASROC	Anti-Submarine Rocket
ASUW	Anti-Surface Warfare

ASW	Anti-Submarine Warfare
beam	extreme width of hull
bhp	brake horsepower (for diesel engines)
BPDMS	Basic Point Defense Missile System
cal	caliber: (1) the diameter of a gun's bore; U.S. naval guns with a diameter of less than 1 inch (25.4 mm) are measured in "calibers"—decimal fractions of an inch, as .50 calibers—or millimeters (mm)
	(2) the nominal length of the gun's bore expressed in multiples of its bore; thus, a 76-mm/62-cal gun has a bore or inner barrel length of 4,712 mm or approximately 185½ inches
CBR	Chemical-Biological-Radiological
CCS	Combat Control System
CINC	Commander in Chief (unified commander)
CIWS	Close-In Weapon System

COD	Carrier Onboard Delivery
comm.	Commissioned
	Note: Some Navy ships are given administrative commissionings at their building yard, being placed "In Commission, Special"; their formal commissioning is then held at a later date in a politically important location. The latter date is listed in this volume.
COTS	Commercial-Off-The-Shelf
CVBG	Carrier Battle Group
DASH	Drone Anti-Submarine Helicopter
decomm.	decommissioned
D/F	Direction Finding
displacement	*light:* displacement of the ship and all machinery without crew, provisions, fuel munitions, other consumables, or aircraft
	standard: displacement of ship fully manned and equipped, ready for sea, including all provisions, munitions, and aircraft, but without fuels
	full load: displacement of ship complete and ready for service in all respects, including all fuels (aviation as well as ship)
DP	Dual Purpose (for use against air and surface targets)
draft	maximum draft of ship at full load, including fixed projections beneath the keel (e.g., sonar dome)
DWT	Deadweight Tonnage (ship's carrying capacity)
ECM	Electronic Countermeasures
ELINT	Electronic Intelligence
ESM	Electronic Support Measures
EW	Electronic Warfare
extreme width	maximum width at or about a carrier's flight deck, including fixed projections (e.g., "gun tubs")
FBM	Fleet Ballistic Missile (early U.S. term for Submarine-Launched Ballistic Missile/SLBM)
FCS	Fire Control System
fiscal year	from 1 October of the calendar year until 30 September of the following year (since June 1976; previously from 1 July through 30 June)
FLIR	Forward-Looking Infrared
FRAM	Fleet Rehabilitation And Modernization
FY	fiscal year
GFCS	Gunfire Control System
GPS	Global Positioning System
GRT	Gross Registered Tons (ship's tonnage measured in total cubic contents, expressed in units of 100 cubic feet or 2.83 m^3)
hp	horsepower
HY	High Yield (steel)
IOC	Initial Operational Capability
IVDS	Independent Variable Depth Sonar
kgst	kilograms static thrust
km/h	kilometers per hour
LAMPS	Light Airborne Multi-Purpose System (helicopter)
LASH	Lighter Aboard Ship
lbst	pounds static thrust
length	*waterline:* length measured at the waterline (this length is generally the same as between perpendiculars [bp])
	overall: maximum length
Mach	speed of sound
MAD	Magnetic Anomaly Detection
manning	the number of personnel assigned to a ship or craft; the term *complement* is no longer used by the U.S. Navy
MarAd	Maritime Administration

MCLWG	Major Caliber Lightweight Gun
MCM	Mine Countermeasures
MEB	Marine Expeditionary Brigade
MEF	Marine Expeditionary Force
MEU	Marine Expeditionary Unit
Mk	Mark
Mod	Modification
MPS	Maritime Prepositioning Squadron
MSC	Military Sealift Command (changed from Military Sea Transportation Service in 1970)
MSTS	Military Sea Transportation Service (established 1 October 1949); changed to MSC in 1970
NATO	North Atlantic Treaty Organization
NDRF	National Defense Reserve Fleet
n.mile	nautical mile (1.852 km)
NOAA	National Oceanic and Atmospheric Administration
NRF	Naval Reserve Force
NSSM	NATO Sea Sparrow Missile
NVR	Naval Vessel Register—the official U.S. Navy list of ships and craft owned by the Navy; known informally as the Navy List
psi	pounds per square inch (1 psi = 0.07 kg/cm^2) (boiler pressure)
RAST	Recovery Assistance, Securing, and Traversing System
RCOH	Refueling/Complex Overhaul
reactors	the first letter of a nuclear reactor's designation indicates the platform (A = aircraft carrier, C = cruiser, D = frigate [DL/DLG], S = submarine); the numeral indicates the sequence of the reactor design by the manufacturer, indicated by the second letter (G = General Electric, W = Westinghouse)
RFA	Royal Fleet Auxiliary (British)
RPV	Remotely Piloted Vehicle (aircraft)
RRF	Ready Reserve Fleet
SABAR	Service Craft And Boat Accounting Report
SAG	Surface Action Group
SAM	Surface-to-Air Missile
SAR	Search And Rescue
SCB	Ships Characteristics Board—a sequential list of Navy ship designs reaching the advanced planning stage; from 1947 to 1964, numbered in a single sequential series from SCB No. 1 (the NORFOLK/CLK 1, later DL 1) through SCB No. 252 (the FLAGSTAFF/PGH 1); from 1964 on, numbered in blocks:

001–099	cruisers
100–199	carriers
200–299	destroyers/frigates
300–399	submarines
400–499	amphibious ships
500–599	mine warfare
600–699	patrol
700–799	auxiliaries
800–899	service craft
900–999	special purpose

The later numbers have as a suffix the fiscal year of prototype, e.g., 400.65 being the LCC of fiscal 1965 design.

SEABEE	Sea Barge
SEAL	Sea-Air-Land (team)
shp	shaft horsepower
SLBM	Submarine-Launched Ballistic Missile
SLEP	Service Life Extension Program
SOSUS	Sound Surveillance System
SRBOC	Super Rapid-Blooming Offboard Chaff
SSM	Surface-to-Surface Missile

status	**AA** = Atlantic Active	str.	Stricken (from the NVR)
	Academic	SUBROC	Submarine Rocket
	AR = Atlantic Reserve	SURTASS	Surveillance Towed Array Sensor System
	GL = Great Lakes (Coast Guard)	SWATH	Small Waterplane-Area Twin Hull (ship)
	ICIR = In Commission, In Reserve	TACAN	Tactical Air Navigation
	MSC-A = Military Sealift Command–Atlantic	TACTAS	Tactical Towed Array Sonar
	MSC-P = Military Sealift Command–Pacific	TAS	Target Acquisition System
	NRF = Naval Reserve Force	TASM	Tomahawk Anti-Ship Missile
	OSIR = Out of Service, In Reserve	TASS	Towed Array Sonar System
	PA = Pacific Active	TLAM	Tomahawk Land-Attack Missile
	PR = Pacific Reserve	UAV	Unmanned Aerial Vehicle
	R&D = Research and Development	UNREP	Underway Replenishment
	TRA = Training	URG	Underway Replenishment Group
	Yard = undergoing major overhaul/conversion	USCGC	U.S. Coast Guard Cutter
STO	Short Takeoff	USNS	U.S. Naval Ship
STOL	Short Takeoff and Landing	USS	U.S. Ship
STOVL	Short Take-Off and Vertical Landing[1]	VDS	Variable Depth Sonar
		VERTREP	Vertical Replenishment
		VLA	Vertical Launch ASROC
		VLS	Vertical Launching System
		VSTOL	Vertical/Short Take-Off and Landing
		VTO	Vertical Take-Off

1. The term VSTOL—for Vertical/Short Take-Off and Landing—was used by the Marine Corps until early 1995, when the less accurate term STOVL was adopted by Headquarters, Marine Corps.

White on gray: The Coast Guard training bark EAGLE (WIX 327) sails past the helicopter carrier NASSAU (LHA 4) during Operation Sail (OPSAIL) 2000 in Hampton Roads, Virginia. The duo also was present two weeks later at the International Naval Review/OPSAIL 2000 in New York harbor on 4 July 2000. (U.S. Navy, PHAA Jason P. Taylor)

CHAPTER 3

Ship Classifications

U.S. Navy ships and most small craft are classified by type, and by sequence within that type. The list of classifications is issued periodically, updating a system that was begun in 1920.

The following are those classifications on the current Secretary of the Navy instruction "Classification of Naval Ships and Craft," which was last revised in 1993. Letter prefixes to the basic symbols are used to indicate:

F   being constructed for foreign government
T-   assigned to Military Sealift Command (formerly Military Sea Transportation Service)
W   Coast Guard cutter

For ships, the suffix N denotes nuclear propulsion; for service craft, the suffix N indicates a non-self-propelled version of a similar self-propelled craft. While the prefix letter W in the list would indicate that Coast Guard classifications are included in the Navy list of classifications, in fact they are not.

There are many inconsistencies in the current classification list. The suffix letter X—which does not appear in the classification list—is used unofficially to indicate new designs or classes, as DDX, LHDX, AKX, and ARX. More-formal designations often exist for several years in official documents and usage before they appear in the ship classification instruction, as in the case of MSH (added to the list in 1982) and LHD (added in 1983).

Parentheses are not used in ship designations.

In the following list, the ships are arranged in the order of the current Navy instruction on classifications; some levels of sub-categorization are deleted here for purposes of readability. Note that combat logistics ships are listed—as combat ships—ahead of mine warfare ships, and separated from other auxiliary ships.

WARSHIP CLASSIFICATIONS

Aircraft Carrier Type

CV	Multipurpose aircraft carrier
CVN	Multipurpose aircraft carrier (nuclear propulsion)

Surface Combatant Type

BB	Battleship
CG	Guided missile cruiser
CGN	Guided missile cruiser (nuclear propulsion)
DD	Destroyer
DDG	Guided missile destroyer
FF	Frigate
FFG	Guided missile frigate
FFT	Frigate (Reserve Training)

Submarine Type

SSN	Submarine (nuclear propulsion)
SSBN	Ballistic missile submarine (nuclear propulsion)

OTHER COMBATANT CLASSIFICATIONS

Patrol Ships

PHM	Patrol combatant missile (hydrofoil)

Amphibious Warfare Type Ships

LHA	Amphibious assault ship (general purpose)
LHD	Amphibious assault ship (multipurpose)
LPD	Amphibious transport dock
LPH	Amphibious assault ship (helicopter)
LKA	Amphibious cargo ship
LSD	Dock landing ship
LST	Tank landing ship
LCC	Amphibious command ship

Combat Logistics Type Ships

AE	Ammunition ship
AF	Store ship
AFS	Combat store ship
AO	Oiler
AOE	Fast combat support ship
AOR	Replenishment oiler

Mine Warfare Type Ships

MSO	Minesweeper—ocean
MCM	Mine countermeasures ship
MCS	Mine countermeasures support ship
MHC	Minehunter, coastal

Coastal Defense Ships

PC	Patrol, coastal

AUXILIARY CLASSIFICATIONS

Mobile Logistic Type Ships

AD	Destroyer tender
AR	Repair ship
AS	Submarine tender

Support Type Ships

ARS	Salvage ship
ASR	Submarine rescue ship
ATF	Fleet ocean tug
ATS	Salvage and rescue ship
ACS	Auxiliary crane ship
AG	Auxiliary general
AGDS	Deep submergence support ship
AGF	Miscellaneous command ship
AGFF	Auxiliary general frigate
AGM	Missile range instrumentation ship
AGOR	Oceanographic research ship
AGOS	Ocean surveillance ship
AGS	Surveying ship
AGSS	Auxiliary research submarine
AH	Hospital ship
AK	Cargo ship
AKB	Auxiliary cargo barge/lighter ship
AKF	Auxiliary cargo float-on/float-off ship
AKR	Vehicle cargo ship
AOG	Gasoline tanker
AOT	Transport oiler
AP	Transport
ARC	Cable repairing ship
AVB	Aviation logistic support ship
AVT	Auxiliary aircraft landing training ship

COMBATANT CRAFT CLASSIFICATION

Patrol Type Craft

PB	Patrol boat
PCF	Patrol craft (fast)
PTF	Fast patrol craft
ATC	Mini-armored troop carrier
PBR	River patrol craft

Amphibious Warfare Type Craft

LCAC	Landing craft, air cushion
LCM	Landing craft, mechanized
LCPL	Landing craft, personnel, large
LCU	Landing craft, utility
LCVP	Landing craft, vehicle, personnel
LWT	Amphibious warping tug
SLWT	Side-loadable warping tug
LSSC	Light SEAL support craft
MSSC	Medium SEAL support craft
SDV	Swimmer delivery vehicle[1]
SWCL	Special warfare craft, light
SWCM	Special warfare craft, medium

SUPPORT CRAFT CLASSIFICATIONS

Dry Docks (non-self-propelled)

AFDB	Large auxiliary floating dry dock
AFDL	Small auxiliary floating dry dock
AFDM	Medium auxiliary floating dry dock
ARD	Auxiliary repair dock
ARDM	Medium auxiliary repair dry dock
YFD	Yard floating dry dock

Tugs (self-propelled)

YTB	Large harbor tug
YTL	Small harbor tug
YTM	Medium harbor tug

Tankers (self-propelled)

YO	Fuel oil barge
YOG	Gasoline barge
YW	Water barge

Lighters and Barges (self-propelled)

CSP	Causeway section, powered
YF	Covered lighter
YFR	Refrigerated covered lighter
YFU	Harbor utility craft
YG	Garbage lighter

Lighters and Barges (non-self-propelled)

CSNP	Causeway section, non-powered
YC	Open lighter
YCF	Car float
YCSS	Cargo semi-submersible barge
YCV	Aircraft transportation lighter
YFN	Covered lighter
YFNB	Large covered lighter
YFNX	Lighter (special purpose)
YFRN	Refrigerated covered lighter
YFRT	Range tender
YGN	Garbage lighter
YOGN	Gasoline barge
YON	Fuel oil barge
YOS	Oil storage barge
YSR	Sludge removal barge
YWN	Water barge

Other Craft (self-propelled)

DSRV	Deep submergence rescue vehicle
DSV	Deep submergence vehicle
NR	Submersible research vehicle (nuclear propulsion)
YAG	Miscellaneous auxiliary service craft
YFB	Ferry boat or launch

---

1. Generally referred to as *SEAL* Delivery Vehicle.

YM	Dredge
YP	Patrol craft, training
YSD	Seaplane wrecking derrick
YTT	Torpedo trials craft

Other Craft (non-self-propelled)

APL	Barracks craft
YD	Floating crane
YDT	Diving tender
YFND	Dry dock companion craft
YFP	Floating power barge
YHLC	Salvage lift craft, heavy
YLC	Salvage lift craft, light
YMN	Dredge
YNG	Gate craft
YPD	Floating pile driver
YR	Floating workshop
YRB	Repair and berthing barge
YRBM	Repair, berthing, and messing barge
YRDH	Floating dry dock workshop (hull)
YRDM	Floating dry dock workshop (machine)
YRR	Radiological repair barge
YRST	Salvage craft tender

Unclassified Miscellaneous

IX	Unclassified miscellaneous unit

COAST GUARD CUTTERS AND BOATS

The cutter designations currently in use for Coast Guard cutters and boats are:

WAGB	Icebreaker
WAGO	Oceanographic cutter
WHEC	High endurance cutter (multimission; 30 to 45 days at sea without support)
WIX	Training cutter
WLB	Offshore buoy tender (full sea-keeping capability; medium endurance)
WLI	Inshore buoy tender (short endurance)
WLIC	Inland construction tender (short endurance)
WLM	Coastal buoy tender (medium endurance)
WLR	River buoy tender (short endurance)
WLV	Light vessel
WMEC	Medium endurance cutter (multimission; 10 to 30 days at sea without support)
WPB	Patrol boat (multimission; 1 to 7 days at sea without support)
WSES	Surface effect ship

The Coast Guard uses the term "icebreaker" for a variety of vessels with the following categories:

Type A	late GLACIER (WAGB 4)
Type B	MACKINAW (WAGB 83) and late Wind class (WAGB)
Type C	Bay class (WTGB 140)
Type D	medium harbor tugs (WYTM)
Type E	small harbor tugs (WYTL)
Type P	Polar (WAGB) class

MARITIME ADMINISTRATION

The following are Maritime Administration design classifications; they were developed in the late 1930s by the Maritime Commission. They are currently assigned only to auxiliary/sealift ships; during World War II, the escort aircraft carriers, frigates, and tank landing ships designed by the Maritime Commission also had these design classifications.

The first letter-number series (e.g., C4) indicates ship type, with the adjacent letter indicating size.

C	Cargo
P	Passenger
R	Refrigerator ("reefer")
S	Special type
T	Tanker
VC	Victory-Cargo

The second letter-number series indicates propulsion:

M	Motor (diesel)
ME2	Motor; 2 shafts (diesel)
MET	diesel-electric; 2 shafts
S	Steam
S2	Steam; 2 shafts

SE	turbo-electric
SE2	turbo-electric; 2 shafts
ST	Steam; 2 shafts

The third letter-number series indicates specific ship design, usually beginning with A1 or 1; later designs have lower-case letters, such as 1b.

The Coast Guard's ALEX HALEY (WMEC 39) is the former Navy EDENTON (ATS 1). Although the Coast Guard cutter classification scheme is based on the Navy scheme, over time it has been extensively amended. The *W* prefix *unofficially* stands for "White-painted ships." (U.S. Coast Guard)

CHAPTER 4

Defense Organization

Increasingly, U.S. military operations are joint, with the Navy and Marine Corps participating with the Army and Air Force in peacekeeping as well as combat operations. Air Force tankers—such as this KC-10A Extender over the Persian Gulf—regularly are called upon to support naval forces. Two F/A-18 Hornets are fueling from the tanker while other planes from the carrier GEORGE WASHINGTON (CVN 73) wait their turn. (U.S. Navy, Lt. Charles Radosta)

The United States has a unified defense establishment responsible for the conduct of military operations—in peace and in war—in support of the national security strategy. The basic structure was established in 1947 and developed during the Cold War, and has undergone several major modifications.

The President—under the provisions of the Constitution—is the commander in chief of the armed forces. The Secretary of Defense, the President's immediate subordinate, serves as the day-to-day decision maker in defense matters. Together, the President and Secretary of Defense—and, in an emergency, their designated alternates—comprise the National Command Authorities (NCA), empowered to command all U.S. combat forces and to release nuclear weapons for operational use.

From the President, the operational chain of command goes through the Secretary of Defense, with orders transmitted to operational commanders through the Chairman of the Joint Chiefs of Staff. The Secretary of Defense and the Chairman of the Joint Chiefs are the principal military advisers to the President. In addition, by statute, the President is assisted by an advisory body called the National Security Council (NSC), which provides advice on a broad range of national security and intelligence matters. Chaired by the President, the permanent members of the NSC are the Vice President; the Secretaries of Defense, State, and Treasury; the Chairman of the Joint Chiefs; and the Director of Central Intelligence. The official who coordinates NSC activities and directs its staff activities is the President's National Security Adviser.

The principal components of the defense establishment are (1) the Department of Defense, (2) the Joint Chiefs of Staff and Joint Staff, (3) the military departments and their subordinate services, and (4) the unified commands. Four of the U.S. military services are within the Department of Defense; the fifth military service, the Coast Guard, is part of the Department of Transportation. That service has responsibilities to both departments (see chapter 30 of this edition of *Ships and Aircraft*).

DEPARTMENT OF DEFENSE

The Department of Defense (DOD) is headed by the Secretary of Defense, a member of the President's cabinet and of the National Security Council. By custom, the Secretary of Defense is a civilian

William S. Cohen, Secretary of Defense since January 1997 (U.S. Navy)

and not a professional military officer.[1]

The principal deputies to the Secretary of Defense are the Deputy Secretary and four Under Secretaries. There are eight Assistant Secretaries of Defense (ASD) and other civilian officials at that level who report directly to the Secretary and Deputy Secretary. The four Under Secretaries, in turn, are supported by 23 persons at the Deputy Under Secretary of Defense (DUSD) and ASD levels (see figure 4-1).[2]

The large staff that supports these officials is the Office of the Secretary of Defense (OSD). There are approximately 500 military personnel and 1,500 civilians assigned to OSD.

There are 14 separate agencies under the Secretary of Defense that support the Department of Defense and the military services. These agencies generally perform functions that affect all U.S. military activities. Of these agencies, eight are headed by military officers (indicated below by asterisks) and six by civilians:

- Ballistic Missile Defense Organization*
- Defense Advanced Research Projects Agency
- Defense Commissary Agency*
- Defense Contract Audit Agency
- Defense Finance and Accounting Service
- Defense Information Systems Agency*
- Defense Intelligence Agency*
- Defense Legal Services Agency
- Defense Logistics Agency*

- Defense Security Cooperation Agency*
- Defense Threat Reduction Agency
- National Imagery and Mapping Agency*
- National Security Agency*
- National Security Service

The Defense Intelligence Agency (DIA), in addition to performing intelligence analysis for OSD, serves as the intelligence staff for the Joint Chiefs of Staff (the equivalent of a J-2 staff). The National Security Agency (NSA) performs electronic intercept and cryptological activities to support the entire U.S. intelligence community as well as the defense establishment. That agency also supervises the cryptologic activities of the Army, Navy, Marine Corps, and Air Force.

Historical: Congress established the War Department in 1789 and the Navy Department in 1798 (see below). These two departments administered their respective services, with the Navy Department administering both the Navy and Marine Corps. The secretaries of these two departments reported directly to the President and were members of the President's cabinet.

This arrangement continued until the National Security Act of 1947, which became effective on 18 September 1947, created the National Military Establishment, along with the National Security Council and Joint Chiefs of Staff. The Departments of the Army, Navy, and Air Force were established as cabinet-level departments, with the newly created Secretary of Defense functioning primarily as a coordinator of these military departments.

In 1949, amendments to the National Security Act established the Secretary of Defense as the principal assistant to the President on defense matters and changed the National Military Establishment to the Department of Defense. These amendments also made the three military departments subordinate to the Department of Defense and removed their secretaries from the cabinet. Subsequent actions by various Secretaries of Defense have taken away many of the decision-making prerogatives of the military departments and assigned them to OSD and to various defense agencies.

The Defense Reorganization Act of 1958 established a new chain of command from the President and Secretary of Defense to the unified and specified commanders in chief, who were given "full operational command" over the forces assigned to them. However, the Secretary of Defense could delegate the Joint Chiefs of Staff to exercise operational control over forces when he deemed it appropriate. Previously, the military departments acted as the executive agencies for the control of their respective forces.

Table 4-1 shows the armed forces personnel authorized for fiscal year 2001. Note that the Navy Department now has a significantly larger active-duty personnel strength than either the Army or Air Force.

TABLE 4-1. DEPARTMENT OF DEFENSE MANPOWER

Service	Active Duty	Reserve and National Guard*	Civilians
Army	480,000	555,000	216,400
Navy	371,300	89,600	192,200
Marine Corps	172,000	39,500	
Air Force	354,400	234,600	161,600
DOD agencies	—	—	114,300
Totals	*1,377,700*	*918,700*	*684,500*

Note: Authorized levels as of the end of fiscal year 2001; numbers are rounded.
* There are Army, Navy, Marine Corps, and Air Force reserve organizations; in addition, there are Army and Air National Guard organizations, which nominally are under state control during peacetime.

---

1. The exception was General of the Army George C. Marshall, who was Chief of Staff of the U.S. Army during World War II (serving from September 1939 to November 1945). He subsequently served as both Secretary of State (1947–1949) and Secretary of Defense (1950–1951).
2. One assistant to each Under Secretary is designated as the Principal Deputy Under Secretary of Defense (PDUSD).

Figure 4-1

Office of the Secretary of Defense

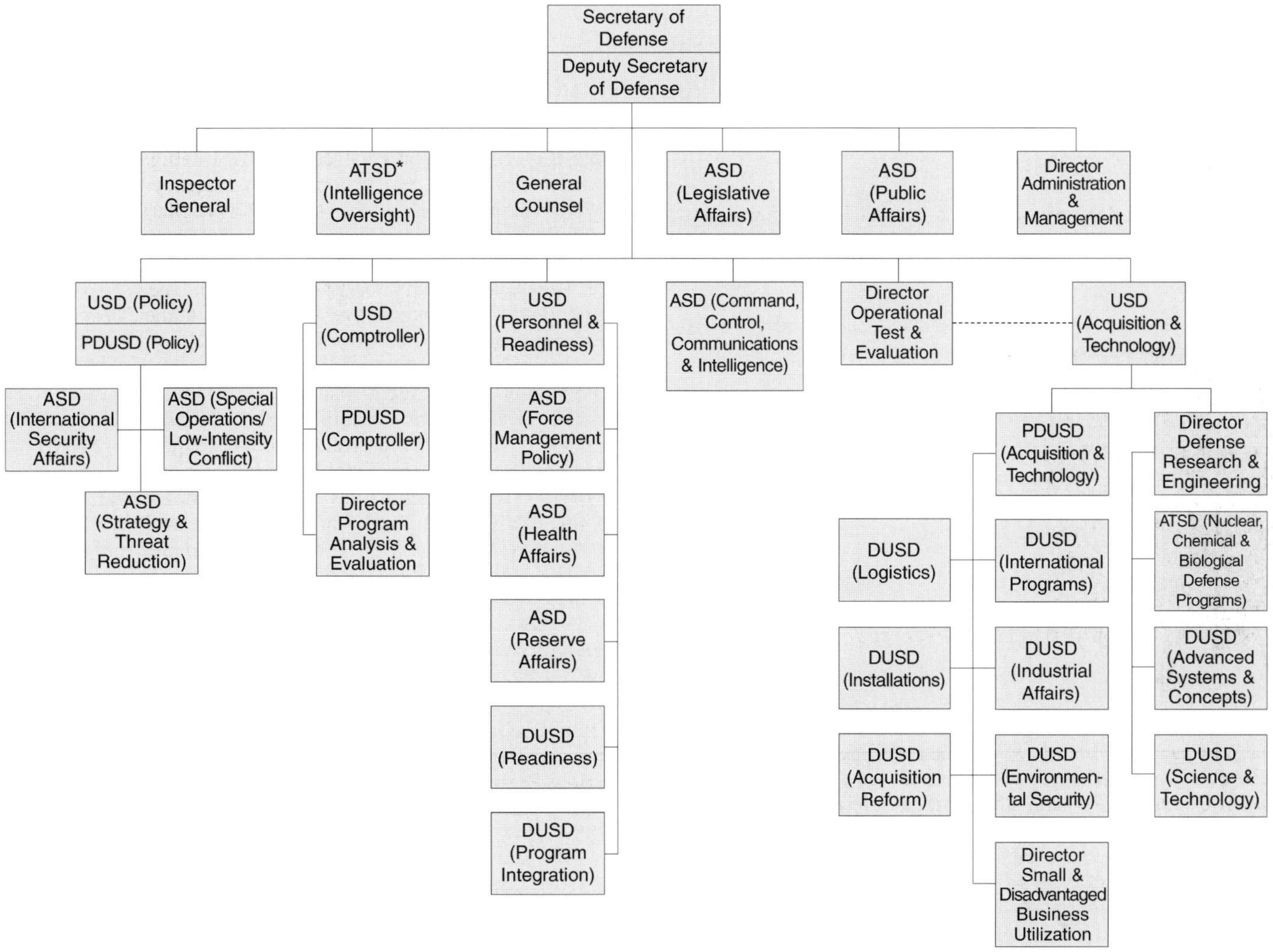

*ATSD = Assistant to the Secretary of Defense

JOINT CHIEFS OF STAFF

The Joint Chiefs of Staff consists of a Chairman, a Vice Chairman, and the military chiefs of the Army, Navy, Air Force, and Marine Corps. The Chairman and Vice Chairman are four-star officers (i.e., general or admiral), as are the military service chiefs.[3]

The Goldwater-Nichols Act of 1986 reduced the role of the members of the Joint Chiefs of Staff and increased the authority of the Chairman, the senior U.S. military officer.[4] The Chairman became the principal military adviser to the Secretary of Defense and the President, and the head of the Joint Staff. Thus the Joint Staff has de facto become a General Staff, something long eschewed by the United States. The JCS collectively serves as the principal military advisers to the President, the Secretary of Defense, and the National Security Council.

The Chairman has a Joint Staff comprised of seven directorates that perform military staff functions for the Joint Chiefs and to some extent for the unified commands. The staff directorates are:

J-1 Manpower and Personnel
J-3 Operations
J-4 Logistics
J-5 Strategic Plans and Policy
J-6 Command, Control, Communications, and Computer Systems
J-7 Operational Plans and Interoperability
J-8 Force Structure, Resources, and Assessment

Note that there is in fact no J-2, with the DOD/JCS intelligence function being carried out by the Defense Intelligence Agency (DIA).

The directors of the JCS staff directorates (and DIA) are three-star officers (i.e., lieutenant general or vice admiral). Their staffs are comprised mostly of military officers from all services. There are approximately 1,200 military personnel and 250 civilians assigned to the Joint Staff. Unlike the former Soviet General Staff and the senior military staffs of some other nations, the officers assigned to the Joint Staff are not professional staff officers, but are assigned from the separate services.

Historical: President Franklin D. Roosevelt and Prime Minister Winston Churchill decided at their wartime meeting in Washington during December 1941–January 1942 to create the Anglo-American Combined Chiefs of Staff. The British component already existed as the Chiefs of Staff Committee; there was no comparable U.S. body of senior military officers.

Without specific executive action or congressional legislation, the senior U.S. military officers met as a body for the first time with their British colleagues to form the Combined Chiefs of Staff on 23 January 1942. At the time, the term "Joint Chiefs of Staff" was

---

3. Four of the 15 chairmen since 1942 have been naval officers:

    Fleet Adm. William D. Leahy   June 1942–Mar 1949
    Adm. Arthur W. Radford   Aug 1953–Aug 1957
    Adm. Thomas H. Moorer   July 1970–June 1974
    Adm. William J. Crowe, Jr.   Oct 1985–Sep 1989

Admiral Leahy's official position was Chief of Staff to the President; he served as the de facto Chairman of the JCS.

4. The Act was sponsored by Sen. Barry Goldwater (R-Ariz.) and Rep. Bill Nichols (R-Ala.).

used for the Americans, although several members were not the chiefs of their services. The JCS initially consisted of the Chief of Naval Operations, Commander in Chief U.S. Fleet, Army Chief of Staff, and Chief of the Army Air Forces.[5]

In July 1942, retired Admiral William D. Leahy was appointed Chief of Staff to the Commander in Chief (Roosevelt) and became de facto Chairman of the JCS. The JCS membership stabilized at four for the remainder of the war.[6] The JCS served both as the U.S. component of the Combined Chiefs of Staff and as the executive body for the direction of U.S. military forces during the war.

The JCS was formally established by the National Security Act of 1947, but not until the 1949 amendments was the position of Chairman authorized. The chairman thereafter rotated, although in no particular order, among the Army, Navy, and Air Force. Some but certainly not all of the chairmen were former chiefs of their services.

In 1952 the Commandant of the Marine Corps was authorized to sit with the JCS and vote on those issues of direct interest to the Marine Corps. In 1979 the Commandant was made a full member of the JCS.

The position of Vice Chairman of the JCS was established in 1987, dictated by the Goldwater-Nichols Act. Previously, when the Chairman was absent, the other members served in his place by rotation. In addition to being a "stand-in" for the Chairman, the Vice Chairman chairs the Joint Requirements Oversight Council (JROC), which has oversight of the acquisition of weapon systems for the military services.

MILITARY DEPARTMENTS

There are three military departments within the Department of Defense—the Army, Navy, and Air Force. Each department is headed by a civilian Secretary, Under Secretary, and several Assistant Secretaries. These are civilian positions, although on occasion a professional officer has been appointed to one of the Assistant Secretary positions.

Reporting directly to the civilian Secretary is the chief of the service assigned to the department, who is the senior military officer of that department (except for officers assigned as Chairman or Vice Chairman of the JCS, who rank above service chiefs). There are two military services within the Navy Department: the Navy and the Marine Corps.

The military departments are responsible for the training, provision of equipment, and administration of their military services. They do not direct military operations, that function having been taken away by the Defense Reorganization Act of 1958. The influence and prerogatives of the military departments have varied considerably in recent years on the basis of the personality, influence, and attitudes of the service secretaries and, to a lesser degree, on the service chiefs.

Historical: The Second Continental Congress authorized the first increment of national troops on 14 June 1775, with their officers responsible to the Congress. The U.S. Constitution of 1789 provided that the President should be Commander in Chief of the Army and Navy, his powers over them exclusive, limited only "by their nature and by the principles of our institutions." On 7 August 1789 the Congress created the War Department.

The U.S. Navy originated with the decision by General George Washington in 1775 to dispatch vessels to prey on British shipping. In October of that year, the Continental Congress established a Naval Committee to acquire and fit out vessels for naval operations. (The following month, the Continental Congress established the Marine Corps.)

At the end of the American Revolution in 1783, the weak and almost bankrupt Congress ordered the Navy to disband. Although the Constitution, adopted in 1789, directed the Congress "to provide and maintain a navy," a separate Navy Department was not considered

necessary, and naval affairs—such as they were—were included under the jurisdiction of the War Department. Not until the Navy Act of 1794, which authorized the procurement of six frigates, was the Navy reestablished, and not until 30 April 1798 did Congress create the Navy Department.[7]

The 1949 amendments to the National Security Act removed the secretaries of the three military departments from the Cabinet and placed them under the supervision of the Secretary of Defense.

UNIFIED COMBATANT COMMANDS

Essentially all U.S. operating forces are assigned to *unified* combatant commands, which plan for military operations, direct exercises and combat and peacekeeping operations, and have operational control of specifically assigned U.S. forces. The 1958 reorganization of the Department of Defense established the chain of command of the operating forces from the National Command Authorities (President and Secretary of Defense) directly to the Commanders in Chief (CINC) of the unified and specified commands. (There are currently no U.S. *specified* commands. That term was applied to commands that had forces assigned from only one military service, with the CINC being from that service.)

The Goldwater-Nichols Act of 1986 greatly strengthened the role and authority of the unified CINCs. Commenting on its influence on the Persian Gulf conflict of 1991, journalist Michael R. Gordon and Marine Lieutenant General Bernard ("Mick") Trainor, also a distinguished journalist, wrote that the Goldwater-Nichols Act

> also strengthened the role of the chairman of the JCS and of field commanders. As a result, [JCS Chairman General Colin L.] Powell wielded power and influence beyond that exercised by previous chairmen. His fellow members of the Joint Chiefs were relegated to onlookers who simply provided the forces. As for [General Norman] Schwarzkopf [Commander in Chief Central Command], he was king of his domain. During the war, no serious attempt was made by any of the services to go around Schwarzkopf. A service chief could not even visit the Gulf without his permission.[8]

There are currently nine unified commands, all of which contain forces from two or more of the military services. Five of the unified commands are responsible for specific geographic areas and four have worldwide functional areas of responsibility (see figure 4-2). The unified command structure is not fixed by law or regulation, and the number of commands and their respective responsibilities periodically are changed at the direction of the President and Secretary of Defense.

Of the geographic commands, the newly established Joint Forces Command (JFCOM), the Pacific Command (PACOM), and the European Command (EUCOM) have major forces assigned to them; the Central Command (CENTCOM) and Southern Command (SOUTHCOM) have primarily planning, command, and control forces assigned on a permanent basis, with specific forces assigned to them by other unified commands during an exercise or a crisis or in wartime. For example, prior to the Iraqi invasion of Kuwait in August 1991, the Central Command was a planning staff of several hundred men and women in the United States. When Operation Desert Shield was initiated in early August 1990, CENTCOM took command of the buildup, with more than 500,000 U.S. military personnel and large numbers of ships, aircraft, and ground units being assigned to it. Subsequently, CENTCOM, in coordination with the commander of Saudi forces, directed Operation Desert Storm, the 1991 assault on Iraq and occupied Kuwait.

Still, in 1993, in a report to the Secretary of Defense on the roles, missions, and functions of the armed forces, General Powell, the Chairman of the Joint Chiefs of Staff, lamented:

> The unified command structure works well overseas, where CINCs with a geographic area of responsibility effectively direct the forces assigned to

---

5. The title of the Chief of the Army Air Forces was changed to Commanding General in March 1942.
6. The position of Chief of Naval Operations was combined with that of Commander in Chief U.S. Fleet in March 1942, giving the JCS just three members—the heads of the Army, Army Air Forces, and Navy. The addition of Admiral Leahy again brought the membership to four.

7. These six frigates included the CONSTITUTION and CONSTELLATION; see chapter 24.
8. Michael R. Gordon and Bernard E. Trainor, *The General's War: The Inside Story of the Conflict in the Gulf* (Boston: Little, Brown, 1995), p. 471.

Figure 4-2

National Defense Command Structure

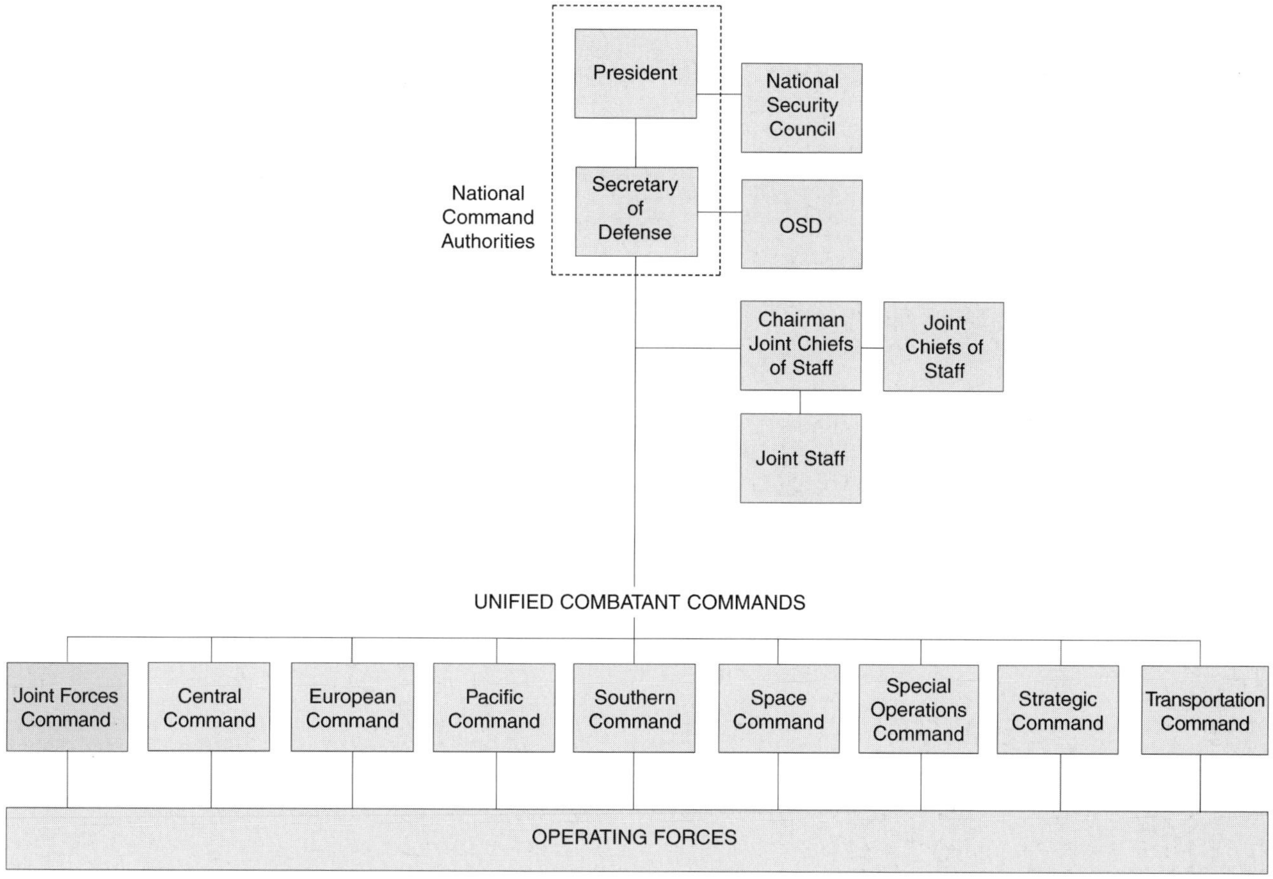

them from the Services in accomplishing a wide range of missions. . . .

But unification has never been achieved in the United States to the same degree as overseas. While forces based in the United States are assigned, by law, to one CINC, many are [also] assigned to overseas CINCs and have limited opportunities to train jointly with the overseas-based forces they would join for military operations in crisis or war.[9]

Twice before, the Joint Chiefs of Staff have attempted to establish a single command to oversee military forces in the United States: In 1961 the U.S. Strike Command (STRICOM) was activated to provide unified control over Army and Air Force units based in the United States, being given responsibility to train forces, develop joint doctrine, and plan for and execute contingency operations as ordered. Subsequently, STRICOM was additionally given geographic responsibility for contingency planning for the Middle East, South Asia, and Africa south of the Sahara. General Powell has noted that "in attempting to fulfill its functional responsibilities as trainer and provider of forces, STRICOM frequently collided with the Services' authority under Title X [U.S. code] to organize, train, and equip forces."[10]

In 1971, Strike Command was replaced by the Readiness Command (REDCOM), which had the same training and readiness functions as STRICOM, but with no geographic areas of responsibility. REDCOM, according to Powell, experienced some of the same resistance by the military services as did its predecessor. Still, over time, REDCOM was given additional responsibilities, including a requirement to plan for and provide Joint Task Force (JTF) headquarters for operations in areas that were not assigned to existing unified commands. What began as REDCOM's Rapid Deployment Joint Task Force (RDJTF) eventually grew into a new unified combat

command, the Central Command (CENTCOM), established in 1983. With headquarters at MacDill Air Force Base in Tampa, Fla., CENTCOM was given responsibility for Southwest Asia and related areas. REDCOM was abolished in 1987.

Subsequently, the U.S. Atlantic Command (LANTCOM) was reorganized on 1 October 1993 as the Atlantic Command (USACOM) to prepare most U.S. continental combat forces for overseas deployment. Significantly, USACOM did not control Pacific Fleet forces based on the U.S. West Coast; those forces—including Marine Forces Pacific—continued to come under the Pacific Command (PACOM). Although there has been increased emphasis on "universal" doctrine and structure for U.S. forces, geography, personality, allies, and other factors make operations in the Pacific very different than the European-Atlantic and other regions.

LANTCOM/USACOM was again reorganized with the establishment of the Joint Forces Command (JFCOM) on 7 October 1999 to control all U.S. forces in the Atlantic area. In addition, JFCOM serves as the DOD agent for joint warfighting experimentation—the creating and exploring of new combat concepts—and provides military assistance to civilian authorities for consequence management of weapons of mass destruction.[11]

(At the same time, responsibility for U.S. military operations in selected waters around Africa and Europe were transferred from JFCOM to EUCOM and CENTCOM, effective 1 October 2000.)

The commanders in chief of the unified forces are four-star officers; some CINC positions rotate among the services, while others are assigned to officers of only one or two services. In late 2000 there were three unified commands under Army generals, four commands under Air Force generals, two commands under Navy admirals, and one command under a Marine general.

---

9. Chairman, Joint Chiefs of Staff, "1993 Report on the Roles, Missions, and Functions of the Armed Forces," 10 February 1993, p. III-3.

10. Ibid.

---

11. I.e., chemical, biological, and nuclear weapons.

Navy SEALs descend from an HH-60H Seahawk onto the deck of the submarine HAMPTON (SSN 767) during an exercise. Army and Air Force special forces have operated from Navy submarines, as have Marines and SEALs. This "interoperability" of special forces has created flexibility in special operations, although some observers contend that this creates some of the duplication in these forces. (U.S. Navy, PH2 Michael W. Pendergrass)

Coast Guard forces operating in forward areas report to the appropriate unified commander.

The unified commands are:

Joint Forces Command (JFCOM): This unified command has geographic responsibility for the North and South Atlantic areas, less the Caribbean and South American coastal areas. The CINC Joint Forces Command is also the NATO Supreme Allied Commander Atlantic, one of the two major NATO military commands, with responsibility for NATO operations in the North Atlantic area. (Until 1985, the Atlantic commander additionally served as CINC Atlantic Fleet.)

The Joint Forces Command—which replaced the previous U.S. Atlantic Command (USACOM)—is the largest U.S. unified command, with responsibility for the readiness of most military forces within the continental United States. JFCOM's principal mission is to develop joint force "packages" of Army, Navy, Air Force, and Marine Corps components that can be rapidly deployed to overseas areas and operate effectively upon arrival in forward areas. Under this concept, major service commands in the United States report to JFCOM for training and deployment; in addition, JFCOM remains the unified or operational commander responsible for the Atlantic Fleet as well as for its readiness and training.

The service component commands under JFCOM are:

- Air Forces Atlantic Command
- Atlantic Fleet (including the Second Fleet)
- Army Forces Command
- Marine Forces Atlantic (II Marine Expeditionary Force)

Headquarters: Norfolk, Va.

Established: 1 December 1947 as Atlantic Command (LANTCOM); 1 October 1993 as U.S. Atlantic Command (USACOM); and 7 October 1999 as JFCOM.

CINC: From its establishment until 1994 CINCLANT/USACOM/LANTCOM has been a Navy officer, except from 31 October 1994 to 24 September 1997, when General John J. Sheehan, USMC, served in this position. (Previously, the Central Command was the only unified command to have had a Marine officer as CINC.) However, in June 2000, Army General William F. Kernan was nominated to become CINC Joint Forces Command.

Central Command (CENTCOM): The Central Command has area responsibility for the Middle East (less Israel, Lebanon, and Syria), southwest Asia (Afghanistan, Iran, and Pakistan), the Persian Gulf and Arabian Sea, and northwest Africa (Egypt, Eritrea, Ethiopia, Kenya, Somalia, and Sudan), and the central Asian states of the former Soviet Union (Kazakhstan, Kyrgyzstan, Tajikistan, Turkmenistan, and Uzbekistan).

The Central Command directed U.S. military operations in the buildup and war in the Persian Gulf War area in 1990–1991 and subsequently in conducting strikes against Iraq (including Operation Desert Fox and the northern and southern "no-fly zones").

The service component commands under CENTCOM are:

- Air Forces
- Army Forces
- Marine Forces
- Naval Forces (including the Fifth Fleet)
- Special Operations Forces

CENTCOM is the direct successor to the U.S. Rapid Deployment Force (see 13th Edition/pages 22–25).

Headquarters: MacDill Air Force Base, Tampa, Fla.

Established: January 1983.

CINC: The Central Command is headed by an Army or Marine officer; the current CINCCENT is General Tommy Franks, USA.

European Command (EUCOM): The area of responsibility for the European Command includes all of Western Europe, portions of the Middle East (Israel, Lebanon, and Syria), the western Slavic and Caucasus states of the former Soviet Union (Armenia, Azerbaijan, Belarus, Georgia, Moldova, and Ukraine), most of Africa, and the Mediterranean. The CINC European Command also serves as the NATO Supreme Allied Commander Europe (SACEUR).

The 1999 campaign against Serbia was directed by SACEUR.

The service component commands under EUCOM are:

- Air Forces Europe
- Army Europe
- Naval Forces Europe (including the Sixth Fleet)
- Special Operations Command

Headquarters: Stuttgart-Vaihingen, Germany.

Established: March 1947.[12]

CINC: The European Command is headed by an Army or Air Force officer; the current CINCEUR is General Joseph W. Ralston, USAF, who previously served as Vice Chairman of the JCS.

Pacific Command (PACOM): The Pacific Command has the largest geographic area of the unified CINCs, with responsibility for the Pacific and Indian Ocean areas (less the Arabian Sea), as well as most of the non-Russian portions of the Asian mainland, Australia, and New Zealand.

The CINC Pacific Command was additionally the CINC Pacific Fleet until 1958.

The service component commands under PACOM are:

- Army Forces Pacific
- Marine Forces Pacific
- Pacific Air Forces
- Pacific Fleet (including the Third and Seventh Fleets)
- Special Operations Command

Headquarters: Camp H. M. Smith, Oahu, Hawaii.

Established: January 1947.

CINC: From its establishment in 1947 PACOM has been headed by a Navy officer. The current CINCPAC is Admiral Dennis C. Blair, USN.

Southern Command (SOUTHCOM): The Southern Command is responsible for operations in Central and South America, including coastal waters, and the Caribbean Sea and Gulf of Mexico.

The command was known as the Caribbean Command (CINC-CARIB) until June 1963.

The service component commands under SOUTHCOM are:

- 12th Air Force
- Army Forces
- Atlantic Fleet (as assigned)
- Special Operations Command

Headquarters: Miami, Fla. SOUTHCOM headquarters previously was located at Quarry Heights, Panama City, Panama; in 1995 it was announced that the headquarters would move to the Coast Guard facility at Richmond Heights in Dade County, Florida, near Miami. (As part of the Panama Canal Treaty, all U.S. military forces had to leave Panama by 31 December 1999; approximately 700 uniformed and civilian personnel at SOUTHCOM Headquarters were involved in the move.)

Established: November 1947.

CINC: The Southern Command historically has been commanded by an Army officer; however, the current CINCSOUTH is General Charles E. Wilhelm, USMC.

Space Command (SPACECOM): U.S. activities and forces in space, including the monitoring of foreign space activities, are under the jurisdiction of SPACECOM. In addition, in 1999 SPACECOM was given responsibility for DOD computer network defense—monitoring and attempting to stop cyber intrusions.[13]

The Army, Navy, and Air Force Space Commands are the principal components of SPACECOM.

Headquarters: Peterson Air Force Base, Colorado Springs, Colo.

Established: September 1985.

CINC: SPACECOM has always been commanded by an Air Force officer; the current CINC is General Ralph E. Eberhart, USAF.

Special Operations Command (SOCOM): SOCOM directs U.S. Special Forces activities throughout the world through the CINCs of the five geographic unified combatant commands. SOCOM differs from all other unified commands by having major budget planning and manpower management responsibilities that are similar to those of the military services.

Its component commands are:

- Air Force Special Operations Command
- Army Special Operations Command
- Naval Special Warfare Command

Headquarters: MacDill Air Force Base, Tampa, Fla.

Established: April 1987.

CINC: CINCSOCOM has been an Army officer until 2000. The current CINC is General Charles R. Holland, USAF.

Strategic Command (STRATCOM): All U.S. land-based and sea-based strategic forces are assigned to STRATCOM. The Strategic Air Command (SAC), a specified command with only Air Force components, was abolished in 1992, with most of its resources being assigned to the newly formed Strategic Command. Also incorporated into STRATCOM was the Joint Strategic Target Planning Staff (JSTPS), a multiservice agency that planned the laydown of U.S. strategic weapons, and various Navy activities related to strategic missile submarine operations.

(Despite some writers stating that the new U.S. Strategic Command combined the separate Air Force and Navy strategic commands, in fact the Navy never had a strategic command; naval strategic forces—carrier-based aircraft and ballistic missile submarines—were assigned to the Atlantic, Pacific, and European unified commands.)

Headquarters: Offutt Air Force Base, Neb.

Established: June 1992.

CINC: STRATCOM has been headed by both Air Force and Navy officers; the current CINC is Admiral Richard W. Mies, USN.

Transportation Command (TRANSCOM): All U.S. military air and sea transport resources are assigned to TRANSCOM. The component commands are:

- Air Mobility Command (Air Force)
- Military Sealift Command (Navy)
- Military Transportation Management Command (Army)

Headquarters: Scott Air Force Base, Ill.

Established: July 1987.

CINC: TRANSCOM has always been commanded by an Air Force officer; the current CINC is General Tony Robertson, USAF.

In addition to the nine unified commands, there are several sub-unified commands and combined commands that have important roles in U.S. defense strategy. Two of these commands are unique and warrant special attention.

---

12. From March 1947 until July 1952 this position was Commander in Chief Europe (CINCEUR), largely a U.S. Army command and only nominally a unified command.

13. This responsibility previously was assigned to Joint Task Force–Computer Network Defense, established in 1998.

The Navy provides sealift for all of the U.S. military services, mostly through the auspices of the Military Sealift Command. Here the MSC-operated combination container/vehicle ship MAERSK CONSTELLATION (T-AKR 2053) unloads U.S. Army vehicles at a Thai port. (U.S. Navy, JO1 Craig P. Strawser)

U.S. Forces Korea (USFK): U.S. Forces Korea—a subordinate command of PACOM—is the joint headquarters through which U.S. combat forces would be sent to the Combined Forces Command, the bi-national command that has operational control over U.S. and Republic of Korea (ROK) forces in South Korea.

The Commander USFK is a U.S. Army general who is also Commander Combined Forces Command with a four-star ROK Army general as his deputy. Additionally, the Commander USFK serves as the CINC United Nations Command and represents the United Nations Security Council on the Korean peninsula.

North American Aerospace Defense Command (NORAD): The North American Aerospace Defense Command is a bi-national combined command of Canadian and U.S. forces. The command is responsible for aerospace warning and air defense control for North America.

CINCNORAD also serves as the CINC U.S. Space Command.

Under the NORAD agreement, CINCNORAD is responsible through the Canadian Chiefs of Staff and the U.S. Chairman of the JCS and the U.S. National Command Authority.

NORAD's command center is located in Cheyenne Mountain, Colo., an underground base that is the centralized collection facility for the worldwide system of sensors to provide the President of the United States and Prime Minister of Canada with warning of air and space threats to North America.

There were previously several specified commands. The more significant ones were: the Strategic Air Command (SAC) and Military Airlift Command (MAC), both comprised of Air Force personnel; Forces Command, comprised of Army personnel. SAC and MAC (previously Military Air Transport Service) were disestablished in 1992, with most of their components transferred to the new Strategic Command and Transportation Command, respectively; and Naval Forces Eastern Atlantic and Mediterranean (NELM), from 1947 to 1963.

Forces Command (FORCECOM), which was responsible for all U.S. Army forces (active and inactive) in the United States, became the Army's component command of the U.S. Atlantic Command (now Joint Forces Command). Established in July 1987, Forces Command was disestablished as a specified command in 1993.

Historical: The official history of the U.S. Joint Chiefs of Staff states: "The surprise attack [on Pearl Harbor] indicated dramatically the difficulties inherent in coordinating responsibility for defense of the whole Hawaiian area. It likewise made President Roosevelt and his advisors determine that there be no uncertainty as to responsibility for protection of the Panama Canal."[14]

Consequently, on 12 December 1941, in meeting with the President, U.S. military leaders established the first unified commands: all U.S. military forces in the Hawaii area were placed under the Commander in Chief Pacific Fleet and those in the Panama area under the CINC Panama (an Army Air Forces officer).

Subsequent U.S. unified commanders were also Allied commanders with responsibility for directing U.S. and British forces in a specific area (with some other Allied forces being present in some commands). The complexity of strategic bombing operations against Germany (including coordination with the British bombers) and later Japan led to the JCS establishing the U.S. Strategic Air Forces in Europe and U.S. Strategic Air Forces in the Pacific. These were all Army–Air Force commands that were operationally outside the control of the respective Allied commanders and, in reality, the first U.S. specified commands.

After World War II, the military departments tended to direct operations of their forces within specific geographic areas. The 1958 defense reorganization gave the unified commands responsibility for all military forces and operations within a specific area and established specified commands when the component forces were all from one service.

CHAPTER 5

Navy Organization

The Navy's leadership is primarily responsible for developing and preparing forces to fight from the sea. The use of naval forces continues at a high tempo in peacetime operations, as well as in crises and conflicts. Tomahawk cruise missiles—as this one being launched from the cruiser LAKE CHAMPLAIN (CG 57)—have become a "weapon of choice" in recent conflicts. (U.S. Navy)

The primary functions of the Navy and Marine Corps are

To organize, train, equip, and provide Navy and Marine Corps forces for the conduct of prompt and sustained combat incident to operations at sea, including operations of sea-based aircraft and land-based naval air components—specifically, forces to seek out and destroy enemy naval forces and to suppress enemy sea commerce, to gain and maintain general naval supremacy, to control vital sea areas and to protect vital sea lines of communication, to establish and maintain local superiority (including air) in an area of naval operations, to seize and defend advanced naval bases, and to conduct such land, air, and space operations as may be essential to the prosecution of a naval campaign.[1]

The Navy does not directly control operating forces except as specifically assigned by the National Command Authorities, Chairman of the Joint Chiefs of Staff, or Commanders in Chief (CINC) of unified combatant commands (see chapter 4 of this edition of *Ships and Aircraft*).

To carry out the above functions, the Navy is part of a dual command structure: (1) an administrative structure that originates with the Secretary of the Navy and the Chief of Naval Operations,

---

1. Department of Defense Directive 5100.1, "Functions of the Department of Defense and Its Major Components," 25 September 1987. This is the latest

iteration of the "roles and missions" statement originally developed at the so-called Key West conference, chaired by Secretary of Defense James Forrestal, in March 1948.

and (2) an operational structure that originates with the unified CINCs. The administrative structure fulfills the institutional need for civilian control and the balancing of service interests by enabling the Navy to support deployed forces without intervening in combat operations directed by the unified command system. The operational structure relieves the fleet and task force commanders from the administrative and procurement workload that would otherwise distract them from their primary task—the command of combat forces.

The Navy has long had a bilinear organization, with squadron and later fleet commanders and, after 1942, the Chief of Naval Operations exercising military command over the operating forces, and the Secretary of the Navy, through civilian assistants and chiefs of the various bureaus and agencies, directing the business, research and development, procurement, and support activities of the Navy. The responsibility for military command of operating forces subsequently has been transferred to the unified commands.

OPERATIONAL ORGANIZATION

The operating forces of the Navy and Marine Corps—like those of the Army and Air Force—are subordinate to unified combatant commands. Most naval forces are assigned to the naval component commanders of three unified commands; their basic command structure is shown in figure 5-1. All component relationships to their unified combatant commands and own services differ.

Unified command	Naval component	Operating fleet
U.S. Joint Forces Command	Atlantic Fleet	Second Fleet
U.S. Central Command	Naval Forces Central Command	Fifth Fleet
U.S. European Command	Naval Forces Europe	Sixth Fleet
U.S. Pacific Command	Pacific Fleet	Third Fleet
		Seventh Fleet

Figure 5-1
Operational Chain of Command

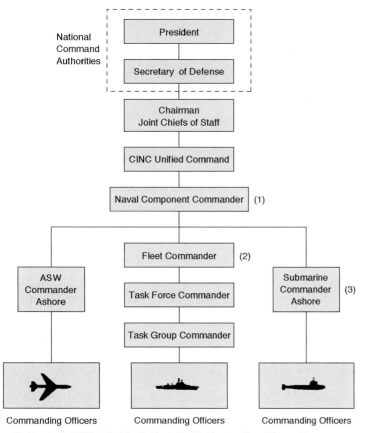

(1) Nominally CINC U.S. Atlantic Fleet, Pacific Fleet, or Naval Forces Europe.
(2) Nominally numbered fleet commander.
(3) Nominally Commander Submarine Force Atlantic Fleet or Submarine Force Pacific Fleet.

Figure 5-2
Fleet Command Structure

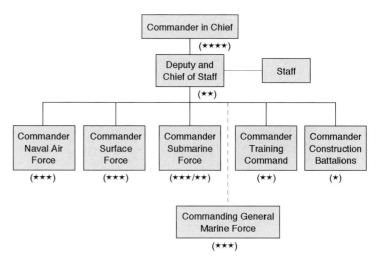

Three naval component commanders are full admirals, while Commander Naval Forces Central Command, who has the additional duty of Commander Fifth Fleet, is a vice admiral; all have shore-based staffs.[2] Several major naval commanders are "double hatted" as NATO commanders.

The Atlantic and Pacific Fleets have similar structures, with subordinate "type" commanders who are responsible for the administration and support of specific ship/aircraft types (see figure 5-2). However, the submarine force commanders additionally are operational commanders. All major type commanders are vice admirals except the Commander Submarine Force Pacific Fleet, who is a rear admiral.

Atlantic Fleet: The CINC Atlantic Fleet functions in both the administrative and tactical chains of command. Until 1986, the position of CINC Atlantic Fleet was an additional duty of the CINC Atlantic Command (who was additionally the NATO Supreme Allied Commander Atlantic). Secretary of the Navy John Lehman separated the command and fleet positions to establish an additional four-star position for flag officers. The Second Fleet is the major operational component of the Atlantic Fleet.

Headquarters: Norfolk, Va.

Pacific Fleet: Like the CINC Atlantic Fleet, the CINC Pacific Fleet functions in both the administrative and operational chains of command. In the latter role (as a naval component commander), he is responsible for naval operations in the Pacific–Indian Ocean areas. The principal operating commands are the Third Fleet and Seventh Fleet.

Headquarters: Pearl Harbor, Hawaii.

Naval Forces Central Command: The Commander Naval Forces Central Command is the naval component commander of CENTCOM, responsible for naval activities in the Arabian Sea, Persian Gulf, Red Sea, and portions of the Indian Ocean. Previously, the Commander Middle East Force, a rear admiral, commanded naval forces in the area under the aegis of CENTCOM. During the 1990–1991 naval buildup and conflict in the Gulf, the Commander Seventh Fleet exercised command of naval forces in the region as the CINCENT naval component commander.

The naval component commander was upgraded to vice admiral in 1992 and additionally designated as the Commander Fifth Fleet in 1995 (see below). The Deputy Commander Naval Forces Central Command, a rear admiral, is at CENTCOM headquarters at MacDill Air Force Base, near Tampa, Fla.

Headquarters: Bahrain.

2. All active duty U.S. Navy admirals and Marine Corps generals are listed, along with their current positions, in the annual May issue of the U.S. Naval Institute *Proceedings* (Naval Review issue) and the annual January issue of *Sea★Power* (Navy League of the United States).

Left: Richard Danzig, Secretary of the Navy since November 1998 (Department of Defense)
Right: Admiral Vernon E. Clark, Chief of Naval Operations since July 2000 (U.S. Navy)

Naval Forces Europe: The CINC Naval Forces Europe is responsible for U.S. naval operations in the European area, especially the Sixth Fleet in the Mediterranean Sea. The CINC simultaneously holds the NATO position of CINC Allied Forces Southern Europe, responsible to the NATO Supreme Allied Commander Europe.

The CINC Naval Forces Europe does not have administrative responsibilities for support of U.S. naval forces in Europe, those functions being under the cognizance of the CINC Atlantic Fleet.

Headquarters: Naples, Italy.

The numbered fleet commanders are vice admirals. Their staffs are normally "split" between the fleet flagship and a component ashore.

Second Fleet: Operating in the Atlantic area, the Second Fleet serves as the NATO strike force, is responsible for anti-submarine operations in the Atlantic, and, increasingly, has operational requirements in the Caribbean area and off Central America. Most ships of the Second Fleet rotate at regular intervals to the Sixth Fleet in the Mediterranean and to the Fifth Fleet in the Persian Gulf area.

Fleet headquarters: Norfolk, Va.
Flagship: MOUNT WHITNEY (LCC 20).

Third Fleet: The Third Fleet operates in the Eastern Pacific and rotates ships to the Seventh Fleet in the Western Pacific–Indian Ocean areas and to the Fifth Fleet. The Third Fleet originally had an anti-submarine orientation, derived from its origins as Anti-Submarine Force Pacific. The growth of Soviet naval capabilities in the Pacific during the 1980s led to an increase in carrier battle force operations in the Third Fleet, with regular North Pacific operations, some within air strike range of Russian bases in Siberia.

Fleet headquarters: Naval Air Station North Island (San Diego), Calif. (Fleet headquarters were shifted from Ford Island in Pearl Harbor to San Diego in August 1991.)

Flagship: CORONADO (AGF 11).

Fifth Fleet: The Commander Naval Forces CENTCOM (NAVCENT) is additionally the Commander Fifth Fleet, that position having been established on 1 July 1995. The fleet has no ships permanently assigned; rather, ships from other fleets that deploy into the area are assigned to the Fifth Fleet. There are up to 15 active Navy/MSC ships in the CENTCOM area at any given time, plus about 25 maritime prepositioning ships and four mine countermeasures ships.

Various task forces are activated within Fifth Fleet, depending upon the ships in the area. For example, Task Force (TF) 50 (Naval Expeditionary Force) is activated when a Carrier Battle Group (CVBG) and Amphibious Ready Group (ARG) are in the area; TF 51 (Amphibious Force) is activated when there is an ARG but no carrier in the area. The normal commanders of these forces retain command, but are additionally assigned to the Fifth Fleet.

Commander TF 53 (Logistics Force) has a permanent staff at Bahrain. He also serves as Commander Service Force for NAVCENT and has control of all underway replenishment ships, tenders, tugs, and the MPS/APF ships in the area.

Four mine countermeasures ships are now homeported at Mina' Sulman, Bahrain. Their crews are rotated from the United States by air every six months. The LA SALLE (AGF 3) previously was flagship of Commander Middle East Force, based at Mina' Sulman.

Headquarters: Bahrain.

Sixth Fleet: The Sixth Fleet operates in the Mediterranean and Black Seas and has both U.S. and NATO responsibilities, the latter as the NATO Striking and Support Forces, Southern Europe. Several NATO allies provide direct support to the Sixth Fleet in terms of shore bases and ASW and reconnaissance forces.

A submarine tender and the fleet flagship are homeported in the Mediterranean, the SIMON LAKE (AS 33) at La Maddalena, Italy, and the LA SALLE at Gaeta, Italy. Most Sixth Fleet ships and aircraft squadrons are on rotation from the Atlantic Fleet; those units normally spend six months in transit and operating in the Mediterranean and Persian Gulf areas, and 12 months in their home port and in Atlantic operations.

Fleet headquarters: Gaeta, Italy.
Fleet flagship: LA SALLE.

Seventh Fleet: The Seventh Fleet has broad responsibilities for naval operations in the Western Pacific and Indian Ocean areas—from the Kamchatka Peninsula of Russian Siberia to the Indian Ocean. Thus the Seventh Fleet has complex and wide-ranging mission requirements with only limited allied support available. The aircraft carrier KITTY HAWK (CV 63), a cruiser-destroyer group, an amphibious group, and two mine countermeasures ships are homeported in Japan.

During the Persian Gulf operations of 1990–1991 (Operations Desert Shield/Desert Storm), the Commander Seventh Fleet became the naval component commander for Central Command.

Fleet headquarters: Yokosuka, Japan.
Flagship: BLUE RIDGE (LCC 19).

Historical: The U.S. Navy's numbered fleets were established from 1942 onward within the U.S. Atlantic and Pacific Fleets. Those in the Atlantic–Mediterranean area were given even numbers; those in the Pacific area received odd numbers. The U.S. numbered fleets were:

First Fleet: Established as the First Task Fleet in 1947 in the Eastern Pacific; changed to the First Fleet in 1950. The fleet was disestablished in 1973.

Second Fleet: Established as the Second Task Fleet in 1947 for operations in the North Atlantic; changed to Second Fleet in 1950.

Third Fleet: Established in 1943 for operations in the Western Pacific. The Third Fleet and the Fifth Fleet generally shared the same naval forces; while one fleet commander and his staff were at sea operating against the Japanese, the other commander and staff would be ashore at Pearl Harbor planning the next operation. The fleet was disestablished in 1946. The Third Fleet was reestablished in 1973 for operations in the Eastern Pacific, the initial staff and operating components being based on Anti-Submarine Force Pacific.

Fourth Fleet: The former U.S. South Atlantic Force, as renamed in 1943. It was disestablished in 1946.

Fifth Fleet: Established in 1944 for operations in the Western Pacific. Disestablished in 1946, the Fifth Fleet was reestablished in 1995 for operations in the Persian Gulf–Indian Ocean area.

Sixth Fleet: Established as the Sixth Task Fleet in 1948 for operations in the Mediterranean; changed to Sixth Fleet in 1950.

Seventh Fleet: The Seventh Fleet was formed in 1943 to provide naval support to operations by General Douglas MacArthur (and called "MacArthur's Navy"). From 1949 to 1950, it was designated the Seventh Task Fleet, after which it was renamed the Seventh Fleet.

Eighth Fleet: Established in 1943 to conduct operations in the Mediterranean; disestablished in 1946.

Ninth Fleet: Designation not used.

Tenth Fleet: A "paper" fleet established on 20 May 1943 in the Navy Department to coordinate anti-submarine warfare under the

The Navy supports a variety of nonmilitary activities. Here divers from Navy Mobile Diving Salvage Unit 2 are briefed aboard the USS GRAPPLE (ARS 53) before diving at the site of a civil airliner crash. (U.S. Navy, PH1 Todd P. Cichonowicz)

direct command of the Chief of Naval Operations and CINC U.S. Fleet, Admiral Ernest J. King.[3]

Eleventh Fleet: Designation not used.

Twelfth Fleet: Established in 1943, with headquarters in London, as the U.S. Navy's planning staff for European operations; disestablished in 1946.

ADMINISTRATIVE ORGANIZATION

The administrative organization of the Navy begins with the Secretary of Defense and then proceeds through the Secretary of the Navy and the Chief of Naval Operations (CNO), as shown in simplified form in figure 5-3. The CNO is "double hatted" as both the uniformed head of the Navy and a member of the Joint Chiefs of Staff.

The Secretary of the Navy and the CNO—as the uniformed head of the Navy—are essentially managers with the task of supporting unified commanders. They are responsible for logistics, personnel management, procurement and maintenance of naval systems and supplies, and research and development.

To accomplish these tasks, the Secretary and the CNO each have staff organizations, with the Secretary's mostly comprised of civilians and the CNO's mostly of naval personnel. The Secretary of the Navy (SECNAV) organization is shown in figure 5-4; several active-duty naval officers hold positions within the SECNAV organization.[4]

The SECNAV officials listed in figure 5-4 handle Marine Corps as well as Navy matters within their areas of responsibility. With the

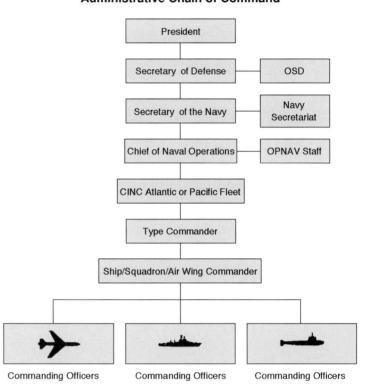

Figure 5-3

Administrative Chain of Command

CNO and his staff, these SECNAV officials are jointly responsible for the administration of numerous commands of the shore establishment; the principal commands, all headed by naval officers, are:

- Bureau of Medicine and Surgery* (★★★)
- Bureau of Naval Personnel* (★★★)
- Naval Air Systems Command (★★★)
- Naval Data Automation Command (captain)
- Naval Doctrine Command (★★)
- Naval Education and Training Command* (★★★)
- Naval Facilities Engineering Command (★)
- Naval Intelligence Command (★)
- Naval Legal Service Command (★★)
- Naval Meteorology and Oceanography Command (★)
- Naval Safety Center (★★)
- Naval Sea Systems Command (★★★)
- Naval Security Group Command (★★)
- Naval Space Command (★)
- Naval Supply Systems Command (★★)
- Naval Telecommunications Command (captain)
- Navy Recruiting Command (★)
- Space and Naval Warfare Systems Command (★★)

The commanders of three of these commands—indicated by asterisks—are "double hatted" on the staff of the Chief of Naval Operations as N093, N1, and N7, respectively (see below). The Naval Space Command also serves as the naval component of the U.S. Space Command and is thus an operational as well as administrative organization.

The Chief of Naval Operations has several deputies and assistants and a large staff historically known as the Office of the Chief of Naval Operations (OPNAV). The most far-reaching reorganization of the U.S. Navy headquarters in almost 50 years, announced on 22 July 1992, changed the OPNAV staff in an effort to downgrade the so-called "platform barons," the vice admirals who directed the submarine, surface, and air "communities" or "unions." The reorganization also eliminated several flag billets, including four vice admirals, and reduced the size of the headquarters staff by about 150 military and civilian positions.

In fall 2000 the CNO initiated a major restructuring of the OPNAV staff (see Addenda). The following discussion reflects the existing structure on the eve of those changes.

---

3. The Battle of the Atlantic was essentially won in May 1943, almost simultaneous with setting up the Tenth Fleet. The delay was caused largely by Admiral King wishing to keep direct control of the U.S. anti-submarine campaign and the bitter controversy between the Army Air Forces and the Navy over the control of land-based anti-submarine aircraft.

4. The rank of military incumbents are shown: ★ = rear admiral (lower half); ★★ = rear admiral; ★★★ = vice admiral; ★★★★ = admiral.

Figure 5-4

Office of the Secretary of the Navy

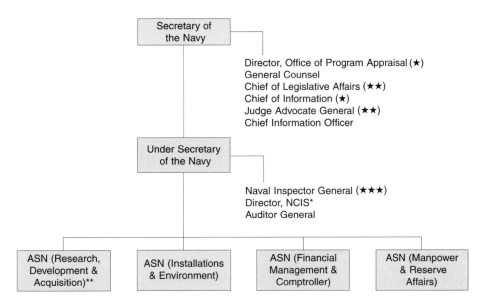

* NCIS = Naval Criminal Investigation Service
** ASN = Assistant Secretary of the Navy

These changes were made, according to the Navy's statement to Congress, because

the dramatic changes that have taken place and are continuing to take place in the world situation have dictated a reduction in the force structure of the U.S. Navy. This reduction also requires that the Navy review how its command and administrative structure is organized. Navy leadership has recognized for some time the need to have a tighter, leaner headquarters organization, better tailored and coordinated to deal with [the Department of Defense] and [Joint Chiefs of Staff] as well as operational staffs.[5]

However, the reorganization reflected a long-standing desire by Department of Defense officials, as well as senior Army and Air Force officers, to bring the Navy's executive staff "into line" with the other services. The new organization more closely aligns the Navy with the Staff of the Chairman of the Joint Chiefs of Staff, as well as the other services. The principal subordinates to the Chief of Naval Operations and their N-series OPNAV codes are shown in figure 5-5.

As a result of the reorganization, ten major divisions now exist within the N8 organization:

N80   Programming Division (★★)
N81   Assessment Division (★★)
N82   Fiscal Management Division (★)
N83   Commander in Chief Liaison Division (★)
N84   ASW Requirements Division (★★)
N85   Expeditionary Warfare Division (USMC ★★)
N86   Surface Warfare Division (★★)
N87   Submarine Warfare Division (★★)
N88   Air Warfare Division (★★)
N89   Special Warfare Division (★)

The earlier system of platform barons, who sought to control their respective communities as fiefdoms, dates to August 1943, when the Deputy CNO for Air was established with responsibility for "the preparation, readiness, and logistic support" of naval aviation. Surface and submarine warfare matters were directed by a single Deputy CNO, who also had general sponsorship responsibilities for aviation ships. However, in 1971, pleading for "equality" by Admiral H. G. Rickover, the head of naval nuclear

propulsion from 1948 until 1992, and the submarine community led the CNO, Admiral Elmo R. Zumwalt, to establish a separate Deputy CNO (OP-02) for submarine warfare in 1971. Zumwalt believed that "setting up the DCNO for Submarines made it easier to deal with the submarine community and with Rickover." This move, in turn, led to OP-03 becoming the Deputy CNO for surface warfare and initiated two decades of intra-Navy or "union" competition as the platform barons competed for resources, political position, and even flag billets. Beyond the competitive aspects of this arrangement, it was easy for non-platform specific programs, such as mine warfare, to "fall through the cracks"—that is, to become lost or underfunded.

Secretary of the Navy Sean O'Keefe, in announcing the 1992 organizational changes, stressed, "One of my primary concerns is ending rivalries and jealousies between the various key warfare fighting communities in the Navy. . . . We believe there can be no jealousy among the fingers of a strong fist. This Navy reorganization will begin the process of bringing our warfare fighters together into a tighter, stronger fist."[6]

Unfortunately, the 1992 reorganization missed opportunities to return anti-submarine warfare programs and mine warfare programs to a realistic staff level, especially when one considers their increasing importance for potential operations in littoral areas. They should have been placed at the same level within N8 as the air, surface, and subsurface offices.

Historical: The first American naval vessel was the schooner HANNAH, which sailed on orders from General George Washington in early September 1775. The HANNAH and other vessels, manned by sailors from the maritime areas of the colonies, particularly Salem, Marblehead, and Beverly, were intended to embarrass the British and capture gunpowder for use by Washington's own forces.[7]

The Continental Navy was founded on 13 October 1775 when the Continental Congress established a naval committee to acquire and fit out vessels for sea and to write appropriate regulations. The following month, the committee purchased two sailing ships and two brigs, and, subsequently, two sloops and two schooners. Esek Hopkins, brother

---

5. Memorandum from Capt. J. R. McCleary, USN, subject: "Reorganization of the Naval Headquarters Staff," 22 July 1992.

6. Press conference at the Pentagon, 22 July 1992.
7. The best single-volume history of the U.S. Navy is *Sea Power: A Naval History* by E. B. Potter and Fleet Adm. Chester W. Nimitz, USN (Annapolis, Md.: Naval Institute Press, 1981).

Figure 5-5

Office of the Chief of Naval Operations

```
                        Chief of Naval
                         Operations
                          (★★★★)              Director, Navy Staff (★)

                           Vice CNO
                           (★★★★)

  Director of Test &    Surgeon      Director of                      Chief
  Evaluation &          General of   Naval        Oceanographer       of
  Technology            the Navy     Reserve      of the Navy         Chaplains
  Requirements (N091)   (N093)       (N095)       (N096)              (N097)
       (★)             (★★★)        (★★)         (★★)                (★)

            DCNO Manpower    Director of    DCNO Plans,      DCNO
            & Personnel      Naval          Policy &         Logistics
            (N1)*            Intelligence   Operations       (N4)
                             (N2)           (N3/N5)
            (★★★)           (★)           (★★★)           (★★★)

                Director, Space        Director,        DCNO Resources,
                Information Warfare,    Naval Training   Warfare
                Command &              (N7)             Requirements &
                Control (N6)                            Assessments (N8)
                   (★★★)               (★★★)           (★★★)
```

* DCNO = Deputy Chief of Naval Operations

of the Rhode Island member of the Naval Committee, was appointed Commander in Chief of the Fleet.

When the American Revolution ended in 1783, the central government saw no need for a fleet and had no means to fund one. By 1785 all U.S. warships had been disposed of. The War Department handled all "naval" matters during this period.

Events of the early 1790s demonstrated a need for a fleet and the Navy Act of 27 May 1794 provided for the acquisition of six frigates. Each frigate was constructed in a separate port:[8]

Ship	Launched	Builder
CHESAPEAKE (36 guns)	1799	Norfolk, Va.[9]
CONGRESS (36 guns)	1799	Portsmouth, N.H.
CONSTELLATION (36 guns)	1797	Baltimore, Md.
CONSTITUTION (44 guns)	1797	Boston, Mass.
PRESIDENT (44 guns)	1799	New York, N.Y.
UNITED STATES (44 guns)	1797	Philadelphia, Pa.

(The CONSTITUTION survives, in active commission, at the Charlestown Naval Shipyard, Boston; see chapter 22.)

The Navy Department was formally established by Act of Congress on 30 April 1798 and the first Secretary of the Navy was Benjamin Stoddart, installed on 18 June 1798. As originally established, the Secretary of the Navy exercised direct control over the Navy's shore establishment, as well as the operating forces.

From 1842 onward, Congress established a series of bureaus to provide effective procurement of ships and supplies, to manage personnel, and to operate shore activities. These bureaus, commanded by naval officers, also reported directly to the Secretary of the Navy. This organizational concept continues today, with the original bureaus having evolved into the modern systems commands and bureaus. However, the systems commands and bureaus now report directly to the Secretary of the Navy *and* the Chief of Naval Operations.

8. These ships are best described in Howard I. Chapelle's *The History of The American Sailing Navy: The Ships and Their Design* (New York: Bonanza Books, 1949).
9. At the time, called Gosport.

The position of Aide for Operations was established in 1890 to provide a flag officer (rear admiral) on the staff of the Secretary of the Navy. He was responsible for ship operations as well as training, planning, intelligence, and logistics and for recommending officer appointments. In 1915, as a result of the war in Europe, the position was changed to Chief of Naval Operations with the rank of full admiral, the first appointee being Admiral William S. Benson.

However, the Aide for Operations and, subsequently, CNO did not direct naval forces afloat. Rather, various squadron and, from 1906, fleet commanders exercised command of ships, with their commands based on geographic areas. In 1919 the position of Commander in Chief U.S. Fleet (CINCUS) was established as the overall commander of U.S. naval forces afloat. The CINCUS—pronounced *SINK*-us—reported to the Secretary of the Navy independent of the Chief of Naval Operations.

The positions of CNO and CINCUS remained separate until Admiral Ernest J. King, who had become Commander in Chief U.S. Fleet in December 1941, was additionally named Chief of Naval Operations in March 1942. From that time on, the CNO had de facto command of operational forces afloat in addition to being the Navy member of the Joint Chiefs of Staff. The position of Commander in Chief U.S. Fleet (whose acronym King had changed to COMINCH—pronounced com-*INCH*) was abolished in October 1945, shortly after World War II.

There have been continual organizational changes within the Navy. Among the more significant, in 1963 the separate technical bureaus were incorporated under a central Naval Material Command headed by the Chief of Naval Material (a full admiral). This had the effect of increasing the influence of the CNO over the bureaus. In 1966 the Secretary of the Navy placed the Naval Material Command (and their subordinate system commands) directly under the CNO, giving him full responsibility for material, personnel, and medical support of the operating forces. Also in this period, the technical bureaus were redesignated as systems commands—air, ship, ordnance, electronic, supply, and so forth.

The intermediate administrative organization of the Naval Material Command was abolished in 1985 by Secretary of the Navy

Sailors prepare to work the flight deck as an F-14 Tomcat lands aboard the Carl Vinson (CVN 70) while the carrier steams in the Persian Gulf. The Navy's activities are worldwide, afloat and ashore. Warships such as the Vinson must be supported by a large training and logistics infrastructure. (U.S. Navy, PHAN Jose Codero)

Lehman. Under his revisions, the Secretary and the CNO exercise joint direction of the existing systems commands (the Naval Air Systems Command, Naval Sea Systems Command, Space and Naval Warfare Systems Command, Naval Facilities Engineering Command, and Naval Supply Systems Command).

The Bureau of Naval Personnel and Bureau of Medicine and Surgery had remained outside of the Naval Material Command. Those bureaus survived with those titles until they were renamed, respectively, the Naval Military Personnel Command in 1978 and the

Naval Medical Command in 1982. Those awkward and bureaucratic titles survived only until 1989, when the traditional bureau names were restored to the two organizations.[10]

----

10. The Bureau of Personnel was created in October 1942, evolving from the Bureau of Navigation (1862) and its predecessor, the Bureau of Ordnance and Hydrography (1842); the Bureau of Medicine and Surgery was one of the five bureaus originally established by Congress in 1842.

Major U.S. Navy–Marine Corps Installations

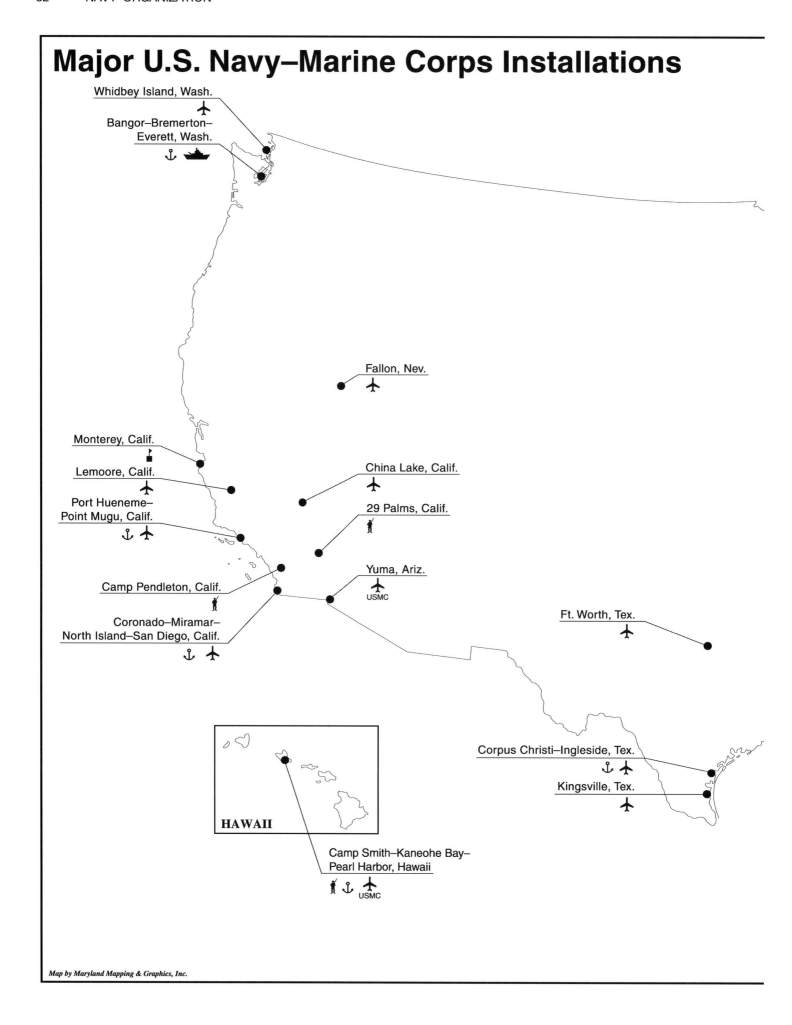

Whidbey Island, Wash.

Bangor–Bremerton–
Everett, Wash.

Fallon, Nev.

Monterey, Calif.

Lemoore, Calif.

China Lake, Calif.

Port Hueneme–
Point Mugu, Calif.

29 Palms, Calif.

Yuma, Ariz.
USMC

Ft. Worth, Tex.

Camp Pendleton, Calif.

Coronado–Miramar–
North Island–San Diego, Calif.

Corpus Christi–Ingleside, Tex.

Kingsville, Tex.

HAWAII

Camp Smith–Kaneohe Bay–
Pearl Harbor, Hawaii
USMC

Map by Maryland Mapping & Graphics, Inc.

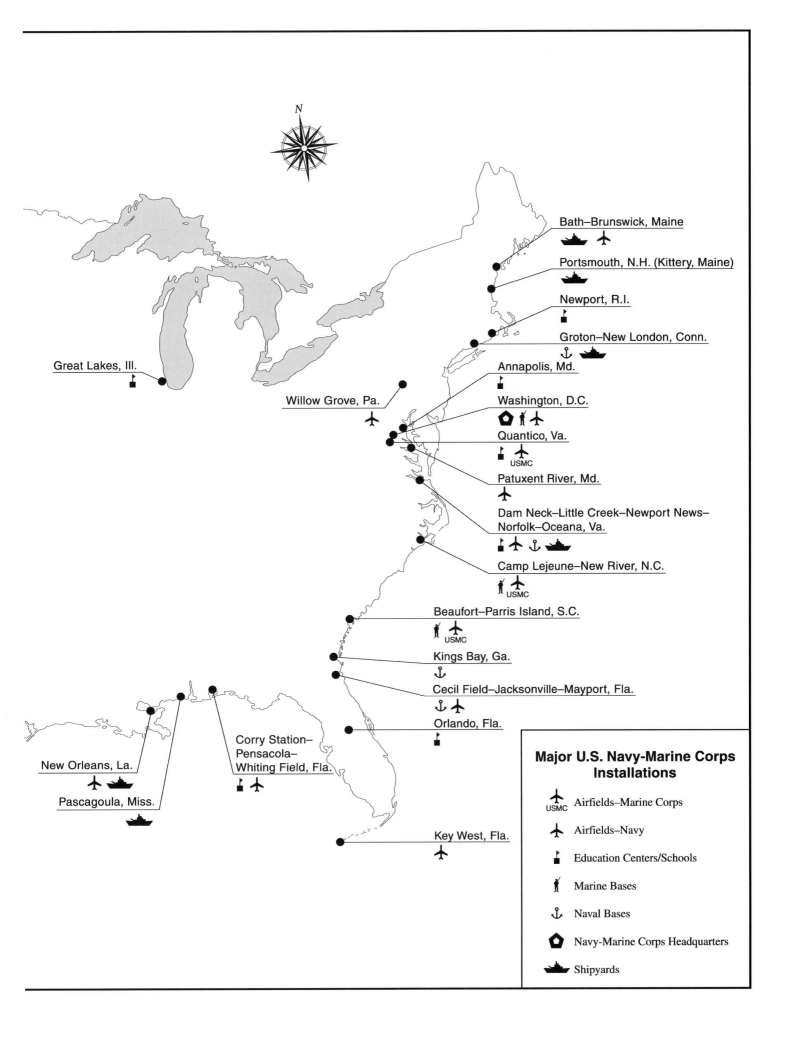

Bath–Brunswick, Maine

Portsmouth, N.H. (Kittery, Maine)

Newport, R.I.

Groton–New London, Conn.

Great Lakes, Ill.

Annapolis, Md.

Willow Grove, Pa.

Washington, D.C.

Quantico, Va.

Patuxent River, Md.

Dam Neck–Little Creek–Newport News–
Norfolk–Oceana, Va.

Camp Lejeune–New River, N.C.

Beaufort–Parris Island, S.C.

Kings Bay, Ga.

Cecil Field–Jacksonville–Mayport, Fla.

Orlando, Fla.

New Orleans, La.

Corry Station–
Pensacola–
Whiting Field, Fla.

Pascagoula, Miss.

Key West, Fla.

**Major U.S. Navy-Marine Corps
Installations**

Airfields–Marine Corps

Airfields–Navy

Education Centers/Schools

Marine Bases

Naval Bases

Navy-Marine Corps Headquarters

Shipyards

CHAPTER 6

Fleet Organization

Different types of naval forces are organized into battle groups, task forces, and fleets. Here the cruiser VINCENNES (CG 49), the destroyers JOHN S. McCAIN (DDG 56) and JOHN CUSHING (DD 985), and the frigate GARY (FFG 51) form a Pacific Fleet "destroyer squadron." The organization of the Atlantic and Pacific Fleets differs considerably, as does that of their components. (U.S. Navy, PH1 Wade McKinnon)

The Navy fleet organization continues to change in the wake of the reduction in air, surface, and submarine forces in the aftermath of the Cold War. Major revisions were made in 1995, developed from the earlier efforts to develop "permanent" carrier battle groups.

As noted in chapter 5 of this edition of *Ships and Aircraft*, all naval forces are assigned to both administrative and operational commands. However, within the new fleet structures, the distinction is becoming blurred. For example, the carrier battle group commander is responsible for both the "workup" and training of his force as well as its forward (overseas) deployment. Similarly, an attempt is made to keep destroyer squadrons together for both workup and deployment. Note that the organizational concept of "destroyer squadron" is ambiguous, with such units being comprised of combinations of cruisers, destroyers, and frigates.

Carrier-based squadrons are assigned to air wings when deployed aboard ship, but to aviation "type" commanders when ashore.

Each battle group nominally consists of an aircraft carrier and two missile cruisers, all located at the same base when possible. However, this is less frequently done as the size of the fleet is reduced; for example, the group staff for Carrier Group 7—the JOHN C. STENNIS (CVN 74) battle group—is at North Island, Calif., while the carrier and one cruiser are homeported at San Diego and the other cruiser is homeported at Pearl Harbor, Hawaii. During pre-deployment workup and training, a destroyer squadron—normally four ships—will join up with the core battle-group elements. From that point on, this seven-ship battle group, along with submarines, if assigned, will train and deploy together. Some carrier battle groups are commanded by the surface warfare admiral in command of a cruiser-destroyer group.

The operational organizations are based primarily on task forces/groups. The Task Force (TF) and Task Group (TG) organizations listed in this chapter under the commanders in chief of the Atlantic and Pacific Fleets are mainly for contingency opera-

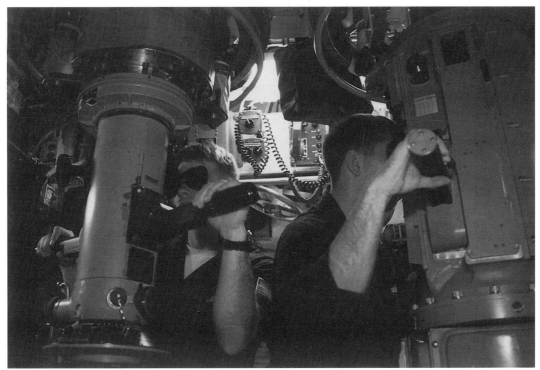

Submarines have been extensively integrated into fleets and battle groups in the post–Cold War period. Most carrier battle groups operate with two attack submarines. An electronics technician *(left)* and officer man the periscopes of the Tucson (SSN 770) as the submarine operates in restricted waters. (U.S. Navy, PH2 Jeffrey S. Viano)

tions; exceptions include the respective submarine force commanders, who have both operational and administrative roles. TF organizations are employed for exercises, for forward deployment operations, and in war.

Naval administrative organizations are asymmetrical; the hierarchy, organization, and composition of units vary within the fleets and from fleet to fleet. Major organizational changes are taking place in the mid-1990s as the size of the active fleet is reduced and organizations are realigned. Ship squadrons that do not have ships assigned are usually operational command staffs that control forward-deployed task forces or groups or training workups.

The Western Hemisphere Group of the Atlantic Fleet, established in 1995, deploys ships for four- and five-month operations, such as Caribbean operations and the South American training cruise UNITAS.

The following tables provide a breakdown of naval organizations and nominal ship assignments as of 2000. Ships assigned to type commanders are indicated under the administrative organizations. Such assignments change regularly as new ships are commissioned, older ships are stricken, and ships are reassigned for overhaul or modernization. Specific aircraft carriers and fleet flagships are identified. The fleet flagships (⚓) are listed under their administrative commands; see chapter 17 for operational details.

The ships listed are active unless indicated as Naval Reserve Force (NRF) ships. Headquarters locations or flagship home ports are indicated, although all ships of a command may not be at the same port. Some ships listed here are under construction but are close enough to completion to warrant their fleet assignment. Note that major Atlantic Fleet units generally have even numbers and Pacific Fleet units use odd numbers.

In the summer of 1992, "permanent" organizations were instituted for the battle groups of the Atlantic and Pacific Fleets. These were to be "transparent" battle groups in the contemporary vernacular, all with essentially the same composition and capabilities, intended to be easily shifted from one unified command to another. Each of the battle groups nominally consisted of one carrier with an embarked carrier air wing; cruisers, destroyers, and frigates; and two attack submarines. The initial compositions of these battle groups as they were established may be found in the 15th Edition/page 36. Those assigned quickly changed as older ships were retired earlier than expected. The current battle group assignments are listed below.

The Marine Force organizations are described in chapter 7 and the naval aviation organization (air wings and squadrons) is provided in chapter 26.

Notes are listed at the end of this chapter.

PACIFIC FLEET

TF 10	Temporary Operations Force
TF 11	Training Force
TF 12	Anti-Submarine Force
TF 14	Submarine Force
TF 15	Surface Force
TF 16	Maritime Defense Zone[1]
TF 17	Naval Air Force
TF 18	Sealift Forces
TF 19	Fleet Marine Force[2]
TF 91	Naval Forces Alaska

THIRD FLEET

TF 30	Battle Force
TF 31	Command and Coordination Force
TF 32	Ready Force
TF 33	Combat Logistics Support Force
TF 34	Submarine Force
TF 35	Surface Combatant Force
TF 36	Amphibious Force
TF 37	Carrier Strike Force
TF 39	Landing Force[2]

SEVENTH FLEET

TF 70	Battle Force
TF 71	Command and Coordination Force
TF 72	Patrol and Reconnaissance Force
TF 74	Submarine Force
TF 75	Surface Combatant Force
TF 76	Amphibious Force
TF 79	Landing Force[2]

CARRIER BATTLE GROUPS

Carrier Group 1	North Island, Calif.
Carrier Group 3	Alameda, Calif.
CVN Abraham Lincoln	Bremerton, Wash.
2 CG	San Diego, Calif.

PACIFIC FLEET (continued)

Carrier Group 5	Yokosuka, Japan
CV Kitty Hawk	Yokosuka, Japan
3 CG	Yokosuka, Japan
Carrier Group 7	North Island, Calif.
CVN John C. Stennis	San Diego, Calif.
1 CG	San Diego, Calif.
1 CG	Pearl Harbor, Hawaii
Cruiser-Destroyer Group 1	San Diego, Calif.
CV Constellation	San Diego, Calif.
2 CG	Pearl Harbor, Hawaii
Cruiser-Destroyer Group 3	San Diego, Calif.
CVN Abraham Lincoln	Everett, Wash.
3 CG	San Diego, Calif.
Cruiser-Destroyer Group 5	San Diego, Calif.
CVN Nimitz	North Island, Calif.
1 CG	San Diego, Calif.

NAVAL AIR FORCE PACIFIC	North Island, Calif.
Carrier Air Wing 2	Miramar, Calif.
Carrier Air Wing 5	Yokosuka, Japan
Carrier Air Wing 9	Lemoore, Calif.
Carrier Air Wing 11	Miramar, Calif.
Carrier Air Wing 14	Miramar, Calif.
Helicopter Tactical Wing	North Island, Calif.
Sea Control Wing	North Island, Calif.
Helicopter Anti-Submarine Wing	North Island, Calif.
Helicopter Anti-Submarine Light Wing	North Island, Calif.
Airborne Early Warning Wing	Miramar, Calif.
Strike Fighter Wing Pacific	Lemoore, Calif.
Patrol and Reconnaissance Force	Kaneohe Bay, Hawaii
PATRECONWING-1	Kamiseya, Japan
PATRECONWING-10	Whidbey Island, Wash.
Electronic Combat Wing	Whidbey Island, Wash.
Strategic Communications Wing 1	Tinker AFB, Okla.
Fleet Air Western Pacific	Atsugi, Japan

Note: Commander Naval Air Force Pacific has administrative control over the aircraft carriers listed with Carrier Battle Groups.

NAVAL SURFACE FORCE PACIFIC	Coronado (San Diego), Calif.
Amphibious Group 1	White Beach, Okinawa
LCC Blue Ridge (⚑ Seventh Fleet)	Yokosuka, Japan
Amphibious Squadron 11	Sasebo, Japan
1 LHA	Sasebo, Japan
1 LPD	Sasebo, Japan
2 LSD	Sasebo, Japan
2 MCM	Sasebo, Japan
Amphibious Group 3	San Diego, Calif.
AGF Coronado (⚑ Third Fleet)	San Diego, Calif.
2 LHA	San Diego, Calif.
2 LHD	San Diego, Calif.
4 LPD	San Diego, Calif.
6 LSD	San Diego, Calif.
Naval Beach Group 1	Coronado, Calif.
Amphibious Construction Battalion 1	Coronado, Calif.
Assault Craft Units 1 and 5	Coronado, Calif.
Beachmaster Unit 1	Coronado, Calif.
Destroyer Squadron 9	Everett, Wash.
1 DDG	Everett, Wash.
3 DD	Everett, Wash.
4 FFG	Everett, Wash.
Destroyer Squadron 15	Yokosuka, Japan
2 DDG	Yokosuka, Japan
2 DD	Yokosuka, Japan
2 FFG	Yokosuka, Japan
Destroyer Squadron 17	San Diego, Calif.
Destroyer Squadron 21	San Diego, Calif.
1 DDG	San Diego, Calif.
1 DD	San Diego, Calif.
3 FFG	San Diego, Calif.
Destroyer Squadron 23	San Diego, Calif.
2 DDG	San Diego, Calif.
3 DD	San Diego, Calif.
1 FFG	San Diego, Calif.

Destroyer Squadron 31	Pearl Harbor, Hawaii
3 DDG	Pearl Harbor, Hawaii
1 DD	Pearl Harbor, Hawaii
2 FFG	Pearl Harbor, Hawaii
Logistic Group Western Pacific	Singapore
Surface Group Pacific Northwest	Everett, Wash.
1 AE	Everett, Wash.
3 AOE	Everett, Wash.
Naval Surface Group Mid-Pacific	Pearl Harbor, Hawaii
2 AO	Pearl Harbor, Hawaii
2 ARS	Pearl Harbor, Hawaii
1 LST (NRF)	Pearl Harbor, Hawaii

Note: Commander Naval Surface Force Pacific has administrative control over the surface combatants listed with Carrier Battle Groups.

SUBMARINE FORCE PACIFIC	PearlHarbor,Hawaii
Submarine Development Group 5	San Diego, Calif.
1 SSN	Bangor, Wash.
1 AGSS	San Diego, Calif.
2 DSRV (submersibles)	North Island, Calif.
1 DSV (submersibles)	San Diego, Calif.
Submarine Group 7	Yokosuka, Japan
1 AS	Guam
Submarine Group 9	Bangor, Wash.
Submarine Squadron 1	Pearl Harbor, Hawaii
7 SSN	Pearl Harbor, Hawaii
Submarine Squadron 3	Pearl Harbor, Hawaii
8 SSN	Pearl Harbor, Hawaii
Submarine Squadron 7	Pearl Harbor, Hawaii
8 SSN 3	Pearl Harbor, Hawaii
Submarine Squadron 11	San Diego, Calif.
7 SSN	San Diego, Calif.
1 ARDM	San Diego, Calif.
Submarine Squadron 17	Bangor, Wash.
8 SSBN	Bangor, Wash.

TRAINING COMMAND PACIFIC	San Diego, Calif.

3RD NAVAL CONSTRUCTION BRIGADE	Pearl Harbor, Hawaii
Mobile Construction Battalions 3, 4, 5, and 40	Port Hueneme, Calif.
Underwater Construction Team 2	Port Hueneme, Calif.

ATLANTIC FLEET

TF 40	Naval Surface Force	
TF 41	Naval Air Force	
TF 42	Submarine Force	
TF 43	Training Command	
TF 44	Coast Guard Forces[1]	
TF 45	Marine Force[2]	
TF 46	Mine Warfare Force	
TF 47	Naval Construction Battalions	
TF 49	Poseidon Operational Test Force	
TF 80	Naval Patrol and Protection of Shipping	
TF 81	Sea Control and Surveillance Force	
TF 82	Amphibious Task Force	
TF 83	Landing Force[2]	
TF 84	ASW Task Force	
TF 85	Mobile Logistic Support Force	
TF 86	Patrol Air Task Force	
TF 87	Tactical Development and Evaluation and Transit Force	
TF 88	Training Force	
TF 89	Maritime Defense Zone[1]	
TF 134	Naval Forces Caribbean	
TF 137	Eastern Atlantic Force	
TF 138	South Atlantic Force	
TF 139	Multilateral Special Operations Force	
TF 142	Operational Test and Evaluation Force	

SECOND FLEET

TF 20	Battle Force
TF 21	Sea Control and Surveillance Force
TF 22	Amphibious Force
TF 23	Landing Force[2]

ATLANTIC FLEET (continued)

TF 24	ASW Task Force	
TF 25	Mobile Logistics Support Force	
TF 26	Patrol Air Force	
TF 28	Caribbean Contingency Force	

CARRIER BATTLE GROUPS

Carrier Group 2	Norfolk, Va.
CVN Harry S. Truman	Norfolk, Va.
1 CG	Norfolk, Va.
Destroyer Squadron 2	Norfolk, Va.
2 DD	Norfolk, Va.
3 DDG	Norfolk, Va.
1 FFG	Norfolk, Va.
Carrier Group 4	Norfolk, Va.
Carrier Group 6	Mayport, Fla.
CV John F. Kennedy	Mayport, Fla.
1 CG	Mayport, Fla.
Destroyer Squadron 24	Mayport, Va.
2 DD	Mayport, Va.
3 DDG	Mayport, Va.
2 FFG	Mayport, Va.
Carrier Group 8	Norfolk, Va.
CVN Theodore Roosevelt	Norfolk, Va.
2 CG	Norfolk, Va.
Destroyer Squadron 28	Norfolk, Va.
2 DD	Norfolk, Va.
2 DDG	Norfolk, Va.
2 FFG	Norfolk, Va.
Cruiser-Destroyer Group 2	Norfolk, Va.
CVN George Washington	Norfolk, Va.
1 CG	Norfolk, Va.
Destroyer Squadron 22	Norfolk, Va.
2 DD	Norfolk, Va.
2 DDG	Norfolk, Va.
2 FFG	Norfolk, Va.
Cruiser-Destroyer Group 8	Norfolk, Va.
CVN Dwight D. Eisenhower	Norfolk, Va.
2 CG	Norfolk, Va.
Destroyer Squadron 26	Norfolk, Va.
4 DDG	Norfolk, Va.
2 FFG	Norfolk, Va.
Cruiser-Destroyer Group 12	Mayport, Fla.
CVN Enterprise	Norfolk, Va.
2 CG	Mayport, Fla.
Destroyer Squadron 18	Norfolk, Va.
2 DD	Norfolk, Va.
2 DDG	Norfolk, Va.
2 FFG	Norfolk, Va.

NAVAL AIR FORCE ATLANTIC

	Norfolk, Va.
Carrier Air Wing 1	Oceana, Va.
Carrier Air Wing 3	Oceana, Va.
Carrier Air Wing 7	Oceana, Va.
Carrier Air Wing 8	Oceana, Va.
Carrier Air Wing 17	Cecil Field, Fla.
Helicopter ASW Wing	Jacksonville, Fla.
Helicopter ASW Light Wing	Mayport, Fla.
Helicopter Tactical Wing	Norfolk, Va.
Airborne Early Warning Wing	Norfolk, Va.
Fighter Wing	Oceana, Va.
Strike Fighter Wing	Oceana, Va.
Sea Control Wing	Cecil Field, Fla.
Patrol and Reconnaissance Force	Norfolk, Va.
PATRECONWING-5	Brunswick, Maine
PATRECONWING-11	Jacksonville, Fla.
Fleet Air Mediterranean	Naples, Italy
Fleet Air Keflavik	Keflavik, Iceland
Fleet Air Caribbean	Roosevelt Roads, P.R.

Note: Commander Naval Air Force Atlantic has administrative control over the aircraft carriers listed with Carrier Battle Groups.

NAVAL SURFACE FORCE ATLANTIC

	Norfolk, Va.
Combat Logistics Squadron 2	Earle Colts Neck, N.J.
4 AOE	Earle Colts Neck, N.J. *and* Norfolk, Va.
2 ARS	Little Creek, Va.

Amphibious Group 2	Little Creek, Va.
LCC Mount Whitney (⚑ Second Fleet)	Norfolk, Va.
2 LHA	Norfolk, Va.
3 LHD	Norfolk, Va.
5 LPD	Norfolk, Va.
7 LSD	Little Creek, Va.
1 LST (NRF)	Little Creek, Va.
8 PC	Norfolk *and* Little Creek, Va.
Amphibious Squadron 2	Little Creek, Va.
Amphibious Squadron 4	Little Creek, Va.
Amphibious Squadron 6	Little Creek, Va.
Amphibious Squadron 8	Little Creek, Va.
Naval Beach Group 2	Little Creek, Va.
Beach Master Unit 2	Little Creek, Va.
Amphibious Construction Battalion 2	Little Creek, Va.
Assault Craft Units 2 and 4	Little Creek, Va.
Naval Inshore Underwater Group 2	Williamsburg, Va.

Note: Commander Naval Surface Force Atlantic has administrative control over the surface combatants listed with Carrier Battle Groups, as well as the Mine Warfare Command and Western Hemisphere Group (below).

MINE WARFARE COMMAND

	Corpus Christi, Texas
MCS Inchon (NRF)	Ingleside, Texas
Mine Countermeasures Squadron 1	Ingleside, Texas
1 MCM	Ingleside, Texas
2 MCM	Sasebo, Japan
2 MCM (NRF)	Ingleside, Texas
1 MHC	Ingleside, Texas
3 MHC (NRF)	Ingleside, Texas
Mine Countermeasures Squadron 2	Ingleside, Texas
3 MCM	Ingleside, Texas
2 MCM (NRF)	Ingleside, Texas
3 MHC (NRF)	Ingleside, Texas
Mine Countermeasures Squadron 3	Ingleside, Texas
2 MCM	Ingleside, Texas
2 MCM	Manama, Bahrain
2 MHC	Manama, Bahrain
3 MHC (NRF)	Ingleside, Texas

WESTERN HEMISPHERE GROUP

	Mayport, Fla.
2 CG	Mayport, Fla.
Destroyer Squadron 6	Pascagoula, Miss.
3 CG	Pascagoula, Miss.
1 FFG	Pascagoula, Miss.
1 FFG (NRF)	Pascagoula, Miss.
1 FFG (NRF)	Norfolk, Va.
Destroyer Squadron 14	Mayport, Fla.
2 DD	Mayport, Fla.
1 FFG	Norfolk, Va.
4 FFG	Mayport, Fla.
2 FFG (NRF)	Mayport, Fla.

SUBMARINE FORCE ATLANTIC

	Norfolk, Va.
Submarine Group 2	Groton, Conn.
1 SSN	Groton, Conn.
2 ARDM	Groton, Conn.
Submarine Squadron 2	Groton, Conn.
5 SSN	Groton, Conn.
NR-1 (submersible)	Groton, Conn.
Submarine Squadron 4	Groton, Conn.
6 SSN	Groton, Conn.
Submarine Squadron 6	Norfolk, Va.
6 SSN	Norfolk, Va.
1 AFDM	Norfolk, Va.
Submarine Squadron 8	Norfolk, Va.
6 SSN	Norfolk, Va.
Submarine Development Squadron 12	Groton, Conn.
5 SSN	Groton, Conn.
Submarine Group 8	Naples, Italy
Submarine Squadron 22	La Maddalena, Italy
1 AS	La Maddalena, Italy
Submarine Group 10	Kings Bay, Ga.
Submarine Squadron 16	Kings Bay, Ga.
5 SSBN	Kings Bay, Ga.
Submarine Squadron 20	Kings Bay, Ga.
5 SSBN	Kings Bay, Ga.

TRAINING COMMAND ATLANTIC

	Norfolk, Va.

ATLANTIC FLEET (continued)

2ND NAVAL CONSTRUCTION BRIGADE   Little Creek, Va.
   Mobile Construction Battalions 1, 7, 13, 14, 20,   Little Creek, Va.
     21, 23, 24, 26, 27, 74, and 133
   Underwater Construction Team 1   Little Creek, Va.

FIFTH FLEET

Manama, Bahrain

   TF 50   Naval Expeditionary Force
   TF 51   Amphibious Force
   TF 53   Logistics Force

   Destroyer Squadron 50/Middle East Force Surface Action Group

SIXTH FLEET

Gaeta, Italy

   TF 60   Battle Force
    TG 60.1   Battle Group 1
    TG 60.2   Battle Group 2
   TF 61   Amphibious Force
   TF 62   Landing Force[2]
   TF 63   Service Force
   TF 66   ASW Force
   TF 67   Maritime Surveillance and Reconnaissance Force
   TF 68   Special Operations Force
   TF 69   Attack Submarine Force

   Note: The Sixth Fleet flagship La Salle (AGF 3) (⚑ Sixth Fleet) is homeported
in Gaeta.

1. Commanded by a Coast Guard officer.
2. Commanded by a Marine Corps officer.

The Moosbrugger (DD 980) operates off the Florida coast as a unit of
the Second Fleet, prior to the ship's 2000 deployment to the
Mediterranean, where the destroyer became a unit of the Sixth Fleet.
The Navy's fleet organization provides a high degree of flexibility.
(U.S. Navy, PH2 Dominick J. Haen)

CHAPTER 7

Marine Forces

Marines train with new tactics and new weapons for a new kind of combat—urban warfare. These Marines, from the 26th Marine Expeditionary Unit (Special Operations Capable), are armed with Heckler & Koch 9-mm MP5N submachine guns as they train for house-to-house operations in Grafenwöhr, Germany. These guns, with 30-round magazines, also are used by Navy SEALs. (U.S. Marine Corps, SSgt. E. V. Walsh)

The Marine Corps is a separate service within the Department of the Navy. The primary mission of the Marine Corps is to provide the unified commanders-in-chief and the Atlantic and Pacific Fleets with combat-ready air-ground task forces to conduct amphibious operations.

The Marine Corps's operating forces consist of:

- Marine Corps Forces (MARFOR)
- Marine Corps Security Forces at naval installations in the United States and abroad
- Marine security guard detachments at embassies and consulates

The commanders of MARFOR Atlantic and Pacific serve as the Marine Corps component commanders to their respective combat commanders and may also serve as commanding generals of Fleet Marine Force (FMF) Atlantic or Pacific. Further, in their roles as Commanding Generals FMF Atlantic and FMF Pacific, they serve as

"type" commanders within the Atlantic and Pacific Fleets, respectively (see figure 5-3 on page 28).

The current Marine Corps strength of 172,000 active-duty personnel and 39,500 reservists compares to a post–Vietnam War peak of approximately 200,000 in the late 1980s. The U.S. Marine Corps is the largest such organization in the world.[1] The Marine Corps has been the only military service within the Department of Defense to achieve its recruiting goals. This may be because the Marine Corps

---

1. At the time of the demise of the Soviet Union in December 1991, the Soviet Naval Infantry or marines consisted of some 18,000 troops. However, in the late 1980s four motorized rifle divisions of the Soviet Ground Forces had been transferred to the Navy and, with the Naval Infantry and Navy-controlled Coastal Missile-Artillery Force (some 14,000 troops), to the Coastal Defense Force within the naval establishment.

   Major naval infantry/marine organizations are maintained by China, South Korea, Taiwan, Thailand, the United Kingdom, and Vietnam.

General James Jones,
Commandant of the Marine
Corps since July 1999
(Department of Defense)

has mostly "trigger pullers," with a relatively small ratio of technical billets compared to the other services.

The Marine Corps has the smallest percentage of women in uniform among the services—less than 6 percent, compared to 15 percent for the Army, 14 percent for the Navy, and 18 percent for the Air Force. Here again, the large proportion within the Marine Corps of infantry and artillery billets, which are closed to women, is likely the key factor.

The Marine Corps no longer provides Marine detachments on board U.S. Navy ships. The last detachment was in the carrier GEORGE WASHINGTON (CVN 73), departing from the ship on 3 April 1998. The detachment consisted of one officer and 25 enlisted Marines; prior to the early-1990s force reductions, Marine carrier detachments numbered two officers and 64 enlisted men.

Marines had been on board U.S. warships virtually without interruption from the Marine Corps's founding in 1775. During the 20th century, they were found on board aircraft carriers, battleships, the larger cruisers (CA/CAG/CB/CL/CLG), and some submarine tenders, the last to provide security for nuclear warheads.

The Marine Corps does not have medical, dental, or chaplain personnel, instead relying upon the Navy to provide these services. These Navy personnel are fully integrated into Marine units and, when in the field, dress in Marine uniforms. In turn, Marine representatives are assigned to all appropriate Navy staffs, including those of the Secretary of the Navy and the Office of the Chief of Naval Operations (OPNAV). A Marine major general serves as the Director of the Expeditionary Warfare Division in OPNAV (code N85) and the lieutenant general who serves as Deputy Chief of Staff for Aviation at Marine Headquarters is additionally assigned as the Principal Adviser, Marine Aviation (code N88M) to the Director of the Air Warfare Division in OPNAV.

Historical: The Marine Corps was established on 10 November 1775 by the Continental Congress, with two battalions of troops being raised who were "good seamen, or so acquainted with maritime affairs as to be able to serve to advantage by sea, when required." Subsequently, Marines have fought at sea and ashore in almost all American conflicts.

The Corps reached a peak strength of 485,000 men and women during World War II, with six divisions and five aircraft wings (plus numerous separate squadrons).

During the 1950s the United States began the practice of maintaining battalion landing teams (and later MEUs) afloat, embarked in amphibious ships, in the Mediterranean, Western Pacific, and, at times, Caribbean and Persian Gulf areas.

From its beginning, the Marine Corps has been a separate service within the Navy Department. The senior Marine officer is the Commandant with the rank of full general. He is a member of the Joint Chiefs of Staff (JCS) and is responsible for the readiness and training of the Marine Corps; he does not have operational command of Marine combat forces except as specifically assigned by the JCS or the Secretary of Defense.

MARINE FORCES

The Marine Forces Atlantic and Pacific are organized as Marine Air-Ground Task Forces (MAGTF) and are either employed as a component of naval expeditionary forces or as part of joint or combined forces.

The U.S. Marine Corps has a significant air arm. These AV-8B Harriers—now being upgraded—are similar to those the Royal Navy used effectively as fighters and attack aircraft in the Falklands conflict in 1982. These Harriers, on the assault ship WASP (LHD 1), are deployed as part of a composite "air group" with troop-carrying and gunship helicopters. (U.S. Marine Corps, Lt. Col. P. Croisetiere)

From 1933 to 1994 the Marines assigned to fleets were designated the Fleet Marine Force (FMF); they provided the tactical and support organizations for amphibious operations. In July 1994 the term FMF was dropped in favor of Marine Forces. The change from FMF to MARFOR was made following Operations Desert Shield/Desert Storm in the Persian Gulf in 1990–1991. During the Gulf campaign, the Marines ashore in Saudi Arabia became the Marine component of the Central Command (CENTCOM), on an equal basis with the Army, Air Force, and Navy components. (The Marine forces afloat in the Gulf were under the Navy component commander.)

The Marine Corps is a "combined arms" force possessing armor and heavy artillery, as well as infantry units and a large tactical air arm including fixed-wing aircraft and helicopters. The Marine Corps is the only such service with its own air arm, except for a small number of helicopters and light fixed-wing aircraft flown by the British and Russian marines. (The U.S. Marine Corps aviation structure is described in chapter 26 of this edition of *Ships and Aircraft* and Marine aircraft are listed in chapter 27.)

The Marine Corps is organized into three ground divisions and three aircraft wings, with a large combat support force formed into three service support groups.[2] The Marine Corps Reserve consists of an additional division, aircraft wing, and support group. The Marine Corps has followed a basic triangular organization since the start of World War II, with each division having three infantry regiments (plus an artillery regiment), each infantry regiment having three rifle battalions, and each battalion having three rifle companies (plus a weapons company).[3]

The combined-arms regiments established in the early 1990s have been replaced by a third infantry regiment with tanks and light armored vehicles formed into separate battalions; see 16th Edition/page 36.

Marine divisions are among the world's largest, with a total strength of 16,911 Marines and 893 Navy personnel. Figures 7-3 through 7-5 at the end of this chapter show the nominal Marine division organization. The division totals vary in actual units because of differing organizations of artillery regiments and personnel shortfalls in some units.

Marine divisions are generally considered to be "light" or "mechanized" combat units. Each tank battalion has 58 M1A1 Abrams tanks mounting a 120-mm gun. Each light armored vehicle battalion has 116 wheeled light armored vehicles, 16 of which mount anti-tank rockets. The Marines also employ AAV-series tracked amphibious vehicles for battlefield transport; however, those vehicles are limited in that role (see chapter 19).

The three Marine artillery regiments (10th, 11th, and 12th Marines) were reorganized in late 1992, with each regiment being assigned three or four direct support battalions, and each battalion having three firing batteries with six M198 155-mm howitzers. However, the artillery regiments were reorganized in the mid-1990s to better support Marine Expeditionary Unit (MEU) deployments; two regiments have four artillery battalions, while the 12th Marine Regiment has only two.

In addition to the M198 heavy towed howitzers, each Marine Expeditionary Force (MEF) has available 48 M101A1 105-mm towed howitzers for use in special contingencies where the 16,000-pound (7,258-kg) M198s are not suitable. The present plan is to retain the M198s in artillery battalions until the Marine Corps receives the lightweight 155-mm howitzer, which weighs less than 9,000 pounds (4,082 kg).[4]

Today, these divisions and wings can be considered primarily administrative structures, as Marine units deploy in MAGTF formations; see below.

---

2. The Marine Corps's strength of three divisions and three aircraft wings is specified in legislation, the only service with that characteristic.

3. In 1988–1989, eight Marine battalions, designated as MEU (Special Operations Capability), were provided with a fourth rifle company. However, the drawdown of Marine strength forced a reduction to three rifle companies in those battalions during 1991.

4. The M198 can be helicopter-lifted only by the CH-53E Super Stallion. The lightweight LW 155 gun can be lifted by the CH-46 Sea Knight and CH-53D Sea Stallion helicopters, as well as by the CH-53E.

Marine divisions have minimal organic combat service support. This is provided by a Force Service Support Group (FSSG) assigned to support each division/wing MEF or simultaneously to four MEUs. Each FSSG has 7,951 Marines and 1,208 Navy personnel (see figure 7-1).

Figure 7-1
Force Service Support Group

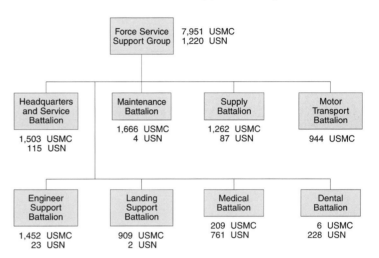

MARINE AIR-GROUND TASK FORCES

The Marine Forces are the amphibious assault component of what are now called Naval Expeditionary Forces—Marine assault units, amphibious ships, supporting carrier task forces, and other forces required to project U.S. military power by sea.

The combined-arms Marine Air-Ground Task Forces (MAGTF)—pronounced "*MAG*-taf"—can be tailored to the size and composition required to meet a broad range of operational requirements, and for transport by various methods. There are four generic types of MAGTFs:

- Marine Expeditionary Unit (MEU)
- Marine Expeditionary Brigade (MEB)
- Marine Expeditionary Force (MEF)
- Special Purpose Force (SPF)

During the 1980s some MEUs underwent special training and qualifications to be designated as Special Operations Capable (SOC). All MEUs are now SOC qualified and are considered capable of carrying out six missions: amphibious raids, security operations (e.g., of an embassy), Noncombat Evacuation Operations (NEO), direct action, humanitarian/civic assistance, and Tactical Recovery of Aircraft and Personnel (TRAP).

Each MAGTF has four fundamental elements that are drawn from the ground divisions, aircraft wings, and support groups as needed; those elements are shown in figure 7-2 and table 7-1.

Figure 7-2
National Marine Air-Ground Task Force Structure

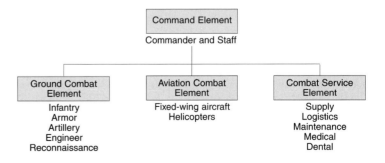

TABLE 7-1. MARINE AIR-GROUND TASK FORCE ORGANIZATIONS

	Marine Expeditionary Force (MEF)	Marine Expeditionary Brigade (MEB)	Marine Expeditionary Unit (MEU)	Special Purpose Force (SPF)
Total personnel	30,000 to 60,000	4,000 to 18,000	1,000 to 4,000	100 to 1,000
Commander	lieutenant general	brigadier general	colonel	varies
Ground combat element	one or more divisions	infantry regiment	infantry battalion	rifle company
Aviation combat element	aircraft wing	aircraft group	composite squadron (helicopters + STOVL)	aviation detachment
Combat service support element	force service support group	brigade service support group	MEU service support group	combat service support detachment
Self-sustainment capability*	60 days	30 days	15 days	as required
Amphibious lift	approx. 50 ships	21 to 26 ships	4 to 6 ships	varies
Major equipment	70 tanks	17 tanks	5 tanks	varies
	147 light armored vehicles	36 light armored vehicles		
	208 assault amphibian vehicles	47 assault amphibian vehicles	12 assault amphibian vehicles	
	12 8-inch (203-mm) howitzers	6 8-inch (203-mm) howitzers		
	108 155-mm howitzers	24 155-mm howitzers	8 155-mm howitzers	
	72 81-mm mortars	24 81-mm mortars	8 81-mm mortars	
	81 60-mm mortars	27 60-mm mortars	9 60-mm mortars	
	288 Dragon anti-tank launchers	96 Dragon anti-tank launchers	32 Dragon anti-tank launchers	
	144 TOW anti-tank launchers*	48 TOW anti-tank launchers*	8 TOW anti-tank launchers*	
	24 Hawk SAM launchers	6 Hawk SAM launchers		
	75 Stinger SAM teams	15 Stinger SAM teams	5 Stinger SAM teams	
	~150 fixed-wing aircraft (STOVL)	~75 fixed-wing STOVL aircraft	6 fixed-wing STOVL aircraft	
	~150 helicopters	~100 helicopters	~20 helicopters	

*Additional TOW launchers are mounted on AH-1 SeaCobra helicopters.

The buildup of MAGTFs from the component "building blocks" is not linear. For example, while a Marine regiment and aircraft group are the ground and air elements of a Marine Expeditionary Brigade, a division-wing team cannot form three MEBs because of the shortfall of command and support units. Thus, the Marine Corps—with three divisions and three wings—can effectively deploy two MEFs or perhaps four MEBs, plus some smaller units.

The Special Purpose Force (SPF) units are employed for both conventional and "unconventional" operations; they can be deployed into forward areas by aircraft, surface ships, or the Navy's transport submarines.

When originally established in the late 1970s, the MAGTFs were not permanent organizations but were to be "task organized for a specific mission and, after completion of that mission, is dissolved."[5] In the 1980s, however, the MAGTF units took on an increasingly permanent structure. This shift came in large part because of commitments to "marrying" Marine combat units with weapons and material in Maritime Prepositioning Ships (MPS) deployed in various ocean areas and prepositioned ashore in Norway. The permanent assignment of MAGTFs to specific prepositioned equipment and to specific geographic areas has reduced the flexibility of Marine units.

During 1992, as a consequence of force level reductions and the lessons learned in Desert Shield/Desert Storm, the Marine Corps began to reform its MAGTF structure. Since 1982, a total of 15 permanent MAGTF command elements have been formed: 3 MEFs, 6 MEBs, and 6 MEUs. With the cutback in personnel strength, all six standing brigade-level (MEB) command elements were deactivated. Instead, when Marine units larger than MEUs deploy, they will be commanded by a forward component of the MEF command element. In a related move, the staffs of the I and II MEF headquarters have been expanded; the III MEF headquarters was deactivated, being replaced by the I MEF (Forward) command element, which retained all of the functions previously found in III MEF.

The standing MEUs are:

Unit	Based at
11th, 13th, 15th	Camp Pendleton, Calif.
22nd, 24th, 26th	Camp Lejeune, N.C.
31st	Okinawa

The MEUs are sized to be carried by a Navy Amphibious Squadron (PHIBRON), which, when combined with the MEU, forms an Amphibious Ready Group (ARG).

MARINE SECURITY FORCES

The Marine Corps Security Force (MCSF) provides security force detachments at various ammunition storage sites, major bases in the United States and overseas, the Naval Academy in Annapolis, Md., and U.S. embassies and consulates abroad. Approximately 200 officers and 5,000 enlisted men and women are assigned to the MCSF.

The security companies, detachments, and "barracks" at more than 100 locations vary considerably in size. The largest such units are the Marine barracks at the Guantánamo Bay (Cuba) naval base and in Washington, D.C. The "Gitmo" barracks has 21 officers and 323 enlisted personnel, and the Washington barracks has 54 officers and 1,000 enlisted personnel; both are commanded by colonels.[6] The Marines in Washington also provide security and honor guards for the White House, provide parades and music for Washington-area events, and support the Marine Corps Schools at Quantico, Va.

The other MCSF units that survive as barracks units are at the Naval Academy in Annapolis and at the fleet support facility at Yokosuka, Japan.

The current MCSF structure was established in late 1987 in response to a directive by the Secretary of the Navy for the reorganization of naval security forces to meet the growing threat of terrorism and to strengthen its ability to detect and defeat attacks targeted at military personnel and their families. The Marine Corps responded by creating two MCSF battalions—Atlantic and Pacific—to supervise the operations of companies and detachments at shore bases around the world. Only the Atlantic battalion survives, with its headquarters at Norfolk, Va. (The Pacific battalion had its headquarters at Mare Island, Calif.)

In addition to the companies and detachments that safeguard various shore facilities, the MCSF battalion also has a Fleet Anti-terrorism Security Team (FAST) company of eight officers and 313 enlisted men. The FAST unit is specially trained and equipped to rescue hostages and contain terrorists. The battalion has a special school to instruct personnel in counter-terrorist operations.

MARINE FORCE MOBILITY

Mobility is a principal of naval operations and is a key characteristic of the Marine Forces. There are several aspects to MARFOR mobility:

Forward afloat forces. Marine units are normally afloat in amphibious ships in forward areas. Normally, one MEU is afloat in the

---

5. Commanding General, Marine Corps Development and Educational Command, *Marine Air-Ground Task Force Doctrine,* FMFM 0-1, June 1978, pp. 1–5.

6. The Guantánamo barracks was the subject of the movie *A Few Good Men* starring Jack Nicholson and Tom Cruise.

cles, equipment, munitions, and provisions for a MEB (see chapter 8). These ships can be sent into a port to be "married" with Marines flown into the area by transport aircraft. While this force does not have the ability to make a forcible entry but requires a friendly port or sheltered unloading area and nearby airfield, the viability of the MPS concept was demonstrated in Operation Desert Shield in August 1991.

Airlift. Marines, like other light combat forces, can be airlifted into an area by transport aircraft. The Marine Corps has a small force of C-130 Hercules transport/tanker aircraft. A sizable troop commitment would require the use of U.S. Air Force transport aircraft.

Aircraft carriers. In 1992 the U.S. Atlantic Command began examining the feasibility of putting Marine *ground* combat troops aboard large-deck carriers. The rationale for such a move was reported as:

- To better justify large-deck carriers by giving them an assault capability
- To provide more fleet flexibility by being able to rapidly embark a Marine assault force in a carrier
- To provide an assault capability in an area without deploying an amphibious ready group, i.e., three to five amphibious ships with an MEU of some 2,000 Marines embarked

Accordingly, in mid-January 1993, 538 Marines embarked in the carrier THEODORE ROOSEVELT (CVN 71) for a month of at-sea training and workup. Designated as a Special-Purpose Marine Air-Ground Task Force (SPMAGTF), the Marines consisted of a rifle company (190 men) from the 3rd Battalion, 6th Marines; a command staff and various detachments, including an 18-man reconnaissance platoon; and a heavy helicopter squadron (HMH-362) with a component from a utility and attack helicopter squadron (HMLA-167), with six CH-53 Sea Stallion and four UH-1N Huey helicopters.[8]

Following the month-long workup, on 11 March 1993, the ROOSEVELT battle group departed Norfolk, steaming for the Mediterranean and a six-month forward deployment as a component of the Sixth Fleet. Aboard the ROOSEVELT—in addition to the 638 Marines—was Carrier Air Wing (CVW) 8. To make space for the Marines and their helicopters, CVW 8 left Air Anti-Submarine Squadron 24, the wing's S-3B Viking squadron, on the beach. Also, Marine squadron VMFA-312, with F/A-18C Hornets, was embarked in the ship in place of the second F-14 Tomcat squadron of CVW 8.

The loss of the Vikings was of particular concern to some Navy planners, because of their anti-submarine prowess as well as their effectiveness for general surveillance and their value as tankers for extending the range of the Hornets. The two latter roles could have been of particular importance as the ROOSEVELT operated in the Adriatic Sea area, supporting the efforts to stop the racial fighting in the former Yugoslavia.

Although the Atlantic Command had at one point envisioned the Marines aboard the ROOSEVELT as a substitution for an Amphibious Ready Group (ARG), in fact an ARG with an MEU embarked was also deployed in the Med. But the focus was on the ROOSEVELT and the 600-man SPMAGTF.

The ROOSEVELT deployment identified a number of problems with Marines aboard large-deck carriers. These included:

(1) *Tactical problems:* Under the new doctrine articulated in the Navy's 1992 policy statement . . . *From the Sea*, the Navy and Marine Corps will "respond to crises and . . . provide the initial, 'enabling' capability for joint operations in conflict—as well as continued participation in any sustained effort." In this context, the forward-deployed Marines are referred to as the "tip of the spear" of the enabling forces.

The concerns about the ROOSEVELT operation centered on that "tip" being a mere 190 Marine riflemen—too small a force to be effective at essentially any level of crisis or conflict. Their largest organic weapons were three 60-mm mortars, six 7.62-mm machine guns, and a few anti-tank weapons—far too few to counter any significant opposition, even in the Third World.

The argument had been made that the support for the SPMAGTF rifle company included the entire carrier air wing. However, this

Marines train aboard the assault ship GUAM (LPH 9) on her last overseas deployment before being decommissioned in 1998. Marines, like these men from the 24th MEU(SOC), train to come ashore—or to board ships—by a variety of means. An AH-1W SeaCobra shares the GUAM's hangar with these Marines. (U.S. Navy, PHAN Rich Williams)

Mediterranean area and one in the Pacific–Indian Ocean area; at times, additional MEUs or larger formations are at sea, in transit to relieve forward-deployed MEUs or for exercises. As a crisis begins to evolve, the afloat MEUs, like other naval forces, can be dispatched to the problem area without creating an intrusion in foreign territory or air space.

Amphibious assault. The Marines have a significant amphibious assault capability, employing helicopters, landing craft, and vehicles from the Navy's amphibious ships. The existing amphibious force has an approximate theoretical lift capacity equivalent to the assault echelon of one MEF, i.e., a reinforced division and the helicopter and STOVL portions of an aircraft wing.[7] (The "assault echelon" is the portion of the force that makes the actual landing: about two-thirds of the troops, one-half the vehicles, and one-quarter of the cargo of the unit.)

Recent reductions in the fleet have seen a decline in the lift capacity to only 2½ MEBs, i.e., reinforced regiments.

Maritime prepositioning. Three squadrons of Maritime Prepositioning Ships (MPS) are forward deployed—one in the Atlantic, one off Diego Garcia in the Indian Ocean, and one off the Mariana Islands in the Western Pacific. Each MPS squadron carries weapons, vehi-

---

7. The term VSTOL for Vertical/Short Take-Off and Landing was used by the Marine Corps until early 1995, when the term STOVL (Short Take-Off and Vertical Landing) was adopted by Headquarters, Marine Corps.

---

8. The aviation personnel totaled about 230 men.

Like the Army and to some extent the Navy, the Marine Corps is increasingly being called upon for humanitarian, peacekeeping, and related noncombat activities. This Marine CH-53D Sea Stallion is evacuating Americans and others from the U.S. Embassy in Tirana, Albania, in March 1977, during one of the continuing crises in the Balkans. Such noncombat evacuations have become a periodic occurrence of the post–Cold War era. (U.S. Navy, PH2 Brett Siegel)

response assumed that the carrier would remain within tactical range of the Marines ashore (see below) and that weather and visibility would permit the carrier aircraft to fly close air support missions.

Such a force had little real combat capability and there was fear that Navy and national planners would commit the small force to a situation far beyond its capabilities. As a senior Marine officer remarked to the author, "This concept could get 600 lightly armed people in trouble in a heartbeat."

(2) *Support problems:* With their limited cargo helicopter capability (six CH-53Ds), even in suitable flying weather the Marines on the ROOSEVELT could not bring ashore heavy trucks and other equipment. While ARGs have helicopters for landing troops, including the heavy-lift CH-53E Super Stallion, they also have air cushion landing craft (LCAC), conventional landing craft (LCM/LCU), and tracked amphibian vehicles (AAV) that could provide seaborne logistics to the troops ashore, regardless of weather conditions.

(3) *Operational problems:* The aircraft carrier with its air wing is one of the most flexible and mobile weapon systems in existence. Should the SPMAGTF be lifted ashore, would the battle group commander be required to remain in the area to provide air support—and possibly air evacuation—for the Marines?

The carrier's flight deck situation also became a problem. Carrier flight decks operate on the basis of launch and recovery cycles that are quite different than those on the helicopter carriers in which Marines normally embarked. This caused problems as the Marine aviators wanted to spread rotors and fly between the normal aircraft cycles, causing major difficulties for the flight deck crewmen.

(4) *Political problems:* Possibly most significant in the long term, it was likely that the embarking Marines in large-deck carriers would have a positive impact on justifying carrier force levels. *If* successful, however, the concept could have led politicians to reconsider the construction of additional amphibious ships, believing that carriers with Marines on board could be substituted for new "amphibs."

There were benefits to be gained and lessons to be learned by such experiments as placing the SPMAGTF aboard the ROOSEVELT. However, the costs and disadvantages far outweighed the benefits and the program was not continued.

MARINE OPERATIONS

The Marines had a major role in the U.S. buildup in the Middle East from August 1990 (Operation Desert Shield) and the subsequent war with Iraq in early 1991 (Operation Desert Storm). With fears that Iraq would launch an assault on Saudi Arabia immediately after consolidating its position in Kuwait, in early August 1990 the President ordered the deployment of U.S. combat forces into Saudi Arabia.

The first squadron of prepositioning ships arrived at the port of Al Jubayl, Saudi Arabia, on 15 August 1990 and was met by troops of the 7th MEB (based on the 7th Marines), airlifted from Twentynine Palms, Calif.[9] Additional Marines followed, by air and sea, with all three MPS squadrons unloading their matériel in Saudi Arabia. When the Gulf War began on 17 January 1991, there were 76,000 Marines "in country" in the 1st and 2nd Marine Divisions, with a massive Marine air force consolidated under the 3rd Marine Aircraft Wing and a large support establishment designated as the 1st Force Service Support Group. The Marine air component in Desert Storm—both on amphibious ships and ashore—totaled 20 fixed-wing and 24 helicopter squadrons, plus detachments of other aviation units.

The entire Marine force within Saudi Arabia was under the command of the I Marine Expeditionary Force, whose commanding general, Lieutenant General Walter E. Boomer, also served as Commander U.S. Marine Force Central Command (MARCENT). Sepa-

9. These were the ships of Maritime Prepositioning Squadron 2. They had been anchored at Diego Garcia in the Indian Ocean and were ordered to get under way for the Persian Gulf on 8 August.

TABLE 7-2. MARINE CORPS BASING

ACTIVE GROUND COMPONENTS

Camp H. M. Smith, Hawaii
  Headquarters Marine Force Pacific

Kaneohe, Hawaii
     3rd Marine Regiment (infantry)
     12th Marine Regiment (artillery)

Camp Pendleton, Calif.
  Headquarters I Marine Expeditionary Force
  1st Marine Division
     1st, 5th Marine Regiments (infantry)
     11th Marine Regiment (artillery)
     1st Combat Engineer Battalion
     3rd Assault Amphibian Battalion
  1st Force Service Support Group

Twentynine Palms, Calif.
     7th Marine Regiment (infantry)
     3rd Tank Battalion
     3rd AA Battalion

Okinawa
  Headquarters III Marine Expeditionary Force (Camp Courtney)
  3rd Marine Division
     4th Regiment (infantry)
  3rd Force Service Support Group

Norfolk, Va.
  Headquarters 4th Marine Expeditionary Brigade (Little Creek)

Camp Lejeune, N.C.
  Headquarters Marine Force Atlantic
  Headquarters II Marine Expeditionary Force
  2nd Marine Division
     2nd, 6th, 8th Marine Regiments (infantry)
     10th Marine Regiment (artillery)
     2nd Tank Battalion
     2nd Assault Amphibian Battalion
     2nd Combat Engineer Battalion
  2nd Force Service Support Group

RESERVE GROUND COMPONENTS

New Orleans, La.
  Headquarters Marine Forces Reserve
  4th Marine Division
  4th Force Service Support Group

Dallas, Texas
     14th Marine Regiment (artillery)

Overland Park, Kans.
  Reserve Support Command

San Rafael, Calif.
     23rd Marine Regiment

Kansas City, Mo.
     24th Marine Regiment

Worcester, Mass.
     25th Marine Regiment

Note: Aviation units are listed in chapter 26.

rate from this command were the 17,000 Marines on board 31 amphibious ships in the Persian Gulf. This afloat force consisted of two separate Marine brigades (4th and 5th MEBs), plus a separate MEU; for political reasons, there was no overall Marine commander assigned for the afloat force. This represented the largest amphibious task force since World War II. (Another 5,000 Marines were embarked in amphibious ships in the eastern Mediterranean.)

During the ground assault against occupied Kuwait and Iraq, the I MEF was to the right wing of the allied line and saw considerable combat. The Marines' shortfall in armored vehicles was a major consideration to allied planners, however, and an Army tank brigade was attacked to the I MEF and, in the field, some Marine units also exchanged their M60A1 tanks for the new M1A1 Abrams tank.[10]

Although the 17,000 afloat Marines were not employed in an amphibious assault, the threat of such a landing did force the Iraqi high command to man several front-line divisions along the coast of Kuwait and away from the main line of defense along the Kuwaiti border. During January 1961, the 5th MEB was landed some 20 miles

10. The Marine Corps completed transition from the M60 to the M1A1 tank in mid-1992.

(32 km) south of the Kuwait-Saudi border, behind the advancing I MEF. Eight air cushion landing craft (LCAC) brought ashore 7,300 Marines along with almost 2,400 tons of vehicles and weapons in less than 24 hours; the ship-to-shore transfer required 55 trips by the LCACs, made in heavy seas with 40-knot winds. Portions of the 4th MEB were subsequently brought ashore.

During Desert Shield/Desert Storm, some 85 percent of the Marine Forces was deployed to Southwest Asia; in addition, 25,710 men and women of the Marine Corps Reserve—61 percent of that force—was mobilized in that period, with many of them sent into the desert with their active-duty counterparts. Then-Commandant A. M. ("Al") Gray declared: "There are four kinds of Marines: those in Saudi Arabia, those going to Saudi Arabia, those who want to go to Saudi Arabia, and those who don't want to go to Saudi Arabia but are going anyway!"

Simultaneous with Desert Shield, a Navy-Marine amphibious force remained off the coast of strife-torn Liberia for seven months, providing security for the U.S. embassy in Sierra Leone. During that operation—code-named Sharp Edge—the Marines helped to evacuate 2,400 American diplomats and citizens. A small Navy amphibious force, with an escorting destroyer, remained off Liberia from the end of May 1990 until early December.

During the buildup in the Gulf, the political crisis in Somalia also boiled over. At the urgent request of the U.S. ambassador in Mogadishu, in the predawn darkness of 4 January 1991, two Marine

Marines wait by a light armored vehicle during an exercise. The Marine in the foreground has a 5.56-mm M16 rifle rigged for laser training. The Marine Corps, with its "warrior ethos," is the only service among the Army, Navy, Marines, and Air Force now attaining its recruiting goals. (U.S. Navy, PH2 Michelle Hammond)

CH-53E Super Stallion helicopters took off from an amphibious ship and carried 70 Marines on a 460-n.mile (852-km) flight to Mogadishu. The CH-53E flight was made with inflight refuelings from Marine KC-130 tankers. The Marines helped to secure the embassy and then the helicopters shuttled out 260 American diplomats and foreign nationals to the amphibious ships GUAM (LPH 9) and TRENTON (LPD 14) to conclude the successful operation, given the codename Eastern Exit.

Following Operation Desert Shield, Navy-Marine amphibious forces were engaged in humanitarian assistance to Kurds in northern Iraq and assisting survivors of flooding in Bangladesh.

Subsequently, the frustrating U.S. attempts to help alleviate the starvation and gang-rule in Ethiopia saw Marines at the forefront of American activities in that ravaged country. While no combat was involved in that humanitarian action, Marines were involved in conflicts with local gangs. After an Army patrol suffered heavy casualties—and with the hunger situation partially alleviated—U.S. forces were hurriedly withdrawn. (The 1992–1994 Somalia operation was an international effort, with large contingents of French and Italian military forces.)

With the decision to have U.S. forces support United Nations/North Atlantic Treaty Organization activities in the Bosnian civil war, Marine F/A-18 Hornet strike fighters have been based on a continuous basis at Aviano, Italy, since April 1994. Periodically, Marine EA-6B Prowlers—as well as Navy Prowlers—have flown from the NATO base. In addition, Marine aircraft have flown from carriers operating in the Adriatic Sea, with a Marine MEU embarked in an amphibious ready group in the Mediterranean–Adriatic area.

When Air Force F-16 fighter pilot Captain Scott O'Grady was shot down by a surface-to-air missile over western Bosnia-Herzegovina on 2 June 1995, the intrepid flier was able to evade capture until 8 June, when he was rescued—by Marines. A TRAP operation was mounted by Marines flying from the MEU embarked in the helicopter carrier KEARSARGE (LHD 3) operating in the Adriatic Sea. Early that morning, CH-53Es lifted off the KEARSARGE's deck—escorted by helicopter gunships and fixed-wing aircraft—and flew the 87 miles (140 km) to the downed pilot's location, pinpointed by his survival radio transmissions. Although the Western press played up O'Grady as a hero, the true heroes were the 57 Marines and 4 Navy hospital corpsmen who flew in to rescue him. The operation was successfully completed without casualties.

Subsequently, in conjunction with the U.S.-led NATO air campaign against Serbia in the spring of 1999, Marine AV-8B Harriers, based aboard ships and ashore, and Marine F/A-18 Hornets and EA-6B Prowlers took part in the air strikes of Operation Allied Force. The afloat MEU was put ashore, but no Allied ground forces were committed in the conflict.

During the 1990s—in addition to continuous forward deployments with naval amphibious/expeditionary forces and participation in conflicts—Marine Forces have been heavily engaged in two other activities: First, Marines have been participating in peacekeeping operations in various parts of the world, from East Timor to the Balkans. While Marines previously carried out similar activities, especially in Central America during the 1920s and 1930s, and even earlier in China, the current peacekeeping operations have become a major factor in U.S. military overseas deployments, training, logistics, and so forth. The Marines have been particularly useful in this role because of their mobility and flexibility when embarked in amphibious ships standing offshore from the crisis area.

Second, beginning in the early 1990s the Marines instituted intensive training programs in urban warfare, the ability to enter a built-up area and successfully operate against entrenched enemy troops or terrorists. Such training also examined the use of Marines to provide humanitarian assistance in the aftermath of natural disaster or terrorist acts. The Marine Corps has had relatively little experience in operations in urban areas, the major exception having been on the Korean peninsula in 1950–1953.

By the late 1990s Marines were carrying out familiarization visits—as well as conducting actual training operations—in major U.S. cities. In Operation Urban Warrior in March 1999, air cushion landing craft and helicopters disgorged some 550 Marines into the abandoned Alameda naval air station in San Francisco Bay for an exercise in operating in a city environment. British and Dutch military personnel observed the operation. Similar exercises, on a smaller scale, have been held in New York City; Monterey, Calif.; Chicago; Jacksonville, Fla.; and Charleston, S.C., as well as at several military bases.

Figure 7-3
Marine Corps Division

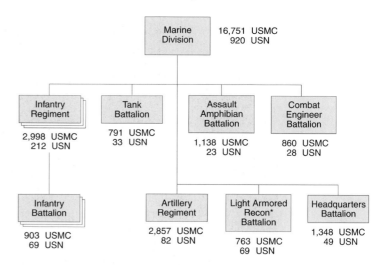

* Recon = Reconnaissance

Figure 7-4
Marine Infantry Battalion

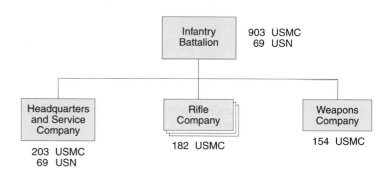

Figure 7-5
Nominal Artillery Regiment

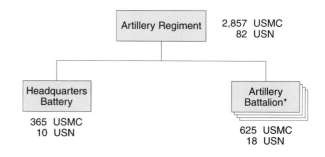

* The 10th and 11th Marine Regiments each have four artillery battalions; the 12th Marine Regiment has two battalions.

MARINE FORCES RESERVE

The Marine Forces Reserve (formerly Maine Corps Reserve) consists of the 4th Marine Division, 4th Marine Aircraft Wing, and 4th Force Service Support Group. These units generally parallel active units in organization, but in some categories have older equipment and lack several service support components. Based on command problems during the reserve callup in Desert Shield/Desert Storm, the Marine Corps in 1992 reorganized its reserves under one command structure.

The Marine Forces Reserve oversees the training, equipping, and leadership of the Marine reserve components.

The principal Marine Forces Reserve units are shown in table 7-2.

Marine reservists have training sessions on a weekly or monthly basis, and for two weeks' duration during the summer. The latter periods include participation in exercises with active units in the United States and overseas.

In 2000 the Marine Forces Reserve had 39,600 officers and enlisted men and women.

Marines rush from an AAVP7A1 assault amphibian vehicle during an exercise. The value of these craft in future amphibious landings is very questionable. Note the appliqué armor fitted to the side of the vehicle. (U.S. Marine Corps)

CHAPTER 8

Military Sealift Command

The Military Sealift Command provides seaborne services for all of the Department of Defense. One of the most important MSC roles in support of the Navy is operating most of the Navy's underway replenishment ships, such as the fleet oiler LARAMIE (T-AO 203), shown here refueling the carrier ENTERPRISE (CVN 65). MSC ships can be easily identified by the blue-and-gold funnel markings. (U.S. Navy, PH3 Brian C. McLaughlin)

Sealift is the term used for the movement of weapons and matériel to forward areas by sea. This aspect of strategic mobility is of increasing importance for future U.S. participation in world affairs as U.S. overseas bases are closed down and the number of troops stationed abroad is reduced. The United States in the early 21st century has fewer bases and troops abroad than at any time since mid-1950, on the eve of the Korean War. While troops can be flown into forward areas, it is prohibitive to consider airlift for overseas buildups in terms of tanks, munitions, fuel, and other war matériel. For example, a C-5 Galaxy cargo aircraft—the largest in U.S. military service—flying from the United States to the Middle East can carry but a single M1-series main battle tank. Further, it is estimated that in a crisis or conflict some 95 percent of the provisions, munitions, and fuels required to support U.S. forces in a forward area would be transported by sea.

The Military Sealift Command (MSC) operates a variety of ships in support of the Department of Defense and the military services.

Under a dual-command concept, the Commander MSC reports both to the Navy chain of command and to the unified Transportation Command. In addition, the Commander MSC reports to the Navy's fleet commanders-in-chief, serving as a "type" commander for MSC-operating ships (see figure 8-1).

The Commander MSC is a vice admiral with his headquarters at the Washington Navy Yard in Washington, D.C. There are MSC area commands—each headed by a Navy captain—located in Norfolk, Va.; Naples, Italy; and Yokohama, Japan. Smaller, sub-area commands are located in other ports.

The Military Sealift Command has approximately 7,500 persons worldwide, most of whom are assigned seagoing jobs. Approximately 1,100 are active-duty Navy personnel, 4,700 are federal employees, and 1,700 are employed by MSC contractors. In wartime the number of contract employees would probably double and up to 1,500 naval reservists would be called to active duty with MSC.

All MSC ships are civilian manned, although many ships have Navy communications and/or technical personnel on board.

The command currently operates some 130 ships, which are allocated to five MSC ship programs; these are designated PM (for Program Manager):

PM 1   Naval Fleet Auxiliary Force (NFAF)
PM 2   Special Mission Ships
PM 3   Prepositioning Ships
PM 4   Ship Introduction
PM 5   Sealift Ships

NAVAL FLEET AUXILIARY FORCE

The MSC currently operates 33 naval auxiliary ships that provide direct support to the fleet. These ships are described in chapter 22 of this edition of *Ships and Aircraft*.

The current NFAF consists of 28 underway replenishment ships (AE/AFS/AO types) and the Navy's five operational fleet tugs (ATF).[1] These ships are operated by civil service mariners, with some ships having a small Navy detachment on board to provide communications and to support ordnance handling and helicopter operations.

In addition, the Navy's two hospital ships, the MERCY (T-AH 19) and COMFORT (T-AH 20), which are maintained in reduced operating status, can be fully activated, crewed, and ready for deployment with MSC operating crews. These are considered both auxiliary and sealift

1. The only Navy-manned underway replenishment ships are eight fast combat support ships (AOE).

Figure 8-1
MSC Command Relationships

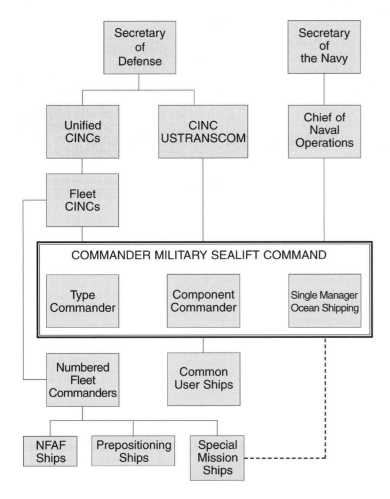

*NFAF = Naval Fleet Auxiliary Force

Vice Admiral Gordon S. Holder, Commander Military Sealift Command since February 1999 (U.S. Navy)

ships, the latter because of their probable deployment to support forward-deployed U.S. ground forces (as in the Gulf War). Further, the hospital ships periodically are activated for forward deployment in peacetime to provide their hospital facilities to other nations.

(Although the Navy's two aviation support ships [AVB] are considered by MSC to be prepositioning ships vice auxiliary ships, because of their being able to support the Marine Forces they are listed with other fleet auxiliary ships in chapter 22.)

SPECIAL MISSION SHIPS

The MSC provides and operates ships to support specialized military activities, especially oceanographic and hydrographic surveys, undersea surveillance, acoustic research, missile range instrumentation, and the collection of telemetry intelligence against foreign missile tests.

About 30 ships operated by MSC are in this category. Of these, 25 are naval auxiliary ships (AGM/AGOR/AGOS/AGS/ARC types). This is a major reduction from the end of the Cold War era, when there were 20 T-AGOS/SURTASS ocean surveillance ships in MSC service plus a large number of research ships. In addition to naval auxiliary ships, several smaller special mission ships that support deep submergence vehicle operations and other projects are listed in this volume as service craft in chapter 24.

Special mission ships are both government-owned ships and chartered vessels, operated by either civil service mariners or contract employees. These ships and craft embark both Navy and civilian scientists and technicians in addition to their civilian crews.

PREPOSITIONING SHIPS

There are currently 37 prepositioning ships operated by the MSC. These ships are kept forward-deployed with equipment, weapons, provisions, potable water, fuels, and other matériel for the Army, Navy, Marine Corps, and Air Force.

Most of these ships—described in chapter 23—are specialized cargo ships that have been extensively converted or built specifically for the prepositioning role. In particular, they are configured for handling heavy military vehicles, containerized cargo, and break-bulk cargo. They are supplemented by standard cargo ships and tankers.[2]

There are three basic categories of prepositioning ships:

(1) *Combat Prepositioning Force (CPF)*. There will soon be 20 MSC-operated Large Medium-Speed Roll-on/Roll-off (LMSR) ships that carry matériel for three Army heavy (mechanized) divisions, equipping up to 17,000 personnel per division for 30 days; this force also includes heavy-lift, float-on/float-off, crane, and cargo ships. Army matériel is loaded in the six prepositioning/LMSR ships of Afloat Prepositioning Squadron (APS) 4 that are deployed in the Persian Gulf/Indian Ocean area.[3]

2. Tankers differ from oilers (or fleet oilers) in that the former are point-to-point petroleum carriers while the latter are rigged for the underway replenishment of ships at sea.
3. The Army designation for this program originally was Army War Reserve (AWR) No. 3.

The Military Sealift Command operates a fleet of Maritime Prepositioning Ships (MPS) that carry matériel and munitions to enable U.S. combat forces to be rapidly introduced into overseas areas. This is the recently completed Cᴘʟ Cʜᴀʀʟᴇs L. Gɪʟʟɪʟᴀɴᴅ (T-AKR 298), a massive, 55,422-ton vehicle and heavy cargo carrier, extensively converted from a Danish-built cargo ship. (Jürg Kürsener)

The LMSR ships are large, medium-speed, roll-on/roll-off (RO/RO) ships that were procured specifically for the CPF role.

(2) *Maritime Prepositioning Ships (MPS)*. There are 13 MSC prepositioning ships assigned to carry the equipment and provisions of three Marine Expeditionary Brigades (MEBs) for 30 days. Each brigade has up to 18,000 Marines. All of these ships are especially configured for MEB equipment.[4]

Three additional ships, designated MPS(E) for "enhanced," carry an expeditionary airfield for use at an advance base, equipment for a Navy mobile construction battalion (Seabee), and a fleet hospital.

MPS Squadron 1 is normally based in the Atlantic area, off the Azores; MPS Squadron 2 at Diego Garcia in the Indian Ocean; and MPS 3 at Guam in the Pacific. In 1994 some ships of MPS Squadron 1 were moved into the Mediterranean in conjunction with U.S. contingency plans for participating in the Bosnian conflict. (Also see the *Operational* notes under Sealift, below.)

(3) *Logistic positioning ships*. Seven MSC-operated cargo ships are prepositioned with a variety of matériel to support U.S. combat operations. This includes Air Force munitions and support equipment, a Navy field hospital, and a variety of military fuels and lubricants. These ships are allocated to the three MPS squadrons.

The two laid-up aviation support ships Wʀɪɢʜᴛ (T-AVB 3) and Cᴜʀᴛɪss (T-AVB 4) are considered to be prepositioning ships. They are based in U.S. ports and can be activated and ready for sea within five days.

Historical: The forward-deployed or prepositioning concept was first introduced on a large scale by Secretary of Defense Robert S. McNamara in the mid-1960s, when he proposed that a force of 30

Fast Deployment Logistic (FDL) ships be constructed in addition to a force of long-range transport aircraft. Congress refused to fund the FDL ships, but the aircraft were developed as the C-5 Galaxy program. However, the Department of Defense did modify several existing cargo ships and tank landing ships (LSTs) to be forward-deployed, carrying munitions and supplies.

SHIP INTRODUCTION

This MSC program is responsible for overseeing ship acquisitions, including the transfer of auxiliary ships from active Navy to MSC status, new ship construction, and conversions and modifications of merchant-type ships.

This program also manages the Department of Defense national defense features program that seeks to provide features in American-flag merchant ships that would make them useful for military sealift. These features include reinforced roll-on/roll-off ramps, strengthened vehicle decks, and heavy cargo cranes.

SEALIFT SHIPS

The MSC sealift program is responsible for the fleet of tankers and dry cargo ships that carry cargo for all Department of Defense agencies and military services. Most of these ships are American-flag commercial vessels that are chartered by the MSC to carry specific cargoes.

For surge sealift, in peacetime, crisis, or war, the MSC first looks to the charter market. If suitable American-flag ships are not available, it can activate Fast Sealift Ships (FSS) or Ready Reserve Force (RRF) ships. The commercial ships are not listed in this volume. The FFS and RRF ships are described in chapter 23.

Fast Sealift Ships. These are the world's fastest cargo ships, acquired in the 1980s specifically to carry Army tanks, armored personnel carriers, and other combat vehicles and trucks. There are

---

4. Along with munitions, supplies, spare parts, lubricants, and other equipment, these ships carry:

123	M1A1 Abrams tanks
154	Bradley armored fighting vehicles
100	armored personnel carriers
24	self-propelled 155-mm howitzers
9	Multiple-Launch Rocket Systems (MLRS)

MSC also operates the Navy's ocean surveillance ships, currently numbering 14 ships. The LOYAL (T-AGOS 22) is one of the newer ships of this type with a Small Waterplane-Area Twin Hull (SWATH) design. Several earlier ocean surveillance ships are employed by other U.S. military services and government agencies, with several others having been transferred to other countries. (U.S. Navy)

eight of these 33-knot roll-on/roll-off ships, which combined can carry the equipment of an Army heavy (mechanized) division.

These ships are kept in U.S. ports and can be activated and under way in four days. (It will take the Army at least that long to transport, by rail, the vehicles from their home bases to ports of embarkation.)

Ready Reserve Force. The RRF consists of almost 80 government-owned ships that are maintained by the Maritime Administration and which can be activated in from four to 20 days.[5] When activated, the RRF ships come under the operational control of the MSC.

There is a variety of ship types in the RRF, including roll-on/roll-off cargo ships, break-bulk ships, barge carriers, auxiliary crane ships, tankers, and two small troop ships (both of which are on loan to academic institutions as training ships). Most of these ships are particularly well suited for handling military cargoes, especially the ten cargo-crane ships (T-ACS), one of which is assigned to an MPS squadron.

These ships are based at various U.S. ports.

Operational: During the U.S. buildup in the Middle East from August 1990 to January 1991 (Operation Desert Shield), MSC-operated or chartered ships carried 95 percent (by weight) of the war matériel moved into the Middle East from the United States and Europe. Undertaken in five months and without hostile interference, it was the largest U.S. military buildup for a single campaign since World War II.

"Sail orders" were issued on 7 August 1990 to the MPS squadrons at Diego Garcia and at Guam, directing them to steam for the Persian Gulf to support Desert Shield. The ships of MPS Squadron 2 began

---

5. The Maritime Administration is an agency of the Department of Transportation (DOT); it was under the Department of Commerce from its establishment in 1950 until transferred to DOT in 1981.

The Navy's research ships, like the ocean surveying ship MATTHEW HENSON (T-AGS 63), also are operated by MSC. These ships carry Navy and civilian scientists and provide data for use in military and civilian activities. Increasingly, the Navy is employing research ships to support civilian projects as a means of keeping those ships in service and available for military work. (U.S. Navy)

unloading on 15 August and the ships from MPS Squadron 1 reached Saudi Arabia on 26 August. Although the Marines were relatively "light" units, the ships did carry M60 tanks and M198 155-mm howitzers, as well as light armored vehicles and amphibian tractors that could serve as armored personnel carriers in the desert. The 11 non-MPS prepositioning ships that were at Diego Garcia began arriving in the Gulf on 17 August to unload their Army and Air Force cargoes. At the same time, MPS Squadron 3 in the Atlantic got under way for the Gulf. (After unloading their prepositioned cargoes, the MPS ships departed the Gulf for U.S. ports and employment in resupply operations.)

In the United States, the eight Fast Sealift Ships (FSS) began loading the Army's 24th Mechanized Infantry Division at Savannah, Ga. The SL-7s, with a maximum speed of 33 knots, were intended to be ready to receive cargo within 96 hours; the first of these RO/RO ships was ready in just 48 hours and all seven met the 96-hour goal. The eighth fast RO/RO ship was in a shipyard for overhaul; she was hastily "put back together" and sailed ten days after the call.

On 27 August—12 days after the first MPS ships arrived—the first fast sealift ships began unloading M1A1 Abrams tanks of the Army's 24th Mechanized Infantry Division in Saudi Arabia. There followed a continuous flow of ships carrying U.S. military equipment. The major bottleneck in the sealift effort was the lack of shore facilities; for example, there were only two loading berths at Savannah to embark the 24th Division, while the massive shipping effort from several U.S. and overseas ports had to be unloaded through only five berths at the Saudi port of Ad Dammam and two at the port of Al Jubail.

More merchant ships followed. On 28 September 1990 the Desert Shield sealift reached a peak with 90 ships at sea—69 en route to the Middle East from the United States and Europe, and 21 "empties" returning for more cargo. Had the ships been evenly spaced on the route from the U.S. East Coast to the Persian Gulf, there would have been one ship every 100 n.miles (185 km). When the "phase II" of Desert Shield was undertaken in November 1990 to build up a U.S. offensive force in the Persian Gulf, a peak of 172 sealift ships at sea was reached on 2 January 1991.

In addition to the merchant ships that already were operational under the aegis of the MSC for Desert Shield/Desert Storm, all of the maritime prepositioning ships and afloat prepositioning ships, the eight fast RO/RO ships (one of which broke down), several ships from the RRF, and 206 operating commercial merchant ships (29 American-flag and 177 foreign-flag) were chartered by the MSC between 10 August 1990 and 18 January 1991 to support Gulf operations. Also activated by the MSC and sent to the Gulf were the two hospital ships and two aviation support ships maintained in standby reserve.

Subsequent to the Gulf War, MSC carried out a massive sealift operation to *remove* thousands of tons of vehicles, munitions, and supplies from Saudi Arabia. Sealift ships have also been employed in small military buildup operations around the world since the Gulf War. Twice, in late 1994 and again in September 1995, prepositioning ships were dispatched to the Persian Gulf during confrontations with Iraq. Also in 1995, 14 RRF ships were activated in support of Operation Uphold Democracy, the U.S. operations in Haiti.

Several RRF ships have been activated to support U.S.–NATO operations in Bosnia and Kosovo. Two, the Cape Diamond (T-AKR 5055) and Cape Race (T-AKR 9960), were activated in June 1995 to carry military supplies for British troops engaged in peacekeeping operations.

Historical: The Military Sealift Command was established in response to a directive issue by the Secretary of Defense in August 1949 making the Secretary of the Navy the single manager for ocean transportation within the defense establishment. Previously, four separate government agencies (including the Army and Navy) controlled oceangoing merchant ships.

The Military Sea Transportation Service (MSTS) was established within the Navy on 1 October 1949. The basis for the new service was the Naval Ocean Transport Service (NOTS). The following year, oceangoing cargo ships and transports of the Army Transportation Corps were transferred to the MSTS. Through 1950, additional Army ships were transferred to the Navy agency. By 1950 the Army had transferred to Navy-MSTS control:

4	AF	refrigerated cargo ships
13	AK	cargo ships
3	AKL	light cargo ships
5	AKV	aircraft cargo ships
41	AP	transports
1	APC	coastal transport
1	ATA	auxiliary tug
1	LST	tank landing ship
2	YO	fuel oil barges

Many of these ships and craft were built for the Navy and subsequently transferred to the Army.

Under the aegis of the MSTS, some of these ships (designated USS) were manned by Navy crews and others (designated USNS) by civilian mariners. Other Navy ships were assigned to the MSTS with Navy crews. Initially, only the civilian-manned ships had the prefix *T-* added to their designations; this later was extended to include Navy-manned ships assigned to the MSTS. Some of the Navy-manned ships were armed. The last Navy crew went ashore in the 1960s, after which all ships were manned by civil service civilian or contract civilian crews.

The MSTS was renamed the Military Sealift Command on 1 August 1970 to bring the name in line with the Air Force's Military Airlift Command (MAC). The Military Airlift Command, however, was a specified command within the defense establishment, while the MSC remained a Navy command, reporting to the Chief of Naval Operations.[6] (The Air Force's Military Air Transport Service [MATS] was renamed the Military Airlift Command on 1 January 1966; it was inactivated on 1 June 1992, with its components being allocated to other Air Force commands.)

On 1 July 1987 the unified Transportation Command (TRANSCOM) was established, with the Military Sealift Command and Military Airlift Command as its principal components. The Commander MSC is a component commander of TRANSCOM.

---

6. A specified command was an organization under the Secretary of Defense and Chairman of the Joint Chiefs of Staff that was comprised mostly of personnel and resources from a single military service.

CHAPTER 9

Naval Personnel

Sailors are the Navy's most important component. Several factors are making men and women more difficult to recruit and retain for Navy service. At the same time, the increasing complexity of ships such as the carrier HARRY S. TRUMAN (CVN 75), submarines, and aircraft demand more competent personnel. One approach to solving the problems created by these situations is to adopt more automation, but that takes time and money. (U.S. Navy, PH1 Patrick J. Chashin)

The decline of U.S. Navy personnel strength since the end of the Cold War has been arrested as the Navy seeks to halt the reduction of the fleet at about 300 ships. The Navy in the year 2000 has just over 371,000 active duty personnel, about 60 percent of the active manpower when the Cold War ended.[1]

But the Navy is hard-pressed to maintain the currently authorized personnel force level. According to Vice Admiral David T. Oliver, the Chief of Naval Personnel in early 1999, the Navy's recruiting and retention situation are "not only our biggest challenges but absolutely fundamental to our success in achieving satisfactory personnel readiness."[2] Oliver admitted that the unanticipated severity of several personnel factors and the application of too few resources too late led to the Navy's recruiting and retention failures. He listed those factors as the very robust economy, enduring low unemployment (a 28-year record), decreasing propensity for military service, and an ever-growing perception among sailors of eroding benefits.

Along with the economic factors, there have been a number of other "dissatisfiers" that have been negatively impacting upon Navy recruiting and retention. These, according to Navy studies, include family separation, adverse working conditions, and lack of spare parts.

The recruiting and retention problems, coupled with the high levels of operational tempo (i.e., forward ship and aviation deployments) are presenting tough challenges to Navy overall personnel readiness. At the beginning of 2000 the Navy had 15,000 empty or "gapped" enlisted billets in the fleet, down from a high of 22,000 in the fall of 1998. These gapped billets were a combination of an inventory shortfall of 3,000 sailors and a distribution shortfall of another 12,000.

As a result of this shortfall, readiness has been severely impacted, with many ships and aviation units deploying at a lower, although still acceptable, level of readiness. Admiral Oliver has called this trend "alarming."

In response to this situation, the Secretary of the Navy and the Chief of Naval Operations have approved a number of aggressive personnel initiatives that, it is hoped, will reduce the immediate manning shortage. Also, Secretary of the Navy Richard Danzig from 1998 sought to initiate several longer-term policies that would improve the quality of life for men and women afloat.

Unfortunately, for much of the 1990s the Navy's leadership failed to realize the long-term implications of the radical force reductions coupled with the Clinton administration's early attitude toward the military services. The primary efforts to "fix" the situation—when belatedly taken—tended to center on increases in military compensation, i.e., basic pay, retirement, bonuses, and special duty payments. While it has been made clear by fleet input and statistical analysis that enhanced military compensation is a fundamental factor in any long-range solution to the Navy's manpower situation, the personnel problems facing the Navy are much deeper. The misuse of Navy personnel and their employment aboard ship and ashore as "cheap labor" has long been taken for granted (see chapter 1 of this edition of *Ships and Aircraft*).

Navy men and women also have been frustrated by shortages of spare parts, having to "cross deck" parts and even aircraft from returning ships to those deploying. Personnel shortages in a given specialty demand more time at sea from those who remain, exacerbating the shortfall when those men and women have an opportunity to leave the service or possibly change their rating.

The percentage of women in the Navy's officer and enlisted ranks is increasing (see below). As of 2000, of 311 active Navy ships, 192 were open to women. Of those, 120, or 63 percent, now have women on board. There have been problems in the integration of crewmen aboard ship, but those problems have been played down or ignored as the Navy's policy in this regard is to "make it work."

Currently the Navy prohibits women from serving in 33,000 positions, about 25,000 of which are aboard submarines. The other

---

1. The planned 600-ship fleet of the Reagan administration would have required some 622,000 personnel for full manning.
2. Statement before the Subcommittee on Personnel, Senate Armed Services Committee, 24 March 1999.

The Navy still offers adventure and travel, as being experienced by these sailors on liberty in the Turkish port of Antalya. But adventure and travel now are available to Americans at relatively low cost, a key factor in recruiting men and women in a society that is relatively affluent with low unemployment rates. (U.S. Navy, PH2 Michael W. Pendergrass)

The U.S. Navy is still manpower-intensive. Here five sailors lift an AMRAAM missile to load it onto an F/A-18C Hornet aboard the carrier CONSTELLATION (CV 64). More automated systems requiring far less people have been proposed for future ships and aircraft, especially the DD 21 land attack destroyer. (U.S. Navy, PH3 Mario P. DeAngelis)

areas are in the SEALs and in jobs that directly support Marine combat forces (i.e., medical, dental, chaplain, and liaison personnel assigned to Marine combat units).[3] In 1999, Secretary Danzig raised the issue of women serving in submarines. He noted that "a majority of this country in 2050 will be what we now call minority," and declared:

> We cannot be out of touch with that change. Congress and political power are changing. More and more, we see the role of women increasing in that regard. As that is the case, realistically, if the submarine force remains a white male bastion, it will wind up getting less and less support when it requires resources, when it has troubles.[4]

Danzig's speech came a few weeks after a Pentagon advisory group on women's issues addressed the issue of submarine service. The Defense Advisory Committee on Women in the Services asked the Navy why its new submarines of the VIRGINIA (SSN 774) class were not being designed to accommodate women. The committee also raised the question of the feasibility of women serving in existing U.S. submarines.[5]

Indicating that Trident missile submarines of the OHIO (SSBN 726) class were the primary candidates for near-term integration of women aboard submarines, Danzig admitted, "There are realities here that are difficult," but pointed out that there were difficulties in integrating women into naval aviation as well as in surface ships. In what some observers considered a first step in integrating women in submarines, during the summer of 1999, for two days at a time, five Trident submarines took women to sea. As part of the summer training program for Naval Reserve Officers Training Corps (NROTC) students, the PENNSYLVANIA (SSBN 735), WEST VIRGINIA (SSBN 736), KENTUCKY (SSBN 737), MARYLAND (SSBN 738), and RHODE ISLAND (SSBN 740) each embarked nine female cadets, with a total of 144 women going to sea in the submarines during the summer.

The Navy's leadership—submariners and non-submariners—have emphatically opposed women aboard submarines. Proponents of women in submarines are quick to point out that Australia and some Scandinavian navies have gender-integrated submarine crews and have designed their subs to provide some privacy. However, those navies that have women serving in submarines have different missions for their submarine forces, with boats typically deploying for

only a few days or weeks at a time. Further, the social structures of those countries are quite different from that of the United States; for example, toilets can be shared by both sexes aboard foreign ships without difficulty.

U.S. submarine crews, by contrast, must endure the intimacy of submarine patrols for months at a stretch. Trident missile submarines deploy for two months at a time, all of it spent under water, with only rare port visits or time alongside a tender. (Attack submarines normally deploy for up to six months accompanying aircraft carrier battle groups, although their cruises are periodically interrupted by port visits.)

Modifications to warships—surface ships or submarines—to accommodate women are expensive, while submarines, even Trident submarines, already have cramped quarters, with some "hot bunking" (sharing of bunks) required aboard attack submarines (SSNs).[6] The assignment of women to SSBNs or SSNs most likely will reduce the heads (toilet facilities) available to enlisted men. For example, a Trident SSBN has two heads for chief petty officers and two large heads for the rest of the enlisted men.[7] Thus, unless the complement of chiefs—approximately 16 on a Trident SSBN—is half women and half men, the larger group would have to do with a lesser ratio of heads; the situation would be even more aggrieved for the approximately 130 junior petty officers and seamen unless the male/female split were 65/65.

Secretary Danzig also raised the question of racial minorities in the submarine forces.[8] He observed that minorities account for just 8 percent of submarine personnel. This compares with about 34 percent Navy-wide (and approximately 32 percent in the Marine Corps). "That's a problem," he said. He explained, "I am not animated by some feeling of affirmative action or political correctness. I am animated by the fundamental perception that we are a democracy. The character of our country is changing. As the character of the country changes, so must the character of our military."

While the Navy—like the other military services—has increasingly more senior minority officers, within the Department of Defense, minority and women officers tend to not do as well in promotions as do white male officers. A Defense study has revealed:

> If we look at the promotion rates of white men and compare that as the benchmark, compare that to white women, to black men and to black women, white women generally do as well as white men beyond the rank of O-4 [lieutenant commander]. . . . Black men do not do as well as white men, and black women do a bit worse than black men.[9]

Another aspect of the minority issue is that most uniformed minority personnel—75 percent, according to a recent Department of Defense study—complain that they have experienced racially offensive behavior.[10] Further, less than one-half of those minority personnel interviewed expressed confidence that complaints of discrimination are thoroughly investigated.

Two other personnel issues are confronting the Navy: First, in January 2000 the Department of Defense agreed that 17-year-olds would not be allowed in combat situations. Under current policy, 17-year-olds can join the U.S. military services with parental permission. However, in bowing to a draft United Nations international treaty on child soldiers, approved in the General Assembly on 21 January, the U.S. government has decided that no 17-year-olds will be placed in potential combat situations.

Actually, this ruling affects only a few hundred Navy enlisted men and women (and even fewer Marines). The largest age bracket for

3. SEAL = Sea-Air-Land (units).
4. Speech to the Naval Submarine League, Arlington, Va., 4 June 1999.
5. The committee—known as DACOWITS—was established in 1951 to assist the armed forces in recruiting quality women for military service. The role of DACOWITS has since evolved into advising the Secretary of Defense on all policies related to women in the military.
6. The cost of adding female facilities aboard surface ships has been estimated at $5,000 for each female berth added to a surface ship, and between $200,000 and $400,000 per female in submarines; see Andrea Stone, "Navy Says Subs Should Keep Hatches Closed to Women," Navy Times, 27 September 1999, p. 14.
7. There are additional heads for the officers.
8. Speech to the Naval Submarine League, 4 June 1999.
9. Remarks by Curtis Gilroy, Director of Special Projects and Research, Office of the Under Secretary of Defense (Personnel and Readiness), Pentagon press conference, 23 November 1999.
10. Robert Suro and Michael A. Fletcher, "Seventy-Five Percent of Military's Minorities See Racism," Washington Post, 23 November 1999, pp. A1, A10.

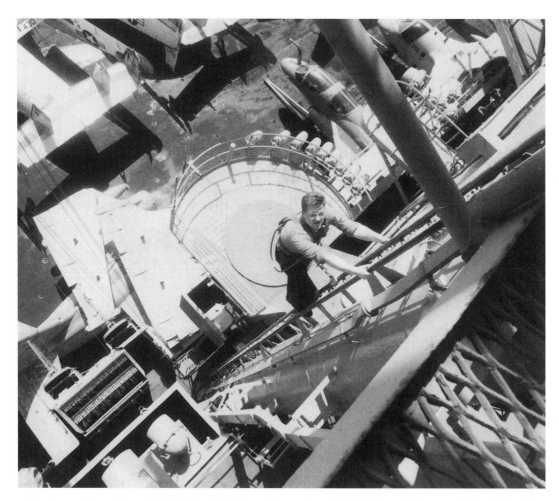

The Navy continues to provide high-tech training and opportunities for its men and women. This electronics technician has been aloft, checking an antenna on the carrier INDEPENDENCE (CV 62) shortly before the ship was decommissioned in 1998. The continued increase in the complexity of combat and support systems is especially evident in aircraft carriers. (U.S. Navy, PHAN John Sullivan)

Navy enlisted personnel is 21 (approximately 24,000 men and women).

The second issue is that of homosexuals in the military. The Clinton administration's "don't ask, don't tell" policy has had mixed reviews, with some critics saying that it has worked as well as it could in the American society and others saying that it has been a complete failure. Both sides of the issue point to the harassment and, in one instance, murder, of men and women suspected by their colleagues of being homosexuals.

The Navy's uniformed leadership has been united in opposition to allowing gays to serve openly in the armed forces. This is based on a number of factors, but especially the crowded living conditions in surface ships and, especially, submarines. This environment is far different than that ashore, whether in barracks, in modern bachelor enlisted and officer quarters, or even in the field.

The Department of Defense has continued to impose classes and "sensitivity training" for military personnel in handling both women in the services and the homosexual issue. The latest came as recently as February 2000, when a new program advised commanders to investigate thoroughly all complaints of "gay-bashing," whether verbal or physical. The policy also warns commanders against turning an investigation into gay-bashing against the person(s) making the complaint, a frequent charge of persons accused of being homosexual under the don't-ask-don't-tell policy. And the homosexual issue has been elevated to the nation's highest political levels through statements and promises of the presidential candidates during the campaign of 2000.

It is not clear to what extent these issues are influencing the shortfalls in Navy (and other service) recruiting and retention. But these issues certainly are adding to the burdens carried on the already heavily laden shoulders of commanding officers.

NAVAL OFFICERS

The Navy also is struggling to retain sufficient officers in the so-called unrestricted line communities—the "warfighters"—made up of aviation, surface, submarine, and special warfare personnel.

According to Vice Admiral Oliver,

> We must retain those mid-career officers and petty officers who are absolutely vital to our day-to-day operations and readiness. These individuals do the vast majority of direct leading, supervising, managing and planning "down on the deck plates." They build cohesion and readiness. They are the trainers who ensure that future generations of warriors are prepared to replace them. These are the people in greatest demand in the private sector and those whom the private sector is prepared to compensate well. These are also the individuals in whom the Navy has made the greatest training and education investments. We must capitalize on that investment and avoid being forced to pay the high costs associated with replacing them prematurely.[11]

The most critical officer retention problems traditionally have been in the aviation, submarine, and medical communities. During the past few years, the special warfare (SEAL) and surface warfare communities also have experienced significant officer shortfalls; the shortfalls in these two categories have been particularly surprising to many observers.

Historically, the special warfare community has enjoyed one of the highest retention rates in the Navy. However, during the past decade it has dropped by more than 20 percent. Since 1996, the annual number of resignations has risen dramatically, and the trend

---

11. Statement before the Subcommittee on Personnel, Senate Armed Services Committee, 24 March 1999.

shows no sign of abating. The SEAL retention rate at the critical seven-year point has fallen to 58 percent from historical levels of greater than 80 percent. The large numbers of resignations at the lieutenant levels and increasing special warfare requirements are having a serious adverse impact on critical senior leadership billets.

To recover from the high loss rates, accessions have been increased, but the decline in retention has prohibited the desired increases at the lieutenant commander and commander levels and will continue to do so.

With regard to surface warfare officers, during the past few years only about 24 percent of the officers that entered the surface warfare community attended department head school. This is 14 percent below the required 38 percent steady-state retention. Since the end of the Cold War, the pool of division officers (i.e., the level below department head) has decreased by 43 percent, while the need for department heads (driven by the replacement of older, manpower-intensive ships with more modern, capable, high-tech ships that are less manpower-intensive) has decreased by only 23 percent.

In the 1980s the retention of department heads averaged 32 percent, and during the height of the post–Cold War drawdown, it fell to a low of 17 percent. Indications are that retention of department heads is now leveling off at about 24 percent. Required retention for the next few years is 34 to 38 percent. This retention shortfall is forcing extensions of 8 to 12 months of sea duty for officers in department head tours, further impacting on surface officer retention and morale.

In all of these categories the Navy is seeking to remedy the recruiting and retention problems primarily with additional bonuses, as well as with general pay increases. Again, the problems appear to be more systemic than money-related, although that is an important factor.

Addressing the pay issue, Vice Admiral Oliver told Congress,

> Our sailors are extremely professional and deeply patriotic. Their love of country, dedicated service and willing acceptance of self-sacrifice are hallmarks of their chosen profession—yes: they all volunteer. Men and women of this calling are understandably reluctant to speak of the monetary value of their service; discussion of money as an instrument of motivation is alien to them and goes against their nature.
>
> In spite of this, the money we pay them (they earn so much more than we can afford) is fundamental to their quality of life. This is even more significant in a Sailor's career decision today than in years past, as a significantly larger number of our sailors are married with families. And while they might expect to endure significant personal sacrifice, self-denial, and even suffering in support of the mission and defense of country, they expect better for their family. Like all Americans, they want their children to have a better life than they did.[12]

With the reduction of Navy personnel at the end of the Cold War, the number of flag officers also has been reduced, although the reductions in this category can be considered token at best (see table 9-1). Of the ten four-star flag officers, all but one are in command or deputy positions:

Chief of Naval Operations
Vice Chief of Naval Operations
CINC Joint Forces Command/Supreme Allied Commander Atlantic (NATO)[13]
CINC Pacific Command
CINC Strategic Command
CINC Pacific Fleet
CINC Atlantic Fleet
CINC Naval forces Europe/CINC Allied Forces Southern Europe (NATO)
Deputy CINC European Command

The tenth four-star flag officer is the Director, Naval Nuclear Propulsion, within the Naval Sea Systems Command. This position was established at the four-star level in 1973 when the incumbent, Vice Admiral H. G. Rickover, was promoted to full admiral. Upon Rickover being relieved of duty in January 1982, Congress estab-

---

12. Statement before the Subcommittee on Personnel, Senate Armed Services Committee, 24 March 1999.
13. CINC = Commander in Chief.

Table 9-1. NAVY FLAG OFFICERS

Rank	Category	1988	1996	2000*
Admirals	Line**	10	8	10
Vice Admirals	Line**	30	26	23
	Engineering	1	—	1
	Aerospace Engineering	—	1	—
	Fleet Support	—	—	1
	Intelligence	—	—	1
	Medical Corps	1	1	—
	Health Care Executive	—	—	1
	Supply Corps	—	1	—
Rear Admirals *Upper Half*	Line**	55	91	58
	Engineering	7	7	3
	Aerospace Engineering	3	3	3
	Cryptology	1	2	1
	Intelligence	2	2	2
	Public Affairs	—	1	—
	Fleet Support	—	1	2
	Oceanography	—	—	1
	Medical Corps	7	3	1
	Health Care Executive	—	8	10
	Dental Corps	1	1	—
	Supply Corps	8	12	6
	Chaplain Corps	1	1	1
	Civil Engineer Corps	3	2	3
	Judge Advocate General's Corps	2	3	3
Rear Admirals *Lower Half*	Line**	144	82	88 + 37
	Engineering	8	5	6 + 2
	Aerospace Engineering	5	4	3 + 2
	Cryptology	2	1	2
	Intelligence	2	3	2 + 1
	Public Affairs	1	1	2 + 1
	Fleet Support	—	3	2 + 3
	Oceanography	3	1	1
	Medical Corps	9	4	2 + 4
	Health Care Executive	—	8	8
	Dental Corps	4	1	1
	Medical Service Corps	2	2	1 + 1
	Nurse Corps	1	1	1
	Supply Corps	11	11	12 + 3
	Chaplain Corps	2	3	2 + 1
	Civil Engineer Corps	4	6	5 + 1
	Judge Advocate General's Corps	1	—	—
	Nurse Corps	1	1	1
Totals ★★★★		10	8	10
★★★		32	29	27
★★		90	137	94
★		199	136	138 + 56

* In the year 2000 column the number after the plus sign indicates selectees; most of those officers are "frocked"—i.e., authorized to assume the title and wear the uniform of a flag officer—but receive the pay of a captain. Selectees are included in the 1988 and 1996 totals.
** Unrestricted Line (URL) officers

Not all Navy jobs are visible: Many men and women work far below deck, like this machinist's mate inspecting a boiler. Sailors work hard and long hours when at sea; Secretary Danzig has worked hard to improve the quality of life for men and women afloat as well as when they are ashore. (U.S. Navy, SN Patrick Horgan)

lished the position at the four-star level. The position continues at that rank despite the massive cutbacks in the numbers of nuclear-propelled surface ships and submarines and the reduction in nuclear propulsion development efforts (see table 9-2).

TABLE 9-2. U.S. NUCLEAR-PROPELLED SHIPS

Ship type		1973	1982	2000	2010*
SSBN	strategic missile submarines	41	32	18	14
SSN	attack submarines	59	89	55	55
CVN	aircraft carriers	1	4	9	11
CGN	missile cruisers	3	9	—	—
NR	research submersibles	1	1	1	1

   * Planned force levels

ENLISTED PERSONNEL

The Navy is an all-volunteer force, the draft having ended in 1973. While post–Cold War cutbacks in personnel strength initially enabled the Navy to accept only enlisted men and women who had a high aptitude for technical training, during the past few years this situation has changed due to the shortfalls in the recruiting and retention of enlisted personnel.

The efforts to correct these shortfalls have primarily been increases in money, both basic pay and bonuses in certain specialties. Some non-monetary approaches are being considered. Rear Admiral Barbara McGann, the Commander Navy Recruiting Command, has outlined plans that are being considered for offering sabbaticals midway in a sailor's career for completing a college degree and for taking in recruits at higher rates (ranks) if they have demonstrated technical skills that the Navy needs.[14]

Secretary of the Navy Danzig also has raised concerns over how the Navy employs sailors as "cheap labor" and over enlisted accommodations in U.S. Navy ships. Studies, according to Danzig, ranks U.S. Navy ships among the least comfortable in all of the NATO navies.

Also, "a greater number of people are damaged today," according to Commander Robert Koffman, the senior medical officer in the carrier CARL VINSON (CVN 70), referring to some of the same trends pervading American society—young men and women who hail from street gangs and broken families.[15]

Historically it has been the chiefs and other petty officers who counseled younger enlistees. Increasingly today, however, commanding officers, executive officers, and command master chief petty officers are holding "bull sessions" with sailors. The burden more and more falls on the senior officers and chiefs of a command because the other petty officers are overburdened with duties (in part because of personnel shortfalls), and the issues affecting military personnel are increasingly complex.

WOMEN IN THE NAVY

Almost 14 percent of the Navy's officers and the same percentage of the Navy's enlisted personnel are women. These are generally similar to the percentages of women in the Army and Air Force, but much larger than the percentages of women in the Marine Corps—4 percent and almost 6 percent, respectively.

The number of women in the military services is expected to continue to increase. More than 80 percent of military positions are now open to women; that number also will increase. Interestingly, by some criteria the pool of women available for military service promises to be better educated than their male counterparts. The proportion of bachelor's degrees awarded to males is now smaller than the

number earned by women; it has dropped from 51 percent in 1980 to 44.9 percent in 1996, the last year for which detailed data are available. This trend applies across the spectrum, including ethnicity and race.[16] If the trend continues, males will earn only 42 percent of the bachelor degrees in 2008.

Similarly, high school graduation rates for males are now lower than for females. Part of the reason may be the large job market for non–high school graduates in the current U.S. economy. Regardless, these factors will affect Navy recruiting as the Navy seeks men and women to sail and support an increasingly complex fleet.

Of concern to the Navy's personnel managers is the impact of large numbers of women in the Navy. This could cause major problems with respect to the impact of pregnancy on crew stability and the Navy's stringent policy of assigning service husbands and wives to the same base or station. A high pregnancy rate among Navy women, especially those in ships' crews, can disrupt operations and also increase medical-care requirements. About 20 percent of the Navy's women are married to Navy men. While the Navy attempts to station the couple at the same installation, that policy becomes increasingly difficult to implement as the number of Navy couples increases.

The Navy has one active-duty vice admiral and 13 active-duty rear admirals who are women (accounting for 4 percent of the Navy's flag officers). The vice admiral, Patricia A. Tracey, is Deputy Assistant Secretary of Defense for Manpower and Personnel Policy; she and seven of the rear admirals are fleet support specialists who hold major staff and shore command assignments. The other rear admirals consist of one engineering duty officer, who is the chief engineer of the Navy, three health care executives, one Nurse Corps officer, and one Supply Corps officer. None of the female flag officers is an unrestricted line officer, i.e., qualified for command at sea.

(The Marine Corps has one female brigadier general, Frances C. Wilson, Commanding General, Marine Corps Base Quantico. Previously the Marine Corps had a female lieutenant general, who has now retired; that officer, selected in March 1996, was Carol A. Mutter, the first woman in the U.S. armed forces to be promoted to three-star rank. The Coast Guard also has female flag officers.)

Historical: Women had long served at sea in U.S. Navy hospital ships and transports. Since 1979 women have also been assigned to noncombatant ships and craft, mostly tenders, repair ships, and fleet oilers. The aircraft carrier DWIGHT D. EISENHOWER (CVN 69) was the first U.S. warship to deploy with women, departing Norfolk, Va., on 20 October 1994 with 367 female officers and enlisteds on board. The ship deployed for six months, operating in the Mediterranean–Adriatic areas.

The first woman to head a Navy aircraft squadron took command of Electronic Warfare Squadron (VAQ) 34 in July 1990, and in December 1990 the first woman took command of a U.S. Navy ship, the salvage ship OPPORTUNE (ARS 41); subsequently female commanding officers have been named to other ships, including destroyers.[17]

NAVAL RESERVE

The Naval Reserve—like the active naval forces—is being reduced following a buildup during the 1980s. The Naval Reserve has several categories of personnel and numerous components. Figure 9-1 shows the basic organizational structure of the Naval Reserve.

The head of the Naval Reserve, currently Rear Admiral John B. Totushek, is "triple-hatted": He serves as Director of the Naval Reserve (code N095) in the Office of the Chief Naval Operations; as Chief of Naval Reserve, primarily for congressional relations; and as Commander Naval Reserve Force, the operational commander.

The Naval Reserve has three principal categories of personnel, totaling approximately 212,000 men and women:

14. Rear Adm. McGann outlined these plans during a presentation at the U.S. Naval Institute's annual meeting, Annapolis, Md., 22 April 1999.
15. Richard J. Newman, "The Navy Tries a Little Shipboard Tenderness," *U.S. News & World Report*, 22 March 1999, p. 26.
16. Department of Education statistics; see Judy Jolley Mohraz, "Missing Men on Campus," *Washington Post*, 16 January 2000, p. B7.
17. Lt. Cdr. Darlene M. Iskra took command of the OPPORTUNE after the ship's previous commanding officer was taken off in a medical emergency; the ship had an all-male crew at the time.

Selected Reserve

16,000	full-time support or Training and Administration of Reserves (TAR)
71,300	assigned to Naval Reserve Force units
225	individuals
3,900	training pipeline

Individual Ready Reserve

109,600	individuals

Standby Reserve

10,800	individuals

The Selected Reserve personnel operate ships and aircraft, provide staff augmentation, and man construction battalions and other specialized units. These personnel normally train 24 days per year, plus serving

Figure 9-1
Naval Reserve Structure

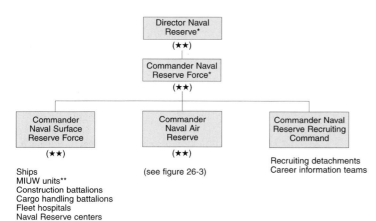

* Same individual
** MIUW = Mobile Inshore Undersea Warfare

two weeks on active duty, and most receive pay for their services. The TAR personnel, along with some other reserve personnel, are on full-time active duty, most in conjunction with training reserves.

During their drill periods, some Selected Reserve personnel participate in Navy day-to-day operational activities. For example, reserve patrol squadrons routinely conduct Anti-Submarine Warfare (ASW) patrols from bases in the United States and overseas during their training periods. These and other reserve air units have regularly flown drug-interdiction missions in the Caribbean and off the U.S. East and West coasts, while reserve transport aircraft regularly carry personnel and cargo between the United States and overseas points.

The Navy activated 21,109 reservists during Operations Desert Storm/Desert Shield, or almost 16 percent of the ready reserve force. Reportedly, 134,000 reservists requested active duty in conjunction with the Gulf buildup (see table 9-3). These reservists were called up mainly for their individual skills, with medical reservists (physicians, nurses, medical service personnel, and corpsmen) accounting for almost one-half of those reservists activated; many of the medical personnel were used to "backfill" positions at U.S. medical facilities while the active duty personnel were sent to the Persian Gulf, and to serve in two reserve field hospitals and two hospital ships deployed in the Gulf area. Cargo handling, construction (Seabee), and Mobile

TABLE 9-3. NAVAL RESERVISTS ACTIVATED, 1990–1991

Category	Available*	Activated**
Medical	19,986	10,452
Ship augmentees	18,687	1,838
Construction	14,731	2,475
Aviation	16,736	1,111
Cargo handling	1,924	961
Military sealift	1,885	469
Other	49,644	3,803
Total	*123,593*	*21,109*

* As of 31 December 1990
** As of 6 June 1991
Source: General Accounting Office, *Operation Desert Shield/Desert Storm: Use of Navy and Marine Corps Reserve* (Washington, D.C.: 1991), p. 3.

The guided missile frigate ESTOCIN (FFG 15) sails off the coast of Puerto Rico during counter-narcotic training exercises. Operations by Naval Reserve Force ships, aircraft, and units and active naval forces are virtually "seamless," in large part because of their similar ships, aircraft, and equipment. The NRF frigates are now operating SH-60B LAMPS III helicopters, as are active surface combatants. (U.S. Navy, JO2 David Rush)

Inshore Undersea Warfare (MIUW) units were sent to the Gulf. (No reserve-manned ships were deployed to the Gulf area; however, portions of nine reserve aircraft squadrons were deployed to Europe and the Middle East during Desert Storm/Desert Shield.)

Subsequently, selected reserve personnel have participated in other U.S. military operations, including the air strikes against Serbian forces in the spring of 1999.

In 2000, the Naval Reserve provided, in terms of personnel:

100 percent of the fleet support airlift squadrons (VR)
100 percent of the MIUW units
98 percent of the naval-control-of-shipping units
93 percent of the cargo-handling units
90 percent of the military sealift
60 percent of the Construction Battalions (Seabees)
53 percent of the intelligence personnel
43 percent of the combat search-and-rescue (SAR) helicopters
40 percent of the fleet hospitals
9 percent of the carrier air wings

In terms of numbers, with approximately 235 aircraft, the Naval Air Reserve provides just over 5 percent of the Navy's aircraft, and with 23 ships, the Naval Reserve constitutes about 7 percent of the U.S. Fleet.

The surface ships of the Naval Reserve Force (NRF) report directly to the active fleet commanders. The Naval Air Reserve Force (tactical air units) reports through the Commander Naval Air Reserve Force to the Chief of Naval Operations. The Chief of Naval Reserve has certain administrative and recruiting functions that support these forces. The headquarters of the Chief of Naval Reserve and the Commander Naval Air Reserve are located in New Orleans, La.

Surface Naval Reserve. The surface Naval Reserve operates a large number of ships of frigate size and smaller. As of late 2000, the following ships were operated by composite active-duty/reserve crews under the aegis of the NRF:

8 FFG 7   OLIVER HAZARD PERRY class
1 LST 1179 NEWPORT class
1 MCS 12   INCHON (IWO JIMA/LPH 2 class)
4 MCM 1   AVENGER class
9 MHC 51   OSPREY class

There is also one reserve small boat squadron with 12 inshore boat units that operates a number of small craft; see chapter 20.

The operation of the carrier JOHN F. KENNEDY (CV 67) as an NRF ship, albeit with mainly an active-duty crew, has been a failure; see chapter 13.

Previous plans to transfer other auxiliary ships to the Naval Reserve have been discarded, as were plans to shift all MHC/MCM-type mine craft to the reserves after one year in the active fleet. Rather, the number of frigates in the Naval Reserve will be reduced as that type of ship is phased out of the active fleet by about 2016 and out of the NRF about 2021.

Naval Air Reserve. The composition of the Naval Air Reserve is described in chapter 26. The Naval Air Reserve currently consists of one carrier air wing (RCVW), plus a large number of land-based squadrons that largely mirror the active fleet in organization and aircraft:

1 VAQ   electronic attack squadron
2 VAW   airborne early warning squadrons
1 VF   fighter squadron
2 VFA   strike fighter squadrons
2 VFC   fighter composite squadrons
7 VP   patrol squadrons
1 VQ   fleet air reconnaissance squadron
4 VR   fleet logistic support squadrons
1 HC   helicopter combat support
         squadron
2 HCS   helicopter combat SAR/special
         warfare support squadrons
2 HS   helicopter ASW squadrons
1 HSL   helicopter light ASW squadron

The Naval Air Reserve has discarded its two light helicopter ASW squadrons that flew the SH-2G LAMPS I helicopters, in favor of one HSL with SH-60B LAMPS III helicopters. These aircraft fly from NRF frigates.

Most reserve air squadrons fly the same type of aircraft as their active duty counterparts, the principal exception being the lack of fixed-wing sea control aircraft (S-3B Viking).

Historical: The naval reserve concept can be traced to the American Revolution, when several of the colonies employed armed merchant ships to resist British military activities within their state waters. By the time of the signing of the Declaration of Independence in July 1776 there were 11 colonies with some form of navy.

During the next century there were various forms of state volunteers, and a volunteer force was established in the Union Navy during the Civil War. Then, beginning in 1888, several states established naval components as part of their state militias. These naval militias were intended for harbor and coastal defense; they had no federal standing, and the rules for applicants and level of competence varied considerably.

Beginning in 1891 the Navy offered to allow state militias to participate in some fleet exercises, and there was soon federal cooperation in a number of training areas. Two years later, the training ship NEW HAMPSHIRE (launched in 1864 although laid down 45 years earlier!) was transferred from the Navy to the New York State Naval Militia.

By the eve of the Spanish-American War of 1898, there were more than 4,000 men in state naval militias. When the conflict erupted, the militias were used to patrol the coasts (there was a perceived threat of a Spanish assault), while thousands more militiamen were taken into the Navy. Their outstanding service in the war led to Navy Department recommendations for the creation of a national Naval Reserve. This was opposed—mostly by state interests—until 1914, when Congress passed legislation that largely placed the naval militias under supervision of the Navy Department. In time of war, they would become part of the Navy (as the state National Guard units would become part of the Army). A year later, in 1915, the U.S. Naval Reserve was established, a reserve force to be comprised of men honorably discharged from the active Navy.

With U.S. entry into World War I in April 1917, the militias were mobilized as the National Naval Volunteers, with almost the total strength of just over 10,000 men coming onto active duty in the Navy. By September 1917 their ranks had grown to almost 17,000 men. These volunteers were consolidated with the Naval Reserve in July 1918, creating the current U.S. Naval Reserve organization. (The states of California, Illinois, and New York continue to maintain state naval forces, whose members are additionally in the Naval Reserve.)

The Naval Reserve had major roles in World War II, the Korean War, and the Vietnam War, as well as periodic operations in NRF and active Navy ships during normal "peacetime" naval operations.

CHAPTER 10

Strategic Missile Submarines

The strategic missile submarine MARYLAND enters port after a deterrent patrol. These large submarines, each carrying 24 Trident ballistic missiles, provide a virtually invulnerable nuclear striking force when at sea. Like other components of the U.S. military establishment, their numbers and role are changing at the start of the 21st century. (1999, Leo Van Ginderen)

In early 2001 the U.S. Navy operated 18 Trident strategic missile submarines of the OHIO class. Four of these submarines—currently the world's largest operational undersea craft—are scheduled to be taken out of service in the next few years to reach the approved force level of 14 submarines carrying 336 Submarine-Launched Ballistic Missiles (SLBM). There are proposals to convert the four SSBNs being retired to combination cruise missile and transport/special forces submarines (see chapter 11 of this edition of *Ships and Aircraft*).

The 18 Trident missile submarines, completed from 1981 to 1997, each carry 24 missiles. The first eight OHIO-class SSBNs are armed with the Trident C-4 missile carrying eight W76 100-kiloton warheads; the ten later submarines have D-5 missiles. Navy planning for the late 1980s envisioned a total of 24 Trident submarines (576 SLBMs), all eventually to be armed with the D-5 missile.

The Trident D-5 has greater range and accuracy in comparison with the C-4, with the D-5 delivering 75 percent more payload than the C-4. The C-4 missile has eight Mk 4 re-entry bodies with eight W76 warheads (each approx. 100 kilotons) while the D-5 has eight Mk 5 re-entry bodies with eight W76 or eight W88 warheads (each W88 approx. 450 kilotons).

An estimate of nuclear weapons currently assigned to U.S. operational forces is provided in table 10-1. The Trident missiles are the only nuclear weapons currently in Navy service. Nuclear Tomahawk Land-Attack Missiles (TLAM-N) and aircraft bombs are available at storage sites in the United States for naval use; however, the lack of realistic training and handling of these weapons makes their effective future use by the Navy doubtful.

Table 10-1 reflects the U.S. reductions based on the START I treaty, which entered into force on 5 December 1994. Under the START II agreement between the United States and Russia, the total number of U.S. strategic nuclear warheads is to be reduced by the year 2007 to no more than 2,250 warheads on missiles (see table 10-2), of which the 14 Trident submarines would carry 336 D-5 missiles with not more than 1,750 warheads (i.e., about five warheads per Trident missile). Under this plan, the four submarines now armed with C-4 missiles that are being retained will be upgraded to the D-5 weapon.

All 500 allowed land-based ICBMs would be downloaded to single warheads. The manned bombers are to consist of B-52H Stratofortress and B-2 "stealth" manned bombers. The B-1B Lancer bombers are considered accountable as nuclear-capable under START I but not START II.

These changes are being planned even though the START II treaty has not been ratified by the Russian Duma (parliament); the U.S. Senate ratified the treaty on 26 January 1996. It is unlikely that Russia will ratify the treaty in the foreseeable future.

There currently are no new types of SSBN or SLBM under development in the United States. The production of Trident D-5 missiles for U.S. submarines is continuing to permit the conversion of four submarines (SSBNs 730–733) to carry the D-5 missile and for the four British Trident-armed submarines of

the VANGUARD class.[1] An updated D-5 missile is planned (see chapter 28).

Beyond the cutback to 14 Trident submarines, the operating tempo of the Trident submarines has been reduced. But no action has been taken on proposals that the Trident force shift from the historic two-crew operating concept to a single crew. While this action could result in considerable financial savings, it would severely reduce Trident submarine time at sea and flexibility in scheduling their deterrent patrols.[2]

The Navy has also conducted a demonstration firing of a Trident D-5 missile in a configuration for carrying a conventional, high-explosive warhead. The tests had been suggested by the Navy's Strategic Systems Project Office as a means of striking time-sensitive, heavily defended, high-value targets. Such a weapon could enable the Navy to retain the four non-strategic submarines for a conventional role. However, there could be significant problems in the concept, such as a nation's early warning system indicating that ballistic missiles were being fired with no way of knowing the intended target or whether they were nuclear or conventional weapons. Further, the modification of existing treaties and their missile counts would be required. Thus, employing Trident SSBNs in a conventional strike role is highly unlikely.

The last of the 41 earlier Polaris-Poseidon ballistic missile submarines, completed from 1959 to 1967, have been decommissioned and stricken except for the transport submarine KAMEHAMEHA (listed in chapter 11). Two retired SSBNs, the DANIEL WEBSTER and SAM

---

1. The British submarines carry 16 Trident D-5 missiles, which are fitted with British-produced W76-type warheads. Only sufficient missiles for three submarines are being procured—58 missiles, including test, training, and spare weapons. British SSBNs go on patrol with some empty tubes. (Previous plans provided for the procurement of 65 missiles.)
2. The only other nations that now maintain continuous SSBN/SLBM patrols are Britain and France; Russian SSBN/SLBM patrols have been sporadic, with no strategic missile submarines at sea at certain times.

TABLE 10-2. U.S. STRATEGIC FORCES UNDER ARMS AGREEMENTS

Weapon	START I (by 5 Dec 2001)	START II (by 31 Dec 2007)
ICBM missiles	550	500
SLBM missiles	432	336
ICBM warheads	not over 2,000	500
SLBM warheads	not over 3,456	not over 1,750
Ballistic missile warheads	not over 4,900	not over 2,250
SSBN submarines	18	14
B-2 bombers	21	21
B-52 bombers	76	76

Source: Secretary of Defense William S. Cohen, *Annual Report to the President and the Congress* (Washington, D.C.: 1999), p. 68.

TABLE 10-1. U.S. NUCLEAR WEAPONS, 2001

	Weapon	Launchers/ Missiles/ Bombers	Total Warheads	Total Megatonnage
ICBM	Minuteman III	500	1,500	404
ICBM	Peacekeeper MX	50	500	150
SLBM	Trident I C-4	192	1,536	154
SLBM	Trident II D-5	240	1,920	336
Bomber	B-2 Spirit	21*	} 1,800	770
Bomber	B-52H Stratofortress	76*		
Fighter	F-15E Eagle**	}	~650	~325
Fighter	F-16 Fighting Falcon**			

*Total number of aircraft; operational aircraft average about 50 percent.
**Fighter-bombers based in Europe and the United States.
Source: The Bulletin of the Atomic Scientists and Natural Resources Defense Council, Washington, D.C.

TABLE 10-3. STRATEGIC MISSILE DEPLOYMENTS

Missile	First patrol begun	Last patrol completed
Polaris A-1	GEORGE WASHINGTON 15 Nov 1960	ABRAHAM LINCOLN 14 Oct 1965
Polaris A-2	ETHAN ALLEN 26 June 1962	JOHN MARSHALL 9 June 1974
Polaris A-3	DANIEL WEBSTER 28 Sep 1964	ROBERT E. LEE 1 Oct 1981*
Poseidon C-3	JAMES MADISON 31 Mar 1971	KAMEHAMEHA and ULYSSES S. GRANT** 1 Oct 1991
Trident C-4	FRANCIS SCOTT KEY 20 Oct 1979	(missile in service)
Trident D-5	TENNESSEE 29 Mar 1990	(missile in service)

*This is the date that the ROBERT E. LEE was taken off alert; she was still at sea at the time, but Polaris patrols officially ended on 1 October 1981.
**The KAMEHAMEHA and ULYSSES S. GRANT were taken off alert on this date; although the submarines were still at sea, returning to port on 15 and 16 October 1981, respectively, their deterrent patrols officially ended on 1 October 1991.

RAYBURN, are retained and immobilized at Charleston, S.C., as Moored Training Ships (MTS) for nuclear propulsion operators.

These submarines were armed with a succession of Polaris missiles (41 submarines), Poseidon missiles (31), and Trident C-4 missiles (12).

The dismantling of nuclear-propelled submarines requires more than a year. Because U.S. Navy nuclear-propelled ships, by law, must have personnel on board until the reactor is permanently closed down and the fuel removed, upon deactivation nuclear ships and submarines are placed "In Commission, In Reserve" (ICIR); these units are listed in this volume as ICIR. After the reactor shutdown requirements have been met, the ships are formally decommissioned and, in recent years, stricken on the same date. Once a ship has been placed in ICIR status, she cannot be returned to service; the ships are officially decommissioned and stricken some six to eight months after the ICIR date. In particular, SSBNs are cut up for scrap to meet disarmament treaty stipulations.

The reactors are "defueled" and removed from the submarines along with other radioactive as well as hazardous materials; the reactors are being "temporarily" buried at Hanford, Wash. Submarines decommissioned on the East Coast are defueled and then towed to Puget Sound for the eventual removal and burial of their reactor compartments and scrapping of the submarines. The submarines are stripped of material that may be of use in the fleet.

The average cost of decommissioning and partially dismantling a nuclear submarine in FY 1999 dollars is $32 million for an SSBN and $26 million for an SSN.

Builders: The Electric Boat Division of General Dynamics in Groton, Conn., built all 18 of the Trident submarines (as well as 17 of the 41 U.S. Polaris-Poseidon submarines). The Polaris submarine program reflected a spectacular U.S. submarine construction effort, with the 41 submarines being completed in a 7½-year period following a highly compressed development period. (In addition to the Polaris submarines, the Navy completed 17 other nuclear-propelled submarines in that period, an average of almost eight nuclear submarines per year.)

Manning: Secretary of the Navy Richard Danzig on 3 June 1999 proposed that consideration be given to assigning women to submarine crews; the Trident SSBNs are the principal candidates for mixed-manning because of their size and accommodations.

Names: The 41 Polaris strategic missile submarines completed from 1960 to 1967 were named for "famous Americans," although several were in fact named for persons never in the American colonies or United States.

The subsequent Trident submarines, completed from 1981 to 1997, are named for states of the Union. Previously, state names were assigned to battleships and, later, to guided missile cruisers (CGNs 36–41). The exception to the state name source for Trident SSBNs was made on 27 September 1983 when the RHODE ISLAND was named for the late Senator Henry M. (Scoop) Jackson, a long-time supporter of nuclear and defense programs.

Operational: About ten of the 18 Trident submarines are normally at sea on deterrent patrols. Each submarine is manned by two complete, alternating crews, designated as blue and gold crews. While one crew is at sea, the other is engaged in training (mostly with system simulators), leave, medical treatment, and other shore activities. The normal deployment patrol (with one crew) is up to 70 days.

The Trident SSBN force is based at Bangor, Wash., for patrols in the North Pacific, and at Kings Bay, Ga., for patrols in the North Atlantic.

As of 1 June 2000, U.S. ballistic missile submarines had completed 3,452 deterrent patrols:

1,245	Polaris
1,182	Poseidon
397	Trident C-4 backfit in older submarines
411	Trident C-4 in OHIO-class submarines
217	Trident D-5 in OHIO-class submarines

This number does not include the 41 patrols conducted by five Regulus-armed guided missile submarines in the North Pacific from 1959 to 1964.[3] There were 1,245 Polaris patrols and 1,182 Poseidon patrols by U.S. submarines. The pioneer GEORGE WASHINGTON conducted the first ballistic missile patrol (see table 10-3).

---

3. The operational Regulus submarines were the TUNNY (SSG 282), BARBERO (SSG 317), GRAYBACK (SSG 574), GROWLER (SSG 577), and HALIBUT (SSGN 587). They deployed with the Regulus I surface-launched cruise missile in the northwest Pacific area from September 1959 to July 1964.

Doing what captains like and sailors don't: Crewmen of the ALABAMA spell out "Bama 50" signifying completion of the submarine's 50th deterrent patrol as the submarine cruises off San Diego. Sailors often are mustered to spell out the names of ports being visited. (2000, U.S. Navy, PH1 Mark A. Correa)

18 STRATEGIC MISSILE SUBMARINES: "OHIO" CLASS

Number	Name	FY	Builder	Start	Laid down	Launched	Commissioned	Status
SSBN 726	OHIO	74	General Dynamics/Electric Boat	19 July 1974	10 Apr 1976	7 Apr 1979	11 Nov 1981	**PA**
SSBN 727	MICHIGAN	75	General Dynamics/Electric Boat	15 Aug 1975	4 Apr 1977	26 Apr 1980	11 Sep 1982	**PA**
SSBN 728	FLORIDA	75	General Dynamics/Electric Boat	27 Feb 1976	9 June 1977	14 Nov 1981	18 June 1983	**PA**
SSBN 729	GEORGIA	76	General Dynamics/Electric Boat	17 Jan 1977	7 Apr 1979	6 Nov 1982	11 Feb 1984	**PA**
SSBN 730	HENRY M. JACKSON	77	General Dynamics/Electric Boat	28 Feb 1978	19 Jan 1981	15 Oct 1983	6 Oct 1984	**PA**
SSBN 731	ALABAMA	78	General Dynamics/Electric Boat	6 Apr 1979	27 Aug 1981	19 May 1984	25 May 1985	**PA**
SSBN 732	ALASKA	78	General Dynamics/Electric Boat	12 Oct 1979	9 Mar 1983	12 Jan 1985	25 Jan 1986	**PA**
SSBN 733	NEVADA	80	General Dynamics/Electric Boat	17 Feb 1981	8 Aug 1983	14 Sep 1985	16 Aug 1986	**PA**
SSBN 734	TENNESSEE	81	General Dynamics/Electric Boat	15 Jan 1982	9 June 1986	13 Dec 1986	17 Dec 1988	**AA**
SSBN 735	PENNSYLVANIA	83	General Dynamics/Electric Boat	29 Nov 1982	2 Mar 1987	23 Apr 1988	9 Sep 1989	**AA**
SSBN 736	WEST VIRGINIA	84	General Dynamics/Electric Boat	21 Nov 1983	18 Dec 1987	14 Oct 1989	20 Oct 1990	**AA**
SSBN 737	KENTUCKY	85	General Dynamics/Electric Boat	13 Aug 1985	18 Dec 1987	11 Aug 1990	13 July 1991	**AA**
SSBN 738	MARYLAND	86	General Dynamics/Electric Boat	22 Mar 1986	18 Dec 1987	10 Aug 1991	13 June 1992	**AA**
SSBN 739	NEBRASKA	87	General Dynamics/Electric Boat	6 June 1987	18 Dec 1987	15 Aug 1992	10 July 1993	**AA**
SSBN 740	RHODE ISLAND	88	General Dynamics/Electric Boat	23 Apr 1988	—	17 July 1993	9 July 1994	**AA**
SSBN 741	MAINE	89	General Dynamics/Electric Boat	4 Apr 1989	—	16 July 1994	29 July 1995	**AA**
SSBN 742	WYOMING	90	General Dynamics/Electric Boat	27 Jan 1990	—	15 July 1995	13 July 1996	**AA**
SSBN 743	LOUISIANA	91	General Dynamics/Electric Boat	15 May 1991	—	27 July 1996	6 Sep 1997	**AA**

Displacement:	16,764 tons standard	ASW weapons:	Mk 48 torpedoes
	18,750 tons submerged	Radars:	BPS-15A surface search on SSBN 726–740
Length:	560 feet (170.7 m) overall		BPS-16 surface search on SSBN 741–743
Beam:	42 feet (12.8 m)	Sonars:	BQQ-6 bow mounted passive
Draft:	36¼ feet (11.05 m)		BQR-15 towed array; being replaced by TB-29
Propulsion:	2 steam turbines (General Electric); approx. 35,000 shp; 1 shaft		BQR-19 active navigation
Reactors:	1 S8G pressurized-water (General Electric)		BQS-13 active
Speed:	approx. 25 knots surface		BQS-15 under-ice
	approx. 25 knots submerged	Fire control:	1 CCS Mk 2 Mod 3
Manning:	163 (15 officers + 148 enlisted)		1 Mk 98 missile FCS
Missiles:	SSBN 726–733: 24 tubes for Trident C-4 SLBM		1 Mk 118 torpedo FCS
	SSBN 734–743: 24 tubes for Trident D-5 SLBM	EW systems:	WLR-8(V)5
Torpedo tubes:	4 21-inch (533-mm) tubes Mk 68 (amidships)		WLR-10

These are the largest submarines to be built in the United States. They were exceeded in size only by the six Soviet Typhoon-class (Project 941) SSBNs, which displace submerged more than three times as much as the OHIOs, and the 11 Oscar-class (Project 949) SSGNs. (Most Typhoons are now being scrapped; the KURSK of the latter class sank in 2000.) The OHIO was laid down nine years after the completion of the previous U.S. strategic missile submarine, the WILL ROGERS.

Incorporation of the D-5 missile in SSBNs 734–736 resulted in a one-year delay in their construction; the SSBN 737 and later submarines were ordered as D-5 ships (see *Missiles* below).

Builders: Note that four submarines of this class were laid down at the Electric Boat yard on the same date. The last four submarines did not have formal keel-layings.

During the mid-1980s Secretary of the Navy John Lehman gave consideration to constructing some Trident submarines at Newport News Shipbuilding; in the event, all were built at Electric Boat.

Class: The origin of the Trident program was the Department of Defense–sponsored STRAT-X study of 1967–1968 to determine future strategic weapon requirements. The study recommended two land-based and two sea-based strategic systems, with one of the latter being the Underwater Long-range Missile System (ULMS). This evolved into the Trident system, the name being changed from ULMS to Trident on 16 May 1972. (One land-based strategic offensive system also was initiated, the MX land-based missile.)

The Trident program lagged considerably behind the schedule established when the weapon system was approved for development in May 1972. The lead submarine was funded in fiscal 1974 with a schedule put forward at that time for constructing an initial series of ten Trident SSBNs at an annual rate of 1-3-3-3, with the last of the ten submarines to be completed by 1982.

The first Trident submarine was ordered on 25 July 1974, with a planned delivery of 30 April 1979. However, the shipyard agreed to attempt to make delivery in December 1977 because of the high priority of the program. Subsequent delays caused by the Navy management of the project, design changes, and problems at the shipyard resulted in the late deliveries of the early submarines, with authorizations for the first ten submarines covering a ten-year period instead of four years.

Navy planning in the early 1980s called for a class of 24 OHIO-class submarines (to be assigned hull numbers SSBN 726–749). These were to replace the 41 Polaris-Poseidon submarines.

The SALT I strategic arms agreement with the Soviet Union in 1972 required the decommissioning of the Polaris A-3 submarines THEODORE ROOSEVELT and ABRAHAM LINCOLN to compensate for the OHIO entering service; those were the first U.S. SSBNs to be decommissioned (see below).

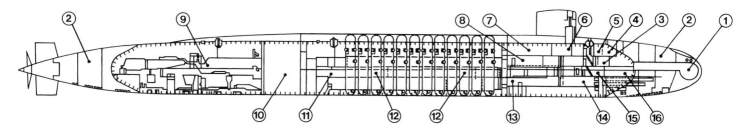

OHIO-class SSBN 1. BQQ-6 sonar sphere 2. Ballast tanks 3. Computer room 4. Radio room 5. Sonar room 6. Command and control center 7. Navigation center 8. Missile control center 9. Engine room 10. Reactor compartment 11. Auxiliary machinery 12. Crew's berthing 13. Crew's mess 14. Torpedo room 15. Wardroom 16. Chief petty officers' quarters (William Clipson)

The NEVADA under way on the surface reveals the long, low lines of the OHIO-class SSBNs. Fourteen of these submarines will remain in service during the first decade of the 21st century. The contemporary Soviet Delta designs had much higher "turtle backs," while the innovative Typhoon SSBN had a highly innovative, multi-hull design. (1999, Leo Van Ginderen)

The OHIO-class submarines were designed for a 30-year service life. Subsequent changes in operational/maintenance cycles and re-evaluation of their material condition have led to a planned 42-year service life.

The OHIO—lead ship of the Trident SSBNs—moored at La Maddalena, Sardinia. Completed in 1981, the OHIO soon will be retired, with the nuclear submarine community hoping to retain her in service as a cruise missile/special operations submarine. (1999, Leo Van Ginderen)

Design: SCB No. 304.74. These are the largest submarines to be built in the West, the size of these craft having been determined by their missile battery and reactor plant. The OHIO-class submarines have a conservative design with the bow sonar dome and amidships torpedo tubes, similar to later attack submarine designs.

The Trident submarines have comfortable accommodations for their crews. Three logistic hatches—in the forward (control-accommodation section), center (missile), and after (engineering) compartments—have escape trunks that can be removed when in port to provide large, six-foot (1.8-m)-diameter resupply and repair openings. These permit the rapid transfer of supply pallets, equipment replacement modules, and even machinery components, allowing a significant reduction in the time required for replenishment and maintenance. (The standard U.S. submarine hatches are 26 inches/0.66 m in diameter.)

These submarines are reported to have a 985-foot (300-m) operating depth.

Electronics: The 14 submarines to be retained are being fitted with the BQQ-10 Acoustic Rapid COTS Insertion (ARCI) sonar update.[4] See the entry for AUGUSTA (SSN 710) in Chapter 11. The first to receive ARCI was the ALASKA in the fall of 2000.

Engineering: The S8G reactor plant was originally intended to provide up to 60,000 shp, having been based on an earlier design for a large, high-speed cruise missile submarine proposed in the early 1970s. Its actual horsepower is publicly reported as being in excess of 30,000 shp.

A land-based prototype of the OHIO plant was installed at West Milton, N.Y.

Reportedly, the OHIO is quieter than the ship's design goals for self-quieting, and at low speeds (i.e., when using natural convection rather than pumps for the circulation of pressurized water in the primary loop) the OHIO may be the quietest U.S. nuclear submarine constructed, except possibly for the SEAWOLF (SSN 21) class.

Missiles: The first eight submarines were completed with a Trident C-4 missile capability. Beginning with the ninth ship they were fitted with the Trident D-5 missile. The D-5 missile will be backfitted into SSBNs 730–733: the first two ships in 2000–2001, and the second two in 2004–2005.

---

4. COTS = Commercial-Off-The-Shelf.

The OHIO fired the first Trident C-4 to be launched from this class on 17 January 1982. The TENNESSEE launched the first D-5 missile from a submarine on 21 March 1989; that missile failed. The first successful Trident D-5 submarine launch (from the TENNESSEE) occurred on 2 August 1989.

Operational: The OHIO made the first operational patrol of this class, from 1 October to 10 December 1982.

The first squadron of eight submarines (Submarine Squadron 17), established on 5 January 1981, operates in the Pacific, based at Bangor, Wash. The second Trident submarine squadron (SubRon 16) operates in the Atlantic, based at Kings Bay, Ga.

These submarines are designed to conduct 70-day patrols interrupted by 25-day overhaul/replenishment periods, during which time the alternating blue/gold crews change over. Under this schedule, the submarines undergo a lengthy overhaul and reactor refueling every ten years.

The LOUISIANA in port with her 24 missile tubes open. The appearance of OHIO-class SSBNs on the surface belies the large size of these submarines—they are as long as the Washington Monument is tall. These submarines have a conventional U.S. design, with sail-mounted diving planes; they cannot operate under the Arctic ice pack. (1997, Leo Van Ginderen)

Early ballistic missile submarines being broken up at the Puget Sound Naval Shipyard. Their reactor compartments and other "hot" components are packaged for temporary burial at Hanford, Wash. The ultimate fate of the radioactive portions of these submarines has been another aspect of the nuclear propulsion controversy. (U.S. Navy)

TABLE 10-4. BALLISTIC MISSILE SUBMARINES

Number	Name	Comm.	Notes
George Washington class (5)			
SSBN 598	George Washington	1959	decomm. 25 Jan 1985; str. 30 Apr 1986
SSBN 599	Patrick Henry	1960	decomm. 25 May 1984; str. 16 Dec 1985
SSBN 600	Theodore Roosevelt	1961	decomm. 28 Feb 1981; str. 1 Dec 1982
SSBN 601	Robert E. Lee	1960	decomm. 1 Dec 1983; str. 30 Apr 1986
SSBN 602	Abraham Lincoln	1961	decomm. 28 Feb 1981; str. 1 Dec 1982
Ethan Allen class (5)			
SSBN 608	Ethan Allen	1961	decomm. 31 Mar 1983; str. 2 Apr 1983
SSBN 609	Sam Houston	1962	decomm./str. 6 Sep 1991
SSBN 610	Thomas A. Edison	1962	decomm. 1 Dec 1983; str. 30 Apr 1986
SSBN 611	John Marshall	1962	decomm./str. 22 July 1992
Lafayette class (31)			
SSBN 616	Lafayette	1963	decomm./str. 12 Aug 1991
SSBN 617	Alexander Hamilton	1963	decomm./str. 23 Feb 1993
Ethan Allen class (continued)			
SSBN 618	Thomas Jefferson	1963	decomm. 24 Jan 1985; str. 30 Apr 1986
Lafayette class (continued)			
SSBN 619	Andrew Jackson	1963	decomm./str. 31 Aug 1989
SSBN 620	John Adams	1964	decomm./str. 24 Mar 1989
SSBN 622	James Monroe	1963	decomm./str. 25 Sep 1990
SSBN 623	Nathan Hale	1963	decomm./str. 31 Mar 1986
SSBN 624	Woodrow Wilson	1963	decomm./str. 1 Sep 1994
SSBN 625	Henry Clay	1964	decomm./str. 5 Nov 1990
SSBN 626	Daniel Webster	1964	decomm./str. 30 Aug 1990; to MTS
SSBN 627	James Madison	1964	decomm./str. 20 Nov 1992
SSBN 628	Tecumseh	1964	decomm./str. 23 July 1993
SSBN 629	Daniel Boone	1964	decomm./str. 18 Feb 1994
SSBN 630	John C. Calhoun	1964	decomm./str. 28 Mar 1994
SSBN 631	Ulysses S. Grant	1964	decomm./str. 12 June 1992
SSBN 632	Von Steuben	1964	decomm./str. 26 Feb 1994
SSBN 633	Casimir Pulaski	1964	decomm./str. 7 Mar 1994
SSBN 634	Stonewall Jackson	1964	decomm./str. 23 Dec 1987
SSBN 635	Sam Rayburn	1964	decomm./str. 31 July 1989; to MTS
SSBN 636	Nathanael Greene	1964	decomm./str. 31 Jan 1987
SSBN 640	Benjamin Franklin	1965	decomm./str. 23 Nov 1993
SSBN 641	Simon Bolivar	1965	decomm./str. 8 Feb 1995
SSBN 642	Kamehameha	1965	in service as SSN (SOF transport)
SSBN 643	George Bancroft	1966	decomm./str. 21 Sep 1993
SSBN 644	Lewis and Clark	1965	decomm./str. 1 Aug 1992
SSBN 645	James K. Polk	1966	decomm./str. 8 July 1999
SSBN 654	George C. Marshall	1966	decomm./str. 24 Sep 1992
SSBN 655	Henry L. Stimson	1966	decomm./str. 5 May 1993
SSBN 656	George Washington Carver	1966	decomm./str. 18 Mar 1993
SSBN 657	Francis Scott Key	1966	decomm./str. 2 Sep 1993
SSBN 658	Mariano G. Vallejo	1966	decomm./str. 9 Mar 1995
SSBN 659	Will Rogers	1967	decomm./str. 12 Apr 1993
SSBN 726–743	Ohio class		

Ballistic missile submarines are numbered in the same series as attack/special-purpose submarines (see chapter 11 for SSN hull numbers). Decommission/strike dates for the original 41 SSBNs are provided; several reflect changes to previous lists, caused in part by ICIR versus decommission dates.

The George Washington class was converted during the design/construction stage from attack submarines of the Skipjack (SSN 585) class. The Ethan Allen submarines were the first U.S. SSBNs designed from the outset as ballistic missile ships.

Eight early SSBNs were briefly reclassified and employed as attack submarines in 1980–1982: SSN 598, 599, 601, 608–611, and 618. They had limited effectiveness in the SSN role because of their sonar, noise levels, and number of torpedoes.

Four ex-missile submarines were converted to support special operations forces: The John Marshall and Sam Houston were extensively converted in 1984–1986 to transport submarines to carry SEALs or other special forces; they were decommissioned in 1991–1992. They were replaced by the Kamehameha and James K. Polk, converted in 1992–1993; the Polk has been decommissioned and the Kamehameha will follow in 2001. The Houston additionally was employed in the mid-1980s as a test platform for the UQQ-2 Surveillance Towed Array Sonar System (SURTASS); the SURTASS is carried by T-AGOS surveillance ships (see chapter 22).

In the transport role, these submarines carried SSN designations; previous, non-nuclear transport submarines were designated, successively, SSP, APSS, and LPSS.

The Sam Rayburn and Daniel Webster were modified (and immobilized) to serve as MTSs to train nuclear propulsion plant operators. Their propellers were removed and their missile tubes filled with concrete. They are officially listed as "floating equipment" by the Navy and are moored at Charleston, S.C.

The Moored Training Submarines (MTS) Daniel Webster *(left)* and Sam Rayburn are immobilized at Charleston, S.C., to train nuclear propulsion operators. Nuclear propulsion training also is given at land-based reactor sites, where portions of nuclear ship reactors are installed for tests and training. (U.S. Navy)

CHAPTER 11

Submarines

The attack submarine SPRINGFIELD crashes through the surface during tests of her emergency ballast-blowing system. A LOS ANGELES–class SSN, the SPRINGFIELD is a highly capable ship, armed with vertical-launch Tomahawk missiles as well as torpedoes. However, a large number of "L.A."-class submarines are being retired long before their nominal 30-year service life. (U.S. Navy)

The attack submarine force in early 2001 consists of just over 50 nuclear-propelled submarines, including one ex-Polaris-Poseidon SSBN employed as a special operations transport (KAMEHAMEHA), one SSN employed in the research and development role (MEMPHIS), and one SSN configured for special ocean search and recovery missions (PARCHE). The approved force level goal is 55 SSNs, increased in January 2000 from the previous goal of 50. In addition, one diesel-electric research submarine, the DOLPHIN, is in service (see chapter 12 of this edition of *Ships and Aircraft*).

An extensively modified submarine of the SEAWOLF class (JIMMY CARTER) is under construction as are the first submarines of the VIRGINIA class. Both classes have been highly controversial.

In addition to new-construction SSNs, the submarine community is proposing the conversion of four Trident-armed submarines of the OHIO (SSBN 726) class to combination cruise missile/Special Operations Force (SOF) submarines. These submarines, to be retired from the strategic missile role in 2002–2004, are discussed below.

The attack submarine force—like strategic missile submarines (SSBN)—has been reduced precipitously since the end of the Cold War. From almost 100 SSNs at the end of the Cold War, the attack submarine force has been reduced to 55 SSNs. This number has been recommended under various Department of Defense studies, beginning with the *Report of the Bottom-Up Review* of October 1993.[1]

However, the Navy's submarine community has stated that 72 SSNs are required to meet current operational commitments, and up to 100 SSNs will be required in the future. The proposed Trident SSGN conversions, under current Department of Defense policies, would be counted against the SSN force level.

The SSGN concept provides considerable promise for a versatile and effective warship. However, there are many questions related to the concept that remain to be answered. Today Tomahawk Land-Attack Missiles (TLAM) are carried primarily in cruisers and destroyers. A loadout of 154 missiles is carried in perhaps three or four cruisers and destroyers. Those surface warships carry out many tasks beyond land attack: anti-air warfare, anti-surface warfare, patrol and interdiction, fire support, etc. Would a unified Commander-in-Chief (CINC) be willing to give up those ships or would he want the SSGNs in addition to those surface ships?

And, with only four SSGNs it would be impossible to keep one missile submarine available in each CINC area on a continuous basis. Deployments of some six months are about the longest possible with the existing personnel situation. Would relief crews then be flown out to the submarines in forward areas, as was done for many years with Polaris and Poseidon submarines? If yes, that would more than double the crew requirements. And, what would happen to missile availability when the SSGNs periodically had to return to U.S. territory for major maintenance and overhaul?

Finally, the land-attack mission often requires a large amount of communications and data-link traffic. This will especially be true with the planned Tactical Tomahawk, a quick-reaction missile. Could an SSGN maintain its clandestine posture and adequately handle the communications requirement? And, today when a TLAM is launched, efforts are made to avoid both friendly and enemy ships—and perhaps certain geographic areas on the first "leg" of the missile's flight.

---

1. The *Report of the Bottom-Up Review,* commissioned by Secretary of Defense Les Aspin, recommended a force of 45 to 55 submarines (p. 57). The subsequent Quarterly Defense Review recommended a 50-SSN force. However, a Department of Defense assessment of SSN missions and force structure late in 1999 concluded that "at least 55 SSNs are needed to ensure the capability to respond to urgent missions of high national interest" (Secretary of Defense William S. Cohen, *Annual Report to the President and the Congress,* February 2000, p. 47).

TABLE 11-1. SUBMARINE FORCE LEVELS (EARLY 2001)

Type	Class/Ship	Comm.	Active*	Building**	Notes
SSN 774	Virginia	2004–	—	2	under construction
SSN 23	Jimmy Carter	2003	—	1	under construction
SSN 21	Seawolf	1997–1998	2	—	
SSN 751	Improved Los Angeles	1988–1996	23	—	
SSN 688	Los Angeles	1976–1989	28	—	1 serves in research role
SSN 683	Parche	1974	1	—	special mission submarine
SSN 642	Kamehameha	1965	1	—	to decommission in 2001

*Some submarines are in the process of "standing down" in preparation for being decommissioned and stricken.
**Submarines authorized through fiscal year 2001.

Data for this flight profile are fed into the missile shortly before launch, based on the launch-ship's own radar/electronic intercept data as well as intelligence from external sources. Again, in certain situations this requirement could be difficult for cruise missile submarines.

With respect to SOF operations, the Navy's last submarine especially configured to carry special operations forces, the Kamehameha, will be retired in 2001. SOF troops also are carried in attack submarines, with seven boats of the Los Angeles class having been modified to carry either a single Dry-Deck Shelter (DDS) or Advanced SEAL Delivery System (ASDS) vehicle (see chapter 12 for submarine names). In addition, the now-building submarine Jimmy Carter and the Virginia class also will be capable of embarking a DDS or ASDS. The later submarines will have "convertible" torpedo rooms, specifically designed for rapid conversion to support SOF personnel with enlarged lockout hatches and storage space for their equipment.

Thus, there will be a large number of SSNs available to support SOF operations without the Trident SSGN conversions. Indeed, some submarine officers believe that the attack submarines—although their SOF capacity is smaller—will be far more effective in SOF operations than SSGNs: first, there will be more SSNs, permitting greater geographic coverage; second, while the SSGNs would normally accommodate 66 SOF personnel, most operations require small numbers of people, from a "few" to perhaps a score to be put ashore or taken off; and third, it will be easier to maneuver and "hide" an SSN than a Trident-size submarine of almost 17,000 tons displacement, about twice as large as an attack submarine.

There also is concern by some Navy planners over whether the SSGNs carrying SEAL teams or other special operations forces would be able to simultaneously perform both roles. An SOF-carrying submarine might have to leave her assigned missile launch "box" or area required by the CINC in order to carry out the SOF assignment or vice versa.

Finally, when operating in the SOF role, the submarine must be clandestine. That may not be possible when communicating (as necessary to update the TLAM targets and confirm readiness) and when launching scores of missiles.

There are also questions being raised about the completion of the Jimmy Carter as a special mission/SOF submarine. For more than a decade, the Seawolfs have been lauded as the world's "best" attack submarines, capable of carrying out littoral as well as blue-water missions vital to the security of the United States. Why is the U.S. Navy taking one-third of the Seawolf class—its best submarines—and converting it to what is essentially a noncombatant role? Although the Jimmy Carter will retain weapons and sensors, a review of the operations of her predecessors—the Parche, Halibut, and earlier Seawolf (SSN 575)—indicates that such search/recovery capabilities will severely limit her employment as an attack submarine.

Could not one of the later Los Angeles–class submarines have been converted to the special mission role? Certainly a "plug" of 30 feet (9.15 m) could be provided—and at far less cost than the Jimmy Carter conversion. (Indeed, the smaller Parche and the earlier Skipjack SSBN "conversions" had far larger sections added.)

Or, is the Seawolf class not truly the "best"? Do we have "enough" high capability SSNs without a third of the class? As this edition went to press, there were still many questions to be answered about the Seawolf class and, especially, the Jimmy Carter configuration.

All Sturgeon and earlier attack submarines have been stricken except for the Parche. The last to be taken out of service (In Commission, In Reserve/ICIR), in early 2001, was the L. Mendel Rivers, which was decommissioned and stricken later in the year. Submarines of the "standard" Los Angeles class are now being decommissioned and stricken to attain the authorized force level of 55 SSNs. Nuclear-propelled submarines cannot be laid up in reserve for possible future reactivation because of the measures necessary for shutting down their reactor plants and removing possibly radioactive components. See the introduction to chapter 10 for details of nuclear submarine deactivation/disposal.

Several submarines of the Ethan Allen and George Washington classes served briefly in the SSN role during the 1980s; they were not successful as SSNs because of their relatively high self-noise levels, limited sonar capability, and few torpedo reloads (see chapter 10).

All diesel-electric combat submarines have been discarded from the U.S. Navy; the diesel-electric research submarine Dolphin remains in service. Several proposals have been made for the U.S. Navy to procure non-nuclear submarines, particularly designs fitted with Air-Independent Propulsion (AIP) to supplement the diesel-electric propulsion plant. Such submarines could carry out some missions as effectively as nuclear units, among them anti-submarine training (against non-nuclear submarine targets), special operations in low-threat areas, and research and development. However, non-nuclear submarine construction has been strongly opposed by the nuclear submarine leadership, as has the construction of conventional submarines in U.S. shipyards for foreign navies.

The last U.S. Navy diesel-electric attack submarine was the Blueback, stricken in 1990 after more than 30 years of service. In 1994 the Litton/Ingalls yard obtained U.S. State Department permission to explore the construction and/or fitting out of submarines in the United States for the Egyptian Navy. That effort was aborted by the objections of the nuclear submarine community. (Previously the yard was involved in the procurement—albeit not construction—of German-built submarines for the Israeli Navy.)

Earlier efforts to construct non-nuclear submarines in the United States for Israel, South Korea, and possibly Australia and Canada, were similarly thwarted by the nuclear submarine community. The senior U.S. submariners feared that the efficacy and relatively low cost of non-nuclear submarines would lead Congress to direct that such craft be procured for the U.S. Navy.

Builders: Two U.S. shipyards construct submarines: Electric Boat/General Dynamics, the successor to the John P. Holland Torpedo Boat Company, which can trace its construction lineage for the U.S. Navy to 1900, when the Navy commissioned the Holland (SS 1) as its first official submarine; and Newport News Shipbuilding, which first built submarines in 1905–1906, completing five craft designed by Simon Lake for the *Russian* Navy. Electric Boat completed the first nuclear submarine, the Nautilus, in 1955; the first Newport News–built nuclear submarine was the Shark of 1961.

In the 1960s, at the height of the Navy's Polaris submarine construction program, there were seven U.S. shipyards building nuclear-propelled submarines:

Electric Boat Company (Conn.)
General Dynamics/Quincy (Mass.)
Ingalls Shipbuilding (Miss.)
Mare Island Naval Shipyard (Calif.)
Newport News Shipbuilding (Va.)
New York Shipbuilding (N.J.)
Portsmouth Naval Shipyard (Maine)

Classification: Beginning with the USS HOLLAND of 1900, all U.S. submarines have been assigned hull numbers in a single series (assigned in 1920), with nine exceptions: the SEAWOLF class (SSN 21–23) and the six undersea craft listed at the end of this chapter (SSK, SST, SSX types). The latter were comparatively small submarines. See page 91 of this edition of *Ships and Aircraft.*

Manning: Most but not necessarily all personnel assigned to a submarine deploy with the craft; several can be left ashore for family, medical, and educational reasons. Still, with rare exceptions, U.S. attack submarines do not have sufficient berths for all enlisted men and "hot bunking" is required. For example, the SEAWOLF is short 12 bunks. When a full torpedo/weapons load is not being carried additional temporary bunks can be fitted in the torpedo room.

Names: Attack submarines have had several name sources. The Navy's first submarine was named for its designer, Irish immigrant schoolteacher John P. Holland, who was living when the craft was accepted by the Navy in 1900. Subsequent U.S. submarines were given "fish" names until 1911, when class letters and numerals were assigned (e.g., A-2). This scheme continued until 1931, at which time fish names were again used (in addition to a scheme of class letter designations and hull numbers).

After World War II the class letter-number names were again used for the small K (hunter-killer) and T (training) submarines, but these subsequently were given fish names. Postwar submarines continued to take fish and other marine-life names until 1971, when the head of the Navy's nuclear propulsion program, Vice Admiral H. G. Rickover, instituted the practice of naming attack submarines for deceased members of Congress who had supported nuclear programs. Four SSNs were so named: GLENARD P. LIPSCOMB, L. MENDEL RIVERS, RICHARD B. RUSSELL, and WILLIAM H. BATES.

The naming source for attack submarines was changed to city names in 1974, with the first being the LOS ANGELES. However, on 9 May 1983, Secretary of the Navy John Lehman directed that the SSN 709 be named HYMAN G. RICKOVER for Admiral Rickover—whom he had helped force to leave the Navy in January 1982. (That was only the second recent U.S. Navy ship to be named for a living person, the first being the carrier CARL VINSON/CVN 70). Lehman's action was intended to prevent Congress from naming an aircraft carrier for Rickover.

The SSN 21 reverted to a fish name for submarines with the SEAWOLF, but the SSN 22 carries a state name, CONNECTICUT, while the SSN 23 is named JIMMY CARTER, the only attack submarine to be named for a president. In the late 1990s, when Secretary of the Navy John Dalton named the CONNECTICUT and JIMMY CARTER, state names were carried by battleships, cruisers, and strategic missile submarines and president names existed for aircraft carriers.

Operational: The primary peacetime SSN missions are intelligence collection, observing potentially hostile surface ships and submarines, and anti-submarine training for air, surface, and submarine forces. One or two SSNs normally deploy overseas with each carrier battle group.

In wartime the primary mission of U.S. attack submarines is to operate against enemy "attack" and strategic missile submarines, as well as carrying out anti-surface-ship, land-attack (with Tomahawk), and mining operations.

Two LOS ANGELES–class SSNs participated in the Gulf War by firing TLAMs against targets in Iraq. Those submarines fired 12 of the 288 (4 percent) of the Tomahawk missiles launched in that conflict, the launches being made primarily for "public relations" purposes although the launchings were valuable to test the concept.

Subsequently, submarines have fired TLAMs in several crises and conflicts, against targets in Afghanistan, Sudan, and Yugoslavia. During Operation Allied Force (the 1999 NATO strikes against Yugoslavia), 238 TLAMs were launched by U.S. surface ships and submarines and the British SSN SPLENDID.[2] Submarines launched about 25 percent of the missiles.

Payload: All U.S. combat submarines (SSBN/SSN) have 21-inch (533-mm) torpedo tubes except for the SEAWOLF class. This diameter has been the standard in U.S. submarines since the submarine AA-2 (SS 60) completed in 1922. The SEAWOLF introduced 26½-inch (670-mm)-diameter torpedo tubes to U.S. submarines.[3] These submarines carry the 21-inch Mk 48 ADCAP (Advanced Capability) torpedo, but the larger-diameter tubes permit quiet, "swim-out" launch of torpedoes. The research submarine MEMPHIS also has been fitted with a single 26½-inch torpedo tube.

The TLAM is launched from standard 21-inch torpedo tubes and from the Vertical Launching System (VLS), which also has 21-inch-diameter launch tubes.

The limitations in the launch envelope caused by this historic reliance on 21-inch tubes led to a Defense Science Board task force on Submarines of the Future, convened in 1998, reporting on the need to greatly increase submarine payload and the means of launching weapons and other payloads.[4] Chaired by John Stenbit, the task force report, published in August 1998, noted:

The next generation SSN must be a highly capable warship with rapid response capability
—It should have flexible payload interfaces with the water, not torpedo tubes, VLS and other special purpose interfaces
—It should not constrain the ship and size of weapons, auxiliary vehicles, and other payloads when they are used

The Stenbit panel was particularly concerned that existing SSN weapon launchers were limited to 21-inch-diameter torpedo tubes, 21-inch VLS tubes, and smaller-diameter countermeasure ejectors.[5] By comparison, Soviet-Russian "attack" submarines have both 21-inch and 26½-inch torpedo tubes, plus—in some SSG/SSGN units—large-diameter missile launching tubes.

Both the Defense Science Board's report and a briefing for industry sponsored by the Navy and the Defense Advanced Research Projects Agency (DARPA) on 10 December 1998, stressed that the VIRGINIA program should continue and evolve: "We should not stop an effective program until we have a superior replacement. . . . We need to get comfortable with the 'flexible interface with the water,' and we need to design and test it."

The next-generation SSN should be a large, nuclear submarine, according to the panel, because "we need to cover the world from the U.S. [at] high transit speed, [with] independent logistics, and endurance" and "to have flexible payloads," meaning a large submarine with a hull 33 to 39 feet (10.0 to 11.9 m) in diameter. However, this submarine must be a "combat" ship, and not simply a "mother" to long-range weapons, sensors, submersibles, and other systems.

2. HMS SPLENDID was the first British warship armed with Tomahawk missiles. The Royal Navy initially procured 65 TLAMs; additional missiles are now on order.
3. The actual internal diameter is 30 inches (762 mm), but there are fixed skids that reduce the usable diameter to 26½ inches.
4. Office of the Secretary of the Navy (Assistant Secretary for Research, Development and Acquisition), Defense Advanced Research Projects Agency, and Chief of Naval Operations (Submarine Warfare Division), "Memorandum of Agreement: A Project to Revise the Payloads and Sensors of Attack Submarines," 19 August 1998.
5. The exception being the three SEAWOLF-class submarines, as mentioned previously, each of which has eight 26½-inch torpedo tubes.

While the panel recommended against the United States developing diesel submarines, it noted:

Just because we choose not to build diesels, we must learn from the development of such ships for
—Technology infusion
—Threat understanding
—Operational development
—Training and tactics for close range engagements

Weapons: All operational U.S. attack submarines carry the Mk 48 ADCAP torpedo for use against surface ships and submarines. These submarines also can carry the Tomahawk missile, launched from standard torpedo tubes or, in the Improved LOS ANGELES and VIRGINIA classes, from 12 VLS tubes.

The Improved LOS ANGELES and later submarines can also launch the Mk 67 Submarine-Launched Mobile Mine (SLMM), carried in place of torpedoes. Harpoon anti-ship missiles previously carried by U.S. submarines have been beached.

The Sea Lance ASW Stand-Off Weapon (SOW) has been canceled. Ostensibly, it was a replacement for the outdated SUBROC (Submarine Rocket), an ASW weapon carrying a nuclear depth bomb launched from 21-inch submarine torpedo tubes that was taken out of service in 1989. With the subsequent cancellation of the Sea Lance, no ASW stand-off weapon is available to U.S. submarines. (The Sea Lance was to have carried either a nuclear depth bomb or the Mk 50 conventional, lightweight torpedo as a warhead, with the latter having development priority.)

The nuclear Tomahawk Land-Attack Missile (TLAM-N) was taken out of service in 1992. It could be launched by surface ships or attack submarines, with 57 LOS ANGELES–class submarines having been configured for launching TLAM-N. Some 350 TLAM-N missiles remain in storage. A Portable Launching System (PLS) has been developed to support placing TLAM-N missiles on board specific SSNs if necessary. The PLS, first delivered to the Navy in fiscal 1999, consists of a laptop computer that connects to the submarine's weapon control system to permit launching TLAM-N. The capability to deploy TLAM-N missiles in submarines, however, will be limited by the requirements to train personnel in handling and launching these weapons.[6]

---

6. See Lt. Michael Kostiuk, USN, "Removal of the Nuclear Strike Option from United States Attack Submarines," *The Submarine Review* (January 1998), pp. 85–90.

(4) GUIDED MISSILE/SPECIAL OPERATIONS SUBMARINES: CONVERTED "OHIO" CLASS

The U.S. submarine community has proposed that the four Trident SSBNs being deleted from the strategic role (due to START limitations; see chapter 10) be converted to guided (cruise) missile/special operations submarines (SSGN). These submarines are:

SSN 726 OHIO
SSN 727 MICHIGAN
SSN 728 FLORIDA
SSN 729 GEORGIA

The OHIO would begin conversion/refueling in January 2003 and the FLORIDA in mid-2004; the two other ships would enter the yard at about 15-month intervals. The conversions would take two years per submarine, including the refuelings (which require about 18 months).

The SSGN conversion would permit at least three different configurations. The submarines' configurations could be changed either in their home ports or selected overseas ports. All variants would have berthing, messing, and limited equipment spaces for 66 Special Operations Forces (SOF) personnel. Former Trident launch tubes nos. 1 and 2 would be permanently modified for SOF lockin/lockout and for attaching Advanced SEAL Delivery System (ASDS) vehicles and Dry Deck Shelters (DDS). The remaining 22 ex-Trident missile tubes would be modified to accept modules/canisters that could store and launch seven TLAMs or other strike missiles. The three configurations are:

• Maximum strike—launch tubes nos. 3 through 24 would each have "seven-pack" missile canisters; all 154 missiles could be fired in six minutes
• Strike/SOF—launch tubes 5 through 24 would be loaded with 140 missiles; launch tubes 3 and 4 would be loaded with SOF stowage canisters; two ASDS vehicles would be carried
• Strike/SOF—same as above with launch tubes 5 and 6 to remain empty or be loaded with additional SOF equipment (these would be blocked by the DDS); launch tubes 7 through 24 would be loaded with 126 missiles

An artist's concept of a Trident SSBN as converted to a cruise missile/special operations submarine (SSGN). In this view, the SSGN has a Dry Deck Shelter (DDS) and Advanced SEAL Delivery System (ASDS) vehicle aft of the sail structure; three Tomahawks are being launched from the submarine's large missile battery. (U.S. Navy)

TABLE 11-2. SSGN CONFIGURATION OPTIONS

Configuration	SOF Troops	Land-Attack Missiles	Tubes for SOF Storage	ASDS/DDS
Maximum Strike	66	154	0	0
Strike/SOF (2 ASDS)	66	140	2	2
Strike/SOF (2 DDS)	66	126	4	2

Some Department of Defense officials have called for the missile tube section to be cut out of the submarines to comply with strategic arms agreements. A new-built TLAM launcher section then could be inserted. The additional cost would be significant (see *Cost,* below). Alternatively, the U.S. government could request from the Soviets a change in existing treaty stipulations, or allow the Trident tubes in the SSGNs to still be counted, reducing actual U.S. submarine launched strategic missiles by 96.

In the SSGN role, each submarine would be manned by a crew of 155 (14 officers + 131 enlisted); the SOF capacity normally would be 66 (14 officers + 52 enlisted). Additional temporary bunks and bunk sharing ("hot bunking") could provide accommodations for up to 102 SOF personnel for short periods.

Classification: Previous U.S. nuclear-propelled submarines as-signed the guided missile classification were the USS HALIBUT (SSGN 587) and SSGNs 594–596 and 607; the latter four submarines were built as ASW submarines of the THRESHER class after cancellation of the Regulus II missile program in 1958. (Several U.S. diesel-electric submarines were designated SSG, both conversions and new-construction submarines.)

Cost: The Navy has estimated the following costs for the four SSGN conversions:

Development and conversion costs	$ 1.994 *billion*
Refueling (reactor cores)	$ .440 *billion*
Total	$ 2.434 *billion*

If the Trident missile section were removed and a new-built TLAM launcher section provided, the additional costs would be about $500 million per submarine, according to Department of Defense estimates.[7]

Manning: It is proposed that as SSGNs the submarines would have two alternating crews, as when they were Trident SSBNs.

Operational: The SSGNs would be based at the Trident home ports of Kings Bay, Ga., and Bangor, Wash.

---

7. All costs in FY 1998 dollars.

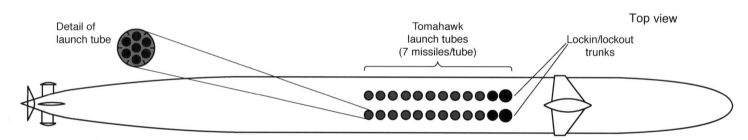

SSGN maximum strike configuration (154 missiles) (Chris Nazelrod)

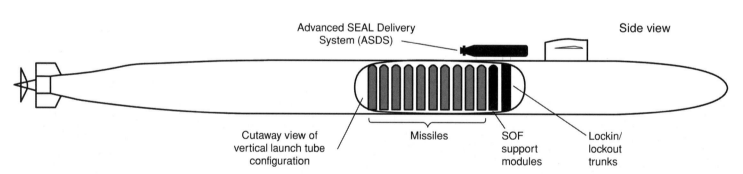

SSGN strike/special operations configuration (140 missiles + 2 ASDS vehicles) (Chris Nazelrod)

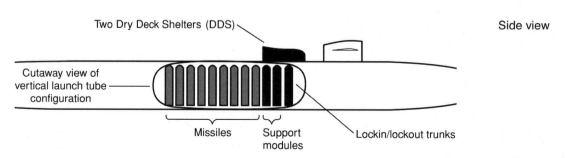

SSGN strike/special operations configuration (126 missiles + 2 DDS) (Chris Nazelrod)

(3 + 27) NUCLEAR-PROPELLED ATTACK SUBMARINES: "VIRGINIA" CLASS

Number	Name	FY	Builder	Laid down	Launch	Commission	Status
SSN 774	VIRGINIA	98	General Dynamics/Electric Boat	2 Sep 1999		2004	building
SSN 775	TEXAS	99	Newport News Shipbuilding	20 Sep 2000		2005	building
SSN 776	HAWAII	01	General Dynamics/Electric Boat	2000		2006	building
SSN 777	NORTH CAROLINA	02	Newport News Shipbuilding	2002		2007	planned
SSN 778	. . . . . .	03					planned
SSN 779	. . . . . .	04					planned
SSN 780	. . . . . .	05					planned
SSN 781–803		06–					planned

Displacement:	7,800 tons submerged		Torpedo tubes:	4 21-inch (533-mm) amidships (27 weapons)
Length:	377 feet (114.94 m) overall		ASW weapons:	Mk 48 ADCAP torpedoes
Beam:	34 feet (10.37 m)		Radars:	BPS-16 surface search
Draft:	30½ feet (9.3 m)		Sonars:	BQG-5A lightweight Wide Aperture Array (WAA)
Propulsion:	2 steam turbines; 25,000 shp; 1 shaft/propulsor			BQQ-6 bow-mounted active/passive (spherical)
Reactors:	1 S9G pressurized-water (General Electric)			BQQ-10 Acoustic Rapid COTS Insertion (ARCI) sonar update[8]
Speed:	25+ knots			minehunting sonar
				TB-16 towed array
Manning:	134 (14 officers + 120 enlisted)			TB-29 thin-line towed array
Missiles:	Tomahawk TLAM launched from torpedo tubes and VLS		EW systems:	WLQ-4(V)1
	12 vertical launch tubes for Tomahawk TLAM			WLY-1

The development of a lower-cost SSN was initiated in 1988–1990 in response to the increasing costs of the SEAWOLF class as well as questions about that submarine's roles and missions. The Navy's goal for the program was to develop a multimission attack submarine that is (1) substantially less expensive than the SEAWOLF design, (2) capable of maintaining U.S. undersea superiority against a reduced but continuing Soviet submarine effort, (3) more capable than the SEAWOLF or Improved LOS ANGELES class for operations in littoral areas, and (4) better able than the SEAWOLF or Improved LOS ANGELES design to incorporate major new submarine technologies as they become available.

In 1990 the Chief of Naval Operations, Admiral Frank B. Kelso II,

proposed a lower-cost SSN, initially given the project name "Centurion." The program was given that name to reflect a submarine for the year 2000.[9] The designation was changed in 1993 to New Attack Submarine (originally NSSN, then briefly NAS, but changed back to NSSN);[10] the lead submarine was given a state name in late 1998 (see *Names* notes, above).

---

8. COTS = Commercial-Off-The-Shelf.
9. There has never been a U.S. Navy ship with the name CENTURION. The Royal Navy has had nine ships named CENTURION since 1650, including two battleships.
10. The term "NAS" was being used within the Department of Defense at the time for National Aerospace Plane.

The VIRGINIA-class SSN will have retractable bow diving planes, a streamlined sail structure, a "chin"-mounted mine-avoidance sonar, and wide aperture arrays fitted along her hull. The VIRGINIA will have 12 vertical-launch tubes forward for Tomahawk missiles, plus four torpedo tubes, the same armament as the later LOS ANGELES class. (U.S. Navy)

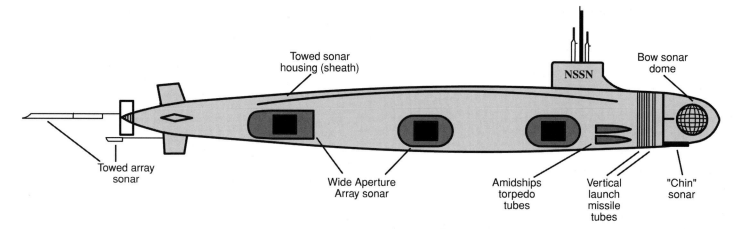

The VIRGINIA-class SSN will have a straightforward design. The use of a Photonics mast alleviates the need for the sail structure to be directly above the control room/attack center, as required in previous submarines with conventional periscopes. Later submarines of the class may have a more effective conformal bow sonar rather than the sphere used in previous SSN classes. (Chris Nazelrod)

The Navy originally announced plans to construct two or three Centurion SSNs per year to maintain a force level of some 80 attack submarines. On 19 March 1991, Secretary of the Navy H. Lawrence Garrett III testified before Congress that

> the Navy face[s] a long term problem of maintaining an adequate force of first line ships when the [SSN] 688 class begins to be retired. As part of an overall effort to seek economies in all our ships and aircraft, I have recently directed the Chief of Naval Operations ... to begin studies for a new submarine that would incorporate the technologies developed for SSN 21 and new technologies, in a smaller, less expensive platform as an option when the LOS ANGELES class submarines reach the end of their service lives after the year 2000. . . . The proposed new submarine will complement the SEAWOLF in the multimission environment of the twenty-first century. While the SEAWOLF design strongly emphasizes ASW capability against the very best projected Soviet submarines, this new submarine design will emphasize capability in other kinds of contingencies. Both of these ships will allow us to maintain an adequate force level as we move past the year 2010.

Through mid-1991 the Navy had maintained that the Centurion/NSSN would be a *complement* to the SEAWOLF rather than a successor. In late June 1991, however, there were reports that the SEAWOLF procurement would cease about the year 2000 to permit acceleration of the new, lower-cost attack submarine.

On 28 August 1992, the Under Secretary of Defense for Acquisition approved concept definition studies for the new attack submarine with the Defense Acquisition Board (DAB) directing the Navy to keep the cost of the Centurion SSN program at $1 *billion* or less per submarine and to examine a variety of attack submarine alternatives for the Centurion (including conventional submarines). The alternatives listed in the directive were largely ignored by Navy planners (see 16th Edition/page 65).

As a result of the DAB review, on 12 January 1994 the Navy was directed to study several nuclear-propelled attack submarine concepts and their impact on the industrial base. On 1 August 1994, the DAB approved Phase I design efforts focused on the authorization of a lead ship in fiscal 1998. However, on 9 December 1994, Secretary of Defense William J. Perry announced a series of budget cutbacks, among them delaying the construction of the third NSSN until fiscal year 2002. The Navy had proposed a building rate of almost two units per year from 2001 onward for a tentative total of 30 NSSNs through fiscal 2014 with some program proposals addressing up to 45 units. The two-per-year rate would be necessary to maintain a force of 55 SSNs.

The VIRGINIA-class submarines will be constructed jointly by the Electric Boat and Newport News shipyards, with assembly and completion being alternated between the yards. (The assembly/completion yard is listed as "builder" in the above class table.) Note that the VIRGINIA has a keel-laying date, reintroducing that ceremony to U.S. submarine construction. The submarines' "keels" are put down at the Electric Boat plant at Quonset Point, R.I.

Builders: The Navy originally planned for Electric Boat to build all submarines of this class, forcing Newport News Shipbuilding out of

submarine construction. Congressional action forced the Navy to accept the participation of both EB and Newport News in the program.

Subsequently, with the Navy's strong encouragement, the two yards proposed a joint construction program, with each yard building portions of all submarines: Newport News Shipbuilding builds the bow, stern, sail, and habitability sections, auxiliary machinery, and weapons handling spaces of all units; Electric Boat builds the pressure hull, command and control spaces, engine room, and main propulsion unit raft for all units. Each yard will build a reactor plant module for alternative submarines and will perform final outfitting, testing, and delivery (see table above).

Cost: In 1994 the Navy estimated that the lead submarine would cost about $3.4 *billion* (including about $1.1 *billion* in nonrecurring design costs) and the fifth and follow-on submarines would cost $1.54 *billion* (in fiscal 1998 dollars). The 1994 study prepared for the Navy estimated the following costs for the first three units:

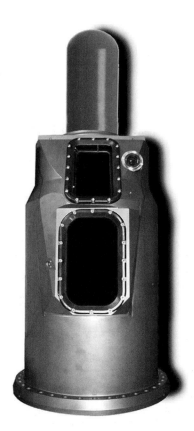

The head of the planned Photonics mast for the SSN VIRGINIA, showing multiple sensor openings and antenna atop the mast.

FY 1998   NSSN No. 1 $2.237 *billion*
FY 1999   NSSN No. 2 $1.843 *billion*
FY 2001   NSSN No. 3 $1.746 *billion*
nonrecurring costs[11] $4.681 *billion*

The fiscal 2001 budget lists the following then-year procurement costs for the second and third units (no outfitting or post-delivery costs are listed):

FY 1999   SSN 775 $1.950 *billion*
FY 2000   (long-lead) $0.746 *billion*
FY 2001   SSN 776 $1.711 *billion*

Design: The VIRGINIA submarines are expected to have an acoustic signature (self-radiated noise) of the same level as the SEAWOLF design. This is in contrast to long-held U.S. Navy belief that the larger the submarine, the quieter the submarine.[12]

The VIRGINIA torpedo room will be configured for the rapid removal of weapon stowage and handling equipment to facilitate the use of the submarine as a special forces (SEAL) transport or possibly for other specialized roles. To further support special forces, one escape hatch will have a nine-man lockin/lockout trunk.

The sail will house an Electronic Support Measures (ESM) mast, multifunction communication masts, and two Photonics

---

11. Nonrecurring costs are for design, research and development, etc.
12. See Rear Adm. W. J. Holland, Jr., USN (Ret.), "Diesel Boats Again?" U.S. Naval Institute *Proceedings* (June 1996), p. 13, and subsequent commentary, especially N. Polmar, "New Approach to Submarines," *Proceedings* (August 1996), pp. 87–88, and Holland (December 1996), pp. 23–24.

masts for improved imaging functions. The Photonics masts are nonpenetrating and replace the conventional (pressure hull–penetrating) periscopes. The system provides several high-resolution color cameras that send visual images to large-screen displays in the ship's control room. Enhanced infrared and low-light-level image enhancement features are provided. The mast also includes an infrared laser range finder.

The pressure hull is being fabricated of HY-100 steel.

In response to criticisms of the NSSN/VIRGINIA design as being too conservative, the Navy developed a series of "technology insertion possibilities" for the class whereby new technologies could be incorporated into successive units of the class. Most, if not all, however, could be incorporated into the earlier SEAWOLF or even LOS ANGELES SSN designs.

Electronics: Space and weight are to be reserved for possible installation of a lightweight Wide Aperture Array (WAA) sonar, considered by the U.S. Navy to be the optimum acoustic sensor for use against the diesel-electric submarine threat in littoral waters.

These submarines will be fitted with the BQQ-10 ARCI sonar, an upgrade to the BQQ-6 (see the AUGUSTA below for details).

Engineering: The reactor core (fuel) for these submarines is expected to last the 30-year service life of the ships.

Missiles: All have 12 vertical launch tubes for Tomahawk missiles fitted forward, between the pressure hull and sonar sphere. In addition, Tomahawk missiles can be launched from the torpedo tubes in this class.

Torpedoes: The VIRGINIAS will stow fewer weapons in the torpedo room/tubes than can the SEAWOLF class.

(1) NUCLEAR-PROPELLED SPECIAL MISSION SUBMARINE: MODIFIED "SEAWOLF" CLASS

Number	Name	FY	Builder	Start	Launch	Commissioned	Status
SSN 23	JIMMY CARTER	92/96	General Dynamics/Electric Boat	12 Dec 1995		2003	building

Displacement:	————	Missiles:	Tomahawk TLAM launched from torpedo tubes
Length:	380⅓ feet (115.9 m) overall	Torpedo tubes:	8 26½-inch (670-mm) amidships (50 weapons)
Beam:		ASW weapons:	Mk 48 ADCAP torpedoes
Draft:	36 feet (10.98 m)	Radars:	BPS-16 surface search
Propulsion:	2 steam turbines (General Electric); approx. 40,000 shp;	Sonars/Fire Control:	BQG-5D hull-mounted Wide Aperture Arrays (WAA)
	1 shaft/propulsor		BQS-24 navigation/ice-avoidance
Reactors:	1 S6W pressurized-water (Westinghouse)		BSY-2 with bow-mounted transducers
Speed:	15 knots surface		TB-16D towed array
	approx. 30 knots submerged		TB-29 towed array
Manning:		EW systems:	BLD-1D/F
Troops:	50 SEALs		WLQ-4(V)1

The JIMMY CARTER was ordered as the third submarine of the SEAWOLF class. In 1999 the Navy directed Electric Boat to modify this submarine for use as a special mission submarine to replace the PARCHE for deep-ocean search, research, and recovery operations. She will also have an enhanced SOF capability. The modifications will add approximately 15 months to the construction of the submarine, which was originally scheduled for delivery on 31 December 2001.

See SEAWOLF-class entry for other program data.

Cost: The SEAWOLF-class submarines are the most costly submarines ever constructed. Precise figures have not been made publicly available by the Navy. In the mid-1970s the estimated cost for a 30-ship SEAWOLF program was $38 *billion* (then-year dollars); in 1999 knowledgeable sources placed the total cost of the SEAWOLF program at almost $16 *billion* for the three submarines of the class.

In 1988 the Navy estimated that the construction of 29 submarines at an eventual production rate of three or four submarines per year would cost $36 *billion*. The Secretary of the Navy's cost ceiling for the program (in fiscal 1985 dollars) was $1.6 *billion* for the lead ship and $1 *billion* for the fifth and later ships; the latter unit cost excludes the cost of constructing the ninth and later ships with HY-130 steel. (These cost estimates do not take into account the welding problems and resulting delays.) In addition, the development cost of the BSY-2 was estimated at $1 *billion*.

The SSN 21 total cost was estimated at $718 million (fiscal 1987 dollars) at the time of contract award; in mid-1994 the estimated cost of the submarine was in excess of $1.1 *billion*. The SSN 22 cost was estimated at $689 million (fiscal 1991) at the time of contract award.

The fiscal 1991 defense appropriation provided $2.4 *billion* to build the SSN 23 and to cover advanced procurement items for follow-on SEAWOLFS. On 18 January 1994 the Chief of Naval Operations, Admiral Kelso, in his briefing "Restructuring Naval Forces," stated that $900 million had already been spent on the SSN 23 and that $1.5 *billion* was required to complete the submarine—an estimated total of $2.4 *billion*. This was prior to the decision to complete the SSN 23 to a modified design.

Design: The JIMMY CARTER is being lengthened by a wide-diameter amidships section. The submarine will be fitted to carry either a DDS or ASDS vehicle plus Remote Operating Vehicles (ROVs). There will be dedicated berthing for SOF personnel as well as stowage space for their equipment.

Names: The SSN 23 introduced a new name source to attack submarines: former (and living) presidents. Jimmy Carter was the first U.S. Naval Academy graduate to be elected president, and he served in a diesel submarine before entering nuclear school. However, he left the Navy before reporting to a nuclear submarine. Still, he was able to campaign on being a "nuclear engineer" during his presidential campaign.

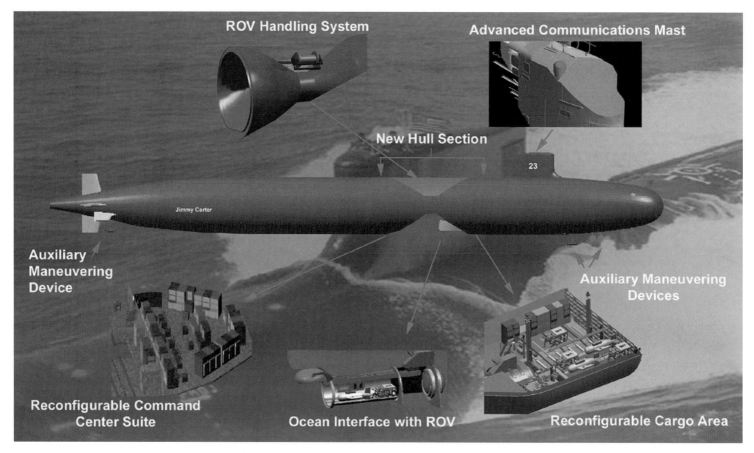

ROV Handling System

Advanced Communications Mast

New Hull Section

Auxiliary Maneuvering Device

Auxiliary Maneuvering Devices

Reconfigurable Command Center Suite

Ocean Interface with ROV

Reconfigurable Cargo Area

The JIMMY CARTER (U.S. Navy)

2 NUCLEAR-PROPELLED ATTACK SUBMARINES: "SEAWOLF" CLASS

Number	Name	FY	Builder	Started	Launched	Commissioned	Status
SSN 21	SEAWOLF	89	General Dynamics/Electric Boat	25 Oct 1989	24 June 1995	19 July 1997	**AA**
SSN 22	CONNECTICUT	91	General Dynamics/Electric Boat	14 Sep 1992	1 Sep 1997	11 Dec 1998	**AA**

Displacement:	7,460 tons surface	Missiles:	Tomahawk TLAM launched from torpedo tubes
	9,137 tons submerged (see *Design* notes)	Torpedo tubes:	8 26½-inch (670-mm) amidships (50 weapons)
Length:	353 feet (107.6 m) overall	ASW weapons:	Mk 48 ADCAP torpedoes
Beam:	40 feet (12.2 m)	Radars:	BPS-16 surface search
Draft:	36 feet (10.98 m)	Sonars/Fire Control:	BQG-5D hull-mounted Wide Aperture Arrays (WAA)
Propulsion:	2 steam turbines (General Electric); approx. 40,000 shp;		BQS-24 navigation/ice-avoidance
	1 shaft/propulsor		BSY-2 with bow-mounted transducers
Reactors:	1 S6W pressurized-water (Westinghouse)		TB-16D towed array
Speed:	15 knots surface		TB-29 towed array
	35 knots submerged (see *Engineering* notes)	EW systems:	BLD-1D/F
Manning:	134 (14 officers + 120 enlisted)		WLQ-4(V)1

The SEAWOLF was developed as a follow-on to the LOS ANGELES class with the primary mission of anti-submarine operations against advanced Soviet submarines. The SEAWOLF was the most controversial U.S. warship program of the 1980s and early 1990s.

The Navy originally planned to construct about 30 submarines of this class, to be authorized in fiscal years 1989 through 2000: one was to be authorized in fiscal 1989, two each in fiscal 1991 and 1992, and an average of 3.3 ships annually in the following years. Subsequent controversy over the design, the issue of concurrent BSY-2 system development and submarine construction, and high costs led to reductions in the program. On 13 August 1990, as a result of a four-month Department of Defense major warship and threat review, the SEAWOLF procurement was reduced to 12 submarines and the production rate was reduced to three submarines every two years (i.e., 1.5 per year). The six-year defense plan submitted to Congress in February 1991 reduced the planned procurement rate to one SSN per year through fiscal 1995; after that there would be a 2-1-2-1 schedule starting in fiscal 1996.

In September 1991 the Chief of Naval Operations, Admiral Kelso, said that he expected only one SEAWOLF per year to be constructed and only until the lead Centurion SSN was authorized; this statement indicated that he did not anticipate a total program of more than seven or eight SEAWOLFS. In January 1992 the Department of Defense announced that the entire SEAWOLF program would be canceled with only the first unit to be completed. The funds previously voted by Congress for the SSN 22 and SSN 23 were to be rescinded.

The SEAWOLF became a political issue when, during the presidential primary campaign of 1992, then-Governor Bill Clinton told Connecticut voters that he would continue production of the SEAWOLF class beyond the first unit; primary candidate Paul Tsongas observed that Clinton, a Democrat, was supporting a defense program that even the Republican president did not wish to continue.

Lobbying by the Navy's nuclear submarine community and support by congressional representatives, especially from Connecticut, led to reversal of the administration's proposal to halt the program with one submarine. Thus two additional submarines were funded.

The SSN 21 delivery was originally scheduled for November 1994; the delivery of the lead ship was delayed by at least six months

The SEAWOLF on her sea trials on 3 July 1996. Since her trials, the SEAWOLF has spent most of the time in the Electric Boat yard, being modified and having problems rectified. The SEAWOLF program is undoubtedly the most controversial submarine program in U.S. Navy history. The band-like devices around her after hull are strain gauges. (1996, General Dynamics)

(to May 1995) due to changes in the BSY-2 system configuration.[13] On 1 August 1991, the Navy announced that massive weld failures had been discovered in the hull that would delay the lead submarine

---

13. The first *Naval Sea Systems Command Monthly Progress Report* issued after the construction contract was awarded listed the SSN 21 projected launch date as 28 January 1994 and completion on 26 May 1995.

The sail of the SEAWOLF has a "fillet" where the leading edge of the sail is faired into the deck. This configuration reduces turbulence as water flows over the hull. (1996, General Dynamics/Jim Brennan)

at least into 1996. The cracks in the welding, which were first discovered in June 1991, required the replacement of all welds made up to that time. The SEAWOLF contract was increased by $58,825,590 to cover the costs of the corrections.

During the SEAWOLF sea trials of 3–4 July 1997, the submarine's flank sonar arrays were damaged. This led to a further delay, with her commissioning in May 1997—2½ years behind the original schedule.

Funding for the SSN 22, authorized in fiscal 1991, was retained by Congress with an additional $540,200,000 to be used for either the third SEAWOLF or some other project to preserve the submarine construction base.

The SSN 23 originally was authorized in 1992, but the Bush administration withheld the funds pending studies of alternative submarine programs. The fiscal 1996 defense budget requested additional funding for the third SEAWOLF to keep the submarine production line at Electric Boat "hot" until the planned New Attack Submarine (NSSN) was authorized in fiscal 1998. The interval between the second SEAWOLF (1991 authorization) and the third (1996) was probably the longest interval between submarine authorizations in U.S. Navy history.

Builders: On 9 January 1989, a fixed-price, incentive-plus-fee contract to build the lead submarine of the SEAWOLF class was awarded to Electric Boat. Construction began on 25 October 1989. The submarine's completion was delayed by several problems, including welding of the HY-100 steel.

The Navy awarded a contract for the SSN 22 to Electric Boat on 3 May 1991. Four days later, Newport News Shipbuilding filed a lawsuit protesting the decision, basing its case on a congressional mandate to preserve a two-yard submarine construction capability.[14] On 31 August 1991 a federal judge voided the contract award with

---

14. On 7 May 1991 the Navy terminated a contract with Newport News Shipbuilding to participate in the design of the Centurion. This was one day after Newport News filed its suit challenging the selection of Electric Boat to build the second SEAWOLF. Navy officials denied that the two events were linked.

The CONNECTICUT at rest. Note the low-lying hull; most of the giant submarine is below the surface. A periscope is almost fully extended. (U.S. Navy)

Electric Boat and directed that the Navy recompete the contract for the second SEAWOLF, which was once again awarded to Electric Boat.

Subsequently, in 1995 Newport News proposed that it could build the New Attack Submarine (i.e., VIRGINIA class) without the Navy having to build the SSN 23 to "bridge" the construction gap between the SSN 22 and the New Attack Submarine, as was required at Electric Boat. This was possible because Newport News had a broader business base than Electric Boat, including the Navy's carrier construction and refueling program, deactivating nuclear cruisers, commercial ship construction and overhaul, and possibly frigate construction for other navies.

Bill Fricks, president of the Newport News yard, told a congressional committee in April 1995 that by taking over the nuclear submarine program it could save the Navy $2 *billion* in the procurement of the first five VIRGINIA SSNs and another $7 to $10 *billion* over the life of the VIRGINIA program of up to 45 submarines.

In the event, the construction of all three submarines of the class was awarded to Electric Boat.

Class: The decision to construct a new SSN class was taken in July 1982. This followed a Navy decision one year earlier *not* to construct a new SSN (see 13th Edition/page 54). When the SEAWOLF was conceived in 1982, the SSN force level goal was increased from 90 to 100 submarines.[15] But from the outset of the SEAWOLF effort, even a cursory look at the program made it apparent that it would be impossible to maintain a 100 SSN force with procurement of the SEAWOLF because of the submarine's high cost.

Classification: The Navy designated this class as SSN 21, indicating an attack submarine for the 21st Century. The subsequent use of that designation as a hull number, and sequential numbers for the two other units of the class, repeat the hull numbers of three previous U.S. submarines (completed in 1912–1913): SS 21 BARRACUDA (also F-2), SS 22 PICKEREL (also F-3), and SS 23 SKATE (also F-4). As these submarines were numbered in the same series as U.S. nuclear submarines, the use of SSN 21, 22, and 23 was a violation of Secretary of the Navy policy and instructions on ship classifications.

Cost: See JIMMY CARTER entry.

---

15. Ninety attack submarines was the Navy's force goal from 1973 to 1981; that goal was never achieved. Before that, the force goal was 120 attack submarines, both diesel-electric and nuclear.

The SEAWOLF on her so-called Bravo sea trials in September 1996. All of her periscopes and masts are fully retracted. The SEAWOLFS are the fastest submarines now in U.S. service. The research submarine ALBACORE (in service 1953–1972) was faster. (1996, General Dynamics/Jim Brennan)

The high-tech SEAWOLF-class SSNs have two helmsmen who operate aircraft-type controls with LED screens presenting navigation data. Traditional "dials and pointers" are located above the LED screens. (1996, U.S. Navy, PHC John E. Gay)

Design: The basic SEAWOLF design was established in 1982–1983. The SEAWOLF design emphasis was on: (1) improved machinery, (2) quieting, and (3) improved combat systems—both sensors and additional weapons.

The SEAWOLF is considered the first "top-to-bottom" U.S. attack submarine design since the SKIPJACK design of the late 1950s. These submarines are slightly faster than the LOS ANGELES class and have more torpedo tubes and more internally stowed weapons; there are no Tomahawk launch tubes external to the pressure hull, as in the later units of the LOS ANGELES class. The design provides for a smaller length-to-beam ratio than the previous U.S. attack submarine classes. A six-surface tail configuration is used with the single propeller shaft common to U.S. SSNs since the late 1950s, but the propeller is a circular shroud or duct similar to the installation in some British TRAFALGAR-class SSNs and (on a smaller scale) the Mk 48 torpedo. The submarines have bow-mounted (vice sail-mounted) diving planes that retract into the bow for under-ice operations.

According to Electric Boat statements, "The SEAWOLF will be less detectable at high speed than a LOS ANGELES class SSN sitting at the pier," and the SEAWOLF is the "world's quietest submarine." Both statements were made before the SEAWOLF was launched.[16]

The submerged displacement listed above (9,150 tons) is the limit imposed by the Secretary of the Navy about 1986. The actual submerged displacement is approximately 9,300 tons. About 150 tons of this is the water trapped in the bow sonar dome, which is normally flooded and closed when the submarine is at sea; however, in this class, to keep within the secretary's ceiling, the sonar dome is "open" to the sea when flooded.

The ninth and subsequent units were to have had HY-130 steel vice the HY-100 steel used in the earlier SEAWOLF-class submarines.

All U.S. submarines from the THRESHER through the LOS ANGELES class were constructed of HY-80 steel.[17] (HY-100 steel was originally proposed for the LOS ANGELES class.)

Electronics: These submarines have the BSY-2 combat system, previously known as SUBACS for Submarine Advanced Combat System (see chapter 29 for characteristics). The BQG-5D WAA system has three rectangular arrays fitted to each side of the submarine's hull.

Changes in the design of the BSY-2 caused redesign of portions of the SEAWOLF. In addition to the large bow spherical array, there are three WAA panels along each side of the submarine.

Engineering: The maximum submerged speed has been officially stated to be 35 knots, making the SEAWOLF class faster than any previous U.S. submarine design. The SEAWOLF is reported to have a maximum "acoustic speed" in excess of 20 knots (i.e., the speed at which the submarine can transit while maintaining a sufficiently low noise level to still employ passive sonar with a narrow-band capability; a comparative Soviet speed was reported at 6 to 8 knots for submarines built in the 1980s).

Immediately after the SEAWOLF's sea trials of 3–4 July 1997, Admiral Bruce DeMars, head of naval nuclear propulsion, declared that the SEAWOLF had gone faster than any previous U.S. submarine.[18] Unofficial reports credited the SEAWOLF with 37 knots on those trials. However, the trials were not conducted over a measured mile, nor was full instrumentation mounted in the submarine, nor was her acoustic coating installed.

Names: The SSN 21 reverted to the practice of using fish names for submarines. The name SEAWOLF was chosen for the lead submarine of this class in 1986 with the assumption that the existing SEAWOLF (SSN 575) would be stricken by the time the new craft was launched; the SSN 575 was stricken on 10 July 1987.

The first SEAWOLF (SS 28), later renamed H-1, ran aground in 1920 off Santa Margarita Island, Calif.; four men died. The submarine sank when she was refloated. The second SEAWOLF (SS 197) was sunk in late 1944 by *U.S.* anti-submarine forces. There were no survivors. She had made 12 successful war patrols in 1942–1944. The third SEAWOLF (SSN 575) was the nation's second nuclear submarine.

The second submarine of this class was named CONNECTICUT. State names previously were used for the 18 Trident missile submarines of the OHIO class, and before that for guided missile cruisers and battleships. The last U.S. ship named CONNECTICUT (BB 18) was stricken in 1923. The state name was assigned to the SSN 22 through the efforts of the Connecticut congressional delegation, to honor the state where one of the two surviving submarine building yards is located. (Subsequently, the SSN 774 was named to honor the home state of the other submarine construction yard.)

Operational: The SEAWOLF was operational from August 1997 to July 1998, carrying out trials, evaluations, and limited exercises; she returned to the EB yard in July 1998 for a 14-month post-shakedown availability. The work included application of anechoic coating to the submarine.

Torpedoes: The Navy originally planned to place the torpedo tubes in the bow of these craft, where they would be less vulnerable to water flow problems during weapon launches at high speed. Following tests, the launch tubes were retained in the amidships position used in all designs since the TULLIBEE and THRESHER classes. Firing tests, however, demonstrated the feasibility of high-speed torpedo firing from amidships tubes and the SEAWOLF design was modified accordingly.

---

16. From "Seawolf," on the reverse of an artist's concept prepared by General Dynamics/Electric Boat Division [n.d.].

17. HY-80 was used in the SKIPJACK class, but the THRESHER was the first to have a complete HY-80 pressure hull, permitting a deeper operating depth.
18. Adm. Bruce DeMars, USN, press conference, New London, Conn., 5 July 1996. Previously the fastest U.S. submarine unquestionably was the research submarine ALBACORE (AGSS 569).

23 NUCLEAR-PROPELLED ATTACK SUBMARINES: IMPROVED "LOS ANGELES" CLASS

Number	Name	FY	Builder	Laid down	Launched	Commissioned	Status
SSN 751	SAN JUAN	83	General Dynamics/Electric Boat	16 Aug 1985	6 Dec 1986	6 Aug 1988	**AA**
SSN 752	PASADENA	83	General Dynamics/Electric Boat	20 Dec 1985	12 Sep 1987	11 Feb 1989	**PA**
SSN 753	ALBANY	84	Newport News Shipbuilding	22 Apr 1985	13 June 1987	7 Apr 1990	**AA**
SSN 754	TOPEKA	84	General Dynamics/Electric Boat	13 May 1986	23 Jan 1988	21 Oct 1989	**PA**
SSN 755	MIAMI	84	General Dynamics/Electric Boat	24 Oct 1986	12 Nov 1988	30 June 1990	**AA**
SSN 756	SCRANTON	85	Newport News Shipbuilding	29 Aug 1986	3 July 1989	26 Jan 1991	**AA**
SSN 757	ALEXANDRIA	85	Newport News Shipbuilding	19 June 1987	23 June 1990	29 June 1991	**AA**
SSN 758	ASHEVILLE	85	Newport News Shipbuilding	9 Jan 1987	24 Feb 1990	28 Sep 1991	**PA**
SSN 759	JEFFERSON CITY	85	Newport News Shipbuilding	21 Sep 1987	17 Aug 1990	29 Feb 1992	**PA**
SSN 760	ANNAPOLIS	86	General Dynamics/Electric Boat	15 June 1988	18 May 1991	11 Apr 1992	**AA**
SSN 761	SPRINGFIELD	86	General Dynamics/Electric Boat	29 Jan 1990	4 Jan 1992	9 Jan 1993	**AA**
SSN 762	COLUMBUS	86	General Dynamics/Electric Boat	7 Jan 1991	1 Aug 1992	24 July 1993	**PA**
SSN 763	SANTA FE	86	General Dynamics/Electric Boat	9 Sep 1991	12 Dec 1992	8 Jan 1994	**PA**
SSN 764	BOISE	87	Newport News Shipbuilding	25 Aug 1988	23 Mar 1991	7 Nov 1992	**AA**
SSN 765	MONTPELIER	87	Newport News Shipbuilding	19 May 1989	23 Aug 1991	13 Mar 1993	**AA**
SSN 766	CHARLOTTE	87	Newport News Shipbuilding	17 Aug 1990	3 Oct 1992	16 Sep 1994	**PA**
SSN 767	HAMPTON	87	Newport News Shipbuilding	2 Mar 1990	28 Sep 1991	6 Nov 1993	**AA**
SSN 768	HARTFORD	88	General Dynamics/Electric Boat	27 Apr 1992	4 Dec 1993	10 Dec 1994	**AA**
SSN 769	TOLEDO	88	Newport News Shipbuilding	6 May 1991	28 Aug 1993	24 Feb 1995	**AA**
SSN 770	TUCSON	88	Newport News Shipbuilding	15 Aug 1991	19 Mar 1994	9 Sep 1995	**PA**
SSN 771	COLUMBIA	89	General Dynamics/Electric Boat	21 Apr 1993	24 Sep 1994	9 Oct 1995	**PA**
SSN 772	GREENVILLE	89	Newport News Shipbuilding	28 Feb 1992	17 Sep 1994	16 Feb 1996	**PA**
SSN 773	CHEYENNE	90	Newport News Shipbuilding	6 July 1992	1 Apr 1995	13 Sep 1996	**PA**

Displacement:	6,300 tons standard except SSN 771–773, 6,330 tons	Sonars:	BQQ-5C/D multifunction bow mounted (being upgraded to
	7,147 tons submerged except SSN 771–773, 7,177 tons		BQQ-5E)
Length:	360 feet (109.7 m) overall		BQQ-10 Acoustic Rapid COTS Insertion (ARCI) sonar update
Beam:	33 feet (10.1 m)		BQR-15 towed array
Draft:	32 feet (9.75 m)		BQR-26 in some units
Propulsion:	2 steam turbines; approx. 30,000 shp; 1 shaft		BQS-13 active
Reactors:	1 S6G pressurized-water (General Electric)		BQS-15 under-ice/mine detection
Speed:	22 knots surface		BSY-1 combat system
	approx. 33 knots submerged		TB-23 and/or TB-29 towed array
Manning:	141 (14 officers + 127 enlisted)	Fire control:	1 CCS Mk 2 Mod 2
Missiles:	Tomahawk SSMs launched from torpedo tubes		1 Mk 117 torpedo FCS
	12 vertical launch tubes for Tomahawk SSM	EW systems:	BRD-7 direction finder
Torpedo tubes:	4 21-inch (533-mm) amidships Mk 67 (25 weapons)		WLR-8(V)
ASW weapons:	Mk 48 ADCAP torpedoes		WLR-9
Radars:	BPS-15A surface search		WLR-12

These are Improved LOS ANGELES–class submarines having Tomahawk vertical launch missile tubes, minelaying and under-ice capabilities, and improved machinery quieting. Submarines of this class are expected to have a service life of 33 years. See the LOS ANGELES–class entry for additional information and notes on these submarines.

Class: The LOS ANGELES class is the world's largest series of nuclear-propelled submarines, with 62 units completed. The "final" program was for 65 units, but the Navy did not request funds for the last four units, instead supporting the SEAWOLF program; however, Congress authorized one of those LOS ANGELES–class submarines (SSN 773).

This is the largest class of submarines built since World War II by any nation except for the Soviet diesel-electric Whiskey class (215 units completed 1949–1957) and Foxtrot class (62 built for Soviet service plus 17 for foreign navies, 1958–1973).

Electronics: These submarines are fitted with the BSY-1 sonar/fire control "combat system." Major problems were encountered in late 1986 in installing the initial system in the SSN 751, resulting in a completion delay of the submarine.

The ASHEVILLE has been fitted with a "chin"-mounted High-Frequency (HF) sonar for shallow-water tactical operations. The system was installed in March 1995.

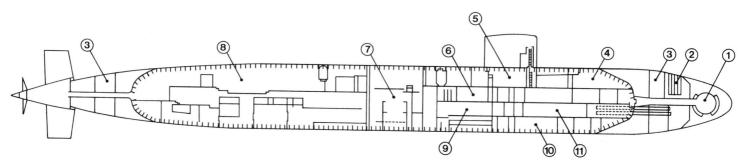

Improved LOS ANGELES–class SSN
1. Sonar BQQ-5 sonar sphere 2. Vertical-launch tubes 3. Ballast tanks 4. Sonar room 5. Control room/attack center 6. Crew's mess 7. Reactor compartment 8. Engine room 9. Auxiliary machinery 10. Battery 11. Torpedo room (William Clipson)

The BQQ-10 Acoustic Rapid COTS Insertion (ARCI) provides an update to the BQQ-5/BQQ-6/BSY-1 sonars; see AUGUSTA, below.

Engineering: These submarines require refueling at 16- to 20-year intervals. The SSN 768 and later units have improved quieting features and two additional stern "fins" (as in the SEAWOLF).

Missiles: All have 12 vertical launch tubes for Tomahawk missiles fitted forward, between the pressure hull and sonar sphere, in space previously used for ballast tanks. In addition, Tomahawk missiles can be launched from the torpedo tubes in this class.

The SANTA FE at Port Canaveral, Florida, shows all 12 hatches open for her vertical-launch tubes for Tomahawk missiles. These weapons greatly enhance SSN capabilities. (1994, John Bouvia)

The ALEXANDRIA entering the port of Zeebrugge, Belgium. Note the towed array sheath on the starboard side of the hull and the absence of sail-mounted diving planes. (1997, Leo Van Ginderen)

The SAN JUAN—lead ship of the Improved LOS ANGELES class—in Arctic ice. Such operations were important during the Cold War because Soviet submarines operated in the Arctic region, often protected from Western ASW aircraft and surface ships by the ice pack. The original 39 LOS ANGELES–class SSNs do not have an under-ice capability. (U.S. Navy)

The GREENVILLE, with crewmen on deck, leaving port. Her sail-mounted sonar arrays are evident. The fitting of retractable bow diving planes in place of sail planes, strengthening of the top of the sail, and other features enable these submarines to operate under the Arctic ice pack. (1999, Leo Van Ginderen)

27 NUCLEAR-PROPELLED ATTACK SUBMARINES
1 NUCLEAR-PROPELLED RESEARCH SUBMARINE } **"LOS ANGELES" CLASS**

Number	Name	FY	Builder	Laid down	Launched	Commissioned	Status
SSN 688	LOS ANGELES	70	Newport News Shipbuilding	8 Jan 1972	6 Apr 1974	13 Nov 1976	**PA**
SSN 689	BATON ROUGE	70	Newport News Shipbuilding	18 Nov 1972	26 Apr 1975	25 June 1977	decomm./str. 13 Jan 1995
SSN 690	PHILADELPHIA	70	General Dynamics/Electric Boat	12 Aug 1972	19 Oct 1974	25 June 1977	**AA**
SSN 691	MEMPHIS	71	Newport News Shipbuilding	23 June 1973	3 Apr 1976	17 Dec 1977	**AA-R&D**
SSN 692	OMAHA	71	General Dynamics/Electric Boat	27 Jan 1973	21 Feb 1976	11 Mar 1978	decomm./str. 5 Oct 1995
SSN 693	CINCINNATI	71	Newport News Shipbuilding	6 Apr 1974	19 Feb 1977	10 June 1978	decomm./str. 29 July 1996
SSN 694	GROTON	71	General Dynamics/Electric Boat	3 Aug 1973	9 Oct 1976	8 July 1978	decomm./str. 7 Nov 1997
SSN 695	BIRMINGHAM	72	Newport News Shipbuilding	26 Apr 1975	29 Oct 1977	16 Dec 1978	decomm./str. 22 Dec 1997
SSN 696	NEW YORK CITY	72	General Dynamics/Electric Boat	15 Dec 1973	18 June 1977	3 Mar 1979	decomm./str. 30 Apr 1997
SSN 697	INDIANAPOLIS	72	General Dynamics/Electric Boat	19 Oct 1974	30 July 1977	5 Jan 1980	decomm./str. 22 Dec 1998
SSN 698	BREMERTON	72	General Dynamics/Electric Boat	6 May 1976	22 July 1978	28 Mar 1981	**PA**
SSN 699	JACKSONVILLE	72	General Dynamics/Electric Boat	21 Feb 1976	18 Nov 1978	16 May 1981	**AA**
SSN 700	DALLAS	73	General Dynamics/Electric Boat	9 Oct 1976	28 Apr 1979	18 July 1981	**AA**
SSN 701	LA JOLLA	73	General Dynamics/Electric Boat	16 Oct 1976	11 Aug 1979	24 Oct 1981	**AA**
SSN 702	PHOENIX	73	General Dynamics/Electric Boat	30 July 1977	8 Dec 1979	19 Dec 1981	decomm./str. 29 July 1998
SSN 703	BOSTON	73	General Dynamics/Electric Boat	11 Aug 1978	19 Apr 1980	30 Jan 1982	decomm./str. 1 Sep 1999
SSN 704	BALTIMORE	73	General Dynamics/Electric Boat	21 May 1979	13 Dec 1980	24 July 1982	decomm./str. 10 July 1998
SSN 705	CITY OF CORPUS CHRISTI	73	General Dynamics/Electric Boat	4 Sep 1979	25 Apr 1981	8 Jan 1983	**AA**
SSN 706	ALBUQUERQUE	74	General Dynamics/Electric Boat	27 Dec 1979	13 Mar 1982	21 May 1983	**AA**
SSN 707	PORTSMOUTH	74	General Dynamics/Electric Boat	8 May 1980	18 Sep 1982	1 Oct 1983	**PA**
SSN 708	MINNEAPOLIS-SAINT PAUL	74	General Dynamics/Electric Boat	20 Jan 1981	19 Mar 1983	17 Mar 1984	**AA**
SSN 709	HYMAN G. RICKOVER	74	General Dynamics/Electric Boat	24 July 1981	17 Aug 1983	8 Sep 1984	**AA**
SSN 710	AUGUSTA	74	General Dynamics/Electric Boat	1 Apr 1982	21 Jan 1984	19 Jan 1985	**AA**
SSN 711	SAN FRANCISCO	75	Newport News Shipbuilding	26 May 1977	27 Oct 1979	24 Apr 1981	**PA**
SSN 712	ATLANTA	75	Newport News Shipbuilding	17 Aug 1978	16 Aug 1980	6 Mar 1982	decomm./str. 1 Sep 1999
SSN 713	HOUSTON	75	Newport News Shipbuilding	29 Jan 1979	21 Mar 1981	25 Sep 1982	**PA**
SSN 714	NORFOLK	76	Newport News Shipbuilding	1 Aug 1979	31 Oct 1981	21 May 1983	**AA**
SSN 715	BUFFALO	76	Newport News Shipbuilding	25 Jan 1980	8 May 1982	5 Nov 1983	**PA**
SSN 716	SALT LAKE CITY	77	Newport News Shipbuilding	26 Aug 1980	16 Oct 1982	12 May 1984	**PA**
SSN 717	OLYMPIA	77	Newport News Shipbuilding	31 Mar 1981	30 Apr 1983	17 Nov 1984	**PA**
SSN 718	HONOLULU	77	Newport News Shipbuilding	10 Nov 1981	24 Sep 1983	6 July 1985	**PA**
SSN 719	PROVIDENCE	78	General Dynamics/Electric Boat	14 Oct 1982	4 Aug 1984	27 July 1985	**AA**
SSN 720	PITTSBURGH	79	General Dynamics/Electric Boat	15 Apr 1983	8 Dec 1984	23 Nov 1985	**AA**
SSN 721	CHICAGO	80	Newport News Shipbuilding	5 Jan 1983	13 Oct 1984	27 Sep 1986	**PA**
SSN 722	KEY WEST	80	Newport News Shipbuilding	6 July 1983	20 July 1985	12 Sep 1987	**PA**
SSN 723	OKLAHOMA CITY	81	Newport News Shipbuilding	4 Jan 1984	2 Nov 1985	9 July 1988	**AA**
SSN 724	LOUISVILLE	81	General Dynamics/Electric Boat	16 Sep 1984	14 Dec 1985	8 Nov 1986	**PA**
SSN 725	HELENA	82	General Dynamics/Electric Boat	28 Mar 1985	28 June 1986	11 July 1987	**AA**
SSN 750	NEWPORT NEWS	82	Newport News Shipbuilding	3 Mar 1984	15 Mar 1986	3 June 1989	**AA**

Displacement:	SSN 688–699:	6,080 tons standard
		6,927 tons submerged
	SSN 700–715:	6,130 tons standard
		6,977 tons submerged
	SSN 716–718:	6,165 tons standard
		7,012 tons submerged
	SSN 719–750:	6,255 tons standard
		7,102 tons submerged
Length:	360 feet (109.7 m) overall	
Beam:	33 feet (10.1 m)	
Draft:	32 feet (9.75 m)	
Propulsion:	2 steam turbines; approx. 30,000 shp; 1 shaft	
Reactors:	1 S6G pressurized-water (General Electric)	
Speed:		
	approx. 33 knots submerged	
Manning:	141 (14 officers + 127 enlisted), except SSN 691: 165	
	(14 officers + 151 enlisted)	
Missiles:	Tomahawk SSMs launched from torpedo tubes	

Torpedo tubes:	4 21-inch (533-mm) amidships Mk 67 (25 weapons)
ASW weapons:	Mk 48 ADCAP torpedoes
Radars:	BPS-15A or BPS-16 surface search
Sonars:	BQQ-5 multifunction bow mounted (BQQ-5E in later and updated units)
	BQR-15 towed array
	BQR-26 in some submarines
	BQS-13 active
	BQS-15 under-ice/mine detection
	TB-16 (BQQ-5A) or TB-23 (BQQ-5D) towed array in later and updated units
Fire control:	SSN 688–719: 1 CCS Mk 2 Mod 0
	SSN 719–725, 750: 1 CCS Mk 2 Mod 1
	1 Mk 117 torpedo FCS
EW systems:	BRD-7 direction finder
	WLR-8(V)
	WLR-9
	WLR-12

These are large attack submarines, originally developed to counter the Soviet Victor fast-attack submarines, which were first completed in 1967–1968. The MEMPHIS is employed as a Research and Development (R&D) platform; she retains her combat capabilities.

The LOS ANGELES submarines are about five knots faster than the previous U.S. STURGEON class, the higher speed being the principal advantage over the earlier class (see *Engineering* notes). However, the LOS ANGELES class is about half again as large in terms of displacement and considerably more expensive (see *Cost* notes). Also, the original LOS ANGELES design lacked the under-ice and minelaying capabilities, both vital for modern submarine warfare. The SSN 756 and later units have a minelaying capability.

The SAN JUAN and later units are considered an "improved" design (see previous listing).

Class: There were originally 39 "straight" LOS ANGELES–class submarines, which were followed by the 23 improved submarines.

The MEMPHIS, formerly a standard SSN, began operating as a full-time "interim" research and development platform in August 1989, the result of congressional criticism of the Navy's failure to pursue advance submarine technology. She provides an at-sea testing environment for the Defense Advanced Research Projects Agency (DARPA), the Navy, and industry. One of the first projects to be evaluated in the MEMPHIS was a nonpenetrating periscope (i.e., mounted on a flexible cable employing fiber optics). In 1993–1994 she underwent extensive modifications to serve in the research role, receiving advanced towed sonar arrays, an oversize logistics hatch to facilitate equipment installation and removal, and a "turtleback" structure for carrying Unmanned Underwater Vehicles (UUVs).

Classification: Submarine hull numbers 726 through 749 were reserved for additional Trident SSBNs. There is no plan to reclassify the MEMPHIS, even though she should properly be designated an SSAN or SSAGN, based on ship classification instructions.

Design: SCB No. 303. The increase in size over the STURGEON class is due primarily to the installation of the larger, more capable S6G reactor plant in an effort to regain the speed loss in the PERMIT and STURGEON classes.

These submarines were designed to be constructed of HY-100 steel; however, they were built with HY-80. The ALBANY and TOPEKA have some hull sections of HY-100 to serve as a materials test bed for the SEAWOLF class; those submarines have not encountered the welding problems sustained by the latter class.

The LOS ANGELES also has improved sonar and fire control systems (that were being retrofitted to the STURGEON class) compared to previous classes. These submarines are not fitted to carry mines, nor are they configured for under-ice operations; these shortcomings are corrected in the Improved LOS ANGELES class.

These submarines originally had berthing for only 95 enlisted men; the remainder used sleeping bags in available space or "hot bunked." Additional berthing has been added, but the ships are considered to be quite crowded in comparison with earlier SSNs.

Electronics: The early submarines were fitted with the Mk 113 (analog) fire control system and could carry the Tomahawk missile, while those with the Mk 117 (digital) cannot carry the SUBROC. All have been refitted with the Mk 117.

The AUGUSTA was fitted with the BQQ-10 Acoustic Rapid COTS Insertion (ARCI) sonar system in 1997. This is an upgrade to the BQQ-5/BQQ-6/BSY-1 "legacy" sonars. The entire submarine force is scheduled to receive the update by the year 2005.

Engineering: The S6G reactor is estimated to have an initial fuel core operating life of 10 to 13 years. According to official Navy statements, with the LOS ANGELES "the speed threshold which had been established by SKIPJACK 18 years earlier was finally surpassed."

Missiles: Tomahawk missiles can be launched from the torpedo tubes in this class. The ATLANTA was the first SSN to deploy with Tomahawk, in November 1983.

Names: Most of the earlier submarines of this class carry names previously borne by cruisers; many later names were carried by lesser warships (e.g., frigates [PF]).

The SSN 705 originally was named CORPUS CHRISTI for the Texas port city of that name. That name was previously borne by the frigate PF 44 (launched in 1943); the seaplane tender ALBEMARLE (AV 5) was converted to a helicopter repair ship (ARVH 1) during the Vietnam War and renamed CORPUS CHRISTI BAY (she was operated by the Military Sealift Command for the Army). After protests from Catholic groups, the SSN 705 name was changed to CITY OF CORPUS CHRISTI on 10 May 1982.

The SSN 708 honors the "twin cities" in Minnesota, which are actually named Minneapolis–St. Paul (vice *Saint* Paul).

The SSN 709 was named for Admiral H. G. Rickover, long-time head of the U.S. Navy's nuclear propulsion program, on 4 March 1983; the move to honor Rickover while he was still alive was, in part, an effort to preempt congressional pressure to name an aircraft carrier for the controversial admiral.

The SSN 719 was named PROVIDENCE in September 1983 to honor the state of Rhode Island after the SSBN 730 (previously the RHODE ISLAND) was renamed HENRY M. JACKSON.

The SSN 757 originally was named ASHEVILLE; the name was changed to ALEXANDRIA on 27 February 1987. The SSN 764 originally was named HARTFORD and the SSN 768 the BOISE; they swapped names on 3 March 1989.

Operational: The LOUISVILLE and PITTSBURGH launched Tomahawk TLAM missiles against targets in Iraq during the 1991 Gulf War. The latter submarine fired the first "war shot" against an enemy by a U.S. submarine since World War II. The LOUISVILLE fired eight missiles and the PITTSBURGH four; this represented 4 percent of the 288 missiles fired in the Gulf War.

The AUGUSTA suffered an underwater collision with a Soviet nuclear-propelled submarine in the North Atlantic in October

The original LOS ANGELES–class SSNs—such as the AUGUSTA shown here—can easily be identified by their sail-mounted diving planes. Those submarines could not carry mines, were unable to operate under ice, and could not operate as deep as the previous U.S. SSNs. The AUGUSTA was lead ship for an upgrade of the LOS ANGELES sonar systems. (1999, Leo Van Ginderen)

1986; she struck a Soviet strategic missile submarine (at least one other Soviet submarine was in the area at the time). Repairs to the AUGUSTA cost $2.7 million.

The BATON ROUGE collided with a Russian nuclear-propelled submarine in the Barents Sea on 11 February 1992. U.S. officials said that the incident occurred in international waters, beyond the 12-n.mile (22.2-km) territorial zone recognized by the United States; Russian officials declared that the collision was off Murmansk, within their territorial waters. Neither submarine was reported to have suffered serious damage and there were no injuries. However, the Navy placed the BATON ROUGE In Commission In Reserve (ICIR) on 11 January 1993 for subsequent disposal.

The CITY OF CORPUS CHRISTI will transfer to the Pacific Fleet in 2001.

The KEY WEST on the surface as part of the CONSTELLATION (CV 64) battle group. This view shows the circular hull form of U.S. attack submarines. The speckled paint scheme of her periscopes and masts reduces their visibility when protruding above the surface. (1997, U.S. Navy, PH3 James W. Olive)

Stern view of the OKLAHOMA CITY, with her rudder hard over. The darker area on her deck is non-skid material to help line-handlers keep their footing. (2000, Leo Van Ginderen)

1 NUCLEAR-PROPELLED SPECIAL MISSION SUBMARINE: MODIFIED "STURGEON" CLASS

Number	Name	FY	Builder	Laid down	Launched	Commissioned	Status
SSN 683	PARCHE	68	Ingalls Shipbuilding	10 Dec 1970	13 Jan 1973	17 Aug 1974	**PA**

Displacement:	6,140 tons surface	Missiles:	Tomahawk SSMs launched from torpedo tubes
	7,140 tons submerged	Torpedo tubes:	4 21-inch (533-mm) amidships Mk 63 (25 weapons)
Length:	401 5/12 feet (122.4 m) overall	ASW weapons:	Mk 48 ADCAP torpedoes
Beam:	31 2/3 feet (9.65 m)	Radars:	BPS-15 surface search
Draft:	35 feet (10.67 m)	Sonars:	BQQ-5 multifunction bow mounted
Propulsion:	2 steam turbines; 15,000 shp; 1 shaft		BQS-13 active
Reactors:	1 S5W pressurized-water (Westinghouse)		towed array
Speed:	approx. 15 knots surface	Fire control:	Mk 117 torpedo FCS
	approx. 28 knots submerged	EW systems:	BRD-7
Manning:	147 (14 officers + 133 enlisted)		WLQ-4E

Built as a unit of the STURGEON class, the PARCHE has been extensively modified to perform ocean-engineering and other "special missions." The PARCHE replaced the HALIBUT in this role in 1976; the SEAWOLF (SSN 575) was also employed for special missions, but had limited effectiveness in this role.

The PARCHE transferred from the Atlantic to the Pacific in October 1976 and underwent modifications at the Mare Island Naval Shipyard for the ocean engineering role. She was refueled and extensively modified at Mare Island from January 1987 to May 1991; these later modifications included the addition of a 100-foot (30.5-m) section forward of the sail to accommodate special search and recovery equipment. The modification is reported to include a claw-like device that can be lowered by cable to recover satellites and other equipment from the ocean floor.

She will be replaced by the JIMMY CARTER about 2004.

Design: SCB No. 300. See 16th Edition/pages 75–77 for additional data.

Electronics: The original BQQ-2 system has been upgraded to the BQQ-5 configuration. She was built with the Mk 113 analog

The PARCHE, showing her lengthened forward section with the small superstructure added ahead of the sail structure. The submarine has been extensively modified for ocean-engineering activities, including deep-ocean search and recovery. The yard tug MANHATTAN (YTB 779) maneuvers alongside off the submarine base at Bangor, Washington. (1994, Ed Offley)

The PARCHE under way at high speed near her home port of Bangor, Wash. Note the raised forward section, where a 100-foot section was installed forward of her sail. The JIMMY CARTER is being completed to a modified design to replace the PARCHE in the search-and-recovery role. (U.S. Navy)

fire control system, which was replaced by the Mk 117 digital system during overhaul.

Operational: The PARCHE relieved the HALIBUT in the special missions role in 1976. The latter submarine participated in Operation Ivy Bells beginning shortly after her completion. In this super-secret U.S. Navy project, nuclear-propelled submarines planted "taps" on seafloor communications cables in the Sea of Ohkotsk between the major submarine base at Petropavlovsk on Kamchatka Peninsula and its surrounding air, naval, and military bases and the mainland of Soviet Siberia.[19]

The PARCHE's special operations have earned the submarine five Presidential Unit Citations and three Navy Unit Citations.

---

19. Details of these submarine operations are provided in Sherry Sontag and Christopher Drew, *Blind Man's Bluff: The Untold Story of American Submarine Espionage* (New York: PublicAffairs, 1998). Ivy Bells was revealed to the Soviets by Ronald W. Pelton, a 14-year employee of the U.S. National Security Agency, who provided the Soviets with intelligence information from January 1980 until his arrest in November 1985. He was subsequently sentenced to life imprisonment.

Details of the PARCHE's sail and forward superstructure. The submarine is covered with anechoic tiles, as are other U.S. SSNs (1994, Ed Offley)

1 NUCLEAR-PROPELLED TRANSPORT SUBMARINE: MODIFIED "LAFAYETTE" CLASS

Number	Name	FY	Builder	Laid down	Launched	Commissioned	Status
SSN 642	KAMEHAMEHA	63	Mare Island Naval Shipyard	2 May 1963	16 Jan 1965	10 Dec 1965	**PA**
SSN 645	JAMES K. POLK	63	General Dynamics/Electric Boat	23 Nov 1963	22 May 1965	16 Apr 1966	decomm./str. 9 July 1999

Displacement:	7,350 tons standard	Torpedo tubes:	4 21-inch (533-mm) Mk 65 (bow)
	8,250 tons submerged	Torpedoes:	Mk 48 ADCAP torpedoes
Length:	425 feet (129.6 m) overall	Radars:	BPS-15 surface search
Beam:	33 feet (10.06 m)	Sonars:	BQR-7E passive detection
Draft:	31½ feet (9.6 m)		BQR-15 towed array
Propulsion:	2 steam turbines; 15,000 shp; 1 shaft		BQR-19 navigation
Reactors:	1 S5W pressurized-water (Westinghouse)		BQR-21 passive array
Speed:	approx. 15 knots surface		BQS-4 active/passive detection
	approx. 25 knots submerged	Fire control:	Mk 113 torpedo/missile FCS
Manning:	144 (14 officers + 130 enlisted)	EW systems:	WLR-8
Troops:	65 SEALs		WLR-10
Missiles:	removed		

These submarines were built to carry the Polaris A-3 SLBM, being subsequently converted in 1972 to carry the Poseidon C-3 missile. (They were not among the 12 LAFAYETTE-class submarines later upgraded to fire the Trident C-4 missile; see chapter 10.)

The KAMEHAMEHA and POLK were converted to serve as transport submarines for special operations forces, such as Navy SEALs, at Mare Island in 1992–1993. They replaced the ex-Polaris submarines SAM

HOUSTON (SSBN/SSN 609) and JOHN MARSHALL (SSBN/SSN 611) in this role. The POLK has since been discarded. The KAMEHAMEHA is scheduled to be withdrawn from active service in October 2001; she should be decommissioned and stricken six to eight months later.

Class: Thirty-one submarines of the LAFAYETTE class were built.

Classification: Changed from SSBN to SSN on 31 August 1992 and 1 October 1993, respectively.

Design: SCB No. 216. As SOF transports, these submarines could each carry two Dry Deck Shelters aft of the sail structure. Each DDS can accommodate a Swimmer Delivery Vehicle (SDV) or be used as a lockout chamber for swimmers.

Internally, all missile support and launch equipment was removed, and air, electrical, internal communications, and drain systems were installed for the DDS. Berthing and sanitary facilities are provided for 65 troops. Some of the former missile tubes are used for SEAL equipment stowage.

Marines crowd the deck of the KAMEHAMEHA during a daylight exercise in the Hawaiian area. At left is an open missile tube hatch, now giving access to the Marines' gear. (1994, U.S. Marine Corps, Cpl. Robert A. Berry)

The former Polaris submarine KAMEHAMEHA as configured as a transport for special operations forces. Each of the two dry deck shelters can accommodate a SEAL delivery vehicle or can be used to lock out SEALs or other special forces. She is to be decommissioned in 2002. (U.S. Navy)

The KAMEHAMEHA at Pearl Harbor with two dry deck shelters fitted amidships. The door of the starboard DDS is partially open. The similar JAMES K. POLK had provided the Atlantic Fleet with a transport submarine. (U.S. Navy)

1 DIESEL-ELECTRIC ATTACK SUBMARINE: "TANG" CLASS

Number	Name	FY	Builder	Laid down	Launched	Commissioned	Status
SS 566	TROUT	48	General Dynamics/Electric Boat	1 Dec 1949	21 Aug 1951	27 June 1952	stricken 19 Dec 1978; see text

Displacement:	2,100 tons standard		Operating depth:	700 feet (213 m)
	2,700 tons submerged		Manning:	88 (8 officers + 80 enlisted)
Length:	287 feet (87.5 m) overall		Torpedo tubes:	8 21-inch (533-mm); 6 Mk 43 bow + 2 Mk 44 stern
Beam:	27⅙ feet (8.3 m)		Torpedoes:	26
Draft:	19 feet (5.8 m)		Radars:	
Propulsion:	3 diesel engines (Fairbanks Morse); 4,500 bhp		Sonars:	BQG-4 PUFFS[20]
	2 electric motors (Westinghouse); 5,600 shp; 2 shafts			BQS-4
Speed:	16 knots surface		Fire control:	Mk 10 torpedo FCS
	16 knots submerged			

The TROUT is the last diesel-electric attack submarine retained by the U.S. Navy. Officially stricken, she is at Key West, Fla., maintained by the Naval Air Warfare Center's Aircraft Division. She is not operational and is considered "floating equipment." The only other diesel-electric submarine retained by the Navy is the active research craft DOLPHIN.

Sold to Iran in 1978, the TROUT (and two sister ships) were retained by the U.S. government because of the overthrow of the Shah in 1979. The two other submarines, the TANG and GUDGEON, were instead transferred to Turkey (see table 11-3). The TROUT was maintained at the Philadelphia Naval Shipyard, then at Newport, R.I., before being towed to Key West in July 1997.

There is considerable interest in reactivating the TROUT as a research platform and for use as an ASW target by naval air and surface forces. The interest in an ASW target by the U.S. Navy—albeit not in the submarine community—is based on the U.S. Navy attack submarine force being all nuclear, with the LOS ANGELES class "smallest" attack submarines in service after the year 2001. The SSNs cannot effectively simulate diesel-electric submarine targets for anti-submarine forces. They are too large, have very different "signatures" than the typical submarines operated by Third World navies, and are operated quite unlike the submarines the Navy could be fighting. Further, the current force level goal of 50 SSNs provides too few sub-marines for training air and surface ASW forces, especially for reserve frigates and maritime patrol aircraft, which have low priority for submarine target time. The shortfall in SSNs for operational assignments have been well publicized of late, with ASW training having a relatively low priority in submarine assignments.[21]

Under current proposals, as a target and research submarine, the TROUT would be manned by a civilian crew (undoubtedly former U.S. Navy submariners). As such, the TROUT would not be subject to U.S. Navy submarine safety regulations, but would be under the cogni-zance of the American Bureau of Shipping, licensed as a commercial "manned submersible."

Class: Six submarines of the TANG class were completed in 1951–1952; see table 11-3 for disposition.

Design: SCB-2A. This design incorporates many features of the German Type XXI design, the most advanced submarine design of World War II.

---

20. PUFFS = Passive Underwater Fire-control System.
21. See Lt. Cdr. Carey Matthews, USNR, "Anti-sub Warfare Calls for Two Russian Diesels," *Navy Times,* 26 February 1996, p. 33; Lt. Jack Shriver, USN, "Developing Real Anti-Diesel Tactics," *Submarine Review* (April 1998), pp. 90–94; and N. Polmar, "Realistic ASW Training," U.S. Naval Institute *Proceedings* (December 1999), pp. 85–86.

The TROUT, retired and awaiting a possible role as a research and target craft, at rest at Key West, Fla. The submarine is under the cognizance of the Naval Air Warfare Center's Key West Detachment. (U.S. Navy)

The TROUT as an active fleet submarine on maneuvers off Guantánamo Bay, Cuba. She and her sister submarines of the TANG class were based on the German Type XXI, the most advanced submarine of World War II. (1965, U.S. Navy)

TABLE 11-3. POST–WORLD WAR II SUBMARINES

Number	Name	Comm.	Notes	Number	Name	Comm.	Notes
K 1 class (2)				SSN 604	HADDO	1964	decomm./str. 12 June 1991
SS 551	BASS		ex-SSK 2 (see below)	SSN 605	JACK	1967	decomm./str. 11 July 1990
SS 552	BONITA		ex-SSK 3 (see below)	SSN 606	TINOSA	1964	decomm./str. 15 Jan 1992
SS 553	(Norwegian KINN)		OSP (Offshore Procurement)	SSN 607	DACE	1964	stricken 1989
SS 554	(Danish SPRINGEREN)		OSP	SSBN 608–611			(see chapter 10)
DOLPHIN type				*THRESHER class (continued)*			
AGSS 555	DOLPHIN	1968		SSN 612	GUARDFISH	1966	decomm./str. 4 Feb 1992
SS 556–562	not used			SSN 613	FLASHER	1966	decomm./str. 14 Sep 1992
TANG class (6)				SSN 614	GREENLING	1967	decomm./str. 18 Apr 1994
SS 563	TANG	1951	to Turkey 1980	SSN 615	GATO	1968	decomm./str. 26 Apr 1996
SS 564	TRIGGER	1952	to Italy 1973	SSBN 616–620			(see chapter 10)
SS 565	WAHOO	1952	stricken 1983 (scrapped)	*THRESHER class (continued)*			
SS 566	TROUT	1952	to Iran 1978 (not transferred; retained by U.S. government)	SSN 621	HADDOCK	1967	decomm./str. 7 Apr 1993
				SSBN 622–636			(see chapter 10)
SS 567	GUDGEON	1952	to Turkey 1983	*STURGEON class (37)*			
SS 568	HARDER	1952	to Italy 1974	SSN 637	STURGEON	1967	decomm./str. 1 Aug 1994
ALBACORE type				SSN 638	WHALE	1968	decomm./str. 25 June 1996
AGSS 569	ALBACORE	1953	stricken 1980 (museum)	SSN 639	TAUTOG	1968	decomm./str. 31 Mar 1997
AGSS 570			completed as SST 1	SSBN 640–645			(see chapter 10)
NAUTILUS type				*STURGEON class (continued)*			
SSN 571	NAUTILUS	1954	decomm. 1980 (museum)	SSN 646	GRAYLING	1969	decomm./str. 18 July 1997
SAILFISH class (2)				SSN 647	POGY	1971	decomm./str. 11 June 1999
SSR 572	SAILFISH	1956	stricken 1978	SSN 648	ASPRO	1969	decomm./str. 3 Mar 1995
SSR 573	SALMON	1956	stricken 1977	SSN 649	SUNFISH	1969	decomm./str. 28 Mar 1997
GRAYBACK class (2)				SSN 650	PARGO	1968	decomm./str. 14 Apr 1995
SSG 574	GRAYBACK	1958	stricken 1984	SSN 651	QUEENFISH	1966	decomm./str. 8 Nov 1991
SEAWOLF type				SSN 652	PUFFER	1969	decomm./str. 12 July 1996
SSN 575	SEAWOLF	1957	stricken 1987	SSN 653	RAY	1967	decomm./str. 16 Mar 1993
DARTER type				SSBN 654–659			(see chapter 10)
SS 576	DARTER	1956	stricken 17 Jan 1990	*STURGEON class (continued)*			
GRAYBACK class (continued)				SSN 660	SAND LANCE	1971	decomm./str. 7 Aug 1998
SSG 577	GROWLER	1958	stricken 1980 (museum)	SSN 661	LAPON	1967	decomm./str. 8 Aug 1992
SKATE class (4)				SSN 662	GURNARD	1968	decomm./str. 28 Apr 1995
SSN 578	SKATE	1957	stricken 1986	SSN 663	HAMMERHEAD	1968	decomm./str. 5 Apr 1995
SSN 579	SWORDFISH	1958	stricken 1989	SSN 664	SEA DEVIL	1969	decomm./str. 16 Oct 1991
BARBEL class (3)				SSN 665	GUITARRO	1972	decomm./str. 29 May 1992
SS 580	BARBEL	1959	decomm. 4 Dec 1989; str. 17 Jan 1990	SSN 666	HAWKBILL	1971	decomm./str. 2000?
				SSN 667	BERGALL	1969	decomm./str. 6 June 1996
SS 581	BLUEBACK	1959	decomm. 1 Oct 1990; str. 30 Oct 1990	SSN 668	SPADEFISH	1969	decomm./str. 11 Apr 1997
				SSN 669	SEAHORSE	1969	decomm./str. 17 Aug 1995
SS 582	BONEFISH	1959	stricken 1989	SSN 670	FINBACK	1970	decomm./str. 28 Mar 1997
SKATE class (continued)				*NARWHAL type*			
SSN 583	SARGO	1958	stricken 1988	SSN 671	NARWHAL	1969	decomm./str. 1 July 1999
SSN 584	SEADRAGON	1959	stricken 1986	*STURGEON class (continued)*			
SKIPJACK class (6)				SSN 672	PINTADO	1971	decomm./str. 26 Feb 1998
SSN 585	SKIPJACK	1959	decomm./str. 19 Apr 1990	SSN 673	FLYING FISH	1970	decomm./str. 16 May 1996
TRITON type				SSN 674	TREPANG	1970	decomm./str. 1 June 1999
SSRN 586	TRITON	1959	to SSN 1961; stricken 1986	SSN 675	BLUEFISH	1971	decomm./str. 31 May 1996
HALIBUT type				SSN 676	BILLFISH	1971	decomm./str. 1 July 1999
SSGN 587	HALIBUT	1960	to SSN 1965; stricken 1986	SSN 677	DRUM	1972	decomm./str. 30 Oct 1995
SKIPJACK class (continued)				SSN 678	ARCHERFISH	1971	decomm./str. 31 Mar 1998
SSN 588	SCAMP	1961	stricken 1988	SSN 679	SILVERSIDES	1972	decomm./str. 21 July 1994
SSN 589	SCORPION	1960	sunk 27 May 1968	SSN 680	WILLIAM H. BATES	1973	decomm./str. 11 Feb 2000
SSN 590	SCULPIN	1961	decomm./str. 3 Aug 1990	SSN 681	BATFISH	1972	decomm./str. 17 Mar 1999
SSN 591	SHARK	1961	decomm./str. 15 Sep 1990	SSN 682	TUNNY	1974	decomm./str. 13 Mar 1998
SSN 592	SNOOK	1961	stricken 1986	SSN 683	PARCHE		(see above listing)
THRESHER class (14)				SSN 684	CAVALLA	1973	decomm./str. 30 Mar 1998
SSN 593	THRESHER	1961	sunk 10 Apr 1963	*GLENARD P. LIPSCOMB type*			
SSN 594	PERMIT	1962	decomm./str. 12 June 1991	SSN 685	GLENARD P. LIPSCOMB	1974	decomm./str. 11 July 1990
SSN 595	PLUNGER	1962	decomm./str. 2 Feb 1990	*STURGEON class (continued)*			
SSN 596	BARB	1963	stricken 1989	SSN 686	L. MENDEL RIVERS	1975	decomm./str. 2001
TULLIBEE type				SSN 687	RICHARD B. RUSSELL	1975	decomm./str. 24 June 1994
SSN 597	TULLIBEE	1960	stricken 1988				
SSBN 598–602			(see chapter 10)	SSN 688–725	LOS ANGELES class		
THRESHER class (continued)				SSBN 726–749	OHIO class		(see chapter 10)
SSN 603	POLLACK	1964	stricken 1989	SSN 750–773	LOS ANGELES class		
				SSN 774–	VIRGINIA class		

U.S. submarine programs reached hull number SS 562 during World War II, with hulls 526–562 being canceled late in the war. Subsequently, five of these numbers were assigned to postwar submarines: three U.S. submarines and two American-financed, foreign-built submarines (Offshore Procurement); two others, to be built in Portugal (SS 556) and Norway (SS 557), were canceled in 1961.

The last war-built submarine on the Naval Vessel Register was the transport submarine SEALION (LPSS 315), decommissioned and laid up in 1970 and stricken in 1977. The last active submarine of World War II construction was the TIGRONE (AGSS 419), which was decommissioned and stricken on 1 July 1975 (correction to date in previous edition).

Note the large number of submarine designs developed and built from the late 1940s into the early 1960s. This was a period of highly innovative thinking in the submarine community, in part while searching for new roles for submarines and exploring the potential impact of emerging technologies on submarine warfare. In particular, the research submarine ALBACORE introduced many of the features found in subsequent undersea craft; in many respects, she was the beginning of the modern submarine era.

The BARBEL-class boats were the last diesel-electric combat submarines built in the United States and the last in U.S. Navy service. They were the first combat submarines to incorporate the ALBACORE's "tear-drop" high-speed hull design.

The GRAYBACK and GROWLER were similar to each other, although their dimensions differed slightly. They carried the Regulus land-attack guided/cruise missile. The GRAYBACK was reconfigured as a transport submarine (redesignated LPSS); she was succeeded in that role by nuclear-propelled submarines.

The pioneer nuclear-propelled submarine NAUTILUS survives as a memorial/museum at Groton, Conn. She was commissioned on 30 September 1954, but did not get under way until 3 January 1955. The NAUTILUS was decommissioned on 3 March 1980, after being defueled and modified at the Mare Island Naval Shipyard, Vallejo, Calif. In 1985 she was towed to Groton and formally transferred to private control on 6 July 1985 for use as a museum.[22]

The special-purpose nuclear submarines TRITON (radar picket) and HALIBUT (guided/cruise missile) were redesignated as SSNs after being withdrawn from their specialized radar picket and guided missile (Regulus) roles. The SEAWOLF, HALIBUT, and PARCHE were modified for deep-ocean search and recovery operations; they carried out "spy" missions.

The SSN 594–596 and 607 were ordered as SSGNs to carry the Regulus II missile. They were reordered as THRESHER-class SSNs on 15 October 1959, following cancellation of the Regulus II guided missile.

The THRESHER was lost on post-overhaul sea trials off New England on 10 April 1963 with all 112 naval personnel and 17 civilians on board. This was the world's first nuclear submarine loss and the worst submarine disaster on record in terms of lives lost.

The SCORPION was lost with all 99 men on board on 27 May 1968 some 400 n.miles (741 km) southwest of the Azores.

---

22. The Navy had decided to moor the ship at the Washington Navy Yard in the nation's capital. However, President Jimmy Carter directed that the ship be moored at New London.

TABLE 11-4. HUNTER-KILLER SUBMARINES

Number	Name/Renamed	Comm.	Notes
SSK 1	K 1/BARRACUDA	1951	to SST 3
SSK 2	K 2/BASS	1951	to SS 551/stricken 1965
SSK 3	K 3/BONITA	1952	to SS 552/stricken 1965

These purpose-built SSKs were small hunter-killer submarines, intended to lie in wait to intercept Soviet submarines off their home ports and in narrow waterways. Several hundred were to have been produced in time of war.

These submarines were originally assigned K-number "names" and were given fish names in 1955. The BASS and BONITA were reclassified SS in 1959 for use in the training role; the BARRACUDA was changed to SST in 1959 for the training role.

In addition to these built-for-the-purpose SSKs, the nuclear-propelled TULLIBEE was built as an SSKN (although designated SSN 597). Seven war-built GATO (SS 212)-class diesel submarines were converted to hunter-killer submarines in the 1950s and redesignated SSK with their SS hull numbers (214, 240–244, and 246).

TABLE 11-5. TRAINING SUBMARINES

Number	Name/Renamed	Comm.	Notes
SST 1	T 1/MACKEREL	1953	stricken 1973
SST 2	T 2/MARLIN	1953	stricken 1973 (museum)
SST 3	BARRACUDA (ex–K 1)	1951	stricken 1973

The SST 1 and 2 were small submarines developed for training and target use. The MACKEREL was ordered as AGSS 570 and completed as the SST 1. Originally assigned T-number "names," they were given fish names in 1956.

The BARRACUDA was changed from SSK 1 to SST 3 after operating as a hunter-killer submarine. She later was reclassified *SS-T3* as a force level adjustment, and then changed back to SST 3.

TABLE 11-6. MIDGET SUBMARINES

Number	Name	In Serv.	Notes
SSX 1	X-1	1955	stricken 1973

The U.S. Navy's lone midget submarine was the X-1, which was based on British X-craft submersibles. She had a closed-cycle/hydrogen-peroxide-diesel propulsion system. SSX 1 was placed "in service," vice in commission, with an officer-in-charge. She is on display at the Naval Academy in Annapolis, Md.

The attack submarine TUCSON and the Canadian frigate TORONTO operate in the Persian Gulf. The submarine's BPS-15 search and navigation radar antenna is visible near the leading edge of the sail. (1998, U. S. Navy, PH2 Jeffrey S. Viano)

CHAPTER 12

Research Submarines and Submersibles

The attack submarine SAND LANCE (SSN 660) has the DSRV AVALON mated to her after hatch as she prepares for a practice rescue operation. A twin-stack tugboat stands by to port. The DSRVs were the most advanced manned submersibles yet developed in terms of sensors and maneuverability. A surface-based rescue system is being developed to replace the DSRVs. (U.S. Navy)

The U.S. Navy operates one dedicated diesel-electric research submarine (the DOLPHIN), one nuclear-propelled research "submersible" (NR-1), and two rescue submersibles (AVALON and MYSTIC), plus a number of small SEAL delivery vehicles, including the new Advanced SEAL Delivery System (ASDS), which in several respects resembles a midget submarine.

Several unmanned submersibles are operated in a number of naval roles. These are classified as Large Scale Vehicles (LSV), Unmanned Underwater Vehicles (UUV), and Remotely Operated Vehicles (ROV).

Classification: The Navy's first deep-diving craft, the bathyscaph TRIESTE, did not have a hull number. When her sphere was married with a more hydrodynamic float and other features as the TRIESTE II, she was designated X-1 and, subsequently, deep submergence vehicle DSV 1.[1]

The DSV 2 through DSV 4 are listed below. The DSV 5 was the unmanned, tethered vehicle NEMO.[2]

---

1. The TRIESTE (with the original sphere and float) is at the Navy Museum at the Navy Yard, Washington, D.C.; the TRIESTE II (as later configured, with new sphere and float) is at the Naval Undersea Museum at Keyport, Wash.
2. On display at San Diego.

Manning: The manning data provided in the submarine descriptions below are the actual number of operating personnel on board these submersibles. The following list indicates the number of Navy personnel assigned to each craft, including maintenance and relief operators.

	Total	Officers	Enlisted
NR-1	26	4	22
AVALON	20	3	17
MYSTIC	20	3	17

Operational: Submarine Development Squadron 5 at Point Loma (San Diego), Calif., operates the rescue submersibles and controls the special-mission submarine PARCHE (SSN 683) and the DOLPHIN. Submarine Group 2 at the Naval Submarine Base New London (Groton), Conn., operates the nuclear submersible NR-1 as well as a number of attack submarines. The NR-1 is based at the Portsmouth Naval Shipyard, Maine.

The rescue submersibles MYSTIC and AVALON are assigned to the Submarine Rescue Unit at Naval Air Station North Island, San Diego, Calif.

1 RESEARCH SUBMARINE: "DOLPHIN"

Number	Name	FY	Builder	Laid down	Launched	Commissioned	Status
AGSS 555	DOLPHIN	61	Portsmouth Naval Shipyard	9 Nov 1962	8 June 1968	17 Aug 1968	**PA**

Displacement:	860 tons standard		Operating depth:	3,000 feet (915 m)
	950 tons submerged		Manning:	48 (4 officers + 44 enlisted) + 5 scientists
Length:	165 feet (50.3 m) overall		Torpedo tubes:	removed
Beam:	$19^5/_{12}$ feet (5.9 m)		Radars:	SPS-53 navigation (portable)
Draft:	16 feet (4.9 m)		Sonars:	BQR-2 passive (bow-mounted)
Propulsion:	2 diesel engines (General Motors 12V71); 850 bhp			BQS-15 active
	1 electric motor (Elliott); 1,650 shp; 1 shaft		Fire control:	none
Speed:	7.5 knots surface			
	15 knots submerged			

The DOLPHIN is an experimental, deep-diving submarine, the last non-nuclear submarine to be built by the U.S. Navy. She has operated at greater depths than any other operational U.S. submarine.

Design: SCB No. 207. The DOLPHIN has a constant-diameter pressure hull with hemisphere heads at both ends; the outside diameter is approximately 15 feet (4.57 m). The submarine has a stepped sail, with the radar antenna, UHF antenna, and single periscope mounted on the upper (rear) step, and the lights, whip antenna, VLF loop antenna, and searchlight mounted on the lower step.

An improved rudder design and other features permit maneuvering without conventional submarine diving planes. There are minimal penetrations of the pressure hull (e.g., only one access hatch) and

built-in safety systems that automatically surface the submarine in an emergency. The single experimental torpedo tube that was originally fitted was removed in 1970. The DOLPHIN has been modified to test HY-130 steel components.

Electronics: Various experimental sonars have been fitted in the DOLPHIN. Her original bow sonar, which had four arrays that could be extended at 90° angles to the submarine's bow–stern axis, has been removed.

Engineering: Submerged endurance is approximately 24 hours; her sea endurance is about 14 days.

Operational: The DOLPHIN's activities have supported research in air–submarine laser communications, deep submergence, sonar, oceanography, and ASW.

The DOLPHIN at rest at San Diego. The craft's only access hatch is in the sail structure.
(1997, Leo Van Ginderen)

The deep-diving DOLPHIN is the only non-nuclear submarine currently in U.S. service. The craft has carried out a variety of research activities in communications, sonar, weapons, and other areas. (U.S. Navy)

SUBMERSIBLES

1 NUCLEAR-PROPELLED RESEARCH SUBMERSIBLE: "NR-1"

Number	Name	FY	Builder	Laid down	Launched	In service	Status
NR-1	(unnamed)	—	General Dynamics/Electric Boat	10 June 1967	25 Jan 1969	27 Oct 1969	**AA**

Displacement:	365.5 tons surface 393 tons submerged	Reactors:	1 pressurized-water
Length:	136 feet (41.46 m) waterline	Speed:	4.5 knots surface 3.5 knots submerged
	$145^3/_4$ feet (44.44 m) overall	Endurance:	210 man-days nominal
	$96^1/_{12}$ feet (29.3 m) pressure hull		330 man-days maximum
Beam:	$12\frac{1}{2}$ feet (3.8)	Operating depth:	3,000 feet (915 m) (see notes)
Draft:	$15^1/_{12}$ feet (4.6 m)	Crew:	11 operators + 2 scientists
Propulsion:	turbo-electric drive with outboard electric motors; 2 propellers		

The NR-1 was originally built as a test platform for a small submarine nuclear power plant, but the craft has often been employed as a deep-ocean research and recovery vehicle. In explaining the craft's importance, Admiral H. G. Rickover, then head of the Navy's nuclear propulsion program, told a congressional committee, "You will be looking at a development that I believe will be as significant for the United States as was the NAUTILUS" (SSN 571).[3] Rickover planned to construct a series of these craft, hence the designation NR-1.

The veil of secrecy surrounding the NR-1 was partially lifted when, on 18 April 1965, President Lyndon Johnson announced the development of the craft. The White House release, citing the severe endurance and space limitations of existing research submersibles, stated:

> The development of a nuclear propulsion plant for a deep submergence research vehicle will give greater freedom of movement and much greater-endurance of propulsion and auxiliary power. This capability will contribute greatly to accelerate man's exploration and exploitation of the vast resources of the ocean.[4]

Beyond her nuclear plant, which gives her a theoretical unlimited underwater endurance, the NR-1's most remarkable feature is her operating depth of 3,000 feet (915 m). (The Navy officially lists the NR-1 operating depth as 2,375 feet; however, Navy statements continually cite a 3,000-foot capability.) While this was not as great as the Navy's other manned research submersibles, their underwater endurance was only a few hours. The NR-1's operating depth is far greater than the U.S. Navy's combat submarines.

The Knolls Atomic Power Laboratory in Schenectady, N.Y., designed the reactor, while the submersible was designed and subsequently built by the Electric Boat yard in Groton.

The NR-1 was launched on 25 January 1969, underwent initial sea trials in August, and was placed in service on 27 October of that year. The Deep Submergence Systems Project (DSSP), the Navy's management office for the NR-1, was not allowed to publicize the craft except to reiterate what was said in President Johnson's statement (which had been prepared by Rickover's office); even the launch photo of the NR-1 had the craft's fixed mast and television camera blanked out. (The camera was provided in place of conventional periscopes.)

The NR-1 is in service—vice in commission—and is commanded by an officer-in-charge rather than a commanding officer. She is towed and supported by the support ship CAROLYN CHOUEST, a leased commercial tender (see chapter 24 of this edition of *Ships and Aircraft*).

3. Adm. H. G. Rickover, USN (Ret.), in *Naval Nuclear Propulsion Program, 1967–1968: Hearings before the Joint Committee on Atomic Energy, Congress of the United States* (Washington, D.C.: Joint Committee on Atomic Energy, 1968), p. 30.
4. Untitled White House press release (Austin, Texas), 18 April 1965.

Class: A Hull Test Vehicle (HTV) was originally proposed as the NR-2 in 1976 by Admiral Rickover, but was never built (see 16th Edition/page 322).

Classification: "NR-1" indicates *N*uclear *R*esearch vehicle although the craft is listed as a "submersible research vehicle" in the Naval Vessel Register.

Cost: The craft was funded as a nuclear-propulsion project rather than as new ship construction. As proposed, the Atomic Energy Commission (now Department of Energy) was to pay for the research and development of the reactor plant and the Navy for the deep-ocean

research vehicle. Admiral Rickover estimated that he could produce the craft for $30 million, the amount available in the management fund of the Navy's Polaris project, which at the time was managing such deep-ocean programs. Rickover stressed to Congress that the NR-1—except for the propulsion plant—would employ existing technology and equipment.

The cost of the NR-1 at launch in 1969 was $67.5 million, plus $19.9 million for oceanographic equipment and sensors and $11.8 million for research and development, a total of $99.2 million. The Navy has never revealed "final" cost figures for the craft. Cost,

The NR-1 at sea—under tow. The nuclear-propelled submersible is usually towed to operating areas by a surface ship or, submerged, by an attack submarine. When developed by Admiral Rickover, the NR-1 was envisioned as the first of a series of such undersea craft; in the event, she was a one-of-a-kind submersible. (1993, Giorgio Arra)

Details of the NR-1's sail structure, with a crewman standing on her starboard sail-mounted diving plane. The submarine has a fixed mast with television-like optics. Note the towing gear fitted to her bow. (U.S. Navy)

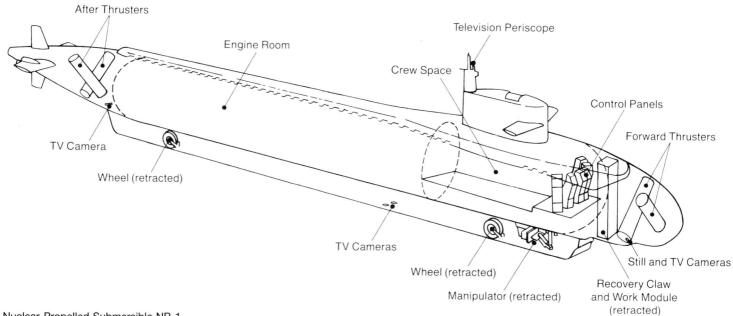

Nuclear-Propelled Submersible NR-1

however, seemed irrelevant in view of the unprecedented capabilities of the NR-1 to carry out research and ocean-engineering work.[5]

Design: The NR-1, generally resembling a conventional submarine, is fabricated of HY-80 steel. She is fitted with two large wheels that permit her to roll and rest on the ocean floor. The retractable tires are normal truck tires with their inner tubes filled with alcohol.

In addition to her twin screws, which provide a submerged speed of 3.5 knots, the craft has paired ducted thrusters forward and aft to provide a high degree of maneuverability. Extensive external lighting, viewing ports, close-range sonars, a remote-controlled mechanical arm, and a recovery cage provide considerable capabilities. The craft carries 22,000 pounds (9,980 kg) of expendable lead shot to provide emergency buoyancy.

Three bunks are provided; crew endurance is limited to a maximum of 30-day missions. There is a warming oven for frozen foods and a hot-drink dispenser.

The NR-1's principal operational limitation is her deployment mobility. Because of her slow speeds, she must be towed to her operating area, either by a surface ship or (underwater) by a nuclear submarine. Her surface towing speed is up to six knots; submerged it is just under four knots.

Electronics: The NR-1 is provided with forward and side-looking sonars; a Doppler sonar is provided to measure over-bottom speed. A BQN-13 rescue pinger beacon is installed.

Engineering: The craft was first refueled during an extensive yard period from November 1990 to November 1992; she is scheduled to be overhauled in 2003 and refueled in 2012, based on a 20-year service life of her reactor core.

Operational: The major NR-1 activities of the Cold War era are still classified. Undoubtedly, she was employed to help maintain the Navy's Sound Surveillance System (SOSUS) and other seafloor installations; she probably also was used to help recover objects that fell to the ocean floor—Soviet as well as American.

Some of her exploits were publicized. For example, in 1976 the NR-1 had a key role in recovering an F-14 Tomcat fighter armed with a then-new Phoenix missile that rolled off the deck of the carrier JOHN F. KENNEDY (CVA 67) and came to rest at a depth of 1,960 feet (598 m). In 1986 the NR-1 participated in the search for wreckage of the crashed space shuttle *Challenger* off Cape Kennedy, Fla.

A few NR-1 exploits were acknowledged only reluctantly. In 1970, for example, the NR-1 participated in installing the NATO-sponsored, eight-nation Azores Fixed Acoustic Range (AFAR). Ob-

viously, a large number of civilians as well as military personnel ashore and afloat were cognizant of the NR-1's participation in the project. When the NR-1 entered Ponta Delgada in the Azores, many civilians in the port saw and probably photographed her. Still, Admiral Rickover objected strongly to the craft being mentioned in press releases or public documents related to AFAR.

With the end of the Cold War, the role of the NR-1 has changed. The Navy, with fewer classified deep-ocean missions, has made the remarkable craft available for civilian scientific and exploration work.

In the spring of 1996 the NR-1 operated off Key Largo, Fla., to support the Jason Project VII, an educational program for youth; in the summer and early fall of 1996, she deployed to Norway to support a Norwegian government request to survey fjords, harbors, shipwrecks, and other undersea obstructions.

From June to late August 1997 the NR-1 operated in the eastern Mediterranean, where, at the behest of the Israeli Navy, she conducted an unsuccessful search for the wreckage of the submarine DAKAR, lost in January 1968 while en route from Britain to Israel. The NR-1's Mediterranean deployment also included exploring the wreck of the BRITANNIC, sister ship of the TITANIC, and searching for Roman wrecks. The latter effort included 19 dives for a total of 403 hours submerged, with 294 hours actually engaged in search, excavating, and recovery operations. Employing a conventional submersible for this work would have required thousands of hours because of the time needed to dive and return to the surface due to the limited battery capacity.

2 DEEP SUBMERGENCE RESCUE VEHICLES: "MYSTIC" CLASS

Number	Name	Launched	Completed
DSRV 1	MYSTIC	24 Jan 1970	6 Aug 1971
DSRV 2	AVALON	1 May 1971	28 July 1972

Builders:	Lockheed Missiles and Space Co., Sunnyvale, Calif.
Weight:	37 tons
Length:	49⅔ feet (15 m) overall
Diameter:	8 feet (2.4 m)
Propulsion:	1 electric motor, 15 shp, 1 propeller mounted in control shroud (see *Engineering* notes)
Speed:	4 knots
Operating depth:	5,000 feet (1,524 m)
Manning:	3 + 24 rescuees

These submersibles were developed after the loss of the submarine THRESHER (SSN 593) in 1963 to provide the capability for rescuing survivors from submarines disabled on the ocean floor beyond their hull collapse depth. The DSRVs provide a long-range, all-weather rescue capability.

5. For a discussion of the trials and tribulations of NR-1 funding, see Capt. W. M. Nicholson, USN (Ret.), "Truth Is in the Eye of the Beholder," U.S. Naval Institute *Proceedings* (June 1995), pp. 10–11.

The MYSTIC and AVALON on wheeled dollies, ready for road or air transportation. The MYSTIC *(left)* has a modified sonar installed in the bow. Note the opening in the starboard side of the MYSTIC for a ducted thruster and the rotating shroud around her propeller. These craft are highly maneuverable. (U.S. Navy)

After lengthy tests and evaluation, both DSRVs were declared fully operational in late 1977.

The two DSRVs will be discarded in the near future. Subsequently, submarine rescue will be based on rescue chambers based on surface ships—the same scheme used by the U.S. Navy from the late 1930s until the availability of these DSRVs.[6] The AVALON

was scheduled to be taken out of service on 1 September 2000; however, the loss of the Soviet SSGN KURSK on 12 August 2000 delayed this action. The MYSTIC was scheduled to be taken out of service about 2005.

Class: Initially 12 rescue vehicles were planned, each able to carry 12 survivors. Subsequently, the vehicle capability was increased to 24 survivors and the proposed number of DSRVs was reduced to six. In the event, only two units were built.

The DSRVs were developed by the Navy's Deep Submergence Systems Project, which also had responsibility for the non-propulsion aspects of the NR-1 and had planned a set of Deep Submergence Search Vehicles (DSSV) that were to have had a 20,000-foot oper-

---

6. The earlier devices were the McCann Rescue Chambers (MRC), in service from the late 1930s. The McCann chamber was used only once on an operational basis with a U.S. submarine, to rescue 33 men from the SQUALUS (SS 192) in 1939; 26 men died when the submarine sank. The operating depth of the chamber initially was 850 feet (259 m), later increased to 1,200 feet (366 m) for some units.

A DSRV is loaded into an Air Force Reserve C-5B Galaxy transport during a rescue exercise. The rescue vehicles were specially designed for air transportation for rapid deployment to the vicinity of a submarine disaster. Subsequently, most NATO submarines could serve as a "mother" submarine to support the DSRV in a rescue operation. (U.S. Navy)

Crewmen check the "mating skirt" of the AVALON. The skirt, which is removed for road and air transport, mates with the hatch of a submarine and is then pumped dry to enable passage between the DSRV and either the carrying "mother" submarine or a disabled submarine. (1992, U.S. Navy)

ating capability. The DSSVs were designed, but neither funded nor built.

Cost: The estimated construction cost of the DSRV 1 was $41 million, and the DSRV 2 cost $23 million. The total development, construction, test, and initial support for these craft have cost in excess of $220 million.

Design: The DSRV consists of three interconnected personnel spheres, each 7½ feet (2.3 m) in diameter, constructed of HY-140 steel, encased in a fiberglass-reinforced plastic shell. The MYSTIC was originally certified only to 3,500 feet for technical reasons; this was subsequently increased to 5,000 feet.

The forward sphere contains the vehicle's controls and is manned by the pilot and co-pilot; the center and after spheres can accommodate 24 survivors and a third crewman. The DSRVs can mate with all U.S. submarines except the DOLPHIN and NR-1.

The DSRVs were configured to be launched and recovered by a submerged attack submarine or by a submarine rescue ship of the PIGEON (ASR 21) class. After launching, the DSRV can descend to the disabled submarine, "mate" with one of the submarine's escape hatches, take on board up to 24 survivors, and return to the "mother" submarine or ASR. The submersible can be air-transported in C-141 or C-5 cargo aircraft, and ground-transported by a special trailer. It is fitted with a remote-control manipulator.

Electronics: The DSRVs are fitted with elaborate search and navigation sonars, closed-circuit television, and optical viewing devices for locating a disabled submarine and mating with the stricken craft's escape hatches.

Engineering: The DSRVs have a single propeller driven by a 15-hp electric motor for forward propulsion. The propeller is in a rotating control shroud, which alleviates the need for rudders and diving planes (which could interfere with a rescue mission). Four ducted thrusters—two vertical and two horizontal, each powered by a 7½-hp electric motor—provide precise maneuvering. The craft has an endurance of five hours at a speed of four knots.

Names: Names were assigned in 1977.

Operational: The DSRV rapid-deployment concept has been tested periodically, employing U.S. and British nuclear-propelled submarines. The DSRVs are based at the North Island Naval Air Station in San Diego. One of the two vehicles is continuously

maintained in a high state of readiness, ready to be flown to a port, loaded onboard a submarine, and taken to the site of a submarine casualty anywhere in the world within 72 hours.

RESEARCH SUBMERSIBLES: MODIFIED "ALVIN" CLASS

The submersible TURTLE (DSV 3) was taken out of service on 1 October 1997 and the SEA CLIFF (DSV 4) on 1 April 1998; the latter craft was then transferred to the Woods Hole Oceanographic Institution on 30 June 1998. See 16th Edition/page 325 for characteristics.

1 RESEARCH SUBMERSIBLE: "ALVIN" CLASS

Number	Name	Launched	Completed
DSV 2	ALVIN	5 June 1964	1965

Builders:	General Mills, Inc., Minneapolis, Minn.
Weight:	16 tons
Length:	22½ feet (6.9 m) overall
Beam:	8 feet (2.4 m); 12 feet (3.7 m) over propeller pods
Speed:	2 knots
Operating depth:	13,124 feet (4,000 m)
Manning:	1 + 2 scientists

The ALVIN is operated by the Woods Hole Oceanographic Institution for the Office of Naval Research, which sponsored construction of the craft.

The ALVIN accidentally sank in 5,050 feet (1,540 m) of water on 16 October 1968 with her sphere being flooded (there were no casualties). She was raised in August 1969 and refurbished from May 1971 to October 1972, and became operational in November 1972. (The research ship MIZAR/T-AGOR 11 and the commercial submersible ALUMINAUT effected the salvage of the ALVIN.)

Classification: Classified DSV 2 on 1 June 1971.

Design: As built, the ALVIN had a single, 7-foot-diameter pressure sphere made of HY-100 steel, which gave her a 6,000-foot operating depth. She was refitted with a titanium sphere in 1971–1972, which increased her capabilities. She is fitted with a remote-control manipulator.

Engineering: A single stern propeller is fitted for forward propulsion; two pod-mounted propellers driven by separate electric motors

The venerable ALVIN continues to serve as a very useful research tool. Shown here being lifted aboard a landing ship, the ALVIN shows her skids for bottom sitting, ducted propeller, and small maneuvering propellers fitted amidships. Two of her viewing ports are evident. (U.S. Navy)

rotate for maneuvering. No through thrusters are fitted. Endurance is one hour at 2.5 knots and eight hours at 1 knot.

Operational: In 1988, the ALVIN aided in the location and photographing of the sunken ocean liner TITANIC.

SEAL DELIVERY VEHICLES

The Navy has two types of SEAL Delivery Vehicles (SDV):[7] The new, "dry" passenger Advanced SEAL Delivery System (ASDS) is entering the fleet and there are about 15 older SDVs that can be carried into forward areas in hangars fitted to attack or special forces transport submarines.

The ASDS vehicles can transport SEALs to their objective in a "dry environment," at higher speed for longer distances than the older vehicles, in which the SEALs are exposed to the open sea.

The Navy Special Warfare organization, which operates the SEAL units, is shown in chapter 20.

---

7. Officially *Swimmer* Delivery Vehicle on the basis of Secretary of the Navy Instruction 5030.1L, "Classification of Naval Ships and Craft." However, they are invariably referred to as SEAL Delivery Vehicles.

ADVANCED SEAL DELIVERY SYSTEMS: ASDS TYPE

Number	Completed	Status
ASDS No. 1	2000	operational
ASDS No. 2		building
ASDS No. 3		building
ASDS No. 4		planned
ASDS No. 5		planned
ASDS No. 6		planned

Builders:	Northrop-Grumman Ocean Systems, Baltimore, Md.
Displacement:	55 tons (dry)
Length:	65 feet (19.8 m) overall
Beam:	6³/₄ feet (2.06 m)
Height:	8¼ feet (2.5 m)
Propulsion:	1 electric motor; 67 hp; 1 propeller
Speed:	8+ knots
Range:	125+ n.miles (231+ km)
Manning:	2 (1 officer + 1 enlisted) + 8 SEALs

These are advanced SDVs that can carry SEALs in a dry environment, providing a "lockout" capability.

An ASDS vehicle can be carried by the proposed cruise missile/special operations transports converted from OHIO (SSBN/SSGN726) submarines (two per submarine); also, the fol-

The long-awaited Advanced SEAL Delivery System (ASDS) vehicles will provide a dry environment for transporting swimmers and special forces from submarines to their objectives. While highly capable, these vehicles will be too few in number to move large numbers of men any great distance. (U.S. Navy)

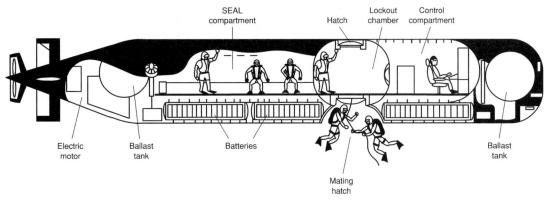

The ASDS vehicle has three compartments: control, lockout, and passenger-cargo spaces. Capable of being carried into forward areas by existing SSNs, the submersible could provide the potential for a number of clandestine missions in littoral operations. (Chris Nazelrod)

lowing attack submarines each can carry a single DDS or ASDS vehicle:

SSN 688	Los Angeles
SSN 690	Philadelphia
SSN 700	Dallas
SSN 701	La Jolla
SSN 715	Buffalo
SSN 766	Charlotte
SSN 772	Greenville[8]
SSN 774	Virginia class
SSN 21	Jimmy Carter

Reportedly, the Navy has a requirement for 11 of the new vehicles, although only six currently are planned for construction.

Design: The ASDS has three compartments—forward control compartment, amidships lockin/lockout chamber, and after SEAL compartment. Top and bottom hatches are provided to the lockin/lockout chamber for both ingress and egress to the vehicle. The vehicle can be carried by C-5 Galaxy or C-17 Skytrain transport aircraft.

Manning: In service, the pilot will be a submarine officer and the copilot a SEAL officer. Up to 16 SEALs could be transported without their diving/breathing gear and weapons.

SEAL DELIVERY VEHICLES: SDV MK VIII TYPE

There are about 15 older SEAL delivery vehicles that can be carried into forward areas in Dry Deck Shelter (DDS) hangars fitted to attack or special operations submarines. These are Mk VIII Mod 1 fiberglass "wet" vehicles, which can carry eight SEALs wearing individual self-contained breathing apparatus, one of whom pilots the vehicle.

8. The Greenville is test submarine for the ASDS vehicle.

A Mk VIII Mod 0 SDV, showing the pilot and passenger compartments open. The acoustic "window" in the bow has been deleted in the conversion to the Mod 1 configuration. The craft has a six-blade propeller powered by battery-supplied electric motors. (U.S. Navy)

Members of SEAL Team 2 conduct exercises with an SDV Mk VIII during training operations in the Caribbean. These submersibles, long the standard "war horse" of SEALs, has severely limited range and capabilities. (1997, U.S. Navy, PH1 Andy McKaskle)

The vehicles are all upgrades of earlier SDVs, with improved propulsion and electronics equipment. The use of more efficient "packaging" has increased their capacity from six to eight SEALs.

A follow-on SDV program was canceled in 1992 because of cost overruns and schedule slippage. That craft was being built by the UNISYS Corp. The ASDS program was developed in its place.

Electronics: A Doppler sonar is provided with a display that presents speed, distance traveled, heading, depth, and other piloting functions.

Propulsion: The SDVs are propelled by 18-hp electric motors with rechargeable silver-zinc batteries.

A Mk VIII Mod 1 SDV being lowered into the water. The pilot's compartment is open and the passenger compartment covers are closed. A swimmer is at the port quarter. These craft can be carried in dry deck shelters mounted on SSNs. (U.S. Navy)

DRY DECK SHELTERS

Dry Deck Shelters (DDS) can house SEAL delivery vehicles and swimmers—a single SDV or 20 SEALs can be accommodated in each shelter. The shelters are mounted on the afterdeck of specially configured attack and transport submarines, the latter carrying one and the former two DDSs. These submarines retain their full suite of weapons and sensors for operations as attack submarines (although there is some loss of speed); they have special fittings, modifications to their air systems, and other features to enable them to carry the shelters. The DDS can be used to transport and launch an SDV or to "lock out" combat swimmers.

A DDS can be installed aboard a submarine in about 12 hours and is air-transportable. The DDS lower hatch is installed over the submarine's after hatch to permit free passage between the submarine and the DDS while the submarine is underwater and approaching the objective area. Then, with the submarine still submerged, the SEALs can exit the DDS and ascend to the surface, bringing with them equipment and rubber rafts, or they can mount an SDV and travel underwater several miles to their objective area.

The DDS has an internal pressure of one atmosphere and can be carried to the test depth of the submarine.

The Navy has six DDSs, the first built by Electric Boat and the remainder by Newport News Shipbuilding; the prototype was delivered in 1982 and the remainder in 1987–1991. The shelters are 38 feet long (11.6 m), have a maximum diameter of 9 feet (2.8 m), and weigh 30 tons. Each DDS has a lockout chamber built into the forward end of the shelter with hatches to the hangar portion of the DDS and to connect to the submarine's escape trunk.

A DDS with a portion of the covering off, revealing, from left, the small hyperbaric chamber, the access sphere, and hangar. These can be easily transferred from one submarine to another by shipyard or floating crane. (U.S. Navy)

A dry deck shelter mounted on the attack submarine SILVERSIDES (SSN 679). The shelters can each carry a single Mk VIII SDV or a variety of rubber rafts and equipment for SEALs or other special forces. The planned SSGN conversions of Trident submarines could each carry two shelters or two ASDS vehicles. (1992, Giorgio Arra)

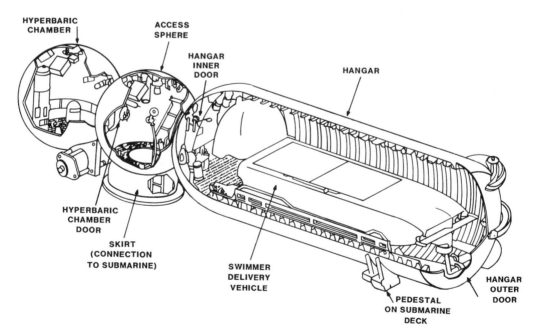

A single dry deck shelter can be carried on several submarines of the LOS ANGELES (SSN 688) class that have had special modifications to support the structure. The proposed Trident SSGN conversions and the specially configured JIMMY CARTER (SSN 23) also will be capable of carrying the DDS.

A dry deck shelter is lifted from the transport submarine SAM HOUSTON (SSN 609) during her brief tenure as a special operations submarine. (U.S. Navy)

LARGE SCALE VEHICLES

One unmanned Large Scale Vehicle (LSV) is being employed to test underwater hull shapes and other features of the SEAWOLF (SSN 21), and another is under construction to simulate VIRGINIA performance. The vehicles operate in Lake Pend Oreille, Idaho, where the Navy has an instrumented test range. The operating depth of the LSVs is not known; the lake has a maximum depth of 1,150 feet (350 m).

When the LSV 2 becomes operational, the LSV 1 is expected to be taken out of service.

1 LARGE SCALE TEST VEHICLE: "CUTTHROAT" TYPE

Number	Name	Complete
LSV 2	CUTTHROAT	2001

Builders:	Newport News Shipbuilding and Electric Boat
Displacement:	196 tons
Length:	111 feet (33.84 m) overall
Beam:	10 feet (3.05 m)
Draft:	
Propulsion:	direct-drive electric motor; 3,000 shp; 1 shaft
Speed:	
Manning:	unmanned

This is the Navy's second LSV, developed to simulate the VIRGINIA design and control features. Hull sections are being built at both submarine yards, to be integrated by Newport News Shipbuilding. The sections will be shipped by truck to Bayview for final assembly.

Design: The LSV 2 will have a significantly lower self-generated noise level than the earlier LSV 1.

Names: The name "Cutthroat"—a trout found in Lake Pend Oreille—was suggested by the student body of the Athol Elementary School in northern Idaho.

1 LARGE SCALE TEST VEHICLE: "KOKANEE" TYPE

Number	Name	Completed
LSV 1	KOKANEE	1988

Builders:	Southwest Research Institute, San Antonio, Texas
Displacement:	155 tons
Length:	$88^5/_6$ feet (27.1 m) overall
Beam:	$10^1/_6$ feet (3.1 m)
Draft:	$9^1/_2$ feet (2.9 m)
Propulsion:	direct-drive electric motor; 3,000 shp; 1 shaft
Speed:	
Manning:	unmanned

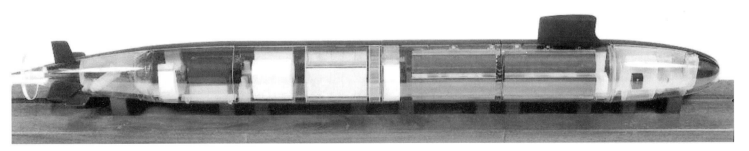

This model of the CUTTHROAT was the only unclassified illustration of the second large-scale test vehicle that was available when this book went to press. The model will evaluate design concepts of the VIRGINIA (SSN 774) class. (Newport News Shipbuilding)

The KOKANEE—the world's largest autonomous, free-swimming submersible—is a submarine design test vehicle operated in Lake Pend Oreille by the acoustic research detachment of the David Taylor Research Center (DTRC, Carderock, Md.). The craft has been employed to test variations of submarine propulsors for the submarine SEAWOLF. Subsequently, the submersible was modified to test an advanced sail structure for possible use in later submarines of the VIRGINIA class.

The LSV concept was proposed by Dr. M. M. Sevik of DTRC in 1972 as an extension of the center's model testing program. The construction contract was awarded in February 1984. The completed vehicle was transported from San Antonio to Bayview by train in October 1987 and dedicated at ceremonies there on 7 March 1988.

Cost: The construction cost of the KOKANEE was $65 million.

Design: The KOKANEE has a conventional submarine configuration with a modified sail or fairwater structure (which can be removed). The forward portion of the submarine contains electric storage batteries; the after portion has the DC electric motor and auxiliary machinery, as well as data recorders, guidance, and navigation equipment.

Engineering: The craft is controlled by onboard computers that are programmed before each test run. Lead-acid batteries are employed. Her endurance is approximately six hours for medium-power runs and two or three hours for full-power runs.

Names: The kokanee is a variety of salmon found in Lake Pend Oreille.

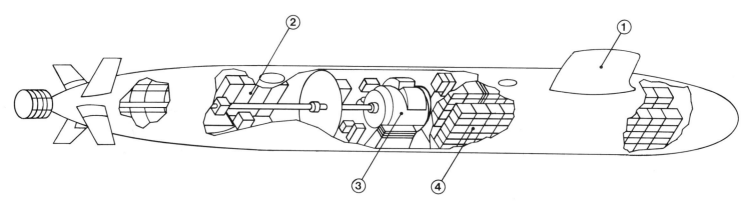

Large Scale Test Vehicle KOKANEE
1. Removable fairwater 2. Data recorders and navigation equipment 3. DC electric motor 4. Batteries (William Clipson)

The KOKANEE immediately after surfacing from a test run in Lake Pend Oreille, Bayview, Idaho. She has been used to test design concepts for the SEAWOLF (SSN 21) class. The craft's hull is gray and the sail structure is red. (U.S. Navy)

UNMANNED UNDERWATER VEHICLES

The U.S. Navy is developing a series of Unmanned UnderwaterVehicles (UUV).[9] Four basic UUV mission areas were identified by the Navy in 1994:

Mine warfare: This mission area has been established as having the most immediate priority for UUV technology. According to the Navy Technology Needs Document of 9 September 1994: "The proliferation of mines, and the willingness of nations to use them, challenges the free movement of U.S. and international shipping, and can impede or deny U.S. power projection in the littoral environment."

The mine warfare UUVs are to search out hostile minefields to determine their area and composition for avoidance, transit, or countermeasures by other naval forces. These vehicles are being fitted with synthetic-aperture, side-scanning sonar with computer-aided detection and classification. They would be delivered to operational areas in a covert manner by attack submarines and would communicate data and images to the host SSN and receive directions using either a fiber-optic (cable) link or wireless acoustic communications.

The Lockheed-developed UUV configured for the minefield surveillance role during in-situ testing (1994, Lockheed)

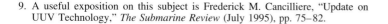

9. A useful exposition on this subject is Frederick M. Cancilliere, "Update on UUV Technology," *The Submarine Review* (July 1995), pp. 75–82.

At the completion of the mission, the UUV would return to the host SSN for underwater recovery.

The UUV program for mine warfare has two phases: The Near-term Mine Reconnaissance System (NMRS) is a submarine-launched mine detection, localization, and classification system delivered in 1999. The NMRS consists of two unmanned vehicles, with appropriate control equipment for the host submarine of the LOS ANGELES class. The vehicles are 21 inches (533 mm) in diameter and are launched and recovered through the torpedo tubes. The NMRS has a forward-looking sonar for obstacle avoidance and initial search capability, with an AQS-14 side-scan sonar for target classification.

It is anticipated that the NMRS will have a service life of about six years, and will be succeeded by the Long-Term Mine Reconnaissance and Avoidance System (LMRS). The LMRS is currently in the conceptual development stage and expected to enter service in FY 2003. The system's vehicles will be deployed and recovered either through SSN torpedoes or the deck-mounted DDS now employed for special operations. It is expected that the LMRS will have significant improvements over the near-term NMRS in terms of sensor performance (swath width, range, and probability of detection), vehicle endurance and control, data processing, and vehicle-to-SSN communications. The expected service life for the LMRS is about 20 years. Five systems currently are planned for procurement.

Surveillance: UUVs in the ocean surveillance role, an extension of the anti-submarine mission, could be programmed to patrol wide ocean areas with passive sensors. Or, they could employed as active sound sources, with reflections of their acoustic pulses being monitored by fixed seafloor Sound Surveillance Systems (SOSUS) or by Surface Towed Array Surveillance Systems (SURTASS).

Intelligence collection: In the intelligence collection role, a UUV would be deployed from a host submarine to ascertain specific information about an area of interest. This could include monitoring of enemy seafloor communications links, as previously undertaken by the U.S. Navy in Operation Ivy Bells.[10]

Tactical oceanography: Monitoring of the underwater environment, both the water column and seafloor, is vital for a variety of naval operations. Bottom surveys by UUVs could be especially important in littoral-area operations.

A number of unmanned underwater vehicles are already in foreign and U.S. naval use. Since the 1960s the U.S. Navy has used cable-controlled torpedo recovery devices, Mk 30 submarine targets, Mk 71 MOSS decoys used by ballistic missile submarines, and tethered mine countermeasures vehicles. There have also been classified deep-ocean search and recovery devices used to exploit Soviet objects lost on the ocean floor. (There are numerous commercial UUV-type vehicles in service as well, most referred to as ROVs or Remote Operating Vehicles. These are used mostly for exploration and support of offshore oilfields. As an indication of the state of the art, some of the commercial vehicles can operate to almost 10,000 feet [3,050 m] and have a 350-hour mission duration at five or six knots.)

The new family of U.S. Navy UUVs will expand the "operational envelope" of underwater drones. The Navy and the Defense Advanced Research Projects Agency (DARPA) initiated a joint advanced-technology UUV program in 1986. Through this effort, DARPA has developed two prototypes for test bed/mission hardware demonstrations. One vehicle took the first mission "package"—a tactical acoustic decoy system developed by Martin Marietta—to sea in 1990 and has since been transferred to the Navy for testing. According to a Navy spokesman, the initial payoff for this UUV would be increased submarine survivability, but it would pave the way for UUV applications to a number of classified submarine scenarios.

The operating Navy is cautious about moving toward UUVs. While most vehicles are considered in the context of enhancing submarine operations, a number of factors make it a problem for submarines themselves to support UUVs, including the limited space, the problem of hull openings, and the difficulty of maintenance on vehicles. If they are sized for torpedo tubes, keeping UUVs aboard submarines displaces torpedoes and missiles. A double-hull submarine configuration might more easily accommodate a UUV, but that design concept is an anathema to the U.S. Navy's nuclear-propulsion leadership. Furthermore, underwater-to-underwater communications are more difficult than those between underwater and surface, air, or satellite platforms.

Surface ships, submarines, and even aircraft (fixed-wing and helicopters) could potentially deploy and recover UUVs. Surface ships would perhaps be the most feasible platform to support UUV operations; however, a preliminary review of vehicle potential indicates that even though some UUVs, such as an area surveillance vehicle, would best be supported by surface ships, for many UUV missions the submarine is the ideal launch/support platform.

---

10. See, for example, Sherry Sontag and Christopher Drew, *Blind Man's Bluff: The Untold Story of American Submarine Espionage* (New York: Public-Affairs, 1998).

CHAPTER 13

Aircraft Carriers

An F/A-18C Hornet is launched from a waist catapult of the carrier JOHN F. KENNEDY during operations in the Persian Gulf. An F/A-18C has just been launched from the ship's starboard catapult and another aircraft is being readied for launch. The flexibility and mobility of aircraft carriers insure their employment for the foreseeable future in support of U.S. political and military interests. (2000, U.S. Navy, PH2 Christian Eskelund)

Aircraft carriers remain the backbone of U.S. conventional naval forces. The U.S. carrier force in early 2001 consists of 12 aircraft carriers—nine nuclear-propelled ships (CVN) and three conventional, oil-burning ships (CV). For the foreseeable future, one of the NIMITZ-class ships (currently the NIMITZ) will be out of service undergoing a lengthy modernization/nuclear refueling.

A tenth nuclear-propelled carrier, the RONALD REAGAN, is under construction. The Department of Defense plans for an additional carrier being authorized in FY 2001 and another in FY 2006.

The JOHN F. KENNEDY was designated as an "operational reserve/ training" ship from 1994 to 2000, but in reality operated and deployed as a standard carrier with a fraction of her crew composed of reserve personnel (see below). However, in September 1999 the decision was made to stop the pretense and change her status from Naval Reserve Force (NRF) to active.

Two additional aircraft carriers of the FORRESTAL class are maintained in reserve ("mothballs"). Because of the complexity of overhauling and updating these ships (radar, communications, etc.) and the size of their crews, it is unlikely that they ever will be recalled to active service.

A force of 15 active carriers is required to provide virtually full-time presence in three key regions where naval presence is considered particularly crucial by the Department of Defense—the Mediterranean, Western Pacific, and Indian Ocean/Persian Gulf. A 12-carrier force can provide a full-time presence in any one of the regions, with a minimum of two-month "gaps" in carrier presence in the other two. With 11 operational carriers—the actual number available for the foreseeable future—the gap in coverage increases. Even this amount of forward-area coverage is possible only by homeporting a carrier in Japan, currently the KITTY HAWK.

The Navy no longer operates a dedicated pilot training ship (AVT). The FORRESTAL was to have replaced the venerable LEXINGTON (CV/AVT 16), an ESSEX/HANCOCK-class carrier completed in 1943, which served in the pilot-training role from 1963 to 1990. However, the FORRESTAL was instead decommissioned as part of the post–Cold War cutback of naval forces (the ship already had been reclassified AVT 59). The "Lex" had succeeded the ANTIETAM (CVS 36), the first large-deck dedicated training carrier, which served in that role from 1957 to 1962. Basic pilot training in carrier landings is now carried out aboard the KENNEDY and, on occasion, other available carriers.

All World War II–built carriers of the MIDWAY and ESSEX/ HANCOCK classes have been retired, the last being the MIDWAY, which was decommissioned in 1992 after 46 years of service.

In addition to the ships described in this chapter, the Navy operates 11 large helicopter carriers called amphibious assault ships (LHA/LHD); these ships are described in chapter 18 of this edition of *Ships and Aircraft*. Amphibious Ready Groups (ARG) centered on an LHA/LHD have been substituted for carrier battle groups in some presence missions. All of the earlier LPH-type helicopter carriers have been stricken except for the INCHON (ex-LPH 12), now employed as a mine countermeasures support ship (MCS 12); see chapter 21.

Aircraft: The composition of carrier air wings is described in chapter 26. Nominal wing strength is provided in this chapter based on a composition of one fighter squadron (VF) and three strike fighter squadrons (VFA), plus electronic attack (VAQ), early warning (VAW), and sea control (VS) fixed-wing aircraft, and anti-submarine (HS) and special operations helicopters.

Builders: Newport News Shipbuilding in Newport News, Va., is the only U.S. shipyard now constructing large aircraft carriers. That yard has built four of the eight oil-burning "super carriers" completed since 1955 (CV 59, 61, 66, and 67), as well as all nuclear-propelled carriers.

The New York Naval Shipyard in Brooklyn, N.Y., built three conventional carriers (CV 60, 62, and 64) and the New York Shipbuilding Corp., in Camden, N.J., built one (CV 63). Those shipyards no longer exist.

The Litton/Ingalls Shipyard in Pascagoula, Miss., constructs LHA/ LHD carrier-type amphibious ships of some 50,000 tons.

Design: Displacements of carriers have continuously increased with new equipment added during overhauls and modernization. The data below have been updated for this edition.

Marines: Aircraft carriers no longer carry permanent Marine Corps security detachments. The last detachment was in the carrier GEORGE WASHINGTON; the unit, with one officer and 25 enlisted men, departed the ship when she returned from deployment on 3 April 1988, ending a tradition of more than 200 years of Marines embarked as part of the ship's company in major U.S. warships. (Previously detachments also were carried onboard battleships and larger cruisers, i.e., CA, CB, CL types.)

Marine carrier detachments embarked in aircraft carriers consisted of two officers and 64 enlisted men until 1993. The Chief of Naval Operations on 28 May 1993 approved a Marine Corps proposal to reduce the size of the detachments and by June 1993 all carrier detachments numbered one officer and 25 enlisted men.

The carrier KITTY HAWK is shown at Pearl Harbor. The oldest aircraft carrier now in service with any navy except for the Brazilian MINAS GERAIS (1945), the KITTY HAWK is homeported at Yokosuka, Japan. In this view, one of her starboard deck-edge elevators is lowered; her bridge structure hosts a variety radar and radio antennas, fire control directors, and a Close-In Weapon System (CIWS). (1998, U.S. Navy, PH1 Spike Call)

TABLE 13-1. CARRIER FORCE LEVELS (EARLY 2001)

Number	Class/Ship	Comm.	Active	Building*	Reserve	Notes
CVN 68	NIMITZ	1975–	8	2	—	nuclear-propelled; 1 "active" ship being refueled/overhauled
CV 63	KITTY HAWK	1961–1968	3	—	—	conventional propulsion
CVN 65	ENTERPRISE	1961	1	—	—	nuclear-propelled
CV 59	FORRESTAL	1957–1959	—	—	2	both in reserve

*Carriers authorized through FY 2001

Marine aircraft squadrons periodically serve aboard aircraft carriers (as well as helicopter carriers). All Marine tactical aircraft are carrier capable, and Marine aviators are trained in carrier operations.

Names: U.S. aircraft carriers traditionally were named for older American warships and battles, following the first carrier being named LANGLEY (CV 1) for aviation pioneer Samuel P. Langley.[1] In 1945 the CVB 42 was named for President Franklin D. Roosevelt, who had died in office; CVA 59 was named for the first Secretary of Defense, James Forrestal, who committed suicide soon after leaving office; and CVA 67 was named for President John F. Kennedy, assassinated while in office. Subsequently, the Navy named the CVN 68 for Fleet Admiral Chester W. Nimitz, who died in 1966, and from that point the naming of carriers became a political issue (see NIMITZ class entry).

Operational: From the late 1940s into the late 1980s, the Navy attempted to operate two carriers forward-deployed in the Mediterranean and three (later two) in the Western Pacific–Indian Ocean region. There was nominally a 1:3 deployment cycle, with the remaining carriers in transit to or from deployment areas, engaged in fleet exercises or other types of training, or in overhaul, which meant a ship was forward-deployed for about six months at a time. The lengthened deployments during the Vietnam War and various crises, however, invariably resulted in lower retention rates—a critical factor in an all-volunteer, high-technology service. Also, the 1:3 cycle did not take into account carriers undergoing the long-term modernization.

The crises and conflicts of the early 1980s, especially the Soviet invasion of Afghanistan (1979) and the Iran-Iraq War (1980–1988) led to more-flexible carrier deployment patterns—called FLEXOPS—with carriers being withdrawn from some areas and spending more time at sea to provide for multi-carrier exercises or to support special operations, as in the continuing crises in Lebanon, the invasion of Grenada in October 1983, operations against Libya in 1986, and Operations Desert Shield/Desert Storm (1990–1991). Carrier deployments thus significantly exceeded the intended ratio of six months' deployment to 12 months in transit/overhaul/port/local operations.

The situation was further exacerbated in the 1990s by the general concern for the Indian Ocean area in the wake of the Gulf War. The steaming distances from U.S. ports to the Indian Ocean require roughly five carriers to maintain one ship on station continuously.

Torpedo countermeasures: U.S. warships have long been fitted with torpedo countermeasures to decoy anti-ship torpedoes. The T-Mk 6 Fanfare, a towed noisemaker, has been phased out of the fleet, succeeded in surface ships by the SLQ-25 Nixie, an advanced towed noisemaker.

However, the revelation in the mid-1980s of several unexpected Soviet submarine and torpedo developments led to a new emphasis on torpedo countermeasures. The Surface Ship Torpedo Decoy (SSTD) system was developed and has been fitted to most active aircraft carriers (see chapter 29). Some carriers have been fitted with 12.75-inch (324-mm) torpedo tubes Mk 32 (in triple mounts) for launching modified Mk 46 torpedoes to counter the Russian Type 65-80 wake-homing torpedo.

NEXT-GENERATION AIRCRAFT CARRIERS

The U.S. Navy initiated a program in 1996 to develop a totally new carrier design—given the designation CVX, for an aircraft carrier of undetermined characteristics. The CVX, according to the Navy's director of air warfare, Rear Admiral Dennis V. McGinn, was being designed on a "clean sheet of paper" and would "feature improved characteristics in selected areas, such as launch and recovery equipment, flight deck layout, C[4]I [Command-Control-Communications-Computers/Intelligence] systems, information networks and propulsion systems. . . . [and] features that will make them more affordable to operate."[2]

The CVX was to be the U.S. Navy's next-generation aircraft carrier, a major divergence from the previous designs. The first ship of the new class was to be funded in fiscal year 2006 and join the fleet about 2013 (to replace the ENTERPRISE). The CVX also promised a more efficient warship, capable of handling advanced aircraft at a faster operating cycle, more efficient aircraft arming techniques (especially requiring less manpower), lower detection signatures (and hence enhanced survivability), overall decreased manning requirements, and significantly lower construction, operating, and modernization costs.

These and other advanced carrier concepts were being studied by the Navy and at the Carrier Innovation Center of the Newport News Shipbuilding. The center was also examining non-nuclear propulsion concepts for the ship, primarily gas turbines, which would be cheaper (even including fuel) and require fewer crewmen with less specialized training than would a nuclear propulsion plant.

But within a few months this "entirely new class" was canceled because of funding shortfalls. Although the Navy never announced a total development and design cost for the CVX, the fiscal 1999 defense program indicated just over $1 *billion* in development and design costs.

The Navy never adequately planned for CVX development costs and never advised Congress of the total funding requirements. Despite this situation, the Navy leadership continued to promote the CVX concept. Indeed, this stance continued in public even after the Chief of Naval Operations, Admiral Jay L. Johnson, announced early in 1998 that the CVX would definitely have nuclear propulsion, a direct contradiction of the "clean sheet" concept.

Johnson's decision ostensibly was based on the draft study *CVX Feasibility* prepared by the Naval Research Advisory Committee (NRAC) in 1997.[3] The report stated that "for maximum availability, the ship should have a nuclear power plant." But the Navy's powerful nuclear propulsion community, led by Admiral Frank (Skip) Bowman, had already decided that nuclear power "is a given" for the CVX, according to a leading defense writer.[4] According to Bowman, "Without this endurance and flexibility [provided by nuclear-propelled carriers], we would be hard put to do what we are doing today."

While the NRAC draft study said that nuclear propulsion provides the "sustained high speed sprint capability . . . necessary if CVX is to be available for rapidly evolving crises," it is interesting to note that a comprehensive study published in June 1994 by the Greenpeace organization concluded:

---

1. The most notable exception to the traditional naming scheme was the SHANGRI-LA (CV 38), so named by the Navy in honor of the April 1942 Doolittle bombing raid on Tokyo and other Japanese cities. After the raid, when journalists asked President Roosevelt where the Doolittle bombers had flown from, he replied "Shangri-La," referring to the mythical Asian kingdom in James Hilton's novel *Lost Horizon*. The Doolittle bombers had in fact flown from the carrier HORNET (CV 8).

2. Rear Adm. Dennis V. McGinn, Director, Naval Air Warfare, Office of the Chief of Naval Operations, *Naval Aviation: Forward Air Power . . . From the Sea* (1998), p. 30. Also see N. Polmar, "Carrier Questions—and Some Answers," U.S. Naval Institute *Proceedings* (April 1998), pp. 103–104.

3. NRAC, comprised of civilian businessmen and scientists, is the principal advisory body to the Secretary of the Navy.

4. Tom Philpott, "Bowman Sees a Smaller Fleet More Reliant on Nuclear Power," in Military Update (syndicated column), 6 November 1997.

The cost of nuclear power is not justified in peacetime or in wartime, in terms of useful military capability. Nuclear ships are more expensive, less available, and only comparable in generating and sustaining air operations. They operate as part of integrated and increasingly joint military missions close to land, and nuclear-powered carriers are not used any differently than their conventional counterparts.[5]

The Greenpeace report based its findings largely on an analysis of three U.S. Navy claims for nuclear-propelled carriers:[6]

- virtually unlimited range at maximum speed
- ability to remain on station indefinitely without refueling
- greater storage capacity for combat consumables, such as bombs and jet fuel

Using Navy data, the report's findings conclude that during the Vietnam and Persian Gulf wars, the period between the two conflicts, and the operation of carriers in crisis response as well as deployments in general, operations have not matched the promises or expectations of nuclear propulsion:

Nuclear-powered carriers do not transit faster to a region, remain longer on-station, or drop significantly more ordnance or launch more aircraft sorties than do conventionally powered carriers. In fact the Navy itself does not appear to distinguish between nuclear and conventional carriers in its operational planning or crisis preparation.[7]

The Greenpeace paper makes additional points against nuclear-propelled carriers, noting that (1) they require more shipyard time, with a related reduction in at-sea time; (2) the costs associated with their uranium fuel cores—from design through disposal—are significant but barely factored into program costs; (3) political liabilities associated with nuclear carriers place limitations on such necessities as foreign port calls, overseas basing, and transit through certain straits and canals; and (4) the current plan to discard the nine nuclear-propelled cruisers will further reduce the potential effectiveness of nuclear carriers.

(Not mentioned in the Greenpeace report, another important factor is the increased cost of nuclear-trained engineering personnel for nuclear carriers compared to those for oil-burning ships. Also, with the demise of the nuclear cruiser force the promotion/command opportunities for those men and women are reduced significantly, which will impact on their recruitment, retention, and cost.)

Despite this acquiescence to the nuclear propulsion community, the CVX program continued to be underfunded by the Navy. Then, in spring 1999, Congress cut almost $100 million from CVX development. Subsequently, a Navy official was reported as saying, "We just cannot afford the investment needed to achieve the hoped for long term savings."[8]

Thus the CVX was scuttled by the Navy.

The next carrier, the unnamed CVN 77, has been described by the Navy as a "transition" ship between the NIMITZ design and the CVX, a term still used as a public relations ploy. The CVN 77 will incorporate some new features, continuing the traditional process of incremental improvements to carriers. Subsequent large aircraft carriers generally will be similar.

Not only is this approach negating the original CVX "clean sheet of paper" concept as earlier espoused by the Navy's leadership, but it ignores the report of the highly innovative study undertaken by the Center for Naval Analyses (CNA) and the Naval Sea Systems Command (NAVSEA) in early 1995. The CNA-NAVSEA effort proposed six design concepts for the CVX; their basic characteristics were described in the previous edition of *Ships and Aircraft* (16th Edition/

pages 89–90). While the aircraft complement carried by most of these designs is significantly less than that of a NIMITZ-class CVN, other, larger carrier concepts have also been suggested; they, too, have been rejected out of hand by the Navy.

MULTIPURPOSE CARRIERS

Separate from the CVN-CVX program, some U.S. naval leaders also see a confluence of the CVN and LHA/LHD designs. In a 1995 book, Admiral William A. Owens, then vice chairman of the Joint Chiefs of Staff, labeled such a development—by the 2020 decade—as "presence" carriers.[9] This union of large carriers and large helicopter carriers also had been proposed by Vice Admiral George R. Sterner, Commander, Naval Sea Systems Command, the Navy official responsible for warship design, development, and construction.[10]

This concept would result in a large carrier that would combine air strike and fighter capabilities with amphibious assault capabilities. While these capabilities may not be compatible in an operational sense, the development of advanced STOVL aircraft (i.e., aircraft that would not require catapults or arresting gear) could ease the interface and support problems. Still, there would be significant operational problems: Would the amphibious component demand that the ship remain offshore in a restricted operating area to support Marines ashore, while the strike/fighter component is needed elsewhere? Will the strike/fighter aircraft and troop-carrying helicopters be compatible on the flight deck? How will missile launches affect flight operations?

More feasible could be the combining of cruiser-destroyer features (e.g., SPY-1 radar, vertical-launch missiles) with an "attack" carrier—a concept used by the Soviet Navy in its KIEV and KUZNETSOV carrier designs.[11]

Admiral Owens has also proposed a merger of the surface combatant (DDG 51) and amphibious ship (LX/LPD 17) designs to produce the "littoral supremacy ship." But his ship would be primarily an amphibious ship (LHA/LHD)—operating helicopters and tilt-rotor aircraft—fitted with vertical-launch missiles forward; it would still have the large docking well of an amphibious ship. The ship, according to Owens,

could provide air and ballistic-missile defense across the littoral, joint-task-force C[3]I, strike and close air support, and direct and indirect fire support [with missiles]. With five to six hundred marines, twenty helicopters, and three or four air-cushioned [*sic*] landing craft . . . it would, as its name suggests, be a very strong asset, allowing the United States to dominate the littoral battle space from a single platform.[12]

But the ship would suffer from the interference of differing missions, support requirements, and so forth. The current operation of a handful of AV-8B Harrier STOVL aircraft from helicopter-carrying LHA/LHD ships is not a reasonable model for such an aviation ship. And as Owens notes:

Such a ship would not be cheap, however, and as an expensive investment that creates something very valuable, the littoral-supremacy ship would pose two perennial problems:
- Would it be too valuable to risk in dangerous areas?
- What would we do with such a specialized ship if the Navy's mission shifted back to sea control?

For these and other reasons, more likely approaches to multipurpose carriers in the coming years would be the Monohull or CGV-series ships, with conventional propulsion, as well as enhanced LHA/LHD designs as follow-on ships to the NIMITZ class.

5. Hans M. Kristensen, William M. Arkin, and Joshua Handler, *Aircraft Carriers: The Limits of Nuclear Power* (monograph), Greenpeace, Washington, D.C., June 1994. Also see N. Polmar, "Nuclear Carrier Questions," U.S. Naval Institute *Proceedings* (September 1994), pp. 121–122.
6. "Navy Kicks Off Campaign to Sell CVN-76 Carrier to Congress," *Inside the Navy* (12 March 1994), pp. 7–8.
7. Kristensen, Arkin, and Handler, *Aircraft Carriers*, p. 3.
8. "Navy Takes New Look at CVX Plan, Cost," *Navy News & Undersea Technology*, 1 June 1998, p. 1.
9. Adm. William A. Owens, USN, *High Seas: The Naval Passage to an Uncharted World* (Annapolis, Md.: Naval Institute Press, 1995), p. 163.
10. Adm. Sterner, presentation at Navy League Sea-Air-Space Symposium, Washington, D.C., 12 April 1995.
11. The latter ship originally was named RIGA, then LEONID BREZHNEV, then TBILISI, and, after the breakup of the Soviet Union, the ADMIRAL FLOTA SOVETSKOGO SOYUZA KUZNETSOV (i.e., Admiral of the Fleet of the Soviet Union Kuznetsov).
12. Owens, *High Seas*, p. 167.

MOBILE OFFSHORE BASES

Another "aircraft carrier" concept is the Mobile Offshore Bases (MOB) concept, which are large, mobile sea bases made up of components towed to a crisis area and assembled at sea. These platforms—referred to in the Bottom-Up Review as "floating islands"—would be capable of handling from 150 to almost 300 aircraft, depending upon type, including C-130 Hercules transports, as well as large amounts of dry and liquid cargoes. Although not directly comparable to aircraft carriers, the MOBs could reduce the requirement for carriers in some areas where there are ample time and resources available to deploy and assemble the platforms.

These platforms would be non-self-propelled. One study by CNA addressed a MOB concept comprising six modules assem-

bled to form a platform 3,000 feet (915 m) long and 300 feet (91.5 m) wide. A MOB concept being developed by the McDermott International and Babcock & Wilcox firms provides for a platform 4,925 feet (1,502 m) long and 500 feet (152 m) wide. The latter design provides for five separate modules to be towed to and assembled at the remote location. The assembled displacement at operating draft would be 1,700,000 tons. Massive amounts of cargo could be carried in the individual sections. The MOB could also be used to rearm surface ships and submarines and to refuel surface ships.

The MOB concept provides for the largest floating structure ever built. However, with available offshore drilling platform and related technology, and the use of subcomponents, there is considered to be little risk in the construction of the platform. The Department of Defense is sponsoring ongoing studies of the MOB concept.

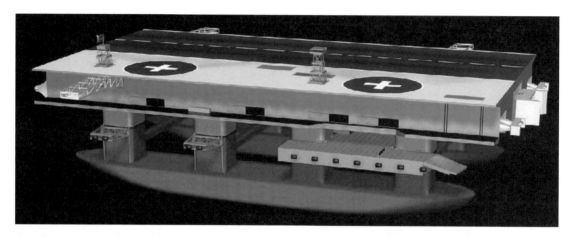

An artist's concept of one of the five semi-submersible base units—each 1,000 feet (305 m) long—that would be assembled to form the mobile offshore base. The assembled MOB could provide an operating and support base for a variety of aircraft, including C-17 Skytrain and C-130 Hercules transports. (McDermott International)

The Mobile Offshore Base (MOB) is being considered by the Department of Defense as a means of supporting aviation at sea when land bases are not available. The massive structure can be towed in sections and assembled in remote areas. Some analysts believe that the MOB could complement or replace aircraft carriers in some areas of long-term U.S. interests. (McDermott International)

8 + 2 NUCLEAR-PROPELLED AIRCRAFT CARRIERS: "NIMITZ" CLASS

Number	Name	FY	Builder	Laid down	Launched	Commissioned	Status
CVN 68	NIMITZ	67	Newport News Shipbuilding, Va.	22 June 1968	13 May 1972	3 May 1975	yard
CVN 69	DWIGHT D. EISENHOWER	70	Newport News Shipbuilding, Va.	15 Aug 1970	11 Oct 1975	18 Oct 1977	**AA**
CVN 70	CARL VINSON	74	Newport News Shipbuilding, Va.	11 Oct 1975	15 Mar 1980	13 Mar 1982	**PA**
CVN 71	THEODORE ROOSEVELT	80	Newport News Shipbuilding, Va.	31 Oct 1981	27 Oct 1984	25 Oct 1986	**AA**
CVN 72	ABRAHAM LINCOLN	83	Newport News Shipbuilding, Va.	3 Nov 1984	13 Feb 1988	11 Nov 1989	**PA**
CVN 73	GEORGE WASHINGTON	83	Newport News Shipbuilding, Va.	25 Aug 1986	21 July 1990	4 July 1992	**AA**
CVN 74	JOHN C. STENNIS	88	Newport News Shipbuilding, Va.	13 Mar 1991	13 Nov 1993	2 Dec 1995	**PA**
CVN 75	HARRY S. TRUMAN	88	Newport News Shipbuilding, Va.	29 Nov 1993	7 Sep 1996	25 July 1998	**AA**
CVN 76	RONALD REAGAN	95	Newport News Shipbuilding, Va.	12 Feb 1998	2001	2003	building
CVN 77	. . . . . .	01	Newport News Shipbuilding, Va.			2007	building
CVN 78	. . . . .	06	Newport News Shipbuilding, Va.			2013	planned
CVN 79	. . . . . .	11	Newport News Shipbuilding, Va.			2018	planned

Displacement:		*Light*	*Full load*
	CVN 68	78,280 tons	101,196 tons
	CVN 69	78,793 tons	101,713 tons
	CVN 70	78,172 tons	101,089 tons
	CVN 71	80,753 tons	103,658 tons
	CVN 72	81,147 tons	104,242 tons
	CVN 73	81,083 tons	104,208 tons
	CVN 74	80,085 tons	103,020 tons
	CVN 75	78,453 tons	101,390 tons
	CVN 76	77,607 tons	98,235 tons

Length: 1,040 feet (317.2 m) waterline
CVN 68: 1,115 feet (339.94 m) overall
CVN 69, 70: 1,098 feet (334.76 m) overall
CVN 71–76: 1,092 feet (332.93 m) overall
Beam: 134 feet (40.85 m)
Flight deck: 252 feet (76.83 m)
Draft: CVN 68–70: 37 feet (11.3 m)
CVN 71–76: 38 $\frac{5}{12}$ feet (11.7 m)
Propulsion: 4 steam turbines (General Electric); 280,000 shp; 4 shafts
Reactors: 2 pressurized-water A4W (Westinghouse)
Speed: 30+ knots

Manning:		*Total*	*Officers*	*Enlisted*
	CVN 68	3,097	158	2,939
	CVN 69	3,124	161	2,963
	CVN 70	3,118	160	2,958
	CVN 71	3,113	161	2,952
	CVN 72	3,102	160	2,942
	CVN 73	3,120	163	2,957
	CVN 74	3,103	161	2,942
	CVN 75	3,093	161	2,932

Flag: approx. 70 (25 officers + 45 enlisted) when embarked
Air wing: approx. 1,700
Aircraft: approx. 70
Catapults: 4 steam Mk 13-1 in CVN 68–71
4 steam Mk 13-2 in CVN 72 and later ships
Elevators: 4 deck edge (85 × 52 feet/25.9 × 15.85 m); 130,000-lb (58,500-kg) capacity
Missiles: 3 8-cell NATO Sea Sparrow launchers Mk 29
Guns: 3 20-mm Phalanx CIWS Mk 16 (3 multibarrel) in CVN 68, 69; 4 guns in later ships
Radars: Furuno 900 navigation (in most ships)
SPS-48E 3-D air search
SPS-49(V)5 air search
SPS-64(V)9 navigation
SPS-67(V)1 surface search
Mk 23 Target Acquisition System (TAS)
Sonars: none
Fire control: 3 Mk 91' missile FCS
EW systems: SLQ-25A Nixie torpedo countermeasures
SLQ-32(V)4

These are the largest warships ever built. Eight ships are in commission, with one more under construction and a tenth ship in the fiscal year 2001 shipbuilding program. Two additional carriers are planned—"transitional" ships to the more advanced (CVX) design. However, it is expected that they will be generally similar to the basic NIMITZ design. Details vary, as improvements have been made in virtually each succeeding ship (see *Design* notes).

When the ninth NIMITZ-class carrier (RONALD REAGAN) is completed in 2003 it will have been 28 years after the completion of the lead ship, the preliminary design of the NIMITZ having begun in 1964—a remarkable and unique life span for a warship design. The NIMITZ class also represents the largest number of carriers built to the

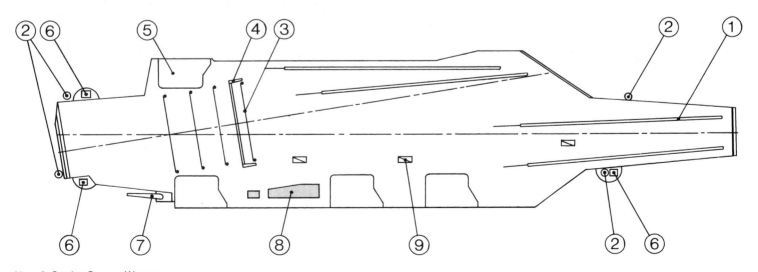

Aircraft Carrier GEORGE WASHINGTON
1. Catapults (4) 2. Phalanx CIWS (4) 3. Arresting wires (4) 4. Barricade 5. Elevators (4) 6. NATO Sea Sparrow (3) 7. Aircraft crane 8. Island structure 9. Bomb elevators (3) (William Clipson)

same basic design since World War II by any nation, except for the U.S. helicopter carriers of the similar TARAWA (LHA 1) and WASP (LHD 1) classes.

The REAGAN was authorized in fiscal 1995, seven years after the previous ship of the class. The CVN 76 was funded after the Cold War ended, having been put forward by the Clinton administration and approved by Congress with relatively little debate and only minor opposition—true testimony to the aircraft carrier's efficacy.

Class: A program to construct the first three CVNs of the NIMITZ class was approved by Secretary of Defense Robert S. McNamara during the Vietnam War as replacements for the three MIDWAY-class carriers to provide a force of 12 large carriers (i.e., CV 59–64, 66, and 67 and CVN 65 and 68–70). The first three ships were delayed

The island structure of the HARRY S. TRUMAN (1998, Jürg Kürsener)

The island structure of the GEORGE WASHINGTON (1999, Jürg Kürsener)

during construction by labor strikes and schedule problems at the Newport News yard. The NIMITZ was seven years from keel laying to commissioning, compared to less than four years for the more complex (eight-reactor) ENTERPRISE.

The CVN 71 was forced on the Carter administration by Congress, overriding a presidential veto in 1980. The CVN 72 and 73 were approved through the efforts of Secretary of the Navy John Lehman early in the Reagan administration—the first time since World War II that two first-line carriers were authorized in the same fiscal year. The Reagan-Lehman naval buildup subsequently gained approval of another two carriers in a single year, the CVN 74 and 75.

The NIMITZ is the first of the class to undergo the Refueling/Complex Overhaul (RCOH) process; the work began at the Newport News yard on 29 May 1998 and was to complete in May 2001.

Classification: The NIMITZ and EISENHOWER were ordered as attack aircraft carriers (CVAN); they were changed to multimission aircraft carriers (CVN) on 30 June 1975. The VINSON and later ships were ordered as CVNs.

Some Navy documents list the CVN 78 as CVX 1 and CVN 79 as CVX 2.

Design: SCB No. 102. The general arrangement of these ships is similar to the previous KITTY HAWK class with respect to flight deck, hangar, elevators, and island structure (e.g., the island structure is aft of the No. 1 and No. 2 elevators with the No. 4 elevator on the port side, aft of the angled deck and opposite the No. 3 elevator on the

The CARL VINSON at Pearl Harbor. These ships can operate some 70 high-performance aircraft. Note the NATO Sea Sparrow launcher and 20-mm Phalanx CIWS mounted on a small sponson on the starboard side of the flight deck; there is another combination mounting to port. (1998, U.S. Navy, PH3 Christopher Hollaway)

starboard side). The angled deck is canted 9° 3′ to port and is $796^2/_3$ feet (242.9 m) long. The hangar deck is 684 feet (208.5 m) long, 108 feet (32.9 m) wide, and 26½ feet (8.1 m) high.

The CVN 71 and later ships incorporate improved magazine protection and modular construction techniques that reduced construction time, the CVN 73 and later ships have improved topside ballistic protection, and the CVN 74 and later units were constructed with HSLA-100 steel. There have also been incremental improvements in the ships' electrical and electronics systems.

"Full load" is maximum displacement after underway replenishment at sea of full ordnance and aviation fuel capacity (previously referred to as "combat load"). The payload includes approximately 2,900 tons of aviation ordnance and up to 3.5 million gallons (13.2 million liters) of jet fuel (JP-5).

Details differ based on individual ships' configuration with respect to maintenance facilities, electronic systems, etc.

Electronics: Several carrier-landing systems are provided: SPN-42A Carrier Controlled Approach (CCA) in the CVN 68–71; SPN-43C marshalling in all ships; SPN-44 landing aid in the CVN 71 and later ships; and two SPN-46 air traffic control in the CVN 72 and later ships.

Periodic proposals to provide these ships with the SPY-1 radar have been turned down on the basis of cost.

Engineering: These carriers have only two reactors, compared to eight in the first nuclear carrier, the ENTERPRISE. The fuel cores in the early ships were estimated to have a service life of at least 13 years (800,000 to 1,000,000 n.miles/1,481,000 to 1,850,350 km); the later cores have been pushed out to 25 years. This means that the later ships would be refueled only once during a service life of 45 to 50 years.

The CVN 77 and later ships are planned to have the improved A5W reactor plant.

Manning: Aircraft carriers were the first U.S. combatant ships to have women assigned as permanent crew members, with the EISEN-HOWER the first to deploy with women, departing Norfolk, Va., on 20 October 1994 with 367 female officers and enlisted women on board. The ship deployed for six months, operating in the Mediterranean Sea.

Missiles: The CVN 68 and 69 were built with the Sea Sparrow Mk 25 missile launchers (with Mk 115 fire control system); they were rearmed with the NATO Sea Sparrow system.

Names: The CVN 68 remembers one of four admirals to hold five-star rank. The Navy's three other Fleet Admirals—William D. Leahy, Ernest J. King, and William F. Halsey—were remembered by guided missile frigates.[13] There were two other ships named for five-star officers: the Polaris submarine SSBN 654, named the GEORGE C. MARSHALL for the World War II Army Chief of Staff and, subsequently, Secretary of State and Secretary of Defense; and the missile range instrumentation ship GEN. H. H. ARNOLD (T-AGM 9), honoring the World War II commander of the Army Air Forces.[14] Thus, of nine five-star officers in U.S. armed forces history, seven have been honored by U.S. ships—only Generals of the Army Omar Bradley and Douglas MacArthur have been slighted.

The CVN 69 was named for General/President Eisenhower; the ship, originally named EISENHOWER, was renamed DWIGHT D. EISENHOWER on 23 May 1970.

The CVN 71–73, 75, and 76 honor former presidents, three of whom previously had ballistic missile submarines named for them: Roosevelt (SSBN 600), Lincoln (SSBN 602), and Washington (SSBN 598). The CVN 72 and 73 were named prior to their start, in part to preempt potential congressional pressure for naming one of those ships for Admiral H. G. Rickover (the SSN 709 was instead named for the admiral).

---

13. Frigates, i.e., DLGs, later designated CG or DDG.
14. The T-AGM 9 was built as the troop transport GEN. R. E. CALLAN (AP 139).

The GEORGE WASHINGTON pulls into the port of Jebel Ali in the United Arab Emirates during the ship's six-month forward deployment. Aircraft carriers have been a principal U.S. instrument of forward presence outside of Europe during the past 50 years. (1998, U.S. Navy, PH3 Erik Kenney)

The DWIGHT D. EISENHOWER at high speed. There is a 20-mm Phalanx CIWS mounted in the "tail gun" position. These Gatling guns and Sea Sparrow missiles provide a minimal, terminal defense against anti-ship cruise missiles. (U.S. Navy)

The CVN 70 and 74 were named for, respectively, the long-time chairman of the House Armed Services Committee who was a major supporter of the U.S. naval buildup on the eve of World War II, and a Navy supporter who served in the House of Representatives from 1947 to 1988.

The CVN 75 was originally named UNITED STATES, after one of the six sailing frigates authorized by Congress in 1794 and the first to be launched; the other ships in the series included the frigates CONSTITUTION and CONSTELLATION. The second UNITED STATES was a battle cruiser (CC 6) laid down in 1920 but canceled; sister ships were completed as the carriers LEXINGTON (CV 2) and SARATOGA (CV 3). The next UNITED STATES was the first "super carrier" (CVA 58), laid down in April 1949 and promptly canceled, leading to the carrier-versus-B-36 controversy. On 2 February 1995 the CVN 75 was renamed for the 33rd president.

Operational: The VINSON shifted to the Pacific Fleet in 1983, the NIMITZ in 1987, the LINCOLN in 1990, and the STENNIS in 1999.

The NIMITZ was to shift home port from Norfolk to San Diego upon completion of her yard period in November 2001.

The forward bomb bay of the DWIGHT D. EISENHOWER is packed with bombs; those in the foreground are 1,000-pound (454-kg) bombs modified to a GBU-16 configuration with laser guidance and control fins. Four elevators carry the bombs to the flight deck, although one normally cannot be used because of its proximity to a catapult. (1998, U.S. Navy, PH2 Shawn Eklund)

The HARRY S. TRUMAN is the latest of the NIMITZ-class carriers to join the fleet. The NIMITZ class has been in production longer than any other carrier design in history, and—despite Navy protestations that the CVX will be a "new ship"—construction of this basic design can be expected well into the 21st century. (1999, U.S. Navy, PHC Cathy Brenneman)

The JOHN C. STENNIS—with most of her air wing on her broad flight deck—steams in the Persian Gulf. The aircraft parked around the after portion of her deck are F-14 Tomcats. Her SH-60F and HH-60H Seahawks are parked next to the island structure (under the "74"), the normal nesting spot for helicopters on U.S. carriers. (1998, U.S. Navy, PH1 James M. Williams)

The GEORGE WASHINGTON tests her countermeasures washdown system during a Chemical, Biological, Radiological (CBR) drill while operating in the Western Atlantic. Although an important capability, the feasibility of using the washdown system with aircraft on deck is doubtful at best. The ship's mobile wrecking crane is parked on the bow. (2000, U.S. Navy, PH1 Robert Catalano)

The HARRY S. TRUMAN maneuvers at high speed. Her empty flight deck clearly reveals her angled flight deck; two flush-deck steam catapults are forward (on either side of the "75") and two more "cats" are in the waist, at the forward end of the angled deck. Two elevators are forward of the island and one aft, with the fourth lift on the port quarter. (1998, U.S. Navy, PHC Tom Wynn)

3 AIRCRAFT CARRIERS: "KITTY HAWK" CLASS AND "JOHN F. KENNEDY"

Number	Name	FY	Builder	Laid down	Launched	Commissioned	Status
CV 63	KITTY HAWK	56	New York Shipbuilding, Camden, N.J.	27 Dec 1956	21 May 1960	29 Apr 1961	**PA**
CV 64	CONSTELLATION	57	New York Naval Shipyard, Brooklyn, N.Y.	14 Sep 1957	8 Oct 1960	27 Oct 1961	**PA**
CV 66	AMERICA	61	Newport News Shipbuilding, Va.	9 Jan 1961	1 Feb 1964	23 Jan 1965	decomm./str. 30 Sep 1996
CV 67	JOHN F. KENNEDY	63	Newport News Shipbuilding, Va.	22 Oct 1964	27 May 1967	7 Sep 1968	**AA**

Displacement:		*Light*	*Full load*
	CV 63	60,933 tons	81,780 tons
	CV 64	61,981 tons	82,538 tons
	CV 67	60,728 tons	82,655 tons
Length:	990 feet (301.9 m) waterline		
	CV 63:	1,069 feet (325.91 m) overall	
	CV 64, 67: 1,073 feet (327.13 m) overall		
Beam:	129¹¹⁄₁₂ feet (39.6 m), except CV 67 128½ feet (39.2 m)		
Flight deck:	282 feet (85.98 m), except CV 67 252 feet (76.8 m)		
Draft:	37 feet (11.3 m)		
Propulsion:	4 steam turbines (General Electric); 280,000 shp; 4 shafts		
Boilers:	8 1,200-psi (83.4-kg/cm²) (Foster Wheeler)		
Speed:	33 knots		
Range:	12,000 n.miles (22,225 km) at 20 knots		
Manning:		*Total*	*Officers* *Enlisted*
	CV 63	3,106	148 2,958
	CV 64	2,950	149 2,801
	CV 67	2,764	136 2,628
Flag:	approx. 70 (25 officers + 45 enlisted) when embarked		
Air wing:	approx. 1,700		

Aircraft:	approx. 70
Catapults:	4 steam C13 in CV 63, 64
	3 steam C13 + 1 steam C13-1 in CV 67
Elevators:	4 deck edge (85 x 52 feet/25.9 x 15.9 m) 130,000-lb (58,500-kg) capacity
Missiles:	2 8-cell NATO Sea Sparrow launchers Mk 29 in CV 64; 3 launchers in other ships
Guns:	4 20-mm Phalanx CIWS Mk 16 (3 multibarrel) in CV 64; 3 guns in other ships
Radars:	Furuno 900 navigation
	SPS-48E 3-D air search
	SPS-49(V)5 air search
	SPS-64(V)9 surface search
	SPS-67(V)1 surface search
	Mk 23 Target Acquisition System (TAS)
Sonars:	none
Fire control:	3 Mk 91 missile FCS
EW systems:	SLQ-29 (SLQ-17 + WLR-8)
	WLR-1H
	WLR-11

These ships have a modified FORRESTAL configuration with improved elevator and flight deck arrangements. The KITTY HAWK was delayed because of shipyard problems, the CONSTELLATION because of a fire on board while under construction, and the KENNEDY because of lengthy debates over whether the ship should have nuclear or conventional propulsion.

The JOHN F. KENNEDY was changed from active status to the Naval Reserve Force (NRF) on 1 October 1994 and from September 1995 served as an "operational reserve/training carrier," providing carrier landing training for pilots while maintaining the capability of deploying as an operational carrier on short notice. However, fleet requirements led to the ship serving as a fully operational carrier, deploying on a regular basis. This was the first time an aircraft carrier has ever been assigned to the NRF, being homeported in Mayport, Fla. (previous AVT training carriers were based at Pensacola, Fla.). However,

the "experiment" in partial reserve manning was unsuccessful and in 2000 she reverted to active status (see *Manning* notes).

The current replacement dates for these ships are:

	To retire	*Replacement*
KITTY HAWK	2008	CVN 77
CONSTELLATION	2003	CVN 79
KENNEDY	2018	CVN 80

Builders: This class includes the last U.S. aircraft carriers (CV/CVN) to be built by shipyards other than Newport News Shipbuilding.

Class: There are three ships in the KITTY HAWK class; the KENNEDY is officially a single ship "type." All four ships were often grouped with the FORRESTAL class in force level discussions.

The KITTY HAWK steams off the coast of Japan, waiting for her air wing to come aboard for carrier qualifications. The Navy has had a carrier homeported in Japan since 1973. When the KITTY HAWK is retired about 2008 it is unlikely that another carrier will be homeported overseas as only one non-nuclear carrier is expected to remain in service, the JOHN F. KENNEDY. (2000, U.S. Navy, PH3 John Sullivan)

The AMERICA was decommissioned and stricken after only 31½ years of service due to high maintenance and overhaul costs caused by thinner hull plating and other cost-reduction methods employed in her construction.

Classification: These ships were originally attack aircraft carriers (CVA). Two ships were changed to multimission carriers (CV) when modified to operate ASW aircraft, the KITTY HAWK on 29 April 1973 and the KENNEDY on 1 December 1974; the CONSTELLATION was changed to CV on 30 June 1975, prior to being modified.

The KITTY HAWK off the coast of Japan with an empty flight deck. Her elevators, catapults, and bomb elevators are clearly visible. There are two bomb elevators forward between the bow catapults and two between the island structure and angled deck. (2000, U.S. Navy, PH3 John Sullivan)

Design: SCB No. 127, 127A, and 127C, respectively. These ships are larger than the FORRESTAL class and have an improved flight deck arrangement, with two elevators forward of the island structure and the port-side elevator on the stern quarter rather than at the forward end of the angled flight deck.

The hangar deck in the KITTY HAWK class is 740 feet (225.6 m) long, 101 feet (30.8 m) wide, and 25 feet (7.6 m) high; in the KENNEDY, the hangar deck is 688 feet (209.75 m) long, 106 feet (32.3 m) wide, and 25 feet (7.6 m) high. The angled decks of the KITTY HAWK and CONSTELLATION are canted 11° 20′ to port and are 722⁷⁄₁₂ feet (220.3 m) long; that of the KENNEDY is canted at 11° and is 754 feet (229.9 m) long. The KENNEDY has her stack angled out to starboard to help carry exhaust gases away from the approach path to the flight deck.

Electronics: Several carrier-landing systems are provided in these ships: SPN-35 blind-landing approach radar, SPN-41 landing aid, SPN-42 carrier-controlled approach, SPN-43C marshalling, and two SPN-46 air traffic control.

The KENNEDY has a bow sonar dome, but no sonar was ever installed.

Manning: Initially, as an NRF/training carrier the JFK was to embark some 600 reserve personnel (about 20 percent of the crew), with most serving aboard the ship for their annual two weeks' active duty for training. It was quickly decided that such assignments would be prohibitively expensive.

Subsequently, the KENNEDY was to embark 277 Naval Reservists for one year periods of active duty. However, after screening of reservist qualifications against billets, only 115 were accepted for service aboard the JFK and only 68 of those reported for duty in March 1999. In addition, some 300 Navy Training and Administration of Reserves (TAR) personnel (full-time reserve personnel) were assigned to the ship.

Missiles: The first three ships were built with two Terrier missile launchers (Mk 10 Mod 3 on the starboard quarter and Mk 10 Mod 4 on the port quarter) with SPQ-55B missile control "searchlight" radars. The KENNEDY originally had three Sea Sparrow Mk 25 launchers and Mk 115 FCS.

Modernization: The KITTY HAWK and CONSTELLATION have been modernized under the SLEP upgrade (see below).

The Secretary of Defense in early 1991 canceled the planned SLEP for the KENNEDY; however, Congress placed language in the fiscal 1991 supplemental appropriation to force the SLEP to be undertaken at the Philadelphia Naval Shipyard.[15] However, Congress voted only $405 million for the KENNEDY work, about one-half the estimated cost of a SLEP. Instead, the Navy undertook a two-year Comprehensive Overhaul (COH) modernization in 1993–1994 (vice about three years for a SLEP), with a cost of $491 million.

	Arrival at yard	Modernization start	Modernization complete
CV 63	7 Apr 1987	28 Jan 1988	31 Aug 1991
CV 64	11 Apr 1990	2 July 1990	10 Mar 1993
CV 67	13 Sep 1993	13 Sep 1993	15 Sep 1995

The SLEP upgrades add an estimated 15 years to the ships' nominal 30-year service life.

Operational: The KITTY HAWK replaced the INDEPENDENCE as the Navy's forward-based carrier at Yokosuka, Japan, the older carrier being homeported there from September 1991 to July 1998. The KITTY HAWK arrived at Yokosuka on 11 August 1998, having traded air wings with the INDEPENDENCE at Pearl Harbor on 18 July 1998.

In a ceremony on 20 November 1998, the KITTY HAWK raised the original Navy jack in place of the standard Navy jack to indicate that she is the longest-serving ship in the fleet (other than the relic CONSTITUTION). The original jack consists of 13 horizontal stripes, alternating red and white, superimposed with a rattlesnake and the motto "Don't Tread On Me." The KITTY HAWK will fly the original Navy jack until she is decommissioned, at which time the jack will be transferred to the "new" oldest serving ship.

---

15. The Philadelphia yard was closed in 1996.

The JOHN F. KENNEDY arriving in New York Harbor. She is fitted with an old-style Tactical Air Navigation (TACAN) "pot," which once adorned the masts of most U.S. carriers, cruisers, and many destroyers. Launch-bridal arrester protrudes from her forward and angled flight decks. (1998, U.S. Navy, PH1 Pat Cashin)

The CONSTELLATION *(foreground)* and KITTY HAWK conduct joint operations in the Western Pacific. The hangar deck openings for her three starboard elevators are visible beneath the flight deck. (1999, U.S. Navy, PH3 Steven Crawford)

1 NUCLEAR-PROPELLED AIRCRAFT CARRIER: "ENTERPRISE"

Number	Name	FY	Builder	Laid down	Launched	Commissioned	Status
CVN 65	ENTERPRISE	58	Newport News Shipbuilding, Va.	4 Feb 1958	24 Sep 1960	25 Nov 1961	**AA**

Displacement:	75,704 tons light	Elevators:	4 deck edge (85 x 52 feet/25.9 x 15.9 m); 130,000-lb (58,500-kg)
	93,284 tons full load		capacity
Length:	1,040 feet (317.07 m) waterline	Missiles:	3 8-cell NATO Sea Sparrow launchers Mk 29
	1,088 feet (331.70 m) overall	Guns:	3 20-mm Phalanx CIWS Mk 16 (3 multibarrel)
Beam:	133 feet (40.5 m)	Radars:	Furuno 900 navigation
Flight deck:	248⅓ feet (75.7 m)		SPS-48E 3-D air search
Draft:	39 feet (11.9 m)		SPS-49(V)5 air search
Propulsion:	4 steam turbines (Westinghouse); approx. 280,000 shp; 4 shafts		SPS-64(V)9 navigation
Reactors:	8 pressurized-water A2W (Westinghouse)		SPS-67(V)1 surface search
Speed:	33 knots		Mk 23 Target Acquisition System (TAS)
Manning:	3,318 (169 officers + 3,149 enlisted)	Sonars:	none
Flag:	approx. 70 (25 officers + 45 enlisted) when embarked	Fire control:	3 Mk 91 missile FCS
Air wing:	approx. 1,700	EW systems:	SLQ-32(V)4
Aircraft:	approx. 70		WLR-1H
Catapults:	4 steam C13-1		

The ENTERPRISE was the world's second nuclear-propelled surface warship and was the world's largest and most expensive warship at the time of her construction. The estimated construction cost was $444 million.

The ship operated in the Pacific from 1965 until early 1990. She arrived at Norfolk on 16 March 1990 in preparation for a three-year refueling/modernization at Newport News Shipbuilding (see *Modernization* notes). She resumed operations with the Atlantic Fleet in 1995.

The "Big E" is scheduled to be retired in fiscal 2013, being replaced by the CVN 78.

Class: Congress provided $35 million in the fiscal 1960 budget for long-lead-time nuclear components for a second aircraft carrier of this type. The Eisenhower administration (1953–1961), however, deferred the project. The next nuclear carrier, the NIMITZ, was not ordered until almost ten years after the ENTERPRISE, with two oil-burning carriers having been constructed in the interim period.

Classification: Originally classified as an attack aircraft carrier (CVAN), the ENTERPRISE was changed to a multimission carrier (CVN) on 30 June 1975.

Design: SCB No. 160. The ENTERPRISE was built to a modified KITTY HAWK design, but in her original configuration she had a distinctive island structure because of the arrangement of "billboard" radar antennas (see *Electronics* notes).

Her hangar deck is 860 feet (262.2 m) long, 107 feet (32.6 m) wide, and 25 feet (7.6 m) high. The angled deck, 755⅚ feet (230.4 m) long, is canted 10° to port.

Electronics: The ENTERPRISE and the cruiser LONG BEACH (CGN 9) were the only ships fitted with the Hughes SPS-32 and SPS-33 fixed-array radars. The radars were difficult to maintain and were replaced during the ENTERPRISE's 1979–1981 modernization with conventional SPS-48 and SPS-49 radars, with a new island structure installed.

Carrier-landing systems provided in the ENTERPRISE are the SPN-41 landing aid, SPN-43C marshalling, and two SPN-46 air traffic control.

Engineering: At the time of her construction, the ENTERPRISE was estimated to have a cruising range of more than 200,000 n.miles (370,400 km) without refueling. On her initial set of fuel cores, the ship traveled 207,000 n.miles (383,365 km).

The two-reactor A1W prototype of the ENTERPRISE propulsion plant was constructed at Arco, Idaho.

Missiles: As built, the ENTERPRISE had neither defensive missiles nor guns, the planned Terrier system having been deleted from the design because of cost. Late in 1967 she was fitted with two Sea Sparrow Mk 25 launchers. During her 1979–1982 overhaul, the NATO Sea Sparrow launchers were installed, as were the Phalanx CIWS.

Modernization: The ENTERPRISE underwent a Refueling/Complex Overhaul (RCOH) modernization and nuclear refueling at Newport News Shipbuilding; she arrived at the yard on 12 October 1990 and the modernization began on 8 January 1991. (Her nuclear plant had been shut down at the Norfolk Naval Base on 15 August 1990 and she was towed to the Newport News yard.)

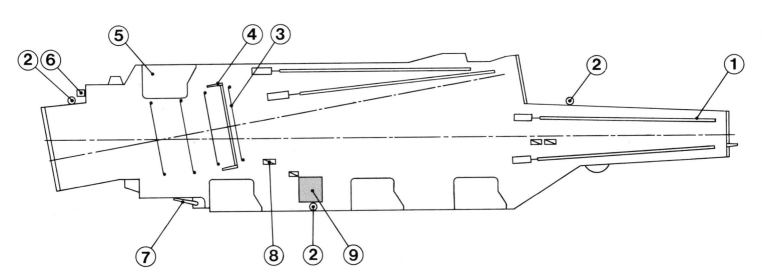

Aircraft Carrier ENTERPRISE
1. Catapults (4) 2. Phalanx CIWS (4) 3. Arresting wires (4) 4. Barricade 5. Elevators (4) 6. NATO Sea Sparrow (3) 7. Aircraft crane 8. Bomb elevators (4) 9. Island structure (William Clipson)

She carried out initial post-overhaul sea trials on 27–30 September 1994. After additional at-sea operations, the carrier returned to Newport News and completed fitting out on 6 December 1994. A post-overhaul yard period followed; she returned to the fleet in July 1995.

Congress authorized $79.5 million in fiscal 1989 and $1.4 *billion* in fiscal 1990 to refuel and upgrade the ship. The actual costs are expected to be approximately $2.5 *billion*. However, the

The forward side of the ENTERPRISE's island structure. The three domes in the foreground are Extremely High Frequency (EHF) communication antennas. (2000, U.S. Navy, PH3 Karl L. Peters)

The after side of the ENTERPRISE's island structure. (1999, Jürg Kürsener)

The "Big E" with CH-46 Sea Knight helicopters "cross-decking" munitions from the aircraft carrier GEORGE WASHINGTON. Munitions are regularly transferred at sea from ships returning to the United States to carriers about to forward deploy. (1999, U.S. Navy, PH3 Sammy Dallal)

extent of the modernization has been reduced because of cost constraints. The refueling was expected to provide cores with a service life of about 20 years, i.e., until about 2115.

Operational: During August–October 1964, the ENTERPRISE, in company with the cruiser LONG BEACH and frigate BAINBRIDGE (DLGN 25/CGN 25), formed all-nuclear Task Force 1. The ships steamed around the world without refueling or replenishing, traveling 32,600 n.miles (60,375 km) in 64 days, including time for

port visits in several countries. They took on no fuel or provisions during the cruise, except for special food for a kangaroo that was picked up in Australia.

The ENTERPRISE shifted to the Pacific Fleet in 1965 and in November of that year began flying air strikes against North Vietnam, becoming the first nuclear ship to enter combat. She remained in the Pacific until 1990, when she returned to the Atlantic in preparation for overhaul at Newport News Shipbuilding.

A row of Marine F/A-18C Hornets undergo maintenance in the hangar deck of the ENTERPRISE as the carrier operates in the Mediterranean. The opening for a deck-edge elevator is visible at far left. The overhead is used to store drop tanks and spare parts. (1999, U.S. Navy, PH3 Karl L. Peters)

2 AIRCRAFT CARRIERS: "FORRESTAL" CLASS

Number	Name	FY	Builder	Laid down	Launched	Commissioned	Status
CV 59	FORRESTAL	51	Newport News Shipbuilding, Va.	14 July 1952	11 Dec 1954	1 Oct 1955	decomm./str. 10 Sep 1993
CV 60	SARATOGA	52	New York Naval Shipyard, Brooklyn, N.Y.	16 Dec 1952	8 Oct 1955	14 Apr 1956	decomm./str. 30 Sep 1994
CV 61	RANGER	53	Newport News Shipbuilding, Va.	2 Aug 1954	29 Sep 1956	10 Aug 1957	PR decomm. 10 July 1993
CV 62	INDEPENDENCE	55	New York Naval Shipyard, Brooklyn, N.Y.	1 July 1955	6 June 1958	10 Jan 1959	PR decomm. 30 Sep 1998

Displacement:		*Light*	*Full load*
	CV 61	60,787 tons	81,003 tons
	CV 62	60,059 tons	80,678 tons
Length:	990 feet (301.8 m) waterline		
	CV 61: 1,067 feet (325.30 m) overall		
	CV 62: 1,070 feet (326.22 m) overall		
Beam:	130 feet (39.6 m)		
Flight deck:	CV 61: 270 feet (82.32 m)		
	CV 62: 263 feet (80.18 m)		
Draft:	CV 61: 37 feet (11.3 m)		
	CV 62: 38 feet (11.59 m)		
Propulsion:	4 steam turbines (General Electric); 280,000 shp; 4 shafts		
Boilers:	8 1,200-psi (83.4-kg/cm^2) (Babcock & Wilcox)		
Speed:	34 knots		
Range:	12,000 n.miles (22,225 km) at 20 knots		
Manning:	approx. 3,126 (147 officers + 2,979 enlisted)		
Flag:	approx. 70 (25 officers + 45 enlisted) when embarked		
Air wing:	approx. 2,000		

Aircraft:	approx. 80
Catapults:	4 steam C7
Elevators:	4 deck edge (63 x 52 feet/19.2 x 15.9 m); 110,000-lb (49,500-kg) capacity
Missiles:	3 8-cell NATO Sea Sparrow launchers Mk 29 in CV 61; 2 launchers in CV 62
Guns:	3 20-mm Phalanx CIWS Mk 16 (3 multibarrel)
Radars:	Furuno 900 navigation
	SPS-48C 3-D air search
	SPS-49(V)5 air search
	SPS-64(V)9 navigation
	SPS-67(V)1 surface search
Sonars:	none
Fire control:	2 Mk 91 missile FCS
EW systems:	SLQ-29 (SLQ-17 + WLR-8)
	WLR-1
	WLR-3
	WLR-11

The FORRESTAL class was the world's first aircraft carrier design to be constructed from the keel up after World War II and the first of the "super carriers." The ships were intended specifically to operate heavy and high-performance turbojet attack aircraft, especially nuclear-armed planes capable of striking the Soviet Union.

Two ships are retained in reserve; it is unlikely that either will ever again see active service because of the complexity and cost of rehabilitating them and their large manning requirements.

Class: The FORRESTAL made her last operational deployment in mid-1991, after which she was to become the Navy's pilot landing training ship. However, she was decommissioned and stricken in 1993 prior to undertaking that role (the FORRESTAL was changed from CV to AVT on 4 February 1992).

Classification: The RANGER and INDEPENDENCE were built as attack aircraft carriers (CVA). The INDEPENDENCE was changed to multimission aircraft carrier (CV) on 28 February 1973 when she was modified to operate S-3A Viking ASW aircraft and SH-3 Sea King ASW helicopters; RANGER was reclassified on 30 June 1975, prior to modification.

Design: SCB No. 80. This class incorporated many design features of the aborted carrier UNITED STATES. The original design provided for an axial (straight) flight deck. The FORRESTAL was modified during construction to incorporate the British-developed angled flight deck. Details of these ships differed considerably.

The hangar deck is 740 feet (225.6 m) long, 101 feet (30.8 m) wide, and 25 feet (7.6 m) high.

Electronics: The RANGER and INDEPENDENCE were fitted with the SPN-41 landing aid, SPN-43A marshalling, SPN-44 landing aid, and two SPN-42 CCA systems.

Guns: These were the last U.S. aircraft carriers built with major gun armament. As built, all ships had eight 5-inch/54-cal DP Mk 42 single guns, mounted in pairs on sponsons, both sides, forward and aft. The forward sponsons were removed from the INDEPENDENCE early in her service because of damage in heavy seas. The RANGER retained her forward sponsons, the only ship of the class to serve primarily in the more placid waters of the Pacific. The after guns were removed as Sea Sparrow launchers became available for these ships.

Modernization: The INDEPENDENCE underwent SLEP modernization intended to add 15 years to her nominal 30-year service live. The SLEP update was undertaken at the Philadelphia Naval Shipyard; she arrived at the yard on 14 April 1985 and began conversion the following day. The SLEP was completed on 30 April 1988.

The SLEP update included rehabilitation of the ship's hull, propulsion, auxiliary machinery, and piping systems, with improved radars, communications equipment, and aircraft launch and recovery systems provided.

The RANGER was the only ship in the four-carrier class not to undergo SLEP modernization.

Operational: The INDEPENDENCE was last homeported in Yokosuka, Japan, having replaced the MIDWAY as the only U.S. aircraft carrier based overseas. The INDEPENDENCE arrived at Yokosuka on 11 September 1991, having traded air wings with the MIDWAY at Pearl Harbor on 15 July 1991. In turn, the INDEPENDENCE was replaced by the KITTY HAWK.

The INDEPENDENCE maneuvers at high speed in the Persian Gulf while operating in support of Operation Southern Watch over southern Iraq. This photo was taken during the ship's last forward deployment. Although laid up in reserve with her sister ship RANGER, it is highly unlikely she will ever be reactivated. (1998, U.S. Navy, PH2 Felix Garza)

TABLE 13-2. POST–WORLD WAR II AIRCRAFT CARRIERS

Number	Name	Comm.	Notes
Midway class (3)			
CVB 41	Midway	1945	decomm. 11 Apr 1992; str. 17 Mar 1997
CVB 42	Franklin D. Roosevelt	1945	stricken 1972
CVB 43	Coral Sea	1947	decomm./str. 30 Apr 1990
CVB 44	(unnamed)		canceled 1943
CVB 56, 57	(unnamed)		canceled 1945
United States class (4*)			
CVA 58	United States		canceled 1949
CVA 59–62	Forrestal class		
CVA 63, 64	Kitty Hawk class		
CVAN 65	Enterprise type		
CVA 66	Kitty Hawk class (continued)		
CVA 67	John F. Kennedy type		
CVN 68–	Nimitz class		

*Four ships were planned; only the CVA 58 was named and ordered.

The three war-built ships of the Midway class originally were designated as "large" carriers (CVB); they were changed to attack carriers (CVA) in 1952 and to multipurpose carriers (CV) in 1975. They were prominent ships in U.S. Cold War operations. Three additional Midway-class carriers (CV 44, 56, and 57) were canceled in 1945. The CV 45–55 were canceled ships of the Essex (CV 9) class.

The Midway was the last World War II–era warship in commission in the U.S. Navy. She was based at Yokosuka, Japan, from 1973 until 1991, the first U.S. carrier ever to be based in a foreign country. (Another U.S. carrier was planned for homeporting in Piraeus, Greece, in the early 1970s, but that proposal was dropped because of problems within the Greek military government.)

The United States was a "heavy" aircraft carrier (CVA); she was authorized in fiscal 1948 and was laid down at Newport News Shipbuilding on 18 April 1949, but canceled on 23 April 1949. Although never completed, her design served as the progenitor of the Forrestal and subsequent large U.S. aircraft carriers. The ship was to have had a standard displacement of 65,000 tons and 80,000 tons full load. Four ships of this class of large carriers, intended primarily to operate nuclear strike aircraft, were planned, with the lead ship to be completed on 1 July 1952.

The Enterprise in the Persian Gulf. Three H-60 Seahawk helicopters are parked on her angled deck, which is otherwise cleared for landings. A large C-2A Greyhound Carrier Onboard Delivery (COD) aircraft, with wings folded back, is parked next to the island. (1999, U.S. Navy, PH3 Timothy S. Smith)

More than 1,000 of the crewmen of the Independence spell out "sayonara" as the carrier prepares to leave her home port of Yokosuka. The carrier returned to the United States for decommissioning; her embarked Carrier Air Wing 5 remained at Naval Air Facility Atsugi to embark in the Kitty Hawk. (1998, U.S. Navy)

CHAPTER 14

Battleships

Still a sight to make one's heart beat faster, the dreadnought Iowa slides under the Newport Bridge en route to the Naval Education and Training Center in Rhode Island. But the Iowa is at the end of a towline, stripped of masts, radar antennas, anti-aircraft guns, and other equipment. Although retained on the Naval Vessel Register, it is highly unlikely she will again see active service. (1998, U.S. Navy)

The Navy retains two battleships in reserve, the Iowa and Wis-consin. These ships have been retained by congressional edict on the basis of pleas by individuals who believe that the dreadnoughts built with 1930s technology can have a role in the 21st century. The battleship era in the U.S. Navy was thought to have ended on 12 January 1995, when the four ships of the Iowa class were stricken from the Naval Vessel Register (NVR). Those four ships had been the world's last operational battleships, all having been returned to active service during the Reagan administration as part of the buildup to a 600-ship fleet under the leadership of Secretary of the Navy John Lehman.

The 1995 decision to strike the four ships from the NVR was a result of the Navy's senior officers realizing that there was no practical role for the ships in future naval operations, while the cost and problems of reactivating the 57,700-ton warships was considered prohibitive. The official strike notice declared they were being disposed of "due to the expenditure necessary to ensure continued, reliable service; the costs of which would be disproportionate to the ships' value."[1]

But the battleship advocates took up arms, ably abetted by several "air power" advocates. This strange alliance came about as both groups opposed the development of the Arsenal Ship, advocated in the early 1990s by then–Chief of Naval Operations Admiral J. M. (Mike) Boorda. The Arsenal Ship gave promise of providing effective long-range support for troops ashore, a role earlier fulfilled by battleships, while air power advocates saw the Arsenal Ship's strike missiles as competition to manned strategic bombers (see appendix E).

As a result of a campaign in the press and letters to Congress by battleship supporters, on 29 June 1995 the Senate Armed Services Committee voted 17 to 3 to retain at least two Iowa-class battleships in mothballs, i.e., on the NVR. The language of the Senate amendment to the FY 1996 defense authorization act directed: "The Secretary of the Navy shall list on the Naval Vessel Register, and maintain on such register, at least two of the Iowa class battleships that were stricken from the register in February [sic] 1995." Further, the amendment proposed that the Secretary maintain two Iowas until the Navy has an "operational surface fire support capability that equals or exceeds the fire support capability that the Iowa class battleships . . . would, if in active service, be able to provide for Marine Corps amphibious assaults and operations ashore." Significantly, the leadership of the Marine Corps did not make strong protests when the battleships were stricken, nor were the Marine leaders particularly vocal in supporting the retention of the ships. The Senate report of 8 July 1995 further stated that these four battleships were the Navy's "only remaining potential source of around-the-clock accurate, high-volume, heavy fire support."

1. Vice Adm. W. A. Earner, USN, Deputy Chief of Naval Operations (Logistics), letter to Secretary of the Navy, subject: "Striking of Iowa Class Battleships," 5 January 1995. Secretary of the Navy John H. Dalton approved the recommendation to dispose of the ships on 12 January 1995.

The Navy did not reinstate the two ships until 30 December 1997, when, under congressional pressure, a memo to do so was promulgated, signed by the Chief of Naval Operations, Admiral Jay Johnson, on 21 January 1998 and by Secretary of the Navy John H. Dalton on 12 February 1998. Thus, two dreadnoughts are back in the Navy. However, in a 26 March 1999 report to Congress, the Navy indicated that it plans to strike the two battleships from the NVR between 2003 and 2005!

NAVAL FIRE SUPPORT

Navy–Marine Corps planning for future amphibious assaults—there has not been a combat assault by U.S. Marines since Inchon, Korea, more than 50 years ago—calls for the assault forces to be launched from over the horizon, anywhere from as far as 50 n.miles (92.65 km) offshore to perhaps 25 n.miles (46.3 km) off the beach. The availability of helicopters, the MV-22 Osprey, and the air-cushion landing craft (LCAC) permit these longer assault ranges. At the same time, there is an increased threat to ships closer inshore from mines and anti-ship missiles, the latter launched from shore cover.

An Iowa-class battleship's 16-inch (406-mm) guns have a maximum range of 27 n.miles (50 km). This range makes the battleship irrelevant for gunfire support unless it can be brought close inshore. In view of the damage sustained by a U.S. helicopter carrier and Aegis cruiser from mines in the Gulf War of 1991, and the two cruise missiles fired against a battleship in that conflict, naval commanders should be reluctant to bring such "high-value" and high-visibility targets close inshore. Even steaming a few miles offshore, the battleship's guns could be irrelevant, as the current amphibious doctrine calls for using helicopters and MV-22s to land assault troops far inshore, away from coastal defenses and closer to their objectives. Programs considered in the late 1980s to develop extended-range munitions for the battleships' 16-inch guns have not been pursued.

Two alternatives are available in the near term in place of the outdated 16-inch guns:

- The 5-inch/62-cal gun that will enter Navy service in 2001 on the destroyer Winston S. Churchill (DDG 81). This gun will fire Extended-Range Guided Munitions (ERGM) rounds out to 63 n.miles (117 km), with the Global Positioning System (GPS) providing an accuracy of between 33 and 66 feet (10 to 20 m).
- Missiles for land attack, initially variants of the Tomahawk Land-Attack Missile (TLAM) and the Land-Attack Standard Missile (LASM). In addition, a Tactical Tomahawk (TACTOM), an improvement of the TLAM, is being developed. These missiles provide improved flexibility for attacking ground targets; they can be carried by all cruisers and destroyers that will be in the fleet after about 2000.

(The 155-mm Vertical Gun for Advanced Ships [VGAS], a 155-mm/52-cal gun with a range of about 100 n.miles [185 km] previously considered for the DD 21 destroyer, has been abandoned. This gun was to have a greater accuracy and a higher rate of fire than ERGMs; however, the initial vertical flight trajectory of the weapon caused operational problems and the decision was made to instead employ a "conventional" 5-inch/64-cal gun[2]; see chapter 28.)

In the long term, i.e., after about 2010, two advanced fire-support weapons are expected to join the fleet: the Advanced Gun System (AGS) and Advanced Land Attack Missile (ALAM). The AGS is specifically intended for the DD 21 land attack destroyer; the ALAM will be compatible with vertical-launch cells in all cruisers and destroyers.

The AGS will fire the 155-mm ERGM round, upgraded to provide a 100-n.mile (185-km) range, as well as the Army's XM982 projectiles and other advanced Army munitions. The XM982 is a fin-stabilized, GPS-guided projectile that can carry submunitions ("bomblets"), anti-armor, or "bunker buster" warheads.

The ALAM has a range objective of 300 n.miles (556 km) and a threshold range (i.e., minimum requirement) of 200 n.miles (370 km). It is intended to carry anti-armor, advanced submunitions, and "complex" unitary warheads.

Both the AGS and ALAM are planned for fleet introduction in fiscal 2008, or shortly before the DD 21. (It had been planned that their introduction would be coincident with the DD 21 joining the fleet, but that ship's delivery schedule was changed in January 2000 to reflect the decision to provide the DD 21 with electric drive.) These weapons are described in chapter 28 of this edition of Ships and Aircraft.

While battleships reactivated in the 1980s each carried 32 Tomahawk missiles, one must recall that a modified destroyer of the Spruance (DD 963) class, while retaining all other weapons and systems, could carry 61 vertical-launch missiles for land attack.

The other problem with the battleships is the cost of reactivating and operating the dreadnoughts. During the Reagan administration, the cost of reactivating the four ships totaled some $1.66 *billion*; the cost of bringing back two ships is expected to be about $650 million according to official statements, but such numbers appear very low in comparison with the 1980s reactivation costs.[3]

Reactivation/modernization of the ships would take 18 to 24 months, assuming shipyard facilities were available. Beyond being activated, the ships would have to be provided with modern (compatible) radars, electronic countermeasures, communications, and other equipment, which may or may not be readily available.

Finding a crew could be even more difficult. There are no U.S. Navy personnel currently qualified in the 16-inch or 5-inch/38-cal guns fitted in the battleships, the Mk 13 fire control systems, 600-pound steam plants, or many of the other systems in the ships. Of course, each warship will require a crew of some 1,600 men (and women if the funds are available for modifying their berthing quarters). Additional crewmen in training, transit, and other assignments will push the total manning requirements for two battleships to about 3,500—enough personnel to operate about ten destroyers of the Arleigh Burke (DDG 51) class.

With the ships reactivated, up to six months of at-sea crew training would be necessary for the battleships to be ready for combat. Thus, the Iowa and Wisconsin could take some 18 months from the order being given until they would be available to the fleet.

Classification: The U.S. Navy's first two steel battleships, the Texas and Maine (both completed in 1895), were not assigned hull numbers. The U.S. Navy classification scheme of 1920 established the designation BB for battleships, with ships in existence at that time being so designated: the Indiana (1895) became BB 1.

The Iowa class reached hull number BB 66 (the canceled Kentucky), with the subsequent, never-started Montana class being assigned hull numbers BB 67–71.

---

2. See N. Polmar, "Arsenal Ship Survives . . . for Now," U.S. Naval Institute *Proceedings* (November 1997), pp. 87–88.

3. Statement of Secretary of the Navy Richard Danzig to Congress, 26 March 1999. The statement estimates the cost of reactivating the Iowa at $221,300,000 and the Wisconsin $430,000,000.

2 BATTLESHIPS: "IOWA" CLASS

Number	Name	Builder	Laid down	Launched	Commissioned	Status
BB 61	IOWA	New York Navy Yard, Brooklyn, N.Y.	27 June 1940	27 Aug 1942	22 Feb 1943	AR; decomm. 26 Oct 1990; museum
BB 62	NEW JERSEY	Philadelphia Navy Yard, Penna.	16 Sep 1940	7 Dec 1942	23 May 1943	decomm. 8 Feb 1991; str. 4 Jan 1999
BB 63	MISSOURI	New York Navy Yard, Brooklyn, N.Y.	6 Jan 1941	29 Jan 1944	11 June 1944	decomm. 31 Mar 1992; str. 12 Jan 1995
BB 64	WISCONSIN	Philadelphia Navy Yard, Penna.	25 Jan 1941	7 Dec 1943	16 Apr 1944	AR; decomm. 30 Sep 1991; museum

Displacement:	48,425 tons standard		Guns:	9 16-inch (406-mm) 50-cal Mk 7 (3 triple)
	57,350 tons full load			12 5-inch (127 mm) 38-cal DP Mk 28 (6 twin)
Length:	860 feet (262.3 m) waterline			4 20-mm Phalanx CIWS Mk 16 (4 multibarrel)
	887¼ feet (270.6 m) overall		Radars:	LN-66 navigation in BB 61
Beam:	108⅙ feet (33.0 m)			SPS-49 air search
Draft:	38 feet (11.6 m)			SPS-64(V) in BB 64
Propulsion:	4 steam turbines (General Electric in BB 61; Westinghouse in BB 64); 212,000 shp; 4 shafts			SPS-67 surface search
			Sonars:	none
Boilers:	8 600-psi (41.7-kg/cm²) (Babcock & Wilcox)		Fire control:	4 Mk 37 GFCS with Mk 25 radar
Speed:	33 knots (see *Engineering* notes)			2 Mk 38 gun directors with Mk 13 radar
Range:	15,000 n.miles (27,780 km) at 15 knots			1 Mk 40 gun director with Mk 26 radar
Manning:	approx. 1,570 (70 officers + 1,500 enlisted)			1 SPQ-9A
Marines:	55 (2 officers + 53 enlisted)		EW systems:	SLQ-25 Nixie torpedo countermeasures
Helicopters:	landing area			SLQ-32(V)3 except (V)4 in BB 64
Missiles:	16 Harpoon SSM (4 quad canisters Mk 141)			
	32 Tomahawk TASM/TLAM (8 quad ABL Mk 143)			

These are the world's only battleships in naval service, albeit laid up in reserve. Originally a class of four ships, all were modernized and recommissioned as part of the naval buildup under the Reagan administration.

The recommissioning of the WISCONSIN in 1988 marked the first time that all four battleships had been in commission since 1955. All have since been retired; when they were stricken from the NVR on 12 January 1995 it marked the first time since 1895 that there were no battleships in the U.S. Navy. Subsequently, Congress forced the Navy to reinstate two ships and on 12 February 1998 the NEW JERSEY and WISCONSIN were reinstated on the NVR. However, because of subsequent interest by the New Jersey congressional delegation on making the NEW JERSEY a memorial/museum, she was again stricken on 4 January 1999, with the IOWA reinstated in her place on the same date. This was done despite the damage to the IOWA's No. 2 16-inch turret (which was inoperative) and the additional time and cost that would be required to reactivate that ship.

The above characteristics reflect the state of the IOWA and WIS-CONSIN at the time of their decommissioning in 1990–1991.

The IOWA is currently in mothballs in Newport, R.I.; her ultimate location has not yet been decided.

The NEW JERSEY, currently moored at the Philadelphia Naval Business Center (formerly Philadelphia Naval Shipyard), will be permanently moored at Camden, N.J.

The MISSOURI is moored off Ford Island in Pearl Harbor, Hawaii, adjacent to the remains of the battleship ARIZONA (BB 39).

The WISCONSIN, previously moored at the Norfolk (Va.) Naval Shipyard, has been moved in 2000 to the Nauticus maritime museum in downtown Norfolk.

Aircraft: These ships were built with two rotating stern catapults and an aircraft crane for handling floatplanes. Three aircraft were normally embarked for scouting and gunfire spotting. The catapults were beached during the Korean War and the ships were assigned utility helicopters. During the Vietnam War, the NEW JERSEY also flew QH-50C "snoopy dash" drones for gunfire spotting.

The IOWA deployed in 1987 with five Pioneer surveillance drones (with a control system that included a radome mounted on the second funnel). The others subsequently were fitted to operate the Pioneer, with the MISSOURI and WISCONSIN flying Pioneer drones for gunfire spotting during the 1991 Gulf War.

One or two utility helicopters are normally embarked. No elevators or aircraft support facilities are provided.

Class: The IOWAs were the world's last battleships to be constructed, although two ships built in the same period were completed after the war: the British VANGUARD (laid down in 1941 and completed in 1946) and the French JEAN BART (laid down in 1939 and completed in 1952).

The U.S. dreadnoughts were exceeded in size and firepower only by the Japanese sister ships YAMATO and MUSASHI, both completed and sunk during World War II. Those ships displaced approximately 70,000 tons full load and had a main battery of nine 18.1-inch (460-mm) guns.

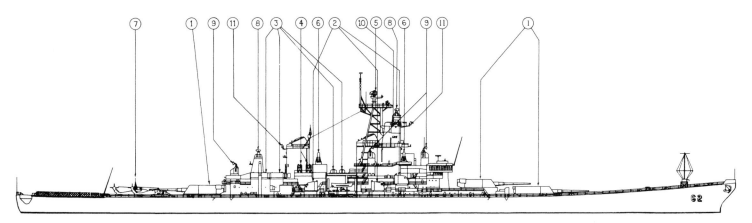

Battleship NEW JERSEY
1. 16-inch triple gun turret (3) 2. 5-inch twin gun mounts (6) 3. Tomahawk quad box launcher (8) 4. Harpoon quad canister launcher (4) 5. SPS-49(V)5 air search radar 6. Phalanx Close-In Weapon System (4) 7. Helicopter landing and parking areas 8. Mk 38 gun fire control radar (2) 9. Mk 37 gun fire control radar (4) 10. SLQ-32(V)3 Electronic Countermeasures (ECM) (2) 11. OE-82 antenna for WSC-3 Satellite Communications (SATCOM) (2) *Note:* The drawing omits the drone control radome antenna atop the after stack and the SPQ-9A gunfire control radar above the upper bridge. (A. D. Baker III)

The NEW JERSEY arriving at Philadelphia, where she is laid up awaiting her move to Camden, N.J., where she will be permanently moored. The battleship was at Bremerton, Wash., when the decision was made to make her a memorial-museum ship in New Jersey, necessitating her being towed through the Panama Canal to the East Coast—at the tax-payers' expense. (1999, U.S. Navy, PHC John F. Williams)

Six ships of the IOWA class were ordered; the ILLINOIS (BB 65) was canceled on 11 August 1945 when 22 percent complete, and construction of the KENTUCKY was suspended on 17 February 1947 when 72.1 percent complete and she was canceled on 22 January 1950 (although the hull was not stricken from the NVR until 9 June 1958).

Five larger battleships of the MONTANA class (BB 67–71) were ordered on 9 September 1940, but none was laid down and the program was canceled on 21 July 1943. They were to have had four triple 16-inch gun turrets, to displace 58,000 tons standard, and to be 903 feet (275.3 m) long. The construction of the MIDWAY (CVB 41)-class aircraft carriers and other priority naval construction programs, as well as the ascendancy of carrier-based aircraft over the battleship gun, caused cancellation of the MONTANA class.

There was speculative press mention of a "super MONTANA" class of some 80,000 tons mounting 20-inch (508-mm) guns with the hull numbers BB 72 to 78; in fact, no battleships beyond the MONTANAS were formally considered by the U.S. Navy.

In the post–World War II period, there were periodic proposals to recommission the IOWAs as well as to convert/modify them for more specialized roles as, for example, guided missile ships (AAW role with Terrier/Talos missiles), fleet command ships, ballistic missile monitors (carrying Polaris SLBMs), or commando/assault ships. In the early 1950s it was intended to complete the KENTUCKY as a guided missile ship carrying the Terrier missile system; however, no work was undertaken on that project.

Design: The design of these ships was constrained by the requirement to transit the Panama Canal (lock width 110 feet/33.5 m).[4]

Armor protection was intended to protect vital areas of the ship from enemy shells fired by guns up to 16-inch. The Class A steel armor belt tapers vertically from 307 mm to 41 mm. There is a lower armor belt of 343 mm aft of the No. 3 main battery turret to protect the propeller shafts (within the hull). Turret faces have 432 mm of armor, turret tops 184 mm, turret backs 305 mm, barbettes up to 295 mm, second armor deck 152 mm, conning tower sides 439 mm, and conning tower top 184 mm.

Electronics: During their 1980s reactivation, the ships were fitted with a cruiser (CG/CGN) communications suite; the WISCONSIN had the most-capable communications suite of the four ships. However, all lacked the Naval Tactical Data System (NTDS), except for the Link 11 receiver and certain other electronic features, of a modern surface combatant.

Engineering: All of these ships achieved 35 knots in service.

Guns: As built during World War II, in addition to the main battery of nine 16-inch guns, these ships carried 20 5-inch/38-cal guns (twin), up to 80 40-mm AA guns (quad), and almost 60 20-mm AA guns (twin and single). The 20-mm weapons were removed after the war and the number of 40-mm guns was successively reduced. (The NEW JERSEY carried only nine 16-inch and 20 5-inch guns during her brief Vietnam reactivation.) Postwar plans to provide twin 3-inch/50-cal AA mounts in place of the quad 40-mm mounts were abandoned.

Four of the original ten 5-inch/38-cal twin gun mounts were removed during the ships' reactivation in the 1980s. Four Phalanx Gatling-type guns were also provided for anti-ship missile defense.

Manning: The NEW JERSEY recommissioning in 1982 marked the first time that Marines had served in a U.S. battleship since the Korean War. The World War II manning of this class was 2,500 to 2,900 men per ship.

Missiles: During the 1970s there was a proposal to provide the IOWAs with the Aegis/SPY-1 AAW weapons system. However, it was discarded at the time as being too costly and was not considered when the ships were recommissioned in the early 1980s. When reactivation plans were being prepared in the 1980s, it was intended to fit the Sea Sparrow Point Defense Missile System (PDMS). However, it was determined that the system could not withstand the overpressure when the 16-inch guns were fired.

Modernization: When reactivated, these ships underwent a limited modernization, including updated communications and radar equipment; sewage holding tanks and habitability features were provided. The Phalanx CIWS defensive system as well as Harpoon and Tomahawk offensive missiles were fitted.

A Phase II modernization was to have added additional Tomahawks fired from vertical launchers, removing the after 16-inch gun turret, and making other upgrades. This proposal was dropped in 1983. (Also proposed was fitting a flight deck aft for VSTOL aircraft operations.)

There have been several proposals to fit these ships as numbered-fleet flagships; however, they have not been so modified or employed.

The IOWA and WISCONSIN were modernized at the Avondale and Litton/Ingalls shipyards.

Operational: All four ships of the class saw extensive combat in the later stages of World War II, mainly as AAW defense ships for fast carriers; in the Korean War (1950–1953), they served primarily as shore bombardment ships. They also served as fleet and force flagships in those conflicts.

The MISSOURI, named for the home state of President Harry S. Truman, was the scene of the Japanese surrender ceremony in Tokyo Bay on 2 September 1945, officially marking the end of World War

---

4. The arguments for recommissioning IOWA-class battleships are found in John F. Lehman, Jr., and William L. Stearman, "Keep the Big Guns," U.S. Naval Institute *Proceedings* (January 2000), pp. 43–47.

The IOWA moored at Newport, R.I., with the carrier FORRESTAL (CV 59) behind her. Both ships probably will become memorial-museums. Note how the carrier's superstructure towers over that of the dreadnought. (1999)

II. Three ships were mothballed after the war, with the MISSOURI retained in partial commission as a training ship.

During her 1968–1969 reactivation for the Vietnam War, the NEW JERSEY made one deployment to the Western Pacific. She was on the "gun line" off South Vietnam for 120 days, during which she fired 5,688 rounds of 16-inch ammunition and 14,891 5-inch rounds. (The NEW JERSEY fired a total of 6,200 main-battery rounds in her 1968–1969 commission, including test and training; by comparison, she fired 771 rounds from 1943 to 1948, and 6,671 during her participation in the Korean War and midshipman cruises from 1950–1957.)

The NEW JERSEY deployed to the Western Pacific in June 1983, but shortly after arrival in the Far East she was ordered to stand off Central America and on 12 September 1983 she transited the Panama Canal into the Caribbean. Later that month she made a hurried trip across the Atlantic and through the Mediterranean to operate off the coast of war-torn Lebanon. The NEW JERSEY fired her 16-inch guns against shore targets near Beirut for the first time on 14 December 1983.

The IOWA suffered an explosion in her No. 2 16-inch gun turret on 19 April 1989, while the ship was operating some 330 n.miles (610 km) off Puerto Rico. One officer and 46 enlisted men in the turret and belowdecks projectile-handling spaces were killed in the explosion and flash fire; 11 sailors in lower powder magazines escaped without harm and those spaces were partially flooded to prevent a powder explosion, which most likely would have destroyed the ship. The damaged gun—center gun of No. 2 turret—was not repaired before the ship was mothballed.

The Navy's investigations concluded that the most probable cause of the disaster was a sabotage-suicide effort by a sailor in the turret. However, subsequent investigation, mainly by the Sandia National Laboratories, concluded that the "foreign materials" that the Navy found in the turret that exploded were normal to battleship turrets, the powder bags were overrammed against the

projectile, and the powder bags were sensitive in that condition. This led to an official Navy apology to the family of the sailor who had been implicated.

The parts needed to rehabilitate the IOWA's No. 2 turret are available with the cost of the repairs estimated at about $8 million. The ships' other guns are in good condition. (Barrel relining is generally needed after firing some 1,500 rounds per barrel. The highest number of rounds fired by any of the guns in the IOWA or WISCONSIN is 418.) There are plenty of shells and powder available: three "shipfills" per ship (i.e., 1,280 16-inch rounds) plus powder, and enough ammunition for two years of training.

The WISCONSIN and MISSOURI participated in Operation Desert Storm in January–February 1991. Operating in the Persian Gulf, the MISSOURI fired 759 16-inch rounds and launched 28 Tomahawk cruise missiles and the WISCONSIN fired 319 16-inch rounds and launched 24 missiles. (Thus 18 percent of the 288 Tomahawks launched in the conflict were from the two battleships.)

During their 1980s reactivation period, the four battleships fired the following 16-inch rounds (Desert Storm included):

IOWA	2,034
NEW JERSEY	2,983
MISSOURI	2,602
WISCONSIN	1,408

The last ship to decommission, the MISSOURI, was present at Pearl Harbor on 7 December 1991 for the commemoration of the 50th anniversary of the Japanese attack that caused American entry into World War II. Subsequently, she steamed into the Long Beach (Calif.) Naval Shipyard on 21 December 1991 for deactivation. She was decommissioned there on 31 March 1992 and then towed to the Bremerton (Wash.) Naval Shipyard for storage until the decision was made by the Secretary of the Navy to permanently moor her at Pearl Harbor.

TABLE 14-1. "IOWA"-CLASS ACTIVE SERVICE

Number	Name	World War II	Korean War	Vietnam War	600-ship fleet
BB 61	IOWA	22 Feb 1943–24 Mar 1949	25 Aug 1951–24 Feb 1958	—	28 Apr 1984–26 Oct 1990
BB 62	NEW JERSEY	23 May 1943–30 June 1948	21 Nov 1950–21 Aug 1957	6 Apr 1968–17 Dec 1969	28 Dec 1982–8 Feb 1991
BB 63	MISSOURI	11 June 1944 ⟵————————⟶ 26 Feb 1955		—	10 May 1986–31 Mar 1992
BB 64	WISCONSIN	16 Apr 1944–1 July 1948	3 Mar 1951–8 Mar 1958	—	22 Oct 1988–30 Sep 1991

The MISSOURI entering Pearl Harbor. She has been placed as a memorial-museum off Ford Island in the center of Pearl Harbor, adjacent to the ARIZONA Memorial. All four of the IOWA-class ships will be permanently moored at U.S. cities. They will bring to eight the number of battleships preserved in the United States. (1998, U.S. Navy, PH2 Kerry Baker)

The WISCONSIN being moored at the Norfolk Naval Shipyard (Portsmouth), Va., before being moored at the Nauticus maritime center in downtown Norfolk. The site of her permanent mooring, opposed by many area residents and businessmen, makes her the dominating feature of the Norfolk skyline. (1996, U.S. Navy, Capt. Robert J. Sitar)

CHAPTER 15

Cruisers and Destroyers

The Aegis missile cruiser THOMAS S. GATES launches an SM-1 Standard-MR missile during exercises in the Caribbean. The later ships of this class—fitted with Vertical Launching Systems (VLS)—are being considered for the theater and national ballistic missile defense roles. All 27 cruisers are scheduled for upgrades to enable them to serve well into the 21st century. (1999, U.S. Navy, JO2 David Rush)

The U.S. Navy is currently authorized a force level of 116 major surface combatants—cruisers, destroyers, and frigates. As of early 2001 the Navy had 27 cruisers and 52 destroyers in active service, in addition to frigates. The frigate force, which is shrinking rapidly, is described in chapter 16 of this edition of *Ships and Aircraft*.

The ARLEIGH BURKE class is in series production—the only major surface combatant now under construction for the U.S. Navy. The so-called Land Attack Destroyer (DD 21)—formerly called the Surface Combatant (SC) 21—is now being developed to succeed the BURKE class on the building ways. Navy long-range planning calls for a new "cruiser" design (CG 21) to follow the DD 21, with the lead ship being delivered in FY 2019.

Although the BURKE class was intended to replace several classes of older cruisers (CG/CGN) and destroyers, the retirements of older ships was accelerated with the end of the Cold War and the current production rate of just under three ships per year is too low to sustain the force goal of 110 to 116 surface combatants proposed by the Department of Defense since 1995.

The roles and configuration of cruisers and destroyers are essentially the same. The blurring of lines between the cruiser and destroyer categories can be seen by the TICONDEROGA class—the only U.S. cruisers now in active commission—which originally were designated as destroyers. The TICONDEROGAS have the same hull and propulsion plant and some of the same combat systems as the destroyers of the SPRUANCE and KIDD classes and essentially the same anti-air system as the ARLEIGH BURKE class. The term "cruiser" now indicates that the ship is commanded by a captain (rather than a commander, as in destroyers).[1]

Cruisers and destroyers have two principal roles: (1) screening carrier battle groups and (2) missile strikes against shore targets.

All U.S. guided missile cruisers (CG) and destroyers (DDG) now in service, except for the first five ships of the TICONDEROGA class, are fitted with Vertical Launching Systems (VLS) missiles, providing considerable weapons flexibility and firepower. Further, all ships of this category have the Aegis/SPY-1 radar and weapons control system. In addition, 24 SPRUANCE-class ships, which are specialized anti-submarine warfare ships, have been fitted with VLS for launching Tomahawk land-attack missiles.

In most respects the TICONDEROGA-class ships are the most capable surface combatants afloat. Their Aegis combat system is undoubtedly the best anti-air missile system in service with any navy, while the ships also have the most capable ASW suite available in the U.S. Navy, the same as in the SPRUANCE-class destroyers.

The 18 conventional cruisers of the LEAHY and BELKNAP classes have been discarded. Those ships, graceful in appearance and capable warships for their time, were decommissioned with the end of the Cold War (as were the Navy's nuclear-propelled cruisers; see below). Also stricken have been the four KIDD-class destroyers, the missile variant of the SPRUANCE class, and the seven SPRUANCE-class destroyers that were not refitted with VLS.

Builders: All U.S. cruisers and destroyers now in service were built by Bath Iron Works in Maine (now owned by General Dynamics) or Litton's Ingalls Shipbuilding yard at Pascagoula, Miss. The keel-laying date for the Ingalls-built ships is the date of the start of erection of the first module on the horizontal building position at the yard; the ships are lowered into the water on a floating dock (launching) and are formally christened at a later date.

Guns: All active cruisers and destroyers have 5-inch (127-mm) guns. No "gun ships" remain in commission; the last two heavy cruisers (CA)—armed with 8-inch (203-mm) guns—have been stricken. At the start of the battleship recommissioning program in the early 1980s, there were proposals to reactivate the two

surviving heavy cruisers, the DES MOINES (CA 134) and SALEM (CA 139), instead of or in addition to the battleships. The Navy rejected those proposals, preferring the larger guns of the more-impressive IOWA (BB 61)-class dreadnoughts. (The two mothballed heavy cruisers were stricken on 9 July 1991 and 12 July 1991, respectively.)

A longer-range 5-inch/62-cal Mk 45 Mod 4 gun fitted for firing advanced munitions is planned for new surface combatants and for retrofitting in older ships (see chapter 28). This weapon replaces the 175-mm gun and Vertical-Launch Gun (VLG) previously considered for the DD 21 class; the latter also is described in chapter 28. The 8-inch Major Caliber Lightweight Gun (MCLWG), at one time proposed for the entire SPRUANCE class, was terminated. The gun was successfully evaluated ashore and at sea in the destroyer HULL in 1975–1979.

During the 1980s and 1990s, cruisers have been fitted with .50-cal/7.62-mm machine guns, 20-mm cannon, and 25-mm Bushmaster Mk 38 "chain" guns for close-in defense against small craft. This armament is especially important for ships deploying into the Persian Gulf area. The weapons are shifted from ship to ship as they forward deploy; accordingly, they are not listed under the specific class entries.

Engineering: All U.S. cruisers and destroyers have aircraft-type gas turbine propulsion.

Names: U.S. cruisers traditionally had been named for major cities in the United States, with the significant exception of the CANBERRA (CA 70, later CAG 2) being named for an Australian cruiser sunk in 1942 while operating with U.S. forces. From 1971 to 1978, six cruisers (DLGN/CGN 36–41) were assigned state names. From 1981, cruisers have been named for famous American battles, although even this scheme was corrupted when the CG 51 was named for a deceased Secretary of the Navy and Secretary of Defense.

U.S. destroyers traditionally have been named for naval heroes and leaders, including deceased secretaries of the Navy, admirals, and inventors. In 1998 the DDG 80 was named ROOSEVELT, honoring President Franklin D. Roosevelt and—to be politically correct—his wife Eleanor. She is the first "first lady" to have a Navy ship named in her honor. (The 32nd president previously was honored by the carrier FRANKLIN D. ROOSEVELT/CVB 42, which was on the Naval Vessel Register from 1945 to 1972.) Historically, past presidents were honored by aircraft carriers (CV/CVN) and strategic missile submarines (SSBN), except for the naming of an attack submarine JIMMY CARTER (SSN 23). Both the DDG 80 and SSN 23 were named by Secretary of the Navy John Dalton (1993–1998).

TABLE 15-1.   CRUISER-DESTROYER FORCE LEVELS (EARLY 2001)

Number	Class/Ship	Comm.	Active	Building*
CG 47	TICONDEROGA	1983–1994	27	—
DDG 51	ARLEIGH BURKE	1991–	30	20
DD 963	SPRUANCE	1975–1983	22	—

* Includes ships authorized through fiscal 2001.

AIR DEFENSE CRUISERS

A new class of "21st century air defense cruisers" (CG 21 design) was identified by the Navy in January 2000. In response to a congressional request for a 30-year shipbuilding forecast, the Navy revealed a long-range proposal for 27 advanced air defense ships to provide a one-for-one replacement of the 27 TICONDEROGA-class Aegis cruisers.

The new cruisers will be built around a new radar, intended to succeed the SPY-1 systems of the Aegis warships. The highly tentative, long-range proposal provides for the lead CG 21 to be funded in fiscal year 2014, followed by two ships in FY 2016 and then three ships annually from FY 2017 through 2024. The lead ship would join the fleet about 2018, at which time the TICONDEROGA would be 35 years old.

---

1. Five nations now have warships rated as cruisers in their fleets: Italy (1 ship), Peru (1), Russia (approx. 7), Ukraine (1), and the United States. The ambiguous "cruiser" category should include two French ships of the SUFFREN class previously rated as "frigates" (DLG); they displace some 6,900 tons full load. No nation currently is building ships rated as "cruisers."

AEGIS COMBAT SYSTEM

The Aegis combat system (Mk 7) is the Navy's primary anti-air/anti-missile warfare system, now provided in U.S. cruisers and destroyers, and some Allied warships.[2] Aegis is the most advanced anti-air system in existence, land-based or naval. During the development of Aegis, a National Security Council study identified "the high priority need of the U.S. Navy for adequate defense against an increasingly sophisticated Soviet anti-ship missile threat."[3] The study went on to report that "the deployment of the Aegis system would offset a primary deficiency in fleet capabilities."

The Aegis system includes the SPY-1 radar, Mk 99 fire control directors (which incorporate the SPG-62 radar), and related computers, displays, weapon control consoles, and power sources. Each of the four SPY-1 fixed antennas or arrays covers over 90° in azimuth from the horizon to zenith as the ship rolls up to 30° and pitches up to 10°. These arrays are about 12½ feet (3.8 m) across with 4,480 energy-radiating elements fixed into each antenna "face."

With conventional, rotating radar antennas, targets are "painted" once each rotation or scan to provide a single positional datum point. Several scans—perhaps requiring 10 to 30 seconds—are required to establish course, speed, altitude, and rate of change of the target. In the Aegis system, computers schedule the pencil-like search beams from the arrays to seek out targets; when a beam dwells on a target the computers schedule several additional beams against the target within a second of initial detection. Thus, a continuous track of the target can be established before a conventional radar antenna could complete a single rotation. The SPY-1 accordingly functions as both a search radar and a fire-control radar, alleviating the time and possible target track loss in a "handover" process between conventional radars. (See chapter 29 for additional details.)

A land-based, partial prototype of the Aegis combat system was installed at the (then) RCA facility at Moorestown, N.J., and shipboard trials were conducted on the missile test ship NORTON SOUND (AVM 1, ex-AV 11).

The Aegis program office in the Naval Sea Systems Command has established its own classification of Aegis ships with variations known as "baselines." The following are the principal baseline characteristics; note that there are some system overlaps in the TICONDEROGA-class cruisers.

Baseline 0: cruisers CG 47, 48	SPY-1A radar Mk 26 launchers UYK-7 computers SH-2F LAMPS I helicopter
Baseline 1: cruisers CG 49–51	SPY-1A radar Mk 26 launchers UYK-7 computers SH-60B LAMPS III helicopter
Baseline 2: cruisers CG 52–58	VLS/Tomahawk SQQ-89 ASW system
Baseline 3: cruisers CG 59–64	SPY-1B radar improved communications
Baseline 4: cruisers CG 65–73	SPY-1B(V) radar SQS-53C sonar UYK-43/44 computers
destroyers DDG 51–67	SPY-1D radar SQS-53C sonar UYK-43/44 computers
Baseline 5: destroyers DDG 68–78	SLQ-32(V)3 EW suite Standard SM-2 Block IV missile JTIDS[4] Combat Direction Finding (DF)
Baseline 6: destroyers DDG 79–90	SPY-1D(V) littoral mod helicopter hangar Evolved Sea Sparrow Missile (ESSM) Theater Ballistic Missile Defense (TBMD) Cooperative Engagement Capability (CEC) UYK-70 displays SM-2 Block IVA (DD 85–90)
Baseline 7: destroyers DDG 91–107	Tomahawk FCS upgrade Theater-Wide TBMD

Beyond the U.S. TICONDEROGA and ARLEIGH BURKE classes of surface combatants, Aegis is being fitted in Japanese and Spanish warships and may be fitted in South Korean ships.

Historical: Aegis evolved from the Typhon anti-aircraft combat system, whose development had begun in 1958 to defend against advanced Soviet aircraft and air-to-surface missiles. Typhon, however, was canceled in 1963 because of technical difficulties and the high cost of the system, which was intended for large, nuclear-propelled "frigates" (DLGN).[5]

The follow-on Advanced Surface Missile System (ASMS) made use of some Typhon technology and sought to use existing missiles—the Terrier, Tartar, and their descendent SM-series. Although development was slower than expected, ASMS became the basis for the Aegis combat system, whose development formally began in December 1969.

BALLISTIC MISSILE DEFENSE

Cruisers and destroyers fitted with the Aegis combat system will have a major role in U.S. development of ballistic missile defense systems. The proliferation of ballistic missile technology—with more than 20 nations now having some form of ballistic or cruise missiles—has sparked a renewed interest in missile defense. In response, the Department of Defense is sponsoring the development of both Theater Air and Missile Defense (TAMD) and National Missile Defense (NMD) programs.

The emphasis in this weapons area is on TAMD systems to protect forward-deployed U.S. forces, as well as allied and friendly forces. This plan envisions time-phased acquisition of multi-tier, interoperable missile defense systems to provide in-depth defense against theater ballistic and cruise missiles. Within this program, the so-called lower-tier systems have the highest priority to defeat short-range ballistic missiles. The Navy's Area Defense System and the Army's Patriot Advanced Capability–3 (PAC-3) are the principal lower-tier programs. (The Air Force also proposes an airborne laser defense program, with five long-endurance aircraft being able to provide two aircraft on 24-hour patrols in a theater; a modified Boeing 747-400 is the proposed aircraft.)

The Navy's Area Defense System will use a reconfigured SPY-1 radar and an upgraded version of the Standard Missile (SM-2 Block IV-A) in existing Aegis warships. This system promises to provide a high degree of effectiveness against ballistic and cruise missile threats in forward coastal areas. Low-rate initial production of Block IV-A missiles began in FY 2000 to support development and operational testing prior to an operational capability expected in FY 2003. Current planning provides for the procurement of 1,500 ship-launched missiles, to be Block IV-A missiles with a new infrared seeker, an adjunct forward-looking fuze, and an improved autopilot.

2. In Greek mythology, Aegis was the name of the shield of Zeus.
3. Quoted in Rear Adm. Wayne E. Meyer, USN, and Capt. Bart Dalla Mura, USN, "Aegis," U.S. Naval Institute *Proceedings* (February 1977), p. 97. Adm. Meyer was head of the Aegis program from 1970 to 1983.
4. JTIDS = Joint Tactical Information Distribution System.
5. The missile test ship NORTON SOUND was fitted with components of the Typhon system and, subsequently, with portions of the later ASMS/Aegis combat system.

(The FY 2000 budget provides for the procurement of 32 PAC-3 missiles and for the first Army unit to be established the following year. The PAC-3 development effort suffered numerous failures and setbacks before scoring two successful intercepts of target missiles in 1999. Obviously the PAC-3 program requires the development and deployment of new radars and fire control systems, and the establishment of new missile-defense units.

(A follow-on lower-tier program in development is the Medium Extended Air Defense System [MEADS] being pursued cooperatively with Germany and Italy. This is planned as a highly mobile missile defense system for use with ground troops. The use of components of the PAC-3 program is expected to reduce costs and development time for the MEADS effort. However, Congress denied the entire $48,500,000 asked by the Clinton administration in the FY 2000 budget request, apparently because of the lack of support by senior military officers.)

Upper-tier missile defense systems, called the Theater High-Altitude Area Defense (THAAD) and Navy Theater-Wide (NTW) systems, are intended to intercept incoming ballistic missiles at high altitudes, permitting the defense of larger areas. The latter also builds on the Aegis combat system, as well as the Navy Area Defense System. Developmental testing of both THAAD and NTW is planned through 2001. The Navy tests include a specialized Aegis-controlled lightweight exoatmospheric projectile.

Both systems will be examined after tests and, based on that assessment, the Department of Defense will allocate upper-tier resources to focus on the more successful system. The objective will be to field an upper-tier defensive system between 2007 and 2010. (The deployment of the upper-tier system could force opponents to rely more on cruise missiles, forcing the deployment of an extensive cruise missile defense system.)

In 1999 a proposal was put forward whereby four TICONDEROGA-class ships would receive an NTW capability consisting of an upgraded Aegis combat system, with a high-powered discriminator radar, and 20 SM-3 versions of the Standard missile per ship. This plan provides for the initial test ship to become operational by 2006, with a fully operational ship to be available the following year.

The SM-3 is an evolved SM-2 Block IV-A booster and sustainer motor supplemented by a third-stage rocket motor and a fourth stage kinetic kill vehicle. The kill vehicle will be guided by an infrared focal-plane array seeker.

The National Missile Defense program is oriented toward the possibility that in the future a rogue nation might possess intercontinental ballistic missiles that could threaten the United States. This possibility, according to the Secretary of Defense, was underscored by the August 1998 attempt by North Korea to launch a satellite on a Taepo Dong–1 (TD-1) missile.[6] That test, which demonstrated some important aspects of ICBM development, most notably multistage separation, showed that North Korea continues to be interested in developing a long-range missile capability. While the U.S. intelligence community had expected a TD-1 launch for some time, it did not anticipate that the missile would have a third stage nor that it would be used to attempt to place a satellite in orbit.

Accordingly, an NMD program is being funded for research and development. On 29 June 1999, President Bill Clinton signed the National Missile Defense Act, which makes it U.S. policy to deploy an NMD system as soon as it becomes technology feasible. The NMD system being developed would have as its primary mission the defense of the United States—all 50 states—against a small number of intercontinental missiles. It would not be capable of defending against a large-scale missile attack.

An initial operational capability for the NMD is proposed for FY 2003. The Department of Defense official in charge of the program has stated that it would be unlikely for a sea-based NMD using the SM-3 missile to be at sea before 2010 or 2011, adding, "The most practical and effective NMD role for a Navy Theater-Wide system

would be to supplement land-based NMD."[7] Rather, the NMD would most likely be a land- or space-based system. The Air Force has proposed a space-based laser system for this role.

Cost: Through 1999, the Navy had spent about $1 *billion* on research, development, and studies related to shipboard ballistic missile defense employing the Aegis combat system. Costs for a limited ABM system deployment range from $2 to $4 *billion*, while a full, national defense system based on Aegis ships would cost up to $19 *billion*, although such estimates are preliminary. (By comparison, a "full" land-based ABM system is said to cost about $10.5 *billion*.)

COOPERATIVE ENGAGEMENT CAPABILITY

The Cooperative Engagement Capability (CEC) is a program to improve battle group Anti-Air Warfare (AAW) and Theater Air Defense (TAD) capabilities by integrating the radar data of several ships and aircraft into a single, real-time, fire-control-quality composite track picture available to all participating ships and aircraft. By simultaneously distributing radar data on airborne threats to each ship within the battle group, CEC extends the range at which a ship can engage hostile missiles to well beyond the radar horizon, significantly improving area, local, and self-defense capabilities. Operating under the direction of a designated commander, CEC will enable a battle group or joint force to act as a single defensive combat system.

The initial CEC operational capability was declared in fiscal year 1996 after a series of tests involving the Aegis cruisers ANZIO and CAPE ST. GEORGE, the aircraft carrier ENTERPRISE (CVN 65), the amphibious assault ship WASP (LHD 1), and P-3C Orion patrol aircraft. The Navy put to sea additional operational CEC systems in 1998 in the Aegis cruisers HUE CITY and VICKSBURG, the carrier JOHN F. KENNEDY (CV 67), and four E-2C Hawkeye radar aircraft. However, the CEC installations in the ANZIO and CAPE ST. GEORGE caused major computer "crashes" and the ships were inoperative for some 16 months while the problems were corrected.

The total CEC-capable force in 2007 is expected to consist of 12 aircraft carriers, 65 Aegis cruisers and destroyers, 12 non-Aegis destroyers, 12 LHA/LHD-type amphibious ships, and 23 LPD/LSD-type amphibious ships, plus E-2C Hawkeye and P-3C Orion aircraft.

NUCLEAR PROPULSION

All nine nuclear-propelled cruisers (CGN) have been stricken, some significantly before the end of their postulated 30-year service life. Their limited weapons systems and the high cost of nuclear refueling led to their premature disposal (i.e., none had VLS, Aegis, or ASW helicopter capability). The decommissioning of the nuclear cruiser force means that the Navy's nuclear-propelled aircraft carriers operate with only oil-burning screening ships.

The nine cruisers and their age at time of decommissioning are indicated below; see table 15-2 for commissioning and decommissioning dates.

		Age at retirement
CGN 9	LONG BEACH	37.9 years
CGN 25	BAINBRIDGE	33.9 years
CGN 35	TRUXTUN	28.3 years
CGN 36	CALIFORNIA	25.5 years
CGN 37	SOUTH CAROLINA	24.8 years
CGN 38	VIRGINIA	18.2 years
CGN 39	TEXAS	15.8 years
CGN 40	MISSISSIPPI	19.0 years
CGN 41	ARKANSAS	17.7 years

The Reagan administration had included a nuclear-propelled cruiser in the last year of the fiscal 1983–1987 shipbuilding plan, but that ship "slipped" into oblivion. According to Navy officials, the

6. Secretary of Defense William S. Cohen, *Annual Report to the President and the Congress* (Washington, D.C., 1999), p. 74. In the 1998 flight test, the TD-1 missile traveled 3,400 n.miles (6,300 km); unofficial estimates contend that a three-stage version of the TD series could travel 4,900 n.miles (9,080 km) with a nuclear warhead.

7. John Harvey, Deputy Assistant Secretary of Defense for Nuclear Forces and Missile Defense Policy, 26 July 1999, quoted in Keith J. Costa, "Citing Secret Study, DoD Official Says Navy NMD Role Unlikely by 2005," *Inside Missile Defense* (11 August 1999), pp. 18–19.

The last nuclear-propelled cruiser in active service was the SOUTH CAROLINA, decommissioned with her sister ship CALIFORNIA in 1999. The nine DLGN/ CGNs, completed between 1962 and 1980, operated primarily as carrier escorts. The latter ships lacked the advanced radars and missile systems of the conventionally propelled Aegis cruisers. (1991, Giorgio Arra)

ship was placed in the long-range program for "planning purposes" and will not be pursued in the near future.

Other than the LONG BEACH, the Navy's nuclear-propelled cruisers were large destroyer or "frigate" (DLGN)-type ships that had been reclassified as cruisers in 1975. The LONG BEACH was the only new-construction cruiser completed by the U.S. Navy in the post–World War II period.

A planned strike cruiser (CSGN) was an outgrowth of the DLGN concept, developed in 1973–1974 as an enlarged carrier escort ship intended specifically to carry the Aegis combat system. They were to have had a full-load displacement of more than 17,000 tons. Up to four CSGNs were considered necessary to screen each carrier.

The cost of the lead strike cruiser in fiscal 1976 was estimated at $1.371 *billion*; the ship was to have been completed in December 1983. After the ship was ignored by Congress, the Naval Sea Systems Command hurriedly developed a strike cruiser Mk II design retaining the same armament but with a flight deck added, presenting a superficial similarity to the Soviet KIEV-class VTOL carriers (see 13th Edition/pages 136–137 for additional details).

The earlier Typhon combat system, precursor to Aegis, was to be fitted in large, nuclear-propelled frigates (DLGN). These ships were to displace approximately 12,000 tons full load in their largest configuration. The lead ship was planned for the FY 1963 shipbuilding program.

The Navy's nuclear propulsion community had long sought all-nuclear escorts for aircraft carriers—up to four cruiser-type ships of 10,000 tons or more for each nuclear carrier. Advocacy by Admiral H. G. Rickover, then head of naval nuclear propulsion, led to Congress specifying in the FY 1975 defense legislation that all future major combatants would have nuclear propulsion (Title VIII of the FY 1975 Military Appropriation Authorization Act, Public Law 93-365, 88 Statute 408).

In the event, the last U.S. nuclear-propelled cruiser was authorized in FY 1975. All subsequent major combatants (cruisers and destroyers) have been gas-turbine-propelled. The only other nation to construct nuclear-propelled surface combatants has been the Soviet Union, completing four ships of the 28,000-ton KIROV class from 1980 to 1996.[8]

See 16th Edition/pages 115–119 for final CGN characteristics.

---

8. The four Soviet nuclear ships underwent name changes with the end of the Soviet regime:

ADMIRAL USHAKOV (ex-KIROV)	comm. 1980
ADMIRAL LAZAREV (ex-FRUNZE)	comm. 1984
ADMIRAL NAKHIMOV (ex-KALININ)	comm. 1988
PETR VELIKIY (ex–YURI ANDROPOV)	comm. 1996

See N. Polmar, *Guide to the Soviet Navy*, 5th Edition (Annapolis, Md.: Naval Institute Press, 1991), pp. 148–152.

The JOHN S. MCCAIN, named for the admiral who commanded the U.S. fast carrier force in World War II and his son, commander in chief of U.S. forces in the Pacific during the Korean War—respectively, the grandfather and father of the U.S. senator of the same name. Unlike most modern cruisers and destroyers, these ships lack a helicopter hangar. (1999, U.S. Navy, PH2 John Collins)

CRUISERS

22 GUIDED MISSILE CRUISERS: IMPROVED "TICONDEROGA" CLASS

Number	Name	FY	Builder	Laid down	Launched	Christened	Commissioned	Status
CG 52	BUNKER HILL	82	Litton/Ingalls, Pascagoula, Miss.	11 Jan 1984	11 Mar 1985	19 Apr 1985	20 Sep 1986	**PA**
CG 53	MOBILE BAY	82	Litton/Ingalls, Pascagoula, Miss.	6 June 1984	22 Aug 1985	12 Oct 1985	21 Feb 1987	**PA**
CG 54	ANTIETAM	83	Litton/Ingalls, Pascagoula, Miss.	15 Nov 1984	14 Feb 1986	19 Apr 1986	6 June 1987	**PA**
CG 55	LEYTE GULF	83	Litton/Ingalls, Pascagoula, Miss.	18 Mar 1985	20 June 1986	11 Oct 1986	26 Sep 1987	**AA**
CG 56	SAN JACINTO	83	Litton/Ingalls, Pascagoula, Miss.	24 July 1985	14 Nov 1986	24 Jan 1987	23 Jan 1988	**AA**
CG 57	LAKE CHAMPLAIN	84	Litton/Ingalls, Pascagoula, Miss.	3 Mar 1986	3 Apr 1987	25 Apr 1987	12 Aug 1988	**PA**
CG 58	PHILIPPINE SEA	84	Bath Iron Works, Maine	8 May 1986	12 July 1987	—	18 Mar 1989	**AA**
CG 59	PRINCETON	84	Litton/Ingalls, Pascagoula, Miss.	15 Oct 1986	25 Sep 1987	17 Oct 1987	11 Feb 1989	**PA**
CG 60	NORMANDY	85	Bath Iron Works, Maine	7 Apr 1987	19 Mar 1988	—	9 Dec 1989	**AA**
CG 61	MONTEREY	85	Bath Iron Works, Maine	19 Aug 1987	23 Oct 1988	—	16 June 1990	**AA**
CG 62	CHANCELLORSVILLE	85	Litton/Ingalls, Pascagoula, Miss.	24 June 1987	15 July 1988	23 July 1988	4 Nov 1989	**PA**
CG 63	COWPENS	86	Bath Iron Works, Maine	23 Dec 1987	11 Mar 1989	—	9 Mar 1991	**PA**
CG 64	GETTYSBURG	86	Bath Iron Works, Maine	17 Aug 1988	22 July 1989	—	22 June 1991	**AA**
CG 65	CHOSIN	86	Litton/Ingalls, Pascagoula, Miss.	22 July 1988	1 Sep 1989	14 Oct 1989	12 Jan 1991	**PA**
CG 66	HUE CITY	87	Litton/Ingalls, Pascagoula, Miss.	20 Feb 1988	1 June 1990	21 July 1990	14 Sep 1991	**AA**
CG 67	SHILOH	87	Bath Iron Works, Maine	1 Aug 1989	8 Sep 1990	—	18 July 1992	**PA**
CG 68	ANZIO	87	Litton/Ingalls, Pascagoula, Miss.	21 Aug 1989	2 Nov 1990	10 Nov 1990	2 May 1992	**AA**
CG 69	VICKSBURG	88	Litton/Ingalls, Pascagoula, Miss.	30 May 1990	2 Aug 1991	12 Oct 1991	14 Nov 1992	**AA**
CG 70	LAKE ERIE	88	Bath Iron Works, Maine	6 Mar 1990	13 July 1991	—	24 July 1993	**PA**
CG 71	CAPE ST. GEORGE	88	Litton/Ingalls, Pascagoula, Miss.	19 Nov 1990	10 Jan 1992	13 June 1992	12 June 1993	**AA**
CG 72	VELLA GULF	88	Litton/Ingalls, Pascagoula, Miss.	22 Apr 1991	30 May 1992	25 July 1992	18 Sep 1993	**AA**
CG 73	PORT ROYAL	88	Litton/Ingalls, Pascagoula, Miss.	20 Nov 1991	20 Nov 1992	5 Dec 1992	9 July 1994	**PA**

Displacement:	8,910 tons standard	Radars:	SPS-49(V)6/7/8 air search
	9,466 tons full load		SPS-55 surface search
Length:	532⅔ feet (162.4 m) waterline		SPS-64(V)9 navigation
	567 feet (172.9 m) overall		(4) SPY-1A multifunction in CG 52–58
Beam:	55 feet (16.75 m)		(4) SPY-1B multifunction in CG 59–73
Draft:	31½ feet (9.6 m)	Sonars:	CG 52–55: SQS-53A bow-mounted
Propulsion:	4 gas turbines (General Electric LM 2500); 80,000 shp; 2 shafts		CG 56–67: SQS-53B bow-mounted
Speed:	30+ knots		CG 68–73: SQS-53C bow-mounted
Range:	6,000 n.miles (11,110 km) at 20 knots		SQR-19 TACTAS
Manning:	387 (28 officers + 359 enlisted) + LAMPS detachment	Fire control:	1 Mk 7 Aegis combat system
Helicopters:	2 SH-60B Seahawk LAMPS III		1 Mk 86 GFCS with SPQ-9A radar
Missiles:	2 61-cell VLS for Standard-MR SM-2/Tomahawk/VLA (ASROC)		4 Mk 99 missile directors with SPG-62 radar
	(122 weapons) Mk 41 Mod 0		1 Mk 116 ASW FCS
	8 Harpoon SSM Mk 141 (2 quad canisters)		SQQ-89(V)3 ASW system in CG 54–73
Guns:	2 5-inch (127-mm) 54-cal DP Mk 45 (2 single)		SWG-1 (Harpoon)
	2 20-mm Phalanx CIWS Mk 16 (2 multibarrel)		SWG-3 (Tomahawk)
	several light machine guns or cannon	EW systems:	SLQ-25 Nixie
ASW weapons:	VLA (ASROC)		SLQ-32(V)3
	6 12.75-inch (324-mm) torpedo tubes Mk 32 (2 triple) for Mk 46 and Mk 50 torpedoes		

These later TICONDEROGA-class cruisers differ from the first five ships in having the Vertical Launch System (VLS) for missiles. The VLS permits them to carry Tomahawk missiles, providing a land-attack capability, as well as more missiles (122 compared to 88) than in the earlier ships (see TICONDEROGA class, below). These are the world's most-capable AAW ships, developed to provide carrier battle group defense against aircraft and anti-ship missiles. In addition, the ships have substantial ASW capabilities.

The Ingalls-built ships are launched from a floating dock; their christening—public relations—ceremony is held at a later date.

The CHANCELLORSVILLE, COWPENS, and VINCENNES (see below) are homeported in Yokosuka, Japan, the only U.S. cruisers based in another country. They are part of the KITTY HAWK (CV 63) carrier battle group.

All 22 ships of this class are planned for the Cruiser Upgrade Program. A variety of weapon and electronic updates are being considered, as well as modernization of the ships' hull, propulsion, and electrical systems.

Class: This is the largest cruiser class built by any Navy in the post–World War II period. The only other cruiser class of this size built by any nation was the 27-ship CLEVELAND (CL 55) class built for the U.S. Navy, completed 1942–1945 (another nine ships were completed as light aircraft carriers [CVL]).

When conceived, the TICONDEROGA class was intended to complement the nuclear-propelled strike cruiser (CSGN), which also was to be fitted with the Aegis AAW system. However, Congress refused to fund the strike cruiser and only the conventionally propelled Aegis ships were built. The Aegis system subsequently was fitted in the ARLEIGH BURKE–class destroyers.

Missiles: The VLS provides these ships with a Tomahawk launch capability. The BUNKER HILL was the first U.S. naval ship, other than the missile test ship NORTON SOUND and experimental surface effect ship SES-100B, to launch a missile at sea from a VLS installation, on 20 May 1986.

Some of these ships will be fitted with the Navy's sea-based Theater Ballistic Missile Defense (TBMD) system, which will employ the Standard SM-2 Block IV-A missile, as a forward, high-altitude interceptor against theater ballistic missile attacks. The LAKE ERIE and PORT ROYAL will be the first ships fitted with TBMD, to conduct at-sea systems tests, help develop doctrine and tactics, and train personnel in TBMD operations.

Modernization: A proposed update for this class includes the provision of 5-foot (1.5-m) blisters on either side along about three-fifths of the ship length; this would provide additional side protection from anti-ship missiles. The shear line of the weather deck would also be raised. The blisters would increase displacement but would reduce maximum speed by less than one knot.

Names: Most of these ship names remember World War II–era aircraft carriers of the ESSEX (CV 9) and INDEPENDENCE (CVL 22) classes (also see WASP/LHD 1–class amphibious ships). The CG 66 is the second U.S. warship to be named for a battle of the Vietnam War; the PELELIU (LHA 5) was originally named DA NANG, but that ship was renamed on 15 February 1978, after the fall of the Republic of South Vietnam to communist forces.

The CG 69 was originally PORT ROYAL; this was changed while under construction. (The CG 65 and 66 did not trade names, as reported in a previous edition.)

Operational: Seven ships of this class fired 105 Tomahawk missiles during Operation Desert Storm (1991):

BUNKER HILL	28 missiles
MOBILE BAY	22 missiles
LEYTE GULF	2 missiles
SAN JACINTO	14 missiles
PHILIPPINE SEA	10 missiles
PRINCETON	3 missiles
NORMANDY	26 missiles

These missiles represented 36 percent of the Tomahawks fired during the conflict.

During the Gulf War, on 18 February 1991 the PRINCETON struck a bottom-laid influence mine that damaged the ship (a second mine was detonated by the explosion of the first). The damage to the PRINCETON required her being towed to port, although at no time was the ship in danger of sinking and most of her combat systems remained operational. (The ship could have proceeded under her own power, but the commanding officer decided on the tow to avoid strain on the ship's hull until an examination could be made in a dockyard.) Repairs were made during a seven-week "availability" at Dubai in the United Arab Emirates, followed by a two-month yard period in the United States.

On 26 June 1993 another 23 Tomahawk missiles were launched against targets in Iraq, nine by the cruiser CHANCELLORSVILLE (and 14 by the destroyer PETERSON).

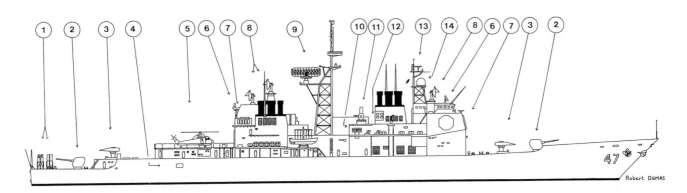

Guided Missile Cruiser TICONDEROGA

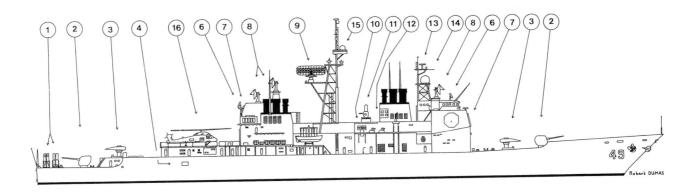

Guided Missile Cruiser VINCENNES

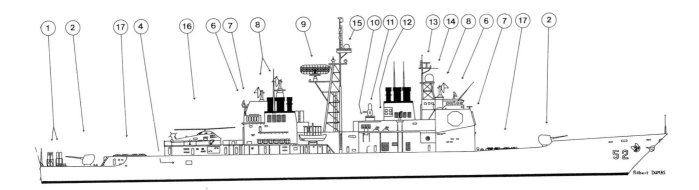

Guided Missile Cruiser BUNKER HILL

1. Harpoon missile canisters (8) 2. 5-inch DP single gun mount (2) 3. surface-to-air missile launcher Mk 26 (2) 4. 12.75-inch triple torpedo tubes Mk 32 (2) 5. SH-2F LAMPS I helicopter 6. OE-82 Satellite Communications (SATCOM) antenna (2) 7. SPY-1 fixed-array radar (4) 8. SPG-62 radar illuminator (4) 9. SPS-49(V)6 air search radar 10. SLQ-32(V)3 Electronic Countermeasures (ECM) (2) 11. Phalanx Close-In Weapon System (2) 12. SUBROC decoy launcher Mk 36 13. SPS-55 surface search radar 14. SPQ-9A surface/gunfire control radar 15. SPS-64(V)9 navigation radar 16. SH-60B LAMPS III helicopter 17. Vertical launching system Mk 41 (2) *Note:* SH-2F LAMPS I is no longer in service. (Robert Dumas)

The cruiser ANTIETAM in Hawaiian waters. These ships will form the backbone of Navy participation in ballistic missile defense efforts. Her missile batteries are located between the 5-inch gun mounts (forward and aft) and the superstructure. (1998, U.S. Navy, PH1 James G. McCarter)

The cruiser ANZIO (left) shows the origins of the Aegis cruiser design as she rests alongside the destroyer HAYLER, the last SPRUANCE-class destroyer. The massive superstructures of these ships give them a large Radar Cross-Section (RCS). (1994, Leo Van Ginderen)

The SAN JACINTO steams in the Persian Gulf, a major operating area of U.S. warships for more than two decades. An SH-60B Seahawk helicopter sits on her flight deck. (1998, U.S. Navy, PH1 James Williams)

5 GUIDED MISSILE CRUISERS: "TICONDEROGA" CLASS

Number	Name	FY	Builder	Laid down	Launched	Christened	Commissioned	Status
CG 47	TICONDEROGA	78	Litton/Ingalls, Pascagoula, Miss.	21 Jan 1980	25 Apr 1981	16 May 1981	22 Jan 1983	**AA**
CG 48	YORKTOWN	80	Litton/Ingalls, Pascagoula, Miss.	19 Oct 1981	17 Jan 1983	16 Apr 1983	4 July 1984	**AA**
CG 49	VINCENNES	81	Litton/Ingalls, Pascagoula, Miss.	20 Oct 1982	14 Jan 1984	18 Apr 1984	6 July 1985	**PA**
CG 50	VALLEY FORGE	81	Litton/Ingalls, Pascagoula, Miss.	14 Apr 1983	23 June 1984	29 Sep 1984	11 Jan 1986	**PA**
CG 51	THOMAS S. GATES	82	Bath Iron Works, Maine	31 Aug 1984	14 Dec 1985	—	22 Aug 1987	**AA**

Displacement:	CG 47, 48 7,019 tons light	ASW weapons:	6 12.75-inch (324-mm) torpedo tubes Mk 32 (2 triple) for Mk 46
	CG 49–51 7,014 tons light		and Mk 50 torpedoes
	CG 47, 48 9,589 tons full load	Radars:	SPS-49(V)6/7/8 air search
	CG 49–51 9,407 tons full load		SPS-53 surface search
Length:	532⅔ feet (162.4 m) waterline		SPS-55 surface search
	567 feet (172.9 m) overall		SPS-64(V)9 navigation
Beam:	55 feet (16.75 m)		(4) SPY-1A multifunction
Draft:	31½ feet (9.6 m)	Sonars:	SQS-53A bow mounted
Propulsion:	4 gas turbines (General Electric LM 2500); 80,000 shp; 2 shafts		SQR-19 towed array
Speed:	30+ knots	Fire control:	1 Mk 7 Aegis combat system
Range:	6,000 n.miles (11,110 km) at 20 knots		1 Mk 86 GFCS with SPQ-9A radar
Manning:	380 (27 officers + 353 enlisted) + LAMPS detachment in CG 49–51		4 Mk 99 missile directors with SPG-62 radar
Helicopters:	2 SH-60B Seahawk LAMPS III in CG 49–51		1 Mk 116 ASW FCS
Missiles:	2 twin Mk 26 Mod 1 launchers for Standard-MR SM-2		SWG-1 (Harpoon)
	(88 weapons)		SWG-3 (Tomahawk)
	8 Harpoon SSM Mk 141 (2 quad canisters)	EW systems:	SLQ-25A Nixie
Guns:	2 5-inch (127-mm) 54-cal DP Mk 45 (2 single)		SLQ-32(V)3
	2 20-mm Phalanx CIWS Mk 16 (2 multibarrel)		
	several light machine guns or cannon		

These first five ships of the TICONDEROGA class have Mk 26 twin-arm missile launchers in lieu of the more-capable VLS in the later 22 ships.

The Ingalls-built ships are launched from a floating dock; their christening—public relations—ceremony is held at a later date. These ships are being considered for the Cruiser Upgrade program, to provide them with updated electric and weapon systems, as well as modernization of their hull, propulsion, and electrical systems.

ASW weapons: As completed, these ships fired the ASROC missile from their forward Mk 26 launcher.

Classification: These ships were changed from guided missile destroyers (DDG with same hull numbers) to guided missile cruisers on 1 January 1980 to better reflect their capabilities and cost.

Design: SCB No. 226. These ships are based on the SPRUANCE design, employing the same hull and propulsion plant. The superstructure has been enlarged to accommodate the Aegis/SPY-1 equipment, with two fixed-array radar antennas on the forward deckhouse facing forward and to starboard, and two on the after deckhouse, facing aft and to port. Internal changes include limited armor plating for the magazine and critical electronic spaces, increases in the ship's service generators from three 2,000 kW to three 2,500 kW, additional accommodations, and additional fuel tanks.

During construction, the design was changed to provide higher exhaust stacks and a bow bulwark, the latter required to reduce water over the bow due to the greater draft compared to the SPRUANCE class.

The VINCENNES and later ships have tripod (vice quadrupod) lattice masts, providing a reduction of some nine tons in topside weight.

Electronics: All ships have the SQR-17 sonar data processor. The SQS-53 series and SQR-19 sonars comprise the SQQ-89(V)3 suite.

Helicopters: These ships have the RAST helicopter-hauldown system (see the OLIVER HAZARD PERRY/FFG 7 class). The sizes of the twin helicopter hangars in these ships vary; they are approximately 39 feet (11.9 m) long, 26½ to 29 feet (8.1 to 8.8 m) wide, and 14⅓ to 15½ feet (4.35 to 4.7 m) high.

The first two ships of this class carried the SH-2F LAMPS I helicopter, now discarded; the CG 49–51 were fitted to carry the SH-60B Seahawk LAMPS III.

Names: The CG 51 is named for a deceased Secretary of the Navy and Secretary of Defense. (Other Secretaries of the Navy are remembered by destroyers and cruisers, the former having been named for secretaries when they were built as DLG "frigates" in the destroyer family; the only other Secretaries of Defense to have had Navy ships named in their honor were James V. Forrestal, also a former Secretary of the Navy, and George C. Marshall.)

Operational: The VINCENNES shot down an Iranian commercial airliner on 3 July 1988 over the southern Persian Gulf. All 290 passengers and crew were killed. The VINCENNES's combat information center had identified the target as probably an Iranian F-14 Tomcat making a dive on the ship. Two Standard missiles were fired.

TABLE 15-2. GUIDED MISSILE CRUISERS

Number	Name	Missile Comm.	Notes
BALTIMORE-class conversions (2)			
CAG 1	BOSTON (ex-CA 69)	1955	reverted to CA 69; str. 1973
CAG 2	CANBERRA (ex-CA 70)	1956	reverted to CA 70; str. 1978
CLEVELAND-class conversions (6)			
CLG 3	GALVESTON (ex-CL 93)	1958	stricken 1973
CLG 4	LITTLE ROCK (ex-CL 92)	1960	changed to CG 4; str. 1977
CLG 5	OKLAHOMA CITY (ex-CL 91)	1960	changed to CG 5; str. 1982
CLG 6	PROVIDENCE (ex-CL 82)	1959	changed to CG 6; str. 1978
CLG 7	SPRINGFIELD (ex-CL 66)	1960	changed to CG 7; str. 1978
CLG 8	TOPEKA (ex-CL 67)	1960	stricken 1973
LONG BEACH type			
CGN 9	LONG BEACH (ex-CLGN/ CGN 160)	1961	decomm./str. 1 May 1995
BALTIMORE/OREGON CITY–class conversions (3)			
CG 10	ALBANY (ex-CA 123)	1962	stricken 1985
CG 11	CHICAGO (ex-CA 136)	1964	stricken 1984
CG 12	COLUMBUS (ex-CA 74)	1962	stricken 1976
CG 13	(unnamed BALTIMORE/OREGON CITY class)		conversion canceled
CG 14	BREMERTON (CA 130)		conversion canceled
CG 15	ROCHESTER (CA 124)		conversion canceled
LEAHY class (9)			
CG 16	LEAHY (ex-DLG 16)	1962	decomm./str. 1 Oct 1993
CG 17	HARRY E. YARNELL (ex-DLG 17)	1963	decomm./str. 29 Oct 1993
CG 18	WORDEN (ex-DLG 18)	1963	decomm./str. 10 Oct 1993
CG 19	DALE (ex-DLG 19)	1962	decomm./str. 23 Sep 1994
CG 20	RICHMOND K. TURNER (ex-DLG 20)	1964	decomm./str. 30 June 1995
CG 21	GRIDLEY (ex-DLG 21)	1963	decomm./str. 21 Jan 1994
CG 22	ENGLAND (ex-DLG 22)	1962	decomm./str. 21 Jan 1994
CG 23	HALSEY (ex-DLG 23)	1963	decomm./str. 28 Jan 1994
CG 24	REEVES (ex-DLG 24)	1964	decomm./str. 12 Nov 1993
BAINBRIDGE type			
CGN 25	BAINBRIDGE (ex-DLGN 25)	1962	decomm./str. 13 Sep 1996
BELKNAP class (9)			
CG 26	BELKNAP (ex-DLG 26)	1964	decomm./str. 15 Mar 1995
CG 27	JOSEPHUS DANIELS (ex-DLG 27)	1965	decomm./str. 22 Jan 1994
CG 28	WAINWRIGHT (ex-DLG 28)	1966	decomm./str. 10 Nov 1993
CG 29	JOUETT (ex-DLG 29)	1966	decomm./str. 28 Jan 1994
CG 30	HORNE (ex-DLG 30)	1967	decomm./str. 4 Feb 1994
CG 31	STERETT (ex-DLG 31)	1967	decomm./str. 24 Mar 1994
CG 32	WILLIAM H. STANDLEY (ex-DLG 32)	1966	decomm./str. 11 Feb 1994
CG 33	FOX (ex-DLG 33)	1966	decomm./str. 15 Apr 1994
CG 34	BIDDLE (ex-DLG 34)	1967	decomm./str. 30 Nov 1993
TRUXTUN type			
CGN 35	TRUXTUN (ex-DLGN 35)	1967	decomm./str. 11 Sep 1995

TABLE 15-2. GUIDED MISSILE CRUISERS (Continued)

Number	Name	Missile Comm.	Notes
CALIFORNIA class (2)			
CGN 36	CALIFORNIA (ex-DLGN 36)	1974	decomm./str. 1999
CGN 37	SOUTH CAROLINA (DLGN 37)	1975	decomm./str. 1999
VIRGINIA class (4)			
CGN 38	VIRGINIA (ex-DLGN 38)	1976	decomm./str. 10 Nov 1994
CGN 39	TEXAS (ex-DLGN 39)	1977	decomm./str. 16 July 1993
CGN 40	MISSISSIPPI (ex-DLGN 40)	1978	decomm./str. 28 July 1997
CGN 41	ARKANSAS	1980	decomm./str. 7 July 1998
CGN 42	(unnamed VIRGINIA class)		canceled
CG 43–46	not used		
CG 47–73	TICONDEROGA class		

World War II cruiser programs reached hull number CL 159 (with hulls 154–159 being canceled in 1945). All heavy (CA), light (CL), and anti-aircraft (CLAA) cruisers were numbered in the same series. One unfinished cruiser hull was completed after the war as the command ship NORTHAMPTON. Begun as a heavy cruiser (CA 125), she was canceled in 1945 when 56.2 percent complete; she was reordered in 1948 and completed as a tactical command ship in 1953 (CLC 1), then changed to a national command ship (CC 1) in 1962. She was finally stricken in 1977.

The guided missile cruiser classifications were established in 1952 to reflect the specialized weapons and AAW roles of these ships. Only one new-construction *cruiser* was built by the U.S. Navy after World War II, the LONG BEACH, ordered as CLGN 160, changed to CGN 160, and completed as CGN 9. The LONG BEACH was the world's first nuclear-propelled surface warship. (The Soviet nuclear-propelled icebreaker LENIN was completed in 1959.) She was also the world's first warship to be built with guided missiles as the main battery, carrying two Terrier surface-to-air launchers forward and a Talos surface-to-air launch aft; no guns were fitted as built (subsequently two 5-inch/38 DP guns and, later, two Phalanx CIWS were installed).

Eleven World War II–built gun cruisers were converted to a missile configuration: two heavy cruisers of the BALTIMORE (CA 68) class and six light cruisers of the CLEVELAND (CL 55) class were converted to combination gun-missile cruisers, the heavy cruisers becoming CAG and the light cruisers CLG; and three other heavy cruisers of the BALTIMORE and CLEVELAND classes were converted to all-missile ships (CG). The all-missile cruisers were referred to as "double-enders."

The two CAGs lost their missile launchers during the Vietnam War and—reverting to the CA designation—served as fire support ships. Four of the CLGs were changed to CG in 1975, although they retained 6-inch and 5-inch gun batteries.

Three additional conversions of this kind were canceled. The conversions and further new cruiser construction were halted in favor of the smaller and comparatively less expensive "frigates" (DLG/DLGN), which could carry most of a cruiser's missile armament.

A total of nine nuclear-propelled cruisers/frigates were built (seven of the latter were reclassified as cruisers in 1975). All have been stricken. In all, 25 guided missile frigates (DLG/DLGN) were changed to cruisers; the ARKANSAS was ordered as CGN 41. The LEAHY-class ships were "double-end" Terrier/Standard-ER missile cruisers with surface-to-air missile launchers forward and aft. They were the smallest U.S. Navy ships to be classified as cruisers in the post–World War II era. The BELKNAP-class ships were "single-end" Terrier/Standard-ER guided missile cruisers. After suffering major damage in a collision with the carrier JOHN F. KENNEDY, the BELKNAP was rebuilt in 1978–1980 and configured as Sixth Fleet flagship; she served in that role until 1995.

TABLE 15-3. HUNTER-KILLER CRUISERS

Number	Name	Notes
CLK 1	NORFOLK	completed as DL 1
CLK 2	NEW HAVEN	deferred 1949; canceled 1951

After World War II, the U.S. Navy established the classification of hunter-killer cruiser (CLK) for a planned class of 12 small cruisers intended for ASW operations against high-speed submarines. Only the lead ship, the NORFOLK, was completed; she was reclassified as a frigate

(DL) while under construction. She was employed mainly in ASW test and evaluation, being decommissioned in 1970 and stricken in 1973.

TABLE 15-4.   FRIGATES/GUIDED MISSILE FRIGATES

Number	Name	Comm.	Notes
NORFOLK type			
DL 1	NORFOLK (ex-CLK 1)	1953	stricken 1973
MITSCHER class (4)			
DL 2	MITSCHER (ex-DD 927)	1953	converted to DDG 35
DL 3	JOHN S. McCAIN (ex-DD 928)	1953	converted to DDG 36
DL 4	WILLIS A. LEE (ex-DD 930)	1954	stricken 1972
DL 5	WILKINSON (ex-DD 930)	1954	stricken 1974
DLG 6–15	FARRAGUT class		changed to DDG 37–46
DLG 16–24	LEAHY class		changed to CG 16–24
BAINBRIDGE type			
DLGN 25	BAINBRIDGE 1962		changed to CGN 25
DLG 26–34	BELKNAP class		changed to CG 26–34
TRUXTUN type			
DLGN 35	TRUXTUN	1967	changed to CGN 35
DLGN 36–37	CALIFORNIA class		changed to CGN 36–37
DLGN 38–40	VIRGINIA class		changed to CGN 38–40

The frigate classification (DL) was established in 1951 for large destroyer-type ships that were designed to operate with fast carrier forces. While initially intended as highly capable ASW ships, with the deployment of missile systems in these ships (as DLG/DLGNs) the emphasis became anti-air warfare, although some ships additionally had the most-capable ASW systems available (i.e., large sonar, helicopter, ASROC).

The hunter-killer cruiser NORFOLK was completed as the DL 1, while four MITSCHER-class ships ordered as destroyers were completed as DL 2–5. These ships were built with an all-gun armament plus the Weapon Alfa ASW rocket launcher and other ASW weapons. The DL 6–8 were changed to DLG in 1956, i.e., before keel laying.

Note that the all-gun frigates and missile-armed frigates were numbered in the same series; in the cruiser, destroyer, and destroyer escort/frigate categories, the missile and non-missile ships were assigned hull numbers in separate series.

The frigate classification was abolished on 30 June 1975, and a new frigate classification (FF/FFG) was established to indicate smaller escort ships (formerly DE/DEG). The FARRAGUT class of DLGs was reclassified as destroyers (DDG); the other DLG/DLGN ships became cruisers (CG/CGN).

The cruiser YORKTOWN with her twin-arm Mk 26 missile launchers visible forward and aft. Vertical launching systems provide a faster rate of fire and more flexible weapons selection. Other than their missile launchers, the two classes of Aegis cruisers are almost identical. (1997, U.S. Navy, PHC John Gay)

The YORKTOWN sails through Narragansett Bay after departing Newport, R.I. The after superstructure's SPY-1 radar antennas face aft and to port; those on the forward superstructure face forward and to starboard. (1997, U.S. Navy, PHC John Gay)

DESTROYERS

(32) LAND-ATTACK MISSILE DESTROYERS: "ZUMWALT" CLASS

Number	Name	FY	Comm.	Status
DDG	ZUMWALT	05	2009	planned
DDG	(3 ships)	06		planned
DDG	(28 ships)	07–21		planned

This is an advanced surface combat being developed as a follow-on to the destroyers of the ARLEIGH BURKE class, to replace the SPRUANCE-class destroyers and TICONDEROGA-class cruisers. The "land-attack" designation reflects the Navy seeking to justify the ship as a component of littoral–joint warfare operations.

Following the lead ship being authorized in 2005, the Navy hopes to construct three ships per year (i.e., the DDG 51 acquisition rate). The decision in January 2000 to provide the ships with electric drive (see *Engineering* notes) led to a one-year delay in starting the program.

Designated SC 21 in the development stage, designs up to 20,000 tons are being considered, although a ship of some 12,000 to 15,000 tons appears more likely. At an early stage in the DD 21/SC 21 program, a variety of concepts were examined, including a missile-armed variant of the SAN ANTONIO (LPD 17), a docking-well amphibious ship of some 23,000 tons full load. In place of the docking well, the ship would have a large VLS battery and advanced electronics, including an advanced version of the SPY-1 multipurpose radar.

The DD 21 program replaces the earlier DD(V) program that sought to determine the characteristics for a new guided missile destroyer intended for construction to begin with the fiscal 1998 shipbuilding program. In the event, it was decided to continue construction of the BURKE class (Flight IIA) into the 21st century.

Cost: The Navy's cost goal is $750 million per ship by the fifth unit; with two shipyards expected to produce the DD 21 class, that cost goal would apply to hull no. 9 or 10. The first few ships will cost approximately $1.5 *billion* per unit. Research and development costs for the DD 21 program are estimated at $3 *billion* to $5 *billion*.

Electronics: It has not yet been decided whether or not the ship will have the Aegis/SPY-1 or a lesser air defense combat system. See entry for Multi-Function Radar (MFR) in chapter 29 of this edition.

Engineering: The Navy Department announced on 6 January 2000 that the DD 21 would be propelled by electric drive and will have an integrated power architecture. Employing electric drive is expected to:

- reduce ship costs
- reduce ship signatures, especially noise
- reduce fuel consumption
- reduce maintenance requirements
- increase available power for sensors and weapons

The key design element of integrated power and integrated architecture is a single-source generator for all ship's power requirements, including propulsion. The primary power source for the DD 21 will most likely be gas turbines, as in contemporary cruisers and destroyers.

However, instead of a reduction gear to convert the turbine power into usable (propulsive) power, the engine will power a generator that produces electricity. The electricity will then be carried by cable to a motor drive. The use of a cable alleviates the requirement for the gas turbines to be aligned with propeller shafts, permitting considerable flexibility in ship design. Further, the turbine can continually be operating at its most fuel-efficient speed, with the motor drive making changes in shaft turns/speed. The main electric motors also will serve as ship's service generators for shipboard electricity.

The U.S. Navy's first electric-drive surface ship was the collier JUPITER (AC 3), commissioned in 1913. That ship subsequently was converted to the Navy's first aircraft carrier, the LANGLEY (CV 1). Later, the Navy constructed the battleship NEW MEXICO (BB 40) and the large aircraft carriers LEXINGTON (CV 2) and SARATOGA (CV 3) with turbo-electric drive (employing steam turbines). During World War II, a large number of destroyer escorts (DE) were built with turbo-electric and diesel-electric drive. Since World War II, no major surface warships were built with electric drive until the DD 21 program.

Manning: The manning goal for the DD 21 is 95 officers and enlisted personnel. The Navy's Program Executive Office (PEO) for DD 21 stated that manning may exceed the target of 95 if

(1) The cost of automation exceeds the cost of maintaining a larger crew
(2) Appropriate workload-reduction technology is unavailable

An artist's stylized concept of a land-attack missile destroyer, showing a ship with a very small RCS, a large vertical-launch missile battery, and two 155-mm long-range guns (one aft of the superstructure). Such a design would be a major departure from previous surface ships, which have substantial RCS and infrared signatures. The DD 21 is shown with conformal radar and communications antennas. (United Defense)

(3) Navy manpower or training situation changes

(4) Holdover shipboard technology, such as the Link 16 system, requires additional personnel

Of the 95-crew goal, about 22 would comprise the ship's LAMPS helicopter detachment.

Missiles: The Navy's VLS goal for the DD 21 is 256 cells. Although other missile-launch systems have been proposed, the DD 21 undoubtedly will have the Mk 41 VLS, as no alternatives are expected to be available by the time construction begins.

IMPROVED "ARLEIGH BURKE" CLASS (FLIGHT III)

The so-called Flight III was a proposed enhancement of the ARLEIGH BURKE design, the principal changes being the provision of a two-helicopter hangar and reduced radar and infrared signatures. This variant would have displaced 10,722 tons full load; weapons and sensors would have been similar to the basic BURKE class except for provision of an improved SPY-1 radar (designated SPY-1E in some publications). Further development of this design was halted in favor of the DD 21/SC 21 program.

2 + 27 GUIDED MISSILE DESTROYERS: IMPROVED "ARLEIGH BURKE" CLASS (FLIGHT IIA)

Number	Name	FY	Builder	Laid down	Launched	Christened	Comm.	Status
DDG 79	OSCAR AUSTIN	94	Bath Iron Works, Maine	9 Oct 1997	7 Nov 1998	—	19 Aug 2000	**AA**
DDG 80	ROOSEVELT	95	Litton/Ingalls, Pascagoula, Miss.	15 Dec 1997	10 Jan 1999	23 Jan 1999	14 Oct 2000	**AA**
DDG 81	WINSTON S. CHURCHILL	95	Bath Iron Works, Maine	7 May 1998	17 Apr 1999	—	2001	building
DDG 82	LASSEN	95	Litton/Ingalls, Pascagoula, Miss.	24 Aug 1998	16 Oct 1999	6 Nov 1999	2001	building
DDG 83	HOWARD	96	Bath Iron Works, Maine	10 Dec 1998	20 Nov 1999	—	2001	building
DDG 84	BULKELEY	96	Litton/Ingalls, Pascagoula, Miss.	10 May 1999	21 June 2000	24 June 2000	2001	building
DDG 85	MCCAMPBELL	97	Bath Iron Works, Maine	15 July 1999	2 July 2000	—	2002	building
DDG 86	SHOUP	97	Litton/Ingalls, Pascagoula, Miss.	13 Dec 1999	2000		2002	building
DDG 87	MASON	97	Bath Iron Works, Maine	20 Jan 2000			2002	building
DDG 88	PREBLE	97	Litton/Ingalls, Pascagoula, Miss.	22 June 2000			2002	building
DDG 89	MUSTIN	98	Litton/Ingalls, Pascagoula, Miss.	2000			2003	building
DDG 90	CHAFEE	98	Bath Iron Works, Maine	5 Nov 2000			2003	building
DDG 91	PINCKNEY	98	Litton/Ingalls, Pascagoula, Miss.				2003	building
DDG 92	MOMSEN	99	Bath Iron Works, Maine				2004	building
DDG 93	CHUNG-HOON	99	Litton/Ingalls, Pascagoula, Miss.				2004	building
DDG 94	NITZE	99	Bath Iron Works, Maine				2004	building
DDG 95	· · · · · ·	00	Litton/Ingalls, Pascagoula, Miss.				2005	building
DDG 96	· · · · · ·	00	Litton/Ingalls, Pascagoula, Miss.				2005	building
DDG 97	· · · · · ·	00	Bath Iron Works, Maine				2005	building
DDG 98	· · · · · ·	01	Litton/Ingalls, Pascagoula, Miss.				2006	building
DDG 99	· · · · · ·	01	Bath Iron Works, Maine				2006	building
DDG 100	· · · · · ·	01	Litton/Ingalls, Pascagoula, Miss.				2006	building
DDG 101	· · · · · ·	02	Bath Iron Works, Maine				2007	planned
DDG 102	· · · · · ·	02	Litton/Ingalls, Pascagoula, Miss.				2007	planned
DDG 103	· · · · · ·	03					2008	planned
DDG 104	· · · · · ·	03					2008	planned
DDG 105	· · · · · ·	04					2009	planned
DDG 106	· · · · · ·	04					2009	planned
DDG 107	· · · · · ·	05					2010	planned

Displacement:	9,217 tons full load	ASW weapons:	VLA (ASROC)
Length:	509 feet (155.18 m) overall		6 12.75-inch (324-mm) torpedo tubes Mk 32 (2 triple) for Mk 46
Beam:	59 feet (18.0 m) waterline		and Mk 50 torpedoes
	66¹¹/₁₂ feet (20.4 m) maximum	Radars:	SPS-64(V)9 navigation
Draft:	30⁷/₁₂ feet (9.3 m)		SPS-67(V)3 surface search
Propulsion:	4 gas turbines (General Electric LM 2500-30); 100,000 shp;		(4) SPY-1D(V) multifunction
	2 shafts	Sonars:	SQS-53C(V)1 bow mounted
Speed:	31 knots	Fire control:	3 Mk 99 illuminators with SPG-62 radar
Range:	4,400 n.miles (8,150 km) at 20 knots		1 Mk 116 ASW control system
Manning:	359 (26 officers + 333 enlisted) + LAMPS detachment of 21		1 Mk 160 GFCS
	(6 officers + 15 enlisted)		SQQ-89(V)10 ASW system
Helicopters:	2 SH-60B/R LAMPS III		SWG-1 (Harpoon)
Missiles:	96-cell VLS for Standard-MR SM-2/Tomahawk/VLA (ASROC)		SWG-3 (Tomahawk)
	Mk 41 Mod 0	EW systems:	SLQ-25A Nixie
Guns:	1 5-inch (127-mm) 54-cal DP Mk 45; 5-inch/62-cal DP Mk 45		SLQ-32(V)3
	Mod 4 in DDG 81 and later ships		
	2 20-mm Phalanx CIWS Mk 15 (2 multibarrel)		

These are Improved ARLEIGH BURKE–class ships, the most significant differences being six additional vertical launch missile cells and full facilities for supporting two SH-60B/R Seahawk helicopters. The Flight IIA ships, however, are larger and do not have Harpoon canisters (as do all other active cruisers and destroyers). These ships are expected to be refitted for the Theater Ballistic Missile Defense (TBMD) role.

The delay in construction of the DD 21 class caused an extension of this class. In February 2000 the Secretary of the Navy restructured the program, reducing procurement to two ships (from three) in fiscal years 2002 and 2003 and extending production with two ships in FY 2004 and one in FY 2005, with the lead ship of the DD 21 design to be procured in FY 2005. The extension of Flight IIA procurement will insure the viability of the surface combatant industrial base for the DD 21 program.

Cost: The following are the fiscal 2001 budget estimates for the latest ships of this class:

	Ship cost	Outfitting	Post-delivery
FY 1999 ships	$0.880 *billion*	$10.9 M	$16.13 M
FY 2000 ships	$0.892 *billion*	$14.4 M	$10.47 M
FY 2001 ships	$1.023 *billion*	$19.2 M	$26.07 M

Design: In addition to the added VLS cells and helicopter facility, the Flight IIA ships have the two after SPY-1 radar "faces" mounted one deck (8 feet/2.4 m) higher than in the earlier ships to improve line-of-sight performance over the after end of the ship. The after superstructure has been extended to accommodate the dual hangar, and the transom also is extended, accounting for the greater length, to accommodate the stern helicopter deck.

These ships have limited steel and Kevlar armor for critical spaces.

Electronics: Beginning with the DDG 79, the SPY-1D radar will be a modified variant to enhance performance in littoral areas (i.e., against background land clutter).

The SQS-53C sonar has been fitted with the Kingfisher modification, i.e., (V)1 modification, for mine detection.

The SQR-19 TACTAS towed array found in earlier ships will not be fitted in these ships, although it could be "reconstituted" if necessary.

Guns: The Winston S. Churchill and later ships will mount the 5-inch/62-cal gun, expected to become operational in 2001. This gun will fire Extended Range Guided Munitions (ERGM) rounds out to 63 n.miles (117 km), with the Global Positioning System (GPS) providing an accuracy of between 33 and 66 feet (10 and 20 m) at maximum range.

Helicopters: The Recovery Assist, Secure, and Traverse (RAST) system is being fitted in these ships. The helicopter hangar doors are of an accordion type, folding upward.

Missiles: The self-loading feature of the two VLS batteries has been deleted in these ships, permitting 32 VLS cells forward and 64 cells aft, for a total of 96 weapons.

The eight-canister Harpoon missile battery found in all other U.S. cruisers and destroyers has been deleted from these ships as a weight-saving measure. However, they could be mounted at a future date between the funnels.

Names: The DDG 81 was originally named Winston Churchill; changed on 3 August 1998.

The Roosevelt during launch-and-recovery operations with an SH-60B Seahawk/LAMPS III helicopter. This Flight IIA version of the Arleigh Burke class has two helicopter hangars, correcting a major shortfall of the first 28 ships of this class. (Litton/Ingalls Shipbuilding)

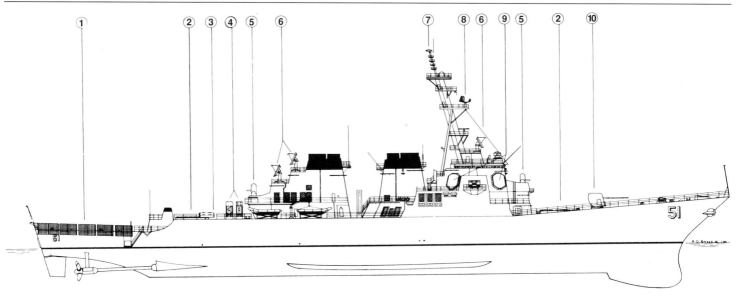

Guided Missile Destroyer Arleigh Burke
1. Helicopter deck 2. Vertical launching system Mk 41 (2) 3. 12.75-inch triple torpedo tubes Mk 32 (2) 4. Harpoon missile canisters (8) 5. Phalanx Close-In Weapon System (2) 6. SPG-62 radar illuminator (3) 7. URN-20 TACAN 8. SPS-67(V)3 surface search/navigation radar (above SPS-64(V) navigation radar) 9. PY-1D fixed-array radar (4) 10. 5-inch DP single gun mount (A. D. Baker III)

28 GUIDED MISSILE DESTROYERS: "ARLEIGH BURKE" CLASS (FLIGHTS I/II)

Number	Name	FY	Builder	Laid down	Launched	Christened	Commissioned	Status
DDG 51	ARLEIGH BURKE	85	Bath Iron Works, Maine	31 July 1986	16 Sep 1989	—	4 July 1991	AA
DDG 52	BARRY	87	Litton/Ingalls, Pascagoula, Miss.	26 Feb 1990	10 May 1991	8 June 1991	12 Dec 1992	AA
DDG 53	JOHN PAUL JONES	87	Bath Iron Works, Maine	8 Aug 1990	26 Oct 1991	—	18 Dec 1993	PA
DDG 54	CURTIS WILBUR	89	Bath Iron Works, Maine	12 Mar 1991	16 May 1992	—	19 Mar 1994	PA
DDG 55	STOUT	89	Litton/Ingalls, Pascagoula, Miss.	12 Aug 1991	16 Oct 1992	24 Oct 1992	13 Aug 1994	AA
DDG 56	JOHN S. MCCAIN	89	Bath Iron Works, Maine	3 Sep 1991	26 Sep 1992	—	2 July 1994	PA
DDG 57	MITSCHER	89	Litton/Ingalls, Pascagoula, Miss.	12 Feb 1992	7 May 1993	15 May 1993	10 Dec 1994	AA
DDG 58	LABOON	89	Bath Iron Works, Maine	24 Mar 1992	20 Feb 1993	—	18 Mar 1995	AA
DDG 59	RUSSELL	90	Litton/Ingalls, Pascagoula, Miss.	27 July 1992	20 Oct 1993	23 Oct 1993	20 May 1995	PA
DDG 60	PAUL HAMILTON	90	Bath Iron Works, Maine	24 Aug 1992	24 July 1993	—	27 May 1995	PA
DDG 61	RAMAGE	90	Litton/Ingalls, Pascagoula, Miss.	4 Jan 1993	11 Feb 1994	23 Apr 1994	22 July 1995	AA
DDG 62	FITZGERALD	90	Bath Iron Works, Maine	9 Feb 1993	29 Jan 1994	—	14 Oct 1995	PA
DDG 63	STETHEM	90	Litton/Ingalls, Pascagoula, Miss.	10 May 1993	17 June 1994	16 July 1994	21 Oct 1995	PA
DDG 64	CARNEY	91	Bath Iron Works, Maine	3 Aug 1993	23 July 1994	—	13 Apr 1996	AA
DDG 65	BENFOLD	91	Litton/Ingalls, Pascagoula, Miss.	27 Sep 1993	9 Nov 1994	12 Nov 1994	30 Mar 1996	PA
DDG 66	GONZALEZ	91	Bath Iron Works, Maine	3 Feb 1994	17 Dec 1994	18 Feb 1995?	12 Oct 1966	AA
DDG 67	COLE	91	Litton/Ingalls, Pascagoula, Miss.	28 Feb 1994	10 Feb 1995	8 Apr 1995	8 June 1996	AA
DDG 68	THE SULLIVANS	92	Bath Iron Works, Maine	27 July 1994	12 Aug 1995	—	19 Apr 1997	AA
DDG 69	MILIUS	92	Litton/Ingalls, Pascagoula, Miss.	8 Aug 1994	1 Aug 1995	28 Oct 1995	23 Nov 1996	PA
DDG 70	HOPPER	92	Bath Iron Works, Maine	23 Feb 1995	6 Jan 1996	—	6 Sep 1997	PA
DDG 71	ROSS	92	Litton/Ingalls, Pascagoula, Miss.	10 Apr 1995	22 Mar 1996	20 Apr 1996	28 June 1997	AA
DDG 72	MAHAN	92	Bath Iron Works, Maine	17 Aug 1995	29 June 1996	—	14 Feb 1998	AA
DDG 73	DECATUR	93	Bath Iron Works, Maine	11 Jan 1996	10 Nov 1996	—	29 Aug 1998	PA
DDG 74	MCFAUL	93	Litton/Ingalls, Pascagoula, Miss.	26 Jan 1996	18 Jan 1997	12 Apr 1997	25 Apr 1998	AA
DDG 75	DONALD COOK	93	Bath Iron Works, Maine	9 July 1996	3 May 1997	—	21 Aug 1998	AA
DDG 76	HIGGINS	93	Bath Iron Works, Maine	14 Nov 1996	4 Oct 1997	—	24 Apr 1999	PA
DDG 77	O'KANE	94	Bath Iron Works, Maine	8 May 1997	28 Mar 1998	—	23 Oct 1999	PA
DDG 78	PORTER	94	Litton/Ingalls, Pascagoula, Miss.	2 Dec 1996	12 Nov 1997	15 Nov 1997	20 Mar 1999	AA

Displacement:	DDG 51: 6,624 tons light	Guns:	1 5-inch (127-mm) 54-cal DP Mk 45
	8,315 tons full load		2 20-mm Phalanx CIWS Mk 15 (2 multibarrel)
	later units: 6,682 tons light	ASW weapons:	VLA (ASROC)
	8,373 tons full load		6 12.75-inch (324-mm) torpedo tubes Mk 32 (2 triple) for Mk 46
Length:	465⅝ feet (142.0 m) waterline		and Mk 50 torpedoes
	504⅓ feet (153.8 m) overall	Radars:	1 SPS-64(V)9 navigation
Beam:	59 feet (18.0 m) waterline		1 SPS-67(V)3/4 surface search
	66¹¹⁄₁₂ feet (20.4 m) maximum		(4) SPY-1D multifunction
Draft:	30⁷⁄₁₂ feet (9.3 m)	Sonars:	SQS-53C(V)1 bow-mounted
Propulsion:	4 gas turbines (General Electric LM 2500-30); 100,000 shp;		SQR-19B TACTAS towed array
	2 shafts	Fire control:	3 Mk 99 illuminators with SPG-62 radar
Speed:	31 knots		1 Mk 116 ASW control system
Range:	4,400 n.miles (8,150 km) at 20 knots		1 Mk 160 GFCS
Manning:	DDG 51–53: 316 (21 officers + 295 enlisted)		SQQ-89(V)4 ASW system
	later units: 337 (22 officers + 315 enlisted)		SWG-1 (Harpoon)
	+ LAMPS detachment 21 (6 officers + 15 enlisted)		SWG-3 (Tomahawk)
Helicopters:	landing deck only	EW systems:	SLQ-25A Nixie
Missiles:	90-cell VLS for Standard-MR SM-2/Tomahawk/VLA (ASROC)		SLQ-32(V)2 in DDG 51–67
	Mk 41 Mod 0		SLQ-32(V)3 in DDG 68–78
	8 Harpoon SSM Mk 141 (2 quad canisters)		

These destroyers emphasize AAW capabilities and are intended to complement Aegis cruisers of the TICONDEROGA class in the air/missile defense of carrier battle groups. Initial plans for a more advanced radar and propulsion plant for these ships were dropped in favor of the propulsion plant in the CG 47/DDG 993/DD 963 classes and a derivative of the CG 47 Aegis radar.

The production DDG 51 units were planned to cost approximately 75 percent the cost of a CG 47–class cruiser. The significant differences in the weapons and sensors for the DDG 51 from the CG 47 are:

- three vice four missile illuminators
- 90 vice 122 VLS missiles
- no helicopter hangar
- no AAW commander/coordination facilities

The lead ship of the class was completed 21 months behind schedule, the original contract with Bath Iron Works requiring delivery in October 1989. The Navy states that the delays were caused by: (1) a 90-day labor strike at Bath Iron Works, (2) corrections to government-furnished information for the main reduction gear, (3) Navy changes to engine room piping, (4) extension of the combat system testing program, and (5) limitations of Bath's design and production capacity.

The CURTIS WILBUR and JOHN S. MCCAIN are homeported in Yokosuka, Japan, as components of the KITTY HAWK battle group.

Builders: In the late 1980s Congress attempted to open construction of the BURKE class to a third shipyard, the most probable candidates being Todd Pacific Shipyards at Long Beach, Calif., and Avondale Shipyards, New Orleans, La. Because of the low production rate that was envisioned at that time, the Navy limited construction to two yards.

Class: Original Navy planning provided for 50 to 60 advanced missile destroyers to be authorized in fiscal 1985–1994 to replace about the same number of older cruisers and destroyers. The Carter administration proposed the construction of 49 ships of this class, while the Reagan administration initially (1981) envisioned a program of 63 ships.

The DDG 51–71 (21 ships) are Flight I and the DDG 72–78 (7 ships) are Flight II. The later ships have a number of combat capability improvements, such as the Joint Tactical Information Distribution System (JTIDS), Tactical Data Information Exchange Subsystem (TADIX), the upgraded SLQ-32(V)3, and the Standard-MR Block IV missile. The later ships also have the ability to refuel and rearm helicopters (see below).

The four Japanese KONGO-class destroyers (completed 1993–1998) are fitted with the Aegis/VLS systems, with a configuration similar to the BURKE class.

Classification: The initial Navy study leading to the preliminary design of this ship, conducted in 1979, used the designation DDX and subsequently DDGX. (Of the various design/capability options developed in the study, subtype 3A was selected for development as the DDG 51.)

Cost: Early cost estimates stipulated $550 million per ship (FY 1982 dollars) for the 6,000-ton ship in series production. Subsequently, in February 1983 the Secretary of the Navy established a cost ceiling of $1.1 *billion* for the lead ship and $700 million each for ships nos. 6 through 10. In early 1987 the Navy estimated the lead ship would cost $1.048 *billion* (in FY 1983 dollars) and the later ships $677 million.

The costs for current ships are shown under the previous entry.

Design: From the outset, these ships were directed by the Chief of Naval Operations to be smaller and less expensive than the DDG/CG 47 design. Early design concepts envisioned a ship as small as 6,000 tons full load displacement.

These are the first U.S. destroyers of post–World War II construction with steel superstructures; that decision was made as a result of the cruiser BELKNAP colliding with an aircraft carrier in 1975 (and not after the loss of a British destroyer to an Argentine-launched Exocet air-to-surface missile in the 1982 conflict in the Falklands). The steel construction provides increased resistance to blast overpressure, fragment, and fire damage plus Electromagnetic Pulse (EMP) protection. The ships have 130 tons of Kevlar armor plating to protect vital spaces.

This is the first class of U.S. Navy ships to be built with the so-called Level III collective protection features against Chemical-Biological-Radiological (CBR) attack. This provides the maximum protection possible within a ship, including berthing, medical, and control spaces. (The second class to be so fitted is the SUPPLY/AOE 6 class.)

The PAUL HAMILTON is an impressive sight cutting through the water with crewmen lining the rails. The lead ship of the Coast Guard's largest cutter class is named simply HAMILTON (WHEC 715) for the first Secretary of the Treasury, Alexander Hamilton; the AOE 7 originally was to be named PAUL HAMILTON. (1999, Leo Van Ginderen)

The ships have been designed with a significantly reduced radar cross-section over previous destroyer-type ships.

Early designs provided for a 61-foot (18.6-m) beam; subsequently it was reduced to 59 feet (18 m).

The DECATUR was the Navy's first environmentally friendly "green ship," having an onboard paper pulper, plastics processor, and other equipment to help reduce, store, and recycle materials such as metal scraps and paper.

Electronics: A derivative of the CG 47 Aegis system is provided, with all four SPY-1D radar "faces" mounted on a single, forward deckhouse.

The SQS-53C sonar has been fitted with the Kingfisher modification—i.e., (V)1 modification—for mine detection.

Engineering: Essentially the same propulsion plant as that in the CG 47/DD 963/DDG 997 classes is fitted in this class. At congressional urging, the Navy looked into the possibility of including a Rankin regenerative system to enhance the efficiency of the gas turbines, but that system was found to require too much internal volume to be practical for the class.

The BURKE reportedly attained 32 knots on sea trials with 103,000 shp. The sustained horsepower for these ships is approximately 90,000 shp.

Guns: The original DDGX proposal called for a gun armament of only two Phalanx CIWS. Subsequently, a single 76-mm OTO Melara Mk 75 gun was provided in the design and later the single 5-inch/54 cal Mk 45 was dictated, in addition to the two CIWS.

Helicopters: These ships have a large helicopter landing area on their fantail and a VERTREP position forward; however, no hangar is provided and helicopters will not normally be deployed in these ships. The DDG 52 and later ships have the RAST hauldown system, plus helicopter refueling and rearming capabilities (adding 58 tons to full load displacement).

Names: In 1983 the not-yet-started DDG 51 was named for Admiral Arleigh Burke, the Chief of Naval Operations from 1955 to 1961. This was the second U.S. ship to be named in recent years for a living person, the first being the CARL VINSON (CVN 70).

The DDG 52 was originally named JOHN BARRY; the name was changed to BARRY on 1 February 1988, back to JOHN BARRY on 9 May 1988, and again back to BARRY on 8 December 1989—further testimony to the confusion in the U.S. Navy ship naming process.

The DDG 68 is named for the five Sullivan brothers killed on 13 November 1942 when the light cruiser JUNEAU (CLAA 52) was sunk by Japanese forces; only ten men from a crew of some 700 survived. The destroyer DD 537 previously carried the name.

The DDG 70 is named for Rear Admiral Grace M. Hopper, USN, a pioneer in developing computer languages. This was only the second U.S. warship to be named for a woman, the first being the HIGBEE (DD 806), honoring the second commandant of the Navy Nurse Corps (1911–1922), also the first woman to be awarded the Navy Cross.

Operational: A terrorist bomb ripped open the destroyer COLE shortly after the warship moored in the port of Aden on 12 October 2000. The blast tore a hole approximately 30 by 40 feet in the port side of the amidships hull. Seventeen sailors—two of them women—were killed outright, and 39 were injured.

The ship, in transit from her home port of Norfolk, Virginia, to the Persian Gulf, had entered Aden in the country of Yemen for a brief refueling stop. As the ship was taking on fuel from a "dolphin" or refueling pier in the center of the harbor a small craft, apparently operated by two men, came alongside the warship. The two men reportedly stood at attention and detonated several hundred pounds of high explosives.

The crew immediately took action to control damage and help the wounded. The ship appears to have been in no immediate danger of sinking although she did take on a slight list. Subsequently, the COLE was loaded aboard the Norwegian heavy-lift ship BLUE MARLIN and returned to the United States. She is being rebuilt at the Litton/Ingalls shipyard where she was built. The reconstruction was expected to take about one year.

The cost of repairs to the COLE was estimated in December 2000 to be $240 million—approximately one-quarter the cost of building the ship.

The CURTIS WILBUR patrolling the Persian Gulf. The BURKE-class ships have relatively broad beams, 12 feet (3.66 m) greater than the larger ships of the TICONDEROGA and SPRUANCE classes. The four SPY-1 radar "faces" are mounted on the corners of the forward superstructure. (1999, U.S. Navy, PHC Mahlon K. Miller)

The JOHN S. MCCAIN in the Persian Gulf. The ship has markings for a Vertical Replenishment (VERTREP) area forward and for both VERTREP and helicopter operations on her fantail. A pair of Rigid Inflatable Boats (RIBs) are stowed on the starboard side of the after superstructure. (1998, U.S. Navy, PH2 Felix Garza)

The sleek lines of the ARLEIGH BURKE class are shown in this waterline view of the GONZALEZ. The stem anchor position helps protect the bow sonar dome; the angled superstructure and funnel sides reduce the ship's radar cross-section. (2000, Leo Van Ginderen)

The STOUT shows the crossed quad banks of Harpoon missile canisters between the after superstructure (topped by a Phalanx CIWS) and the after VLS battery. The ship's 12.75-inch torpedo tubes are mounted outboard of the after VLS battery. (1999, Leo Van Ginderen)

24 DESTROYERS: "SPRUANCE" CLASS

Number	Name	FY	Builder	Laid down	Launched	Commissioned	Status
DD 963	SPRUANCE	70	Litton/Ingalls, Pascagoula, Miss.	27 Nov 1972	10 Nov 1973	20 Sep 1975	**AA**
DD 964	PAUL F. FOSTER	70	Litton/Ingalls, Pascagoula, Miss.	6 Feb 1973	23 Feb 1974	21 Feb 1975	**PA**
DD 965	KINKAID	70	Litton/Ingalls, Pascagoula, Miss.	19 Apr 1973	25 May 1974	10 July 1976	**PA**
DD 966	HEWITT	71	Litton/Ingalls, Pascagoula, Miss.	23 July 1973	24 Aug 1974	25 Sep 1976	**PA**
DD 967	ELLIOT	71	Litton/Ingalls, Pascagoula, Miss.	15 Oct 1973	19 Dec 1974	22 Jan 1977	**PA**
DD 968	ARTHUR W. RADFORD	71	Litton/Ingalls, Pascagoula, Miss.	14 Jan 1974	1 Mar 1975	16 Apr 1977	**AA**
DD 969	PETERSON	71	Litton/Ingalls, Pascagoula, Miss.	29 Apr 1974	21 June 1975	9 July 1977	**AA**
DD 970	CARON	71	Litton/Ingalls, Pascagoula, Miss.	1 July 1974	24 June 1975	1 Oct 1977	**AA**
DD 971	DAVID R. RAY	71	Litton/Ingalls, Pascagoula, Miss.	23 Sep 1974	23 Aug 1975	19 Nov 1977	**PA**
DD 972	OLDENDORF	72	Litton/Ingalls, Pascagoula, Miss.	27 Dec 1974	21 Oct 1975	4 Mar 1978	**PA**
DD 973	JOHN YOUNG	72	Litton/Ingalls, Pascagoula, Miss.	17 Feb 1975	7 Feb 1976	20 May 1978	**PA**
DD 974	COMTE DE GRASSE	72	Litton/Ingalls, Pascagoula, Miss.	4 Apr 1975	26 Mar 1976	5 Aug 1978	decomm./str. 5 June 1998
DD 975	O'BRIEN	72	Litton/Ingalls, Pascagoula, Miss.	9 May 1975	8 July 1976	3 Dec 1977	**PA**
DD 976	MERRILL	72	Litton/Ingalls, Pascagoula, Miss.	16 June 1975	1 Sep 1976	11 Mar 1978	decomm./str. 26 Mar 1998
DD 977	BRISCOE	72	Litton/Ingalls, Pascagoula, Miss.	21 July 1975	18 Dec 1976	3 June 1978	**AA**
DD 978	STUMP	72	Litton/Ingalls, Pascagoula, Miss.	22 Aug 1975	21 Mar 1977	19 Aug 1978	**AA**
DD 979	CONOLLY	74	Litton/Ingalls, Pascagoula, Miss.	29 Sep 1975	3 June 1977	14 Oct 1978	decomm./str. 18 Sep 1998
DD 980	MOOSBRUGGER	74	Litton/Ingalls, Pascagoula, Miss.	3 Nov 1975	23 July 1977	16 Dec 1978	decomm./str. 15 Dec 2000
DD 981	JOHN HANCOCK	74	Litton/Ingalls, Pascagoula, Miss.	16 Jan 1976	28 Sep 1977	10 Mar 1979	decomm./str. 6 Oct 2000
DD 982	NICHOLSON	74	Litton/Ingalls, Pascagoula, Miss.	20 Feb 1976	29 Nov 1977	12 May 1979	**AA**
DD 983	JOHN RODGERS	74	Litton/Ingalls, Pascagoula, Miss.	12 Aug 1976	25 Feb 1978	14 July 1979	decomm./str. 4 Sep 1998
DD 984	LEFTWICH	74	Litton/Ingalls, Pascagoula, Miss.	12 Nov 1976	8 Apr 1978	25 Aug 1979	decomm./str. 27 Mar 1998
DD 985	CUSHING	74	Litton/Ingalls, Pascagoula, Miss.	2 Feb 1977	17 June 1978	20 Oct 1979	**PA**
DD 986	HARRY W. HILL	75	Litton/Ingalls, Pascagoula, Miss.	1 Apr 1977	10 Aug 1978	17 Nov 1979	decomm./str. 29 May 1998
DD 987	O'BANNON	75	Litton/Ingalls, Pascagoula, Miss.	24 June 1977	25 Sep 1978	15 Dec 1979	**AA**
DD 988	THORN	75	Litton/Ingalls, Pascagoula, Miss.	29 Aug 1977	14 Nov 1978	16 Feb 1980	**AA**
DD 989	DEYO	75	Litton/Ingalls, Pascagoula, Miss.	14 Oct 1977	20 Jan 1979	22 Mar 1980	**AA**
DD 990	INGERSOLL	75	Litton/Ingalls, Pascagoula, Miss.	16 Dec 1977	10 Mar 1979	12 Apr 1980	decomm./str. 24 July 1998
DD 991	FIFE	75	Litton/Ingalls, Pascagoula, Miss.	6 Mar 1978	1 May 1979	31 May 1980	**PA**
DD 992	FLETCHER	75	Litton/Ingalls, Pascagoula, Miss.	24 Apr 1978	16 June 1979	12 July 1980	**PA**
DD 997	HAYLER	78	Litton/Ingalls, Pascagoula, Miss.	22 Oct 1980	27 Mar 1982	5 Mar 1983	**AA**

Displacement:	7,410 tons light 9,250 tons full load	ASW weapons:	6 12.75-inch (324-mm) torpedo tubes Mk 32 (2 triple) for Mk 46 and Mk 50 torpedoes
Length:	528¹¹⁄₁₂ feet (161.25 m) waterline 563⅙ feet (171.7 m) overall	Radars:	Mk 23 Target Acquisition System (TAS) in most ships SPS-40B/C/D/E air search, except SPS-49(V)2 in DD 997
Beam:	55 feet (16.8 m)		SPS-53 or SPS-64(V)9 or LN-66 navigation
Draft:	29 feet (8.8 m)		SPS-55 surface search
Propulsion:	4 gas turbines (General Electric LM 2500); 86,000 shp; 2 shafts		SPS-64(V)9 navigation
Speed:	32.5 knots	Sonars:	SQS-53B bow-mounted, except SQS-53C in DD 978
Range:	6,000 n.miles (11,112 km) at 20 knots 3,300 n.miles (6,112 km) at 30 knots		SQR-19A/B TACTAS towed array in most ships
Manning:	approx. 325 (21 officers + 304 enlisted) (see *Manning* notes) + LAMPS detachment 21 (6 officers + 15 enlisted)	Fire control:	1 Mk 86 GFCS with SPG-60 and SPQ-9A radars 1 Mk 91 missile FCS 1 Mk 116 ASW FCS
Helicopters:	2 SH-60B/R Seahawk LAMPS III		SQQ-89(V)1 ASW system
Missiles:	1 8-cell NATO Sea Sparrow launcher Mk 29		SWG-1 (Harpoon)
	1 21-cell RAM missile launcher Mk 49 in DD 967, 972, 973, 977, 978, 982, 985, 987, 988, 991, 992	EW systems:	SWG-3 (Tomahawk) SLQ-25A Nixie
	8 Harpoon SSM Mk 141 (2 quad canisters)		SLQ-32(V)3
	61-cell VLS for Tomahawk/VLA (ASROC) Mk 41 Mod 0		SLQ-34 Classic Outboard DF in 16 ships
Guns:	2 5-inch (127-mm) 54-cal DP Mk 45 (2 single) 2 25-mm Bushmaster cannon Mk 38 (2 single) in some ships 2 20-mm Phalanx CIWS Mk 16 (2 multibarrel) 4 12.7-mm machine guns		

The SPRUANCES originally were built as specialized ASW ships. They have since been provided with an anti-ship capability in the form of the Harpoon missile and, subsequently, with a long-range anti-ship/land-attack capability through the installation of Tomahawk missiles. (These are the only ships rated as "destroyers" to carry the Tomahawk.) Seven ships had Armored Box Launchers (ABL) mounted forward of the bridge for eight Tomahawk missiles; the 24 other ships had a 61-cell VLS fitted forward of the bridge (replacing ASROC launcher and magazine). The ABLs subsequently were removed in the mid-1990s, prior to the ships being decommissioned in 1998.

The four stricken KIDD-class missile destroyers and the TICONDEROGA-class missile cruisers have the same hull, propulsion, and auxiliary systems.

The CUSHING and O'BRIEN are homeported in Yokosuka, Japan, as part of the KITTY HAWK carrier battle group.

The seven non-VLS ships have been decommissioned and stricken (same dates); five are scheduled for scrapping, the DD 979 is being held for possible assignment as a memorial, and the DD 986 is retained as a "logistic support asset" (i.e., spare-parts source).

ASW weapons: As built, these ships had a Mk 16 ASROC launcher forward of the bridge (with reload capability); it was removed with the installation of VLS.

Builders: The entire SPRUANCE class was contracted with a single shipyard to facilitate design and mass production. A contract for the development and production of 30 ships was awarded on 23 June 1970 to a new yard established by the Ingalls Shipbuilding Division of Litton Industries at Pascagoula. Labor and technical problems delayed the construction of these ships. The 31st ship was placed under contract in 1979 (see *Class* notes).

Class: The SPRUANCE-class destroyers were developed as replacements for the large number of World War II–built general purpose destroyers of the ALLEN M. SUMNER (DD 692) and GEARING (DD 710) classes that reached the end of their service lives in the mid-1970s. In addition to these 31 ships, four similar ships were ordered with the Mk 26/Standard AAW missile system for the Iranian Navy, but were completed as the U.S. KIDD class, accounting for hull numbers DD 993–996.

The last ship of this class (DD 997) was ordered on 29 September 1979. This ship was one of two authorized (one funded) by Congress with the proviso that, in the wording of the Senate Committee on Armed Services, "the committee does not intend for these funds to be used for acquisition of two standard DD 963–class destroyers; rather, it is the committee's intention that these ships be the first element in a new technology approach to the problems of designing surface escorts. The standard [DD] 963 class design should be modified to substantially increase the number of helicopter aircraft carried." This feature could permit the eventual modification of the ships to operate VSTOL aircraft as well. However, the Navy chose to build the ship as a standard SPRUANCE, and no additional ships were funded by Congress. (The ship was initially listed as DDH 997 in Navy working papers.)

The JOHN HANCOCK and MOOSBRUGGER were the first VLS-configured ships to be decommissioned and stricken, both in late 2000. Additional ships will be discarded as improved BURKE-class destroyers join the fleet.

Design: SCB No. 224. The original concept for this class provided for an AAW missile version (DXG) as well as the ASW version (DX); these designs became the KIDD and SPRUANCE classes, respectively.

The SPRUANCE design provided for the subsequent installation of additional weapon systems, specifically the Mk 26 missile launcher (and subsequently the Mk 41 VLS) forward, with removal of the ASROC launcher, and aft with removal of the Sea Sparrow launcher (see *Missiles* notes). In addition, the forward 5-inch gun could be replaced by the now-canceled 8-inch Mk 71 Major Caliber Lightweight Gun.

The Mk 16 ASROC launchers have been removed. They could be automatically reloaded, with a vertical magazine providing 16 reloads. The Sea Sparrow launcher is reloaded "by hand," with a total of 24 Sea Sparrow missiles carried.

The RADFORD was refitted with an Advanced Enclosed Mast/Sensor (AEM/S) structure in place of her mainmast during a refit at the Norfolk Naval Shipyard in 1997. Built by Litton/Ingalls, the mast is fabricated of nonmetallic material and envelops the normal suite of radar and communications antennas; it is 93 feet (28.3 m) high and, at its widest point, 31 feet (9.4 m) in diameter.[9] The mast reduces the ship's radar cross-section and improves sensor performance. The mast project cost $23 million.

---

9. The mast is fabricated of 5-inch (127-mm)-thick sandwiches of circuit boards and Polyvinyl Chloride (PVC) foam with a hollow core; the mast's sides are flat to reduce radar reflections. The mast provides access to all installed electronics through an enclosed ladder.

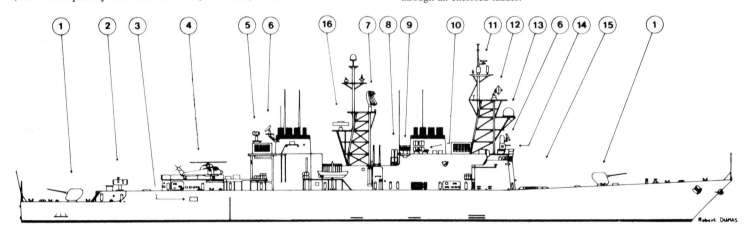

Destroyer SPRUANCE
1. 5-inch DP single gun mount (2) 2. NATO Sea Sparrow missile launcher Mk 29 3. 12.75-inch triple torpedo tubes Mk 32 (2) 4. LAMPS helicopter 5. Mk 91 Mod 0 radar director for Sea Sparrow missiles 6. OE-82 SATCOM antenna (2) 7. SPS-40 air search radar 8. Harpoon missile canisters (8) 9. SLQ-32(V)2 ECM antenna (2) 10. SRBOC decoy launcher (4) 11. SPS-55 surface search radar 12. SPG-60 gun/missile control radar 13. SPQ-9A gun fire control radar 14. Phalanx CIWS (2) 15. vertical launching system Mk 41 16. Mk 23 TAS radar (Robert Dumas)

The JOHN HANCOCK, showing the massive superstructure block of the SPRUANCE class. The after 5-inch gun is hidden by deck clutter, just aft of the eight-cell NATO Sea Sparrow launcher. The superstructure and masts give these ships—and the derivative TICONDEROGA class—a very large RCS. (1999, Leo Van Ginderen)

Electronics: As built, these ships had the SLQ-32(V)2; it was subsequently upgraded to (V)3 configuration.

The Mk 23 TAS is not provided in three ships: DD 985, 988, and 992.

Original plans provided for these ships to have the SQS-35 Independent Variable Depth Sonar (IVDS) in addition to their bow-mounted SQS-53. The IVDS was deleted because of the effectiveness of the SQS-53. The decision was subsequently made to fit these ships with the SQR-19 TACTAS; the SQR-19 is not fitted in six ships: DD 969, 972, 982, 985, 988, and 989.

The ARTHUR W. RADFORD, showing the ship's massive Advanced Enclosed Mast/Sensor (AEM/S) structure fitted in place of her lattice-pole main-mast. Her portside helicopter hangar is open, revealing an SH-60B Seahawk. (1998, Leo Van Ginderen)

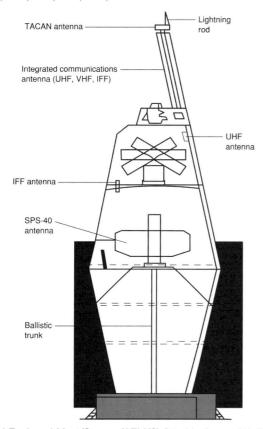

Advanced Enclosed Mast/Sensor (AEM/S) fitted in ARTHUR W. RADFORD. (Chris Nazelrod)

The NICHOLSON, moments before launching Tomahawk Land-Attack Missiles (TLAM) against targets in Iraq on 18 December 1998. The ship was steaming in the Persian Gulf at the time. A 21-cell RAM launcher is fitted on her fantail. (1998, U.S. Navy, PH1 Todd Cichonowicz)

The STUMP was fitted with the engineering development model of the SQS-53C sonar; the MOOSBRUGGER was refitted with the SQS-53B sonar and was the first Navy ship to have the SQQ-89 system.

Four ships were fitted with the SQR-15 TASS; it had been removed by 1992.

Engineering: These were the first U.S. Navy major surface combatants to have gas-turbine propulsion as their main propulsion. Gas turbines previously had been installed in Navy patrol combatants (the PGM/PG 84 class) and in the Coast Guard HAMILTON (WHEC 715) class, as well as some RELIANCE (WMEC 615)-class cutters.

The SPRUANCE-class ships have four LM 2500 gas turbines, which are modified TF39 aircraft turbofan engines. One engine can propel the ships at about 19 knots, two engines at about 27 knots, and three or four engines can provide speeds in excess of 30 knots. The engines have a maximum rating of 86,000 shp; 80,000 shp is the sustained rating.

Guns: Bushmaster "chain guns" are fitted in some ships when they forward deploy, especially to the Persian Gulf area.

Helicopters: The sizes of the twin helicopter hangars in these ships vary; they are 49 to 54 feet (14.9 to 16.5 m) long, 21 to 23½ feet (6.4 to 7.2 m) wide, and at least 16 feet (4.9 m) high.

Manning: The crews of these ships vary from 319 to 350 (20–22 officers + 308–328 enlisted).

Missiles: The Mk 41 VLS installation, which replaces the ASROC launcher and magazine, carries vertical-launch ASROCs, thus reducing the number of Tomahawks that can be loaded from a normal loadout of 61 missiles.

All ships were to have RAM missiles fitted to their Sea Sparrow launchers (four missiles per cell in two of the eight cells). The DAVID R. RAY in the late 1980s evaluated the RAM Ex-31 (Mk 49) launcher; subsequently, the launcher is being fitted on 12 ships (those listed above, plus the DD 997 in 2001).

Operational: Five ships of this class fired Tomahawk missiles during Operation Desert Storm:

CARON	2 missiles
FIFE	60 missiles
LEFTWICH	8 missiles
PAUL F. FOSTER	40 missiles
SPRUANCE	2 missiles

These 112 missiles were 39 percent of the Tomahawks fired during the Gulf War. The FOSTER fired the first Tomahawk missile and hence the "opening shot" of the Gulf War on 17 January 1991. Apparently the FIFE had 61 missiles, but one was simply not required.

In subsequent Tomahawk attacks against Iraq in January 1993, 45 missiles were launched by the destroyers CARON, HEWITT, and STUMP, and on 26 June 1993 the PETERSON launched 14 missiles (with the cruiser CHANCELLORSVILLE launching nine missiles in the later strike).

The DAVID R. RAY in port. An antenna dome is installed on the main deck at the face of the bridge structure, to starboard. The forward Phalanx CIWS is atop the bridge, also to starboard. This class of ships formed the basis for the KIDD and TICONDEROGA classes of missile ships. (1999, Leo Van Ginderen)

The ARTHUR W. RADFORD with the distinctive AEM/S structure. Future warships, such as the DD 21 land-attack missile destroyer, will have conformal or enclosed radar/communications antennas to reduce the ship's RCS. Shortly after this photo was taken, in February 1999 the RADFORD was heavily damaged in a nighttime collision with the Saudi tanker SAUDI RIYADH off the Virginia Capes. (U.S. Navy)

The differing hull forms of the SPRUANCE-KIDD-TICONDEROGA classes and the ARLEIGH BURKE class are evident from the TICONDEROGA *(left)* and LABOON. Although the BURKE-class ships have an angled superstructure to reduce their RCS, their guns, masts, and radars create major radar returns. (1996, U.S. Navy, Don S. Montgomery)

TABLE 15-5. GUIDED MISSILE DESTROYERS

Number	Name	Comm.	Notes
GYATT type			
DDG 1	GYATT (ex-DD 712)	1956	stricken as DD 712 in 1969 (see text)
CHARLES F. ADAMS class (23)			
DDG 2	CHARLES F. ADAMS	1960	decomm./str. 20 Nov 1992
DDG 3	JOHN KING	1961	decomm. 30 Mar 1990; str. 12 Jan 1993
DDG 4	LAWRENCE	1962	decomm. 30 Mar 1990; str. 16 May 1990
DDG 5	CLAUDE V. RICKETTS	1962	decomm. 31 Oct 1989; str. 1 June 1990
DDG 6	BARNEY	1962	decomm. 17 Dec 1990; str. 20 Nov 1992
DDG 7	HENRY B. WILSON	1960	decomm. 2 Oct 1989; str. 26 Jan 1990
DDG 8	LYNDE MCCORMICK	1961	decomm. 1 Oct 1991; str. 20 Nov 1992
DDG 9	TOWERS	1961	decomm. 1 Oct 1990; str. 1 Oct 1990
DDG 10	SAMPSON	1961	decomm. 24 June 1991; str. 20 Nov 1992
DDG 11	SELLERS	1961	decomm. 31 Oct 1989; str. 20 Nov 1992
DDG 12	ROBISON	1961	decomm. 1 Oct 1991; str. 20 Nov 1992
DDG 13	HOEL	1962	decomm. 1 Oct 1990; str. 20 Nov 1992
DDG 14	BUCHANAN	1962	decomm. 1 Oct 1991; str. 20 Nov 1992
DDG 15	BERKELEY	1962	decomm. 1 May 1992; str. 30 Sep 1992
DDG 16	JOSEPH STRAUSS	1963	decomm. 1 Feb 1990; to Greece 1 Oct 1990
DDG 17	CONYNGHAM	1963	decomm. 29 Oct 1990; str. 30 May 1991
DDG 18	SEMMES	1962	decomm. 12 Sep 1991; to Greece 12 Sep 1991
DDG 19	TATNALL	1963	decomm. 18 Jan 1991; str. 12 June 1993
DDG 20	GOLDSBOROUGH	1963	decomm./str. 29 Apr 1993; to Australia 17 Sep 1993
DDG 21	COCHRANE	1964	decomm. 1 Oct 1990; str. 20 Nov 1992
DDG 22	BENJAMIN STODDERT	1964	decomm. 20 Dec 1991; str. 20 Nov 1992
DDG 23	RICHARD E. BYRD	1964	decomm. 27 Apr 1990; to Greece 1 Oct 1991
DDG 24	WADDELL	1964	decomm. 1 Oct 1992; to Greece 1 Oct 1992
DDG 25–27			built for Australia
DDG 28–30			built for West Germany
Converted FORREST SHERMAN class (4)			
DDG 31	DECATUR (ex-DD 936)	1956	stricken 1988 (test ship)
DDG 32	JOHN PAUL JONES (ex-DD 932)	1956	stricken 1986
DDG 33	PARSONS (ex-DD 949)	1959	stricken 1984
DDG 34	SOMERS (ex-DD 947)	1959	stricken 1988
Converted MITSCHER class (2)			
DDG 35	MITSCHER (ex-DL 2)	1968	stricken 1978
DDG 36	JOHN S. MCCAIN (ex-DL 3)	1969	stricken 1978
FARRAGUT class (10)			
DDG 37	FARRAGUT (ex-DLG 6)	1960	decomm. 31 Oct 1989; str. 20 Nov 1992
DDG 38	LUCE (ex-DLG 7)	1961	decomm. 1 Apr 1991; str. 20 Nov 1992
DDG 39	MACDONOUGH (ex-DLG 8)	1961	decomm. 23 Oct 1992; str. 30 Nov 1992
DDG 40	COONTZ (ex-DLG 9)	1960	decomm. 2 Oct 1989; str. 6 May 1993
DDG 41	KING (ex-DLG 10)	1960	decomm. 28 Mar 1991; str. 20 Nov 1992
DDG 42	MAHAN (ex-DLG 11)	1960	decomm. 15 June 1993; str. 15 June 1993
DDG 43	DAHLGREN (ex-DLG 12)	1961	decomm. 31 July 1992; str. 20 Nov 1992
DDG 44	WILLIAM V. PRATT (ex-DLG 13)	1961	decomm. 30 Sep 1991; str. 20 Nov 1992
DDG 45	DEWEY (ex-DLG 14)	1959	decomm. 31 Aug 1990; str. 20 Nov 1992
DDG 46	PREBLE (ex-DLG 15)	1960	decomm. 15 Nov 1991; str. 20 Nov 1992
DDG 47–50 TICONDEROGA class			changed to CG 47–50
DDG 51–106 ARLEIGH BURKE class			
KIDD class (4)			
DDG 993	KIDD	1981	decomm./str. 12 Mar 1998
DDG 994	CALLAGHAN	1981	decomm./str. 31 Mar 1998
DDG 995	SCOTT	1981	decomm./str. 10 Dec 1998
DDG 996	CHANDLER	1982	decomm./str. 24 Sep 1999

The guided missile destroyer classification was established in 1956. The first DDG was the GEARING-class destroyer GYATT (DD 712), fitted with a twin Terrier SAM launcher aft, replacing the ship's after 5-inch twin gun mount; two twin gun mounts were retained forward. The GYATT became DDG 712 on 3 December 1956 and DDG 1 on 23 April 1957; she reverted to DD 712 on 1 October 1962 with removal of her missile system.

All subsequent DDGs were fitted with the smaller Tartar (later Standard-MR) missile system until the FARRAGUT-class frigates were reclassified as destroyers in 1975, those ships being armed with the Terrier/Standard-ER missile. The ten FARRAGUT-class frigates were single-end missile ships; the first three ships were ordered as all-gun frigates (DL), and the COONTZ was the first ship ordered with missiles (DLG). They were changed from DLG to DDG in 1975.

Six ADAMS-class DDGs built for Australia and West Germany in U.S. shipyards were assigned U.S. hull numbers.

Four all-gun destroyers of the FORREST SHERMAN class and two frigates of the MITSCHER class were converted to DDGs with the installation of a Mk 13 Tartar launcher aft; gun armament was retained forward.

The four KIDD-class destroyers—originally ordered for the Iranian Navy during the Shah's reign—had DD-series hull numbers with the DDG prefix. All four ships were decommissioned and stricken on the same date. Negotiations for their transfer to Greece halted with the Greek Navy reportedly seeking MEKO frigates from Germany. The KIDDS probably will go to Taiwan. These ships had only 16 to 18 years of service when decommissioned. See 16th Edition/pages 128–130 for characteristics.

The first four ships of the TICONDEROGA class, ordered as DDGs, were reclassified as cruisers in 1980.

The SPRUANCE-class destroyer O'BRIEN shows some of the mass of electronic systems fitted in these anti-submarine/land-attack ships. Note the stem anchor ready for release. (1999, Leo Van Ginderen)

The end of the Cold War caused the premature retirement of 11 destroyers—four KIDD-class DDGs and seven SPRUANCE-class DDs. This is the CALLAGHAN, one of four modified SPRUANCE destroyers fitted with Mk 26 twin-rail missile launchers forward and aft. (1995, Giorgio Arra)

The DDGs of the KIDD class—including the CALLAGHAN shown here—retained the twin SH-60 helicopter hangar and flight deck as well as the twin 5-inch/54-cal guns of the SPRUANCE class. These were the most-capable U.S. destroyers prior to the ARLEIGH BURKE class. (1995, Giorgio Arra)

The MERRILL was one of seven SPRUANCE-class DDs not refitted with vertical-launch missiles. There were two Armored Box Launchers (ABL) forward for eight Tomahawk missiles. The ship's other missile systems were eight Harpoons (amidships) and a NATO Sea Sparrow launcher aft. (1997, Leo Van Ginderen)

TABLE 15-6. POST–WORLD WAR II DESTROYERS

Number	Name	Comm.	Notes
DD 927–930	MITSCHER class		completed as DL 2–5
	FORREST SHERMAN class (18)		
DD 931	FORREST SHERMAN	1955	stricken 27 July 1990
DD 932	JOHN PAUL JONES	1956	to DDG 32; stricken 1985
DD 933	BARRY	1956	to floating equipment 1983; museum
DD 934	(ex-Japanese HANAZUKI)		war prize
DD 935	(ex-German T-35)		war prize
	SHERMAN class (continued)		
DD 936	DECATUR	1956	to DDG 31; str. 1988, retained as test ship
DD 937	DAVIS	1957	stricken 27 July 1990
DD 938	JONAS INGRAM	1957	stricken 1983
DD 939	ex-German Z-39		war prize
	SHERMAN class (continued)		
DD 940	MANLEY	1957	stricken 1 June 1990
DD 941	DU PONT	1957	stricken 1 June 1990
DD 942	BIGELOW	1957	stricken 1 June 1990
DD 943	BLANDY	1957	stricken 27 July 1990
DD 944	MULLINNIX	1958	stricken 26 July 1990
DD 945	HULL	1958	stricken 1983
DD 946	EDSON	1958	stricken 1989
DD 947	SOMERS	1959	to DDG 34
DD 948	MORTON	1959	stricken 7 Feb 1990
DD 949	PARSONS	1959	to DDG 33
DD 950	RICHARD S. EDWARDS	1959	stricken 7 Feb 1990
DD 951	TURNER JOY	1959	stricken 13 Feb 1990
DD 952–959	CHARLES F. ADAMS class		completed as DDG 2–9
DD 960	(Japanese AKIZUKI)		OSP (Offshore Procurement)
DD 961	(Japanese TERUZUKI)		OSP
DD 962	(ex-British CHARITY)		to Pakistan 1958 (SHAH JAHAN)
DD 963–992	SPRUANCE class		
	KIDD class		
DD 993	(Iranian KOUROSH)		completed as U.S. DDG 993
DD 994	(Iranian DARYUSH)		completed as U.S. DDG 994
DD 995	(Iranian ARDESHIR)		canceled 1976
DD 996	(Iranian NADER)		completed as U.S. DDG 995
DD 997	(Iranian SHAPOUR)		canceled 1976; reassigned to SPRUANCE class
	SPRUANCE class (continued)		
DD 997	HAYLER		
	KIDD class (continued)		
DD 998	(Iranian ANOUSHIRVAN)		completed as U.S. DDG 996

U.S. World War II destroyer programs reached hull number DD 926 (with hulls DD 891–926 being canceled in 1945). Many ships built during the war subsequently were reclassified as escort destroyers (DDE), hunter-killer destroyers (DDK), radar picket destroyers (DDR), and experimental destroyers (EDD). One GEARING-class ship was converted to a missile configuration (DDG 712) to evaluate the Terrier system in a destroyer-size ship and subsequently was changed to DDG 1 (and reverted to DD 712 in 1962 when the Terrier launcher was beached). All except the missile-ship conversions retained their DD hull numbers in their new roles.

As indicated in table 15-6, several war prizes and foreign-built ships had DD-series hull numbers, as did one British destroyer transferred to Pakistan with U.S. funds.[10] Two destroyers built for the Japanese Maritime Self-Defense Force in Japan with U.S. funds under the Offshore Procurement (OSP) program had U.S. hull numbers.

The FORREST SHERMAN class was halted at 18 ships in favor of building the ADAMS-class DDGs, which had a similar design with a Mk 11 or Mk 13 launcher aft in place of gun mounts. The BARRY is retained as a museum ship, being reclassified as "floating equipment" in 1983; since 2 February 1984 the ship has been permanently moored at the Washington Navy Yard. Adjacent to the Navy Museum, the BARRY is manned by one officer and 15 enlisted active-duty Navy personnel.

On 5 September 2000, during a routine maintenance operation, the BARRY's hull began leaking; subsequent material inspection showed that the ship was no longer safe for visitors. She probably will be disposed of in the near future.

The EDSON was transferred to the INTREPID (CVS 11) Sea-Air Museum in New York City on 30 June 1989. The JONAS INGRAM, stripped of weapons and radars, served as a test hulk at the Philadelphia Naval Shipyard; she was sunk as a target in 1988. The MULLINNIX was sunk as a target in 1992.

The stricken DECATUR serves as a test hulk for the Ship Self-Defense System (SSDS), operating out of the Naval Surface Warfare Center, Port Hueneme Division, Calif. She currently is being used in tests of the RAM missile (see chapter 24).

The SOMERS served as a target hulk for the Naval Air Weapons Center at Point Mugu, Calif., and was sunk as a target on 22 July 1998.

Six missile-armed ships of the SPRUANCE class ordered by Iran were assigned destroyer hull numbers by the U.S. Navy (DDG 993–998). Two ships were canceled, with one of their hull numbers being subsequently reassigned to the 31st SPRUANCE-class ship.

---

10. While three Axis destroyers were given DD numbers, U.S. warship designations were not assigned to the Japanese battleship NAGATO, Japanese light cruiser SAKAWA, German heavy cruiser PRINZ EUGEN, and several German and Japanese submarines acquired after World War II. The German CA was assigned the designation IX 300 (and was sunk in Bikini atomic bomb tests of 1946 along with the NAGATO and SAKAWA). The German supply ship CONECUH became the IX 301 and, subsequently, saw U.S. Navy service as the replenishment ship AO/AOR 110.

CHAPTER 16

Frigates

The frigate—such as the SAMUEL B. ROBERTS shown here with the carrier GEORGE WASHINGTON (CVN 73) and submarine BALTIMORE (SSN 704)—is expected to disappear from the U.S. Fleet in about two decades. The U.S. Navy's frigates were designed primarily to counter Soviet submarine threats, but have demonstrated a high degree of flexibility. (1996, U.S. Navy, PH1 Greg Pinkley)

The frigate has become the least important U.S. Navy warship in the post–Cold War era. As of early 2001 the Navy had 27 frigates in active service and eight frigates assigned to the Naval Reserve Force, all of the OLIVER HAZARD PERRY class. The frigate is expected to disappear entirely from the active fleet by fiscal year 2016 and entirely from the U.S. fleet in 2021. No frigate-type ships are under construction or proposed.

Procured in large numbers to combat the threat posed by Soviet submarines, the number of frigates was reduced precipitously with the collapse of the Soviet Union. The number of frigates in the Cold War era peaked in 1985 with 115 ships in service (94 active and 21 Naval Reserve Force ships). Although the PERRY-class frigates are considered multipurpose ships because of their Standard-MR surface-to-air and Harpoon anti-ship missiles and their major helicopter capability, their predecessors were highly specialized for the ASW mission.

Despite the higher speed and missile capabilities of the PERRY-class frigates, these ships are still not capable of serving as effective escorts for carrier battle groups in wartime. These ships can also fire

Harpoon anti-ship missiles from their Mk 13 missile launcher, albeit at the expenses of anti-air missiles in their magazine.

As Navy force levels are reduced to 116 surface combatants (cruisers, destroyers, and frigates), the emphasis will be on the more-capable cruisers and destroyers. No frigate-type ships are under construction, the last ship of the PERRY class having been completed in 1989.

The argument can—and has—been made that frigates in fact *should* have an important role in post–Cold War naval operations because of the value of such ships in exercises and operations with coalition partners, with many allied nations having frigates as their major warships, and the value of frigate-size warships in littoral operations.[1] However, it is highly unlikely that severely limited Navy funds for operations and maintenance will be expended on frigates.

---

1. See, for example, Capt. Donald Loren, USN, "(Not Quite) The (Almost) End of the Frigate," U.S. Naval Institute *Proceedings* (October 1996), p. 41, and N. Polmar, "The (Almost) End of the Frigate," *Proceedings* (July 1995), pp. 81–82.

In the mid-1980s the Navy began the design of an advanced frigate for construction in the 1990s to replace the KNOX and earlier frigate classes. That effort, however, was canceled in 1986 by the Deputy Chief of Naval Operations (Surface Warfare) because of the large size of those designs.

During the late 1970s the Navy proposed the construction of a class of small frigates (design designation FFX) for use by the Naval Reserve Force. The ships were intended to augment the PERRY-class ships in the ASW role in low-threat areas. A class of some 12 ships was planned, with the lead ship intended for authorization in FY 1984. For several reasons, however, the FFX class was not started. Subsequently, the Naval Reserve Force was provided with frigates of the KNOX and PERRY classes to replace the aging destroyers of the GEARING (DD 710) class previously assigned to the NRF.

Classification: This type of warship was officially classified as "escort vessel" (DE) from its inception in the U.S. Navy in 1941, although the DE type invariably was called "destroyer escort"—often in official publications. Only in the early 1950s—as the Soviet submarine threat emerged and DE production began to accelerate—were these ships generally referred to as escort vessels. (At that time the term "frigate" was applied to large destroyer-type ships designated DL/DLG.) Subsequently, missile-armed escort ships were designated DEG and the escort research ship GLOVER became AGDE. All escort ships were changed to "frigate" (FF/FFG/AGFF) on 30 June 1975.

Guns: Beginning during the 1990–1991 crisis and war in the Persian Gulf, several PERRY-class frigates were fitted with .50-cal machine guns and 25-mm Bushmaster Mk 38 "chain" guns for close-in defense against small craft. The weapons are shifted from ship to ship as they forward deploy; accordingly, they are not listed under the specific class entries.

Names: Because the frigate ship type evolved from the World War II–era destroyer escort (DE), they have destroyer-type names. The HAROLD E. HOLT remembers the deceased Australian prime minister who supported U.S. policy in the Vietnam War.

35 GUIDED MISSILE FRIGATES: "OLIVER HAZARD PERRY" CLASS

Number	Name	FY	Builder	Laid down	Launched	Commissioned	Status
FFG 7	OLIVER HAZARD PERRY	73	Bath Iron Works, Maine	12 June 1976	25 Sep 1976	17 Dec 1977	decomm. 20 Feb 1997; str. 3 May 1999
FFG 8	MCINERNEY	75	Bath Iron Works, Maine	16 Jan 1978	4 Nov 1978	15 Dec 1979	**AA**
FFG 9	WADSWORTH	75	Todd Shipyards, San Pedro, Calif.	13 July 1977	29 July 1978	28 Feb 1980	**NRF-P**
FFG 10	DUNCAN	75	Todd Shipyards, Seattle, Wash.	29 Apr 1977	1 Mar 1978	24 May 1980	decomm. 17 Dec 1994; str. 5 Jan 1998; to Turkey
FFG 11	CLARK	76	Bath Iron Works, Maine	17 July 1978	24 Mar 1979	9 May 1980	decomm./str. 31 Dec 1999; to Poland 22 Mar 2000
FFG 12	GEORGE PHILIP	76	Todd Shipyards, San Pedro, Calif.	14 Dec 1977	16 Dec 1978	15 Nov 1980	**NRF-P**
FFG 13	SAMUEL ELIOT MORISON	76	Bath Iron Works, Maine	4 Dec 1978	14 July 1979	11 Oct 1980	**NRF-A**
FFG 14	SIDES	76	Todd Shipyards, San Pedro, Calif.	7 Aug 1978	19 May 1979	30 May 1981	**NRF-P**
FFG 15	ESTOCIN	76	Bath Iron Works, Maine	2 Apr 1979	3 Nov 1979	10 Jan 1981	**NRF-A**
FFG 16	CLIFTON SPRAGUE	76	Bath Iron Works, Maine	30 July 1979	16 Feb 1980	21 Mar 1981	decomm. 2 June 1995; str. 4 Sep 1997; to Turkey
FFG 19	JOHN A. MOORE	77	Todd Shipyards, San Pedro, Calif.	19 Dec 1978	20 Oct 1979	14 Nov 1981	decomm. 2000; to Turkey
FFG 20	ANTRIM	77	Todd Shipyards, Seattle, Wash.	21 June 1978	27 Mar 1979	26 Sep 1981	decomm. 8 May 1996; str. 4 Sep 1997
FFG 21	FLATLEY	77	Bath Iron Works, Maine	13 Nov 1979	15 May 1980	20 June 1981	decomm. 11 May 1996; to Turkey
FFG 22	FAHRION	77	Todd Shipyards, Seattle, Wash.	1 Dec 1978	24 Aug 1979	16 Jan 1982	decomm./str. 31 Mar 1998; to Egypt
FFG 23	LEWIS B. PULLER	77	Todd Shipyards, San Pedro, Calif.	23 May 1979	15 Mar 1980	17 Apr 1982	decomm./str. 18 Sep 1998; to Egypt
FFG 24	JACK WILLIAMS	77	Bath Iron Works, Maine	25 Feb 1980	30 Aug 1980	19 Sep 1981	decomm./str. 13 Sep 1996; to Bahrain
FFG 25	COPELAND	77	Todd Shipyards, San Pedro, Calif.	24 Oct 1979	26 July 1980	7 Aug 1982	decomm./str. 18 Sep 1996; to Egypt
FFG 26	GALLERY	77	Bath Iron Works, Maine	17 May 1980	20 Dec 1980	5 Dec 1981	decomm./str. 14 June 1996; to Egypt
FFG 27	MAHLON S. TISDALE	78	Todd Shipyards, San Pedro, Calif.	19 Mar 1980	7 Feb 1981	13 Nov 1982	decomm. 27 Sep 1996; str. 20 Feb 1998; to Turkey
FFG 28	BOONE	78	Todd Shipyards, Seattle, Wash.	27 Mar 1979	16 Jan 1980	15 May 1982	**NRF-A**
FFG 29	STEPHEN W. GROVES	78	Bath Iron Works, Maine	16 Sep 1980	4 Apr 1981	17 Apr 1982	**NRF-A**
FFG 30	REID	78	Todd Shipyards, San Pedro, Calif.	8 Oct 1980	27 June 1981	19 Feb 1983	decomm./str. 25 Sep 1998; to Turkey
FFG 31	STARK	78	Todd Shipyards, Seattle, Wash.	24 Aug 1979	30 May 1980	23 Oct 1982	decomm. 7 May 1999
FFG 32	JOHN L. HALL	78	Bath Iron Works, Maine	5 Jan 1981	24 July 1981	26 June 1982	**AA**
FFG 33	JARRETT	78	Todd Shipyards, San Pedro, Calif.	11 Feb 1981	17 Oct 1981	2 July 1983	**PA**
FFG 34	AUBREY FITCH	78	Bath Iron Works, Maine	10 Apr 1981	17 Oct 1981	9 Oct 1982	decomm. 12 Dec 1997; str. 3 May 1999
FFG 36	UNDERWOOD	79	Bath Iron Works, Maine	3 Aug 1981	6 Feb 1982	29 Jan 1983	**AA**
FFG 37	CROMMELIN	79	Todd Shipyards, Seattle, Wash.	30 May 1980	1 July 1981	18 June 1983	**PA**
FFG 38	CURTS	79	Todd Shipyards, San Pedro, Calif.	1 July 1981	6 Mar 1982	8 Oct 1983	**NRF-P**
FFG 39	DOYLE	79	Bath Iron Works, Maine	23 Oct 1981	22 May 1982	21 May 1983	**AA**
FFG 40	HALYBURTON	79	Todd Shipyards, Seattle, Wash.	26 Sep 1980	13 Oct 1981	7 Jan 1984	**PA**
FFG 41	MCCLUSKY	79	Todd Shipyards, San Pedro, Calif.	21 Oct 1981	18 Sep 1982	10 Dec 1983	**PA**
FFG 42	KLAKRING	79	Bath Iron Works, Maine	19 Feb 1982	18 Sep 1982	20 Aug 1983	**AA**
FFG 43	THACH	79	Todd Shipyards, San Pedro, Calif.	6 Mar 1982	18 Dec 1982	17 Mar 1984	**PA**
FFG 45	DE WERT	80	Bath Iron Works, Maine	14 June 1982	18 Dec 1982	19 Nov 1983	**AA**
FFG 46	RENTZ	80	Todd Shipyards, San Pedro, Calif.	18 Sep 1982	16 July 1983	30 June 1984	**PA**
FFG 47	NICHOLAS	80	Bath Iron Works, Maine	27 Sep 1982	23 Apr 1983	10 Mar 1984	**AA**
FFG 48	VANDEGRIFT	80	Todd Shipyards, Seattle, Wash.	13 Oct 1981	15 Oct 1982	24 Nov 1984	**PA**
FFG 49	ROBERT G. BRADLEY	80	Bath Iron Works, Maine	28 Dec 1982	13 Aug 1983	11 Aug 1984	**AA**
FFG 50	JESSE L. TAYLOR	81	Bath Iron Works, Maine	5 May 1983	5 Nov 1983	1 Dec 1984	**AA**
FFG 51	GARY	81	Todd Shipyards, San Pedro, Calif.	18 Dec 1982	19 Nov 1983	17 Nov 1984	**PA**
FFG 52	CARR	81	Todd Shipyards, Seattle, Wash.	26 Mar 1982	26 Feb 1983	27 July 1985	**AA**
FFG 53	HAWES	81	Bath Iron Works, Maine	22 Aug 1983	17 Feb 1984	9 Feb 1985	**AA**
FFG 54	FORD	81	Todd Shipyards, San Pedro, Calif.	16 July 1983	23 June 1984	29 June 1985	**PA**
FFG 55	ELROD	81	Bath Iron Works, Maine	21 Nov 1983	12 May 1984	6 July 1985	**AA**
FFG 56	SIMPSON	82	Bath Iron Works, Maine	27 Feb 1984	31 Aug 1984	9 Nov 1985	**AA**
FFG 57	REUBEN JAMES	82	Todd Shipyards, San Pedro, Calif.	19 Nov 1983	8 Feb 1985	22 Mar 1986	**PA**
FFG 58	SAMUEL B. ROBERTS	82	Bath Iron Works, Maine	21 May 1984	8 Dec 1984	12 Apr 1986	**AA**
FFG 59	KAUFFMAN	83	Bath Iron Works, Maine	8 Apr 1985	29 Mar 1986	21 Feb 1987	**AA**
FFG 60	RODNEY M. DAVIS	83	Todd Shipyards, San Pedro, Calif.	8 Feb 1985	11 Jan 1986	9 May 1987	**PA**
FFG 61	INGRAHAM	84	Todd Shipyards, San Pedro, Calif.	30 Mar 1987	25 June 1988	5 Aug 1989	**PA**

Displacement:	2,769 tons light, except 3,210 tons for ships with LAMPS III modification
	3,658 tons full load, except 3,900–4,100 tons for ships with LAMPS III modification
Length:	413 feet (125.9 m) waterline
	445 feet (135.6 m) overall, except 455¼ feet (138.8 m) for ships with LAMPS III modification
Beam:	45 feet (13.7 m)
Draft:	21¹¹⁄₁₂ feet (6.7 m)
Propulsion:	2 gas turbines (General Electric LM 2500); 40,000 shp; 1 shaft
Speed:	29 knots (sustained; see *Engineering* notes)
Range:	5,000 n.miles (9,260 km) at 18 knots
	4,200 n.miles (7,778 km) at 20 knots
Manning:	*active ships*
	approx. 201 (16 officers + 185 enlisted) + LAMPS detachment 21 (6 officers + 15 enlisted)
	NRF ships
	approx. 162 active (14 officers + 148 enlisted) + 76 reserve (46 officers + 72 enlisted)
Helicopters:	1 or 2 SH-60B Seahawk LAMPS III in FFG 8, 28, 29, 32, 33, 35–61
	1 SH-2G LAMPS I in FFG 9, 12–15
Missiles:	1 single Mk 13 Mod 4 launcher for Standard-MR SAM/Harpoon SSM (40 weapons); see *Missiles* notes

Guns:	1 76-mm/62-cal AA Mk 75
	1 20-mm Phalanx CIWS Mk 16 (multibarrel) in active ships and FFG 13
ASW weapons:	6 12.75-in (324-mm) torpedo tubes Mk 32 (2 triple) for Mk 46 torpedoes; provision for Mk 50 torpedoes in 13 ships (see *Anti-submarine* notes)
Radars:	SPS-49(V)4 air search, except SPS-49(V)5 in FFG 50, 51, 53, 55, 56, and 61
	SPS-55 surface search
Sonars:	SQS-56 keel-mounted
	SQR-19 TACTAS towed array, except none in FFG 51, 52, 54
Fire control:	1 Mk 13 weapon direction system
	1 Mk 92 weapons FCS, except Mk 92 Mod 6 CORT in FFG 36, 47, 48, 50–55, 57, 59, 61 (not in FFG 56, as stated in previous edition)
	1 STIR radar
	SQQ-89(V)2 ASW system in active ships
	SYS-2(V)2 Integrated Automatic Detection and Tracking (IADT) system in FFG 50, 61
EW systems:	SLQ-25A Nixie in FFG 36, 47, 51–53, 55, 57–60
	SLQ-32(V)2, except SLQ-32(V)5 with Sidekick in FFG 29, 32, 36, 40, 45–59, 61

This is the third largest class of major surface warships to be built by any nation since World War II, with 51 ships completed for the U.S. Navy between 1977 and 1989; additional ships for foreign navies were built in the United States and in other countries (see *Class* notes). The Soviet SKORYY class of destroyers was larger, with 72 ships completed between 1950 and 1954, and the U.S. ARLEIGH BURKE (DDG 51) class currently is planned at more than 60 ships.

The PERRY class was initiated in the early 1970s—together with the planned Sea Control Ship (SCS)—to provide a viable capability for defending Sea Lines of Communications (SLOC) against Soviet air and submarine attacks. After the cutbacks in the DX/DXG program (i.e., SPRUANCE/DD 963) class, the FFG 7 class additionally was looked upon as a replacement for GEARING (DD 710)-class destroyers that were being retired.

These frigates lack the large, hull-mounted active/passive sonar and ASROC launcher of previous U.S. frigate classes. However, their towed-array and ability to support two large LAMPS III helicopters make them useful ASW ships. In addition, they have a surface-to-air missile system, a feature lacking in all but six of the previous U.S. post–World War II frigates.[2] And, despite their

relatively light construction, according to the reference work *Combat Fleets of the World*, "The soundness of the design has permitted the expansion [of capabilities], and the ships have proven remarkably sturdy."[3]

Sixteen ships have been decommissioned through the end of 2000; all remaining units except the INGRAHAM are scheduled to be decommissioned by 2019, with that ship to follow in 2021. Most of these ships are expected to be transferred to other navies.

The GARY and VANDEGRIFT are homeported in Yokosuka, Japan.

Anti-submarine: The only ship-mounted ASW weapons are Mk 32 torpedo tubes, with the SH-60B helicopters being their primary ASW weapon. These are the first U.S. surface combatants that have been built without ASROC since that weapon became available in the early 1960s.

Thirteen ships—FFG 40, 43, 46, 47, 50–56, 58, and 59—have been fitted with the Flexible Universal Storage System (FUSS) to permit the storage of Penguin air-to-surface missiles and Mk 50 torpedoes (in addition to Mk 46 torpedoes).

Class: Early U.S. Navy planning provided for approximately 75 ships of this class. Shipbuilding programs of the early 1970s reduced the number of ships to be built in "later" years, in part because of the

---

2. The point-defense missile systems fitted in a number of previous frigates did have a limited anti-air capability but were intended primarily to defeat incoming Styx-type anti-ship cruise missiles.

3. A. D. Baker III, *Combat Fleets of the World, 2000–2001* (Annapolis, Md.: Naval Institute Press, 2000), p. 939.

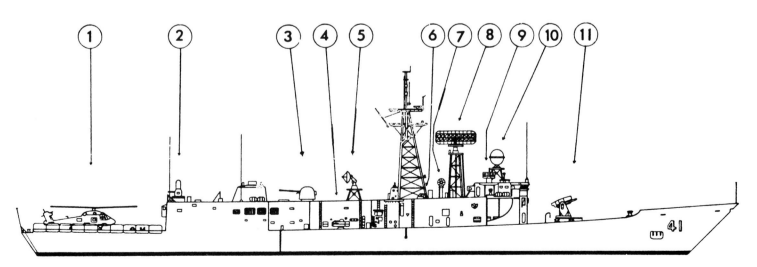

Guided Missile Frigate MCCLUSKY
1. SH-60 LAMPS III helicopter 2. Phalanx CIWS 3. 76-mm AA gun mount 4. 12.75-inch triple torpedo tubes Mk 32 (2) 5. STIR fire control radar
6. SRBOC decoy launcher (2) 7. OE-82 Satellite Communications (SATCOM) antenna (2) 8. SPS-49(V)4/5 air search radar 9. SLQ-32(V)2 ECM antenna (2) 10. Mk 92 fire control radar 11. Surface-to-air missile launcher Mk 13 (Robert Dumas)

planned FFX, a smaller frigate intended specifically for NRF operation (see below).

The last Carter administration five-year plan, for fiscal 1982–1986, deleted all FFG 7 construction after one ship in the 1983 program. However, the Reagan administration's shipbuilding program put forward in January 1982 for FY 1983–1987 provided for 12 additional FFGs; Congress approved the two ships in the fiscal 1983 budget but the Reagan administration's subsequent five-year plan (FY 1984–1988) deleted all further frigate construction, thus halting the FFG 7 program at 50 ships. Congress subsequently funded one additional ship (FFG 61) in the fiscal 1984 budget specifically for construction at the Todd–San Pedro yard.

The Todd-Seattle yard built four ships of this class for the Australian Navy (given the U.S. designations FFG 17, 18, 35, and 44), delivered from 1980 to 1983. Additional ships of this design have been constructed in Australia (two ships), Spain (seven), and Taiwan (eight) for their respective navies. Thus, the total number of ships built to the PERRY design is 72.

Nineteen ships were assigned to the NRF at various times; ten ships remain in this role (mobilization category A). The NRF ships are listed below, with the home ports for the current NRF ships identified:

		To NRF	NRF location[4]
FFG 7	PERRY	31 May 1984	
FFG 9	WADSWORTH	30 June 1985	San Diego, Calif.
FFG 10	DUNCAN	13 Jan 1984	
FFG 11	CLARK	30 Sep 1985	
FFG 12	PHILIP	18 Jan 1986	San Diego, Calif.
FFG 13	MORISON	30 June 1986	Mayport, Fla.
FFG 14	SIDES	9 Aug 1986	San Diego, Calif.

4. Ships currently assigned to the NRF.

FFG 15	ESTOCIN	30 Sep 1986	Norfolk, Va.
FFG 16	SPRAGUE	31 Aug 1984	
FFG 19	MOORE	30 Jan 1987	San Diego, Calif.
FFG 20	ANTRIM	30 Jan 1987	
FFG 21	FLATLEY	30 Nov 1987	
FFG 22	FAHRION	30 Sep 1988	
FFG 23	PULLER	1 June 1987	
FFG 25	COPELAND	30 Sep 1989	
FFG 27	TISDALE	31 Jan 1988	
FFG 28	BOONE	30 Sep 1998	Mayport, Fla.
FFG 29	GROVES	1 Apr 1997	Pascagoula, Miss.
FFG 38	CURTS	15 Sep 1998	San Diego, Calif.

The NRF is being stabilized at eight ships until the demise of the frigate force. By 2003 all eight NRF frigates are expected to be assigned to the Western Hemisphere Group to carry out operational tasks such as counterdrug operations.

The transfer of the JACK WILLIAMS and GALLERY to NRF status was canceled in July 1990.

Classification: When conceived, these ships were designated "patrol frigates" (PF), a designation previously applied to a series of smaller, World War II–era ships (PF 1–102) and postwar coastal escorts that were constructed specifically for foreign transfer (PF 103–108). The PERRY was designated PF 109 until changed to "frigate" FFG 7 on 30 June 1975.

Design: SCB No. 261. During their design phase, the Chief of Naval Operations, Admiral Elmo R. Zumwalt, placed constraints on the ships' cost, displacement, and crew size:

- $50 million in then-year dollars
- 3,530 tons full load
- 185 crew (17 officers + 168 enlisted)

The TAYLOR refuels from the carrier JOHN F. KENNEDY (CV 67) in the Atlantic while operating with the carrier battle group. Although designed as convoy and amphibious group escorts, PERRY-class ships have been effective in battle group operations. The TAYLOR's port hangar is open; two large SH-60 LAMPS III helicopters can be accommodated in these ships. (1999, U.S. Navy, PH2 Keith Murphy)

All three parameters were exceeded, although the design did arrest the upward trend in frigate (DE/FF) cost, size, and manning requirements.

Note the short interval between the PERRY's keel laying and launching due to modular construction; fabrication of modules began on 17 December 1974. These ships were designed for modular assembly to facilitate mass production. All major components were tested at sea or in land facilities before completion of the lead ship. Space and weight were reserved for fin stabilizers, which were installed during construction in FFG 36 and later units.

Early designs provided for a single hangar aft with twin funnels ("split" by the hangar). The design was revised to provide separate, side-by-side hangars to accommodate two SH-60B helicopters (see *Helicopters* notes). The hangars vary in size; they are approximately 41 to 46 feet (12.5 to 14 m) long, each 13⅔ to 16 feet (4.2 to 4.9 m) wide, and 13½ to 15½ feet (4.1 to 4.7 m) in height. In addition to the fantail landing area, the ships have a VERTREP area forward.

Electronics: The STIR (Separate Target Illumination Radar) is a modified SPG-60 radar. The Sperry Corporation had lobbied Congress and the Navy to install a phased-array radar in the later ships of this class, with a backfit to the earlier ships. However, the cost was considered prohibitive by the Navy.

The INGRAHAM was completed with an improved combat system developed by Sperry/Unisys referred to as CORT (Coherent Receiver/Transmitter). It consists of the Mk 92 Mod 6 fire control system with the SYS-2(V)2 automatic tracking system. The ship's SPS-49(V)5 digital radar has enhanced ECM capabilities. A similar CORT refit followed in 11 other ships.

The Sidekick ECM installation provides an active countermeasures capability to the otherwise passive SLQ-32(V)2; suites so modified are redesignated SLQ-32(V)5.

The SQR-18A towed array sonar is fitted in the NRF ships and the SQR-19 TACTAS towed-array sonar is provided in the active units and FFG 7. The first ship to be built with the SQR-19 was the ELROD, with the array to be backfitted in the earlier ships. The limited capabilities of the hull-mounted SQS-56 will make these ships rely primarily on the towed array for effective ASW.

The NICHOLAS was provided with the Kingfisher modification to the SQS-26 sonar for mine detection.

Several ships (FFG 9, 31, 32, 36, 38, 42, 43, 47–55, and 57–61) have been fitted with a passive countermeasures system (formerly Outlaw Bandit) to reduce the ship's radar cross-section to enhance survivability.

Engineering: These ships have two LM 2500 gas turbine main propulsion engines and can attain 25 knots on one engine. On trials, some ships reportedly have reached 36 knots. The maximum rated horsepower is 41,000; the sustained shp is shown above.

The ships have two 350-hp, electric-drive, retractable auxiliary propulsion pods for precise maneuvering; they also provide a "come-home" capability at six knots in the event of main propulsion failure. They are fitted with four 1,000-kilowatt diesel ship's service generators, thus lacking the elaborate silencing of the SPRUANCE-class destroyers, which have gas turbine generators.

Guns: Early designs addressed a variety of guns for these ships, among them a twin 35-mm rapid-fire gun in place of the later 76-mm gun and CIWS. These are the first U.S. surface combatants built since the early 1960s without a 5-inch gun.

Helicopters: These were the first U.S. ships fitted with a helicopter haul-down system. The MCINERNEY was modified to serve as test ship for the RAST hauldown system and conducted FFG sea trials with the SH-60B in 1981. It permits the recovery of helicopters with the ship rolling through 28° and pitching up to 5°. RAST was backfitted in those ships completed prior to the TAYLOR (ships that have LAMPS III capability), with that ship being the first to be completed with the RAST system.

The NRF-operated ships are intended to take aboard an SH-2G LAMPS I helicopter operated by the Naval Air Reserve (squadrons HSL-84 and HSL-94).

Manning: The original complement was to be 179 (12 officers + 167 enlisted); this was increased to 185 (17 officers + 168 enlisted) by the time the design was completed. The crews of active ships vary considerably, from 13 to 19 officers, and from 184 to 215 enlisted men, in addition to LAMPS detachments.

Missiles: In early 2000 the Navy revealed that plans for replacing the Mk 13 launcher with a Rolling Airframe Missile (RAM) missile launcher were being considered. While RAM is a close-in defense weapon compared to the limited area capabilities of the Standard-MR launched by the Mk 13, which also can launch the

The McCLUSKY shows the large, block-like superstructure of the OLIVER HAZARD PERRY–class frigates. The Navy is proposing replacement of the Mk 13 missile launcher forward with a RAM missile launcher for close-in defense when operating in littoral waters. That change would delete the ships' Harpoon anti-ship capability as well as their limited area air defense. (1998, U.S. Navy, PH1 Spike Call)

The GARY departs the naval base at San Diego, Calif. The 76-mm gun mount is lost among the clutter atop the superstructure; the triple torpedo tubes are on the main deck, in the ship's waist. The Phalanx CIWS is atop the large hangar structure. (1998, U.S. Navy, PH2 Ted Banks)

Harpoon anti-ship missile, the threat from anti-ship cruise missiles in littoral operating areas is forcing the Navy to reevaluate shipboard defenses.

Operational: While operating in the Persian Gulf on the night of 17 May 1987, the STARK was struck by two Exocet missiles launched by an Iraqi Mirage F1 aircraft that mistook the frigate for an Iranian ship. The STARK suffered 37 dead as one of the missile warheads detonated, with unexpended fuel in both setting fires and causing heavy damage. The STARK's crew fought fires for 24 hours and at one point the accumulation of water on board from fire-fighting efforts caused the ship to list 16°. (The STARK was able to return to the United States under her own power and underwent months of repairs at the Litton/Ingalls yard from November 1987 to August 1988. The repairs cost an estimated $90 million.)

The SAMUEL B. ROBERTS struck an Iranian-laid mine in the Persian Gulf on 14 April 1988. The ship suffered a 22-foot (6.7-m) gash in the side and a 9-foot (2.7-m) tear in the bottom, her superstructure cracked, the ship's gas turbines were knocked from their mountings, and there was heavy flooding; ten sailors were injured, but there were no fatalities. (After emergency repairs, on 1 July 1988 the crippled ROBERTS departed the Gulf on board the Dutch-flag heavy-lift ship MIGHTY SERVANT 2; the frigate was brought back to the United States and underwent 18 months of repairs at Bath Iron Works in 1988–1989. The repairs cost an estimated $37.5 million.)

TABLE 16-1. GUIDED MISSILE ESCORTS/FRIGATES

Number	Name	Comm.	Notes
BROOKE class (6)			
DEG 1	BROOKE	1966	decomm. 16 Sep 1988; to Pakistan 8 Feb 1989
DEG 2	RAMSEY	1967	decomm. 1 Sep 1988; str. 13 Sep 1994
DEG 3	SCHOFIELD	1968	decomm. 8 Sep 1988; str. 13 Sep 1994
DEG 4	TALBOT	1967	decomm. 30 Sep 1988; to Pakistan 31 May 1989
DEG 5	RICHARD L. PAGE	1967	decomm. 30 Sep 1988; to Pakistan 31 Mar 1989
DEG 6	JULIUS A. FURER	1967	decomm. 10 Nov 1988; to Pakistan 31 Jan 1989

These ships were built as guided missile escorts (DEG); their classification was changed to guided missile frigate (FFG) in 1975.

The BROOKE-class frigates were identical to the GARCIA class, except with a Mk 22 single-arm launcher for Tartar/Standard-MR missiles in place of the second 5-inch gun. Additional ships of this configuration were planned but not built because of the significantly higher costs of the missile variants compared to all-gun ASW frigates and their limited magazine capacity (16 missiles).

The TALBOT conducted at-sea tests of the gun, fire control, and sonar systems for the PERRY class.

The four ships loaned to Pakistan have been returned to U.S. custody and stricken:

	Returned	*Stricken*
BROOKE	2 Jan 1994	2 Jan 1994
TALBOT	11 Dec 1993	29 Nov 1993
PAGE	15 Jan 1994	15 Jan 1994
FURER	11 Dec 1993	2 Jan 1994

TABLE 16-2. POST–WORLD WAR II ESCORTS/FRIGATES

Number	Name	Comm.	Notes	Number	Name	Comm.	Notes
DEALEY class (13)				DE 1064	LOCKWOOD	1970	decomm. 27 Sep 1993; str. 27 Sep 1993
DE 1006	DEALEY	1954	to Uruguay 1972				
DE 1007–1013			OSP French frigates	DE 1065	STEIN	1972	decomm. 19 Mar 1992; str. 11 Jan 1995; to Mexico
DEALEY class (continued)				DE 1066	MARVIN SHIELDS	1971	decomm. 2 July 1992; str. 11 Jan 1995; to Mexico
DE 1014	CROMWELL	1954	stricken 1972				
DE 1015	HAMMERBERG	1955	stricken 1973	DE 1067	FRANCIS HAMMOND	1970	decomm. 2 July 1992; str. 11 Jan 1995
DE 1016–1019			OSP French frigates				
DE 1020			OSP Italian frigate	DE 1068	VREELAND	1970	decomm. 30 June 1992; to Greece 25 July 1992
DEALEY class (continued)				DE 1069	BAGLEY	1972	decomm. 30 Sep 1991; str. 11 Jan 1995
DE 1021	COURTNEY	1956	stricken 1973				
DE 1022	LESTER	1957	stricken 1973	DE 1070	DOWNES	1971	decomm. 5 June 1992; str. 11 Jan 1995
DE 1023	EVANS	1957	stricken 1973				
DE 1024	BRIDGET	1957	stricken 1973	DE 1071	BADGER	1970	decomm. 20 Dec 1991; str. 11 Jan 1995; sunk as target
DE 1025	BAUER	1957	stricken 1973				
DE 1026	HOOPER	1958	stricken 1973				
DE 1027	JOHN WILLIS	1957	stricken 1972				
DE 1028	VAN VOORHIS	1957	stricken 1972	DE 1072	BLAKELY	1970	to NRF 11 June 1983; decomm. 15 Nov 1991; str. 11 Jan 1995
DE 1029	HARTLEY	1957	to Colombia 1972				
DE 1030	JOSEPH K. TAUSSIG	1957	stricken 1972	DE 1073	ROBERT E. PEARY	1972	decomm. 7 Aug 1992; to Taiwan 7 Aug 1992
DE 1031			OSP Italian frigate				
DE 1032			OSP Portuguese frigate	DE 1074	HAROLD E. HOLT	1971	decomm. 2 July 1992; str. 11 Jan 1995
CLAUD JONES class (4)							
DE 1033	CLAUD JONES	1959	to Indonesia 1974	DE 1075	TRIPPE	1970	decomm./to Greece 30 July 1992
DE 1034	JOHN R. PERRY	1959	to Indonesia 1973	DE 1076	FANNING	1971	decomm./to Turkey 31 July 1992
DE 1035	CHARLES BERRY	1959	to Indonesia 1974	DE 1077	OUELLET	1970	decomm. 6 Aug 1993; str. 11 Jan 1995; to Thailand 27 Nov 1996
DE 1036	MCMORRIS	1960	to Indonesia 1974				
BRONSTEIN class (2)				DE 1078	JOSEPH HEWES	1971	to NRF 30 Sep 1991; decomm./ to Taiwan 30 June 1994
DE 1037	BRONSTEIN	1963	decomm. 13 Dec 1990; str. 4 Oct 1991; to Mexico 16 Nov 1993				
				DE 1079	BOWEN	1971	to NRF 30 Sep 1991; decomm./ to Turkey 3 June 1994
DE 1038	MCCLOY	1963	decomm. 14 Dec 1990; str. 4 Oct 1991; to Mexico 16 Nov 1993	DE 1080	PAUL	1971	decomm. 14 Aug 1992; str. 11 Jan 1995; to Turkey
				DE 1081	AYLWIN	1971	decomm. 15 May 1992; str. 11 Jan 1995; to Taiwan 29 Apr 1998
DE 1039			OSP Portuguese frigate				
GARCIA class (10)				DE 1082	ELMER MONTGOMERY	1971	decomm./str. 30 June 1993; to Turkey 13 Dec 1993
DE 1040	GARCIA	1964	to Pakistan 1989				
DE 1041	BRADLEY	1965	to Brazil 1989	DE 1083	COOK	1971	to NRF 1 Oct 1989; decomm. 30 Apr 1992; to Taiwan 31 May 1994
DE 1042			OSP Portuguese frigate				
GARCIA class (continued)							
DE 1043	EDWARD MCDONNELL	1965	stricken 15 Dec 1992	DE 1084	MCCANDLESS	1972	to NRF 31 Dec 1991; decomm./ to Turkey 6 May 1994
DE 1044	BRUMBY	1965	to Pakistan 1989				
DE 1045	DAVIDSON	1965	to Brazil 1989	DE 1085	DONALD B. BEARY	1972	to NRF 30 Sep 1991; decomm./ to Turkey 20 May 1994
DE 1046			OSP Portuguese frigate				
GARCIA class (continued)				DE 1086	BREWTON	1972	decomm. 2 July 1992; to Taiwan 23 July 1992
DE 1047	VOGE	1966	stricken 15 Dec 1992				
DE 1048	SAMPLE	1968	to Brazil 1989	DE 1087	KIRK	1972	decomm./to Taiwan 6 Aug 1993
DE 1049	KOELSCH	1967	to Pakistan 1989	DE 1088	BARBEY	1972	to NRF 15 Jan 1991; decomm. 20 Mar 1992; to Taiwan 21 June 1994
DE 1050	ALBERT DAVID	1968	to Brazil 1989				
DE 1051	O'CALLAHAN	1968	to Pakistan 1989				
KNOX class (46)				DE 1089	JESSE L. BROWN	1973	to NRF 31 Dec 1991; decomm. 27 July 1994; str. 11 Jan 1995; to Egypt
DE 1052	KNOX	1969	decomm. 14 Feb 1992; str. 11 Jan 1995				
DE 1053	ROARK	1969	decomm. 14 Dec 1991; str. 11 Jan 1995	DE 1090	AINSWORTH	1973	to NRF 30 Sep 1990; decomm./ to Turkey 27 May 1994
DE 1054	GRAY	1970	decomm. 30 Sep 1991; str. 11 Jan 1995	DE 1091	MILLER	1973	to NRF 17 Jan 1982; decomm. 15 Oct 1991; str. 11 Jan 1995; to Turkey
DE 1055	HEPBURN	1969	to NRF 1 Oct 1989; decomm. 20 Dec 1991				
DE 1056	CONNOLE	1969	decomm./to Greece 30 Aug 1992	DE 1092	THOMAS C. HART	1973	decomm./to Turkey 30 Aug 1993
DE 1057	RATHBURNE	1970	decomm. 14 Feb 1992; str. 11 Jan 1995	DE 1093	CAPODANNO	1973	decomm./to Turkey 30 July 1993
				DE 1094	PHARRIS	1974	decomm. 15 Feb 1992; str. 11 Jan 1995
DE 1058	MEYERKORD	1969	to NRF 30 Sep 1989; decomm. 14 Dec 1991; str. 11 Jan 1995				
DE 1059	W. S. SIMS	1970	to NRF 30 Sep 1990; decomm. 6 Sep 1991; str. 11 Jan 1995; to Turkey	DE 1095	TRUETT	1974	to NRF 31 Dec 1991; decomm. 30 July 1994; str. 11 Jan 1995; to Thailand 29 Apr 1998
DE 1060	LANG	1970	to NRF 17 Jan 1982; decomm. 12 Dec 1991; str. 11 Jan 1995	DE 1096	VALDEZ	1974	decomm. 16 Dec 1991; str. 11 Jan 1995
DE 1061	PATTERSON	1970	to NRF 15 June 1983; decomm. 30 Sep 1991; str. 11 Jan 1995	DE 1097	MOINESTER	1974	to NRF 31 Dec 1991; decomm. 28 July 1994; str. 11 Jan 1995; to Egypt 25 Mar 1998
DE 1062	WHIPPLE	1970	decomm. 14 Feb 1992; str. 11 Jan 1995	DE 1098–1107 KNOX class			canceled 1968–1969
				GLOVER type			
DE 1063	REASONER	1971	decomm./to Turkey 28 Aug 1993	FF 1098	GLOVER (ex-AGDE 1)	1965	decomm. 15 June 1990; to MSC; str. 20 Nov 1992 (see text)

U.S. World War II destroyer escort programs reached hull number DE 1005 (with DE 801–1005 being canceled in 1943). After the war, 43 destroyer escorts were converted to radar picket escorts (DER)—seven for the tactical fleet role and 36 for strategic early warning of a Soviet bomber attack against the continental United States. A few were modified to an escort control (DEC) configuration to support amphibious landings. These ships retained their original DE hull numbers in their new roles. (During the war, 96 DEs were converted to high speed transports, designated in the series APD 37–139; the APD 1–36 were converted World War I–era destroyers.)

The first postwar DEs actually were envisioned as successors to the war-built, steel-hulled submarine chasers (PC/PCE). With the start of the postwar programs in the early 1950s, these ships were reclassified as ocean escorts (DE), partly to avoid confusion with escort destroyers (DDE). In 1975 all existing U.S. escort vessels (DE/DEG/DER) were reclassified as frigates (FF/FFG/FFR).

U.S. hull numbers were assigned to 17 ships built in Europe with American funding (under the Offshore Procurement or OSP program). Thirteen U.S. ships of the DEALEY design (DE 1006, 1014, 1015, and 1021–1030) were completed between 1954 and 1957, and ships of the CLAUD JONES design (DE 1033–1036) were completed in 1959–1960. Both of these designs were intended for mass production in wartime, especially by small shipyards. Significantly, while the massive World War II–era DE program included large numbers of diesel-propelled ships, in the postwar era only the four ships of the JONES class were diesel, the remainder being steam/geared powered until the advent of the PERRY class (gas turbine).

The two-ship BRONSTEIN class (DE 1037, 1038) introduced several new ASW capabilities to U.S. frigates—drone helicopters, ASROC, and the large SQS-26 bow-mounted sonar. They were armed with 3-inch guns; the subsequent BROOKE, GARCIA, and KNOX classes had 5-inch guns, with the PERRY class returning to smaller-caliber, 76-mm weapons.

Of the GARCIA class, the O'CALLAHAN was returned from Pakistan on 14 November 1993, the GARCIA on 13 November 1994, and the BRUMBY and KOELSCH on 19 August 1994. All were stricken on the same dates.

The KNOX class, with 46 ships completed, was the largest class of surface combatants to be constructed in the West after World War II until the PERRY-class frigates. The KNOX DE/FFs were criticized for their large size (comparable to World War II–era destroyers) with a single propeller shaft and limited AAW/ASUW capabilities. The latter limitation was partially corrected with the Harpoon missile fired from the ASROC launcher.

All PERRY-class ships on loan at the time were stricken from the NVR on 11 January 1995. The MILLER, PAUL, and W. S. SIMS were transferred to Turkey for cannibalization to support other ships of this class in Turkish service; they were subsequently scrapped.

The GLOVER was built as an experimental frigate with a modified propeller configuration. The ship was commissioned in 1965 as the AGDE 1; subsequently changed to AGFF 1 and then FF 1098, she was decommissioned and again assigned to the research role with the auxiliary designation T-AGFF 1 on 15 June 1990, being operated from that date by the Military Sealift Command. She was the only truly armed MSC ship, having a 5-inch gun at the time of her transfer.

The sterns of the WADSWORTH *(left)* and MCCLUSKY show the opening in their stern counters for the SQR-19 TACTAS (round opening) and the SLQ-25A Nixie torpedo countermeasures. A few PERRY-class ships are not fitted with those systems. These are single-screw ships, a cause of criticism of their design. (1997, U.S. Navy)

CHAPTER 17

Command Ships

The Third Fleet flagship CORONADO enters Seattle, Wash., to participate in a major waterfront fair. The Navy's fleet flagships provide an important political presence during port visits in the United States as well as overseas. They are increasingly hard-pressed to carry out their primary command ship mission because of the growth of flagship equipment and staffs. (1999, U.S. Navy, PH2 Christopher Mobley)

The U.S. Navy has four fleet-level command ships in service: the MOUNT WHITNEY, flagship of Commander, Second Fleet, in the Atlantic; CORONADO, flagship of Commander, Third Fleet, in the Eastern Pacific; LA SALLE, flagship of Commander, Sixth Fleet, in the Mediterranean; and BLUE RIDGE, flagship of Commander, Seventh Fleet, in the Western Pacific.

Two new-construction "joint command ships" are planned for construction, to be authorized in FY 2004 and 2005 under current Department of Defense planning, to replace the four existing LCC/AGF command ships. At this writing, it was not known if additional JCCs would be constructed in later years to provide four replacement ships, or if amphibious ships (most likely) or other ships would be modified to serve in the fleet flagship role. In planning documents, the planned ships are given the unofficial designation JCC.

The four numbered fleets generally had cruisers for flagships from the end of World War II until the 1970s. However, the cruisers now in service do not have major flag facilities and accommodations. The last specially configured cruiser-flagship, the BELKNAP (CG 26), had been partially converted in 1978–1980 to accommodate a portion of the Sixth Fleet staff, while retaining a full missile cruiser capability; she was decommissioned in 1995.

The four battleships of the IOWA (BB 61) class reactivated in the 1980s were not fitted to serve as major flagships.

Classification: The BLUE RIDGE and MOUNT WHITNEY retain their amphibious command ship LCC designation in the fleet command ship role; the miscellaneous flagships (AGF) retain their previous LPD hull numbers with the AGF designation.

Names: Amphibious command ships (AGC/LCC) have traditionally been assigned the names of American mountains and mountain ranges. The AGFs retain their amphibious ship names.

2 AMPHIBIOUS COMMAND SHIPS: "BLUE RIDGE" CLASS

Number	Name	FY	Builder	Laid down	Launched	Commissioned	Status
LCC 19	BLUE RIDGE	65	Philadelphia Naval Shipyard	27 Feb 1967	4 Jan 1969	14 Nov 1970	**PA**
LCC 20	MOUNT WHITNEY	66	Newport News Shipbuilding, Va.	8 Jan 1969	8 Jan 1970	16 Jan 1971	**AA**

Displacement:	16,790 tons light	Flag:	approx. 250
	18,646 tons full load	Troops:	LCC 19: 16 (1 officer + 15 enlisted)
Length:	579¹¹⁄₁₂ feet (176.8 m) waterline	Helicopters:	landing area only
	636⁵⁄₁₂ feet (194.0 m) overall	Missiles:	removed
Beam:	82 feet (25.0 m)	Guns:	2 25-mm Bushmaster cannon Mk 38 (2 single)
Extreme width:	108 feet (32.9 m)		2 20-mm Phalanx CIWS Mk 16 (2 multibarrel)
Draft:	28⅚ feet (8.8 m)		4 .50-cal machine guns (4 single)
Propulsion:	1 steam turbine (General Electric); 22,000 shp; 1 shaft	Radars:	SPS-40E air search
Boilers:	2 600-psi (41.7-kg/cm²) (Foster Wheeler)		SPS-48C 3-D search
Speed:	22 knots (20 knots sustained)		SPS-64(V)9 navigation
Range:	13,500 n.miles (25,000 km) at 16 knots		SPS-65(V)1 surface search
Manning:	LCC 19: 784 (42 officers + 742 enlisted)	Fire control:	removed
	LCC 20: 717 (43 officers + 674 enlisted)	EW systems:	SLQ-25A Nixie
			SLQ-32(V)3

These are large command ships, the only U.S. Navy ships to be designed from the outset specifically for the amphibious command ship role. The Navy's earlier command ships could not operate with the 20-knot amphibious ships built from the 1960s onward. Both of these ships are now employed as fleet flagships.

The BLUE RIDGE is homeported in Yokosuka, Japan, having relieved the cruiser OKLAHOMA CITY (CG 5) in October 1979 as flagship of the Seventh Fleet. The MOUNT WHITNEY is based at Norfolk, Va.

Class: A third ship of this class (AGC 21) was planned, to have been configured for service as both an amphibious flagship and fleet flagship; she was canceled.

Classification: These ships were originally classified as amphibious force flagships (AGC); they were changed to amphibious command ships (LCC) on 1 January 1969.

Design: SCB No. 400. The hull and propulsion machinery are similar to that of the IWO JIMA (LPH 2)-class helicopter carriers. The command ship facilities originally provided in this class were for a Navy amphibious task force commander and a Marine assault force commander and their staffs. Their designed flag/staff accommodations were for 200 officers and 500 enlisted men.

The ships have large open deck areas to provide for optimum antenna placement. There is a helicopter landing area aft, but no hangar. (A small vehicle hangar is serviced by an elevator.) Davits provide stowage for five LCPL/LCVP-type personnel craft, plus a ship's launch.

Guns: The early designs for this ship provided for six 3-inch/50-cal AA Mk 33 guns in twin mounts; two pair forward of the bridge structure in enclosed gun houses were fitted, but the third pair on the forecastle were not installed. The two 3-inch mounts were removed in 1992.

Phalanx CIWS were long scheduled for installation in these ships. Two CIWS were provided in the BLUE RIDGE in 1985, mounted forward on a small deckhouse fitted on the main deck and a sponson at the stern (increasing length approximately 16 feet/4.9 m); the same installation was fitted in MOUNT WHITNEY in 1987.

Helicopters: An SH-3 Sea King is usually assigned to each ship.

Missiles: Two 8-tube Sea Sparrow BPDMS launchers were fitted abaft of the bridge structure in 1974. They were re-

moved from both ships in 1992, as were the two Mk 115 missile fire control systems.

Operational: In addition to the Seventh Fleet staff, the BLUE RIDGE carriers a Marine communications detachment. For exercises, the BLUE RIDGE normally embarks the staffs of Commander, Amphibious Group 1/Amphibious Force Seventh Fleet (48 officers + 95 enlisted), and the Commander, III Marine Expeditionary Force/Landing Force Seventh Fleet (80 officers + 127 enlisted).

The MOUNT WHITNEY, in addition to the Second Fleet staff, for exercises carries the staff of Amphibious Group 2 (26 officers + 47 enlisted) and a Marine communications detachment (1 officer + 15 enlisted).

AMPHIBIOUS COMMAND SHIPS

Amphibious command ships—originally called amphibious force flagships—reached hull number AGC 18 during World War II. Fourteen C2-type merchant ships were completed as command ships (AGCs 1–3, 5, and 7–17); one transport was converted to that role (AGC 4), as was one small seaplane tender, the BISCAYNE (AGC 18, ex-AVP 11). In addition, six large Coast Guard cutters of the "Secretary" class were reconfigured as flagships in 1944–1945, but only one was reclassified: the DUANE (AGC 6, ex-WPG 33). After the war, the six ships, rated as 327-foot (99.7-m) cutters by the Coast Guard, reverted to multimission ships.

Five surviving C2-type ships were changed from AGC to LCC on 1 January 1969. The last war-era AGC to see active naval service was the ELDORADO (AGC/LCC 11), decommissioned in 1973.

The civilian yacht WILLIAMSBURG, which served as a gunboat (PG 56) from 1941 to 1945, was assigned as the presidential yacht after World War II, being redesignated AGC 369 on 10 November 1945. She served in that role for President Truman and (for one cruise) President Eisenhower. The WILLIAMSBURG was decommissioned in 1953 and stricken in 1962.

The WILLIAMSBURG was then employed as a civilian oceanographic research ship from 1962 to 1986. Now abandoned in Italy, efforts are under way to return her to the United States for preservation and possible use as an excursion vessel.

The MOUNT WHITNEY at anchor (with national ensign at stern). Note the bridge extensions, boat stowage, and the antenna arrays fitted in this class. They have had sponsons installed on their stern counter to mount a Phalanx CIWS. Their original armament was 3-inch/50-cal AA guns in twin mounts. (1999, Leo Van Ginderen)

The MOUNT WHITNEY in her current configuration, with the large lattice mast previously mounted forward of her bridge structure deleted. The antenna rigs of these ships change periodically as communications gear is updated. The proposed follow-on JCC ships could be even larger, as staffs are being increased and more equipment is being provided to command centers. (U.S. Navy)

The BLUE RIDGE in the Far East. She has a VIP-configured SH-3 Sea King on her helicopter deck; these ships have no helicopter hangar. The large lattice mast previously mounted forward has been removed. Built as amphibious force flagships (AGC), they have long and effectively served as fleet flagships. (1997, Leo Van Ginderen)

1 MISCELLANEOUS FLAGSHIP: CONVERTED "AUSTIN" CLASS

Number	Name	FY	Builder	Laid down	Launched	Comm.	Status
AGF 11 (ex-LPD 11)	CORONADO	64	Lockheed Shipbuilding & Constn., Seattle, Wash.	3 May 1965	30 July 1966	23 May 1970	**PA**

Displacement:	11,050 tons light	Helicopters:	1 SH-3 Sea King
	16,912 tons full load	Missiles:	none
Length:	568¾ feet (173.4 m) overall	Guns:	2 20-mm Phalanx CIWS Mk 16 (2 multibarrel)
Beam:	84 feet (25.6 m)		2 12.7-mm machine guns (2 single)
Draft:	23⁷⁄₁₂ feet (7.2 m)	Radars:	SPS-10F surface search
Propulsion:	2 steam turbines (De Laval); 24,000 shp; 2 shafts		SPS-40E air search
Boilers:	2 600-psi (41.7-kg/cm²) (Foster-Wheeler)		SPS-64(V)9 navigation
Speed:	21 knots	Fire control:	local control only
Range:	7,700 n.miles (14,260 km) at 20 knots	EW systems:	SLQ-32(V)2
Manning:	457 (24 officers + 433 enlisted)		WLR-1H intercept
Flag:			

The CORONADO was built and served as an amphibious ship until 1980 when she was modified to serve as a temporary flagship to permit the Middle East flagship LA SALLE to undergo a lengthy overhaul at the Philadelphia Naval Shipyard. Subsequently, after overhaul in 1983–1984, she became flagship of the Sixth Fleet in August 1985 and was homeported in Gaeta, Italy. The CORONADO replaced the destroyer tender PUGET SOUND (AD 38) as Sixth Fleet flagship.

In June 1986, with the BELKNAP assigned as Sixth Fleet flagship, the CORONADO departed the Mediterranean and the following month shifted to the Pacific to become flagship for Commander, Third Fleet (then based at Pearl Harbor). Prior to breaking his flag in the CORONADO on 26 November 1986, the Commander, Third Fleet, had flown his flag ashore since the end of World War II. In August 1991 the Commander, Third Fleet, sailing on board the CORONADO, shifted her home port to Naval Air Station North Island at San Diego, Calif.

Classification: The classification of the CORONADO was changed from LPD 11 to AGF 11 on 1 October 1980.

Conversion: The CORONADO's telescoping hangar is 49½ feet (15.1 m) long, 18½ feet (5.6 m) wide, and 17⅔ feet (5.4 m) high; it expands to a length of about 75 feet (22.9 m). The ship retained a docking well until her 1997–1998 overhaul, when the well was rebuilt. The well now contains a three-deck, 35,000-square-foot (3,255-m²) space for command and control facilities, and accommodations for 220 personnel.

Design: SCB No. 187C. See AUSTIN (LPD 4) listing for additional details. The ship is similar to but larger than the LA SALLE.

Guns: Phalanx CIWS have been installed on an extension of the bridge structure, forward to port, and amidships on the starboard side. The two 3-inch/50-cal Mk 33 AA twin gun mounts previously carried in the AGF role were removed in the early 1990s.

The CORONADO largely retains her LPD configuration. She can be readily identified as an AGF by her array of antennas with a lattice mast fitted aft of her superstructure. Her two Phalanx CIWS are situated on a platform forward and between her masts. A VIP-configured SH-3 Sea King is on her helicopter deck, aft of her hangar. (1997, Leo Van Ginderen)

1 MISCELLANEOUS FLAGSHIP: CONVERTED "RALEIGH" CLASS

Number	Name	FY	Builder	Laid down	Launched	Commissioned	Status
AGF 3 (ex-LPD 3)	La Salle	61	New York Naval Shipyard	2 Apr 1962	3 Aug 1963	22 Feb 1964	**AA**

Displacement:	8,040 tons light	Flag:	
	14,650 tons full load	Helicopters:	1 SH-3G Sea King
Length:	500 feet (152.4 m) waterline	Missiles:	none
	521¾ feet (159.0 m) overall	Guns:	2 25-mm Bushmaster cannon Mk 38 (2 single)
Beam:	84 feet (25.6 m)		2 20-mm Phalanx CIWS Mk 16 (2 multibarrel)
Draft:	22 feet (6.7 m)		2 12.7-mm machine guns (2 single)
Propulsion:	2 steam turbines (De Laval); 24,000 shp; 2 shafts	Radars:	SPS-10F surface search
Boilers:	2 600-psi (41.7-kg/cm²) (Babcock & Wilcox)		SPS-40E air search
Speed:	21.6 knots (20 knots sustained)		SPS-64(V)9 navigation
Range:	9,600 n.miles (17,780 km) at 16 knots	Fire control:	local control only
	16,500 n.miles (30,558 km) at 10 knots	EW systems:	SLQ-32(V)3
Manning:	455 (24 officers + 431 enlisted)		WLR-1H

The La Salle was converted from an amphibious ship specifically to serve as flagship for Commander, U.S. Middle East Force (now Commander, U.S. Naval Forces, Central Command). In November 1994, she replaced the cruiser Belknap as flagship of the Sixth Fleet in the Mediterranean.

Class: The La Salle was one of three amphibious transport docks of the Raleigh (LPD 1) class.

Classification: She was built as LPD 3 and served as an amphibious ship until 1 July 1972 when she was changed to AGF 3.

Conversion: The ship was converted to a flagship in 1972, with command and communication facilities, a helicopter hangar, and additional air conditioning. The amidships hangar is 47⁵⁄₁₂ feet (14.6 m) long, 18¹⁄₁₂ feet (5.5 m) wide, and 19¹⁄₃ feet (5.9 m) high.

Design: SCB No. 187A.

Guns: Phalanx CIWS have been installed amidships, port and starboard. The two 3-inch (76-mm) 50-cal Mk 33 AA twin gun mounts previously mounted as an AGF have been deleted.

Operational: The La Salle operated in the Persian Gulf–Indian Ocean area from 1972 to 1980, when she was relieved by the Coronado. The La Salle underwent an extensive overhaul at the Philadelphia Naval Shipyard from December 1980 to September 1982. After that overhaul, she in turn relieved the Coronado as flagship of the Middle East Force on 16 June 1983 at Mina' Sulman, Bahrain. She served in that role during the Persian Gulf War, shifting to the Mediterranean in late 1994 to serve as Sixth Fleet flagship; she is homeported at Gaeta, Italy.

In 1984, in response to mining of the Red Sea by a Libyan merchant ship, the La Salle operated RH-53D Sea Stallion mine countermeasures helicopters.

Prior to the conversion of the La Salle, the flagship of the Commander, Middle East Force, had been small seaplane tenders of the Barnegat (AVP 10) class from the time that command was established in the late 1940s (see below).

The La Salle, showing the additional structure built into the ship's docking well. A small lattice mast is immediately forward of the structure, adjacent to the ship's large crane. An alternative to a new-design JCC could be the construction of modified amphibious ships of the San Antonio (LPD 17) class, although they may be too small for command ships. (1999, Leo Van Ginderen)

The LA SALLE at Malta. She retains her original pole mast, in contrast to the forward lattice mast of the CORONADO. The LA SALLE's two Phalanx CIWS mounts are amidships, port and starboard; here OE-82 SATCOM antennas are mounted on her mast, below her radar antennas. (1996, Leo Van Ginderen)

FLEET/NATIONAL COMMAND SHIPS

In addition to the two amphibious command ships (AGC/LCC) listed above, in the post–World War II era the Navy has built one ship and converted another specifically for use as major command ships. A third such ship was planned for conversion.

Construction of the heavy cruiser NORTHAMPTON (CA 125) was canceled in 1945 when 56.2 percent complete. She was reordered in 1948 and completed as a tactical command ship (CLC 1) in 1953. After operating as a fleet flagship, she was reconfigured to serve as a National Emergency Command Post Afloat (NECPA) in 1961 (redesignated CC 1). She was decommissioned in 1970 and laid up in reserve until stricken in 1977.

The light aircraft carriers WRIGHT (CVL 49) and SAIPAN (CVL 48), completed in 1946–1947, were similarly chosen for conversion to the NECPA role. The WRIGHT, designated AVT 7 while in reserve, was converted to a national command ship in 1962–1963 and became CC 2. She operated in the NECPA role until 1970 when she was laid up in reserve; she was stricken in 1977. The SAIPAN, designated AVT 6 while in reserve after World War II, began conversion to CC 3 in 1964, but was instead completed as a major communications relay ship in 1966 (renamed ARLINGTON and designated AGMR 2).

In the NECPA role, these ships were to provide afloat facilities for the president in the event of a national emergency or war. (A more interesting—although not undertaken—proposal was to convert the large, nuclear-propelled submarine TRITON/SSRN 586 to an underwater NECPA.)

In the fiscal 1953 conversion program, the unfinished large (battle) cruiser HAWAII (CB 3) was authorized for conversion to a fleet command ship (CBC), but no work was undertaken on that project other than the removal of her main battery turrets and it was ultimately canceled. She would have been an enlarged version of the command ship NORTHAMPTON.

MISCELLANEOUS FLAGSHIPS

From 1949 until 1965 the Navy rotated small seaplane tenders (AVP) as flagships for U.S. forces in the Persian Gulf area: the DUXBURY BAY (AVP 38), GREENWICH BAY (AVP 41), and VALCOUR (AVP 55). Subsequently, on 15 December 1965 the VALCOUR was reclassified as a miscellaneous flagship (AGF 1) specifically for that role and was homeported in Bahrain, alleviating the need to rotate flagships. She was replaced in that role by the LA SALLE in 1972. The Middle East AVP/AGF flagships were painted white to help counter the intense heat of the Persian Gulf.

Since 1994 various U.S. cruisers and destroyers operating in the Gulf area have served as flagship for the Commander, Naval Forces, U.S. Central Command; the first was the destroyer FLETCHER (DD 992), in 1994.

The CORONADO departing Pearl Harbor for the multinational exercise RIMPAC '98. The CORONADO has not had as extensive modifications for the AGF role as has the older LA SALLE. (1998, U.S. Navy, PH2 August Sigur)

CHAPTER 18

Amphibious Warfare Ships

Amphibious ready groups—centered on LHA/LHD helicopter/STOVL carriers—have had major roles in supporting U.S. military and peacekeeping operations in the post–Cold War era. Here the PELELIU takes aboard one of her LCUs off East Timor as U.S. Marines provide support to United Nations peacekeeping forces on the island. (1999, U.S. Navy, PH3 Michael Townsend)

The U.S. Navy's amphibious lift in early 2001 consists of 37 ships in active service and two assigned to the Naval Reserve Force (NRF), the latter manned by composite active/reserve crews (see table 18-1). Four additional amphibious-type ships (LCC/LPD) are employed as command ships for fleet/force commanders and are not available to provide amphibious lift (see chapter 17 of this edition of *Ships and Aircraft*). One former LPH, the INCHON, has been converted to a mine countermeasures support ship (now MCS 12).

TABLE 18-1. AMPHIBIOUS WARFARE SHIPS (EARLY 2001)

Type	Class/Ship	Commissioned	Active	NRF	Reserve	Building*
LHD 1	WASP	1989–	6	—	—	1
LHA 1	TARAWA	1976–1980	5	—	—	—
LPD 17	SAN ANTONIO	2003–	—	—	—	6
LPD 4	AUSTIN	1965–1971	11	—	—	—
LSD 49	HARPERS FERRY	1995–1998	4	—	—	—
LSD 41	WHIDBEY ISLAND	1985–1992	8	—	—	—
LSD 36	ANCHORAGE	1969–1972	3	—	—	—
LST 1179	NEWPORT	1969–1972	—	1	4	—
LKA 113	CHARLESTON	1968–1970	—	—	5	—

*Ships authorized through FY 2001

In addition, nine older amphibious ships (LKA/LST) are being maintained in reserve to offset the rapid retirement of older "amphibs" and delays in procurement of the SAN ANTONIO–class LPDs.

Currently under construction are a helicopter/dock ship assault ship (LHD) and a new class of amphibious transport docks (LPD). Additional LHDs will be constructed starting in FY 2001 to begin replacing the TARAWA-class LHAs. The Department of Defense did not plan authorization for this ship until FY 2005; however, in 1999 Congress voted long-lead-time procurement for the ship in the FY 2000 budget with full funding for FY 2001.

In the later stages of the Cold War, the U.S. Navy/Marine requirement for amphibious lift was 60-plus ships capable of carrying the assault elements of a Marine Expeditionary Force (MEF) plus a Marine Expeditionary Brigade (MEB; see chapter 7). In 1991—when the Soviet Union collapsed—the Navy had 60 amphibious ships in active commission, plus three NRF ships.

The post–Cold War requirement is for sufficient amphibious ships to lift three MEBs. This is significantly less than the previous MEF + MEB requirement because a MEF, in addition to having the rough equivalent of three MEBs as ground combat elements, contains numerous command, combat support, and other support components.

In reality, since the mid-1990s the lift capacity has been about two and a half MEBs *if* essentially all amphibious ships were available—a total lift capacity of perhaps 25,000 troops. This is a theoretical capability, however, as it is impossible to assemble more than perhaps three Amphibious Ready Groups (ARG) in a given area in less than two to three months. (During the five-month buildup for the Persian Gulf conflict of January 1991, the Navy assembled 31 amphibious ships embarking a MEB plus a separate MEU—a total of some 17,000 troops.)

The Navy currently has 12 Amphibious Ready Groups, each normally consisting of three or four ships. Each ARG can embark a Marine Expeditionary Unit (MEU), i.e., a reinforced Marine battalion with complementary command, aviation, and support units totaling some 2,000 officers and enlisted personnel. The ARG carries helicopters, landing craft (LCU), air cushion landing craft (LCAC), and amphibious assault vehicles (AAV—"amphibious tractors") that can land the combat components of the MEU. Note that only 11 LHA/LHD helicopter carriers currently are available, severely limiting the helicopter/STOVL capabilities of one ARG.

By 2010 each ARG will be standardized at three ships:

1 LHA/LHD
1 LPD
1 LSD

Normally, two or three ARGs are forward deployed: one in the Atlantic–Mediterranean area, one in the Persian Gulf–Indian Ocean area, and/or one in the Western Pacific area. The other ARG ships are in transit, working up (with MEUs), or in overhaul. One ARG (four ships) is forward based in Sasebo, Japan.

Aircraft: A nominal LHA/LHD "air wing" consists of a Marine composite squadron of 18 CH-46 Sea Knight, 4 CH-53 Sea Stallion, and 4 AH-1W SeaCobra helicopters, plus a couple of UH-1N Huey command/utility helicopters. These ships regularly operate AV-8B Harrier STOVL fixed-wing attack aircraft. They also can operate Unmanned Aerial Vehicle (UAV)-type aircraft. No catapults or arresting gear is fitted in the LHA/LHD-type ships.

Guns: Beginning in the 1980s, LSD- and LPD-type amphibious ships were fitted with .50-cal/7.62-mm machine guns, 25-mm Bushmaster Mk 38 "chain" guns, and 20-mm cannon for close-in defense against small craft; this armament suite was especially important for ships deploying into the Persian Gulf.

All 3-inch/50-cal (76-mm) guns have been removed from surviving amphibious ships except for NEWPORT-class LSTs and CHARLESTON-class LKAs, all in reserve. The 5-inch/54-cal (127-mm) guns previously fitted in the TARAWA-class LHAs have been removed.

Historical: The Reagan administration's buildup of amphibious ships in the 1980s was the third major "spurt" of amphibious ship construction since World War II. The first, during the Korean War, produced the LSD 28 and LST 1156 classes (23 ships); the second, in the Kennedy–Johnson administrations of the early 1960s, produced the LCC 19, LHA 1, LKA 112, LPD 12, LSD 36, and LST 1179 classes (49 ships).

The third postwar amphibious ship buildup effort began with the WHIDBEY ISLAND, the first amphibious ship authorized for the U.S. Navy in a decade. That ship was funded by Congress in fiscal 1981 over the objections of the Carter administration. With the Reagan administration entering the White House in January 1981, amphibious ship construction was accelerated. This third amphibious buildup included the WASP, WHIDBEY ISLAND, and HARPERS FERRY classes. Eighteen ships of these three classes were funded in the fiscal 1984–1993 shipbuilding programs.

Table 18-2 shows the capacity of current amphibious ships.

Names: Amphibious assault ships (LPH/LHA) are named for battles fought by Marines; the LHD series, however, carries the names of World War II–era aircraft carriers, which in turn were named for earlier Navy ships and battles.

Amphibious cargo ships (LKA) and tank landing ships (LST) are named for counties and parishes, the latter being the equivalent of counties in the state of Louisiana.[1]

---

1. When LSTs were first assigned names on 1 July 1955, all names had the suffix "County" or "Parish." This naming scheme was continued until the advent of the NEWPORT and several of her sister ships, which do not have suffixes.

The PELELIU, barely under way. The "notches" in her forward flight deck indicate where she originally mounted 5-inch/54-cal guns. The deck-edge elevator, on the port side, is at the flight-deck level. (U.S. Navy)

TABLE 18-2. NOMINAL AMPHIBIOUS LIFT CAPABILITIES

Class	Troops	Vehicle space (square feet)	Cargo space (cubic feet)	Helicopter spots[a]	LCAC spots[b]
LHD 1	1,685	20,900	109,000	46	3
LHA 1	1,710	25,400	105,900	41	1
LPH 2[c]	1,490	3,400	49,500	26	—
LPD 17	720	25,000	25,000	6	2
LPD 4	[d]	12,000	40,000	4	1
LSD 49 CV	400	16,600	50,700	2	2
LSD 41	450	13,500	5,100	0	4
LSD 36	300	15,200	1,400	0	3
LST 1179	350	17,300	3,400	0	—
LKA 113	210	32,900	66,100	0	—

[a] Hangar and flight deck capacity (CH-46E equivalents) for ships that normally embark helicopters
[b] Docking well capacity
[c] Included for comparative purposes; none on the current Naval Vessel Register
[d] LPD 4–6, 14, 15 can accommodate 930 troops; LPD 7–10, 12, 13 can accommodate 840 troops, the reduction to provide space for flag accommodations

Amphibious transport docks (LPD) are named for cities that honor explorers and pioneers.

Dock landing ships (LSD) carry the names of historic sites and cities.

Operational: Amphibious Squadron 11 is the Navy's only permanently forward-deployed Amphibious Squadron (PHIBRON). It consists of four ships: one LHD, one LPD, and two LSDs. The squadron was initially activated in July 1966 and then comprised seven ships homeported in Long Beach, Calif., with VALLEY FORGE (LPH 8) as flagship. The squadron was "reactivated" on 30 September 1992 to provide a forward-deployed PHIBRON in the Far East.

PHIBRON 11 embarks the 31st Marine Expeditionary Unit (MEU), which is forward-deployed to Okinawa.

6 + 2 AMPHIBIOUS ASSAULT SHIPS: "WASP" CLASS

Number	Name	FY	Builder	Laid down	Launched	Christened	Commissioned	Status
LHD 1	WASP	84	Litton/Ingalls Shipbuilding, Pascagoula, Miss.	30 May 1985	4 Aug 1987	19 Sep 1987	6 July 1989	**AA**
LHD 2	ESSEX	86	Litton/Ingalls Shipbuilding, Pascagoula, Miss.	20 Mar 1989	7 Jan 1991	16 Mar 1991	17 Oct 1992	**PA**
LHD 3	KEARSARGE	88	Litton/Ingalls Shipbuilding, Pascagoula, Miss.	6 Feb 1990	26 Mar 1992	16 May 1992	16 Oct 1993	**AA**
LHD 4	BOXER	89	Litton/Ingalls Shipbuilding, Pascagoula, Miss.	8 Apr 1991	13 Aug 1993	13 Aug 1993	11 Feb 1995	**PA**
LHD 5	BATAAN	91	Litton/Ingalls Shipbuilding, Pascagoula, Miss.	22 June 1994	15 Mar 1996	18 May 1996	20 Sep 1997	**AA**
LHD 6	BONHOMME RICHARD	93	Litton/Ingalls Shipbuilding, Pascagoula, Miss.	18 Apr 1995	14 Mar 1997	14 Mar 1997	15 Aug 1998	**PA**
LHD 7	IWO JIMA	96	Litton/Ingalls Shipbuilding, Pascagoula, Miss.	12 Dec 1997	4 Feb 2000	25 Mar 2000	2001	building
LHD 8	. . . . . .	02	Litton/Ingalls Shipbuilding, Pascagoula, Miss.					planned

Displacement:	28,233 tons light	Elevators:	2 deck edge (50 x 45 feet/15.2 x 13.7 m)
	40,535 tons full load	Missiles:	2 8-cell NATO Sea Sparrow missile launchers Mk 29
Length:	777⅝ feet (237.1 m) waterline		2 21-cell RAM missile launchers Mk 49
	844 feet (257.3 m) overall	Guns:	2 20-mm Phalanx CIWS Mk 15 (3 multibarrel)
Beam:	106 feet (32.3 m) waterline		8 12.7-mm machine guns M2HB (8 single)
Extreme width:	140 feet (42.7 m)	Radars:	Mk 23 Target Acquisition System (TAS)
Draft:	26⅔ feet (8.1 m)		SPS-48E 3-D air search
Propulsion:	2 steam turbines; 77,000 shp; 2 shafts		SPS-49(V)5 air search
Boilers:	2 600-psi (41.7-kg/cm²) (Combustion Engineering)		SPS-64(V)9 navigation
Speed:	24 knots (22 knots sustained)		SPS-67(V)3 surface search
Range:	9,500 n.miles (17,594 km) at 20 knots	Fire control:	2 Mk 91 missiles FCS
Manning:	1,146 (62 officers + 1,084 enlisted)		1 SYS-2(V)3 weapon control system
Troops:	1,700	EW systems:	SLQ-25A Nixie
Aircraft:	*amphibious role:* approx. 30 CH-46 Sea Knight and CH-53 Sea Stallion helicopters + 6 AV-8B Harrier STOVL		SLQ-32(V)3
			SRS-1 combat D/F
	carrier role: approx. 20 AV-8B Harrier STOVL + 6 SH-60 ASW helicopters		

These ships and the similar TARAWA class are the world's largest amphibious ships. The only larger ships that have been employed in this role were the converted ESSEX (CV 9)-class fleet carriers that operated in the LPH role (see below). The WASP class initially was planned as helicopter-carrying amphibious ships that would be smaller and less costly than the TARAWA class. In the event, the basic LHA design was adopted, with the following principal differences: (1) increased Harrier STOVL aircraft support capability; (2) movement of the stern elevator to the starboard side of the flight deck; (3) redesign of the docking well to accommodate three LCACs with an LPD/LSD stern gate vice the sectional, "split" gate of the LHA; and (4) modification of the self-defense armament.

The ESSEX is homeported in Sasebo, Japan, having relieved the BELLEAU WOOD as the forward-based helicopter carrier in mid-2000.

Class: An eighth LHD originally was planned during the late 1990s for inclusion in the Navy's fiscal 2005 shipbuilding program. However, Congress provided $880 million for design and material procurement for the LHD 8 in fiscal years 1999–2001 with total procurement expected to cost $1.5 *billion*. The remaining funds are expected to be provided by Congress in the fiscal 2002 budget.

The Department of Defense released $400 million to Litton/Ingalls on 28 July 2000 for the ship.

The LHD 8 will have a modified design with gas turbines and a hybrid electric propulsion system.

Classification: During the preliminary design stage these ships were designated LHDX. These ships should correctly have been designated sequentially in the LHA series as the differences in the two types are minor.

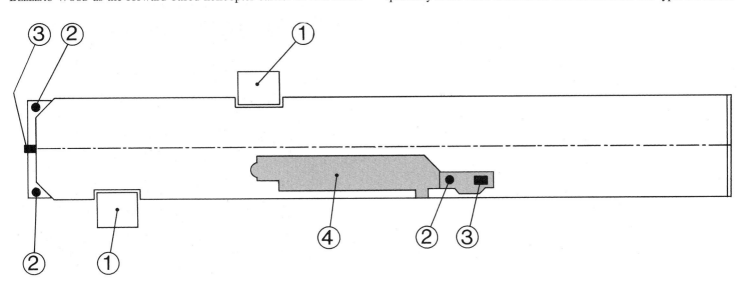

Amphibious Assault Ship WASP
1. Deck-edge elevator (2) 2. Phalanx CIWS (2) 3. NATO Sea Sparrow missile launcher Mk 29 (2) 4. Island structure

Cost: The BONHOMME RICHARD is officially listed as a fiscal 1993 ship, although only advance funds were provided in fiscal 1993 ($303.1 million) and the majority of the funds came in fiscal 1994 ($893.8 million). The ship also required outfitting and post-delivery funding, a total cost of about $1.2 *billion.*

Design: The basic configuration of these ships is similar to the LHA 1 class; however, they have less vehicle storage space and bulk cargo space, but carry more aircraft and the arrangement of the docking well permits more air-cushion landing craft to be embarked (three LCACs can be embarked); alternatively, the well can hold 12 LCM(6)s or six LCM(8)s or two LCU 1610s. The LHDs also have communications and certain command spaces moved into the hull (vice island structure in the LHAs) for better protection.

Although intended from the outset to operate Harriers as well as helicopters, these ships do not have ski-jump ramps to assist STOVL operations because the size of the flight deck is considered sufficiently large to enable rolling takeoffs for even heavily laden STOVL aircraft.

Medical facilities include beds for 600 patients, with six operating rooms and extensive dental facilities.

Electronics: Fitted with SPN-35A marshalling and SPN-43B and SPN-47 aircraft approach/control radars.

Engineering: Maximum horsepower is indicated above; the sustained shp is 70,000.

Missiles: The RAM launchers were added to the first six ships after completion; one of the original CIWS mounts was deleted with missile installation.

Names: These ships honor World War II–era fleet carriers (CV/CVL) and, in some cases, earlier Navy ships. The WASP recalls both the CV 7, which was sunk in 1942, and her namesake, the CV 18.

The BONHOMME RICHARD is named for the carrier CV 31—although that ship was named BON HOMME RICHARD (three words)—and the original frigate BONHOMME RICHARD, commanded by John Paul Jones in 1779 during her heroic battle with the British frigate SERAPIS.

The IWO JIMA is named for the Navy's first helicopter carrier (LPH 2) and the penultimate U.S. amphibious assault of World War II.

Troops: An additional 190 troops can be embarked for short transits (i.e., several days).

The ESSEX off the coast of southern California while carrying out trials of the MV-22 Osprey tilt-rotor aircraft. The MV-22 will replace the tired Marine CH-46E Sea Knight helicopters. (2000, U.S. Navy, PH3 Jamie D. Hernandez)

The BATAAN in the Atlantic, her flight deck crowded with Marine helicopters and, aft of the island structure, AV-8B Harrier STOVL aircraft. Belowdecks are several hundred Marines. The LHDs are easily distinguished from the LHAs by the later ships having their SPS-48E radar antennas on their forward mast and by their elevator arrangement. (1999, U.S. Navy, PH3 M. Dennis Timms)

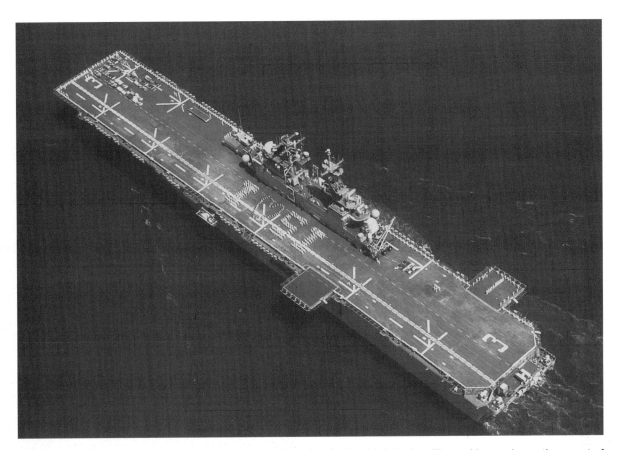

The KEARSARGE shows off her carrier configuration as she arrives in New York Harbor. These ships are larger than most of the world's "aircraft carriers" and displace more than the original fleet carriers of the ESSEX (CV 9) class, for which the LHDs are named. Note the elevator arrangement. (1998, U.S. Navy, PH1 Pat Cashin)

The docking well of the KEARSARGE with an LCAC in the after portion of the well. Three LCACs can be accommodated. Having a "wet well" is expensive in terms of space, machinery, and ship cost; neither the LCACs nor assault amphibian vehicles require a wet well to come aboard or be launched from a ship. (1994, Leo Van Ginderen)

The hangar deck of the KEARSARGE provides space for storage and maintenance of aircraft, such as this Marine CH-53E Sea Stallion shown being "stuffed" into the hangar. The procedure is referred to as a *stuffex*. The aircraft's rotors are folded back; the inflight refueling probe protrudes forward. (1999, U.S. Marine Corps, CWO Seth Rossman)

5 AMPHIBIOUS ASSAULT SHIPS: "TARAWA" CLASS

Number	Name	FY	Builder	Laid down	Launched	Christened	Comm.	Status
LHA 1	TARAWA	69	Litton/Ingalls Shipbuilding, Pascagoula, Miss.	15 Nov 1971	1 Dec 1973	1 Dec 1973	29 May 1976	**PA**
LHA 2	SAIPAN	70	Litton/Ingalls Shipbuilding, Pascagoula, Miss.	21 July 1972	18 July 1974	20 July 1974	15 Oct 1977	**AA**
LHA 3	BELLEAU WOOD	70	Litton/Ingalls Shipbuilding, Pascagoula, Miss.	5 Mar 1973	11 Apr 1977	11 June 1977	23 Sep 1978	**PA**
LHA 4	NASSAU	71	Litton/Ingalls Shipbuilding, Pascagoula, Miss.	13 Aug 1973	21 Jan 1978	28 Jan 1978	28 July 1979	**AA**
LHA 5	PELELIU	71	Litton/Ingalls Shipbuilding, Pascagoula, Miss.	12 Nov 1976	25 Nov 1978	6 Jan 1979	3 May 1980	**PA**

Displacement:	33,536 tons light		Aircraft:	approx. 30 CH-46 Sea Knight and CH-53 Sea Stallion +
	39,967 tons full load			6 AV-8B Harrier STOVL
Length:	777⅔ feet (237.1 m) waterline		Elevators:	1 deck edge (50 × 34 feet/15.2 × 10.3 m)
	833¾ feet (254.2 m) overall			1 stern (59¾ × 34¾ feet/18.2 × 10.6 m)
Beam:	106 feet (32.3 m)		Missiles:	2 21-cell RAM launchers Mk 49
Extreme width:	132 feet (40.2 m)		Guns:	2 20-mm Phalanx CIWS Mk 15 (2 multibarrel)
Draft:	26 feet (7.9 m)			8 12.7-mm machine guns M2 (8 single)
Propulsion:	2 steam turbines (Westinghouse); 77,000 shp; 2 shafts		Radars:	Mk 23 Target Acquisition System (TAS)
Boilers:	2 600-psi (41.7-kg/cm²) (Combustion Engineering)			SPS-40E air search
Speed:	24 knots (22 knots sustained)			SPS-48E 3-D air search
Range:	10,000 n.miles (18,520 km) at 20 knots			SPS-64(V)9 navigation
Manning:	LHA 1: 1,063 (58 officers + 1,005 enlisted)			SPS-67(V)3 surface search
	LHA 2: 1,067 (58 officers + 1,009 enlisted)		Fire control:	1 Mk 86 GFCS with SPG-60 and SPQ-9A radars
	LHA 3: 1,058 (58 officers + 1,000 enlisted)			2 Mk 115 missile FCS
	LHA 4, 5: 1,064 (58 officers + 1,006 enlisted)			1 SWY-2 weapon control system (RAM)
Troops:	1,700		EW systems:	SLQ-25A Nixie
				SLQ-32(V)3

The TARAWA-class ships combine the capabilities of several types of amphibious ships in a single hull. In addition, these ships periodically have operated AV-8 Harrier STOVL aircraft and OV-10 Bronco STOL aircraft.

Note that the TARAWA was christened on the same date that she was launched ("floated off" her assembly dock).

The BELLEAU WOOD was homeported at Sasebo, Japan, the flagship for the ships of Amphibious Group 1 based there, until replaced by the ESSEX in mid-2000.

Class: Nine ships of this class were originally planned in the early 1960s. The Navy announced on 20 January 1971 that LHA 6–9 would not be constructed (they were formally canceled on 9 February 1971).

Design: SCB No. 410. Special features of this class include an 18-foot (5.5-m) section of the mast that is hinged to permit passage under bridges; a 5,000-square-foot (450-m²) training and acclimatization room to permit troops to exercise in a controlled environment; the vehicle storage decks connected by ramps to the flight deck and

docking well; and five cargo elevators to move equipment between the holds and flight deck. Extensive command and communications facilities are provided for an amphibious force commander.

The hangar deck is 820 feet (250 m) long and 78 feet (23.8 m) wide, with a 20-foot (6.1-m) overhead.

The stern docking well is 268 feet (81.7 m) long and 78 feet (23.8 m) wide and can accommodate four LCU 1610 landing craft or seven LCM(8)s or 17 LCM(6)s or 45 AAV/LVTP-7 amphibian vehicles. Because of the arrangement of the docking well, only one LCAC can be carried. In addition, 35 amphibian vehicles can be carried on the third deck of an LHA.

Extensive medical facilities are provided, including three operating rooms and bed space for 300 patients.

Electronics: SPN-35 aircraft marshalling and SPN-43B approach/control radars are fitted.

Engineering: Maximum horsepower is indicated above; the sustained shp is 70,000. A 900-hp through-tunnel thruster is fitted in the forward part of the hull to assist in maneuvering while launching landing craft.

The ships' boilers are the largest ever manufactured in the United States.

Guns: As built, these ships were armed with three single 5-inch 54-cal DP guns. One gun and one Sea Sparrow launcher were removed from each ship in the early 1990s to provide space for the UAV control station. The two other guns were deleted about 1997. The gunfire control system and associated radars had been retained when this edition went to press.

Missiles: These ships originally had two Sea Sparrow BPDMS Mk 25 launchers (one in LHA 2), controlled by two Mk 71 directors with Mk 115 radars. These have been replaced by two RAM launch-

ers, beginning with the PELELIU and BELLEAU WOOD being refitted in 1992.

Names: The PELELIU was originally named DA NANG; the ship was renamed on 15 February 1978 after the fall of the Republic of (South) Vietnam to communist forces.

Operational: The NASSAU evaluated the "sea control" configuration for these ships during a 1981 deployment, when she successfully operated 19 AV-8A Harrier STOVL aircraft; that same year, the TARAWA made the first extended deployment of an amphibious ship with Harriers on board, carrying six AV-8A aircraft during a deployment to the Western Pacific. Subsequent studies showed that an LHA in the sea control role could effectively operate 20 Harriers plus four to six SH-60B LAMPS III helicopters.

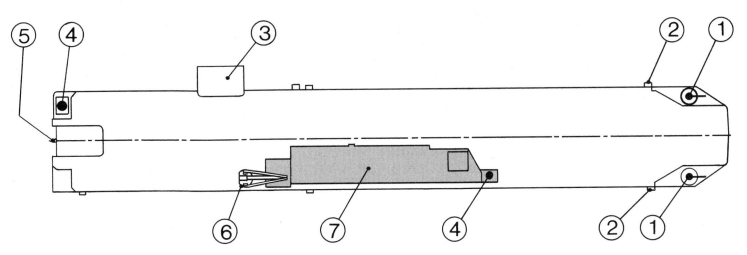

TARAWA

1. Former position of 5-inch DP single gun mount (2) 2. 20-mm cannon Mk 67 (6) 3. Deck-edge elevator 4. Phalanx CIWS (2) 5. Stern elevator 6. Aircraft crane 7. Island structure

The NASSAU entering Malta's Grand Harbor. The LHA/LHD design has vertical sides above the waterline. The hangar deck opening for the deck-edge elevator is visible above the tug. The LHAs were the Navy's last amphibious ships to mount 5-inch guns. (1999, Leo Van Ginderen)

The PELELIU with her crew manning the rail. She has CH-46E Sea Knights parked forward and CH-53E Sea Stallions and AV-8B Harriers on the after flight deck. The hull opening for her deck-edge and stern elevators are visible; the latter, above the docking well, proved a difficult arrangement, which was changed in the LHDs. (U.S. Navy)

Table 18-3. AMPHIBIOUS ASSAULT SHIPS

Number	Name	LPH Comm.	Notes
Converted COMMENCEMENT BAY *class*			
LPH 1	BLOCK ISLAND (ex-CVE 106)		conversion canceled
IWO JIMA *class (7)*			
LPH 2	IWO JIMA	1961	decomm. 14 July 1993; str. 24 Sep 1993
LPH 3	OKINAWA	1962	decomm./str. 17 Dec 1992
Converted ESSEX *class (3)*			
LPH 4	BOXER (ex-CV 21)	1959	stricken 1969
LPH 5	PRINCETON (ex-CV 37)	1959	stricken 1970
Converted CASABLANCA *class*			
LPH 6	THETIS BAY (ex-CVE 90)	1956	stricken 1966
IWO JIMA *class (continued)*			
LPH 7	GUADALCANAL	1963	decomm./str. 31 Aug 1994
Converted ESSEX *class (continued)*			
LPH 8	VALLEY FORGE (ex-CV 45)	1961	stricken 1970
IWO JIMA *class (continued)*			
LPH 9	GUAM	1965	decomm./str. 25 Aug 1998
LPH 10	TRIPOLI	1966	decomm./str. 15 Sep 1995
LPH 11	NEW ORLEANS	1968	decomm. 1 Oct 1997; str. 23 Oct 1998
LPH 12	INCHON	1970	converted to MCS 12

The LPH classification for amphibious assault ship was established in 1955. (The U.S. Navy designation LPH has *never* signified "Landing Platform Helicopter," as used in some documents.) The World War II–era escort carrier BLOCK ISLAND was to have been LPH 1, but her conversion was canceled. Three large aircraft carriers of the ESSEX (CV 9) class subsequently were modified to LPHs, as was the escort carrier THETIS BAY. The smaller ship had been designated as a helicopter assault carrier (CVHA 1) at the start of her 1955–1956 conversion; she was changed to LPH to avoid confusion and budget competition with the CV-type aircraft carriers.

Three ESSEX LPHs previously were designated CV/CVA/CVS. In addition to the three ESSEX-class ships changed to LPH, the TARAWA (CVS 40) operated extensively with Marine helicopters in the late 1950s.

The IWO JIMA class represented an improved World War II–type escort carrier design with accommodations for a Marine battalion and a helicopter squadron. These ships also operated Harrier STOVL aircraft. Unlike the Royal Navy's commando carriers from the 1960s and the later TARAWA/WASP classes, the LPHs did not carry landing craft, except that LCVP davits were provided in the INCHON. The GUAM served as an interim Sea Control Ship (SCS) in 1971–1972. Several ships have operated in the mine countermeasures role, operating CH-53/MH-53/RH-53 helicopters in the MCM role.

After being stricken, the GUAM was transferred to the NDRF; the TRIPOLI was transferred to U.S. Army custody for use in rocket tests, although when this edition went to press she was still moored at the former Mare Island Naval Shipyard in California. The INCHON has been converted to a mine countermeasures support ship (see chapter 21; see 16th Edition/pages 157–159 for LPH 2 class characteristics).

(12) AMPHIBIOUS TRANSPORT DOCKS: "SAN ANTONIO" CLASS

Number	Name	FY	Builder	Laid down	Launch	Comm.	Status
LPD 17	SAN ANTONIO	96	Avondale Industries, New Orleans, La.	11 Dec 2000	2002	2003	building
LPD 18	NEW ORLEANS	99	Avondale Industries, New Orleans, La.	16 July 2000	2002	2004	building
LPD 19	MESA VERDE	00	Bath Iron Works, Maine			2005	building
LPD 20	GREEN BAY	00	Avondale Industries, New Orleans, La.			2005	building
LPD 21	. . . . . .	01	Bath Iron Works, Maine			2006	building
LPD 22	. . . . . .	01	Avondale Industries, New Orleans, La.			2006	building
LPD 23	. . . . . .	02	Avondale Industries, New Orleans, La.			2007	planned
LPD 24	. . . . . .	02	Bath Iron Works, Maine			2007	planned
LPD 25	. . . . . .	03	Avondale Industries, New Orleans, La.			2008	planned
LPD 26	. . . . . .	03	Avondale Industries, New Orleans, La.			2008	planned
LPD 27	. . . . . .	04	Bath Iron Works, Maine			2009	planned
LPD 28	. . . . . .	04	Avondale Industries, New Orleans, La.			2009	planned

Displacement:	24,900 tons full load	Guns:	3 25-mm Bushmaster cannon Mk 38 (3 single)
Length:	684 feet (208.5 m) overall		4 12.7-mm machine guns Mk 26 (2 single)
Beam:	105 feet (31.9 m)	Radars:	Mk 23 Target Acquisition System (TAS)
Draft:	23 feet (7.0 m)		SPS-48E 3-D air search (in initial units; new D-band radar
Propulsion:	4 turbocharged diesel engines; 40,000 shp; 2 shafts		in later ships)
Speed:	25 knots maximum (22 knots sustained)		SPS-64(V)9 navigation
Range:			SPS-67(V)3 surface search
Manning:	420 (24 officers + 396 enlisted)	Fire control:	1 SPQ-9B radar
Troops:	720		1 SWY-2 weapon control system (RAM)
Helicopters:	6	EW systems:	SLQ-25A Nixie
Missiles:	2 21-cell RAM launchers Mk 49 (also see *Missile* notes)		SLQ-32(V)3

The LPD is a development of the dock landing ship (LSD) design, which had its origins in World War II; the LPD design provides for increased troop and vehicle capacity and a relatively small docking well. These ships have fixed helicopter decks above the docking well (the LSDs have removable decks). They carry Marines into forward areas and unload them by landing craft and vehicles carried in their docking well, and by using helicopters provided mainly from amphibious assault ships.

The LPD 17 class is described by the Navy as the functional replacement for 41 older ships: 11 LPDs, 5 LSDs, 20 LSTs, and 5 LKAs.

The class was designated LX during the design phase.

The Navy's 1996 competition for the "winner-take-all" contract for these ships was won by a consortium led by Avondale Shipyards and Bath Iron Works; accordingly, eight ships will be built at the Avondale yard and four at the Bath yard.

Class: The Navy originally proposed a program of 27 LX-type ships to operate with 17 LSD and 15 LHA/LHD ships to provide a MEF + MEB lift capability; however, the reduced amphibious lift goals have led to a 12-ship LX/LPD 17 program.

Cost: The following are the 2000 cost estimates for the ships of this class.

	Ship cost	Outfitting
FY 1999 ships	$632.9 M	unknown
FY 2000 ships	$1,504.4 M	$12.2 M
FY 2001 ships	$755.0 M	$23.8 M

In addition, minimal research and development funding is provided for these ships ($1.3 million in FY 1999 and 2000 and $2.6 million for two ships in FY 2001).

Design: Compared to the previous LPD 4 class, these ships are larger and have considerably more vehicle storage space, at the cost of reduced bulk cargo space; they accommodate two LCACs in the docking well, compared to one in the earlier ships. Two helicopter landing spots are provided; the hangar, built into the superstructure, can accommodate six helicopters.

The LPD 17 will have a 124-bed medical facility with two operating rooms.

Electronics: These LPDs will be fitted with a Cooperative Engagement Capability (CEC).

Missiles: The forward RAM launcher is on the port side of the forward superstructure; the amidships RAM launcher is on the starboard side of the after superstructure.

Space and weight are reserved for possible future installation of the Evolved Sea Sparrow Missile (ESSM) in a vertical-launch system (modified Mk 41 with 16 launch cells) just ahead of the superstructure.

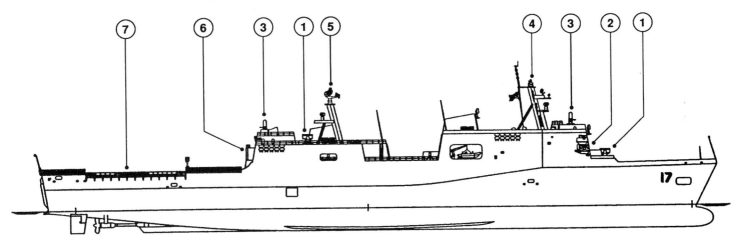

Amphibious Transport Dock SAN ANTONIO
1. RAM missile launcher Mk 49 (2) 2. SLQ-32(V)3 ECM (2) 3. Phalanx CIWS (2) 4. SPS-64(V)9 navigation radar 5. SPS-49(V)5 air search radar
6. Helicopter hangar 7. Helicopter deck

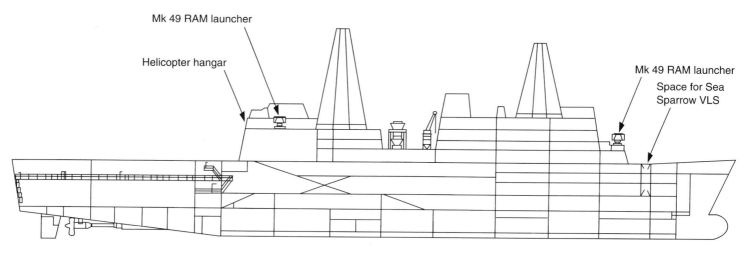

Mk 49 RAM launcher

Helicopter hangar

Mk 49 RAM launcher

Space for Sea
Sparrow VLS

Amphibious Transport Dock SAN ANTONIO

An artist's depiction of the SAN ANTONIO. She will be the largest amphibious ship built in the United States except for the LHA/LHD helicopter/STOVL carriers. The SAN ANTONIO retains the basic LSD/LPD design that dates to World War II. The hangar, however, is an integral part of the superstructure. (U.S. Navy)

11 AMPHIBIOUS TRANSPORT DOCKS: "AUSTIN" CLASS

Number	Name	FY	Builder	Laid down	Launched	Commissioned	Status
LPD 4	AUSTIN	62	New York Naval Shipyard	4 Feb 1963	27 June 1964	6 Feb 1965	**AA**
LPD 5	OGDEN	62	New York Naval Shipyard	4 Feb 1963	27 June 1964	19 June 1965	**PA**
LPD 6	DULUTH	62	New York Naval Shipyard	18 Dec 1963	14 Aug 1965	18 Dec 1965	**PA**
LPD 7	CLEVELAND	63	Ingalls Shipbuilding, Pascagoula, Miss.	30 Nov 1964	7 May 1966	21 Apr 1967	**PA**
LPD 8	DUBUQUE	63	Ingalls Shipbuilding, Pascagoula, Miss.	25 Jan 1965	6 Aug 1966	1 Sep 1967	**PA**
LPD 9	DENVER	63	Lockheed SB & Constn., Seattle, Wash.	7 Feb 1964	23 Jan 1965	26 Oct 1968	**PA**
LPD 10	JUNEAU	63	Lockheed SB & Constn., Seattle, Wash.	23 Jan 1965	12 Feb 1966	12 July 1969	**PA**
LPD 12	SHREVEPORT	64	Lockheed SB & Constn., Seattle, Wash.	27 Dec 1965	25 Oct 1966	12 Dec 1970	**AA**
LPD 13	NASHVILLE	64	Lockheed SB & Constn., Seattle, Wash.	14 Mar 1966	7 Oct 1967	14 Feb 1970	**AA**
LPD 14	TRENTON	65	Lockheed SB & Constn., Seattle, Wash.	8 Aug 1966	3 Aug 1968	6 Mar 1971	**AA**
LPD 15	PONCE	65	Lockheed SB & Constn., Seattle, Wash.	31 Oct 1966	30 May 1970	10 July 1971	**AA**

Displacement:	9,128 tons light		Flag:	90 in LPD 7–10, 12, 13
	16,585 to 17,595 tons full load		Helicopters:	landing area and hangar, except no hangar in LPD 4
Length:	568¾ feet (173.4 m) overall		Missiles:	none
Beam:	84 feet (25.6 m)		Guns:	2 25-mm Bushmaster cannon Mk 38 (2 single)
Draft:	23 to 23⁷/₁₂ feet (7.0 to 7.2 m)			2 20-mm Phalanx CIWS Mk 15 (2 multibarrel)
Propulsion:	2 steam turbines (De Laval); 24,000 shp; 2 shafts			8 12.7-mm machine guns M2HB (8 single)
Boilers:	2 600-psi (41.7-kg/cm²) (Foster-Wheeler, except Babcock &		Radars:	SPS-10F surface search
	Wilcox in LPD 5, 12)			SPS-40B air search, except SPS-40E in LPD 13
Speed:	21 knots			SPS-64(V)9 navigation
Range:	7,700 n.miles (14,260 km) at 20 knots		Fire control:	removed
Manning:	approx. 402 (28 officers + 374 enlisted)		EW systems:	SLQ-25A Nixie
Troops:	930 in LPD 4–6, 14, 15; 840 in LPD 7–10, 12, 13			SLQ-32(V)1

These ships are enlarged versions of the previous RALEIGH-class LPDs.

The JUNEAU is homeported at Sasebo, Japan.

Aircraft: These ships have deployed with up to six CH-46 Sea Knights embarked for short-term operations. They are rated as being able to deploy with up to four cargo helicopters (CH-46 or CH-53), but this can only be achieved with a helicopter carrier in company to provide maintenance and other support on a sustained basis.

Builders: The DULUTH was completed at the Philadelphia Naval Shipyard after the closing of the New York Naval Shipyard; she was reassigned to Philadelphia on 24 November 1965.

Class: An additional ship of this class (LPD 16) was provided in the fiscal 1966 shipbuilding program, but construction was deferred in favor of the LHA program and the ship officially was canceled on 25 February 1969.

The CORONADO (LPD 11) of this class was modified for use as a flagship in late 1980 and reclassified AGF 11.

Design: LPDs 4–10 are SCB No. 187B, and LPDs 11–13 are SCB No. 187C, which was changed to No. 402 for LPD 14 and 15 under the new SCB numbering scheme.

The LPD 7–10, 12, and 13 are configured as amphibious squadron flagships and have an additional bridge level, plus flag berthing space and communications equipment. The docking well in these ships is 168 feet (51.2 m) long and 50 feet (15.2 m) wide; it can accommodate one

LCAC, or one LCU and three LCM(6)s, or nine LCM(6)s, or four LCM(8)s, or 28 AAV/LVTP-7 amphibian vehicles. In addition, two LCM(6)s or four LCVP/LCPLs are normally carried on the helicopter deck, and up to 16 amphibian vehicles can be parked on the main deck.

One 30-ton-capacity crane and six 4-ton cranes are provided.

Guns: As built, these ships had eight 3-inch (76-mm) 50-cal AA Mk 33 guns in twin mounts. Two mounts were removed in the late 1970s and two in the early 1990s. They had Mk 56 and Mk 63 GFCS.

Helicopters: These ships have a fixed flight deck above the docking well, with two landing spots. All except the AUSTIN are fitted with a hangar, varying from 58 to 64 feet (17.7 to 19.5 m) in length, 18½ to 24 feet (5.6 to 7.3 m) in width, and 17½ to 19 feet (5.3 to 5.8 m) in height; the hangars have an extension that can expand to provide a length of approximately 80 feet (24.4 m).

Modernization: A Service Life Extension Program (SLEP) was developed for these ships to permit them to operate 10 to 15 years beyond a nominal 30-year service life. In addition to general improvements, they were to be fitted with the SPS-67 radar in place of the SPS-10 and to be modified to carry two LCACs; their aviation capabilities were also to be improved. However, budget constraints and congressional opposition to the program caused cancellation of the program.

The PONCE at the Norfolk (Va.) naval base. Her basic design is similar to that of the LSDs, the principal external difference being that the LPD flight deck is an integral part of the hull in comparison to the removable deck of the LSD. The PONCE has an expandable helicopter hangar, showing here fully extended. (1999, Jürg Kürsener)

The CLEVELAND, with an extra bridge level to serve as flagship for an amphibious squadron. Her forward Phalanx CIWS is mounted on a platform forward of the bridge on the port side; the amidships gun is on the starboard side, outboard of the mast. (1998, U.S. Navy)

The OGDEN, lifting a boat aboard with her boat crane. The hangar is partially retracted and a CH-53 Sea Stallion sits on her flight deck. The LPD design differs from the LSD in the former ship having a larger troop/vehicle capacity and a smaller docking well. (1998, Leo Van Ginderen)

TABLE 18-4. AMPHIBIOUS TRANSPORT DOCKS

Number	Name	Comm.	Status
RALEIGH class (3)			
LPD 1	RALEIGH	1962	decomm. 13 Dec 1991; str. 25 Jan 1992
LPD 2	VANCOUVER	1963	decomm. 27 Mar 1992; str. 8 Apr 1997
LPD 3	LA SALLE	1964	converted to AGF 3
LPD 4–16	AUSTIN class		
LPD 17–28	SAN ANTONIO class		

After being stricken on 25 January 1992, the RALEIGH was transferred to NDRF on 23 July 1992. She was retained for use as a non-destructive target by the Atlantic Fleet, but was sunk as a target on 4 December 1994.

The LA SALLE served in the amphibious role until converted to a miscellaneous flagship in 1972.

4 DOCK LANDING SHIPS: "HARPERS FERRY" CLASS

Number	Name	FY	Builder	Laid down	Launched	Commissioned	Status
LSD 49	HARPERS FERRY	88	Avondale Industries, New Orleans, La.	15 Apr 1991	16 Jan 1993	7 Jan 1995	**PA**
LSD 50	CARTER HALL	90	Avondale Industries, New Orleans, La.	11 Nov 1991	2 Oct 1993	30 Sep 1995	**AA**
LSD 51	OAK HILL	91	Avondale Industries, New Orleans, La.	21 Sep 1992	11 June 1994	8 June 1996	**AA**
LSD 52	PEARL HARBOR	93	Avondale Industries, New Orleans, La.	27 Jan 1995	24 Feb 1996	30 May 1998	**PA**

Displacement:	11,894 tons light	Helicopters:	landing area
	16,695 tons full load	Missiles:	2 21-cell RAM launchers Mk 49 in LSD 49
Length:	579¹¹⁄₁₂ feet (176.8 m) waterline	Guns:	2 25-mm Bushmaster cannon Mk 38 (2 single)
	609⁵⁄₁₂ feet (185.8 m) overall		2 20-mm Phalanx CIWS Mk 15 (2 multibarrel)
Beam:	84 feet (25.6 m)		8 12.7-mm machine guns M2 (8 single)
Draft:	19¾ feet (6.0 m)	Radars:	1 SPS-49(V)5 air search
Propulsion:	4 diesel engines (Colt-Pielstick 16 PC2.5V400); 41,600 bhp; 2 shafts		1 SPS-64(V)9 navigation
			1 SPS-67(V)1 surface search
Speed:	22 knots	Fire control:	1 SWY-2 weapon control system in LSD 49
Range:	approx. 8,000 n.miles (14,816 km) at 20 knots	EW systems:	SLQ-25A Nixie
Manning:	333 (21 officers + 312 enlisted)		SLQ-32(V)2
Troops:	400		

These ships are similar to the WHIDBEY ISLAND–class LSDs, but with a smaller docking well to provide space for increased troop, vehicle, cargo, and helicopter capacity. Navy planning documents refer to the class as LSD 41CV (CV for *Cargo Variant*).

An additional 100 troops can be embarked for short durations (i.e., several days).

Class: The Navy originally planned a class of six ships: the four above ships, plus the LSD 53 and LSD 54; the latter were canceled. The LSD 52 originally was funded in FY 1992 but the funds were rescinded by the Bush administration; Congress again funded the ship in FY 1993.

Design: The docking well is 180 feet (54.9 m) by 50 feet (15.2 m); it can accommodate two LCACs or one LCU or four LCM(8)s or nine LCM(6) landing craft.

A 30-ton-capacity crane is provided; an eight-ton cargo elevator is fitted to service the helicopter deck.

Engineering: Maximum horsepower is given above; sustained shp is 34,600.

Missiles: These ships will probably be fitted with the RAM missile system.

Names: LSDs are named for historic sites. Harpers Ferry, W.Va., was site of a government arsenal that insurrectionist-abolitionist John Brown captured in 1859, a prelude to the American Civil War.

The LSD 52 honors the *site* of the Japanese surprise attack on the U.S. Fleet on 7 December 1941, and not the attack itself.

The HARPERS FERRY "dressed"—all decked out with bunting and her signal flags. Her superstructure is a massive block of accommodations and working spaces. Her forward Phalanx CIWS is visible on a large platform forward of the bridge; the second Phalanx is at the after end of the superstructure. (1999, Leo Van Ginderen)

The HARPERS FERRY–class LSDs continue the lines of these most useful ships that began with the ASHLAND (LSD 1), completed in 1943. The LSDs' removable helicopter platforms are visible in most views in this chapter. (1995, Avondale Industries, Ricky Kellum)

The HARPERS FERRY takes aboard an LCAC. Classified as the cargo variant of the WHIDBEY ISLAND design, this class has a smaller docking well, which allows the additional internal space to be used for cargo. (1995, Avondale Industries, Ricky Kellum)

The COMSTOCK at rest. The two heavy cranes are used for handling the heavy cargo and vehicles needed by Marine combat units. With portions of the landing deck removed, they can load cargo into LCACs and LCUs in the docking well. (1999, Leo Van Ginderen)

8 DOCK LANDING SHIPS: "WHIDBEY ISLAND" CLASS

Number	Name	FY	Builder	Laid down	Launched	Commissioned	Status
LSD 41	WHIDBEY ISLAND	81	Lockheed Shipbuilding, Seattle, Wash.	4 Aug 1981	10 June 1983	9 Feb 1985	**AA**
LSD 42	GERMANTOWN	82	Lockheed Shipbuilding, Seattle, Wash.	5 Aug 1982	29 June 1984	8 Feb 1986	**PA**
LSD 43	FORT McHENRY	83	Lockheed Shipbuilding, Seattle, Wash.	10 June 1983	1 Feb 1986	8 Aug 1987	**PA**
LSD 44	GUNSTON HALL	84	Avondale Industries, New Orleans, La.	26 May 1986	27 June 1987	22 Apr 1989	**AA**
LSD 45	COMSTOCK	85	Avondale Industries, New Orleans, La.	27 Oct 1986	16 Jan 1988	3 Feb 1990	**PA**
LSD 46	TORTUGA	85	Avondale Industries, New Orleans, La.	23 Mar 1987	15 Sep 1988	17 Nov 1990	**AA**
LSD 47	RUSHMORE	86	Avondale Industries, New Orleans, La.	9 Nov 1987	6 May 1989	1 June 1991	**PA**
LSD 48	ASHLAND	86	Avondale Industries, New Orleans, La.	4 Apr 1988	11 Nov 1989	9 May 1992	**AA**

Displacement:	12,434 tons standard		Troops:	560
	15,745 tons full load		Helicopters:	landing area
Length:	580 feet (176.8 m) waterline		Missiles:	2 21-cell RAM launchers Mk 49 in LSD 41
	609^{5}/$_{12}$ feet (185.8 m) overall		Guns:	2 25-mm Bushmaster cannon Mk 38 (2 single)
Beam:	84 feet (25.6 m)			2 20-mm Phalanx CIWS Mk 15 (2 multibarrel)
Draft:	19^{7}/$_{12}$ feet (6.0 m)			8 12.7-mm machine guns M2HB (8 single)
Propulsion:	4 diesel engines (SEMT-Pielstick 16 PC2.5 V400); 41,600 bhp;		Radars:	SPS-64(V)9 navigation
	2 shafts			SPS-49(V)1 air search in LSD 41–45; (V)5 in LSD 46–48
Speed:	22 knots			SPS-67(V)1 surface search
Range:	8,000 n.miles (14,816 km) at 20 knots		Fire control:	1 SWY-2 weapon control system (RAM) in LSD 41
Manning:	LSD 41, 44, 46: 310 (21 officers + 289 enlisted)		EW systems:	SLQ-25A Nixie
	LSD 42, 43, 47: 317 (21 officers + 296 enlisted)			SLQ-32(V)1
	LSD 45: 312 (21 officers + 291 enlisted)			
	LSD 48: 320 (21 officers + 299 enlisted)			

These ships were built to replace the THOMASTON-class LSDs and to provide increased lift for air-cushion landing craft.

The GERMANTOWN and FORT McHENRY are homeported in Sasebo, Japan.

Class: Navy planning in the early 1980s called for nine or ten ships of this class to replace the LSD 28 class; the number was subsequently increased to 12 ships through the fiscal 1988 shipbuilding program. However, the decision was made in the mid-1980s to instead produce eight LSD 41s and six LSD 41 cargo variants (HARPERS FERRY class) in place of 12 units of this design.

Design: The docking well is 440 feet (134.1 m) long and 50 feet (15.2 m) wide; it can accommodate 4 LCACs, or 3 LCU or 10 LCM(8) or 21 LCM(6) landing craft, or 64 AAV/LVTP-7 amphibian vehicles. In addition, several LCVP/LCPL-type landing craft are normally carried on deck.

The ships are fitted with one 60-ton-capacity crane and one 20-ton crane. No helicopter hangar or support facilities are provided.

Engineering: These are the first U.S. ships powered by medium-speed diesel engines. Of French design, the diesels are produced under license by the Fairbanks Morse Division of Colt Industries. The maximum horsepower is given above; sustained shp is 33,600.

Missiles: These ships are being fitted with the RAM missile system. The WHIDBEY ISLAND conducted trials with the RAM system (one launcher) in June 1993 using radar inputs from the Phalanx VPS-2 search and track radar.

The RUSHMORE shows the massive block superstructure of modern LSDs. These ships carry cargo, troops, and landing craft or vehicles for Marine operations. (1997, Leo Van Ginderen)

The Comstock maneuvering at slow speed. The large stern gate is evident, showing the spacing between the ship's hull and the removable helicopter deck. These ships are very flexible with respect to payloads that they can carry in their docking wells. (1996, Leo Van Ginderen)

3 DOCK LANDING SHIPS: "ANCHORAGE" CLASS

Number	Name	FY	Builder	Laid down	Launched	Commissioned	Status
LSD 36	Anchorage	65	Ingalls Shipbuilding, Pascagoula, Miss.	13 Mar 1967	5 May 1968	15 Mar 1969	**PA**
LSD 37	Portland	66	General Dynamics, Quincy, Mass.	21 Sep 1967	20 Dec 1969	3 Oct 1970	**AA**
LSD 38	Pensacola	66	General Dynamics, Quincy, Mass.	12 Mar 1969	11 July 1970	27 Mar 1971	stricken 30 Sep 1999 (see notes)
LSD 39	Mount Vernon	66	General Dynamics, Quincy, Mass.	29 Jan 1970	17 Apr 1971	13 May 1972	**PA**
LSD 40	Fort Fisher	67	General Dynamics, Quincy, Mass.	15 July 1970	22 Apr 1972	9 Dec 1972	decomm./str. 27 Feb 1998

Displacement:	8,200 tons light		Troops:	336
	13,680 tons full load		Helicopters:	landing area
Length:	534 feet (162.8 m) waterline		Missiles:	none
	553¼ feet (168.66 m) overall		Guns:	2 25-mm Bushmaster cannon Mk 38 (2 single)
Beam:	85 feet (25.9 m)			2 20-mm Phalanx CIWS Mk 15 (2 multibarrel)
Draft:	20 feet (6.1 m)			6 12.7-mm machine guns M2HB6 (single)
Propulsion:	2 steam turbines (De Laval); 24,000 shp; 2 shafts		Radars:	SPS-10F surface search
Boilers:	2 600-psi (41.7-kg/cm²) (Foster-Wheeler, except Combustion Engineering in LSD 36)			SPS-40B/D air search
				SPS-64(V)9 navigation
Speed:	22 knots (20 knots sustained)		Fire control:	removed
Range:	14,000 n.miles (25,940 km) at 12 knots		EW systems:	SLQ-25A Nixie
Manning:	322 (18 officers + 304 enlisted)			SLQ-32(V)1

These LSDs were part of the large amphibious ship construction program of the early 1960s and were to supplement the LPDs and LHAs by carrying additional landing craft to an assault area.

The Pensacola was placed "in commission, in reserve" on 22 September 1999 and stricken eight days later; she will be transferred to another country.

Design: SCB No. 404. The docking well is 430 feet (131.1 m) long and 50 feet (15.2 m) wide; it can accommodate 4 LCACs or 3 LCUs or 9 LCM(8)s or 52 AAV/LVTP-7 amphibian vehicles. Another 15 amphibian vehicles can be stowed on a "mezzanine"

deck. A removable helicopter deck is fitted over the docking well. Several additional landing craft are normally stowed on deck.

Two 50-ton-capacity cranes are fitted. No helicopter hangar or support facilities are provided.

Guns: As built, these ships had eight 3-inch/50-cal Mk 33 guns in twin mounts; one amidships mount and the Mk 56 and Mk 63 GFCS were removed in 1977. An additional 3-inch twin mount was deleted with installation of the two Phalanx CIWS in the 1980s. The remaining 3-inch guns were deleted in the early 1990s.

The MOUNT VERNON and other surviving LSDs of the ANCHORAGE class will be discarded in the near future as the Navy reduces the number of ships in each amphibious squadron to one LHA/LHD and two LPD/LSD types. The Phalanx CIWS mountings are high in these ships, forward and aft of the pole mast. (1998, Leo Van Ginderen)

The stern aspect of the MOUNT VERNON, showing one of her large 50-ton-capacity cranes. (1995, Giorgio Arra)

TABLE 18-5. POST–WORLD WAR II DOCK LANDING SHIPS

Number	Name	Comm.	Notes
THOMASTON class (8)			
LSD 28	THOMASTON	1954	decomm. 1984; str. 24 Feb 1992
LSD 29	PLYMOUTH ROCK	1954	decomm. 1983; str. 24 Feb 1992
LSD 30	FORT SNELLING	1955	decomm. 1984; str. 24 Feb 1992
LSD 31	POINT DEFIANCE	1955	decomm. 1983; str. 24 Feb 1992
LSD 32	SPIEGEL GROVE	1956	decomm. 1989; str. 13 Dec 1989
LSD 33	ALAMO	1956	decomm. 28 Sep 1990; to Brazil 20 Nov 1990
LSD 34	HERMITAGE	1956	decomm. 1989; to Brazil 1989
LSD 35	MONTICELLO	1957	decomm. 1985; str. 24 Feb 1992
LSD 36–40	ANCHORAGE class		
LSD 41–48	WHIDBEY ISLAND class		
LSD 49–52	HARPERS FERRY class		

After the tank landing ship (LST), the dock landing ship was in many respects the most innovative amphibious ship developed during World War II. Establishing the basic design for future LSD/LPD classes, the ASHLAND (LSD 1) had a large superstructure forward and a docking well that took up most of her hull, with machinery fitted in the side walls of the dock. The wartime ASHLAND program embraced LSD 1–27, with the LSD 9–12 being built for Britain.

12 TANK LANDING SHIPS: "NEWPORT" CLASS

Number	Name	FY	Laid down	Launched	Commissioned	Status
LST 1179	NEWPORT	65	1 Nov 1966	3 Feb 1968	7 June 1969	decomm. 30 Sep 1992
LST 1180	MANITOWOC	66	1 Feb 1967	4 June 1969	24 Jan 1970	decomm. 30 June 1993; to Taiwan 14 July 1995
LST 1181	SUMTER	66	14 Nov 1967	13 Dec 1969	20 June 1970	decomm. 30 Sep 1993; to Taiwan 14 July 1995
LST 1182	FRESNO	66	16 Dec 1967	20 Sep 1968	22 Nov 1969	PR; decomm. 8 Apr 1993
LST 1183	PEORIA	66	22 Feb 1968	23 Nov 1968	21 Feb 1970	decomm. 28 Jan 1994
LST 1184	FREDERICK	66	13 Apr 1968	8 Mar 1969	11 Apr 1970	**NRF-P**
LST 1185	SCHENECTADY	66	2 Aug 1968	24 May 1969	13 June 1970	decomm. 10 Dec 1993
LST 1186	CAYUGA	66	28 Sep 1968	12 July 1969	8 Aug 1970	decomm. 26 Aug 1994; to Brazil 26 Aug 1994
LST 1187	TUSCALOOSA	66	23 Nov 1968	6 Sep 1969	24 Oct 1970	PR; decomm. 18 Feb 1994
LST 1188	SAGINAW	67	24 May 1969	7 Feb 1970	23 Jan 1971	decomm./str. 28 June 1994; to Australia 24 Aug 1994
LST 1189	SAN BERNARDINO	67	12 July 1969	26 Mar 1970	27 Mar 1971	decomm./str. 30 Sep 1995; to Chile 30 Sep 1995
LST 1190	BOULDER	67	6 Sep 1969	22 May 1970	4 June 1971	AR; decomm. 28 Feb 1994
LST 1191	RACINE	67	13 Dec 1969	15 Aug 1970	9 July 1971	PR; decomm. 2 Oct 1993
LST 1192	SPARTANBURG COUNTY	67	7 Feb 1970	11 Nov 1970	1 Sep 1971	decomm./str. 16 Dec 1994; to Malaysia 16 Dec 1994
LST 1193	FAIRFAX COUNTY	67	28 Mar 1970	19 Dec 1970	16 Oct 1971	decomm./str. 17 Aug 1994; to Australia 27 Sep 1994
LST 1194	LA MOURE COUNTY	67	22 May 1970	13 Feb 1971	18 Dec 1971	decomm./str. 17 Nov 2000
LST 1195	BARBOUR COUNTY	67	15 Aug 1970	15 May 1971	12 Feb 1972	decomm. 30 Mar 1992
LST 1196	HARLAN COUNTY	67	7 Nov 1970	24 July 1971	8 Apr 1972	decomm. 14 Apr 1995; to Spain 14 Apr 1995
LST 1197	BARNSTABLE COUNTY	67	19 Dec 1970	2 Oct 1971	27 May 1972	decomm. 26 Aug 1994; to Spain 26 Aug 1994
LST 1198	BRISTOL COUNTY	67	13 Feb 1971	4 Dec 1971	5 Aug 1972	decomm./str. 29 July 1994; to Morocco 16 Aug 1994

Builders:	LST 1179–1181: Philadelphia Naval Shipyard	Manning:	*active ships:* approx. 262 (15 officers + 247 enlisted)
	LST 1182–1198: National Steel & SB, San Diego		*NRF ships:* 191 active (11 officers + 180 enlisted) + approx. 70
Displacement:	4,975 tons light		reservists
	8,576 tons full load	Troops:	430
Length:	522⅛ feet (159.2 m) overall	Helicopters:	landing area
	561⅙ feet (171.3 m) over derrick arms	Guns:	1 20-mm Phalanx CIWS Mk 15 (multibarrel) in LST 1179–1183,
Beam:	69½ feet (21.2 m)		1187, 1189, 1194 (see *Guns* notes)
Draft:	5¹¹⁄₁₂ feet (1.8 m) forward		4 12.7-mm machine guns M2HB (4 single)
	17½ feet (5.3 m) aft	Radars:	SPS-10F surface search
Propulsion:	6 diesel engines (General Motors 16-645-E5 in LST		SPS-64(V)9 navigation
	1179–1181; Arco 16-251 in others); 16,500 bhp; 2 shafts	Fire control:	removed
Speed:	22 knots (20 knots sustained)	EW systems:	none
Range:	14,250 n.miles (26,400 km) at 14 knots		

These ships represented the ultimate design in landing ships that could be "beached." However, they generally unload onto pontoon causeways. They depart from the traditional LST bow-door design to obtain a hull design for a sustained speed of 20 knots.

Four ships are laid up in reserve in Mobilization Category B, intended for reactivation within 180 days. Five ships have served in the Naval Reserve Force (NRF); two currently are in NRF status. The decommissionings and shifts of these ships to NRF in 1992–1995 mark the first time since 1942 that there have not been LSTs in the active U.S. amphibious force.

	To NRF
LST 1182	30 Sep 1990
LST 1184	31 Jan 1995
LST 1190	1 Dec 1980
LST 1191	15 Jan 1981
LST 1194	30 Sep 1995

Ten NEWPORT-class LSTs have been transferred to other navies. The LST 1193 departed from Little Creek, Va., en route to Australia on 15 August 1994 as a U.S. Navy ship carrying a combined U.S. (150) and Australian (20) crew; she was decommissioned and stricken en route to Sydney. In Australian service, the LST 1188 and 1193 began a 1995–2000 conversion to serve as training and helicopter support ships; they support Army Black Hawk helicopters, as well as Navy S-70B-2 Seahawk helicopters, the latter flown from Australian frigates of the OLIVER HAZARD PERRY (FFG 7) design.

The Israeli Navy's plan to acquire an LST of this class for conversion to a small craft tender did not come to fruition.

Class: Twenty ships of this class were completed from 1969 to 1972. Seven additional ships were planned for the fiscal 1971 shipbuilding program, but they were canceled.

The FREDERICK is one of the last two LSTs in U.S. Navy service. These are large, graceful ships, little resembling the superstructure-aft configuration of their predecessors. Note the large "horns" to support the ramp; there is a tunnel through the superstructure, connecting the forward and after main deck areas. (1999, Leo Van Ginderen)

Design: SCB No. 405. The design provides bow and stern ramps for unloading tanks and other vehicles. The aluminum bow ramp is 112 feet (34.1 m) long and is handled over the bow by the twin, fixed derrick arms. Vehicles can be driven between the main deck forward and aft through a passage in the superstructure. The stern ramp permits unloading AAV/LVTP-type amphibious vehicles directly into the water while the ships are under way or "mating" the LST to landing craft or a pier. They can carry 2,000 tons of vehicles or cargo, but only 500 tons when beaching. The tank (lower) deck can accommodate 23 AAV/LVTP-7 amphibian vehicles or 41 2½-ton 6×6 cargo trucks; another 29 trucks can be carried on the main (upper) deck. Two 10-ton-capacity cranes are fitted amidships.

Four LCVP/LCPL-type landing craft are carried in amidships davits. Four pontoon causeway sections can be carried on the hull, amidships. There is a large helicopter landing area aft, but no hangar or support facilities.

Electronics: In the 1970s the Navy planned to provide the SLQ-32(V)1 in these ships; however, EW systems will not be installed. (A few ships do have chaff launchers, originally planned for the entire class.)

Guns: These ships all were built with four 3-inch 50-cal guns in twin mounts atop the superstructure; their Mk 63 GFCS were removed in 1977–1978. The 3-inch guns were removed from all active ships in the 1990s. One Phalanx CIWS has been mounted above the bridge; a planned second Phalanx was not installed.

Missiles: There were proposals in the 1980s to mount the Army's Assault Ballistic Rocket System (ABRS) on some or all of these ships for the fire support role; none was installed.[2]

Names: The first 13 ships of the NEWPORT class did not have county or parish name suffixes, as had all previous named LSTs. County and parish names were assigned to 158 existing LSTs on 1 July 1955 (36 Japanese-manned T-LSTs were not named). All subsequent LSTs were assigned names when built.

Operational: Congress had wanted both NRF ships to be based in Hawaii, to be able to transport Marine and Army equipment from Oahu to the island of Hawaii for training. The FREDERICK is based at Pearl Harbor.

The LA MOURE COUNTY was assigned to the NRF and based at Little Creek, Va., when on 12 September 2000 she ran aground on an underwater mountain off the coast of Chile. There were no personnel casualties, but the ship was severely damaged. Consequently, the ship was decommissioned and stricken.

---

2. The ABRS also was proposed for installation in the reactivated battleships of the IOWA (BB 61) class in the early 1980s. The ABRS, an area bombardment weapon, has a range of some 32,000 yards (29,270 m). Research was under way to increase the projectile range to some 50 n.miles (92.65 km).

The FREDERICK shows her stern gate and anchor, helicopter landing area, asymmetric funnels, and boat booms (aft of the funnels) in this overhead view. (1999, Leo Van Ginderen)

The LA MOURE COUNTY with her stern door open. The side of the ship is configured for transporting pontoon causeways, to connect the ship's bow ramp to the beach. (1999, Leo Van Ginderen)

TABLE 18-6. POST–WORLD WAR II TANK LANDING SHIPS

Number	Name	Comm.	Notes
TALBOT COUNTY class (2)			
LST 1153	TALBOT COUNTY	1947	stricken 1973
LST 1154	TALLAHATCHEE COUNTY	1949	converted to AVB 2
LST 1155	(unnamed)		canceled 1946
TERREBONNE PARISH class (15)			
LST 1156	TERREBONNE PARISH	1952	to Spain 1971
LST 1157	TERRELL COUNTY	1954	to Greece 1977
LST 1158	TIOGA COUNTY	1953	stricken 1973
LST 1159	TOM GREEN COUNTY	1953	to Spain 1972
LST 1160	TRAVERSE COUNTY	1953	to Peru 1984
LST 1161	VERNON COUNTY	1953	to Venezuela 1973
LST 1162	WAHKIAKUM COUNTY	1953	stricken 1973
LST 1163	WALDO COUNTY	1953	to Peru 1984
LST 1164	WALWORTH COUNTY	1953	to Peru 1984
LST 1165	WASHOE COUNTY	1953	to Peru 1984
LST 1166	WASHTENAW COUNTY	1953	converted to MSS 2
LST 1167	WESTCHESTER COUNTY	1954	to Turkey 1974
LST 1168	WEXFORD COUNTY	1954	to Spain 1971
LST 1169	WHITFIELD COUNTY	1954	to Greece 1977
LST 1170	WINDHAM COUNTY	1954	to Turkey 1973
DE SOTO COUNTY class (7)			
LST 1171	DE SOTO COUNTY	1958	to Italy 1972
LST 1172	(unnamed)		canceled 1955
LST 1173	SUFFOLK COUNTY	1957	stricken 1989
LST 1174	GRANT COUNTY	1957	to Brazil 1973
LST 1175	YORK COUNTY	1957	to Italy 1972
LST 1176	GRAHAM COUNTY	1958	to AGP 1176
LST 1177	LORAIN COUNTY	1958	stricken 1989
LST 1178	WOOD COUNTY	1959	stricken 1989
LST 1179–1198	NEWPORT class		

From December 1942 to June 1945, a total of 1,052 LSTs were completed for the U.S. Navy (numbered LST 1–1152, with 100 units being canceled). All were of the same basic design. Three larger, improved LSTs with steam-turbine propulsion were ordered late in the war; two were completed: the LST 1153 and 1154 (all other U.S. LSTs have had diesel propulsion).

The TALLAHATCHEE COUNTY was converted to an advance aviation base ship (AVB 2), to provide support for patrol planes operating from remote airfields in the Mediterranean. (Earlier the ALAMEDA COUNTY/LST 32 served as the AVB 1.) The designation AVB subsequently was assigned to two merchant ships converted to support Marine aviation deployments overseas (see chapter 22).

The TERREBONNE PARISH–class LSTs were the Navy's first post–World War II tank landing ship design. All were in Navy service until decommissioned in 1970, except the WALWORTH COUNTY in 1971; the LSTs 1158, 1160, and 1162–1165 then served with the Military Sealift Command in 1972–1973 (designated T-LST).

The WASHTENAW COUNTY was reclassified as a "minesweeper special" (MSS 2) and used as an pressure-mine countermeasures craft to sweep mines in North Vietnamese waters (stricken in 1973).

The DE SOTO COUNTY class was the last U.S. Navy LST design with traditional bow doors and ramp, and superstructure aft. The GRAHAM COUNTY was converted to a gunboat support ship (AGP 1176) to service the ASHEVILLE (PG 84)-class ships operating in the Mediterranean; the WOOD COUNTY was to have been converted to support the PEGASUS (PHM 1)-class hydrofoil missile craft, but her conversion was canceled in 1977; she was to have been designated AGHS 1178.

5 AMPHIBIOUS CARGO SHIPS: "CHARLESTON" CLASS

Number	Name	FY	Builder	Laid down	Launched	Commissioned	Status
LKA 113	CHARLESTON	65	Newport News SB & DD Co., Va.	5 Dec 1966	2 Dec 1967	14 Dec 1968	AR
LKA 114	DURHAM	65	Newport News SB & DD Co., Va.	10 July 1967	29 Mar 1968	24 May 1969	PR
LKA 115	MOBILE	65	Newport News SB & DD Co., Va.	15 Jan 1968	19 Oct 1968	29 Sep 1969	PR
LKA 116	SAINT LOUIS	65	Newport News SB & DD Co., Va.	3 Apr 1968	4 Jan 1969	22 Nov 1969	PR
LKA 117	EL PASO	65	Newport News SB & DD Co., Va.	22 Oct 1968	17 May 1969	17 Jan 1970	AR

Displacement:	10,000 tons light		Troops:	approx. 225
	20,700 tons full load		Helicopters:	landing area only
Length:	549¾ feet (167.6 m) waterline		Missiles:	none
	576 feet (175.6 m) overall		Guns:	6 3-inch (76-mm) 50-cal AA Mk 33 (3 twin), except 4 guns in
Beam:	62 feet (18.9 m)			LKA 113, 117
Draft:	27¹¹⁄₁₂ feet (8.5 m)			2 20-mm Phalanx CIWS Mk 15 (2 multibarrel) in LKA 113, 117
Propulsion:	1 steam turbine (Westinghouse); 22,000 shp; 1 shaft		Radars:	LN-66 navigation, except SPS-64(V)9 in LKA 115
Boilers:	2 600-psi (41.7-kg/cm²) (Combustion Engineering)			SPS-10F surface search
Speed:	20 knots		Fire control:	local control only for 3-inch guns
Range:	9,600 n.miles (17,800 km) at 16 knots		EW systems:	SLQ-25A Nixie in LKA 117
Manning:	approx. 363 (25 officers + 338 enlisted)			SLQ-32(V)1

These ships carry heavy equipment and supplies for amphibious assaults. They are configured for rapid unloading of equipment into landing craft and helicopters.

During 1979–1981 four of the ships were shifted to the NRF; they were returned to active Navy service in the early 1980s to improve amphibious readiness in response to the crises in the Persian Gulf, Lebanon, and Caribbean areas. All were decommissioned in 1992–1994. The LKA 113 was transferred to the NDRF on 29 September 1992, but was reacquired by the Navy on 31 May 1994; she was never struck from the Naval Vessel Register.

	To NRF	*Returned to active fleet*	*Decomm.*
LKA 113	21 Nov 1979	18 Feb 1983	27 Apr 1992
LKA 114	1 Oct 1979	1 Oct 1982	25 Feb 1994
LKA 115	1 Sep 1980	30 Sep 1983	4 Feb 1994
LKA 116	—	—	2 Nov 1992
LKA 117	1 Mar 1981	1 Oct 1982	21 Apr 1994

All five ships are in reserve Category B, suitable for activation within 180 days. The plan to assign the LKA 115 and 117 to a Reduced Operating Status (ROS), manned with 50-man nucleus crews and capable of being reactivated within five days, was canceled because of funding limitations; they were to have been assigned to the Military Sealift Command.

Classification: These ships were ordered as attack cargo ships (AKA). The CHARLESTON was changed to LKA on 14 December 1968 and the others on 1 January 1969.

Design: SCB No. 403. This is the first class of ships designed specifically for this role; all previous ships of the AKA/LKA type were converted from or built to merchant designs.

These ships have a large helicopter landing area aft, but no hangar or maintenance facilities. There are two 78-ton-capacity booms, two 40-ton booms, and eight 15-ton booms. The ships normally carried as deck cargo 4 LCM(8)s, 5 LCM(6)s, 2 LCVPs, and 2 LCPLs.

Engineering: Maximum horsepower is shown above; sustained shp is 19,250.

Guns: As built, four 3-inch twin gun mounts were installed. One mount was removed from each ship, as was the Mk 56 GFCS, in 1977–1978; subsequently, a second 3-inch twin mount is being removed for the installation of the CIWS.

Two Phalanx CIWS are fitted in these ships. One CIWS is fitted forward, to port of the remaining forward 3-inch gun mount, and the other Phalanx is fitted on the superstructure in place of the starboard 3-inch gun mount.

The Navy is retaining the five CHARLESTON-class amphibious cargo ships in reserve because of their valuable break-bulk cargo capability. Here the EL PASO is lowering an LCM landing craft, one of several carried by these ships. The EL PASO has a Phalanx CIWS on the bow and a second on the starboard bridge wing; only she and the CHARLESTON were so armed. (1991, Giorgio Arra)

TABLE 18-7. POST–WORLD WAR II AMPHIBIOUS CARGO SHIPS

Number	Name	Comm.	Notes
Mariner class			
AKA 112	TULARE	1956	(see text)
LKA 113–117	CHARLESTON class		

The TULARE was acquired by the Navy while under construction as a Mariner-class merchant ship (C4-S-1a). Built as AKA 112, she was changed to LKA 112 on 1 January 1969. The TULARE was decommissioned in 1981 and placed in the NDRF, reinstated on the Naval Vessel Register in 1984, and again stricken on 31 August 1992.

In addition to the three Mariner-class amphibious ships listed here, two other ships of that class (AG 153, AG 154) became support ships for the Polaris program.[3] One ship of this design remains on the Navy List as a missile range instrumentation ship: the OBSERVATION ISLAND (T-AGM 23).

---

3. Thirty ships of the Mariner class were completed to this design for commercial service in 1952–1955. The design was developed by the U.S. Maritime Administration to compete with the foreign trend toward larger and faster cargo ships.

TABLE 18-8. POST–WORLD WAR II ATTACK TRANSPORTS

Number	Name	Comm.	Notes
Mariner class			
APA 248	PAUL REVERE	1958	stricken/to Spain 1980
APA 249	FRANCIS MARION	1961	stricken/to Spain 1980

Attack transports carried troops and landing craft. Both ships were acquired while under construction as Mariner-class cargo ships. Initially designated APA, they were changed to LPA on 1 January 1969.

FIRE SUPPORT SHIPS

In World War II, numerous production landing ships were modified during construction or converted to the fire support role for amphibious landings (LCIG/LCIM/LCIR/LCSL/LSMR). One inshore fire support ship was constructed after the war, the CARRONADE (IFS 1), an improved LSMR with a single 5-inch gun and several rapid-fire rocket launchers; the CARRONADE was commissioned in 1955 and stricken in 1973. Her designation was changed to LFR on 1 January 1969, as were the surviving war-built LSMRs. (The CARRONADE and three LSMRs saw active service in the Vietnam War.)

There have been subsequent proposals to build fire support ships (IFS/LFR/LFS), but none has been authorized. The recommissioning of the four battleships of the IOWA (BB 61) class in the 1980s made consideration of such ships superfluous during the naval buildup of that decade. The aborted arsenal ship was intended to provide such fire support at longer ranges with cruise/ballistic missiles (see appendix E).

CHAPTER 19

Landing Craft and Vehicles

An LCAC air-cushion landing craft comes aboard the assault ship PELELIU (LHA 5) during operations in the Persian Gulf. These craft are invaluable for rapidly moving vehicles, equipment, and stores from ship to shore. The current LCAC force is being upgraded and the force of conventional LCU landing craft is to be replaced. (1999, U.S. Navy, PH3 John LoGrande)

The U.S. Navy operates several hundred landing craft. All landing craft are operated by Navy personnel. The assault amphibian vehicles (formerly amphibious tractors), operated by the Marine Corps, are listed in the latter section of this chapter.

The larger air-cushion landing craft (LCAC) and utility landing craft (LCU) are usually identified by "hull" numbers. The smaller landing craft are identified by the ship, unit, or base to which they are assigned.

Numerous LCUs have been transferred to other navies, reclassified, or stricken. Others serve as test support craft (IX), ferry boats (YFB), and harbor utility craft (YFU); they are described in chapter 24 of this edition of *Ships and Aircraft*. The U.S. Army operates several LCUs—in the same designation series as the Navy craft—as well as LCMs; see chapter 32.

The amphibious forces also operate warping tugs (LWT) and side-loading warping tugs (SLWT), which are used to move pontoon causeways in amphibious areas. They can be transported to forward areas by amphibious ships. Additional landing craft of the smaller types are laid up in various forms of storage.

LANDING CRAFT

91 AIR-CUSHION LANDING CRAFT: LCAC TYPE

Number	FY	In service	Status*	Number	FY	In service	Status*	Number	FY	In service	Status*
LCAC 1	82	14 Dec 1984	ROS	LCAC 32	86	1 May 1991	ACU-5	LCAC 63	91	30 Sep 1993	ACU-5
LCAC 2	82	22 Feb 1986	SLEP	LCAC 33	86	4 June 1991	ACU-5	LCAC 64	91	27 Oct 1993	ACU-5
LCAC 3	82	9 June 1986	ROS	LCAC 34	89	31 May 1992	ACU-4	LCAC 65	91	24 Nov 1993	ACU-5
LCAC 4	83	13 Aug 1986	SLEP	LCAC 35	89	31 May 1992	ACU-4	LCAC 66	91	31 Dec 1993	NCSL
LCAC 5	83	26 Nov 1986	ROS	LCAC 36	89	1 May 1992	ACU-4	LCAC 67	91	25 Feb 1994	ACU-4
LCAC 6	83	1 Dec 1986	ROS	LCAC 37	89	31 July 1991	ACU-4	LCAC 68	91	25 Mar 1994	ACU-4
LCAC 7	84	18 Mar 1987	SLEP	LCAC 38	89	6 Sep 1991	ACU-4	LCAC 69	91	29 Apr 1994	ACU-4
LCAC 8	84	3 June 1987	SLEP	LCAC 39	89	30 Sep 1991	ACU-4	LCAC 70	91	5 June 1994	ACU-4
LCAC 9	84	26 June 1987	SLEP	LCAC 40	89	5 Nov 1991	ACU-4	LCAC 71	91	21 June 1994	ACU-4
LCAC 10	84	4 Sep 1987	ROS	LCAC 41	89	27 Nov 1991	ACU-4	LCAC 72	91	28 July 1994	ACU-5
LCAC 11	84	7 Dec 1987	ROS	LCAC 42	89	20 Dec 1991	ACU-5	LCAC 73	92	28 Sep 1994	ACU-5
LCAC 12	84	23 Dec 1987	ROS	LCAC 43	89	21 Feb 1992	ACU-5	LCAC 74	92	10 Nov 1994	ACU-5
LCAC 13	85	30 Sep 1988	ACU-5	LCAC 44	89	29 Feb 1992	ACU-5	LCAC 75	92	6 Jan 1995	ACU-5
LCAC 14	85	3 Nov 1988	ACU-5	LCAC 45	89	26 Mar 1992	ACU-5	LCAC 76	92	14 Feb 1995	ACU-5
LCAC 15	85	20 Sep 1988	ACU-4	LCAC 46	89	8 May 1992	ACU-4	LCAC 77	92	31 Mar 1995	ACU-4
LCAC 16	85	4 Nov 1988	ACU-5	LCAC 47	89	24 June 1992	ACU-5	LCAC 78	92	23 May 1995	ACU-4
LCAC 17	85	1989	ACU-5	LCAC 48	89	17 July 1992	ACU-5	LCAC 79	92	20 July 1995	ACU-5
LCAC 18	85	1989	ROS	LCAC 49	90	16 Oct 1992	ACU-4	LCAC 80	92	23 Aug 1995	ACU-5
LCAC 19	85	May 1990	ACU-4	LCAC 50	90	28 Feb 1993	ACU-4	LCAC 81	92	25 Oct 1995	ACU-5
LCAC 20	85	Sep 1990	ACU-4	LCAC 51	90	June 1993	ACU-4	LCAC 82	92	13 Dec 1995	ACU-5
LCAC 21	85	1990	SLEP	LCAC 52	90	2 Sep 1992	ACU-5	LCAC 83	92	29 Feb 1996	ACU-4
LCAC 22	86	Nov 1990	ROS	LCAC 53	90	10 July 1992	ACU-4	LCAC 84	92	25 Apr 1996	ACU-4
LCAC 23	86	15 June 1991	ACU-5	LCAC 54	90	30 Oct 1992	ACU-4	LCAC 85	93	25 July 1996	ACU-4
LCAC 24	86	1 Mar 1990	ACU-5	LCAC 55	90	30 Nov 1992	ACU-4	LCAC 86	93	26 Sep 1996	ACU-4
LCAC 25	86	29 June 1990	SLEP	LCAC 56	90	8 Jan 1993	ACU-5	LCAC 87	93	20 Nov 1996	ACU-4
LCAC 26	86	July 1990	ACU-4	LCAC 57	90	26 Feb 1993	ACU-5	LCAC 88	93	20 Feb 1997	ACU-4
LCAC 27	86	24 Aug 1990	ACU-4	LCAC 58	90	31 Mar 1993	ACU-5	LCAC 89	93	15 Apr 1997	ACU-4
LCAC 28	86	12 Oct 1990	ACU-4	LCAC 59	90	30 Apr 1993	ACU-5	LCAC 90	93	24 Oct 1997	ACU-5
LCAC 29	86	18 Dec 1990	ACU-5	LCAC 60	90	4 June 1993	ACU-4	LCAC 91	93	Dec 2000	trials
LCAC 30	86	19 Dec 1990	ROS	LCAC 61	91	30 July 1993	ACU-5				
LCAC 31	86	27 Feb 1991	ACU-5	LCAC 62	91	31 Aug 1993	ACU-5				

* NCSL = Naval Coastal Systems Laboratory, Panama City, Fla.; ROS = Reduced Operating Status; SLEP = Service Life Extension Program

Builders:	Bell-Aerospace/Textron Marine Systems, New Orleans, La., except LCAC 15–23, 34–36, 49–51 by Avondale Gulfport Marine, La.	Propulsion/lift:	4 gas turbines (Avco-Lycoming TF-40B); 15,820 shp; 2 shrouded propellers and 2 bow thrusters/4 centrifugal lift fans	
Displacement:	102.2 tons light	Speed:	50 knots maximum on cushion	
	169 tons full load		40+ knots with payload on cushion in sea state 2	
	184 tons overload		30+ knots with payload on cushion in sea state 3	
Length:	81 feet (24.7 m) overall (structure)		25 knots maximum on hull	
	87¹¹/₁₂ feet (26.8 m) on cushion	Range:	200 n.miles (370 km) at 40 knots with payload	
Beam:	43⅔ feet (13.3 m) (structure)	Manning:	5 (enlisted)	
	47 feet (14.3 m) on cushion	Troops:	24	
Draft:	3 feet (0.9 m) structure	Guns:	(see notes)	
		Radars:	navigation	

These landing craft are the first advanced-technology surface ships to be produced in series by the U.S. Navy. They carry heavy vehicles and cargo from amphibious ships onto the beach at higher speeds and for longer distances than can conventional landing craft.

Modifications are required for these craft to carry the improved (and heavier) M1 Abrams tanks now in Marine Corps service. The older LCACs require rehabilitation, and a Service Life Extension Program (SLEP) began in FY 2000 to extend the LCACs' service life by 20 to 30 years.

The SLEP process, being carried out at Textron Marine and Land Systems in New Orleans, La., will increase reliability and reduce maintenance requirements by providing state-of-the-art components, improved engines, and increased fuel capacity. All LCACs except the LCAC 91 are planned for SLEP upgrade, the last to be completed about 2016; the LCAC 91 was built to SLEP standards, hence the delay in her completion.

As of 2000, 36 LCACs are assigned to each of the assault craft units (with several ACU-5 craft being based at Sasebo, Japan), ten are

Operational: In the Pacific Fleet, Naval Beach Group 1, based at the Naval Amphibious Base Coronado (San Diego), Calif., has Assault Craft Unit (ACU) 1, which operates conventional landing craft, and ACU-5 at Camp Pendleton, Calif., which operates LCACs. In the Atlantic Fleet, Naval Beach Group 2 at Little Creek (Norfolk), Va., has ACU-2 for conventional landing craft and ACU-4 for LCACs.

in reserve–Reduced Operating Status (ROS), seven are undergoing SLEP, and the LCAC 66 is employed for test and evaluation.

Builders: Lockheed Shipyard in Seattle, Wash., originally was the second source for LCAC construction; however, beginning in June 1988 that firm divested itself of shipbuilding activities and the Gulfport Marine division of Avondale Industries took over the Lockheed contracts.

Class: The original Navy–Marine plan was to acquire 107 LCACs to support an amphibious assault force of one Marine Expeditionary Force (MEF) plus one Marine Expeditionary Brigade (MEB). In early 1984 the Department of Defense announced a plan for "at least 90" units, although the 107 force-level goal was listed in official documents through fiscal 1991. The fiscal 1993 Department of Defense budget request provided for the final seven LCACs, for a total of 91 units.

Design: The Navy began development of air-cushion craft in 1960. The LCAC design is based on the JEFF(B), one of two competitive prototypes delivered to the Navy in 1977.

The LCAC has a modular design, which facilitates construction, maintenance, and damage repairs. The craft are fully "skirted"; they

Men of an Explosive Ordnance Disposal (EOD) team drag their rubber boat onto the rear ramp of an LCAC after having been dropped into the Adriatic Sea from a helicopter during an exercise. The team, based aboard the amphibious ship KEARSARGE (LHD 3), was supporting Operation Allied Force. (1999, U.S. Navy, CWO Seth Rossman [USMC])

are amphibious and can clear land obstacles up to 4 feet (1.2 m) high. Bow and stern ramps are fitted. The cargo deck area is 81 feet (24.7 m) × 27 feet (8.2 m), totaling 1,809 square feet (162.8 m^2).

The design payload is 120,000 pounds (54,545 kg) with a maximum overload of 150,000 pounds (68,182 kg). The LCAC initially could accommodate one M1 tank or four Light Armored Vehicles (LAV) or three AAV7/LVTP-7 amphibian vehicles (two AAVs if appliqué armor is fitted) or two M198 155-mm towed howitzers.

The control compartment is located on the starboard side, with an aircraft-type cockpit with the operator seated on the far right, the engineer in the center, and navigator on the left.

Design problems occurred with the early craft; operational tests revealed that the craft shipped water that could cause electrical shorts and interrupt operations. The early craft have been modified and the Navy did not request additional units in the fiscal 1987–1988 budgets because the five units completed to that time would require additional testing before modifications could be developed.

All units were built with composite (ceramic tile) armor for the control station module; the LCAC 34 and later units have one engine on each side armored, with the LCAC 61 and subsequent units having additional engine armor. Armor, modular arrangement, and redundancy provide a relatively high degree of survivability.

Electronics: The modified LN-66 is combined with a Unisys-developed system to provide multiple functions.

Engineering: The gas turbines are fitted in modules, two per side. The clutch/gearbox system permits a high degree of flexibility. Two engines are normally employed for propulsion and two for lift; under emergency conditions, one engine can provide propulsion and one can provide lift. The craft have a high degree of maneuverability and can turn 180° within their own length.

The propellers are four-blade, 11¾-foot (3.6-m)-diameter, reversible, each fitted with two rudders; the lift fans are 5¼ feet (1.6 m) in diameter.

Guns: No armament is fitted. However, three mounting positions are provided: one for a 7.62-mm M60 machine gun, and two for a 7.62-mm M60 or .50-cal M2HB machine gun or 40-mm Mk 19 grenade launcher.

Mine countermeasures: In December 1993 the decision was made to provide a packaged Mine Countermeasures (MCM) capability for use by LCACs. Operational test and evaluation began with the reconfigured LCAC 66 in February 1994 at Panama City, Fla. Fitted with MCM gear, this craft is sometimes referred to as a Multipurpose Air-Cushion Vehicle (MCAC). It can be modified to employ the Mk 104, Mk 105, and Mk 106 MCM systems and M-58 line charges, the latter to be eventually replaced by the SABER line charge system. Towing speed for the Mk 104/105/106 systems is 25 knots. The AQS-14 minehunting sonar can also be fitted.

(The Royal Navy conducted MCM trials with the 55-ton BH7 Mk 2 hovercraft [pennant P 235] in 1983. An enlarged, specialized BH7 Mk 20 hovercraft configured for the MCM role—using U.S. helicopter equipment—was designed but not procured.)

Operational: Each LCAC is commanded by a craftmaster, a chief petty officer, who also pilots the craft; the other crewmen are the engineer, navigator, load master, and deck seaman.

The LCACs are assigned in approximately equal numbers to ACU-4 at Little Creek (Norfolk), and ACU-5 at Camp Pendleton, Calif. ACU-4 was established in 1987 and ACU-5 in 1983.

The LCACs can be carried in the following amphibious ships (number carried per ship in parentheses): LHD (3), LHA (1), LPD 17 (2), LPD 4 (1), LPD 1 (1), LSD 49 (2), LSD 41 (4), and LSD 36 (3).

Seventeen LCACs were deployed on board amphibious ships participating in Operation Desert Storm in January–February 1991. All were "mission ready" and operated in day and night exercises and administrative (noncombat) landings with 100 percent availability. (This was precisely one-half the number of LCACs in service at the time.)

Three LCACs normally are carried by each Amphibious Ready Group (ARG).

The heavily laden LCAC 52 "flies" along the coast of California during an amphibious exercise. While very useful for amphibious operations, these craft are highly vulnerable to detection and attack because of their radar, acoustic, and infrared signatures. (1997, U.S. Navy, PH2 Michael D. Degner)

A "travel lift" moves the LCAC 84 at Assault Craft Unit 4 at Little Creek (Norfolk), Va. The LCACs can move on their own when ashore, as well as when afloat and on sand or ice. Indeed, they can come aboard a ramp-fitted ship without requiring a docking well. (1999, U.S. Navy, ETC R. S. Richard)

UTILITY LANDING CRAFT: NEW CONSTRUCTION

A replacement LCU class is planned, with 35 units to be delivered from fiscal year 2005 through 2011. The new LCU will be capable of lifting up to 225 tons of cargo or (for short trips) 400 combat-loaded troops. Maximum speed will be between 20 and 25 knots in sea state 3.

Issues being addressed in the LCU design include enhanced navigation for over-the-horizon operations, armor, and Chemical-Biological-Radiological (CBR) protection.

A procurement contract for the lead units is planned for FY 2004.

39 UTILITY LANDING CRAFT: "LCU 1610" CLASS

Number	Assignment*	Number	Assignment*	Number	Assignment*
LCU 1614	NADC, Key West, Fla.	LCU 1643	ACU-2	LCU 1658	ACU-2
LCU 1616	ACU-1	LCU 1644	ACU-2	LCU 1659	ACU-2
LCU 1617	ACU-1	LCU 1645	ACU-2	LCU 1660	ACU-2
LCU 1619	ACU-1	LCU 1646	ACU-1	LCU 1661	ACU-2
LCU 1624	ACU-1	LCU 1647	NADC, Key West, Fla.	LCU 1662	ACU-2
LCU 1627	ACU-1	LCU 1648	ACU-1	LCU 1663	ACU-2
LCU 1629	ACU-1	LCU 1649	ACU-2	LCU 1664	ACU-2
LCU 1630	ACU-1	LCU 1650	ACU-2	LCU 1665	ACU-1
LCU 1631	ACU-1	LCU 1651	ACU-1	LCU 1666	ACU-1
LCU 1632	ACU-1	LCU 1653	ACU-2	135CU8501	reserve training; Buffalo, N.Y. (ex-LCU 1680)
LCU 1633	ACU-1	LCU 1654	ACU-2		
LCU 1634	ACU-1	LCU 1655	ACU-2	135CU8502	reserve training; Tampa, Fla. (ex-LCU 1681)
LCU 1635	ACU-1	LCU 1656	ACU-2		
LCU 1641	ACU-1	LCU 1657	ACU-2		

*ACU = Assault Craft Unit; EOD = Explosive Ordnance Disposal; NAB = Naval Amphibious Base; NADC = Naval Air Development Center

Builders:	LCU 1616–1619, 1623, 1624: Gunderson Bros, Portland, Ore. LCU 1626, 1629, 1630: Southern SB, Slidell, La. LCU 1627, 1628, 1631–1635: General Ship & Engine Works, East Boston, Mass. LCU 1643–1645: Marinette Marine, Wisc. LCU 1646–1666: Defoe SB, Bay City, Wisc. LCU 1680, 1681: Moss Point Marine, Escatawpa, Miss.	Draft: Propulsion:	6¹¹/₁₂ feet (2.1 m) 4 diesel engines (General Motors Detroit 6-71), 1,200 bhp, except LCU 1646 and later units: 4 General Motors 12V71N, 1,700 bhp; 2 Kort-nozzle propellers
Displacement:	190 tons light 390 tons full load, except LCU 1680, 1681: 404 tons	Speed: Range: Manning:	11 knots 1,200 n.miles (2,222 km) at 8 knots with payload 6 (enlisted), except LCU 1680, 1681: 14 (2 officers + 12 enlisted)
Length: Beam:	134¾ feet (41.1 m) overall 29¾ feet (9.1 m)	Troops: Guns: Radars:	8 2 20-mm cannon or 2 .50-cal machine guns M2 (2 single) SPS-69 Pathfinder navigation

These are improved LCUs with 15 units (LCU 1610–1624) having been completed in 1959–1960 and the remainder from 1967 to 1976, except the LCU 1680 and 1681 in 1987.

Class: This class originally consisted of hull numbers LCU 1610–1624 and 1627–1681.

The LCU 1680 and 1681 were built to a modified design. The LCU 1667–1679 went to the U.S. Army.

The LCU 1621, 1623, and 1628 have been converted to auxiliary swimmer delivery vehicles (ASDV) to support diving operations and others became service craft (YFU); both types are described in chapter 24.

Classification: Two LCUs assigned to Naval Reserve training activities have hull registry numbers.

Design: The LCU 1610–1624 were SCB No. 149. The LCU 1627 and later units were SCB No. 149B (new series SCB No. 406).

These LCUs have a "drive-through" configuration with bow and stern ramps, and a small, starboard-side island structure housing controls and accommodations. Previous LCU/LCT-type landing craft had a small deck structure aft. They are welded-steel construction; the mast folds down for entering the well decks of amphibious ships.

The cargo capacity is one M1 Abrams tank or up to about 190 tons of cargo or, for short distances, 350 to 400 troops.

Engineering: The LCU 1621 had vertical shafts fitted with vertical-axis, cycloidal, six-blade propellers; all other units have Kort-nozzle propellers. The LCU 1680 and 1681 were built with improved engines, which have been backfitted into the LCU 1646 and later units.

Guns: Weapons are not normally fitted in these craft.

Operational: Most LCUs are assigned to Assault Craft Units 1 and 2, as indicated above. The LCU 1641 is used as a training minelayer; fitted with a stern mine rail and a recovery crane.

The LCU 1627 in the Western Pacific. Assault Craft Unit 1 maintains four of these craft at Sasebo, Japan, to support the Japan-based Amphibious Ready Group (ARG). The others are the LCU 1629, LCU 1630, LCU 1634, and LCU 1651. Other LCUs forward deploy with ARGs based in the United States. (1999, U.S. Navy)

The white-painted LCU 1647, currently assigned to support and research duties with the Naval Air Warfare Center's detachment in Key West, Fla. Note the heavy crane fitted aft. Three other, extensively modified LCUs serve as support craft for combat swimmers; see chapter 24. (U.S. Navy)

The LCU 1635 while supporting United Nations peacekeeping forces in East Timor. Normally embarked in the amphibious ship PELELIU (LHA 5), the LCU 1635 and LCU 1646 were detached for 15 and 30 days, respectively, to support the peacekeepers. Here Australian troops supervise unloading trucks and rollers. (1999, U.S. Navy)

Details of the bridge structure of the LCU 1645. The craft's radar "pot" and mast fold down when being taken aboard amphibious ships. The LCU 1645 was coming into the docking well of the SAIPAN (LHA 2) at Rota, Spain, when this photo was taken. (1998, U.S. Navy, RM3 Jeffrey Tiemann)

3 UTILITY LANDING CRAFT: "LCU 1466" CLASS

Number	Assignment
119WB1561 (ex-LCU 1561, YFU 61)	Naval Station Roosevelt Roads, P.R.
LCU 1580 (ex-Army VERA CRUZ)	on loan to Maritime Administration
LCU 1590 (ex-Army SPOTSYLVANIA)	Mobile Diving and Salvage Unit 2

Displacement:	180 tons light
	360 tons full load
Length:	119 feet (39.0 m) overall
Beam:	34 feet (10.4 m)
Draft:	6 feet (1.8 m)
Propulsion:	3 geared diesel engines (Gray Marine 64 YTL); 675 bhp; 3 shafts
Speed:	8 knots
Range:	700 n.miles (1,300 km) at 7 knots with payload
Manning:	6 (enlisted)
Troops:	8
Guns:	removed
Radars:	navigation

These are the survivors of a large series of LCUs. The LCU 1580 supports the National Defense Reserve Fleet (NDRF) at Suisun Bay (Vallejo), Calif. These craft were completed in 1954.

Class: This class covered hull numbers LCU 1466–1609, with 14 units (LCU 1594–1607, completed in 1955) constructed in Japan under the Offshore Procurement (OSP) program for foreign service. Other ships of this design were built for the U.S. Army.

Numerous U.S. units were transferred to other nations; others became service craft (YFU).

Classification: The LCU 1466–1503 were ordered as utility landing ships (LSU) on 31 October 1951; they were reclassified as LCUs on 15 April 1952.

Design: SCB No. 25. These craft have a deckhouse-aft configuration.

Guns: Built with gun "tubs" on either side of the bridge structure for .50-cal machine guns or 20-mm cannon.

An LCU 1466–class landing craft carrying three Marine M48 Patton tanks (with turrets turned to the rear) during a landing exercise. Many of these craft were operated by the Army as well as the Navy. The craft has only a bow ramp; twin 20-mm cannon are fitted on either side of the bridge. (U.S. Navy)

POST–WORLD WAR II TANK LANDING CRAFT

Tank landing craft designs LCT(1), (2), (3), and (4) were British. The first U.S. design was the LCT(5), with LCT 1–500 being completed in 1942; many were transferred to Great Britain. The LCT(6) followed, with nos. 501–1465 being completed in 1943–1944; a few went to Britain and six became coastal minehunters, designated AMc(U) 1–6.[1] The LCT(6) had an "island" structure on the port side, introducing the "drive-through" design to landing craft. The American LCT(7) nos. 1501–1830 were oceangoing craft, completed as medium landing ships (LSM/LSMR). The British LCT(8) was a similar oceangoing craft.

In 1949 the surviving LCT(6)s were reclassified as utility landing ships (LSU), keeping their LCT hull numbers. Landing craft nos. 1466–1503 were ordered in 1951 as LSUs but changed to LCU in May 1952. Subsequent LCUs followed in sequence, bypassing the numbers initially assigned to the LCT(7) series.

Approx. 75 MECHANIZED LANDING CRAFT: LCM(8) MK 3, MK 5

Weight:	34 tons light
	121 tons full load
Length:	73⁷/₁₂ feet (22.4 m) overall
Beam:	21 feet (6.4 m)
Draft:	4⁷/₁₂ feet (1.4 m) aft
Propulsion:	4 diesel engines (General Motors Detroit 6-71); 1,300 bhp; 2 shafts (see *Engineering* notes)
Speed:	12 knots
Range:	150 n.miles (278 km) at 12 knots
Manning:	5 (enlisted)
Guns:	none (see notes)

These are standard landing craft intended to carry vehicles and cargo. Their capacity is 58 tons of cargo or light vehicles. No accommodations are provided in these or other LCM-type craft.

Most of these craft are assigned to Assault Craft Units 1 and 2.

Engineering: Most have four GM 6-71 diesels; a few have two of the larger GM 12V71 diesels. The last 20 units (delivered 1991–1992) have GM 8V92N engines.

Guns: A pair of .50-cal machine guns can be fitted.

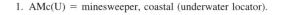

1. AMc(U) = minesweeper, coastal (underwater locator).

An LCM(8) from Assault Craft Unit 1 being hoisted aboard ship. These so-called "Mike" boats are still in use, mostly at naval bases and stations. (U.S. Navy)

An LCM(8) assigned to the Naval Amphibious Base in Coronado (San Diego), Calif. Bow ramps vary in these craft. The mast protruding from the conning position mounts a navigation light. (Giorgio Arra)

An LCM(8) from Assault Craft Unit 2 off Norfolk, Va. A glass-windowed cover is installed over the conning position. LCMs and smaller landing craft are identified by their parent unit, base, or ship. (Giorgio Arra)

Approx. 25 MECHANIZED LANDING CRAFT: LCM(8) MK 2, MK 4

Weight:	36.5 tons light
	106.75 tons full load
Length:	74 1/12 feet (22.6 m) overall
Beam:	21 1/12 feet (6.4 m)
Draft:	4 1/2 feet (1.4 m)
Propulsion:	4 diesel engines (General Motors); 1,300 bhp; 2 shafts
Speed:	12 knots
Range:	150 n.miles (278 km) at 12 knots
Manning:	5 (enlisted)
Guns:	none

These are aluminum versions of the steel-hulled LCM(8) originally developed for use with the CHARLESTON (LKA 113)-class amphibious cargo ships (Mk 2). Subsequently, additional units were ordered for use aboard maritime prepositioning ships (Mk 4).

Cargo capacity is 65 tons of cargo or light vehicles.

Engineering: Some units have been refitted with Kort nozzles.

Approx. 60 MECHANIZED LANDING CRAFT: LCM(6) TYPE

Weight:	26.7 tons light
	62.35 tons full load
Length:	56 feet (17.1 m) overall
Beam:	14 1/3 feet (4.4 m)
Draft:	3 5/8 feet (1.2 m)
Propulsion:	2 diesel engines (Gray Marine 64HN9 or General Motors 8V71); 625 bhp; 2 shafts
Speed:	12 knots
Range:	130 n.miles (240 km) at 9 knots
Manning:	5 (enlisted)
Guns:	none

Additional units of this type serve in various support roles. Numerous LCMs of this type were converted to riverine combat craft during the Vietnam War. Of the above total, about ten are normally carried aboard amphibious ships.

Of welded steel construction, they can carry 34 tons of cargo or, for short distances, 120 troops.

Engineering: The above horsepower and speed are for the General Motors engines; those with Gray Marine have 450 bhp and can make 10 knots.

Approx. 130 LANDING CRAFT PERSONNEL LIGHT (LCPL): MK 11, MK 12, MK 13

Weight:	10 tons full load
Length:	36 feet (11.0 m) overall
Beam:	13 feet (4.0 m)
Draft:	3 1/2 feet (1.1 m)
Propulsion:	1 diesel engine (General Motors 8V71); 350 bhp; 1 shaft (see notes)
Speed:	17 knots
Range:	150 n.miles (278 km) at 15 knots
Manning:	3 (enlisted)
Guns:	none (see notes)

These small landing craft are used for passenger transport and for the control of other landing craft. About 100 are currently carried in amphibious ships, with the remainder assigned to shore activities.

LCPLs are built of fiberglass-reinforced plastic. They carry 17 passengers or two tons of cargo.

Engineering: The Mk 13 LCPLs have Cummins lightweight engines fitted.

Guns: During the Vietnam War, several LCPLs were armed with one or more .50- and .30-cal machine guns and employed for inshore patrol (some with a navigation radar fitted).

Approx. 10 LANDING CRAFT VEHICLE AND PERSONNEL (LCVP): MK 7

Weight:	13.5 tons full load
Length:	35 3/4 feet (10.9 m) overall
Beam:	10 1/2 feet (3.2 m)
Draft:	3 1/2 feet (1.1 m)
Propulsion:	1 diesel engine (Gray Marine 64HN9); 225 bhp; 1 shaft
Speed:	10 knots
Range:	110 n.miles (204 km) at 8 knots
Manning:	2 or 3 (enlisted)
Guns:	none

These small landing craft can be carried by amphibious ships. Most of these are currently aboard "amphibs."

LCVPs are built of wood or fiberglass-reinforced plastic. They have a bow ramp and can carry light vehicles or four tons of cargo or 40 troops.

A "short-hull" LCM(6) traveling at high speed (Giorgio Arra)

An LCM(6) modified to serve as a tender at the Naval Surface Warfare facility in Florida. A life raft canister is fitted alongside the elevated pilothouse. (1990, Giorgio Arra)

An LCVP from the command ship BLUE RIDGE (LCC 19). Two or three sailors usually operate these craft. (Giorgio Arra)

AMPHIBIOUS WARPING TUGS

The Navy operates a large number of these craft, which are fabricated from pontoon sections. They are used to ferry material from amphibious and Maritime Prepositioning Ships (MPS) to shore, to install amphibious fuel and water transfer systems, and to maneuver and support causeways. One warping tug (SLWT) and three or four powered causeway sections (CSP) are carried by many MPS vessels; with some equipment removed and the A-frame lowered, the tugs can be side-loaded on tank landing ships of the NEWPORT (LST 1179) class.

The tugs are operated by Amphibious Construction Battalions (ACB) under the Commanders, Naval Beach Group 1 (Coronado, Calif.) and Naval Beach Group 2 (Norfolk, Va.).

21 SIDE-LOADABLE WARPING TUGS

Builders:	Oregon Iron Works, Klackamas, Ore.
Displacement:	100 tons light
Length:	80 feet (24.38 m) overall
Beam:	22 feet (6.71 m)
Draft:	
Propulsion:	2 diesel engines (GM Detroit Diesel 6V92); 860 bhp; all-azimuth propulsors
Speed:	5 knots
Range:	
Manning:	

These units were delivered in 1994–1995. Each consists of 36 sections that can be easily taken apart and reassembled.

3 SIDE-LOADABLE WARPING TUGS

Number	Number	Number
SLWT 4013	SLWT 4014	SLWT 4015

Builders:	PACECO, Gulfport, Miss.
Weight:	110 tons loaded
Length:	84 feet (25.6 m) overall
Beam:	21¼ feet (6.48 m)
Draft:	2⅔ feet (0.8 m)
Propulsion:	2 turbocharged diesel engines (GM Detroit Diesel 8V71TI); 850 bhp; 2 waterjet propulsion units with 360° rotating nozzles with 12,500 lbs (5,625 kg) thrust
Speed:	8.5 knots
Range:	75 n.miles (140 km)
Manning:	8 (enlisted)

These side-loadable warping tugs are modular, consisting of 33 replaceable pontoon "cans" that are bolted together, plus three engine modules, a small control station, and an A-frame lifting device. They can be connected as "pushers" to between one and six unpowered pontoon causeways to form barge ferries; each causeway can carry 100 tons of containerized cargo or vehicles. Without the A-frame and minor modifications, these craft are designated as causeway sections, powered (CSP); that designation is now found on the Navy's ship classification list (see chapter 3).

The SLWT has a double-drum, diesel-powered A-frame/winch (turbocharged Detroit Model 4-53T) with a lifting capacity of 12 tons. Fitted with 1,120-pound (504-kg) stern anchor. Fuel capacity is 625 gallons (2,375 liters).

Classification: In the fleet, these craft are (incorrectly) referred to as side-loading warping tugs (SLWT).

An SLWT from ACB 1 is seen beaching at Coronado. Note the control station (offset to starboard), removable mast, and A-frame. (1992, U.S. Navy, Tom Hollinberger)

The SLWT 35 from ACB 1 serves as a pusher for pontoon causeways with Marine trucks parked on the pontoons. (1992, U.S. Navy, Tom Hollinberger)

The SLWT 35 from Amphibious Construction Battalion 1 pushes two pontoon causeways laden with several Marine trucks. These "tugs" and pontoon causeways are necessary for unloading amphibious ships and, in some situations, Maritime Prepositioning Ships (MPS). (1992, U.S. Navy, Tom Hollinberger)

1 AMPHIBIOUS WARPING TUG

Number
LWT 1 (also 85WT681)

Builders:	Campbell Machine Works, San Diego, Calif.
Weight:	61 tons light
Length:	85 feet (25.9 m) overall
Beam:	22 feet (6.7 m)
Draft:	6¹¹/₁₂ feet (2.1 m)
Propulsion:	2 diesel engines (GM Detroit Diesel 8V71); 420 bhp; 2 steerable propellers
Speed:	9 knots
Range:	
Manning:	6 (enlisted)

Two units of this aluminum-construction design were delivered in 1970. The LWT 2 (85WT682) has been discarded, but this unit has been retained (correction to previous edition).

LANDING VEHICLES

Assault Amphibian Vehicles (AAV) are used by the Marine Corps for assault landings and for subsequent movement ashore. The Marine Corps currently operates 1,057 assault amphibian vehicles of the AAV7 series. Most of these are troop carriers (AAVP7); 79 are configured as command vehicles (AAVC7) and 53 as recovery/repair vehicles (AAVR7).

An Advanced Amphibian Assault Vehicle (AAAV) is under development. The Defense Acquisition Board, the Pentagon's major review agency for new weapon programs, on 15 March 1995 approved moving the AAAV from the initial concept and exploration phase into the demonstration and validation phase, and a contract for prototypes was awarded in June 1996.

Increasingly, the Marines have employed these vehicles on land, as well as for ship-to-shore movement. The AAV/LVT is limited in its usefulness as an armored personnel carrier because of (1) its high noise level, (2) the height of the vehicle, (3) treads that are susceptible to damage during heavy overland use, (4) slow speed over certain types of terrain, and (5) light armor. Also, there is now no effective method of protecting the troops in the AAV7 vehicles from CBR weapons attack.

The Marine Corps has three battalions and two lesser units that operate amphibian tractors. These are:

- Combat Assault Battalion on Okinawa to support the 3rd Marine Division (1 amphibian company)

Figure 19-1
Marine Assault Amphibian Battalion

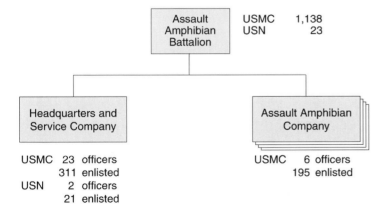

- 2nd Assault Amphibian Battalion at Camp Lejeune, N.C., to support the 2nd Marine Division (4 amphibian companies)
- 3rd Assault Amphibian Battalion at Camp Pendleton, Calif. (3 amphibian companies)
- Company D, 3rd Assault Amphibian Battalion, at Twentynine Palms, Calif.
- Combat Support Company, at Kaneohe Bay, Hawaii (1 platoon)

Note that the battalion on Okinawa is a *combat* unit, with two tank companies in addition to the amphibian company. The standard amphibian battalion has a total of 1,161 personnel and 233 amphibian vehicles—213 AAVP7s, 14 AAVC7s, and 6 AAVR7s (see figure 19-1).

The 2nd and 3rd Battalions are each capable of simultaneously lifting the assault elements of a Marine Expeditionary Brigade (i.e., reinforced regiment), while the 1st Battalion can provide lift for a Marine Expeditionary Unit (i.e., reinforced battalion).

There are additional AAVs forward deployed on board the maritime prepositioning ships. Additional AAVs are assigned to the Marine Corps Reserve and are in the pipeline for maintenance, training, etc.

The service life of the present AAV7 "family" of vehicles was expected to end in the mid-1980s. However, the failure to gain approval for a follow-on amphibian vehicle led the Marines to embark on an extensive Service Life Extension Program (SLEP) for existing vehicles (with modified vehicles receiving the designation suffix A1).

There have been two previous proposed successors to the AAV7/LVTP-7: the landing assault vehicle (LVA), initiated in 1973 and canceled in 1979, followed by the advanced tracked landing vehicle, designated LVT(X). The abortive LVT(X), which was canceled in 1985, is described in the 13th Edition/page 212.

Classification: The AAV7 series was previously designated landing vehicle tracked, personnel, or LVTP-7. The term AAV was adopted in the 1970s as a "sexy" designation for the next generation of assault amphibian vehicle. In 1985 the designation LVTP and the term amphibious tractor ("amtrac") were discarded from AAV terminology.

Modernization: The AAV7 SLEP upgrade program included the following changes:

- Replacing the existing gun turret, which mounts a single .50-cal M85 machine gun, with an electric-drive turret mounting a 40-mm grenade launcher Mk 19 as well as the older but more reliable .50-cal machine gun M2.
- An advanced mine-clearing system that fires explosive "snakes" for detonating ground mines. The system—including a possible later version with fuel-air explosive—can be installed on top of a tractor.
- A limited CBR alarm and protection system.
- Appliqué steel armor that can be bolted onto the vehicle by the crew. This P-900 armor will defeat 14.7-mm gunfire. The armor weighs 3,500 pounds (1,591 kg), which the vehicle can easily handle—in fact, the weight actually improves the water stability of the craft. A lighter, improved armor is in development.
- A bow plane that extends when the craft is in the water to reduce the tendency to push down into seas.
- An automatic fire sensor and suppression system to reduce the possibility of fuel fires in the troop compartment.
- Improved transmission and suspension.
- A magnetic heading device.

These improvements add weight to the vehicle, but this is not a concern because of the craft's great payload. More critical is space, with the changes reducing the troop capacity to perhaps 21 riflemen; if crew-served weapons—such as mortars—are carried, the troop capacity is even less.

An advanced propulsion system that will provide enhanced mobility is being considered. A rotary engine of about 750 hp with all-electric drive has been evaluated in a prototype AAV7.

ADVANCED AMPHIBIAN ASSAULT VEHICLE

Weight:	approx. 74,000 pounds (33,566 kg) fully loaded
Length:	27⅚ feet (8.48 m) on land
	37 feet (11.28 m) in water
Width:	12 feet (3.66 m)
Height:	10 feet (3.05 m)
Propulsion:	1 diesel engine (MTU MT883 Ra-523); 2,600 hp in water mode, 800 hp in land mode; tracked running gear on land; 2 waterjets in water
Speed:	45 mph on land
	20 knots in 3-foot (0.91-m) waves
Range:	300 miles (483 km) on land
	75 miles (120 km) in water
Crew:	3
Troops:	18
Guns:	1 30-mm Bushmaster II cannon M242 (300 rounds ready + 600 stowed)
	1 7.62-mm machine gun M240 (800 rounds ready + 1,600 stowed)

The development of an Advanced Amphibian Assault Vehicle (AAAV) "remains our primary developmental research effort," according to the commandant of the Marine Corps.[2] This development program seeks to provide a high-speed tracked vehicle to move assault troops from amphibious ships beyond the horizon to inland objectives.

The Marine AAAV program envisions a "high-speed" sea craft

---

2. Gen. A. M. Gray, USMC, testimony before the House Armed Services Committee, 21 February 1991.

with the land mission capabilities of the U.S. Army's Bradley Armored Fighting Vehicle (AFV).

The Marine Corps plans to procure 1,013 AAAVs to replace the AAV7s. Two groups, United Defense (formerly FMC Corporation's Ground Systems Division, which built all AAV7s) and General Dynamics's Land Systems Division teamed with AAI Corp., competed for the development of the new vehicle. Following tests with demonstration vehicles, General Dynamics was selected to produce 15 prototype vehicles—13 troop carriers and 2 command-and-control vehicles. Full-scale production is to begin in FY 2006 with a unit price of $6.6 million and a total program price—for development and procurement—estimated $7.5 *billion*.

The first AAAV prototype was delivered in August 1999. Under the January 2000 schedule, production will begin in fiscal year 2004, with 35 units funded that year and 66 in FY 2005.

Design: The GD-AAI design has a planing hull. GD-AAI has produced three AAV technology test beds under contract to the Navy, with the last—called a Propulsion System Demonstrator (PSD)—achieving a planing speed of 25 mph (40 km/h) for 33 n.miles (61 km) in trials with a top speed of 45 mph (72.4 km/h); vehicle weight was 57,000 pounds (25,855 kg). The craft had a Cummins VTA 903T diesel engine and (for high water speed) a General Electric LM 120/T700/TC7 gas turbine engine. Such a combat vehicle, with a crew of three, could carry 15 troops.

The AAAV will have the Global Positioning System (GPS), Forward-Looking Infrared (FLIR), and night-vision devices for nav-

The prototype AAAV, without appliqué armor. The lower panels open to serve as chines when the craft is waterborne. (1999, General Dynamics/Land Systems)

AAAV No. 1, showing the turret mounting the 30-mm Bushmaster II cannon and 7.62-mm machine gun (1999, General Dynamics/Land Systems)

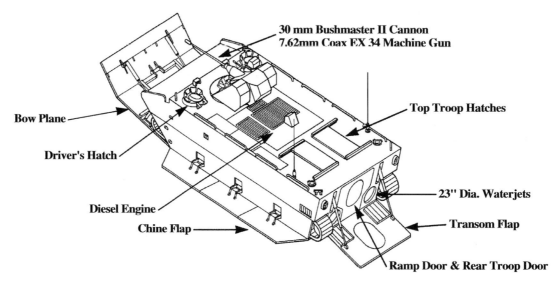

30 mm Bushmaster II Cannon
7.62mm Coax EX 34 Machine Gun
Bow Plane
Driver's Hatch
Diesel Engine
Chine Flap
Top Troop Hatches
23" Dia. Waterjets
Transom Flap
Ramp Door & Rear Troop Door

Advanced Amphibian Assault Vehicle

igating, targeting, and intelligence collection. In place of troops, the vehicle can carry 5,130 pounds (2,327 kg) of cargo.

Guns: The 25-mm cannon and 7.62-mm machine gun are coaxially mounted in a turret atop the vehicle.

925 PERSONNEL VEHICLES: AAVP7A1 SERIES (FORMERLY LVTP-7)

Weight:	38,450 pounds (17,477 kg) empty
	50,350 pounds (22,886 kg) loaded
Length:	26 feet (7.9 m) overall
Width:	10¾ feet (3.3 m)
Height:	10¼ feet (3.1 m)
Draft:	5⅔ feet (1.7 m)
Propulsion:	turbo-supercharged diesel engine (Cummins VT400); 400 hp; tracked running gear on land; 2 waterjets in water (3,025 lbst each)
Speed:	40 mph maximum, 20–30 mph cruise on land
	8.4 mph maximum, 8 mph cruise in water
Range:	300 miles at 25 mph on land
	approx. 55 miles at 8 mph in water
Crew:	3 (enlisted)
Troops:	18
Guns:	1 .50-cal machine gun M2
	1 40-mm grenade launcher Mk 19

The AAVP7 is a full-tracked, amphibian vehicle, providing an over-the-beach capability for landing troops and equipment through heavy surf. It is the world's only vehicle capable of operating in rough seas and plunging surf (up to ten feet high). Several hundred are being modernized and are designated AAV7A1 (see below).

These vehicles were designed and manufactured by the Ordnance Division of FMC Corporation, San Jose, Calif. They are also used by the Marine forces of Argentina, Brazil, Italy, South Korea, Spain, and Thailand.

Armament: The LVTP-7 was designed to mount a 20-mm cannon coaxially with a machine gun; however, because of development problems, the cannon was deleted. The current .50-cal machine gun is co-mounted with a 40-mm grenade launcher in a 360° powered turret; the turret holds 200 .50-cal rounds and 98 40-mm rounds.

A mine clearance kit can be fitted for clearing beach obstacles. This consists of a rack launcher firing three 350-foot-long explosive line charges. Detonation is controlled by wire from within the vehicle.

Class: The prototypes for the LVTP-7 design were 15 LVTPX-12 vehicles delivered to the Marines in 1967–1968. These were followed by a production run of 965 LVTP-7s delivered from 1970 to 1974, plus the specialized LVTC and LVTR vehicles described below. In

Marines check out their AAVP7A1 while aboard the landing ship HARPERS FERRY (LSD 41). There are separate hatches for the driver, gunner, and vehicle commander. (1993, Hughes Missile System)

AAVP7A1 assault vehicles—fitted with appliqué armor—drive along the beach at Vladivostok in the Russian Far East during a joint exercise with the Russian Navy called Cooperation from the Sea. A Russian landing ship is at left. (1994, U.S. Navy, PH1 Charles W. Alley)

Chilean Marines race from the rear of an AAVP7A1 during a joint U.S.-Chilean amphibious exercise in Chile. Appliqué armor is fitted to the vehicle. (1996, U.S. Navy)

An AAVP7A1 assault vehicle prepares to come aboard the SHREVEPORT (LPD 12) during Exercise Agile Provider. These vehicles are low in the water when at sea. (1994, U.S. Navy, PH1 Robert N. Scoggin)

addition, one LVTE-7 prototype of an assault engineer/mine clearance vehicle was delivered in 1970, but none were series-produced. Additional vehicles have been produced for use by the maritime prepositioning forces.

Design: The LVTP-7 was designed to replace the LVTP-5-series amtracs and offered increased land and water speeds and more range, with less vehicle weight. In lieu of troops, the newer vehicle can carry 10,000 pounds (4,545 kg) of cargo. The LVTP-7 has a rear door and ramp for loading/unloading troops and cargo; it can turn 360° within its own length on land or in water.

Modernization: The SLEP-upgraded vehicles were designated LVTP-7A1 prior to the change to AAV7A1. The first updated vehicles were delivered to the Marine Corps on 24 October 1983.

79 COMMAND VEHICLES: AAVC7A1 SERIES (FORMERLY LVTC-7)

Weight:	40,187 pounds (18,267 kg) empty
	44,111 pounds (20,050 kg) loaded
Crew:	12 (3 vehicle crew, 5 radiomen, 4 unit commander and staff)
Troops:	none
Guns:	1 7.62-mm machine gun M60D

Except as indicated above, the AAVC7 command vehicle characteristics are similar to those of the basic AAV7 series. Eighty-five of these vehicles were originally procured for use as command vehicles in amphibious landings. Additional vehicles were procured in the 1980s.

These vehicles are fitted with radios, cryptographic equipment, and telephones. Seventy-seven of the original vehicles are being modernized to the 7A1 configuration.

53 RECOVERY/REPAIR VEHICLES: AAVR7A1 SERIES (FORMERLY LVTR-7)

Weight:	47,304 pounds (21,502 kg) empty
	49,853 pounds (22,660 kg) loaded
Crew:	5 (3 vehicle crew, 2 mechanics)
Troops:	none
Guns:	1 7.62-mm machine gun M60D

Except as indicated above, the characteristics of the recovery/repair vehicle are similar to the AAV7 series. Sixty of these vehicles were originally procured for the recovery of damaged amtracs during amphibious landings. Additional units were procured during the 1980s. They are fitted with a 6,000-pound (2,727-kg)-capacity telescoping boom-type crane and 30,000-pound (13,636-kg) pull winch, plus maintenance equipment.

An "amtrac," shown carrying Marines in the assault on occupied Kuwait during the Persian Gulf conflict. The troops have hung their gear from the vehicle, whose name is "Pressure Point." (1991, U.S. Navy, CWO Ed Bailey)

The turret of an AAVP7A1 showing the .50-cal machine gun and 40-mm grenade launcher. Previous generations of "amtracs" included vehicles armed with heavier guns, including howitzers up to 105 mm. (1991, U.S. Navy, CWO Ed Bailey)

An AAVP7A1 employed ashore as an armored personnel carrier. The roof plates are open, and Marines with their M16 rifles are at the ready in the troop compartment. (FMC Corporation)

An AAVR7A1 vehicle with its crane raised. There is a towing winch at the rear of the vehicle, above the ramp. (FMC Corporation)

POST–WORLD WAR II AMPHIBIOUS TRACTORS

The U.S. Marine Corps procured 18,620 "amtracs" of various LVT/ LVTA models during World War II. The first postwar LVT design produced for the Marine Corps was the LVTP-5 troop carrier and its derivatives: the LVTH-6, mounting a 105-mm howitzer; LVTE-1 engineer vehicle; LVTC-1 command vehicle; and LVTR-1 recovery vehicle. A total of 1,332 of these vehicles were manufactured between 1951 and 1957.

This series was followed by the LVT-7 (now AAV7) series.

The Navy-manned LCAC 77 races ashore with equipment for the 26th Marine Expeditionary Unit (MEU), providing assistance to earthquake victims at Hersek, Turkey. The Navy-Marine amphibious team provides a flexible and useful military-humanitarian tool for supporting U.S. political-military interests. But the capabilities of one or two MEUs in a combat situation are severely limited. (1999, U.S. Navy, CWO Seth Rossman [USMC])

The LCU 1635 and LCU 1646 while detached to assist United Nations peacekeeping forces on East Timor. The Navy is planning to procure 35 new LCU-type craft as replacements for outdated utility landing craft. LCUs still are needed for landing vehicles and bulk cargo. Although the current LCUs are considered capable of independent operations for ten days, the LCU 1635 and LCU 1646 operated independently for much longer in 1999. (1999, U.S. Navy)

CHAPTER 20

Patrol and Special Warfare Craft

A corvette-size warship—usually called the "streetfighter"—intended specifically for littoral operations has been proposed for the U.S. Navy. Such ships, procured in large numbers, would carry out blockades, perform surveillance functions, support special forces, and support amphibious landings and other operations. (From a painting by Jim Stilphen)

The role of special warfare craft in the U.S. Navy has increased significantly in the post–Cold War era with the U.S. Navy's emphasis on littoral warfare and special operations forces. The CYCLONE-class ships are the first major patrol craft to be built for the U.S. Navy in a decade and replace smaller, less-capable craft. There is some Navy interest in pursuing the development of an advanced fast patrol craft—that interest having been initiated after Congress directed that the Navy consider the procurement of such craft.

Historically, the U.S. Navy has shown little interest in small combatants in peacetime, in part because of the emphasis on long-range, blue water operations that supported the Navy's primary missions, and also because of the belief that the tactics and craft needed for coastal and inshore operations could be rapidly developed in wartime.

The CYCLONE class comprises the Navy's third post–World War II "large" patrol-series ships to be built. The Navy's six hydrofoil missile craft have been discarded, most after little more than a decade of operational service. Designed as Cold War attack craft to counter Soviet warships in coastal areas (such as the Aegean Sea), they were never forward-deployed and spent virtually all of their service in the Caribbean area engaged in anti-drug operations. Also discarded have been the ASHEVILLE-class patrol gunboats produced in the 1960s. Those ships participated in offshore patrol operations during the Vietnam War.

The Navy evaluated several advanced technology combat craft in the 1960s and produced several hundred coastal and riverine patrol and support craft. Those, too, have been discarded, except for a few craft operated by Special Boat Unit 22 (see below). During the Vietnam War, the lack of a capability in small combatant craft forced the Navy to procure Norwegian-built fast patrol boats and to adopt commercial designs for naval use. The Navy subsequently sought to keep abreast of small craft design and during the early 1980s U.S. yards delivered a series of Navy-designed missile craft (PCG/PGG types) to Saudi Arabia, as well as smaller inshore and riverine combat craft to several other countries.

During 1998 the Navy gave serious consideration to proposals to the transfer up to one-half of the CYCLONE class to the Coast Guard, which would have operated the ships in support of both the U.S. Special Operations Command and Coast Guard requirements. After considerable discussion, the PCs were retained in Navy service until one unit was transferred in 2000 (see below).

Operations of Navy special warfare forces are under the control of the U.S. Special Operations Command, a unified command responsible for the employment of all U.S. special operations forces (see chapter 4 of this edition of *Ships and Aircraft*).

The CYCLONE class of 14 ships followed a series of failures in U.S. Navy efforts during the 1980s to develop patrol/special warfare craft. The earlier craft had the design designations PBM, PCM, SWCM (Sea Viking), SWCX, and PXM, the last being a hydrofoil patrol craft.[1]

Armament: No anti-submarine weapons are carried by U.S. patrol craft.

Classification: The smaller, unnamed patrol boats and craft are individually designated by their hull length, hull type, calendar year of construction, and consecutive hull of that type built during the year. Thus, 68PB842 indicates the second 68-foot PB-type craft built in 1984. The first two letters in this scheme are generally used in the designation:

AT   armored troop carrier
HS   harbor security
PB   patrol boats
RP   river patrol boat

Operational: Navy special warfare ships and craft are assigned to the Naval Special Warfare Command, which supports the U.S. Special Operations Command. The six major special warfare units are located at the Naval Amphibious Base Coronado (San Diego), Calif., and the Naval Amphibious Base Little Creek (Norfolk), Va.

Special Boat Squadrons 1 and 2 control all surface craft operations. Special Boat Unit (SBU) 22 is oriented to riverine operations, with worldwide responsibility for that mission. (The unit is located at the John C. Stennis Space Flight Center in Mississippi. The riverine-oriented SBU-26 was disestablished in December 1998.)

The two Naval Special Warfare Groups direct the Navy's SEAL teams, special warfare units, and SEAL Delivery Vehicle Teams (SDVT) 1 and 2. The SDVT vehicles are described in chapter 12. The SEAL teams and SDVTs are deployed worldwide, with major U.S. naval forces and detachments deployed at Stuttgart, Germany; Rodman, Panama; Roosevelt Roads, Puerto Rico; Rota, Spain; Guam; and Bahrain.

The Naval Special Warfare Development Group manages the test, evaluation, and development of technology applicable to these forces. The Naval Special Warfare Center serves as the "schoolhouse" for basic and advanced special warfare training, including SEAL training.

There is also a Naval Reserve program that provides augmentation and other support to the active commands.

LITTORAL COMBAT CRAFT: "STREETFIGHTER" CONCEPT

A new concept of small combatants has been proposed for acquisition by the U.S. Navy. Although the U.S. Navy has rejected "corvette"-size warships—between patrol craft and frigates—since World War II, there is significant support for the construction of such warships configured specifically for littoral operations.[2] The name "streetfighter" has been used for this warship concept.

One of the more senior supporters of the streetfighter concept has been Vice Admiral Arthur K. Cebrowski, President of the Naval War College. He has written that such a ship

> exploits new sensor capabilities and such platforms as unmanned or autonomous air, surface, and subsurface vehicles; a family of numerically larger but physically different surface ships; and submarines capable of contributing substantively to both access and power projection. Streetfighter is intended to gain and sustain access in the face of an adversary's sophisticated (or not so sophisticated) area-denial strategy.[3]

Envisioning large numbers of these ships operating in littoral waters, supporters of the streetfighter concept contend that these ships would enable larger, more vulnerable warships to stand farther offshore, providing covering support for these smaller warships. The streetfighters would use advance hull forms and stealth techniques, with modular adaptability permitting the same basic hulls to be fitted for specific roles. One writer on the subject—calling it a "guerrilla warfare ship"—has listed these missions for the ship:

- littoral battlespace domination
- maritime embargo
- precision engagement
- surface and subsurface surveillance and choke point traffic monitoring
- interdiction of littoral traffic
- commerce raiding
- Special Forces delivery and extraction
- protection of the amphibious assault lines of communications, which will extend over the horizon[4]

Nevertheless, at this writing there is no Navy plan or program for the design and procurement of such ships. Further, the Navy's surface warfare community is highly apprehensive that a large-scale streetfighter program would divert funding from large surface combatants (i.e., the DD 21 design).

Still, looking at the mine, missile, and non-nuclear submarine threats in the littoral areas, and the limited number of traditional warships that can be afforded under existing budget projects, the streetfighter concept becomes attractive.

1. See 13th Edition/page 221 and 14th Edition/pages 227–228 for program notes.

2. Since the sailing ship era, the only corvettes acquired by the U.S. Navy were 18 ARABIS- or Flower-class ships acquired in 1942–1943. Designated PG 62–71, 86, 87, 89, and 92–96, the first ten were built in British shipyards and eight in Canadian yards.

3. Vice Adm. A. K. Cebrowski, USN, and Capt. Wayne P. Hughes, USN (Ret.), "Rebalancing the Fleet," U.S. Naval Institute *Proceedings* (November 1999), p. 34.

4. Lt. Cdr. Dave Weeks, USNR, "Combatant for the Littorals," U.S. Naval Institute *Proceedings* (November 1999), p. 27.

Figure 20-1

Naval Special Warfare

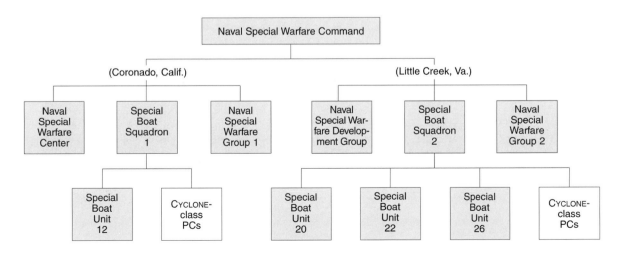

13 COASTAL PATROL SHIPS: "CYCLONE" CLASS

Number	Name	FY	Laid down	Launched	Commissioned	Status
PC 1	CYCLONE	90	22 June 1991	1 Feb 1992	7 Aug 1993	to Coast Guard
PC 2	TEMPEST	90	30 Sep 1991	4 Apr 1992	21 Aug 1993	**AA**
PC 3	HURRICANE	90	20 Nov 1991	6 June 1992	15 Oct 1993	**PA**
PC 4	MONSOON	90	15 Feb 1992	10 Oct 1992	22 Jan 1994	**PA**
PC 5	TYPHOON	90	15 May 1992	3 Mar 1993	12 Feb 1994	**AA**
PC 6	SIROCCO	90	20 June 1992	29 May 1993	11 June 1994	**AA**
PC 7	SQUALL	90	17 Feb 1993	28 Aug 1993	4 July 1994	**PA**
PC 8	ZEPHYR	90	6 Mar 1993	3 Dec 1993	15 Oct 1994	**PA**
PC 9	CHINOOK	91	16 June 1993	6 Feb 1994	28 Jan 1995	**AA**
PC 10	FIREBOLT	91	17 Sep 1993	10 June 1994	10 June 1995	**AA**
PC 11	WHIRLWIND	91	4 Mar 1994	9 Sep 1994	1 July 1995	**PA**
PC 12	THUNDERBOLT	91	9 June 1994	2 Dec 1994	7 Oct 1995	**PA**
PC 13	SHAMAL	91	22 Sep 1994	3 Mar 1995	27 Jan 1996	**AA**
PC 14	TORNADO	96	25 Aug 1998	24 June 1999	24 June 2000	**AA**

Builders:	Bollinger Shipyards, Lockport, La.		Manning:	28 (4 officers + 24 enlisted)
Displacement:	331 tons full load		Troops:	9 (SEALs or other passengers)
Length:	157⁵/₁₂ feet (48.0 m) waterline		Missiles:	hand-held Stinger point-defense missile launchers
	170½ feet (52.0 m) overall		Guns:	2 25-mm Bushmaster cannon Mk 38 (2 single)
Beam:	25 feet (7.6 m)			2 .50-cal machine guns M2HB (2 single)
Draft:	7 ⅚ feet (2.4 m)			2 7.62-mm machine guns M60 (2 single)
Propulsion:	4 diesel engines (Paxman Valenta 16VRP-200); 13,400 bhp;			2 40-mm grenade launchers Mk 19 (2 single)
	4 shafts		Radars:	2 Sperry RASCAR 2500 surface search (S and X bands)
Speed:	35 knots		Sonars:	Wesmar side-scanning (HF)
Range:	2,000 n.miles (3,700 km) at 12 knots		EW systems:	APR-39A(V)1 radar warning receiver

These are small combatants intended for coastal interdiction and the support of special operations forces, primarily Navy SEALs. They were specifically intended as replacements for the Navy's over-age PB Mk III craft.

The CYCLONE class was "designed to cost," hence a readily available foreign design was adopted. According to the reference work *Combat Fleets of the World*, these ships "have limited endurance for their size, and their combat systems and ammunition allowance do not compare well with those of similar ships in most other navies."[5]

---

5. A. D. Baker III, *Combat Fleets of the World, 1998–1999* (Annapolis, Md.: Naval Institute Press, 1998), p. 1031.

In anticipation of completion of the TORNADO, the CYCLONE was decommissioned on 28 January 2000 and transferred to the Coast Guard on 29 January 2000 at the Coast Guard Yard in Curtis Bay, Md. Most of the Navy crew of the CYCLONE was transferred to the newer craft. According to unofficial reports, the CYCLONE was transferred to avoid the Navy having to stand up another PC crew.

Armament: These ships were to be fitted with the Stabilized Weapon Platform System (SWPS), installed on the fantail. The SWPS could launch a variety of missiles, including the Hellfire, Stinger, and Hydra-70, with a co-mounted 25-mm or 30-mm cannon, a television camera, a laser rangefinder and designator, and a Forward-Looking Infrared (FLIR) sensor. In the event, the system was not installed.

The TORNADO on trials with a Coast Guard patrol craft. The PC 14 introduces a new stern configuration to these craft, which will be backfitted in several units beginning with the SHAMAL. The stern ramp and gates facilitate the recovery of Rigid Inflatable Boats (RIB) at high speed. (2000, Bollinger Shipyards)

The CYCLONE ammunition allowance is:

Stinger SAM	6 ready missiles
25-mm cannon	2,000 rounds
.50-cal machine gun	2,000 rounds
7.62-mm machine gun	2,000 rounds
grenade launcher	1,000 rounds

Builders: The building yard previously was named Bollinger Machine Shop & Shipyard.

Class: The Navy planned to construct 16 of these ships when the program was defined in the late 1980s; by the time the lead ship was ordered, the program had been reduced to 13 units. Bollinger was awarded a contract for the construction of eight ships with an option for five additional units on 3 August 1990; the five-ship option was exercised on 19 July 1991.

In the fiscal 1996 budget, without a Navy request and although not included in the Department of Defense shipbuilding plan, Congress funded $20 million for advance procurement of another ship of the CYCLONE class as a political benefit for the shipyard area, with full funding expected in the fiscal 1997 budget.

Classification: These ships were originally designated PBC for patrol boat, coastal; this was changed to PC for patrol, coastal, on 25 July 1991.

The classification PC originated in World War I as the *hull numbers* for a series of 110-foot (33.5-m) wood-hull submarine chasers given *names* in an SC series. Beginning in 1940, a series of steel-hull submarine chasers were built with PC designations, and in October 1942 all wood-hull submarine chasers were given SC hull numbers.

The World War II steel-hull program reached hull number PC 1603 (completed in 1944); most were 173-foot (52.7-m) oceangoing craft designated PC, although the PCE/PCS/SC types shared the same numbering series. Postwar ships with PC/PCE designations built in U.S. and foreign shipyards, all for use by foreign navies, took the series to PC 1646. The PC 1647 and 1648 were canceled; thus, the new construction U.S. PCs should properly have begun with hull number PC 1647 or 1649—not PC 1.

The TORNADO with her stern gate open, showing the RIB recovery system. High-speed recovery reduces the exposure of both the PC and the SEALs to enemy fire. (2000, Bollinger Shipyards)

The original stern configuration of the CYCLONE class provided for a small hydraulic crane to lift RIBs, and a "step" built into the stern counter to assist SEALs in boarding their RIBs and coming back aboard the PCs. (1994, Bollinger Shipyards)

Design: The PC hull/propulsion design is based on the Vosper Thornycroft–built missile craft of the *Ramadan* class constructed for the Egypt (six units completed 1981–1982), Oman (four units completed 1982–1989), and Kenya (two units completed 1987).

The U.S. ships have steel hulls with aluminum superstructures; one-inch (25-mm) appliqué armor is fitted to portions of the superstructure for protection against small arms fire. Their endurance is ten days.

A single 20-foot (6.1-m) rigid inflatable swimmer delivery craft normally is carried by each PC. Earlier it also was planned to carry two 15½-foot (4.7-m) combat rubber raiding craft on each PC.

Electronics: The ships have two Mk 52 chaff/decoy launchers. An Identification Friend or Foe (IFF) transponder, but no interrogator, is fitted.

Manning: Although originally intended to be commanded by lieutenants, in fact these ships are commanded by lieutenant commanders.

Names: These ships are named for weather phenomena.

Operational: These ships were initially placed "In Commission, Special" at the Bollinger yard to permit a Navy crew to take the ships to ports where they were placed in "In Commission, Full," the formal commissioning ceremony (listed above). The CYCLONE was the first U.S. Navy ship ever to be placed in commission at the U.S. Naval Academy, Annapolis, Md. The SIROCCO was commissioned at the Washington (D.C.) Navy Yard. She was the first U.S. Navy ship to be placed in commission at the yard—the Navy's oldest—since the steam/sail corvette NIPSIC was commissioned on 11 October 1879, the last of 22 ships that were constructed at the Washington Navy Yard.

The first four ships of the class participated in the U.S. occupation of Haiti in 1994; the MONSOON ran aground during coastal patrol activities. During the operations off Haiti, the boats carried up to 25 SEALs while on multiday patrols.

The first overseas deployment of this class began on 21 April 1995, when the TYPHOON and SIROCCO departed Norfolk for operations in the Baltic and Mediterranean Seas.

The SQUALL operating off Oahu, Hawaii. Based on a Vosper Thornycroft design, the PCs have severe operational limitations. Still, they were built and entered service following the failure of several U.S. small combat designs to come to fruition. (1998, U.S. Navy, PH3 Christopher Hollaway)

The SQUALL at sea. Her superstructure blocks, lattice mast, and railings (especially those on the walkways connecting the superstructure blocks) combine to give the PCs a very large radar cross-section. (1998, U.S. Navy, PH3 Christopher Hollaway)

The shaft and propeller arrangement on the SHAMAL. Note the shape of the propeller blades. (2000, Bollinger Shipyards)

20 SPECIAL OPERATIONS CRAFT: SOC MK V TYPE

Builders:	Trinity-Halter Marine, Gulfport, Miss.
Displacement:	approx. 75 tons full load
Length:	82 feet (25.0 m) overall
Beam:	17 feet (5.18 m)
Draft:	5 feet (1.52 m)
Propulsion:	2 diesel engines (MTU 16V396 TE94); 4,770 hp; 2 waterjets
Speed:	50+ knots
Range:	600 n.miles (1,112 km) at 35 knots
Manning:	5 (enlisted)
Troops:	16 (SEALs or other passengers)
Guns:	combinations of .50-cal machine guns M2HB, 7.62-mm machine guns M60E, and 40-mm grenade launchers Mk 19
Radars:	navigation

The Trinity-Halter design won the Navy's competition with the Peterson Builders' Mk V Sea Stalker design for a special warfare craft (see 16th Edition/pages 188–189).

A special operations craft Mk V at high speed. Another long-delayed program, the SOCs replaced the long-serving 65-foot (19.8-m) PBs used by SEALs. Mounts for machine guns are fitted aft. (1999, Leo Van Ginderen)

The after aspect of a special operations craft Mk V. These craft carry a RIB on their stern. Up to 16 SEALs can crowd aboard these craft. (1999, Leo Van Ginderen)

These craft support special operations forces: the insertion and extraction of special forces (primarily SEALs), and limited coastal patrol and interdiction operations. The first two craft were delivered in August 1995 and the last in 2000.

Design: These craft are fabricated of aluminum. Up to four combat rubber raiding craft can be carried. They can be air transported by C-5 Galaxy aircraft (two craft plus their support equipment).

Operational: Twelve Mk V craft are assigned to Special Boat Squadron (SBR) 1 at Coronado and eight to SBR-2 at Little Creek.

The stern of a special operations craft Mk V, showing the RIB recovery ramp and stowage position. There are four machine gun mounts aft. (1999, Leo Van Ginderen)

PATROL BOATS: PB MK IV TYPE (SEA SPECTRE)

All patrol boats of the 68½-foot (20.85-m) Mk IV type have been stricken; see 16th Edition/pages 189–190 for characteristics.

PATROL BOATS: PB MK III TYPE (SEA SPECTRE)

All of these 65-foot (19.8-m) patrol craft have been stricken; see 16th Edition/page 190 for characteristics.

SEVERAL HIGH SPEED BOATS: HSB TYPE

Weight:	14,600 lbs (6,622.5 kg) without payload
	19,100 lbs (8,664 kg) full load
Length:	40 feet (12.2 m) overall
Beam:	9 feet (2.74 m)
Draft:	3 feet (0.9 m)
Propulsion:	2 gasoline engines; 1,160 hp; 2 stern propellers
Speed:	55+ knots
Range:	175 n.miles (324 km)
Manning:	3 (enlisted)
Troops:	12 SEALs
Guns:	(see notes)
Radars:	navigation

The boats are used by naval special warfare forces for short-range SEAL insertion/extraction operations; they also have a limited coastal patrol and interdiction.

Design: These craft are fabricated of glass-reinforced vinylester resin. Two boats, with their trailers, can be carried by a C-5 Galaxy or C-141 Starlifter transport.

Guns: A variety of guns and grenade launchers can be carried by embarked SEALs.

21 ARMORED TROOP CARRIERS: MINI-ATC (MATC) TYPE

Builders:	Marinette Marine, Wisc.
	Tacoma Boatbuilding, Wash.
Weight:	22,000 pounds (9,979 kg) light
	29,500 pounds (13,381 kg) full load
Length:	36 feet (11.0 m) overall
Beam:	12¾ feet (3.9 m)
Draft:	3½ feet (1.0 m)
Propulsion:	2 diesel engines (General Motors 8V53N); 566 bhp; 2 waterjets
Speed:	25+ knots
Range:	200+ n.miles (370+ km)
Manning:	3 or 4 (enlisted)
Troops:	16
Guns:	(see notes)
Radars:	LN-66 navigation

The MATC was developed from lessons learned in the Vietnam War and are intended for clandestine operations during riverine campaigns. They have low radar signatures and quiet engines.

These craft were built between 1972 and 1979.

Design: The MATCs have aluminum hulls and ceramic armor. At high speed, they have a 1-foot (0.3-m) draft. They can carry two tons of cargo.

Guns: Up to seven machine guns and grenade launchers can be mounted on this craft.

A mini-ATC under way in San Francisco Bay (1988, Giorgio Arra)

A mini-ATC without the radar "pot" fitted (1988, Giorgio Arra)

RIGID INFLATABLE BOATS: RIB TYPE

Weight:	17,400 lbs (7,893 kg)
Length:	35¹¹/₁₂ feet (10.95 m) overall
Beam:	10⁷/₁₂ feet (3.23 m)
Draft:	2¹¹/₁₂ feet (0.89 m)
Propulsion:	2 turbocharged diesel engines (Caterpillar 3126); 2 propellers
Speed:	40+ knots
Range:	200 n.miles (370 km)
Manning:	3 (enlisted)
Troops:	8 SEALs
Guns:	(see notes)
Radars:	Furuno 841 navigation

Rigid Inflatable Boats (RIB) are employed by SEALs for ship-to-shore insertion/extraction. These craft are faster and quieter and have a greater range than previous boats; also, troops being carried are subjected to less spray than in previous boats. An entire SEAL squad can be transported in these craft.

Design: The RIB hull is a deep "V" fabricated of fiberglass and Kevlar.

Guns: Two mounts are provided for machine guns or grenade launchers.

A standard RIB-type craft employed by special forces. Some have the radar "pot" aft. Note the machine gun fitted forward and the amidships "cockpit." (1998, Leo Van Ginderen)

RIB-type craft with radar fitted aft. This photo was taken as SEALs were en route to inspect a Danish cargo ship as part of the United Nations embargo of Iraq. The U.S. Coast Guard also uses these craft. (1994, U.S. Navy, PH1 Richard Piening)

24 RIVERINE PATROL BOATS: PBR MK 2 TYPE

Builders:	Uniflite, Bellingham, Wash.
Displacement:	7.5 tons light
	8.9 tons full load
Length:	32 feet (9.75 m) overall
Beam:	11²/₃ feet (3.6 m)
Draft:	2⁷/₁₂ feet (0.8 m)
Propulsion:	2 diesel engines (General Motors 6V53 or 6V53T or 4-53N); 430 bhp; 2 waterjets
Speed:	24 knots
Range:	150 n.miles (278 m) at 23 knots
Manning:	4 or 5 (enlisted)
Missiles:	none
Guns:	1 60-mm mortar Mk 4 in some units
	1 25-mm Bushmaster cannon Mk 38
	1 .50-cal machine gun
	1 40-mm grenade launcher Mk 19
Radars:	navigation

These heavily armed craft were developed for riverine warfare in Vietnam. All are operated by the Naval Reserve Force. These craft were delivered from 1965 through 1974.

Class: More than 500 PBRs were built in 1965–1973, with most transferred to South Vietnam after being used by the U.S. Navy. Additional units were built for the U.S. Navy in the early 1980s (with GM 4-53N diesel engines). Subsequently, replacement hulls have been procured commercially for refit/replacement of existing boats in a one-for-one "swap" procedure. The newer boats are being provided with GM 6V53T engines.

The 31RP66108, 31RP7023, and 31RP9999—not included in the above type totals—are at the Naval Historical Center at the Washington Navy Yard.

A PBR Mk 2, one of the types of riverine craft that were widely used in the Vietnam War. (1988, Giorgio Arra)

A PBR Mk 2 under way in San Francisco Bay. The Coast Guard aids-to-navigation boat 55101 is in the background. (1988, Giorgio Arra)

Design: These craft have fiberglass hulls and ceramic armor. They can be transported in C-5 Galaxy cargo aircraft.

Engineering: The waterjet propulsion enables the boats to operate in shallow and debris-filled water with a very high degree of maneuverability.

LIGHT PATROL BOATS: PBL TYPE

Weight:	6,500 pounds (2,948 kg) fully loaded
Length:	25 feet (7.62 m) overall
Beam:	8⁷⁄₁₂ feet (2.6 m)
Draft:	1½ feet (0.46 m)
Propulsion:	2 outboard gasoline engines; 2 propellers
Speed:	30+ knots
Range:	160 n.miles (296 km)
Manning:	3 (enlisted)
Troops:	several
Guns:	(see notes)
Radars:	navigation

These are lightly armed Boston Whaler–type craft employed for riverine and coastal patrol and interdiction.

Design: These craft can be carried by C-130 Hercules and larger aircraft, or by sling under helicopters.

Guns: Each craft has three positions for mounting various machine guns and grenade launchers.

COMBAT RUBBER RAIDING CRAFT: CRRC TYPE

Weight:	265 pounds (120 kg)
Length:	15⁵⁄₁₂ feet (4.7 m) overall
Beam:	6¼ feet (1.9 m)
Draft:	2 feet (0.61 m)
Propulsion:	1 outboard gasoline engine; 55 hp
Speed:	18+ knots
Range:	60+ n.miles (111 km)
Manning:	1 (enlisted)
Troops:	8 SEALs
Guns:	none
Radars:	none

These Combat Rubber Raiding Craft (CRRC) are used for clandestine insertion/extraction of SEAL forces. They can be carried and launched from submarines and aircraft, as well as from surface ships and craft.

An 18-gallon (68-liter) fuel bladder is fitted to the craft.

Marines recover a combat rubber raiding craft aboard a submarine. An outboard motor is fitted onto the stern. (1994, U.S. Marine Corps, Cpl. Robert A. Berry)

73 HARBOR SECURITY BOATS: HSB TYPE

Number	Number	Number
24HS8701	24HS8733–24HS8735	24HS8801–24HS8810
24HS8703–24HS8709	24HS8738–24HS8745	24HS8813–24HS8825
24HS8711–24HS8728	24HS8748–24HS8750	24HS8901–24HS8910

Builder:	Peterson Builders, Sturgeon Bay, Wisc.
Displacement:	2.5 tons light
	3.8 tons full load
Length:	24 feet (7.3 m) overall
Beam:	7⁷⁄₁₂ feet (2.3 m)
Draft:	5⅙ feet (1.6 m)
Propulsion:	2 diesel engines (Volvo Penta AGAD 41A); 2 outboard drives
Speed:	22.5 knots
Range:	
Manning:	4 (enlisted)
Guns:	(see notes)
Radars:	none

Light patrol boats—based on the Boston Whaler design—are used in an exercise in Paraguay. A tripod-mounted radar "pot" is fitted in the stern of these craft. Several machine guns and grenade launchers can be mounted. (1996, U.S. Navy)

These craft are employed for harbor patrol at various bases, shipyards, and forward operating areas. Aluminum construction. No armament is provided, but light machine guns can be mounted.

Class: Originally 75 craft were in this series, numbered 24HS8701–24HS8750 and 24HS8801–24HS8825. All were built in 1988–1989.

A harbor security boat in the Persian Gulf (1991, U.S. Navy)

A harbor security boat in the Persian Gulf patrolling against Iraqi and Iranian floating mines and swimmers (1991, U.S. Navy)

GUIDED MISSILE CRAFT: EX-SOVIET TARANTUL I CLASS

The former East German missile craft HIDDENSEE is now a museum/exhibition ship at Battleship Cove in Fall River, Mass. Completed in 1995, the ship was built in the Soviet Union for service in the East German Navy. She was transferred to the U.S. Navy in 1992 for trials and evaluation.

Listed as "floating equipment" and designated 185NS9201, the craft was operated by the Naval Air Warfare Center at Patuxent River, Md., until 18 April 1996. She was transferred to Battleship Cove on 20 October 1996. (The HIDDENSEE was not transferred to the Sea-Air-Space Museum in New York City, as earlier proposed.)

The HIDDENSEE was a Tarantul I–class missile craft; see 16th Edition/page 194 for characteristics.

PATROL COMBATANTS, MISSILE (HYDROFOIL): "PEGASUS" CLASS

Number	Name	Comm.	Notes
PHM 1	PEGASUS	1977	
PHM 2	HERCULES	1983	
PHM 3	TAURUS	1981	decommissioned and stricken 30 July 1993
PHM 4	AQUILA	1982	
PHM 5	ARIES	1983	
PHM 6	GEMINI	1983	

These were high-speed, heavily armed missile craft, originally intended to conduct sea control operations in restricted seas. However, from their completion they were employed primarily in anti-drug operations in the Caribbean area.

Class: This design was one of the new warship types initiated by Admiral Elmo R. Zumwalt as Chief of Naval Operations (1970–1974). A class of at least 30 missile craft of this type were planned. When Zumwalt left office, the Navy's leadership reduced the program to only the prototype; however, congressional pressure led to the first "flight" of six ships, already funded, being completed. See 15th Edition/pages 197–198 for characteristics.

The CYCLONE-class PCs ZEPHYR *(foreground),* SQUALL, and HURRICANE cruise off San Diego, Calif. These craft primarily support special operations forces. Unfortunately, they do not have stealth characteristics. Some of the PCs have camouflage markings. (1997, U.S. Navy, PH2 Jeffrey S. Viano)

CHAPTER 21

Mine Countermeasures Ships and Craft

The mine countermeasures support ship INCHON steaming with a covey of U.S. and allied mine countermeasures ships; an MH-53E Sea Dragon flies overhead. The U.S. Navy is attempting to shift from such ships to MCM devices to be carried in surface ships and submarines. (1998, U.S. Navy)

The U.S. Navy is belatedly making major improvements in Mine Countermeasures (MCM) capabilities and in mine countermeasure systems that will be organic to submarines, surface combatants, and amphibious ships, as well as MCM ships and helicopters.

Questions about the fundamental ability of the U.S. Navy to cope with modern mine warfare problems came following difficulties in earlier MCM programs, the mining of the supertanker BRIDGETON in the first convoy escorted by U.S. forces in the Persian Gulf in 1987, the mining of the U.S. frigate SAMUEL B. ROBERTS (FFG 58) in the Gulf in 1988, and the damage inflicted by mines on the helicopter carrier TRIPOLI (LPH 10) and the Aegis cruiser PRINCETON (CG 59) in the Gulf in 1991.

According to the U.S. Navy's official history of the Persian Gulf conflict, *Shield and Sword*, the captain of one Aegis cruiser, Captain Steve Woodall, said, "I could make [an Iraqi] airplane a memory . . . [but] the most appreciable threat to us [was] just hitting a mine."[1] The result was the ludicrous scenes of Aegis cruisers—the most advanced surface warships afloat—with a sailor perched in the bow with binoculars, searching the water for mines!

The problems of locating and destroying Iraqi mines, the superiority of foreign mine countermeasures ships, the complications caused by the "command-control picture," and the shortcomings of the command staff for the U.S. mine countermeasures group led General Norman Schwarzkopf to declare that the Navy's "very, very antiquated mine-sweeping fleet . . . frankly, just could not get the job done." Vice Admiral Stanley Arthur, commander of U.S. naval forces in the Gulf, concluded that "everybody in the world had better minesweepers out there than I did."[2]

Thus, even with the demise of the Soviet Union as a military threat to the United States, sea mines remain a major threat to the maritime operations of the United States and other nations. The Department of Defense report on the Persian Gulf conflict stated:

> Operation Desert Shield and Desert Storm highlighted the dangers that sea mines pose to naval forces. Mines will continue to pose a difficult problem. Refocusing our national defense strategy away from the European theater and toward regional contingencies has exposed a gap in U.S. mine warfare capability that our European allies were previously expected to fill.[3]

No additional mine countermeasures ships are planned by the U.S. Navy, the emphasis now being on so-called organic MCM capabilities. The current force of 26 MCM ships falls short of providing the Navy's minimum goal for mine countermeasures capabilities. That goal, as stated in 1991, was 45 new MCM/MHC ships, plus helicopters. (Studies of wartime requirements indicate a need for at least 60 mine countermeasures ships, with the high end of estimates in the hundreds, much too large a force for American peacetime budgets—or interest.)

1. Dr. Edward J. Marolda and Dr. Robert J. Schneller, Jr., *Shield and Sword: The United States Navy and the Persian Gulf War* (Washington, D.C.: Naval Historical Center, 1998), p. 205.

2. Marolda and Schneller, *Shield and Sword*, p. 263.
3. Department of Defense, *Conduct of the Persian Gulf Conflict* (Washington, D.C.: GPO, 1991), pp. 6–9.

In response to these shortfalls, difficulties, and criticism, the U.S. Navy is developing an array of organic MCM systems that can be carried by warships into forward areas without the need for specialized MCM ships. These currently include:

- *Airborne Mine Neutralization System (AMNS):* The AMNS is an expendable, remotely operated mine neutralization device that will be compatible with HH-60 and SH-60 Seahawk and CH-60 Knight Hawk helicopters. It currently is in the engineering and manufacturing development phase, employing off-the-shelf technologies to the extent possible. The system is scheduled to become operational late in 2003. The prime contractors are Lockheed Martin and Atlas (Germany).
- *Airborne Laser Mine Detection System (ALMDS):* This is an electro-optical mine-detection system using an aircraft-mounted laser to detect floating and anchored mines. This capability was successfully demonstrated during an operational assessment in 1995 (employing an SH-2F LAMPS I helicopter). An interim contingency capability has been developed employing Naval Reserve SH-2G helicopters. The program goal is to integrate the ALMDS into the HH-60 and SH-60R Seahawk force. The prime contractor for the contingency system is the Kaman Corp.
- *Remote Minehunting System (RMS):* Designed specifically for MCM operations in littoral areas, these devices are intended for use by surface ships (see below). The prime contractor is Lockheed Martin.
- *Unmanned Underwater Vehicles (UUV):* Intended for use by attack submarines, two UUV systems are under development: the Near-term Mine Reconnaissance System (NMRS) and the Long-term Mine Reconnaissance System (LMRS). These are tethered and untethered systems, respectively (see chapter 12 of this edition of *Ships and Aircraft* for descriptions). The prime contractor is Northrop Grumman.

The Navy's conventional MCM force has completed its long-delayed modernization, with new ships and helicopters (MH-53E) entering the fleet. In early 2001 the surface MCM force consists of 14 mine countermeasures ships (MCM) and 12 coastal minehunters (MHC).

The current MCM buildup was initiated under the Reagan-Lehman naval program of the early 1980s. After an almost 30-year hiatus in the series production of minesweepers, two new ship classes were initiated: the AVENGER-class MCM ships and the CARDINAL-class air-cushion minehunters (MSH). Both the MCM and MSH encountered major construction problems, with the latter being canceled and the OSPREY-class MHC, adopted from the Italian LERICI design, built in place of the CARDINAL class.

(All of the U.S. minesweepers of the MSO and MSC types built during the Korean War era have been stricken, although many continue to serve in other navies. The smaller MSB and COOP mine countermeasures craft are also gone, with a single exception.)

Air-cushion landing craft (LCAC) can also be employed to undertake mine countermeasures operations in shallow water (see chapter 19).

The helicopter carrier INCHON has been converted to an MCM support ship. There has long been a need for such a ship to enhance the effectiveness and on-station time of deployed MCM forces, both surface ships and helicopters. Only one such support ship is now envisioned until the end of the next decade.

Two Airborne MCM squadrons are operational: Helicopter Mine Countermeasures Squadron (HM) 14 at Norfolk, Va., and HM-15 at NAS Corpus Christi, Texas.[4] Both squadrons fly the MH-53E Sea Dragon helicopter, with 12 aircraft per squadron. In addition, reserve Light Helicopter Anti-submarine Squadron (HSL) 94 at NAS Willow Grove, Pa., flies the SH-2G LAMPS I helicopter fitted with the ALMDS.

Reserve MCM helicopter squadrons HM-18 and HM-19 have been disestablished, with their personnel integrated with the active duty squadrons. Similarly, HM-12, the MCM readiness/transition training squadron, was disestablished, with the Marine Corps now being responsible for all H-53 pilot and air crew training. See chapter 26 for details of MCM helicopter squadrons.

TABLE 21-1. MINE WARFARE SHIPS (EARLY 2001)

Type	Ship/Class	Commissioned	Active	NRF
MCS 12	INCHON	1970	—	1
MCM 1	AVENGER	1987–1994	10	4
MHC 51	OSPREY	1992–1999	3	9

These MCM forces have the primary missions of clearing U.S. waters and strategic choke points and clearing paths for amphibious assaults. It should be noted that the helicopters have a limited night-flying capability and marginal detection capabilities against bottom-laid mines.

Almost all surface minesweepers and one of the two helicopter MCM squadrons are based at the mine warfare complex at NAS Corpus Christi and the adjacent base at Ingleside, Texas. The headquarters for the Mine Warfare Command is located at the air station.

The move to Ingleside began following the Navy's announcement in May 1991 that all MCM forces would be relocated there. In a report to the Secretary of the Navy issued on 27 December 1991, the General Accounting Office attacked the Navy's plan, criticizing the Navy for not spending enough time analyzing the issue and indicating that the costs of the relocation could be prohibitive. (The Mine Warfare Command and several mine warfare ships previously were based at Charleston, S.C.)

The move to Ingleside was commended by the Navy in 1992 as improving efficiency. However, there has been criticism of the move based primarily on (1) removing mine warfare ships and personnel from the major fleet operating bases, thus inhibiting the exchange of ideas; (2) making exercises with the fleet more difficult and costly; and (3) increasing transits to and from forward operating areas—a significant factor for the relatively low-speed MCM forces.

In response, the Navy has based two MCMs at Sasebo, Japan, and two MCMs and two MHCs are homeported in the Persian Gulf. Proposals to base MCMs in Astoria, Ore., and Pearl Harbor, Hawaii, have not been pursued.

Mine countermeasures: The MCM and MHC classes both use a hull-mounted Variable Depth Sonar (VDS) as their primary means of mine detection and the cable-controlled SLQ-48 Mine Neutralization System (MNS) for examination and clearing of the mines (see description at end of this chapter).[5]

Names: The larger minesweepers have adjective names and smaller units have bird names. The use of bird names dates to World War I and was continued for most U.S. minesweepers into the 1950s, except that the larger destroyer-minesweepers (DMS series) retained their destroyer names.

Operational: U.S. minesweepers in the Persian Gulf escorted Kuwaiti tankers and other merchant ships during the Iran-Iraq conflict in the late 1980s and again in 1990–1991 during the Desert Shield/Desert Storm operations. The Navy sent four MSOs as well as MSBs to the Persian Gulf in 1988 and sent the AVENGER, GUARDIAN, and three MSOs into the Gulf in 1990–1991.

The MCM support ship INCHON undertook her first deployment from March to July 1999, steaming to the Adriatic Sea where she served as flagship of Mine Squadron 2, composed of the INCHON; the MCM ships AVENGER, CHAMPION, DEVASTATOR, and SCOUT; HM-15; Helicopter Combat Support Squadron (HC) 8 Detachment 1; and components of Explosive Ordnance Disposal (EOD) Mobile Unit 6.

The entire U.S. Navy surface ship/craft MCM force was originally scheduled to be operated by the Naval Reserve Force (NRF). However, following the mine countermeasures effort in Operation Desert Storm, the decision was made to retain ten of the AVENGER-class ships in the active fleet. Four of those large MCM ships and all but one of the smaller OSPREY-class ships are operated by the Naval Reserve Force with a composite active-reserve crew.

---

4. The status of the naval airfield at Norfolk was downgraded from a separate Naval Air Station to a detachment of NAS Oceana, Va., in 1998.

5. The MNS previously was referred to as the MNV (Mine Neutralization Vehicle).

The fantails of mine countermeasures ships are crowded with reels, sweep gear, hoisting devices, and so forth. These MCMs are at Ingleside, Texas, being rigged for heavy weather. The basing of most of the U.S. mine warfare forces at Ingleside removes them from day-to-day fleet operations and increases their transit time to and from exercise areas. (U.S. Navy)

1 MINE COUNTERMEASURES SUPPORT SHIP: CONVERTED "IWO JIMA" CLASS

Number	Name	FY	Builder	Laid down	Launched	LPH comm.	MCS completed	Status
MCS 12 (ex-LPH 12)	INCHON	66	Ingalls Shipbuilding, Pascagoula, Miss.	8 Apr 1968	24 May 1969	20 June 1970	30 June 1996	**NRF-A**

Displacement:	11,000 tons light		Troops:	approx. 150 aviation personnel
	18,340 tons full load			approx. 75 explosive ordnance disposal personnel
Length:	556 feet (169.5 m) waterline		Aircraft:	8 MH-53E Sea Dragon MCM helicopters
	602¼ feet (183.6 m) overall			2 CH-46D Sea Knight cargo helicopters
Beam:	83⅔ feet (25.5 m) waterline		Elevators:	2 deck edge (50 × 34 feet/15.2 × 10.4 m)
Extreme width:	104 feet (31.7 m)		Missiles:	removed
Draft:	26 feet (7.9 m)		Guns:	4 25-mm Bushmaster cannon Mk 38 (4 single)
Propulsion:	1 steam turbine (Westinghouse); 23,000 shp; 1 shaft			2 20-mm Phalanx CIWS Mk 15 (2 multibarrel)
Boilers:	2 600-psi (41.7-kg/cm²) (Combustion Engineering)			4 .50-cal machine guns M2HB (4 single)
Speed:	23 knots (21 knots sustained)		Radars:	SPS-40E air search
Range:	16,600 n.miles (30,743 km) at 11.5 knots			SPS-64(V)9 navigation
	10,000 n.miles (18,520 km) at 20 knots			SPS-67(V)1 surface search
Manning:	active 505 (36 officers + 469 enlisted)		Fire control:	removed
	reserve 177 (5 officers + 172 enlisted)		EW systems:	SLQ-25 Nixie
				SLQ-32(V)3

The INCHON was converted from an IWO JIMA–class helicopter carrier (amphibious assault ship) to a mine countermeasures support ship to operate MCM helicopters and to provide services to mine countermeasures ships. She was the last of the seven IWO JIMA–class ships to be completed (see chapter 18).

Early supporters of this program sought a ship that could (1) support and provide underway replenishment for MCM ships,

(2) provide command and control facilities for MCM operations, and (3) carry and operate MH-53E helicopters. Prior to selection of the INCHON, the Navy had considered the conversion of two dock landing ships of the AUSTIN (LPD 4) class for this role. The LPD conversions would have provided a limited transport capability for MHC-type ships. However, their command and control and helicopter support facilities were too limited for the MCS role.

The INCHON—the largest ship ever to carry a mine warfare designation—can embark an MCM squadron commander and his staff and can provide alongside services for four MCM/MHC-type ships, as well as supporting her embarked helicopters. The ship is manned by a composite active-reserve crew; she is homeported at Ingleside, Texas, and technically is assigned to the Naval Reserve Force.

A second LPH conversion was tentatively planned for the period 2005–2010, but a suitable hull is unlikely to be available in that period. Current Navy planning provides for a second MCS to be funded in fiscal year 2014.

Classification: LPH 12 was changed to MCS 12 on 24 May 1996; the ship properly should have been designated MCS 8 (see table 21-2).

Conversion: The ship was converted to the MCM support role at the Ingalls Shipyard in Pascagoula, with the conversion beginning on 6 March 1995 and being completed 28 May 1996; fitting out was completed 30 June 1996. The ship was not decommissioned during her conversion.

Her conversion included an upgrade of command and control facilities, removal of the larger self-defense weapons (see below), and modification of the hangar bay to stow MCM-related equipment.

Design: The LPH project number was SCB No. 157. The INCHON was the only IWO JIMA (LPH 2)-class ship with boat davits for carrying four LCVP-type landing craft.

The hangar and flight decks can accommodate 11 MH-53E helicopters. The ship's medical facilities include 12 beds. In the MCS role, the ship can provide over-the-stern refueling of mine countermeasures ships while under way and alongside refueling while stationary. (As an LPH the ship could carry 1,500+ troops.)

Electronics: The ship has SPN-35A marshalling and SPN-43B aircraft approach systems.

Guns/missiles: As built, the ship had four 3-inch Mk 33 twin gun mounts, two forward of the island structure and two on the after corners of the flight deck. Two gun mounts were replaced in the 1970s by two Sea Sparrow BPDMS Mk 25 launchers; the remaining pair of twin gun mounts was removed during the MCS conversion, as were the Sea Sparrow launchers.

Operational: Several ships of this class had previously operated helicopters in the countermeasures role off North Vietnam (1973), in the Suez Canal (1974–1975), and in the Persian Gulf (1991).

The INCHON's first deployment as an MCS was in March 1997 to the Baltic and Mediterranean to participate in Blue Harrier, a large NATO mine countermeasures exercise, and other exercises. From March to July 1999 she deployed to the Adriatic in support of NATO operations against Serbia/Yugoslavia and to provide humanitarian assistance to refugees from Kosovo.

This view of the INCHON shows her portside elevator at the flight-deck level, a platform for handing MCM gear over the side, a stowed LCVP, and, on her port quarter, a Phalanx CIWS. The size of the MH-53E helicopters demands highly efficient flight deck and air operations teams. (U.S. Navy)

TABLE 21-2. MINE WARFARE COMMAND AND SUPPORT SHIPS

Number	Name	Comm.	MCS comm.	Former*
MCS 1	CATSKILL	1944	1967	LSV 1, CM 6, AP 106
MCS 2	OZARK	1944	1967	LSV 2, CM 7, AP 107
MCS 3	OSAGE	1944	—	LSV 3, AN 3, AP 108
MCS 4	SAUGUS	1945	—	LSV 4, AN 4, AP 109
MCS 5	MONITOR	1944	—	LSV 5
MCS 6	ORLEANS PARISH	1945	(1952)	LST 1069
MCS 7	EPPING FOREST	1943	1962	LSD 4
MCS 8–11	not used			
MCS 12	INCHON	1970	1996	LPH 12

*AN = net laying ship; AP = transport; CM = minelayer; LPH = amphibious assault ship; LSD = dock landing ship; LST = tank landing ship; LSV = vehicle landing ship

The designation MCS was established in 1956 for mine countermeasures ship; this subsequently was changed to mine warfare command and support ship. The CATSKILL and OZARK were converted in 1963–1967; their sister ships LSV 3–5 were not converted and remained laid up in "mothballs" while carrying the MCS designation.

The ORLEANS PARISH supported minesweepers from 1952 to 1960, being redesignated MCS 6 in 1959. After serving in the mine warfare role, she was transferred to the MSTS in 1966 (redesignated T-LST 1069) for use as a cargo ship and sold to the Philippines in 1976.

The INCHON is the last of the IWO JIMA–class helicopter carriers in service. These were the world's first ships built specifically as helicopter carriers. Forward on the INCHON's deck are two CH-46 Sea Knight helicopters; the others are MH-53E Sea Dragons used for MCM. (U.S. Navy)

14 MINE COUNTERMEASURES SHIPS: "AVENGER" CLASS

Number	Name	FY	Builder	Laid down	Launched	Commissioned	Status
MCM 1	AVENGER	82	Peterson Builders, Sturgeon Bay, Wisc.	3 June 1983	15 June 1985	12 Sep 1987	**NRF-A**
MCM 2	DEFENDER	83	Marinette Marine, Marinette, Wisc.	1 Dec 1983	4 Apr 1987	30 Sep 1989	**NRF-A**
MCM 3	SENTRY	84	Peterson Builders, Sturgeon Bay, Wisc.	8 Oct 1983	20 Sep 1986	6 Oct 1990	**NRF-A**
MCM 4	CHAMPION	84	Marinette Marine, Marinette, Wisc.	28 June 1984	15 Apr 1989	8 Feb 1991	**NRF-A**
MCM 5	GUARDIAN	84	Peterson Builders, Sturgeon Bay, Wisc.	8 May 1985	20 June 1987	16 Dec 1989	**PA**
MCM 6	DEVASTATOR	85	Peterson Builders, Sturgeon Bay, Wisc.	9 Feb 1987	11 June 1988	6 Oct 1990	**AA**
MCM 7	PATRIOT	85	Marinette Marine, Marinette, Wisc.	31 Mar 1987	15 May 1990	13 Dec 1991	**PA**
MCM 8	SCOUT	85	Peterson Builders, Sturgeon Bay, Wisc.	8 June 1987	20 May 1989	15 Dec 1990	**AA**
MCM 9	PIONEER	85	Peterson Builders, Sturgeon Bay, Wisc.	5 June 1989	25 Aug 1990	7 Dec 1992	**AA**
MCM 10	WARRIOR	86	Peterson Builders, Sturgeon Bay, Wisc.	25 Sep 1989	8 Dec 1990	30 Dec 1992	**AA**
MCM 11	GLADIATOR	86	Peterson Builders, Sturgeon Bay, Wisc.	7 May 1990	29 June 1991	4 June 1993	**AA**
MCM 12	ARDENT	90	Peterson Builders, Sturgeon Bay, Wisc.	22 Oct 1990	16 Nov 1991	18 Sep 1993	**Gulf**
MCM 13	DEXTROUS	90	Peterson Builders, Sturgeon Bay, Wisc.	11 Mar 1991	20 June 1992	9 July 1994	**Gulf**
MCM 14	CHIEF	90	Peterson Builders, Sturgeon Bay, Wisc.	19 Aug 1991	12 June 1993	5 Nov 1994	**AA**

Displacement:	1,195 tons light 1,312 tons full load	Speed:	13.5 knots
Length:	212¾ feet (64.85 m) waterline 224¼ feet (68.4 m) overall	Range: Manning:	MCM 1–4: active 71 (7 officers + 64 enlisted) + reserve 12 (1 officer + 11 enlisted)
Beam:	38¹¹⁄₁₂ feet (11.9 m)		MCM 5–14: 82 (7 officers + 75 enlisted)
Draft:	11¼ feet (3.4 m)	Guns:	2 .50-cal machine guns M2HB (2 single)
Propulsion:	MCM 1, 2: 4 diesel engines (Waukesha L-1616); 2,280 bhp; 2 shafts	Radars:	SPS-55 surface search Furuno or Raytheon navigation
	MCM 3–14: 4 diesel engines (Isotta-Fraschini ID36 SS 6V-AM); 2,600 bhp; 2 shafts (see notes)	Sonars:	SQQ-32(V)3 mine detection
	2 low-speed motors (Hansome); 400 shp (geared to propellers)		

These are relatively large mine countermeasures ships intended to locate and destroy mines that cannot be countered by conventional minesweeping techniques.

The AVENGER class has suffered a number of design and construction problems. The first two ships were fitted with American engines from existing stocks; the engines were installed improperly and subsequently tests revealed a potential fire hazard from lubricating oil leakage through the turbocharger into the exhaust stack. This engine design had been blamed for a series of fires in previous minesweepers. In addition, the Italian engines planned for the later MCMs initially failed in their endurance tests and passed only after modifications.

The MCMs are also overweight—one of two planned DC generators for sweep gear and minehunting had to be deleted because of space/weight problems—and the ships have had electronic interference problems. During Operation Desert Storm in 1991, the AVENGER suffered continuous problems with both main engines and generator as she hunted mines in the Persian Gulf. There are indications that her acoustic signature was greater than expected.

The AVENGER was ordered on 29 June 1982, becoming the first large minesweeper under construction for the U.S. Navy since the ASSURANCE (MSO 521) was completed 25 years earlier. The AVENGER was almost two years behind her original contract schedule; the follow-on ships also were late.

The SCOUT shows the utilitarian configuration of the AVENGER-class MCMs. The OE-82 SATCOM antennas are visible atop the bridge and aft of the tapered stack; the large winch for the SQQ-32 mine detecting sonar is forward of the bridge. (1999, Leo Van Ginderen)

Four of these ships have been transferred to NRF status, with ten retained in active service.

The GUARDIAN and PATRIOT have been based at Sasebo, Japan, since January 1996. The ARDENT and DEXTROUS are homeported in the Persian Gulf, based at Manama, Bahrain; the latter deployed to the Gulf in 2000 with two MHCs. All other ships are based at Ingleside, Texas.

Class: The Navy originally planned a two-year "program gap" between the fiscal 1982 lead ship and four ships in fiscal 1984. Subsequently, the Navy sought to accelerate the program with four ships in fiscal 1983. Congress, citing problems with the MCM design, instead funded only one ship in fiscal 1983 and directed the Navy to develop a second source shipyard (i.e., Marinette).

Design: The MCM design is similar to previous MSO classes. The hulls are constructed of fiberglass-sheathed wood (laminated oak framing, Douglas fir planking and deck sheathing with reinforced fiberglass covering). One MNS vehicle can be carried, in addition to conventional sweep gear.

The MCM concept has undergone several changes in the past two decades, having originally been proposed in the late 1970s as an oceangoing ship to protect U.S. strategic missile submarines against Soviet deep-ocean mines. A Small Waterplane Area Twin Hull (SWATH) design was considered for that concept to provide improved sea-keeping in northern waters. Under that concept, the MCMs would have operated in pairs, towing sweep gear between them. Nineteen of these ships were proposed, to have displaced 1,640 tons and with a length of 265 feet (80.8 m).

Electronics: Fitted with the SSN-2(V) precise navigation system and SYQ-13 navigation/command system; the improved SYQ-15 is to replace the latter system.

Early ships were fitted with the SQQ-30 variable-depth minehunting sonar. This equipment, an upgraded SQQ-14, has severe limitations and is replaced in later ships by the SQQ-32; the SQQ-32 has

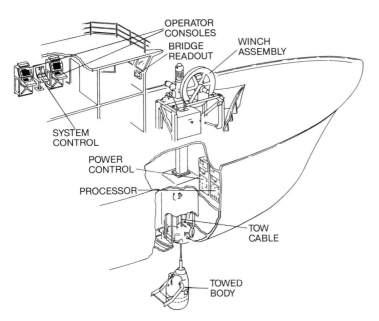

An SQQ-32 arrangement in MCM/MHC-type ships (William Clipson)

Floats or "pigs" used to steam sweep gear on the fantail of the DEFENDER. Hydraulic cranes for handling sweep gear are between the floats, in their stowed position. When the ship anchors, the national ensign will be flown from the stern. (1993, Leo Van Ginderen)

The CHIEF at speed. The U.S. Navy's traditional neglect of mine countermeasures resulted in a 30-year interval between the completion of the last MSO for the U.S. Navy and the first of the successor AVENGER-class MCMs. (U.S. Navy)

been backfitted into the earlier ships. In 1990 the AVENGER was hurriedly refitted with the engineering development model of the SQQ-32 for operations in the Persian Gulf. Deployed to the Gulf (with several MSOs), the AVENGER detected the first Manta bottom mine to be discovered, but the ship then suffered mechanical and power-generation problems and was forced to withdraw from the mined area.

Engineering: All ships have four very-low-magnetic-signature diesel engines for propulsion; electrical power for the minesweeping gear is provided by gas turbines. The low-speed motors are geared to the propellers. A 350-hp bow thruster is fitted for precise maneuvering. The maximum minehunting speed is 5 knots.

Congress directed that the MCM 10–14 would have American-made diesel engines; nevertheless, foreign engines were procured for them.

Names: Navy publicity at the time of the commissioning of the CHIEF stated that the ship was named "in honor of the chief petty officers" of the Navy. In reality, the ship was named (on 3 July 1990) along with several other MCMs to "commemorate the service of World War II minecraft that saw significant service. . . . CHIEF (MCM 14) commemorates CHIEF (AM 315), [which] earned five battle stars in World War II." In turn, the AM 315 was named for "the head or leader of a group," according to the U.S. Naval Historical Center.

Operational: The first overseas deployment of this class was by the AVENGER, which was sent to the Persian Gulf for Operations Desert Shield/Desert Storm; she was transported to the area by a heavy-lift ship along with three MSOs.[6] The AVENGER returned to the United States in June 1991 (under her own power).

OCEAN MINESWEEPERS: "ACME" CLASS

Number	Name	Comm.	Notes
MSO 508	ACME	1956	decomm. 1970; str. 1976
MSO 509	ADROIT	1957	decomm. 12 Dec 1991; str. 8 May 1992
MSO 510	ADVANCE	1958	decomm. 1970; str. 1976
MSO 511	AFFRAY	1958	decomm./str. 31 Dec 1992

6. The four mine warfare ships were carried by the Dutch heavy-lift ship SUPER SERVANT 3, which departed Norfolk on 29 August 1990 and arrived at Bahrain on 3 October 1990. The use of a heavy-lift ship saved debilitating wear-and-tear on the MCM ships and crews during the long transit.

This was an improved ocean minesweeper design, based on the earlier AGILE and AGGRESSIVE classes. The four ships built for the U.S. Navy have been stricken; ADROIT and AFFRAY were assigned to the Naval Reserve Force in their later years. Seven additional ships (MSO 512–518) were built for allied navies.

The ADROIT participated in Operation Desert Storm in 1991.

OCEAN MINESWEEPERS: "AGILE" AND "AGGRESSIVE" CLASSES

Number	Name	Comm.	Notes
MSO 427	CONSTANT*	1954	decomm. 30 Sep 1992; str. 9 Mar 1994
MSO 433	ENGAGE*	1954	decomm. 30 Dec 1991; str. 20 Apr 1992
MSO 437	ENHANCE*	1954	decomm. 13 Dec 1991; str. 21 Feb 1992
MSO 438	ESTEEM*	1954	decomm./str. 20 Sep 1991
MSO 439	EXCEL*	1955	decomm. 30 Sep 1992; str. 28 Mar 1994
MSO 440	EXPLOIT*	1954	decomm. 16 Dec 1993; str. 28 Mar 1994
MSO 441	EXULTANT*	1954	decomm. 30 June 1993; str. 9 Mar 1994
MSO 442	FEARLESS*	1955	decomm. 23 Oct 1990; str. 28 Oct 1990
MSO 446	FORTIFY*	1954	decomm. 31 Aug 1992; str. 9 Mar 1994
MSO 448	ILLUSIVE*	1955	decomm. 30 Mar 1990; str. 1 June 1990
MSO 449	IMPERVIOUS*	1955	decomm. 12 Dec 1991 str. 18 Mar 1992
MSO 455	IMPLICIT*	1954	decomm./to Taiwan 30 Sep 1994 (str. 29 Nov 1994)
MSO 456	INFLICT*	1954	decomm. 30 Mar 1990; str. 23 May 1990
MSO 464	PLUCK*	1954	decomm. 29 Nov 1990; str. 16 Jan 1991
MSO 488	CONQUEST*	1955	decomm./str. 29 June 1994; to Taiwan 3 Aug 1994
MSO 489	GALLANT*	1955	decomm./str. 29 Apr 1994; to Taiwan 3 Aug 1994
MSO 490	LEADER	1955	decomm. 12 Dec 1991; str. 18 Mar 1992
MSO 492	PLEDGE*	1956	decomm./str. 31 Jan 1994; to Taiwan 3 Aug 1994

* Ships assigned to the Naval Reserve Force prior to disposal

All ocean minesweepers of the massive Korean War–era program have been discarded. Fifty-eight ships of this design were built for the U.S. Navy (MSO 421–449, 455–474, and 488–496); another 28 ships were built for allied navies (MSO 450–454, 475–487, and 498–507), with the MSO 497 being canceled. The above list contains those ships stricken since 1990.

All three ships of the similar ABILITY class (MSO 519–521) built for the U.S. Navy have been discarded. The MSO 522 of that design was built for foreign use.

Operational: The IMPERVIOUS, INFLICT, and LEADER were deployed to the Persian Gulf in 1990–1991, participating in Desert Storm.

The RAVEN entering the port of Baltimore, Md., for her formal commissioning ceremony. Another manifestation of U.S. neglect of mine countermeasures, the OSPREY class was developed from an Italian design. (1998, U.S. Navy)

12 COASTAL MINEHUNTERS: "OSPREY" CLASS

Number	Name	FY	Builder	Start*	Launched	Commissioned	Status
MHC 51	OSPREY	86	Intermarine USA, Savannah, Ga.	16 May 1988	23 Mar 1991	20 Nov 1993	**AA**
MHC 52	HERON	89	Intermarine USA, Savannah, Ga.	7 Apr 1989	21 Mar 1992	6 Aug 1994	**NRF-A**
MHC 53	PELICAN	89	Avondale Industries, New Orleans, La.	6 May 1991	27 Feb 1993	18 Nov 1995	**NRF-A**
MHC 54	ROBIN	90	Avondale Industries, New Orleans, La.	28 Jan 1992	11 Sep 1993	11 May 1996	**NRF-A**
MHC 55	ORIOLE	90	Avondale Industries, New Orleans, La.	8 May 1991	22 May 1993	16 Sep 1995	**NRF-A**
MHC 56	KINGFISHER	91	Avondale Industries, New Orleans, La.	24 Mar 1992	18 June 1994	26 Oct 1996	**NRF-A**
MHC 57	CORMORANT	91	Avondale Industries, New Orleans, La.	8 Apr 1992	21 Oct 1995	12 Apr 1997	**NRF-A**
MHC 58	BLACKHAWK	92	Intermarine USA, Savannah, Ga.	12 May 1992	27 Aug 1994	11 May 1996	**NRF-A**
MHC 59	FALCON	92	Intermarine USA, Savannah, Ga.	3 Apr 1993	3 June 1995	8 Feb 1997	**NRF-A**
MHC 60	CARDINAL	92	Intermarine USA, Savannah, Ga.	1 Feb 1994	9 Mar 1996	18 Oct 1997	**Gulf**
MHC 61	RAVEN	93	Intermarine USA, Savannah, Ga.	4 May 1994	28 Sep 1996	5 Sep 1998	**Gulf**
MHC 62	SHRIKE	93	Intermarine USA, Savannah, Ga.	1 Aug 1995	24 May 1997	31 May 1999	**NRF-A**

*These ships do not have a formal keel laying

Displacement:	803 tons light	Speed:	12 knots
	918 tons full load	Range:	1,500 n.miles (2,780 km) at 10 knots
Length:	174⅙ feet (53.1 m) waterline	Manning:	MHC 51 51 (5 officers + 46 enlisted)
	187¾ feet (57.25 m) overall		others active 46 (5 officers + 41 enlisted)
Beam:	35¹¹/₁₂ feet (10.95 m)		reserve 6 (1 officer + 5 enlisted)
Draft:	9½ feet (2.9 m)	Guns:	2 .50-cal machine guns M2HB (2 single)
Propulsion:	2 diesel engines (Isotta-Fraschini ID36 SS 6V-AM); 1,160 bhp; 2 cycloidal propellers	Radar:	SPS-64(V)9 navigation
	2 180-shp hydraulic motors for quiet operation	Sonar:	SQQ-32(V)3 mine detection

These ships are intended for harbor clearance, port breakout, and deep-water coastal mine countermeasures. This class was developed in place of the canceled CARDINAL-class of air-cushion minehunters.

The OSPREY is in active commission; the others are assigned to the NRF. All are based at Ingleside, Texas, except for the CARDINAL and RAVEN, based at Manama, Bahrain, from 1 September 2000.

Class: Congress added one ship to the Bush administration's request for two MHCs each in the fiscal 1992 and 1993 programs, reflecting an increase in concern over the U.S. Navy's mine countermeasures capabilities. Still, only 12 MHCs have been procured even though the initial program called for 17 ships. The follow-on enlarged MHC(V) program was canceled in 1991.

The Italian Navy procured four similar ships of the LERICI class, completed in 1985; additional ships were built in Italy for Malaysia and Nigeria. The U.S. design is slightly larger to accommodate U.S. sonars, MNS, and navigation gear; also, a different propulsion system is provided.

Classification: The MHC designation originated in the early 1950s as AMC(U)—mine vessel underwater locator. Those ships were intended to locate and plot mines for subsequent destruction by minesweepers. The BITTERN (MHC 43), completed in 1957, was built for the purpose on a 144-foot (43.9-m) MSC hull with a full-load displacement of 350 tons; the planned series production of similar MHCs was canceled.

The AMC(U) 1–6 were converted LCT(6)s; the AMC(U) 7–11 and 15–42 were converted LSI(L)s; the AMC(U) 12 and 13 were converted coastal survey ships (AGSC), which in turned had been converted from YMS motor minesweepers; the AMC(U) 14 was a converted AMC, originally built as a PCS; and the AMC(U) 44–50 were converted YMS minesweepers.

The designation AMC(U) was changed to coastal minehunter (MHC) on 7 February 1955.

Design: These are the first U.S. Navy ships to be constructed of Glass-Reinforced Plastic (GRP), a material long used in foreign mine countermeasures craft. They are the world's largest MCM ships to be constructed entirely of GRP.

The hull is a solid, continuous monocoque structure, with no longitudinal or transverse framing.

The ships are fitted with the SYQ-13 tactical navigation/command system. One MNS vehicle is carried.

At-sea endurance is 15 days.

Engineering: They are fitted with a 180-shp bow thruster.

Operational: The CARDINAL and RAVEN were transferred from Ingleside to the Persian Gulf in July–August 2000 on board the merchant ship BLUE MARLIN. The two MHCs are now homeported at Manama, Bahrain, along with two larger MCMs.

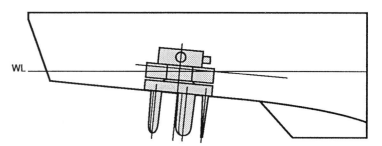

A diagram of the Voith Schneider propeller arrangement in the OSPREY-class ships. This arrangement provides a very high degree of maneuverability.

POST–WORLD WAR II MINESWEEPERS

A large number of minesweepers of various types have been built by the U.S. Navy since World War II, beginning with the massive ocean minesweeper (AM/MSO) and coastal minesweeper (AMS/MSC) series built in the early 1950s. During the 1960s a large number of smaller riverine sweep craft were developed for use in the Vietnam War (all of which have been discarded, as have all previous ships and craft).

The various types of post–World War II minesweepers are discussed in the 13th Edition (pages 236–237) and earlier editions of *Ships and Aircraft.*

CRAFT OF OPPORTUNITY PROGRAM

The Navy developed the Craft of Opportunity Program (COOP) in the 1980s to provide a mine countermeasures capability for U.S. ports, employing fishing craft and small patrol-type craft. The Navy initially sought to cancel the program in 1990, although Congress continued to fund it for the next few years. One unit survives: the CT-15 (ex-YP 662). Built in 1959, she is a former Naval Academy seamanship training craft. See 16th Edition/pages 204–205 for characteristics.

Classification: Note that CT (for COOP Trainer) was not an "official" designation; a hyphen is used in the designation. Several CT numbers were used twice.

The SHRIKE under way, showing the unusual hull form. Both the MCM and MHC designs feature advanced hull materials and low-magnetic-signature propulsion machinery to reduce their vulnerability to magnetic-influence mines. (U.S. Navy)

MINESWEEPING BOATS

The Navy's long-serving minesweeping boats (MSB) have all been discarded from the MCM role, the last in 1993. See 16th Edition/page 204 and, for characteristics, 14th Edition/pages 241–242.

UNMANNED CATAMARAN MINESWEEPERS

The two Swedish-built unmanned minesweepers acquired by the U.S. Navy in February 1991 have been discarded. For the past several years, they were located at Ingleside, Texas. Their upkeep was halted in 1997 as a cost-cutting measure and they were removed from the Navy's list of "floating equipment" in the fall of 1999.

See 16th Edition/page 207 for characteristics (photo on page 206).

MINE WARFARE SYSTEMS

MINE NEUTRALIZATION SYSTEM

One SLQ-48 Mine Neutralization System (MNS) vehicle is carried aboard ships of the AVENGER and OSPREY classes. Formerly called the Mine Neutralization Vehicle (MNV), the device is controlled and powered through a 3,500-foot (1,067-m) cable. A closed-circuit television and close-range sonar provide viewing of objects detected by shipboard sonar; the sonar range against mines is approximately 1,000 yards (915 m). The vehicle can then cut the cables of moored mines or plant a small explosive charge to detonate bottom mines; the two charges carried by the MNS each have 85 pounds (38.5 kg) of high explosives.

The Navy took delivery of 67 systems from Honeywell (subsequently Alliant Techsystems) between 1987 and 1995. The SLQ-48 was used extensively during Operation Desert Storm in 1991.

Weight:	2,750 lb (1,247 kg)
Length:	12½ feet (3.8 m)
Width:	3 feet (0.9 m)
Height:	3 feet (0.9 m)
Propulsion:	2 electric motors; 30 hp
Speed:	6 knots

An SLQ-48 mine neutralization vehicle is lowered into the sea. These vehicles are carried by both MCM and MHC mine countermeasures ships. (Alliant Techsystems)

SLQ-38 MECHANICAL CABLE-CUTTING SWEEPS

Mechanical or "Oropesa" wire sweeps of various types are fitted in the AVENGER class to counter moored buoyant (cable) mines. The SLQ-38 can be rigged from one or both sides of an MCM or can be used in conjunction with a second MCM.

Wire cable cutters cut the mooring cable and the mine is destroyed by gunfire when it bobs to the surface. During normal one-ship operations, the SLQ-38 can sweep a path 250 yards (228.6 m) wide; a two-MCM sweep can cover 500 yards (457 m).

SLQ-37 MAGNETIC/ACOUSTIC INFLUENCE SWEEP SYSTEM

Installed in the AVENGER class, the SLQ-37 consists of a Mk 5 "straight-tail" magnetic sweep combined with the earlier Mk 4(V) and/or Mk 6(B) acoustic sweeps. This system can be configured several ways to counter specific types of minefields.

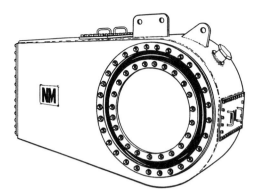

Mk 6 towed acoustic device (also designated TB [Towed Body] 26)

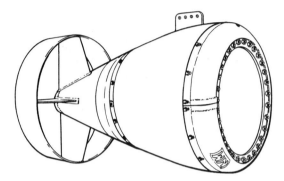

Mk 4 towed acoustic device (also designated TB 27)

AIRBORNE SYSTEMS

A variety of airborne MCM systems are available for use by MH-53E Sea Dragon helicopters. These are:

- *ALQ-141 acoustic system:* This airborne mine countermeasures system is an underwater towed body providing electronic countermeasures to counter new mine threats. The towed device and associated electronics have distinct surveillance and sweep-to-detonate modes.
- *A Mk 2(G) acoustic sweep:* The device—also known as "rattle bars"—consists of parallel pipes or bars, towed broadside-on, at speeds from four to ten knots. This produces a Bernoulli effect between the bars, causing them to bang together to produce medium- to high-frequency acoustic energy.

  The A Mk 2(G) was used by helicopters during Operation End Sweep in North Vietnam in 1973 and in Operation Desert Storm in the Persian Gulf in 1991.
- *AN 37U mechanical sweep:* This is a variable-depth towed mechanical sweep system capable of countering moored mines in both deep and shallow water.
- *AQS-14 sonar:* This is a helicopter-towed, active minehunting sonar developed for the earlier RH-53D Sea Stallion helicopter. It is a multibeam, side-looking sonar with electronic beamforming. The system consists of three parts: a stabilized underwater vehicle, an electro-mechanical tow cable, and a console in the helicopter. The underwater vehicle, almost 10 feet (3 m) long, can be maintained at a fixed depth above the sea floor or below the surface; the thin, coaxial cable is armored and nonmagnetic. The sonar information is presented on two continuous "waterfall" acoustic displays.

  The system became operational in 1984 and its first operational use came in August of that year during Operation Intense Look, the Red Sea/Gulf of Suez mine crisis.[7]
- *Mk 103 mechanical sweep:* This helicopter-towed system for sweeping bottom-moored mines consists of a tow wire, sweep wires (with explosive-actuated cutters), floats, a depressor, and float pendants (for visual location of the floats). This is similar to the conventional sweep gear long used by surface minehunters.

---

7. Beyond minehunting, the AQS-14 was used successfully from helicopters in January 1992 to locate cyanide containers on the ocean floor.

- *Mk 104 acoustic sweep:* This airborne system consists of a cavitating disk within a venturi tube, driven by two self-rotating disks. The Mk 104 is towed behind a helicopter or can be attacked to the Mk 105 sled to provide a combination acoustic/magnetic system.

Weight:	180 pounds (81.65 kg)
Length:	49 inches (1.2 m)
Width:	26 inches (660 mm)
Height:	35 inches (890 mm)

- *Mk 105 magnetic sweep:* The Mk 105 is a helicopter-towed hydrofoil sled. It is fitted with a gas turbine generator to power its magnetic sweep gear. The sled is typically towed at 20 to 25 knots, about 450 feet (137 m) behind the helicopter; the sled becomes foilborne at about 13 knots. Twin magnetic tails, consisting of open-electrode magnetic sweeps about 600 feet (183 m) long, are towed behind the sled. A combination of influence sweeps can be achieved by the addition of a Mk 104 or A Mk 2(G) acoustic system to the sweep array (see Mk 106).

  The vehicle is launched and recovered from a surface ship or shore base, hooked to a hovering helicopter. The helicopter can refuel the sled during a mission.

  Operational since 1970, the Mk 105 was used during Operation End Sweep in 1973, the Suez Canal sweeps of 1974–1975, and Operation Desert Storm in 1991. The systems are being upgraded for improved reliability and performance. The following are sled characteristics:

Weight:	original	5,907 lb (2,679 kg) dry
		748 lb (339 kg) fuel
	upgraded	7,259 lb (3,293 kg) dry
		1,741 lb (790 kg) fuel
Length:	27½ feet (8.38 m)	
Width:	11½ feet (3.5 m) at float	
	16½ feet (5.0 m) at top foil tip	

- *Mk 106 acoustic/magnetic sweep:* The Mk 106 is a helicopter-towed acoustic/magnetic sweep consisting of the Mk 105 sled with a Mk 104 attached to one of the magnetic tails. The Mk 106 combination was used extensively during the MCM operations in the Red Sea and Gulf of Suez.
- *Shallow Water Influence Minesweeping System (SWIMS):* This is a self-contained, high-speed, shallow-water magnetic influence sweeping device developed in the 1990s. It is 10 feet (3.05 m) long and 20 inches (508 mm) in diameter and can be transported and deployed by an MH-53E helicopter. The system emulates magnetic signatures of the platforms in transit through an assault area, as well as conducting generic minesweeping operations. Designed to operate in shallow water at speeds up to 40 knots, it can be towed as a single unit or in tandem.
- *SPU-1W Magnetic Orange Pipe (MOP):* The MOP is a magnetized pipe, filled with Styrofoam for buoyancy, designed to cause magnetically activated mines to detonate. A modern version of the World War II–era "iron rail" sweep, the MOP was

A Mk 105 sled in an HM-14 hangar. When on land or aboard ship, wheels can be fitted to the sleds. Note the electrical generator fitted atop the sled.

developed for use as an initial sweep mechanism for helicopters during Operation End Sweep in North Vietnamese waters. Magnetic mines, laid there by U.S. naval aircraft, were so sensitive that they would have been triggered by and destroyed the Mk 105 sleds towed by helicopters. The MOP also was used to sweep waters too shallow for the Mk 105 sled.

A single helicopter can tow up to three MOPs in tandem to enhance sweep effectiveness.

Weight: 1,000 pounds (453.6 kg)
Length: 30 feet (9.15 m)
Diameter: 10¾ inches (273 mm)

MARINE MAMMAL SYSTEMS

The U.S. Navy has developed a fully operational minehunting capability known as the Marine Mammal Systems (MMS) that employs trained bottlenose dolphins and sea lions when hardware is inadequate or personnel safety is an issue. Dolphins are used because of their exceptional biological sonar that is unmatched by hardware sonars in detecting objects in the water column and on the ocean floor. Sea lions are used because of their highly sensitive underwater directional hearing and low-light-level vision. Both of these marine mammals are trainable for tasks and are capable of repetitive diving.

The mammals are assigned to the Navy's Explosive Ordnance Disposal (EOD) mobile units. Each "system" has four to eight mam-

Swimmers from Helicopter MCM Squadron (HM) 14 prepare a Mk 105 hydrofoil sled for use during operations in the Persian Gulf. The hydrofoils at the ends of the sled fold down when the craft is being towed by a helicopter. (1991, U.S. Navy)

A sea lion attaches a pendant to a practice bottom mine during a marine mammal training exercise. The pendant, attached to a float, marks the mine's location for subsequent examination and disposal by other means. (U.S. Navy)

mals, an officer-in-charge, and several enlisted personnel. The mammal units can be transported by aircraft, helicopter, and land vehicles and can be maintained on board an amphibious ship. For example, in the multinational RIMPAC 94 exercise, dolphins and their supporting personnel and equipment were based on the amphibious ship JUNEAU (LPD 10). The mammals—two Mk 4 dolphins and four Mk 7 dolphins—lived in specially designed saltwater pools kept in the ship's docking well. Operating one at a time, the dolphins then swam to the operating area, accompanied by their handlers riding in small boats.

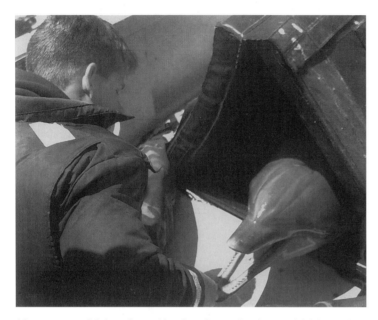

After a successful day of searching for mines, a bottlenose dolphin receives a treat from one of his handlers. Although these mammals regularly operate in the open sea, they invariably return to the "good life" of Navy food and accommodations. (1995, U.S. Navy, PH1 Stephen Batiz)

The MMS mammals have also been used for waterfront security, including at the 1996 Republican Convention in San Diego, Calif. The current systems are:

- *Mk 4:* a dolphin searching system that detects and marks the location of moored mines. It is assigned to EOD Mobile Unit 3 at Coronado, Calif.
- *Mk 5:* a sea lion exercise-mine recovery unit that operates training mines fitted with acoustic pingers. The sea lions can locate these mines in depths to 1,000 feet (305 m) and attach a recovery device. The unit is assigned to EOD Mobile Unit 3 and EOD Mobile Unit 6 at Charleston, S.C.
- *Mk 6:* a dolphin and swimmer detection system that can detect and mark the location of an intruder. The system was used in Vietnam in 1970–1971 and in the Persian Gulf in 1987–1988. It is assigned to EOD Mobile Unit 3.
- *Mk 7:* a dolphin mine search system that can detect and mark the location of mines on the ocean floor. The system is configured specifically to support amphibious operations. The system is attached to EOD Mobile Unit 3.

REMOTE MINEHUNTING SYSTEM

The Navy's WLD-1(V)1 remote minehunting system is an unmanned undersea vehicle configured to hunt mines. It is intended to be carried in surface ships and, at some future date, also could be deployed from helicopters or fixed-wing aircraft. The WLD-1(V)1—based on the Remote Minehunting Operational Prototype (RMOP)—is planned to alleviate the need for specialized mine countermeasures ships to accompany task forces operating in littoral waters where there is a high threat of encountering hostile mines.

As shown in the accompanying diagram and photo, the device has a torpedo-like body with a fixed "sail" that contains a navigation light, antenna for its controls/sensors, and snorkel for its diesel engine. The RMOP had a Reason SeaBat 6012 forward-looking sonar for mine detection in its "keel," and towed an AQS-14 helicopter

Holding pens for marine mammals are erected in the docking well of the amphibious ship JUNEAU (LPD 10). Here, members of Explosive Ordnance Disposal (EOD) Unit 3 feed a bottlenose dolphin amid a clutter of RIBs, tanks, and other gear. (1998, U.S. Navy, PH1 "Spike" Call)

minehunting sonar. The destroyers JOHN YOUNG (DD 973) and CUSH-ING (DD 985) carried out trials with prototype vehicles.

The system employs Global Positioning System (GPS) navigation and, after launching from a mother ship, conducts its mission in a semi-autonomous manner, running preprogrammed tracks. Sonar and mission data are displayed to the operator aboard the mother ship in real time. Aboard ship, the sonar operator identifies and classifies contacts that are detected by the vehicle's sonar.

The vehicle can operate for 24 hours at a speed of five knots before it requires refueling and servicing aboard its mother ship. (Of course, helicopter recovery should be possible.) Upon completion of a mission, the vehicle winches the AQS-14 sonar body into a stowed position. The vehicle can be refueled, checked, and begin another mission in less than an hour.

Development of the system began in September 1993. Earlier versions were designated RMOP and RMS, for Remote Minehunting System. It is planned for installation in the later destroyers of the ARLEIGH BURKE (DDG 51) class, beginning with the DDG 91.

The RMOP vehicle for the WLD-1(V)1 unmanned minehunting system. The device is planned for use aboard surface combatants, initially the later destroyers of the ARLEIGH BURKE (DDG 51) class. (2000, Lockheed Martin)

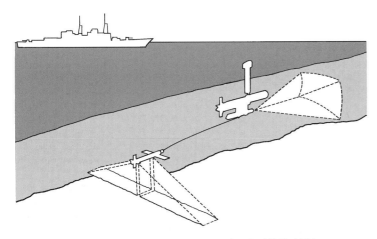

A diagram showing the operational concept for the WLD-1(V)1 unmanned minehunting system. The device is shown here being controlled by a destroyer several miles away.

The mine countermeasures ship SENTRY *(foreground)* and KINGFISHER under way in the Gulf of Mexico. At the time, they were en route from their homeport of Ingleside, Texas, to the Great Lakes and a series of fleet exercises in the Atlantic. (2000, U.S. Navy, PH1 Charlo Whorton)

CHAPTER 22

Auxiliary Ships

The fast combat support ship DETROIT replenishes the carrier ENTERPRISE (CVN 65) and, at right, the frigate NICHOLAS (FFG 47) during operations in the Mediterranean Sea. Navy-manned and civilian-manned auxiliary ships under the aegis of the Military Sealift Command enable the Navy's surface forces to operate at long distances with minimal reliance on overseas bases. (1999, U.S. Navy, PHAN Karl L. Peters)

Auxiliary ships provide support to the "fighting fleet." There are a large number of different types of specialized auxiliary ships in U.S. naval service. Most Navy auxiliary ships are operated as the Naval Fleet Auxiliary Force of the Military Sealift Command (MSC) with civilian crews; Navy communications personnel and other specialists are assigned to some MSC ships. Only 14 auxiliary ships listed in this chapter are manned by active-duty Navy crews: eight replenishment ships (AOE), four salvage ships (ARS), and two submarine tenders (AS).

Sealift ships—although nominally considered to be auxiliary ships—are described in chapter 23 of this edition of *Ships and Aircraft*.

Like other components of the Navy, the roster of auxiliary ships has been slashed in the post–Cold War reductions. In particular the tender force has been all but eliminated; only two submarine tenders remain in active service, compared to nine destroyer tenders and 11 submarine tenders in commission in 1990.

Only one auxiliary ship is under construction in 2001, a surveying ship (T-AGS). A new class of underway replenishment ships (T-ADC) is being developed to replace existing Underway Replenishment (UNREP) ships.

Almost all of the large numbers of auxiliary ships built in the 1940s and 1950s have been discarded from active naval service.

Classification: Auxiliary ships are listed in this chapter in alphabetical order according to classification. The U.S. Navy arranges auxiliary ships according to function, with the categories being:

(1) Combat Logistic Type Ships: Ships that have the capability to provide underway replenishment to fleet units[1]
    (a) Underway Replenishment: AE, AFS, AO, AOE

---

1. These are considered warship/combatant ships.

TABLE 22-1. AUXILIARY SHIPS (EARLY 2001)

Type		Active				Reserve	Building[a]
		Total	Navy	MSC	Academic		
AD	Destroyer tenders	—	—	—	—	2	—
AKE	Underway replenishment ships	—	—	—	—	—	(see text)
AE	Ammunition ships	7	—	7	—	—	—
AFS	Combat store ships	6	—	6	—	—	—
AG	Miscellaneous auxiliaries	2	—	2	1[b]	—	—
AGM	Missile range instrumentation ships	2	—	2	—	—	—
AGOR	Oceanographic research ships	12	—	6	6	—	—
AGOS	Ocean surveillance ships	12	—	12	—	—	1
AGS	Surveying ships	10	—	10	—	—	—
AH	Hospital ships	—	—	—	—	2	—
AO	Oilers	16	—	14[b]	—	2	—
AOE	Fast combat support ships	8	8	—	—	—	—
ARC	Cable ships	1	—	1	—	—	—
ARS	Salvage ships	4	4	—	—	—	—
AS	Submarine tenders	4	2	—	—	2	—
ATF	Fleet tugs	7	—	5	2[c]	—	—
AVB	Aviation logistic ships	—	—	—	—	2	—

[a]Ships authorized through fiscal 2001.
[b]One ship assigned as prepositioning ship.
[c]Ships on commercial loan.

(2) Mobile Logistic Type Ships: Ships that have the capability to provide underway replenishment to fleet units and/or provide direct material support to other deployed units operating far from home base
  (a) Material Support: AS
(3) Support Type Ships: Ships designed to operate in the open ocean in a variety of sea states to provide general support to either combatant forces or shore based establishments (includes smaller auxiliaries which, by the nature of their duties, rarely leave inshore waters)
  (a) Fleet Support: ARS, ATF
  (b) Other Auxiliaries: ACS, AG, AGF, AGM, AGOR, AGOS, AGSS, AH, AK, AKB, AKR, AOG, AOT, AP, ARC, AVB

Although overly simplistic, this scheme does attempt to indicate the types of support the various auxiliaries provide to the fleet. This Navy scheme was initiated in 1978.

Several ships officially classified as auxiliaries are listed elsewhere in this volume and are not included in table 22-1: AGFs (miscellaneous command ships) are described in chapter 17 and AGSSs (auxiliary submarines) in chapter 12.

Guns: Large Navy-manned auxiliaries have a minimal armament of 20-mm Gatling guns for close-in self-defense. No active auxiliary ships retain the 5-inch guns that populated such ships from the late 1930s onward, nor the 3-inch guns that were common in auxiliary ships from the early 1940s.

None of the ships operated by the Military Sealift Command are armed.

Missiles: The AOE replenishment ships are the only U.S. Navy auxiliary ships that are armed with guided missiles.

Names: The historic naming scheme for auxiliary ships, like those for combatants, has undergone a considerable degree of corruption during the past few years, mainly for political purposes (see comments under various auxiliary ship headings).

Operational: Auxiliary ships are operated by the active Navy and MSC, the latter with civil service or contractor civilian crews. Aux-

iliary ships are no longer assigned to the Naval Reserve Force (NRF), which previously manned several salvage ships (ARS) with composite active-reserve crews.

Several Navy ships are on loan to academic institutions that are conducting naval research projects.

The Maritime Administration holds title to all state maritime academy training ships, most of which are former U.S. Navy ships.

MSC ships have the prefix "USNS" for U.S. Naval Ship and the prefix "T-" is appended to their hull numbers.

Status: Navy ships are decommissioned; MSC (civilian-manned) ships taken out of service are placed "Out of Service, In Reserve" (OSIR).

AUXILIARY CRANE SHIPS

The auxiliary crane ships (ACS) are listed with sealift ships; see chapter 23. The Navy's one previous ship in this general category was the ex-battleship KEARSARGE (BB 5, redesignated IX 16 and then AB 1). Completed in 1900, the KEARSARGE was converted in 1920, being fitted with a 250-ton-capacity crane and hull blisters to provide more stability; she was non-self-propelled. In 1941 she was renamed CRANE SHIP NO. 1 when the name KEARSARGE was assigned to the carrier CV 12 (subsequently renamed HORNET) and then to the CV 33. The crane ship was stricken in 1955 and sold for scrap.

DESTROYER TENDERS

Destroyer tenders have served the U.S. Navy from 1898 (DIXIE/AD 1) until 1996, when the last active ship was decommissioned. These ships provided all manner of support to destroyers and other surface ships.

Names: Destroyer tenders were named for geographic areas, except for the SAMUEL GOMPERS, which honored a labor leader.

2 DESTROYER TENDERS: "SAMUEL GOMPERS" CLASS

Number	Name	FY	Launched	Commissioned	Status
AD 37	SAMUEL GOMPERS	64	14 May 1966	1 July 1967	decomm. 27 Oct 1995; str. 7 Apr 1999
AD 38	PUGET SOUND	65	16 Sep 1966	27 Apr 1968	AR; decomm. 27 Jan 1996
AD 41	YELLOWSTONE	75	27 Jan 1979	28 June 1980	decomm. 31 Jan 1996; str. 7 Apr 1999
AD 42	ACADIA	76	28 July 1979	6 June 1981	PR; decomm. 16 Dec 1994
AD 43	CAPE COD	77	2 Aug 1980	17 Apr 1982	decomm. 29 Sep 1995; str. 7 Apr 1999
AD 44	SHENANDOAH	79	6 Feb 1982	15 Aug 1983	decomm. 13 Sep 1996; str. 7 Apr 1999

Builders:	AD 38	Puget Sound Naval Shipyard, Wash.	Boilers:	2 600-psi (41.7-kg/cm^2) (Combustion Engineering)
	AD 42	National Steel & Shipbuilding, San Diego, Calif.	Speed:	20 knots (18 knots sustained)
Displacement:	AD 38	13,600 tons light	Range:	
	AD 42	13,318 tons light	Manning:	AD 38 625 (42 officers + 583 enlisted)
	AD 38	20,500 tons full load		AD 42 631 (47 officers + 584 enlisted)
	AD 42	20,224 tons full load	Helicopters:	landing area (see *Design* notes)
Length:		620 feet (189.02 m) waterline	Guns:	2 40-mm grenade launchers Mk 19 (2 single)
		643⅝ feet (196.3 m) overall		4 20-mm cannon Mk 67 (2 single) in AD 38;
Beam:		85 feet (25.9 m)		2 guns in AD 42
Draft:		22½ feet (6.9 m)	Radars:	LN-66 navigation
Propulsion:		2 steam turbines (De Laval); 20,000 shp; 1 shaft		SPS-10 surface search

These were the Navy's only destroyer tenders designed and built after World War II. They were configured to support modern surface combatants, including ships with nuclear and gas turbine propulsion. They are similar to the L. Y. SPEAR–class submarine tenders.

Two ships are being maintained in reserve, one on each coast.

Class: The AD 39 was authorized in the fiscal 1969 shipbuilding program but was canceled prior to the start of construction because of cost overruns in other new ship programs. The AD 40 was authorized in fiscal 1973 but was not built. An AD 45 was planned for the fiscal 1980 program but was not funded. Two additional tenders planned for fiscal 1987 and 1988 were deleted from the five-year program of January 1984.

The AD 41 and later ships are officially considered the YELLOWSTONE class; they are similar and hence are combined in this entry.

Design: The SAMUEL GOMPERS was SCB No. 244; subsequent ships were No. 700 in the new SCB series.

A landing platform and hangar for DASH helicopters were provided in the AD 37 and 38.[2] The later ships had helicopter decks only.

The ships have two 30-ton-capacity cranes and two 6½-ton cranes.

Guns: As built, the AD 37 and 38 had a single 5-inch/38-cal DP gun forward with a Mk 56 GFCS; this armament was removed. Plans to install NATO Sea Sparrow missile launchers in these ships were dropped.

Operational: The PUGET SOUND served as flagship of the U.S. Sixth Fleet from May 1980 to August 1985, when relieved by the command ship CORONADO (AGF 11). When serving as the Sixth Fleet flagship, the PUGET SOUND was homeported at Gaeta, Italy. As fleet flagship, the PUGET SOUND carried some 225 flag personnel.

---

2. DASH = Drone Anti-Submarine Helicopter.

The PUGET SOUND is one of two destroyer tenders retained in reserve. With the ACADIA, she is the last of a once numerous auxiliary ship type in the U.S. Navy. Her massive hull holds repair ships, and provisions, parts, and munitions stowage, as well as accommodations for a crew of skilled machinists and artisans. (1991, Giorgio Arra)

The PUGET SOUND—like other tender-type ships—has large cranes for handling parts, provisions, and weapons for her brood. Large side ports open to provide direct access to ships moored alongside. (1991, Giorgio Arra)

TABLE 22-2. DESTROYER TENDERS

Number	Name	Comm.	Notes
Dixie class (5)			
AD 14	DIXIE	1940	stricken 1982
AD 15	PRAIRIE	1940	decomm./str. 26 Mar 1993
C3-S1-N2 type (1)			
AD 16	CASCADE	1943	stricken 1974
Dixie class (continued)			
AD 17	PIEDMONT	1944	str. 1982; to Turkey 1982
AD 18	SIERRA	1944	decomm./str. 29 Oct 1993
AD 19	YOSEMITE	1944	decomm./str. 27 Jan 1994
C3 cargo type (2)			
AD 20	HAMUL (ex-AK 20)		stricken 1963
AD 21	MARKAB (ex-AK 31)		to AR 23
AD 22–25	KLONDIKE class		modified C3 design
AD 26–31	SHENANDOAH class		modified C3 design
AD 32	NEW ENGLAND (ex-AS 28)		canceled 1945
AD 33	SHENANDOAH class		canceled 1945
AD 34	ALCOR (ex-AR 10, AG 34)		stricken 1946
AD 35, 36	SHENANDOAH class		(AD 35 canceled 1945)
AD 37–44	SAMUEL GOMPERS class		

World War II destroyer tenders reached hull number AD 36, with the AD 32, 33, and 35 being canceled at the end of World War II. The AD 32 was to have been a one-of-a-kind tender. Several of the war-built ships served into the 1990s, hence they are listed above. During their very long careers, these ships were modernized to support surface warships fitted with ASROC, DASH, improved electronics, nuclear propulsion, and so forth.

Three destroyer tenders were reclassified as repair ships: KLON-DIKE (AD 22) to AR 22 in 1960, MARKAB (AD 21) to AR 23 in 1959, and GRAND CANYON (AD 28) to AR 28 in 1971.

REPLENISHMENT/CARGO SHIPS

(12) UNDERWAY REPLENISHMENT SHIPS: NEW CONSTRUCTION

Number	Name	FY	Launched	Commissioned	Status
T-AKE 1	LEWIS AND CLARK	00			building
T-AKE 2	SACAGAWEA	01			building
T-AKE	(2 ships)	02			planned
T-AKE	(2 ships)	03			planned
T-AKE	(3 ships)	04			planned
T-AKE	(3 ships)	05			planned

Builders:
Displacement: 35,400 tons full load
Length: 689 feet (210 m) overall
Beam: 106 feet (32.31 m)
Draft: 29½ feet (9.0 m)
Propulsion:
Speed: 20 knots
Range: 14,000 n.miles (16,130 km) at 20 knots
Manning: (civilian)
Helicopters: 2 VERTREP helicopters
Guns: none
Radars:

This is a planned class of 12 underway replenishment ships. They are intended to operate independently to replenish naval ships with dry cargo, provisions, munitions, and spare parts. In this role they would eventually replace T-AE ammunition ships and T-AFS combat stores ships. A T-AKE and an oiler of the HENRY J. KAISER class operating together could provide a carrier battle group with the replenishment capability of an AOE fast combat support ship.

The contract award for the program to a single shipyard was expected to be made early in 2001.

Classification: During planning these ships were designated T-ADC(X) for replenishment/dry cargo ship. Changed to T-AKE in the fall of 2000 although that designation was not yet added to the official classification list.

Cost: The lead ship in FY 2000 is listed with a construction cost of $440 million, plus $13.1 million for research and development costs. The 12-ship class is expected to cost a total of $12 *billion.*

Design: These ships are designed to carry 5,900 tons of dry cargo and 2,350 tons of fuel (18,000 barrels—10,500 barrels of ship fuel and 7,500 barrels of JP-5 aviation fuel).

Names: The Secretary of the Navy announced on 27 October 2000 that these ships would be named for "legendary explorers." The name Lewis and Clark previously was assigned to the strategic missile submarine SSBN 644.

The second ship honors the Shoshone woman living in North Dakota who served as guide and interpreter for Meriwether Lewis and William Clark during their 1804–1806 expedition into the northwest region of the United States.

AMMUNITION SHIPS

These ships carry a vast variety of munitions for surface combatants and aircraft carriers. They are capable of underway replenishment of warships.

Names: Ammunition ships carry the names of explosives and volcanoes.

AMMUNITION SHIPS: MODIFIED "KILAUEA" CLASS

The planned ammunition ships of the modified KILAUEA class (AE 36–40) were deferred in favor of the construction of additional AOE-type replenishment ships. With the lead ship initially planned for the fiscal 1986 shipbuilding program, the ships were continually delayed until, when the program was halted, one ship was planned for fiscal 1991, one for fiscal 1992, two for fiscal 1993, and one for fiscal 1994.

These ships were to have been slightly larger than the KILAUEA class, with gas turbine propulsion (two LM 2500s); see 14th Edition/pages 250–251 for characteristics.

7 AMMUNITION SHIPS: "KILAUEA" CLASS

Number	Name	FY	Launched	Commissioned	To MSC	Status
T-AE 26	KILAUEA	65	9 Aug 1967	10 Aug 1968	1 Oct 1980	**MSC-P**
T-AE 27	BUTTE	65	9 Aug 1967	29 Nov 1968	3 June 1996	**MSC-A**
T-AE 28	SANTA BARBARA	66	23 Jan 1968	11 July 1970	30 Sep 1998	**MSC-A**
AE 29	MOUNT HOOD	66	17 July 1968	1 May 1971	—	decomm./str. 13 Aug 1999
T-AE 32	FLINT	67	9 Nov 1970	20 Nov 1971	4 Aug 1995	**MSC-P**
T-AE 33	SHASTA	67	3 Apr 1971	26 Feb 1972	1 Oct 1997	**MSC-P**
T-AE 34	MOUNT BAKER	68	23 Oct 1971	22 July 1972	18 Dec 1996	**MSC-A**
T-AE 35	KISKA	68	11 Mar 1972	16 Dec 1972	1 Aug 1996	**MSC-P**

Builders:	AE 26, 27	General Dynamics, Quincy, Mass.	
	AE 28, 29	Bethlehem Steel, Sparrows Point, Md.	
	AE 32–35	Ingalls Shipbuilding, Pascagoula, Miss.	
Displacement:	9,238 tons light		
	19,937 tons full load		
Length:	563⅚ feet (171.9 m) overall		
Beam:	81 feet (24.7 m)		
Draft:	27¹¹⁄₁₂ feet (8.5 m)		
Propulsion:	3 steam turbines (General Electric); 22,000 shp; 1 shaft		
Boilers:	3 600-psi (41.7-kg/cm²) (Foster Wheeler)		

Speed:	22 knots (20 knots sustained)
Range:	18,000 n.miles (33,336 km) at 11 knots
	10,000 n.miles (18,520 km) at 20 knots
Manning:	125 civilian + 23 or 24 Navy (1 officer + 22 or 23 enlisted)
Helicopters:	2 UH-46 Sea Knight
Guns:	removed
Radars:	SPS-10F surface search
	SPS-64(V)9 navigation
EW systems:	removed

These are high-capability underway replenishment ships, fitted with the FAST system for the rapid transfer of missiles and other munitions.

Seven of these were being taken out of Navy commission and transferred to the Military Sealift Command for operation by civilian crews with Navy communications and helicopter detachments. The MOUNT HOOD was decommissioned and stricken without transfer to MSC (as had been planned for 1998); she is being scrapped.

Design: SCB No. 703. The KILAUEA design provides for the ship's main cargo spaces forward of the superstructure with a helicopter landing area aft. A hangar approximately 50 feet (15.2 m) long, 15½ to 17½ feet (4.7 to 5.3 m) wide, and 16⅔ to 17¾ feet (5.1 to 5.4 m) high is built into the superstructure. Cargo capacity is approximately 6,500 tons.

Guns: As built, the ships had eight 3-inch/76-cal Mk 33 guns in twin mounts with two Mk 56 GFCS. Their armament was reduced during the late 1970s; the Navy-manned ships lost their last two 3-inch gun mounts in the late 1980s when two Phalanx CIWS were installed.

Upon transfer to MSC, the ships were totally disarmed and their SLQ-25 Nixie and SLQ-32(V)1 electronic systems were removed.

The lead ship of the KILAUEA class barely under way. All seven active ammunition ships are operated by MSC civilian crews. A UH-46 Sea Knight helicopter for Vertical Replenishment (VERTREP) sits on the KILAUEA's helicopter deck. (1995, Giorgio Arra)

The KILAUEA at rest. She has kingposts forward for underway replenishment; there are cargo booms aft. (1997, Leo Van Ginderen)

The SHASTA in port (with a KNOX/FF 1052–class frigate behind her). The SHASTA's two helicopter hangars are open. As Navy ships, such fleet auxiliaries were almost always armed; MSC ships are not fitted with guns or missiles. (1998, Leo Van Ginderen)

TABLE 22-3. POST–WORLD WAR II AMMUNITION SHIPS

Number	Name	Comm.	Notes
AE 20	FOMALHAUT (ex-AK 22)	1942	stricken 1962
SURIBACHI class (5)			
AE 21	SURIBACHI	1956	decomm. 2 Dec 1994; str. 12 Dec 1996
AE 22	MAUNA KEA	1957	decomm. 30 June 1995; str. 12 Dec 1996
AE 23	NITRO	1959	decomm. 28 Apr 1995; str. 14 Aug 1995
AE 24	PYRO	1959	decomm. 31 May 1994; str. 8 Apr 1997
AE 25	HALEAKALA	1959	decomm./str. 10 Dec 1993
AE 26–29	KILAUEA class		
AE 30	VIRGO (ex-AKA 20)	1943	stricken 1971
AE 31	CHARA (ex-AKA 58)	1944	stricken 1972
AE 32–35	KILAUEA class		

The AE program of World War II reached AE 19. The AE 20 was a C1-A (diesel) cargo ship (ex-AK 22), which was changed to attack cargo ship AKA 5 in 1943, reverted to AK 22 in 1944, and changed to AE in 1948. Similarly, the later AE 30 and 31 were former attack cargo ships; their heavy booms for lifting vehicles and landing craft facilitated their use as ammo ships. They both were stricken as AKAs in 1960–1961, reinstated on the Naval Vessel Register (NVR) in 1965, and recommissioned as AEs in 1966.

The SURIBACHI class (AE 21–25) was designed specifically for underway replenishment of munitions; the three later ships also were referred to as the NITRO class (the AE 21 and 22 were SCB No. 114; AEs 23–25 were SCB 114A). The MAUNA KEA was transferred to the Naval Reserve Force in 1979 and the PYRO in 1980; however, the heavy operating tempo in the Indian Ocean–Persian Gulf areas led to their being returned to the active fleet in 1982.

STORE SHIPS

These ships carried refrigerated stores and general cargo for the underway replenishment of ships at sea; they were generally referred to as "reefers." Their role in the fleet was taken over by the more versatile AFS/AOE/AOR types.

World War II–era store ships reached AF 47. All postwar ships were based on merchant designs. Most were of the R-series, indicating refrigerated holds; for example, the R2 was the reefer variant of the C2 design. By 1990 all had been stricken except one ship of the R3-S-4a type.

STORE SHIPS: "RIGEL" CLASS

Number	Name	Comm.	To MSC	Status
T-AF 58	Rigel	1955	23 June 1975	decomm. 9 Sep 1992; str. 16 May 1994
AF 59	Vega	1955	—	stricken 1977

The Rigel was the last store ship in naval service; she and her sister ship Vega were the Navy's largest reefers. They were the Navy's only designed-for-the-purpose store ships, being built to a modified R3-S-4a merchant design; they were similar to the AE 21 design.

COMBAT STORES SHIPS

These ships combined the capabilities of early store ships (AF), stores-issue ships (AKS), and aviation store ships (AVS), carrying refrigerated and dry stores as well as parts and other cargo for underway replenishment of ships at sea. They do not carry bulk petroleum products as do the AOE/AOR replenishment ships.

Names: British-built combat stores ships are named for celestial bodies; U.S.-built ships have city names, except that the Mars honors the Roman god of war.

3 COMBAT STORES SHIPS: EX-BRITISH STORES SUPPORT SHIPS

Number	Name	Launched	Completed	U.S. In Service	Status
T-AFS 8	Sirius	7 Apr 1966	22 Dec 1966	17 Jan 1981	**MSC-A**
T-AFS 9	Spica	22 Feb 1967	21 Mar 1967	4 Nov 1981	**MSC-P**
T-AFS 10	Saturn	16 Sep 1966	10 Aug 1967	30 Sep 1984	**MSC-A**

Builders:	Swan Hunter & Wighman Richardson, Wallsend-on-Tyne (England)	Propulsion:	1 turbocharged diesel engine (Wallsend-Sulzer 8RD76); 12,700 bhp; 1 shaft
Displacement:	9,010 tons light	Speed:	19 knots
	16,792 tons full load	Range:	27,500 n.miles (50,930 km) at 12 knots
Length:	489⅝ feet (149.35 m) waterline		11,000 n.miles (20,372 km) at 19 knots
	523¼ feet (159.5 m) overall	Manning:	107 civilian + 49 Navy (5 officers + 44 enlisted)
Beam:	72 feet (22.0 m)	Helicopters:	2 UH-46 Sea Knight or SA 330J Puma
Draft:	25½ feet (7.8 m)	Radars:	2 . . . navigation

These ships are former Royal Navy replenishment ships, acquired by the U.S. Navy because of the increased logistics demands of maintaining two carrier battle groups in the Persian Gulf–Indian Ocean area following the crises and conflicts in that region that began with the Iranian revolution of 1979. The ships previously were operated as Royal Fleet Auxiliary (RFA) ships with civilian crews.

With the purchase of the third British ship, the Navy dropped plans to construct an additional AFS of the Mars class under the FY 1987 shipbuilding program.

Class: This was a three-ship class, their British names being Lyness, Tarbatness, and Stromness, respectively. The Lyness was originally acquired by the U.S. government on a bare-boat charter for one year on 17 January 1981, at which time she was placed in U.S. service (renamed Sirius); she was acquired by the Navy on 1 March 1982.

The Tarbatness was acquired on time charter on 30 September 1981, changed to bare-boat charter on 4 November 1981 and at that time placed in U.S. service (renamed Spica). She was acquired by the Navy on 30 September 1982.

The Stromness was acquired on 1 October 1983 (renamed Saturn).

The Sirius and Spica were purchased under the fiscal 1982 program at a total cost of $37 million. The Saturn was purchased in fiscal 1984 for $13 million (plus $3.1 million in spare parts for the entire class).

Helicopters: The Saturn conducted flight tests with the SA 330J Puma as a Vertical Replenishment (VERTREP) helicopter off the Virginia coast on 20–21 December 1999. The Puma will be employed aboard these ships in the VERTREP role because of the shortfall in Navy UH-46 Sea Knight helicopters. The Pumas are operated by a commercial helicopter services firm.

Modernization: In U.S. service, the ships have been modernized with the provision of improved communication and UNREP facilities, plus automated data processing. All have been fitted with twin helicopter hangars.

The British-built Spica, one of three sister ships in U.S. service. A Navy UH-46 Sea Knight is on the helicopter deck. A shortage of those "birds" has led MSC to contract for civilian-operated Pumas to operate from these ships. There are replenishment rigs forward and amidships. (1997, Leo Van Ginderen)

After aspect of the SATURN, showing the ship's twin helicopter hangars. The funnel—like those on all MSC ships—has *(from top)* black, gray, blue, and gold stripes. These ships were never U.S. Navy manned, and hence were never armed in U.S. service. (1999, Leo Van Ginderen)

Another view of the SPICA at anchor. Refueling hoses are visible hanging on the forward kingpost. AFS-type ships carry small quantities of fuel and bulk lubricants. (1997, Leo Van Ginderen)

5 COMBAT STORES SHIPS: "MARS" CLASS

Number	Name	FY	Launched	Commissioned	To MSC	Status
T-AFS 1	Mars	61	15 June 1963	21 Dec 1963	1 Feb 1993	PR; OSIR 18 Feb 1998
AFS 2	Sylvania	62	15 Aug 1963	11 July 1964	—	decomm. 26 May 1994; str. 5 Jan 1995
T-AFS 3	Niagara Falls	64	26 Mar 1966	29 Apr 1967	23 Sep 1994	**MSC-A**
AFS 4	White Plains	65	23 July 1966	23 Nov 1968	—	decomm. 17 Apr 1995; str. 24 Aug 1995
T-AFS 5	Concord	65	17 Dec 1966	27 Nov 1968	15 Oct 1992	**MSC-P**
T-AFS 6	San Diego	66	13 Apr 1968	24 May 1969	11 Aug 1993	AR; OSIR 10 Dec 1997
T-AFS 7	San Jose	67	12 Dec 1969	23 Oct 1970	2 Nov 1993	**MSC-A**

Builders:	National Steel & Shipbuilding, San Diego, Calif.	Boilers:	3 600-psi (41.7-kg/cm^2) (Babcock & Wilcox)
Displacement:	9,200–9,400 tons light	Speed:	21 knots
	16,070 tons full load	Range:	18,000 n.miles (33,336 km) at 11 knots
Length:	529⅝ feet (161.5 m) waterline		10,000 n.miles (18,520 km) at 20 knots
	580⅝ feet (177.1 m) overall	Manning:	125 civilian + 49 Navy (5 officers + 44 enlisted)
Beam:	79 feet (24.1 m)	Helicopters:	2 UH-46 Sea Knight
Draft:	24 feet (7.3 m)	Guns:	removed
Propulsion:	2 steam turbines (De Laval, except Westinghouse in AFS 6);	Radars:	LN-66 navigation
	22,000 shp; 1 shaft		SPS-10 surface search

These are large, built-for-the-purpose underway replenishment ships combining the capabilities of store ships (AF) and stores-issue ships (AKS). All ships of this class were originally in active Navy service; six were transferred to MSC operation with civilian crews (the Sylvania and White Plains were decommissioned while in Navy commission). During modification for MSC operation, their cargo handling capabilities were enhanced (e.g., with additional cargo elevators).

Class: Three additional ships of this class were originally planned in the fiscal 1977–1978 shipbuilding programs; they were not requested by the administration in those years.

Design: The AFS 1–3 were SCB No. 208; the later ships were No. 705 in the later SCB series. These ships have five cargo holds (one refrigerated) with a 7,000-ton cargo capacity. A large helicopter deck is fitted with a hangar 46¾ to 51 feet in length and 16 to 23 feet wide.

Electronics: When Navy manned, these ships had the SLQ-32(V)1 ECM system and SLQ-25 Nixie towed acoustic torpedo decoy.

Engineering: Two boilers are normally used for full-power steaming, with the third shut down for maintenance.

Guns: These ships were completed with four 3-inch twin gun mounts, one pair of mounts forward and a second pair aft of the funnel. Two mounts were deleted from all ships except the White Plains during the late 1970s; all ships lost their Mk 56 GFCS as well as their SPS-40 air-search radar.

The White Plains carried eight 3-inch guns into the mid-1980s when she beached two twin mounts in favor of two Phalanx CIWS. The other ships were to be similarly rearmed. All guns were removed for MSC service (i.e., from all ships except Sylvania).

The Concord was the first of five of the seven Mars-class replenishment ships to be civilian-manned under the aegis of the Military Sealift Command. In MSC service these ships have been able to carry out forward replenishments of naval ships without difficulty. The new T-AKE design will replace these ships. (U.S. Navy)

The NIAGARA FALLS, one of three MARS-class combat stores ships retained in naval service. The ubiquitous UH-46 Sea Knight is on her helicopter deck. The ship has three replenishment kingposts forward, two amidships. (1997, Leo Van Ginderen)

The NIAGARA FALLS with one of her two helicopter hangars open and a UH-46 on the helicopter deck. Virtually all spare parts, munitions, and provisions can be transferred by helicopter during VERTREP operations. (1997, Giorgio Arra)

The NIAGARA FALLS under way. Note the massive deckhouse structures of these ships, mostly for accommodations. The hull is filled with machinery and store holds. (1997, Giorgio Arra)

MISCELLANEOUS AUXILIARIES

Only one ship is in naval service under the designation of miscellaneous auxiliary. A second ship—the infamous deep-ocean salvage ship GLO-MAR EXPLORER—remains on the Naval Vessel Register in a loan status, being used by a commercial firm as a deep-sea drilling platform.

1 SOUND TRIALS SHIP: "HAYES"

Number	Name	FY	Launched	Commissioned	Status
T-AG 195 (ex-T-AGOR 16)	HAYES	67	2 July 1970	21 July 1971	**MSC-A**

Builders:	Todd Shipyards, Seattle, Wash.		Speed:	12 knots
Displacement:	2,329 tons light		Range:	6,000 n.miles (11,112 km) at 12 knots
	4,037 tons full load		Manning:	19 civilian + 30 technicians
Length:	220 feet (67.1 m) waterline		Helicopters:	no facilities
	246 5/12 feet (75.1 m) overall		Radars:	Raytheon TM 1650/6X navigation
Beam:	75 feet (22.9 m)			Raytheon TM 1660/12S navigation
Draft:	22 feet (6.7 m)			
Propulsion:	diesel-electric (3 Caterpillar 3516 geared diesels); 5,400 shp; 2 shafts			

The HAYES is a catamaran, built specifically for use as an oceanographic research ship. She has been converted to an acoustic research ship to replace the sound barge MONOB ONE (YAG 61) in support of noise measuring of nuclear-propelled submarines. In her new role the HAYES can transport, deploy, and retrieve acoustic arrays and conduct acoustic research. She is operated by an MSC civilian crew.

Following service as an oceanographic research ship (T-AGOR 16), the HAYES was laid up from 1983 until conversion to a sound trials ship began in 1989. The conversion was completed and she was returned to service on 19 June 1992.

The HAYES operates in the Exuma Sound in the Bahama Islands under sponsorship of the David Taylor Research Center. She is homeported at Port Canaveral, Fla.

Classification: Changed from T-AGOR 16 to T-AG 195 on 20 March 1989.

Conversion: The HAYES was to have been converted to a sound trials ship under a contract awarded on 20 February 1987 to the Tacoma Boatbulding Co., in Tacoma, Wash. Conversion began on 27 August 1989, but the contract with Tacoma was terminated and the ship was towed to the Puget Sound Naval Shipyard on 1 December 1990 for completion at that yard. Placed in MSC service in 1992.

Design: SCB No. 726. The HAYES has two hulls, each with a 24-foot (7.3-m) beam, spaced 27 feet (8.2 m) apart for an overall ship beam of 75 feet (22.9 m). Berthing and messing spaces are located in the forward superstructure "block," while the laboratories are located aft.

The catamaran design provides a stable work platform with a large, open deck area; also, a centerline well makes it possible to lower research equipment into sheltered water between the two hulls. Some sea-keeping problems were encountered in the design and it has not been repeated. In particular, the HAYES suffered excessive pitching in her AGOR role and was not considered particularly successful as a seagoing research ship.

The HAYES was built simultaneously with the catamaran submarine rescue ships of the PIGEON (ASR 21) class. This design differs considerably from the Small Waterplane Area Twin-Hull (SWATH) design employed for ocean surveillance ships (AGOS); see below.

Electronics: The ship conducts noise measurements with a towed array, with a towing speed of 3 to 10 knots.

Engineering: The AG conversion included providing a high degree of automation in the engineering spaces; the original four high-speed diesel engines driving controllable-pitch propellers were replaced. An auxiliary 165-hp diesel engine is provided in each hull to permit a "creeping" speed of 2 to 4 knots with main propulsion shut down.

The HAYES, which supports the research and development of advanced acoustic sensors in addition to work on submarine noise suppression efforts. Catamaran designs have not been efficient for large, oceangoing ships. (1992, courtesy Capt. David W. Muir/USNS HAYES)

The HAYES, following an extensive conversion to a sound trials ship. The ship now meets the very stringent self-generated noise levels required to measure other ships' self-generated noises specified in Navy noise reduction programs. (1992, courtesy Capt. David W. Muir/USNS HAYES)

NAVIGATION RESEARCH SHIP: CONVERTED OILER

Number	Name	Acquired by Navy	T-AGM in service	Notes
T-AG 194	VANGUARD	1947	1966	OSIR 7 July 1997; str. 13 Dec 1999

This ship was built as a merchant tanker (MISSION SAN FERNANDO); she was acquired by the Navy in 1947 and placed in service as a fleet oiler (AO 122) with the Naval Transportation Service, then transferred to MSTS service when that agency was created in 1949 (changed to T-AO 122). Subsequently, she was in and out of service as the oiler/tanker requirements changed: to the National Defense Reserve Fleet (NDRF) in 1955; stricken on 22 June 1955; reacquired by the Navy on 21 June 1956; stricken and returned to the NDRF on 4 September 1957; reac-

quired by the Navy on 28 September 1964 for conversion to T-AGM 19 and renamed MUSCLE SHOALS. She was again renamed VANGUARD in 1965. Later employed as a navigation test ship for Trident strategic missile submarines, her designation was changed to T-AG 194 in 1980.

The three AGMs of this type—Maritime Administration T2-SE-A2—were the largest of the 23 range instrumentation ships operated by the United States. See 16th Edition/pages 218–219 for characteristics.

1 HEAVY LIFT SHIP: "GLOMAR EXPLORER"

Number	Name	Launched	Completed	Status
AG 193	GLOMAR EXPLORER	1 Nov 1972	July 1973	loan

Builders:	Sun Shipbuilding and Dry Dock, Chester, Pa.
Displacement:	63,300 tons full load
Tonnage:	39,705 DWT
	27,445 GRT
	18,511 tons net
Length:	556$^{11}/_{12}$ feet (169.8 m) waterline
	618¾ feet (188.7 m) overall
Beam:	115⅔ feet (35.3 m)
Draft:	46$^{11}/_{12}$ feet (14.3 m)
Propulsion:	diesel-electric (5 Nordberg diesel engines; 6 General Electric motors); 13,200 shp; 2 shafts
Speed:	10.8 knots
Range:	
Manning:	approx. 180 civilian
Helicopters:	landing area
Radars:	2 . . . navigation

The GLOMAR EXPLORER was built and operated by the Central Intelligence Agency specifically to lift the remains of a Soviet Golf-class (Project 629) ballistic missile submarine (SSB) that sank in the mid-Pacific in 1968. The ship lifted the forward portion of the submarine from a depth of 3 miles (4.8 km) in 1974 in a clandestine operation given the code-name Operation Jennifer. (The ship's cover story was a seafloor mining operation under the aegis of millionaire Howard Hughes through the Summa Corporation for his Global Marine Development firm.)

The ship was acquired by the Navy on 30 September 1976 and placed on the NVR; she was transferred to the Maritime Administration on 17 January 1977 and laid up in the National Defense Reserve Fleet in Suisun Bay, Calif. Subsequent Navy efforts to sell the ship failed and in 1978 she was leased to Global Marine Development, Inc., for a commercial seafloor mining venture; she was to be operated by the Lockheed Missiles and Space Company in that role. However, that lease was terminated and the ship was returned to Navy control on 25 April 1980 and again assigned to the Maritime Administration on the same date.

In late 1979 it was planned to provide the ship to the National Science Foundation as a deep-sea drilling ship. After modification she was to have the capability of drilling into the earth at an operating depth of approximately 15,000 feet (4,573 m). That project was not funded.

Since 2 July 1996 the ship has been on loan to Chevron U.S.A. Production Company. In August 1998 the ship drilled to a record 7,718 feet (2,353 m) on the initial exploratory test well in the Gulf of Mexico's Atwater Valley Block No. 118, about 175 n.miles (324 km) southeast of New Orleans. The ship remains on the Naval Vessel Register.

Classification: When acquired by the Navy in 1976, the GLOMAR EXPLORER was assigned hull number AG 193.

Cost: The cost of the ship at the time of construction was estimated at approximately $350 million. Certain related equipment and the cost of the HMB-1 submersible barge and personnel brought the total project cost to an estimated $550 million.

Design: The ship was designed specifically to lift the sunken Golf-class submarine from a depth of 16,500 feet (5,030 m), employing a heavy lift system including a grappling claw that could be attached to the ship clandestinely by a submersible barge (designated

The GLOMAR EXPLORER as configured for deep-ocean lift. The ship has since been modified and currently is employed as a deep-sea drilling ship. The associated HMB-1 submersible barge is being used to support the SEA SHADOW project (see chapter 24). A photo of the GLOMAR EXPLORER as laid up in the NDRF appears in the 13th Edition/page 249.

HMB-1). Reportedly the barge would also have been used to hide the Soviet submarine had the entire 330-foot (100.6-m) submarine been salvaged. In the event, the portion salvaged could be accommodated in a large underwater hangar or "moon pool" within the GLOMAR EXPLORER.

Engineering: Three bow and two stern thrusters are fitted with an automatic position-keeping system to permit precise maneuvering or holding directly over an object on the ocean floor.

Names: As built, the ship was named HUGHES GLOMAR EXPLORER. Although no Navy name was ever assigned, she is listed in the Naval Vessel Register and other official documents as the GLOMAR EXPLORER.

Operational: The GLOMAR EXPLORER arrived at the submarine lift site on 4 July 1974 and during the month-long operation lifted the forward portion of the submarine. The amidships section containing three SS-N-5 ballistic missiles with nuclear warheads was not salvaged. However, torpedoes were recovered, including two reported to have nuclear warheads. The remains of the submarine were studied within the GLOMAR EXPLORER, then cut apart and packaged for further analysis or jettisoned.

This was the deepest and most complex salvage operation ever undertaken by any nation.

SONAR TRIALS SHIP: "GLOVER"

The GLOVER was authorized as a miscellaneous auxiliary (AG 163), completed in 1965 as an escort research ship (AGDE 1), and reclassified as a frigate research ship (AGFF 1) on 30 June 1975. The ship was used primarily for research into the 1970s, after which the ship became as an operational frigate, being reclassified FF 1098 on 1 October 1979 (assigned the hull number of a canceled KNOX-class frigate).

She was again changed to AGFF and designated T-AGFF 1 on 15 June 1990 as a sonar trials ship; she was reconfigured as trials ship for the wide-aperture array sonar and placed in MSC service on 15 June 1991. The forward 5-inch gun mount was retained in MSC service—the only MSC-operated warship.

The GLOVER was placed out of service on 28 September 1992 and transferred to the NDRF on that date; she was stricken on 18 August 1994.

MISCELLANEOUS AUXILIARIES

A variety of ships were designated as miscellaneous auxiliaries to fulfill a number of auxiliary and research functions. At the end of World War II, the AG series had reached hull no. 120. In the postwar period, the series reached AG 195, plus two ocean minesweepers that served as miscellaneous auxiliaries with their MSO hull numbers: ALACRITY (MSO/AG 520) and ASSURANCE (MSO/AG 521).

Of the AG-series ships on the Naval Vessel Register in 1990, the hydrographic research ship KINGSPORT (T-AG 164) was stricken on 31 January 1984 and laid up in the James River (Va.) group of the NDRF; she was *again* stricken on 20 August 1990 due to a Navy records error (and later sold for scrap). The small surveying ship S. P. LEE (T-AG 192) was loaned to the U.S. Geological Survey in February 1974. The ship was carried on the NVR in a lease status until taken out of service on 1 August 1992; she was stricken on 1 October 1992 and transferred to Mexico on 7 December 1992.

DEEP SUBMERGENCE SUPPORT SHIPS

The hybrid missile test/support ship POINT LOMA (T-AGDS 2) was taken out of MSC service and stricken on 1 October 1993; she was transferred to the NDRF on 4 October 1993.

The POINT LOMA was built as an Arctic cargo ship fitted with a docking well; she originally was named POINT BARROW and designated T-AKD 1. As an AGDS, she supported the deep-diving bathyscaph TRIESTE II. See 15th Edition/pages 233–234 for characteristics.

(The previous TRIESTE II support ship, the modified floating dry dock WHITE SANDS/ARD 20, was briefly assigned the hull number AGDS 1.)

INTELLIGENCE COLLECTION SHIPS

The U.S. Navy converted ten cargo hulls to intelligence collection ships in the 1960s; a large force of these platforms was planned to supplement aircraft, submarines, and surface warships employed in that role. The conversions were to be the equivalent of the large force of Soviet intelligence collection ships (AGI).

Converted for the collection of Signals Intelligence (SIGINT), these ships were manned by Navy personnel but operated under the aegis of the National Security Agency, with some civilian specialists on board. Their "cover" was the collection of oceanographic and other environmental information, although their real role was readily apparent from their operations and electronic antennas. The ships carried a minimal armament of machine guns and small arms. The ships were designated AGER for environmental research ship or AGTR for technical research ship.

Three FS/AKL-type cargo ships were converted to this role (AGER 1–3), as were five larger ships of the Liberty and Victory classes (AGTR 1–5).[3] Two smaller cargo-type ships also were

---

3. The similar MARK (ex-AKL 12, ex-AG 143, ex-U.S. Army FS 214) was transferred to Taiwan in 1971; she later served as the intelligence collection ship WU KANG.

employed by the U.S. government in the intelligence role in the 1960s, the PRIVATE JOSEPH E. VALDEZ (AG 169) and SERGEANT JOSEPH E. MULLER (AG 171).

The U.S. specialized intelligence ship program was abandoned after the Israeli attack on the LIBERTY (AGTR 5) in 1967 and the capture of the PUEBLO (AGER 2) by North Korea in 1968. The PUEBLO remains listed as "Active, In Commission" on the Naval Vessel Register, although the ship has been interned since she was captured on 23 January 1968 while some 12 n.miles (22.2 km) off the coast of Wonsan in international waters. The ship remains at Wonsan, having been opened in 1995 for selective tourist visits.

One former repair ship also served in the intelligence collection role: the SPHINX (ARL 24, ex-LST 963). She was the last of several score LSTs converted to various types of repair and support ships to be operated by the U.S. Navy. Originally completed in 1944, she was in service from 1944 to 1947, 1950 to 1956, and again from 1967 to 1971 as an ARL. The SPHINX was recommissioned in 1985 for employment as an intelligence collection ship to operate off Central America to intercept radio and radar emissions from Marxist Nicaragua. The ship was decommissioned and stricken on 19 June 1989 and transferred to the NDRF on 15 June 1990.

MISSILE RANGE INSTRUMENTATION SHIPS

The Navy and Air Force designated 24 merchant-type ships to serve as missile range instrumentation ships to support various U.S. research, space, and missile programs. One, the OBSERVATION ISLAND, remains in naval service. A list of all 24 range instrumentation ships appears in table 22-4.

Names: Missile range instrumentation ships (AGM) have a variety of name sources, including cities, "range" names (RANGE SENTINEL/T-AGM 22), and missile project names (REDSTONE/T-AGM 20), while some of the ships previously "owned" by the Air Force honor generals (GENERAL H. H. ARNOLD/T-AGM 9). The OBSERVATION ISLAND retains the name assigned when she supported the Polaris program.

1 MISSILE RANGE INSTRUMENTATION SHIP: CONVERTED SURVEILLANCE SHIP

Number	Name	FY	Launched	In service	Status
T-AGM 24	INVINCIBLE	82	1 Nov 1986	30 Jan 1987	**MSC-P**

Builders: Tacoma Boatbuilding, Wash.

In 2000 the Navy announced that the ocean surveillance ship INVINCIBLE (T-AGOS 10) would be converted to a missile range instrumentation ship. See page 252 for characteristics.

1 MISSILE RANGE INSTRUMENTATION SHIP: MARINER CLASS

Number	Name	Launched	Commissioned	Status
T-AGM 23 (ex-AG 154)	OBSERVATION ISLAND	15 Aug 1953	5 Dec 1958	**MSC-A**

Builders:	New York Shipbuilding, Camden, N.J.	Speed:	20 knots
Displacement:	13,060 tons light	Range:	17,000 n.miles (31,500 km) at 13 knots
	16,076 tons full load	Manning:	65 civilian + 60 technicians
Length:	563 feet (171.6 m) overall	Helicopters:	no facilities
Beam:	76 feet (23.2 m)	Radars:	Raytheon 1650/9X navigation
Draft:	29⅝ feet (9.1 m)		Raytheon 1660/12S navigation
Propulsion:	2 steam turbine (General Electric);		SPQ-11 missile tracking
	22,000 shp; 1 shaft		. . . missile tracking
Boilers:	2 600-psi (41.7-kg/cm²) (Combustion Engineering)		

The OBSERVATION ISLAND is a former missile test ship now employed as a range instrumentation ship, primarily to monitor Russian missile tests in the Western Pacific. The ship was built for commercial cargo service, being completed in February 1954; after brief operation, she was laid up in the National Defense Reserve Fleet in November 1954. She was transferred to the Navy on 10 September 1956 for conversion to a missile test ship for the Polaris SLBM and was commissioned in 1958; she was subsequently modified to launch the Poseidon missile. After completion of the Poseidon development program, the ship was decommissioned on 25 September 1972 and again laid up in the NDRF.

The OBSERVATION ISLAND was reacquired for conversion to a missile range instrumentation ship on 18 August 1977. Converted 1979–1981, she is now operated by MSC with a civilian crew in support of Air Force and NASA activities in the Pacific.

The only other missile range instrumentation ship remaining on the NVR is the VANGUARD, serving as a miscellaneous auxiliary.

Class: Five Mariner-class merchant ships were acquired by the Navy, with three being converted to amphibious assault ships (AKA 112, APA 248, APA 249) and two—the COMPASS ISLAND (AG 153) and OBSERVATION ISLAND—to support ships for the Polaris program. A third Mariner was planned to support the Polaris effort (AG 155), but was not acquired. The COMPASS ISLAND was configured to test strategic missile submarine navigation systems; she was stricken in 1981.

Classification: The OBSERVATION ISLAND originally was classified YAG 57 for naval service; this was changed to AG 154 on 19 June 1956, being listed as EAG 154 until 1 April 1968 when the ship was "reclassified" as AG 154 to avoid confusion with her "E" prefix. The ship was changed to T-AGM 23 on 1 May 1979.

Conversion: The ship was converted to AGM configuration at the Maryland Shipbuilding & Dry Dock Co., Baltimore, Md., from July 1977 to April 1981. She was fitted with the Cobra Judy phased-array radar (SPQ-11) aft and two radar spheres were installed atop her superstructure.

Design: As an AG, she was fitted with two SLBM launch tubes.
Engineering: Two bow thrusters are fitted for precise position-keeping.
Names: Her merchant name was EMPIRE STATE MARINER.

The OBSERVATION ISLAND is the last of five Marine-class ships acquired by the Navy for conversion to amphibious and research ships. The OBSERVATION ISLAND now serves as a missile range instrumentation ship, tracking U.S., Russian, Chinese, and North Korean missile and space launches in the Pacific area. (1993, Giorgio Arra)

The OBSERVATION ISLAND with the massive Cobra Judy phased array facing aft. The Cobra Judy can rotate to port and starboard. Like most research and missile range instrumentation ships, the OBSERVATION ISLAND is rarely photographed. (1993, Giorgio Arra)

MISSILE RANGE INSTRUMENTATION SHIP: VICTORY CLASS

Number	Name	APA comm.	T-AGM in service	Notes
T-AGM 22	RANGE SENTINEL	1944	1971	OSIR 7 Sep 1995; str. 3 May 1999

The RANGE SENTINEL was the former Navy attack transport SHER-BURNE (APA 205), converted to a missile range instrumentation ship. She was the last of eight Victory-type ships (T-AGM 1, 3–8, and 22) to serve in that role. She was converted between October 1969 and October 1971 to a support ship for Poseidon and later Trident missile test firings. See 16th Edition/pages 222–223 for characteristics.

TABLE 22-4. MISSILE RANGE INSTRUMENTATION SHIPS

Number	Name	In service	Notes
T-AGM 1	RANGE TRACKER	1961	ex-AG 160; VC2-S-AP3 type
T-AGM 2	RANGE RECOVERER	1962	ex-AG 161; ex-FS 278
T-AGM 3	LONGVIEW	1960	ex-AK 238; VC2-S-AP3 type
T-AGM 4	RICHFIELD	1959	ex-AK 253; VC2-S-AP2 type
T-AGM 5	SUNNYVALE	1960	ex-AK 256; VC2-S-AP3 type
T-AGM 6	WATERTOWN	1961	VC2-S-AP3 type
T-AGM 7	HUNTSVILLE	1961	VC2-S-AP3 type
T-AGM 8	WHEELING	1964	VC2-S-AP3 type
T-AGM 9	GEN. H. H. ARNOLD	1963	ex-AP 139; C4-S-A1 type
T-AGM 10	GEN. HOYT S. VANDENBERG	1963	ex-AP 145; C4-S-A1 type
T-AGM 11	TWIN FALLS VICTORY	1964	VC2-S-AP3 type; AGM conversion canceled; to AGS 37
T-AGM 12	AMERICAN MARINER	1964	EC2 type
T-AGM 13	SWORD KNOT	1964	C1-M-AV1 type
T-AGM 14	ROSE KNOT	1964	C1-M-AV1 type
T-AGM 15	COASTAL SENTRY	1964	ex-AK 212; C1-M-AV1 type
T-AGM 16	COASTAL CRUSADER	1964	C1-M-AV1 type; to AGS 36
T-AGM 17	TIMBER HITCH	1964	C1-M-AV1 type
T-AGM 18	SAMPAN HITCH	1964	C1-M-AV1 type
T-AGM 19	VANGUARD	1966	ex-AO 122; T2-SE-A2 type
T-AGM 20	REDSTONE	1966	ex-AO 114; T2-SE-A2 type
T-AGM 21	MERCURY	1966	ex-AO 126; T2-SE-A2 type
T-AGM 22	RANGE SENTINEL	1971	ex-APA 205; VC2-S-AP5 type
T-AGM 23	OBSERVATION ISLAND	1981	ex-AG 154; C4-S-1a type
T-AGM 24	INVINCIBLE	2000	ex-T-AGOS 10

The in-service dates listed above are as Navy/USAF missile range instrumentation ships. The Navy acquired 13 merchant and naval ships and the Air Force ten ships (AGM 9–18) to support military and NASA missile/space operations, providing a worldwide telemetry and communications network. All of the ships except the AGM 11 eventually were operated by MSC for the Navy, Air Force, and NASA.

The ten USAF ships initially were operated on the Atlantic Missile Range by contractor personnel under contract to that service; the ships were transferred to MSC on 28 April 1964. Some immediately were taken out of service.

The conversion of the AGM 11 to a surveying ship (AGS 37) was canceled.

The submersible support ship POINT LOMA (AGDS 2) also served as a range instrumentation ship (see page 242).

OCEANOGRAPHIC RESEARCH SHIPS

Oceanographic research ships perform a broad spectrum of basic ocean research. A major U.S. oceanographic research/surveying ship construction program has recently been completed to replace the large number of such ships procured in the 1960s. The older ships had reached the end of their effective service lives and are technologically inadequate for modern oceanographic operations. Their replacement ships are multimission designs.

Navy AGORs carry out military research and also are a part of the University-National Oceanographic Laboratory System (UNOLS). The UNOLS program is funded primarily by the National Science Foundation (approximately 75 percent) and the Office of Naval Research (approximately 13 percent), with the remainder funded by other federal and state organizations. The UNOLS organization, chartered in 1972, has 59 federal and state agencies as members, of which 20 operate oceanographic research ships. Table 22-6 lists the UNOLS ships of 100 feet (30.5 m) or greater length, other than those of the Navy, Coast Guard, and National Oceanic and Atmospheric Administration (NOAA). The Coast Guard and NOAA ships, as well as those of the National Science Foundation, are listed in chapters 30 through 32 of this volume.

All active Navy research ships are operated by civilian crews under the aegis of MSC.

The former oceanographic research ship HAYES (T-AGOR 16) has been converted to a sound trials ship and reclassified T-AG 195 (see page 240).

The unique, Navy-owned Floating Instrument Platform (FLIP) is described in chapter 24.

Names: Oceanographic research ships generally are named for oceanographers and Navy oceanographic officers.

3 OCEANOGRAPHIC RESEARCH SHIPS: "THOMAS G. THOMPSON" CLASS

Number	Name	FY	Launched	In service	Status
AGOR 23	THOMAS G. THOMPSON	87	27 July 1990	8 July 1991	**Academic**
AGOR 24	ROGER REVELLE	93	20 Apr 1995	11 June 1996	**Academic**
AGOR 25	ATLANTIS	94	1 Feb 1996	3 Mar 1997	**Academic**

Builders:	Trinity/Halter Marine, Moss Point, Miss.
Displacement:	2,155 tons light
	3,250 tons full load
Length:	243 feet (74.09 m) waterline
	274 feet (83.5 m) overall
Beam:	53 feet (16.16 m)
Draft:	19 feet (5.79 m)
Propulsion:	diesel-electric (3 diesel generators/ Caterpillar 3516TA, 2 electric motors/ General Motors CD6999); 6,000 shp; 2 all-azimuth propellers
Speed:	15 knots
Range:	11,300 n.miles (20,940 km) at 12 knots
Manning:	20 civilian + 35–40 scientists and technicians
Helicopters:	no facilities
Radars:	. . . navigation
Sonar:	Krupp-Atlas seafloor mapping

These oceanographic research ships are especially suited to support Navy research laboratories, academic institutions, and commercial contractors involved in Navy projects (replacing the CONRAD-class ships). The program was designated AGX during the design phase. A fourth ship of this class, the RONALD H. BROWN (AGOR 26), was built for NOAA; see chapter 31.

The lead ship, the THOMPSON, was laid down on 29 March 1989.

Design: The ships were built to commercial standards. They are specially designed for extended at-sea operations and are fitted with a dynamic positioning system to maintain station during research activities. Four laboratory/accommodation vans can be carried on deck in addition to more than 4,000 square feet (372 m^2) of laboratory space. Their endurance is 60 to 70 days.

The AGOR 23 is configured for oceanographic research and coastal survey.

Engineering: In addition to three diesel generators for propulsion, the ships have three ship's service power generators (3508TA) and one emergency generator (3406TA).

The ships are fitted with azimuth or Z-drives with 360° directional propellers; there is also a 360°, 1,180-shp bow thruster to provide precise station keeping.

Names: The AGOR 23 initially was to be named EWING; the AGOR 24 originally was named REVELLE. The AGOR 25 remembers two previous oceanographic research ships operated by Woods Hole (Mass.) Oceanographic Institution, the ATLANTIS I and ATLANTIS II.

Operational: The THOMPSON is operated by the University of Washington (state), replacing her namesake, the former AGOR 9 (subsequently IX 517); the REVELLE by the Scripps Institution of Oceanography in La Jolla, Calif.; and the ATLANTIS by Woods Hole.

1 OCEANOGRAPHIC RESEARCH SHIP: "GYRE" CLASS

Number	Name	FY	Launched	Delivered	Status
AGOR 22	MOANA WAVE	71	18 June 1973	16 Jan 1974	**Academic**

Builders:	Trinity/Halter Marine, New Orleans, La.
Displacement:	946 tons light
	1,190 tons full load
Length:	204⅙ feet (62.25 m) overall
Beam:	36 feet (11.0 m)
Draft:	14½ feet (4.4 m)
Propulsion:	2 geared diesel engines (Caterpillar); 1,700 bhp; 2 shafts
Speed:	12.5 knots (11.5 knots sustained)
Range:	8,000 n.miles (14,816 km) at 10 knots
Manning:	13 civilian + 19 scientists
Helicopters:	no facilities
Radars:	. . . navigation

The ROGER REVELLE, the second of a new class of large oceanographic research ships. All U.S. Navy ships of this category are operated by civilian academic institutions. (1998, Leo Van Ginderen)

The THOMAS G. THOMPSON shows the clean, sharp lines of this latest class of oceanographic research ships. The THOMPSON and her sister ships replace the CONRAD-class AGORs completed in the 1960s. (1991, Trinity/Halter Marine)

The MOANA WAVE was one of two small "utility" research ships built specifically for use by academic research institutions. She was laid down on 9 October 1972.

She is operated for the Oceanographer of the Navy by the Hawaii Institute of Geophysics, having been assigned to that institution upon completion. During the early 1980s the MOANA WAVE was employed for at-sea testing of the T-AGOS/SURTASS towed sonar array.

Class: The GYRE (AGOR 21), completed in 1973, was immediately assigned to Texas A&M University for operation. She was stricken on 17 August 1992 and transferred on the same date to the school.

Design: SCB No. 734. This design is based on the design of a commercial offshore oil-rig resupply ship. The open deck aft provides space for special-purpose vans and research equipment. Endurance is 40 to 50 days.

Engineering: A 175-hp bow thruster is fitted.

Modifications: The MOANA WAVE conducted trials in 1979–1984 with satellite communications equipment and with the towed SUR-TASS array for the T-AGOS program. In 1984–1985 the ship was lengthened, with a deckhouse built aft.

Class: The AGOR 19 and 20 of this design were authorized in the fiscal 1968 shipbuilding program, but their construction was canceled.

Design: SCB No. 710. Although these ships have the same SCB number as the CONRAD class, they are quite different. A bow observation dome is fitted. Endurance is 35 to 40 days.

Engineering: These ships were built with a single diesel engine driving two cycloidal (vertical) propellers through long, internal shafts; the forward propeller is located just behind the bow observation dome and the after propeller is just in front of the rudder. The ships could hold a fixed position in heavy seas with winds up to 35 knots. Cycloidal propulsion—controlled by a "joystick"—allowed the ship to be propelled in any direction and to turn up to 360° in their own length. This type of propulsion also allowed precise station keeping and slow speeds without the use of auxiliary propulsion units.

The ships experienced transmission system difficulties with their original propulsion plant. They were re-engined in 1988–1991 to the configuration described above. They now have azimuth or Z-drives with 360° directional propellers.

Modernization: Both ships were extensively modernized when re-engined in 1988–1991.

Operational: The KNORR helped to locate the wreck of the British liner TITANIC in the North Atlantic on 1 September 1985 using a remote-controlled search submersible.

The MOANA WAVE as a research ship. She previously was employed as a test ship for the T-AGOS/SURTASS program (see 14th Edition/page 266). In addition to cranes and other lifting gear, she now has a housing amidships for lowering equipment into the sea. (1991, Leo Van Ginderen)

The MELVILLE (*above*) and similar KNORR have an unusual configuration. Their "mack"—combination mast and stack—structure is amidships, with an enclosed lookout position. These ships are well equipped for their academic research roles under Navy sponsorship. (1989, Giorgio Arra)

2 OCEANOGRAPHIC RESEARCH SHIPS: "MELVILLE" CLASS

Number	Name	FY	Launched	Commissioned	Status
AGOR 14	MELVILLE	66	10 July 1968	27 Aug 1969	**Academic**
AGOR 15	KNORR	66	21 Aug 1968	14 Jan 1970	**Academic**

Builders:	Defoe Shipbuilding, Bay City, Mich.
Displacement:	1,915 tons standard
	2,670 tons full load
Tonnage:	2,100 GRT
Length:	279 feet (85.1 m) overall
Beam:	46⅓ feet (14.1 m)
Draft:	15 feet (4.6 m)
Propulsion:	diesel-electric (4 diesel generators); 3,000 shp; 3 azimuth propellers (1 forward retractable, 2 aft)
Speed:	14 knots
Range:	12,000 n.miles (22,224 km) at 12 knots
Manning:	24 civilian + 34 scientists
Helicopters:	no facilities
Radars:	. . . navigation

These ships are large research ships. The MELVILLE is operated by the Scripps Institution of Oceanography and the KNORR by the Woods Hole Oceanographic Institution, both for the Office of Naval Research under the technical control of the Oceanographer of the Navy. They were assigned to those institutions upon completion.

The MELVILLE was laid down on 12 July 1967 and the KNORR on 9 August 1967.

Stern aspect of the research ship KNORR (1991, Woods Hole Oceanographic Institution)

TABLE 22-5. NAVY OCEANOGRAPHIC RESEARCH SHIPS

Number	Name	In service	Notes
AGOR 1	Josiah Williard Gibbs	1958	ex-AVP 51; to Greece
AGOR 2	H. U. Sverdup	1960	built in Norway
AGOR 3	Robert D. Conrad	1962	to NDRF 1989
AGOR 4	James M. Gilliss	1962	to Mexico 1982
AGOR 5	Charles M. Davis	1963	to New Zealand 1970
AGOR 6	Sands	1964	to Brazil 1974
T-AGOR 7	Lynch	1965	decomm. 21 Oct 1991; str. 6 Nov 1991
T-AGOR 8	Eltanin	1961	ex-T-AK 270; C1-ME2-13a type; to Argentina
AGOR 9	Thomas G. Thompson	1965	to IX 517 in 1989
AGOR 10	Thomas Washington	1965	decomm. 1 Aug 1992; to Chile 28 Sep 1992
AGOR 11	Mizar	1962	ex-T-AK 272; C1-ME2-13a type
T-AGOR 12	De Steiguer	1969	decomm./to Tunisia 2 Nov 1992
T-AGOR 13	Bartlett	1969	decomm./to Morocco 26 July 1993
AGOR 14, 15	Melville class		
AGOR 16	Hayes	1971	to T-AG 195
AGOR 17	Chain	1958	ex-ARS 20; str. 1977
AGOR 18	Argo	1960	ex-ARS 27; str. 1970
AGOR 19			canceled 1969
AGOR 20			canceled 1969
AGOR 21, 22	Gyre class		
AGOR 23–26	Thomas G. Thompson class		

The above in-service dates are as oceanographic research ships.

The AGOR 2 was built for the Norwegian government with U.S. offshore procurement funds. The nine Conrad-class ships (AGORs 3–7, 9, 10, 12, and 13) were the U.S. Navy's first purpose-built oceanographic research ships. The highly capable Eltanin and Mizar were extensively converted from Arctic cargo ships.

TABLE 22-6. UNIVERSITY-NATIONAL OCEANOGRAPHIC LABORATORY SYSTEM

Name	Operating Agency*	Built	Length
Alpha Helix	NSF	1966	134½ ft (41.0 m)
Cape Hatteras	NSF	1981	135 ft (41.15 m)
Cape Henlopen	University of Delaware	1976	120 ft (36.6 m)
Edwin Link	Harbor Branch Oceanographic Institution	1982	168 ft (51.2 m)
Endeavor	NSF	1993	183⅔ ft (56.0 m)
Healy	USCG	1999	419⅝ ft (128.0 m)
Longhorn	University of Texas	1971	105 ft (32.0 m)
Maurice Ewing	NSF	1983	239⁵⁄₁₂ ft (73.0 m)
New Horizon	Scripps Institution of Oceanography	1978	170 ft (51.8 m)
Oceanus	NSF	1994	176¹¹⁄₁₂ ft (53.9 m)
Pelican	Louisiana Universities Marine Consortium	1985	105 ft (32.0 m)
Point Sur	NSF	1981	135 ft (41.15 m)
Polar Sea	USCG	1978	399 ft (121.65 m)
Polar Star	USCG	1976	399 ft (121.65 m)
Ronald H. Brown	NOAA (AGOR 26)	1997	274 ft (83.5 m)
Seaward Johnson	Harbor Branch Oceanographic Institution	1994	203⅓ ft (62.0 m)

*NOAA = National Oceanic and Atmospheric Administration (see chapter 31); NSF = National Science Foundation (see chapter 32); USCG = U.S. Coast Guard (see chapter 30).

Only non-Navy owned UNOLS ships of 100 feet (30.5 m) and larger are listed in the table above; there are a few smaller, coastal research ships in service. The Coast Guard no longer operates specialized oceanographic cutters (WAGO); hence, only that service's three icebreakers are listed here. Only NOAA's flagship, the Ronald H. Brown, is listed as part of the UNOLS fleet; another 15 ships are in the NOAA fleet, most configured for nautical charting and fisheries research.

The Robert D. Conrad, as laid up in the James River (Va.) NDRF. The ship was transferred to the Maritime Administration/NDRF on 4 October 1989; the ship's title was transferred to MarAd on 1 May 1999. (1990, Leo Van Ginderen)

OCEAN SURVEILLANCE SHIPS

These ships are configured for operating the Surveillance Towed Array Sensor System (SURTASS), a submarine detection system intended to supplement the seafloor Sound Surveillance System (SOSUS). The ships were designed to operate where SOSUS coverage is inadequate or where the seafloor arrays are damaged or destroyed. SURTASS data are sent via satellite link to shore facilities for processing and further transmission to ASW forces; however, the ships can provide "raw" acoustic data to ASW ships in the area. (The SURTASS concept differs from the TACTAS system in that the latter are tactical hydrophone arrays towed by warships to supplement hull-mounted sonars.)

The SURTASS carried by the later ocean surveillance ships is being supplemented by a Low-Frequency Active (LFA) system, considered suitable for effective submarine detection in shallow/littoral areas as well as deep-ocean areas.

The initial Navy planning for the T-AGOS/SURTASS program called for 18 ships. This was later reduced to 12 ships due to fiscal constraints; however, because of the success of the early ships and the increasing Soviet submarine threat, in the late 1980s the Navy sought a force of 39 surveillance ships—the 18 monohull ships of the STALWART class, four SWATH-P ships, and five SWATH-A ships.

In January 1992 the Navy announced its intention to dispose of all monohull T-AGOS ships by 1997 because of budget constraints, although the decline of the Russian submarine threat is usually cited for this action.[4] Accordingly, the planned force level was reduced to nine SWATH-type ships. Subsequently, contractual and construction problems with the first of the larger SWATH-P ships led to a delay in procuring the five ships of this design.

These ships are not armed.

Costs: In 1992, as the Navy revised its T-AGOS force planning, it stated the cost of the SWATH acquisition program as $487 million for the first five SWATH ships (T-AGOS 19–23) and $674 million for the last four ships, i.e., a total of $1.2 *billion.* At that time, annual operating costs were postulated as:

$6.3 million for monohull ships
$7.0 million for SWATH-P ships
$7.7 million for SWATH-A ships

Electronics: The UQQ-2 SURTASS array is a flexible, tube-like structure some 2,600 feet (793 m) long containing numerous hydrophones towed with a 6,000-foot (1,829-m) cable. It is neutrally buoyant when at depth, with the depth being varied to compensate for environmental conditions. Typical array operating depths are 500 to 1,500 feet (152 to 457 m).

Data from the hydrophone array are generated at a very high data rate. The information is "pre-processed" on board the T-AGOS and sent at a much lower rate, reduced by a factor of ten, via satellite to shore stations. The data rate from ship to shore is about 32,000 bits (32 kilobits) per second.

Names: Surveillance ships have names that convey traits of capability or accomplishment.

Operational: The massive decommissioning of T-AGOS ships is taking place despite the Navy's inability to meet certain surveillance operational requirements. For example, early in 1994 Rear Admiral James Prout, the Deputy Chief of Staff for Resources, Requirements, and Assessment of the U.S. Pacific Fleet told the Senate Armed Services Committee: "We were recently unable to support a U.S. Central Command request for full-time deployment of a T-AGOS ship to the Persian Gulf for surveillance purposes."[5]

1 OCEAN SURVEILLANCE SHIP: SWATH-A DESIGN

Number	Name	FY	Launched	In service	Status
T-AGOS 23	IMPECCABLE	90	25 April 1998	2001	building

Builders:	Halter Marine, Moss Point, Miss.
Displacement:	5,362 tons full load
Length:	232 feet (70.73 m) waterline
	281½ feet (85.8 m) overall
Beam:	95¾ feet (29.2 m)
Draft:	26 feet (7.9 m)
Propulsion:	diesel-electric (4 diesel generators); 5,000 shp; 2 shafts
Speed:	12 knots sustained
Range:	8,000 n.miles (14,816 km) at 15 knots
Manning:	25 civilian + 25 Navy technicians
Helicopters:	no facilities
Radars:	. . . navigation
Sonars:	Low-Frequency Active (LFA)
	UQQ-2 SURTASS

This was an enlarged SWATH ship intended to conduct SURTASS missions in higher sea states, specifically for operations in high-latitude areas; they are intended to operate through sea state 6 on all headings and sea state 7 on best heading.

A class of four ships originally was planned. The IMPECCABLE was ordered from American Shipbuilding, Tampa, Fla., on 28 March 1991.

---

4. See *Undersea Surveillance: Navy Continues to Build Ships Designed for Soviet Threat* (Washington, D.C.: General Accounting Office, December 1992).

5. Barbara Starr, "SOSUS Suffers as USN Stretches Its Funding," *Jane's Defence Weekly* (26 March 1994), p. 3.

An artist's concept of the IMPECCABLE, the "ultimate" U.S. Navy T-AGOS design. Delays in the construction of the lead ship ended initial plans to produce a five-ship class (T-AGOS 23–27). The projection from the stern is to keep the towed array clear of the propellers. (U.S. Navy)

However, work was halted due to contractual problems with the Tampa yard.[6] (She originally was to have been laid down in December 1993, launched in March 1994, and completed in January 1995.) The unfinished hull was transferred from the Tampa yard to Halter Marine for completion; she was placed on the ways there on 21 January 1996.

The IMPECCABLE was formally christened and named in ceremonies at Halter Marine on 1 November 2000—2½ years after her launch.

It is unlikely that additional ships of this class will be constructed in the near term.

Design: The Small Waterplane Area Twin-Hull form was evaluated in the research craft KAIMALINO (see chapter 24). The SWATH concept differs from that of a catamaran, which has two conventional ship hulls joined together; the SWATH design provides two fully submerged underwater hulls with structures rising through the water to support the ship's superstructure.

The SWATH design provides a high degree of ship stability in rough waters and a large deck space. It was adopted because the monohull T-AGOS ships experienced sea-keeping difficulties in northern latitudes during winter. Endurance is planned to be 50 to 60 days.

Engineering: Fitted with two 360° thrusters for station keeping.

4 OCEAN SURVEILLANCE SHIPS: "VICTORIOUS" CLASS (SWATH-P)

Number	Name	FY	Launched	In service	Status
T-AGOS 19	VICTORIOUS	87	2 May 1990	13 Aug 1991	**MSC-P**
T-AGOS 20	ABLE	89	14 Feb 1991	24 Mar 1992	**MSC-A**
T-AGOS 21	EFFECTIVE	89	26 Sep 1991	28 Jan 1993	**MSC-P**
T-AGOS 22	LOYAL	89	19 Sep 1992	1 July 1993	**MSC-A**

Builders:	McDermott, Morgan City, La.
Displacement:	2,676 tons light
	3,438 tons full load
Length:	190⅔ feet (58.1 m) waterline
	234½ feet (71.5 m) overall
Beam:	93½ feet (28.5 m)
Beam of "box":	80½ feet (24.5 m)
Draft:	25 feet (7.6 m)
Propulsion:	diesel-electric (4 Caterpillar-Kato 3512-TA diesel generators; 2 General Electric motors); 3,200 bhp; 2 shafts
Speed:	16 knots; 9.6 knots array towing speed
Range:	3,000 n.miles (5,556 km) at 10 knots
Manning:	T-AGOS 19 20 civilian + 5 Navy technicians
	T-AGOS 20, 22 19 civilian + 5 Navy technicians
	T-AGOS 21 18 civilian + 5 Navy technicians
Helicopters:	no facilities
Radars:	. . . navigation
Sonars:	Low-Frequency Active (LFA)
	UQQ-2 SURTASS

These are improved, SWATH-configured SURTASS ships.

A contract was awarded to the McDermott firm in October 1986 for the detailed design and construction of the lead ship of this class, the VICTORIOUS, which was laid down on 12 April 1988.

Design: These are the world's first operational military ships with the SWATH design. The design is based on the Navy's research/range support ship KAIMALINO.

Mission endurance is 90 days.

Engineering: The ships' steering system uses a pair of angled rudders aft and a pair of angled canards forward; two azimuth thrusters are fitted forward.

Operational: The SURTASS data are transmitted from the T-AGOS via satellite link to shore facilities for processing and further transmission to ASW forces; however, the ships can provide "raw" acoustic data to ASW ships in the area.

The LOYAL was operating in the Barents Sea in August 2000 when the Russian submarine KURSK was lost. At the time, the U.S. ship was conducting surveillance of a Russian naval exercise, as were two U.S. attack submarines (SSNs).

The stern of the VICTORIOUS, showing the twin five-blade propellers. The torpedo-like submerged hulls have a streamlined appearance, but a SWATH is built for stability, not for speed. (1990, McDermott)

The twin, submerged hulls of the VICTORIOUS have stabilizing fins facing inward, both forward and aft. Twin anchors are set into the bow of the ship. (1990, McDermott)

---

6. The American Shipbuilding Corp. also defaulted on the construction of two Navy oilers (T-AO 191 and 192); see page 260.

The VICTORIOUS was the Navy's first SWATH surveillance ship. The twin, submerged-hull configuration provides enhanced sea-keeping in northern waters. Near the end of the Cold War, the Navy had planned to replace the monohull T-AGOS 1–18 with a force of SWATH ships. (1990, McDermott)

The SWATH design provides the ABLE with extensive working space amidships. No helicopter facilities or combat capabilities are provided in these ships. VERTREP spaces are marked on the deck, amidships, port and starboard. (U.S. Navy)

8 OCEAN SURVEILLANCE SHIPS: "STALWART" CLASS

Number	Name	FY	Launched	In service	Status
T-AGOS 1	STALWART	79	7 Nov 1983	9 Apr 1984	**MSC-A**
T-AGOS 3	VINDICATOR	80	1 June 1984	20 Nov 1984	**MSC-A**
T-AGOS 6	PERSISTENT	81	6 Apr 1985	11 Aug 1985	**MSC-A**
T-AGOS 7	INDOMITABLE	81	16 July 1985	1 Dec 1985	**MSC-A**
T-AGOS 8	PREVAIL	81	7 Dec 1985	5 Mar 1986	**MSC-A**
T-AGOS 9	ASSERTIVE	82	20 June 1986	12 Sep 1986	**MSC-P**
T-AGOS 12	BOLD	82	22 May 1989	20 Oct 1989	**MSC-A**
T-AGOS 16	CAPABLE	86	28 Oct 1998	9 June 1989	**MSC-A**

Builders:	Tacoma Boatbuilding, Wash.
Displacement:	1,600 tons light
	2,285 tons full load
Tonnage:	1,584 GRT
	786 DWT
Length:	203⅔ feet (62.1 m) waterline
	224 feet (68.3 m) overall
Beam:	43 feet (13.1 m)
Draft:	15 feet (4.6 m)
Propulsion:	diesel-electric (4 Caterpillar D-398B diesel generators with General Electric motors); 3,200 bhp; 2 shafts
Speed:	11 knots; 2 to 3 knots towing array
Range:	3,000 n.miles (5,556 km) at 11 knots + 90 days on station at 3 knots
Manning:	T-AGOS 1, 7, 16 18 civilian + 18 Navy technicians
	T-AGOS 8, 9, 12 18 civilian + 5 Navy technicians
Helicopters:	no facilities
Radars:	1 or 2 . . . navigation
	SPS-40 in T-AGOS 16
	SPS-49(V)3 in T-AGOS 1, 3, 6, 7
Sonars:	UQQ-2 SURTASS in T-AGOS 8, 9, 12

These are monohull SURTASS ships. The program suffered from significant cost increases over original estimates and equipment failures, resulting in a several-year delay beyond the original 1974 schedule.

Only six ships remain in active service, operated by the Military Sealift Command. The T-AGOS 8, 9, and 12 were retained in MSC service during the massive force reduction; the T-AGOS 3, 6, and 10 were taken out of service and, subsequently, returned to MSC operation.

Class: Originally a class of 18 ships (see the complete list in table 22-7). A plan to provide six of the ships withdrawn from the T-AGOS role to the Coast Guard was rejected by that service because of the ships' slow speed and lack of a helicopter capability.

The VINDICATOR and PERSISTENT were to have been the first receiving Coast Guard modifications. Instead they were transferred back to the Navy and reactivated for anti-drug patrols in the Caribbean (manned by MSC).

Seven ships were scheduled for transfer to NOAA.

The CONTENDER was transferred to the Merchant Marine Academy, Kings Point, N.Y., for service as a training ship (renamed KINGS POINTER).

The INVINCIBLE was assigned as a missile range instrumentation ship (T-AGM 24).

Design: The T-AGOS hull is similar to that of the T-ATF 166 class. For MSC operation, a high degree of crew habitability is provided, including single staterooms for all crewmen with three single and four double staterooms for technicians. There are four additional berths in the T-AGOS 1–12 and seven additional berths in the later ships. The T-AGOS 13–18 also have a larger SURTASS operations center and modified machinery layout.

Endurance is rated at 98 days (see *Operational* notes).

Engineering: The four diesel generators drive two main propulsion motors. A bow thruster powered by a 550-hp electric motor is fitted for station keeping. There are special features to reduce machinery noise.

Manning: Navy manning data list nine Navy personnel assigned to each T-AGOS ship; the numbers listed here are based on MSC data.

Names: T-AGOS 11 was originally named DAUNTLESS, T-AGOS 12 was VIGOROUS, and T-AGOS 17 was INTREPID; all were renamed while under construction.

Operational: Early Navy planning provided for these ships to have 90-day patrol periods plus 8 days in transit, resulting in more than 300 days at sea per year. This intensity of operations was rejected by MSC as impractical and unrealistic; a patrol duration of 60 to 74 days was subsequently undertaken.

The BOLD barely under way. In 1998–1999 she became the first T-AGOS to be modified for littoral operations; she has been refitted with a twin-line towed array, a surface ship tracking capability, and a communications upgrade. (1992, Giorgio Arra)

The PERSISTENT as refitted with an SPS-49(V)3 air search radar, on a tripod mast aft of her twin funnel. At right is the SPS-40 air search radar fitted in the CAPABLE. (2000, Leo Van Ginderen)

TABLE 22-7. OCEAN SURVEILLANCE SHIPS

Number	Name	In service	OSIR	Notes
STALWART *class (18)*				
T-AGOS 1	STALWART	1984		(see above)
T-AGOS 2	CONTENDER	1984	1 Oct 1992	str. 11 Dec 1992; to Merchant Marine Academy, Kings Point, N.Y.
T-AGOS 3	VINDICATOR	1984	30 Mar 1993	str. 30 Mar 1993; reactivated 26 Aug 1999
T-AGOS 4	TRIUMPH	1985	20 June 1994	stricken 6 Jan 1995
T-AGOS 5	ASSURANCE	1985	28 Mar 1994	stricken 6 Jan 1995; to Portugal 30 Sep 1999
T-AGOS 6	PERSISTENT	1985	11 Oct 1994	str. 6 Jan 1995; reactivated 26 Aug 1999
T-AGOS 7	INDOMITABLE	1985		(see above)
T-AGOS 8	PREVAIL	1986		(see above)
T-AGOS 9	ASSERTIVE	1986		(see above)
T-AGOS 10	INVINCIBLE	1986	6 Feb 1995	str. 9 May 1995; reactivated 13 Mar 1998; to T-AGM 24
T-AGOS 11	AUDACIOUS	1989	30 Nov 1995	stricken 30 Nov 1995; to Portugal 9 Dec 1996
T-AGOS 12	BOLD	1989		(see above)
T-AGOS 13	ADVENTUROUS	1988	1 June 1992	str. 3 June 1992; to NOAA 5 June 1992; to MarAd 27 Feb 1996
T-AGOS 14	WORTHY	1989	17 Mar 1993	to Geological Survey 17 Mar 1993; to U.S. Army 25 Mar 1993; str. 20 May 1993 (see chapter 32)
T-AGOS 15	TITAN	1989	31 Aug 1993	to NOAA 31 Aug 1993; str. 3 Sep 1993
T-AGOS 16	CAPABLE	1989		(see above)
T-AGOS 17	TENACIOUS	1989	3 Feb 1995	str. 6 Feb 1997; to New Zealand 10 Oct 1996
T-AGOS 18	RELENTLESS	1990	17 Mar 1993	to NOAA 17 Mar 1993; str. 20 May 1993
T-AGOS 19–22	VICTORIOUS class			
T-AGOS 23	IMPECCABLE class			

SURVEYING SHIPS

Surveying ships conduct ocean surveys and collect data in support of fleet operations and systems development. All Navy surveying ships are operated by the Military Sealift Command under the sponsorship of the Naval Oceanographic Command. They have civilian crews.

Names: Surveying ships generally are named for oceanographers and Navy oceanographic officers. The PATHFINDER commemorates the Coast and Geodetic Survey ship by that name that was operated by the Navy (as AGS 1) during World War II.

5 + 1 OCEAN SURVEYING SHIPS: "PATHFINDER" CLASS

Number	Name	FY	Launched	In service	Status
T-AGS 60	PATHFINDER	90	4 Oct 1993	5 Dec 1994	**MSC**
T-AGS 61	SUMNER	90	28 Feb 1994	30 May 1995	**MSC**
T-AGS 62	BOWDITCH	90	15 Oct 1994	30 Dec 1995	**MSC**
T-AGS 63	MATTHEW HENSON	94	21 Oct 1996	20 Feb 1998	**MSC**
T-AGS 64	BRUCE C. HEEZEN	97	25 Mar 1999	13 Jan 2000	**MSC**
T-AGS 65	MARY SEARS	99	19 Oct 2000	2002	building

Builders:	Halter Marine, Moss Point, Miss.
Displacement:	2,800 tons light (see Design notes)
	5,100 tons full load
Length:	328 feet (100.0 m) overall
Beam:	58 feet (17.7 m)
Draft:	19 feet (5.8 m)
Propulsion:	diesel engines; 8,000 bhp; 2 azimuth propellers
Speed:	16 knots
Range:	
Manning:	T-AGS 60–63 28 civilian + 27 scientists/technicians
	T-AGS 64 25 civilian + 27 scientists/technicians
Helicopters:	no facilities
Radars:	. . . navigation

This class of ships is intended for long-range ocean survey and research. Research for a variety of ocean sciences can be conducted. Their design is based on the AGOR 23, with the third ship having special features for ice operations.

The PATHFINDER and SUMNER both were laid down on 30 January 1991. The MARY SEARS was laid down on 28 July 1999.

Design: Details differ. The ships have 3,500 square feet (325.5 m^2) of deck working space and 4,000 square feet (372 m^2) of laboratory space; in addition, four 20-foot (6.1-m) containers can be carried to provide additional laboratory spaces.

Engineering: These ships are propelled and steered through a Z-drive arrangement to all-azimuth thrusters. The elimination of conventional reduction gears and long propeller shafts frees space for other uses while the Z-drive provides excellent maneuverability and station keeping for survey and research activities. Retractable bow thrusters are fitted.

2 COASTAL SURVEYING SHIPS: "JOHN McDONNELL" CLASS

Number	Name	FY	Launched	In service	Status
T-AGS 51	JOHN McDONNELL	87	13 Dec 1990	15 Nov 1991	**MSC-A**
T-AGS 52	LITTLEHALES	87	14 Feb 1991	10 Feb 1992	**MSC-A**

Builders:	Trinity/Halter Marine, Moss Point, Miss.
Displacement:	2,000 tons full load
Length:	190 feet (57.9 m) waterline
	208⅙ feet (63.5 m) overall
Beam:	45 feet (13.7 m)
Draft:	14 feet (4.3 m)
Propulsion:	diesel engines; 1 shaft
Speed:	16 knots sustained
Range:	13,800 n.miles (25,535 km) at 16 knots
Manning:	23 civilian + 11 scientists
Helicopters:	no facilities
Radars:	. . . navigation

Both of these coastal surveying ships were laid down on 10 November 1988. They are used to collect bathymetric/hydrographic data in shallow and deep water. They carry small survey launches.

1 OCEAN SURVEYING SHIP: "WATERS"

Number	Name	FY	Launched	In service	Status
T-AGS 45	WATERS	90	6 June 1992	26 May 1993	**MSC-P**

Builders:	Avondale Industries, New Orleans, La.
Displacement:	12,208 tons full load
Length:	442 feet (134.75 m) overall
Beam:	69 feet (21.0 m)
Draft:	21⅙ feet (6.45 m)
Propulsion:	diesel-electric; 7,400 shp; 2 shafts
Speed:	13.2 knots sustained
Range:	
Manning:	32 civilian + 60 civilian technicians
Helicopters:	no facilities
Radars:	. . . navigation

The Sᴜᴍɴᴇʀ, one of a series of new ocean surveying ships. Note the equipment for handling research gear over the stern. A large crane is fitted amidships. (1997, Leo Van Ginderen)

The Pᴀᴛʜꜰɪɴᴅᴇʀ is fitted with cranes and other lifting devices for handling research and surveying gear. Whereas all Navy oceanographic research ships are operated by academic institutions, all ocean surveying ships are operated by the Military Sealift Command. (U.S. Navy)

The Lɪᴛᴛʟᴇʜᴀʟᴇs (above) and sister ship Jᴏʜɴ McDᴏɴɴᴇʟʟ are the smallest of the several classes of AGOR/AGS research ships that were initiated in the late 1980s. (1991, Trinity/Halter Marine)

The JOHN MCDONNELL *(left)* and LITTLEHALES, a two-ship class (1992, Anderson & Rizzo)

The WATERS is one of the Navy's largest surveying/research ships. The ship has a single large square funnel aft for diesel exhausts. The WATERS replaced the long-serving and highly effective deep-ocean survey ship MIZAR. (1993, Giorgio Arra)

This is a large, multifunction surveying ship constructed to replace the MIZAR (T-AGOR 11). The ship is capable of performing bathymetric, oceanographic, and hydrographic surveys and is able to launch and recover a variety of remotely operated vehicles.

The keel for the WATERS was laid down on 21 May 1991.

Design: Fitted with bow and stern thrusters for precise maneuvering.

OCEAN SURVEYING SHIPS: "MAURY" CLASS

Number	Name	In service	Notes
T-AGS 39	MAURY	1989	OSIR/str. 28 Oct 1994
T-AGS 40	TANNER	1990	OSIR/str. 14 Jan 1994

These were built-for-the-purpose ocean survey ships, acquired to replace the outdated BOWDITCH and DUTTON. They were the largest purpose-built U.S. Navy research ships, designed to conduct primarily hydrographic, magnetic, and gravity surveys.

The MAURY and TANNER were discarded after unprecedentedly short service lives; they were taken out of service and stricken on the same dates. The TANNER suffered major engineering problems and was taken out of service after having steamed only 166,000 n.miles (307,600 km).

The MAURY was transferred to the California Maritime Academy on 4 May 1996 and renamed GOLDEN BEAR (in place of the H. H. HESS; see below). The TANNER was transferred to the Maine Maritime Academy on 6 October 1997 and renamed STATE OF MAINE.

OCEAN SURVEYING SHIP: "H. H. HESS"

The large surveying ship H. H. HESS (T-AGS 38) was taken out of service on 5 February 1992, transferred to the NDRF on 21 February 1992, and stricken on 28 July 1992. She was to have been transferred to the California State Maritime Academy as a training ship, but was rejected because of a burned-out boiler.

The HESS was built as a merchant ship, launched in 1964, and acquired by the Navy in 1976 for conversion to an ocean surveying ship.

2 SURVEYING SHIPS: "SILAS BENT" CLASS

Number	Name	FY	Launched	In service	Status
T-AGS 26	SILAS BENT	63	16 May 1964	23 July 1965	OSIR 29 Sep 1995; to Turkey 29 Sep 1995
T-AGS 27	KANE	64	20 Nov 1965	19 May 1967	**MSC-A**
T-AGS 33	WILKES	67	31 July 1969	28 June 1971	OSIR 9 Aug 1995; to Tunisia 29 Sep 1995
T-AGS 34	WYMAN	67	30 Oct 1969	3 Nov 1971	**MSC-A**

Builders:	T-AGS 27 Christy Corp., Sturgeon Bay, Wisc.
	T-AGS 34 Defoe Shipbuilding, Bay City, Mich.
Displacement:	1,790 to 1,935 tons light
	T-AGS 27 2,558 tons full load
	T-AGS 34 2,420 tons full load
Length:	265 feet (80.8 m) waterline
	285⅓ feet (87.0 m) overall
Beam:	48 feet (14.6 m)
Draft:	15 feet (4.6 m)
Propulsion:	diesel-electric (2 Alco diesel engines; Westinghouse or General Electric motors); 3,600 bhp; 1 shaft
Speed:	14 knots
Range:	5,800–6,300 n.miles (10,742–11,668 km) at 14 knots
	8,000 n.miles (14,816 km) at 13 knots
Manning:	T-AGS 26 32 civilian + 26 scientists
	T-AGS 27, 33 50 civilian + 26 scientists
	T-AGS 34 41 civilian + 20 scientists
Helicopters:	no facilities
Radars:	Raytheon TM 1650/9X navigation
	Raytheon TM 1660/12S
Sonars:	BQN-17 in T-AGS 34

These ships were designed specifically for surveying operations. They differ in detail. All four ships were operated by MSC, with some supporting the Navy's SOSUS program.

Two have been transferred to other navies; the remaining two ships are expected to be discarded in the near future.

Design: The first two ships are SCB No. 226; the WILKES is No. 725 in the new series and WYMAN No. 728.

Electronics: The WYMAN is fitted with the SQN-17 bottom survey system.

Engineering: These ships have 350-hp bow propulsion units for precise maneuvering and station keeping.

The KANE is typical of a useful class of small surveying ships that are, nevertheless, reaching the end of their effective service lives. The KANE has lifting devices for handling surveying gear. (1994, Leo Van Ginderen)

The WYMAN, which has a clear fantail (i.e., no crane or derrick) (1991, Giorgio Arra)

OCEAN SURVEYING SHIPS: "CHAUVENET" CLASS

Number	Name	In service	Notes
T-AGS 29	CHAUVENET	1970	OSIR 7 Nov 1992; str. 30 Nov 1992
T-AGS 32	HARKNESS	1971	OSIR/str. 15 Mar 1993

These British-built surveying ships were designed specifically for the U.S. Navy. They were the U.S. Navy's first purpose-built surveying ships.

The CHAUVENET was transferred to the Texas State Maritime Academy and renamed TEXAS CLIPPER II. The HARKNESS was transferred to the National Defense Reserve Fleet on 29 March 1993 for retention as a "spare parts" store for the TEXAS CLIPPER II.

TABLE 22-8. POST–WORLD WAR II SURVEYING SHIPS

Number	Name	In service	Notes
AGS 15	TANNER	1946	ex-AKA 34; S4-SE2-BE1 design
AGS 16	MAURY	1946	ex-AKA 36; S4-SE2-BE1 design
AGS 17	PURSUIT	1950	ex-MSF 108
AGS 18	REQUISITE	1950	ex-MSF 109
AGS 19	SHELDRAKE	1952	ex-AM 62
AGS 20	PREVAIL	1952	ex-MSF 107
AGS 21	BOWDITCH	1958	VC2-S-AP3 type
AGS 22	DUTTON	1958	VC2-S-AP3 type
AGS 23	MICHELSON	1958	VC2-S-AP3 type
AGS 24	SERRANO	1960	ex-ATF 112
AGS 25	KELLAR	1968	to Portugal 1972
AGS 26, 27	SILAS BENT class		
AGS 28	TOWHEE	1964	ex-MSF 388
AGS 29	CHAUVENET	1970	
AGS 30	SAN PABLO	1948	ex-AVP 30
AGS 31	S. P. LEE	1968	to AG 192 (see above)
AGS 32	HARKNESS	1971	
AGS 33, 34	SILAS BENT class		
AGS 35	SGT GEORGE D. KEATHLEY	1967	ex-APc 117; C1-M-AV1 type; to Taiwan 1972
AGS 36	COASTAL CRUSADER	—	ex-AGM 16; C1-M-AV1 type
AGS 37	TWIN FALLS	—	ex-AGM 11; VC2-S-AP3 type
AGS 38	H. H. HESS	1976	C4-S-1a type
AGS 39, 40	MAURY class		
AGS 41–44	not used		
AGS 45	WATERS	1993	
AGS 46–49	not used		
AGS 50	REHOBOTH	1948	ex-AVP 50
AGS 51	JOHN MCDONNELL	1992	
AGS 52	LITTLEHALES	1992	
AGS 53–59	not used		
AGS 60–65	PATHFINDER class		

The above in-service dates are as oceanographic surveying ships. World War II–era surveying ships reached hull number AGS 14. The designations AGSc 12–15 were used for coastal surveying ships (assigned in the same series as the AGS type). The SAN PABLO and REHOBOTH retained their seaplane hull numbers as surveying ships, throwing the AGS numbering scheme out of sequence and leading to confusion.

The three former Victory-type merchant ships (AGS 21–23), acquired by the Navy in 1957 and converted for seafloor charting and magnetic surveys to support the Navy's SSBN programs, have been stricken.

The TWIN FALLS was never converted and the COASTAL CRUSADER, reclassified AGS in 1969, was not put into service as a surveying ship.

HOSPITAL SHIPS

The Department of Defense during the early 1980s decided to provide two hospital ships to support the deployment of U.S. forces overseas in conventional combat operations. Several alternatives were considered, including merchant ship conversions and new construction.

The candidates for conversion included the superliner UNITED STATES, laid up since her final transatlantic voyage in November 1969. The 990-foot (301.8-m) liner, completed in 1952, carried up to 2,000 passengers and was designed from the outset for conversion to a transport for 14,000 troops. In the AH role, she would have had 2,000 to 2,500 beds.

(The UNITED STATES attained 46.4 knots on her classified sea trials; she averaged 35.59 knots on her maiden transatlantic voyage—the fastest oceangoing merchant ship ever built. The ship, now privately owned, has been stripped and is immobilized in Philadelphia.)

Names: Hospital ships are assigned "benevolent" names.

2 HOSPITAL SHIPS: CONVERTED TANKERS

Number	Name	Launched	In service	Status
T-AH 19	MERCY	19 July 1975	15 Dec 1986	MSC ROS-5
T-AH 20	COMFORT	12 Feb 1976	1 Dec 1987	MSC ROS-5

Builders:	National Steel and Shipbuilding, San Diego, Calif.
Displacement:	24,752 tons light
	69,360 tons full load
Length:	854⅚ feet (260.6 m) waterline
	894 feet (272.6 m) overall
Beam:	105¾ feet (32.25 m)
Draft:	32⅚ feet (10.0 m)
Propulsion:	1 steam turbine (General Electric); 24,500 shp; 1 shaft
Boilers:	2
Speed:	17.5 knots
Range:	13,400 n.miles (24,817 km) at 17.5 knots
Manning:	*ROS* 16 civilian + 58 Navy communications and support
	(6 officers + 52 enlisted)
	Active 63 civilian + 58 Navy + 1,100 medical/dental
	(see *Manning* notes)
Patients:	900+ beds (see *Conversion* notes)
Helicopters:	landing area
Radars:	. . . navigation
	SPS-67 surface search

These ships are former commercial tankers that have been fully converted to support U.S. forward-deployed troops. They were delivered as tankers to commercial customers on 19 February 1976 and 23 July 1976, respectively.

These are the first ships of the type in U.S. service since the SANCTUARY was decommissioned in March 1974; at that time the SANCTUARY was serving as a naval dependents support ship.

They are intended to be based at U.S. ports in Reduced Operating Status (ROS); in crisis or wartime they would be assigned medical staffs from military hospitals and go to sea with five days' notice. The MERCY is based at San Diego, Calif., and the COMFORT at Baltimore, Md. (The MERCY shifted her home port from Oakland, Calif., in 1997.)

Conversion: Both ships were converted at the National Steel and Shipbuilding yard in San Diego; the T-AH 19 conversion was authorized in fiscal 1983 (begun July 1984) and the T-AH 20 in fiscal 1984 (begun April 1985).

As hospital ships, they have 12 operating rooms, four X-ray rooms, a pharmacy, a blood bank, an 80-bed intensive care facility, and 920 other beds; up to 1,000 additional patients can be accommodated for limited care. The ships are designed to handle a peak admission rate of 300 patients in 24 hours with surgery required by 60 percent of the admissions and an average patient stay of five days. The ships are designed to take aboard casualties primarily by helicopter; there is a limited capability for taking on casualties from boats on the port side.

There are facilities for preparing 7,500 meals daily and distilling 75,000 gallons (285,000 liters) of fresh water daily.

Design: Maritime Administration T8-S-100b type.

Manning: The ships operate as Medical Treatment Facilities in ROS; upon full mobilization, each ship would be manned by 1,156 Navy personnel.

Names: The merchant names of the ships were WORTH and ROSE CITY, respectively.

Operational: The MERCY operated in the Philippines as a hospital facility from March to June 1987. She was staffed with 375 medical personnel, representing all of the U.S. military services as well as the Public Health Service. The ship treated almost 63,000 patients during the three-month period.

Both ships were activated in August 1990 in response to the Kuwaiti crisis. They departed their respective home ports on 13 August; the COMFORT arrived in the Persian Gulf on 8 September and the MERCY on 14 September. They were initially manned by some 450 medical personnel assigned from the naval hospitals at Oakland, Calif., and Bethesda, Md.; this staff was subsequently augmented by about 700 additional personnel from the hospitals who were flown to the Middle East to rendezvous with the ships. Both ships were in the Persian Gulf during Operations Desert Shield/Desert Storm.

The COMFORT was sent to Jamaica in June 1994 to support Haitian refugee processing; she subsequently sailed to the U.S. naval base at Guantánamo Bay, Cuba, to support Haitian and Cuban refugees interned there. She returned to her home port of Baltimore in July 1994.

The COMFORT was reactivated to take part in Baltic Challenge 98, an air-naval exercise conducted in July 1998 in the Baltic Sea as part of the NATO Partnership for Peace program. The United States and 11 European nations participated in the two-week exercise.

Both ships undertake periodic sea trials.

The MERCY at her home port, the naval submarine base at San Diego, Calif. Although often listed with sealift ships, the MERCY and her sister ship COMFORT are the latest in a long line of Navy and Army hospital ships. (1997, U.S. Navy, PH2 Felix Garza, Jr.)

The MERCY shows the high sides of these converted tankers. The principal means of bringing casualties aboard these ships is by helicopter. (1999, Leo Van Ginderen)

CARGO SHIPS

No cargo ships remain on the Naval Vessel Register except for sealift ships (see chapter 23).

The last "straight" cargo ship on the NVR was the MIRFAK (T-AK 271), completed in 1957; she was stricken on 21 February 1992. The MIRFAK was one of three small cargo ships designed for Arctic operations (C1-ME2-13a type). Her sister ships ELTANIN (AK 270) and MIZAR (AK 272) were converted to the AGOR 8 and 11, respectively.

FLEET BALLISTIC MISSILE SUPPLY SHIPS

These cargo ships—usually referred to as AK(FBM)s—were configured to support U.S. Polaris/Poseidon/Trident I submarine tenders. They carried strategic missiles, fuel oil (for tenders), diesel oil (for tenders and submarines), spare parts, and provisions to tenders at Holy Loch, Scotland; Rota, Spain; and Apra Harbor, Guam. The ships were manned by MSC civilian crews with Navy security detachments. There was no further need for these supply ships after the concentration of U.S. Trident missile submarines at Kings Bay, Ga., and Bremerton, Wash.

FBM SUPPLY SHIP: "VEGA"

Number	Name	In service	Notes
T-AK 286	VEGA	1983	OSIR 28 Apr 1994; str. 7 Nov 1998

The VEGA was a one-of-a-kind AK(FBM). Built for commercial service, she was launched in 1960 and, after brief merchant service, was laid up until acquired by the Navy in 1981. She was a C3-S-33a-type merchant ship; two sister ships were to be converted to surveying ships (T-AGS 39 and 40), but Congress directed that new ships be constructed for that role. Accordingly, the two ships served instead as maritime prepositioning ships (NORTHERN LIGHT/T-AK 284 and SOUTHERN CROSS/T-AK 285); see chapter 23.

FBM SUPPLY SHIPS: CONVERTED VICTORY TYPE

Number	Name	In service	Notes
T-AK 259	ALCOR	1952	stricken 1968
T-AK 260	BETELGEUSE	1952	stricken 1974
T-AK 279	NORWALK	1963	stricken 1979
T-AK 280	FURMAN	1963	OSIR 1981; str. 13 Apr 1992
T-AK 281	VICTORIA	1965	stricken 1986
T-AK 282	MARSHFIELD	1970	OSIR 1 Oct 1992; str. 30 Nov 1992

These are former VC2-S-AP3 merchant ships built during World War II; they were extensively converted to support deployed FBM submarine tenders. The ALCOR and BETELGEUSE originally served as fleet supply ships carrying general cargo.

The FURMAN was further modified in 1982–1983 to transport undersea cable. The ship was operated by MSC under the sponsorship of the Naval Space and Warfare Systems Command.

OILERS

Oilers—also referred to as fleet oilers—provide underway replenishment of naval forces. These ships differ from tankers, which provide point-to-point transfer of fuels, at times replenishing oilers at sea (see chapter 23).

All active Navy oilers are operated by MSC civilian crews.

Names: Oilers historically have been named for rivers with Indian names. The lead ship of the latest class, the HENRY J. KAISER, is named for an American industrialist and World War II master shipbuilder; the succeeding eight ships of the class are named for industrialists, engineers, and naval architects—after which Indian names were assigned to the final nine ships of the class.

16 FLEET OILERS: "HENRY J. KAISER" CLASS

Number	Name	FY	Launched	In service	Status
T-AO 187	HENRY J. KAISER	82	5 Oct 1985	19 Dec 1986	**MSC MPS-2**
T-AO 188	JOSHUA HUMPHREYS	83	22 Feb 1986	3 Apr 1987	OSIR 29 June 1996
T-AO 189	JOHN LENTHALL, JR.	84	9 Aug 1986	25 June 1987	**MSC-A**
T-AO 190	ANDREW J. HIGGINS	84	17 Jan 1987	22 Oct 1987	OSIR 6 May 1996
T-AO 191	BENJAMIN ISHERWOOD	85	15 Aug 1988		canceled 1993
T-AO 192	HENRY ECKFORD	85	14 Aug 1989		canceled 1993
T-AO 193	WALTER S. DIEHL	85	10 Oct 1987	13 Sep 1988	**MSC-P**
T-AO 194	JOHN ERICSSON	86	21 Apr 1990	19 Mar 1991	**MSC-P**
T-AO 195	LEROY GRUMMAN	86	3 Dec 1988	2 Aug 1989	**MSC-A**
T-AO 196	KANAWHA	87	22 Sep 1990	10 Dec 1991	**MSC-A**
T-AO 197	PECOS	87	23 Sep 1989	13 July 1990	**MSC-P**
T-AO 198	BIG HORN	88	2 Feb 1991	21 May 1992	**MSC-A**
T-AO 199	TIPPECANOE	88	16 May 1992	8 Feb 1993	**MSC-P**
T-AO 200	GUADALUPE	89	5 Oct 1991	25 Sep 1992	**MSC-P**
T-AO 201	PATUXENT	89	23 July 1994	22 June 1995	**MSC-A**
T-AO 202	YUKON	89	6 Feb 1992	25 Mar 1994	**MSC-P**
T-AO 203	LARAMIE	89	6 May 1995	7 May 1996	**MSC-A**
T-AO 204	RAPPAHANNOCK	89	14 Jan 1995	7 Nov 1995	**MSC-P**

Builders:	Avondale Shipyards, New Orleans, La., except T-AO 191 and 192 by Pennsylvania Shipbuilding (Pa.) and American Shipbuilding, Tampa, Fla.	Range:	6,000 n.miles (11,112 km) at 20 knots
Displacement:	9,500 tons light / 40,700 tons full load	Manning:	81 civilian + 23 Navy (1 officer + 22 enlisted), except T-AO 194, 197, 200: 66 civilian + 23 Navy; T-AO 187: 27 civilian (no Navy personnel)
Tonnage:	26,500 deadweight	Helicopters:	landing area
Length:	649¾ feet (198.1 m) waterline / 677½ feet (206.6 m) overall	Guns:	none (see notes)
Beam:	97½ feet (29.7 m)	Radars:	2 . . . navigation
Draft:	36 feet (11.0 m)	EW systems:	(see *Electronics* notes)
Propulsion:	2 diesel engines (Colt-Pielstick 10PC4.2V); 32,540 bhp; 2 shafts		
Speed:	20 knots		

These fleet oilers/UNREP ships were built to civilian specifications. Although civilian manned, they operate regularly with forward-deployed battle groups. This class provides the only fleet oilers currently in naval service. The lead ship was laid down on 22 August 1984.

The KAISER currently serves as a Maritime Prepositioning Ship (MPS). She is assigned to Maritime Prepositioning Squadron 2, normally moored at Diego Garcia in the Indian Ocean and manned by a civilian crew of 23. Since 31 January 1995 the ship has carried JP-4 fuel for military aircraft. She previously operated as a fleet tanker.

Builders: Contracts for the construction of the T-AO 191, 192, 194, and 196 were awarded to Pennsylvania Shipbuilding in 1985–1986; those contracts were canceled on 31 August 1989 for default on construction. The first two ships were towed to the Philadelphia Naval Shipyard in October 1989, and subsequently were transferred to American Shipbuilding (Tampa) for comple-

tion; they were reordered on 16 November 1989. The T-AO 194 and 196, for which assembly had not yet begun, were awarded to Avondale for construction.

The two ships towed to the Tampa yard were, according to shipyard officials there, "a mess." The yard sued the Navy because of the ships' condition. The Navy argued it was forced to send the ships to the yard because of political pressure and that the yard did not have the trained work force to complete the ships. Despite additional congressional funding to the Tampa yard, the ships were not completed and the Navy terminated the contract on 15 August 1993. The ships were then towed to the James River (Va.) NDRF anchorage. The ISHERWOOD was 95.3 percent complete and the ECKFORD 84 percent complete when canceled. The government had paid Pennsylvania Shipbuilding $331 million and American Shipbuilding $102 million for the two ships. They are not completed and there is no plan to finish them.

The LARAMIE shows the superstructure-aft configuration of the KAISER-class oilers; note the massive size of the superstructure, which provides comfortable accommodations for the ship's civilian mariners. There is a helicopter deck aft, but no hangar as in other types of replenishment ships. (1999, Leo Van Ginderen)

Design: These are midsize petroleum carriers with a 180,000-barrel cargo capacity; in addition, they can carry 25,000 gallons (95,000 liters) of lubrication oil as bulk cargo, plus 105,000 gallons (399,000 liters) of potable water and 88,000 gallons (334,400 liters) of boiler feed water. The ships have seven UNREP stations.

The PATUXENT and later ships are the first "double hulled" oilers built for MSC operation.

The ships have a limited UNREP capacity for dry stores as well as fuels, with a tunnel for forklift trucks running through the superstructure to permit cargo to be carried aft to the helicopter deck. Crew requirements have been increased by about ten from the early designs; space is also provided for another ten transient personnel.

Electronics: Space and weight are reserved for SLQ-25 Nixie torpedo countermeasures. However, no SLQ-32 installation is planned.

Guns: There are provisions to mount 20-mm Phalanx CIWS on the bow and after superstructure in wartime.

Names: The ANDREW J. HIGGINS honors an American industrialist who pioneered the development and construction of effective landing craft in World War II. (The destroyer HIGGINS/DDG 76 honors a U.S.

Marine Corps officer, Colonel William Higgins, kidnapped by terrorists in Lebanon in 1988 and subsequently murdered.)

FLEET OILERS: "CIMARRON" CLASS

Number	Name	Comm.	Status
AO 177	CIMARRON	1981	decomm./str. 15 Dec 1998
AO 178	MONONGAHELA	1981	decomm./str. 30 Sep 1999
AO 179	MERRIMACK	1981	decomm./str. 18 Dec 1998
AO 180	WILLAMETTE	1982	decomm./str. 30 Mar 1999
AO 186	PLATTE	1983	decomm./str. 30 June 1999

These were the last U.S. Navy fleet oilers in active commission. They were a class of five ships built to Navy (vice Maritime Administration) design. They could provide two complete refuelings to a conventional aircraft carrier and six to eight accompanying escort ships. All five ships were lengthened or "jumboized" in 1989–1992.

See 16th Edition/pages 237–239 for characteristics.

Classification: Hull numbers 182–185 were assigned to the Falcon-class transport tankers (T-AOT), and the USNS POTOMAC is T-AOT 181 (see chapter 23).

The KANAWHA at rest. The massive size of her superstructure is evident here. There is a helicopter control position atop the superstructure, aft of the funnel. (1997, Jürg Kürsener)

The RAPPAHANNOCK—the last fleet oiler constructed—pulls alongside the carrier KITTY HAWK (CV 63) during operations off the coast of Japan. The RAPPAHANNOCK is riding high in the water, indicating that she has little oil to transfer to the KITTY HAWK. (2000, U.S. Navy, PH3 John Sullivan)

FLEET OILERS: "NEOSHO" CLASS

Number	Name	Comm.	Notes
T-AO 143	NEOSHO	1954	OSIR 10 Aug 1992; str. 16 Feb 1994
T-AO 144	MISSISSINEWA	1955	OSIR 30 July 1991; str. 16 Feb 1994
T-AO 145	HASSAYAMPA	1955	OSIR 2 Oct 1991; str. 16 Feb 1994
T-AO 146	KAWISHIWI	1955	OSIR 31 July 1992; str. 7 Nov 1994
T-AO 147	TRUCKEE	1955	OSIR 21 Oct 1991; str. 18 July 1994
T-AO 148	PONCHATOULA	1956	OSIR 1 Apr 1992; str. 31 Aug 1992

These were the first fleet oilers built for the U.S. Navy after World War II. They were large, graceful, heavily armed ships, built to a Navy (vice Maritime Administration) design. They were configured as service squadron flagships. All were originally active Navy-manned ships; transferred to MSC for civilian manning in 1976–1980.

FLEET OILERS: "MISPILLION" CLASS

Number	Name	Comm.	Notes
T-AO 105	MISPILLION	1945	OSIR 8 Feb 1990; str. 15 Feb 1995
T-AO 106	NAVASOTA	1946	OSIR 2 Oct 1991; str. 2 Jan 1992
T-AO 107	PASSUMPSIC	1946	OSIR/str. 17 Dec 1991
T-AO 108	PAWCATUCK	1946	OSIR/str. 21 Sep 1991
T-AO 109	WACCAMAW	1946	OSIR/str. 11 Oct 1989

These were the last of a large class of twin-screw naval oilers built during World War II as Navy fleet oilers (Maritime Administration T3-S2-A1/A3 design). The above five ships comprised the A3 series. They were "jumboized" (enlarged) in the mid-1960s to increase their cargo capacity. All five were transferred from the active Navy to MSC with civilian manning in 1973–1975, subsequently taken out of service and transferred to the NDRF, and later stricken.

Class: A total of 23 ships of the T3 designs was delivered to the Navy (AO 51–64, 68–72, 97–100, and 105–109); see the CIMARRON class below.

Designation: The WACCAMAW was intended for conversion to a replenishment oiler (AOR 109); the conversion was not undertaken.

FLEET OILERS: "CIMARRON" CLASS

Number	Name	Comm.	Notes
AO 51	ASHTABULA	1943	decomm. 1982; str. 6 Sep 1991
T-AO 57	MARIAS	1944	OSIR 1982; str. 11 Dec 1992
T-AO 62	TALUGA	1944	OSIR 1983; str. 21 Feb 1992
AO 98	CALOOSAHATCHEE	1945	decomm. 1989; str. 18 July 1994
AO 99	CANISTEO	1945	decomm. 1989; str. 31 Aug 1992

These were fleet oilers of the T3-S2-A1 type. Three ships (Navy manned) were "jumboized" (enlarged) in the mid-1960s to increase their carrying capacity. Two ships were transferred to MSC operation in 1972–1973. All were assigned to the NDRF after being taken out of service.

POST–WORLD WAR II OILERS

War-built fleet oilers reached hull AO 109. The ex-German submarine tender DITHMARSCHEN (built in 1938) became the USS CONECUH (IX 301) after the war; her designation was later changed to AO 110 and subsequently, because of ordnance and stores capability, to AOR 110. (The AOR classification was established in 1952 as fleet replenishment tanker to provide "one stop" fuel and munitions replenishment. The classification AOR was reestablished as replenishment oiler in 1964.)

AO 111–142 were Mission-class T2 merchant tankers operated by the MSTS/MSC. The MISSION CAPISTRANO (AO 112) was converted to a sonar trials ship (AG 162).

AO 143–148 were the NEOSHO class, built specifically as naval fleet oilers (see above).

AO 149–152 were large tankers of the MAUMEE class built specifically for MSTS/MSC service and subsequently designated AOT (see chapter 23). The similar AMERICAN EXPLORER was built for merchant use, but upon completion was acquired by the Navy as AO 165.

AO 153–164 were commercial T2 tankers acquired during the 1956 Suez crisis for MSTS operations; they were stricken in 1957–1958.

AO hull numbers 166 and 167 were reserved for planned Mission-class "jumbo" conversions (i.e., civilian merchant tankers).

AO 168–176 were the Sealift-class tankers built for MSC operation (see chapter 23).

AO 177–180 and 186 are the CIMARRON class built specifically for naval service (see above).

AO 181 was assigned to the POTOMAC, constructed from portions of an earlier POTOMAC (AO 150) (see chapter 23).

AO 182–185 were merchant tankers taken over for naval use (see chapter 23).

AO 187–204 are the HENRY J. KAISER class (see above).

FAST COMBAT SUPPORT SHIPS

These ships are intended to operate as part of fast carrier battle groups, providing petroleum products, munitions, and other supplies to aircraft carriers and their screening surface combatants. In practice, they combine the functions of fleet oilers (AO) and ammunition ships (AE) and, to a limited extent, the combat stores ships (AFS).

Names: The AOE 1–4 are named for cities, and the AOE 6–10 carry the names of earlier supply ships (AE/AF/IX types).

FAST COMBAT SUPPORT SHIPS: IMPROVED DESIGN

Displacement:	48,000–50,000 tons full load
Length:	approx. 754⅓ feet (230.0 m) overall
Beam:	approx. 105 feet (32.0 m)
Draft:	approx. 37¾ (11.5 m)
Propulsion:	4 gas turbines (General Electric LM 2500) with electric drive; 2 shafts
Speed:	26 knots
Range:	
Manning:	
Helicopters:	3 UH-46 Sea Knight

An improved multi-product stores ship—tentatively designated AOE(V)—was being designed as a follow-on to the SUPPLY class. The new ship was to be slightly larger, with enhanced munitions-carrying capacity. Also, the AOE(V) was proposed as the first modern U.S. Navy ship to have electric drive.

The design effort was canceled in 1991. Sixteen AOE(V)s were listed in preliminary planning for the class, with the first unit to be requested in the fiscal 1993 budget, to be completed in 1997. These ships were to replace the ammunition ships (AE) of the NITRO and SURIBACHI classes and, subsequently, the combat stores ships (AFS) of the MARS and LYNESS classes.

4 FAST COMBAT SUPPORT SHIPS: "SUPPLY" CLASS

Number	Name	FY	Launched	Commissioned	Status
AOE 6	SUPPLY	87	6 Oct 1990	26 Feb 1994	**AA**
AOE 7	RAINIER	89	28 Sep 1991	1 Dec 1994	**PA**
AOE 8	ARCTIC	90	30 Oct 1993	11 Sep 1995	**AA**
AOE 10	BRIDGE	93	24 Aug 1996	31 Mar 1998	**PA**

Builders:	National Steel, San Diego, Calif.
Displacement:	19,700 tons light
	48,800 tons full load
Length:	730 feet (222.56 m) waterline
	754¾ feet (230.1 m) overall
Beam:	107 feet (32.6 m)
Draft:	39 feet (11.9 m)
Propulsion:	4 gas turbines (General Electric LM 2500); 100,000 shp; 2 shafts
Speed:	26 knots
Range:	
Manning:	AOE 6, 7 497 (27 officers + 470 enlisted)
	AOE 8 494 (27 officers + 467 enlisted)
	AOE 10 506 (27 officers + 479 enlisted)
Helicopters:	3 UH-46 Sea Knight
Missiles:	1 8-cell NATO Sea Sparrow launcher Mk 29
Guns:	2 25-mm Bushmaster cannon Mk 38 (2 single)
	2 20-mm Phalanx CIWS Mk 15 (2 multibarrel)
	4 .50-cal machine guns (4 single)
Radars:	SPS-64(V)9 navigation
	SPS-67(V) surface search
Fire control:	1 Mk 25 Target Acquisition System (TAS)
	2 Mk 95 missile FCS
EW systems:	SLQ-25 Nixie
	SLQ-32(V)3

These are large, multi-product replenishment ships. They are based on the SACRAMENTO design, the principal difference in the two classes being in their propulsion plants. Note that the later ships are smaller.

The lead ship, the SUPPLY, was laid down on 24 February 1989. The first three ships suffered major delays, caused mainly by delays in delivery of reduction gears, a major propulsion system component. All four ships were delivered behind schedule. Related to these delays has been a major increase in cost. In August 1991 the Navy stated that the ships will cost 30 percent more than original estimates.

Class: The AOE 9 was authorized in fiscal 1992; tentatively named CONECUH, her construction was deferred, and the funds were employed to pay for shipbuilding cost overruns. The ship was reauthorized in fiscal 1993 as the AOE 10.

Design: The cargo capacity is 156,000 barrels of petroleum products, plus 1,800 tons of munitions, 400 tons of refrigerated provisions, and 250 tons of dry stores.

This is the second class of U.S. Navy ships to be built with the so-called Level III collective protection features against Chemical-Biological-Radiological (CBR) attack, the first having been the ARLEIGH BURKE (DDG 51)-class destroyers. Level III provides the maximum protection possible within a ship, including berthing, medical, and control spaces.

Manning: In March 2000 the Navy announced that the SUPPLY would be assigned 17 Civil Service steward/utilitymen to carry out food service and laundry functions aboard the ship. This is believed to be the first time civilians have been assigned to the actual crew in a commissioned Navy ship (i.e., USS).

The program, which will replace 24 sailors normally assigned to the ship, will evaluate the feasibility of such assignments in the future. During the year-long trial, the SUPPLY was to deploy for about six months with the GEORGE WASHINGTON (CVN 73) battle group to the Mediterranean area. The SUPPLY is the only ship involved in the trial.

Names: The AOE 10 is named for the first U.S. Navy ship built from the keel up as a store ship, the AF 1; she, in turn, was named for Commodore Horatio Bridge, the first Chief of the Bureau of Provisions and Clothing, established in 1842, and a pioneer in fleet supply.

The AOE 7 originally was named PAUL HAMILTON; while the AOE 7 under construction, that name was assigned to the destroyer DDG 60.

The RAINIER at anchor. The ship's broad stern is topped by a helicopter deck; there is a two-bay helicopter hangar, topped by a helicopter control station. (1996, Giorgio Arra)

The ARCTIC sails the Ionian Sea while supporting the THEODORE ROOSEVELT (CVN 71) battle group. The large AOEs were designed specifically to operate with carrier battle groups, providing fuels, provisions, and munitions in forward areas. (1999, U.S. Navy, JO1 Andrew Thomas)

The RAINIER at speed. She has a Phalanx CIWS forward, another aft, and other close-in defensive weapons, including a NATO Sea Sparrow launcher. SLQ-32(V)3 ECM antennas are atop the bridge wings. These are the only auxiliary ships with a self-defense capability. (1996, Giorgio Arra)

4 FAST COMBAT SUPPORT SHIPS: "SACRAMENTO" CLASS

Number	Name	FY	Launched	Commissioned	Status
AOE 1	SACRAMENTO	61	14 Sep 1963	14 Mar 1964	**PA**
AOE 2	CAMDEN	63	29 May 1965	1 Apr 1967	**PA**
AOE 3	SEATTLE	65	2 Mar 1968	5 Apr 1969	**AA**
AOE 4	DETROIT	66	21 June 1969	28 Mar 1970	**AA**

Builders:	Puget Sound Naval Shipyard, Bremerton, Wash., except AOE 2 at New York Shipbuilding, Camden, N.J.
Displacement:	18,700 tons light
	53,600 tons full load
Length:	770 feet (234.75 m) waterline
	794¾ feet (242.4 m) overall
Beam:	107 feet (32.6 m)
Draft:	38 feet (11.6 m)
Propulsion:	2 steam turbines (General Electric); 100,000 shp; 2 shafts
Boilers:	4 600-psi (41.7-kg/cm^2) (Combustion Engineering)
Speed:	27.5 knots (26 knots sustained)
Range:	10,000 n.miles (18,520 km) at 17 knots
	6,000 n.miles (11,112 km) at 26 knots
Manning:	AOE 1, 2 568 (27 officers + 541 enlisted)
	AOE 3, 4 569 (27 officers + 542 enlisted)
Helicopters:	2 UH-46 Sea Knight
Missiles:	1 8-cell NATO Sea Sparrow launcher Mk 29
Guns:	2 20-mm Phalanx CIWS Mk 15 (2 multibarrel)
	4 .50-cal machine guns (4 single)
Radars:	SPS-10F surface search
	SPS-40E air search in AOE 1, 2
	SPS-64(V)9
Fire control:	2 Mk 95 missile FCS
	1 Mk 23 TAS in AOE 3
EW systems:	SLQ-25 Nixie
	SLQ-32(V)2 or 5

These are the world's largest underway replenishment ships, designed to provide a carrier battle group with full fuels, munitions, dry and frozen provisions, and other supplies. Plans to modernize (SLEP) these ships beginning about FY 2000 have been dropped.

Class: The AOE 5 of this class was planned for the fiscal 1968 program but canceled on 4 November 1968.

Design: SCB No. 196. These ships can carry 156,000 barrels of fuels, 2,100 tons of munitions, 250 tons of dry stores, and 250 tons of refrigerated stores. They have highly automated cargo-handling equipment.

A large helicopter deck is fitted aft with a three-bay hangar for VERTREP helicopters. Each bay is 47 to 52 feet (14.3 to 15.85 m) long, 17 to 19 feet (5.2 to 5.8 m) wide, and 18 to 18½ feet (5.5 to 5.6 m) high.

Electronics: The hull has provision for the SQS-26 sonar, but it has not been installed. The earlier WLR-1 ECM system has been replaced by the SLQ-32 system.

Engineering: The first two ships were provided with the main propulsion machinery produced for the canceled battleship KENTUCKY (BB 66).

Guns: As built, these ships were armed with eight 3-inch guns in twin mounts and associated Mk 56 GFCS. The armament was reduced in the mid-1970s and a NATO Sea Sparrow launcher was installed forward. The remaining 3-inch guns have been removed, with two Phalanx CIWS being fitted to each ship.

The SACRAMENTO, the first of the massive AOE "one-stop" replenishment ships. These are larger and considerably more capable than the AOR-type replenishment ships, all of which have been retired. (1995, Giorgio Arra)

The SACRAMENTO in the western Pacific, under way at slow speed. The superstructures of the newer SUPPLY-class ships are considerably different from the first four AOEs. (1995, Giorgio Arra)

Details of the SACRAMENTO, showing the NATO Sea Sparrow launcher forward, the two associated Mk 95 FCS antennas mounted atop the bridge, and, visible atop the starboard bridge wing, the SLQ-32 ECM antenna. The SUPPLY class has a lattice mast abaft the bridge in place of the SACRAMENTO's pole mast. (1995, Giorgio Arra)

REPLENISHMENT OILERS

These ships combined the capability of a fleet oiler (AO) with a limited capability for the services of an ammunition ship (AE) and combat stores ship (AFS).

REPLENISHMENT OILERS: "WICHITA" CLASS

Number	Name	Comm.	Notes
AOR 1	WICHITA	1969	decomm. 12 Mar 1993; str. 15 Feb 1995
AOR 2	MILWAUKEE	1969	decomm. 27 Jan 1994; str. 8 Apr 1997
AOR 3	KANSAS CITY	1970	decomm. 7 Oct 1994; str. 8 Apr 1997
AOR 4	SAVANNAH	1970	decomm. 28 July 1995; str. 29 Oct 1998
AOR 5	WABASH	1971	decomm. 30 Sep 1994; str. 8 Apr 1997
AOR 6	KALAMAZOO	1973	decomm. 16 Aug 1996; str. 29 Oct 1998
AOR 7	ROANOKE	1976	decomm./str. 6 Oct 1995

These are smaller variations of the AOE-type ships. All were decommissioned and stricken within a few years of the end of the Cold War.

The AORs were Navy-manned ships and were armed; all had hangars and flight decks to support two UH-46 Sea Knight cargo helicopters for vertical replenishment operations.

See 16th Edition/pages 243–244 for characteristics.

REPAIR SHIPS

These ships provided major repairs to ship hulls, machinery, and equipment. They did not carry the weapons and specialized stores and parts stocked on destroyer, submarine, and seaplane tenders.

The Navy planned a new class of repair ships to replace the VULCAN-class ships, with the lead ship included in the fiscal 1994 shipbuilding program and then slipped to fiscal 1998. This class was to eventually replace older destroyer tenders (AD) as well as the VULCAN-class repair ships.

In the event, the plan was canceled in the early 1990s when the decision was made to dispose of all repair ships, as well as most of the tenders. Only two large repair ships, the VULCAN and JASON, were in active U.S. Navy service in the 1990s.

TABLE 22-9. REPAIR SHIPS

Number	Name	Comm.	Notes
VULCAN class (4)			
AR 5	VULCAN	1941	decomm. 30 Sep 1991; str. 28 July 1992
AR 6	AJAX	1943	decomm. 31 Dec 1986; str. 16 May 1989
AR 7	HECTOR	1944	decomm. 31 Mar 1987; to Pakistan 20 Apr 1989
AR 8	JASON	1944	decomm./str. 24 June 1995
AR 9–21	World War II program		
Reclassified destroyer tenders (3)			
AR 22	KLONDIKE (ex-AD 22)	1945	stricken 1974
AR 23	MARKAB (ex-AD 21)	1941	stricken 1976
AR 24–27	not used		
AR 28	GRAND CANYON (AD 28)	1946	stricken 1978

World War II repair ships reached hull AR 21. Three destroyer tenders (AD) were reclassified as repair ships after the war, indicating their employment in general repair and support work. Two retained their AD hull numbers.

The large VULCAN-class ships were highly capable repair ships, although they lacked the ability to support more-sophisticated weapon and electronic systems. These ships served well into the Cold War era. The VULCAN class was one of three series of large tender-type ships begun in the late 1930s, the others being the DIXIE (AD 14) and FULTON (AS 11) classes. The JASON was completed as a heavy hull repair ship (ARH 1); she was reclassified as AR 8 in 1957.

Numerous specialized repair ships were built/converted during World War II; none remain on the NVR. Most of these ships were converted from LSTs. Their designations were:

ARB	battle damage
ARG	internal combustion engines
ARL	landing craft
ARV	aircraft
ARVA	aircraft—airframes
ARVE	aircraft—engines

CABLE REPAIR SHIPS

The Navy's cable ships support SOSUS and other underwater cable activities. In addition, cable ships conduct special oceanographic and acoustic surveys in support of the Naval Electronic Systems Command under the Oceanographer of the Navy. (Commercial ships are also used under contract to support U.S. seafloor cable installations.)

Names: Cable ships are assigned mythological names.

1 CABLE REPAIR SHIP: "ZEUS"

Number	Name	FY	Launched	In service	Status
T-ARC 7	ZEUS	79	30 Oct 1982	19 Mar 1984	**MSC-P**

Builders:	National Steel and Shipbuilding, San Diego, Calif.
Displacement:	8,297 tons light
	14,225 tons full load
Length:	454 feet (138.4 m) waterline
	502½ feet (153.2 m) overall
Beam:	73⅙ feet (22.3 m)
Draft:	23⅝ feet (7.3 m)
Propulsion:	diesel-electric (5 General Motors EMD diesel engines); 12,500 shp; 2 shafts
Speed:	15.8 knots
Range:	10,000 n.miles (18,520 km) at 15 knots
Manning:	53 civilian + 6 Navy (enlisted) + 15 civilian technicians
Helicopters:	no facilities
Radars:	2 . . . navigation

The ZEUS was the first cable ship built specifically for use by the U.S. Navy. Two ships of this type were planned to replace the now-stricken THOR and AEOLUS. The second ship of the class was planned for the FY 1986 budget, but was not requested.

The ZEUS was delayed because of design and construction problems; her keel was laid down 1 June 1981. She is operated by MSC under sponsorship of the Naval Space and Warfare Systems Command.

The Navy personnel are communications specialists.

Design: The ship can lay up to 1,000 miles (1,610 km) of cable in depths down to 10 miles (16 km).

Electronics: The ZEUS is fitted with the SSN-2 precision seafloor navigation system.

Engineering: Two 1,200-hp bow and two 1,200-hp stern thrusters are fitted for station keeping while handling cables.

The ZEUS is the only cable ship to have been constructed specifically for U.S. naval use. Commercial cable ships also support the Navy's SOSUS seafloor acoustic detection system and Air Force missile impact sensors on the ocean floor. The ZEUS has cable sheaves in her bow and stern, and massive holds for the stowage of cable. (1991, Giorgio Arra)

The stern cable sheaves of the ZEUS are visible in this view. The ship does not have a helicopter platform. (1990, Giorgio Arra)

TABLE 22-10.   CABLE REPAIR SHIPS

Number	Name	Comm.*	Notes
ARC 1	Protunus (ex-LSM 275)	1952	to Portugal 1959
T-ARC 2	Neptune	1953	OSIR 24 Sep 1991; str. 20 Aug 1992
T-ARC 3	Aeolus (ex-AKA 47)	1955	stricken 1985
T-ARC 4	Thor (ex-AKA 49)	1956	stricken 1978
ARC 5	Yamacraw (ex-WARC 333)	1948	stricken 1965
T-ARC 6	Albert J. Myer	1963	OSIR 13 Feb 1994; str. 7 Nov 1994

* Commissioned or in service as cable ships.

A war-built landing ship completed in 1944, the ARC 1, after brief service as a cable ship, was transferred to Portugal, where she was converted to a diving tender.

Two war-built attack cargo ships were converted to cable ships; new names were assigned. The Neptune and Myer were built-for-the-purpose cable ships initially intended for Army use. Both ships were completed in 1946 and laid up in Maritime Administration reserve. The Myer was acquired by the Navy in 1952 and the Neptune in 1953 to support the SOSUS program; they were placed in Navy commission (as ARC 2 and 6) and operated as commissioned ships (USS). The Myer was transferred outright to the Navy and the Neptune on loan until permanently acquired in 1966. Both ships were transferred to MSC operation (as T-ARCs) in 1973.

The ex-Army Maj Gen Arthur Murray was acquired by the Navy in 1945 as the USS Trapper (ACM 9). She was transferred to the Coast Guard in 1948 and renamed Yamacraw (WARC 333). She was then retransferred to the Navy in 1959, commissioned as ARC 5, and was engaged largely as an underwater research ship.[7]

SALVAGE SHIPS

These ships are fitted for deep-sea salvage and towing operations. In addition to naval salvage activities, the Navy has a national responsibility for the salvaging of all U.S. ships, both government and private (Public Law 80-513). These ships, along with the ATS-type tugs, are the principal diver support ships of the Navy.

Names: Salvage ships are named for terms related to diving and salvage activities.

SALVAGE SHIPS: NEW CONSTRUCTION

A new class of ARS-type ships was planned to replace the older ARS/ASR-type ships in the salvage, heavy towing, and diving roles. The lead ship was scheduled for authorization in the fiscal 1994 shipbuilding program. However, the program was canceled in the early 1990s.

4 SALVAGE SHIPS: "SAFEGUARD" CLASS

Number	Name	FY	Launched	Commissioned	Status
ARS 50	Safeguard	81	12 Nov 1983	17 Aug 1985	PA
ARS 51	Grasp	82	21 Apr 1984	14 Dec 1985	AA
ARS 52	Salvor	82	28 July 1984	14 June 1986	PA
ARS 53	Grapple	83	8 Dec 1984	15 Nov 1986	AA

Builders:	Peterson Builders, Sturgeon Bay, Wisc.
Displacement:	2,725 tons light
	3,193 tons full load
Length:	240 feet (73.15 m) waterline
	254^{11}/$_{12}$ feet (77.7 m) overall
Beam:	51 feet (15.5 m)
Draft:	15^{5}/$_{12}$ feet (4.7 m)
Propulsion:	4 geared diesel engines (Caterpillar D399 BTA); 4,200 bhp; 2 shafts (Kort-nozzle propellers)
Speed:	13.5 knots
Range:	8,000 n.miles (14,816 km) at 12 knots
Manning:	110 (7 officers + 103 enlisted)
Helicopters:	VERTREP area
Guns:	2 .50-cal machine guns (2 single)
Radars:	Raytheon 1900 navigation
	SPS-64(V)9 navigation

These ships replaced several of the long-serving salvage ships of the Escape class in the salvage and towing roles.

The Safeguard is homeported in Sasebo, Japan; the only other U.S. auxiliary ships homeported outside of the continental United States are the submarine tenders Emory S. Land and Frank Cable.

Design: The ships are fitted for towing and heavy lift, with a limited diving support capability. A 40-ton-capacity boom is fitted aft and a 7.5-ton boom is located forward.

Engineering: A 500-hp bow thruster is provided.

Operational: In July 1990 the Grasp salvaged an S-3B Viking anti-submarine aircraft off the coast of Virginia from a depth of more than 10,000 feet (3,050 m). The aircraft had crashed at sea during a takeoff from the carrier John F. Kennedy (CV 67) on 7 October 1989.

Subsequently, the Grasp had a major role in the salvage of TWA flight 800 (a Boeing 747) off Long Island, N.Y., in 1996 and the recovery of the plane and remains of John F. Kennedy, Jr., off Martha's Vineyard, Mass., on 16 July 1999.

The Grapple helped to recover debris from the EgyptAir flight 990 (a Boeing 767) that crashed off Rhode Island on 31 October 1999.

The Grapple returns to Newport, R.I., after recovering the cockpit voice recorder from the crash site of the EgyptAir Flight 990. These are the last tug/salvage/rescue-type ships to be manned by U.S. naval personnel. They are highly capable ships. (1999, U.S. Navy, PH2 Brian McFadden)

The Salvor's stern aspect shows the ship's work area on the fantail. (1996, Giorgio Arra)

---

7. ACM = auxiliary minelayer.

The SALVOR shows the unusual SAFEGUARD-class design. The ship's bow and stern facilitate deep-sea, four-point mooring to keep the ship over a salvage target. There are booms forward and aft, with a pair of work-boats stowed amidships. (1996, Giorgio Arra)

SALVAGE AND RESCUE SHIPS: "EDENTON" CLASS

Number	Name	Comm.	Notes
ATS 1	EDENTON	1971	decomm. 29 Mar 1996; to Coast Guard
ATS 2	BEAUFORT	1972	decomm. 8 Mar 1996; to S. Korea 29 Aug 1996
ATS 3	BRUNSWICK	1972	decomm. 8 Mar 1996; to S. Korea 29 Aug 1996

These British-built oceangoing tugs had extensive salvage and diving capabilities. They are one of two classes of auxiliary ships to be constructed in British shipyards for the U.S. Navy, the other being the two ships of the CHAUVENET (T-AGS 29) class. The more-recently acquired British-built store ships (T-AFS) were constructed for RFA service.

The EDENTON has been resurrected as the Coast Guard cutter ALEX HALEY (WMEC 39), being transferred to that service on 18 November 1997. The BEAUFORT and BRUNSWICK were transferred to South Korea on 29 August 1996; both were stricken on 12 December 1996 and delivered in July 1997.

See 16th Edition/p. 248 for characteristics.

Classification: ATS originally indicated salvage tug; it was changed to salvage and rescue ship on 16 February 1971.

SALVAGE SHIPS: "DIVER" AND "BOLSTER" CLASSES

Number	Name	Comm.	Notes
ARS 8	PRESERVER*	1944	decomm. 7 Aug 1992; str. 16 Mar 1994
ARS 38	BOLSTER*	1945	decomm./str. 24 Sep 1994
ARS 39	CONSERVER	1945	decomm./str. 1 Apr 1994
ARS 40	HOIST*	1945	decomm./str. 30 Sep 1994
ARS 41	OPPORTUNE	1945	decomm. 30 Apr 1993; str. 5 Aug 1993
ARS 42	RECLAIMER*	1945	decomm./str. 16 Sep 1994
ARS 43	RECOVERY	1946	decomm./str. 30 Sep 1994

* ships assigned to the Naval Reserve Force prior to disposal.

Seven ARS-type ships survived into the 1990s, testimony to the excellence of their design. Four ships were transferred to the Naval Reserve Force (NRF) in 1979–1986 and manned by composite active-reserve crews; they are indicated with asterisks above. The PRESERVER and CONSERVER were decommissioned on 30 September 1986; both ships were recommissioned on 26 September 1987 for salvage and anti-drug patrol duties in the Caribbean. The PRESERVER then shifted to NRF in exchange for the HOIST on 30 April 1989, with the latter returning to active service.

Class: Originally these two similar classes included 23 ships: ARS 5–9, 19–28, 33, 34, and 38–43 (plus the canceled ARS 44–49). The

lead ship of this design was the DIVER (ARS 5); after she was sold in 1949, the Navy listed ESCAPE as the class name. The BOLSTER and later ships were considered a separate class, but the differences were minimal (e.g., beam, fuel capacity).

Two ships of these classes were converted to oceanographic ships: the CHAIN (AGOR 17, ex-ARS 20) and ARGO (AGOR 18, ex-SNATCH/ARS 27). Three other ships served with the Coast Guard: ESCAPE (ARS 6/WMEC 6), SHACKLE (ARS 9/WMEC 167), and SEIZE (ARS 26/WMEC 168).

SUBMARINE TENDERS

Submarine tenders have extensive maintenance shops for various submarine systems and equipment, as well as considerable weapon and provision storage. Tenders also provide hospital facilities, as well as extra berths for submarine relief personnel.

These are the only tender-type ships now in active U.S. Navy service.

Names: Submarine tenders had a variety of name sources—mostly mythological figures (PROTEUS) and submarine pioneers (SIMON LAKE). The CANOPUS (AS 34) remembered an earlier CANOPUS (AS 9) lost in the Philippines in 1942.

3 SUBMARINE TENDERS: "EMORY S. LAND" CLASS

Number	Name	FY	Launched	Commissioned	Status
AS 39	EMORY S. LAND	72	4 May 1977	7 July 1979	**AA**
AS 40	FRANK CABLE	73	14 Jan 1978	5 Feb 1980	**PA**
AS 41	McKEE	77	16 Feb 1980	15 Aug 1981	AR; decomm. 1 Sep 1999

Builders:	Lockheed Shipbuilding and Construction, Seattle, Wash.
Displacement:	13,842 tons light
	22,650 tons full load
Length:	620 feet (189 m) waterline
	645⅔ feet (196.9 m) overall
Beam:	85 feet (25.9 m)
Draft:	25½ feet (7.8 m)
Propulsion:	1 steam turbine (De Laval); 20,000 shp; 1 shaft
Boilers:	2 650-psi (43.6-kg/cm²) (Combustion Engineering)
Speed:	20 knots (18 knots sustained)
Range:	7,600 n.miles (14,075 km) at 18 knots
Manning:	AS 39, 41 620 (65 officers + 555 enlisted)
	AS 40 619 (64 officers + 555 enlisted)
Flag:	69 (25 officers + 44 enlisted)
Helicopters:	VERTREP area
Guns:	4 20-mm cannon Mk 67 (4 single)
	2 40-mm grenade launchers Mk 19 (2 single)
Radars:	SPS-10 surface search
	1 . . . navigation

Two of these ships are the only tenders remaining in active U.S. Navy service. These are improved versions of the L. Y. SPEAR–class tenders, with the later ships fitted specifically to support the LOS ANGELES (SSN 688)-class attack submarines. Up to four SSNs can be supported alongside simultaneously.

The LAND is homeported at La Maddalena, Sardinia, supporting U.S. Sixth Fleet submarines operating in the Mediterranean; the CABLE is homeported at Guam, supporting U.S. ships assigned to the Seventh Fleet in the Western Pacific. The only other U.S. auxiliary ship homeported outside of the continental United States is the salvage ship SAFEGUARD at Sasebo, Japan.

The McKEE was "ceremonially" decommissioned at Guam on 16 July 1999; the ship then sailed for Norfolk, Va., where she was officially decommissioned on 1 September 1999.

Design: SCB No. 737. Fitted with a 30-ton-capacity crane and two 5-ton traveling cranes. Medical facilities include an operating room, dental clinic, and 23-bed ward.

The Emory S. Land departs Norfolk, Va., for the Mediterranean, where she is now homeported. She tends to U.S. submarines in the Sixth Fleet, as well as on occasion to the needs of surface ships. The Land and Frank Cable are the only tender-type ships now in active U.S. Navy service. (1999, Jürg Kürsener)

The Frank Cable, homeported at Guam, provides support for U.S. submarines and surface ships operating in the Western Pacific. Major support of U.S. ships in "WestPac" is accomplished in Japanese shipyards. In this view, the Cable's boats and cranes are stowed. (1996, Giorgio Arra)

SUBMARINE TENDERS: "L. Y. SPEAR" CLASS

Number	Name	Comm.	Notes
AS 36	L. Y. Spear	1970	decomm. 6 Sep 1996; str. 31 May 1999
AS 37	Dixon	1971	decomm. 15 Dec 1995; str. 18 Mar 1996

These were the U.S. Navy's first submarine tenders designed specifically to support nuclear-propelled attack submarines. The Dixon was placed "Out of Commission, Special" on 7 August 1995 and "Out of Commission, Full" on the above date. See 16th Edition/pages 248–250 for characteristics.

Class: The AS 38 of this design was authorized in the fiscal 1969 budget but was not built because of funding shortages in other ship programs; the ship was canceled on 27 March 1969.

1 SUBMARINE TENDER: "SIMON LAKE" CLASS

Number	Name	Comm.	Notes
AS 33	Simon Lake	1964	AR; decomm. 10 Sep 1999
AS 34	Canopus	1965	decomm. 30 Nov 1996; str. 30 May 1995

Builders:	Puget Sound Naval Shipyard, Bremerton, Wash.
Displacement:	12,000 tons light
	19,934 tons full load
Length:	643¾ feet (196.3 m) overall
Beam:	85 feet (25.9 m)
Draft:	28½ feet (8.7 m)
Propulsion:	1 steam turbine (De Laval); 20,000 shp; 1 shaft
Boilers:	2 650-psi (43.6-kg/cm²) (Combustion Engineering)
Speed:	18 knots
Range:	7,600 n.miles (14,075 km) at 18 knots
Manning:	612 (62 officers + 550 enlisted)
Helicopters:	VERTREP area
Guns:	4 20-mm cannon Mk 67 (4 single)
Radars:	LN-66 navigation
	SPS-10 surface search

These were two of the four tenders constructed specifically to service fleet ballistic missile submarines. In addition, the World War II–built tender Proteus was converted to support SSBNs.

Class: The AS 35 of this design was authorized in fiscal 1965 but construction was deferred and the ship was not built. That ship would have provided one tender for each of five Polaris SSBN squadrons, with a sixth tender in overhaul or transit. However, the Polaris SSBN program was reduced from the proposed 45 to 41 submarines and only four squadrons were formed, with four tenders built (AS 31–34) plus one conversion (AS 19).

Operational: The Simon Lake was the last submarine tender to be based at Holy Loch, Scotland, where the U.S. Navy maintained an SSBN base from 1961 until 1992. Subsequently she was homeported

at La Maddalena as a tender for U.S. submarines operating in the Mediterranean (relieved by the Emory S. Land).

SUBMARINE TENDERS: "HUNLEY" CLASS

Number	Name	Comm.	Notes
AS 31	Hunley	1962	decomm. 30 Sep 1994; str. 30 May 1995
AS 32	Holland	1963	decomm./str. 30 Sep 1996

These were the first tenders designed specifically to service fleet ballistic missile submarines. The Holland was placed "Out of Commission, Special" on 13 April 1996 and "Out of Commission, Full" on the above date. See 16th Edition/page 252 for characteristics.

TABLE 22-11. POST–WORLD WAR II SUBMARINE TENDERS

Number	Name	Comm.	Notes
Fulton class (7)			
AS 11	Fulton	1941	decomm. 17 May 1991; str. 20 Dec 1991
AS 12	Sperry	1942	stricken 1982
AS 13, 15	converted cargo ships		
Fulton class (continued)			
AS 15	Bushnell	1943	stricken 1980
AS 16	Howard W. Gilmore	1944	stricken 1980
AS 17	Nereus	1960	stricken 1971
AS 18	Orion	1943	decomm./str. 30 Sep 1993
AS 19	Proteus	1944	to IX 518 (see notes)
AS 20–26	converted cargo ships		
AS 27–30	redesignated AD 30–33		
AS 31, 32	Hunley class		
AS 33–35	Simon Lake class		
AS 36–38	L. Y. Spear class		
AS 39–41	Emory S. Land class		

Submarine tenders reached hull number AS 30 during World War II. The long-serving Fulton-class tenders were similar to the contemporary Dixie (AD 14)-class destroyer tenders and Vulcan (AR 5)-class repair ships. The ships had been modernized but had a limited capability to support nuclear-propelled attack submarines.

The Proteus was rebuilt and lengthened in 1959–1960 to service Polaris missile submarines and served in that role at Holy Loch, Scotland; Rota, Spain; and Apra Harbor, Guam. She then served as a general repair ship at Diego Garcia. She was decommissioned and stricken on 30 September 1992, but reinstated on the Naval Vessel Register on 1 February 1994 as the IX 518 (see chapter 24).

The Navy is retaining two submarine tenders, including the Simon Lake *(above),* and two destroyer tenders laid up in reserve. The Lake was one of four tenders built and one converted specially to support ballistic missile submarines (SSBN). (1995, Leo Van Ginderen)

SUBMARINE RESCUE SHIPS

All submarine rescue ships have been stricken. These ships carried out general salvage and diving duties and were configured to carry the McCann submarine rescue chamber. The large PIGEON and ORTOLAN also could carry two of the Deep Submergence Rescue Vehicles (DSRV; see chapter 12) and were fitted with the fleet's most advanced deep diving system (Mk II).

SUBMARINE RESCUE SHIPS: "PIGEON" CLASS

Number	Name	Comm.	Notes
ASR 21	PIGEON	1973	decomm./str. 31 Aug 1992
ASR 22	ORTOLAN	1973	decomm./str. 30 Mar 1995

These ships were constructed specifically to carry DSRVs and to support deep-ocean diving operations with the Mk II deep-dive system. They were large catamaran ships. Their completion was delayed by problems in design, construction, and fitting out.

The PIGEON class was developed after the loss of the submarine THRESHER (SSN 593) in 1963 to provide an ASR/DSRV force for submarine rescue down to the collapse depth of contemporary submarines; up to ten ASRs were planned, but delays and funding constraints reduced the program to two ships. (The DSRVs also are carried by SSNs.)

SUBMARINE RESCUE SHIPS: "CHANTICLEER" CLASS

Number	Name	Comm.	Notes
ASR 9	FLORIKAN	1943	decomm. 2 Aug 1991; str. 3 Sep 1991
ASR 13	KITTIWAKE	1946	decomm./str. 30 Sep 1994
ASR 14	PETREL	1946	decomm. 30 Aug 1991; str. 9 Oct 1991
ASR 15	SUNBIRD	1950	decomm./str. 30 Sep 1993

These were the last of a series of large, tug-type ships fitted for salvage and helium-oxygen diving operations. They had a limited submarine rescue capability employing the McCann chamber. The first ASRs were converted Bird-class minesweepers built in World War I, hence the fowl names for these ships.

The SUNBIRD was accepted by the Navy on 15 January 1947 and towed (inactivated) to the Charleston Naval Shipyard; she was not commissioned for 3½ years.

Class: There were originally seven ships in this class: ASR 7–11, 13, and 14 (plus the canceled ASR 15–18). The ASR 12, 19, and 20 were converted fleet tugs (ATF 99, 164, and 165, respectively). The ASR 1–6 were converted World War I–built minesweepers.

OCEANGOING TUGS

The Navy uses primarily harbor tugs to handle port tug duties (see chapter 24). The ATS-series salvage and rescue ships (formerly salvage tugs) are listed with salvage ships in this chapter (see page 269).

Names: Tugs have Indian tribe names.

7 FLEET TUGS: "POWHATAN" CLASS

Number	Name	FY	Launched	In service	Status
T-ATF 166	POWHATAN	75	24 June 1978	15 June 1979	on loan
T-ATF 167	NARRAGANSETT	75	28 Nov 1978	9 Jan 1979	on loan
T-ATF 168	CATAWBA	75	22 Sep 1979	28 May 1980	**MSC-P**
T-ATF 169	NAVAJO	75	20 Dec 1979	13 June 1980	**MSC-P**
T-ATF 170	MOHAWK	78	5 Apr 1980	16 Oct 1980	**MSC-A**
T-ATF 171	SIOUX	78	30 Oct 1980	12 May 1981	**MSC-P**
T-ATF 172	APACHE	78	20 Dec 1980	30 July 1981	**MSC-A**

Builders:	Marinette Marine, Wisc.
Displacement:	2,000 tons standard
	2,260 tons full load
Length:	225¹¹⁄₁₂ feet (68.9 m) waterline
	240¹⁄₁₂ feet (73.2 m) overall
Beam:	42 feet (12.8 m)
Draft:	15 feet (4.6 m)
Propulsion:	diesel-electric (2 General Motors EMD 20 645X7 diesel engines); 4,500 shp; 2 shafts (Kort-nozzle propellers)
Speed:	15 knots
Range:	10,000 n.miles (18,520 km) at 13 knots
Manning:	16 civilian + 4 Navy (enlisted) + 20 transients
Helicopters:	VERTREP area
Radars:	SPS-53 surface search
	Raytheon TM 1660/12S navigation

These are oceangoing tugs based on a commercial design. They have replaced the war-built ATFs in the active fleet. The new ATF differs from the ASR and ATS types because it lacks the salvage and diving equipment of the earlier ships and has a limited towing capability. A portable Mk 1 Mod 1 diving/decompression module can be loaded on the stern of these ships.

The POWHATAN was leased to a commercial salvage firm, the Donjon Marine Co. of Hillside, N.J., on 26 February 1999 for a period of five years. The wheel house was reconfigured for civilian use, and other, minor modifications have been made.

The NARRAGANSETT was leased on 15 October 1999.

Design: SCB No. 744. These craft are easily distinguished by their side-by-side funnels and low, open sterns. The Navy personnel are communications specialists; the transients are salvage and diving specialists. There is a 10-ton-capacity crane.

In wartime, two 20-mm guns and two .50-cal machine guns can be fitted.

Engineering: The ships have a 300-hp bow thruster.

The APACHE, the last fleet tug built for the U.S. Navy. Most Navy ocean towing and salvage operations are undertaken by civilian ships under Navy charter. Two of the POWHATAN-class ATFs have been loaned to commercial firms that operate them under MSC contracts. (1999, Leo Van Ginderen)

The MOHAWK under way with several containers—and the ship's gangway—on the open stern. There is a crane amidships. These are most useful ships, limited only by their small numbers. (1996, Leo Van Ginderen)

FLEET TUGS: "CHEROKEE" CLASS

Number	Name	Comm.	Notes
ATF 91	SENECA	1943	str. 1985; trials ship (immobilized)
ATF 105	MOCTOBI	1944	decomm. 1985; str. 7 Feb 1995
ATF 110	QUAPAW	1944	decomm. 1985; str. 26 Jan 1995
ATF 113	TAKELMA	1944	decomm. 20 Feb 1992; str. 30 June 1992
ATF 149	ATAKAPA	1944	decomm. 1981; str. 21 Feb 1992
ATF 158	MOSOPELEA	1945	decomm. 1981; str. 21 Feb 1992
ATF 159	PAIUTE	1945	decomm. 7 Aug 1992; str. 14 Feb 1995
ATF 160	PAPAGO	1945	decomm. 28 July 1992; str. 14 Feb 1995

These were the last of a class of 48 large oceangoing tugs, many of which saw extensive combat service in World War II. All of the above ships were laid up in the NDRF after being decommissioned except for the SENECA, which was reacquired from the NDRF on 21 November 1985 for use as an immobilized trials craft at the David Taylor Research Center, Annapolis, Md.

The PAIUTE was decommissioned on 23 August 1985 and the PAPAGO on 28 June 1985. They were recommissioned into active naval service for anti-drug patrols in the Caribbean on 23 August 1985 and 28 June 1985, respectively, and again decommissioned in 1992.

Ships of this class served in the U.S. Coast Guard as well as several foreign navies.

Class: The AT 64–76 and 81–118 were built to the same basic design, the principal differences being in their engineering plant. The class was officially known as the CHEROKEE (ATF 66) class after the loss of the NAVAJO (AT 64) in 1943 and the SEMINOLE (AT 65) in 1942. Later ships are unofficially referred to as the ABNAKI (ATF 96) class.

Classification: These ships all were ordered with the AT designation. The AT 66 and later ships were changed to ATF on 15 May 1944.

AVIATION LOGISTIC SHIPS

These ships provide maintenance and logistic support for aircraft in forward areas. The AVB 3 and 4 are operated by MSC with civilian crews.

The previous AVB 1 and 2 were tank landing ships converted to support land-based patrol aircraft from unimproved airfields and seaplanes in the Mediterranean area; they were Navy manned in the AVB role. The ALAMEDA COUNTY (LST 32) became the AVB 1 and, after she was stricken in 1962, the TALLAHATCHIE COUNTY (LST 1154) became the AVB 2.

Names: The current aviation logistic ships are named for aviation pioneers. (The two LST/AVB conversions retained their landing ship names.)

2 AVIATION LOGISTIC SUPPORT SHIPS: "SEABRIDGE" CLASS

Number	Name	Built	In service	Status
T-AVB 3	WRIGHT	1970	14 May 1986	MSC-ROS-A
T-AVB 4	CURTISS	1969	18 Aug 1987	MSC-ROS-P

Builders:	Ingalls Shipbuilding, Pascagoula, Miss.
Displacement:	12,409 tons light
	27,580 tons full load
Length:	559⅝ feet (170.7 m) waterline
	600 ¹¹⁄₁₂ feet (183.2 m) overall
Beam:	90 feet (27.4 m)
Draft:	34 feet (10.4 m)
Propulsion:	2 steam turbines (General Electric); 30,000 shp; 1 shaft
Boilers:	2 (Combustion Engineering)
Speed:	23.6 knots
Range:	9,000 n.miles (16,668 km) at 23.6 knots
Manning:	37 civilian
Troops:	300+
Helicopters:	landing area (forward)
Radars:	2 navigation

These ships were converted from RO/RO-container ships to provide support for Marine aviation in forward areas. The ships are normally at ports in the United States and partially loaded with a Marine intermediate maintenance unit; the WRIGHT is normally based at Philadelphia, Pa., and the CURTISS at Port Hueneme, Calif. During war or crisis periods, the remainder of the unit and personnel would be loaded on board and the ships deployed to forward areas to support Marine tactical aircraft.

The majority of the maintenance unit's facilities used ashore are packaged mainly in standard freight containers. Access ladders, scaffolding, and shipboard electrical power and other services will permit the unit to function while embarked in the ship.

Most of the embarked troops are with the maintenance unit; the remainder are communications and other support personnel.

Conversion: The WRIGHT was converted from December 1984 to May 1986 and the CURTISS from December 1985 to August 1987; both ships were converted at Todd Shipyards in Galveston, Texas.

Design: MarAd C5-S-78a type. The ships are combination RO/RO and self-sustaining container ships. The conversion included fitting a helicopter deck above the two forward holds; the deck can be removed to permit full access to the holds with the use of offboard cranes.

The CURTISS *(above)* and WRIGHT provide extensive maintenance and parts stowage facilities for Marine fixed-wing aircraft and helicopters. The amidships cargo areas can be stacked with aviation support containers. (U.S. Navy)

There are seven cargo holds, with the No. 7 hold, aft, having troop berthing and mess facilities installed above it. As a maintenance ship, the AVB can embark 300 standard containers, plus 52 access modules; in the resupply role, 684 containers can be carried. There is 35,000 square feet (3,150 m^2) of vehicle storage space provided. The ships are fitted with ten 30-ton-capacity booms (which can be joined to form 60-ton lifts); a single 70-ton Stuelcken boom is also installed.

Names: The ships' original merchant names, YOUNG AMERICA and GREAT REPUBLIC, respectively, were changed when they were acquired by the Navy for conversion to AVB.

UNCLASSIFIED MISCELLANEOUS SHIPS

These ships (designated IX) are officially considered to be service craft (see chapter 24).

The WRIGHT with a Marine CH-53 Sea Stallion on her helicopter deck. The T-AVBs are generally considered to be sealift ships, being intended to primarily support forward-deployed Marine aviation units. (U.S. Navy)

The fleet oiler LARAMIE sends paired fuel hoses over to the carrier ENTERPRISE during refueling operations in the Atlantic. Relatively high-speed replenishments are a daily activity in the U.S. Navy. All "straight" oilers (AO) are operated by civilian crews under the aegis of MSC. (2000, U.S. Navy, PH3 Brian C. McLaughlin)

CHAPTER 23

Sealift Ships

Vehicles of the U.S. Army's 1st Cavalry Division rolls down the stern ramp of the PFC WILLIAM A. SODERMAN at Rijeka, Croatia. The SODERMAN is one of 20 Large Medium-Speed Roll-on/Roll-off (LMSR) ships procured in the late 1990s to enhance U.S. military sealift. Beginning in the early 1980s under the Reagan administration, the U.S. government has built a realistic sealift capability. (1998, U.S. Navy)

Sealift ships provide point-to-point transportation for cargo, including dry and liquid cargoes, of all of the U.S. military services and Department of Defense agencies. Also included in this category are the forward-deployed or prepositioned merchant ships that carry guns, vehicles, munitions, provisions, fuels, field hospitals, and other supplies for U.S. troops that are to be flown into forward areas to "marry up" with the matériel.

All sealift ships are operated by civilian crews under the control of the Military Sealift Command (MSC). Navy-owned ships have the prefix USNS (U.S. Naval Ship). Most of the other ships are under long-term charter from their owners and have the prefixes M/V (Motor Vessel) for diesel ships or SS (Steam Ship) for those with steam turbines. The two maritime academy training ships on the MSC register are designated TS (Training Ship). See *Status* notes for individual ships.

A breakdown of the specific ships in various categories of sealift is provided in chapter 8 of this edition of *Ships and Aircraft*. Ships in this chapter are arranged in the following order by type:

Type	*Designation*
Cargo ships	T-AK
Container ships	T-AK, T-AKR
Crane ships	T-ACS
Fast Sealift Ships (FSS)	T-AKR
Float-On/Float-Off (FLO/FLO) ships	T-AK
Gasoline tankers	T-AOG
Lighter-Aboard-Ship (LASH) ships	T-AK
Prepositioning ships	T-AK, T-AKR
Range support ships	(none)
Roll-On/Roll-Off (RO/RO) vehicle cargo ships	T-AKR
Sea Barge (SEABEE) ships	T-AK
Transport oilers	T-AOT
Troop transports	T-AP

Within these categories the ships are listed on the basis of size (length), except that crane ships, the only category in which all ships are assigned Navy hull numbers, are listed by their hull numbers.

The following status comments are used in the individual ship entries:

Academic	on loan to maritime school
APS	Afloat Prepositioning Ship
FSS	Fast Sealift Ship
MPS	Maritime Prepositioning Ship[1]
NDRF	National Defense Reserve Fleet[2]
ROS	Reduced Operating Status
RRF	Ready Reserve Force
Sealift	ocean transportation (active)

Ships placed in ROS are laid up in reserve in four- or five-day readiness for reactivation, with cadre crews of ten and nine personnel, respectively, who maintain the ships. Those ships assigned to the RRF are laid up in reserve; most are kept ready to be reactivated in between ten and 30 days (the number of days is indicated under *Status* in the following class tables).

Ships indicated by **Sealift** are active, engaged in point-to-point ocean transportation. In addition to the ships so indicated, several FSS and RRF ships periodically are activated and employed in this role for special operations and exercises.

In addition to the ships listed below, two hospital ships (T-AH), two aviation support ships (T-AVB), and one fleet oiler (T-AO) listed in chapter 22 are generally included in the sealift category, as they are intended to support forward-deployed forces.

Classification: There are two types of hull numbers used in this chapter: the four-digit Navy Ships and Aircraft Supplementary Data Tables (SASDT) numbers that are assigned for accounting purposes and are not actual hull numbers in the normal context, and the one- to three-digit numbers that are traditional Navy hull numbers, assigned when the ship is ordered and part of the ship designation scheme that began in 1920.

The Maritime Administration's code scheme for American-built merchant ship designs is explained in chapter 3. A few ships constructed in the United States to private designs do not have MarAd designations.

Electronics: All ships listed here have one or (usually) two navigation radars of commercial types.

Guns/Missiles: These ships are not armed.

Helicopters: The prepositioning ships and the eight converted SL-7 fast sealift ships have helicopter landing decks. Some other sealift ships have open areas that could be used in an emergency.

Manning: All sealift ships area manned by civilian mariners. Several prepositioning ships are fitted as squadron flagships, carrying a squadron commodore and small Navy planning/communications staff. Some prepositioning ships have small numbers of civilian maintenance personnel to check equipment and handle embarked landing craft/pontoon barges.

Prepositioning ships also have facilities for embarking small numbers of troops (primarily maintenance and unloading personnel).

Operational: Maritime-prepositioned matériel was used by all of the U.S. military services in the Persian Gulf conflict of 1990–1991. The first U.S. ground combat units brought into Saudi Arabia with tanks, heavy artillery, and so forth were two Marine Expeditionary Brigades (MEB) that married up with MPS squadrons. The third MPS squadron followed. In addition, several APF ships were at Diego Garcia, loaded with field hospitals, Air Force and Army equipment, and potable water.

Status: A large number of MSC/RRF ships were transferred to the NDRF, under the aegis of the Maritime Administration, in 1994 because of funding shortages. Their readiness is far lower than when in MSC/RRF status.

The NDRF ships would take considerably longer to reactivate than RRF ships. On a periodic basis, they are "broken out" of RRF and "exercised" by employing them in cargo-carrying for the Department of Defense.

1. MPS squadron is indicated, e.g., MPS-1.
2. Administered by the Maritime Administration of the Department of Transportation.

CARGO SHIPS

These are primarily break-bulk cargo ships. While of limited value in modern commercial shipping operations, these ships have considerable military utility.

2 CARGO SHIPS: C5-S-75a TYPE

Number	Name	Launched	To RRF	Status
T-AK 2039	Cape Girardeau (ex-President Adams, Alaskan Mail)	1968	15 Mar 1988	MSC ROS-5
T-AK 5051	Cape Gibson (ex-President Jackson, Indian Mail)	1968	15 Mar 1988	MSC ROS-5

Builders:	Newport News Shipbuilding, Va.
Displacement:	31,995 tons full load
Tonnage:	15,949 GRT
	Cape Girardeau 22,273 DWT
	Cape Gibson 22,216 DWT
Length:	582⅓ feet (177.55 m) waterline
	604⅚ feet (184.4 m) overall
Beam:	82⅙ feet (25.05 m)
Draft:	35 feet (10.7 m)
Propulsion:	2 steam turbines (General Electric); 24,000 shp; 1 shaft
Boilers:	2 (Babcock & Wilcox)
Speed:	21 knots
Range:	14,000 n.miles (25,928 km) at 20.8 knots
Manning:	47 civilian

These break-bulk cargo ships can carry 409 containers in addition to dry and refrigerated cargo and 17,000 barrels of liquid cargo. There are accommodations for 22 passengers. One 70-ton-capacity boom and 20 20-ton and four 15-ton cranes are fitted.

Class: The Cleveland (T-AK 851) of this design has been discarded.

1 CARGO SHIP: C5-S-78a TYPE

Number	Name	Launched	To RRF	Status
T-AK 1014	Cape Nome (ex-Rapid, American Rapid, Red Jacket, Mormacstar)	26 Sep 1969	7 Dec 1987	MSC RRF-10

Builders:	Ingalls Shipbuilding, Pascagoula, Miss.
Displacement:	27,980 tons full load
Tonnage:	11,757 GRT
	15,694 DWT
Length:	559⅚ feet (170.7 m) waterline
	601⅓ feet (183.3 m) overall
Beam:	90 feet (27.4 m)
Draft:	34 feet (10.4 m)
Propulsion:	2 steam turbines (General Electric); 30,000 shp; 1 shaft
Boilers:	2 (Combustion Engineering)
Speed:	23.6 knots
Range:	12,000 n.miles (22,224 km) at 23.6 knots
Manning:	34 civilian

The Cape Nome is a combination break-bulk/container ship with a capacity of 70 containers. She is an especially attractive, superstructure-aft ship with three kingposts supporting cargo booms.

Design: There is a stern door and ramp for vehicle loading/unloading.

The CAPE GIRARDEAU in reduced operating status. She is a useful ship, combining break-bulk, container, and liquid cargo capabilities in a relatively fast hull. (1998, Leo Van Ginderen)

1 COMBINATION CARGO SHIP: DANISH-BUILT

Number	Name	Launched	Status
T-AKR 2053	MAERSK CONSTELLATION (EX-ELIZABETH MAERSK)	1980	**MSC Sealift**

Builders:	Odense Staalskibsvaerft A/S, Lindo, Denmark
Displacement:	approx. 34,069 tons
Tonnage:	20,529 GRT
	21,050 DWT
Length:	551¾ feet (168.2 m) waterline
	598 feet (182.3 m) overall
Beam:	90 feet (27.4 m)
Draft:	32 feet (9.75 m)
Propulsion:	2 diesel engines (Sulzer); 15,960 bhp; 1 shaft
Speed:	18.5 knots
Range:	
Manning:	21 civilian

The MAERSK CONSTELLATION is a combination container/vehicle ship, chartered by MSC on 30 November 1988. The ship is fitted with stern ramp and has four 30-ton and two 16-ton cranes. She can carry 566 containers.

4 CARGO SHIPS: C4-S-58a TYPE

Number	Name	Launched	To RRF	Status
T-AK 5009	CAPE ANN	12 May 1962	Mar 1980	MSC RRF-10
T-AK 5010	CAPE ALEXANDER	7 July 1962	Apr 1980	MSC ROS-5
T-AK 5011	CAPE ARCHWAY	15 Sep 1962	Apr 1980	MSC RRF-10
T-AK 5012	CAPE ALAVA	24 Mar 1962	Apr 1980	NDRF
T-AK 5013	CAPE AVINOF	8 Dec 1962	Apr 1980	MSC ROS-5

Builders:	Ingalls Shipbuilding, Pascagoula, Miss.
Displacement:	18,560 tons full load
Tonnage:	11,309 GRT
	12,932 DWT
Length:	540¹¹/₁₂ feet (164.9 m) waterline
	571⅚ feet (174.35 m) overall
Beam:	75⅙ feet (22.9 m)
Draft:	30⅝ feet (9.4 m)
Propulsion:	2 steam turbines (General Electric or Westinghouse); 16,500 shp; 1 shaft
Boilers:	2
Speed:	21.5 knots
Range:	13,300 n.miles (24,632 km) at 20 knots
Manning:	39 civilian
Helicopters:	landing deck in CAPE ANN and CAPE AVINOF

These large break-bulk cargo ships were built for Farrell Lines specifically for the East African trade, with special dehumidifying equipment to prevent cargo sweating and odor permeation. They are fitted with one 60-ton-capacity boom and six 10-ton and 14 5-ton cranes. Two ships were fitted with a helicopter deck aft and other enhancements upon being taken over by MSC.

Class: The CAPE ALAVA was downgraded from RRF-30 to NDRF on 1 October 2000.

Engineering: Normal horsepower is indicated above; the maximum is 19,250 shp. Several ships have exceeded their designed speed (above); the AFRICAN NEPTUNE (now T-AK 5011) averaged 22.48 knots on the 6,786 n.mile trip from New York to Cape Town, South Africa.

The CAPE NOME with a full load of containers. Her array of cargo booms marks her as a break-bulk cargo ship; note that the second of three kingposts is "split." (1991, Leo Van Ginderen)

The CAPE ALEXANDER emitting white smoke while under way. Some of the ships of this type have light helicopter platforms aft. (1991, Leo Van Ginderen)

4 CARGO SHIPS: C4-S-1 TYPE

Number	Name	Launched	To RRF	Status
T-AK 5022	CAPE JOHN (ex-SANTA ANA)	18 Aug 1962	May 1980	MSC ROS-5
T-AK 5029	CAPE JACOB (ex-CALIFORNIA)	28 July 1961	Dec 1980	MSC RRF-20
T-AK 5075	CAPE JOHNSON (ex-MORMACSAGA, M. M. DANT)	5 May 1962	29 Feb 1988	MSC ROS-5
T-AK 5077	CAPE JUBY (ex-MORMACSEA, HAWAII)	9 Feb 1962	July 1988	MSC ROS-5

Builders:	CAPE JOHN, CAPE JUBY	National Steel and Shipbuilding, San Diego, Calif.
	others	Newport News Shipbuilding, Va.
Displacement:	22,629 tons	
Tonnage:	SANTA ANA	12,724 GRT
		14,376 DWT
	CAPE JOHNSON	12,724 GRT
		14,467 DWT
	others	12,691 GRT
		14,321 DWT

Length:	528⁵⁄₁₂ feet (161.1 m) waterline
	565 feet (172.25 m) overall
Beam:	76 feet (23.2 m)
Draft:	32 feet (9.75 m)
Propulsion:	2 steam turbines (General Electric); 17,500 shp; 1 shaft
Boilers:	2 (Foster Wheeler)
Speed:	20.75 knots
Range:	12,600 n.miles (23,335 km) at 20 knots
Manning:	44 civilian, except CAPE JOHN 41 civilian, CAPE JACOB 37 civilian

These are break-bulk cargo ships, the first two built for States Steamship Co. and the latter two (*Mormac* prefix ships) for the Moore-McCormack Lines.

Design: One 60-ton-capacity boom, ten 20-ton cranes, two 10-ton cranes, and ten 5-ton cranes.

Engineering: Normal horsepower is indicated above; the maximum is 19,200 shp.

The CAPE JUBY at Norfolk shortly after she was chartered by the Military Sealift Command. These ships have a standard kingpost arrangement with a heavy, 60-ton-capacity boom on the third kingpost. (1988, U.S. Navy)

CARGO SHIPS: C4-S-57a TYPE

Number	Name	Launched	To RRF	Status
T-AK 2016	PIONEER COMMANDER (ex-AMERICAN COMMANDER)	20 Dec 1962	June 1982	NDRF
T-AK 2018	PIONEER CONTRACTOR (ex-AMERICAN CONTRACTOR)	22 Mar 1963	Sep 1981	NDRF

Builders:	Bethlehem Steel, Quincy, Mass.
Displacement:	21,053 tons full load
Tonnage:	11,164 GRT, except PIONEER COMMANDER 11,105 GRT
	13,535 DWT
Length:	529 feet (161.28 m) waterline
	560¹¹/₁₂ feet (171.0 m) overall
Beam:	75¹/₁₂ feet (22.9 m)
Draft:	32¹/₆ feet (9.8 m)
Propulsion:	2 steam turbines (Bethlehem); 16,500 shp; 1 shaft
Boilers:	2 (Foster Wheeler)
Speed:	21 knots
Range:	12,000 n.miles (22,224 km) at 21 knots
Manning:	43 civilian

Details of these ships differ. Built for the United States Lines, they carry a mixed load of dry cargo, refrigerated provisions, and 8,000 barrels of liquid cargo.

Class: The PIONEER CRUSADER (T-AK 2019) of this type was downgraded on 7 May 1998 from RRF to "no status," being simply retained in reserve.

Both surviving ships (above) were downgraded from RRF-30 to NDRF on 1 October 2000.

Design: They have one 70-ton boom and several smaller cranes.

Engineering: Normal horsepower is indicated above; the maximum is 18,150 shp. The merchant AMERICAN CHARGER of this design set a 1963 speed record of 24.9 knots across the Atlantic (3,718 n.miles/6,890 km).

1 TRAINING SHIP ⎫ 4 CARGO SHIPS ⎬ C4-S-66a TYPE

Number	Name	Launched	To RRF	Status
T-AK 5056	CAPE BRETON	4 June 1966	May 1985	MSC RRF-10
T-AK 5057	CAPE BOVER	12 Feb 1966	Apr 1985	MSC ROS-5
T-AK 5058	CAPE BORDA	16 Apr 1966	Apr 1985	MSC ROS-5
T-AK 5059	CAPE BON	16 July 1965	July 1985	**Academic**
T-AK 5060	CAPE BLANCO	10 July 1965	July 1985	MSC ROS-5

Builders:	Avondale Shipyards, New Orleans, La.
Displacement:	21,840 tons full load
Tonnage:	10,723 GRT
	14,662 DWT
Length:	514¾ feet (156.9 m) waterline
	539⅝ feet (164.6 m) overall
Beam:	76 feet (23.2 m)
Draft:	32⅔ feet (9.95 m)
Propulsion:	2 steam turbines (De Laval or Westinghouse); 15,500 shp; 1 shaft
Boilers:	2 (Foster Wheeler)
Speed:	21 knots
Range:	13,660 n.miles (25,300 km) at 20 knots
Manning:	38 civilian

These break-bulk cargo ships carry 4,000 barrels of liquid cargo in addition to dry cargo.

Design: Fitted with one 80-ton capacity boom and 20 small booms.

Status: The LETITIA LYKES (T-AK 2043) of this type was returned to commercial merchant service.

The CAPE BON, formerly in the RRF category, relieved the PATRIOT STATE (T-AP 1000) as the Massachusetts Maritime Academy's training ship in December 1999. When fully converted to the training ship role, she will be designated T-AP 1003.

The CAPE BRETON, showing the unusual small, paired funnels of this ship type. (1995, Leo Van Ginderen)

The CAPE BOVER under way. These ships also have an unusual kingpost-boom arrangement. (1991, Giorgio Arra)

2 COMBINATION CARGO SHIPS: GERMAN-BUILT

Number	Name	Launched	Status
T-AK 9655	GREEN RIDGE (ex-WOERMAN MERCUR, CAROL MERCUR, SLOMAN MERCUR)	1979	**MSC MPS-2**
T-AK 2050	GREEN WAVE (ex-WOERMAN MIRA, SLOMAN MIRA)	1980	**MSC Sealift**

Builders:	Howaldtswerke (HDW), Kiel, West Germany
Displacement:	18,178 tons full load
Tonnage:	GREEN RIDGE 5,805 GRT
	9,549 DWT
	GREEN WAVE 9,521 GRT
	12,487 DWT
Length:	479¹/₁₂ feet (146.1 m) waterline
	507 feet (154.6 m) overall
Beam:	69¾ feet (21.25 m)
Draft:	24½ feet (7.45 m)
Propulsion:	2 diesels (Krupp-MaK); 10,000 bhp; 1 shaft
Speed:	18 knots
Range:	14,400 n.miles (26,669 km) at 17 knots
Manning:	21 civilian

These ships are similar, but not identical, combination break-bulk and container ships, originally chartered by MSC mainly for Greenland and Antarctic resupply, the GREEN WAVE in August 1984 and the GREEN RIDGE in October 1988. Both ships have ice-strengthened hulls, and each can carry 543 containers. They are fitted with six 25-ton-capacity cranes, four of which can be "ganged" to lift 80 tons from hold No. 4.

The GREEN WAVE in Arctic waters. She has containers stacked four-high amidships and rides low in the water from a full load. She has a self-unloading capability with six cranes. Her bulbous bow is partially visible. (1988, U.S. Navy)

CARGO SHIPS: C3-S-37c TYPE

Number	Name	Launched	To RRF	Status
T-AK 5036	CAPE CHALMERS	6 Dec 1962	Nov 1984	NDRF
T-AK 5041	CAPE COD	11 July 1962	Nov 1984	NDRF

Builders:	Bethlehem Steel, Sparrows Point, Baltimore, Md.
Displacement:	18,560 tons full load
Tonnage:	9,296 GRT
	12,684 DWT
Length:	470 feet (143.29 m) waterline
	494¾ (150.8 m) overall
Beam:	69⅙ feet (21.1 m)
Draft:	32 feet (9.75 m)
Propulsion:	2 steam turbines (General Electric); 11,000 shp; 1 shaft
Boilers:	2 (Combustion Engineering or Foster Wheeler)
Speed:	18.75 knots
Range:	18,300 n.miles (33,892 km) at 17.75 knots
Manning:	34 to 40 civilian

Break-bulk cargo ships built for the Lykes Brothers Steamship Co., these ships carry 8,000 barrels of liquid cargo. This was the first series of U.S. oceangoing cargo ships to be built after World War II by a private shipping company.

Class: All eight ships of this class have now been downgraded from formal RRF status to "no status," and simply retained in reserve:

		to NDRF
T-AK 5036	CAPE CHALMERS	1 Oct 2000
T-AK 5037	CAPE CANSO	1 Apr 1994
T-AK 5039	CAPE CLEAR	4 Dec 1996
T-AK 5038	CAPE CHARLES	8 Dec 1992
T-AK 5040	CAPE CANAVERAL	7 Oct 1994
T-AK 5041	CAPE COD	1 Oct 2000
T-AK 5042	CAPE CARTHAGE	7 May 1998
T-AK 5043	CAPE CATOCHE	7 Oct 1994

Design: Twin risers resembling kingposts serve as stacks. Each ship is fitted with one 60-ton-capacity boom and 20 smaller booms.

CARGO SHIPS: C3-S-37d TYPE

Number	Name	Launched	To RRF	Status
T-AK 2036	GULF TRADER	28 Dec 1963	Nov 1984	NDRF
T-AK 5044	GULF BANKER	5 Oct 1963	Nov 1984	NDRF
T-AK 5045	GULF FARMER	3 Aug 1963	Nov 1984	NDRF

Builders:	Avondale Shipyards, New Orleans, La.
Displacement:	17,210 tons full load
Tonnage:	8,970 GRT, except GULF TRADER 8,988 GRT
	11,367 DWT, except GULF TRADER 11,368 DWT
Length:	470 feet (143.29 m) waterline
	494⅔ feet (150.8 m) overall
Beam:	69⅙ feet (21.1 m)
Draft:	30¹/₁₂ feet (9.2 m)
Propulsion:	2 steam turbines (General Electric, except GULF TRADER Westinghouse); 10,000 shp; 1 shaft
Boilers:	2 (Combustion Engineering)
Speed:	18.75 knots
Range:	12,000 n.miles (22,224 km) at 17.75 knots
Manning:	45 civilian

These are break-bulk cargo ships built for the Gulf and South American Steam Ship Co.

Class: The GULF SHIPPER (T-AK 2035) and GULF MERCHANT (T-AK 5046) of this type have been discarded.

The GULF FARMER was downgraded from RRF-30 to NDRF on 7 May 1998; the GULF TRADER and GULF BANKER on 1 October 2000.

Design: These ships have twin exhaust risers (stacks) that resemble kingposts. Their machinery spaces are well aft. They have one 66-ton-capacity boom and two 15-ton, two 10-ton, and ten 5-ton derricks.

Engineering: Normal horsepower is indicated above; the maximum is 11,000 shp.

The GULF TRADER shows another unusual arrangement of kingposts and cargo booms. Twin funnels are abaft the bridge structure. Additional cargo booms are aft. (1990, Giorgio Arra)

CARGO SHIPS: C3-S-46a TYPE

Number	Name	Launched	To RRF	Status
T-AK 5008	BANNER	1961	Jan 1983	NDRF
T-AK 5019	COURIER	1962	Aug 1983	NDRF

Builders:	BANNER National Steel and Shipbuilding, San Diego, Calif.
	COURIER Sun Shipbuilding and Dry Dock, Chester, Pa.
Displacement:	19,400 tons full load
Tonnage:	BANNER 10,659 GRT
	12,629 DWT
	COURIER 11,000 GRT
	12,705 DWT
Length:	469¹¹⁄₁₂ feet (143.3 m) waterline
	493 feet (150.3 m) overall
Beam:	73 feet (22.25 m)
Draft:	30½ feet (9.3 m)
Propulsion:	2 steam turbines (General Electric); 13,750 shp; 1 shaft
Boilers:	2 (Babcock & Wilcox)
Speed:	20 knots
Range:	18,000 n.miles (33,336 km) at 18.5 knots
Manning:	39 civilian

These are break-bulk cargo ships built for American Export/Isbrandtsen Lines. The COURIER has been modified to carry containers in addition to break-bulk cargo.

Class: The BUYER (T-AK 2033) of this type was transferred from MSC/RRF-30 to the NDRF on 7 October 1994; the BANNER and COURIER were transferred on 1 October 2000.

Design: The ships have machinery and large superstructure aft, with an amidships bridge structure. They are fitted with one 60-ton-capacity boom and 20 smaller booms and cranes.

Engineering: Normal horsepower is indicated above; the maximum is 13,750 shp.

Names: Note that there was previously a tanker named COURIER in MSC service.

1 CARGO SHIP: C3-S-33a TYPE

Number	Name	Launched	To RRF	Status
T-AK 284	NORTHERN LIGHT	Apr 1961	Oct 1984	MSC RRF-10
T-AK 5016	LAKE	5 Jan 1961	Mar 1977	NDRF
T-AK 5018	SCAN	21 Mar 1961	Feb 1977	NDRF
T-AK 5074	CAPE CATAWBA	1960	Feb 1987	NDRF

Builders:	Sun Shipbuilding and Dry Dock, Chester, Pa., except CAPE CATAWBA by Todd Shipyards, San Pedro, Calif.
Displacement:	18,365 tons full load
Tonnage:	NORTHERN LIGHT 9,361 GRT
	12,537 DWT
Length:	457⅚ feet (139.6 m) waterline
	485¹¹⁄₁₂ feet (148.15 m) overall
Beam:	68 feet (20.7 m)
Draft:	28½ feet (8.7 m)
Propulsion:	1 steam turbine (General Electric); 11,000 shp; 1 shaft
Boilers:	2 (Combustion Engineering)
Speed:	19 knots
Range:	14,000 n.miles (25,928 km) at 18 knots
Manning:	41 civilian

These were commercial cargo ships built for Moore-McCormack Lines. After merchant service, they were laid up in the NDRF. The NORTHERN LIGHT and SOUTHERN CROSS (T-AK 285) were acquired by the Navy in April 1980 for use as prepositioning ships in the Indian Ocean; they were placed in service on 22 April 1980 and 1 May 1980,

The BANNER, moored in the Elizabeth River, Va., awaiting crisis or war. These ships have an amidships bridge structure, with their machinery aft. (1987, U.S. Navy)

respectively. Their sister ship VEGA was acquired in April 1981 for conversion to an SSBN supply ship (T-AK 286); see chapter 22. Two other ships were acquired for conversion to surveying ships but instead the Congress directed new construction ships.

The NORTHERN LIGHT was laid up by MSC on 26 April 1984 and the SOUTHERN CROSS on 13 September 1984 (correction to previous edition). The SOUTHERN CROSS was transferred from MSC/RRF to the NDRF on 7 October 1994.

The LAKE, SCAN, and CAPE CATAWBA were transferred from RRF-30 to NDRF on 1 October 2000.

Design: The NORTHERN LIGHT has a modified bow that makes her slightly longer than other ships of this design. Both ex-T-AK ships are ice-strengthened for Arctic operations.

Classification: The NORTHERN LIGHT retains her Navy hull number.

Engineering: Normal horsepower is shown above; the maximum is 12,100 shp.

Status: The PRIDE (T-AK 5017) and SOUTHERN CROSS (T-AK 285) were transferred from MSC/RRF to the NDRF on 1 April 1994 and 7 October 1994, respectively. The NORTHERN LIGHT and SOUTHERN CROSS were U.S. Naval Ships when active.

The NORTHERN LIGHT, typical of the several hundred C3-type merchant ships built in the United States from the late 1960s to replace the massive World War II merchant ship program. Note the large, distinctive funnel of this subtype. (1992, Leo Van Ginderen)

The STRONG TEXAN is an unusual ship: Short and broad, the Dutch-built ship was rebuilt at a U.S. shipyard into a heavy lift ship by fitting her with two 160-ton-capacity cranes that can work in tandem. Here, the STRONG TEXAN is carrying 34 house trailers belonging to the U.S. Army's 1302nd Medium Port Command. (1996, U.S. Navy, courtesy *Sealift* magazine)

1 HEAVY LIFT CARGO SHIP: DUTCH-BUILT

Number	Name	Launched	Status
T-AKR 9670	STRONG TEXAN (ex-DOCK EXPRESS TEXAS, HAPPY RUNNER)	1976	**MSC Sealift**

Builders:	Arnhemsche Schipswerf Maats, Arnhem, the Netherlands
Displacement:	approx. 4,200 tons full load
Tonnage:	1,382 GRT
	2,776 DWT
Length:	244 feet (74.4 m) waterline
	268⅓ feet (81.82 m) overall
Beam:	51½ feet (15.7 m)
Draft:	18¼ feet (5.55 m)
Propulsion:	2 diesel engines (Stork-Kromhout 9F-CHD240); 2,500 bhp; 2 shafts
Speed:	12 knots
Range:	
Manning:	11 civilian

This is a small heavy lift/cargo/vehicle ship. She has one 160-ton capacity crane and ramps for loading/unloading vehicles.

CARGO SHIP: NORWEGIAN-BUILT

The Norwegian-built cargo ship NOBLE STAR (T-AK 5076) has been discarded. The ship was chartered in 1988 and, loaded with a 500-bed deployable field hospital (330 containers), was deployed to Diego Garcia in November 1989 as part of the Afloat Prepositioning Force. The ship's field hospital was deployed during Operations Desert Shield/Desert Storm. She briefly was reassigned to general MSC operation on 30 September 1993, but has since been discarded.

CARGO SHIPS: C3-S-76a TYPE

The three cargo ships of this type have been taken out of MSC/RRF and assigned to the NDRF: the DEL VIENTO (T-AK 5026) and DEL VALLE (T-AK 5050) on 7 October 1994 and the DEL MONTE (T-AK 5049) on 1 April 1994. The ships were break-bulk cargo ships built for Delta Line.

CARGO SHIPS: C3-S-38a TYPE

The four cargo ships of this type in MSC/RRF were transferred to the NDRF on 7 October 1994: ADVENTURER (T-AK 5005), AIDE (T-AK 5006), AMBASSADOR (T-AK 5007), and AGENT (T-AK 5008). They were break-bulk cargo ships originally built for the American Export/Isbrandtsen Lines.

CARGO SHIP: JAPANESE-BUILT

The ADVANTAGE (T-AK 9652) has been taken out of MSC service. She was employed as a prepositioned ammunition ship, carrying Air Force munitions.

CONTAINER SHIPS

Container capacity is measured in standard (TEU) containers, which are $8 \times 8 \times 20$ feet ($2.4 \times 2.4 \times 6.1$ m).[3]

2 CONTAINER SHIPS: GERMAN-BUILT

Number	Name	Launched	In service	Status
T-AKR 9718	LT COL CALVIN P. TITUS (ex-ALBERT MAERSK)	1975	31 Mar 1994	**MSC MPS-3**
T-AKR 9966	SP5 ERIC G. GIBSON (ex-ADRIAN MAERSK)	1975	31 Mar 1994	**MSC MPS-3**

Builders:	Blohm + Voss, Hamburg, West Germany
Displacement:	approx. 50,000 tons full load
Tonnage:	40,600 GRT
	30,461 DWT
Length:	725⁵⁄₁₂ feet (221.16 m) waterline
	784⅚ feet (239.28 m) overall
Beam:	100¼ feet (30.56 m)
Draft:	37¾ feet (11.52 m)
Propulsion:	1 diesel engine (Burmeister & Wain–Hitachi 8L90GBE); 31,800 bhp; 1 shaft
Speed:	21 knots
Range:	
Manning:	21 civilian

These ships were chartered on 31 March 1994 from the Danish firm Maersk. They can accommodate 1,600 containers on the forward third of ship or alternatively provide a total of 45,000 square feet (4,050 m²) of vehicle space. They carry Army matériel; both are normally moored at Guam.

Each ship has two 40-ton-capacity cranes and is fitted with a bow thruster.

Names: Both ships honor Army Medal of Honor winners.

---

3. TEU = Twenty-foot (6.1-m) Equivalent Unit.

The CAPT STEVEN L. BENNETT fully loaded with her deck cargo in protective "cocoons" (2000, U.S. Navy)

1 CONTAINER SHIP: KOREAN-BUILT

Number	Name	Launched	In service	Status
T-AK 4296	Capt Steven L. Bennett	1984	1999	**MSC MPS-1**

Builders:	
Displacement:	52,878 tons full load
Tonnage:	
Length:	687 feet (209.45 m) overall
Beam:	100 feet (30.49 m)
Draft:	38½ feet (11.74 m)
Propulsion:	
Speed:	18 knots
Range:	
Manning:	21 civilian

The BENNETT was acquired to preposition Air Force munitions in the Mediterranean area.

Names: Some Navy lists refer to the ship as STEVEN BENNETT; however, the full name and rank are on the ship.

1 CONTAINER SHIP: "CHOUEST" TYPE

Number	Name	Launched	In service	Status
(none)	Margaret B. Chouest		Nov 1995	**MSC Sealift**

Builder:	North American Shipbuilding, Larose, La.
Displacement:	12,923 tons full load
Length:	319¹¹⁄₁₂ feet (97.54 m) overall
Beam:	60 feet (18.29 m)
Draft:	19 feet (5.79 m)
Propulsion:	2 diesels (Bergens Mek); 10,800 bhp; 2 shafts
Speed:	16 knots
Range:	
Manning:	14 civilian

This small container ship, built specifically for MSC charter operations, replaced the CLEVELAND. She operates in the Western Pacific–Indian Ocean areas.

Design: The ship has a superstructure-forward design with a large, open cargo deck amidships. She can carry 286 standard containers. Two container handling cranes are located on her starboard side.

CRANE SHIPS

These ships are intended to provide an unloading capability for other sealift ships when port facilities are not available. Moored alongside a loaded merchant ship, a T-ACS can lift cargo onto a pier or into landing craft or barges alongside.

Each crane ship has two or three pairs of 30-ton cargo cranes; the cranes can be paired to lift 30 tons. Thus, one crane can lift a fully loaded container, two cranes an M1-series main battle tank, and four cranes working together a 105-ton floating causeway.

The C6-S-1 container ship AMERICAN BANKER was to become the T-ACS 11 and the C6-S-MA1xb container ship AMERICAN RESERVIST was to have become the T-ACS 12.

One crane ship is assigned to an MPS squadron; the others are in reserve.

Names: These ships have state nicknames.

2 AUXILIARY CRANE SHIPS: C6-S-MA60d TYPE

Number	Name	Launched	To RRF	Status
T-ACS 9	Green Mountain State (ex-American Altair, Mormacaltair)	20 Aug 1964	24 Sep 1990	MSC ROS-5
T-ACS 10	Beaver State (ex-American Draco, Mormacdraco)	14 Jan 1965	1995	MSC ROS-5

Builders:	Ingalls Shipbuilding, Pascagoula, Miss.
Displacement:	16,600 tons light
	22,900 tons full load
Tonnage:	14,000 GRT (as built)
	12,763 DWT (as built)
Length:	634⅚ feet (193.55 m) waterline
	665¾ feet (203.0 m) overall
Beam:	75¹⁄₁₂ feet (22.9 m)
Draft:	31½ feet (9.6 m)
Propulsion:	2 steam turbines (General Electric); 19,000 shp; 1 shaft
Boilers:	2 (Combustion Engineering)
Speed:	21 knots
Range:	17,000 n.miles (31,485 km) at 20 knots
Manning:	64 civilian

These converted container ships could accommodate 649 containers.

Conversion: The GREEN MOUNTAIN STATE was converted at Nor-

The GREEN MOUNTAIN STATE, like most of the auxiliary crane ships, is a converted C6-series cargo ship. The subtypes of these ships and the three C5-type crane ships differ in dimensions and details. (1990, Leo Van Ginderen)

folk Shipbuilding Co. in February–March 1989. The BEAVER STATE began conversion to a crane ship on 28 February 1989 at the Norfolk (Va.) Shipbuilding Co.; slowed by lack of funding, the conversion was canceled on 12 January 1990 and she was transferred to MarAd for layup on 9 April 1990. The conversion was resumed in 1992 at the Charleston Naval Shipyard.

Both ships are fitted with three sets of twin 30-ton-capacity cranes.

Engineering: They are fitted with highly automated engineering plants. Several ships of this design exceeded 24 knots when new.

2 AUXILIARY CRANE SHIPS: C6-S-MA1xb TYPE

Number	Name	Launched	To RRF	Status
T-ACS 7	DIAMOND STATE (ex-PRESIDENT TRUMAN, JAPAN MAIL)	8 Aug 1961	8 Feb 1989	MSC ROS-5
T-ACS 8	EQUALITY STATE (ex-AMERICAN BUILDER, PHILIPPINE MAIL, SANTA ROSA, PRESIDENT ROOSEVELT, WASHINGTON MAIL)	6 Jan 1962	24 May 1989	MSC ROS-5

Builders:	Todd Shipyards, San Pedro, Calif.
Displacement:	15,138 tons light
Tonnage:	16,518 GRT (as built)
	19,871 DWT (as built)
Length:	632$\frac{11}{12}$ feet (192.95 m) waterline
	667$\frac{5}{6}$ feet (203.6 m) overall
Beam:	76 feet (23.2 m)
Draft:	33$\frac{1}{4}$ feet (10.1 m)
Propulsion:	2 steam turbines (General Electric); 22,000 shp; 1 shaft
Boilers:	2 (Combustion Engineering)
Speed:	20 knots
Range:	14,000 n.miles (25,930 km) at 20 knots
Manning:	

These are former container ships that could accommodate 625 containers.

Conversion: The T-ACS 7 was converted November 1987–December 1988 and T-ACS 8 converted January 1988–February 1989 at the Tampa (Fla.) Shipbuilding Co. They are fitted with three sets of twin 30-ton-capacity cranes.

The DIAMOND STATE, showing her massive, paired cranes. These ships can carry a large amount of cargo. (1999, Leo Van Ginderen)

3 AUXILIARY CRANE SHIPS: C5-S-MA73c TYPE

Number	Name	Launched	To RRF	Status
T-ACS 4	GOPHER STATE (ex-EXPORT LEADER)	1973	27 Oct 1987	**MSC MPS-3**
T-ACS 5	FLICKERTAIL STATE (ex-LIGHTNING)	1969	28 Dec 1987	MSC ROS-5
T-ACS 6	CORNHUSKER STATE (ex-STAGHOUND)	1969	29 Mar 1988	MSC ROS-5

Builders:	Bath Iron Works, Maine
Displacement:	15,060 tons light
	25,000 tons full load
Tonnage:	16,445 DWT
Length:	581$\frac{2}{3}$ feet (177.35 m) waterline
	609$\frac{5}{6}$ feet (185.9 m) overall
Beam:	91$\frac{1}{6}$ feet (27.8 m)
Draft:	30 feet (9.1 m)
Propulsion:	2 steam turbines; 17,500 shp; 1 shaft
Boilers:	2 (Babcock & Wilcox)
Speed:	20 knots
Range:	9,340 n.miles (17,300 km) at 20 knots
Manning:	35 civilian + 6 maintenance personnel in GOPHER STATE

These are former container ships.

Conversion: All three ships were converted at Norfolk (Va.) Shipbuilding Co.—the T-ACS 4 from October 1986 to October 1987, T-ACS 5 from December 1986 to February 1988, and T-ACS 6 from March 1987 to April 1988. They were fitted with two sets of twin 30-ton-capacity cranes.

Operational: The T-ACS 4, as the mercantile EXPORT LEADER, served as test ship for the Arapaho project of operating and supporting military helicopters from a merchant ship. The 1982 evaluation was totally successful, albeit conducted on a limited scale. (During a 40-hour at-sea period, 178 day and 45 night landings were logged by several helicopter types.)

In early 1990 the FLICKERTAIL STATE and GOPHER STATE were activated and fitted with collective protection spaces for defense against Chemical-Biological-Radiological (CBR) effects. They then carried more than 100,000 artillery projectiles filled with nerve agents from Nordenham, Germany, to Johnston Island in the Pacific. The voyage, from 22 September to 6 November 1990 (via Cape Horn), was under the escort of two guided missile cruisers and was made without incident. The ships were subsequently employed in Desert Shield.

The GOPHER STATE was assigned to the Army's prepositioning force on 30 September 1994.

The GOPHER STATE and other crane ships of this series have their navigation bridge forward; their machinery is aft, with a helicopter landing deck on the fantail. (1994, Leo Van Ginderen)

3 AUXILIARY CRANE SHIPS: C6-S-MA1qd TYPE

Number	Name	Launched	To RRF	Status
T-ACS 1	KEYSTONE STATE (ex-PRESIDENT HARRISON)	2 Oct 1965	May 1984	MSC ROS-5
T-ACS 2	GEM STATE (ex-PRESIDENT MONROE)	22 May 1965	Oct 1985	MSC ROS-5
T-ACS 3	GRAND CANYON STATE (ex-PRESIDENT POLK)	23 Jan 1965	Oct 1986	MSC ROS-5

Builders:	National Steel and Shipbuilding, San Diego, Calif.
Displacement:	28,660 tons full load
Tonnage:	17,128 GRT
	13,600 DWT
Length:	632^{11}/₁₂ feet (192.95 m) waterline
	668½ feet (203.8 m) overall
Beam:	76⅙ feet (23.2 m)
Draft:	33 feet (10.1 m)
Propulsion:	2 steam turbines (General Electric); 19,250 shp; 1 shaft
Boilers:	2 (Foster Wheeler)
Speed:	20 knots
Range:	13,000 n.miles (24,075 km) at 20 knots
Manning:	64 civilian

These ships can each accommodate 303 containers.

Conversion: The T-ACS 1 was converted by Bay Shipbuilding, Sturgeon Bay, Wisc., from March 1983 to May 1984; T-ACS 2 by Continental Marine, San Francisco, Calif., from October 1984 to October 1985; and T-ACS 3 by Dillingham Corp., San Francisco, from October 1985 to October 1987. All have been fitted with three sets of twin 30-ton-capacity cranes.

The KEYSTONE STATE, the first of the auxiliary crane ships. There are two sets of cranes forward of the superstructure and a third set aft. (1995, Leo Van Ginderen)

FAST SEALIFT SHIPS

These highly capable ships are maintained in U.S. Atlantic and Gulf Coast ports, ready for the rapid loading of Army or Marine equipment and sailing to crisis/war areas. They were employed in the Gulf War.

8 FAST SEALIFT SHIPS: CONVERTED SL-7 TYPE

Number	Name	Launched	In service	Status
T-AKR 287	ALGOL (ex-SEA-LAND EXCHANGE)	22 Sep 1972	19 June 1984	MSC FSS
T-AKR 288	BELLATRIX (ex-SEA-LAND TRADE)	30 Sep 1972	10 Sep 1984	MSC FSS
T-AKR 289	DENEBOLA (ex-SEA-LAND RESOURCE)	10 May 1973	7 Oct 1985	MSC FSS
T-AKR 290	POLLUX (ex-SEA-LAND MARKET)	18 May 1973	31 Mar 1986	MSC FSS
T-AKR 291	ALTAIR (ex-SEA-LAND FINANCE)	28 Apr 1973	13 Nov 1985	MSC FSS
T-AKR 292	REGULUS (ex-SEA-LAND COMMERCE)	18 Dec 1972	28 Aug 1985	MSC FSS
T-AKR 293	CAPELLA (ex-SEA-LAND McLEAN)	9 Sep 1971	1 July 1984	MSC FSS
T-AKR 294	ANTARES (ex-SEA-LAND GALLOWAY)	13 May 1972	12 July 1984	MSC FSS

Builders:	T-AKR 287, 289, 293 Rotterdamsche Dry Dock Maats, Rotterdam, the Netherlands T-AKR 288, 291 Rheinstahl Nordseewerke, Emden, West Germany T-AKR 290, 292, 294 A.G. Weser, Bremen, Germany
Displacement:	31,017 tons light 55,425 tons full load
Tonnage:	T-AKR 287, 288 25,915 DWT T-AKR 289 25,169 DWT T-AKR 290 24,212 DWT T-AKR 291, 292 25,595 DWT T-AKR 293 25,407 DWT T-AKR 294 24,270 DWT
Length:	893 feet (272.26 m) waterline 946⅙ feet (288.5 m) overall
Beam:	105½ feet (32.2 m)
Draft:	36⅔ feet (11.2 m)
Propulsion:	2 steam turbines (General Electric); 120,000 shp; 2 shafts
Boilers:	2 (Foster Wheeler)
Speed:	33 knots
Range:	12,200 n.miles (22,594 km) at 27 knots
Manning:	42 civilian
Helicopters:	landing area

These are the world's fastest oceangoing merchant ships. Together they can carry almost all of the equipment of an Army mechanized division.

The ships are former high-speed merchant ships of the SL-7 class built for the SeaLand Corporation in European shipyards. They have been converted to Fast Sealift Ships (FSS) that can carry U.S. military cargoes with an extensive Roll-On/Roll-Off (RO/RO) capability. They are operated by civilian charter crews.

The ships were available because they were found to be uneconomical for commercial operation at the time, due to high fuel costs. The average cost per ship to the Navy was $34.6 million.

Classification: During the planning stage, these ships were designated T-AKRX. Upon acquisition, they were designated T-AK and assigned hull numbers in the cargo ship (AK) series; however, upon conversion to RO/RO configuration, they were changed to T-AKR but retained the AK-series hull numbers. T-AK 287 changed to T-AKR on 19 June 1984; T-AK 288 on 10 September 1984; T-AK 289–292 on 1 November 1983; and T-AK 293 and 294 on 30 June 1984.

Conversion: Four ships were converted with fiscal 1982 funds and four with fiscal 1984 funds: the T-AKR 287, 288, and 292 at National Steel and Shipbuilding, San Diego, Calif.; T-AKR 289 and 293 at Pennsylvania Shipbuilding, Chester, Pa.; and T-AKR 290, 291, and 294 at Avondale Shipyards, New Orleans, La.

These ships have approximately 185,000 square feet (16,650 m²) of vehicle space. They retain a major container capability, with provision for special racks for loading heavy material, including trucks and tanks (being lifted on and off vice RO/RO). Side ports and heavy ramps are provided on both sides of the ship. Twin 35-ton-capacity cranes are fitted forward and twin 50-ton cranes aft. Through limited arcs, they can provide a combined lift of 70 and 100 tons, respectively.

A helicopter landing deck amidships can accommodate the largest U.S. military helicopters (Marine/Navy CH-53E, Army CH-47 Chinook). The four cargo decks beneath the landing deck are connected by ramps and can accommodate helicopters, the first with a height of 19½ feet (5.95 m) and the others 13½ feet (4.1 m).

In addition to the RO/RO and helicopter space, the ships can each accommodate other vehicles, plus 78 35-foot (10.7-m) flat racks and 46 containers. There is a tunnel in the amidships deck structure for trucks up to 5-ton capacity to permit passage between the forward and after cargo areas.

Design: As built, the 33-knot SL-7s were the fastest cargo ships ever constructed for U.S. merchant service.

The REGULUS at slow speed. All eight of the fast sealift ships were deployed in 1990 for Operation Desert Shield, carrying U.S. Army equipment to the Persian Gulf. They are the fastest large merchant ships afloat. (1995, Leo Van Ginderen)

Names: These ships are assigned traditional Navy cargo ship names (i.e., stars and constellations), reflecting their acquisition on bare-boat charter versus the time charter of maritime prepositioning ships. Most names previously were carried by store ships (AF).

Operational: All eight ships participated in Operations Desert Shield/Desert Storm in 1990–1991, being activated in August 1990. The ANTARES, which had suffered previous machinery problems, had an engine breakdown in the eastern Atlantic during the initial lift of Desert Shield in August 1990. She was towed into a Spanish port and her cargo was shifted to other sealift ships.

Status: These ships are USNS.

The BELLATRIX, showing the twin-funnel arrangement of these ships. The type is unusual—albeit not unique—in that eight ships were constructed at three shipyards in three countries. (1993, Leo Van Ginderen)

The fast sealift ships CAPELLA *(left)* and ANTARES, laid up at Baltimore, Md. Note the flat stern counter, after cranes, and massive superstructure blocks. (1999, Kevin Clarke)

FLOAT-ON/FLOAT-OFF (FLO/FLO) SHIPS

These ships can be ballasted down to permit small ships and craft to be floated on and off.

1 FLO/FLO SHIP: CONVERTED TANKER

Number	Name	Launched	To RRF	Status
T-AK 2062	AMERICAN CORMORANT (ex-FERNCARRIER, KOLLBRIS)	1975	Oct 1985	**MSC MPS-2**

Builders:	Eriksbergs Mek. Verkstads, Gothenburg, Sweden
Displacement:	70,692 tons full load
Tonnage:	10,195 GRT
	51,269 DWT
Length:	738⅙ feet (225.1 m) overall
Beam:	135 feet (41.15 m)
Draft:	32⅔ feet (10.0 m); flooded 65¾ feet (20.05 m)
Propulsion:	1 diesel engine (Eriksberg–Burmeister & Wain 10K84EF); 25,000 bhp; 1 shaft
Speed:	16 knots
Range:	23,700 n.miles (43,892 km) at 13 knots
Manning:	20 civilian + 6 maintenance personnel

The AMERICAN CORMORANT has a lifting deck 394 feet (120.1 m) long and 135 feet (41.15 m) wide that can be submerged by ballasting the ship to about 65 feet (19.8 m), at which point the lifting deck is 26 feet (7.9 m) below the surface. Small craft, heavy equipment, and barges up to a total of approximately 45,000 tons can then be positioned over the ship, which is then deballasted. The ship can also carry 25 long (40-foot/12.2-m) containers on her fantail.

This ship was built as a tanker (133,000 deadweight tons) and was laid up almost immediately because of the international shipping glut. She was converted in 1981–1982 at the Gotaverken Cityvarvet yard in Sweden to her current configuration. During the modification process, she was lengthened by 180 feet (54.9 m).

Status: The ship was purchased by the U.S. firm American Automar in 1985 (and renamed).

The AMERICAN CORMORANT, showing her tanker lines with the cut-out main deck. The ship has a red hull. (1993, Leo Van Ginderen)

The AMERICAN CORMORANT, loaded with Army barges, landing craft, and a floating crane. Several foreign-flag FLO/FLO ships have been employed under charter by MSC to carry U.S. minesweepers to and from the Persian Gulf, and to bring back the mine-damaged frigate SAMUEL B. ROBERTS (FFG 58) and the destroyer COLE (DDG 67), damaged in a terrorist attack. (1994, Leo Van Ginderen)

1 FLO/FLO SHIP: GERMAN-BUILT

Number	Name	Launched	To RRF	Status
T-AK 9205	STRONG VIRGINIAN (ex-ST. MAGNUS, JOLLY INDACO)	1984	July 1992	**MSC MPS-2**

Builders:	Bremer Vulkan A.G., Bremen-Vegesack, West Germany
Displacement:	31,390 tons full load
Tonnage:	16,169 GRT
	21,541 DWT
Length:	475⅔ feet (145.01 m) waterline
	511¹¹⁄₁₂ feet (156.06 m) overall
Beam:	105 feet (32.03 m)
Draft:	29⁷⁄₁₂ feet (9.02 m)
Propulsion:	2 diesel engines (MaK 6M601AK); 16,320 bhp; 2 shafts
Speed:	16.5 knots
Range:	
Manning:	19 civilian + 6 maintenance personnel

The ship was to be taken out of service in 2000.

GASOLINE TANKERS

These are small tankers. The type was developed during World War II to carry gasoline and aviation fuels for aircraft, motor torpedo boats, and other special craft.

Classification: The Military Sealift Command often lists these ships as standard tankers (T-AOT); however, they are carried on the Naval Vessel Register as T-AOG and hence that is their official designation.

1 GASOLINE TANKER: "TONTI" CLASS (T1-M-BT2)

Number	Name	Launched	To RRF	Status
T-AOG 78	NODAWAY	15 May 1945	30 Sep 1985	MSC RRF-10

Builders:	Todd Shipyards, Houston, Texas
Displacement:	2,060 tons light
	6,060 tons full load
Tonnage:	4,000 DWT
Length:	309 feet (94.21 m) waterline
	325⅙ feet (99.2 m) overall
Beam:	48⅙ feet (14.7 m)
Draft:	19 feet (5.8 m)
Propulsion:	2 diesels (Nordberg); 1,400 bhp; 1 shaft
Speed:	10 knots
Range:	5,500 n.miles (10,186 km) at 10 knots
Manning:	45 civilian

The NODAWAY is the lone survivor of the large number of small gasoline tankers built during World War II for naval and merchant service. The ship originally was placed in Military Sea Transportation Service (MSTS) service on 7 September 1950. She was taken out of naval service on 22 July 1984 and assigned to MSC/RRF on 30 September 1985; she was then transferred to the NDRF on 7 October 1994 but reacquired for the RRF on 1 October 1995. She is berthed at Tsuneishi, Japan.

Class: Five ships of this specific design were built as merchant tankers, all of which were acquired by the Navy in 1950 and assigned to the MSTS (later MSC) as T-AOG 76–80. The AOG 64–75, the last gasoline tankers in the Navy's World War II program, were similar (T1-M-BT1 design).

The RINCON (T-AOG 77), sister ship to the NODAWAY, shows the conventional tanker lines of the standard gasoline tanker design. These ships generally carry aviation fuels. (U.S. Navy)

2 GASOLINE TANKERS: "ALATNA" CLASS (T1-MET-24a)

Number	Name	Launched	To RRF	Status
T-AOG 81	ALATNA	6 Sep 1956	July 1957	MSC RRF-10
T-AOG 82	CHATTAHOOCHEE	4 Dec 1956	Oct 1957	MSC RRF-10

Builders:	Bethlehem Steel, Staten Island, N.Y.
Displacement:	2,367 tons light
	7,300 tons full load
Tonnage:	4,933 DWT
Length:	290 feet (88.41 m) waterline
	302 feet (92.1 m) overall
Beam:	61 feet (18.6 m)
Draft:	19 feet (5.8 m)
Propulsion:	diesel-electric (4 Alco diesels; Westinghouse electric motors); 4,000 shp; 2 shafts
Speed:	13 knots
Range:	5,760 n.miles (10,667 km) at 10 knots
Manning:	approx. 25 civilian

This two-ship class was built specifically for the support of U.S. military activities in the Arctic. Both ships were operated by the MSTS (later MSC) from their completion until taken out of service on 8 August 1972 and laid up in the NDRF. The ships were reacquired by the Navy on 10 May 1979 and 24 May 1979, respectively, and reactivated for MSC service to replace older AOGs; the ALATNA was placed in MSC service on 3 February 1983 and the CHATTAHOOCHEE on 11 January 1982.

They again were taken out of service on 25 January 1985 and placed in the MSC Ready Reserve Force in April 1985 and January 1985, respectively. Both ships were transferred from the RRF to the NDRF on 7 October 1994. They were reacquired for the RRF on 1 October 1995.

They are berthed at Tsuneishi, Japan.

Design: These ships have ice-strengthened hulls and icebreaking prows and other features for Arctic operation (similar to the ELTANIN/AK 270 class). Their cargo capacity is 30,000 barrels of petroleum products, plus some 2,700 tons of dry cargo. A small helicopter platform was fitted aft in their original configuration.

The long-serving gasoline tankers ALATNA *(left)* and CHATTAHOOCHEE are laid up in Tsuneishi, Japan. They were built for Arctic operations, to support U.S. radar stations in remote areas. (U.S. Navy, courtesy *Sealift* magazine)

LIGHTER-ABOARD-SHIP (LASH) SHIPS

These merchant ships carry large, fully loaded barges or lighters that can be floated or lifted on and off the ship. This scheme speeds up loading and unloading and allows cargo to be handled at ports where piers or wharves are unavailable. The two principal barge-carrying designs are known as LASH (Lighter Aboard Ship) and SEABEE (Sea Barge); the former ships use cranes to lift barges to the cargo decks and the latter have large stern elevators.

SEABEE ships maintained by MSC are listed on page 311.

3 LASH CARGO SHIP: C9-S-81d TYPE

Number	Name	Launched	To RRF	Status
T-AK 5070	CAPE FLATTERY (ex-DELTA NORTE)	19 May 1973	June 1987	MSC RRF-10
T-AK 5073	CAPE FAREWELL (ex-DELTA MAR)	27 Jan 1973	Apr 1987	MSC RRF-10
T-AK 2049	GREEN VALLEY (ex-BUTTON GWINNETT)	1974	—	**MSC MPS-2**

Builders:	Avondale Shipyards, New Orleans, La.
Displacement:	62,314 tons full load
Tonnage:	
Length:	797⅙ feet (243.0 m) waterline 893⅓ feet (272.35 m) overall
Beam:	100 feet (30.56 m)
Draft:	40⅚ feet (12.4 m)
Propulsion:	2 steam turbines (De Laval); 32,000 shp; 1 shaft
Boilers:	2 (Combustion Engineering)
Speed:	22.75 knots
Range:	15,000 n.miles (27,780 km) at 22 knots
Manning:	24 civilian

These LASH ships can carry 89 preloaded barges. A small tug is also embarked to help maneuver barges alongside. Fitted with a 510-ton traveling crane.

1 LASH SHIP: JAPANESE-BUILT

Number	Name	Launched	Status
T-AK 9204	JEB STUART (ex-ATLANTIC FOREST)	1970	**MSC MPS-2**

Builders:	Sumitomo Heavy Industries, Uraga, Japan
Displacement:	approx. 65,000 tons
Tonnage:	33,221 GRT 49,858 DWT
Length:	771½ feet (235.2 m) waterline 857⅓ feet (261.4 m) overall
Beam:	106⅝ feet (32.6 m)
Draft:	39¾ feet (12.13 m)
Propulsion:	1 diesel engine (Sumitomo-Sulzer 9RND90; 26,000 bhp; 1 shaft
Speed:	18 knots
Range:	29,920 n.miles (55,440 km) at 18 knots
Manning:	23 civilian

Chartered in July 1992, this ship was assigned to MSC operations on 30 September 1993. She can carry 80 LASH barges, handled by a 510-ton traveling crane.

3 LASH SHIPS: C8-S-81b TYPE

Number	Name	Launched	To RRF	Status
T-AK 5061	CAPE FEAR (ex-AUSTRAL LIGHTNING, LASH ESPAÑA)	9 Jan 1971	Sep 1985	MSC RRF-10
T-AK 5071	CAPE FLORIDA (ex-DELTA CARIBE, LASH TURKIYE)	10 Oct 1970	Feb 1987	MSC RRF-10
T-AK 2064	GREEN HARBOUR (ex-WILLIAM HOOPER)	1972		**MSC MPS-2**

Builders:	Avondale Shipyards, New Orleans, La.
Displacement:	44,606 tons full load
Tonnage:	26,456 GRT 29,820 DWT
Length:	723⅚ feet (220.7 m) waterline 819⅚ feet (249.9 m) overall
Beam:	100 feet (30.5 m)
Draft:	40¾ feet (12.4 m)
Propulsion:	2 steam turbines (De Laval); 32,000 shp; 1 shaft
Boilers:	2 (Babcock & Wilcox or Combustion Engineering)
Speed:	22.5 knots
Range:	13,000 n.miles (24,076 km) at 22.5 knots
Manning:	24 civilian

These are former LASH barge carriers that were modified (prior to MSC charter) to combination barge/container ships. They can carry 71 to 77 standard cargo barges or some 840 containers, except the GREEN HARBOUR, which can carry 1,000 containers.

A 30-ton-capacity traveling crane is fitted for handling containers and a 446-ton-capacity traveling barge crane is fitted. Two 5-ton cranes are also installed.

These ships are similar to the larger C9-S-81d barge carriers.

Class: These were highly innovative ships; 11 were built to this design. Several ships of this type previously operated by MSC have been laid up in the NDRF or returned to commercial service.

The AUSTRAL RAINBOW of this type was discarded in February 2000. Previously loaded as a prepositioning ship and assigned to MPS Squadron 2, she was transferred to strategic sealift operations in April 1998.

The CAPE FLATTERY shows the long, clean lines of LASH ships. The containers on her "deck" are actually in lighters, moved and lowered over the stern by the massive overhead traveling crane. (1995, Leo Van Ginderen)

The AUSTRAL RAINBOW—a recently discarded C8-type LASH ship—was similar to the C9-type LASH ships, but smaller. The C8 ships have two massive traveling cranes to move fully laden lighters. There are two small lighter-handling tugs near the stern, carried as "deck cargo" and lowered into the water by crane. (U.S. Navy)

PREPOSITIONING SHIPS

Twenty Large Medium-Speed RO/RO (LMSR) ships are being procured by conversion and new construction for the forward prepositioning of Army vehicles, artillery, munitions, and provisions. In addition, two additional ships are providing enhanced capabilities for the 13 Maritime Prepositioning Ships (MPS) that were procured in the 1980s to carry Marine Corps matériel. The new ships—designated MPS(E)—carry matériel for an expeditionary airfield, a Navy mobile construction battalion (Seabee), and a fleet hospital.

Names: The 15 MPS/MPS(E) ships are named for Marine Corps recipients of the Medal of Honor.

Seventeen of the 20 LMSR ships listed below are named for Medal of Honor recipients of the Army and Marine Corps; the Bob Hope honors a great American comedian who long entertained U.S. troops throughout the world, and the Fisher is named for an Air Force hero, Major Bernard F. Fisher, who received the Medal of Honor in Vietnam in 1966.

2 LMSR PREPOSITIONING SHIPS: "GORDON" CLASS

Number	Name	Launched	In service	Status
T-AKR 296	MSgt Gary I. Gordon (ex-Jutlandia)	1972	23 Aug 1996	**MSC APS-4**
T-AKR 298	Cpl Charles L. Gilliland (ex-Selandia)	1972	23 May 1997	**MSC APS-4**

Builders:	Denmark
Displacement:	55,422 tons full load
Tonnage:	
Length:	954 feet (290.85 m) overall
Beam:	105⅝ feet (32.25 m)
Draft:	35¾ feet (10.9 m)
Propulsion:	3 slow-speed diesel engines (1 Burmeister & Wain 12K84EF, 26,000 bhp; 2 Burmeister & Wain 9K84EF, 39,000 bhp); 3 shafts
Speed:	24 knots
Range:	12,000 n.miles (22,235 km) at 24 knots
Manning:	30 civilian + 5 maintenance personnel
Troops:	accommodations for 50 troops

These conversions to LMSR configurations, authorized in fiscal 1993, were undertaken at Newport News Shipbuilding, Va., both beginning in October 1993.

Design: These ships were modified and lengthened at the Hyundai shipyard in Ulsan, South Korea, in 1984. Their cargo capacity is 334,055 feet^2 (31,067 m^2). A bow thruster is fitted.

Status: These ships are U.S. Naval Ships (USNS).

5 + 2 LMSR PREPOSITIONING SHIPS: "WATSON" CLASS

Number	Name	FY	Launched	In service	Status
T-AKR 310	Watson	93	26 July 1997	23 June 1998	**MSC APS-4**
T-AKR 311	Sisler	95	28 Feb 1998	1 Dec 1998	**MSC APS-4**
T-AKR 312	Dahl	95	2 Oct 1998	13 July 1999	**MSC**
T-AKR 313	Red Cloud	96	7 Aug 1999	2000	**MSC**
T-AKR 314	Charlton	97	11 Dec 1999	2000	**MSC**
T-AKR 315	Watkins	97	28 July 2000	2001	building
T-AKR 316	Pomeroy	98	2001	2001	building

Builders:	National Steel and Shipbuilding, San Diego, Calif.
Displacement:	62,968 tons full load
Tonnage:	
Length:	951⁵/₁₂ feet (290.0 m) overall
Beam:	105¾ feet (32.24 m)
Draft:	34 feet (10.37 m)
Propulsion:	2 gas turbines (General Electric LM2500-30); 64,000 shp; 2 shafts
Speed:	24 knots
Range:	12,700+ n.miles (23,530+ km) at 24 knots
Manning:	30 civilian + 5 maintenance personnel in Sisler only
Troops:	accommodations for 50 troops
Helicopters:	landing area

These ships are similar to the Bob Hope design, but with gas turbine propulsion. These ships are being constructed following studies after the Gulf War of 1991.

Design: These ships have approximately 394,000 feet^2 (36,642 m^2) of cargo space.

Engineering: These ships and the Lance Cpl Roy M. Wheat are the only prepositioning ships with gas turbine propulsion; most have diesel engines, while a few have steam turbines.

Names: The Red Cloud remembers Army Corporal Mitchell Red Cloud, Jr., who posthumously received the nation's highest military award for action in the Korean War.

Status: These ships are USNS.

The MSgt Gary I. Gordon is another conversion from a merchant ship to a massive vehicle/cargo ship for carrying military matériel. These ships have unusual hull lines; there is a large vehicle ramp aft and helicopter landing areas forward of the bridge structure. Also see photo in Addenda. (U.S. Navy)

The SISLER is one of the mammoth LMSR prepositioning ships being added to the U.S. sealift force. After many decades of niggardly support for sealift, the U.S. Congress has now funded a realistic heavy lift capability. These are machinery-aft ships. (1999, Leo Van Ginderen)

The SISLER, showing the ship's bulbous bow that increases performance and reduces fuel consumption. Her cranes can be paired for heavy lift requirements. These ships have a massive stern ramp and two side ramps for rapidly unloading vehicles. (1999, Leo Van Ginderen)

The stern quarter of the SISLER. The WATSON class LMSRs are similar to the contemporary BOB HOPE class, but with gas turbines in place of medium-speed diesel engines. The speed and range of the two designs are comparable. (1999, Leo Van Ginderen)

4 + 3 LMSR PREPOSITIONING SHIPS: "BOB HOPE" CLASS

Number	Name	FY	Launched	In service	Status
T-AKR 300	Bob Hope	93	29 May 1995	18 Nov 1998	**MSC APS-4**
T-AKR 301	Fisher	94	21 Oct 1997	5 Aug 1999	**MSC**
T-AKR 302	Seay	94	25 June 1998	Mar 2000	**MSC**
T-AKR 303	Mendonca	96	25 May 1999	July 2000	**MSC**
T-AKR 304	Pililaau	97	28 Jan 2000	2001	building
T-AKR 305	Brittin	98	2000	2002	building
T-AKR 306	MSGT Roy B. Benavidez	99	2001	2002	building

Builders:	Avondale Industries, New Orleans, La.
Displacement:	35,500 tons light
	62,069 tons full load
Tonnage:	26,569 DWT
Length:	950 feet (289.63 m) overall

Draft:	34⅔ feet (10.57 m)
Propulsion:	4 medium-speed diesel engines (Colt Pielstick 10 PC4.2V); 65,160 bhp; 1 shaft
Speed:	24 knots
Range:	12,000+ n.miles (22,235+ km) at 24 knots
Manning:	30 civilian + 5 maintenance personnel
Troops:	accommodations for 50 troops
Helicopters:	landing area

These ships are similar to the Watson class but with diesel propulsion. The Bob Hope was laid down on 31 May 1995.

Design: Approximately 380,000 feet^2 (35,340 m^2) of cargo space is provided in these ships.

Status: These ships are USNS.

The Bob Hope (1999, Leo Van Ginderen)

The Bob Hope (1999, Leo Van Ginderen)

Beam:	105⅚ feet (32.27 m)

The Bob Hope *(above)* and Watson classes have similar appearances. The LMSR ships have Navy-series hull numbers. (1999, Leo Van Ginderen)

The Pililaau as launched, showing the ship's bow configuration and the two ducted thrusters in her bow. The thrusters enable the ship to hold steady in a stream or against a pier while unloading. (2000, Litton Avondale Industries)

3 LMSR PREPOSITIONING SHIPS: "SHUGHART" CLASS

Number	Name	Launched	In service	Status
T-AKR 295	SGT 1ST CLASS RANDALL D. SHUGHART (ex-LAURA MAERSK)	1981	7 May 1996	**MSC APS-4**
T-AKR 297	SGT 1ST CLASS RODNEY J. T. YANO (ex-LEISE MAERSK)	1981	8 Feb 1997	**MSC APS-4**
T-AKR 299	PFC WILLIAM A. SODERMAN (ex-LICA MAERSK)	1981	11 Nov 1997	**MSC Sealift**

Builders:			Speed:	24 knots
Displacement:	54,298 tons full load		Range:	12,000 n.miles (22,235 km) at 24 knots
Tonnage:			Manning:	30 civilian + 5 maintenance personnel
Length:	906¾ feet (276.45 m) overall		Troops:	accommodations for 50 troops
Beam:	105⁷/₁₂ feet (32.2 m)		Helicopters:	landing area
Draft:	34⅚ feet (10.62 m)			
Propulsion:	1 slow-speed diesel engine (Burmeister & Wain 12L90 GFCA); 46,653 bhp; 1 shaft			

These ships are conversions to the LMSR configuration. They were funded under the fiscal 1993 conversion program. All were converted at the National Steel yard in San Diego, Calif.; the SHUGHART began conversion in June 1994, the YANO in December 1994, and the SODERMAN in April 1995.

Design: These ships were modified and lengthened at the Hyundai shipyard in Ulsan, South Korea, in 1987. Their cargo capacity is 312,461 feet² (29,059 m²). Bow and stern thrusters are fitted.

Status: These ships are USNS. Note that the SODERMAN initially was employed in general cargo carrying. The ship is being configured as a third MPF(E)—Maritime Prepositioning Force (Enhancement)—ship (see below).

The Sgt 1st Class Randall D. Shughart was the first LMSR ship to enter service. Here, the ship moves slowly through the harbor at San Diego, Calif. (1999, Leo Van Ginderen)

The Shughart on sea trials, riding high in the water. The ship has a vehicle ramp on each side (abreast the second set of cranes) in addition to the stern ramp. (1996, National Steel and Shipbuilding)

1 ENHANCED MARITIME PREPOSITIONING SHIP: "WHEAT"

Number	Name	Launched	In service	Status
T-AK 3016	Lance Cpl Roy M. Wheat (ex-Bazaliya)		2000	**MSC MPS**

Builders:	Black Sea Shipyard, Nikolayev, Ukraine	Propulsion:	2 gas turbines; 47,020 shp; 1 shaft
Displacement:	50,570 tons full load	Speed:	22 knots
Tonnage:		Range:	11,000+ n.miles (20,383+ km) at 22 knots
Length:	863¾ feet (263.34 m) overall	Manning:	30 civilian + 12 maintenance
Beam:	98⅓ feet (29.98 m)	Troops:	accommodations for 100 troops
Draft:	35 1/12 feet (10.7 m)		

The Wheat, Soderman, and Martin are officially listed as MPF(E) ships, assigned to support the MPS squadrons. This ship was converted by the Bender Shipbuilding and Repair yard at Mobile, Ala.

Design: The ship has 127,000 feet² (11,811 m²) of deck space; 960 standard containers can be carried.

3 MARITIME PREPOSITIONING SHIPS: CONVERTED WATERMAN CLASS (C7-S-133a)

Number	Name	Launched	Start conv.	In service	Status
T-AK 3005	SGT MATEJ KOCAK (ex-JOHN B. WATERMAN)	1981	Mar 1983	5 Oct 1984	**MSC MPS-1**
T-AK 3006	PFC EUGENE A. OBREGON (ex-THOMAS HEYWOOD)	1982	Nov 1982	15 Jan 1985	**MSC MPS-1**
T-AK 3007	MAJ STEPHEN W. PLESS (ex-CHARLES CARROLL)	1983	Mar 1983	1 May 1985	**MSC MPS-1**

Builders:	Sun Shipbuilding and Dry Dock, Chester, Pa., except PLESS by General Dynamics, Quincy, Mass.	Propulsion:	2 steam turbines; 30,000 shp; 1 shaft
Displacement:	15,000 tons light	Boilers:	2
	48,754 tons full load	Speed:	20 knots
Length:	821 feet (250.3 m) overall	Range:	13,000 n.miles (24,076 km) at 20 knots
Beam:	105½ feet (32.2 m)	Manning:	26 or 27 civilian + 3 maintenance personnel, except no maintenance personnel in PLESS
Draft:	32⅙ feet (9.8 m)	Troops:	accommodations for 100 troops
		Helicopters:	landing area

These ships were previously commercial container ships operated by the Waterman Corp. They were acquired specifically for conversion to the MPS role and were designated T-AKX during the planning stage; they are under 25-year charter.

Conversion: As built, these ships were 695 feet (211.9 m) overall with a full load displacement of 38,975 tons. A 126-foot (38.4-m) midbody section was inserted and the ships were reconfigured for 152,524 square feet (13,727 m²) of vehicle cargo space to carry 540 standard cargo containers, 1,544,000 gallons (5.8 million liters) of bulk fuels, and 94,780 gallons (360,164 liters) of potable water. The ships are fitted with vehicle ramps and cranes to provide a self-unloading capability.

All three ships were converted to the MPS role by the National Steel yard in San Diego, Calif.

The PFC EUGENE A. OBREGON, with an empty main deck. Two helicopter spots are marked on the raised helicopter deck. Unlike UNREP ships, these prepositioning ships cannot easily move cargo from holds to helicopters. (1989, Giorgio Arra)

The SGT MATEJ KOCAK, anchored off of Norfolk. These ships have two pairs of heavy cranes forward, as well as a traveling crane forward for handling containers. (1998, Giorgio Arra)

5 MARITIME PREPOSITIONING SHIPS: DANISH-BUILT

Number	Name	Launched	Start conv.	In service	Status
T-AK 3000	CPL LOUIS J. HAUGE JR. (ex-ESTELLE MAERSK)	3 Aug 1979	Jan 1984	7 Sep 1984	**MSC MPS-2**
T-AK 3001	PFC WILLIAM B. BAUGH JR. (ex-ELEO MAERSK)	1979	Jan 1983	30 Oct 1984	**MSC MPS-2**
T-AK 3002	PFC JAMES ANDERSON JR. (ex-EMMA MAERSK)	23 Mar 1979	Oct 1983	26 Mar 1985	**MSC MPS-2**
T-AK 3003	1ST LT ALEX BONNYMAN JR. (ex-EMILIE MAERSK)	3 Aug 1979	Jan 1984	26 Sep 1985	**MSC MPS-2**
T-AK 3004	PVT FRANKLIN J. PHILLIPS (ex-PVT HARRY FISHER, EVELYN MAERSK)	12 Oct 1979	Apr 1984	12 Sep 1985	**MSC MPS-2**

Builders:	Odense Staalskibsvaerft, Lindo, Denmark	Speed:	17.5 knots
Displacement:	28,249 tons light	Range:	10,800 n.miles (20,000 km) at 17.5 knots
	46,484 tons full load	Manning:	25 to 27 civilian + 3 maintenance personnel, except 14
Length:	755½ feet (230.3 m) overall		maintenance in PHILLIPS
Beam:	90¹/₁₂ feet (27.5 m)	Flag:	25 Navy in PHILLIPS
Draft:	32¹/₁₂ feet (9.8 m)	Troops:	accommodations for 77 troops
Propulsion:	1 diesel (Sulzer 7RND 76M); 16,800 bhp; 1 shaft	Helicopters:	landing area

These are former Maersk Line combination container and RO/RO vehicle cargo ships that were acquired by the U.S. government specifically for conversion to the MPS role. The ships were designated T-AKX during the design stage.

The PHILLIPS is flagship of MPS Squadron 3.

Conversion: During conversion, a new 157½-foot (48-m) midsection was added to each ship (original length 598¹/₁₂ feet/182.3 m with a deadweight tonnage of 29,182 tons). In the MPS role, they have 120,080 square feet (10,807 m^2) of vehicle storage space and can carry up to 332 standard freight containers, 1,283,000 gallons (4.8 million liters) of bulk fuels, and 65,000 gallons (247,000 liters) of potable water. Ramps and cranes provide a limited self-unloading capability.

The HAUGE, ANDERSON, and PHILLIPS were converted by the Bethlehem Steel yard at Sparrows Point, Md.; the BAUGH and BONNYMAN by the Bethlehem Steel yard in Beaumont, Texas.

Names: 1ST LT ALEXANDER BONNYMAN JR. was changed to 1ST LT ALEX BONNYMAN JR. on 4 March 1986. The PVT HARRY FISHER was changed to PVT FRANKLIN S. PHILLIPS, the former being the pseudonym used by Phillips when he won the Medal of Honor. Note that the T-AKR 301 is named FISHER.

The CPL LOUIS J. HAUGE JR., showing how the heavy lift cranes are paired in these ships. Military containers are stowed on the forward deck. (1991, Leo Van Ginderen)

1 ENHANCED MARITIME PREPOSITIONING SHIP: "MARTIN"

Number	Name	Launched	In service	Status
T-AK 3015	1ST LT HARRY L. MARTIN (ex-TARAGO)		Apr 2000	**MSC MPS**

Builders:	
Displacement:	47,519 tons full load
Tonnage:	
Length:	754 feet (229.88 m) overall
Beam:	105¾ feet (32.24m)
Draft:	33⅔ feet (10.26 m)

Propulsion:	1 diesel engine; 25,345 bhp; 1 shaft
Speed:	17 knots
Range:	16,000 n.miles (29,650 km) at 17 knots
Manning:	24 civilian + 12 maintenance
Troops:	accommodations for 100 troops

The MARTIN was converted to the MPF(E) role at the Atlantic Drydock Co., Jacksonville, Fla.

Design: The ship has 127,000 square feet (11,811 m^2) of deck space; 767 standard containers can be carried.

The PFC WILLIAM B. BAUGH JR. at Portsmouth, Va. The ship is riding high in the water even though a large amount of deck cargo is being carried. (1990, Leo Van Ginderen)

5 MARITIME PREPOSITIONING SHIPS: "BOBO" CLASS (C8-M-MA134j)

Number	Name	Launched	In service	Status
T-AK 3008	2ND LT JOHN P. BOBO	19 Jan 1985	14 Feb 1985	**MSC MPS-1**
T-AK 3009	PFC DEWAYNE T. WILLIAMS	18 May 1985	6 June 1985	**MSC MPS-3**
T-AK 3010	1ST LT BALDOMERO LOPEZ	26 Oct 1985	21 Nov 1985	**MSC MPS-3**
T-AK 3011	1ST LT JACK LUMMUS	22 Feb 1986	6 Mar 1986	**MSC MPS-3**
T-AK 3012	SGT WILLIAM R. BUTTON	17 May 1986	18 May 1986	**MSC MPS-3**

Builders:	General Dynamics, Quincy, Mass.
Displacement:	22,700 tons light
	40,846 tons full load
Tonnage:	44,543 GRT
	26,523 DWT
Length:	673 feet (205.2 m) overall
Beam:	105½ feet (32.2 m)
Draft:	29½ feet (9.0 m)
Propulsion:	2 diesels (Stork Werkspoor 18TM410V); 26,400 bhp; 1 shaft
Speed:	17.7 knots
Range:	11,100 n.miles (20,557 km) at 17.7 knots
Manning:	29 or 30 civilian + 3 maintenance personnel, except
	9 maintenance personnel in BOBO and LUMMUS
Flag:	20 Navy personnel in BOBO and LUMMUS
Troops:	accommodations for 100 troops
Helicopters:	landing area

These new-construction ships were classified T-AKX during planning stages. Each of these ships carries equipment and supplies for about a quarter of a MAB for 30 days. Although built specifically for the MPS role, they are under 25-year charter.

The first two ships were laid down in 1983; the others in 1984.

The BOBO is flagship of MPS Squadron 1 and the LUMMUS is flagship of MPS Squadron 2.

Design: These ships have 162,500 square feet (14,625 m²) of vehicle deck space and can carry 1,605,000 gallons (6 million liters) of break-bulk petroleum products, plus 81,770 gallons (310,726 liters) of potable water. Up to 522 containers can be carried. A stern ramp is fitted for unloading vehicles into landing craft and onto piers, and there are five 39-ton-capacity cranes fitted.

Engineering: These ships achieved 18.8 knots on trials; above is the sustained speed. A 1,000-hp bow thruster is fitted to permit maneuvering alongside a pier without the aid of tugs.

The PFC DEWAYNE T. WILLIAMS at Norfolk. When forward deployed, the ship's holds are stuffed with munitions, vehicles, and equipment for Marine expeditionary forces. The heavy cranes and stern ramp provide a self-unloading capability. (1998, Jürg Kürsener)

The 1ST LT JACK LUMMUS is typical of the original 13 maritime prepositioning ships placed in MSC service to carry Marine vehicles, weapons, and equipment. These ships have a raised helicopter deck above their stern, above the main vehicle unloading ramp. (1995, Giorgio Arra)

RANGE SUPPORT SHIPS

These two ships provide logistics support for the tracking stations of the Atlantic Missile Range. Both ships are homeported in New Orleans, La.

1 RANGE SUPPORT SHIP: "SEACOR CLIPPER"

Number	Name	Launched	Status
(none)	SEACOR CLIPPER (ex-NICOR CLIPPER)	20 Apr 1982	**MSC Sealift**

Builders:	Moss Point Marine, Escatawpa, Miss.
Displacement:	2,746 tons full load
Tonnage:	428 GRT
	1,200 DWT
Length:	253¹¹/₁₂ feet (77.4 m) overall
Beam:	44 feet (13.4 m)
Draft:	13 feet (4.0 m)
Propulsion:	2 diesel engines (General Motors EMD 12-567C); 2,700 bhp; 2 shafts
Speed:	10 knots
Range:	
Manning:	9 civilian

This is a small, open-deck cargo ship employed to support U.S. space tracking and research facilities on Caribbean islands. The ship was chartered by MSC on 6 May 1987.

Design: The ship was built as an offshore oil rig supply vessel. A stern ramp is fitted for carrying small vehicles. A bow thruster is also fitted.

1 RANGE SUPPORT SHIP: "SEA MARK III"

Number	Name	Launched	Status
(none)	SEA MARK III		**MSC Sealift**

Builder:	
Displacement:	
Length:	150 feet (45.73 m) overall
Beam:	50 feet (15.24 m)
Draft:	9¼ feet (2.8 m)
Propulsion:	
Speed:	
Range:	
Manning:	4 civilian

ROLL-ON/ROLL-OFF CARGO SHIPS

These are vehicle cargo ships with strengthened cargo decks for carrying heavy vehicles and side and/or stern ramps for loading and unloading vehicles. They are extremely important for the sealift of modern ground combat forces.

3 RO/RO CARGO SHIPS: JAPANESE/NORWEGIAN-BUILT

Number	Name	Launched	To RRF	Status
T-AKR 5066	CAPE HUDSON (ex-BARBER TIAF)	1979	Nov 1986	MSC ROS-4
T-AKR 5067	CAPE HENRY (ex-BARBER PRIAM)	1979	Sep 1986	MSC ROS-5
T-AKR 5068	CAPE HORN (ex-BARBER TØNSBERG)	1979	Dec 1986	MSC ROS-4

Builders:	CAPE HUDSON	Mitsubishi, Nagasaki, Japan
	CAPE HENRY	Kaldnes Mek., Versted A/S, Tønsberg, Norway
	CAPE HORN	Tangen Verft, Kragerø, Norway
Displacement:	approx. 47,200 tons full load	
Tonnage:	CAPE HUDSON	21,976 GRT
	CAPE HENRY	21,747 GRT
	CAPE HORN	22,090 GRT
Length:	693¾ feet (211.5 m) waterline	
	749½ feet (228.5 m) overall	
Beam:	105⅝ feet (32.3 m)	
Draft:	35⁵/₁₂ feet (10.8 m)	
Propulsion:	1 diesel engine (Mitsubishi-Sulzer in CAPE HENRY; Burmeister & Wain in others); 30,700 bhp (30,150 bhp in CAPE HUDSON); 1 shaft	
Speed:	21 knots	
Range:	24,300 n.miles (45,000 km) at 17 knots	
Manning:	27 civilian	

All three of these large combination RO/RO-container ships were purchased on 1 June 1986. Their details vary. They can carry vehicles or 1,607–1,626 containers. They all have one 40-ton-capacity crane forward (the superstructure is aft).

Status: All three ships were assigned to the Army's prepositioning force on 30 September 1994.

The CAPE HENRY, one of the three largest specialized roll-on/roll-off ships in the Military Sealift Command. The three ships of this type were built in three yards in two countries. (1994, Leo Van Ginderen)

The CAPE HORN at Antwerp, Belgium. These ships have a massive, angled stern ramp. They are vital for U.S. overseas operations because of the huge number of vehicles in U.S. Army units. (1994, Leo Van Ginderen)

The CAPE HUDSON, like many other modern RO/RO ships, has a superstructure aft configuration. There is a tunnel through the superstructure (port side) to permit vehicles to move from the forward deck to the stern. (1996, Leo Van Ginderen)

The CAPE WASHINGTON (above) and her sister ship CAPE WRATH are among the most ungainly looking ships afloat. They have a high freeboard, low bridge structure amidships, and short funnel aft. (1994, Leo Van Ginderen)

2 RO/RO CARGO SHIPS: POLISH-BUILT

Number	Name	Launched	To RRF	Status
T-AKR 9961	CAPE WASHINGTON (ex-HUAL TRANSPORTER)	1981	5 Apr 1994	MSC ROS-5
T-AKR 9962	CAPE WRATH (ex-HUAL TRADER, HOEGH TRADER)	1982	30 Sep 1994	MSC ROS-5

Builders:	Stocznia imeni Komuny Paryskiej, Gdynia, Poland
Displacement:	approx. 55,000 tons
Tonnage:	CAPE WASHINGTON 23,597 GRT
	32,695 DWT
	CAPE WRATH 20,563 GRT
	32,722 DWT
Length:	642 feet (195.76 m) waterline
	697⅓ feet (212.6 m) overall
Beam:	105¹¹⁄₁₂ feet (32.28 m)
Draft:	38⅙ feet (11.63 m)
Propulsion:	1 diesel engine (Cegielski-Sulzer 6RND 90/155); 17,400 bhp; 1 shaft
Speed:	17 knots
Range:	
Manning:	

The CAPE WASHINGTON was acquired for the RRF on 7 April 1993 and the CAPE WRATH on 14 May 1993. Both initially were assigned to the Army's Afloat Prepositioning Force (APF) on 30 September 1994.

These ships are former automobile carriers (capacity was 6,000 cars), designed to carry vehicles (loaded/unloaded through side doors and quarter doors/ramps). Their capacity is 1,203 containers or vehicles.

The ships have ice-strengthened hulls and are fitted with bow thrusters.

2 RO/RO CARGO SHIPS: JAPANESE-BUILT

Number	Name	Launched	To RRF	Status
T-AKR 5082	CAPE KNOX (ex-NEDLLOYD ROUEN, ROUEN)	1978	July 1996	MSC ROS-4
T-AKR 5083	CAPE KENNEDY (ex-NEDLLOYD RRFARIO, RRFARIO)	1979	June 1996	MSC ROS-4

Builders:	Nippon Kokan, Tsurumi, Japan
Displacement:	36,450 tons full load
Tonnage:	21,144 GRT
	29,218 DWT
Length:	695⅔ feet (212.1 m) overall
Beam:	105¹¹⁄₁₂ feet (32.29 m)
Draft:	35⅙ feet (10.72 m)
Propulsion:	1 diesel engine (Sumitomo-Sulzer 8RND90M); 25,400 bhp; 1 shaft
Speed:	19 knots
Range:	
Manning:	

The lowered stern ramp of the CAPE WRATH, seen while the ship was at Antwerp. The single funnel is offset to starboard; it has red-white-blue stripes, not the black-gray-blue-gold stripes common to most MSC ships. (1994, Leo Van Ginderen)

Both of these ships were acquired for the RRF in February 1995. They have a large stern door and two angled stern ramps and can each carry 1,550 standard containers or vehicles. A bow thruster is fitted.

The CAPE KENNEDY *(above)* and CAPE KNOX have a single large stern door with two vehicle ramps. The top of the ship's bulbous bow is visible. (1997, Leo Van Ginderen)

1 RO/RO CARGO SHIP: "CALLAGHAN"

Number	Name	Launched	In service	Status
T-AKR 1001	ADM. WM. M. CALLAGHAN	17 Oct 1967	19 Dec 1967	MSC ROS-4

Builders:	Sun Shipbuilding and Dry Dock, Chester, Pa.
Displacement:	26,573 tons full load
Tonnage:	13,500 GRT
	24,471 DWT
Length:	633⁵/₁₂ feet (193.12 m) waterline
	694¼ feet (211.66 m) overall
Beam:	92 feet (28.1 m)
Draft:	29 feet (8.8 m)
Propulsion:	2 gas turbines (General Electric LM2500); 40,000 shp; 2 shafts
Speed:	26 knots
Range:	12,000 n.miles (22,224 km) at 20 knots
Manning:	28 civilian

The CALLAGHAN was an early RO/RO ship, the first built for the U.S. Navy; the ship was laid down on 17 October 1967. However, she was operated under charter to the MSTS/MSC rather than under outright Navy ownership. The ship was operated by the MSTS/MSC in that status for almost two decades until being purchased outright in 1986. She was assigned to the RRF in May 1987.

The ship has 167,537 square feet (15,078 m²) of vehicle storage space, with four side ports and a stern ramp for rapid loading and unloading, and is fitted with two 120-ton-capacity booms and 12 booms with a capacity of 5 to 10 tons. She can offload some 750 vehicles in 27 hours.

Engineering: The CALLAGHAN was the first all-gas-turbine ship constructed for the U.S. Navy. The engines were originally two Pratt & Whitney FT-4 (rated at 25,000 shp each); these were replaced in 1977 by the widely used LM 2500.

Name: The ship is named for Admiral William M. Callaghan, the first commander of the Military Sea Transportation Service (predecessor to MSC), from 1949 to 1952. He was retired and employed by American Export lines, which built the ship, when she was named in his honor by the firm.

Status: The CALLAGHAN was taken out of service and transferred to the RRF on 31 May 1987 after almost 20 years of continuous MSC service. She was transferred to MarAd on 25 June 1987 for layup, but subsequently returned to ROS. The ship has the prefix GTS for Gas Turbine Ship.

The venerable ADM. WM. M. CALLAGHAN—the first RO/RO ship acquired by the U.S. Navy—was purchased specifically to move Army vehicles between the United States and Europe. There are cargo holds forward; vehicles are loaded/unloaded through side ports as well as the stern ramp. (1985, Leo Van Ginderen)

4 RO/RO CARGO SHIPS: C7-S-95a TYPE

Number	Name	Launched	To RRF	Status
T-AKR 10	CAPE ISLAND (ex-MERCURY, ILLINOIS)	21 Dec 1976	Nov 1993	MSC ROS-4
T-AKR 11	CAPE INTREPID (ex-JUPITER, LIPSCOMB LYKES, ARIZONA)	1 Nov 1975	Apr 1986	MSC ROS-4
T-AKR 5062	CAPE ISABEL (ex-CHARLES LYKES, NEVADA)	15 May 1976	June 1986	MSC ROS-5
T-AKR 5076	CAPE INSCRIPTION (ex-TYSON LYKES, MAINE)	24 May 1975	Sep 1987	MSC ROS-5

Builders:	Bath Iron Works, Maine
Displacement:	14,222 tons light
	33,765 tons full load
Tonnage:	13,156 GRT
	19,172 DWT
Length:	639⅝ feet (195.1 m) waterline
	684¾ feet (208.8 m) overall
Beam:	102 feet (31.1 m)
Draft:	32¹⁄₁₂ feet (9.8 m)
Propulsion:	2 steam turbines (General Electric); 37,000 shp; 2 shafts
Boilers:	2 (Babcock & Wilcox)
Speed:	24 knots
Range:	12,600 n.miles (23,335 km) at 23 knots
Manning:	36 civilian, except 41 in CAPE ISLAND

These ships were built for commercial service by the Lykes Brothers Steamship Co. They are RO/RO vehicle carriers, with side ports and a stern ramp for rapidly loading and unloading vehicles. They can also carry containers and 728 tons of liquid cargo.

The MERCURY and JUPITER were acquired by the Navy on long-term charter in 1980 for use as prepositioning ships in the Indian Ocean. Note that they were assigned standard Navy hull designations; they were placed in service on 3 June 1980 and 7 May 1980, respectively.

The MERCURY was taken out of service and transferred to the NDRF on 30 April 1993, renamed CAPE ISLAND and assigned to RRF on 22 November 1993, and subsequently placed in MSC service. The JUPITER was transferred to MarAd (Suisun Bay) on 23 April 1986, assigned to the RRF on 2 May 1986, and renamed in 1993.

Status: The MERCURY and JUPITER were USNS.

The CAPE INTREPID—shown here as the USNS JUPITER—has a deck load of military containers. (U.S. Navy)

The CAPE ISLAND—long the USNS MERCURY—has a small crane forward. The larger crane visible aft is on the adjacent pier. The RO/RO ships are among the most important sealift ships because of the large numbers of vehicles used by U.S. military services. (1990, Leo Van Ginderen)

2 RO/RO CARGO SHIPS: CANADIAN-BUILT

Number	Name	Launched	To RRF	Status
T-AKR 5077	CAPE LAMBERT (ex-FEDERAL LAKES, AVON FOREST)	1973	Nov 1987	MSC RRF-10
T-AKR 5078	CAPE LOBOS (ex-FEDERAL SEAWAY, LAURENTIAN FOREST, GRAND ENCOUNTER)	1972	Mar 1988	MSC RRF-10

Builders:	Port Weller Dry Dock, St. Catharines, Ontario, Canada
Displacement:	30,375 tons full load
Tonnage:	15,005 GRT
	20,545 DWT
Length:	621⅓ feet (189.4 m) waterline
	681⅚ feet (207.9 m) overall
Beam:	75⅙ feet (22.9 m)
Draft:	30½ feet (9.3 m)
Propulsion:	2 diesel engines (Crossley-Pielstick); 18,000 bhp; 2 shafts
Speed:	19 knots
Range:	6,000 n.miles (11,112 km) at 17.5 knots
Manning:	27 civilian

These ships were built as newsprint and vehicle carriers and were purchased on 5 June 1987. They are ice-strengthened for operations on the Great Lakes. The ships have side doors with two vehicle ramps and are fitted with a bow thruster. They have 189,937 square feet (17,094 m²) of vehicle space.

5 RO/RO CARGO SHIPS: FRENCH/SWEDISH-BUILT

Number	Name	Launched	To RRF	Status
T-AKR 5051	CAPE DUCATO (ex-BARRANDUNA)	1972	Dec 1985	MSC ROS-4
T-AKR 5052	CAPE DOUGLAS (ex-LALANDIA)	1973	Nov 1985	MSC ROS-4
T-AKR 5053	CAPE DOMINGO (ex-TARAGO)	1973	Oct 1985	MSC ROS-4
T-AKR 5054	CAPE DECISION (ex-TOMBARRA)	1973	Oct 1985	MSC ROS-4
T-AKR 5055	CAPE DIAMOND (ex-TRICOLOR)	1972	Oct 1985	MSC ROS-4

Builders:	T-AKR 5051, 5052, 5054: Eriksberg M/V, Lindholmen, Sweden
	T-AKR 5053, 5055: Ch. de France, Dunkerque, France
Displacement:	35,173 tons full load
Tonnage:	23,972 to 24,437 GRT
	21,299 to 21,398 DWT
Length:	633⅝ feet (193.24 m) waterline
	680¼ feet (207.4 m) overall
Beam:	97 feet (29.57 m)
Draft:	31½ feet (9.59 m)
Propulsion:	*French-built* 3 diesel engines (Ch. d'Atlantic-Pielstick); 28,890 bhp; 1 shaft
	Swedish-built 3 diesel engines (Lindholmen-Pielstick); 27,000 bhp; 1 shaft
Speed:	22 knots
Range:	26,000 n.miles (48,180 km) at 20.6 knots
Manning:	27 civilian

These are combination cargo ships, able to carry heavy vehicles, as well as 1,327 containers. They are fitted with bow and stern thrusters.

The CAPE LOBOS as laid up in the James River (Va.) reserve group of the NDRF. The kingposts are on the ship moored alongside. The design has the bulbous bow common to many modern merchant ships. (1989, Leo Van Ginderen)

The CAPE DECISION at Antwerp. Large numbers of ventilators are fitted on her deck to clear exhaust fumes from the ship's garage decks. She has no side ports, only the large stern ramp. (1993, Leo Van Ginderen)

Status: The CAPE DECISION and CAPE DOUGLAS were assigned to the Army's APF on 30 September 1994. (In addition to Army combat equipment, the CAPE DOUGLAS carries a 300-bed field hospital.)

1 RO/RO CARGO SHIP: FRENCH-BUILT

Number	Name	Launched	Status
T-AK 9881	BUFFALO SOLDIER (ex-MONET)	1975	**MSC MPS-2**

Builders:	Ch. Navals de la Ciotat, la Ciotat, France
Displacement:	approx. 36,000 tons full load
Tonnage:	26,409 GRT 19,669 DWT
Length:	$639\frac{11}{12}$ feet (195.1 m) waterline $669\frac{7}{12}$ feet (204.15 m) overall
Beam:	$87\frac{1}{12}$ feet (26.55 m)
Draft:	$35\frac{1}{4}$ feet (10.74 m)
Propulsion:	2 diesel engines (SEMT-Pielstick 18PC2 5V 4000); 1 shaft
Speed:	19 knots
Range:	
Manning:	23 civilian

This ship was chartered in 1992 from a French firm; she was assigned to MSC-Atlantic on 30 September 1993. Primarily a vehicle carrying ship, she can accommodate 637 containers. She is now in the Pacific/Indian Ocean.

Class: The AMERICAN MERLIN (T-AK 9301) of this type has been discarded.

Conversion: Both ships were lengthened from their original $538\frac{1}{6}$ feet (164.07 m) overall.

1 RO/RO CARGO SHIP: SWEDISH-BUILT

Number	Name	Launched	To RRF	Status
T-AKR 5069	CAPE EDMONT (ex-PARRALLA)	1971	Apr 1987	MSC ROS-4

Builders:	Eriksberg M/V, Lindholmen, Sweden
Displacement:	approx. 32,000 tons full load
Tonnage:	13,355 GRT 20,224 DWT
Length:	$602\frac{1}{2}$ feet (183.7 m) waterline $652\frac{11}{12}$ feet (199.02 m) overall
Beam:	$94\frac{1}{6}$ feet (28.7 m)
Draft:	$31\frac{1}{2}$ feet (9.6 m)
Propulsion:	3 diesel engines (Eriksberg-Pielstick 18PC2V 400); 25,920 bhp; 1 shaft
Speed:	19 knots
Range:	17,000 n.miles (31,500 km) at 19 knots
Manning:	32 civilian

The CAPE EDMONT is a combination vehicle and container ship that can carry 1,212 containers. The ship has 118,325 square feet (10,649 m^2) of vehicle space and is fitted with a bow thruster. She was assigned to the RRF on 10 April 1987.

3 RO/RO CARGO SHIPS: JAPANESE-BUILT

Number	Name	Launched	To RRF	Status
T-AKR 9678	CAPE RISE (ex-SAUDI RIYADH, SEASPEED ARABIA)	1977	15 Nov 1994	MSC ROS-5
T-AKR 9679	CAPE RAY (ex-SAUDI MAKKAH, SEASPEED ASIA)	1977	17 Dec 1994	MSC ROS-4
T-AKR 9960	CAPE RACE (ex-G AND C ADMIRAL, SEASPEED AMERICA)	1977	11 Sep 1994	MSC ROS-4

Builders:	Kawasaki Heavy Industries, Sakaide, Japan
Displacement:	
Tonnage:	14,825 GRT 22,735 DWT
Length:	591 feet (180.22 m) waterline $647\frac{5}{6}$ feet (197.52 m) overall
Beam:	$105\frac{5}{6}$ feet (32.26 m)
Draft:	$32\frac{5}{6}$ feet (10.0 m)
Propulsion:	2 diesel engines (Kawasaki-MAN 14V 52/55A); 28,000 bhp; 1 shaft
Speed:	19.75 knots
Range:	
Manning:	

These ships, combination vehicle and container carriers, were acquired: the RISE on 9 August 1993, the RAY on 20 April 1993, and the RACE on 28 April 1993. They can carry 1,315 containers and are fitted with bow and stern thrusters.

The BUFFALO SOLDIER has an unusual configuration—a self-loading container and vehicle carrier (with large stern ramp). Like many other MSC cargo/prepositioning ships, she was lengthened for naval service. (U.S. Navy)

1 RO/RO CARGO SHIP: SWEDISH-BUILT

Number	Name	Launched	To RRF	Status
T-AK 2044	Cape Orlando (ex-American Eagle, Zenit Eagle, Finneagle)	1981	12 Sep 1994	MSC ROS-4

Builders:	Kockums AB, Malmö, Sweden
Displacement:	approx. 30,000 tons full load
Tonnage:	15,632 GRT
Length:	593 feet (180.8 m) waterline 635¼ feet (199.2 m) overall
Beam:	91⅚ feet (28.0 m)
Draft:	29½ feet (9.0 m)
Propulsion:	2 diesel engines (Cegielski-Sulzer 6RND68M); 21,500 bhp; 1 shaft
Speed:	22 knots
Range:	16,800 n.miles (31,130 km) at 19 knots
Manning:	20 civilian

The Cape Orlando was acquired for RRF as the American Eagle; on charter since 22 August 1983, she was purchased by MSC in December 1992 and renamed in 1993.

This is a large ship with bridge forward and twin funnels aft. The Cape Orlando can carry 1,040 containers or vehicles, with 116,669 square feet (10,500 m^2) of vehicle parking area. Vehicles are loaded/unloaded via stern ramps. There are two bow thrusters.

Class: Two other ships of this type have been discarded by MSC: the American Condor and American Falcon (no hull numbers assigned).

The Cape Orlando at rest. The ship was earlier chartered by the British Ministry of Defence, at which time she was renamed American Eagle. The ship's superstructure is far forward; there are twin funnels aft. (1997, Leo Van Ginderen)

2 RO/RO CARGO SHIPS: ITALIAN-BUILT

Number	Name	Launched	To RRF	Status
T-AKR 9666	Cape Vincent (ex-Taabo Italia, Merzario Italia)	1984	19 Aug 1994	MSC ROS-4
T-AKR 9701	Cape Victory (ex-Merzario Britannia)	1984	2 Sep 1994	MSC ROS-4

Builders:	Fincantieri, Genoa, Italy
Displacement:	approx. 27,000 tons
Tonnage:	22,423 GRT 21,439 DWT
Length:	566¾ feet (172.8 m) waterline 631¾ feet (192.6 m) overall
Beam:	87 feet (26.55 m)
Draft:	27¾ feet (8.47 m)
Propulsion:	1 diesel engine (GMT-Sulzer 6RNB 66/140); 11,850 bhp; 1 shaft
Speed:	16 knots
Range:	21,000 n.miles (38,900 km) at 16 knots
Manning:	

The Cape Vincent was acquired for the RRF on 13 May 1993 and Cape Victory on 2 April 1993. The ships can carry 1,306 containers or vehicles, loaded/unloaded via a stern ramp. They are fitted with a bow thruster.

3 RO/RO CARGO SHIPS: GERMAN/JAPANESE-BUILT

Number	Name	Launched	To RRF	Status
T-AKR 112	Cape Texas (ex-Lyra, Reichenfels)	1977	19 Aug 1944	MSC ROS-5
T-AKR 113	Cape Taylor (ex-Thekwini, Cygnus, Rabenfels)		27 July 1994	MSC ROS-5
T-AKR 9711	Cape Trinity (ex-Santos, Canadian Forest, Radbod, Norefjord, Rheinfels)		21 Nov 1994	MSC ROS-4

Builders:	Cape Taylor	Sasebo Heavy Industries, Japan
	others	Howaldtswerke, Kiel, West Germany
Displacement:	Cape Texas	9,870 tons light 24,555 tons full load
	others	26,455 tons full load
Tonnage:	14,174 GRT 15,075 DWT	
Length:	583⅚ feet (178.0 m) waterline 627⅚ feet (191.29 m) overall, except Cape Texas 634⅙ feet (193.33 m)	
Beam:	89¼ feet (27.2 m)	
Draft:	28⅙ feet (8.6 m)	
Propulsion:	2 diesel engines (MAN 9L 52/55A heavy-oil); 18,980 bhp; 1 shaft	
Speed:	20.5 knots	
Range:	22,600 n.miles (41,880 km) at 16.5 knots	
Manning:	49 civilian	

These are large RO/RO ships purchased in December 1992 and acquired in 1993. The Cape Texas initially operated in MSC service as the USNS Lyra. These ships can accommodate 340 containers, plus vehicles. Their hulls are ice-strengthened.

The CAPE TEXAS has a conventional RO/RO appearance, with superstructure aft, side ports, and a stern ramp. Like other ships of this type, the CAPE TEXAS has (twin) square funnels aft. (1994, Giorgio Arra)

1 RO/RO CARGO SHIP: C4-ST-67a TYPE

Number	Name	Launched	Commissioned	Status
T-AKR 9	METEOR (ex-SEA LIFT)	18 Apr 1965	19 May 1967	MSC RRF-10

Builders:	Lockheed Shipbuilding and Construction, Seattle, Wash.
Displacement:	9,154 tons light
	21,480 tons full load
Tonnage:	16,467 GRT
	12,326 DWT
Length:	499½ feet (152.28 m) waterline
	540 feet (164.7 m) overall
Beam:	83⅔ feet (25.5 m)
Draft:	29 feet (8.8 m)
Propulsion:	2 steam turbine (De Laval); 19,400 shp; 2 shafts
Boilers:	2
Speed:	22 knots
Range:	10,000 n.miles (18,520) at 20 knots
Manning:	56 civilian

The METEOR, originally named SEA LIFT, was built specifically as a RO/RO ship for naval service. She was authorized in the fiscal 1963 naval shipbuilding program and laid down on 19 May 1964. The ship has four side ramps, a stern ramp, and 87,735 square feet (7,896 m²) of vehicle space. She was assigned to the Rapid Deployment Force (RDF) in 1980–1981, then placed in the RRF on 30 October 1985.

Classification: Authorized as T-AK 278 but changed to T-LSV 9 while under construction, the ship was changed again to vehicle cargo ship T-AKR 9 on 14 August 1969.

The LSV 1–6 were World War II–built vehicle landing ships, all of which served under other designations. The TAURUS (LSV 8) was the former AK 273; she had been begun as the FORT SNELLING (LSD 23). Note that the later SL-7 conversions to rapid response ships have AK-series hull numbers with the AKR type designation.

Design: The METEOR was one of the few ships to have both an SCB (No. 236) and MarAd design number.

Names: Changed from SEA LIFT to METEOR on 12 September 1975 to avoid confusion with the Sealift-class tankers (T-AOT 168–176).

Status: The METEOR was a U.S. Naval Ship until transferred to the RRF in 1985.

The long-serving METEOR, a combination cargo-RO/RO ship. The ship has a small funnel abreast of the bridge structure. (1999, Leo Van Ginderen)

1 RO/RO CARGO SHIP: C3-ST-14a TYPE

Number	Name	Launched	In service	Status
T-AKR 7	COMET	31 July 1957	27 Jan 1958	MSC RRF-10

Builders:	Sun Shipbuilding and Dry Dock, Chester, Pa.
Displacement:	8,175 tons light
	18,286 tons full load
Tonnage:	13,792 GRT
	10,111 DWT
Length:	465 feet (141.77 m) waterline
	499 feet (152.2 m) overall
Beam:	78 feet (23.8 m)
Draft:	29⅙ feet (8.9 m)
Propulsion:	2 steam turbines (General Electric); 13,200 shp; 2 shafts
Boilers:	2 (Babcock & Wilcox)
Speed:	18 knots
Range:	12,000 n.miles (22,235 km) at 18 knots
Manning:	44 civilian

The COMET was built specifically for naval service, laid down on 15 May 1956. She can accommodate some 700 vehicles in her two after holds; the two forward holds are intended for general cargo. Vehicle space totals 83,613 square feet (7,525 m^2).

The COMET was assigned to the RRF in March 1985.

Classification: The COMET originally was classified T-AK 269; she was changed to vehicle cargo ship T-LSV 7 on 1 June 1963 and again to T-AKR 7 on 1 January 1969.

Status: The COMET was a U.S. Naval Ship prior to transfer to MarAd on 15 March 1985.

SEA BARGE (SEABEE) SHIPS

3 SEABEE SHIPS: C8-S-82a TYPE

Number	Name	Launched	To RRF	Status
T-AKR 5063	CAPE MAY (ex-ALMERIA LYKES)	1972	July 1986	MSC ROS-5
T-AKR 5064	CAPE MENDOCINO (ex-DOCTOR LYKES)	1972	Oct 1986	MSC RRF-10
T-AKR 5065	CAPE MOHICAN (ex-TILLIE LYKES)	1973	Sep 1986	MSC ROS-5

Builders:	General Dynamics, Quincy, Mass.
Displacement:	18,880 tons light
	57,290 tons full load
Tonnage:	21,667 GRT
	38,410 DWT
Length:	721⅓ feet (219.9 m) waterline
	873¾ feet (266.39 m) overall
Beam:	105⅝ feet (32.3 m)
Draft:	39 1/12 feet (11.9 m)
Propulsion:	2 steam turbines (General Electric); 36,000 shp; 1 shaft
Boilers:	2 (Babcock & Wilcox)
Speed:	20.5 knots
Range:	14,300 n.miles (26,484 km) at 19.25 knots
Manning:	39 civilian

These ships can each carry 38 cargo barges.

Design: The ships are fitted with a 2,000-ton-capacity elevator at the stern for loading and unloading fully laden barges. In addition, they can carry 4,000 barrels (CAPE MOHICAN capacity is 11,000 barrels) of liquid cargo.

The COMET was another early cargo-RO/RO ship. Her two portside vehicle ports are clearly visible. (1982, Leo Van Ginderen)

The CAPE MOHICAN shows the long, straight lines of this barge-carrying design. The bridge structure straddles the barge well. The machinery is fitted in the sidewalls. (1991, Leo Van Ginderen)

The CAPE MOHICAN, showing the bridge, twin funnels, and barge well (1999, Leo Van Ginderen)

TRANSPORT OILERS

In addition to the tankers listed below, the Navy-built fleet oiler HENRY J. KAISER (T-AO 187) is employed as a prepositioning ship with MPS-2 (see page 260).

Four ships are fitted with the OPDS (Offshore Petroleum Discharge System) to transfer fuel ashore without pier facilities; they are fitted with a 4-mile (6.5-km) flexible floating pipeline.

2 TRANSPORT OILERS: "CHESAPEAKE" CLASS

Number	Name	Launched	To RRF	Status
T-AOT 5084	CHESAPEAKE (ex-HESS VOYAGER)	1964	20 July 1991	MSC ROS-5
T-AOT 9101	PETERSBURG (ex-SINCLAIR TEXAS, CHARLES KURZ, KEYSTONE)	1963	1 Aug 1991	**MSC MPS-3**

Builders:	Bethlehem Steel, Sparrows Point, Baltimore, Md.
Displacement:	approx. 65,000 tons full load
Tonnage:	CHESAPEAKE 27,015 GRT 50,826 DWT PETERSBURG 27,469 GRT 50,072 DWT
Length:	704⅚ feet (214.9 m) waterline 736⅙ feet (224.4 m) overall
Beam:	102⅚ feet (31.2 m)
Draft:	39¾ feet (12.1 m)
Propulsion:	2 steam turbines (Bethlehem); 15,000 shp; 1 shaft
Boilers:	2
Speed:	15 knots
Range:	
Manning:	38 civilian in PETERSBURG

These are large merchant tankers and, with the similar MOUNT WASHINGTON, the largest ships in MSC in terms of displacement. The PETERSBURG was assigned to the RRF on 30 September 1994 and subsequently activated for service with an MPS squadron. Both ships are fitted with OPDS.

1 TRANSPORT OILER: "MOUNT WASHINGTON"

Number	Name	Launched	To RRF	Status
T-AOT 5076	MOUNT WASHINGTON	1963	30 Oct 1989	MSC ROS-5

Builders:	Bethlehem Steel, Sparrows Point, Baltimore, Md.
Displacement:	approx. 65,800 tons full load
Tonnage:	27,412 GRT 47,751 DWT
Length:	706⅚ feet (215.5 m) waterline 736⅙ feet (224.4 m) overall
Beam:	102⅚ feet (31.2 m)
Draft:	40¼ feet (12.3 m)
Propulsion:	2 steam turbines (Bethlehem); 21,500 shp; 1 shaft
Boilers:	2
Speed:	17.5 knots
Range:	
Manning:	

This is a large commercial tanker, similar to the CHESAPEAKE and PETERSBURG (see above), but with more powerful turbines. The ship is fitted with OPDS.

Status: The MOUNT VERNON (T-AOT 3009) of this design was transferred from MSC/RRF to the NDRF on 7 October 1994.

1 TRANSPORT OILER: FALCON CLASS

Number	Name	Launched	To RRF	Status
T-AOT 5005	MISSION CAPISTRANO (ex-COLUMBIA, FALCON LADY)	12 Sep 1970	Mar 1988	MSC RRF-20

Builders:	Ingalls Shipbuilding, Pascagoula, Miss.
Displacement:	45,877 tons full load
Tonnage:	20,751 GRT 37,874 DWT
Length:	637⅚ feet (194.5 m) waterline 672⅙ feet (204.9 m) overall
Beam:	89⅙ feet (27.2 m)
Draft:	36¼ feet (11.0 m)
Propulsion:	2 diesel engines (Crossley-Pielstick 16 PC-2V400); 16,000 bhp; 1 shaft
Speed:	16.5 knots
Range:	16,000 n.miles (29,632 km) at 16.5 knots
Manning:	23 civilian

This ship served on MSC charter from 1974 to 1983 under the name COLUMBIA (designated T-AOT 182); see *Class* notes and 13th Edition/page 288 for additional data. Her cargo capacity is 303,000 barrels.

Class: Three other tankers of this class were returned to their owners in 1983–1984 after MSC service: NECHES (T-AOT 183), HUDSON (T-AOT 184), and SUSQUEHANNA (T-AOT 185).

This ship should not be confused with the earlier MISSION CAPISTRANO (AO 112, later AG 162), a World War II–built T2-SE-A2 fleet oiler.

Classification: The ship was designated T-AO 182 upon being chartered by MSC; this was changed to T-AOT in 1979.

1 TRANSPORT OILER: "AMERICAN OSPREY"

Number	Name	Launched	To RRF	Status
T-AOT 5075	AMERICAN OSPREY (ex-GULF PRINCE)	1958	June 1987	MSC RRF-30

Builders:	Bethlehem Steel, Sparrows Point, Baltimore, Md.
Displacement:	44,840 tons full load
Tonnage:	20,143 GRT 34,723 DWT
Length:	660 11/12 feet (201.5 m) overall
Beam:	89 11/12 feet (27.4 m)
Draft:	36 1/12 feet (11.0 m)
Propulsion:	2 steam turbines (Bethlehem); 15,000 shp; 1 shaft
Boilers:	2 (Foster Wheeler)
Speed:	17 knots
Range:	14,000 n.miles (25,928 km) at 17 knots
Manning:	37 civilian

The AMERICAN OSPREY is a former merchant tanker modified at Alabama Dry Dock Co. in 1987–1988 to carry a barge-launching device and four-point mooring system to be used when transferring fuel to shore without pier facilities. She served in the APF until November 1998.

1 TRANSPORT OILER: "MISSION BUENAVENTURA"

Number	Name	Launched	To RRF	Status
T-AOT 1012	MISSION BUENAVENTURA (ex-SPIRIT OF LIBERTY)	1968	Oct 1987	MSC RRF-20

Builders:	Bethlehem Steel, Sparrows Point, Baltimore, Md.
Displacement:	46,243 tons full load
Tonnage:	20,947 GRT 38,851 DWT
Length:	629 11/12 feet (192.0 m) waterline 660 feet (201.2 m) overall
Beam:	90⅙ feet (27.5 m)
Draft:	38¼ feet (11.7 m)
Propulsion:	2 steam turbines (Bethlehem); 15,000 shp; 1 shaft
Boilers:	2 (Foster Wheeler)
Speed:	16.5 knots
Range:	12,000 n.miles (22,224 km) at 16.5 knots
Manning:	26 civilian

This ship has a cargo capacity of 326,000 barrels.

The PETERSBURG. The massive reels and the flexible piping on her deck are part of the Offshore Petroleum Discharge System (OPDS). (1998, Leo Van Ginderen)

The AMERICAN OSPREY. Visible on her deck is the OPDS. The AMERICAN OSPREY has the traditional tanker configuration, with an amidships bridge structure and machinery aft. (U.S. Navy)

The POTOMAC, her bunkers empty, riding high in the water. The OPDS is visible on her deck. The POTOMAC has a bridge-aft configuration. (1996, Leo Van Ginderen)

1 TRANSPORT OILER: "POTOMAC"

Number	Name	Launched	In service	Status
T-AOT 181	POTOMAC	(see notes)	12 Jan 1976	**MSC MPS-2**

Builders:	Sun Shipbuilding and Dry Dock, Chester, Pa.
Displacement:	7,333 tons light
	34,800 tons full load
Tonnage:	15,739 GRT
	27,908 DWT
Length:	591⅙ feet (180.2 m) waterline
	619⅝ feet (189.0 m) overall
Beam:	83½ feet (25.5 m)
Draft:	33⁷⁄₁₂ feet (10.2 m)
Propulsion:	1 steam turbine (Westinghouse); 20,460 shp; 1 shaft
Boilers:	2 (Combustion Engineering)
Speed:	18.5 knots
Range:	18,000 n.miles (33,336 km) at 18 knots
Manning:	37 civilian

The POTOMAC was constructed with midbody and bow sections built to mate with the stern section of an earlier tanker named POTOMAC (T-AO 150). The "new" tanker was named SHENANDOAH and operated under commercial charter to MSC for several years until she was purchased on 12 January 1976. At that time, the ship was renamed POTOMAC and designated T-AO 181; the designation was changed to T-AOT 181 on 30 September 1978.

The ship was contractor-operated by MSC with a civilian crew. She was taken out of service on 26 September 1983, placed in the RRF on 5 March 1984, and subsequently assigned to the MPS Force. (The original POTOMAC was launched on 8 October 1956; she was partially destroyed by fire on 3 October 1961, but the stern section and machinery were relatively intact; she was originally of the T5-S-12a type.)

The ship's cargo capacity is 200,000 barrels and she is fitted with OPDS.

Class: Three other tankers of the original POTOMAC design have been discarded:

Ship		Notes
T-AOT 149	MAUMEE	stricken from NDRF on 13 Apr 1992
T-AOT 151	SHOSHONE	to NDRF 7 Oct 1994
T-AOT 152	ex-YUKON	stricken from NDRF on 13 Apr 1992; the name YUKON dropped on 9 May 1989 to make the name available for the T-AO 202

Design: The MAUMEE has an ice-strengthened bow. The T-AO(T) 149 and T-AO(T) 150 were of the T5-S-12a type.

Status: The POTOMAC was a U.S. Naval Ship prior to transfer to the RRF.

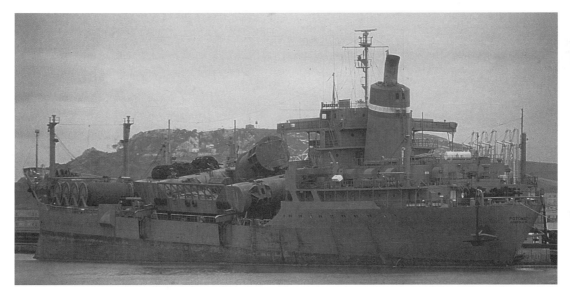

The POTOMAC, shown in a laid-up condition before being reactivated for assignment to Maritime Prepositioning Squadron 2 (1996, Leo Van Ginderen)

5 TRANSPORT OILERS: MODIFIED T5 TYPE

Number	Name	Launched	In service	Status
T-AOT 1121	GUS W. DARNELL (ex-OCEAN FREEDOM)	10 Aug 1985	11 Sep 1985	**MSC Sealift**
T-AOT 1122	PAUL BUCK (ex-OCEAN CHAMPION)	1 June 1985	11 Sep 1985	**MSC Sealift**
T-AOT 1123	SAMUEL L. COBB (ex-OCEAN TRIUMPH)	2 Nov 1985	15 Nov 1985	**MSC Sealift**
T-AOT 1124	RICHARD G. MATTHIESEN (ex-OCEAN SPIRIT)	15 Feb 1986	18 Feb 1986	**MSC Sealift**
T-AOT 1125	LAWRENCE H. GIANELLA (ex-OCEAN STAR)	19 Apr 1986	22 Apr 1986	**MSC Sealift**

Builders:	American Shipbuilding, Tampa, Fla.	Beam:	90 feet (27.4 m)	
Displacement:	9,000 tons light	Draft:	34 feet (10.4 m)	
	39,624 tons full load	Propulsion:	1 diesel (Mitsubishi or Ishikawajima-Sulzer 5RTA-76); 15,300 bhp; 1 shaft	
Tonnage:	19,037 GRT			
	30,150 DWT	Speed:	16 knots	
Length:	587⅓ feet (179.1 m) waterline	Range:	12,000 n.miles (22,224 km) at 16 knots	
	614⅝ feet (187.45 m) overall	Manning:	23 civilian	

These are build-and-charter oilers constructed specifically for naval service, although initially contracted for commercial service. The lead ship was laid down on 26 December 1983.

Builders: Major components for these ships were built by the American Shipbuilding Co. at Lorain, Ohio, and Nashville, Tenn.

Design: Modified T-5 design with ice-strengthened hulls. The cargo capacity is 238,400 barrels in the first three ships and 239,500 barrels in the last two units.

Engineering: The first two ships have Mitsubishi diesels; the others, Ishikawajima.

The LAWRENCE H. GIANELLA, one of two tankers of this type provided with an UNREP capability. The portside location of the refueling stations facilitates the fueling of aircraft carriers, which have starboard island structures. This enables the carrier's commanding officer to monitor the evolution. (1993, Leo Van Ginderen)

1 TRANSPORT OILER

Number	Name	Launched	Status
T-AOT 1201	ALLEGIANCE (ex-NEW YORK SUN)	1980	**MSC Sealift**

Builders:	
Displacement:	44,000 tons full load
Tonnage:	
Length:	612 feet (186.59 m) overall
Beam:	90 feet (27.44 m)
Draft:	37 feet (11.28 m)
Propulsion:	
Speed:	
Range:	
Manning:	20 civilian

1 COASTAL TRANSPORT OILER: NORWEGIAN-BUILT

Number	Name	Launched	Status
T-AOT 94	VALIANT (ex-SETA, CHIMBORAZO, THOMONA)	1973	**MSC Sealift**

Builders:	Kleven Mek. Verksted A/S, Ulsteinvik, Norway
Displacement:	approx. 10,600 tons full load
Tonnage:	4,375 GRT
	7,634 DWT
Length:	396 feet (120.76 m) overall
Beam:	52 7/12 feet (16.03 m)
Draft:	22 2/3 feet (6.9 m)
Propulsion:	2 diesel engines (MaK 6M453AK); 4,200 bhp; 1 shaft
Speed:	13.5 knots
Range:	10,000 n.miles (18,530 km) at 13.5 knots
Manning:	15 civilian

This ship is a small tanker, a successor to the Navy-built gasoline tankers (AOG) operated by MSC. She has an ice-strengthened hull.

TRANSPORT OILERS: SEALIFT CLASS

Number	Name	In service	Returned to Owner
T-AOT 168	SEALIFT PACIFIC	1974	15 Feb 1995
T-AOT 169	SEALIFT ARABIAN SEA	1975	2 Mar 1995
T-AOT 170	SEALIFT CHINA SEA	1975	18 Apr 1995
T-AOT 171	SEALIFT INDIAN OCEAN	1975	2 May 1995
T-AOT 172	SEALIFT ATLANTIC	1974	4 Apr 1995
T-AOT 173	SEALIFT MEDITERRANEAN	1974	18 Apr 1995
T-AOT 174	SEALIFT CARIBBEAN	1975	4 Apr 1995
T-AOT 175	SEALIFT ARCTIC	1975	4 Apr 1995
T-AOT 176	SEALIFT ANTARCTIC	1975	4 Apr 1995

These ships were built specifically for MSC to replace 16 World War II–era tankers of the T2 type. The ships were contractor-operated under bare-boat charter for MSC with civilian crews for a 20-year period. All were returned to their owners in 1995. By that time, the condition of the ships was marginal for safe and efficient service.

Classification: The ships' designation was changed from T-AO to T-AOT on 30 September 1978.

TRANSPORT OILER: T5-S-RM2a TYPE

The AMERICAN EXPLORER (T-AOT 165) was built for merchant use, but upon completion she was acquired by the Navy. The ship is similar to the MAUMEE-class ships. She was transferred from MSC/RRF to the NDRF on 7 October 1994.

TRANSPORT OILERS: T6-M-98a TYPE

The four large tankers of this class were returned to civilian owners: PATRIOT (T-AOT 1001), RANGER (T-AOT 1002), ROVER (T-AOT 1006), and COURIER (T-AOT 1007).

TRANSPORT OILERS: OVERSEAS CLASS

These four have been returned to their owners: OMI CHAMPION (no number), OVERSEAS ALICE (T-AOT 1203), OVERSEAS VALDEZ (T-AOT 1204), and OVERSEAS VIVIAN (T-AOT 1205). All were in active MSC service or served in the APF.

TRANSPORT OILERS: "SUAMICO" CLASS (T2-SE-A1)

The last of the Navy-operated, World War II–built T2 tankers, the SAUGATUCK (T-AOT 75), was stricken on 15 February 1995. Ships of this class were begun as merchant tankers but were acquired by the Navy in 1942–1943 and completed as fleet oilers (AO) and Navy manned. After World War II, they were employed in the tanker role by the MSTS (later MSC).

Class: The TALLULAH (T-AOT 50), CACHE (T-AOT 67), MILLICOMA (T-AOT 73), and SCHUYLKILL (T-AOT 76) were stricken on 4 March 1988.

Classification: The SAUGATUCK was changed from T-AO to T-AOT on 30 September 1978 (while laid up).

Status: The SAUGATUCK was laid up in NDRF on 5 November 1974.

TRANSPORT OILERS: MISSION TYPE (T2-SE-A2)

The MISSION SANTA YNEZ (T-AOT 134) was the last survivor retained in reserve of the Mission series of merchant tankers built late in

World War II and acquired by the Navy after the war. Delivered as a merchant tanker on 13 March 1944 and acquired by the Navy for use as a tanker on 22 October 1947, the MISSION SANTA YNEZ was laid up in the NDRF on 6 March 1975 (changed to T-AOT on 30 September 1978); she was stricken on 1 November 1990.

Class: The Mission class encompassed the AO 111–137; other fleet oilers and tankers (transport oilers) of this design were in naval service during and after World War II.

TROOP TRANSPORTS

The two troop transports listed below are employed as state maritime academy training ships. Although they remain available for immediate use as transports under the jurisdiction of MSC, their small troop capacities make it highly unlikely that they would be recalled in that role.

The other major U.S. state maritime academy training ships that are former U.S. Navy auxiliaries are:

State	Ship	Formerly
California	GOLDEN BEAR	USNS MAURY (T-AGS 39)
Maine	STATE OF MAINE	USNS TANNER (T-AGS 40)
Texas	TEXAS CLIPPER II	USNS CHAUVENET (T-AGS 29)

In addition, the former sonar ship CONTENDER (T-AGOS 2) serves as a training ship for the U.S. Merchant Marine Academy in Kings Point, N.Y.; she is named KINGS POINTER.

1 TROOP TRANSPORT: C5-S-MA1ua TYPE

Number	Name	Launched	In service	Status
T-AP 1001	EMPIRE STATE (ex-CAPE JUNCTION, MORMACTIDE, OREGON)	16 Sep 1961	3 Jan 1990	**Academic**

Builders:	Newport News Shipbuilding and Dry Dock, Va.
Displacement:	22,629 tons full load
Tonnage:	9,298 GRT (before conversion)
	12,691 DWT (before conversion)
Length:	528⅓ feet (161.1 m) waterline
	564¹¹⁄₁₂ feet (172.2 m) overall
Beam:	76⅙ feet (23.2 m)
Draft:	31⁷⁄₁₂ feet (9.6 m)
Propulsion:	2 steam turbines (General Electric); 17,500 shp; 1 shaft
Boilers:	2 (Foster Wheeler)
Speed:	20 knots
Range:	
Manning:	107 civilian + 684 cadets

This cargo ship was acquired on 14 October 1988 from the NDRF for conversion to a training ship for the New York State Maritime Academy, replacing the former USNS BARRETT (T-AP 196). She was converted by Bay Shipbuilding, Bay City, Wisc., refitted with classrooms and berthing for students.

The ship was laid down on 1 March 1961, assigned to MSC/RRF, and assigned as a school ship in 1990.

The New York state training ship EMPIRE STATE at Portsmouth, England. Most state training ships carry their state's nickname. (1993, Leo Van Ginderen)

TROOP TRANSPORT: S5-S-MA49c TYPE

Number	Name	Launched	Status
T-AP 1000	PATRIOT STATE (ex-SANTA MERCEDES)	30 July 1963	NDRF

Builders:	Bethlehem Steel, Sparrows Point, Baltimore, Md.
Displacement:	approx. 20,500 tons full load
Tonnage:	11,188 GRT
	9,376 DWT
Length:	508⅝₁₂ feet (155.0 m) waterline
	544¹¹⁄₁₂ feet (166.1 m) overall
Beam:	79⅙ feet (24.1 m)
Draft:	29 feet (8.9 m)
Propulsion:	2 steam turbines (General Electric); 19,800 shp; 2 shafts
Boilers:	2 (Babcock & Wilcox)
Speed:	20 knots
Range:	7,000 n.miles (12,964 km) at 20 knots
Manning:	74 civilian + 165 cadets

This is a former passenger/cargo liner modified for use as a school ship by the Massachusetts Maritime Academy. She can carry 175 containers. About 120 cadets were normally embarked for training cruises. She was relieved as the Massachusetts Maritime Academy training ship by the CAPE BON (T-AK 5059) in December 1999; see page 279. (The CAPE BON will become T-AP 1003.)

She was laid down on 29 October 1962.

Class: The PATRIOT STATE is one of four similar ships completed in 1963 for the Grace Lines for the Central/South American trade.

Design: As built, the ship was a combination passenger-cargo ship with accommodations for 119 passengers.

Engineering: The above horsepower is the maximum; normal is 18,000 shp.

The Massachusetts state training ship PATRIOT STATE. In an emergency these state training ships could be employed as troop transports, although such employment is unlikely because of their small troop capacity. (1993, Giorgio Arra)

TROOP TRANSPORTS: "BARRETT" CLASS (P2-S1-DN3 TYPE)

Number	Name	In service	Notes
T-AP 196	EMPIRE STATE V (ex-USNS BARRETT)	1952	stricken 1 July 1973
T-AP 197	BAY STATE (ex-USNS GEIGER)	1952	stricken 1 Apr 1983
T-AP 198	STATE OF MAINE (ex-USNS UPSHUR)	1952	stricken 2 Apr 1973

These veteran troop transports have been discarded and are laid up in the NDRF. The three ships of this design were begun as combination passenger-cargo liners for the American President Lines; they were taken over by the Navy during construction and completed as troop transports. All three were placed in naval service in 1952 with the MSTS and operated by civilian crews.

All were laid up in the NDRF in 1973, having been the last large transports operated by the Military Sealift Command. Subsequently they were transferred on loan to state maritime schools—the BARRETT to the New York Maritime Academy, the GEIGER to the Massachusetts Maritime Academy, and the UPSHUR to the Maine Maritime Academy—and renamed. The ex-GEIGER was severely damaged by an engine room fire in 1981 and was not returned to service.

The ships are not suitable for reactivation.

TROOP TRANSPORTS: ADMIRAL TYPE (P2-SE2-R1)[4]

All transports of this design have been stricken. Ten ships of this design (AP 120–129) were completed in 1944–1945. Several units served as barracks ship (designated IX); see chapter 24.

The last units to be stricken—the GEN ALEXANDER M. PATCH (T-AP 122), GEN SIMON B. BUCKNER (T-AP 123), and GEN MAURICE ROSE (T-AP 126)—had been laid up in the NDRF and were stricken on 20 August 1990. The GEN NELSON M. WALKER (T-AP 125) was stricken on 25 January 1981 and was donated to Life International for conversion to a civilian hospital ship; when this edition went to press, she remained laid up in the James River NDRF.

TROOP TRANSPORTS: GENERAL TYPE (P2-S2-R2)

All transports of this design have been stricken. Eleven ships of this design (AP 110–119 and 176) were completed as troop ships in 1943–1945. The last unit to be stricken, the GEN JOHN POPE (T-AP 110), had been laid up in the NDRF and was stricken on 26 October 1990.

---

4. As built, these ships had "admiral" names. They were transferred to the Army in 1946 and renamed for generals; when they were transferred back to the Navy on 1 March 1950, following establishment of the Military Sea Transportation Service, they retained their Army-assigned names.

Flat racks are used in sealift ships to load vehicles and equipment in place of standard containers. Here flat racks containing Army trucks and trailers are being loaded aboard ship. (U.S. Navy)

CHAPTER 24

Service Craft

Service craft and "floating equipment" come in all sizes and shapes. The largest ship in these categories is the ex-DECATUR (ex-DDG 31/DD 936), now employed as a Self-Defense Test Ship (SDTS). The oldest U.S. "warship" still in service except for the sail frigate CONSTITUTION, the ex-DECATUR is fitted with some of the Navy's latest self-defense weapons and electronics. (U.S. Navy)

The U.S. Navy operates a couple hundred service craft, both self-propelled and non-self-propelled. Most service craft are at naval bases in the United States, with a few overseas. These craft perform a variety of fleet and base support functions.

In addition, two special research platforms are arbitrarily listed at the beginning of this chapter, the self-defense test ship DECATUR and the signature-reduction (stealth) research ship SEA SHADOW.

Also listed in this chapter are the Navy's miscellaneous unclassified ships with the IX designation, which are officially classified as service craft. Although the relic CONSTITUTION has dropped her designation of IX 21, she is included below in her sequential position for historical reasons. (The sailing corvette CONSTELLATION, formerly IX 20, is not listed in this volume; she is not owned by the U.S. government nor is she the original frigate built in 1797; see CONSTITUTION entry.)

The former Coast Guard buoy tender WHITE BUSH (WLM 542), decommissioned in 1985, was assigned to Navy control in the Bremerton-Keyport, Wash., area and informally listed as IX 542; however, she was never officially given that designation and was sold for scrap on 9 July 1995.

Only the self-propelled service craft are described below, with a few exceptions; i.e., all IX-series ships are provided to present a complete listing. The non-self-propelled units are indicated by an arrow (↓).

The Navy's manned submersibles and floating dry docks, officially classified as service craft, are listed in chapters 12 and 25, respectively, of this edition of *Ships and Aircraft*.

Classification: Most service craft have Y-series designations, that letter having been established when these were considered yard craft; they were also known as district craft, from being assigned to the now defunct naval districts. Some service craft have hull registry numbers (length + type designation + serial); a few have both. For example, the TWR 821 has the hull registry number 120TR821.

Only Y-series service craft are listed in the Naval Vessel Register (NVR). All service craft are found in the Service Craft And Boat Accounting Report (SABAR).

Guns: Service craft are not armed. The Naval Academy's seamanship training craft (YP) can be armed with light weapons for use as harbor patrol craft, while some of the utility cargo carriers (YFU) and barracks ships (APB) were armed for service in the Vietnam War. The IX 515/SES-200 has carried out trials with a number of weapons.

Helicopters: The "mini-carrier" IX 514 is the only service craft with a helicopter capability.

Operational: Most service craft are manned by Navy personnel. Those assigned to the Naval Command, Control, and Ocean Surveillance Center at San Diego, Calif., and a few other service craft are operated by civilian personnel. Several service craft acquired or leased during the 1990s are manned by contractor personnel.

1 SELF-DEFENSE SYSTEMS TEST SHIP: EX-"FORREST SHERMAN" CLASS

Number	Name	Launched	Commissioned	Status
(ex-DDG 31, DD 936)	DECATUR	15 Dec 1955	7 Dec 1956	**Active**

Builder:	Bethlehem Steel, Quincy, Mass.
Displacement:	approx. 4,000 tons full load
Length:	407 feet (124.09 m) waterline
	418⁵/₁₂ feet (127.57 m) overall
Beam:	45⅙ feet (13.77 m)
Draft:	
Propulsion:	2 diesel engines (Harbormaster); all-azimuth drives
Speed:	10 knots
Missiles:	1 8-cell NATO Sea Sparrow launcher Mk 29
Guns:	1 20-mm Phalanx CIWS Mk 16 (multibarrel)
Radars:	HFSWR air-search
	R70A navigation
Fire control:	1 Mk 23 TAS (Target Acquisition System)
EW systems:	SLQ-32(V)3
Manning:	approx. 50

The former destroyer DECATUR has been configured to test shipboard self-defenses, both active and passive. She can operate both manned or under radio-control. The ship is expected to operate at sea for one month per quarter to test and evaluate shipboard defensive systems and tactics.

Originally completed as one of 18 all-gun destroyers of the FORREST SHERMAN (DD 931) class, the DECATUR was one of four ships converted to a guided missile configuration in 1965–1967. She was decommissioned on 30 June 1983 and stricken on 16 March 1988.

The DECATUR subsequently was converted to a test platform in 1989–1994 at the Puget Sound Naval Shipyard and at the Naval Surface Weapons Center at Port Hueneme, Calif. Her masts and superstructure have been extensively modified; a helicopter platform is fitted aft. All original guns, torpedo tubes, and ASW weapons have been deleted.

Classification: Originally DD 936; changed to DDG 31 on 15 September 1966.

The ship has "E 31" painted on the hull; she is referred to as EDD 31 and as SDTS (Self-Defense Test Ship).

Electronics: The ship retains her SQS-23 sonar; it is inactive.

Engineering: The ship's steam-turbine propulsion plant is inactive.

UNCLASSIFIED AUXILIARY SHIPS

Unclassified ship designations reached hull number IX 235 at the end of World War II. The series was continued after the war, beginning with the designation IX 300, assigned to the German heavy cruiser PRINZ EUGEN, thus creating a gap in IX hull numbers from 236 to 299.

The postwar IX series reached hull number 310 when—in 1967—the extensively converted ELK RIVER (LSMR 501) was placed in this category and classified IX with her previous hull number. Subsequent craft were given 500-series designations, creating a second major sequential gap in IX hull numbers from 311 to 500.

Thus, there has been an official disregard for the IX numerical series, which dated back to December 1941. (The IX symbol for unclassified vessels was used by the Navy from 1920 without specific hull numbers being assigned.)

The non-self-propelled YFND 5 (formerly YFN 268), a diving tender, was changed to IX 530 on 6 September 2000.

The IX 521, 522, 524, and 525 are floating dry docks; they are listed in chapter 25. The only other craft "missing" in the following listings between hulls IX 501 and IX 529 is the IX 505—the former medium harbor tug YTM 759—which was stricken in 1977.

1 STEALTH RESEARCH SHIP: "SEA SHADOW"

Number	Name	In service	Status
IX 529	SEA SHADOW	1985	**Active**

Builders:	Lockheed Missiles and Space Co., Sunnyvale, Calif.
Displacement:	560 tons full load
Length:	164 feet (50.0 m) overall
Beam:	68 feet (20.73 m)
Draft:	14 feet (4.27 m)
Propulsion:	diesel-electric (2 General Motors Detroit 12V149 TI diesel engines); 1,600 shp; 2 shafts
Speed:	13 knots sustained
	15 knots maximum
Range:	2,250 n.miles (4,170 km) at 9 knots
Manning:	12 Navy-civilian + 12 technicians

The SEA SHADOW was built as a test platform for several surface ship technologies, among them ship control, automation, structures, seakeeping, and—especially—signature reduction. The program was sponsored by the Navy, the Advanced Research Projects Agency (ARPA), and Lockheed.[1] Results of the signature reduction research have been used in the ARLEIGH BURKE (DDG 51) class and Small Waterplane-Area Twin Hull (SWATH)-configured ocean surveillance ships (T-AGOS 19–23).

The SEA SHADOW was not intended as the prototype for a stealth warship.

---

1. ARPA subsequently was renamed the Defense Advanced Research Projects Agency (DARPA).

The ex-DECATUR has SLQ-32 ECM antennas atop her bridge and various radars and other electronic antennas atop her lattice masts. A NATO Sea Sparrow missile launcher is aft of the second stack, a Phalanx CIWS atop her after deckhouse, and a helicopter platform is over her fantail. All of these systems were installed for her SDTS role. (U.S. Navy)

Builders: The craft was designed and built by the Lockheed "Skunk Works," which developed the U-2, SR-71 Blackhawk, and F-117A stealth fighter, among other projects. Construction began in 1983 inside of the covered floating dock HMB-1.[2]

Classification: The SEA SHADOW was classified as IX 529 on 15 March 2000.

Cost: The Navy states that the cost of the SEA SHADOW program was $195 million, including ship construction costs of $50 million.

Design: The SEA SHADOW has a SWATH configuration with twin submerged hulls. The diesel engines are fitted in the "fuselage" and the electric motors in the submerged hulls.

The angled fuselage and supports for the twin submerged hulls help reflect radar signals. Anechoic coatings have been used on the craft to further deter radar detection.

A small, retractable radar is fitted atop the control station. There are no fixed projections from the hull.

---

2. HMB = Hughes Mining Barge. This dock was developed for use with the deep-ocean salvage ship GLOMAR EXPLORER (AG 193); see page 241. The HMB-1 is 5,800 tons full load with a length of 323$\frac{11}{12}$ feet (98.75 m), beam of 105 feet (32.00 m), and draft of 8 feet (2.44 m); when ballasted down to receive the SEA SHADOW, her draft is increased to 42 feet (12.80 m).

The SEA SHADOW shortly after being reactivated in 1999 to continue research into ship design and technologies. Here, she is getting under way in San Francisco Bay at dusk in preparation for an exercise with Third Fleet units. A radar "pot" is raised above the "cockpit." (1999, U.S. Navy)

The SEA SHADOW under way. The SWATH craft has twin hulls beneath the surface. There are hatches forward and aft in the angled superstructure. All masts and other projects retract into the superstructure to reduce the craft's Radar Cross-Section (RCS). (Lockheed Martin)

Operational: The SEA SHADOW conducted exclusively nighttime test runs off the coast of southern California in 1985–1986, after which funding shortages led to the craft being laid up. She was then stored in floating dock HMB-1 at Redwood City in the San Francisco Bay area.

At-sea testing was resumed in April 1993 off Santa Cruz Island and, subsequently, in San Francisco Bay, until she was again laid up in the HMB-1 in May 1995. The first daylight test run of the SEA SHADOW—with publicity—was made on 11 April 1993.

The ship was reactivated in February 1999 to test signature-reduction concepts for the DD 21 program.[3]

3. See David Abel, "Navy Stealthy about Details of 'Sea Shadow' Ship," *Defense Week,* 2 August 1999, p. 7.

The SEA SHADOW inside her support platform HMB-1. The platform partially submerges for the stealth craft to enter or depart; it can then be pumped out to raise itself and the SEA SHADOW up and out of the water to provide access to the lower areas of the craft. (Lockheed Martin)

The SEA SHADOW entering the support platform HMB-1. The island structure of the carrier JOHN C. STENNIS (CVN 74) is off to starboard. The hull, island structure, and innumerable antennas of a modern aircraft carrier provide a massive RCS. (1993, U.S. Navy)

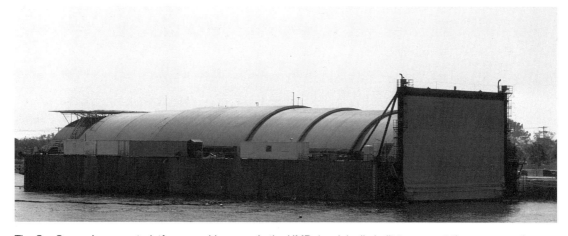

The SEA SHADOW's support platform—and hangar—is the HMB-1, originally built to support the recovery of a Soviet missile submarine by the GLOMAR EXPLORER (AG 193). The designation *HMB* indicated Hughes Mining Barge, part of the cover for the GLOMAR EXPLORER as a seafloor mining operation by Howard Hughes. (1999, Leo Van Ginderen)

1 SUPPORT CRAFT ↓

Number	Launched	In service	Status
IX 528 (ex-YRDH 1)	3 Sep 1943	2 Dec 1943	**Active**

Builder:	Associated Shipbuilding, Seattle, Wash.
Displacement:	460 tons light
	750 tons full load
Length:	150 feet (45.73 m) waterline
	151 feet (46.0 m) overall
Beam:	34 feet (10.37 m)
Draft:	6 feet (1.83 m)
Propulsion:	non-self-propelled (diesel generator)
Manning:	47 (1 officer, 46 enlisted)

Assigned to the Naval Surface Warfare Center's detachment at Puget Sound, Wash.

Classification: Built as a non-self-propelled floating workshop (YR 55); changed to floating workshop (hull) (YRDH 1) during World War II and to IX 528 on 7 April 1999.

1 SUPPORT CRAFT ↓

Number	Launched	In service	Status
IX 527 (ex-YFN 1259)		1 June 1982	**Active**

Builder:	Steel Style
Displacement:	
Length:	110 feet (33.54 m) waterline
	110 feet (33.54 m) overall
Beam:	35 feet (10.67 m)
Draft:	8 feet (2.44 m)
Propulsion:	non-self-propelled (diesel generator)
Manning:	

Assigned to the Naval Surface Warfare Center's detachment at Puget Sound, Wash.

Classification: Changed from YFN 1259 to IX 527 on 7 April 1999.

1 WORK BARGE ↓

Number	Launched	In service	Status
IX 526 (ex-YRST 1)	17 Jan 1945	13 Feb 1945	**Active**

Builder:	Everett-Pacific, Everett, Wash.
Displacement:	700 tons light
	2,700 tons full load
Length:	260 feet (79.27 m) waterline
	261 feet (79.57 m) overall
Beam:	48 feet (14.63 m)
Draft:	9 feet (2.74 m)
Propulsion:	non-self-propelled (diesel generator)
Manning:	
Accommodations:	86 (15 officers + 71 enlisted)

The craft is employed as a work barge at San Diego, Calif.

The barge was built as the YFN 723 and subsequently was changed to YFNB 12, YDT 11, and YRST 1. It was changed again, to IX 526, on 1 October 1975.

1 TRAINING CRAFT

Number	Launched	In service	Status
IX 523 (ex-YOG 93)	8 Sep 1945	8 Feb 1946	**Active**

Builders:	R.T.C. Shipbuilding, Camden, N.J.
Displacement:	440 tons light
	1,390 tons full load
Length:	174 feet (53.0 m) overall
Beam:	33 feet (10.1 m)
Draft:	13 feet (4.0 m)
Propulsion:	1 diesel engine (General Motors); 640 bhp; 1 shaft
Speed:	11 knots
Manning:	23 (1 officer + 22 enlisted)

This a former self-propelled gasoline barge, assigned to the Fleet Training Group, Norfolk, Va.

Two sister ships, the last YOGs in Navy service, have been stricken, the YOG 78 on 31 July 1995 and the YOG 88 on 19 May 1997.

Classification: Changed to IX 523 on 25 November 1996.

Design: As a YOG, her cargo capacity was 6,570 barrels.

1 BARRACKS SHIP ↓

Number	Launched	Commissioned	Status
IX 520 (ex-APL 19)	6 Aug 1944	14 Oct 1944	**Active**

Builder:	Tampa Shipbuilding Co., Tampa, Fla.
Displacement:	2,660 tons light
Length:	260 feet (79.27 m) waterline
	261⅙ feet (79.62 m) overall
Beam:	49⅙ feet (14.99 m)
Draft:	
Propulsion:	non-self-propelled (diesel generator)
Manning:	
Troops:	686 (6 officers + 680 enlisted)

Built as a non-self-propelled barracks ship. She was stricken in 1993 but reinstated on the NVR on 16 August 1996. She is used as an accommodations barge at the Norfolk Naval Shipyard.

Classification: Changed from APL 19 to IX 520 on 16 August 1996.

1 SUPPORT BARGE ↓

Number	Launched	In service	Status
IX 519 (ex-YC 1643)		1 Mar 1991	**Active**

Builder:	Orange Shipbuilding, Orange, Texas
Displacement:	115 tons light
	659 tons full load
Length:	110 feet (33.54 m) waterline
	110 feet (33.54 m) overall
Beam:	32 feet (9.75 m)
Draft:	7 feet (2.13 m)
Propulsion:	non-self-propelled (diesel generator)
Manning:	

Ordered in 1989 as an open, steel barge. The craft is employed to support the LA SALLE (AGF 3), flagship of the Sixth Fleet. The barge is carried by the LA SALLE and employed as an alongside landing stage for small boats.

Classification: Changed to IX 519 on 1 March 1993.

BARRACKS SHIP: EX-SUBMARINE TENDER ↓

Number	Name	Commissioned	Status
IX 518 (ex-AS 19)	ex-PROTEUS	31 Jan 1944	to MARAD 24 Sep 1999

The PROTEUS originally was a submarine tender of the FULTON (AS 11) class. She was in active service as a tender from 1944 to 26 September 1947, when she was decommissioned and placed "in service." The ship provided support to submarines at New London, Conn., until January 1955, when she was taken in hand for extensive conversion to support Polaris fleet ballistic missile submarines; she was recommissioned on 8 July 1960. She served in that role until the 1980s and was subsequently employed in general repair and support activities for surface ships as well as submarines.

The PROTEUS was decommissioned and stricken on 30 September 1992. Her status was changed from "strike" to "In Service, In Reserve" on 1 February 1994 for use as a barracks ship at the Puget Sound Naval Shipyard, Bremerton, Wash., replacing the GEN HUGH J. GAFFEY (see page 326).

She was transferred to the Maritime Administration in 1999 and towed to Suisun Bay, Calif., in preparation for scrapping. When this edition went to press, she had not been stricken from the NVR.

Classification: Changed from AS 19 to IX 518 on 1 February 1994 (at time her name was deleted).

1 ESCORT SHIP: EX-OCEANOGRAPHIC RESEARCH SHIP

Number	Name	FY	Launched	In service	Status
IX 517 (ex-AGOR 9)	GOSPORT	63	18 July 1964	4 Sep 1965	**Active**

Builders:	Marinette Marine, Wisc.
Displacement:	1,088 tons light
	1,400 tons full load
Length:	195⅝ feet (59.7 m) waterline
	208⅝ feet (63.7 m) overall
Beam:	37 feet (11.3 m)
Draft:	16 feet (4.9 m)
Propulsion:	diesel-electric (2 Cummins diesels); 10,000 shp; 1 shaft
Speed:	13.5 knots
Range:	12,000 n.miles (22,235 km) at 9 knots
Manning:	civilian
Radars:	. . . navigation

This is a former CONRAD (AGOR 3)-class oceanographic research ship. She was employed in support of submarines undergoing trials after overhaul at the Mare Island Naval Shipyard, Calif., from 1990 until early 1995. Since then, she has been operating at the Norfolk Naval Shipyard. Her future status is undetermined.

The GOSPORT replaced a former Army tug named PACIFIC ESCORT (designated 143WB8401, ex-Army LT 535).

As an AGOR, the ship was operated by the University of Washington (state). All research equipment has been removed.

Class: Nine ships of this class were built for Navy's Military Sealift Command (MSC) and academic use: AGOR 3–7, 9, 10, 12, and 13 (see page 248).

Classification: Changed to IX 517 on 11 December 1989.

Design: SCB No. 185. A retractable bow propulsor provides speeds up to 6.5 knots in "quiet" conditions for research.

Engineering: The large stack contains a small diesel exhaust funnel and provides space for a small, 620-hp gas turbine engine used to provide "quiet" power when noise generated by the main propulsion machinery could interfere with research activities. The gas turbine can be linked to the propeller shaft for speeds up to 6.5 knots. There is also a retractable bow propeller pod that allows precise maneuvering.

Name: Originally named THOMAS G. THOMPSON as an AGOR; name changed to PACIFIC ESCORT in 1989 and to GOSPORT in April 1997.

1 CLASSROOM BARGE ↓

Number	Name	Built	In service	Status
IX 516	(none)	1976	15 Apr 1988	**Active**

Builder:	McDermott Shipyard, Morgan City, La.
Displacement:	3,122 tons light
	3,476 tons full load
Length:	302¾ feet (92.28 m) overall
Beam:	90 feet (27.43 m)
Draft:	22 feet (6.7 m)
Propulsion:	non-self-propelled (diesel generator)
Manning:	

The IX 516 is a classroom barge employed at the Naval Nuclear Power Training Unit, Goose Creek (Charleston), S.C. There is a three-story deckhouse on the barge containing classrooms; the structure is 241 feet (73.5 m) long, 72 feet (21.95 m) wide, and 35 feet (10.7 m) high.

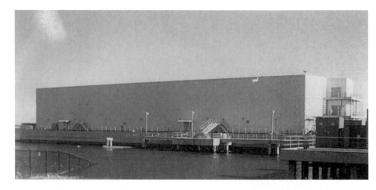

The IX 516 is a floating classroom for nuclear propulsion technicians. The craft has emergency power generators but normally uses shore electrical power. (1990, U.S. Navy)

The THOMAS G. THOMPSON—now the GOSPORT—as an oceanographic research ship. She now is employed in utilities duties, awaiting her final disposition. (1986, Giorgio Arra)

1 SURFACE EFFECTS SHIP: "SES-200"

Number	Launched	In service	Status
IX 515 (ex-SES-200, WSES 1)	Dec 1978	Feb 1979	**Active**

Builders:	Bell-Halter, New Orleans, La.
Displacement:	187 tons light
	243 tons full load
Length:	159¹⁄₁₂ feet (48.5 m) overall
Beam:	42⁷⁄₁₂ (13.0 m)
Draft:	6 feet (1.8 m) on hull
	5 feet (1.5 m) on cushion
Propulsion:	2 diesel engines (MTU 16V396 TB94); 5,720 bhp; 2 waterjets
Lift:	2 diesel engines (MTU 6V396 TB83); 1,400 bhp; 4 centrifugal fans
Speed:	16 knots on hull in sea state 0
	14 knots on hull in sea state 3
	40+ knots on cushion in sea state 0
	27 knots on cushion in sea state 3
Range:	2,950 n.miles (5,463 km) at 30 knots in sea state 0
	2,400 n.miles (4,445 km) at 25 knots in sea state 3
Manning:	22 (2 officers + 20 enlisted)
Guns:	(see notes)
Radars:	2 Decca navigation

The SES-200 was built as a prototype for U.S. Navy and Coast Guard evaluation. The craft was designed by Bell Aerospace and built by Halter Marine. After completion, the craft was leased to the U.S. Coast Guard for trials (beginning January 1980) and then transferred back to the U.S. Navy (from 1982) for continued trials. Following her conversion (see below), the craft was again evaluated by the Coast Guard in late 1984.

In Coast Guard service, the craft was named DORADO and designated WSES-1. (Subsequently, the Coast Guard purchased three similar craft; see chapter 32.)

The experimental surface effects ship SES-200 in her current configuration. The U.S. Navy has not proceeded with SES development as has the Russian Navy, which has developed a corvette-size SES, the Dergach class. (Textron Marine Systems)

The SES-200 at rest (1989, Giorgio Arra)

The craft was again placed in U.S. Navy service on 24 September 1982. She is assigned to the Naval Surface Warfare Center and based at the Naval Air Station Patuxent River, Md.[4]

Classification: The hull number IX 515 was assigned on 11 May 1987; previously the craft was listed as "floating equipment."

Conversion: In January 1982, the craft was returned to Bell-Halter, where she was cut in half and a 50-foot (15.2-m) midships section was installed. The modified craft was accepted by the Navy on 24 September 1982.

Two additional lift fans were installed in 1984. Her propulsion plant was upgraded from September 1987 through 1988, with the older propulsion system being replaced by the current diesel engines and waterjet propulsion in 1990.

Engineering: The original characteristics and propulsion plant are described in the 14th Edition/pages 355–356. The waterjet propulsion is the Swedish KaMeWa system.

Guns: The ship was fitted in 1986–1987 with an Ex-25 25-mm Sea Vulcan rotary-barrel (Gatling) gun to evaluate the effectiveness of such weapons on high-speed craft, especially against slow-moving targets.

Missiles: In 1989 the craft evaluated the LTV-developed Crossbow weapons pedestal, which can be used to launch a variety of short-range missiles.

Operational: In 1985–1986 the craft carried out trials and demonstrations in several European countries and Canada. The craft conducted visits to several South American ports in 1987.

The SES-200, showing the craft's broad stern (1989, Giorgio Arra)

1 HELICOPTER TRAINING CRAFT: EX-YFU TYPE

Number	Name	In service	To IX	Status
IX 514 (ex-YFU 79)	(none)	1968	Mar 1986	**Active**

Builders:	Pacific Coast Engineering, Alameda, Calif.
Displacement:	220 tons light
	380 tons full load
Length:	125 feet (38.1 m) overall
Beam:	36 feet (11.0 m)
Draft:	7½ feet (2.3 m)
Propulsion:	2 diesel engines (General Motors 6-71); 1,000 bhp; 2 shafts
Speed:	8 knots
Manning:	12 (2 officers + 10 enlisted)
Radars:	1 Decca navigation

The YFU 79 was converted in 1985–1986 for use as a helicopter landing ship to train helicopter pilots. Placed in service on 31 March 1986, she operates in the Gulf of Mexico, based at the Naval Air Station Pensacola, Fla.

---

4. The Naval Surface Warfare Center was formerly the Naval Ship Research and Development Center, with headquarters at Carderock, Md.

The helicopter landing training craft IX 514 off Pensacola, Fla. The TH-57C SeaRanger is flown by student pilots, practicing landings aboard the world's "smallest aircraft carrier." During the Vietnam War, smaller U.S. LCMs were fitted with flight decks. (Bell Helicopter Textron)

Classification: Changed from YFU to IX on 31 March 1986.

Helicopters: The flight deck landing area is 57⅚ feet (17.6 m) long and 28 feet (8.5 m) wide. There is no helicopter parking area or hangar on the craft nor is a refueling capability provided. Lighting is installed for night landings.

1 RADIATION TEST BARGE ↓

Number	In service
IX 513	June 1988

Builders:	Eastern Marine, Panama City, Fla.
Displacement:	approx. 2,200 tons full load
Length:	120 feet (36.57 m) overall
Beam:	90 feet (27.43 m)
Draft:	15 feet (4.57 m)
Propulsion:	non-self-propelled (diesel generator)
Manning:	

The IX 513 is an unmanned barge used to produce electric pulse to evaluate ships' Electro-Magnetic Pulse (EMP) protection under a program named Empress II. The craft has a 150-foot (45.7-m),

The Empress II radiation test barge IX 513. Tests to determine electromagnetic effects on ships have become controversial due to the efforts of environmental groups. (1990, Leo Van Ginderen)

four-leg support structure for a 188½-foot (57.5-m)-diameter pulse transmission antenna ring. A pulse of 7 million volts can be generated by the craft's two diesel generators.

Delayed by builder problems and environmental impact concerns, the barge began pulse tests against warships in 1990 off the coast of North Carolina; she was subsequently moved to the Gulf of Mexico.

MISSILE TEST BARGE ↓

The Trident D-5 missile test barge IX 512 (ex-BD 6651) was stricken on 13 December 1995. This was a former U.S. Army floating crane converted for simulation of Trident D-5 missile launches. Known as the Simulated Underwater Partial Launch System (SUPLS) II, the craft is fitted with a single Trident missile tube. The 52-ton-capacity crane is retained.

The craft was operated off San Clemente Island, Calif.

BARRACKS SHIPS: EX-TROOP TRANSPORTS (P2-SE2-R1) ↓

Number	Name	AP Comm.	Notes
IX 507 (ex-AP 121)	GEN HUGH J. GAFFEY	1944	stricken 26 Oct 1993
IX 510 (ex-AP 127)	GEN WILLIAM O. DARBY	1945	stricken 26 Oct 1993

These former Admiral-class transports were employed as immobilized barracks ships during the 1980s. Built as naval transports, they were transferred to the Army in 1946 and subsequently assigned to the Navy's newly established Military Sea Transportation Service (MSTS) on 1 March 1950. As troop transports, the AP 121 could carry 4,680 troops and the AP 127 could carry 4,985 troops.

The GAFFEY was stricken from the NVR on 9 January 1969. The ship was reacquired by the Navy on 1 November 1978 for conversion to a barracks ship and reclassified IX 507; she was assigned to the Bremerton Naval Shipyard for the crews of aircraft carriers undergoing conversion and modernization.

The DARBY was operational as a transport from completion until laid up in National Defense Reserve Fleet (NDRF) ready reserve status on 1 July 1967. She was reacquired from the NDRF on 27 October 1981 (reclassified IX 510 on that date) for use as a barracks ship; after being modified, she was towed to the Norfolk Navy Yard to house crews of ships undergoing conversion and modernization, with the status "Out of Service, In Reserve" (OSIR). She was again laid up in the NDRF on 23 April 1991.

Only the ships' accommodations and messing spaces were rehabilitated. The ships were not capable of steaming in their final condition.

EXPLOSIVES DAMAGE-CONTROL BARGE

The unnamed IX 509, a non-self-propelled barge configured to support explosives testing, was stricken on 18 December 1992. The craft had been placed in service in 1979.

1 TEST OPERATIONS SUPPORT SHIP: EX-LCU TYPE

Number	Name	In service	Status
IX 508 (ex-LCU 1618)	ORCA	1 June 1959	**Active**

Builders:	Gunderson Bros., Portland, Ore.
Displacement:	190 tons light
	390 tons full load
Length:	134¾ feet (41.1 m) overall
Beam:	29¾ feet (9.1 m)
Draft:	6⅝ feet (2.1 m)
Propulsion:	4 diesel engines (General Motors 6-71); 1,200 bhp; 2 shafts
	(Kort nozzles)
Speed:	11 knots
Range:	1,200 n.miles (2,222 km) at 11 knots
Manning:	

This craft is configured to support test operations at the Naval Command, Control, and Ocean Surveillance Center at San Diego. Formerly an LCU 1610–class landing craft, the craft served for several years in the test support role before being changed to IX 508 on 1 December 1979.

Electronics: Modified in 1978 to conduct trials with the NAVSTAR satellite Global Positioning System.

Names: ORCA is an unofficial name for the craft.

The test operations ship ORCA is an extensively rebuilt LCU. Such service and support craft are rarely seen or photographed. (1990, U.S. Navy)

RESEARCH SUPPORT SHIP: EX-YFU TYPE

Number	Name	In service	Status
IX 506 (ex-YFU 82)	SEA LION	1968	stricken 21 Aug 1997

This former harbor utility craft was extensively rebuilt for use as a research platform by the Naval Command, Control, and Ocean Surveillance Center at San Diego (replacing the YTM 759).

She was changed from YFU 82 to IX 506 on 1 April 1978.

See 16th Edition/page 302 for characteristics.

2 BARRACKS SHIPS: MODIFIED LST DESIGN ↓

Number	Name	Launched	Commissioned	Status
IX 502 (ex-APB 39)	MERCER	17 Nov 1944	19 Sep 1945	**Active**
IX 503 (ex-APB 40)	NUECES	6 May 1945	30 Nov 1945	**Active**
IX 504 (ex-APB 37)	ECHOLS	30 July 1945	(1 Jan 1947)	OSIR/str. 22 Dec 1995

Builders:	Boston Navy Yard, Mass.
Displacement:	2,190 tons light
	3,640 tons full load
Length:	328 feet (100.0 m) overall
Beam:	50 feet (15.25 m)
Draft:	11 feet (3.4 m)
Propulsion:	2 diesel engines (General Motors 12-267); 1,600 bhp; 2 shafts
	(see *Engineering* notes)
Speed:	10 knots
Manning:	198 (12 officers + 186 enlisted) as APB
Troops:	approx. 900
Guns:	removed

These ships were built to provide accommodations and support for small craft. All three were completed as barracks ships (APL, later APB). They were modified in 1975–1976 to serve at shipyards for crews of ships being built or in overhaul and were changed from APB to IX at that time.

Two ships were placed in commission upon original completion; the ECHOLS was placed in service. All three ships were laid up in reserve after World War II. The MERCER and NUECES were recommissioned in 1968 for service in the Vietnam War. They were rearmed at that time with two 3-inch/50-cal AA guns (single), eight 40-mm AA guns (quad), and several machine guns. As modified to support riverine forces in South Vietnam, they had crews of 12 officers and 186 enlisted men and could accommodate 900 troops and small-craft crewmen. Both ships were again laid up from 1969–1971 until reactivated in 1975 as barracks ships; the MERCER is at San Diego and the NUECES is at the U.S. Naval Ship Repair Facility, Yokosuka, Japan.

The ECHOLS was reactivated and placed in service on 1 February 1976 as a barracks ship for the crews of new-construction SSBNs at the General Dynamics/Electric Boat yard in Groton, Conn.; she was subsequently stricken.

Class: There were originally six ships of this class, APB 35–40.

Classification: APL/APB 39 changed to IX 502 and APL/APB 40 to IX 503 on 1 November 1975; APL/APB 37 changed to IX 504 on 1 February 1976.

Engineering: Their propulsion plants are not operational.

Guns: As built, these ships had eight 40-mm AA guns in quad mounts.

The barracks ship MERCER at San Francisco. Barracks ships provide mess and berthing facilities for the crews of ships undergoing construction, overhaul, or conversion. (1986, Giorgio Arra)

BARRACKS SHIP: EX-MEDIUM ROCKET LANDING SHIP ↓

Number	Name	Commissioned	Status
IX 501 (ex-LSMR 501)	ELK RIVER	1945	stricken 13 Aug 1999

The ELK RIVER was converted from a rocket landing ship to a test and training ship for deep-sea diving and salvage. She was operated in that role by the Naval Ocean Systems Center (NOSC), San Diego, from 1969 until 1986. Her specialized equipment was removed in 1986 and the ship was relegated to service as a barracks hulk at San Diego.

See 16th Edition/page 303 for characteristics.

Class: The ELK RIVER was the last of 48 medium landing ships (LSM) completed as or converted to rocket fire support ships (LSMR 401–412 and 501–536). All other ships of this type have been stricken, the last three LSMRs having been used in the Vietnam War (redesignated IFS for inshore fire support ships with their LSMR hull numbers).

A total of 558 LSM-type ships were completed 1944–1946; the design originally was designated LCT(7).

Classification: Changed from LSMR to IX on 1 April 1967.

1 SONAR TEST BARGE ↓

Number	Name	IX in service	Status
IX 310	(none)	1 Apr 1971	**Active**

The IX 310 consists of two non-self-propelled barges moored in Lake Seneca, N.Y., for sonar research by the Naval Undersea Warfare Center at Newport, R.I. (formerly Naval Underwater Sound Laboratory). They were built in 1970.

SOUND TRIALS SHIP: "MONOB ONE"

The MONOB ONE (ex-IX 309, YW 87) has been reclassified as the YAG 61 and subsequently stricken (see below).

TORPEDO TRIALS SHIP: EX-CARGO SHIP

The torpedo trials ship NEW BEDFORD (IX 308, ex-AKL 17) was stricken on 4 April 1995. See 16th Edition/pages 303–304 for characteristics.

1 SAILING FRIGATE: "CONSTITUTION" ↓

Number	Name	Launched	Commissioned	Status
(ex-IX 21)	CONSTITUTION	21 Oct 1797	July 1798	**Active**

Builders:	Hartt's Shipyard, Boston, Mass.
Displacement:	2,200 tons standard
Length:	175 feet (53.35 m) waterline
	204 feet (62.2 m) billet head to taffrail
Beam:	43½ feet (13.3 m)
Draft:	22½ feet (6.85 m)
Masts:	fore 198 feet (60.4 m)
	main 220 feet (67.0 m)
	mizzen 171½ feet (52.6 m)
Speed:	13+ knots (under sail)
Manning:	54 (2 officers + 52 enlisted) as relic; up to 500 as frigate (including 55 Marines)
Guns:	several smooth-bore cannon (see notes)

The CONSTITUTION is the oldest U.S. ship in Navy commission and the oldest warship still known to be afloat. Her original commissioning date is not known; she first put to sea on 23 July 1798. She is now moored as a relic at the Charlestown Naval Shipyard in Boston, Mass. (She is afloat, unlike the older VICTORY, Lord Admiral Nelson's flagship at the battle of Trafalgar, which is preserved in concrete at the naval dockyard in Portsmouth, England.)

Her keel was laid down on 1 November 1794.

No sails are fitted; her designed sail area was 42,710 square feet (3,844 m²). Once a year, usually on 4 July, she is taken out into Boston Harbor under tow and "turned around," so that her masts do not bend from the effects of sun and wind. At noon on 4 July, the CONSTITUTION traditionally fires a 21-gun salute from her forward 24-pounder long guns.

Class: The CONSTITUTION was one of six sail frigates built under an act of Congress of 1794. The CONSTELLATION (38 guns), built under the same act and launched on 7 September 1797, was broken up at the Gosport shipyard (Norfolk), Va., in 1852–1853; almost simultaneously, a sailing corvette of that name was built in the same yard. That ship served in the Navy (designated IX 20 in 1941) until her transfer in 1954 to a private group in Baltimore, Md., where she is maintained.[5]

Classification: The CONSTITUTION was classified as an "unclassified" ship in 1920 (IX without a hull number). She became IX 21 on 8 December 1941 and carried that classification until 1 September 1975 when it was withdrawn because, according to Navy officials, the designation "tended to demean and degrade the CONSTITUTION through association with a group of insignificant craft of varied missions and configurations."

Design: Three-masted sail frigate designed by Joshua Humphreys. The ship was built at Edmond Hartt's shipyard in Boston; she was rebuilt several times, but her basic lines and configuration have been retained.

Guns: The CONSTITUTION was authorized as a 44-gun frigate, but was in fact completed with a larger gun battery. The ship was usually overgunned, with an early armament consisting of 30 long 24-pounders, 20 to 22 long 12-pounders, and 2 long 24-pounder

---

5. Until 1991, the preserving organization contended that the Baltimore CONSTELLATION was the frigate of 1797, despite extensive evidence to the contrary. The issue was decisively addressed and the Baltimore ship proven to be the 1853 vessel in an analysis by Dana M. Wegner, et al., of the Navy's David Taylor Research Center (*Fouled Anchors: The Constellation Questions Answered,* September 1991).

The CONSTITUTION in her normal habitat in Boston Harbor. She is the oldest warship in commission and afloat. (1996, U.S. Navy, PH3 David G. Schmidt)

The CONSTITUTION under sail on her 200th anniversary—for the first time in 116 years. During her brief cruise, she was accompanied by the destroyer RAMAGE (DDG 61) and frigate HALYBURTON (FFG 40), with an overhead salute by the Blue Angels flight demonstration squadron. (1997, U.S. Navy)

chase guns. This heavy armament overloaded and strained the ship; still, she could have accommodated up to 60 guns.

The number and types of guns varied considerably during her service as a frigate.

Names: The ship was named OLD CONSTITUTION from 1 December 1917 until 4 July 1925 while the name CONSTITUTION was assigned to a battle cruiser (CC 5); the cruiser was never completed and the name reverted to this ship.

Operational: As a sail frigate, the CONSTITUTION fought in the Quasi-War with France, against the Barbary pirates, and in the War of 1812 against Great Britain.

The ship has been at Boston since 7 May 1934, following a sailing tour of 90 ports on the U.S. Atlantic, Pacific, and Gulf coasts from 1931 to 1934.

The CONSTITUTION hosts more than one million visitors per year.

On 21 July 1997 the CONSTITUTION was towed from Boston to Marblehead, Mass., a distance of 17 n.miles (31.5 km). There the tow lines were cast off and the ship set sail for the first time since 1881. However, she is not considered to be a self-propelled ship in her current status.

Y-SERIES SERVICE CRAFT

SOUND TRIALS SHIP: "DEER ISLAND"

The sound trials ship DEER ISLAND (YAG 62), a former oilfield supply ship built in 1966, was stricken on 2 August 1996. She was acquired by the Navy on 15 March 1982. The craft was used for sound testing by the Naval Surface Warfare Center (formerly David Taylor Research Center), operating from Port Everglades, Fla.

SOUND TRIALS SHIP: "MONOB ONE"

The MONOB ONE—so named for *Mobile Noise Barge*—was converted to a sound trials configuration (YAG 61) in 1969 and placed in service in June 1970 for the David Taylor Research Center and later the Naval Surface Warfare Center, operating from Port Canaveral, Fla. She was stricken on 2 August 1996. The ship was built as YW 87 and reclassified IX 309 and, subsequently, YAG 61.

1 TORPEDO TRIALS CRAFT: "YF 852" CLASS

Number	Launched	Completed	Status
YF 885	1 May 1945	1 July 1945	Reserve

Builder:	Defoe Shipbuilding, Bay City, Mich.
Displacement:	160 tons light
	650 tons full load
Length:	132 feet (40.24 m) waterline
	133 feet (40.55 m) overall
Beam:	31 feet (9.45 m)
Draft:	9 feet (2.74 m)
Propulsion:	diesel
Speed:	
Range:	
Manning:	

This steel-hulled craft is the lone survivor of several covered lighters converted to torpedo trials craft. She was laid up in reserve on 23 August 1990 (not stricken as previously reported).

Class: The other YFs converted to torpedo trials craft have been discarded: the YF 862 in 1985 and the Kodiak (YF 866) in 1989.

FERRYBOATS

Two ferryboats in service at Pearl Harbor, Hawaii, were stricken on 25 June 1999, the Wa'a Hele Honua (YFB 83) and Moku Holo Hele (YFB 87). They were rendered redundant by the construction of a bridge-causeway to Ford Island in the center of the harbor. See 16th Edition/page 305 for characteristics.

All former LCU 1610–class utility landing craft modified in 1969 for use as ferryboats have been stricken: YFB 89 (ex-LCU 1638), YFB 90 (ex-LCU 1639), and YFB 91 (ex-LCU 1640) on 9 October 1992 and YFB 88 (ex-LCU 1636) on 30 June 1993.

2 FERRYBOATS: EX-ARMY LANDING CRAFT

Number	Name	Launched	In service	Status
YFB 94			1954	**Active**
YFB 1504	(ex-Hampton Roads)		1954	**Active**

Builder:	Avondale Shipyard, Westwego, La.
Displacement:	180 tons light
	347 tons full load
Length:	105 feet (32.01 m) waterline
	115 1/12 feet (35.08 m) overall
Beam:	34 feet (10.36 m)
Draft:	5 1/4 feet (1.60 m)
Propulsion:	3 diesel engines (GM Gray Marine 64YTL); 675 bhp; 3 shafts
Speed:	8 knots
Manning:	

These were LCU 1466–class landing craft built specifically for Army service. Three of these craft were transferred to the Navy in the early 1990s for use at Guantánamo Bay—these two units and the YFB 95.

Class: This class originally consisted of hulls LCU 1466–1609, with 14 units built in Japan with U.S. funding for foreign use: the LCU 1594–1601 for Taiwan and the LCU 1602–1607 for Japan. The U.S. Navy and Army operated the remainder of the craft.

The YFB 94 and YFB 95, both former Army LCUs, were stricken from the NVR on 3 March 1998 and 24 April 1996, respectively. The YFB 94 was reinstated on the NVR on 25 June 1999.

2 FERRYBOATS: "WINDWARD" CLASS

Number	Name	Launched	In service	Status
YFB 92	R. W. Huntington	Oct 1993	30 Jan 1995	**Active**
YFB 93	William H. Allen	Dec 1993	30 Jan 1995	**Active**

Builder:	Bender Shipbuilding & Repair, Mobile, Ala.
Displacement:	200 tons light
Length:	136 feet (41.46 m) overall
Beam:	36 feet (10.98 m)
Draft:	11 feet (3.35 m)
Propulsion:	2 diesel engines (GM 12V-71); 720 bhp; 2 shafts
Speed:	10 knots
Manning:	4 + 80 passengers

These craft were built specifically for use at the naval base at Guantánamo Bay. They can carry 15 civilian automobiles or two M1A1 Abrams main battle tanks.

Names: Both were unofficially renamed in 1996—YFB 92 is the ex-Windward and YFB 93 the ex-Leeward.

10 SPECIAL-PURPOSE LIGHTERS: "YFNX 35" TYPE

Number	Completed	To YFNX	Status
YFNX 35 (ex-YFN 1283)	1 June 1954	1 Nov 1992	**Active**
YFNX 36 (ex-YFN 1263)	1 June 1982	1 Nov 1992	**Active**
YFNX 37 (ex-YFN 1198)	1 July 1964	1 Nov 1992	**Active**
YFNX 39 (ex-YFN 1276)	1 Apr 1988	1 Nov 1992	**Active**
YFNX 40 (ex-YC 1519)	27 June 1977	1 Feb 1994	**Active**
YFNX 42 (ex-YFN 1255)	1 Nov 1982		**Active**
YFNX 43 (ex-YFN 1271)	1 Aug 1982		**Active**
YFNX 44	16 May 1994		**Active**
YFNX 45	16 May 1994		**Active**
YFNX 46	29 June 1994		**Active**

Builders:	
Displacement:	340 tons light
Length:	153 feet (46.65 m) overall
Beam:	
Draft:	
Propulsion:	diesel
Speed:	
Manning:	

These are self-propelled special-purpose craft that have been converted from non-self-propelled lighters; most have maneuvering engines. Details and configurations vary. All have steel hulls.

Class: YFNX 38 was stricken on 29 February 1996 and YFNX 41 on 4 April 1995.

1 SPECIAL-PURPOSE LIGHTER: YFNX TYPE

Number	Completed	To YFNX	Status
YFNX 24 (ex-YFN 1215)	1 Jan 1965	1 June 1966	**Active**

Builders:	
Displacement:	144 tons light
	694 tons full load
Length:	126 feet (38.4 m) overall
Beam:	32 5/8 feet (10.0 m)
Draft:	8 feet (2.44 m)
Propulsion:	diesel
Speed:	
Manning:	

This is a special-purpose craft that has been converted from a non-self-propelled lighter. The YFNX 24 is configured as a berthing barge for divers. She has a steel hull.

Class: YFNX 23 was stricken on 2 September 1993, YFNX 25 on 29 December 1997, YFNX 26 on 29 July 1994, and YFNX 31 (ex-YFN 1249) on 9 November 1999. YFNX 32 (ex-YRBM 7) was reclassified as YRBM 7 on 1 May 1992.

1 SPECIAL-PURPOSE LIGHTER: YFNX TYPE

Number	Name	Completed	To YFNX	Status
YFNX 30 (ex-YFN 1186)	Sea Turtle	1 Mar 1952	1 Jan 1973	**Active**

Builders:	
Displacement:	200 tons light
Length:	111 1/2 feet (34.0 m) overall
Beam:	32 5/8 feet (10.0 m)
Draft:	5 7/12 feet (1.7 m)
Propulsion:	diesel
Speed:	
Manning:	

The Sea Turtle is assigned to the Naval Command, Control, and Ocean Surveillance Center San Diego and supports the Curv II recovery vehicle.[6] The Sea Turtle has a steel hull.

Names: Sea Turtle is an unofficial name.

---

6. CURV = Cable-controlled Underwater Research Vehicle.

The SEA TURTLE, with a canvas covering over a triple Mk 32 torpedo tube mounting on her 01 level, aft of the bridge (1990, U.S. Navy)

The YFNX 30, unofficially named SEA TURTLE, is a unique research support craft operated by the Naval Command, Control, and Ocean Surveillance Center at San Diego. (1986, Giorgio Arra)

3 SPECIAL-PURPOSE LIGHTERS: YFNX TYPE

Number	Completed	To YFNX	Status
YFNX 15 (ex-YNg 22)	1 June 1941	1 Mar 1965	**Active**
YFNX 20	1 June 1952	1 Mar 1965	**Active**
YFNX 22	1 June 1941	1 Mar 1965	**Active**

Builders:	
Displacement:	160 tons light
Length:	$109^{11}/_{12}$ feet (33.5 m) overall
Beam:	$32^{5}/_{6}$ feet (10.0 m)
Draft:	$5^{7}/_{12}$ feet (1.7 m)
Propulsion:	diesel; 1 shaft
Speed:	
Manning:	

These are steel-hulled, self-propelled special-purpose craft, having been converted from non-self-propelled lighters.

The YFNX 15 was built as a non-self-propelled gate craft (originally YNg 22).

Class: The YFNX 4 was stricken on 13 December 1995 and YFNX 23 on 2 September 1993. The YFNX 7 was on loan to the Coast Guard, based at Governors Island, N.Y.; she was stricken on 4 April 1995.

1 TORPEDO TRIALS CRAFT: CONVERTED LIGHTER

Number	Name	Completed	To YFRT	Status
YFRT 520 (ex-YF 520)	POTENTIAL	1 Aug 1943	1965	Reserve

Builders:	Erie Concrete & Steel, Pa.
Displacement:	300 tons light
	650 tons full load
Length:	133 feet (40.5 m) overall
Beam:	30 feet (9.1 m)
Draft:	9 feet (2.7 m)
Propulsion:	2 diesel engines (Caterpillar D379); 600–800 bhp; 2 shafts
Speed:	9.5 knots
Torpedo tubes:	3 12.75-inch (324-mm) Mk 32 (triple)
Manning:	

The POTENTIAL was converted from a YF-type lighter to a torpedo trials configuration. She was laid up in reserve on 21 June 1991.

Class: The similar YFRT 451 and YFRT 287 were stricken on 15 November 1993 and 3 March 1998, respectively.

Names: POTENTIAL is an unofficial name.

The POTENTIAL—officially the YFRT 520—is now laid up. She is shown in Dabob Bay, Wash. There is a triple Mk 32 torpedo tube mounting aft of the bridge. (1969, U.S. Navy)

1 HARBOR UTILITY CRAFT: "LCU 1610" CLASS

Number	Launched	Completed	Status
YFU 83	1 Feb 1971	1 Apr 1971	**Active**

Builders:	Defoe Shipbuilding, Bay City, Mich.
Displacement:	190 tons light
	390 tons full load
Length:	$134^{3}/_{4}$ feet (41.0 m) overall
Beam:	$29^{3}/_{4}$ feet (9.0 m)
Draft:	6 feet (1.8 m)
Propulsion:	4 diesel engines (General Motors 6-71); 2,000 bhp; 2 shafts (Kort nozzles)
Speed:	11 knots
Manning:	8 (enlisted)

The YFU 83 was built as a harbor utility craft. All other YFUs of this design were converted landing craft of the LCU 1610 class. She is assigned to the Naval Station Roosevelt Roads, P.R.

Class: The class originally consisted of the YFU 83 and 97–102. The YFU 97 was reclassified as LCU 1611 on 15 June 1990, and the YFU 100 and YFU 102 were stricken on 18 June 1991.

1 HARBOR UTILITY CRAFT: "LCU 1608" CLASS

Number	Launched	Completed	Status
YFU 91 (ex-LCU 1608)	1 June 1957	1 July 1957	**Active**

Builders:	Defoe Shipbuilding, Bay City, Mich.
Displacement:	351 tons full load
Length:	115⅙ feet (35.1 m) overall
Beam:	34 feet (10.4 m)
Draft:	5 feet (1.5 m)
Propulsion:	3 diesels (Gray Marine 64 HN12); 675 bhp; 3 shafts (Kort nozzles)
Speed:	8 knots
Manning:	8 (enlisted)

The YFU 91 is a coastal cargo craft with a cargo capacity of 183 tons, assigned to the Naval Station Roosevelt Roads, P.R.

Classification: Changed from LCU to YFU 91 on 1 July 1970.

The YFU 91 with the superstructure-aft configuration of the early LCU/LCT-type landing craft. She shows wear and tear, typical of the Navy's hard-working service craft. (1999, Leo Van Ginderen)

1 HARBOR UTILITY CRAFT: "YFU 71" CLASS

Number	Launched	Completed	Status
YFU 81	1 July 1968	1 Sep 1968	Reserve

Builders	Pacific Coast Engineering Co., Alameda, Calif.
Displacement:	220 tons light
	380 tons full load
Length:	125 feet (38.1 m) overall
Beam:	38 feet (11.0 m)
Draft:	7½ feet (2.4 m)
Propulsion:	2 diesel engines (General Motors 6-71); 1,000 bhp; 2 shafts (Kort nozzles)
Speed:	8 knots
Manning:	12 (2 officers + 10 enlisted)

This craft was constructed specifically for use as a coastal cargo craft in the Vietnam War, one of 12 units built to a modified commercial design (YFU 71–82), completed in 1967–1968. Cargo capacity is 300 tons. The craft has been laid up at Roosevelt Roads, P.R., since 1 October 1978.

Class: The YFU 71–77 and 80–82 were transferred to the U.S. Army in 1970 for use in South Vietnam; they were returned to the Navy in 1973. YFU 74 and YFU 75 were stricken in 1986. YFU 71, 72, 76, and 77 were transferred to the Department of the Interior in 1984; YFU 76 and 77 subsequently transferred to the government of the Marshall Islands in 1987.

The YFU 82 became the IX 506 and the YFU 79 became the IX 512.

Guns: During their service in Vietnam waters, these craft each had two or more .50-cal machine guns fitted.

The YFU 81, another superstructure-aft variant of the LCU/LCT design (1999, Leo Van Ginderen)

SELF-PROPELLED DREDGES

All Navy self-propelled dredges have been stricken: the YM 32 on 17 January 1990, YM 35 on 31 July 1995, YM 17 on 13 December 1995, and YM 33 on 3 August 1998.

See 16th Edition/page 307 for characteristics.

FUEL OIL BARGES

All self-propelled fuel oil barges have been stricken:

YO 46 class: CASING HEAD (YO 47) was stricken on 21 August 1997.

YO 65 class: YO 130 was immobilized and changed to YON 130 on 5 September 1990, and the YO 203 was immobilized and changed to the YON 320 on 1 February 1994. The YO 129 was stricken on 25 March 1994, YO 220 and YO 223 on 19 May 1997, and YO 230 on 9 October 1997.

YO 153 class: The YO 153 was stricken on 27 March 1992.

See 16th Edition/page 308 for characteristics.

GASOLINE BARGES

All self-propelled gasoline barges have been stricken. The last units, of the YOG 5 class, were: YOG 78, stricken on 31 July 1995; YOG 88, stricken on 19 May 1997; and YOG 93, changed to IX 523 in 1996.

See 16th Edition/page 308 for characteristics.

A trio of YPs shows the simple lines of these craft. In theory, in wartime they could be armed for harbor patrol duties; see following page. (1999, Leo Van Ginderen)

25 SEAMANSHIP TRAINING CRAFT: "YP 676" CLASS

Number	Launched	In service	Status
YP 676	9 Apr 1984	1 Nov 1984	**Active**
YP 677	23 June 1984	1 Dec 1984	**Active**
YP 679	11 Dec 1984	3 June 1985	**Active**
YP 680	23 Mar 1985	30 July 1985	**Active**
YP 681	1 June 1985	11 Oct 1985	**Active**
YP 682	3 Aug 1985	19 Nov 1985	**Active**
YP 683	19 June 1986	21 Oct 1986	**Active**
YP 684	14 Aug 1986	21 Oct 1986	**Active**
YP 685	25 Sep 1986	25 Nov 1986	**Active**
YP 686	25 Oct 1986	8 Dec 1986	**Active**
YP 687	17 Mar 1987	22 May 1987	**Active**
YP 688	13 Mar 1987	22 May 1987	**Active**
YP 689	20 Mar 1987	10 June 1987	**Active**
YP 690	17 Apr 1987	10 June 1987	**Active**
YP 691	19 May 1987	2 July 1987	**Active**
YP 692	18 June 1987	27 July 1987	**Active**
YP 693	14 Aug 1987	22 Sep 1987	**Active**
YP 694	21 Sep 1987	27 Oct 1987	**Active**
YP 695	26 Oct 1987	1 Dec 1987	**Active**
YP 696	31 Mar 1988	1 May 1988	**Active**
YP 697	1 Feb 1988	26 May 1988	**Active**
YP 698	29 Mar 1988	16 June 1988	**Active**
YP 699	11 Apr 1988	30 June 1988	Reserve
YP 700	12 May 1988	21 July 1988	**Active**
YP 701	14 June 1988	9 Aug 1988	**Active**
YP 702	19 July 1988	2 Sep 1988	stricken 20 Nov 1998

Builders:	YP 676–682	Peterson Builders, Sturgeon Bay, Wisc.
	YP 683–702	Marinette Shipbuilding, Marinette, Wisc.
Displacement:	172 tons full load	
Length:	101⅔ feet (31.0 m) waterline	
	108 feet (32.9 m) overall	
Beam:	24 feet (7.3 m)	
Draft:	5¾ feet (1.75 m)	
Propulsion:	2 diesel engines (General Motors 12V71N); 875 bhp; 2 shafts	
Speed:	12 knots	
Range:	1,500 n.miles (2,778 km) at 12 knots	
Manning:	6 (2 officers + 4 enlisted) + 24 students	

The YP 698 maneuvers in Chesapeake Bay while training Naval Academy midshipmen. A second YP, whose mast is visible, steams in the wake of the YP 698. (U.S. Navy)

These are seamanship training craft. They have wood hulls; the deckhouse and pilot house are aluminum. The YP 686 is fitted for oceanographic research studies, and the YP 679 is engaged in work for the Office of Naval Research (ONR).

Class: The YP 678 and YP 679 were stricken on 20 November 1998; however, the YP 679 was reinstated on 25 June 1999 for use by ONR.

Electronics: All are fitted with NAVSAT and Loran C receivers, as well as a navigation radar and fathometer.[7]

Operational: All active units are employed for seamanship training at the Naval Academy, Annapolis, Md., except for the YP 696, assigned to the Naval Air Station Pensacola, Fla., and the YP 697 and YP 701 at the Naval Torpedo Station Keyport, Wash.

The YP 699 was laid up at Pensacola on 3 May 1999.

SEAMANSHIP TRAINING CRAFT: "YP 654" CLASS

All craft of this class have been stricken. The class originally consisted of 22 units, the YP 654–675. Seventeen units (YP 654, 659–666, and 668–675) were reclassified as mine countermeasures craft under the COOP program. The YP 655–658 were stricken on 12 February 1993, and the YP 667 on 4 February 1994.

See 16th Edition/page 309 for characteristics.

1 SEAPLANE WRECKING DERRICK: "YSD 11" CLASS

Number	Launched	Completed	Status
YSD 74	5 June 1943	15 July 1944	**Active**

Builders:	Pearl Harbor Navy Yard, Hawaii
Displacement:	240 tons light
	270 tons full load
Length:	104 feet (31.7 m) overall
Beam:	31⅙ feet (9.5 m)
Draft:	4 feet (1.2 m)
Propulsion:	2 diesels (Superior); 640 bhp; 2 shafts
Speed:	6 knots
Manning:	15 (enlisted)

This is a small, self-propelled floating crane, with a steel hull and fitted with a 10-ton-capacity crane. She is active at Pearl Harbor.

YSDs are called "Mary Anns."

Class: YSD 53 was stricken in May 1991 and YSD 63 on 15 July 1993.

---

7. NAVSAT = Navigation Satellite.

The "Mary Ann" YSD 63 chugging along. Only the YSD 74 of this class survives. "Mary Anns" of this class have been in the fleet since about 1930. (1977, Giorgio Arra)

49 LARGE HARBOR TUGS: "YTB 760" CLASS

Number	Name	Launched	Completed	Status
YTB 760	Natick	28 Feb 1961	30 June 1961	**Active**
YTB 761	Ottumwa	30 May 1961	9 Oct 1961	**Active**
YTB 763	Muskegon	8 Aug 1962	19 Apr 1963	**Active**
YTB 764	Mishawaka	3 Jan 1963	19 Apr 1963	**Active**
YTB 765	Okmulgee	18 Apr 1963	25 July 1963	**Active**
YTB 766	Wapakoneta	11 June 1963	25 July 1963	**Active**
YTB 767	Apalachicola	26 Oct 1963	9 June 1964	**Active**
YTB 769	Chesaning	5 Feb 1964	16 June 1964	**Active**
YTB 770	Dahlonega	23 Mar 1964	4 Aug 1964	**Active**
YTB 771	Keokuk	21 May 1964	23 Aug 1964	**Active**
YTB 775	Wauwatosa	19 May 1965	21 June 1965	**Active**
YTB 776	Weehawken	8 June 1965	22 Oct 1965	**Active**
YTB 777	Nogalesen	24 June 1965	22 Oct 1965	**Active**
YTB 779	Manhattan	15 July 1965	1 Dec 1965	**Active**
YTB 781	Niantic	7 Sep 1965	10 Nov 1965	**Active**
YTB 782	Manistee	20 Oct 1965	1 Feb 1966	**Active**
YTB 783	Redwing	12 Nov 1965	1 Feb 1966	**Active**
YTB 784	Kalispell	13 Dec 1965	4 May 1966	**Active**
YTB 787	Kittanning	29 Mar 1966	19 May 1966	**Active**
YTB 789	Tomahawk	5 May 1966	7 June 1966	**Active**
YTB 791	Marinette	10 Apr 1967	10 June 1967	**Active**
YTB 793	Piqua	25 Apr 1967	10 July 1967	**Active**
YTB 794	Mandan	30 Apr 1968	15 Oct 1968	**Active**
YTB 795	Ketchikan	11 June 1968	6 Nov 1968	**Active**
YTB 796	Saco	3 July 1968	8 Jan 1969	**Active**
YTB 797	Tamaqua	14 Aug 1968	26 Jan 1969	**Active**
YTB 798	Opelika	21 Aug 1968	30 Jan 1969	**Active**
YTB 806	Tuskegee	15 Apr 1970	2 Oct 1970	**Active**
YTB 807	Massapequa	27 May 1970	30 Nov 1970	**Active**
YTB 808	Wenatchee	7 July 1970	21 Dec 1970	**Active**
YTB 810	Anoka	15 Apr 1971	31 Aug 1971	**Active**
YTB 812	Accomac	8 June 1971	17 Nov 1971	**Active**
YTB 813	Poughkeepsie	23 July 1971	27 Nov 1971	**Active**
YTB 814	Waxahachie	9 Sep 1971	2 Jan 1972	**Active**
YTB 815	Neodesha	6 Oct 1971	2 Jan 1972	**Active**
YTB 818	Mecosta	26 Mar 1973	25 June 1973	**Active**
YTB 820	Wanamassa	4 May 1973	12 July 1973	**Active**
YTB 821	Tontocany	16 May 1973	28 July 1973	**Active**
YTB 822	Pawhuska	7 June 1973	10 Sep 1973	**Active**
YTB 823	Canonchet	10 July 1973	23 Sep 1973	**Active**
YTB 824	Santaquin	13 Aug 1973	30 Sep 1973	**Active**
YTB 828	Catahecassa	29 May 1974	16 Aug 1974	**Active**
YTB 829	Metacom	19 June 1974	21 Sep 1974	**Active**
YTB 831	Dekanawida	12 Sep 1974	31 Oct 1974	**Active**
YTB 832	Petalesharo	3 Oct 1974	17 Nov 1974	**Active**
YTB 833	Shabonee	29 Oct 1974	16 Dec 1974	**Active**
YTB 834	Negwagon	27 Mar 1975	19 May 1975	**Active**
YTB 835	Skenandoa	3 Apr 1975	10 June 1975	**Active**
YTB 836	Pokagon	9 Apr 1975	24 June 1975	**Active**

Builders:		
	YTB 760, 761	Jakobson Shipyard, Oyster Bay, N.Y.
	YTB 763–766, 801, 802	Southern Shipbuilding, Slidell, La.
	YTB 767, 769–771	Mobile Ship Repair, Ala.
	YTB 775–777, 818–836	Marinette Marine, Wisc.
	YTB 803, 806–815	Peterson Builders, Sturgeon Bay, Wisc.

Displacement:	283 tons light
	356 tons full load
Length:	109 feet (33.2 m) overall
Beam:	30½ feet (9.3 m)
Draft:	13½ feet (4.1 m)
Propulsion:	1 diesel engine (Fairbanks-Morse 38D8⅛); 2,000 bhp; 1 shaft
Speed:	12.5 knots
Range:	2,000 n.miles (3,704 km) at 12 knots
Manning:	10–14 (enlisted)

These tugs are all in active service. They are fitted with small commercial navigation radars.

Class: The similar YTB 837 and 838 were transferred to Saudi Arabia in 1975.

Dispositions of other units of the class: Eufaula (YTB 800) transferred to the NDRF on 9 November 1992; Tonkawa (YTB 786) to NDRF on 18 November 1992; Nashua (YTB 774) stricken on 6 May 1994; Arcata (YTB 768) and Palatka (YTB 801) stricken on 4 April 1995; Tuscumbia (YTB 762) to NDRF on 11 September 1995; Pushmataha (YTB 830) stricken on 2 October 1995; Ahoskie (YTB 804) stricken on 10 October 1995; Natchitoches (YTB 799) stricken on 13 October 1995; Iuka (YTB 819) stricken on 19 October 1995; Winnemucca (YTB 785) stricken on 20 December 1995; Cheraw (YTB 802) and Chetek (YTB 827) stricken on 29 February 1996; Wapato (YTB 788) stricken on 25 April 1996; Apopka (YTB 778) stricken on 26 June 1996; Hyannis (YTB 817) and Washtuena (YTB 826) stricken on 21 August 1997; Saugus (YTB 780), Ocala (YTB 805), and Wathena (YTB 825) stricken on 28 October 1997; Menominee (YTB 790) stricken on 4 September 1998; Antigo (YTB 792) stricken on 25 June 1999; and Nanticoke (YTB 803), Agawam (YTB 809), Houma (YTB 811), and Campti (YTB 816) stricken on 9 November 1999.

Design: SCB No. 147A. These and other Navy harbor tugs are used for towing and for maneuvering ships in harbors. Their masts fold down to facilitate working alongside large ships.

Tugs are also equipped for firefighting.

Names: Named tugs honor American towns and small cities.

LARGE HARBOR TUGS: "YTB 756" CLASS

All of these 109-foot (33.2-m), 409-ton harbor tugs have been stricken. Tugs stricken during the 1990s were: Pontiac (YTB 756) on 18 November 1992, Bogalusa (YTB 759) on 7 August 1996, Oshkosh (YTB 757) on 25 April 1996, and Paducah (YTB 758) on 25 June 1999.

See 16th Edition/page 311 for characteristics.

The Chesaning at Norfolk, Va. These tugs have folding masts to facilitate working under a ship's overhang; there is a large, open working space aft. A small navigation radar is fitted atop the bridge. (1999, Jürg Kürsener)

The HOUMA awaiting a ship's arrival. These tugs have fenders wrapped around the bow and rollers on the superstructure to protect them from larger ships. (1999, Leo Van Ginderen)

The DEKANAWIDA moving at a rapid clip to rendezvous with a larger ship to help her maneuver. Only one of the smaller, once-numerous YTL small harbor tugs remains in service. (1999, Leo Van Ginderen)

LARGE HARBOR TUGS: "YTB 752" CLASS

The last harbor tugs of this design, similar to the YTB 760 class, have been stricken: MARIN (YTB 753) on 21 May 1991 and EDENSHAW (YTB 752) on 5 May 1994.

See 16th Edition/page 311 for characteristics.

1 SMALL HARBOR TUG: "YTL 422" CLASS

Number	Name	Launched	Completed	Status
YTL 602	(none)	26 July 1945	5 Oct 1945	**Active**

Builders:	Robert Jacob, City Island, N.Y.
Displacement:	70 tons light
	80 tons full load
Length:	62 feet (18.9 m) waterline
	66⅙ feet (20.2 m) overall
Beam:	17 feet (5.2 m)
Draft:	5 feet (1.5 m)
Propulsion:	1 diesel engine (Hoover); 375 bhp; 1 shaft
Speed:	10 knots
Manning:	6 (enlisted)

The YTL 602 is the lone survivor in Navy service of several hundred small tugs built during World War II. Many served in foreign navies. The YTL 602 is active at the Portsmouth Naval Shipyard, Kittery, Maine.

Classification: The YTLs originally were classified YT with the same hull number. YTL originally meant harbor tug, *little*.

MEDIUM HARBOR TUGS

All surviving YTM-type tugs have been stricken except the ex-YTM 404, which is now designated 100WB8501 and serves at the Naval Station Roosevelt Roads, P.R. She was reclassified on 1 December 1985.

The YTM 394 was stricken on 31 December 1985 (correction to previous edition).

2 TORPEDO TRIALS CRAFT: "YTT 9" CLASS

Number	Name	Launched	Completed	Status
YTT 9	CAPE FLATTERY	5 May 1989	28 Sep 1990	stricken 13 Aug 1999
YTT 10	BATTLE POINT	17 Aug 1989	11 Nov 1990	**Active**
YTT 11	DISCOVERY BAY	22 Feb 1990	19 Apr 1991	**Active**
YTT 12	AGATE PASS	6 Sep 1990	1 July 1991	stricken 13 Aug 1999

Builders:	McDermott Shipyard, Morgan City, La.
Displacement:	1,000 tons light
	1,200 tons full load
Length:	186½ feet (56.85 m) overall
Beam:	40 feet (12.2 m)
Draft:	10½ feet (3.2 m)
Propulsion:	diesel-electric (1 Cummins VTA-28 diesel engine); 1,250 shp;
	2 all-azimuth drives
Speed:	11 knots
Torpedo tubes:	2 21-inch (533-mm) Mk 59 (fixed single; submerged)
	3 12.75-inch (324-mm) Mk 32 (triple)
Manning:	31 + 9 technicians

These are specialized torpedo trials craft that were to replace the IX and YFRT craft now employed in this role. A 350-hp bow thruster is fitted. Electric drive on batteries permits quiet operation for launching acoustic-homing torpedoes.

The craft are assigned to the Naval Undersea Warfare Center, Keyport, Wash. The AGATE PASS was never put in service but was laid up in reserve at the Bremerton Naval Shipyard upon completion; the CAPE FLATTERY was stricken after only nine years of service. Thus, these two craft provided the Navy with little return for its investment.

Classification: These craft were originally planned as YFRT type, but were built as YTT. The classification YTT originally indicated torpedo testing barge.

The YTT 1–4 were built in 1912–1916; the YTT 5–7 were of World War II construction. All were non-self-propelled barges. The designation YTT 8 was not assigned.

The BATTLE POINT, with the CAPE FLATTERY astern, at Keyport, Wash., the Navy's principal torpedo testing facility. They have cranes forward and aft for recovering torpedoes and handling specialized underwater recovery devices. (1990, U.S. Navy)

The CAPE FLATTERY. The broad working area aft is flanked by the craft's twin engine exhausts. Two bar-type radar antennas sit atop the large deckhouse. (1990, U.S. Navy)

WATER BARGES

These craft were similar to the YO/YOG types, being employed to carry fresh water for ships. The last two units were the YW 98, stricken on 10 September 1991, and the YW 127, stricken on 18 April 1994.

The similar YW 87 was converted to the MONOB ONE (YAG 61, ex-IX 309).

MISCELLANEOUS SHIPS AND CRAFT

These craft do not have Y-series designations; some have hull registry numbers (length + type designation + serial). The ships and craft in this section are listed according to length.

Classification: The type designations used below are:

NS	Non-Standard (commercial design)
UB	Utility Boat
WB	Work Boat

The definition of the designation "C" does not appear in the SABAR directory.

3 AUXILIARY SWIMMER DELIVERY VESSELS: MODIFIED LCUs

Number	Built	Status
ASDV 1 (ex-LCU 1621)	1960	**Active;** Naval Amphibious Base Coronado (San Diego), Calif.
ASDV 2 (ex-LCU 1623)	1960	**Active;** Naval Special Warfare Group 2
ASDV 3 (ex-LCU 1628)	1967	**Active;** Special Boat Unit 12

Builders:	Southern Shipbuilding, Slidell, La.
Displacement:	approx. 210 tons light
	approx. 390 tons full load
Length:	134¾ feet (41.1 m) overall
Beam:	29¾ feet (9.1 m)
Draft:	6¹¹/₁₂ feet (2.1 m)
Propulsion:	4 diesel engines (GM Detroit Diesel 6-71); 1,200 shp; 2 Kort-nozzle propellers
Speed:	11 knots
Range:	1,200 n.miles (2,222 km) at 8 knots
Manning:	10 to 14 (enlisted)
Guns:	removed
Radars:	1 SPS-69 navigation

These are modified utility landing craft of the LCU 1610 class; they are employed to support training operations for SEALs and other Navy swimmers.

As ASDVs, they are fitted with a decompression chamber and associated air compressors, storage flasks, and an electric generator. Manning varies from 10 to 14 enlisted personnel, depending on whether or not the training operation requires use of the decompression chamber. Sleeping accommodations are provided for embarked personnel. A crane is fitted for handling rubber rafts.

Operational: The ASDVs 2 and 3 are based at Little Creek (Norfolk), Va.

The ASDV 3 retains the LCU lines, but has several shelters and diving equipment on her former tank deck. (1998, Leo Van Ginderen)

1 SUBMERSIBLE SUPPORT SHIP: "KELLIE CHOUEST"

Number	Name	Completed	In service	Status
(none)	KELLIE CHOUEST	1 Mar 1996	17 Mar 1996	**Active**

Builder:	North American Shipbuilding, Larose, La.
Displacement:	1,575 tons full load
Length:	310 feet (94.51 m) overall
Beam:	52 feet (15.85 m)
Draft:	15 feet (4.57 m)
Propulsion:	2 diesel engines; 3,900 bhp; 2 shafts
Speed:	
Manning:	

This is one of several submersible support tenders provided to the Navy under a contract with the Military Sealift Command (MSC) by the Edison Chouest Offshore Co. of Galliano, La. Most were built as offshore oilfield support ships.

The in-service date above is the date of charter by MSC.

1 ACOUSTIC RESEARCH SHIP: "COREY CHOUEST"

Number	Name	Completed	In service	Status
(none)	COREY CHOUEST	1974	14 Nov 1991	**Active**

Builders:	Ulstein Hatlo A/S, Ulsteinvik, Norway
Displacement:	approx. 3,900 tons full load
Tonnage:	1,597 GRT
	1,800 DWT
Length:	265¹¹/₁₂ feet (81.08 m) overall
Beam:	59⅛ feet (18.04 m)
Draft:	14⅛ feet (4.32 m)
Propulsion:	2 diesel engines (Atlas-MaK 6M453AK); 4,000 bhp; 2 shafts
Speed:	13.75 knots
Manning:	approx. 16 civilian + 30 technicians

A former offshore oilfield cargo/pipe carrying ship, the COREY CHOUEST provides diver support.

Names: Her commercial names were FAR COMET and TENDER COMET.

Operational: The COREY CHOUEST is employed in research in the Hawaii area in the development of Low-Frequency Active (LFA) sonar systems. During 1997–1998 she conducted studies of low-frequency sound on marine mammals.

(The COREY CHOUEST's sister ship AMY CHOUEST was chartered by MSC from 1990 to 1993 for acoustic research.)

The KELLIE CHOUEST provides support to the Navy's rescue submersibles AVALON (DSRV 2) and MYSTIC (DSRV 1). A DSRV is in the ship's "docking well," which has a lift for raising the submersibles out of the water. (U.S. Navy)

The KELLIE CHOUEST has an unusual configuration. She serves as a tender for the Navy's DSRVs but also can handle other undersea vehicles and equipment. Most of the Chouest-series ships have red hulls and buff superstructures. (1998, Leo Van Ginderen)

CONSTRUCTION PLATFORM: "SEACON"

Number	Name	Launched	Completed	Status
(ex-YFNB 330)	SEACON	22 Mar 1945	25 Oct 1945	to Mexico Nov 1998

This ship was converted from a barge to transport rockets for NASA and subsequently was converted in 1974–1976 by the Norfolk Ship-building and Dry Dock Co. to serve as a seagoing work ship. The craft was towed to work positions and can use her own engines for propulsion and maneuvering within the work area.

See 16th Edition/page 315 for characteristics.

The SEACON is a "work ship" configured for seafloor work, another unique Navy service craft. (1992, Giorgio Arra)

1 SUBMERSIBLE SUPPORT SHIP: "LANEY CHOUEST"

Number	Name	In service	Status
(none)	LANEY CHOUEST	1985	Discarded

Builders:	North American Shipbuilding, Larose, La.
Displacement:	2,700 tons full load
Tonnage:	497 GRT
	1,200 DWT
Length:	234 feet (71.33 m) overall
Beam:	50 feet (15.2 m)
Draft:	14⅙ feet (4.33 m)
Propulsion:	3 diesel engines (GM); 9,210 bhp; 3 shafts
Speed:	16 knots
Manning:	13 civilian + 40 technicians

This former oilfield support craft was chartered by the Navy to support the submersibles DSV 3 and DSV 4 in Submarine Development Group 1 at San Diego. With the disposal of those craft, the LANEY CHOUEST was returned to the Edison Chouest Offshore firm in September 1998.

Design: The ship has a large lifting device aft and an ice-strengthened hull. Three thrusters are fitted for station keeping. A sonar is fitted for tracking submersibles approaching the ship.

1 SUBMERSIBLE SUPPORT SHIP: "CAROLYN CHOUEST"

Number	Name	Completed	In service	Status
(none)	CAROLYN CHOUEST	1994	1994	**Active**

Builders:	North American Shipbuilding, Larose, La.
Displacement:	1,599 tons full load
Length:	238 feet (72.56 m) overall
Beam:	52 feet (15.85 m)
Draft:	17 feet (5.18 m)
Propulsion:	2 diesel engines; 2,440 bhp; 2 shafts
Speed:	12 knots
Manning:	13 civilian + 45 technicians/passengers

This former oilfield support craft was chartered by the Navy to support the nuclear-propelled submersible NR-1. The CAROLYN CHOUEST provides berthing for NR-1 support personnel and services and undertakes surface towing of the submersible.

The LANEY CHOUEST, acquired by the Navy to support the DSV 3 and DSV 4, which have now been discarded. The crane on the stern swings out to lift submersibles out of the water and into the amidships hangar. (U.S. Navy)

The CAROLYN CHOUEST, support ship for the nuclear submersible NR-1, off Key Largo, Fla. (1995, U.S. Navy, PH1 G. Hurd)

1 FORMER SPACE BOOSTER RECOVERY SHIP: "INDEPENDENCE"

Number	Name	Launched	In service	Status
(none)	INDEPENDENCE	27 Feb 1985	1988	**Active**

Builders:	Halter Marine, Moss Point, Miss.
Displacement:	1,798 tons full load
Length:	182 feet (55.47 m) waterline
	199^{11}/$_{12}$ feet (60.96 m) overall
Beam:	40 feet (12.2 m)
Draft:	13½ feet (4.1 m)
Propulsion:	diesel (2 Cummins KTA 3067-M); 2,500 bhp; 2 shafts + 2
	all-azimuth thrusters (1,000 shp each)
Speed:	13 knots
Range:	8,500 n.miles (15,750 km) at 11 knots
	7,800 n.miles (14,450 km) at 13 knots
Manning:	13 civilian + 14 scientists/technicians

Built for the U.S. Air Force to recover solid-propellant missile boosters from off Vandenberg Air Force Base, Calif., the INDEPENDENCE was transferred to the Navy in 1988 and operated by the Naval Facilities Engineering Center at Port Hueneme, Calif. She can carry 338 tons of deck cargo aft, including laboratory vans, and is fitted with a 22-ton-capacity crane.

2 TRIALS SUPPORT CRAFT

Number	Name	Completed	Status
192UB8701	RANGER	1981	**Active**
192UB8702	NAWC 38	1981	**Active**

Builders:	McDermott Shipyard, New Iberia, La.
Displacement:	approx. 1,800 tons full load
Length:	191^{11}/$_{12}$ feet (58.52 m) overall
Beam:	40 feet (12.19 m)
Draft:	14 feet (4.27 m)
Propulsion:	2 diesel engines (GM 12-645-E6); 3,000 bhp; 2 shafts
Speed:	12 knots
Range:	
Manning:	NAWC 38 8 civilian + 22 technicians

Both ships were acquired in 1986 to support ship trials. The NAWC 38 (ex-SEA LEVEL NO. 7) operates from Key West, Fla., for the Naval Air Warfare Center's Key West Detachment. The RANGER (ex-SEACOR RANGER, SEA LEVEL NO. 27) is employed on the Anglo-American Atlantic Undersea Test and Evaluation Center (AUTEC) range, Andros Island, Bahamas. She replaces the IX 306 (former U.S. Army FS 221).

The trials support craft NAWC 38. She previously had a crane fitted on her fantail. (1991, Giorgio Arra)

1 SUBMERSIBLE SUPPORT SHIP: "DOLORES CHOUEST"

Number	Name	In service	Status
(none)	DOLORES CHOUEST	1978	**Active**

Builders:	North American Shipbuilding, Larose, La.
Displacement:	1,650 tons full load
Length:	228 feet (69.51 m) overall
Beam:	40 feet (12.2 m)
Draft:	12½ feet (3.81 m)
Propulsion:	2 diesel engines (Caterpillar D399-SCAC); 2,250 bhp; 2 shafts
Speed:	13 knots
Manning:	9 civilian + 30 technicians

The ship is configured to support DSRV rescue submersibles and is under Navy charter in the Pacific area.

Name: The name DOLORES CHOUEST is painted on the ship, although most documents refer to the ship as DELORES CHOUEST.

The DOLORES CHOUEST is another specialized support ship on long-term lease to the Navy. (U.S. Navy)

1 SONOBUOY TRIALS CRAFT: "ACOUSTIC PIONEER"

Number	Name	Completed	Status
180WB8701	ACOUSTIC PIONEER	1981	**Active**

Builders:	Halter Marine, Moss Point, La.
Displacement:	approx. 1,500 tons full load
Length:	179¹¹/₁₂ feet (54.86 m) overall
Beam:	40 feet (12.2 m)
Draft:	14 feet (4.3 m)
Propulsion:	2 diesel engines (EMD 12-567BC); 2,500 bhp; 2 shafts
Speed:	12 knots
Manning:	

Formerly the oilfield supply boat SEPTEMBER MORN, the ACOUSTIC PIONEER was acquired by the Navy in 1987 and employed by the Naval Avionics Development Center at St. Croix in the Virgin Islands for sonobuoy testing. She is now based at Key West, Fla., operated by the Naval Air Warfare Center's Key West Detachment.

A 300-hp through-hull thruster is fitted in the bow.

The ACOUSTIC PIONEER, now employed as a support craft at the Naval Air Development Center's detachment in Key West, Fla. (U.S. Navy)

3 RESEARCH CRAFT: "ASHEVILLE" CLASS

Number	Name	Launched	PG comm.	To DTRC	Status
165NS761 (ex-PG 94)	ATHENA I	8 June 1968	8 Nov 1969	21 Aug 1975	**Active**
165NS762 (ex-PG 98)	ATHENA II	4 Apr 1970	5 Sep 1970	3 Oct 1977	**Active**
165NS763 (ex-PG 100)	LAUREN	19 June 1970	6 Feb 1971	1990	**Active**

Builders:	Tacoma Boatbuilding, Wash.
Displacement:	approx. 265 tons full load
Length:	164½ feet (50.2 m) overall
Beam:	23¾ feet (7.2 m)
Draft:	9½ feet (2.9 m)
Propulsion:	CODOG: 2 diesel engines (Cummins VT12-875M), 1,400 bhp; 1 gas turbine (General Electric LM 1500), 12,500 shp; 2 shafts
Speed:	16 knots on diesel engines; 40+ knots on gas turbines
Range:	2,400 n.miles (4,445 km) at 14 knots on diesel engines
	325 n.miles (602 km) at 37 knots on gas turbines
Manning:	

These are former ASHEVILLE-class patrol combatants/gunboats employed in the research role. They are the last of a class of 17 in U.S. naval service. These three ships were transferred on the dates indicated to the David Taylor Research Center (DTRC) for use in various offshore research projects; they are based at Panama City, Fla.

The DOUGLAS was stricken on 1 October 1977 for transfer to DTRC to be placed in service as the ATHENA III. She was instead discarded in 1984 but retained in storage at Little Creek, Va., for possible foreign transfer. She was reacquired and converted in 1991–1992 for use as a test ship in the Athena program, although given the name LAUREN.

All weapons have been removed.

Class: Originally a class of 17 gunboats (PGM/PG 84–101), completed from 1966 to 1970. See 16th Edition/page 195 for class disposition.

Classification: When assigned to DTRC, these ships were reclassified as service craft without specific hull designations; the NVR lists the ATHENA I and ATHENA II as being reclassified as service craft on

1 August 1975 and 1 October 1977, respectively. The LAUREN is listed as having been stricken on 1 October 1977.

Design: These ships have aluminum hulls with fiberglass superstructures.

Names: Their names as gunboats were CHEHALIS, GRAND RAPIDS, and DOUGLAS, respectively.

Operational: These ships have participated in a variety of research projects. Possibly the most unusual was one in which the ATHENA II, at maximum speed, towed an in-flight MH-53E helicopter backwards to help assess flight envelope characteristics. Other trials have included sonars and mine countermeasures gear.

The ATHENA I, showing the extension forward of her bridge. The ATHENA I and II have orange hulls with white superstructures. The ATHENA I does not have the "I" after her name as painted on the bow. (1991, Giorgio Arra)

The ATHENA II pulling away from a pier. There is a laboratory van amidships, along with winches and lift equipment. (1989, Giorgio Arra)

The ATHENA II, with a rounded bridge face. All three craft are employed for research and development work by the David Taylor Research Center. (1991, Giorgio Arra)

1 SALVAGE TENDER: "SOTOYOMO" CLASS

Number	Name	Launched	Commissioned	Status
142NS9201 (ex-ATA 213)	KEYWADIN	9 Apr 1945	1 June 1945	**Active**

Builder:	Gulfport Boiler & Welding Works, Port Arthur, Texas
Displacement:	
Length:	133⅔ feet waterline
	143 feet overall
Beam:	33⅝ feet
Draft:	13⅙ feet
Propulsion:	diesel-electric (1 GM diesel engine 12-278A); 1 shaft
Speed:	13 knots
Manning:	

This is the only auxiliary tug (ATA) remaining in U.S. naval service. The KEYWADIN is used for fire and salvage training by Mobile Diving and Salvage Unit 2 at Little Creek, Va.

Three of the other ATAs are used as salvage training hulks by other Navy diving and salvage activities. Only the KEYWADIN has a hull number. The KEYWADIN was decommissioned in 1970 and transferred to the NDRF in 1971; she was reacquired for naval service in 1992.

Class: Originally, the SOTOYOMO class consisted of 70 ships: ATA 121–125, 146, 170–213, and 219–238.

Two sister ships are used as salvage hulks—the TUNICA (ATA 179), decommissioned and transferred to the NDRF in 1962, and the NAVIGATOR (ATA 203), transferred in 1960. They are sunk and salved in training exercises. The ACCOKEEK (ATA 181), previously used in this role, was sunk in the Gulf of Mexico as part of an artificial reef on 9 July 2000.

1 SONOBUOY TRIALS CRAFT: "ACOUSTIC EXPLORER"

Number	Name	Completed	In service	Status
111NS8801	ACOUSTIC EXPLORER	Dec 1981	1988	**Active**

Builder:	Eastern Marine, Panama City, Fla.
Displacement:	
Length:	125 feet (38.1 m) overall
Beam:	30 feet (9.14 m)
Draft:	4⅔ feet (1.42 m)
Propulsion:	2 diesel engines; 2 shafts
Speed:	
Manning:	

The ACOUSTIC EXPLORER is the former oilfield supply boat STRONG BRIO, acquired by the Navy and employed by the Naval Avionics Development Center at St. Croix in the Virgin Islands for sonobuoy testing.

The sonobuoy trials craft ACOUSTIC EXPLORER (1998, Leo Van Ginderen)

1 TRIALS SUPPORT TENDER: "SUB SIG II"

Number	Name	Launched	In service	Status
(none)	SUB SIG II		Aug 1967	**Active**

Builder:	Saint John Shipbuilding & Dry Dock, N.B., Canada
Displacement:	approx. 520 tons full load
Tonnage:	177 GRT
Length:	97 feet (29.57 m) waterline
	107¹¹⁄₁₂ feet (35.97 m) overall
Beam:	28¼ feet (8.64 m)
Draft:	11 feet (3.35 m)
Propulsion:	1 diesel engine (Caterpillar); 765 bhp; 1 shaft
Speed:	11 knots
Manning:	

A converted stern trawler, the SUB SIG II (for "Submarine Signal") is used for active acoustic propagation trials.

Names: The ship's commercial name was SCOTIA PORT.

1 HULL FORM RESEARCH SHIP: "SLICE"

Number	Name	Launched	In service	Status
(none)	SLICE	Nov 1996	1997	**Active**

Builder:	Honolulu Shipyard Division, Pacific Marine, Hawaii
Displacement:	180 tons full load
Length:	105 feet (32.01 m) overall
Beam:	55 feet (16.77 m)
Draft:	14 feet (4.27 m)
Propulsion:	2 diesel engines (MTU 16V396 TB 94); 6,850 bhp; 2 propulsion pods
Speed:	23–27 knots cruise (varies with payload)
	30 knots maximum
Range:	850 n.miles (1,575 km) at cruise speed
Manning:	2 civilian + 4 trials technicians

The SLICE is a test platform for a variation of the SWATH (Small Waterplane-Area Twin Hull) configuration. Funded jointly by the Office of Naval Research and Pacific Marine and Supply Co., the SLICE is based on the design for an interisland ferry. The craft is capable of towing a "trailer" platform, also supported on four struts/pods.

The Navy is considering the highly effective SLICE design for a class of coastal combatants to succeed the CYCLONE (PC 1) class, although no such program had been structured when this edition went to press.

Design: The SLICE has four supporting struts/pods that penetrate the air–water interface to provide lift at high speeds. The *forward* pods contain the diesel engines and are fitted with 7¼-foot (2.2-m) controllable-pitch propellers; the after pods carry fuel and/or ballast. A fifth strut could be fitted to provide a third propeller pod. The pods are 40 feet (12.20 m) in length and 8 feet (2.44 m) in diameter.

The SWATH configuration provides a large, open deck and considerable internal cargo volume suitable for cargo or missiles. The design/propulsion system provides for low wake observability. The hull is built of aluminum.

A quadrupod hull configuration of the SLICE test ship, which offers considerable potential for small ships (Lockheed Martin)

The SLICE test ship at high speed; a Kaman K-Max helicopter practices vertical replenishment techniques with a high-speed craft. Note the ship's large open deck, suitable for the installation of weapons or accommodations for Special Forces or other specialized equipment. (Lockheed Martin)

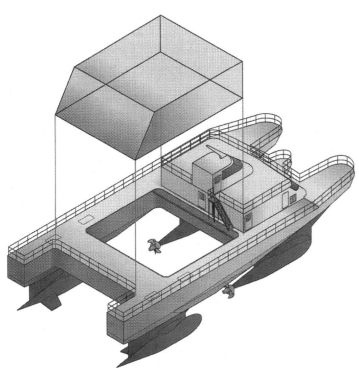

A schematic of the SLICE configuration, showing the supporting struts/pods; propellers are fitted to the forward pair. The amidships section can be changed for handling special payloads, or fitted with a specially configured deckhouse or equipment. (Lockheed Martin)

1 RANGE SUPPORT SHIP (SWATH): "KAIMALINO"

Number	Name	Launched	In service	Status
90WB8701	KAIMALINO	7 Mar 1973	1973	**Active**

Builder:	Coast Guard Yard, Curtis Bay, Md.
Displacement:	228 tons full load
Length:	88⅓ feet (26.9 m) overall
Beam:	46½ feet (14.2 m)
Draft:	15¼ feet (4.65 m)
Propulsion:	CODOG: 2 diesel engines (GM 6-71); 160 bhp; 2 gas turbines (General Electric T64-6B); 5,000 shp; 2 shafts
Speed:	22 knots
Range:	1,500 n.miles (2,778 km) at 5 knots on diesel engines
	450 n.miles (833 km) at 17 knots on gas turbines
Manning:	10 civilian + 6 technicians

A SWATH/Semi-Submerged Platform (SSP) research ship, the KAIMALINO has had a long career as a test platform. She was discarded in 1994 after 20 years of operation testing the SWATH configuration and serving as an underwater test range support ship. She was laid up at San Diego until reactivated in 1997 for trials in conjunction with the SLICE program (see above).

The SWATH design subsequently was adopted for the SEA SHADOW stealth research ship and for later ocean surveillance ships (T-AGOS 19–23).

Classification: The craft is also known as SSP 1.

Conversion: The KAIMALINO was modified at the Dillingham Shipyard in Hawaii in 1980–1981. The craft was enlarged from 190 to 228 tons through the addition of fiberglass buoyancy modules. Plans to further enlarge the ship to some 600 tons were not carried out.

Design: The SWATH design provides for extensive stability and a large working/payload deck area. It differs from that of a catamaran, which has two conventional ship hulls joined together. The KAIMALINO has two fully submerged, torpedo-shaped hulls, each 6½ feet (2.0 m) in diameter, with vertical struts penetrating the water to support the superstructure and deck. The ship's flight deck area is 3,400 square feet (306 m²).

The KAIMALINO has a hull-stabilizing fin connecting the two submerged hulls and two small canard fins forward, one inboard on each hull. There is an opening in the craft's main deck for lowering search and recovery devices. (The opening is covered over for helicopter operations.) The beam listed above is the maximum over both hulls.

Up to 16 tons of mission equipment can be carried.

Engineering: Two T64 aircraft-type gas turbine engines provide propulsion power. Two Detroit diesel engines (8V-71T) are installed for auxiliary propulsion.

Helicopters: The KAIMALINO conducted tests in 1976 on the feasibility of landing helicopters on SSP/SWATH-type ships in high sea states at speeds up to 25 knots. The operations with an SH-2F LAMPS I were completely successful.

Torpedoes: In 1982 the KAIMALINO was fitted with triple Mk 32 torpedo tubes for tests of lightweight ASW torpedoes.

The KAIMALINO at rest. Unlike a hydrofoil, a SWATH or SSP remains high above the water when not under way. (1999, Leo Van Ginderen)

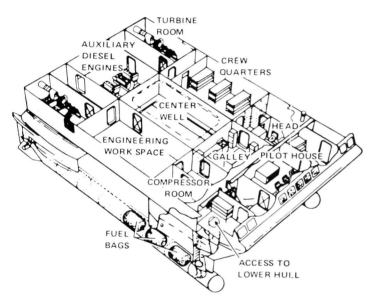

The interior arrangement of the KAIMALINO. SWATH configurations provide relatively high cube for a given displacement. Although SWATH hulls are very stable, they are relatively slow compared to SLICE and monohull configurations.

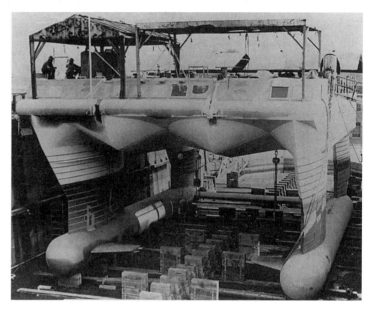

The KAIMALINO in dry dock, showing her twin, torpedo-like submerged hulls. Compare this arrangement with the SWATH T-AGOS surveillance ships (chapter 22). (1973, U.S. Navy)

1 PATROL BOAT: EX-COAST GUARD CUTTER

Number	Name	Commissioned
95NS8801 (ex-WPB 95310)	VENTURE	15 Dec 1953

Builders:	Coast Guard Yard, Curtis Bay, Md.
Displacement:	87 tons standard
	105 tons full load
Length:	95 feet (29.0 m) overall
Beam:	19 feet (5.8 m)
Draft:	6 feet (1.8 m)
Propulsion:	4 diesel engines (Cummins VT-12-M-700); 2,300 bhp; 2 shafts
Speed:	20 knots
Range:	2,600 n.miles (4,820 km) at 9 knots
	460 n.miles (850 km) at 20 knots
Manning:	8 (enlisted)
Radar:	SPS-64(V)1 navigation

Formerly the Coast Guard cutter CAPE WASH, this is the last of the 95-foot Cape class units in U.S. service. She was stricken from the Coast Guard on 1 June 1987 and transferred to the Navy for use at the submarine base in Bangor, Wash., as a patrol-escort craft for submarines going to and returning from sea.

Class: Four ships of this class were transferred to the Navy. Of the others, the VANGUARD (ex-CAPE HEDGE/WPB 95311) was returned to the Coast Guard for transfer to Mexico in 1990; unnamed 95NS8902 (ex-CAPE JELLISON/WPB 95317) was transferred from the Navy to the Sea Scouts at San Diego in 1993; and unnamed 95NS8901 (ex-CAPE ROMAINE/WPB 95319) was discarded in 1993.

The KAIMALINO at speed with an SH-2F LAMPS I helicopter on her flight deck. Although dated, this is perhaps the best photo ever taken of the ship. (1976, U.S. Navy)

TORPEDO/WEAPON RETRIEVERS

These craft support torpedo testing and submarine practice torpedo launches. The designations TR, TWR (torpedo weapon retriever), and TRB (torpedo recovery boat) are used for these craft. The names listed are unofficial.

These craft have stern ramps and—in some units—hydraulic cranes, for recovering torpedoes. They are arranged below according to size.

2 TORPEDO RECOVERY CRAFT | EX-OILFIELD SUPPORT CRAFT
1 SONOBUOY-TORPEDO TRIALS SHIP |

Number	Name	Completed
180NS8201	HUGO	Jan 1982
180NS8202	HUNTER	Jan 1981
180NS9201	RANGE ROVER	Jan 1980

Builders:	McDermott Shipyard, New Iberia, La., except HUNTER by Quality Shipbuilders, Moss Point, Miss.
Displacement:	approx. 1,500 tons full load
Length:	180 feet (54.86 m) overall
Beam:	40 feet (12.2 m)
Draft:	12¼ feet (3.73 m)
Propulsion:	2 diesel engines (Caterpillar D399 SCAC); 2,250 bhp; 2 shafts
Speed:	12 knots
Range:	
Manning:	

These are former oilfield support vessels. Two ships were acquired for the torpedo recovery role; both are assigned to the Atlantic Fleet Weapons Training activity at Roosevelt Roads, P.R. The RANGE ROVER serves as a trials ship at the Anglo-American AUTEC range, Andros Island, Bahamas. Details of the ships differ.

Names: Commercial names were CRYSTAL PELHAM, NOLA PELHAM, and LOUISE PELHAM, respectively.

The torpedo recovery craft HUNTER heading to an exercise area (1999, Leo Van Ginderen)

A pair of 120-foot missile retrievers at Tyndall Air Force Base near Panama City, Fla., before their transfer to the Navy (1991, U.S. Air Force)

5 MISSILE RETRIEVERS: EX-AIR FORCE CRAFT

Number	Name	Completed
126NS8801 (ex-MR-120-8801)		
MR-120-8802		
MR-120-8803		1988–1989
MR-120-8004	SEADOG	
MR-120-8805		

Builders:	Swiftships, Morgan City, La.
Displacement:	91 tons light
	133 tons full load
Length:	117⅓ feet (35.78 m) overall
Beam:	24⅔ feet (7.51 m)
Draft:	6¾ feet (2.06 m)
Propulsion:	4 diesel engines (Detroit Diesel 16V92 MTA); 5,600 bhp; 4 shafts
Speed:	30 knots
Range:	600 n.miles (1,111 km) at 27 knots
Manning:	10 (enlisted)

These retrieval craft are employed to recover practice missiles. They were built for the U.S. Air Force and were transferred to the Navy in 1996. Most retain their Air Force numbers; the MR-120-8004 was named at Port Hueneme (and carries the base designation SL-120).

The ships can carry 20 tons of cargo. They are of aluminum construction.

6 TORPEDO RETRIEVERS: 120-FOOT TYPE

Number	Name	Launched	Completed
TWR 821	SWAMP FOX	17 Oct 1984	4 Nov 1985
TWR 823	PORPOISE	4 May 1985	6 Dec 1985
TWR 832		22 Mar 1986	3 July 1986
TWR 833		4 Apr 1986	3 July 1986
TWR 841		15 Aug 1986	18 Oct 1986
TWR 842	NARWHAL	22 Sep 1986	24 Dec 1986

Builders:	Marinette Marine, Wisc.
Displacement:	174 tons standard
	213 tons full load
Length:	120 feet (36.6 m) overall
Beam:	25 feet (7.6 m)
Draft:	12 feet (3.65 m)
Propulsion:	2 diesel engines (Caterpillar D 3512); 2,350 bhp; 2 shafts
Speed:	16 knots
Range:	1,700 n.miles (3,150 km) at 16 knots
Manning:	15 (1 officer + 14 enlisted)
Radar:	Canadian Marconi LN-66 navigation

These are improved torpedo retrievers capable of recovering and carrying up to 14 Mk 48 torpedoes. All are active except the TWR 832, laid up in reserve.

Class: Originally a class of ten units: TR 821–825, 831–833, 841, and 842. The TWR 824 and 831 were sunk by Hurricane Hugo at Roosevelt Roads. The TWR 822 and 835 were stricken in 1997.

Classification: These craft have SABAR (Service Craft And Boat Accounting Report) designations consisting of the prefix 120 + TR + the above numbers; thus, TWR 821 has the SABAR designation 120TR821.

Design: A stern ramp and crane are provided for torpedo recovery. Endurance is seven days.

The SWAMP FOX is typical of the later series of U.S. Navy torpedo recovery craft. She has various awards painted on her deckhouse, indicating outstanding performance. (1994, Giorgio Arra)

1 TORPEDO AND DECOY RECOVERY SHIP: "RANGEMASTER"

Number	Name	Launched	In service
110WB8501	RANGEMASTER	1981	1985

Builder:	Steiner Fabricators, Bayou LaBatre, Ala.
Displacement:	
Tonnage:	99 GRT
Length:	110 feet (33.53 m) overall
Beam:	26 feet (7.92 m)
Draft:	11½ feet (3.51 m)
Propulsion:	1 diesel engine; 1 shaft
Speed:	
Manning:	

The RANGEMASTER was built as a crewboat for RCA to support Navy contract work. She was purchased by the Navy in 1985 for use at the AUTEC Range for torpedo and decoy recovery.

4 TORPEDO WEAPON RETRIEVERS: 100-FOOT TYPE

Number	(SABAR)	Name	Completed
TWR 1	(100C13728)	DIAMOND	
TWR 3	(100C13729)	CONDOR	Sep 1963
TWR 6	(100C14251)	FERRET	Mar 1966
TWR 771	(100TR771)	PHOENIX	Dec 1978

Builders:	Peterson Builders, Sturgeon Bay, Wisc.
Displacement:	110 tons light
	165 tons full load
Length:	102 feet (31.1 m) overall
Beam:	21 feet (6.4 m)
Draft:	7¾ feet (2.4 m)
Propulsion:	4 diesel engines (GM 12V-149); 1,600 bhp; 2 shafts
Speed:	17 knots
Range:	1,920 n.miles (3,556 km) at 10 knots
Manning:	15 (enlisted)

These torpedo retrievers are based on the PGM 59–class motor gunboat design.

Class: Stricken units of this type are CRAYFISH (TWR 682) in 1991, TWR 711 (unnamed) in 1994, and LABRADOR (TWR 681) in 1995.

Design: Of steel construction, the craft are fitted with a stern recovery ramp and can carry 17 tons of torpedoes.

The PHOENIX, also wearing several award insignia on her bridge, is another of these most-useful torpedo and weapon retrieval craft. The twin-funnel configuration permits a large area for torpedo recovery and stowage. A rubber raft is stowed aft. (1998, Leo Van Ginderen)

2 TORPEDO RETRIEVERS: 85-FOOT TYPE

Number	(SABAR)	Name	Completed
TWR 7	(85TR762)	CHAPARRAL	1975
TWR 8	(85TR761)	ILIWAI	1975

Builders:	Tacoma Boatbuilding, Wash.
Displacement:	
Length:	85 feet (25.9 m) overall
Beam:	18⅔ feet (5.7 m)
Draft:	5⅔ feet (1.7 m)
Propulsion:	4 diesel engines; 2 shafts
Speed:	18 knots
Manning:	

The TWR 7 was laid up at San Diego in 1992, but returned to service (at Pearl Harbor) in 1997. These craft each can carry eight torpedoes (22,000 pounds/9,979 kg). They are of aluminum construction.

The CHAPARRAL at high speed. Note the engine exhaust arrangement (port and starboard). (1985, Giorgio Arra)

4 MISSILE RETRIEVERS: EX-AIR FORCE CRAFT

Number	(SABAR)	Completed
TWR 4 (ex-MR-85-1608)	85NS9001	1967
(ex-MR-85-1603)	85NS9601	1967
HM-8		1967
HM-9		1967

Builders:	Swiftships, Morgan City, La.
Displacement:	90 tons full load
Length:	85 feet (25.91 m) overall
Beam:	18 feet (5.49 m)
Draft:	5⅙ feet (1.57 m)
Propulsion:	2 diesel engines (GM Detroit 16V92); 2 shafts
Speed:	17 knots
Range:	400 n.miles (740 km) at 17 knots
Manning:	10 (enlisted)

These craft were built for the U.S. Air Force as weapon retrievers and were transferred to the Navy in 1990–1996. The HM designations are assigned by Port Hueneme.

The ex-Air Force MR-85-1603, a missile retriever now employed by the Navy (U.S. Air Force)

A 72-foot torpedo retriever at San Diego (1986, Giorgio Arra)

2 TORPEDO RETRIEVERS: 85-FOOT TYPE

Number	(SABAR)	Completed
TR 651	(85TR651)	July 1965
TR 654	(85TR654)	Jan 1967

Builders:	Tacoma Boatbuilding, Wash.
Displacement:	61 tons full load
Length:	85 feet (25.9 m) overall
Beam:	18⅔ feet (5.69 m)
Draft:	5⅔ feet (1.73 m)
Propulsion:	2 diesel engines (GM 16V-71); 1,160 bhp; 2 shafts
Speed:	21 knots
Manning:	8 (enlisted)

These craft are of aluminum construction and can carry eight torpedoes (22,000 pounds/9,979 kg).

Two craft have been stricken: the TR 653 and TR 761. Two similar patrol craft, built without stern ramps, have the SABAR designations 85C14252 and 85C14253.

4 TORPEDO RETRIEVERS: 72-FOOT MK 2 TYPE

Number	(SABAR)	Completed
TRB 32	(72TR645)	Mar 1966
TRB 33	(72TR652)	Aug 1966
TRB 36	(72C4560)	Feb 1961
TRB 37	(72C9426)	Oct 1961

Builders:	
Displacement:	53 tons full load
Length:	72⅙ feet (22.0 m) overall
Beam:	17 feet (5.2 m)
Draft:	4⅓ feet (1.3 m)
Propulsion:	8 diesel engines; 1,300 bhp; 2 shafts
Speed:	18 knots
Range:	180 n.miles (333 km) at 18 knots
Manning:	7 (enlisted)
Radar:	SPS-69 navigation

This series of torpedo recovery craft was to be replaced by the new, 120-foot craft, but was retained because of the shortfall in TRs. These wooden-construction craft can carry 24,000 pounds (10,886 kg) of torpedoes.

They were built with SPS-53 radars; these subsequently were replaced by the SPS-69.

Two units have been stricken: the TWR 10 (72TR653) and TWR 31 (72C3211).

5 TORPEDO RETRIEVERS: 65-FOOT TYPE

Number	(SABAR)	Name	Completed
TR 671			Oct 1967
TRB 5	(65TR675)	HARRIER	July 1968
TR 6	(65TR676)	PEREGRINE	July 1968

Builders:	
Displacement:	34.8 tons full load
Length:	65 feet (19.8 m) overall
Beam:	17¼ feet (5.25 m)
Draft:	3⅝ feet (1.2 m)
Propulsion:	2 diesel engines (GM 12V71); 1,800 bhp; 2 shafts
Speed:	18.7 knots
Range:	280 n.miles (518 km) at 18.7 knots
Manning:	6 (enlisted)

This basic 65-foot design was also used for Navy utility and air-sea rescue boats. These aluminum-construction craft can carry four Mk 48 torpedoes.

Two units were stricken in 1996: the SEA HAWK (TR 673) and ALBATROSS (TR 4/65TR674); both were transferred for use by Sea Scouts.

A 65-foot torpedo recovery craft bringing aboard a Mk 48 torpedo (1986, Giorgio Arra)

A flock of YTB harbor tugs takes refuge at the piers at Norfolk, Va., during a blizzard. These small, hard-working craft usually are under way, helping to move big ships and pushing and pulling the multitude of barges at a naval base. (2000, U.S. Navy, PH2 Michael W. Pendergrass)

MISCELLANEOUS SHIPS AND CRAFT

Several hundred small craft, including various launches, work boats, and ship's boats, are in service at various U.S. naval stations and bases and aboard ships. There are also numerous pollution control and sampling craft.

NON-SELF-PROPELLED SERVICE CRAFT

The following are the approximate numbers of various types of non-self-propelled service craft listed on the Naval Vessel Register; almost all are in service. The YCF transports railroad cars; some of the YD floating cranes have maneuvering propulsion.

Only four of these ships have names: PHOEBUS (YDT 14), SUITLAND (YDT 15), TOM O'MALLEY (YDT 16), and THE BIG W (YSR 6). The non-self-propelled craft are tallied below. For characteristics, see A. D. Baker III, *Combat Fleets of the World, 2000–2001* (Annapolis, Md.: Naval Institute Press, 2000), pages 986–999.

12	APL	Barracks craft
183	YC	Open lighters
1	YCF	Car float
7	YCV	Aircraft transportation lighters
42	YD	Floating cranes
4	YDT	Diving tenders
109	YFN	Covered lighters
11	YFNB	Large covered lighters
4	YFND	Dry dock companion craft
3	YFP	Floating power barges
3	YGN	Garbage lighters
1	YLC	Salvage lift craft
1	YNG	Gate craft
14	YOGN	Gasoline barges
41	YON	Fuel oil barges
11	YOS	Oil storage barges
1	YPD	Floating pile driver
23	YR	Floating workshops
5	YRB	Repair and berthing barges
37	YRBM	Repair, berthing, and messing barges
4	YRDH	Floating dry dock workshops (hull)
2	YRDM	Floating dry dock workshops (machinery)
5	YRR	Radiological repair barges
2	YRST	Salvage craft tenders
7	YSR	Sludge removal barges
5	YWN	Water barges

In addition, the Navy owns a unique oceanographic research craft known as FLIP that warrants description (see page 349).

Barracks craft APL 15 (1999, Leo Van Ginderen)

Open lighter YC 829 (1998, Leo Van Ginderen)

Covered lighter YFN 1267 (1997, Leo Van Ginderen)

Crane barge YD 251 (1999, Leo Van Ginderen)

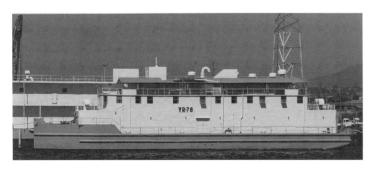

Floating workshop YR 78 (1997, Leo Van Ginderen)

Repair, berthing, and messing barge YRBM 39 (1998, Leo Van Ginderen)

Floating dry dock workshop (machinery) YRDM 5 (1999, Leo Van Ginderen)

Sludge removal barge YSR 39 (1992, Stefan Terzibaschitsch)

1 FLOATING INSTRUMENTATION PLATFORM: "FLIP" ↓

Number	Name	Launched	In service
(none)	FLIP	22 June 1962	6 Aug 1962

Builder:	Gunderson Brothers, Portland, Ore.
Displacement:	700 tons full load
Length:	359^{11}/$_{12}$ feet (109.73 m) overall
Beam:	28 feet (8.53 m)
Draft:	12½ feet (3.81 m) horizontal
	280 feet (85.37 m) vertical
Propulsion:	non-self-propelled (see *Engineering* notes)
Manning:	5 + 11 technicians

The FLIP, ballasted down, has 55 feet of her "bow" above water. Note the radar reflector and bar-type search radar antenna fitted on the above-water portion of the FLIP. The horizontal waterline is visible on the bow. (Scripps Institution of Oceanography)

The FLIP is a unique research craft—basically a long cylinder that can be "flipped" to a vertical position, with the upper portion above sea level and the lower portion providing sensors at various levels within the water column. It has a "ship bow" to facilitate towing (towing speed is up to 10 knots).

The FLIP was built to support Navy submarine/ASW research; subsequently it has been used for a variety of ocean research projects. The craft is Navy owned and, since entering service, has been operated by the Scripps Institution of Oceanography's Marine Physical Laboratory, part of the University of California, in La Jolla, Calif.

The FLIP has an at-sea endurance of up to 30 days without replenishment.

A similar, unmanned Navy project was SPAR (Seagoing Platform for Acoustic Research), in use in the latter 1960s. This platform was 354 feet (107.93 m) in length and 16 feet (4.88 m) in diameter, and displaced 1,370 tons in the horizontal position and 1,720 tons ballasted in the vertical position; the platform operated with a draft of 302 feet (92.07 m).

Engineering: The craft is non-self-propelled but has a 60-horsepower thruster for station keeping. She is towed to operating areas and can drift free or be anchored to the ocean floor.

Names: FLIP is an acronym for Floating Instrumentation Platform.

The FLIP in the horizontal position, for towing and mooring when in port. The 360-foot instrument platform has been in service for almost four decades. (Scripps Institution of Oceanography)

CHAPTER 25

Floating Dry Docks

The RESOLUTE servicing the OKLAHOMA CITY (SSN 723) at Norfolk, Va. Most of the Navy's active floating dry docks now support submarines. Submarines in dry dock generally have their propellers shrouded to prevent people from viewing their propeller configurations, a key factor in submarine quieting. The RESOLUTE is a three-piece steel dock. (1999, Jürg Kürsener)

The Navy operates floating dry docks at several bases in the continental United States for the repair and maintenance of surface ships and submarines. These are non-self-propelled docks, but have electrical generators to provide power for their lighting, tools, and equipment. Normally they operate with a flotilla of non-self-propelled barges that provide specialized services, such as messing and berthing, for the docks themselves and for ships being dry docked.

Like the Navy's ships and service craft, the number of dry docks has been reduced in the post–Cold War era. The floating docks in this chapter are arranged according to their classification. The docks in active Navy service have their locations indicated; several others are operated by foreign navies and commercial firms on lease from the Navy. Class totals are for docks in U.S. Navy service and laid up in reserve, plus the single YFD-type dock in Coast Guard service.

Floating dry docks officially are considered to be service craft; they are listed in both the Naval Vessel Register (NVR) and Service Craft and Boat Accounting Report (SABAR).

Classification: IX 521, 522, 524, and 525 were assigned to AFDB dock sections in 1996–1997. The rationale for this change has not been revealed by the Navy, and it adds further to the recent confusion of Navy ship and service craft classifications.

Many existing U.S. floating dry docks were reclassified on 1 August 1946, several of which remain on the NVR:

World War II	Post-1946
ABSD	AFDB
ARD	AFDL/ARD
ARDC	AFDL[1]
AFD	AFDL
YFD	AFDM and YFD

Design: All U.S. Navy floating dry docks are open-ended, through-type docks except for the ARD-series. The ARDs are distinctive in being closed at one end by a ship-shaped bow.[2]

The large ABSD/AFDB-series docks are sectional, to facilitate disassembly and towing. Mounted on their hull sections—which are called "pontoons"—these docks have side or "wing" walls that fold down for storage or towing. These wing walls can be easily shifted between pontoons in the event of damage.

The lift capacities listed in this chapter are nominal; much heavier ships can be lifted if the distribution of ship weight is favorable.

Guns: No floating dry docks are armed, although some were originally fitted to mount light anti-aircraft guns.

Names: Floating dry docks were unnamed until the 1960s. Dry docks that service nuclear-propelled submarines have been given the names of towns and cities associated with nuclear power; most of the others that are named have positive trait names.

Operational: Operational Navy docks are manned by Navy personnel.

---

1. Initially these were referred to as AFDL(C).
2. The ARD-type docks are also referred to as "Camel docks" for a ship of that name that was gutted and fitted with a stern gate in 1700 to serve as a dock at the Russian harbor of Kronshtadt (off St. Petersburg). The project was undertaken by a captain in the Royal Navy because of the lack of docking facilities at Kronshtadt (which is now a major Russian naval base).

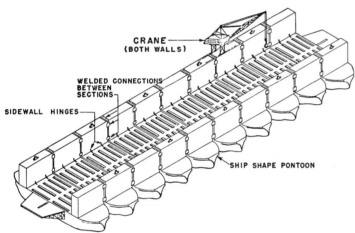

A TEN-SECTION AFDB CONFIGURATION

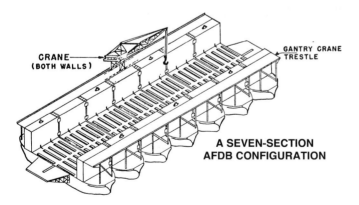

A SEVEN-SECTION AFDB CONFIGURATION

1 LARGE FLOATING DRY DOCK SECTION: "AFDB 4" CLASS

Floating dock AFDB 7 section F was transferred to the Army's Corps of Engineers in 1966 for use as a floating power plant at Kwajalein atoll (Marshall Islands) in conjunction with anti-ballistic missile tests. The dock was fitted with two gas turbine generators (General Electric 7LM1500) to produce 22 megawatts. The Army named her ANDREW J. WEBER.

The dock section subsequently was used in the Philippines from 1968 until 1972, when it was moved to Guam. It was then moved to Pearl Harbor for further storage.

9 LARGE AUXILIARY FLOATING DRY DOCK SECTIONS: "AFDB 1" CLASS

Number	Former	Name	Sections	In service	Status
	AFDB 1	ARTISAN	B, E	1 July 1943	Reserve 1 Mar 1987
IX 521	AFDB 1		D	1 July 1943	Reserve 1 Mar 1987
IX 522	AFDB 2		D	1 Apr 1944	Reserve 1 Mar 1987
	AFDB 2		E, H, I	1 Apr 1944	Reserve 24 Mar 1987
IX 524	AFDB 2		F	1 Apr 1944	Reserve 25 Apr 1997
IX 525	AFDB 1		C	1 Apr 1944	**Active**

Builders:	Mare Island Navy Yard, Vallejo, Calif.[3]
Displacement:	15,400 tons per section
Length:	approx. 93 feet (28.35 m) overall per section
	approx. 82½ feet (25.15 m) on pontoon per section
Width:	256 feet (78.05 m)
Width clear inside:	133⁷⁄₁₂ feet (40.73 m)
Draft:	9 feet (2.74 m) light surface
	68 feet (23.78 m) maximum submerged

These are the remains of seven huge advanced base sectional docks (ABSD 1–7) built by the Navy during World War II. They were intended to be towed in sections to advance bases to be assembled and service the Navy's largest warships. The ABSD 1 and ABSD 2 were the largest, being ten-section docks intended to lift battleships of the IOWA (BB 61) class and aircraft carriers of the MIDWAY (CVB 41) class. Later designated as large auxiliary floating dry docks AFDB 1 and AFDB 2, their sections are the only ABSD/AFDB floating dock sections remaining on the NVR.

Of the nine remaining sections of these docks, all are in reserve at Pearl Harbor except IX 525 (AFDB 2 section H), in service at the Pacific Missile Range Facility, Kekaha, Hawaii. AFDB 1 sections B through E were stricken on 27 October 1986; they remain laid up at Pearl Harbor in Navy custody and are listed on the NVR as being in reserve. AFDB 2 sections D, E, F, H, and I were stricken on 27 October 1986 but reacquired in March 1987.

Class: The Navy constructed seven advanced base sectional docks (ABSD) in World War II:

	Sections	Lift capacity
ABSD 1, 2	10	90,000 tons
ABSD 3	9	81,000 tons
ABSD 4–7	7	55,000 tons

The ABSD 1 was completed in 1943, the ABSD 2–6 in 1944, and the ABSD 7 in 1945. A planned eighth ABSD was canceled.

AFDB 1 section I was sold for scrap in 1979 and sections A, F, G, H, and J were stricken in 1987.

AFDB 2 section C was sunk as a target in 1987 and sections A, B, G, and J were stricken in 1989 and transferred to the state of Washington.

AFDB 3 was transferred to the state of Maine in 1982 for use by the Bath Iron Works at Portland, Maine.

AFDB 4 was stricken in 1989 and transferred to the Port of Portland, Ore.

AFDB 5 was transferred to the city of Port Arthur, Texas, in 1984 for use by Todd Shipyards Corp.

---

3. The ABSD sections were erected and assembled at Mare Island; they were fabricated by commercial firms.

AFDB 6 was stricken in 1975 and transferred to the Industrial Investment Corp. in Bermuda.

AFDB 7 sections A through E and G were loaned to the Brownsville Navigation District, Brownsville, Texas; the fate of section F is unknown.

Classification: These docks were originally designated ABSD with the same hull numbers; they were reclassified AFDB in August 1946.

Design: Steel construction. The large wing walls can support cranes and, as built, anti-aircraft guns (authorized armament when built was a twin 40-mm Bofors AA mount on each section).

The ABSD 1–3 had the capacity to lift any World War II–era U.S. warship, including the MIDWAY-class large aircraft carriers. The ABSD 4–7 could lift IOWA-class battleships and ESSEX (CV 9)-class aircraft carriers.

Names: Names were assigned to two of these docks in the 1960s: the AFDB 1 became ARTISAN and the AFDB 7 became LOS ALAMOS.

Operational: AFDB 7 sections A-B-C-D were reactivated from the reserve fleet in 1961 and towed across the Atlantic in February–March 1961 for use at the Holy Loch (Scotland) SSBN refit base; AFDB 7 sections were in use at Holy Loch for 30 years until the forward base there was disestablished in 1992.

Some sections of these docks were held at times in the National Defense Reserve Fleet (NDRF).

LARGE AUXILIARY FLOATING DRY DOCK: CIVILIAN-BUILT

The unnamed AFDB 9 is a civilian-built, two-section dock acquired by the Navy in 1974. She has been on commercial lease since 14 June 1993, operated by the Metro Machine Corp. in Norfolk, Va.

The AFDB 9 was taken over by the Navy and placed on the NVR effective 12 July 1990. The dock had been operated by the Pennsyl-

vania Shipbuilding Co. and was acquired by the Navy when that firm defaulted on Navy contracts.

See 16th Edition/page 327 for characteristics.

LARGE AUXILIARY FLOATING DRY DOCK: GERMAN-BUILT

The floating dock MACHINIST (AFDB 8) is a single-piece dock acquired by the Navy in 1985. She was towed to Subic Bay in the Philippines for operation beginning in March 1986; with the withdrawal of U.S. forces from the Philippines, she was towed to Pearl Harbor in 1992. The MACHINIST was stricken on 23 April 1997 and approved for sale.

See 16th Edition/page 327–328 for characteristics.

1 SMALL AUXILIARY FLOATING DRY DOCK: "AFDL 1" CLASS

Number	Name	In service	Status
AFDL 6	DYNAMIC	Mar 1944	**Active**

Builders:	Chicago Bridge and Iron, Calif.
Sections:	1
Lift capacity:	1,000 tons
Length:	200 feet (61.0 m) overall
Width:	64 feet (19.5 m)
Width clear inside:	45 feet (13.7 m)
Draft:	3⁵⁄₁₂ feet (1.0) light
	28½ feet (8.7) maximum submerged
Manning:	24 (1 officer + 23 enlisted)

The AFDL 6 is the last dock of this type in Navy service. She is operational at Little Creek, Va.

Class: See table 25-1 for class listing.

Design: One-piece, steel construction. The AFDL 1–type docks originally were intended to service minesweeper-size ships (AM/MSF/MSO).

Two sections of an AFDB *(top)* and the ADEPT *(foreground)* at Subic Bay. The wing walls of the AFDBs fold down for towing and storage. The AFDL 23 still had gun tubs that held anti-aircraft guns during World War II. (U.S. Navy)

The now-retired ARTISAN, with six sections assembled, at Subic Bay, Philippines. Another AFDB section—with sidewalls raised—is being overhauled within the dock. All AFDBs were similar except for their assembled length. (U.S. Navy)

Water begins to rise above the positioning blocks in the RESOLUTE. The dock will be submerged to provide sufficient clearance for a submarine to float into the dock, after which it will be pumped out to lift the submarine high and dry. (1996, U.S. Navy, PH2 Richard Rosser)

TABLE 25-1. SMALL AUXILIARY FLOATING DRY DOCKS

Number	Name	In service	Lift (tons)	Notes
AFDL 1 class (28)				
AFDL 1	ENDEAVOR	1943	1,000	to Dominican Republic 1986
AFDL 2		1943	1,000	stricken 15 Nov 1981
AFDL 3		1943	1,000	to U.S. Army 1946–1948; commercial lease 1973
AFDL 4		1943	1,000	to Brazil 1966; purchased 1977
AFDL 5		1944	1,000	to China (Taiwan) 1948
AFDL 6	DYNAMIC	1944	1,000	active (see above)
AFDL 7 class (5)				
AFDL 7	ABILITY	1944	1,900	sold 1 July 1982 (scrapped)
AFDL 1 class (continued)				
AFDL 8		1944	1,000	stricken 1 Dec 1981 (sunk as an artificial reef)
AFDL 9		1943	1,000	str. 15 July 1982; sold 1 Oct 1982 (scrapped)
AFDL 10		1943	1,000	to Philippines 1978; str. 13 July 1987
AFDL 11		1944	1,000	to Cambodia (Khmer Republic) 1971
AFDL 12		1943	1,000	commercial lease (disposal 1 July 1984)
AFDL 13		1943	1,000	to South Vietnam; str. 1 Oct 1983
AFDL 14 not used				
AFDL 15		1943	1,000	commercial lease; str. 18 Dec 1983
AFDL 16		1943	1,000	commercial lease; str. 15 Aug 1986; sold 1 June 1982 (scrapped)
AFDL 17		1943	1,000	sold Jan 1971 (scrapped)
AFDL 18		1944	1,000	sold Dec 1962
AFDL 19		1944	1,000	(disposal 1 Apr 1983)
AFDL 20		1944	1,000	to Philippines 1961; purchased 1980
AFDL 21		1944	1,000	commercial lease; str. 31 March 1989
AFDL 7 class (continued)				
AFDL 22		1944	1,900	to South Vietnam; str. 1 July 1985 (disposal same date; see notes)
AFDL 23	ADEPT	1944	1,900	commercial lease 15 July 1994
AFDL 1 class (continued)				
AFDL 24		1944	1,000	to Philippines 1948; purchased 1980
AFDL 25	UNDAUNTED	1944	1,000	str. 13 Mar 1996 (disposal 19 May 1997)
AFDL 26		1944	1,000	to Paraguay 1977; purchased 1977
AFDL 27		1944	1,000	sold May 1961 (scrapped)
AFDL 28		1944	1,000	to Mexico 1973; purchased 1978
AFDL 29		1944	1,000	commercial lease; str. 15 July 1985; sold 1 Aug 1983 (scrapped)
AFDL 30		1944	1,000	sold 1 June 1979 (scrapped)
AFDL 31		1943	1,000	loan to Coast Guard 1943; listed as YFD 83 (see below)
AFDL 7 class (continued)				
AFDL 32		1944	1,900	scuttled 1945; str. 1946
AFDL 33		1944	1,900	to Peru 1959; purchased 1980
AFDL 34 class (13)				
AFDL 34		1944	2,800	to Taiwan 1959
AFDL 35		1944	2,800	sold 1 Jan 1974 (scrapped)
AFDL 36		1944	2,800	to China (Taiwan) 1947
AFDL 37		1944	2,800	commercial lease; sold 1 Dec 1981 (scrapped)
AFDL 38		1944	2,800	commercial lease (disposal 1 Oct 1981)
AFDL 39		1944	2,800	to Brazil 1966; purchased 1981
AFDL 40		1944	2,800	commercial lease; str. 30 June 1987; to Philippines 30 June 1990
AFDL 41		1944	2,800	sold 1983
AFDL 42		1944	2,800	sold 15 Jan 1975 (scrapped)
AFDL 43		1944	2,800	sold 29 May 1979 (scrapped)
AFDL 44		1944	2,800	to Philippines 1969; purchased 1980
AFDL 45		1945	2,800	commercial lease (disposal 1981)
AFDL 46		1945	2,800	target at Bikini 1946; scuttled 1946; str. 1947
AFDL 47 type				
AFDL 47	RELIANCE	1946	6,500	ex-ARD 33; commercial lease 15 July 1991
AFDL 48 type				
AFDL 48	DILIGENCE	1956	4,000	commercial lease; str. 28 Aug 1986
AFDL 49 type				
AFDL 49				canceled 1958

Table 25-1 represents an attempt to list all AFDL-type floating docks. Navy records are incomplete. Some docks were stricken and some were not; the term "disposal" is used in the NVR and is provided above when no strike date is known.

The AFDL 1–6, 8–13, 15–21, and 24–31 originally were designated AFD (mobile floating dry docks); these were one-piece steel docks. The AFDL 34–46 originally were ARDC 1–13; they were one-piece reinforced-concrete docks.[4] Only seven of these docks were given names. All are one-piece steel docks except the AFDL 34–46.

The AFDL 47 was the largest U.S. Navy single-piece "through"-type floating dock.

The AFDL 13 and AFDL 22 were taken over by Communist forces on 30 April 1975 with the fall of the South Vietnamese government. The AFDL 25 was taken back from commercial lease in June 1984, refitted, and towed to Guantánamo Bay to replace the AFDL 1; the dock was stricken in 1996.

2 MEDIUM AUXILIARY FLOATING DRY DOCKS: "AFDM 3" CLASS

Number	Name	In service	Status
AFDM 7 (ex-YFD 63)	SUSTAIN	Jan 1945	lease
AFDM 10 (ex-YFD 67)	RESOLUTE	1945	**Active**

Builders:	Everett Pacific Shipbuilding, Everett, Wash.
Sections:	3
Lift capacity:	18,000 tons
Length:	622 feet (189.6 m) overall
Width:	124 feet (37.8 m)
Width clear inside:	93 to 96 feet (28.35 to 29.27 m)
Draft:	6⅙ feet (1.9 m) light
	52¾ feet (16.1 m) maximum submerged
Manning:	AFDM 7 143 (4 officers + 139 enlisted)
	AFDM 10 150 (6 officers + 144 enlisted)

These are three-piece, steel docks. The AFDM 7 was taken out of service on 21 October 1997 and laid up in the NDRF at Fort Eustis, Va.; she was extensively overhauled in 1991–1992 by the Bethlehem Steel yard at Sparrows Point, Baltimore, Md. She was leased to a commercial firm in 1999. The AFDM 10 supports Submarine Squadron 8 at Norfolk, Va.

Classification: These docks initially were classified as yard floating dry docks (YFD).

Design: Originally intended to dock destroyers, light cruisers, and escort carriers.

1 MEDIUM AUXILIARY FLOATING DRY DOCK: "AFDM 1" CLASS

Number	Name	In service	Status
AFDM 2 (ex-YFD 4)	(unnamed)	1 Oct 1942	reserve 16 May 1995

Builders:	
Sections:	3
Lift capacity:	15,000 tons
Length:	615⅔ feet (187.7 m) overall
Width:	116 feet (35.4 m)
Width clear inside:	87½ feet (26.7 m)
Draft:	5¾ feet (1.75 m) light
	49¾ feet (15.2 m) maximum submerged
Manning:	

This is a three-section steel dock. The dock was leased to Halter Marine, Gulfport, Miss., on 1 September 1992. She was returned to Navy custody on 16 May 1995 and promptly placed in storage in the NDRF at Beaumont, Texas.

She is scheduled to be transferred to Venezuela.

Design: Originally intended to dock destroyers, light cruisers, and escort carriers.

---

4. Concrete was used in the construction of ARDC and some YFD floating dry docks because of the steel shortage during World War II.

TABLE 25-2.   MEDIUM AUXILIARY FLOATING DRY DOCKS

Number	Name	In service	Lift (tons)	Notes
AFDM 1 class (2)				
AFDM 1 (ex-YFD 3)		1942	15,000	commercial lease; str. 1 Sep 1986 (scrapped)
AFDM 2 (ex-YFD 4)		1942	15,000	reserve (see above)
AFDM 3 class (11)				
AFDM 3 (ex-YFD 6)		1943	18,000	commercial lease 1983
AFDM 4		1943	18,000	
AFDM 5 (ex-YFD 21)	RESOURCEFUL	1943	18,000	str. 22 Aug 1997 (disposal 6 Apr 1997)
AFDM 6 (ex-YFD 62)	COMPETENT	1944	18,000	str. 21 Aug 1997
AFDM 7 (ex-YFD 63)	SUSTAIN	1945	18,000	commercial lease 1999
AFDM 8 (ex-YFD 64)	RICHLAND	1944	18,000	str. 22 Aug 1997 (disposal 6 Apr 1997)
AFDM 9 (ex-YFD 65)		1945	18,000	commercial lease; str. 31 Dec 1987 (disposal 2 Aug 1989)
AFDM 10 (ex-YFD 67)	RESOLUTE	1945	18,000	active (see above)
AFDM 11 (ex-YFD)				canceled 1945
AFDM 12 (ex-YFD)				canceled 1945
AFDM 13 (ex-YFD 85)				canceled 1945
AFDM 14 type				
AFDM 14 (ex-YFD 71)	STEADFAST	1945	14,000	str. 7 Feb 1999 (disposal 25 Aug 1999)

These all were three-piece steel docks, originally designated YFD. Only six of the docks were given names.

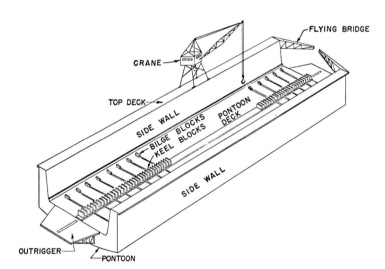

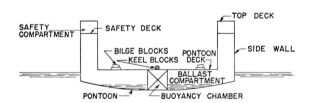

Typical floating dry dock configuration

TABLE 25-3.   AUXILIARY REPAIR DRY DOCKS

Number	Name	In service	Lift (tons)	Notes
ARD 2 class (8)				
ARD 2		1942	3,500	to Mexico 1963
ARD 3				canceled
ARD 4				canceled
ARD 5	WATERFORD	1942	3,500	str. 1 Oct 1997; to Chile 10 Mar 1999
ARD 6		1943	3,500	to Pakistan 1961; str. 24 Nov 1997
ARD 7	WEST MILTON	1943	3,500	str. 23 Aug 1990 (disposal 23 Jan 1992)
ARD 8		1943	3,500	to Peru 1961; purchased 1980
ARD 9		1943	3,500	to Taiwan 1977; purchased 1981
ARD 10		1943	3,500	str. 1972 (scrapped)
ARD 11		1943	3,500	to Mexico 1974
ARD 12 class (21)				
ARD 12		1943	3,500	to Turkey 1971; purchased 1987
ARD 13		1943	3,500	to Venezuela; purchased 1977
ARD 14		1943	3,500	to Brazil 1963; purchased 1980
ARD 15		1944	3,500	to Mexico 1971; purchased 1981
ARD 16		1944	3,500	sold 1 Mar 1973 (scrapped)
ARD 17		1944	3,500	to Ecuador 1951; purchased 1980
ARD 18		1944	3,500	converted to ARDM 3
ARD 19		1944	3,500	converted to ARDM 1
ARD 20		1944	3,500	
ARD 21		1944	3,500	to Taiwan
ARD 22	WINDSOR	1944	3,500	to Taiwan 1976; purchased 1995
ARD 23		1944	3,500	to Argentina; purchased 1993
ARD 24		1944	3,500	to Ecuador; purchased 1982
ARD 25		1944	3,500	to Chile 1960; purchased 2000
ARD 26		1944	3,500	converted to ARDM 2
ARD 27		1944	3,500	sold 1 Sep 1974 (scrapped)
ARD 28		1944	3,500	sold 1 Feb 1981 (scrapped)
ARD 29	ARCO	1944	3,500	to Iran 1977
ARD 30	SAN ONOFRE	1944	3,500	str. 21 Aug 1997; to Mexico 2000
ARD 31		1944	3,500	to U.S. Air Force
ARD 32		1944	3,500	to Chile 1970; str. 25 June 1992; purchased 2000
ARD 33			3,500	reclassified AFDL 47
ARD 34–36				canceled 1945
ARD 37 type				
ARD 37				canceled 1956

These were one-piece steel dry docks. All ARD-type docks have been stricken, the last in active U.S. Navy service being the SAN ONOFRE; she was inactivated on 29 September 1995. (See 15th Edition/page 369 for characteristics.)

The 2,200-ton-capacity ARD 1 was placed in service in 1934. All subsequent ARDs were of the same design. They were intended to dock World War II–era destroyers and submarines; the ARD 12 and later docks were slightly longer and could accommodate tank landing ships (LST). Three ARDs were converted to support Polaris/Poseidon missile submarines (and changed to ARDM).

Only five of these docks were named, all for sites associated with nuclear energy development. The same name source was used for ARDM-type docks.

2 MEDIUM AUXILIARY REPAIR DOCKS: "ARDM 4" CLASS

Number	Name	In service	Status
ARDM 4	SHIPPINGPORT	27 Jan 1979	**Active**
ARDM 5	ARCO	27 Feb 1986	**Active**

Builders:	ARDM 4 Bethlehem Steel, Sparrows Point, Md.
	ARDM 5 Todd Shipyards, Seattle, Wash.
Sections:	1
Lift capacity:	7,800 tons
Length:	492 feet (150.0 m) overall
Width:	96 feet (29.3 m)
Width clear inside:	64 feet (19.5 m)
Draft:	54½ feet (16.6 m) maximum submerged
Manning:	ARDM 4 131 (6 officers + 125 enlisted)
	ARDM 5 130 (5 officers + 125 enlisted)

These were the first floating dry docks built for the U.S. Navy specifically to support nuclear-propelled submarines. The SHIPPINGPORT is operational at the Naval Submarine Base New London, and the ARCO is operational at the Naval Submarine Base (Point Loma) San Diego supporting Submarine Squadron 11.

Class: Authorized in the fiscal 1975 and 1983 naval shipbuilding programs. A third, similar dock planned for fiscal year 1984 was not built.

1 MEDIUM AUXILIARY REPAIR DOCK: CONVERTED "ARD 12" CLASS

Number	Name	In service	Status
ARDM 1 (ex-ARD 19)	OAK RIDGE	1 Mar 1944	**Active**

Builders:	Pacific Bridge, Alameda, Calif.
Sections:	1
Lift capacity:	8,000 tons
Length:	541 feet (164.9 m) overall
Width:	81 feet (24.7 m)
Width clear inside:	58 feet (17.7 m)
Draft:	7 feet (2.1 m) light
	42⅝ feet (13.1 m) maximum submerged
Manning:	179 (5 officers + 174 enlisted)

Three ARD 12–class docks were converted in the 1960s to service Polaris/Poseidon missile submarines.

The OAK RIDGE is active at the Naval Submarine Base New London, Conn. Two sister docks have been stricken; see below.

The SHIPPINGPORT at New London, Conn., with an attack submarine being serviced (1996, Leo Van Ginderen)

The ARCO at San Diego, Calif. There are traveling cranes on the wing walls. The crane at left is on a barge alongside the dock. (1996, Leo Van Ginderen)

TABLE 25-4.   MEDIUM AUXILIARY REPAIR DRY DOCKS

Number	Name	In service	Lift (tons)	Notes
Converted ARD 12 class (3)				
ARDM 1	OAK RIDGE	1944	8,000	active (see above)
ARDM 2	ALAMOGORDO	1944	8,000	stricken 23 Nov 1993
ARDM 3	ENDURANCE	1944	8,000	stricken 31 July 1995
ARDM 4 class (2)				
ARDM 4	SHIPPINGPORT	1979	7,800	active (see above)
ARDM 5	ARCO	1986	7,800	active (see above)

These five docks were specifically intended to support nuclear-propelled submarines. The first three units were converted from ARD-type docks in the 1960s.

The ARDM 2 is scheduled to be transferred to Greece.

1 YARD FLOATING DRY DOCK: "YFD 83"

Number	In service	Status
YFD 83 (ex-AFDL 31)	1 Dec 1943	Active (USCG)

Builders:	Foundation Co., Kearney, N.J.
Sections:	1
Lift capacity:	1,000 tons
Displacement:	800 tons light
Length:	200 feet (61.0 m) overall
Width:	64 feet
Width clear inside:	45 feet (13.7 m)
Draft:	3⁵/₁₂ feet (1.1 m) light
	28½ feet (8.7 m) maximum submerged
Manning:	

The YFD 83 has been on loan to the Coast Guard since 1943 for use at the Coast Guard yard at Curtis Bay, Md. She was reclassified AFDL 31 with other YFDs, but was listed as YFD in Coast Guard service.

Several other YFDs are on commercial lease.

YARD FLOATING DRY DOCKS

The Navy built 81 docks designated YFD from 1942 onward. (The YFD 1 and YFD 2 were completed in 1900 and 1905, respectively.)[5] The YFDs varied in size and type (one to six sections) and were constructed of steel, wood, and concrete to several different designs.

Units disposed of since 1990 are listed below (lift capacity in parentheses):

YFD 69 (14,000 tons)   commercial lease 1 Feb 1995
YFD 70 (14,000 tons)   commercial lease 16 Apr 1996

---

5. The YFD 1 was towed to Pearl Harbor in 1940. She was sunk on 7 December 1941 (with the destroyer SHAW/DD 373); both were salvaged and the YFD 1 continued to serve throughout the war. The YFD 2—unofficially named the DEWEY dock—was towed to the Philippines; she served there until scuttled in early 1942 to prevent her capture by the Japanese.

The ARCO, resting high and dry at the submarine base at Point Loma (San Diego), California. The dock was built specifically to support nuclear-propelled submarines. (1999, Leo Van Ginderen)

CHAPTER 26

Naval Aviation

An F-14B Tomcat from VF-102 streaks skyward from a waist catapult of the carrier GEORGE WASHINGTON (CVN 73) during operations in the Persian Gulf. A pair of F/A-18C Hornets in the foreground are being readied for flight; the wisp of steam indicates the bow catapults also are being used. (U.S. Navy, PH3 Brian Fleske)

U.S. Naval Aviation consists of the aviation organizations and activities of the Navy and Marine Corps. The naval air training organization also supports the Coast Guard.

The strength and structure of U.S. naval aviation have been reduced at a precipitous rate during the 1990s.[1] U.S. naval aviation comprises more than 4,000 aircraft, in both active and reserve units. This number includes "pipeline," research, and training aircraft. The current active aircraft inventory is listed in table 26-1. (U.S. Coast Guard aircraft are listed separately; see chapter 30 of this edition of *Ships and Aircraft*.)

Furthermore, in the post–Cold War era, the Navy's carrier air wings are being reshaped to meet the changing operational requirements—and the failure of the Navy to develop a long-range/all-weather attack aircraft. At the same time, according to the head of the Naval Strike and Air Warfare Center, "the challenges to Naval Aviation Readiness . . . are mounting with reduced forces—a higher percentage of assets at sea, a higher percentage deployed, a resultant compression of the management cycle, higher aircraft utilization rates, increased maintenance demands, and certainly a higher [personnel/operational tempo] accompanying the reduction in our turn-around time."[2]

---

1. Details of the current U.S. naval aviation structure are provided in Richard R. Burgess, "US Navy," *World Air Power Journal* 37 (Summer 1999), pp. 124–157; Tony Holmes, "United States Navy Today: Part 1: The Carrier Air Wing," *Air International* (August 1999), pp. 100–106; and Richard R. Burgess, "United States Navy Today: Part 2: Operational Land-based Units," *Air International* (October 1999), pp. 210–218. Another invaluable source is the annual feature "The Year in Review," published in the July–August issue of *Naval Aviation News*.

2. Rear Adm. Bernard J. Smith, USN, statement before the Subcommittee on Military Readiness and Personnel, National Security Committee, House of Representatives, 4 March 1997.

The Navy currently operates 12 aircraft carriers, following the aborted effort to employ the JOHN F. KENNEDY as an "operational reserve/training" ship. Flying from their flight decks are ten active carrier air wings (CVW) and one reserve air wing (CVWR). The current force is based on the Department of Defense's Bottom-Up Review of 1993 and subsequent quadrennial reviews. (By comparison, during the 1980s the Navy briefly had 14 active wings as part of the Reagan-Lehman naval buildup, with a 15th wing planned but not activated; in addition, there were two reserve air wings at the time.)

To sustain 11 active air wings and one reserve air wing, the Navy has restructured carrier aviation, reducing the number of fighter-attack aircraft per carrier and "necking down" the different types of aircraft in the wings.[3] With the change, each wing has 50 strike fighter aircraft: 14 F-14 Tomcats and 36 F/A-18 Hornets, except that two wings will have a second F-14 squadron to act as "place holders" until the fleet introduction of the F/A-18E Hornet in 2001.[4]

Because of the shortage of F/A-18 squadrons, up to four Marine Corps F/A-18 squadrons have been assigned to Navy carrier wings at various times during the past decade. In addition, a Marine F/A-18 squadron is assigned to the reserve air wing. (Occasionally a Marine VMAQ squadron has also been assigned to a carrier air wing during this period.) This, of course, reduces the training time that the Marine squadrons have for combined operations with ground combat forces—their primary purpose for existing.

Gone from the carrier wings is the Grumman A-6E Intruder, the last "straight" attack aircraft (VA) in the fleet.[5] While many lament the passing of the Intruder, with its large payload and all-weather capability, the Navy had failed to develop a follow-on attack aircraft despite several efforts—the A-6F and A-6G variants of the Intruder, A-12 Avenger, AX concept, and several more proposals. Fortunately, the large number of vertical-launch missile ships in the fleet now carrying Tomahawks, and in the future more-advanced missiles, can provide an effective sea-based, long-range strike capability.

At the start of the post–Cold War era, the last LTV A-7E Corsairs, the penultimate Navy attack aircraft, were discarded. Their combat finale was the Gulf War, with the Navy's last two A-7E squadrons flying from the carrier JOHN F. KENNEDY in that 1991 conflict.

At the same time, the Boeing–McDonnell Douglas–Northrop F/A-18 has proven to be a highly effective fighter and strike aircraft—and readily interchangeable (changing roles with the flick of a switch). While the existing carrier-based F/A-18C variants have less range than desired for many mission scenarios, the improved F/A-18E will have greater range, albeit in a larger aircraft that costs considerably more and has encountered many difficulties in development.

Meanwhile, the venerable Grumman F-14 Tomcat continues to fly in carrier air wings. The Tomcat remains one of the most capable fighter aircraft in the sky as it approaches three decades of first-line service with the Navy. Several upgrades have provided enhanced air-to-air as well as long-delayed air-to-ground capabilities, the latter in the form of laser guidance, LANTIRN, and the ability to carry several guided missiles, as well as "iron bombs."[6] LANTIRN provides the F-14 with an autonomous target-designation capability for day/night attacks at from high/low altitudes. The first LANTIRN-equipped F-14 squadron was VF-103, which went aboard the ENTERPRISE in June 1996.

The F-14 has been retrofitted with enhanced defensive counter-measure systems (improved chaff and the ALR-67 threat warning receiver), a night-vision capability, and the ubiquitous Global Positioning System (GPS).

In addition, F-14s will continue to provide the only manned tactical-reconnaissance capability in the fleet, with each F-14 squadron having several aircraft fitted to carry the TARPS camera pod.[7] The Gulf War and post–Cold War operations have demonstrated that despite high-flying U-2 spy planes, Unmanned Aerial Vehicles

(UAV), and satellites, the low-flying photo-reconnaissance planes still provide invaluable intelligence. The TARPS is fitted with a digital imaging system and data link to provide near-real-time imagery to commanders ashore and aboard ship.

But the F-14's days are numbered. The F/A-18E joins the fleet in 2001 and within a decade that aircraft and the two-seat F/A-18F should completely replace the F-14 in air wings. By that time, the F-14 will have been in the fleet for almost 40 years, having entered service in 1973.

Thus, by about 2010 the carrier air wings will have 50 FA-18C, E, and F Hornets for the fighter and strike roles, with the older C-model Hornets being phased out in favor of the F/A-18E. Beyond the first decade of the 21st century, the Joint Strike Fighter (JSF) is envisioned joining the fleet, providing a multirole stealth aircraft to complement the F/A-18.[8] However, the JSF promises to be a controversial program and the Navy may have "all" F/A-18 air wings well into the next century.

Beyond fighter and strike aircraft, carrier air wings operate several special-purpose planes:

Electronic attack: A four-plane EA-6B Prowler electronic attack squadron (VAQ) is assigned to each air wing. The Prowler design evolved from the A-6 Intruder. The effectiveness of the Prowler in Electronic Countermeasures (ECM) was demonstrated by the decision by the Air Force to retire its EF-111A Raven ECM aircraft, to be replaced by Navy land-based EA-6B squadrons augmented with some Air Force personnel.

Airborne Early Warning (AEW): Each carrier air wing has a four-plane squadron flying the E-2C Hawkeye AEW aircraft to provide early warning and command-and-control functions. These planes are continuously undergoing equipment upgrades to enhance their mission capabilities.

Sea control: The eight-plane sea control squadrons (VS) flying from carriers have the S-3B Viking. These aircraft are no longer assigned to the Anti-Submarine Warfare (ASW) role. Rather, "sea control" is a euphemism for the aircraft's relegation to surface surveillance and aerial tanking roles (the latter caused by the loss of A-6E and KA-6D Intruders that served as tankers in carrier air wings).

Helicopter anti-submarine warfare: A similar situation is occurring in helicopter ASW (HS). Each carrier wing has an HS squadron of four SH-60F and two HH-60H Seahawk helicopters. The SH-60F variants are specialized ASW aircraft; the HH-60H variants are configured for combat Search-and-Rescue (SAR) and the support of special forces.

Both the SH-60F and SH-60B helicopters—which are based on surface combatants—are being modified to the SH-60R configuration. This upgrade will extend the life of the helicopters while providing them with more sensors and anti-ship missiles, the Penguin and Hellfire. Their new capabilities will detract from their availability and training for the ASW role.

The HH-60H will be succeeded by the CH-60—a "new" helicopter combining the Army's UH-60 Black Hawk airframe with the SH-60 Seahawk dynamic components. The multirole CH-60 will be used in the cargo, utility, combat SAR, utility, and Airborne Mine Countermeasures (AMCM) roles, the last of these providing the Airborne Mine Neutralization System (AMNS) to carrier battle groups (see chapter 21). The CH-60 also will replace the Navy's UH-46 Sea Knight in the Vertical Replenishment (VERTREP) role aboard replenishment ships.

Signals Intelligence (SIGINT): The ES-3A variant of the Viking was phased out of service in 1998. One or two of these SIGINT aircraft—in service only since 1995—were assigned to forward-deployed carriers to provide battle group commanders with tactical intelligence. The ES-3A—unofficially called Shadow—replaced the long-serving EA-3B Skywarrior in the carrier-based SIGINT role. (Battle group commanders also are provided with SIGINT from land-based EP-3E Orions, submarines, surface combatants, and SIGINT satellites.)

---

3. "Neck down" is the naval aviation term for a fewer number of aircraft or missiles replacing a larger number of types.

4. The designation F/A-18 is somewhat controversial; see page 388–389.

5. See N. Polmar, "No More Intruders," U.S. Naval Institute *Proceedings* (September 1996), pp. 87–88.

6. LANTIRN = Low-Altitude Navigation and Targeting Infrared for Night.

7. TARPS = Tactical Air Reconnaissance Pod System.

8. See N. Polmar, "Next Generation Strike Fighter," U.S. Naval Institute *Proceedings* (January 1997), pp. 89–90. The JSF program is the successor to the Joint Advanced Strike Technology (JAST) program.

The future of the special-mission aircraft is unclear. There have been proposals to eventually replace the EA-6B Prowler with an ECM version of the two-seat F/A-18F Hornet. This seems logical, as it will provide an ECM aircraft that can accompany F/A-18 strikes.

The potential replacement for the other special-mission aircraft is now being addressed by the Common Support Aircraft (CSA) study, an ongoing, multiyear effort by the Navy to determine replacements for the S-3B Viking, ES-3 Shadow, E-2C Hawkeye, and the C-2A Greyhound (the last is a land-based cargo aircraft that delivers people, mail, and high-priority cargo to carriers at sea).

The Navy envisions a CSA-derived aircraft entering service in 2012. This is not the first attempt to develop a common support aircraft. For example, the earlier Advanced Tactical Support (ATS)

concept was a Navy plan for a "totally new start" aircraft to replace the E-2, EA-6B, S-3, and ES-3, while possibly providing new capabilities to support carrier battle groups. ATS aircraft was conceived in the late 1980s with funding for advanced development provided by Congress until fiscal 1991, when all ATS funding was deleted and the project terminated.

The V-22 Osprey VSTOL aircraft was at one point considered a viable candidate for the ATS role until Secretary of Defense Dick Cheney canceled the V-22 program in 1989. In the ATS role, the V-22 would have had the valuable attributes of being independent of flight deck cycles on large carriers and capable of operating from large surface combatant and amphibious ships. Although the V-22 has been resurrected and is in production, there does not appear to be

TABLE 26-1. ACTIVE U.S. NAVAL AIRCRAFT (MID-2000)

Aircraft Type*	Total	Navy Active	Navy Reserve	Marine Active	Marine Reserve	Pipeline	Aircraft Type*	Total	Navy Active	Navy Reserve	Marine Active	Marine Reserve	Pipeline
Attack							T-39G Sabreliner	8	8	—	—	—	—
AV-8B Harrier	130	5	—	113	—	12	T-39N Sabreliner	17	14	—	—	—	3
NAV-8B Harrier	1	1	—	—	—	—	T-44A King Air	55	45	—	—	—	10
Fighter/Strike Fighter							T-45A Goshawk	74	67	—	—	—	7
YF-4J Phantom	1	1	—	—	—	—	T-45C Goshawk	34	33	—	—	—	1
F-5E Tiger II	31	—	17	—	9	5	TA-4J Skyhawk	7	7	—	—	—	—
F-5F Tiger II	4	—	3	—	1	—	TAV-8B Harrier	16	1	—	15	—	—
F-14A Tomcat	52	39	—	—	—	13	TC-12B Huron	20	16	—	—	—	4
NF-14A Tomcat	3	3	—	—	—	—	TC-18F	2	2	—	—	—	—
F-14B Tomcat	72	52	—	—	—	20	TC-130G Hercules**	1	1	—	—	—	—
NF-14B Tomcat	1	1	—	—	—	—	TE-2C Hawkeye	2	2	—	—	—	—
F-14D Tomcat	46	29	—	—	—	17	*Utility/Miscellaneous*						
NF-14D Tomcat	4	3	—	—	—	1	NU-1B Otter	1	1	—	—	—	—
F/A-18A Hornet	191	47	40	26	38	40	U-6A Beaver	2	2	—	—	—	—
NF/A-18A Hornet	2	2	—	—	—	—	UC-12B Huron	37	20	6	6	3	2
F/A-18B Hornet	31	17	3	4	—	7	RC-12F Huron	2	2	—	—	—	—
F/A-18C Hornet	412	283	—	76	—	53	UC-12F Huron	10	6	—	4	—	—
NF/A-18C Hornet	2	2	—	—	—	—	RC-12M Huron	2	2	—	—	—	—
F/A-18D Hornet	141	35	—	81	—	25	UC-12M Huron	10	10	—	—	—	—
NF/A-18D Hornet	3	2	—	—	—	1	UP-3A Orion	4	3	—	—	—	1
F/A-18E Hornet	10	9	—	—	—	1	*Rotary-Wing*						
F/A-18F Hornet	8	5	—	—	—	3	MV-22 Osprey	5	1	—	4	—	—
Patrol/Sea Control							AH-1W SeaCobra	194	6	—	130	37	21
P-3B Orion	2	2	—	—	—	—	AH-1Z SeaCobra	2	—	—	—	—	2
P-3C Orion	226	123	39	—	—	64	HH-1N Huey	25	18	—	7	—	—
NP-3C Orion	1	—	—	—	—	1	UH-1N Huey	101	3	—	70	16	12
NP-3D Orion	12	8	—	—	—	4	UH-1Y Huey	2	—	—	—	—	2
S-3B Viking	112	93	—	—	—	19	SH-2G Seasprite	12	—	12	—	—	—
Electronic/Special Purpose							SH-3H Sea King	2	2	—	—	—	—
E-2C Hawkeye	68	52	9	—	—	7	UH-3H Sea King	50	40	9	—	—	1
E-6A Mercury	7	6	—	—	—	1	VH-3A Sea King	2	2	—	—	—	—
E-6B Mercury	9	9	—	—	—	—	NVH-3A Sea King	1	1	—	—	—	—
EA-6B Prowler	119	78	4	13	4	20	VH-3D Sea King	11	—	—	8	—	3
EP-3E Orion	11	10	—	—	—	1	TH-6B Cayuse	6	5	—	—	—	1
Cargo/Transport							CH-46D Sea Knight	26	24	—	—	—	2
C-2A Greyhound	37	28	—	—	—	9	CH-46E Sea Knight	230	—	—	178	25	27
C-9B Skytrain	17	—	10	2	—	5	HH-46D Sea Knight	42	26	—	8	—	8
DC-9 Skytrain	12	—	9	—	—	3	UH-46D Sea Knight	11	9	—	—	—	2
C-12C Super King Air	4	4	—	—	—	—	CH-53D Sea Stallion	44	—	—	36	—	8
C-20D Gulfstream III	2	—	2	—	—	—	CH-53E Super Stallion	154	1	—	106	16	31
C-20G Gulfstream IV	5	—	3	—	—	2	MH-53E Sea Dragon	41	24	7	4	—	6
C-26D	7	5	—	—	—	2	TH-57B SeaRanger	44	44	—	—	—	—
UC-35	2	—	—	—	—	2	TH-57C SeaRanger	76	75	—	—	—	1
DC-130A Hercules	1	—	—	—	—	1	OH-58C Cayuse	4	4	—	—	—	—
KC-130F Hercules	36	1	—	28	—	7	YCH-60S	1	—	—	—	—	1
NC-130H Hercules	1	—	—	—	—	1	HH-60H Seahawk	39	19	14	—	—	6
KC-130R Hercules	14	—	—	11	—	3	SH-60B Seahawk	160	129	—	—	—	31
C-130T Hercules	20	—	18	—	—	2	SH-60F Seahawk	74	60	1	—	—	13
KC-130T Hercules	28	—	—	—	26	2	SH-60R Seahawk	3	—	—	—	—	3
VP-3A Orion	5	4	—	—	—	1	NSH-60B Seahawk	2	2	—	—	—	—
CT-39G Sabreliner	1	—	—	—	—	1	YSH-60F Seahawk	1	1	—	—	—	—
Training							UH-60A Black Hawk	2	2	—	—	—	—
T-2C Buckeye	95	89	—	—	—	6	VH-60N Seahawk	8	—	—	6	—	2
T-34C Turbomentor	309	278	—	2	—	29	*Research/Experimental*						
NT-34C Mentor	1	1	—	—	—	—	X-26A	2	2	—	—	—	—
T-38A Talon	10	10	—	—	—	—	*Totals*	4,001	2,080	164	963	192	602
T-39D Sabreliner	1	1	—	—	—	—							

* Drone (radio-control) target aircraft are not included; there currently are four QF-4N Phantoms and 17 QF-4S Phantoms in this category.
** TC-130G is a Marine aircraft assigned to the Chief of Naval Air Training to support the Blue Angels.

a major effort to adopt the Bell-Boeing VSTOL aircraft to special-mission configurations.

The Navy had also identified two other potential roles for the ATS: (1) airborne battle management, having the computer power and other facilities to enable a force commander or tactical action officer to direct operations from above the force, and (2) the "missileer" concept. First advanced in the 1960s with the never-built Douglas F6D aircraft, the missileer concept provides for a relatively low-performance aircraft to remain on station for long periods with advanced air-to-air missiles to intercept incoming attackers.

Accordingly, many questions remain concerning the future composition of carrier air wings. The reduction to 50 fighter and strike aircraft and the demise of the A-6E Intruder reduce the strike capabilities of the carriers, yet the F-14 Tomcat upgrades and the versatility of the F/A-18 Hornet increase the effectiveness of the carrier force because of their mission flexibility and greater survivability in a hostile environment. There are also many critical questions about the JSF project and, if past multiservice aircraft projects are a guide, there will be rough waters ahead for that program.

Finding answers to these questions is important to the future of the Navy. As the Director of Air Warfare wrote recently, "Our twelve aircraft carriers and embarked air wing mix of 50 high performance multiple mission capable strike fighters, and [24] tactical support aircraft, makes the striking air wing's power unmatched in terms of flexibility, accuracy and sustainability."[9]

In this chapter, current wings and squadrons are listed, along with those disestablished after 1 January 1990; for the latter, the official disestablishment dates are listed, not the ceremonial dates, which usually differ by a few days.

NAVAL AIR ORGANIZATION

All naval aviation units belong to an administrative organization and most units also belong to tactical organizations. For example, a strike fighter squadron (VFA) is administratively under a strike fighter "type" wing commander while at its home base; when deployed on board a carrier, the squadron comes under the air wing commander embarked in that ship. Similarly, a patrol squadron (VP) is under the patrol "type" wing commander while in the United States, but if deployed in a forward area would be under a fleet commander and his subordinate air commander.

The administrative organization is headed by the Director, Air Warfare Division, in the Office of the Chief of Naval Operations,[10] and extends through the Commander, Naval Air Force Atlantic Fleet (NAVAIRLANT), and Commander, Naval Air Force Pacific Fleet (NAVAIRPAC), and their respective wing type commanders. Details of naval air administrative organization are provided in chapter 6.

Navy wings and squadrons are officially "established" and "disestablished" and are not in commission; however, records and ceremonies continually use the terms "commission" and "decommission." The Marine Corps uses the terms "activated" and "deactivated" for its aviation units.

In addition to the numbered wings and squadrons described in this chapter, in 1995–1996 the aircraft at various test facilities were organized into two test wings. Naval Test Wing Atlantic comprises four squadrons, all based at Naval Air Station (NAS) Patuxent River, Md.: the Naval Rotary Wing Test Squadron, Naval Strike Aircraft Test Squadron, Naval Force Aircraft Test Squadron, and Naval Test Pilot School. Naval Test Wing Pacific has two squadrons: Naval

Weapons Test Squadron Point Mugu and Naval Weapons Test Squadron China Lake (both in California).

UNIT DESIGNATIONS

Naval air units are designated in two systems of abbreviations: pronounceable acronyms, and simpler letter-number combinations. Accordingly, Fighter Squadron 2 is known as both FITRON TWO and VF-2. The latter series is used in this volume and is summarized in table 26-2.

All naval aviation units have the prefix V for heavier-than-air or H for helicopter. Previously Z was employed for lighter-than-air (airship/blimp) units.

The V prefix for naval aircraft types and subsequently for aviation units dates from 1922. VF indicated fighter squadron, VA attack squadron, ZP airship patrol squadron, and so forth. (The last U.S. Navy airship, a Goodyear ZPG-2W, was taken out of service in 1962.) Subsequently, H was introduced as the helicopter type letter for aircraft (HNS-1) in 1943 and for squadrons in 1947 (the first naval helicopter squadron was Marine Corps HMX-1, followed in 1948 by Navy HU-1 and HU-2). Marine units have the letter M added as the second letter of aviation unit designations.[11]

---

11. The H, V, and Z were also used for ship designations—hence CV for aircraft carrier, AV for seaplane tender, and AZ for airship tender. Subsequently, H was used for helicopter-carrying ships in CVHA, CVHE, LPH, LHA, and LHD.

TABLE 26-2. NAVAL AVIATION DESIGNATIONS*

CVW	Carrier Air Wing
CVWR	Reserve Carrier Air Wing
HC	Helicopter Combat Support Squadron
HCS	Helicopter Combat Search and Rescue/Special Warfare Support Squadron
HM	Helicopter Mine Countermeasures Squadron
HMH	(Marine) Heavy Helicopter Squadron
HMLA	(Marine) Light Attack Helicopter Squadron
HMM	(Marine) Medium Helicopter Squadron
HMX	(Marine) Helicopter Squadron
HS	Helicopter Anti-Submarine Squadron
HSL	Light Helicopter Anti-Submarine Squadron
HT	Helicopter Training Squadron
MAG	Marine Aircraft Group
MAW	Marine Aircraft Wing
MCAF	Marine Corps Air Facility
MCAS	Marine Corps Air Station
NAF	Naval Air Facility
NAS	Naval Air Station
VAQ	Electronic Attack Squadron
VAW	Carrier Airborne Early Warning Squadron
VC	Fleet Composite Squadron
VF	Fighter Squadron
VFA	Strike Fighter Squadron
VFC	Fighter Composite Squadron
VMAQ	(Marine) Electronic Attack Squadron
VMF	(Marine) Fighter Squadron
VMFA	(Marine) Fighter-Attack Squadron
VMFA(AW)	(Marine) Fighter-Attack Squadron (All-Weather)
VMGR	(Marine) Refueler-Transport Squadron
VMM	(Marine) Medium-Lift Squadron**
VMR	Marine Search and Rescue Squadron
VP	Patrol Squadron
VPU	Patrol Squadron—Special Projects Unit
VQ	Fleet Air Reconnaissance Squadron or Strategic Communications Squadron
VR	Fleet Logistics Support Squadron
VRC	Fleet Logistics Support (COD) Squadron***
VS	Sea Control Squadron
VT	Training Squadron
VX	Air Test and Evaluation Squadron
VXN	Oceanographic Development Squadron

  * Marine squadrons add the letter T as a suffix for readiness/training units.
  ** Designation for MV-22 Osprey squadron.
*** Carrier Onboard Delivery.

---

9. Rear Adm. Dennis McGinn, USN, in *Worldwide Challenges to Naval Strike Warfare* (Washington, D.C., 1997), p. 28.
10. This position was originally established in 1944 as the Deputy Chief of Naval Operations (Air), a three-star billet; the title was changed to Assistant Chief of Naval Operations (Air Warfare) in 1987. The position was again changed, to Director, Air Warfare Division, on 10 August 1992 and was downgraded to a two-star billet.

UNIT CODES

Most naval aviation organizations have two-letter identification codes that are displayed on aircraft tail fins and, in some marking schemes, on wings; training wings have single-letter designations, while air stations and other special organizations use a number-letter scheme.

Beginning in 1946 the Navy used single-letter codes to identify specific ships to which the planes were attached—e.g., *B* for BOXER (CV 21), *F* for FRANKLIN D. ROOSEVELT (CVB 42)—with land-based units having two-letter codes. The system was revised in 1957 to provide the current fleet "split," with the first letter indicating the fleet assignment: *A* to *M* for Atlantic and *N* to *Z* for Pacific. The letters *I* and *O* are not used to avoid confusion with numerals. The unit code AF was dropped because of confusion with *Air Force* (AF had been used by Carrier Air Group 6, which then took code letters AE).

The code letters AD and NJ now are worn by several Fleet Readiness Squadrons (FRS). Those letters were formally assigned to Combat Readiness Carrier Air Wing 4 and Combat Readiness Carrier Air Wing 12, respectively. Both of those wings were disestablished on 1 June 1970, but some of their squadrons survived in the Atlantic and Pacific Fleets.

Within carrier air wings, the squadrons are identified by blocks of numbers and colors, with the individual aircraft identified by numbers within the block. The block numbers (e.g., 100, 200) are aircraft flown by the wing commander and the first of each series (e.g., 101, 201) are flown by squadron commanding officers. The number blocks are assigned as:

Side number	Squadron type	Color code	Aircraft
1XX	VF	insignia red	F-14
2XX	VFA	orange-yellow	F/A-18
3XX	VFA	light blue	F/A-18
4XX	VFA	international orange	F/A-18
50X	VAQ	light green	EA-6B
60X	VAW	black	E-2C
61X	HS	black	HH-60H, SH-60F
7XX	VS	black	S-3B

Thus, the third E-2C Hawkeye assigned to the carrier CARL VINSON has NH (for CVW-11) on its tails and 603 on its forward fuselage and wings.

CARRIER AIR WINGS

The Navy currently has ten active and one reserve carrier air wings (CVW/CVWR). The reserve carrier air wing flies first-line aircraft and is suitable for deployment on board carriers. In addition, most Marine Corps combat aircraft are carrier-capable and all Marine aviators are carrier trained.

The composition of carrier air wings continues to change. Into the 1980s the standard wing had two fighter squadrons (24 F-14A), two light attack squadrons (24 A-7E), and one medium attack squadron (10 A-6E, plus 4 KA-6D tankers), in addition to specialized ASW, AEW, and ECM/electronic strike aircraft squadrons.

During the 1980s, with the introduction of the F/A-18 Hornet strike fighter, the Navy evaluated several air wing variations. For example, the so-called "ROOSEVELT air wing" (evaluated aboard the CVN 71) had double the number of A-6E Intruder aircraft, accommodated by reducing the numbers of fighters and strike fighters (the F/A-18 having replaced the A-7E). Under this plan, the A-6Es would have been succeeded in service by improved models of the Intruder (A-6F or A-6G) and, subsequently, by the A-12 Avenger. The cancellation of the A-12 in early 1991 and overall budget reductions forced the Navy to drop this plan.

Subsequently, the Navy has gone to a smaller, but more flexible, strike fighter wing with one F-14 squadron and three F/A-18

TABLE 26-3. CARRIER AIR WINGS (EARLY 2001)

Air Wing	Code	Carrier	Squadrons[a]	
CVW-1	AB	THEODORE ROOSEVELT	VF-102	VAQ-137
			VFA-82	VAW-123
			VFA-86	VS-32
			VMFA-251	HS-11
CVW-2	NE	CONSTELLATION	VF-2	VAQ-131
			VFA-137	VAW-116
			VFA-151	VS-38
			VMFA-323	HS-2
CVW-3	AC	HARRY S. TRUMAN	VF-32	VAQ-130
			VFA-37	VAW-126
			VFA-105	VS-22
			VMFA-312	HS-7
CVW-4		disestablished 1 June 1970		
CVW-5[b]	NF	KITTY HAWK	VF-154	VAQ-136
			VFA-27	VAW-115
			VFA-192	VS-21
			VFA-195	HS-14
CVW-6	AE	disestablished 1 Apr 1992		
CVW-7	AG	JOHN F. KENNEDY	VF-11	VAQ-140
			VF-143	VAW-121
			VFA-131	VS-31
			VFA-136	HS-5
CVW-8	AJ	ENTERPRISE	VF-14	VAQ-141
			VF-41	VAW-124
			VFA-15	VS-24
			VFA-87	HS-3
CVW-9	NG	JOHN C. STENNIS	VF-211	VAQ-138
			VFA-146	VAW-112
			VFA-147	VS-33
			VMFA-314	HS-8
CVW-10	NM	disestablished 1 June 1988		
CVW-11	NH	CARL VINSON	VF-213	VAQ-135
			VFA-22	VAW-117
			VFA-94	VS-29
			VFA-97	HS-6
CVW-12		disestablished 1 June 1970		
CVW-13	AK	disestablished 1 Jan 1991		
CVW-14	NK	ABRAHAM LINCOLN	VF-31	VAQ-139
			VFA-25	VAW-113
			VFA-113	VS-35
			VFA-115	HS-4
CVW-15	NL	disestablished 31 Mar 1995		
CVW-16	AK	disestablished 30 June 1971		
CVW-17	AA	GEORGE WASHINGTON	VF-103	VAQ-132
			VFA-34	VAW-125
			VFA-81	VS-30
			VFA-83	HS-15
CVW-18 not used				
CVW-19		disestablished 30 June 1977		
CVWR-20	AF	(Reserve)[c]	VFA-201	VAQ-209
			VFA-203	VAW-78
			VFA-204	HS-75
			VMFA-142	
CVW-21	NP	disestablished 12 Dec 1975		
CVW-22 to CVW-29 not used				
CVWR-30	ND	(Reserve) disestablished 31 Dec 1994		

[a] HS = Helicopter ASW Squadron, VAQ = Electronic Attack Squadron, VAW = Carrier Airborne Early Warning Squadron, VF = Fighter Squadron, VFA = Strike Fighter Squadron, VMFA = Marine Fighter-Attack Squadron, VS = Sea Control Squadron

[b] CVW-5 is based at NAF Atsugi, Japan. The wing flew from the carrier MIDWAY (CV 41) from 1973 to 1991, when it was shifted in its entirety to the INDEPENDENCE; subsequently, the wing was transferred to the KITTY HAWK in 1998. While assigned to the MIDWAY, the wing did not have F-14 Tomcats or S-3 Vikings because of the ship's size and lack of an ASW command center. A detachment of three Marine RF-4B Phantoms from VMFP-3 had provided the ship with a photo-reconnaissance capability until 1986, when the MIDWAY wing shifted from F-4 Phantom fighters to F/A-18 Hornets. Upon joining the "INDY" in 1991, CVW-5 gained two F-14 squadrons and an S-3 squadron, becoming the last wing to receive those aircraft.

[c] Reserve Carrier Air Wings 20 and 30 were established 1 April 1970 to improve the readiness of reserve squadrons. A month later, on 1 May, two reserve ASW air groups, CVSGR-70 and CVSGR-80, were established.

squadrons, except that two wings have a second F-14 unit in place of a third F/A-18 unit. Thus, most carrier air wings have:

Units	Aircraft
1 VF fighter squadron	14 F-14 Tomcat
3 VFA strike fighter squadrons	36 F/A-18 Hornet
1 VAQ electronic attack squadron	4 EA-6B Prowler
1 VAW airborne early warning	4 E-2C Hawkeye
1 VS sea control squadron	8 S-3B Viking
1 HS helicopter ASW squadron	6 HH-60H, SH-60F Seahawk[12]

On 13 January 1992 the Secretary of the Navy directed that the Navy and Marine Corps more closely integrate Marine tactical aviation into carrier air wings. The memorandum directed that the Navy and Marine Corps "undertake innovative measures to enhance the efficiency of naval aviation through the closer integration . . . ," especially of Marine fighter-attack (VMFA) and electronic warfare (VMAQ) squadrons, to reduce Navy aircraft requirements by at least 140 planes in those categories.

(Marine tactical squadrons periodically have operated from aircraft carriers since November 1931, when Marine scouting squadron VS-15M went aboard the carrier Lexington/CV 2 and VS-14M went aboard the Saratoga/CV 3 for fleet operations; they remained in those carriers until November 1934.)

In addition to wing aircraft, forward-deployed carriers generally operate one or two C-2A Greyhound COD aircraft.

Historical: The designation carrier air wing (CVW) was established on 20 December 1963 in place of carrier air group (CVG).[13] Air group designations had reached No. 153 during World War II, albeit with several gaps in the series.

The designation ASW carrier air group (CVSG) was established on 1 April 1960 for aircraft assigned to ASW carriers (CVS); those ships were phased out in the late 1960s and early 1970s, and the last CVSG was disestablished on 30 June 1973. The ASW groups were numbered from CVSG-50 to CVSG-62. When the ASW carrier air groups were phased out, the fixed-wing and helicopter ASW aircraft went aboard the larger attack aircraft carriers, which became simply CV/CVN vice CVA/CVAN.

Replacement air groups (RAG) became combat readiness air wings (CRAW) in 1963, but those were phased out over the next few years, the last on 30 June 1973. Some of their squadrons survive, known officially as Fleet Readiness Squadrons (FRS). These provide transition training to introduce pilots and air crewmen to fleet aircraft.

The CV/CVN concept originally was intended for the "swing wing" concept, wherein a carrier could be loaded with an emphasis of fighter, attack, or ASW aircraft. This was not followed in practice, as standard wings were organized to the extent possible for all carriers. (However, in a demonstration of the swing-wing concept, in October 1971 the carrier Saratoga operated 37 ASW aircraft—21 S-2E Trackers and 16 SH-3D Sea Kings—plus 20 fighters, 9 attack aircraft, and 8 special-mission aircraft.)[14]

Specialized reconnaissance aircraft were phased off carrier decks in the late 1970s as the RA-5C Vigilante and RF-8G Photo Crusader were retired, the active fleet's last "recce" squadrons being RVAH-7, disestablished on 30 September 1979, and VFP-63, disestablished on 30 June 1982. Marine RF-4B Phantoms subsequently provided a limited photographic reconnaissance capability on some carriers pending the availability in the early 1980s of the TARPS for the F-14 Tomcat on the larger carriers. (The Naval Air Reserve flew the RF-8G Photo Crusader until 1987.) The TARPS pod, however, flown by nonspecialized reconnaissance pilots, does not provide the quality or quantity of tactical reconnaissance that was possible with the RA-5C; this shortfall was keenly felt during Operation Desert Storm in 1991. According to the U.S. Director of Naval Intelligence, the

TARPS "was totally inadequate" in providing sufficient and timely bomb damage assessment during that operation.[15]

Carrier air wings staffs average 15 officers and 21 enlisted personnel, except that Atsugi-based CVW-5 has 24 officers and 31 enlisted personnel assigned. See the specific squadron entries for their personnel strength.

PATROL AND RECONNAISSANCE FORCES

Patrol and Reconnaissance Wings (PATRECONWINGs) direct the operations of the Navy's patrol squadrons (VP), with East Coast squadrons assigned to Patrol and Reconnaissance Force Atlantic Fleet (PATRECONFORLANT) at NAS Norfolk, Va., and West Coast squadrons assigned to Patrol and Reconnaissance Force Pacific (PATRECONFORPAC) at MCAF Kaneohe Bay, Hawaii.[16] (PATRECONFORPAC was previously designated Patrol Wings Pacific Fleet; as such, its headquarters were previously at NAS Moffett Field, Calif., south of San Francisco; the command moved to NAS Barbers Point, Hawaii, on 1 July 1993 and to Kaneohe Bay on 1 July 1999.)

These "forces" previously were designated Patrol Wings (PATWINGs); the Atlantic wing command and subordinate units were redesignated on 1 March 1999, and the Pacific wing and subordinate units on 1 June 1999.

TABLE 26-4. PATROL AND RECONNAISSANCE WINGS

Commands/Wings	Location	Squadrons
PATRECONFORLANT	Norfolk, Va.	VP-30*
PATRECONWING-5	Brunswick, Maine	VP-8
		VP-10
		VP-26
		VPU-1
PATRECONWING-11	Jacksonville, Fla.	VP-5
		VP-16
		VP-45
	Rota, Spain	VQ-2
PATRECONFORPAC	Kaneohe Bay, Hawaii	VP-4
		VP-9
		VP-47
		VPU-2
PATRECONWING-1	Kamiseya, Japan	(see text)
PATRECONWING-10	Whidbey Island, Wash.	VP-1
		VP-40
		VP-46
		VQ-1

* VP-30 is the P-3 Orion fleet readiness squadron.

The P-3 Orion squadrons and detachments of PATRECONFORLANT operate in the Atlantic, Caribbean, and Mediterranean areas. Pacific and Indian Ocean VP operations are directed by PATRECONFORPAC, which also has direct control over VP squadrons in Hawaii as well as VPU-1. PATRECONWING-1 directs the VP squadrons that rotate to the Western Pacific.

Patrol Wing 2 in the Pacific was disestablished on 30 September 1993; the wing had been established at NAS Ford Island (Pearl Harbor) on 1 October 1937. The Navy had planned to reestablish the wing at Kaneohe Bay with the 1998–1999 move of VP squadrons to that base; in the event, the wing was not reestablished. (Kaneohe Bay was a patrol plane base before and during World War II.)

Additional information on VP squadrons is provided below.

Historical: On 30 June 1973 Fleet Air Wings 1 and 2 were redesignated Patrol Wings 1 and 2. This was the end of the use of the Fleet Air Wing designation and beginning of the Patrol Wing designation, which had been used prior to World War II.

12. These will be replaced by the SH-60R, an SH-60B or SH-60F modified to a common, multisensor ASW configuration.
13. The term "CAG" (for Commander Air Group) is still used to refer to an air wing commander.
14. In 1960–1961, in an earlier example of a swing-wing concept in response to Soviet "saber-rattling," U.S. carriers in the Mediterranean and Far East unloaded their fighter aircraft to embark more nuclear strike aircraft.

15. Rear Adm. Thomas A. Brooks, USN, comments at a luncheon of the Naval and Maritime Correspondents Circle, Washington, D.C., 15 July 1991.
16. NAS Norfolk was officially changed to the Air Detachment Norfolk (Chambers Field) of NAS Oceana, Va., on 24 November 1998. However, for clarity, NAS Norfolk is used throughout this edition.

NAVAL AVIATION SQUADRONS

ATTACK SQUADRONS

Squadron	Aircraft	Notes
VA-22	A-7E	to VFA-22 on 4 May 1990
VA-27	A-7E	to VFA-27 on 24 Jan 1991
VA-34	A-6E	to VFA-34 on 30 Sep 1996
VA-35	A-6E	disestablished 31 Jan 1995
VA-36	A-6E	disestablished 31 Mar 1994
VA-37	A-7E	to VFA-37 on 28 Nov 1990
VA-42	A-6E, TC-4C, T-34C	disestablished 30 Sep 1994
VA-46	A-7E	disestablished 30 June 1991
VA-52	A-6E	disestablished 31 Mar 1995
VA-55	A-6E	disestablished 1 Jan 1991
VA-65	A-6E	disestablished 31 Mar 1993
VA-72	A-7E	disestablished 30 June 1991
VA-75	A-6E	disestablished 31 Mar 1997
VA-85	A-6E	disestablished 30 Sep 1994
VA-94	A-7E	to VFA-94 on 28 June 1990
VA-95	A-6E	disestablished 31 Oct 1995
VA-97	A-7E	to VFA-97 on 25 Jan 1991
VA-105	A-7E	to VFA-105 on 17 Dec 1990
VA-115	A-6E	to VFA-115 ON 30 Sep 1996
VA-122	A-7E	disestablished 31 May 1991
VA-128	A-6E, TC-4C	disestablished 30 Sep 1995
VA-145	A-6E	disestablished 1 Oct 1993
VA-155	A-6E	disestablished 30 Apr 1993
VA-165	A-6E	disestablished 30 Sep 1996
VA-176	A-6E	disestablished 30 Oct 1992
VA-185	A-6E	disestablished 30 Aug 1991
VA-196	A-6E	disestablished 21 Mar 1997

A UH-46D Sea Knight from the ammunition ship FLINT (T-AE 32) delivers ordnance to the carrier KITTY HAWK during replenishment operations off the coast of Japan. The Navy and Marine Corps operate more H-46s than any other type of rotary-wing aircraft. (U.S. Navy, DM3 Chris Roell)

The A-6E Intruder, U.S. Navy's last specialized attack aircraft, was retired from the fleet in December 1996 when Attack Squadron (VA) 75 completed a deployment aboard the carrier ENTERPRISE. The disestablishment of the VA-75 "Sunday Punchers" marked the end of the plane's 34-year operational career.[17] With the demise of the Intruder, the attack role has been taken over by bomb- and missile-carrying variants of the F-14 Tomcat fighter and the F/A-18 Hornet strike fighter.

Historical: U.S. carriers have operated attack aircraft since 15 November 1946, when the squadron designation VA was established to replace the previous carrier-based bombing (VB), bombing-fighting (VBF), and torpedo (VT) squadrons. The VA designation was used for "light" attack squadrons flying the A-1 Skyraider, A-4 Skyhawk, and A-7 Corsair, as well as for "medium" attack units flying the A-6 Intruder.

After 1991 all attack squadrons flew the A-6E Intruder, except for two transition/readiness squadrons, VA-42 and VA-128, which also flew specialized trainers.

All A-7E squadrons were disestablished or converted to VFA units. Squadrons VA-46 and VA-72 in the Atlantic were the Navy's last A-7E Corsair squadrons; their demise was delayed because of the Persian Gulf War (during which they flew from the KENNEDY). Both squadrons were disestablished in 1991.[18] This ended the 25-year career of the Corsair as a first-line Navy attack aircraft. (It continued in service briefly in special-purpose roles; it was not flown by the Marine Corps.) Squadrons VA-122, VA-125, and VA-174 were the A-7E readiness/transition squadrons.

15 ELECTRONIC ATTACK SQUADRONS

Squadron	Aircraft	Name/Notes
VAQ-33	various	disestablished 1 Oct 1993
VAQ-34	various	disestablished 1 Oct 1993
VAQ-35	various	established 14 Aug 1991; disestablished 1 Oct 1993
VAQ-128	EA-6B	Fighting Phoenix (NL); established 1 Oct 1997
VAQ-129	EA-6B	Vikings (NJ)
VAQ-130	EA-6B	Zappers
VAQ-131	EA-6B	Lancers
VAQ-132	EA-6B	Scorpions
VAQ-133	EA-6B	Wizards (NL); disestablished 1 June 1992; reestablished 1 April 1996
VAQ-134	EA-6B	Garudas (NL)
VAQ-135	EA-6B	Black Ravens
VAQ-136	EA-6B	Gauntlets
VAQ-137	EA-6B	Rooks (NL); disestablished 30 Sep 1994; reestablished 1 Oct 1996
VAQ-138	EA-6B	Yellowjackets
VAQ-139	EA-6B	Cougars
VAQ-140	EA-6B	Patriots
VAQ-141	EA-6B	Shadowhawks
VAQ-142	EA-6B	Gray Wolves (NL); disestablished 1 July 1991; reestablished 1 Apr 1997
VAQ-143	EA-6B	to establish 2002 (?)

All front-line electronic attack (VAQ) squadrons have four EA-6B Prowlers. There are ten active and one reserve carrier-based squadrons. In addition, there are one fleet readiness squadron (NJ) and five land-based VAQ squadrons (NL), the latter providing ECM support to Army, Navy, Air Force, and Marine air operations. The fifth land-based VAQ is to "stand up" about 2002, following experience in the Kosovo air campaign the previous year. (The Marine Corps has three VMAQ squadrons.)

The formation of land-based VAQ squadrons was the result of the late 1995 decision by the Department of Defense to replace the Air Force's 24 EF-111A Raven ECM aircraft with Navy ECM aircraft. The Air Force retired its last EF-111 on 2 May 1998 and inactivated the 429th Electronic Combat Squadron at Cannon AFB, N.M., on 19 June 1998, marking the transition to the EA-6B as the nation's only specialized ECM aircraft. To meet this requirement, the planned disestablishment of VAQ-134 on 30 September 1995 was canceled

17. The last A-6E carrier landing occurred aboard the ENTERPRISE in February 1997.
18. The A-7D variant was flown by the Air Force Reserve until 1993; several other countries also fly A-7 variants.

An EA-6B Prowler from VAQ-137 is readied on the deck of the GEORGE WASHINGTON. The Prowler's two cockpit canopies are open; a HARM anti-radar missile and an ALQ-99 electronic countermeasures pod are visible under the right wing; another ALQ-99 pod is fitted under the fuselage. (U.S. Navy, PH3 Brian Fleske)

and three disestablished VAQ squadrons were stood up: VAQ-128, -133, and -142. These four Prowler squadrons each have the equivalent of one Air Force crew—a pilot and three ECM officers—with other Air Force personnel on their staffs.

All Navy EA-6B units are based at NAS Whidbey Island, Wash., except for VAQ-136, based at NAF Atsugi, Japan. VAQ-129 provides EA-6B readiness training for Navy and Marine Prowler crews. All Navy electronic attack squadrons report to Electronic Attack Wing Pacific Fleet (changed from Electronic Combat Wing Pacific Fleet on 30 March 1998).

Designation: VAQ formerly indicated tactical electronic warfare squadron; this was changed to electronic attack squadron on 30 March 1998.

Historical: VAQ-132 was the first squadron to receive the EA-6B, in July 1971. VAQ-129, -131, and -132 were previously heavy attack squadrons (VAH-10, -4, and -2, respectively); they were changed to VAQ in 1968–1970, when they shifted from EKA-3B Skywarriors to EA-6B aircraft. VAQ-130 was formerly early warning squadron VW-13, redesignated VAQ in 1968. Most of the other VAQs were built up from EKA-3B detachments that operated from forward-deployed carriers.

Manning: Most VAQ squadrons have 28 officers and 153 enlisted personnel. In July 1990, VAQ-34 became the first U.S. military aviation squadron to be commanded by a woman.

Operational: During the Kosovo campaign of 1999, 10½ of 19 active and reserve Navy and Marine electronic attack squadrons—each with four aircraft—were forward deployed (the half-squadron being a two-plane detachment from reserve squadron VAQ-209). At the height of the campaign, six squadrons were flying from Aviano, Italy, in support of Operation Allied Force, two squadrons were forward deployed aboard carriers, one squadron was supporting the "no-fly" zone over southern Iraq from Saudi Arabia, and one squadron was flying "no-fly" operations over northern Iraq from a base in Turkey. In addition, a Marine Prowler squadron was ashore in Japan.[19]

---

19. See Robert Holzer, "More Military Operations Keep Prowler Fleet Busier Than Ever," *Navy Times* (3 May 1999), p. 10; and Capt. Lloyd E. Bonzo, USMC, "Parting with the Prowler," U.S. Naval Institute *Proceedings* (August 1999), pp. 36–37.

11 AIRBORNE EARLY WARNING SQUADRONS

Squadron	Aircraft	Name/Notes
VAW-88	E-2C	disestablished 31 Dec 1994
VAW-110	E-2C, C-2A	disestablished 30 Sep 1994
VAW-112	E-2C	Golden Hawks
VAW-113	E-2C	Black Hawks
VAW-114	E-2C	disestablished 31 Mar 1995
VAW-115	E-2C	Liberty Bells (ex-Sentinels)
VAW-116	E-2C	Sun Kings
VAW-117	E-2C	Wallbangers
VAW-120	E-2C, C-2A, TE-2C	Greyhawks (ex-Hummers) (AD)
VAW-121	E-2C	Bluetails
VAW-122	E-2C	disestablished 31 Mar 1996
VAW-123	E-2C	Screwtops
VAW-124	E-2C	Bear Aces
VAW-125	E-2C	Tigertails
VAW-126	E-2C	Seahawks
VAW-127	E-2C	disestablished 30 Sep 1991

The ten deploying AEW squadrons are assigned to carrier air wings, each with four E-2C Hawkeye aircraft. VAW-120 provides readiness training.

The Pacific VAW squadrons are assigned to Airborne Early Warning Wing Pacific Fleet and are based at NAS Point Mugu, Calif., except VAW-115, based at NAF Atsugi (having changed name upon assignment to INDEPENDENCE in 1991). The West Coast VAQ units previously were based at NAS Miramar, Calif. (which was changed to MCAS Miramar on 1 October 1997). The Atlantic squadrons are assigned to Airborne Early Warning Wing Atlantic at NAS Norfolk.

Designation: The two readiness AEW squadrons—VAW-110 and VAW-120—were designated RVAW until 1 May 1983, when they dropped the *R* prefix; they were the only readiness squadrons with that prefix.

Historical: The first carrier AEW squadrons were VAW-1 and VAW-2, commissioned in 1948 to provide aircraft detachments to Pacific and Atlantic carriers, respectively. (AEW aircraft had earlier flown from carriers and a land-based squadron, VPW-1, had been established in 1948.)

The current VAW structure dates from 1967, when seven AEW squadrons numbered in sequence were established. Previously

An E-2C Hawkeye from VAW-113 launches from the carrier ABRAHAM LINCOLN (CVN 72). The Hawkeye has been in production longer than any other Navy aircraft still being procured. (U.S. Navy, PHAN Michael B.W. Watkins)

VAW-11, -12, -13, and -33 provided AEW detachments to carriers, while Barrier Squadron Pacific and AEW Wing Atlantic operated land-based WV/EC-121 Warning Star aircraft as part of the North American air defense efforts until 1965.

Manning: Most VAW squadrons have 29 officers and 133 enlisted personnel.

2 FLEET COMPOSITE SQUADRONS

Squadron	Code	Aircraft	Name/Notes
VC-1	UA	F/A-18, CH-53A, VP-3A	disestablished 30 Sep 1992
VC-5	UE	F/A-18, SH-3G	disestablished 31 Aug 1992
VC-6	JG	(none assigned)	Skeet of the Fleet (ex-Skeeters)
VC-8	GF	UH-3H	Redtails
VC-10	JH	F/A-18	disestablished 14 Aug 1993

Composite squadrons provide utility services for the fleet, noncombat photography, aerial target services, radar calibration, and transport. Two now-disestablished VC squadrons had combat missions: VC-1 and VC-10 had F/A-18 Hornets that had the additional role of air defense for Hawaii and Guantánamo Bay, Cuba, respectively. (They previously flew A-4E and TA-4J Skyhawks, as did VC-8.)

VC-6 at NAS Norfolk flies no aircraft, but operates air and surface target drones. There are permanent VC-6 detachments at the Fleet Combat Training Center in Dam Neck, Va., and at the Naval Amphibious Base, Little Creek, Va. Five smaller, mobile detachments operate in the Atlantic–Mediterranean areas and periodically deploy with U.S. ships operating around South America in the UNITAS exercises.

VC-8 at Naval Station (NS) Roosevelt Roads, P.R., provides services to Atlantic fleet training and weapon test activities.

Historical: The current VC squadrons comprise the third series of composite squadrons in the fleet. From 1943 to 1945 the Navy had 83 composite squadrons (VC) that operated from escort carriers.

Beginning in 1948, six VC squadrons were formed with nuclear-strike aircraft (flying P2V-3C Neptunes and AJ Savages); those squadrons became heavy attack squadrons (VAH) in 1955–1956. At the same time, several ASW squadrons were formed but were redesignated VS (see page 371).

On 1 July 1965 the Navy's utility squadrons (VJ and later VU) were changed to VC, with VU-1, -5, -6, -8, and -10 being redesignated as fleet composite squadrons (VC).

VC-2 (Oceana, Va.) and VC-7 (Miramar, Calif.) were disestablished in 1980, and VC-3 (North Island, Calif.), which flew DC-130A Hercules to launch aerial drones, was disestablished in 1981.

13 FIGHTER SQUADRONS

Squadron	Aircraft	Name/Notes
VF-1	F-14A	disestablished 30 Sep 1993
VF-2	F-14D*	Bounty Hunters
VF-11	F-14B	Red Rippers
VF-14	F-14A	Tophatters
VF-21	F-14A	disestablished 31 Jan 1996
VF-24	F-14A	disestablished 31 Aug 1996
VF-31	F-14D*	Tomcatters
VF-32	F-14B*	Swordsmen
VF-33	F-14A	disestablished 1 Oct 1993
VF-41	F-14A	Black Aces
VF-43	F-5E/F, A-4E, F-16N, F-21A, T-2C	disestablished 1 July 1994
VF-45	A-4E, TA-4J	disestablished 31 Mar 1996
VF-51	F-14A	disestablished 31 Mar 1995
VF-74	F-14B	disestablished 30 Apr 1994
VF-84	F-14A*	disestablished 1 Oct 1995
VF-101	F-14A/B/D, T-34C	Grim Reapers (AD)
VF-102	F-14B*	Diamondbacks
VF-103	F-14B*	Jolly Rogers
VF-111	F-14A*	disestablished 31 Mar 1995
VF-114	F-14A	disestablished 30 Apr 1993
VF-124	F-14A/D, T-34C	disestablished 30 Sep 1994
VF-126	TA-4J, F-5E/F, F-16N	disestablished 1 Apr 1994
VF-142	F-14B	disestablished 30 Apr 1995
VF-143	F-14B*	World Famous Dogs (see *Name* notes)
VF-154	F-14A*	Black Knights
VF-211	F-14A*	Flying Checkmates
VF-213	F-14D*	Black Lions

* TARPS-capable squadrons.

A TA-4J Skyhawk from Training Wing 2 is launched from the carrier GEORGE WASHINGTON on 29 September 1999. A short time later, the long-serving TA-4J was retired from the Naval Air Training Command and, subsequently, from VC-8, ending 44 years of service in U.S. naval aviation. (U.S. Navy, PH3 Johnnie Robbins)

There are 12 fighter squadrons (VF) assigned to carrier air wings, plus one readiness training squadron, VF-101; all fly the F-14 Tomcat.

With arrival of the F/A-18E Hornet in the fleet in 2001, the number of F-14 squadrons will be reduced to one per carrier air wing (i.e., ten). Subsequently, the JSF will replace those squadrons during the second decade of this century.

The F-14 squadrons each have 14 aircraft assigned; in one F-14 squadron on each carrier there are three aircraft wired for the TARPS reconnaissance package, which can be installed or removed in a few hours. (VF-211 was the first squadron to deploy with TARPS, in early 1982 on board the CONSTELLATION.)

All F-14 squadrons are assigned to Strike Fighter Wing Atlantic Fleet and are based at NAS Oceana, Va., except for VF-154 at NAS Atsugi. Previously, West Coast fighter squadrons were at NAS Miramar, Calif. F-14 readiness training is provided by VF-101. (The West Coast F-14 readiness unit, VF-124, was disestablished in 1994.)

The Naval Strike and Air Warfare Center, established in 1995 at Fallon, Nev., replaces the Strike Warfare Center ("Strike University") and Fighter Weapons School ("Top Gun"). Top Gun had begun as a VF-121 detachment and became a separate command on 1 July 1972. The Strike and Air Warfare Center operates aircraft to help develop fleet tactics; "students" bring their own aircraft to the center. Currently assigned to the center are eight F-14A, 25 F/A-18A, four F/A-18B, and four SH-60F.

Historical: VF-43 (Oceana), VA-45 (Key West, Fla.), and VF-126 (Miramar) previously provided adversary training, with the last also providing instrument training. VA-45 was changed to VF-45 on 7 February 1985.

VF-191 and VF-194 were established in 1986 for the Navy's 14th carrier air wing. However, the two squadrons were disestablished in 1988. Plans to establish "new" VF-191 and VF-194 as F-14D squadrons were canceled when VF-11 and VF-31 became available because CVW-6 was disestablished when the FORRESTAL was named as the training carrier. Those two VF squadrons were then shifted to the West Coast.

The MIDWAY flew the Navy's last two active F-4 Phantom squadrons (VF-151 and VF-161), which stood down as Phantom units in 1986; the squadrons then became VFA-151 and VFA-161 flying the F/A-18. The last Phantom fleet-readiness squadron was VF-171, disestablished in 1984. All Navy-Marine readiness training in the Phantom was then being undertaken by VMFAT-101 at MCAS

Yuma, Ariz. (VF-121, the West Coast F-4 readiness squadron, was disestablished in 1980; it had been the Navy's first squadron to fly the F-4.)

Manning: Most VF squadrons have 33 or 34 officers and about 235 enlisted personnel.

Names: VF-143 was the World Famous Pukin' Dogs from 1949 until 1994, when "Pukin'" was deleted, another casualty of political correctness.

25 STRIKE FIGHTER SQUADRONS

Squadron	Aircraft	Name	Notes
VFA-15	F/A-18C	Valions	former VA-15
VFA-22	F/A-18C	Fighting Redcocks	former VA-22
VFA-25	F/A-18C	Fist of the Fleet	former VA-25
VFA-27	F/A-18C	Chargers	former VA-27
VFA-34	F/A-18C	Blue Blasters	former VA-34
VFA-37	F/A-18C	Bulls	former VA-37
VFA-81	F/A-18C	Sunliners	former VA-81
VFA-82	F/A-18C	Marauders	former VA-82
VFA-83	F/A-18C	Rampagers	former VA-83
VFA-86	F/A-18C	Sidewinders	former VA-86
VFA-87	F/A-18C	Golden Warriors	former VA-87
VFA-94	F/A-18C	Mighty Shrikes	former VA-94
VFA-97	F/A-18A	Warhawks	former VA-97
VFA-105	F/A-18C	Gunslingers	former VA-105
VFA-106	F/A-18A/B/C/D, T-34C	Gladiators (AD)	former VA-106
VFA-113	F/A-18C	Stingers	former VA-113
VFA-122	F/A-18E/F	Redcocks (NJ)	
VFA-125	F/A-18A/B/C/D, T-34C	Rough Riders (NJ)	former VA-125
VFA-127	A-4, F-5	Desert Bogeys	former VA-127; disestablished 31 Mar 1996
VFA-131	F/A-18C	Wildcats	
VFA-132	F/A-18A		disestablished 1 June 1992
VFA-136	F/A-18C	Knighthawks	
VFA-137	F/A-18C	Kestrels	
VFA-146	F/A-18C	Blue Diamonds	former VA-146
VFA-147	F/A-18C	Argonauts	former VA-147
VFA-151	F/A-18C	Fighting Vigilantes	former VF-151
VFA-192	F/A-18C	World Famous Golden Dragons	
VFA-195	F/A-18C	Dambusters	former VA-195

An F-14A Tomcat from VF-154 is readied for launch from the carrier KITTY HAWK (CV 63); an F/A-18 Hornet is also readied for launch from a waist catapult. The Tomcat is the last "straight" fighter, although later variants have a strike capability. (U.S. Navy, PHAN Mara McCleaft)

All carrier air wings have two or three strike fighter squadrons (VFA), each with 12 F/A-18 aircraft. VFA-97 is the last fleet squadron flying the F/A-18A model, having been delayed in being updated to the F/A-18C. VFA-122—a readiness squadron—is the first Navy F/A-18E unit; it was established on 1 October 1998. Beginning in 2001, all carrier air wings are to have four F/A-18 squadrons.

Currently there are 22 squadrons assigned to carrier air wings, and three readiness training squadrons: VFA-106, VFA-122, and VFA-125. Shortfalls in fleet squadrons have been met by assigning four Marine F/A-18 squadrons to carrier air wings (see table 26-3). The Atlantic F/A-18 squadrons are assigned to Strike Fighter Wing Atlantic Fleet; all are based at NAS Oceana except for VFA-82 and VFA-86, which moved to MCAS Beaufort, S.C., in late 1999. All Pacific squadrons are under Strike Fighter Wing Pacific Fleet and based at NAS Lemoore, Calif., except for VFA-27, VFA-192, and VFA-195, which are based at NAF Atsugi.

Designation: The Marine Corps has had fighter-attack squadrons (VMFA) since the introduction of the F-4 Phantom into squadron service in 1963. The Navy designation VFA originally indicated fighter attack squadron; this was changed in 1983 to strike fighter to emphasize the attack role.

Historical: The first F/A-18 squadron was VFA-125, established on 13 November 1980 as the F/A-18 readiness squadron for training Navy and Marine pilots and ground crews; VFA-125's first aircraft was delivered in February 1981. A second F/A-18 readiness squadron, VFA-106, subsequently stood up in October 1985 at NAS Cecil Field (Jacksonville), Fla.

VFA-75 and VFA-113 were the Navy's first F/A-18 fleet squadrons, shifting from the A-7E Corsair to the F/A-18 in March–June 1983. Most F/A-18 squadrons are former A-7E Corsair units (VA), with two F-14 squadrons (VF-151, VF-161) transitioning to F/A-18s and more VA and VF squadrons scheduled to shift to F/A-18s. VFA-161 was disestablished in 1987.

VFA-127 provided adversary training.

Manning: Most VFA squadrons have 25 officers and 186 enlisted personnel.

Operational: The Navy operates more F/A-18 Hornets than any other aircraft type. The aircraft had its combat debut in the strikes against Libya in 1986; it has been active in subsequent U.S. peacekeeping and combat operations.

13 PATROL SQUADRONS

Squadron	Code	Aircraft	Name/Notes
VP-1	YB	P-3C	Screaming Eagles
VP-4	YD	P-3C	Skinny Dragons
VP-5	LA	P-3C	Mad Foxes
VP-6	PC	P-3C	disestablished 31 May 1993
VP-8	LC	P-3C	Tigers
VP-9	PD	P-3C	Golden Eagles
VP-10	LD	P-3C	Red Lancers
VP-11	LE	P-3C	disestablished 15 Jan 1997
VP-16	LF	P-3C	War Eagles
VP-17	ZE	P-3C	disestablished 31 Mar 1995
VP-19	PE	P-3C	disestablished 31 August 1991
VP-22	QA	P-3C	disestablished 31 Mar 1994
VP-23	LJ	P-3C	disestablished 7 Dec 1994
VP-24	LR	P-3C	disestablished 13 Apr 1995
VP-26	LK	P-3C	Tridents
VP-30	LL	P-3C, VP-3A	Pro's Nest
VP-31	RP	P-3C	disestablished 1 Nov 1993
VP-40	QE	P-3C	Fighting Marlins
VP-44	LM	P-3C	disestablished 28 June 1991
VP-45	LN	P-3C	Pelicans
VP-46	RC	P-3C	Grey Knights
VP-47	RD	P-3C	Golden Swordsmen
VP-48	SF	P-3C	disestablished 26 June 1991
VP-49	LP	P-3C	disestablished 1 Mar 1994
VP-50	SG	P-3C	disestablished 30 June 1992
VP-56	LQ	P-3C	disestablished 28 June 1991

There are 12 active patrol squadrons (VP), each flying eight aircraft, plus a P-3 Orion readiness training squadron. This is half the number of VP squadrons in the active fleet from the early 1970s until 1991. VP-30, with some 30 aircraft, provides training for all P-3 users; the Pacific Fleet readiness squadron was VP-31.

Patrol squadrons are assigned to PATRECONFORLANT and PATRECONFORPAC; see table 26-4 for squadron assignments and bases.

Designation: VP indicated patrol squadron from 1922 to 1944, when patrol and multiengine land-based bombing squadrons were redesignated patrol bombing squadrons (VPB). The squadrons reverted to VP on 15 May 1946.

Historical: VP-8 was the first P3V/P-3 Orion squadron, receiving the aircraft in 1962. Previously VP units flew P2V/P-2 Neptunes and P5M/P-5 Marlin flying boats.

F/A-18 Hornets crowd the flight deck of the carrier THEODORE ROOSEVELT (CVN 71). The F/A-18C in the foreground—from VFA-15—joined other planes from Carrier Air Wing 8 in strikes during Operation Allied Force. There are more F/A-18s in naval aviation than any other aircraft type. (Lt. Bradley K. Silva)

Manning: Most VP squadrons are manned by 68 officers and 299 enlisted personnel.

Operational: VP squadrons—active and reserve—regularly deploy in whole or detachments to Roosevelt Roads, P.R.; Keflavik, Iceland; Sigonella, Sicily; Jidda, Saudi Arabia; Masirah, Oman; Diego Garcia; Misawa, Japan; and Kadena, Okinawa. (Previous deployments to Adak, Alaska; Bermuda; Lajes, Azores; Rota, Spain; Cubi Point, Philippines; and Agana, Guam, have ceased.)

2 SPECIAL PROJECTS PATROL SQUADRONS

Squadron	Code	Aircraft	Name
VPU-1	OB	P-3B/C	Ancient Order of the Buzzard
VPU-2	SP	P-3C, UP-3A	Wizards

These two squadrons fly specially modified electronic surveillance variants of the Orion. They often operate with the tail codes of other squadrons. VPU-1's unit code is unofficial, being derived from "Order of the Buzzard"; VP-2's code is derived from Special Projects. VPU-1 is based at NAS Brunswick, under Patrol and Reconnaissance Wing 5; VPU-2 is at MCAF Kaneohe Bay under Patrol and Reconnaissance Force Pacific Fleet.

Designation: VPU was patrol squadron special projects unit; VPU-1 changed to special projects patrol squadron on 8 April 1988, and VPU-2 on 14 April 1998.

Manning: VPU-1 has 29 officers and 163 enlisted personnel; VPU-2 has 29 officers and 178 enlisted.

2 FLEET AIR RECONNAISSANCE SQUADRONS

Squadron	Code	Aircraft	Name/Notes
VQ-1	PR	P-3C, EP-3E, UP-3A/B	World Watchers
VQ-2	JQ	P-3C, EP-3E	Batmen
VQ-5	SS	S-3B, ES-3A	disestablished 30 July 1999
VQ-6	ET	ES-3A	disestablished 30 Sep 1999
VQ-11	LP	P-3C, EP-3J	disestablished 31 Mar 2000

VQ-1 and VQ-2 provide electronic surveillance in direct support of fleet operations and carry out special reconnaissance along the borders of foreign territory. They each fly six ELINT-configured EP-3E Orions, plus support and training aircraft.

VQ-1, based at NAS Whidbey Island, is under PATRECONWING-10; VQ-2, based at NS Rota, Spain, is under Fleet Air Mediterranean (at Naples, Italy).

VQ-5 at NAS North Island and VQ-6 at NAS Jacksonville, Fla., flew the ES-3A Sea Shadow as carrier-based ELINT aircraft.[20] The squadrons were established in 1991. The ES-3A replaced the EA-3B Skywarrior ("Whale"), with one or two aircraft assigned to forward-deployed aircraft carriers. VQ-2 retired the last EA-3B operated by a VQ squadron in September 1991. VQ-1 and VQ-2 and other electronic intelligence "assets" took over the collection role of the ES-3A aircraft.

---

20. "Sea Shadow" was an unofficial name; the aircraft retained the name Viking in official documentation. Note that the unit code ET is also assigned to Marine helicopter squadron HMM-262.

A P-3C Orion from VP-10 overflies Mt. Etna during a training flight over Sicily. U.S.-based patrol squadrons, including reserve units, regularly deploy overseas. At the time, the Orions of the Red Lancers squadron were on a six-month deployment to NAS Sigonella, Sicily. (U.S. Navy, PHAN Alesha A. Stanaitis)

VQ-11 was established on 1 July 1997 to help train fleet personnel in electronic warfare. The squadron, based at NAS Brunswick, Maine, had one P-3C and two EP-3J Orions, the latter fitted with a variety of emitters to simulate hostile communications intrusion, deception, and jamming. The squadron had a brief career.

Designation: VQ was changed from electronic countermeasures squadron to fleet air reconnaissance squadron on 1 January 1960.

Historical: VQ-1 was established as Electronic Countermeasures Squadron 1 at NAS Iwakuni, Japan, on 1 June 1955, initially flying P4M-1Q Mercator aircraft; VQ-2 was established as ECM Squadron 2 on 1 September 1955 at Port Lyautey, Morocco, first flying the P4M-1Q and the A3D-1Q (EA-3B) aircraft. Previously PB4Y-2 Privateer and PBM Mariner aircraft were employed in the ELINT role.

Operational: VQ-2 flew both EP-3s and EA-3Bs in support of Desert Shield/Desert Storm in 1990–1991; the latter were the last operational combat-environment flights by the venerable Skywarrior.

3 STRATEGIC COMMUNICATION SQUADRONS

Squadron	Code	Aircraft	Name
VQ-3	TZ	E-6B	Ironmen (ex-TACAMOPAC)
VQ-4	HL	E-6B	Shadows
VQ-7	(none)	EC-18B	Roughnecks

VQ-3 and VQ-4, designated fleet air reconnaissance squadrons, fly the E-6 Mercury, a navalized version of the Boeing 707-320B airframe. They provide LF/VLF communications relay to strategic missile submarines under a program known as TACAMO (Take Charge And Move Out); in addition, in the E-6B configuration these aircraft replace the Air Force EC-135 "Looking Glass" strategic command post aircraft. The last EC-135 was retired on 25 September 1998.

Sixteen E-6B aircraft are flown by these squadrons, replacing 22 EC-130Q Hercules aircraft.

VQ-3 and VQ-4 are under the Navy Strategic Communications Wing 1, which was established on 1 May 1992, the year both squadrons moved to Tinker Air Force Base (AFB), outside of Oklahoma City, Okla. Operationally they are under the U.S. Strategic Command. (Previously, VQ-3 was at NAS Barbers Point and VQ-4 at NAS Patuxent River, Md.) The two squadrons "forward deploy"

aircraft to Travis AFB, Calif.; Offutt AFB, Neb.; and NAS Patuxent River to fly operational patrols.

Two similar 707-320B aircraft—designated TC-18F—are operated by the Naval Training Support Unit at Tinker AFB in Oklahoma to train E-6 pilots. The unit was redesignated VQ-7 on 1 November 1999.

During 2000 structural problems were found in the squadron's TF-18Fs and they were withdrawn from service. In their place VQ-7 borrowed Air Force EC-18B aircraft for transition training to the E-6B (see photo page 376).

Historical: VQ-3 transitioned from the EC-130Q Hercules to the E-6A Hermes in 1989–1990, and VQ-4 in 1991–1992. The last EC-130Q TACAMO flight, by a VQ-4 "Herk," was on 7 May 1992.

2 FLEET LOGISTIC SUPPORT SQUADRONS

Squadron	Code	Aircraft	Name/Notes
VR-22	JL	C-130F, KC-130F	disestablished 31 Mar 1993
VR-24	JM	C-2A, CT-39G	disestablished 31 Jan 1993
VRC-30	RW	C-2A, UC-12B	Providers (ex-Truckin' Traders)
VRC-40	CD	C-2A	Rawhides
VRC-50	RG	C-2A, US-3A, C-130	disestablished 7 Oct 1994

The two surviving fleet logistic support squadrons (VRC) deliver passengers, mail, and high-priority parts to carriers at sea. The Navy's straight transport squadrons (VR) have been phased out, their role taken over by Naval reserve VR units and the Air Force's Air Mobility Command (formerly Military Airlift Command).

VRC-30 is at NAS North Island under AEW Wing Pacific Fleet and VRC-40 is under AEW Atlantic Fleet at NAS Norfolk. The assignment of the C-2A Carrier Onboard Delivery (COD) aircraft to the E-2C Hawkeye wings is based on the similarity of their aircraft.

The disestablishment of VRC-50 led to setting up VRC-30 Detachment 5 at NAF Atsugi, to provide CODs to support carriers in the Western Pacific. The turboprop C-2A is not normally based aboard carriers because of the aircraft's large size.

The KC-130F "Herks" of VR-22 were the Navy's only land-based tanker aircraft. VRC-50 flew the Navy's three US-3A Viking COD aircraft. VAW-110 took over readiness training for the C-2 from VRC-30; subsequently, VRC-30 provides transition/readiness training for the UC-12 Super Air King for the Navy.

An S-3B Viking from VS-32 refuels F/A-18s from the carrier JOHN F. KENNEDY (CV 67) during operations over the Persian Gulf. Inflight refueling is a primary function of sea control squadrons, which have discarded their traditional ASW role. (U.S. Navy)

Designation: The VR squadrons were originally transport squadrons (VR) and were changed to fleet tactical support squadrons (VR) on 15 July 1957. They became fleet logistic support squadrons on 1 April 1976.

Historical: The first Navy transport squadron was VR-1, established on 9 March 1942; it was disestablished in October 1978.

The first COD squadron was VRC-40, established on 1 July 1960. The first COD aircraft were converted TBM Avengers, intended to fly nuclear bomb components from forward bases to aircraft carriers.

Manning: Approximately 12 officers and 100 enlisted personnel are assigned to most squadrons.

11 SEA CONTROL SQUADRONS

Squadron	Aircraft	Name/Notes
VS-21	S-3B	Fighting Redtails
VS-22	S-3B	Checkmates
VS-24	S-3B	Scouts
VS-27	S-3B	(AD) disestablished 30 Sep 1994
VS-28	S-3B	disestablished 1 Oct 1992
VS-29	S-3B	Screaming Dragonfires (ex-Vikings)
VS-30	S-3B	Diamond Cutters
VS-31	S-3B	Topcats
VS-32	S-3B	Maulers
VS-33	S-3B	Screwbirds
VS-35	S-3B	Blue Wolves
VS-37	S-3B	disestablished 31 Mar 1995
VS-38	S-3B	Red Griffins
VS-41	S-3B	Shamrocks (NJ)

The Navy's ten operational sea control squadrons each fly eight S-3B Viking aircraft. During the 1980s these units—then called ASW squadrons—had ten aircraft; in the 1990s this was reduced to six for a short period; eight are now assigned to each VS squadron. These aircraft are no longer employed in ASW operations but are used for surface surveillance, aerial refueling, and utility functions.

VS-41 at NAS North Island provides readiness training for the S-3 community; previously VS-27 at NAS Cecil Field provided S-3 readiness/transition services for the Atlantic Fleet. (VS-30 was an S-2 Tracker readiness training squadron; it became an operational squadron upon transitioning to the S-3A in 1976.)

Viking squadrons are subordinate to their respective fleet Sea Control Wings, operating out of North Island and Jacksonville, except VS-21 is based at NAF Atsugi.

Designation: The 13 VS units in service on 16 September 1993 were changed from anti-submarine squadrons (VS) to sea control squadrons, reflecting their more versatile operational capabilities.

Historical: Specialized carrier-based ASW squadrons were formed in World War II, most designated as composite squadrons (VC). In April 1950 eight VC squadrons were changed to air anti-submarine squadrons (VS); each flew 18 TBM-3E Avengers. Four of the squadrons had previously been attack units (VA), which were changed to VC on 1 September 1948.

Manning: VS squadrons have 33 officers and 180 enlisted personnel.

16 TRAINING SQUADRONS

Command	Aircraft	Name	Training	Location/Notes
TRAINING WING 1 (A)				NAS Meridian, Miss.
VT-7	T-45C	Strike Eagles	Advanced strike	
VT-9*	T-2C	Tigers	Intermediate strike	
VT-23	T-45C	Professionals	Advanced jet	disestablished 30 Sep 1999
TRAINING WING 2 (B)				NAS Kingsville, Texas
VT-21	T-45A	Fighting Redhawks	Intermediate/ advanced jet	
VT-22	T-45A	Golden Eagles	Intermediate/ advanced jet	
TRAINING WING 3 (C)				disestablished 31 Aug 1992
VT-24	TA-4J			disestablished 30 Oct 1992
VT-25	TA-4J			disestablished 30 Oct 1992
VT-26	T-2C			disestablished 29 May 1992
TRAINING WING 4 (G)				NAS Corpus Christi, Texas
VT-27	T-34C	Boomers	Primary flight	
VT-28	T-34C	Rangers	Primary flight	
VT-31	T-44A	Wise Owls	Advanced maritime	
VT-35	TC-12B	Stingrays	Multiengine	
TRAINING WING 5 (E)				NAS Milton, Fla.
VT-2	T-34C	Doer Birds	Primary flight	
VT-3	T-34C	Red Knights	Primary flight	
VT-6	T-34C	Shooters	Primary flight	
HT-8	TH-57B/C	Eight Ballers	Helicopter	
HT-18	TH-57B/C	Vigilant Eagles	Helicopter	
TRAINING WING 6 (F)				NAS Pensacola, Fla.
VT-4	T-34C, T-39G	Mighty Warbucks	NFO**	
VT-10	T-34C, T-39G	Wildcats	NFO	
VT-86	T-2C, T-39N	Sabrehawks	Advanced NFO	

* VT-19 was redesignated VT-9 on 1 October 1998.
** NFO = Naval Flight Officer (i.e., the "backseater").

These 16 squadrons provide fixed-wing training for Navy, Marine Corps, Coast Guard, Air Force, and foreign military pilots and air crewmen under the direction of the Naval Air Training Command at NAS Corpus Christi, Texas. VT-3 provides primary flight training for U.S. Air Force pilots and VT-31 provides training to Air Force cargo/transport pilots.

There are currently three Air Force Flying Training Squadrons (FTS) that train Navy pilots:

Squadron	Aircraft	Training	Location
35th FTS	T-37	Primary	Reese AFB, Texas
52nd FTS	T-1A	E-6B	Reese AFB, Texas
562nd FTS	Boeing 737	Advanced NFO	Randolph AFB, Texas

The T-45 and T-2C are carrier capable and enable students to practice landings aboard aircraft carriers. VT-21 began operating the long-delayed T-45 Goshawk in early 1992; the plane finally replaced the long-serving TA-4J Skyhawk in 1999, VT-7 being the last U.S. Navy squadron with that aircraft.

VT-31 and VT-35 train Navy, Marine, and Coast Guard pilots in multiengine turboprop aircraft; it also trains Air Force C-130 pilots.

VT-86 trains Naval Flight Officers (NFO), as well as Air Force Weapon System Operators (WSO) for B-1, B-2, and F-15 bomber/strike aircraft. The T-39N aircraft of VT-86 are refurbished Sabreliners used to train NFOs. They are flown and maintained by contractor personnel, having replaced T-47A aircraft that were operated under a similar arrangement.

Designation: The letters *T* and *HT* (helicopter) have been used for naval aircraft designations since shortly after World War II; however, VT and HT were not used for squadron designations until 1 May 1960, when 17 training units were redesignated as training squadrons (VT). From the 1920s until 15 November 1946, the designation VT indicated torpedo squadron.

Note that HT squadrons are numbered in the same series as VT squadrons.

Historical: VT-7 was the last U.S. training squadron to fly the A-4

Skyhawk. The diminutive and highly versatile aircraft had entered Navy service as the A4D-1 in September 1956; the TA-4J two-seat trainer entered service in 6 June 1969. The aircraft is still flown by several other countries.

HT-8 traces its history to HTU-1, established in 1950 and changed to HTG-1 in 1957 and to HT-8 in 1960. HT-18 was established in 1972.

1 FLIGHT DEMONSTRATION SQUADRON

Code	Aircraft	Name
BA	F/A-18A/B, TC-130G	Blue Angels

The Blue Angels is the Navy–Marine Corps flight demonstration team, performing throughout the United States to encourage aviation recruiting. The unit currently flies early-model F/A-18 Hornets—eight F/A-18A and one two-seat F/A-18B. The F/A-18s are not normally capable of carrier operations, have had their guns removed, and are provided with smoke generators, improved flight control systems, and additional navigation equipment.

A Marine-owned C-130 Hercules is assigned to the team as a support aircraft; it is now designated TC-130G. (A Marine "Herk" has been assigned to the unit since December 1970.)

The tail code BA is not shown on Blue Angels aircraft; they have blue-and-gold livery with large numerals indicating the aircraft place in formation. "Fat Albert"—the nickname for the TC-130G—has Blue Angels livery with "Marines" on wing surfaces and "United States Marines" on the fuselage.

Historical: The unit was established on 18 April 1946; it was named the Blue Angels soon afterwards—for a New York City night club. The unit stood down in 1950–1951 for the start of the Korean War, with its pilots forming the cadre of VF-191. Reestablished, it was formally designated the Flight Demonstration Squadron on 1 December 1973.

The "Blues" have flown a succession of first-line naval aircraft: F6F-5 Hellcat, F8F-1 Bearcat, F9F-2 and F9F-5 Panther, F9F-6 Cougar, F11F-1 Tiger, F-4J Phantom, A-4F Skyhawk, and, since November 1986, the F/A-18 Hornet.

Operational: The first carrier "trap" and launch by a Blue Angel aircraft from a carrier occurred on 11 November 1998 when Commander Patrick Driscoll, the team leader, landed an F/A-18A aboard and took off from the HARRY S. TRUMAN.

2 AIR TEST AND EVALUATION SQUADRONS

Squadron	Code	Aircraft	Name/Notes
VX-1	JA	P-3C, S-3B, SH-60B/F	ASW Pioneers
VX-4	XF	TA-4J, F-14A/D, F/A-18A	disestablished 30 Sep 1994
VX-5	XE	TA-4J, A-6E, EA-6B, AV-8B, F/A-18, AH-1W	disestablished 29 Apr 1994
VX-9	XE	AV-8B, EA-6B, F-14D, F/A-18, AH-1W	Vampires (ex-Evaluators)

These squadrons test and evaluate air weapon systems; they fly a variety of aircraft. VX-1 at NAS Patuxent River specializes in operational test and evaluation of airborne ASW under the cognizance of Naval Air Force Atlantic Fleet.

VX-9 at NAS China Lake, Calif., specializes in fighter-attack aircraft, air-to-surface weapons and tactics, and electronic countermeasures programs. It is directly subordinate to Naval Air Force Pacific Fleet. VX-9 was established on 30 April 1994 by the merger of VX-4 from Point Mugu, Calif., and VX-5 at China Lake; their successor unit was appropriately designated VX-9. The VX-9 detachment at Point Mugu uses the tail code XF.

Designation: Two specialized development squadrons—VXE-6 and VXN-8—were numbered in the basic VX series (see below).

Historical: VX-1 had two predecessors: The Aircraft Experimental and Development Squadron was established at NAS Anacostia in Washington, D.C., on 13 August 1942. Subsequently, on 1 April 1943 an Air Anti-Submarine Development Detachment was established at Quonset Point, R.I.; this unit was recommissioned as Anti-Submarine Development Squadron 1 in 1946. These units underwent several name changes, and their functions eventually were combined, with Air Test and Evaluation Squadron 1 adopted on 1 January 1969. The squadron was moved to NAS Patuxent River on 15 September 1973.

Figure 26-1
Naval Aviation Pilot Training

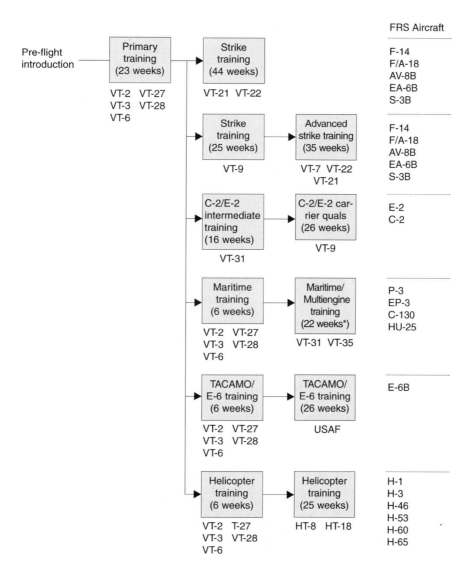

* 25 weeks for USAF pilots

Figure 26-2
Naval Aviation NFO Training

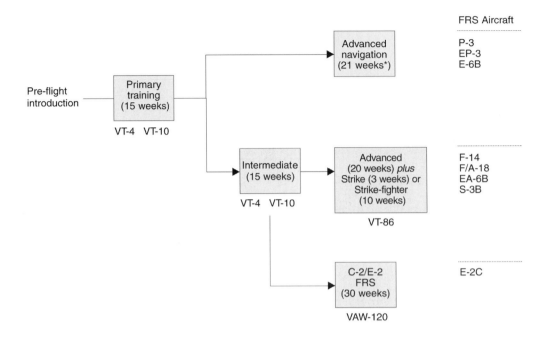

* Training at 562nd Flying Training Squadron, Randolph AFB, Texas

ANTARCTIC DEVELOPMENT SQUADRON

Squadron	Code	Aircraft	Notes
VXE-6	XD	LC-130F/R, UH-1N	disestablished 31 Mar 1999

The Navy's only squadron dedicated to aerial support of U.S Antarctic operations—VXE-6, long known as the "Puckered Penguins"—has been disestablished. (In its final days the squadron was known as the "Ice Pirates.") Based at Point Mugu, Calif., it provided support of U.S. Antarctic programs sponsored by the National Science Foundation. The squadron flew from McMurdo when operating in Antarctica.

The Antarctic support role has been taken over by the Air National Guard's 109th Airlift Wing, Schenectady, N.Y. Flying ski-equipped LC-130 Hercules transports, the 109th Airlift Wing has operated in the northern and, subsequently, southern polar regions since 1975. It is now the only U.S. military aviation unit flying ski-fitted "Herks."

VXE-6 flew two LC-130F and five LC-130R Hercules at the time it was disestablished; it was the last active-duty Navy squadron to fly the C-130. Prior to February 1996 the squadron also flew UH-1N Huey helicopters equipped with skis. Helicopter support is now provided under contract by a commercial firm.

Designation: Squadron VXE-6 was originally established as Air Development Squadron 6 (VX-6) on 17 January 1955, specifically for Antarctic operations (Operation Deep Freeze); the squadron was redesignated VXE-6 on 1 January 1969.

Historical: The U.S. Navy has had aviation interests in the Antarctic since 1928 when retired Commander Richard E. Byrd took four civilian aircraft on his first expedition to the South Pole.[21] Major Navy support began with Byrd's 1939–1940 expedition, and on his 1947–1948 expedition there were 19 Navy fixed-wing aircraft and four helicopters, including six R4D/C-47 transports that flew into Antarctica from the aircraft carrier PHILIPPINE SEA (CV 47).

---

21. On 21 December 1928, while Byrd was on the expedition, Congress promoted him to the rank of rear admiral on the retired list.

OCEANOGRAPHIC DEVELOPMENT SQUADRON

Squadron	Code	Aircraft	Notes
VXN-8	JB	RP-3D, UP-3A	disestablished 1 Oct 1993

VXN-8 at NAS Patuxent River operated five RP-3D Orion aircraft in support of worldwide research projects: Project Magnet was a gravity and geomagnetic study, Project Birdseye an ice reconnaissance and physical oceanography study, and Project Seascan an aerial oceanographic effort.

Some of the squadron's programs have been taken over by aircraft sponsored by the Naval Research Laboratory (NRL) in Washington, D.C., which operates five research-configured NP-3D aircraft in support of worldwide scientific research projects. Based at NAS Patuxent River, the NRL Orions are extensively modified P-3A/B/C models that support research into gravity and ocean floor spreading, basic and advanced electronic warfare, space sensing applications, spaceborne radar, laser projects, and optical systems. These aircraft have "NRL" and the American flag on their tail fins (no code letters); they are painted orange and white.

Historical: VXN-8 had its beginnings as Airborne Early Warning Training Unit Atlantic Fleet which, in 1951, was assigned Project Magnet. Projects Birdseye and Outpost Seascan were assigned in 1962 and Project Jenny in July 1965. The last was to provide radio and television broadcasts to South Vietnam pending the completion of ground facilities. Subsequently, the unit became the Oceanographic Airborne Survey Unit and, on 1 July 1967, Air Development Squadron (VX) 8. It was changed to VXN-8 in January 1969.

7 HELICOPTER COMBAT SUPPORT SQUADRONS

Squadron	Code	Aircraft	Name/Notes
HC-1	UP	SH-3G/D/H, CH-53E	disestablished 29 Apr 1994
HC-2	HU	VH-3A, UH-3H	Circuit Riders
HC-3	SA	CH/HH-46D	Packrats
HC-4	HC	MH-53E	Black Stallions
HC-5	RB	CH/HH/UH-46D	Providers (ex–Night Riders)
HC-6	HW	CH/HH/UH-46D	Chargers
HC-8	BR	CH/HH/UH-46D	Dragon Whales
HC-11	VR	CH/HH/UH-46D, UH-3H	Gunbearers
HC-16	BF	SH-3D, UH-1N	disestablished 1 Apr 1994

A Blue Angels F/A-18A Hornet is prepared for launching from the HARRY S. TRUMAN (CVN 75)—the jet-blast deflector is raised behind the aircraft. On 11 November 1998 the first landing and takeoff aboard a carrier was made by a Blue Angels aircraft. (U.S. Navy)

Most of these squadrons provide helicopter detachments for Search and Rescue (SAR) and Vertical Replenishment/Vertical Onboard Delivery (VERTREP/VOD) operations in direct support of the fleet. Atlantic units report to Helicopter Tactical Wing Atlantic Fleet, Pacific units to Helicopter Tactical Wing Pacific Fleet.

HC-2 at NAS Norfolk is both an operational and fleet readiness training squadron. It has H-3 Sea Kings for VIP transport, including ferry service between Norfolk and the Pentagon; it also has UH-3H detachments at Bahrain and Naples to provide helicopters for the Commander Fifth Fleet and Commander Sixth Fleet, respectively.

HC-3 and HC-11 are at NAS North Island, with HC-3 conducting all Navy readiness/transition training for the H-46 Sea Knight. The squadron provides a helicopter for Commander Third Fleet.

HC-4 at NAS Sigonella, Sicily, provides logistics support for the Sixth Fleet with MH-53Es (having previously flown the CH-53E).The MH-53Es came from reserve HM-18 and HM-19 when those units combined with active MCM units.

HC-5 at Anderson AFB on Guam provides detachments to the Seventh Fleet for VERTREP operations; the squadron, with 12 Sea Knights, also flies a variety of secondary missions on Guam, including SAR, medical evacuation, VIP transport, and support of local police agencies.

HC-6 and HC-8 at NAS Norfolk support Atlantic Fleet ships, with the latter squadron providing UH-46 helicopters to the MCM support ship INCHON (MCS 12).

HC-9 was a reserve unit when disestablished in 1990 (see below).

Historical: The progenitor of these squadrons was VX-3, the Navy's first helicopter squadron, established in 1947.[22] The following year, on 1 April 1948, VX-3 was split into helicopter utility squadrons HU-1 and HU-2, on the East and West Coasts, respectively. All helicopter utility squadrons (HU) were changed to combat support squadrons (HC) on 1 July 1965.

2 HELICOPTER MINE COUNTERMEASURES SQUADRONS

Squadron	Code	Aircraft	Name/Notes
HM-12	DH	CH/MH-53E	disestablished 30 Sep 1994
HM-14	BJ	MH-53E	Vanguard
HM-15	TB	MH-53E	Blackhawks

HM-14 at NAS Norfolk and HM-15 at NAS Corpus Christi, Texas, are Airborne Mine Countermeasures (AMCM) squadrons, comprised of active and reserve personnel. Originally HM-14 and HM-16 were established in 1978 for operational deployments, but HM-16 subsequently was disestablished and HM-15 established at NAS Alameda, Calif., for Pacific operations. (A four-helicopter detachment from HM-15 previously was deployed to Cubi Point in the Philippines until U.S. forces withdrew from that country.)

Both MCM squadrons are assigned to Helicopter Tactical Wing Atlantic Fleet.

Squadron HM-12 at Norfolk provided AMCM readiness training until disestablished in 1994. AMCM flight training is now provided by Marine HMT-302 at MCAS New River, N.C.

Reserve HM-18 and HM-19 have been disestablished and their aircraft and personnel were merged with HM-14 and HM-15 on 1 March 1995 and 5 November 1994, respectively. This was the first complete merger of active and reserve aviation squadrons in the U.S. Navy.

Historical: The Navy used helicopters for mine-spotting in the Korean War (1950–1953), and beginning in September 1966 squadrons HC-6 and HC-7 provided RH-3A Sea King detachments for mine countermeasures operations. Those helicopters flew from the MCM support ships CATSKILL (MCS 1) and OZARK (MCS 2).

HM-12 was established on 1 April 1971 as the world's first helicopter mine countermeasures squadron. Initially flying Navy and Marine CH-53A Sea Stallions and then the specialized RH-53D, HM-12 operated off North Vietnam in 1972 (Operation End Sweep), at the northern end of the Suez Canal in 1974 (Nimbus Star) and again in 1975 (Nimbus Stream), and in the Red Sea in 1984. These squadrons flew MH-53E helicopters in the Persian Gulf area in the late 1980s (escorting Kuwaiti merchant ships) and in Operation Desert Storm and the subsequent mine cleanup.

Manning: HM-14 and HM-15 each are manned by 36 officers and 506 enlisted personnel.

---

22. During World War II, the Coast Guard undertook helicopter development for the Navy.

A U.S. Air Force EC-18B being used by Navy squadron VQ-7 to train E-6B TACAMO pilots. The EC-18B is a Boeing 707-320 series aircraft extensively modified for tracking, recording, and retransmitting telemetry signals. The Air Force's 452d Flight Test Squadron flies EC-135E and EC-18B aircraft in that role. (U.S. Air Force)

11 HELICOPTER ANTI-SUBMARINE SQUADRONS

Squadron	Aircraft	Name/Notes
HS-1	SH-3G/H, SH-60F	disestablished 30 June 1997
HS-2	SH-60F, HH-60H	Golden Falcons
HS-3	SH-60F, HH-60H	Tridents
HS-4	SH-60F, HH-60H	Black Knights
HS-5	SH-60F, HH-60H	Night Dippers
HS-6	SH-60F, HH-60H	Indians
HS-7	SH-60F, HH-60H	Dusty Dogs and Shamrocks
HS-8	SH-60F, HH-60H	Eight Ballers
HS-9	SH-3H	disestablished 30 April 1993
HS-10	SH-60F, HH-60H	Warhawks (RA)
HS-11	SH-60F, HH-60H	Dragonslayers
HS-12	SH-3H	disestablished 30 Nov 1994
HS-14	SH-60F, HH-60H	Chargers
HS-15	SH-60F, HH-60H	Red Lions
HS-17	SH-3H	disestablished 30 June 1991

Helicopter ASW squadrons are assigned to all carrier air wings, with each of the ten carrier squadrons flying four SH-60F Seahawks and two HH-60H combat SAR variants. The squadrons provide combat search and rescue, vertical replenishment, passenger transfer, and support to special operations as well as ASW.

Atlantic squadrons are based at NAS Jacksonville under Helicopter Anti-Submarine Wing Atlantic Fleet; Pacific units are at NAS North Island under Helicopter Anti-Submarine Wing Pacific Fleet, except that HS-14 is at NAF Atsugi.

HS-10 has consolidated all SH-60/HH-60 readiness/transition training for the Navy.

Note that HS-8 and HT-8 have the same name. HS-7 uses *two* names.

Historical: Previously, HS units flew the SH-3H Sea King; HS-7 made the last SH-3H deployment, aboard the EISENHOWER in early 1995. The first fleet squadron to receive the SH-60F was HS-2, taking delivery in March 1990; beginning with HS-6 in September 1990, these squadrons were additionally provided with two HH-60H combat SAR helicopters.

The Navy's first helicopter ASW squadron was HS-1, established on 3 October 1951, flying the Sikorsky HO4S-1 helicopter.

Manning: HS squadrons have 23 officers and 157 enlisted personnel.

12 LIGHT HELICOPTER ANTI-SUBMARINE SQUADRONS

Squadron	Code	Aircraft	Name/Notes
HSL-30	HT	SH-2F	disestablished 30 Sep 1993
HSL-31	TD	SH-2F	disestablished 31 July 1992
HSL-32	HV	SH-2F	disestablished 31 Jan 1994
HSL-33	TF	SH-2F	disestablished 29 Apr 1994
HSL-34	HX	SH-2F	disestablished 30 Nov 1993
HSL-35	TG	SH-2F	disestablished 4 Dec 1992
HSL-36	HY	SH-2F	disestablished 30 Sep 1992
HSL-37	TH	SH-60B	Easy Riders
HSL-40	HK	SH-60B	Airwolves
HSL-41	TS	SH-60B	Seahawks
HSL-42	HN	SH-60B	Proud Warriors
HSL-43	TT	SH-60B	Battlecats
HSL-44	HP	SH-60B	Swamp Foxes
HSL-45	TE	SH-60B	Wolfpack
HSL-46	HQ	SH-60B	Grand Masters
HSL-47	TY	SH-60B	Saberhawks
HSL-48	HR	SH-60B	Vipers
HSL-49	TX	SH-60B	Scorpions
HSL-51	TA	SH-60B, UH-3H	Warlords

The HSL squadrons provide detachments of two ASW helicopters for deployments aboard cruisers, destroyers, and frigates. Each operational squadron has 10 to 13 aircraft. HSL-51 operates UH-3H helicopters to support the Commander Seventh Fleet. HSL-40 and HSL-41 are fleet readiness squadrons.

Atlantic squadrons are based at NS Mayport, Fla., under Helicopter Anti-Submarine Wing Light Atlantic Fleet; Pacific units are at NAS North Island under Helicopter Anti-Submarine Wing Light Pacific Fleet, except that HSL-51 is at NAF Atsugi. HSL-51 was established in October 1991 to operate helicopters from Japan-based ships.

The seven squadrons flying the SH-2F Seasprite have been disbanded; those aircraft flew from active frigates of the KNOX (FF 1052) class and a few cruisers and destroyers. (Reserve HSL-60 now provides helicopters for reserve frigates of the OLIVER HAZARD PERRY/ FFG 7 class.)

Historical: The first Seahawk squadron was HSL-41, established on 21 January 1983 at NAS North Island as the SH-60B readiness training squadron; the first SH-60B fleet squadrons were established the following year.

The first SH-2D LAMPS were assigned to helicopter combat support squadrons HC-4 and HC-5, which were redesignated HSL-30 and HSL-31, respectively, on 1 March 1972. The last SH-2F deployment was from HSL-33 in 1994.

Manning: Most HSL squadrons have 40 officers and 136 enlisted personnel.

An MH-53E Sea Dragon from HM-15 operates from the mine countermeasures support ship INCHON (MCS 12). These large helicopters dwarf the INCHON, the last of the helicopter carriers of the IWO JIMA (LPH 2) class. (U.S. Navy)

NAVAL AIR STATIONS/NAVAL AVIATION SUPPORT ACTIVITIES

Code	Aircraft	Activity
A	HH-1N	NAS Meridian, Miss.
F	UC-12B, UH-3H	NAS Pensacola, Fla.
G	UC-12B, HH-1N	NAS Corpus Christi, Texas
6M	UC-12B	Naval Support Activity Memphis, Tenn.
7A	UC-12B, UH-3H	NAS Patuxent River, Md.
7C	UC-12B/M	NAS Norfolk, Va.
7E	UC-12B	NAS Jacksonville, Fla.
7F	HH-1N	NAS Brunswick, Maine
7G	UC-12B, UH-3H	NAS Whidbey Island, Wash.
7H	UC-12B, HH-1N	NAS Fallon, Nev.
7M	UC-12B	NAS North Island, Calif.
7Q	UC-12B, UH-3H	NAS Key West, Fla.
7R	UH-3H	NAS Oceana, Va.
7S	UC-12B, HH-1N	NAS Lemoore, Calif.
8A	UC-12F	NAF Atsugi, Japan
8C	UC-12M, VP-3A	NAS Sigonella, Sicily
8D	UC-12M	NS Rota, Spain
8E	RC-12M	NS Roosevelt Roads, P.R.
8F	UC-12B, HH-1N	NS Guantánamo, Cuba
8G	UC-12M	NAF Mildenhall, England
8H	UC-12F	NAF Kadena, Okinawa
8M	UC-12F	NAF Misawa, Japan
8N	UC-12B	NAF El Centro, Calif.
8U	(none)	NS Mayport, Fla.
(none)	C-26D	Naval Support Activity Naples, Italy
(none)	UC-12B	Administrative Support Unit Bahrain

These are utility and light transport aircraft assigned to the bases and helicopters assigned to the activities indicated above.

NAVAL AIR WARFARE CENTER

Squadron	Aircraft
Naval Force Warfare Aircraft Test Squadron	E-2C, C-2A, KC-130F, NC-130H, P-3C, UP-3A, NP-3C/D, S-3B, T-34C, NT-34C
Naval Strike Aircraft Test Squadron	EA-6B, F-14A, NF-14A/D, F/A-18A/B/C, NF/A-18A/C/D
Naval Rotary-Wing Aircraft Test Squadron	AH-1W, UH-1N, NVH-3A, CH-46E, CH-53E, TH-57C, SH-60B/F, NSH-60B, HH-60H, YSH-60F
Naval Test Pilot School	F/A-18B, NP-3D, T-2C, T-38A, NU-1B, U-6A, C-12C, TH-6B, OH-58C, UH-60A, NSH-60B, X-26A

These commands are subordinate to the Naval Air Warfare Center and the center's Aircraft Division at NAS Patuxent River. The three test squadrons were established on 21 July 1995.

NAVAL AIR WARFARE CENTER

Squadron	Aircraft
Naval Weapons Test Squadron China Lake	F-14A, F/A-18A/C/D, NF/A-18D, AV-8B, NAV-8B,TAV-8B, T-39D, AH-1W, HH-1N
Naval Weapons Test Squadron Point Mugu	YF-4J, QF-4N/S, NF-14A/B/D, NP-3D

These squadrons are under the Naval Air Warfare Center's Weapons Division. The squadrons are based at NAS China Lake and NAS Point Mugu. Both squadrons were established on 8 May 1995.

NAVAL COASTAL SYSTEMS CENTER

Squadron	Aircraft
(none)	HH-1N, MH-53E

The Naval Coastal Systems Center at Panama City, Fla., is responsible for the development of mine countermeasures systems.

NAVAL AIR RESERVE

The Naval Air Reserve operates approximately 235 aircraft. These are organized primarily into one carrier air wing, eight maritime patrol squadrons, and several helicopter and transport squadrons. All air reserve units are assigned to the Naval Air Reserve Force based at New Orleans, La. The major air reserve subordinate commands are the Reserve Patrol Wing (NAS Norfolk), which controls the VP squadrons; the Reserve Helicopter Wing (NAS North Island), which directs the HCS, HSL, and HS squadrons; and the Reserve Fleet Logistics Support Wing (NAS Fort Worth, Texas), which controls the VR squadrons.

Squadrons within the reserve carrier air wing are designated in sequence based on the wing designation, except for the AEW squadron. Non-carrier air wing squadrons have designations in the standard Navy squadron numerical series. The VF and VFA squadrons are normally assigned 12 aircraft each, the VAQ and VAW squadrons four each. There are no fixed-wing ASW aircraft (S-3 Vikings) assigned to the wing; an SH-3 Sea King squadron could provide ASW helicopters for the wing.

One reserve helicopter anti-submarine squadron flies SH-60B LAMPS III helicopters, which operate from Naval Reserve Force (NRF) frigates. Three reserve HAL/HC squadrons have been merged to form two combat support squadrons (HCS).

TABLE 26-5. RESERVE CARRIER AIR WINGS

Wing	Code	Squadron	Aircraft	Name	Base/Notes
CVWR-20	AF	VFA-201	F/A-18A	Hunters	NAS Fort Worth, Texas
		VF-202	F-14A	Superheats	disestablished 31 Dec 1994
		VFA-203	F/A-18A	Blue Dolphins	NAS Fort Worth, Texas
		VFA-204	F/A-18A	River Rattlers	NAS New Orleans, La.
		VA-205	A-6E, KA-6D	Green Falcons	disestablished 31 Dec 1994
		VAQ-209	EA-6B	Star Warriors	NAF Washington, D.C.
		VAW-77	E-2C	Night Wolves	NAS Atlanta, Ga.
		VAW-78	E-2C	Fighting Escargots	NAS Norfolk, Va.
		VFC-12	F/A-18A/B	Fighting Omars	NAS Oceana, Va.
		VFC-13	F-5E/F	Saints	NAS Fallon, Nev.
CVWR-30	ND				disestablished 31 Dec 1994
		VF-301	F-14A	Flying Infernos	disestablished 31 Dec 1994
		VF-302	F-14A	Stallions	disestablished 31 Dec 1994
		VFA-303	F/A-18	Golden Hawks	disestablished 31 Dec 1994
		VA-304	A-6E, KA-6D	Firebirds	disestablished 31 Dec 1994
		VFA-305	F/A-18	Lobos	disestablished 31 Dec 1994
		VAQ-309	EA-6B	Axemen	disestablished 31 Dec 1994
		VAW-88	E-2C	Cornpickers	disestablished 31 Dec 1994

One reserve carrier air wing now exists. The second was a casualty of the end of the Cold War. Note that non-carrier squadrons VFC-12 and VFC-13 are assigned to the wing.

Historical: The two reserve carrier air wings (CVWR) were established on 1 April 1970.

ATTACK SQUADRONS

All reserve VA squadrons have been disestablished. Six reserve VA squadrons—three per wing—flew the A-7E; the last was VA-204, which became VFA-204 on 1 May 1991. Two squadrons (VA-205 and VA-304) traded in their Hornets for A-6E and KA-6D Intruders; the four others shifted to F/A-18 Hornets (see below). Earlier, all six squadrons flew the trouble-plagued A-7B model, and before that the A-4 Skyhawk. KA-6D tankers were assigned to these units to replace the KA-3B Skywarrior in the inflight refueling role.

FIGHTER SQUADRONS

Four reserve fighter squadrons shifted to the F-14A Tomcat in the 1980s, which replaced the F-4 Phantom. The last naval squadron to fly the Phantom was VF-202, which transitioned from the F-4S to the F-14A in early 1987.[23] All reserve fighter squadrons have been disbanded.

3 STRIKE FIGHTER SQUADRONS

The F/A-18 Hornet replaced the A-7E Corsair in four attack squadrons, which became VFA. VA-303 became the first Naval Reserve squadron to fly the F/A-18 Hornet, acquiring its first aircraft in 1985. The two F/A-18 squadrons assigned to CVWR-30 have been disestablished.

2 FIGHTER COMPOSITE SQUADRONS

The two reserve composite fighter squadrons—VFC-12 and VFC-13—are assigned to CVWR-20. They provide air combat maneuver training for reserve and active fighter and attack squadrons. Both squadrons previously flew A-4F Skyhawks; they switched to F/A-18s in 1992–1993, and VFC-13 subsequently shifted to the nimble F-5E/F Tigers to simulate MiG-type fighter aircraft.

Prior to being assigned to CVWR-20, the squadrons were assigned tail codes AF and UX, respectively.

Designation: These squadrons were previously designated VC-12 and VC-13, respectively; they were changed to VFC on 22 April 1988 to reflect their emphasis on adversary training.

An SH-60F Seahawk unloads cargo on the carrier GEORGE WASHINGTON during a vertical replenishment operation with the fast combat support ship SUPPLY (AOE 8). The SH-60 Seahawks are employed in a variety of roles in addition to ASW. (U.S. Navy, AN Scott Campbell)

---

23. The Phantom flew in the Marine air reserve into 1992.

Figure 26-3

Naval Air Reserve Force

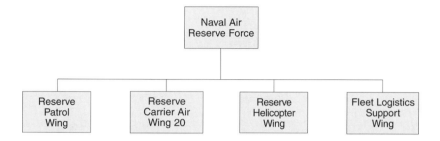

```
          ┌─────────────────┐
          │   Naval Air     │
          │ Reserve Force   │
          └────────┬────────┘
     ┌─────────┬───┴────┬──────────┐
┌────────┐ ┌────────┐ ┌────────┐ ┌──────────┐
│ Reserve│ │ Reserve│ │ Reserve│ │   Fleet  │
│ Patrol │ │Carrier │ │Helicop.│ │ Logistics│
│  Wing  │ │Air Wing│ │  Wing  │ │  Support │
│        │ │   20   │ │        │ │   Wing   │
└────────┘ └────────┘ └────────┘ └──────────┘
```

RECONNAISSANCE SQUADRONS

The last specialized Navy reconnaissance squadron, VFP-206, flying the RF-8G Photo Crusader, was disestablished on 1 April 1987. This was a light photo-reconnaissance squadron. The unit was based at NAF Washington, D.C. Subsequently, F-14 Tomcat fighters provided a photo-reconnaissance capability with TARPS pods, but that capability has been lost with the demise of the F-14/VF units.

1 ELECTRONIC ATTACK SQUADRON

VAQ-209 and VAQ-309 were established in 1977 and 1979, respectively, to provide the reserve air wings with an organic ECM capability. The reserve VAQ squadrons flew the EA-6A Intruder until 1989 when they shifted to the more capable EA-6B Prowler.

Only VAQ-209 survives. It is additionally assigned the Navy's electronic aggressor role with the disestablishment of active squadron VAQ-33. VAQ-209 is based at NAF Washington, located at Andrews Air Force Base in a nearby Maryland suburb.

2 AIRBORNE EARLY WARNING SQUADRONS

The first E-2C variant of the Hawkeye to be flown by the reserves was assigned to VAW-78 in 1983; VAW-88 began receiving the E-2C in 1986. VAW-88 was later disestablished, and VAW-77 was established on 1 October 1995. Both VAW-77 and VAW-78 have assisted in U.S. drug enforcement surveillance efforts, as have active Navy AEW squadrons. VAW-77 is considered a land-based squadron although assigned to CVWR-20 (it uses the tail code AF).

Designation: Note that VAW-78 and VAW-88, both established in 1970, were not numbered in the standard CVWR designation scheme.

Mechanics from HS-14 check their SH-60 Seahawk helicopters aboard the carrier KITTY HAWK. Although hangar decks provide a protective environment for aircraft maintenance, the large number of aircraft embarked in U.S. carriers requires work also be performed on the flight deck. (U.S. Navy, PHAN Mara McCleaft)

7 PATROL SQUADRONS

Squadron	Code	Aircraft	Name	Location/Notes
VP-60	LS	P-3B	Cobras	disestablished 1 Sep 1994
VP-62	LT	P-3C	Broad Arrows	NAS Jacksonville, Fla.
VP-64	LU	P-3C	Condors	NAS Willow Grove, Pa.
VP-65	PG	P-3C	Tridents	NAS Point Mugu, Calif.
VP-66	LV	P-3C	Liberty Bells	NAS Willow Grove, Pa.
VP-67	PL	P-3B	Golden Hawks	disestablished 30 Sep 1994
VP-68	LW	P-3C	Black Hawks	disestablished 31 Dec 1996
VP-69	PJ	P-3C	Totems	NAS Whidbey Island, Wash.
VP-90	LX	P-3B	Lions	disestablished 30 Sep 1994
VP-91	PM	P-3C	Black Cats	disestablished 1 Apr 1999
VP-92	LY	P-3C	Minutemen	NAS Brunswick, Maine
VP-93	LH	P-3B	Executioners	disestablished 30 Sep 1994
VP-94	LZ	P-3C	Crawfish	NAS New Orleans, La.

These squadrons each fly six Orion patrol aircraft (down from nine). The reserve P-3s regularly supplement active squadrons in U.S. and overseas operational deployments. The reserve VP strength has been reduced from its long-standing Cold War strength of 13 squadrons to seven.

All remaining squadrons fly the P-3C variant; the first to transition to the P-3C from the P-3B was VP-62. The last reserve-flown P-3A was retired by VP-69 in October 1990. VP-67 was the last squadron to fly the SP-2H Neptune, completing transition to the Orion in 1979.

VP-66 received the two EP-3J aircraft previously flown by VAQ-33 in 1993. They were then transferred to VQ-11, an active squadron.

Two VP master Augmentation Units (VP-MAU) were based at NAS Brunswick (code LB) and NAS Moffett Field (code PS). These units—with P-3C, UP-3A, and TP-3A Orions—trained crews to augment fleet VP squadrons and often operated detachments overseas, with VP-MAU Moffett Field operating one aircraft and crew in Desert Storm. The two units were disestablished on 30 June 1991 and 30 September 1991, respectively.

14 FLEET LOGISTICS SUPPORT SQUADRONS

Squadron	Code	Aircraft	Name	Location/Notes
VR-1	JK	2 C-20D, 1 CT-39	Starlifters	NAF Washington. D.C.; established 1 May 1997
VR-46	JS	3 C-9B, DC-9	Peach Airlines	NAS Atlanta, Ga.
VR-48	JR	2 C-20G	Capital Skyliners	NAF Washington, D.C.
VR-51	RV	C-9B	Flaming Hookers	disestablished 30 Sep 1994
VR-51	RG	2 C-20G	Windjammers	MCAF Kaneohe, Hawaii; established 1 June 1997
VR-52	JT	4 DC-9	Taskmasters	NAS Willow Grove, Pa.
VR-53	WV	4 C-130T	Capital Express	NAF Washington, D.C.; established 1 Oct 1993
VR-54	CW	4 C-130T	Revelers	NAS New Orleans, La.; established 1 June 1991
VR-55	RU	4 C-130T	Bicentennial Minuteman	NAS Point Mugu, Calif.
VR-56	JU	4 C-9B	Globemasters	NAS Norfolk, Va.
VR-57	RX	4 C-9B, DC-9	Conquistadors	NAS North Island, Calif.
VR-58	JV	4 C-9B	Sun Seekers	NAS Jacksonville, Fla.
VR-59	RY	4 C-9B, DC-9	Lone Star Express	NAS Fort Worth, Texas
VR-60	RT	DC-9	Volunteer Express	disestablished 1 Apr 1995
VR-61	RS	4 DC-9	Islanders	NAS Whidbey Island, Wash.
VR-62	JW	2 C-130T	Downeasters	NAF Brunswick, Maine

These squadrons provide transport support for active and reserve Navy activities within the United States and, on a limited basis, overseas. Reserve VR squadrons report to Fleet Logistics Support Wing, NAS Dallas.

The C-9B Skytrain and the similar (commercial) DC-9 provide long-range logistics support for naval activities; four squadrons fly the C-130T Hercules, the only Navy squadrons with that aircraft except for test and evaluation squadrons and the Blue Angels. VR-1 and VR-48 in the nation's capital provide C-20 Gulfstreams for VIP flights. These squadrons have multiple crews for their aircraft; VR aircraft totals are indicated above because the numbers assigned to each squadron vary.

Historical: VR-48 previously flew the C-131H Samaritan, the last one being retired in mid-1990.

Names: VR-62 was nicknamed "Motowners" while based at NAS Detroit, Ill., and then "Mass Transit" while at NAS South Weymouth, Mass., before moving to NAS Brunswick.

1 HELICOPTER COMBAT SUPPORT SQUADRON

Squadron	Code	Aircraft	Location/Notes
HC-9	NW	HH-3A	disestablished 31 July 1990
HC-85	NW	UH-3H	NAS North Island, Calif.

HC-85 operates utility helicopters. Previously designated HS-85, the squadron moved from Alameda to North Island in 1994 to replace squadron HC-1 providing target/torpedo recovery off San Clemente Island. The squadron received Sea Kings specially modified for recovery operations and was redesignated HC-85 on 1 October 1994. The squadron is assigned to the Reserve Helicopter Wing.

HC-9 was the Navy's only active combat SAR unit, flying armed and armored HH-3A Sea Kings. Established in 1975, the squadron was disestablished on 31 July 1990, with its mission passing to two reserve squadrons, HCS-4 and HCS-5.

Note that all reserve helicopter squadrons have the code letter NW.

Designation: HC-9 was numbered in the standard (active) Navy HC designation series.

2 HELICOPTER COMBAT SAR/SPECIAL WARFARE SUPPORT SQUADRONS

Squadron	Code	Aircraft	Name	Location
HCS-4	NW	HH-60H	Red Wolves	NAS Norfolk, Va.
HCS-5	NW	HH-60H	Firehawks	NAS Point Mugu, Calif.

These squadrons were established in 1989 to provide combat SAR and special warfare support for active and reserve operations. Each squadron flies eight HH-60H Seahawk helicopters. During Desert Shield/Desert Storm in 1990–1991, these two squadrons deployed HH-60H helicopters as a joint unit into Saudi Arabia for combat SAR operations.

The HH-60H is the Navy's only dedicated combat SAR helicopter; it is also integrated into active HS anti-submarine squadrons. (The Coast Guard flies the HH-60J SAR-configured version of the Blackhawk/Seahawk helicopter.)

The HCS squadrons took over the functions of reserve helicopter light attack squadrons HAL-4 and HAL-5, which flew the HH-1K Huey in support of riverine and special operations, and of helicopter composite squadron HC-9, which flew the HH-3A in the combat SAR role. The reserve HALs also had anti-terrorist support roles, working with SEAL units.

Historical: HAL-4 and HAL-5 were established in 1976–1977 as helicopter gunship units. The Navy's only active gunship unit was HAL-3, established in 1967 and disestablished in 1972 after extensive service in Vietnam. HCS-4 was established with HAL-4 personnel and aircraft when the latter squadron was disestablished on 1 October 1989.

HELICOPTER MINE COUNTERMEASURES SQUADRONS

Squadron	Code	Aircraft	Notes
HM-18	NW	RH-53D/MH-53E	disestablished 4 Mar 1995
HM-19	NW	RH-53D/MH-53E	disestablished 5 Nov 1994

Reserve mine countermeasures squadron HM-18 was established in 1986 and HM-19 in 1989. They initially flew the RH-53D Sea Stallion helicopter and were transitioning to the MH-53E Sea Dragon when the decision was made to merge them with active MCM squadrons HM-14 and HM-15, respectively.

1 HELICOPTER ANTI-SUBMARINE SQUADRON

Squadron	Code	Aircraft	Name	Location/Notes
HS-75	NW	SH-60F, HH-60H	Emerald Knights	NAS Jacksonville, Fla.
HS-85	NW	SH-3H		changed to HC-85

HS-75 flies ASW and combat SAR helicopters capable of operating from carriers with the reserve carrier air wing.

1 LIGHT HELICOPTER ANTI-SUBMARINE SQUADRON

Squadron	Code	Aircraft	Name	Location/Notes
HSL-60	NW	SH-60B		NS Mayport, Fla.
HSL-74	NW	SH-2F		disestablished 1 Apr 1994
HSL-84	NW	SH-2G	Thunderbolts	disestablished 2000
HSL-94	NW	SH-2G	Titans	disestablished 2000

Three helicopter squadrons flying the SH-2F/G LAMPS I have been closed down in favor of a new squadron flying the SH-60B LAMPS III from NRF frigates. The new squadron is based at NS Mayport, Fla. The HSL-60 designation is based on the helicopter designation.

The three disestablished squadrons previously were designated HS and flew the SH-3G Sea King. HS-74 transitioned to HSL for LAMPS operations on 1 January 1985, HS-84 on 1 March 1984, and HS-94 on 1 October 1985.

HSL-94 helicopters were fitted with the Magic Lantern laser mine-detection system beginning in December 1996. With the demise of the squadron, the Magic Lantern will be carried by MH-53E mine countermeasures helicopters.

CHIEF OF NAVAL AIR RESERVE

The Chief of Naval Air Reserve has several aircraft assigned, which are based at various air stations.

Code	Aircraft	Activity
7B	UC-12B	NAS Atlanta, Ga.
7D	UC-12B	NAS Fort Worth, Texas
7N	UC-12B	NAF Washington, D.C.
7W	UC-12B	NAS Willow Grove, Pa.
7X	UC-12B	NAS New Orleans, La.

MARINE AVIATION

The U.S. Marine Corps currently operates about 950 aircraft in three active aircraft wings, plus almost 200 aircraft in a reserve wing. It is the only marine force in the world with a major air arm.[24]

During the 1990s Marine aviation completed a major force upgrade, with the advanced AV-8B Harrier replacing the earlier AV-8A/C Short Take-Off/Vertical Landing (STOVL) aircraft, and variants of the F/A-18 Hornet strike fighter replacing all A-4 Skyhawk, A-6 Intruder, and RF-4 and F-4 Phantom aircraft.[25] The F/A-18 has become the most numerous fixed-wing aircraft in the Marine Corps, as it has in the Navy. However, the Marines fly the two-seat F/A-18D variant, a type so far eschewed by the Navy.

The Marine Corps is now acquiring the long-delayed MV-22 Osprey tilt-rotor STOVL aircraft (which can land and take off only in a vertical mode).

In the longer term, the Marine Corps will be a key participant in the Joint Strike Fighter (JSF) program, which is now the Marine Commandant's number-one procurement priority. The STOVL variant of the JSF will replace the AV-8B and is also

planned for acquisition by the Royal Navy to replace its carrier-based Harriers.

Operational: Marine aviation had a major role in the Gulf War during January–February 1991, with most Marine aircraft flying from shore bases in Saudi Arabia. Marine aircraft also took part in enforcement of the "no fly" zones over northern and southern Iraq and in the air campaign against Serbia and Serbian forces in Kosovo in 1999.

ORGANIZATION

Marine Aviation is under the Deputy Chief of Staff for Aviation, a lieutenant general at Marine Corps Headquarters.

The Marine Aircraft Wing (MAW) is the principal Marine aviation command. The wings vary in size and composition. An active wing has a theoretical strength of 325 aircraft of all types; however, only the 2nd and 3rd MAWs actually have full aircraft assignments.

The 1st MAW is based at Iwakuni, Japan, and Futenma, Okinawa, with most of its aircraft provided on six-month rotation from the other aviation commands, including the newly established 1st MAW Aviation Support Element (Kaneohe Bay), formerly MAG-24, at MCAF Kaneohe Bay, Hawaii. Wing headquarters is at Camp Butler (Futenma), Japan.

The 2nd MAW, with headquarters at Cherry Point, N.C., has aircraft squadrons based on the East Coast, while the 3rd MAW, with headquarters at MCAS Miramar, Calif., has its squadrons on the West Coast and at Yuma, Ariz.

In addition to aircraft groups, a Marine aircraft wing contains:

- *Marine Wing Headquarters Squadron:* Provides command, administration, and camp facilities for the wing headquarters.
- *Marine Air Control Group:* Provides communications, air control, and air support squadrons for the operation of the wing; it also contains a low-altitude air defense battalion (with 90 Stinger missile teams). The air support squadron provides control and coordination for aircraft operating in direct support of Marine ground forces.
- *Marine Wing Support Group:* Provides fixed-wing and helicopter maintenance, as well as mess, medical, supply, transportation, weather, and airfield services for the wing's components.

An aircraft wing is generally paired with a reinforced division to form a Marine Expeditionary Force (MEF), an aircraft group with a reinforced regiment to form a Marine Expeditionary Brigade (MEB), and a composite squadron with a reinforced battalion to form a Marine Expeditionary Unit (MEU); see chapter 7.

Marine aviation units—like ground units—have Navy chaplain, medical, and dental personnel assigned.

Unlike Navy aircraft wings, in which the principal subordinate command is the squadron, the Marine aircraft wings have several groups, as shown in figure 26-4, which depicts a notional Marine aircraft wing with five aircraft groups. The Marine aircraft groups each control specific aircraft squadron types, i.e., fighter and attack, and helicopters (see figures 26-5 and 26-6). Several aircraft are attached to wing headquarters and support squadrons.

A composite squadron generally consists of 4 CH-53, 12 CH-46, 4 AH-1, and 2 UH-1N helicopters deployed aboard an LHA/LHD and accompanying amphibious ships. Additionally, AV-8B Harriers may be assigned to the squadron, depending upon mission and aircraft and ship availability.

UNIT DESIGNATIONS

The Marine Corps uses the standard naval squadron designation scheme, except that the second letter *M* is used to indicate Marine aviation squadrons; the suffix *T* indicates Marine readiness-transition squadrons.

---

24. Britain's Royal Marines fly helicopters and light fixed-wing aircraft, while Russia's Naval Infantry has some helicopters assigned.
25. The term VSTOL—for Vertical/Short Take-Off and Landing—was used by the Marine Corps until early 1995, when the less accurate term STOVL was adopted by Headquarters, Marine Corps.

Figure 26-4

Notional Marine Aircraft Wing

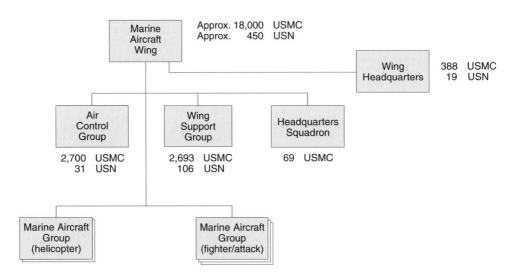

Figure 26-5

Notional Marine Aircraft Group

(Fighter/Attack)

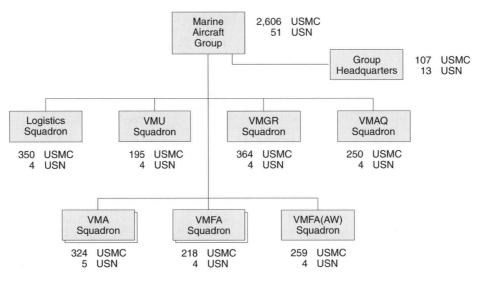

Figure 26-6

Notional Marine Aircraft Group

(Helicopter)

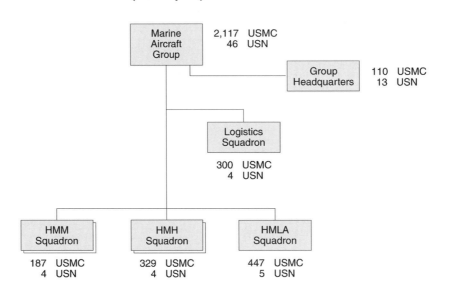

TABLE 26-6. MARINE AIRCRAFT WINGS

Marine Aircraft Wing/Group	Squadron	Aircraft
1st MARINE AIRCRAFT WING		
MAG-12 (Iwakuni, Japan)	VMA	(from 3rd MAW)[a]
	VMAQ	(from 2nd MAW)[a]
	VMFA	(from 2nd MAW)[a]
	VMFA	(from 3rd MAW)[a]
	VMFA(AW)	(from 3rd MAW)[a]
	VMFA-212	F/A-18C
MAG-36 (Futenma, Japan)	HMH	(from 3rd MAW)[a]
	HMLA	(from 3rd MAW)[a]
	VMGR-152	KC-130F
	HMM-262	CH-46E
	HMM-265	CH-46E
1st MAW Aviation Support		
Element (Kaneohe)[b]	HMH-362	CH-53D
	HMH-363	CH-53D
	HMH-463	CH-53D
	HMT-301	CH-53D
2nd MARINE AIRCRAFT WING		
MAG-14 (Cherry Point, N.C.)	VMAQ-1	EA-6B
	VMAQ-2	EA-6B
	VMAQ-3	EA-6B
	VMAQ-4	EA-6B
	VMAT-203	AV-8B, TAV-8B
	VMA-223	AV-8B
	VMA-231	AV-8B
	VMGR-252	KC-130F/R
	VMGRT-253	KC-130F
	VMA-542	AV-8B
	VMU-2	(UAVs)
MAG-26 (New River, N.C.)	HMM-162	CH-46E
	HMM-263	CH-46E
	HMLA-269	AH-1W, UH-1N
	HMT-302	CH-53E, MH-53E
	HMM-365	CH-46E
	HMH-464	CH-53E
MAG-29 (New River, N.C.)	HMLA-167	AH-1W, UH-1N
	VMMT-204	MV-22
	HMM-261	CH-46E
	HMM-264	CH-46E
	HMM-266	CH-46E
	HMH-461	CH-53E
MAG-31 (Beaufort, S.C.)	VMFA-115	F/A-18A
	VMFA-122	F/A-18A
	VMFA(AW)-224	F/A-18D
	VMFA-251	F/A-18C
	VMFA-312	F/A-18C
	VMFA(AW)-332	F/A-18D
	VMFA(AW)-533	F/A-18D
3rd MARINE AIRCRAFT WING		
MAG-11 (Miramar, Calif.)	VMFAT-101	F/A-18A/B/C/D
	VMFA(AW)-121	F/A-18D
	VMFA(AW)-225	F/A-18D
	VMFA-232	F/A-18C
	VMFA(AW)-242	F/A-18D
	VMFA-314	F/A-18C
	VMFA-323	F/A-18C
	VMGR-352	KC-130F/R
MAG-13 (Yuma, Ariz.)	VMA-211	AV-8B
	VMA-214	AV-8B
	VMA-311	AV-8B
	VMA-513	AV-8B
	VMU-1	(UAVs)
MAG-16 (Miramar, Calif.)[c]	HMM-161	CH-46E
	HMM-163	CH-46E
	HMM-165	CH-46E
	HMM-166	CH-46E
	HMH-361	CH-53E
	HMH-462	CH-53E
	HMH-465	CH-53E
	HMH-466	CH-53E
MAG-39 (Camp Pendleton, Calif.)	HMLA-169	AH-1W, UH-1N
	HMLA-267	AH-1W, UH-1N
	HMM-164	CH-46E
	HMM-268	CH-46E
	HMM-364	CH-46E
	HMT-303	AH-1W, UH-1N
	HMLA-367	AH-1W, UH-1N
	HMLA-369	AH-1W, UH-1N

[a] Aircraft units rotated from 2nd and 3rd MAWs.
[b] MAG-24 was changed to 1st Marine Aircraft Wing Aviation Support Element Kaneohe Bay on 30 September 1994. Its fixed-wing tactical squadrons were reassigned to other MAGs.
[c] Formerly at MCAS Tustin, Calif., which was closed in 1999.

8 MARINE ATTACK SQUADRONS

Squadron	Code	Aircraft	Name/Notes
VMAT-203	KD	AV-8B/TAV-8B	Hawks
VMA-211	CF	AV-8B	Wake Island Avengers
VMA-214	WE	AV-8B	Black Sheep
VMA-223	WP	AV-8B	Bulldogs
VMA(AW)-224	WK	A-6E	changed to VMFA(AW)-224
VMA-231	CG	AV-8B	Ace of Spades
VMA(AW)-242	DT	A-6E	to VMFA(AW)-242 14 Dec 1990
VMA-311	WL	AV-8B	Tomcats
VMA-331	VL	AV-8B	deactivated 30 Sep 1992
VMA(AW)-332	EA	A-6E	to VMFA(AW)-332 16 June 1993
VMA-513	WF	AV-8B	Flying Nightmares
VMA(AW)-533	ED	A-6E	to VMFA(AW)-533 1 Oct 1992
VMA-542	CR	AV-8B	Flying Tigers

Marine attack squadrons have been reduced to eight units, including a readiness squadron (VMAT-203), all flying the AV-8B Harrier. They converted from the A-4 Skyhawk and A-6 Intruder; other squadrons that flew those two aircraft have been deactivated or converted to the F/A-18 Hornet.

Harrier squadrons initially had 15 aircraft; all were subsequently increased to 20, by now reduced while Harriers are being "remanufactured."

Historical: VMA-513 was the first operational Harrier squadron, with AV-8A deliveries beginning in April 1971; all AV-8A/C models of the Harrier have been retired. VMA-331 was the first AV-8B squadron, established at Cherry Point on 30 January 1985.

The A-6 was flown by the Marines from 1964 until 20 October 1993, when VMA(AW)-332 retired its last A-6E. (Six squadrons plus VMAT-202 had flown the Intruder.)

The A-4 was flown by the Marines from 1957 until 1992.

4 MARINE ELECTRONIC ATTACK SQUADRONS

Squadron	Code	Aircraft	Name
VMAQ-1	CB	EA-6B	Screaming Banshees
VMAQ-2	CY	EA-6B	Panthers (see *Names* notes)
VMAQ-3	MD	EA-6B	Moon Dogs
VMAQ-4	RM	EA-6B	Seahawks

The Marine Corps formed four EW squadrons in 1992, replacing the single active duty squadron (VMAQ-2 with code CY) and the reserve squadron VMAQ-4 (RM). VMAQ-1 and VMAQ-3 were established on 1 July 1992; VMAQ-4 was deactivated as a reserve unit on 1 October 1992 and reactivated as an active unit the following day. Each of the squadrons has four EA-6B Prowlers assigned.

All four squadrons are at MCAS Cherry Point and provide aircraft or detachments to the 1st and 3rd Wings.

Historical: The Marine Corps originally operated EW and photo-reconnaissance aircraft in three composite reconnaissance squadrons (VMCJ); they were deactivated in 1975 and their aircraft allocated to VMAQ-2 and VMFP-3. VMAQ-2 flew the EA-6A Intruder and then the EA-6B Prowler, providing detachments to the aircraft wings and occasionally to Navy carrier wings.

Names: VMAQ-2 was named the "Playboys" until 1999; the name change was another example of political correctness. Also given up was the squadron's historic and well-known Playboy bunny symbol.

An AV-8B Harrier lifts off from the amphibious assault ship Essex (LHD 2). These aircraft provide a potent combat capability in limited conflict situations. (U.S. Navy, PH3 Jason A. Pylarinos)

15 MARINE FIGHTER-ATTACK SQUADRONS

Squadron	Code	Aircraft	Names/Notes
VMFAT-101	SH	F/A-18	Sharpshooters
VMFA-115	VE	F/A-18A	Silver Eagles
VMFA(AW)-121	VK	F/A-18D	Green Knights; former VMA(AW)-121
VMFA-122	DC	F/A-18A	Crusaders
VMFA-124		F/A-18A	deactivated 1 Dec 1995
VMFA-212	WD	F/A-18C	Lancers
VMFA(AW)-224	WK	F/A-18D	Bengals
VMFA(AW)-225	CE	F/A-18D	Vikings; former VMFP-3
VMFA-232	WT	F/A-18C	Red Devils
VMFA-235	DM	F/A-18C	deactivated 30 June 1996
VMFA(AW)-242	DT	F/A-18D	Bats; former VMA(AW)-242
VMFA-251	DW	F/A-18C	Thunderbolts
VMFA-312	DR	F/A-18C	Checkerboards
VMFA-314	VW	F/A-18C	Black Knights
VMFA-323	WS	F/A-18C	Death Rattlers
VMFA(AW)-332	EA	F/A-18D	Moonlighters
VMFA-333	DM	F/A-18C	deactivated 31 Mar 1992
VMFA-451	VM	F/A-18C	deactivated 31 Jan 1997
VMFA-531	EC	F/A-18C	deactivated 31 Mar 1992
VMFA(AW)-533	ED	F/A-18D	Nighthawks; former VMA(AW)-533

The F/A-18 Hornet succeeded the F-4 Phantom in Marine fighter-attack squadrons. All remaining Marine fighter squadrons have made the transition to the F/A-18 Hornet, the first being VMFA-314, which shifted to the F/A-18 in January 1983. In addition to former VMFA and VMA squadrons that now fly the F/A-18C, five A-6E (VMA[AW]) squadrons transitioned to the two-place F/A-18D variant. These planes also replaced OA-4M and TA-4F Skyhawks in the tactical air control role.

VMFA-212 is one of only two fixed-wing aircraft squadrons permanently assigned to the 1st Marine Aircraft Wing.

VMFAT-101 provides readiness training.

VMFA squadrons each have 12 aircraft.

Historical: Marine fighter squadrons flew the F-4 from 1961 to 1988. On 1 August 1962 the F-4 squadrons were changed from VMF(AW) to the current VMFA. Proposals to provide the F-14 Tomcat to at least four Marine squadrons were canceled in August 1975 at the request of the Marine Corps (freeing up funds for the procurement of the AV-8A Harrier).

MARINE PHOTO-RECONNAISSANCE SQUADRONS

The last photo-reconnaissance squadron in service with the Navy or Marine Corps was VMFP-3, which was deactivated on 1 October 1990. It was the only Navy or Marine squadron to fly the RF-4B Phantom (the U.S. Air Force and several foreign air forces flew other RF-4 variants).

VMFP-3 flew 21 of the reconnaissance-configured Phantoms. Detachments from the squadron were provided to the other wings (and to the carrier MIDWAY's air wing).

4 MARINE REFUELER-TRANSPORT SQUADRONS

Squadron	Code	Aircraft	Names/Notes
VMGR-152	QD	KC-130F	
VMGR-252	BH	KC-130F/R	Heavy Haulers
VMGR-352	QB	KC-130F/R	Raiders
VMGRT-253	GR	KC-130F	

These squadrons fly KC-130 Hercules aircraft to provide transport for ground forces and for inflight refueling. Each VMGR squadron is authorized 12 aircraft. The single Marine TC-130G "Herk" supports the Navy-Marine Blue Angels flight demonstration team.

VMGRT-253 provides readiness training.

VMGR-152 is one of only two fixed-wing aircraft squadrons permanently assigned to the 1st Marine Aircraft Wing.

1 MARINE MEDIUM-LIFT SQUADRON

Squadron	Code	Aircraft	Notes
VMMT-204	GX	MV-22	former HMT-204

This squadron is the Marine Corps's transitional training squadron for the MV-22 Osprey STOVL aircraft, successor to the CH-46 and CH-53A/D helicopters. HMT-204, previously the Marine CH-45E readiness squadron, was redesignated VMMT-204 on 10 June 1999.

MARINE OBSERVATION SQUADRONS

Squadron	Code	Aircraft	Notes
VMO-1	ER	OV-10D	deactivated 31 July 1993
VMO-2	UU	OV-10D	deactivated 31 July 1993

A Marine HMMWV is lowered to the flight deck of the amphibious assault ship SAIPAN (LHA 2) by an MV-22B Osprey during trials of the aircraft, which will replace CH-46 Sea Knight helicopters in Marine service. (U.S. Navy, PH1 Tina M. Ackerman)

The two Marine observation squadrons flew the Short Take-Off and Landing (STOL)-capable OV-10 Bronco. Unlike previous Marine observation aircraft, the Bronco could be heavily armed. Twelve aircraft were assigned to each squadron. (The Navy's lone light attack squadron, VAL-4, flew Broncos during the Vietnam War.)

The VMO mission was taken over by the F/A-18D units.

Operational: OV-10 aircraft periodically operated from LHA/LHD helicopter carriers, as well as large aircraft carriers. (They were not fitted with arresting hooks.)

1 MARINE SEARCH AND RESCUE SQUADRON

Squadron	Code	Aircraft
VMR-1	5C	C-9B, C-12B, HH-46D

VMR-1 at MCAS Cherry Point provides worldwide air transport for the Marine Corps with two Huron and two Skytrain II aircraft; the squadron also has three Sea Knights configured for the SAR mission in support of the 2nd Marine Aircraft Wing.

All other Marine air stations and facilities place their SAR aircraft under local Headquarters Squadrons. VMR-2 was briefly in existence at MCAS Miramar but was renamed Headquarters Squadron in 1999.

Historical: During the World War II era, the designation VMR indicated Marine transport squadron.

2 MARINE UNMANNED AERIAL VEHICLE SQUADRONS

Squadron	Code	Aircraft
VMU-1	FZ	UAVs
VMU-2	FF	UAVs

Two Marine Unmanned Aerial Vehicle (UAV) squadrons were established on 15 January 1996, VMU-1 at MCAS Yuma and VMU-2 at MCAS Cherry Point. Previously Marine UAVs were operated by remotely piloted vehicle companies. (Each company consisted of 10 Marine officers, 56 Marine enlisted personnel, and 1 Navy hospital corpsman.)

Earlier UAV platoons were the primary drone operating units.

12 MARINE HEAVY HELICOPTER SQUADRONS

Squadron	Code	Aircraft	Names/Notes
HMT-301	SU	CH-53D	Windwalkers
HMT-302	UT	CH/MH-53E	Phoenix
HMH-361	YN	CH-53E	Pineapples
HMH-362	YL	CH-53D	Ugly Angels
HMH-363	YZ	CH-53D	Lucky Red Lions
HMH-366	HH	CH-53D	deactivated Sep 2000
HMH-461	CJ	CH-53E	Sea Stallions
HMH-462	YF	CH-53E	Heavy Haulers
HMH-463	YH	CH-53D	
HMH-464	EN	CH-53E	Condors
HMH-465	YJ	CH-53E	Warhorses
HMH-466	YK	CH-53E	Wolfpack

These 12 squadrons fly the three-engine CH-53E Super Stallion or two-engine CH-53D Sea Stallion. Each squadron has eight helicopters. The first CH-53E squadron was HMH-464, activated at New River on 27 February 1981.

HMT-301 provides CH-53D readiness training and HMT-302 is the CH/MH-53E readiness/transition squadron for both the Navy and Marine Corps, including Airborne Mine Countermeasures (AMCM) personnel for the Navy. Navy personnel are assigned to HMT-302, which took over the Navy training role in 1994.

Operational: HMT-301 is assigned the code US according to official documents, but the squadron uses SU on its aircraft.

7 MARINE UTILITY AND ATTACK HELICOPTER SQUADRONS

Squadron	Code	Aircraft	Names
HMLA-167	TV	AH-1W, UH-1N	
HMLA-169	SN	AH-1W, UH-1N	Vipers
HMLA-267	UV	AH-1W, UH-1N	Black Aces
HMLA-269	HF	AH-1W, UH-1N	Sea Cobras
HMT-303	QT	AH-1W, UH-1N, HH-1N	
HMLA-367	VT	AH-1W, UH-1N	Scarfaces
HMLA-369	SM	AH-1W, UH-1N	

The Marine light (HML) and attack (HMA) helicopter squadrons were combined beginning on 1 April 1986 to facilitate the deployment of detachments of combined troop-carrying/command UH-1N Huey helicopters and AH-1W SeaCobra gunships. The last of these squadrons transitioned from the AH-1J/T to the AH-1W model in the early 1990s. Each unit has 18 AH-1W and nine UH-1N helicopters.

HMT-303 provides helicopter readiness training for both helicopter types. With the disestablishment of Navy HC-16 in 1994 all Navy-Marine HH-1N/UH-1N training was assigned to HMT-303.

15 MARINE MEDIUM HELICOPTER SQUADRONS

Squadron	Code	Aircraft	Names
HMM-161	YR	CH-46E	The First
HMM-162	YS	CH-46E	Golden Eagles
HMM-163	YP	CH-46E	Ridgerunners
HMMT-164	YT	CH-46E	Flying Clamors
HMM-165	YW	CH-46E	White Knights
HMM-166	YX	CH-46E	Sea Elk
HMT-204	GX	MV-22	redesignated VMMT-204 on 10 June 1999
HMM-261	EM	CH-46E	Bulls
HMM-262	ET	CH-46E	Flying Tigers
HMM-263	EG	CH-46E	Red Lions
HMM-264	EH	CH-46E	Black Knights
HMM-265	EP	CH-46E	
HMM-266	ES	CH-46E	Griffins
HMM-268	YQ	CH-46E	Red Dragons
HMM-364	PF	CH-46E	Purple Foxes
HMM-365	YM	CH-46E	Blue Knights

Each medium helicopter squadron flies 12 Sea Knight helicopters, reduced from 18 in some units. The CH-46 is scheduled for eventual replacement by the MV-22 Osprey tilt-rotor aircraft.

HMT-164 provides all CH-46E readiness/transition training.

Designation: Due to an administrative oversight, HMM-262 and Navy VQ-6 both have the same tail code—ET. VQ-6 was assigned the code after HMM-262 was inadvertently omitted from the official code assignment chart.

Historical: HMM-161 was the first Marine tactical helicopter squadron, established on 15 January 1951, flying the Sikorsky HRS-1.

1 MARINE HELICOPTER SQUADRON

Squadron	Code	Aircraft
HMX-1	MX	UH/VH-1N, VH-3D, VH-60N, CH-46E, CH-53E, VH-60A

This unique squadron, at MCAS Quantico, Va., fulfills a variety of development and operational functions, including providing helicopter transport for the President with the VH-3D Sea King and VH-60A Blackhawk.[26] With the President embarked, a helicopter is designated "Marine One."

HMX-1 is the only Marine unit to operate the H-60 Black Hawk/Seahawk helicopter.

Designation: HMX-1 is officially Marine Helicopter Squadron 1; "Experimental" is no longer a part of its designation.

Historical: This squadron—originally designated Marine Helicopter Experimental Squadron 1 or Marine Development Squadron 1—was established on 1 December 1947 to develop helicopter assault tactics for the Marine Corps. HMX-1 began providing helicopter transportation for presidents in September 1957, when an HUS-1 (UH-34) from HMX-1 carried President Dwight D. Eisenhower from Newport, R.I., to NAS Quonset Point, Conn. In 1976 the Marine Corps was given sole responsibility for the helicopter transport of the President.

Manning: More than 700 personnel are assigned to HMX-1.

MARINE AIR RESERVE

The Marine Air Reserve consists of the 4th Marine Aircraft Wing, plus a few detachments. The wing, organized similarly to the active MAWs, has just over 100 aircraft in 13 squadrons.

In addition to the aircraft squadrons indicated for the 4th MAW, there are various wing command and support aircraft, as well as a detachment of C-12 utility aircraft. (The wing headquarters has the tail code EZ.)

TABLE 26-7. 4th MARINE AIRCRAFT WING

Group	Squadron	Code	Aircraft	Location
MAG-41				NAS Fort Worth, Texas
	VMFA-112	MA	F/A-18A	NAS Fort Worth, Texas
	VMGR-234	QH	KC-130T	NAS Fort Worth, Texas
MAG-42				NAS Atlanta, Ga.
	VMFA-142	MB	F/A-18A	NAS Atlanta, Ga.
	HMLA-773	MP	AH-1W, UH-1N	NAS Atlanta, Ga.
	HMM-774	MQ	CH-46E	NAS Norfolk, Va.
	HMLA-775[a]	WR	AH-1W, UH-1N	NAS New Orleans, La.
MAG-46				MCAS Miramar, Calif.
	VMFA-134	MF	F/A-18A	MCAS Miramar, Calif.
	VMFT-401	WB	F-5E/F	MCAS Yuma, Ariz.
	HMM-764	ML	CH-46E	Edwards AFB, Calif.
	HMH-769	MS	CH-53E	Edwards AFB, Calif.
	HMLA-775	WR	AH-1W, UH-1N	MCAS Camp Pendleton, Calif.
MAG-49				NAS Willow Grove, Pa.
	VMFA-321	MG	F/A-18A	NAF Washington, D.C.
	VMGR-452	NY	KC-130	Stewart ANGB, N.Y.[b]
	HMH-772	MT	CH-53E	NAF Washington, D.C.

[a] Detachment from squadron is at Camp Pendleton, Calif.
[b] ANGB = Air National Guard Base.

MARINE ATTACK SQUADRONS

Reserve squadron VMA-131 was the last Navy-Marine squadron to fly the single-seat A-4 Skyhawk, retiring its last A-4M "Scooter" in 1992. The squadron—thereafter held in service by congressional edict—was deactivated on 30 December 1998.

VMA-133 and VMA-322 flying the A-4M Skyhawk were deactivated on 30 September 1992.

---

26. The Army name for the H-60A series is Black Hawk (two words).

MARINE ELECTRONIC WARFARE SQUADRONS

VMAQ-4 became an active EW squadron in 1992.

MARINE FIGHTER SQUADRONS

VMF-112 was the last U.S. Navy-Marine squadron to fly the versatile Phantom, the F-4S variant in this instance. The squadron converted to F/A-18s in late 1992.

Fighter readiness training squadron VMFT-401 was activated in 1986 to provide adversary training aircraft for active and reserve Marine squadrons. The squadron initially flew 13 F-21A Kfir fighters leased from Israel Aircraft Industries from June 1987 until September 1989. They were replaced by 12 F-5E Tiger II and one F-5F aircraft for adversary training.

MARINE OBSERVATION SQUADRONS

The last Marine OV-10 Bronco unit, VMO-4, was deactivated on 30 July 1994.

MARINE HEAVY HELICOPTER SQUADRONS

HMH-769 was activated on 1 April 1993 from Detachment A of HMH-772.

MARINE UTILITY AND ATTACK HELICOPTER SQUADRONS

HMA-767 was changed to HMLA-767 on 1 August 1994, HMA-773 to HMLA-773 on 1 July 1994, and HMA-775 to HMLA-775 on 1 August 1994.

HML-771 at NAS South Weymouth, Mass., flying the UH-1N, was deactivated on 1 August 1994, and HML-776 at NAS Glenview, Ill., also flying the UH-1N, was deactivated on 1 July 1994.

MARINE CORPS AIR STATION AIRCRAFT

These are mostly administrative and training aircraft, both fixed-wing (UC-12B, CT-39G) and helicopter (HH-46D, HH-1N) types.

Code	Location
5A	NAF Washington, D.C.
5B	MCAS Beaufort, S.C.
5C	MCAS Cherry Point, N.C.
5D	MCAS New River, N.C.
5F	MCAS Futenma, Okinawa
5G	MCAS Iwakuni, Japan
5T	MCAS El Toro, Calif.
5Y	MCAS Yuma, Ariz.

A C-9B Skytrain from VMR-1 is typical of these DC-9 series aircraft flown by the Navy and Marine Corps. Some will be replaced by the C-40A Airlifter now being procured by the naval services. (U.S. Marine Corps)

CHAPTER 27

Naval Aircraft

An F/A-18C Hornet is readied for launch from the carrier THEODORE ROOSEVELT during air operations over former Yugoslavia. A catapult safety observer is giving the "thumbs up" signal. The Navy, Marine Corps, and Coast Guard operate their aircraft from ships and shore bases. (U.S. Navy, PH2 Donné McKissic)

This chapter describes the aircraft flown by Naval Aviation—the U.S. Navy and Marine Corps—as well as the Coast Guard. The Unmanned Aerial Vehicle (UAV), formerly referred to as Remotely Piloted Vehicle (RPV), or drone programs are described at the end of this chapter.

The procurement of naval aircraft, both types and numbers, was severely reduced following the end of the Cold War. Severe budget constraints, technical problems, and the Navy's mismanagement of aircraft programs have caused the cancellation of several aircraft. By the beginning of the 21st century, however, there had been a turn-around in aircraft procurement rates as part of the "recapitalization" of the Navy and Marine Corps. Indeed, the *planned* fiscal year 2003 aircraft procurement of 131 aircraft is more than twice the rate of the nadir year of fiscal 1991, when only 65 aircraft were authorized.

However, in presenting the fiscal year 2000–2005 defense procurement plan to Congress in January 2000, the Clinton administration announced a significant reduction in naval aircraft procurement in comparison to the plan given to Congress one year earlier. In FY 2000 the aircraft buy increased from 86 to 98—a gain of 12 aircraft. But the planned FY 2001–2005 procurement now totals 612 aircraft compared to 682 one year ago, a loss of 70 naval aircraft.

Further, the procurement of increased numbers of aircraft in later years is always a questionable situation because higher costs and other factors generally result in the procurement of fewer weapons, ships, or aircraft than originally planned. This can be expected to occur because of the increased cost of the significantly larger F/A-18E/F compared to the earlier F/A-18s and the cost of development and initial procurement of the Joint Strike Fighter (JSF).

Ten aircraft currently are being procured by the Navy and Marine Corps:

Aircraft	Prime contractor	Type
F/A-18E/F Hornet	McDonnell Douglas[1]	strike-fighter
E-2C Hawkeye	Northrop Grumman	airborne early warning
T-6A Texan	Raytheon/Beech	trainer
T-45 Goshawk	British Aerospace/ McDonnell Douglas	trainer
KC-130J Hercules	Lockheed Martin	transport
C-40A Airlifter	Boeing	transport
UC-35A	Beech	utility
C-37 Gulfstream	Gulfstream	utility
MV-22 Osprey	Bell/Boeing	assault (STOVL)
CH-60S	Sikorsky	helicopter

(Aircraft currently in production for the Navy and Marine Corps are indicated by asterisks in the subsequent aircraft entries.)

The T-6A was developed as the Joint Primary Aircraft Training System (JPATS). Both the T-6 and V-22 are joint programs with the Air Force.

Table 27-1 lists the current aircraft procurement plan for the Navy and Marine Corps as of January 2000. Beyond these new procurement aircraft, in the 21st century the Navy and Marine Corps plan to procure the Joint Strike Fighter. The JSF is a joint Air Force–Navy–Marine–Royal Navy program.

Both the V-22 STOVL aircraft and the JSF offer the promise of foreign procurement. However, the future of the JSF can be considered precarious. The Air Force seeks the continued production of its controversial F-22 Raptor stealth fighter. Efforts to continue the procurement of that aircraft can only detract from interest in the JSF. At the same time, the Air Force is seeking to increase the *fighter* capabilities of the JSF at the expense of its effectiveness as a *strike* aircraft. This could result in an aircraft that would be so analogous to the F-22 that there would be insufficient rationale (and funds) for Air Force procurement of the JSF.

Similarly, the Navy's interest in the JSF is tempered by the desire to procure the F/A-18E/F aircraft, which have suffered

---

1. Now part of Boeing.

technical problems as well as increasing costs. Here again, the acquisition of the F/A-18E/F could have the effect of delaying the JSF and dissipating Navy interest in the aircraft.

This is in stark contract to the Marine Corps and Royal Navy, to whom the JSF is critical if those services are to continue fixed-wing aircraft operations from small carriers (i.e., LHA/LHD amphibious ships in the U.S. Navy). The various U.S. and British Harrier variants are aging and will need replacement in a decade.

In addition to new aircraft procurement, there are two major aircraft upgrade programs underway in U.S. naval aviation: the provision of enhanced AV-8B Harrier attack aircraft, and the conversion of SH-60B and SH-60F Seahawk anti-submarine helicopters to the SH-60R configuration.

Historically, the Marine Corps and Coast Guard have flown Navy aircraft; however, during the 1980s both the Marines and Coast Guard sponsored the procurement of aircraft not acquired by the Navy, principally the AV-8 Harrier series for the Marines and the HU-25 Guardian reconnaissance aircraft and HH-65 Dolphin helicopter for the Coast Guard. All of those procurement programs have been completed, although the HH-65 helicopters are being re-engined. (The original AV-8A Harrier has been replaced in Marine service by the advanced AV-8B aircraft.)

U.S. naval aircraft in service after 1990 are listed below, even if they have subsequently been discarded.

AIRCRAFT DESIGNATIONS

U.S. military aircraft are designated in a scheme adopted on 18 September 1962. It is relatively simple, with prefix and suffix letters providing extensive detail. Nevertheless, confusion persists as the old and new schemes are mixed or written incorrectly.

For example, the McDonnell Douglas F-4B Phantom was often written incorrectly as F4B—which was a Boeing fighter of the 1920s. Similarly, the F4F Wildcat of World War II fame is often written incorrectly as F-4F, which is the U.S. designation used for F-4 Phantoms configured for West Germany. The phasing out of most pre-1996 aircraft, however, is alleviating this problem.

There have also been major corruptions of the system by the services. The most numerous aircraft in the Navy–Marine Corps inventory—the F/A-18 Hornet—carries an unofficial designation that

---

TABLE 27-1 U.S. NAVY–MARINE CORPS AIRCRAFT PROCUREMENT

	FY 97 Actual	FY 98 Actual	FY 99 Actual	FY 00 Actual	FY 01 Planned	FY 02 Planned	FY 03 Planned	FY 04 Planned	FY 05 Planned
F/A-18E/F	—	20	30	36	42	45	48	48	48
F/A-18C/D	36	24	12	—	—	—	—	—	—
E-2C	—	4	3	3	5	5	5	—	—
T-6A	—	—	—	12	21	24	24	24	24
T-45	12	15	15	15	12	4	—	—	—
KC-130J	—	—	—	1	2	2	2	—	1
C-40A	—	—	—	1	—	1	—	—	1
C-37	—	—	—	—	1	—	—	1	1
UC-35	—	—	—	2	—	1	—	1	1
MV-22	—	—	—	11	16	19	28	28	28
CH-60S	—	1	5	17	15	16	24	24	20
HH-60H	17	—	—	—	—	—	—	—	—
SH-60B	7	—	—	—	—	—	—	—	—
CH/MH-53E	12	12	—	—	—	—	—	—	—
Total	84	76	65	98	114	117	131	126	124
Remanufactured Aircraft									
AV-8B "Plus"	4	4	4	11	10	—	—	—	—
SH-60R	—	—	—	7	4	8	25	27	27
AH-1Z/UH-1Y	—	—	—	—	—	5	17	24	36
Total	4	4	4	18	14	13	42	51	63

violates the prescribed designation scheme. In 1975—three years before the first Hornet flew—Vice Admiral William D. Houser, then Deputy Chief of Naval Operations (Air), determined that the designation F-18 would be used for the fighter variant and A-18 for the attack variant.[2] However, on 5 September 1978, shortly before the first Hornet flight, Houser's successor, Vice Admiral Frederick C. Turner, wrote to the Commander, Naval Air Systems Command, stating his preference for the designation F/A-18, which did not follow the official aircraft designation guidance:

> My choice, F/A-18, would be based not so much on conformance with existing directives as with the necessity to designate this aircraft so that it truly reflects its multimission nature. Certainly the designation F-18 is in consonance with the tri-service instruction . . . . I prefer to continue [with F/A-18] even though it may be one that receives its legitimacy through use rather than directive.[3]

The U.S. military services do not follow the 1962 designation system in other respects as well. For example, a new helicopter series was established, beginning with H-1 (formerly the HU-1); that series reached only H-6 before the services began adding to the abandoned Air Force series with H-54 and above. More severe violations have been made by the Air Force, with fighter-series numbers above F-111 being assigned despite the new series that had begun with the F-1 and carried through to the F-23.

Similarly, the 1962 system dictated that the "next" training aircraft be designated T-41. That was done, and successive training aircraft reached number T-47. Under the 1962 system, the Navy's T2V-1 Sea Star, a navalized version of the T-33, became the T-1. However, in 1992 the Air Force began receiving a new undergraduate pilot training aircraft, which it designated the T-1A Jayhawk. This probably was the most flagrant violation of the 1962 Department of Defense directive on designations.

The T-2 was a Navy training aircraft, formerly the T2J Buckeye. The Air Force has subsequently added the designation T-3 to the list, the T-3A Firefly being a flight screening aircraft.

Modifications to aircraft, which have in the past added a new suffix numeral or letter, now have such confusing designations as the P-3C Update III, EA-6B ICAP, and EP-3E Aries II aircraft. Also, whereas the original 1962 scheme used the prefix M for missile-carrying aircraft, the prefix M now indicates multipurpose aircraft, as for the MH-53E Sea Dragon helicopter.

Historical: From 1922 to 1962, the Navy had its own designation scheme that indicated the aircraft mission, sequence of that aircraft type produced by the manufacturer, manufacturer, and (after a hyphen) model and modification. Thus AD-2N indicated the first series of attack aircraft (A) built by Douglas (D), the second model (2), modified for night operation (N); the second Douglas attack aircraft was A2D, the third A3D, and so forth.

That scheme became unwieldy as the number of manufacturers of naval aircraft increased. For example, the letter *F* was used for Grumman (as in the F9F) because *G* was already assigned to Gallaudet; *Y* for Consolidated (as in PBY) because *C* was used by Curtiss and, later, Cessna and Culver as well; and *A* for Brewster (as in F2A) because *B* was assigned to Boeing and, later, Beech and Budd Manufacturing. Also, the same aircraft flown by different services had different designations. The famed Boeing B-29 Superfortress had the Navy designation P2B, the North American B-25 was used by the Navy and Marine Corps as the PBJ, and the McDonnell Phantom II entered service as the F4H in the Navy and F-110 in the Air Force.

The U.S. Air Force and Army used different designation schemes for their respective aircraft after the establishment of the Air Force as a separate service in 1947. (Previously, from 1941 to 1947, what became the U.S. Air Force was the U.S. Army Air Forces.)

Under the unified scheme of 1962, all existing and new naval aircraft were redesignated. The Navy-flown AD Skyraider became the first plane in the new attack series, the A-1. The Navy's TF Trader started the new cargo series as the C-1. The FJ Fury became the F-1, the T2V Sea Star the T-1, and the UC-1 Otter the U-1.[4]

There was no P-1 or S-1, as the new system picked up the Navy's P2V Neptune and S2F Tracker as the P-2 and S-2, respectively. The improved P3V Orion was the obvious candidate for P-3 and the P5M Marlin, the Navy's last combat flying boat, for P-5. The designation P-4 was used, albeit briefly, for the drone versions of the Privateer (the P4Y-2K, formerly PB4Y-2). The designations P-4 and P-6 are sometimes cited as having been reserved for the P4M Mercator and the P6M Seamaster, but the last of the combination piston-turbojet Mercators were gone by 1962 and the turbojet Seamaster flying boat had been canceled in 1959. The next patrol aircraft was to be the P-7 (which was the canceled Long-Range Air Anti-Submarine Warfare Capable Aircraft).

The 1962 system also introduced the mission designation of special electronic E-series aircraft. The first two planes were Navy: the WF-2 Tracer became the E-1B and the W2F-1 Hawkeye the E-2A.

Variations of the previous Air Force X (for experimental) and V (for Vertical/Short Take-Off and Landing/VSTOL) designations remained, but official records differ as to which aircraft were part of the old or new series. The Marine AV-8 Harrier is officially in the V series, the designation A-8 apparently being avoided to reduce confusion. In the V series, however, the Ryan "flying jeep" had already been designated XV-8. But the latter program never took off, and hence the "8" spot is firmly held by the successful Harrier series.

Planes that were used by both services, such as the Albatross seaplane (Navy UF), generally took on the existing Air Force numerical designation (U-16, formerly SA-16). But the Phantom was recent enough to be given a new designation, the now-familiar F-4, and not the Air Force F-110.

Helicopters proved a more confusing issue, because the Army also had its own helicopter designation system before 1962 in addition to those of the Navy–Marine Corps and Air Force. The Sea Knight was the Navy HRB, while the Army called the helicopter the HC-1A (HC for helicopter—cargo). This became the H-46 in the new scheme. The Army's HU-1 Iroquois (HU for helicopter—utility) started the new helicopter series as the H-1, with most of the Army and Air Force designations being merged to form the new H series. Navy helicopters were "stuck in" where there were gaps. The Kaman HU2K became the H-2 and the Sikorsky HSS-2 the H-3, but the Navy-Marine HSS-1/HUS, being similar to the Army–Air Force H-34, took on that designation. Further, after the new H-series reached H-6, the military reverted to simply adding to the larger numerical series, i.e., H-54 and above.

The accompanying diagram explains the current aircraft designation scheme.

Names: The U.S. military services assign popular names to aircraft. Those carrying a previously used name take a Roman numeral suffix, although in reality these are meaningless because the earlier aircraft has already been discarded by the time the "II" aircraft enters service.

The following contemporary aircraft have such a suffix:

AV-8B Harrier II
C-9B Skytrain II
T-6 Texan II

2. Vice Adm. Houser, "Memorandum for the Chief of Naval Operations," Memo 05/187 (30 Oct 1975).
3. Vice Adm. Turner, "Memorandum for the Commander, Naval Air Systems Command," ser. 506C5/781084, 5 Sep 1978. A full discussion of the designation issue may be found in James P. Stevenson, *The Pentagon Paradox: The Development of the F-18 Hornet* (Annapolis, Md.: Naval Institute Press, 1993). This excellent book is a program history of the F/A-18.

4. The U-2 spy plane was given a utility designation in an effort to hide its real purpose.

Figure 27-1
Aircraft Designations

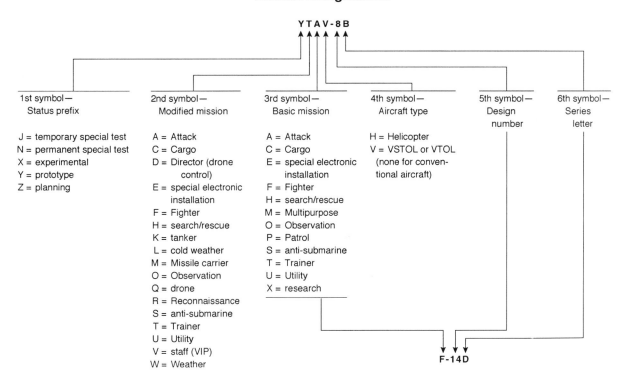

NOTE: Letters I and O are not used as series letters to avoid confusing them with numerals.

AIRCRAFT MARKINGS

Navy and Marine Corps aircraft normally feature the following markings:

- *Unit markings:* Indicative of wing, squadron, or base assignment, these consist of letters or letter-number combinations on the tail fin or after body of the aircraft; see chapter 26 of this edition of *Ships and Aircraft* for unit codes.
- *Side numbers:* Generally on the fuselage and upper right and lower left wing surfaces, these indicate the aircraft position in a squadron or other unit. The side number sequence for carrier air wings is shown on page 383.
- *Bureau numbers:* Assigned to all Navy and Marine Corps aircraft in the sequence of their procurement, these numbers are used on the aircraft's after fuselage or tail; on transports, the last three digits are sometimes used as their side numbers. "Bureau" refers to the Bureau of Aeronautics, which directed naval aircraft procurement from 1921 to 1959, when it became the Bureau of Naval Ordnance and subsequently, in 1966, the Naval Air Systems Command. However, the term "bureau" continues in use.
- *National insignia:* The U.S. national insignia consists of a white star within a blue circle, with white rectangles on either side, the rectangles having a red horizontal stripe and blue border. All naval aircraft have the national insignia on both sides of the fuselage, with fixed-wing aircraft also having it on the upper left and lower right wing surfaces. Most U.S. tactical aircraft now have low-visibility national markings (i.e., no color).

Coast Guard aircraft have the national insignia or American flag on their tail fin. Some U.S. Navy Carrier Onboard Delivery (COD) and other transport aircraft also have the American flag on their fin. Coast Guard aircraft wear that service's wide orange and narrow blue stripe insignia on the forward fuselage with the Coast Guard crest on the orange stripe. These aircraft have a four-digit side number based on their (Coast Guard) procurement sequence.

ATTACK AIRCRAFT

Specialized attack aircraft have been phased out of naval aviation, except for the AV-8B Harrier, which the Marine Corps will operate well into the 21st century.

The last Navy "straight" attack aircraft was the A-6E Intruder, which was taken out of squadron service in 1996. Retirement of the A-6E ended the 50-year history of VA aircraft in the U.S. Navy. (TA-4J Skyhawks, training variants of the famed A-4 light attack aircraft, remained in service until 1999.) Attack missions now are carried out by the multipurpose F/A-18 Hornet and the F-14 Tomcats that have a limited strike capability.

Several efforts to develop a specialized successor to the A-6 Intruder have been aborted or stillborn. The latest was the Navy's A/F-X program, initiated in the early 1990s after the demise of the AX. The A/F-X was a study effort that quickly fell victim to another paper airplane, the so-called Joint Attack Fighter (JAF), an Air Force–sponsored conceptual aircraft. The JAF was to have a range of about 500 n.miles (926 km) carrying a payload goal of four internal air-to-air missiles and up to four 2,000-pound (907-kg) air-to-surface weapons carried externally.

The F-14 and early F/A-18 aircraft will be succeeded by the JSF. See Joint Strike Fighter under Fighter Aircraft.

A-12 AVENGER

The A-12 Avenger was intended to replace the A-6E Intruder as the "medium" all-weather strike aircraft in carrier air wings. It was also to replace the A-6E in five Marine attack squadrons, but the Marine Corps early in the program decided to forgo the A-12 in favor of flying the two-seat F/A-18D in the all-weather attack role.

The A-12 program was formally initiated in 1984 with the first of six A-12 prototypes originally scheduled to fly in June 1990; at the time the aircraft was canceled in 1991, the first flight was expected to occur in March 1992. At that point, carrier trials were expected in late 1992 or early 1993, with an Initial Operational Capability (IOC) of 1996.

The Navy and Department of Defense canceled the A-12 program on 7 January 1991, citing "the inability of the contractors to design,

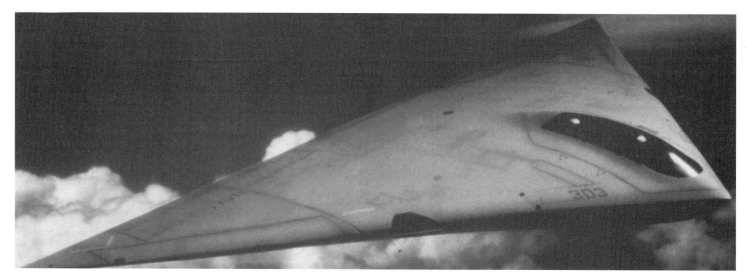

An artist's concept of the controversial and ill-fated A-12 Avenger attack aircraft. Control surfaces on the stealthy A-12 included "elevons" or "flaperons" and pairs of spoilers, plus a single trailing-edge control surface between the elevons. With no vertical tail surfaces, the A-12 would have depended upon differential use of the elevons and/or spoilers for yaw control. (General Dynamics)

develop, fabricate, assemble, and test A-12 aircraft within the contract schedule and to deliver an aircraft that meets contract requirements." Also cited were major cost overruns and misrepresentations by the Naval Air Systems Command; the latter resulted in several officers being censured.[5] Subsequently, General Dynamics and McDonnell Douglas sued the government for improper termination of their contract. On 9 December 1994, the U.S. Court of Federal Claims ruled, "Testimony and other evidence at trial showed that the A-12 contract was not terminated because of contractor default. The contract was terminated because the Office of the Secretary of Defense withdrew support and funding from the A-12. Prior to that, the Navy did not believe that the contractors' performance justified termination for default."

The design and cost of the A-12 were highly classified until January 1990, when a "slip" in congressional testimony led to revelations that the 620-plane program was to have a unit cost of $96.2 million, making it the most expensive Navy aircraft yet built.[6] Peak A-12 production for the run of 620 aircraft was to be 36 units in fiscal 1994. When the Marine Corps was also planning to buy the A-12, the procurement goal was 858 aircraft.

The Air Force had been forced by the Defense Department to join the A-12 program to develop a deep-strike aircraft to succeed the F-111 and F-15E Strike Eagle in that role. Production of the Air Force version—called the Advanced Tactical Aircraft (ATA)—was deferred in 1990 to beyond 1997. The Air Force had planned to buy 400 ATA variants of the aircraft.

See 16th Edition/pages 363–365 for characteristics.

Design: The A-12 was to be a low-observable, or stealth, aircraft with a flying-wing configuration sans major tail-fin structures. The official artist's drawings of the A-12—heavily retouched—showed a classic delta flying-wing configuration with the "fuselage" extending slightly rearward from the trailing edge; the wing has a leading-edge sweep of about 48°. There were two large, trapezoidal inlets for the engines just aft and below the leading edges of the wing; no afterburners were fitted. The tandem-seat cockpit was close to the nose of the aircraft, which was sharply pointed and "blended" into the leading edge of the wing. The aircraft was to have been fitted with a digital fly-by-wire control system.

The weapons load—up to 12,000 pounds (5,443 kg)—was to be carried internally. The A-12 would have had folding wings for carrier stowage. Other features were to include superior range and payload

over the A-6E, a low flight-to-maintenance ratio (expected to be four times better than the A-6E's ratio), and dual-function radar/FLIR (Forward-Looking Infrared) search and tracking system.

Designation: The designation A-12 previously was assigned by the Central Intelligence Agency to the supersonic aircraft that was the progenitor of the YF-12 fighter aircraft and SR-71 Blackbird reconnaissance aircraft.

Names: The name Avenger was assigned to honor President George Bush, who had flown TBM Avenger torpedo planes in World War II; he was reported to be the Navy's youngest wartime pilot.

AV-8B HARRIER

The AV-8B is a highly capable STOVL attack aircraft flown by Marine attack squadrons.[7] Since 1996 the Harrier has been the only "straight" attack aircraft (VA/VMA) in naval aviation. The aircraft operates from amphibious ships and has flown from large aircraft carriers.

---

7. The designation STOVL in place of VSTOL for the AV-8B Harrier was made by the Deputy Chief of Staff/Aviation, Headquarters, U.S. Marine Corps, in March 1995.

The AV-8B Harrier can be distinguished from the AV-8A variant by its massive air intakes for the F402-RR-408 Pegasus turbofan engine that provides both thrust and lift. Note the retracted refueling probe above the port intake. The underwing weapon pylons are evident in this view of a VMA-223 aircraft. (Ted Carlson)

---

5. The Commander, Naval Air Systems Command, was retired and the program's manager and executive officer were transferred, the two latter officers also receiving administrative letters of censure.
6. See, for example, "A-12 Disclosure," *Aviation Week & Space Technology,* 15 January 1990, p. 15.

The AV-8B has replaced the A-4M Skyhawk and AV-8A Harrier aircraft in Marine VMA squadrons. During the Carter administration (1977–1981), the Department of Defense sought to have the Marines procure the F/A-18 Hornet as a replacement for the A-4M, but the Marines—with congressional support—held fast to the AV-8B program.[8] The Marine Corps originally planned to procure 336 operational AV-8B aircraft, plus four full-scale development aircraft in addition to the two YAV-8B prototypes converted from AV-8A aircraft. Procurement was revised downward to the actual production of 256 AV-8B models and 20 of the two-seat TAV-8B trainers, the last procurement being in fiscal 1991.

Design: The AV-8B differs from the earlier AV-8A Harrier flown by the Marines in having a supercritical wing shape, larger trailing-edge flaps, drooped ailerons, strakes under the gun pods, redesigned engine intakes, strengthened landing gear, and a more-powerful engine, providing twice the payload of the AV-8A with up to 9,200 pounds (4,173 kg) of external stores. The aircraft has one external 25-mm gun pack faired into the underfuselage, with one underfuselage and six wing points available for bombs, rockets, missiles, or 300-gallon (1,140-liter) fuel tanks.

The wings of the AV-8B are constructed predominately of composites that save weight without losing strength. Compared to AV-8A, the AV-8B has 15 percent greater wing area and can carry 75 percent more fuel in its wing tanks. The AV-8B has six wing stores stations (compared to four on AV-8A), plus an updated engine, composite material in some fuselage areas, an elevated cockpit and canopy to improve visibility, redesigned engine intakes, and improved avionics.

The AV-8B aircraft has the ASB-19(V)3 angle-rate bombing system. Those aircraft delivered after September 1989 are night-attack capable, being fitted with nose-mounted FLIR, pilot night-vision goggles, Head-Up Display (HUD) and color head-down displays, and digital moving-map system. Aircraft delivered from 1993 ("Harrier II Plus") have the APG-65 multimode synthetic aperture radar and the improved Pegasus 408 engine; the aircraft is also 17 inches (0.43 m) longer in the forward fuselage and weighs some 900 pounds (408 kg) more than the improved (radar-equipped) AV-8B. In addition, earlier AV-8B aircraft are being "remanufactured" to the "Plus" configuration.

Also fitted are the ALR-67 radar warning receiver and the pod-mounted ALQ-164 Electronic Countermeasures (ECM) system.

The two-seat TAV-8B differs from the standard AV-8B in having an enlarged forward fuselage and canopy and a vertical fin extension. The two aircraft have a 90 percent component commonality.

Operational: The 86 Marine AV-8B Harriers participating in Operation Desert Storm in 1991 flew 3,380 combat sorties. (Earlier Harriers flown by Britain's Royal Navy and Royal Air Force from VSTOL carriers achieved remarkable results in both the fighter and attack roles in the 1982 Falklands conflict.)

---

8. In the event, during the Reagan administration (1981–1989) Secretary of the Navy John Lehman procured both the AV-8B and the F/A-18 for the Marine Corps.

An EAV-8B variant—being delivered to the Spanish Navy for carrier use—takes on fuel from a U.S. Air Force KC-10 Extender over the Atlantic; the Harrier is fitted with two 300-gallon (1,136-liter) ferry tanks. Naval aircraft increasingly are supported by Air Force tankers. (Boeing/McDonnell Douglas)

A two-seat TAV-8B Harrier at rest with both canopies open while on the tarmac at MacDill Air Force Base, Fla. The after cockpit is raised above the forward, student cockpit. (John Bouvia)

A pair of AV-8B Harriers from VMA-231 in flight. Note the retracted outrigger wheels under the wings; their tail cones contain the ALR-67 Radar Warning Receiver (RWR). British Harriers saw considerable combat in the Falklands War (1982) as did U.S. Marine Harriers in the Gulf War (1991). (Boeing)

Status: Operational; no longer in production but early AV-8B aircraft are being "remanufactured." First flight: YAV-8B on 9 November 1978; AV-8B on 5 November 1981; Harrier II Plus in September 1992. IOC: Marine AV-8Bin January 1985 (VMA-331); Harrier II Plus in August 1993 (VMA-542).

(Britain's Royal Air Force procured essentially the same aircraft as the AV-8B, designated GR.Mk 5 and the night-attack GR.Mk 7 variants; the British T.Mk 10 variants are similar to the TAV-8B. AV-8B variants are also flown from VSTOL aircraft carriers by Italy and Spain; earlier Sea Harriers are flown from two Indian ships.)

Characteristics for the AV-8B "Plus":

Manufacturer:	McDonnell Douglas and British Aerospace
Crew:	(1) pilot (2 in TAV-8B)
Engines:	1 Rolls-Royce F402-RR-408 Pegasus turbofan; 23,800 lbst (10,795 kgst)
Weight:	empty 12,922 lbs (5,861 kg)
	maximum T/O VTO 19,550 lbs (8,868 kg)
	STO 31,000 lbs (14,060 kg) with 1,200-ft (366-m) takeoff run
Dimensions:	length AV-8B 46 ft 4 in (14.12 m)
	TAV-8B 50 ft 3 in (15.32 m)
	wingspan 30 ft 4 in (9.25 m)
	wing area 230 ft² (21.37 m²)
	height 11 ft 7¾ in (3.55 m)
Speed:	maximum 580 knots (1,075 km/h) at sea level
Ceiling:	50,000 ft (15,244 m)
Range:	radius 150 n.miles (278 km) with 12 500-lb (227-kg) bombs with 1 hour loiter in STO mode
	600 n.miles (1,110 km) with 7 500-lb bombs in STO mode
	ferry 2,560 n.miles (4,740 km) with 4 300-gallon (1,140-liter) drop tanks
Armament:	1 25-mm cannon GAU-12/U (multibarrel; 300 rounds)
	11,920 lbs (5,407 kg) bombs, missiles, and/or drop tanks, including Sidewinder AAMs
Radar:	APG-65

AV-8A HARRIER

The Harrier was the first VSTOL aircraft to enter first-line service with the U.S. armed forces. The British-developed Harrier was procured for three Marine attack squadrons. The Marines deemed it a success despite a high accident rate; several surviving AV-8A aircraft were upgraded to the AV-8C and two AV-8A Harriers were converted to YAV-8B prototypes for the Harrier II. All AV-8A/C aircraft have been discarded.

The Marine Corps took delivery of 102 single-seat AV-8A (British GR.Mk 50) and eight two-seat TAV-8A (British T.Mk 4) aircraft from 1971 to 1976, with McDonnell Douglas as the American support contractor.

See 14th Edition/pages 403–404 for characteristics.

A-7 CORSAIR

The Corsair was a carrier-based, light attack aircraft in Navy service from 1966 to 1991. It saw extensive combat in the Vietnam War. The last two A-7E squadrons (VA-46 and VA-72) flew in the Gulf War; both units were disbanded in May 1991. The last naval air reserve units to fly the A-7E traded in their Corsairs for the F/A-18 Hornet in April 1991. The Marine Corps did not fly the A-7.

The A-7E was replaced in Navy carrier air wings by the F/A-18. Production of the A-7 ended in 1983 with 1,551 Corsairs delivered—997 for the U.S. Navy, 459 A-7D and 30 two-seat A-7K for the U.S. Air Force, and 65 A-7H and TA-7H models for Greece. Two A-7D models were upgraded to YA-7F prototypes for an improved close air support aircraft, but no large-scale conversion followed. Many former U.S. Navy aircraft were modified for foreign use.

Sixty U.S. Navy versions were the two-seat TA-7C with dual controls (converted from A-7A and A-7C aircraft). A proposed RA-7E with reconnaissance pods was dropped in favor of the F-14/TARPS, and a proposed twin-engine A-7 variant lost out in the concept stage to the F/A-18 as the new Navy attack aircraft.

See 14th Edition/pages 404–405 for characteristics.

A-6 INTRUDER

A highly versatile attack aircraft, the Intruder was the U.S. Navy's most capable carrier-based aircraft with respect to weapons payload and was able to carry out all-weather, day/night strikes. The aircraft was to have been succeeded by the A-12 Avenger.

Navy and Marine Corps Intruders flew combat missions in the Vietnam War as well as the Persian Gulf conflict of 1991. The last Navy A-6E squadrons were disbanded in December 1996; the last Marine A-6E squadrons were disbanded in 1993. The last carrier operations by the plane took place when four A-6Es "trapped" and launched from the EISENHOWER in February 1997.

A total of 679 A-6 aircraft were produced, plus five A-6F prototypes and 191 electronic warfare variants. The KA-6D tankers (all converted from earlier aircraft) had avionics deleted from the after fuselage to provide space for reel; up to five 500-gallon (1,900-liter) drop tanks could be carried to permit the transfer of up to 21,000 pounds (9,525 kg) of fuel. The EA-6A Intruder and EA-6B Prowler electronic warfare variants were derived from the basic Intruder (see Electronic Aircraft). A KA-6H tanker based on the enlarged EA-6B airframe was proposed as a successor to the KA-6D but none was procured.

Designation: Originally designated A2F; changed to A-6 in 1962. See 16th Edition/pages 366–367 for characteristics.

A-4 SKYHAWK

See TA-4J Skyhawk under Training Aircraft.

A-3 SKYWARRIOR

The Douglas A3D (later A-3) was developed as a long-range, carrier-based nuclear strike aircraft. The Skywarrior survived its intended successor, the A3J (later A-5) Vigilante. The A3D—known as the "Whale"—was the largest aircraft to operate regularly from an aircraft carrier, the tanker version having a carrier takeoff weight of more than 80,000 pounds (36,288 kg).

The aircraft was used in the Vietnam War in a variety of roles, including conventional bombing attacks.

The Navy took delivery of 282 Douglas-built Skywarriors of all variants, including 25 A3D-2Q/EA-3B specialized Electronic Intelligence (ELINT) collection aircraft; other straight attack variants subsequently were modified to Electronic Warfare (EW)/ECM configurations. The ELINT version was the last flown by the Navy, having been assigned to squadrons VQ-1 and VQ-2 from 1959 until 1991. (From 1987 until 1991, they were restricted to operations only from land bases.) The last Skywarrior was retired from VQ-2 in September 1991.

(The Air Force flew the similar B-66 Destroyer in the bomber, electronic, reconnaissance, weather, and research roles; B-66 production totaled 206 aircraft.)

Designation: Originally designated A3D; changed to A-3 in 1962. See 14th Edition/pages 415–416 for characteristics.

FIGHTER AIRCRAFT

The Navy now flies the F-14 Tomcat in the fighter role and both the Navy and Marine Corps fly the multipurpose F/A-18 Hornet. With the halt in both the procurement and remanufacture of the F-14, the F/A-18 alone eventually will fill the fighter role for both services.

The proposed Naval Advanced Tactical Fighter (NATF) was essentially stillborn, being considered unaffordable by the Navy's leadership (see below). Still, proposals were put forward for a carrier-capable variant of the Air Force's Advanced Technology Fighter (ATF), now the Lockheed Boeing F-22. The Navy's record for adopting non-Navy-developed aircraft for carrier use made it highly unlikely that there would be a navalized F-22.

The JSF is being developed in place of the NATF for the Navy and Marine Corps.

JOINT STRIKE FIGHTER

The Joint Strike Fighter (JSF) is being developed as a multipurpose aircraft for U.S. and British service. The JSF program as currently configured is planned to produce more than 3,000 aircraft for the U.S. Air Force (2,000), Navy (300), and Marine Corps (650), and the Royal Navy (60). In those air arms, the JSF could replace the:

AV-8B Harrier
F-14 Tomcat
F-15 Eagle
F-16 Fighting Falcon
F/A-18C/D Hornet
F-117A stealth strike aircraft
RN Harrier
RAF GR.Mk 7 Harrier

Several other air forces also have expressed interest in the JSF program, with Denmark, the Netherlands, and Norway having become "associated partners" of the JSF program.

A successful JSF program could lead to the U.S. armed forces having only three fighter-type aircraft by the second decade of the 21st century: the F/A-18E/F Hornet, F-22 Raptor, and JSF.

As now envisioned, JSF production—scheduled to begin in 2005 for the U.S. Air Force—could be worth more than $150 *billion* to the firms that build the planes. The massive outlay to develop and produce the JSF will be the largest U.S. weapons procurement of the first decade of the 21st century.

Two industrial teams are producing competitive prototypes for the JSF program, the team leaders being Boeing and Lockheed Martin. A third team, led by McDonnell Douglas (in collaboration with Northrop Grumman and British Aerospace) was dropped from the competition in November 1996.

Each of the two remaining teams is producing Concept Demonstrator Aircraft (CDA); the Boeing entry is designated X-32 and Lockheed Martin's is the X-35. Each team is producing one conventional JSF aircraft and one STOVL version for flight demonstrations. Flight testing was to begin in 2000.

The JSF designs proposed by the competitors differ considerably: The Boeing design is the more radical, with a high trapezoidal wing. Significantly, Boeing has not built fighter-attack aircraft in the jet age, but the firm points to its bomber and commercial experience, where it is without equal in the West.

The X-35A concept demonstration aircraft developed by the Lockheed Martin Skunk Works. That organization previously built super-secret aircraft, among them the U-2, A-12 Oxcart, and SR-71 Blackbird spy planes, as well as the first U.S. jet-propelled fighter, the P-80 Shooting Star. (Lockheed Martin)

The Boeing X-32A concept demonstration aircraft, showing some of the differences in configuration from the Lockheed Martin design. Both JSF designs will have land-based, carrier-based, and STOVL variants. (Boeing)

The Lockheed Martin X-35A technology demonstrator in flight. The aircraft took to the skies for the first time on 24 October 2000. In both JSF programs the A model will be land-based, the B model will be STOVL, and the C model will be carrier-based. (Lockheed Martin)

The Lockheed Martin JSF has a more traditional configuration, somewhat resembling existing fighter designs. Lockheed Martin has extensive experience in stealth aircraft and won the Air Force's 1981 competition for the ATF, now the F-22. That aircraft has the F119 engine—to be used in the JSF—which some analysts believe gives that firm a significant advantage in the contest. Further, Lockheed Martin has claimed two significant advantages over the Boeing entry: (1) an additional 100-n.mile (183-km) radius and (2) increased potential supply of electrical power to run sensor payloads or a laser weapon.[9]

(McDonnell Douglas had developed what was considered the riskiest JSF design: an aircraft with no vertical tail surfaces and with separate engines for forward thrust and for vertical takeoff and landing. McDonnell Douglas is a leading producer of fighter aircraft, and partner with British Aerospace in the highly successful Harrier program.)[10]

The JSF aircraft is intended to be suitable for three air services and the Royal Navy with 90 percent commonality of the four variants and only 10 percent differences for separate service needs. This will be difficult. The Marine Corps and Royal Navy have a requirement for the STOVL configuration, for operation from their specialized aircraft carriers. While the Air Force would find a short-field operational capability attractive, the Navy must have certain features in its aircraft for conventional carrier operation (strengthened fuselage, catapult attachment points, improved landing gear, and so forth).

Past efforts at developing multiservice tactical aircraft have not been marked by success. The most illustrious example was the 1960s effort to produce the triservice fighter (TFX) for the Air Force, Navy, and Marine Corps tactical roles, and for the strategic bomber role. The resulting F-111 had a lackluster career as a tactical strike (*not* fighter) aircraft, while the Navy rejected their F-111B variant as being unsuitable for carrier operation and that rejection ended possible Marine Corps procurement. The proposed British procurement of the F-111 was stillborn, although the Royal Australian Air Force acquired the F-111 and still flies that aircraft.[11]

Similarly, several land-based tactical aircraft proposed for naval (carrier) use have also been less than a total success, with most of the examples of such efforts having been British. In sharp contrast, carrier-based aircraft that have been adopted for land operation have had marked success, among them the F-4 Phantom, A-3 Skywarrior (as the B-66 Destroyer), A-4 Skyhawk, and A-7 Corsair. Indeed, the Phantom ranks as having achieved the second highest production rate of any Western combat aircraft since World War II even though it was designed specifically for carrier operation. (Among combat aircraft, only the F-86 Sabre/FJ Fury has been produced in larger numbers since World War II.)

In addition to the concern of many aviation specialists (including aviators) that a single aircraft will not effectively serve all four users, there also is apprehension about the Navy's role in the management of the JSF, which is being developed under the aegis of a joint project office. The U.S. Navy has experienced major problems of late in the development of advanced aircraft, as evidenced by failures to produce the A-12 Avenger, AX, and AF-X—all planned follow-on aircraft to the A-6 Intruder—and the P-7 LRAACA maritime patrol aircraft and

9. David A. Fulghum, "LockMart Expands JSF Range, Payload," *Aviation Week & Space Technology*, 8 November 1999, p. 56.

10. McDonnell Douglas produced the F-23, an advanced fighter that lost to the F-22 in the Air Force ATF competition.

11. Major variants of the F-111 Aardvark were the EF-111 electronic countermeasures aircraft, FB-111 strategic bomber, and RF-111 reconnaissance aircraft. The EF-111 was the last variant flown by the U.S. Air Force and was replaced by the Navy-Marine EA-6B Prowler.

An artist's concept of a Boeing JSF on the deck of a U.S. carrier. The STOVL variant of the JSF will be flown from carriers by the U.S. Marine Corps and Royal Navy, replacing the Harrier STOVL aircraft in both services. (Boeing)

the lengthy delays in adapting the British Hawk trainer aircraft for Navy use as the T-45 Goshawk.[12]

Beyond the requirement that no JSF variant may differ more than 10 percent from the basic design, the program's ground rules demand that the maximum price per copy is not to exceed $30 million; all variants must have low-observable (stealth) characteristics, including an internal weapons bay; and all must employ F119 engines produced by the Pratt & Whitney Division of United Technologies (used by the F-22 aircraft).

With respect to stealth characteristics, the JSF is intended to have a Radar Cross-Section (RCS) slightly larger than the radar signature of the F-22 Raptor at a fraction of the cost. The reduction is to be achieved through shaping, construction materials, and skin coatings. An equivalent signature is the radar reflection from a perfectly electrically conducting metal sphere the size of a golf ball.[13]

The weapons bay will be an unusual feature for carrier-based aircraft, with previous naval jet fighters and light/medium attack aircraft carrying their weapons on external pylons and attachment points. In contrast, Air Force tactical strike aircraft—largely developed to carry nuclear weapons—tend to have internal weapon bays. The internal bay usually permits higher speeds and enhances stealth. In the Marine Corps and British variants of the JSF, the weapons bay may be smaller because of the VTOL requirement.

The JSF will not be a low-level attack aircraft but will operate above the kill zones of small arms and shoulder-launched missiles. This tactic will require that the planes employ stand-off tactical missiles and guided bombs. The availability of data links to offboard sensors (unmanned aerial vehicles, satellites, other aircraft, ground forces) will provide the JSF with precision targeting data for these stand-off weapons.

Thus, the challenges to the JSF competitors are considerable. But the payoff will be the only large-scale production of a Western

An overhead view of the Boeing JSF X-32A concept demonstration aircraft. The delta wing configuration is part of the "shaping" that helps to reduce the aircraft's radar cross-section, as do radar-absorbing materials used in the plane's fabrication. (Boeing)

---

12. LRAACA = Long-Range Air Anti-submarine Warfare Capable Aircraft.
13. See David A. Fulghum, "JSF Reflection Is Golf Ball–Sized," *Aviation Week & Space Technology,* 15 February 1999, pp. 27, 30.

The first flight of a JSF demonstrator took place on 18 September 2000 when the Boeing X-32A took to the air. The aircraft flew from Air Force Plant No. 42 in Palmdale, Calif., to Edwards Air Force Base, Calif., to begin flight tests. The Lockheed Martin X-35A JSF was expected to fly a few weeks later. (Boeing, Kevin Flynn)

tactical aircraft for the next two decades or more. The "proof" of their success will be seen in 2008, when the first aircraft are scheduled to enter service.

Designation: The X-32 and X-35 JSF concept demonstrators have the suffix letter *A* for the conventional variant and *B* for the STOVL variant.

NAVAL ADVANCED TACTICAL FIGHTER

The Naval Advanced Tactical Fighter (NATF)—the planned long-term replacement for the F-14 Tomcat—was originally envisioned by the Navy as a navalized version of the F-22, which had been developed for the U.S. Air Force by the team of Lockheed, General Dynamics, and Boeing. A senior official of Lockheed said that the company planned to "give the NATF a swing-wing like the F-14. The swing-wing will let us optimize the plane for the best performance in different [speed and altitude] regions." The official admitted that there would be a penalty for the swing-wing, but performance and stealth would be enhanced in combat environments. Also, Lockheed was to look at producing a two-seat aircraft for the Navy (the basic F-22 is a single-seat plane) and increasing the fuel-carrying capacity of the Navy aircraft by 50 percent compared to the Air Force version. Other changes envisioned for the naval aircraft would be additional avionics and engines modified to resist corrosion in a salt-water environment. In short, said the Lockheed official, "The NATF will be designed to a completely different set of requirements."[14]

By early 1991—about the time of the Air Force selection of the F-22 ATF design—the Navy reached the decision that development and production of a naval ATF was unaffordable.

---

14. "Lockheed NATF Design Will Be Swing-wing," *Navy News,* 4 February 1991, pp. 1–2.

*F/A-18E/F HORNET

This advanced Hornet series—unofficially referred to as the Super Hornet—is being produced for the Navy and Marine Corps as the principal fighter-attack aircraft for both services. The F/A-18E is a single-seat aircraft and the F/A-18F is a two-seat variant; they are successors, respectively, to the F/A-18C and F/A-18D. Both variants are now in production.

Officials of Boeing–McDonnell Douglas point to several advantages of the F/A-18E/F over the previous C/D variants:

- increased range
- increased payload
- enhanced maneuverability
- 10-knot (18.5-km/hour) slower speed on landing approach
- easier to fly

The requirement for an enhanced F/A-18 was first mentioned in a 15 July 1987 memorandum from Secretary of Defense Caspar Weinberger to the Secretaries of the Navy and Air Force noting that, because the next-generation Navy attack aircraft and a replacement for the Air Force's F-16 fighter could not be available "for many years," the Navy should study derivatives of the F/A-18 and the Air Force should study F-16 upgrades as interim replacements.

In selecting the F/A-18E as the next-generation carrier-based fighter over several alternatives, including resumed production of the F-14D, Secretary of Defense Dick Cheney, in a letter to Senator Christopher Bond dated 29 July 1991, said that the F/A-18E "was the clear choice over the F-14" based on reliability, safety, and fewer maintenance personnel and operating costs. "It is three times more reliable, twice as easy to maintain, and has a safety record which is 50 percent better, requires about 25 [percent] fewer maintenance

An F/A-18E Hornet—unofficially called a Super Hornet—streaks over the Naval Air Weapons Station at China Lake, Calif. A pair of dummy Sidewinder missiles are affixed to the wingtips of this aircraft from squadron VX-9. (U.S. Navy)

Another view of the same F/A-18E from VX-9. The E/F variants resemble the earlier Hornets, but are significantly larger and are fitted with more powerful engines and improved avionics. Still, the later aircraft suffer from a number of shortcomings, especially range/payload. (U.S. Navy)

personnel, and costs about 25 percent less to operate per flight hour." Cheney concluded: "When combined, these factors clearly show that the FA-18E/F is the more cost-effective aircraft."

Subsequently, the F/A-18E/F program has encountered several delays and higher-than-expected costs while, according to the General Accounting Office (GAO),

the operational deficiencies in the F/A-18C/D that the Navy cited in justifying the F/A-18E/F either have not materialized or can be corrected with nonstructural changes to the C/D. Furthermore, E/F operational capabilities will only be marginally improved over the C/D model. In addition, although the E/F will have increased range over the C/D model, the C/D's range will exceed the range required by the E/F's system specifications and the E/F's range increase is achieved at the expense of its aerial combat performance. Also, modifications to increase the E/F's

payload have created a problem when weapons are released from the aircraft that may reduce the E/F's potential payload capability.[15]

Separate from the problems identified in the lengthy GAO report, on the seventh flight of the first F/A-18E aircraft (4 March 1996), a "wing-drop" phenomenon was detected. During certain high-speed maneuvers, the aircraft's wing would dip uncontrollably, caused by turbulence in the air passing over the wing.

15. General Accounting Office, *Navy Aviation: F/A-18E/F Will Provide Marginal Operational Improvements at High Cost,* NSIAD-96-98 (June 1996), pp. 4–5.

A two-seat F/A-18F showing the three pylons under each wing for weapons or fuel tanks; there also are fuselage attachment points (a centerline-mounted drop tank is shown here) and there are wingtip rails for Sidewinder AAMs. (Boeing)

A two-place F/A-18F is launched from a waist catapult of the carrier ABRAHAM LINCOLN during advanced carrier trials of the F/A-18E/F conducted in April 2000. There are five F/A-18E and two F/A-18F aircraft in the flight test program. (U.S. Navy)

Almost two years were required to develop a correction to the Hornet's wing-drop problem, amidst fears that an entirely new wing would have to be designed—a possible "show stopper" for the entire F/A-18E/F program. A variety of modifications—in aircraft software as well as design—were proposed. The fix proved to be perforated panels 5 feet (1.52 m) in length and made of composite material fitted in each wing. The fix led to Secretary of Defense William Cohen approving low-rate production of the F/A-18E/F in April 1998.

The original Navy–Marine Corps requirement was for 1,000 aircraft; however, by the mid-1990s the E/F procurement goal had been reduced to just under 800 aircraft. Procurement began with the fiscal 1998 budget, with all 800 aircraft to be acquired by 2015. The production number is based on a squadron requirement (including readiness units) of 630 aircraft plus 60 pipeline aircraft and about 100 aircraft for attrition through the year 2020. In addition, five F/A-18E and two F/A-18F aircraft were built specifically for the flight test program.

The F/A-18 team—Boeing–McDonnell Douglas and Northrop Grumman—also are studying the feasibility of an EW/ECM variant of the two-seat F/A-18F to replace the EA-6B Prowler (see Electronic Aircraft).

Design: The E/F models are based on an enlarged and upgraded F/A-18C/D design. Compared to the earlier series, the E/F variants have a center section plug, a 25 percent larger wing, and improved engines with 35 percent more thrust. The F414 engine is a derivative of the F404 used in earlier F/A-18s. Two additional wing stores stations provide a total of 11 on the fuselage and wings, plus two wingtip stations for the Sidewinder AAM.

The E/F aircraft are fitted with the ALE-50 towed missile countermeasures system, more expendable chaff, and flare countermeasures.[16] They are able to accommodate an inflight refueling pod to permit the aircraft to serve in a limited tanker role while carrying two 480-gallon (1,817-liter) drop tanks.

The "spotting factor" or footprint on the carrier deck is 23 percent larger for the F/A-18E than for the F/A-18C.

Status: In production. First flight: F/A-18E on 29 November 1995; F/A-18F on 1 April 1996. Planned IOC in 2001.

---

16. The ALQ-50 is an interim system until the Navy fields the Integrated Defensive Electronic Countermeasures (IDECM) system with a fiber-optic towed decoy.

Characteristics for the F/A-18E:

Manufacturer:	Boeing–McDonnell Douglas and Northrop Grumman
Crew:	F/A-18E (1) pilot
	F/A-18F (2) pilot, bombardier/navigator
Engines:	2 General Electric F414-GE-400 turbofan; 22,000 lbst (9,979 kgst) each
Weight:	empty 30,500 lbs (13,835 kg)
	maximum T/O 66,000 lbs (29,937 kg)
Dimensions:	length 60 ft 4 in (18.38 m)
	wingspan 44 ft 8 ½ in (13.63 m) with Sidewinder AAMs fitted
	wing area 500 ft² (45 m²)
	height 15 ft 10 in (4.83 m)
Speed:	maximum 1,028 knots (1,900 km/h) at 37,000 ft (11,280 m); Mach 1.8
Range:	radius 200 n.miles (370 km) in fighter role with 1.8 hours on station (2 Sidewinders + 4 AMRAAMs)
	420 n.miles (778 km) in fighter escort role (2 Sidewinders + 2 AMRAAMs)
	475 n.miles (880 km) in interdiction role (2 Sidewinders + 4 1,000-lb/454-kg bombs)
Ceiling:	50,000 ft (15,244 m)
Armament:	1 20-mm Vulcan cannon M61A1 (multibarrel; 400 rounds)
	up to 17,750 lbs (8,051 kg) of bombs, rockets, missiles, and external tanks
Radar:	APG-73

F/A-18C/D HORNET

The Hornet is a strike-fighter aircraft flown by the Navy and Marine Corps in significantly larger numbers than any other naval aircraft. Carrier air wings have three VFA/VMFA squadrons flying the F/A-18.[17]

The F/A-18 replaced the F-14 Tomcat and A-7 Corsair aboard carriers; in the Marine Corps, the F/A-18 replaced the F-4S Phantom fighter, A-6E Intruder and A-4M Skyhawk attack aircraft, and RF-4B Phantom and OA-4 Skyhawk special-purpose aircraft.

The development of the F/A-18 came as a result of pressure by Congress for the Navy to obtain a lightweight fighter to complement the F-14 in carrier air wings. Congress originally had directed the Navy to select the winner of the Air Force's lightweight fighter competition of the mid-1970s between the General Dynam-

---

17. A few wings have two F-14 squadrons and two F/A-18 squadrons.

An F/A-18C from VFA-94 during Operation Southern Watch, the enforcement of sanctions against Iraq. The squadron was aboard the carrier CARL VINSON during her 1999 deployment to the Persian Gulf. Two Sidewinders and four AMRAAMs, plus an internal 20-mm Vulcan gun, comprise the aircraft's armament. (U.S. Navy, Lt. Steve Lightstone)

ics YF-16 and Northrop YF-17 prototypes. The Air Force selected the F-16 for production; the Navy selected the YF-17, but made major modifications, leading to the F/A-18 developed jointly by McDonnell Douglas and Northrop. The naval aircraft failed to fully achieve its range/payload goals in the attack role.

The original F/A-18 procurement plan was for 11 development aircraft and 1,366 production planes for 24 Navy attack and six fighter squadrons and 12 Marine fighter squadrons, plus 332 aircraft in reserve units and 142 attrition and pipeline aircraft; the actual procurement was less (see *Status* notes).

The Navy–Marine Corps Blue Angels flight demonstration team began flying the F/A-18 in 1987. These are early, development models of the Hornet that are not carrier capable.[18]

The F/A-18 has been a controversial program because of the initial Marine decision to procure the AV-8B Harrier instead of the F/A-18 for the attack role, higher-than-predicted F/A-18 costs, and the F/A-18 having less range than the A-7. However, the aircraft's widespread use has had positive cost and support impact, and its

18. See page 373 for previous Blue Angel aircraft.

performance in Operation Desert Storm (1991) equaled its manufacturers' performance promises.

Design: A twin-engine, single- or two-seat aircraft, the F/A-18 is characterized by its high maneuverability, the ability to operate in either the fighter or attack role with the push of a button, and comparatively low maintenance requirements. The initial versions were the F/A-18A strike-fighter and TF-18 two-seat trainer, the latter now referred to as the F/A-18B. The F/A-18C is an improved single-seat aircraft and the F/A-18D is a two-seat aircraft with a weapons officer in the rear seat (no flight controls).

The twin-engine aircraft is distinguished by twin tail fins and swept leading wing edges. The F/A-18 has wingtip Sidewinder AAM positions, as well as three fuselage and four wing stations for weapons and sensor/guidance pods. A variety of bombs, missiles, and rockets can be carried, including up to four 2,000-pound (907-kg) bombs.

Initially, the F/A-18 flew with a pod-mounted FLIR developed specifically for the F/A-18 (the AAS-38). The F/A-18C/D models delivered after October 1989 have a night-attack capability based on a FLIR sensor called TINS (Thermal Imaging Navigation Set), designated ARR-50, and an improved HUD. The F/A-18s delivered through mid-1994 have the APG-65 multimode synthetic aperture radar.

The rear aspect of an F/A-18C from VMFA-251 being catapulted from the GEORGE WASHINGTON. The plane's engines are on afterburner. All fixed-wing aircraft except STOVLs are catapult launched from U.S. aircraft carriers, with all supercarriers having four steam catapults. (U.S. Navy, PH3 Sammy Dallal)

An F/A-18C Hornet at rest aboard the GEORGE WASHINGTON. The aircraft is fitted with three 300-gallon (1,140-liter) drop tanks. (U.S. Navy, PH3 Lisa Marcus)

A Marine F/A-18C from VMFA-251 during Operation Southern Watch. The Marine squadron was assigned to the carrier GEORGE WASHINGTON's air wing to compensate for the Navy's shortfall of Hornet squadrons. The outer wing panels fold for handling and stowage aboard ship. (U.S. Navy, PH3 Erik Kenney)

Some Marine D variants are configured for the Advanced Tactical Air Reconnaissance System (ATARS). The system, which can be installed in modified aircraft, provides real- and near-real-time photo-reconnaissance, with a limited data-link capability to transmit images to ground and shipboard facilities. This is the long-awaited replacement for the RF-4B Phantom reconnaissance aircraft. Two Marine F/A-18D Hornets fitted with ATARS entered combat operations over Kosovo on 26 May 1999. Plans call for a total purchase of 31 tactical reconnaissance conversion kits, 24 data-link pods, and seven squadron ground stations. Deliveries will continue through 2002, with each 12-plane VMFA(AW) squadron to have four ATARS "packages."

Designation: The initial Navy order for 11 development aircraft used the designation YF-18. The designation F/A-18A was used for initial single-seat aircraft and F/A-18B for those with tandem seating. See page 389–390 for further discussion of the F/A-18 designation.

Operational: More F/A-18s participated in the Persian Gulf War (January–February 1991) than any other fixed-wing naval aircraft, with 13 Navy VFA and 7 Marine VMFA squadrons—plus Canadian Forces—flying the Hornet. The 90 Navy F/A-18s flew 4,449 combat sorties and 84 Marine F/A-18s flew 5,239 sorties; these amounted to almost one-third of the 29,363 Navy-Marine combat sorties flown in the Gulf War (including fixed-wing aircraft and helicopter).

On 17 January 1991 two Navy F/A-18C aircraft shot down two Iraqi MiG-21 fighters using both Sparrow and Sidewinder missiles.[19]

Status: Operational; in production. First flight: F/A-18A on 18 November 1978; F/A-18B on 25 October 1979; F/A-18C on 18 November 1978; F/A-18D on 6 May 1988. IOC: Navy F/A-18A in February 1981 (VFA-125); Marine F/A-18A in March 1983 (VMFA-314); F/A-18D in May 1991 (VMFA[AW]-121). Through 30 September 2000, 1,048 F/A-18s of the A/B/C/D variants were delivered to the U.S. Navy and Marine Corps, ending production of these aircraft. In addition, 483 are being delivered to foreign air forces (including aircraft assembled, mostly with U.S. components, in Australia, Finland, and Switzerland). Almost all F/A-18A/B models have been retired from U.S. service.

Australia, Canada, Finland, Kuwait, Malaysia, Spain, and Switzerland have purchased the F/A-18 for land-based operation. (A proposed Northrop F-18L land-based variant has not been procured.)

---

19. On 17 January 1991, the two Navy F/A-18 Hornets from the carrier SARATOGA—on a bombing mission, each carrying four 2,000-pound (907-kg) bombs—were able to engage two Iraqi MiG-21 fighters. Both of the Iraqi planes which were shot down with air-to-air missiles, after which the F/A-18s were able to continue their bombing mission, not having had to jettison their bombs to engage the enemy planes.

An F/A-18C from VFA-86 about to plug in to a drogue streamed by an Air Force KC-10 Extender during an air-to-air fueling over the Persian Gulf. (U.S. Navy, Lt. Chuck Radosta)

Aviation ordnancemen work on an M61A1 Vulcan cannon on the carrier JOHN C. STENNIS steaming in the Persian Gulf. These six-barrel Gatling guns are fitted in F/A-18 and F-14 aircraft. (U.S. Navy, PH2 Robert M. Baker)

Characteristics for the F/A-18C:

Manufacturer:	McDonnell Douglas and Northrop	
Crew:	F/A-18C (1) pilot	
	F/A-18D (2) pilot, bombardier/navigator	
Engines:	2 General Electric F404-GE-400 turbofan; 16,000 lbst (7,258 kgst) each; F404-GE-402 engines with 17,700 lbst (8,029 kgst) in fiscal 1992 and later aircraft	
Weight:	empty	23,050 lbs (10,455 kg)
	normal T/O	36,710 lbs (16,651 kg) fighter mission
		49,224 lbs (22,328 kg) attack mission
Dimensions:	length	56 ft (17.07 m)
	wingspan	37 ft 6 in (11.43 m)
		40 ft 5 in (12.31 m) with Sidewinder AAMs fitted
	wing area	400 ft² (37.16m²)
	height	15 ft 3½ in (4.66 m)
Speed:	maximum	1,028 knots (1,900 km/h) at 37,000 ft (11,280 m); Mach 1.8
Ceiling:	50,000 ft (15,240 m)	
Range:	radius	200 n.miles (370 km) in fighter role with 1 hour on station (2 Sidewinders + 4 AMRAAMs)
		303 n.miles (565 km) in fighter escort role (2 Sidewinders + 2 AMRAAMs)
		277 n.miles (513 km) in interdiction role (2 Sidewinders + 4 1,000-lb/454-kg bombs)
Armament:	1 20-mm Vulcan cannon M61 (multibarrel; 570 rounds)	
	2 Sidewinder + 4 Sparrow/AMRAAM AAMs in fighter role	
	or 2 Sidewinder AAMs + 17,000 lbs (7,711 kg) of bombs, missiles, or rockets in attack role	
Radar:	APG-65 or APG-73	

A pair of F/A-18D aircraft from VMFA(AW)-121 are fitted with the Advanced Tactical Air Reconnaissance System (ATARS) in their modified nose sections. This system is a belated replacement for the RF-4B Phantom photo aircraft, the last of which were retired in 1992. (Boeing)

F-16N FIGHTING FALCON

The Navy flew 26 modified F-16C Fighting Falcon fighters in the adversary training role (replacing the F-21A Kfir). The service took delivery of 22 single-seat F-16N and four two-seat TF-16N aircraft in 1987–1988. These aircraft were grounded beginning in 1991 because of structural cracking in the center fuselage. They were then disposed of.

The F-16 is the standard U.S. Air Force lightweight fighter, which also is flown by several allied air forces. The Navy F-16Ns were similar to the Air Force F-16C variant, but did not have the M61 20-mm Vulcan cannon; also, the Navy planes were fitted with the APG-66 radar of the earlier Air Force F-16A/B aircraft and had a more advanced engine.

See 15th Edition/pages 402–403 for characteristics.

F-14 TOMCAT

The F-14 was the standard U.S. Navy carrier-based fighter of the 1970s and 1980s, with two squadrons assigned to each standard carrier air wing. Today most U.S. carrier wings have one F-14 squadron and a few have two squadrons, pending the availability of additional F/A-18s. Eventually the F-14 will be replaced aboard carriers by the F/A-18E and, subsequently, the JSF.

Designed to intercept Soviet long-range strike aircraft, in several respects the F-14 remains the most capable long-range, all-weather fighter aircraft in service with any air force.

One VF squadron in each carrier can employ the F-14 in the photo-reconnaissance role with the standard aircraft fitted with the removable TARPS (Tactical Air Reconnaissance Pod System). The TARPS package—a KS-87 frame camera, a KA-99 panoramic camera, and an

An F-14B Tomcat from VF-143 flies over the Swiss Alps during a NATO training symposium. Operating from the GEORGE WASHINGTON, the plane shows the graceful lines of the Tomcat, one of the most attractive military aircraft now flying. It is the last VF-type aircraft flown by U.S. Naval Aviation. (U.S. Navy, Lt. Lee Turner)

AAD-5 infrared line scanner—can be fitted to or removed from the aircraft in a few hours.

The F-14 also was planned for Marine Corps use, but that service turned it down, in part because of the decision to procure the AV-8A Harrier.

Design: A two-seat aircraft, the F-14 has variable-geometry wings that sweep back automatically as the aircraft maneuvers during flight; they extend for long-range flight and landings, sweeping back for high-speed flight (and carrier stowage). The normal sweep range is 20° to 68°, with a 75° "oversweep" position provided for shipboard hangar stowage; sweep speed is 7.5° per second.

The F-14 has the long-range AWG-9 radar, which can detect hostile aircraft out to more than 87 n.miles (161 km) and simulta-

neously track up to 24 targets, and the Phoenix missile, which can engage targets more than 52 n.miles (96.5 km) away. The basic F-14 suite includes the ALR-45 and ALR-50 radar warning receivers, ALE-29 and ALE-39 chaff/flare dispensers, and ALQ-100 deception jamming pod. A forward-looking AXX-1 television camera is fitted for long-range visual detection.

All surviving F-14s are being fitted with the AAQ-14 LANTIRN (Low Altitude Navigation and Targeting Infrared for Night) targeting pod for aiming laser-guided munitions. (The first F-14 squadron to receive LANTIRN was VF-103, which deployed aboard the carrier ENTERPRISE in July 1996.)

Up to 14,500 pounds (6,577 kg) of external stores can be carried by the F-14. The aircraft originally had a total of four fuselage missile positions (4 Sparrow or 4 Phoenix) and two wing positions

With wings swept back, an F-14A from VF-154 streaks low over Okinawa. The Tomcat, assigned to the KITTY HAWK's Japan-based air wing, has a Phoenix AAM under the left wing; drop tanks are fitted under both of the aircraft's elongated engine nacelles. (U.S. Navy, PH1 Chris Desmond)

An F-14B flies over coral reefs in the Caribbean during a brief deployment to the Naval Station at Roosevelt Roads, P.R. The plane is from VF-102. The F-14's wings are swept back for high-speed flight. When aboard ship, they are swept back to facilitate handling and stowage. (U.S. Navy)

(4 Sidewinder or 2 Sparrow or 2 Phoenix). Subsequently, the F-14B/D have been fitted with racks for "iron bombs" and laser-guided bombs (GBU); the F-14D also has pylon adapters for HARM and Harpoon air-to-surface missiles, as well as iron bombs and GBUs.[20] With a reduced missile load, the aircraft can carry fuel tanks or a TARPS.

Only about 80 F-14A variants originally were to have been procured; subsequent aircraft were to have been the F-14B with F401-PW-400 engines, with a later F-14C additionally to have an avionics upgrade. In the event, only the F-14A model was produced through the mid-1980s. (The Navy had planned an F-14 upgrade with improved engines and air-to-surface weapons in the 1970s, but those programs were halted

because of the lack of funds.) Engine problems plagued the F-14A, and the F-14A+ variants were fitted with F110-GE-400 engines (formerly F101 DFE), but were otherwise similar to the basic F-14A. The F-14A+ designation was changed to F-14B in 1991 (previously, one F-14A had been reengined and designated F-14B).

The follow-on F-14D has the synthetic-aperture APG-71 radar and other improvements, including a capability for the AMRAAM missile. It retained the F-14B's F110-GE-400 engines. The F110 engines provide an increased radius (deck-launched intercept) from 135 n.miles (250 km) to 210 n.miles (390 km) and maximum catapult weight increase from 59,000 pounds (26,762 kg) to 74,000 pounds (33,566 kg).

The decision to procure 324 F-14D models with the F110 engines and upgraded avionics was made in early 1984. In April 1989, new procurement was halted by the Department of Defense in favor of the "remanufacture" of 400 earlier F-14 aircraft; subsequently, in 1991 the Navy decided to remanufacture only 104 F-14A to the F-14D configuration by the year 1997, the cutback having been made in an unsuccessful effort to garner funds for new F-14D production. In the event, only 37 new F-14D aircraft and 18 F-14A upgrades to full F-14D configuration were procured.

---

20. GBU = Guided Bomb Unit, referring to the guidance package fitted to Mk 82 (500-lb), Mk 83 (1,000-lb), and Mk 4 (2,000-lb) bombs.

An F-14B from VF-32 aboard the ENTERPRISE shows the Tomcat's Television Camera Set (TCS) and Infrared Search and Track (IRST) sensor under the nose, and the opening for the 20-mm M61A1 Vulcan cannon (beneath the side number *101*). The refueling probe retracts into the right side of the aircraft's nose. (U.S. Navy)

An F-14A assigned to VX-9 conducts an inflight refueling from an Air Force KC-10 Extender. Sidewinder AAMs are mounted under the Tomcat's wings. Air Force tankers—KC-10 and KC-135—use rigid booms to refuel most Air Force aircraft, but can stream drogues for Navy probe-and-drogue refueling systems. (U.S. Navy, MSgt. Joe Cupido [USAF])

An F-14A from VF-41 launches from the THEODORE ROOSEVELT. Both afterburners are on, adding thrust to the catapult stroke. Steam catapults in these ships have launched A-3 Skywarriors, a non-afterburning aircraft and, with a takeoff weight of more than 80,000 pounds (36,288 kg), the largest to regularly operate from U.S. carriers. (U.S. Navy, PH3 Shawn M. Boyer)

The F-14C variant was to have been a development of the original (engine update) F-14B with improved avionics. Several research variants are designated NF-14D.

Operational: The 99 F-14 aircraft participating in Desert Storm flew 4,124 combat sorties. On 6 February 1991, an F-14A shot down an Iraqi Mi-8 Hip helicopter with a Sidewinder missile. This was one of three Navy air-to-air kills in the conflict (the other two were made by F/A-18s).

The first use of the Tomcat in the air-to-ground role in combat occurred on 5 September 1995 when an F-14A from the carrier THEODORE ROOSEVELT dropped two 2,000-pound (907-kg) bombs on Serb positions in Bosnia.

Status: Operational; no longer in production. First flight: F-14A on 21 December 1970; F-14B (F-14A engine conversion) on 29 Sep-

tember 1986; F-14A+ on 24 November 1987. IOC: F-14A in January 1973 (VF-124); F-14D in November 1990.

The last F-14 was delivered in May 1992. A total of 632 aircraft were produced for the U.S. Navy: 557 F-14A (including development models), 38 F-14A+ (redesignated F-14B), and 37 new F-14D variants. Subsequently, the following F-14A conversions were undertaken: 1 to F-14B (engine change only in 1973), 32 to F-14A+, 3 to F-14D electronic test bed aircraft, and 18 to F-14D.

An additional 80 F-14A aircraft were built for Iran; 79 were delivered in 1976–1979 and one was retained by Grumman because of the Iranian revolution.

Characteristics for the F-14A:

Manufacturer:	Grumman	
Crew:	(2) pilot, radar-intercept officer	
Engines:	F-14A	2 Pratt & Whitney TF30-P-414A turbofan; 20,900 lbst (9,480 kgst) each with afterburning
	F-14B/D	2 General Electric F110-GE-400 turbofans; 27,000 lbst (12,150 kg) each with afterburning
Weight:	empty	40,104 lbs (18,191 kg)
	takeoff	59,714 lbs (27,086 kg) with 4 Sparrow/AMRAAM AAMs
		70,764 lbs (32,098 kg) with 6 Phoenix AAMs
		74,349 lbs (33,724 kg) maximum
Dimensions:	length	62 ft 8 in (19.1 m)
	wingspan	64 ft 1½ in (19.54 m) unswept
		38 ft 2½ in (11.65 m) swept back
	wing area	565 ft² (52.49 m²)
	height	16 ft (4.88 m)
Speed:	maximum	1,342 knots (2,485 km/h) at altitude
		793 knots (1,468 km/h) at low level
	maximum cruise	550 knots (1,019 km/h)
Ceiling:	50,000+ ft (15,240+ m)	
Range:	radius	approx. 500 n.miles (925 km) in strike role
		925 n.miles (1,715 km) in air intercept role
	ferry	1,740 n.miles (3,220 km) with 2 267-gallon (1,015-liter) drop tanks
Armament:	1 20-mm Vulcan cannon M61 (multibarrel; 676 rounds) *and*	
	2 Phoenix + 3 Sparrow/AMRAAM + 2 Sidewinder AAMs + 2 267-gallon (1,015-liter) drop tanks	
or	4 Phoenix + 2 Sparrow/AMRAAM + 2 Sidewinder AAMs + 2 267-gallon drop tanks	
or	6 Phoenix + 2 Sidewinder AAMs + 2 267-gallon drop tanks	
or	6 Sparrow/AMRAAM + 2 Sidewinder AAMs + 2 267-gallon drop tanks	
Radar:	F-14A	AWG-9
	F-14D	APG-71

Photographer's mates on the GEORGE WASHINGTON remove a Tactical Air Reconnaissance Pod System (TARPS) from an F-14. Although the improved TARPS is a capable reconnaissance system, the pilots of TARPS aircraft are "fighter jocks" with little training and experience in the art of reconnaissance. (U.S. Navy)

Mechanics maintain an F-14B from VF-143 aboard the JOHN C. STENNIS during operations in the Persian Gulf. Modern naval aircraft require large numbers of maintenance and support personnel as well as specialized test equipment, tools, and spare parts. (U.S. Navy, PH2 Clint Beaird)

F-5E/F TIGER II

The F-5E/F variant of the F-5 lightweight fighter is flown by the Navy as an air combat maneuvering/adversary training aircraft. The aircraft was the penultimate design in a long series of trainer/fighter aircraft developed by Northrop, primarily for Third World markets. (The much-improved F-5G was redesignated F-20.)

Design: The F-5E Tiger is a single-seat aircraft and the F-5F a two-seat version, both with two turbojet engines. Sidewinder AAMs can be carried on the wingtips and there are one fuselage and four wing stations for ordnance. The aircraft is not carrier capable.

Status: Operational; no longer in production. First flight: F-5A on 30 July 1959; F-5E on 11 August 1972.

More than 3,000 F-5 fighters and similar T-38 Talon trainers have been built for the U.S. Air Force and some 25 foreign nations. The U.S. Navy has 32 F-5E variants and 4 F-5F aircraft (plus 11 T-38s) to simulate Russian fighter aircraft in adversary training. The Marines previously flew the F-5E/F in reserve adversary training squadron VMFT-401.

Manufacturer:	Northrop		
Crew:	F-5E (1) pilot		
	F-5F (2) pilot, student		
Engines:	2 General Electric J85-GE-21B turbojet; 5,000 lbst (2,268 kgst) each with afterburning		
Weight:	empty	F-5E	9,723 lbs (4,410 kg)
		F-5F	10,576 lbs (4,797 kg)
	maximum T/O	F-5E	24,722 lbs (11,214 kg)
		F-5F	25,152 lbs (11,409 kg)
Dimensions:	length	F-5E	47 ft 4¾ in (14.45 m)
		F-5F	51 ft 4 in (15.65 m)
	wingspan	26 ft 8 in (8.13 m)	
	wing area	186 ft² (17.3 m²)	
	height	F-5E	13 ft 4 in (4.06 m)
		F-5F	13 ft 1¾ in (4.01 m)
Speed:	maximum	Mach 1.64 at 36,000 ft (10,975 m)	
Ceiling:	51,800 ft (15,790 m)		
Range:	radius	570 n.miles (1,056 km) with 2 Sidewinder AAMs	
		1,545 n.miles (2,861 km) with external tanks	
Armament:	none		
Radar:	APQ-159		

An F-5E Tiger II in Marine markings. Both the Navy and Marine Corps have flown the F-5E and two-seat F-5F to provide stand-ins for high-performance MiG-21 type aircraft in their training programs. (Northrop, Michael Benolkin)

In Navy markings, this F-5E shows the stub wings and twin engines of the Tiger II aircraft. In naval service these aircraft are camouflaged, reflecting the paint scheme of many Third World air forces. (Northrop, Michael Benolkin)

F-4 PHANTOM

Long the principal all-weather, multipurpose fighter of the Navy and Marine Corps, all F-4 Phantoms have been retired from Navy and Marine combat squadrons, replaced by the F-14 Tomcat in Navy fighter squadrons (VF) and by the F/A-18 Hornet in Marine fighter-attack squadrons (VMFA).

There is a single YF-4J aircraft in service at Naval Weapons Test Squadron, NAS Point Mugu, Calif., for flight tests. Additional Phantoms designed QF-4N/S are in use as radio-controlled target drones.

McDonnell Douglas produced 5,211 Phantom aircraft for U.S. and foreign service, while Japan built 138 F-4EJ variants, including 11 from parts produced by McDonnell Douglas. Production ended in 1979; the last of 1,264 aircraft delivered to the Navy and Marine Corps were completed in December 1971 (including 46 of the RF-4B reconnaissance variant). The principal U.S. naval production versions were the F-4B and F-4J, which subsequently were upgraded to the F-4N and F-4S, respectively. The Phantom is no longer in service with the U.S. Air Force, but is flown by several other nations.[21]

The last Navy squadron to fly the Phantom, reserve VF-202, retired its last F-4S in early 1987; the last Marine unit, also flying the F-4S, was reserve VMFA-112, which phased out its last Phantoms in mid-1992. All RF-4B reconnaissance variants have been retired from Marine service, the last in 1992.

Designation: Originally designated F4H by the Navy and F-110 by the Air Force; the designation of both was changed to F-4 in 1962.

See 14th Edition/pages 401–402 for characteristics.

---

21. The Royal Navy also flew Phantoms from aircraft carriers, with the F-4K being Britain's last non-VSTOL carrier-based fighter-attack aircraft; all have been discarded.

MARITIME PATROL/ANTI-SUBMARINE AIRCRAFT

The U.S. Navy has a requirement for 300 land-based maritime patrol aircraft for active and reserve patrol squadrons, plus special-purpose aircraft (EP-3, RP-3, etc.). This requirement compares to more than 400 P-3 aircraft in service in 1990 and 230 P-3 aircraft operational in the year 2000 (plus EP-3 electronic, NP-3D research, VP-3 transport, and UP-3 utility aircraft). All first-line patrol aircraft are P-3C variants (with various levels of the Update series of modernization.)

Following cancellation of the P-7 LRAACA program in 1990, the Navy has been examining options to meet future requirements for maritime patrol aircraft. The most likely options are to resume production of an updated P-3 Orion variant or to "remanufacture" P-3 aircraft into an improved P-3H configuration. The proposed P-3H variant would have the Update IV avionics, survivability enhancements, extended-range Harpoon capability, and a larger sonobuoy capacity.

(P-3 production ended in the United States in 1995 with eight aircraft for South Korea; P-3 production continued a while longer in Japan.)

P-7A LRAACA

The P-7 Long-Range Air Anti-Submarine Warfare Capable Aircraft (LRAACA) was intended as a replacement for the P-3 Orion in the maritime patrol and ASW roles. Development and procurement of the P-7 was canceled by the Navy on 20 July 1990 because the contractor, Lockheed Aeronautical Systems of Burbank, Calif., "failed to make adequate progress toward completion of all contract phases, which were to have resulted in the delivery of two prototype aircraft in April and December 1992." Two prototypes and 125 production aircraft were to have been delivered from 1994 through 2001.

In the mid-1980s the Navy held a competition for the P-3 replacement, with the Lockheed design and proposals based on the Boeing 757 and McDonnell Douglas MD-90 airframes competing. The mod-

The YF-4J Phantom, assigned to tests work, is shown over the Caribbean. The Phantom was produced in greater numbers than any other Western combat aircraft of the Cold War era, except for the F-86 Sabre/FJ Fury series. The refueling probe, above the right engine intake, is in the process of retracting after an inflight refueling. (U.S. Navy, JO1 David Rush)

ified P-3 design submitted by Lockheed was selected in October 1988 on the basis of acquisition and life-cycle costs, according to the Navy.[22] The $3.5 *billion* program was badly needed at Lockheed, with the last P-3 Orion then scheduled to come off the production line in September 1991 and few other aircraft on the Lockheed order book. Lockheed subsequently experienced major cost problems with the P-7 program, as well as some technical difficulties. In March 1989—shortly before cancellation—the estimated acquisition cost for 125 P-7A aircraft was about $7.9 *billion* with an estimated production cost of $56.7 million per aircraft. The technical problems were particularly perplexing to observers because the Lockheed design was in several respects an enlarged P-3, with less technical innovation than the competitive designs.

The LRAACA bore a strong resemblance to the P-3 Orion; there was to be a large internal weapons bay plus 12 wing hard points for weapons. The four GE-38 engines were estimated to have 25 percent lower fuel consumption over the aircraft operating envelope compared with the P-3's T56 engines. The improved performance was due in part to five-blade composite propellers.

Initial Navy planning was for 125 aircraft plus two prototypes, but more aircraft were anticipated, in addition to eventual foreign orders. The German government in April 1988 announced that it planned to select the P-7 to replace its Dassault-Breguet Atlantic ASW aircraft for long-range maritime patrol duties.

See 16th Edition/pages 375–376 for characteristics.

P-3 ORION

The Orion is a long-range maritime reconnaissance and ASW aircraft, with the Harpoon anti-ship missile providing a surface attack capability. The P-3C Orion serves in all active and reserve Navy patrol squadrons (VP/VPU), with several specialized ELINT, research, and utility variants also in naval service—a current total of some 250 aircraft.

The decision not to procure the P-7 will require further upgrades to the P-3 force. P-3s are expected to remain in U.S. Navy patrol squadrons at least through 2015.

Design: The Orion was adapted from the commercial Electra transport with a lengthened fuselage and other design modifications.

---

22. Boeing proposed a modified version of the 757 twin-engine commercial transport and McDonnell Douglas a modified MD-87 twin-engine transport, the latter with ultra-high-bypass-ratio engines. Gulfstream Aerospace had also proposed a twin-engine, wide-body Gulfstream-IV for the LRAACA program, but it was not accepted as a viable competitor.

It is powered by four turboprop engines. Up to 15,000 pounds (6,804 kg) of rockets, missiles, mines, ASW torpedoes, or nuclear depth bombs can be carried in the internal weapons bay and on ten wing pylons. The P-3C aircraft are fitted to carry the Harpoon. (In the early 1970s some P-3B variants were fitted to carry the AGM-12 Bullpup missile.) The plane's ASW equipment includes radar, the tail-mounted ASQ-81 MAD, and 48 external (fuselage) sonobuoy chutes plus four inflight reloadable (internal) chutes; a total of 84 buoys are normally carried.

The P-3C variants have undergone a series of modernizations: Update I of the mid-1970s included a computer upgrade, the Omega navigation system, additional tactical displays, and a new tactical program for computer-aided analysis of incoming data. Update II, introduced in 1977, had additional navigation capabilities and provision for the Harpoon anti-ship missile. The latest improvement series is Update III, introduced in 1984, which provides an IBM Proteus signal processor system and new avionics. An Update IV that will further improve EW, radar, and acoustic systems has been developed. Plans to provide an inflight refueling capability have not been pursued.

Several specialized P-3 variants are in service. The EP-3E and EP-3J are listed separately under Electronic Aircraft. Thirteen NP-3D aircraft are flown in various research configurations by the Navy; these were previously designated RP-3A/D, EP-3A/B, and several UP-3A test bed variants. The Navy also flies five UP-3A/B and three VP-3A "bob-tailed" (i.e., sans the MAD "stinger") aircraft as executive transports and support aircraft. Two WP-3D are operated by the National Oceanic and Atmospheric Administration (NOAA) of the Department of Commerce; several UP-3A aircraft have been on loan from the Navy to the Customs Service for anti-drug surveillance since October 1985 (those aircraft have been fitted with an APG-53 radar, as in the Air Force F-15 fighter, one with an APS-125 radar with rotodome antenna, as in the E-2C, and one with an APS-138 radar); and NASA flies one P-3B.

A planned P-3G maritime patrol/ASW aircraft for the U.S. Navy was to have had new engines and updated avionics. (This aircraft was incorrectly identified as a P-3F in some official documents; six P-3F variants were produced for Iran.) The procurement of 125 P-3G models in fiscal 1990–1995 was envisioned; however, the Navy did not pursue the P-3G option because only Lockheed responded to the Navy's request for a proposal, and the P-7 LRAACA was developed in its place. Proposals were also being considered to re-engine and upgrade the avionics of the P-3C force, with a possible enlargement of the weapons bay to carry extended-range Harpoon missiles internally—that upgrade being labeled P-3H.

A P-3C Orion from VP-45. There is no plan to replace the venerable Orions in the maritime patrol/ASW role. Low-visibility markings were instituted for U.S. naval aircraft during the Vietnam War; however, the policy and visibility of aircraft markings vary considerably. (U.S. Navy)

Future upgrades for the P-3C may include the APS-137 Inverse Synthetic Aperture Radar (ISAR); Cluster Ranger, a long-range, day/night electro-optical imaging system; upgrading the AAR-36 infrared system to improve effectiveness against small targets, both day and night; new tactical displays; a UHF satellite communications system; and Maverick air-to-surface missiles.

Designation: Originally designated P3V; changed to P-3 in 1962.

Status: Operational; no longer in production. First flight: aerodynamic airframe on 19 August 1958; YP-3A on 25 November 1959; P-3A on 15 April 1961; YP-3C on 18 September 1968. IOC: P-3A in August 1962 (VP-8); P-3C in 1969.

Lockheed facilities at Burbank and Palmdale, Calif., delivered a total of 551 Orions to the U.S. Navy. The last U.S. Navy Orion to be produced was a P-3C, delivered on 17 April 1990. (The last Palmdale aircraft was a CP-140A for the Canadian Forces, completed in May 1991; the eight P-3C aircraft for South Korea were delivered by the Lockheed-Martin facility at Marietta, Ga., in 1995.) Kawasaki in Japan assembled five airframes produced by Lockheed and, under

Sonobuoys are loaded into dispensers of a P-3C Orion. These devices are launched from these 48 external dispensers, as well as from four chutes that can be reloaded in flight. (U.S. Navy, PH2 August Sigur)

A P-3C Orion shows the comely lines of the aircraft, adapted from the commercial Electra airliner. (Chris Buhlmann)

A P-3C from VP-10 approaches Mt. Etna during the squadron's six-month deployment to NAS Sigonella, Sicily. The Italian airfield supports a number of U.S. and other NATO air operations in the Mediterranean area. VP-10 is based at NAS Brunswick, Maine. (U.S. Navy, PHAN Alesha A. Stanaitis)

license, built more than 100 P-3C, EP-3, UP-3C, and UP-3D aircraft for the Japanese Maritime Self-Defense Force.[23]

Almost 200 aircraft—new and ex-U.S. Navy—are flown by Australia, Canada, Iran, Japan, South Korea, the Netherlands, New Zealand, Norway, Portugal, Spain, and Thailand. Numerous upgrade programs are under way for the non-U.S. aircraft.

Characteristics for the P-3C:

Manufacturer:	Lockheed	
Crew:	(10) command pilot, 2 pilots, flight engineer, navigator/communications officer, tactical coordinator, 3 systems operators, 1 technician + provision for 2 additional observers	
Engines:	4 Allison T56-A-14 turboprop; 4,910 ehp each[24]	
Weight:	empty	61,491 lbs (27,892 kg)
	normal T/O	135,000 lbs (61,236 kg)
	maximum T/O	142,000 lbs (64,411 kg)
Dimensions:	length	116 ft 10 in (35.61 m)
	wingspan	99 ft 8 in (30.37 m)
	wing area	1,300 ft² (120.77 m²)
	height	33 ft 8½ in (10.29 m)
Speed:	maximum	411 knots (761 km/h) at 15,000 ft (4,573 m)
	cruise	330 knots (611 km/h) at 25,000 ft (7,622 m)
	loiter	200 knots (370 km/h) with two engines shut down
Ceiling:	28,300 ft (8,628 m)	
Range:	radius 1,346 n.miles (2,493 km) with 13 hours on station	

Armament:

	in weapons bay		on wings
	8 Mk 46/50 torpedoes	+	4 Mk 46/50 torpedoes
or	2 2,000-lb mines	+	4 Mk 46/50 torpedoes
or	4 1,000-lb mines	+	4 Mk 46/50 torpedoes
or	8 Mk 46/50 torpedoes	+	16 5-inch rockets

Radar:	EP-3B/E	APS-20
	P-3B	APS-80
	P-3C	APS-115

---

23. The single Japanese UP-3C is an inflight electronic systems test bed aircraft; the UP-3D aircraft support fleet EW training.

24. ehp = equivalent horsepower—a measure of the propulsive power of a turboprop engine, made up of shaft horsepower (shp) plus additional power due to residual jet thrust.

S-3B VIKING

The S-3 Viking is a carrier-based surveillance/tanker aircraft with one eight-plane squadron serving on board each carrier. The Viking replaced the S2F/S-2 Tracker as the Navy's ship-based, fixed-wing ASW aircraft.

From 1993 the S-3B was considered a "sea control" vice ASW aircraft, and in the mid-1990s the ASW equipment and operators were removed. Thus configured, they are employed in ocean surveillance, anti-shipping (with Harpoon and Maverick air-to-surface missiles), and aerial tanking (with external drogue pod and fuel tanks) missions. The last role is particularly significant because of the demise of the KA-6D Intruder tanker aircraft and the relatively short range of the F/A-18 Hornet.

All surviving aircraft are of the S-3B configuration.

Design: The S-3 was designed to be within the approximate dimensions of the piston-engine Tracker, but to be faster and to carry more advanced ASW equipment. The internal weapons bay, sized to hold four lightweight ASW torpedoes, can carry 2,400 pounds (1,089 kg) of weapons or auxiliary fuel tanks. There are also two wing pylons, which in the S-3B are upgraded to carry the Harpoon anti-ship missile. The S-3B has an improved acoustic processor and the improved APS-137 ISAR radar, with a major avionics upgrade program for 124 S-3B aircraft begun in 1995. (ASW systems included the ASQ-81 MAD, FLIR, and 60 sonobuoys in fuselage chutes.) The wings and tail fin fold for carrier stowage.

Five preproduction S-3A aircraft were modified to a US-3A cargo configuration for operation from carriers in the Western Pacific and Indian Ocean; those planes were taken out of service in the early 1990s (see 15th Edition/pages 414–415). A KS-3 tanker configuration was proposed, as well as pod tanks and a drogue system for the US-3A variant; however, no development of a specialized tanker was undertaken.

Sixteen S-3A aircraft were converted to the ELINT role and were designated ES-3A (see entry under Electronic Aircraft).

Two S-3B Vikings from VS-33—at the time, aboard the carrier NIMITZ—operate over the Persian Gulf. The Vikings were developed and initially flew as ASW aircraft. In the post–Cold War era they are employed as surveillance/tanker aircraft and are used as bombers and minelayers in low-threat areas. (U.S. Navy, PH2 Matthew J. Magee)

Operational: S-3A/B aircraft served as ground-attack aircraft in low-threat areas during Operation Desert Storm. The 41 Vikings participating in that conflict flew 1,674 combat sorties.

Status: Operational; no longer in production. First flight of S-3A on 21 January 1972. IOC of S-3A in February 1974 (VS-41).

The last of 187 S-3A aircraft was completed in 1978. About 160 were upgraded to S-3B by 1994. Proposals for additional S-3 production have not come to fruition.

Manufacturer:	Lockheed	
Crew:	(2) pilot, copilot + 2 technicians/passengers	
Engines:	2 General Electric TF34-GE-400 turbofan; 9,275 lbst (4,207 kgst) each	
Weight:	empty	26,783 lbs (12,149 kg)
	maximum T/O	52,539 lbs (23,832 kg)

Dimensions:	length	53 ft 4 in (16.26 m)	
	wingspan	68 ft 8 in (20.93 m)	
	wing area	598 ft² (55.56 m²)	
	height	22 ft 9 in (6.94 m)	
Speed:	maximum	440 knots (814 km/h) at sea level	
	cruise	347+ knots (644+ km/h)	
	loiter	208 knots (386 km/h) at 20,000 ft (6,098 ft)	
Ceiling:	40,000 ft (12,195 m)		
Range:	patrol	2,300+ n.miles (4,260+ km)	
	ferry	3,000+ n.miles (5,556+ km)	
Armament:[25]	*in weapons bay*		*on wings*
	4 Mk 46/50 torpedoes	+	6 500-lb (227-kg) bombs
or	4 500-lb bombs	+	6 500-lb bombs
Radar:	APS-137 ISAR		

25. Armament shown was for the ASW role.

A tired and worn-looking S-3B from VS-22 aboard the ENTERPRISE patrols over southern Iraq as part of Operation Southern Watch. (U.S. Navy, PH2 Michael W. Pendergrass)

An S-3B from VS-22 embarked in the ENTERPRISE refuels another Viking from the squadron over the Persian Gulf. The refueling drogue is streamed from a pod under tanker Viking's left wing. (U.S. Navy, PH2 Michael W. Pendergrass)

An S-3B from VS-31 comes aboard the JOHN C. STENNIS. The Viking has a HARM anti-radar missile under its right wing and a refueling pod under the left wing. (U.S. Navy, Lt. Wayne S. Grazio)

ELECTRONIC AIRCRAFT

U.S. naval electronic aircraft have two distinct types of designations: those with E-series designations that were designed specifically for an electronic mission (e.g., E-2C, E-6B), and those that have been adopted from other aircraft types and have an E-prefix to their original designation (e.g., EA-6B, EP-3E). In this subsection all electronic aircraft are listed in alphabetical sequence by designation, which is not their chronological order.

In addition to the electronic aircraft discussed here, the Customs Service flies Airborne Early Warning (AEW)-configured P-3 Orions and the Coast Guard evaluated an AEW-configured C-130 Hercules.

COMMON SUPPORT AIRCRAFT

The Common Support Aircraft (CSA) is intended to provide a single aircraft to fulfill the carrier-based surveillance, control, and support roles, replacing the C-2A, E-2C, ES-3A, KA-6D, and S-3B aircraft. It is envisioned as a single aircraft design that could carry different mission suites of sensors and avionics.

A 1993 Naval Aviation study concluded that a "neck down" of follow-on aircraft was the only affordable procurement strategy for future naval aircraft. The CSA will require a 2012 initial operational capability at the latest.

The CSA program replaces several earlier, unsuccessful efforts to develop a single aircraft for these diversified roles. The immediately previous effort was the Advanced Tactical Support (ATS) aircraft, which the Navy also viewed as a "totally new start." The ATS aircraft was conceived in the late 1980s and funding for advanced development was provided by Congress until fiscal 1991, when all ATS funding was deleted and the project terminated.

The V-22 Osprey STOVL aircraft was at one point considered a viable candidate for the ATS role until Secretary of Defense Cheney canceled the V-22 program in 1989. In the ATS role, the V-22 was to have the valuable attributes of being independent of flight deck cycles on large carriers and capable of operating from large surface combatant and amphibious ships.

The Navy had also considered two other potential roles for the ATS: (1) airborne battle management, having the computer power and other facilities to enable a force commander or tactical action officer to direct operations from above the force, and (2) the "missileer" concept. First advanced in the 1960s with the never-built Douglas F6D aircraft, the missileer would provide for a relatively low-performance aircraft to remain on station for long periods with advanced air-to-air missiles to intercept incoming attackers.

E-6A/B MERCURY

This aircraft has replaced the EC-130 Hercules in the TACAMO (Take Charge And Move Out) role of providing VLF radio relay to strategic missile submarines at sea. In addition, in the late 1990s these aircraft (upgraded to the E-6B configuration) replaced 27 Air Force EC-135 aircraft in the "Looking Glass" program, providing airborne control of U.S. land-based strategic weapons with the Airborne Launch Control System (ALCS). In this role, the aircraft carry joint Navy–Air Force operational teams.

The original E-6A was a modified Boeing 707-320B airframe, which also served as the airframe for the E-3 AWACS (Airborne Warning And Control System); the C-135/KC-135/VC-137/EC-18/E-8A aircraft are similar.

Design: The Navy had proposed a competition of available airframes to replace the EC-130 in the TACAMO role; however, only

The E-6B Mercury combines the historic Navy TACAMO role with the Air Force "Looking Glass" airborne launch control of strategic weapons. The "B" modification to the Mercury is readily identified by the dorsal "hump" housing additional electronics and other, minor external modifications. (U.S. Navy)

the Boeing Company responded, proposing the modified Boeing 707-320B airframe. The E-6 has the familiar lines of the Boeing 707-series commercial transports, but is fitted with four large GE/SNECMA turbofan engines. (The engine oil tanks have been enlarged to provide for increased flight endurance.)

In the TACAMO role, the E-6 has essentially the same communications equipment as the EC-130Q, with two trailing-wire antennas, one almost 5,000 feet (1,524 m) and the other some 30,000 feet (9,146 m) in length; only the shorter wire is electrically charged, with energy re-radiating off of the longer wire. Wingtip pods on the E-6 contain satellite communication antennas. The aircraft are hardened against Electro-Magnetic Pulse (EMP) effects. They retain the inflight refueling receptacle for the Air Force flying-boom refueling system. Normal mission duration is 16 hours; with inflight refueling, that can be extended to 72 hours.

Status: Operational; no longer in production. First flight of E-6A in February 1987. IOC: E-6A in August 1989 (VQ-3), with first operational mission completed on 31 October 1989; E-6B in October 1998.

The E-6 program consisted of one prototype aircraft, which has been upgraded to full operational capability, and 15 production aircraft. The prototype was delivered in 1987; that aircraft was recon-

figured as a standard E-6A and "redelivered" in 1992. The last E-6A aircraft was delivered on 7 May 1992. Subsequently all aircraft are being upgraded to the E-6B configuration with the last scheduled to be completed by 2003.

Manufacturer:	Boeing	
Crew:	E-6A (14) 4 flight crew + 6 mission crew + 4 relief crew	
	E-6B (22)	
Engines:	4 General Electric/SNECMA CFM-56-2A-2 high-bypass turbofan; 24,000 lbst (10,886 kgst) each	
Weight:	empty	172,795 lbs (78,380 kg)
	maximum T/O	342,000 lbs (155,131 kg)
Dimensions:	length	150 ft 4 in (45.82 m)
	wingspan	148 ft 4 in (45.22 m)
	wing area	3,050 ft² (283.4 m²)
	height	42 ft 5 in (12.93 m)
Speed:	cruise	441 knots (817 km/h)
	maximum	527 knots (977 km/h)
Ceiling:	42,000 ft (12,805 m)	
Range:	6,600 n.miles (12,223 km)	
	radius 1,000 n.miles (1,852 km) with 10.5 hours loiter on station	
Radar:	APS-133 weather	

An E-6B reveals its origins in the Boeing 707 transport design. These aircraft are assigned to Navy Strategic Communications Wing 1 and its two subordinate squadrons, VQ-3 and VQ-4. (U.S. Navy)

An E-2C Hawkeye from VAW-126 makes a touch-and-go landing aboard the carrier THEODORE ROOSEVELT. The Hawkeye force is continually undergoing upgrades, but no replacement carrier-based AEW aircraft is foreseen. (U.S. Navy, PH2 Johnny Grasso)

*E-2C HAWKEYE

The Hawkeye is an AEW aircraft developed for carrier operation. The E-2C variant is considered by many authorities the most capable radar warning and aircraft control plane now in service. A four-plane squadron is provided to each carrier, having replaced the piston-engine WF/E-1 Tracer in AEW squadrons.

Procurement continues through fiscal year 2003 at the rate of five aircraft per year. Previously planned rebuilding of the aircraft has been canceled in favor of new E-2C aircraft; a "hot" production line will facilitate continued foreign sales.

Design: The Hawkeye's most distinctive feature is the 24-foot (7.3-m)-diameter, saucer-like radome for the APS-125 or APS-145 UHF radar. The radome revolves freely in the airstream at the rate of six revolutions per minute. It provides sufficient lift to offset its own weight in flight and on board ship can be lowered to facilitate aircraft handling. The E-2C represents primarily an avionics upgrade over the previous E-2A/B variants (which had the APS-96 radar). Beginning with the fiscal 1986 procurement, the E-2C is being upgraded to T56-A-427 engines, providing improved flight safety with some increase in aircraft weight.

An E-2C from VAW-126 prepares for takeoff from the THEODORE ROOSEVELT. The Hawkeye's wings fold back and the rotodome can be lowered for shipboard stowage. The Hawkeye and C-2A Greyhound are the only fixed-wing propeller (turboprop) aircraft aboard U.S. carriers. (U.S. Navy, PH2 Donné McKissic)

The APS-120 radar with overland surveillance capability was installed in E-2C aircraft initially. Electronic upgrades have included the APS-125 radar, which has an effective aircraft detection range of some 240 n.miles (444.5 km) and adds an overwater capability; the aircraft can simultaneously track more than 250 air targets and control up to 30 interceptors. The ALR-73 passive detection system is also installed. Subsequently, the more-capable APS-145 radar has been provided to E-2C aircraft.

Designation: Originally designated W2F; changed to E-2 in 1962.

Operational: During Operation Desert Storm, the 27 E-2C aircraft on U.S. carriers flew 1,183 operational sorties.

Status: Operational; in production. First flight: E-2A on 21 October 1960; E-2C on 20 January 1971. IOC: E-2A in January 1964 (VAW-11); E-2C in November 1973 (VAW-123).

Fifty-nine E-2A aircraft were delivered from 1960 to 1967; all have been retired. The E-2B was a designation assigned but not popularly used for E-2A aircraft with upgraded computers. Two E-2A development aircraft were modified to a YE-2C configuration; these and two early production E-2C aircraft were later employed as trainers (TE-2C).

The Navy has approximately 65 E-2C aircraft and two TE-2C in service. A small number of E-2C aircraft were transferred to the Coast Guard in 1987 and to the Customs Service in 1989 for anti-drug operations. The aircraft is also flown by Egypt, France, Israel, Japan, Singapore, and Taiwan (the last receiving E-2B aircraft, designated E-2T for transfer; these are subsequently being upgraded to E-2C capability with APS-145 radar). The French Navy flies its E-2Cs from the carrier CHARLES DE GAULLE; the other nations fly the aircraft from land bases.

Manufacturer:	Grumman	
Crew:	(5) pilot, copilot, combat information center officer, air controller, radar operator or technician	
Engines:	2 Allison T56-A-422 turboprop; 4,591 shp each	
Weight:	empty	37,678 lbs (17,090 kg)
	maximum T/O	51,569 lbs (23,392 kg)
Dimensions:	length	57 ft 7 in (17.56 m)
	wingspan	80 ft 7 in (24.58 m)
	wing area	700 ft² (65.03 m²)
	height	18 ft 4 in (5.59 m)
Speed:	maximum	326 knots (603 km/h)
	cruise	269 knots (499 km/h)
Ceiling:	30,800 ft (9,390 m)	
Range:	radius	200 n.miles (370 km) with 6 hours on station
	ferry	1,525 n.miles (2,820 km)
Armament:	none	
Radar:	APS-125 or APS-145	

An E-2C from VAW-120, the transition–readiness training squadron for all E-2C airborne early warning and C-2 carrier onboard delivery flight crews. AD and NJ are the tail codes for all Navy fleet readiness squadrons. (Peter B. Mersky)

EA-6B PROWLER

The EA-6B is an electronic strike aircraft based on the now-departed A-6 Intruder attack aircraft. The EA-6B has significantly more EW/ECM capabilities than previous carrier-based electronic aircraft. Four-plane VAQ squadrons flying the Prowler are normally assigned to each carrier air wing, with several additional Navy and Marine squadrons being land based. The Prowler is the only U.S. fixed-wing electronic strike/countermeasures aircraft, having replaced previous naval aircraft, as well as the Air Force's EF-111A Aardwark, in that role.

The upgraded Prowler is the world's most capable, combat-proven tactical jamming aircraft.

The Prowler is scheduled for retirement about 2015, at which time a replacement electronic strike aircraft is expected to be operational. An F/A-18G variant of the Hornet has been proposed for use by the Marine Corps and possibly by the Navy as an EA-6B replacement (see below).

Design: The Prowler has the basic Intruder configuration, with an enlarged cockpit for two additional crew members. There is a distinctive electronics pod mounted atop the tail fin, and up to five jamming pods and two fuel tanks can be carried on fuselage and wing pylons. The weight of internal avionics/EW equipment totals 8,000 pounds (3,636 kg), in addition to 950 pounds (431 kg) carried on each of five pylons. Normally five ALQ-99 pods are carried, each with two

An EA-6B Prowler from VAQ-130 is launched from the carrier ENTERPRISE. Prowlers—land- and carrier-based—provide the only U.S. tactical electronic countermeasures capability. The Prowler could be easily distinguished from the now-discarded A-6 Intruder by the ECM aircraft's electronics pod mounted on the tail fin. (U.S. Navy, PH2 Damon J. Moritz)

An EA-6B is prepared for launch aboard the JOHN C. STENNIS. The aircraft has an ALQ-99 ECM pod and fuel tank under its left wing. On patrol these aircraft normally carry HARM anti-radar missiles that home on enemy radar transmissions. Note the position of the fixed inflight refueling probe. (U.S. Navy, PH3 Robert Baker)

jamming transmitters, although a 300-gallon drop tank can be substituted for each pod. Since 1986, EA-6B aircraft have been configured to carry the HARM anti-radar missile, their first "hard kill" armament (the Air Force EF-111A did not carry weapons).

The EA-6B has undergone a number of EW system upgrades since the original configuration. These modifications were given the designations EXCAP (Expanded Capability), in service from 1973 to 1985; ICAP (Improved Capability), first delivered in 1976; ICAP II, first delivered in 1984; and ADVCAP (Advanced Capability), entering service in 1994. The ADVCAP was terminated in 1994, however, after examination of the ICAP II aircraft in view of predicted post–Cold War threats. These upgrades responded to changing foreign radar/SAM threats and have been incorporated into new-production EA-6B aircraft.

The ADVCAP upgrades included adding the low-band ALQ-149 communications ECM, providing two additional ALE-39 chaff/flare dispensers (a total of four), fitting the J52-P-409 engine to increase allowable landing weight by about 2,000 pounds (907 kg) and decrease stall speed, increasing the number of wing pylons to seven, and adding a GPS (Global Positioning System) receiver. In addition, the

jammer pods have been successively upgraded from the basic ALQ-99 to the A/B/C configurations, primarily to increase reliability.

Designation: Originally designated A2F-1Q; changed to EA-6B in 1962.

Names: The EA-6B name was changed from Intruder to Prowler in February 1972.

Operational: During Operation Desert Storm, the 27 Navy EA-6B aircraft flew 1,126 combat sorties from carriers and the 12 Marine EA-6B aircraft in the area flew 511 sorties from shore bases.

Status: Operational; no longer in production. First flight: converted A-6A on 25 May 1968; production EA-6B in November 1970. IOC in January 1971 (VAQ-129). Grumman produced 170 EA-6B aircraft built for the U.S. Navy and Marine Corps through June 1991, when production ended. Three A-6A Intruder airframes were modified to serve as development aircraft for the EA-6B program.

Manufacturer:	Grumman
Crew:	(4) pilot, 3 electronic countermeasures officers[26]
Engines:	2 Pratt & Whitney J52-P-408 turbojet; 11,200 lbst (5,080 kgst) each
Weight:[27]	empty 32,162 lbs (14,589 kg)
	normal T/O 54,461 lbs (24,704 kg)
	maximum T/O 65,000 lbs (29,480 kg)
Dimensions:	length 59 ft 10 in (18.24 m)
	wingspan 53 ft (16.15 m)
	wing area 528.9 ft² (49.1 m²)
	height 16 ft 3 in (4.95 m)
Speed:	maximum 532 knots (986 km/h) at sea level
	cruise 420 knots (777 km/h)
Ceiling:	41,000 ft (12,500 m)
Range:	700 n.miles (1,296 km)
Armament:	2 HARM ASM
Radar:	APQ-129

EA-6A INTRUDER

This variant of the carrier-based Intruder had a built-in Electronic Countermeasures (ECM) suite to detect and jam hostile radars, primarily for suppressing anti-aircraft missile systems. The aircraft was developed specifically for Marine Corps use; it was succeeded in Marine service by the more-capable EA-6B Prowler beginning in

An EA-6B from VAQ-141 is launched from the Theodore Roosevelt during Operation Allied Force in May 1999. The Prowler was en route to support NATO air strikes over Kosovo and Serbia. Because of the large number of strike aircraft available, no HARM missiles were mounted. (U.S. Navy, PH2 Johnny Grasso)

---

26. The ECMO in the right forward seat (next to the pilot) also serves as navigator.
27. Normal takeoff weight, speed, ceiling, and range while carrying five jammer pods.

An EA-6B from VAQ-132 being readied for flight aboard the Dwight D. Eisenhower. This Prowler has ALQ-99 ECM pods beneath both wings and under the fuselage; two drop tanks are on the inboard wing pylons. (U.S. Navy)

1977. It was flown by the Navy only in the research and development and training roles.

The EA-6A differed from the later and larger EA-6B Prowler in having only one ECM operator (vice three in the EA-6B) and significantly less electronics equipment.

Seven A-6A Intruder attack aircraft were converted to the EA-6A configuration, followed by the production of 21 EA-6A aircraft delivered by Grumman from 1965. In service from December 1965 (with VMCJ-2), the last EA-6A in service was a Navy aircraft (of VAQ-33), which was retired in 1993.

Designation: Originally designated A2F-1H; changed to EA-6A in 1962.

See 15th Edition/pages 419–420 for characteristics.

EC-24A

The single EC-24A flown by the Navy in the EW simulation/jamming role in support of weapons development and fleet exercises was discarded in 1992. The aircraft, a converted commercial DC-8 Series 54F, was placed in service in November 1987 and operated and supported by a contractor.

This four-turbofan transport was the only U.S. military aircraft given a C-24 series designation. It became operational in 1987.

See 15th Edition/page 421 for characteristics.

EC-130V HERCULES

The EC-130V was an AEW conversion of an HC-130H Hercules aircraft developed for U.S. Coast Guard evacuation. It had a large rotating radome (rotodome) for the APS-125 radar of the type fitted in the E-2C Hawkeye.[28]

---

28. The aircraft should properly have been redesignated EC-130H; however, that designation was already in use for the U.S. Air Force "Compass Call" electronic jamming aircraft.

Flight testing for the aircraft began in July 1991; it was handed over to the Coast Guard on 16 October 1991 for a one-year evaluation. The Coast Guard referred to the project as a High-Endurance Surveillance (HES) aircraft, given the nickname "Delphi." The initial funding for the project was based on the aircraft's potential value in counter-drug surveillance operations.

After Coast Guard tests the aircraft was transferred to the Air Force. Subsequently, it was retransferred to the Navy and—redesignated NC-130H—is assigned to the Naval Force Warfare Aircraft Test Squadron at NAS Patuxent River, Md.

See 15th Edition/pages 421–422 for characteristics.

EC-130Q HERCULES

The EC-130Q aircraft were C-130 transports extensively modified for the TACAMO role of communications relay with strategic missile submarines (SSBN). These aircraft had the USC-13 airborne VLF communications suite with a trailing wire antenna. The E-6A Mercury replaced the 22 TACAMO "Herks" in squadrons VQ-3 and VQ-4.

F/A-18G HORNET

A variant of the two-seat F/A-18D has been proposed by Boeing–McDonnell Douglas as a replacement for the EA-6B Prowler electronic attack aircraft. The aircraft would identify, jam, and, if feasible, launch missiles against hostile radars. The Marine Corps is especially interested in an F/A-18 variant as a replacement for the EA-6B; the Navy also will require a replacement after the year 2015. To meet that replacement date, the first F/A-18G would have to enter service about 2010.

While the F/A-18 has the advantages of being carrier capable and already in service with the Navy and Marine Corps, there is the serious question of whether one ECM officer (plus the pilot) is

An artist's view of an F/A-18G Hornet launching a HARM missile. This variant of the Hornet is being proposed as a successor to the EA-6B Prowler. The basic loadout for such an aircraft would be up to five jamming pods, four HARM missiles, and two Sidewinder or other AAMs on wingtip rails. Only one electronic warfare officer would be carried in addition to the pilot. (Boeing)

adequate in place of three ECM officers (plus pilot) in the EA-6B. However, the F/A-18G could be a temporary successor.

Like the EA-6B, the F/A-18G would carry HARM anti-radar missiles, as well as JSOW, SLAM-ER, and JDAM weapons.

The nickname "Growler" is being used informally for the F/A-18G.

Boeing has published the following characteristics for an electronics variant of the F/A-18. No gun would be fitted; in addition to radar, the aircraft would have the ALQ-99 jamming system, as well as other intercept and jamming systems and various data links. Six wing and one fuselage pylon would be provided—up to five for ALQ-99 pods and the others for missiles or external fuel tanks.

Crew:	(2) pilot, electronic countermeasures officer	
Engines:	2 General Electric F414-GE-400 turbofans; 22,000 lbst (9,979 kgst) each	
Weight:	empty	32,642 lbs (14,806 kg)
	maximum T/O	66,000 lbs (29,937 kg)
Dimensions:	length	60 ft 4 in (18.38 m)
	wingspan	44 ft 8½ in (13.63 m) over wingtip pods
	wing area	500 ft² (45 m²)
	height	16 ft (4.88 m)
Ceiling:	50,000 ft (15,244 m)	

EP-3J ORION

The Navy's single EP-3J is employed to simulate hostile electric emissions for fleet exercises.

Two P-3B aircraft were modified in 1992 to the EP-3J configuration (initially flown by reserve squadron VP-66; now flown by active VQ-11). The aircraft were fitted with the USQ-113 communications intrusion and deception system and can carry the ALE-43, ALQ-167, ALQ-170, and AST-4/6 pods.

See page 411 for basic characteristics.

EP-3E ORION

These are P-3 Orions extensively modified for ELINT collection. The 11 aircraft in service were P-3C variants converted to the EP-3E Aries II configuration, replacing earlier EP-3E Aries I aircraft.

The Aries II variants (flown by squadrons VQ-1 and VQ-2) have automatic electronic and communication intercept/analysis equipment to provide fleet and task force commanders with real-time intelligence. The aircraft have the ALR-52 multiband frequency-measuring receiver and/or ALR-60 Deepwell communications intercept/analysis system, and the ALR-76 combined ESM (Electronic Support Measures)/radar warning system.

(The Japanese Maritime Self-Defense Force acquired six Kawasaki-produced EP-3 variants for ELINT missions.)

See page 411 for basic characteristics.

An EP-3E Orion configured for ELINT collection. Flown by VQ-1, the aircraft has a radome under the fuselage and antenna "canoes" mounted in the dorsal and ventral positions; the tail MAD stinger has been "bobbed." Low-visibility markings usually are worn during ELINT operations. (U.S. Navy, R. Hepp)

A P-3 modified to an AEW configuration, flown by the U.S. Customs Service as part of the effort to suppress drug smuggling and illegal immigration. The Customs Service took delivery of six Orions in the AEW configuration from 1988 to 2000. Lockheed Martin has sought to sell similar aircraft to other countries. (Lockheed Martin)

P-3 ORION AEW VARIANTS

Nine P-3 Orion aircraft are in U.S. service in AEW configurations—one flown by the Navy and eight by the Customs Service, the latter employed primarily in efforts to counter drug smuggling.

The first aircraft was a modified P-3B, exchanged by Lockheed to the Royal Australian Air Force (RAAF) for a new-production P-3C Orion. Following Customs Service trials in 1988, that aircraft was acquired by that service as was a second modified P-3B AEW aircraft also exchanged with the RAAF for a P-3C.

Subsequently the Customs Service acquired six additional P-3 AEW aircraft, the last two delivered by Lockheed Martin in 2000. The surveillance radars fitted in the Customs Service aircraft—all of which are in service—are:

No. 1	APS-125
No. 2–4	APS-138
No. 5–8	APS-145

The Navy's AEW-configured aircraft is a rebuilt NP-3D operated by the Naval Research Laboratory in Washington, D.C. That aircraft, fitted with an extensively modified APS-145 radar, is based at NAS Patuxent River, Md.

See page 411 for basic characteristics.

One P-3 modified to an AEW configuration is flown under the auspices of the Naval Research Laboratory; the other aircraft of this configuration are operated by the Customs Service. The single Navy P-3/AEW aircraft has red trim markings. (U.S. Navy)

An ES-3A Viking *(foreground)*—generally referred to as Sea Shadow—and an S-3B Viking from the carrier ENTERPRISE operate over the Persian Gulf in 1999. The ES-3A, from VQ-6 Detachment Alfa, was on one of the last deployments of that aircraft, which was discarded soon afterwards. The aircraft are preparing to land aboard the "Big E"; their arresting hooks are lowered but not their landing gear. (U.S. Navy, PH2 Michael W. Pendergrass)

ES-3A VIKING (SEA SHADOW)

The Navy converted 16 S-3A Viking carrier-based ASW aircraft to an ES-3A configuration to serve as electronic surveillance aircraft. One or two planes—from Electronic Reconnaissance Squadrons (VQ) 5 and 6—normally operated from each forward-deployed aircraft carrier. Sometimes labeled TASES for Tactical Airborne Signal Exploitation System, the aircraft's missions were (1) electronic warfare reconnaissance (i.e, surveillance), (2) over-the-horizon targeting, and (3) airborne tactical command, control, communications, and intelligence.

The last ES-3A aircraft was taken out of service in 1999. A year earlier, the Navy had stated that the aircraft supports "all facets of Navy, Marine Corps, and joint operations," seeking out electronic emissions from potential hostile radars and intercepting communications, and "the ES-3A has already demonstrated tremendous reliability and safety, as well as a robust mission capability."[29] Shortly thereafter, the decision was made to retire the aircraft to save operating funds.

The ES-3A aircraft, delivered to the fleet in 1995–1996, were long-delayed replacements for the Navy's EA-3B Skywarrior. For more than a decade, the Navy had sought a replacement to the EA-3B. Now, in place of the ES-3A, carrier battle group commanders will employ land-based aircraft, primarily the EP-3E Aries II aircraft flown by squadrons VQ-1 and VQ-2.

See page 412 for basic characteristics.

Names: The aircraft is generally called Shadow or Sea Shadow, although the names were not officially assigned.

Status: No longer operational. First flight: prototype ES-3A conversion (NS-3A aerodynamic prototype) on 7 September 1989; second conversion, with a full electronics suite, on 21 January 1992. IOC on 9 May 1992 (VQ-5). All delivered in 1992–1993 to squadrons VQ-5 and VQ-6.

NKC-135A STRATOTANKER

The Navy's two NKC-135A aircraft employed in the EW simulation/jamming role in support of weapons development and fleet exercises were discarded in 1992. They replaced a pair of modified EB-47E Stratojet bombers previously flown in this role; the two NKC-135A aircraft entered Navy service in 1977–1978 and were contractor operated.

The aircraft were modified Boeing 707/Air Force KC-135A tankers, originally fitted with inflight refueling equipment. They were modified by the Air Force for research work, with their refueling equipment removed. Further modifications by the Navy included removal of some of the body fuel cells to provide equipment bays, replacement of the weather track radar with a sea search unit, provision of wing pylons for electronic pods, and an EW officer/navigator station in the cargo cabin area. Each aircraft carried about 12,500 pounds (5,670 kg) of electronic equipment on board and had two wing pylons providing a greater jamming capability than any other aircraft then flying.

Operational: The two NKC-135A and the single EC-24 aircraft were operated by contractor personnel for the Fleet Electronic Warfare Support Group (FEWSG) to provide ECM training for naval forces. These planes had Navy markings but did not carry FEWSG's GD tail code. Squadrons VAQ-33, VAQ-34, and VAQ-35 also operated under FEWSG.

See 14th Edition/page 416 for characteristics.

---

29. Office of the Chief of Naval Operations, *Naval Aviation: Forward Air Power . . . From the Sea* (Washington, D.C., 1988), p. 45.

OBSERVATION/RECONNAISSANCE AIRCRAFT

OV-10D BRONCO

The last Marine observation squadrons flying the OV-10D Bronco were deactivated in 1993, with the last OV-10D transferred from the Marine Corps to the Bureau of Alcohol, Tobacco, and Firearms on 24 July 1994. The aircraft's Short Take-Off and Landing (STOL) characteristics permitted limited flight operations from LHA/LPH-type ships without the use of catapults or arresting gear. (Trials also were flown from fleet carriers.)

The turboprop Bronco was developed during the Vietnam War as a multipurpose Counterinsurgency (COIN) aircraft; the Navy also flew the Bronco during the Vietnam War. The Navy and Marine Corps took delivery of 114 aircraft from 1967 to 1969, with additional OV-10s going to the U.S. Air Force and foreign services. Former Marine OV-10D aircraft—stripped of their weapons—were transferred to the Bureau of Alcohol, Tobacco, and Firearms; the Bureau of Land Management; and the California Forestry Department.

RF-4B PHANTOM

The Marine Corps operated one squadron of RF-4B photo-reconnaissance aircraft. These aircraft were similar to the now-discarded F-4B version of the Phantom; 46 of this variant were produced. All RF-4B reconnaissance variants have been retired from Marine service, the last in 1992.

The U.S. Navy never flew the reconnaissance version of the Phantom, although Marine RF-4s flew from the carrier MIDWAY until 1986, when the ship's fighter and attack squadrons transitioned to the F/A-18 Hornet. Reconnaissance variants of the F-4 were flown by the U.S. Air Force and foreign air forces.

Designation: Reconnaissance variants of the Phantom were originally designated F4H-1P; this was changed to RF-4B in 1962.

CARGO/TRANSPORT AIRCRAFT

*C-40A AIRLIFTER

The Navy will procure a small number of Boeing 737-700 cargo/transport aircraft as partial replacements for the C-9B/DC-9 Skytrain force. The first aircraft is being procured under the fiscal year 2000 budget.

Design: The C-40A has a conventional, swept-wing configuration with engines mounted under the wing and a conventional tail configuration. In the all-passenger role, the aircraft can carry 121 passengers (the same as the commercial 737-700); in the all-cargo role, it can lift eight standard cargo pallets. The aircraft also can be configured as a "combi" for 70 passengers and three cargo pallets.

Status: Operational. First flight of 737-700 on 9 February 1997. The aircraft is in production for commercial users.

Manufacturer:	Boeing	
Crew:	(4) pilot, copilot, 2 flight crewmen + 121 passengers	
Engines:	2 General Electric CFM56-7B high-bypass turbofan; 24,000 lbst (10,886 kgst) each	
Weight:	empty	
	maximum T/O	171,000 lbs (77,565 kg)
Dimensions:	length	110 ft 4 in (33.6 m)
	wingspan	112 ft 7 in (34.3 m)
	wing area	
	height	41 ft 2 in (12.5 m)
Speed:	cruise	460 knots (853 km/h)
Ceiling:	40,600 ft (12,370 m)	
Range:	3,000 n.miles (5,555 km) in passenger configuration	
Radar:	navigation/weather	

The Navy's first C-40A Airlifter takes to the air for the first time on 14 April 2000. The aircraft, to replace Naval Air Reserve C-9B and DC-9 transports, is readily convertible to several passenger-cargo configurations. (Boeing)

A C-40A in Navy livery, as seen by a Boeing artist. The Navy and Marine Corps probably will take delivery of large numbers of this versatile transport, based on the 737-700 design. (Boeing)

*C-37 GULFSTREAM V

This is an updated C-20 Gulfstream VIP aircraft (see below). The Air Force operates several C-37A aircraft as VIP transports. Three of these aircraft are being procured by the Navy.

Manufacturer:	Gulfstream Aerospace
Crew:	(5) pilot, copilot, 3 flight crewmen + 12 passengers
Engines:	2 BMW Rolls-Royce BR710A1-10 turbofan; 14,900 lbst (6,760 kgst) each
Weight:	empty 47,601 lbs (21,592 kg)
	maximum T/O 90,500 lbs (41,051 kg)
Dimensions:	length 96 ft 5 in (29.40 m)
	wingspan 93 ft 6 in (28.51 m)
	wing area
	height 25 ft 10 in (7.88 m)
Speed:	
Ceiling:	51,000 ft (15,550 m)
Range:	
Radar:	navigation

*UC-35A

The UC-35A is a medium-range executive and priority cargo aircraft that is planned for procurement by the Navy beginning in fiscal 2001. This will be a Commercial-Off-The-Shelf (COTS) procurement of the Cessna Citation 560 Ultra V aircraft.

Manufacturer:	Beech (Raytheon)
Crew:	(2) pilot, copilot + 8 passengers
Engines:	2 Pratt & Whitney JT15D-5D turbofan; 3,045 lbst (1,380 kgst) each
Weight:	empty
	maximum T/O 16,500 lbs (7,484 kg)
Dimensions:	length
	wingspan
	wing area
	height
Speed:	maximum cruise 450 knots (833 km/h)
	cruise 330 knots (610 km/h)
Ceiling:	45,000 ft (13,720 m)
Range:	1,800 n.miles (3,330 km)
Radar:	navigation

C-20 GULFSTREAM

Gulfstream VIP transport aircraft are flown by the Navy and Coast Guard (the Marine Corps no longer operating this type aircraft). The Navy has two C-20D Gulfstream III variants and four C-20G Gulfstream IV aircraft, and the Coast Guard flies a single C-20B. The last replaces the long-serving VC-11A Gulfstream II.

Design: Designed for the commercial market, the Gulfstreams are swept-wing, T-tail aircraft, with twin engine pods mounted on the after fuselage. Winglets are fitted (5 feet 4¼ inches high). Seats can be removed from the C-20G for carrying up to 4,500 pounds (2,041 kg) of cargo, handled through a large cargo door on the right side, forward.

Navy plans to acquire three additional G variants configured for EW/ECM training, to have been designated EC-20F, were dropped.

Gulfstream Aerospace has proposed a maritime patrol/ASW variant of the improved Gulfstream IV; the Royal Danish Navy flies the Gulfstream III in a maritime/fisheries patrol variant.

Status: Operational. First flight: Gulfstream III on 24 December 1979; Gulfstream IV on 19 September 1985. The Coast Guard's C-20B became operational in 1995. Variants of the C-20 are also flown by the Air Force and Army.

Characteristics for the C-20D (see p. 425 for C-20G characteristics):

Manufacturer:	Gulfstream Aerospace
Crew:	(2) pilot, copilot + 19 passengers
Engines:	2 Rolls-Royce Spey Mk 511-8 turbofan; 11,400 lbst (5,171 kgst) each
Weight:	empty 32,000 lbs (14,515 kg)
	maximum T/O 69,700 lbs (31,616 kg)
Dimensions:	length 83 ft 1 in (25.32 m)
	wingspan 77 ft 10 in (23.72 m)
	wing area 934.6 ft^2 (86.83 m^2)
	height 24 ft 4½ in (7.43 m)
Speed:	maximum cruise 500 knots (927 km/h)
	cruise 441 knots (817 km/h)
Ceiling:	45,000 ft (13,720 m)
Range:	
Radar:	weather radar

A Beech-Cessna Citation 560 Ultra V aircraft in civilian markings. The Navy's UC-35A executive transport will be similar.

A Naval Air Reserve C-20G Gulfstream from Washington, D.C.–based VR-48 with its right-side cargo door open (Gulfstream Aerospace)

A C-20G from reserve squadron VR-48 taking off and retracting its landing gear. The C-20G has "bent" wingtips or "winglets" that improve performance. (Gulfstream Aerospace)

The Coast Guard's C-20B streaks over the coast near Elizabeth City, N.C., site of the Coast Guard's "transition" training facility. The lone Coast Guard C-20B is a VIP transport used by that service and officials of the Department of Transportation. Coast Guard aircraft wear the same orange and blue stripes as cutters and small boats. (U.S. Coast Guard, PA1 Telfair Brown)

Characteristics for the C-20G:

Manufacturer:	Gulfstream Aerospace	
Crew:	(4) pilot, copilot, 2 flight crewmen + 26 passengers	
Engines:	2 Rolls-Royce Tay Mk 611-8 turbofan; 13,850 lbst (6,282 kgst) each	
Weight:	maximum T/O	74,600 lbs (33,838 kg)
Dimensions:	length	88 ft 4 in (26.92 m)
	wingspan	77 ft 10 in (23.73 m)
	wing area	
	height	24 ft 5 in (7.44 m)
Speed:	maximum	490 knots (907 km/h) at 35,000 ft (10,670 m)
Range:	4,225 n.miles (7,820 km)	
Ceiling:	45,000 feet (13,720 m)	
Radar:	weather radar	

A UC-12B Huron from NAS Jacksonville, Fla., being refueled at Norfolk. The Army-assigned name Huron is not usually used by the Navy; the aircraft's commercial name Super King Air or "Super King" is heard more often. (Peter B. Mersky)

C-12/UC-12 HURON

The Navy and Marine Corps fly large numbers of the military version of the Super King Air for transport and utility purposes.

Design: The aircraft's twin turboprop engines are mounted far forward on the low wing; the aircraft has a T-tail, compared with the conventional tail configuration of the smaller T-44A King Air trainer. The payload is 2,000 pounds (907 kg) of cargo or eight passengers.

More than 2,800 aircraft of this basic design have been produced, most for civilian use. This is the only fixed-wing aircraft flown by the U.S. Army, Navy, Marine Corps, and Air Force (plus the Army National Guard and Marine Corps Reserve). Almost 70 of these aircraft are flown by the Navy and Marine Corps in the C-12, UC-12B, RC-12F, RC-12M, and UC-12M variants, with the UC-12B being the most widely used. The RC variants are fitted with a surface search radar.

Characteristics for the UC-12B:

Manufacturer:	Beech	
Crew:	(2) pilot, copilot + 8 passengers	
Engines:	2 Pratt & Whitney PT6A-41 turboprop; 850 shp each	
Weight:	empty	7,869 lbs (3,569 kg)
	loaded	12,500 lbs (5,670 kg)
Dimensions:	length	43 ft 9 in (13.34 m)
	wingspan	54 ft 6 in (16.61 m)
	wing area	
	height	14 ft 6 in (4.42 m)
Speed:	maximum cruise	270 knots (500 km/h)
	cruise	227 knots (420 km/h)
Ceiling:	31,000 ft (9,451 m)	
Range:	1,760 n.miles (3,260 km)	
Radar:	none	

VC-11A GULFSTREAM II

The Coast Guard's single VC-11A, the only such aircraft in U.S. government service, was retired in 1995. It was flown in the executive transport role and based at Washington, D.C.

The Grumman-built aircraft had entered Coast Guard service in July 1968. It was suffering from structural integrity problems, communications limitations, and insufficient range and passenger capacity for current requirements. Accordingly, it has been replaced by a C-20B Gulfstream.

See 15th Edition/page 427 for characteristics.

A UC-12B from VRC-30 with landing gear down. Navy transports usually have the American flag on their tail fin(s). The numerals *1327* are the last four digits of the aircraft's serial or "BuAer" number—161327.

C-9B/DC-9 SKYTRAIN

The C-9B is the naval version of the commercial DC-9 Series 30 medium-range passenger/cargo aircraft and is convertible to the cargo or passenger transport roles. Both military (C-9B) and commercial (DC-9) versions are in naval service.

All Skytrains are flown by the Naval Air Reserve, except for a single C-9B flown by the Marine Corps. The C-9B/DC-9 replaced the long-serving C-118 Liftmaster (formerly R6D). The U.S. Air Force flies the C-9A Nightingale in the medical evacuation role and the VC-9C as an executive transport. McDonnell Douglas has proposed a maritime patrol/ASW variant of the aircraft (company designation P-9D); it would have General Electric Unducted Fan (UDF) turboprop-type engines.

Design: This sleek-looking, swept-wing transport has a T-tail with the turbofan engines in nacelles mounted on the after fuselage. The cargo compartment can accommodate eight standard 88 × 108-inch (2.2 × 2.7-m) cargo pallets. The payload is 32,444 pounds (14,717 kg) or 90 passengers.

Status: Operational. First flight of DC-9 Series 30 on 1 August 1966. IOC in Naval Air Reserve in 1976.

Manufacturer:	McDonnell Douglas	
Crew:	(5) pilot, copilot, crew chief, 2 attendants + 90 passengers	
Engines:	2 Pratt & Whitney JT8D-9 turbofan; 14,500 lbst (6,577 kgst) each	
Weight:	empty	59,706 lbs (27,083 kg) in cargo configuration
		65,283 lbs (29,612 kg) in transport configuration
	maximum T/O	110,000 lbs (49,896 kg)
Dimensions:	length	119 ft 4 in (36.37 m)
	wingspan	93 ft 5 in (28.47 m)
	wing area	1,000 ft² (92.97 m²)
	height	27 ft 6 in (8.38 m)
Speed:	maximum	500 knots (927 km)
	cruise	438 knots (811 km)
Ceiling:	37,000 ft (11,280 m)	
Range:	2,540 n.miles (4,700 km) with 10,000 lbs (4,536 kg) cargo	
Radar:	weather radar	

VC-4 GULFSTREAM I

The Coast Guard continues to operate a single VC-4A as an executive transport. The Navy and Marine Corps have discarded the several TC-4C trainers previously employed to train A-6E Intruder bombardier/navigators.

Developed as a business executive aircraft, the Gulfstream I is a low-wing, twin turboprop aircraft with the long nacelles common to Rolls-Royce engines. The cabin is pressurized.

Status: Operational. First flight: Gulfstream I on 14 August 1958; TC-4C on 14 June 1967. IOC of VC-4A in March 1963.

Grumman produced 190 Gulfstream I commercial aircraft, plus the single Coast Guard VC-4A and nine TC-4C aircraft for the Navy and Marine Corps. The T-41A (later TC-4B) was a navigation training version of the Gulfstream I ordered by the Navy, but that entire program was canceled prior to deliveries.

A second VC-4A planned for the Coast Guard was not acquired.

Manufacturer:	Grumman	
Crew:	(2) pilot, copilot + 10 to 14 passengers	
Engines:	2 Rolls-Royce Dart Mk 529-8X turboprop; 2,210 shp each	
Weight:	empty	24,575 lbs (11,147 kg)
	loaded	36,000 lbs (16,330 kg)
Dimensions:	length	63 ft 9 in (19.43 m)
	wingspan	78 ft 6 in (23.92 m)
	wing area	610.3 ft² (56.7 m²)
	height	22 ft 9 in (6.94 m)
Speed:	maximum	300 knots (927 km) at 25,000 ft (7,625 m)
	cruise	250 knots (463 km) at 25,000 ft (7,625 m)
Ceiling:	33,600 ft (10,240 m)	
Range:	2,210 n.miles (4,088 km)	
Radar:	navigation	

A C-9B Skytrain II in Marine markings. The four active and two reserve Marine refueler-transport squadrons (VMGR) fly the KC-130 Hercules. Two C-9Bs normally are assigned to Marine Search and Rescue Squadron (VMR) 1. (McDonnell Douglas, Harry Gann)

A C-9B from reserve squadron VR-56 showing the aircraft's large cargo door. The Navy's Skytrain IIs are flown only by reserve squadrons; the active VR squadrons fly C-130 Hercules for long-range transport. (Peter B. Mersky)

The Coast Guard's lone VC-4A Gulfstream I still flies as an executive transport, based at Miami. The Navy has retired its TC-4C Academe trainers, used to train Navy and Marine Corps bombardier/navigators for the A-6E Intruder. (U.S. Coast Guard)

C-2A GREYHOUND

The Greyhound is a second-generation built-for-the-purpose COD aircraft, having been derived from the E-2 Hawkeye AEW aircraft. Nineteen C-2A models were originally procured.

In the late 1970s, the Navy developed a plan to produce 24 new COD aircraft beginning in fiscal 1983 to replace the existing C-1A and, eventually, early C-2A aircraft. The principal candidate for the new COD—designated VCX for planning purposes—was a variant of the S-3A Viking, with several early aircraft having been modified to a US-3A COD configuration. The decision, however, was to procure 39 additional C-2A aircraft (with the first of these "reprocured" aircraft making its first flight on 4 February 1985); the principal difference in the later aircraft was uprated engines.

Design: The cargo aircraft has the E-2's wings, power plant, and tail configuration, but a larger fuselage and rear-loading ramp. This last feature permits the carrying of high-cube cargo, including some aircraft engines. The cargo capacity is 675 cubic feet (20.25 m³), and the payload is 10,000 pounds (4,536 kg) of cargo or 26 passengers.

The wings fold for carrier stowage, although these planes are not assigned to carrier wings.

Status: Operational. First flight on 18 November 1964. IOC in December 1966 (VRC-50). Total C-2A production (both "batches") was 58 aircraft. Thirty-eight remain in Navy service.

Manufacturer:	Grumman
Crew:	(3) pilot, copilot, flight engineer + 26 passengers or 20 litters
Engines:	2 Allison T56-A-425 turboprop; 4,910 shp each
Weight:	empty 31,250 lbs (14,175 kg)
	loaded 54,382 lbs (24,668 kg)
Dimensions:	length 56 ft 8 in (17.27 m)
	wingspan 80 ft 7 in (24.57 m)
	wing area 700 ft² (65.03 m²)
	height 15 ft 11 in (4.85 m)
Speed:	maximum 305.5 knots (566 km/h) at 30,000 ft (9,146 m)
	cruise 257 knots (476 km/h) at 30,000 ft (9,146 m)
Ceiling:	33,500 ft (10,210 m)
Range:	normal 1,042 n.miles (1,930 km)
	maximum 1,560 n.miles (2,890 km)
Radar:	navigation radar

A C-2A Greyhound from VRC-30 landing aboard the carrier Abraham Lincoln shows the COD aircraft's resemblance to its progenitor, the E-2 Hawkeye. The C-2A and E-2C are the only fixed-wing propeller aircraft aboard U.S. aircraft carriers. Both planes will remain in service for the foreseeable future. (U.S. Navy, PHAN Michael B. Watkins)

A C-2A from VRC-30 showing the squadron's colorful (black-and-orange) tail insignia. Most naval aircraft have their unit code letters on the tail surfaces, with VRC-30 aircraft being one of the few exceptions. The arresting hook retracts under the rear door ramp. (U.S. Navy, Lt. James Muse)

A C-2A from VRC-40 with engines turned up on a rain-swept runway at Norfolk. The rear ramp is lowered, permitting the rapid loading and unloading of cargo and personnel. The second tail fin from the left does not have a rudder as do the others. (Peter B. Mersky)

A C-2A from VR-30 unfolding its wings while taxiing on the flight deck of the Abraham Lincoln. This COD aircraft has the squadron letters RW on the outer tail fins; the American flag is on the inner fins, another variation on naval aircraft markings. (Lt. Corrine Kelley)

C-131H SAMARITAN

The last Navy-flown C-131 was retired in 1990. The C-131 was flown by the Navy/Naval Reserve as a transport and by the Coast Guard (HC-131), the latter also having been discarded. The Convair-built, twin-engine aircraft was also flown by the Air Force as a transport and specialized trainer (T-29).

Designation: Originally designated R4Y by the Navy; the Air Force C-series designation was adopted in 1962.

See 14th Edition/page 424 for characteristics.

*C-130/KC-130 HERCULES

The Hercules or "Herk" is the most widely flown military cargo/transport aircraft in the West. The Naval Air Reserve flies 19 C-130 cargo aircraft and the Marine Corps has 34 aircraft with active squadrons and 22 with the Marine Air Reserve. An additional Herk owned by the Marine Corps is assigned to the Blue Angels flight demonstration team.

The aircraft assigned to Marine refueler-transport squadrons (VMGR) are all KC variants, fitted for inflight refueling as well as for cargo/transport operations.

The Navy has retired the ski-equipped LC-130F/R Hercules flown in support of Antarctic research programs; those were the last C-130s flown by the active Navy. The Navy's EC-130Q TACAMO aircraft have been retired from the strategic communications role, replaced by the E-6A Mercury.

The Coast Guard employs the HC-130H as a long-range search and surveillance aircraft.

Design: The basic C-130 is a four-engine, high-wing cargo aircraft with the main landing gear in pods to provide a clear fuselage cargo space; a rear ramp provides access to the cargo compartment and can be opened in flight for parachuting troops or equipment.

The Marine KC-130F/R/T aircraft can accommodate removable aluminum tanks for 3,600 gallons (13,680 liters) of fuel in the cargo area; two refueling drogues can be streamed simultaneously. Two KC-130T-30 stretched aircraft delivered in 1991 to reserve squadron VMGR-452 have two fuselage plugs adding a total of 14¾ feet (4.5 m) to the fuselage length. The KC-130R has a payload of

An HC-130H Hercules low over the water, a normal operating mode for these Coast Guard long-range search aircraft. The service's "Herks" carry out a vast number of missions, among them SAR, illegal drug interdiction, law enforcement, and international ice patrol, while also transporting cargo and personnel. (U.S. Coast Guard, PAC Tom Gillespie)

26,913 pounds (12,208 kg) of cargo or 92 troops; the KC-130J can lift a payload of 41,790 pounds (18,952 kg).

The improved KC-130J variant has more-powerful Allison AE2100 D3 engines (6,000 shp each), digital avionics, and improved reliability.

One Marine TC-130G is equipped as a maintenance center to support the Navy-Marine Blue Angels flight demonstration team, carrying a crew of seven, plus 30 maintenance personnel; it is nicknamed "Fat Albert" after a characterization of comedian Bill Cosby. The TC-130G is a converted Navy EC-130G delivered in 1991; the previous Fat Albert was a KC-130F.

Coast Guard HC-130H aircraft carry air-dropped rescue and salvage gear. The HC-130H has increased range, flare launchers, and other improvements over the C-130B aircraft they replaced. (Characteristics are similar to the KC-130R described below.) The HC-130H aircraft have been retrofitted with the APS-137 ISAR radar; they also have APN-215 weather radar, and an external SAMSON sensor pod containing a FLIR can be fitted to these aircraft.

A Marine KC-130 tanker simultaneously refuels two F/A-18D Hornet strike-fighters while an F/A-18C Hornet awaits its turn. Marine "Herks" also are used to carry troops and cargo. (U.S. Marine Corps)

A KC-130T flown by Marine reserve squadron VGMR-452 shows the shape of one of the latest variants of the prolific Hercules production line. Non-tanker-configuration C-130T aircraft are flown by the Naval Air Reserve. (Lockheed Martin)

A floatplane configuration of the standard C-130 has been proposed by Lockheed Martin. The asymmetrical floats can be installed in any variant of the C-130, permitting the aircraft to land and take off from sheltered waters. This artist's concept shows a float-configured C-130J aircraft. (Lockheed Martin)

A single Coast Guard Hercules was converted to an AEW configuration for Coast Guard evaluation, redesignated an EC-130V. It was discarded after evaluation.

Lockheed Martin has proposed a floatplane variant of the C-130 for both military and civil use (see photo).

Designation: The Navy-Marine variants of the Hercules were originally designated GV-1; the designation was changed to C-130 in 1962.

Operational: A KC-130F conducted carrier landings and take-offs from the FORRESTAL in 1963 without the use of arresting gear or catapults. C-130s have also been employed to evaluate aerial minelaying.

Status: Operational; in production. First flight of a YC-130 on 23 August 1954. Production of KC-130J aircraft for the Marine Corps is being undertaken on a sporadic basis, with delivery of the first aircraft in 2001.

The Hercules is believed to have been in production longer than any other aircraft in history. It is currently flown by some 60 air forces, as well as numerous civil operators. The U.S. Air Force has some 450 in active and reserve squadrons, in a variety of configurations.

Characteristics for the KC-130R:

Manufacturer:	Lockheed Martin	
Crew:	(5) pilot, copilot, navigator, flight engineer, radio operator/loadmaster + 92 troops	
Engines:	4 Allison T56-A-15 turboprop; 4,591 shp each	
Weight:	empty	75,368 lbs (34,187 kg)
	loaded	109,744 lbs (49,780 kg)
	maximum T/O	155,000 lbs (70,308 kg)
Dimensions:	length	99 ft 5 in (30.32 m)
	wingspan	132 ft 7 in (40.42 m)
	wing area	1,745 ft² (162.12 m²)
	height	38 ft 3 in (11.66 m)
Speed:	maximum	302 knots (560 km/h) at 19,000 ft (5,790 m)
	cruise	288 knots (533 km/h)
Ceiling:	25,000 ft (7,622 m)	
Range:	radius	2,564 n.miles (4,749 km) with maximum payload
		1,000 n.miles (1,852 km) in tanker role with 32,140 lbs (14,579 kg) of fuel for transfer
Radar:	APN-59B	

CT-39G SABRELINER

A few CT-39G aircraft are employed to transport high-priority cargo and passengers for the Marine Corps, the Navy having discarded its aircraft of this type.

The T-39 was long used in the training role, having been employed to train bombardier/navigators and radar intercept officers (see Training Aircraft).

Designation: The low, swept-wing configuration of the CT-39 has two turbojet engine nacelles mounted on the after fuselage. The aircraft is not carrier capable. The CT-39 aircraft carry a crew of three and seven passengers. These were modified commercial Sabreliner Series 40 (E) and 60 (G) aircraft, acquired specifically for the transport role and never used as trainers. One T-39D was fitted as the test bed for the F/A-18 Hornet's APG-65 radar. The aircraft was also used by the Air Force.

Status: North American produced 12 of their Sabre 60 series as the CT-39G.

Manufacturer:	North American Rockwell	
Crew:	(3) pilot, copilot, crewman + 7 passengers	
Engines:	2 Pratt & Whitney J60-P-3A turbojet; 3,000 lbst (1,361 kgst) each	
Weight:	loaded	17,760 lbs (8,056 kg)
Dimensions:	length	43 ft 9 in (13.33 m)
	wingspan	44 ft 5 in (13.53 m)
	wing area	342.6 ft² (31.83 m²)
	height	16 ft (4.88 m)
Speed:	375 knots (695 km/h)	
Ceiling:		
Range:	2,500 n.miles (4,630 km)	
Radar:	navigation	

The Marine Corps flies two CT-39G Sabreliners as transport and utility aircraft. The Navy is phasing out its Sabreliners and the Marines will follow. (McDonnell Douglas, Harry Gann)

CASA 212

The Coast Guard operated a single CASA 212 as a utility transport, flying from Miami, Fla. This is a utility transport, employed in large numbers around the world by commercial, government, and military organizations. The Coast Guard has discarded the aircraft.

See 16th Edition/page 393 for characteristics.

UTILITY AIRCRAFT

HU-25 GUARDIAN

The Guardian is an all-weather, medium-range search and surveillance aircraft flown by the Coast Guard. It replaced the HU-16 Albatross and HC-131 Samaritan aircraft.

Design: This aircraft is a modification of the French-developed commercial Falcon 20G. It has two turbofan engines mounted in nacelles outboard of the after fuselage, an arrangement similar to the T-39 Sabreliner. In addition to crew and passengers, 3,200 pounds

(1,452 kg) of rescue supplies are carried. A galley and toilet are provided.

The ATF3-6 engines have been difficult and expensive to support.

Seven aircraft were modified with the AIREYE sensor system with infrared/ultraviolet line scanners in an underwing pod and an APS-131 Side-Looking Airborne Radar (SLAR) in a fuselage pod, a television camera, and other equipment for pollution reconnaissance; these were redesignated HU-25B in 1989.

Nine other aircraft were fitted with the APG-66 multimode radar, which provides detection of aircraft out to 80 n.miles (148 km), and FLIR; they were redesignated HU-25C in 1989.

Status: Operational. IOC in the Coast Guard in February 1982. The last of 41 aircraft were delivered in 1984. (The Guardian Jet Corporation was a jointly owned subsidiary of Dassault-Breguet and Pan American.)

As part of the downsizing of Coast Guard fixed-wing aircraft, beginning in 1994 several of these aircraft were placed in storage. Similar French-built Mystère-Falcon aircraft are flown in a variety of roles by several air forces.

An HU-25B Guardian fitted with the Aireye sensor system to detect oil pollution, with antennas mounted in a "canoe"-type pod under the fuselage. Russian aircraft and satellites have been similarly fitted. (U.S. Coast Guard)

An HU-25 at rest, with a Coast Guard HC-130H Hercules in the background. The French-designed Guardians have been difficult and expensive to maintain. (U.S. Coast Guard, PA1 Eric Eggen)

Manufacturer:	Dassault-Breguet and Guardian Jet	
Crew:	(5) pilot, copilot, drop master, avionics man, air crewman + 3 passengers + 4 litters	
Engines:	2 Garrett AiResearch ATF3-6-2C turbofan; 5,538 lbst (2,512 kgst) each	
Weight:	empty	19,000 lbs (8,618 kg)
	maximum T/O	33,510 lbs (15,200 kg)
Dimensions:	length	56 ft 3 in (17.15 m)
	wingspan	53 ft 6 in (16.30 m)
	wing area	450 ft² (41.80 m²)
	height	17 ft 5 in (5.32 m)
Speed:	maximum	461 knots (854 km/h) at 40,000 ft (12,195 m)
Ceiling:	42,000 ft (12,805 m)	
Range:	2,250 n.miles (4,167 km) with 30 minutes on station	
Radar:	APS-127 search/weather radar except APG-66 in eight HU-25C aircraft	
	plus APS-131 SLAR in eight HU-25B aircraft	

U-11A AZTEC

All Navy and Marine U-11A utility aircraft have been discarded. Twenty were acquired in 1960 for use by naval air stations. The aircraft was modified from the commercial Piper Aztec, which was also used by the U.S. Army and other countries.

See 14th Edition/page 420 for characteristics.

U-6A BEAVER

Two de Havilland DHC-2 aircraft are in service at the U.S. Naval Test Pilot School at NAS Patuxent River, Md. This is a rugged aircraft, used largely in the Arctic region with wheels, floats, or skis.

These Beavers are the oldest aircraft type flown by the U.S. Navy.

Design: The DHC-2 has a straightforward design with a single radial engine, high-wing configuration, and fixed landing gear. The seats for seven passengers can be easily removed to provide for carrying cargo.

Designation: Flown by the Army, Navy, and Air Force with the designation L-20A until 1962, when it was changed to U-6A.

Status: Operational. First flight in August 1947. A total of 1,631 aircraft were produced, of which 980 went to the U.S. armed forces.

Manufacturer:	de Havilland (Canada)	
Crew:	(2) pilot, copilot + 7 passengers	
Engines:	1 Pratt & Whitney R-985 radial piston; 450 hp	
Weight:	empty	2,850 lbs (1,293 kg)
	maximum T/O	5,099 lbs (2,313 kg)
Dimensions:	length	30 ft 3 in (9.22 m)
	wingspan	48 ft (14.63 m)
	wing area	250 ft² (23.2 m²)
	height	9 ft (2.74 m)
Speed:	cruise	141.5 knots (262 km/h)
Ceiling:	17,991 ft (5,485 m)	
Range:	637 n.miles (1,180 km)	
Radar:	none	

Two U-6A Beaver utility aircraft are flown by the Naval Test Pilot School (NTPS). This aircraft continues to fly in civil service in remote areas. (U.S. Navy)

NU-1B OTTER

A single de Havilland DHC-3 Otter is in service at the U.S. Naval Test Pilot School. This is a rugged aircraft, largely used in Arctic region with wheels, floats, or skis.

Design: This is an enlarged version of the U-6A/DHC-2 (see above). Their appearance is similar.

Designation: Initially given the Navy designation UC-1; this was changed to U-1 in 1962.

Status: Operational. First flight on 12 December 1951. Almost half of the de Havilland production of some 460 aircraft went to the U.S. Air Force and a few to the Navy as the U-1.

Manufacturer:	de Havilland (Canada)	
Crew:	(2) pilot, copilot + 10 passengers	
Engines:	1 Pratt & Whitney R-1340-S1H1-G radial piston; 600 hp	
Weight:	empty	4,431 lbs (2,010 kg)
	maximum T/O	8,000 lbs (3,629 kg)
Dimensions:	length	41 ft 10 in (12.75 m)
	wingspan	58 ft (17.68 m)
	wing area	375 ft² (34.84 m²)
	height	12 ft 7 in (3.84 m)
Speed:	cruise	120 knots (222 km/h)
Ceiling:	18,795 ft (5,730 m)	
Range:	820 n.miles (1,520 km)	
Radar:	none	

A single NU-1B Otter utility aircraft also is flown by NTPS. The school operates a variety of fixed-wing and rotary-wing aircraft to train pilots, mainly from the Navy and Marine Corps but also from the other U.S. services, foreign air forces, and some civilian agencies. (U.S. Navy)

TRAINING AIRCRAFT

*T-6A TEXAN

The T-6A Texan is the aircraft component of the Joint Primary Aircraft Training System (JPATS), an Air Force–Navy program to develop a new training aircraft for production after the year 2000. The Air Force is the lead service for JPATS development.

In naval service, the T-6A will replace the T-34, and in Air Force service it replaces the T-37. The service requirements are for 339 and 372 aircraft, respectively, for a total program of 711 aircraft, plus three prototypes. Production is expected to be completed about 2020.

The Raytheon Aircraft Company's Beech Mk II was selected as the JPATS aircraft in June 1995. Six other aircraft types competed for the JPATS role.

Design: The T-6 is a single-engine, turboprop aircraft with tandem seating. It is derived from the Swiss-built Pilatus PC-9 aircraft. This is a straight-wing aircraft with a pressurized cockpit and ejection seats.

Designation: The next designation in the trainer series at the time of the JPATS selection was T-48. However, the Air Force assigned the designation T-6 in remembrance of the North American AT-6/T-6 Texan trainer (which was also used as a limited attack aircraft); the Navy designation of that trainer was SNJ. The Navy procured more than 4,000 SNJs during World War II, with the last being retired in 1968.

Status: In production for U.S. Navy and Air Force. First flight: engineering prototype JPATS in September 1992; T-6A on 15 July 1995.

Manufacturer:	Beech (Raytheon)	
Crew:	(1) pilot + 1 student	
Engines:	1 Pratt & Whitney PT6A-68 turboprop; 1,700 shp	
Weight:	empty	approx. 3,715 lbs (1,685 kg)
	maximum T/O	approx. 7,055 lbs (3,200 kg)
Dimensions:	length	33 ft 4¾ in (10.175 m)
	wingspan	33 ft 2½ in (10.12 m)
	wing area	16.9 ft² (1.57 m²)
	height	
Speed:	270 knots (500 km/h) at sea level	
Range:	approx. 886 n.miles (1,642 km)	
Ceiling:	25,000 ft (7,620 m)	
Armament:	none	
Radar:	none	

The first T-6A Texan trainers are going to the Air Force, as is this one shown in USAF markings. This aircraft will replace the Navy's T-34 trainer. The use of the same designation and name of a World War II–era aircraft will only confuse future aviation buffs, writers, and historians. (Raytheon/Beech)

The Beech Mk II trainer, prototype for the T-6A Texan, shows the excellent visibility of this nimble aircraft. (Raytheon/Beech)

TC-4C ACADEME

The Navy previously operated several TC-4C trainers for A-6E Intruder bombardier/navigators. These aircraft were discarded in 1995 in anticipation of the A-6E being phased out of Navy service in 1996. The Marines transferred their TC-4s to the Navy. The Coast Guard retains its single, long-serving VC-4A Gulfstream VIP transport. (All variants of the aircraft in military service are generally referred to as Gulfstreams; the Coast Guard aircraft officially retains the name Gulfstream I.)

The TC-4C variants had a simulated A-6E cockpit with pilot and bombardier/navigator positions in the after section of the fuselage, plus four identical bombardier/navigator training consoles. In addition to the A-6E radar (upgraded from the original APQ-92 and APQ-88 radars), these planes had the Target Recognition Attack Multiple-sensor (TRAM) and FLIR fitted in the A-6Es.

The T-41A (later TC-4B) was a navigation training version of the Gulfstream I. That program was canceled before delivery.

See 15th edition/pages 428–429 for characteristics.

T-1A JAYHAWK

The Navy operates a small number of Air Force–owned T-1A trainers. These aircraft are used interchangeably with the T-39N Sabreliners for advanced Naval Flight Officer (NFO) training. These are a military version of the Beech 400A business jet.

Status: First flight of the Beech 400A on 22 September 1989. IOC in the U.S. Air Force in January 1993. Air Force production totaled 180 aircraft.

Manufacturer:	Beech (Raytheon)	
Crew:	(1) pilot + 2 students	
Engines:	2 Pratt & Whitney Canada JT15D-5 turbofan; 2,900 lbst (1,315 kgst) each	
Weight:	empty	1,852 lbs (840 kg)
	maximum T/O	3,350 lbs (1,520 kg)
Dimensions:	length	31 ft 2 in (9.5 m)
	wingspan	33 ft 4 in (10.16 m)
	wing area	
	height	11 ft 7 in (3.53 m)
Speed:	maximum cruise	114 knots (210.8 km/h)
Ceiling:	18,000 ft (5,490 m)	
Range:	458 n.miles (848 km)	
Radar:	none	

A Navy-operated T-1A Jayhawk trainer. In the post–Cold War period, there has been an increase in joint Navy–Air Force flight training for several aircraft types. The Navy does not own any Jayhawks. (U.S. Navy)

T-47A CITATION

The Navy's T-47 trainers, a modified commercial Cessna Citation II Model 500 design, have been discarded. The Navy employed 15 T-47A aircraft in training squadrons VT-10 and VT-86 to train NFOs; the T-47 replaced the T-39 Sabreliner in that role. The T-47 was contractor maintained and operated.

See 14th Edition/page 426 for characteristics.

*T-45 GOSHAWK

The T-45 Goshawk is the Navy's basic undergraduate jet training aircraft, replacing the T-2C and TA-4J. It is a variant of British Aerospace's Hawk Series 60 trainer. Despite using an off-the-shelf aircraft, the first flight of a U.S. Navy Goshawk took place almost five years behind the original schedule. Employing the T-45 reduces flight training by about 15 hours per student compared to the previously used T-2C/TA-4J. The first student pilots flew in the T-45A on 11 February 1994.

The Navy initially planned to procure 253 carrier-capable T-45A trainers and 54 land-based T-45B variants; however, Congress directed that they all be T-45A "wet" models. Accordingly, the current program provides for a total of 268 training aircraft and two prototypes (plus 32 flight simulation devices). Developed by Hawker Siddeley Aviation before it was merged into British Aerospace, the Hawk entered Royal Air Force service in 1976 and is also flown by several other air forces. The U.S. Navy's program was originally designated VTX-TS—VTX for a new training aircraft and TS for Training System, i.e., the simultaneous development of simulators and related training equipment.

Initial T-45 flight tests revealed several shortcomings; among other changes, the original Adour Mk 861/F405-RR-400 engine

was replaced in production aircraft with the Adour Mk 871/F405-RR-401.

Design: The T-45 is a low, swept-wing aircraft with relatively small air intakes beneath the cockpit. The vertical tail surface is forward of the horizontal surfaces.

The U.S. Navy's Goshawks differ from the British Hawk design in having a small ventral fin, an arresting hook, and modified wing, landing gear, and speed brakes. Endurance is approximately four hours. Leading-edge slats are fitted to bring carrier approach speeds within acceptable limits. A pylon is fitted under each wing for small bombs, rockets, or drop tanks; there is also a provision for a centerline store.

The wing and after-fuselage sections of the T-45A are built in Britain by British Aerospace, and Rolls-Royce produces the engines in Britain. (The Hawk continues in production in Britain.)

Names: The name Goshawk was previously assigned to the Navy's Curtiss-built F11C fighter of the 1930s.

Status: Operational; in production. First flight: British T.Mk 1 on 21 August 1974; T-45A on 16 April 1988. IOC in 1994 (VT-21). The British Hawk is flown by ten other countries.

A T-45C from Training Wing 1 comes aboard the GEORGE WASHINGTON. Note the twin nose wheels of the aircraft's tricycle landing gear. The Goshawk was adapted from a widely flown British trainer/light attack aircraft. (U.S. Navy, PH3 Corey Lewis)

Manufacturer:	British Aerospace and McDonnell Douglas		
Crew:	(1) pilot + 1 student		
Engines:	1 Rolls-Royce Adour Mk 871/F405-RR-401 turbofan; 5,845 lbst (2,651 kgst)		
Weight:	empty	9,834 lbs (4,461 kg)	
	maximum T/O	14,081 lbs (6,387 kg)	
Dimensions:	length	35 ft 9 in (10.89 m) + probe	
	wingspan	30 ft 9¾ in (9.39 m)	
	wing area	179.6 ft² (9.39 m²)	
	height	13 ft 6⅛ in (4.12 m)	
Speed:	maximum	529 knots (980 km) at 8,000 ft (2,439 m)	
Ceiling:	42,500 ft (12,957 m)		
Range:	700 n.miles (1,296 km)		
	ferry	1,600 n.miles (2,963 km) with external tanks	
Armament:	25-lb (11-kg) Mk 76 target bombs and 2.75-inch (70-mm) rockets		
Radar:	none		

A T-45A Goshawk from Training Wing 2 is readied for launch from the carrier GEORGE WASHINGTON off the Atlantic Coast. The lack of a designated training carrier forces training operations to be conducted aboard whatever CV/CVN is available at the time. The Goshawk's second cockpit—normally for the instructor—is unoccupied. (U.S. Navy, PH3 Corey Lewis)

A T-45A during the aircraft's carrier trials aboard the JOHN F. KENNEDY. The aircraft's hook still is engaged in the arresting wire and its dive brakes are open. The numeral *1* on the tail fin is nonstandard; training aircraft carry their Training Wing letters. (McDonnell Douglas)

Another view of aircraft 1 landing aboard the KENNEDY, its arresting hook still engaged. At the time the "JFK" was designated as a reserve-training carrier. That scheme was unsuccessful, as sufficient reservists were not available to fill the needed positions. (McDonnell Douglas)

T-44A KING AIR

The T-44A was procured as a replacement for the TS-2/US-2 Tracker employed in the multiengine training role.

Design: The aircraft is a modification of the commercial King Air 90, with a straight wing mounting twin turboprop engines relatively far forward and a conventional tail configuration. The aircraft can be configured as a transport carrying two pilots and three passengers. During development, the military version was designated VTAM(X).

Status: Operational. First flight of the T-44A in January 1977. From April 1977, the Navy took delivery of 61 T-44A aircraft, all being assigned to squadrons VT-21 and VT-31; only the latter squadron now flies the T-44A.

The U.S. Army procured unpressurized versions as the U-21A, while the Air Force obtained one as the UC-6A for special missions and one VC-6 as a VIP transport.

A T-44A King Air *(background)* and a T-34C Turbomentor from Training Wing 4 fly in formation over Corpus Christi, Texas. The King Air wears a rear admiral's flag; in an earlier aviation era, aircraft actually flew such flags when admirals were on board. The Army and Air Force also flew variants of the T-34 and T-44. (U.S. Navy)

Manufacturer:	Beech	
Crew:	(3) pilot, copilot, instructor + 2 students	
Engines:	2 Pratt & Whitney of Canada PT-6A-34B turboprop; 550 hp each	
Weight:	empty	6,326 lbs (2,869 kg)
	maximum T/O	9,650 lbs (4,377 kg)
Dimensions:	length	35 ft 6 in (10.82 m)
	wingspan	50 ft 3 in (15.32 m)
	wing area	293.9 ft^2 (27.3 m^2)
	height	14 ft 3 in (4.33 m)
Speed:	cruise	240 knots (444 km) at 15,000 ft (4,573 m)
Ceiling:	29,500 ft (8,994 m)	
Range:	1,265 n.miles (2,343 km)	
Radar:	navigation	

A T-44A from Training Wing 2's squadron VT-31, which provides intermediate multiengine and maritime multiengine training. The squadron also flies the TC-12B variant of the Huron transport/utility aircraft. (U.S. Navy)

T-39D/N SABRELINER

The Navy operates several of the long-serving T-39s to train NFOs who fly in the F-14, S-3B, and two-seat variants of the F/A-18 aircraft. The T-39N is a basic T-39A upgraded with advanced radar and the same engines as the CT-39E/G. It is flown only by training squadron VT-86. A single T-39D also remains in service.

Eight CT-39G aircraft are in service, principally as a Marine utility-transport aircraft; see page 430.

Design: The T-39 has a low, swept-wing configuration with two turbojet engine nacelles mounted on the after fuselage. The aircraft is not carrier capable.

One of the few T-39N Sabreliner aircraft assigned to the training role for instructing Naval Flight Officers (NFO). These Navy aircraft are contractor flown and maintained for Training Wing 6's squadron VT-86. (U.S. Navy)

The N variant is distinguished from the basic T-39A by being fitted with the Westinghouse APG-66NT radar, a modification of the APG-68 currently installed in several combat aircraft. The T-39N also has engine thrust reversers.

Designation: Originally flown by the Navy as the T3J; the designation was changed to T-39 in 1962.

Status: Operational. First flight: modified commercial Sabreliner on 16 September 1958; T-39A in June 1960; T-39D in December 1962. The first of 17 T-39N aircraft were delivered in late 1991; these were converted civil Sabre 40 aircraft. The aircraft are flown by Tracor Flight Services, Inc., under contract to the Navy.

Characteristics of the T-39N:

Manufacturer:	North American Rockwell	
Crew:	(1) pilot + 2 instructors, 3 students	
Engines:	2 Pratt & Whitney J60-P-3A turbojet; 3,000 lbst (1,361 kgst) each	
Weight:	maximum T/O	approx. 18,000 lbs (8,165 kg)
Dimensions:	length	44 ft (13.41 m)
	wingspan	44 ft 6 in (13.57 m)
	wing area	342 ft^2 (31.77 m^2)
	height	16 ft (4.88 m)
Speed:	maximum	481 knots (892 km/h)
	cruise	435 knots (806 km/h)
Ceiling:	45,000 ft (13,720 m)	
Range:		
Radar:	APG-66NT	

T-38A TALON

The T-38 is the standard U.S. Air Force trainer, flown in small numbers by the Navy for test pilot proficiency and air combat maneuver training. It is closely related to the design of the Northrop F-5 Freedom Fighter and F-5E/F/G (now F-20) Tiger II aircraft.

Status: The YT-38 first flew in April 1959. More than 1,187 were produced, most for the U.S. Air Force, which still flies more than 500 of the aircraft in the training role; others remain in foreign service. The Air Force also flew an AT-38B attack version. The U.S. Navy took delivery of 18 aircraft.

Manufacturer:	Northrop	
Crew:	(1) pilot + 1 student	
Engines:	2 General Electric J85-GE-5A turbojet; 3,850 lbst (1,746 kgst) each with afterburner	
Weight:	empty	7,594 lbs (3,445 kg)
	maximum T/O	12,000 lbs (5,443 kg)
Dimensions:	length	46 ft 10 in (14.13 m)
	wingspan	25 ft 3 in (7.7 m)
	wing area	170 ft^2 (15.80 m^2)
	height	12 ft 11 in (3.92 m)
Speed:	maximum cruise	547 knots (1,014 km/h) at 40,000 ft (12,195 m)
	economical cruise	516 knots (956 km/h) above 40,000 ft
Ceiling:	53,600 ft (26,341 m)	
Range:	1,140 n.miles (2,111 km)	
Radar:	none	

A T-38A Talon, camouflaged for adversary training with VF-43. All Navy Talons now are assigned to the Naval Test Pilot School. The Navy operated few T-38s; the U.S. Air Force and foreign services flew many hundreds of these nimble trainers. (Robert L. Lawson)

T-34C TURBOMENTOR

The Turbomentor is the Navy's primary and basic flight training aircraft. A few T-34C aircraft are used for recruiting and utility activities.

The turboprop T-34C model has replaced the earlier piston-engine aircraft in Navy service. The plane is not carrier capable.

The Navy selected the Beechcraft Model 45 as a primary trainer in 1953, leading to procurement of the T-34A/B/C series. Two T-34B aircraft were converted to YT-34C prototypes (with the turboprop engine) in 1973.

Names: The piston-engine T-34 aircraft had the name Mentor.

Status: Operational. First flight of the YT-34C on 21 September 1973. IOC of the T-34C in July 1976. A total of 352 T-34C aircraft were delivered from 1976 to 1988. (The earlier, piston-engine aircraft have been retired.) T-34 variants are no longer flown by the U.S. Air Force.

Manufacturer:	Beech	
Crew:	(1) pilot + 1 student	
Engines:	1 Pratt & Whitney of Canada PT6A-25 turboprop; 400 shp	
Weight:	empty	2,940 lbs (1,334 kg)
	maximum T/O	4,300 lbs (1,950 kg)
Dimensions:	length	28 ft 8½ in (8.75 m)
	wingspan	33 ft 3⅞ in (10.16 m)
	wing area	179.6 ft² (16.69 m²)
	height	9 ft 7 in (2.92 m)
Speed:	maximum	223 knots (413 km/h) at 5,335 ft (1,627 m)
	cruise	214.5 knots (397 km/h) at 5,335 ft
Ceiling:	30,000 ft (9,146 m)	
Range:	740 n.miles (1,370 km)	
Radar:	none	

The T-34C Turbomentor continues to serve in Navy training squadrons. The aircraft was procured in large numbers by the Navy and Air Force as a basic training aircraft, originally in piston-engine variants named simply Mentor. (Beech)

TC-18F

The Navy owns two training variants of the Boeing 707 to prepare air crewmen for the E-6B Mercury TACAMO aircraft. Both TF-18F aircraft were flown in this role in 1987–1991 and again from 1993, the "break" in service caused by lack of funding, when they were grounded.

They again were grounded in 2000 because of structural problems. Two Air Force EC-18B aircraft are being flown in their place by "training" squadron VQ-7.

Status: Operational. Assigned to Navy Strategic Communications Wing 1.

Manufacturer:	Boeing	
Crew:	(2) pilot, flight engineer + 2 students	
Engines:	4 Pratt & Whitney JT3D turbofan	
Weight:	empty	135,000 lbs (61,236 kg)
	normal T/O	225,000 lbs (102,060 kg)
	maximum T/O	326,000 lbs (147,873 kg)
Dimensions:	length	152 ft 11 in (46.62 m)
	wingspan	145 ft 9 in (44.435 m)
	wing area	
	height	42 ft 5½ in (12.94 m)
Speed:		
Range:		
Ceiling:	42,000 ft (12,800 m)	
Armament:	none	
Radar:	APS-133 weather	

One of the two TC-18F training aircraft previously flown by Navy Strategic Communications Wing 1 to train E-6 Mercury TACAMO/Looking Glass pilots. The aircraft's JT3D turbofans are much smaller than the F108-CF-100 turbofans of the Mercury. (U.S. Navy)

T-2C BUCKEYE

The T-2C variant of the Buckeye is used by the Navy for undergraduate jet pilot training, with a few aircraft also flown by fleet readiness squadrons (for spin recovery training), the Navy's aggressor training squadron, and the Naval Test Pilot School. It is being replaced in the Navy by the T-45 Goshawk.

Design: The Buckeye has straight wings, generally with wingtip tanks fitted, with the twin engines buried in the bottom of the fuselage. Wing pylons can be fitted for carrying small bombs, rockets, or gun pods. The aircraft is carrier capable.

The T-2A was a single-engine aircraft and the T-2B/C were similar with twin engines; all earlier aircraft have been phased out of U.S. naval service. A T-2D variant was developed from the T-2C for the Venezuelan Navy, and a T-2E attack variant for the Greek Air Force.

Designation: Originally designated T2J; changed to T-2 in 1962.

Status: Operational. The Navy took delivery of 217 T-2A and 97 T-2B aircraft before procuring 231 T-2C variants from 1969 to 1975.

The aircraft's service life has been extended from 7,500 to 12,000 hours, at considerable cost, pending availability of the T-45.

Only training squadrons VT-26 and VT-86 currently fly the T-2C in the undergraduate jet training program.

Manufacturer:	North American Rockwell	
Crew:	(1) pilot + 1 student	
Engines:	2 General Electric J85-GE-4 turbojet; 2,950 lbst (1,338 kg) each	
Weight:	empty	8,115 lbs (3,681 kg)
	maximum T/O	13,191 lbs (5,983 kg)
Dimensions:	length	38 ft 3½ in (11.67 m)
	wingspan	38 ft 1½ in (11.62 m) over wingtip tanks
	wing area	255 ft² (23.69 m²)
	height	14 ft 10 in (4.51 m)
Speed:	maximum	460 knots (853 km/h) at 25,000 ft (7,622 m)
Ceiling:	45,500 ft (13,970 m)	
Range:	908 n.miles (1,683 km)	
Armament:	up to 640 lbs (290 kg) of bombs or rockets on 2 wing stations + wingtip tanks	
Radar:	none	

A T-2C Buckeye from Training Wing 1/VT-9 comes aboard the carrier GEORGE WASHINGTON during carrier qualifications off the Atlantic coast. Only two training squadrons now fly the Buckeye. (U.S. Navy, PH3 Brian Fleske)

A T-2C Buckeye from Training Wing 1. Most Buckeyes have been replaced in the Naval Aviation training program by the T-45 Goshawk. (U.S. Navy)

A T-2C Buckeye from VT-9 with the arresting hook in the retracted position. These twin-engine trainers normally have wingtip tanks fitted. (U.S. Navy)

A TA-4J Skyhawk from VT-9 makes one of the last carrier landings by a Skyhawk during qualifications aboard the GEORGE WASHINGTON on 30 September 1999. Parked alongside the angled deck is another TA-4J and two T-2C Buckeyes. The Skyhawk was a most versatile and long-lived carrier aircraft. (U.S. Navy, PH3 Johnnie Robbins)

TA-4J SKYHAWK

The Skyhawk was developed in the early 1950s as a lightweight, daylight-only, nuclear strike aircraft for attacking the Soviet Union. The aircraft subsequently evolved into a highly versatile attack aircraft, widely used by the Navy and Marine Corps, as well as by several foreign air forces. It survived in Navy service in the TA-4J configuration as a training and utility aircraft until 2000.

The TA-4J variant has been replaced by the T-45 Goshawk.

Designation: Originally designated A4D; changed to A-4 in 1962.

Status: A total of 2,960 A-4s were built for U.S. and foreign use, of which 555 were two-seaters, including 293 TA-4J aircraft for the Naval Air Training Command. The last delivery was an A-4M for the Marine Corps in 1979; this was one of the longest production runs of any combat aircraft in history. The last U.S. combat aircraft were Marine A-4M variants, the last retired on 30 June 1992. Many A-4s survive in foreign air forces.

See 16th Edition/pages 399–400 for TA-4J characteristics.

ROTARY-WING AIRCRAFT

JOINT TRANSPORT ROTORCRAFT

The Joint Transport Rotorcraft (JTR) is a proposed program to develop the next-generation military helicopter suitable for use by all U.S. military services. The JTR is envisioned as primarily a replacement for the CH-47 Chinook, flown mainly by the Army, and the CH-53 Sea Stallion, flown by the Navy, Marine Corps, and Air Force. The new helicopter would have an IOC of about 2015.

JOINT ROTARY-WING AIRCRAFT

The Joint Rotary-wing Aircraft (JRA) is being proposed by the Marine Corps as an eventual replacement for the AH-1W SeaCobra and UH-1N Huey helicopters. The JRA would be available after the year 2015.

*MV-22 OSPREY

The MV-22 Osprey is a high-speed, rotary-wing aircraft currently being produced for the Marine Corps assault role as a replacement for the CH-46E Sea Knight and CH-53D Sea Stallion. In addition, the Air Force plans to procure the CV-22 as a special operations aircraft and the Navy had plans to procure the HV-22 for the Search-And-Rescue (SAR) role. The aircraft also has the potential for both the AEW and ASW missions, but at this writing the Navy had no development plans for those variants.

The Navy–Marine Corps had the lead in developing the aircraft under the project designation JVX. The Marine Corps initially planned to procure 552 aircraft for vertical assault and the Navy an additional 50 for combat SAR.[30] The other Navy missions could have added some 200 to 300 additional aircraft to the Navy program. The Air Force at one point envisioned a buy of 80 aircraft for special operations and the Army about 230 for medical evacuation as well as for Special Electronic Mission Aircraft (SEMA). Thus, the V-22 program could have reached 900 to 1,200 aircraft.

The Army and Air Force withdrew from the program in the late 1980s, and on 25 April 1989 Secretary of Defense Cheney eliminated all funding for the Navy-Marine program. At the time, his staff proposed a replacement force of 602 MV-22s with a combination of 376 CH-53E and 590 H-60 helicopters. Department of Defense opposition to the V-22 continued as late as September 1994, but the Marine Corps opposed all alternatives to the V-22 and Congress continued to support and fund the V-22 program.

Production is now approved for a Marine buy of 360 MV-22s, Air Force procurement of 50 CV-22s, and 48 HV-22s for the Navy—a total acquisition of 458 aircraft. To help compensate for the delays in procurement, Marine MV-22 procurement has been accelerated to a rate of 30 aircraft per year beginning in fiscal 2003.

Design: The V-22, developed from the XV-15A technology-demonstration aircraft, has twin rotor-engine nacelles mounted on a connecting wing. The nacelles rotate to a horizontal position for conventional aircraft flight and are vertical for vertical takeoff and landing or for hover.

The basic aircraft has an internal cargo capacity of 10,000 pounds (4,536 kg) and an external (slung) capacity of 15,000 pounds (6,804 kg). Rolling takeoffs and landings are the normal operating mode, although VTOL operations are feasible. Thus, the design has the advantages of both a conventional aircraft and helicopter. An inflight refueling probe is provided.

---

30. The original Marine requirement was based on:

16 HMM squadrons × 15 aircraft	240
2 reserve squadrons × 15 aircraft	30
2 HMT squadrons × 20 aircraft	40
1 VMX squadron × 15 aircraft	15
RDT&E, pipeline, 20-year attrition	227

The Marine Corps has proposed a gunship variant of the MV-22 that could carry a variety of guns, rockets, and missiles. The proposed Navy SV-22 would carry Mk 50 ASW torpedoes and operate a number of anti-submarine sensors, including APS-137 radar, dipping sonar, sonobuoys, and FLIR.

The Royal Navy has expressed interest in the AEW variant of the V-22 for operation from the INVINCIBLE-class VSTOL carriers. That AEW aircraft would loiter at about 15,000 feet (4,500 m) and would have a radius of some 200 n.miles (370 km) with 2.5 hours on station; inflight refueling could extend the on-station time to 5.5 hours. The aircraft would carry the APS-138 or APS-145 radar. (Potential U.S. Navy AEW configurations provided for conformal-array radars on the fuselage of the aircraft.)

Operational: The No. 4 development aircraft began shipboard flight trials on the WASP (LHD 1) on 4 December 1990; they were highly successful.

Status: In production. First flight of the MV-22 on 19 March 1989; first full conversion flight on 14 September 1989. IOC is planned for 2001.

Six development aircraft have been built (two were lost in crashes).

Manufacturer:	Bell-Boeing
Crew:	(3) pilot, copilot, crew chief + 24 troops
Engines:	2 Allison T406-AD-400 turboshaft; 6,150 shp each (continuous rating 5,890 shp)
Weight:	maximum T/O 60,500 lbs (27,443 kg)
Dimensions:	fuselage length 56 ft 10 in (17.33 m)
	span 46 ft 6 in (14.18 m) over engine nacelles
	height 17 ft 4 in (5.28 m)
	rotor diameter 36 ft (10.98 m)
	aircraft width 84 ft 6 in (25.76 m), including rotor blades
Speed:	dash approx. 300 knots (156 km/h)
	maximum cruise approx. 260 knots (483 km/h) at 18,000 ft (5,488 m)
Ceiling:	30,000+ ft (9,146+ m)
Range:	radius 200 n.miles (370 km) with 24 troops
	50 n.miles with 8,300 lbs (3,765 kg) external cargo
	ferry 1,720 n.miles (3,185 km) without refueling
Radar:	none

Marines from the 2nd Reconnaissance Battalion, 2nd Marine Expeditionary Force, parachute from an MV-22 Osprey over Camp Lejeune, N.C. The Osprey's engine nacelles are angled at about 45° as the aircraft moves forward at a slow speed. The aircraft has a large rear cargo door. (U.S. Navy, Vernon Pugh)

An MV-22 prepares to land aboard the amphibious assault ship Saipan (LHA 2) during flight tests off the Atlantic coast. The MV-22 can make limited rolling takeoffs and landings, but the engine nacelles cannot be in a horizontal mode. (U.S. Navy, PH1 Tina M. Ackerman)

A development MV-22 during an inflight refueling demonstration with an Air Force KC-135 Stratotanker. The MV-22's engine nacelles are in the horizontal, high-speed flight configuration as the aircraft closes with the tanker, which streams a refueling drogue from its fixed refueling boom. (Bell)

A development model of the MV-22 on a deck-edge elevator of the amphibious assault ship Wasp (LHD 1). The aircraft's engine nacelles and rotor blades are in the stowed position. (Bell)

HH-65A DOLPHIN

The French-designed Dolphin is flown by the Coast Guard in the short-range SAR role. It replaced the HH-52A. The HH-65A is flown in larger numbers than any other Coast Guard aircraft.

Developed by Aérospatiale as model SA 366G Dauphin, the helicopter was selected in a Coast Guard competition in 1979.

Those HH-65A helicopters that embark in icebreakers are fitted with skis in addition to their standard landing gear, giving them more stability for snow and ice operations.

Design: This is a streamlined helicopter with fully retractable landing gear, twin turboshaft engines, and a fan-in-fin *fenestron* tail rotor (i.e., an 11-blade tail rotor within a shroud). Engine problems led to replacement of the original LTS101 with Allison-Garrett LHTEC T800-800 turboshaft engines, the first being replaced in 1991.

In Coast Guard service they have a 3.5-million candlepower searchlight, an infrared system, and droppable rescue equipment. Maximum mission endurance is four hours.

Status: First flight: SA 360 on 2 June 1972; SA 366G/HH-65A (prior to installation of avionics) on 23 July 1980. IOC in the Coast Guard in November 1984.

The Coast Guard has procured 96 Dolphins, with deliveries delayed from an originally planned IOC of late 1981 because of engine problems.

Several nations fly the helicopter in the military role, with some variants fitted with anti-ship missiles and ASW equipment. The Israeli Navy procured for shipboard evaluation two H-65A helicopters that were funded by the United States; the procurement of 20 additional helicopters by Israel followed, all built by Aérospatiale to HH-65A standards.

Manufacturer:	Aérospatiale	
Crew:	(3) pilot, copilot, crewman + 3 passengers	
Engines:	2 Allison-Garrett LHTEC T800-800 turboshaft; 1,200 shp each	
Weight:	empty	5,992 lbs (2,718 kg)
	maximum T/O	9,200 lbs (4,173 kg)
Dimensions:	fuselage length	37 ft 6 in (11.43 m)
	overall length	43 ft 9 in (13.33 m)
	height	12 ft 9 in (3.89 m)
	main rotor diameter	39 ft 2 in (11.9 m)
Speed:	maximum 175 knots (324 km/h)	
	cruise 139 knots (257 km/h)	
Ceiling:	7,510 ft (2,290 m) hover IGE[31]	
	5,340 ft (1,627 m) hover OGE	
Range:	radius 152 n.miles (280 km) with 30 minutes loiter	
	maximum 410 n.miles (760 km)	
Radar:	none	

---

31. IGE = In Ground Effect; OGE = Out of Ground Effect.

An HH-65A Dolphin in flight with landing gear retracted. The helicopter has the unusual fenestron in place of a conventional tail rotor. Coast Guard aircraft carry their serial number vice unit number. (U.S. Coast Guard)

An HH-65A helicopter en route to conduct a survey after Hurricane Bret came ashore in Texas in August 1999. The landing gear is extended; the rescue hoist is visible on the right side, above the large sliding door. (U.S. Coast Guard, PA3 Bridget Hieronymus)

*CH-60S

The CH-60S is a cargo version of the Seahawk series, especially developed for use in Vertical Replenishment (VERTREP) operations. In addition to VERTREP, the CH-60S will be capable of performing the SAR and Mine Countermeasures (MCM) roles. The Navy is planning to procure approximately 250 helicopters to replace that service's UH-46D Sea Knight, H-3 Sea King, and H-1 Huey helicopters.

The principal competitor to the CH-60S was a Kaman single-engine helicopter designated K-MAX®, which conducted extensive VERTREP tests from Navy ships. (K-MAX® helicopters are in commercial service.)

Design: The prototype CH-60S is a modified UH-60L Black Hawk, transferred to the Navy in 1997 and redesignated YCH-60. The production aircraft are based on the UH-60L, with two T700 engines and certain SH-60 dynamic systems, including the gear box and flight controls. An External Stores Support System (ESSS), consisting of removable four-station pylons, can be fitted to the CH-60; the ESSS can carry additional fuel tanks to increase ferry range.

The CH-60 can lift 10,000 pounds (4,536 kg) of cargo externally by sling. The external lift capacity of the standard UH-60L is 9,000 pounds (4,082 kg).

Names: The name Knighthawk has been unofficially used with this helicopter. Note that the Army tends to use two-word names for its H-60 series helicopters, the Navy one word.

Status: IOC in 2000. First flight CH-60S on 27 January 2000.

The U.S. Army and National Guard have more than 1,500 H-60 series helicopters in service. The helicopter is also flown by the Air Force, primarily for special operations, and in smaller numbers by the Marine Corps (VH-60N) and Coast Guard (HH-60J), as well as the armed forces of several other nations.

The prototype CH-60S VERTREP helicopter demonstrates its lift capacity. The hybrid "Hawk" beat out the smaller, single-engine Kaman K-MAX for this role. Maintenance and training are simplified because of the large number of SH-60 and HH-60 helicopters in Navy service. (Sikorsky)

Manufacturer:	Sikorsky	
Crew:	(4) pilot, copilot, 2 crewmen + 13 passengers	
Engines:	2 General Electric T700-GE-401C turboshaft; 1,900 shp each	
Weight:	empty	11,516 lbs (5,224 kg)
	loaded	17,432 lbs (7,907 kg)
	maximum T/O	22,000 lbs (9,979 kg)
Dimensions:	fuselage length	
	overall length	
	height	
	main rotor diameter	
Speed:	maximum cruise	
	cruise	
Ceiling:		
Range:		
Radar:	none	

SH-60R SEAHAWK

The SH-60R is a multipurpose variant of the Seahawk, "remanufactured" from SH-60B LAMPS III, SH-60F ASW, and HH-60H SAR helicopters. The remanufacture includes a Service Life Extension Program (SLEP); installation of ISAR, low-frequency dipping sonar, and an upgraded computer; and provision for Penguin and Hellfire Air-to-Surface Missiles (ASM) as well as ASW torpedoes.

Navy plans call for the remanufacture of some 250 SH-60B, SH-60F, and HH-60H aircraft to the SH-60R by about 2012. The basic characteristics are similar to the SH-60B/F.

Status: First flight in 1999.

VH-60N "WHITE TOP"

The Marine Corps flies eight VH-60 variants of the H-60 series as executive transports. Assigned to squadron HMX-1 at Quantico, Va., these are "white top" helicopters that provide transportation for the president and other senior national officials. They replaced VH-1A Huey helicopters previously employed in this role. When the president is embarked in one of these helicopters, it is designated "Marine One."

Design: The VH-60N is fitted with a weather radar, cabin soundproofing, and Electromagnetic Pulse (EMP) hardening and has a VIP interior configuration.

Names: These helicopters do not have an official name; they are generally referred to as "White Tops."

Status: IOC on 30 November 1988.

A VH-60N "White Top," configured as an executive transport flown by Marine squadron HMX-1. Eight of these helicopters are available for the President and other VIPs. This relatively lightweight variant has only a single tail wheel, positioned farther aft than on the SH-60 variants. (Sikorsky)

Manufacturer:	Sikorsky	
Crew:	(4) pilot, copilot, flight engineer, radio operator + passengers	
Engines:	2 General Electric T700-GE-700 turboshaft; 1,560 shp each	
Weight:	empty	11,284 lbs (5,118 kg)
	loaded	16,994 lbs (7,708 kg)
Dimensions:	fuselage length	50 ft ¾ in (15.26 m)
	overall length	64 ft 10 in (19.76 m)
	height	16 ft 10 in (5.13 m)
	main rotor diameter	53 ft 8 in (16.36 m)
Speed:	maximum	160 knots (296 km/h)
	maximum cruise	145 knots (268 km/h)
Ceiling:	19,000 ft (5,790 m)	
	9,500 ft (2,896 m) hover IGE	
	10,400 ft (4,390 m) hover OGE	
Range:	323 n.miles (600 km) with 30 minutes loiter	
Radar:	weather	

HH-60J JAYHAWK

The HH-60J is the Coast Guard's medium-range SAR variant of the ubiquitous Black Hawk/Seahawk helicopter series. The HH-60J replaced the HH-3F Pelican and CH-3E Sea King in Coast Guard service. The Jayhawk is flown in larger numbers than any Coast Guard aircraft except the HH-65A helicopter.

Design: The HH-60J configuration is similar to the Navy's SH-60F variants, with generally the same characteristics, except that the HH-60J can be fitted with three external fuel tanks for long-range operations. The helicopter has an external lift of 4,000 pounds (1,814 kg).

Like all H-60 series helicopters, the HH-60J has a fixed, tail-wheel landing gear. It can operate on board the 12 Famous (WMEC 270)-

An HH-60J Jayhawk flying fast and low. The H-60 designation suffix "J" and name Jayhawk are both duplicative of existing aircraft—the Japanese variant of the SH-60 and the T-1A Jayhawk, respectively. (U.S. Coast Guard, PA2 Joe Dye)

An HH-60J with the large right-side door open; a left-side opening permits stretchers to be easily loaded. These aircraft have a weather radome protruding from the nose, as do other variants of the H-60. They have a fixed landing gear. (U.S. Coast Guard)

class Coast Guard cutters and larger ships. The helicopter has a FLIR and a large searchlight.

Standard SH-60F data apply except as indicated below.

Designation: The Japanese Maritime Self-Defense Force flies the SH-60J and UH-60J helicopters, the former a copy of the U.S. SH-60B Seahawk ASW aircraft and the latter a utility variant. The J indicates Japanese, in an improper use of the suffix letter.

Status: Operational. IOC 60J in July 1991. The Coast Guard procured 42 Jayhawks through 1995.

Manufacturer:	Sikorsky
Engines:	2 General Electric T700-GE-401C turboshaft; 1,900 shp each
Crew:	(4) pilot, copilot, 2 crewmen + 6 rescuees
Weight:	maximum T/O 21,884 lbs (9,927 kg)
Range:	radius 300 n.miles (556 km) with 45 minutes loiter
Radar:	Bendix RDR-1300C weather

HH-60H SEAHAWK

The HH-60H is the Navy's combat SAR variant of the H-60 series. It has replaced the HH-3A Sea King as a specialized SAR helicopter. The HH-60H variants are flown by reserve squadrons HCS-4 and HCS-5, and all carrier HS squadrons are assigned two HH-60H variants (in addition to four SH-60F helicopters).

These helicopters can carry eight SEALs and their equipment when operating in support of special operations.

Design: The HH-60H variants have the APR-39 radar warning receiver, ALE-39 chaff/flare dispenser, and ALQ-144 infrared jammer, as well as sophisticated communications gear. Although initially armed with machine guns, proposals are being considered to additionally provide these helicopters with 2.75-inch (70-mm) rockets and Hellfire missiles, with a growth potential for air-to-air missiles. Other planned upgrades to the HH-60 include a FLIR/laser designator–range finder.

Standard SH-60B/F data apply, except as indicated below.

Status: Operational. First flight on 17 August 1988. IOC in July 1989 (HCS-5).

Manufacturer:	Sikorsky
Crew:	(3) pilot, copilot, crew chief + rescuees
Range:	radius 252 n.miles (465 km)
Armament:	2 7.62-mm machine guns M60D (8,000 rounds)
Radar:	none

Details of an HH-60H from squadron HCS-4 with a 7.62-mm, six-barrel GAU-2B/A Minigun mounted in the door. Alternatively, conventional 7.62-mm machine guns can be fitted in both side doors. (Peter B. Mersky)

SH-60B/F SEAHAWK

In naval service, the Seahawk is primarily an ASW helicopter, with the SH-60B the helicopter component of the Navy's ship-based LAMPS III ASW and over-the-horizon targeting system, and the SH-60F a carrier-based ASW aircraft. Both types are being remanufactured to provide the multipurpose SH-60R variant (see above).

The SH-60B is embarked in active cruisers, destroyers, and frigates in two-plane detachments from HSL squadrons; the SH-60F is

An HH-60H Seahawk assigned to HS-8 prepares for a fast-rope exercise with an Explosive Ordnance Disposal (EOD) team aboard the carrier John C. Stennis. There is a FLIR tracker ball mounted on the nose of the helicopter. (U.S. Navy)

An SH-60B Seahawk from HSL-47 hovers over the cruiser Ticonderoga (CG 47) during a Hot In-Flight Refueling (HIFR) evolution. The circular radome under the nose identifies the SH-60B variant. The H-60 helicopters have a fixed landing gear. (U.S. Navy, JO2 Ty Swartz)

combined with two HH-60H Seahawks in six-plane HS squadrons aboard aircraft carriers.

The following ships were configured to each carry two SH-60B helicopters:

25	CG 47	TICONDEROGA class
24	DD 963	SPRUANCE class
26	FFG 7	OLIVER HAZARD PERRY class

In addition, the Improved ARLEIGH BURKE (DDG 51)-class ships carry the SH-60, as will the DD 21 land-attack destroyer.

Design: The Seahawk is adopted from the UH-60A Black Hawk, the U.S. Army's basic transport helicopter. The SH-60B carries 2,000 pounds (907 kg) of avionics, including the ALQ-142 ESM sensor (similar to the SLQ-32 found on most U.S. surface warships); this system permits the helicopter to provide over-the-horizon detections and missile targeting for the launching ship. The helicopter also has a 25-sonobuoy dispenser, APS-124 radar, FLIR, ASQ-81 MAD, and UYS-1(V)2 Proteus acoustic processor. No dipping sonar is fitted in the SH-60B. Beginning in 1990, the SH-60B variants have been fitted to carry the Penguin anti-ship missile. Some helicopters will be further modified to fire the Hellfire missile. From 1995, these helicopters are also being fitted to mount a 7.62-mm M60D machine gun,

An SH-60F from HS-5 lowers an AQS-13F dipping sonar. The ship-generated noises near a carrier battle group require the use of active dipping sonar rather than passive sonobuoys for submarine detection. (U.S. Navy)

AAR-47 missile detection system, ALE-39 chaff/flare dispenser, and ALQ-144 infrared jammer.

A YSH-60B was modified in 1984 to test the AQS-13F active dipping sonar and automated flight control system for the SH-60F. The carrier-based SH-60F has an AQS-13F dipping sonar with a 1,500-foot (457-m) cable; the radar, MAD, sonobuoys, and some other equipment of the SH-60B has been deleted. The UYS-1(V)2 acoustic processor is fitted in the F variants.

Early plans called for a crew of four in the SH-60B, but in the event, the aircraft has three crewmen. Although designed to carry nuclear depth bombs, the Seahawks have not been "wired" for this weapon. The IBM corporation was the prime contractor for the LAMPS III/SH-60B, the first time that the airframe manufacturer did not perform this role for a U.S. Navy helicopter; Sikorsky is the prime for the SH-60F variant.

Designation: LAMPS = Light Airborne Multi-Purpose System, a term originally coined for the SH-2 LAMPS I helicopter (see below). The LAMPS II was a design study that did not reach fruition.

Status: Operational; no longer in production. First flight: YUH-60 test bed on 17 October 1974; prototype SH-60B on 12 December 1979. IOC: Navy SH-60B in September 1983 (HSL-41); SH-60F in June 1989 (HS-10).

Australia, Greece, Spain, and Turkey have purchased the SH-60B or the commercial-sale S-70 Seahawk, while Japan is producing the SH-60J for shipboard use and the UH-60J for land basing. (A total of 17 nations other than the United States fly military variants of H-60/S-70 helicopters.)

Manufacturer:	IBM/Sikorsky
Crew:	(3) pilot, copilot/airborne tactical officer, sensor operator
Engines:	2 General Electric T700-GE-401 turboshaft; 1,690 shp each; helicopters procured after 1988 have 2 T700-GE-401C turboshaft (1,900 shp each)
Weight:	empty 13,648 lbs (6,191 kg)
	loaded 19,500 lbs (8,845 kg) in ASW role
	18,000 lbs (8,165 kg) in Harpoon targeting role
	21,000+ lbs (9,526+ kg) in utility role
Dimensions:	fuselage length 50 ft (15.26 m)
	overall length 64 ft 10 in (19.76 m)
	height 17 ft 2 in (5.23 m)
	main rotor diameter 53 ft 8 in (16.36 m)
Speed:	maximum cruise 126 knots (233 km/h)
Ceiling:	19,000 ft (5,790 m)
	9,500 ft (2,896 m) hover IGE
	10,400 ft (4,390 m) hover OGE
Range:	radius 50 n.miles (92.5 km) with 3 hours loiter
	150 n.miles (278 km) with 1 hour loiter
Armament:	2 Mk 46/50 ASW torpedoes or 2 Penguin anti-ship missiles
Radar:	APS-124 in SH-60B (none in SH-60F)

Carrying two dummy Mk 46 ASW torpedoes, an SH-60B hovers for the camera. Outboard of the starboard torpedo is a towed MAD antenna in its stowed position. This is the only H-60 variant to have the APS-124 radar, mounted in a circular radome between the main landing gear. (Sikorsky)

An early OH-58 Kiowa light observation helicopter of the type flown by the NTPS. The helicopter was procured in large numbers by the U.S. Army. The TH-57 SeaRanger is similar. (Bell)

OH-58C KIOWA

Four diminutive OH-58C helicopters are assigned to the Naval Test Pilot School. The H-58 series was the losing entry in the Army's 1961 Light Observation Helicopter (LOH) competition. Despite its loss to the OH-6, the Bell 206/OH-58 design became a commercial success and the Navy ordered 40 as TH-57 SeaRangers for basic helicopter flight training (see below). Subsequently, the Army reopened the LOH competition and placed an initial order for 2,200 OH-58s.

Design: This is a single-engine light helicopter with landing skids, a two-blade main rotor, and an anti-torque tail rotor mounted on the left side of the tailboom.

Several hundred OH-58A helicopters were updated to the OH-58C configuration.

Status: Operational. First flight of the OH-58A on 10 January 1966. IOC of the TH-57A in 1968.[32] The H-58 series remains in service in large numbers with the U.S. Army.

Manufacturer:	Bell
Crew:	(2) pilot, copilot + 2 passengers
Engines:	1 Allison T63-8-720 turboshaft; 420 shp
Weight:	empty
	maximum T/O
Dimensions:	length 32 ft 7 in (9.93 m)
	height 9 ft 6½ in (2.91 m)
	rotor diameter 35 ft 4 in (10.77 m)
Speed:	
Ceiling:	
Range:	
Radar:	none

TH-57 SEARANGER

The SeaRanger is a training version of the commercial Bell 206 JetRanger series. See OH-58C (above) for program details.

Design: The TH-57 is fitted with dual controls. The TH-57C models have improved avionics and controls; these are upgraded TH-57A variants (designation changed to TH-57C in February 1983).

Status: IOC: TH-57A in 1968; TH-57C in November 1982.

The Navy purchased 40 off-the-shelf commercial aircraft as the TH-57A in 1968; subsequently, 89 improved TH-57C models were procured in the 1980s. The latter replaced the TH-1L Hueys in the training role.

Manufacturer:	Bell	
Crew:	(1) pilot + 4 students	
Engines:	1 Allison T63-A-700 turboshaft; 317 shp	
Weight:	empty	1,464 lbs (664 kg)
	maximum T/O	3,000 lbs (1,361 kg)
Dimensions:	fuselage length	32 ft 7 in (9.94 m)
	overall length	41 ft (12.5 m)
	height	9 ft 7 in (2.91 m)
	main rotor diameter	35 ft 4 in (10.78 m)
Speed:	maximum 120 knots (222 km)	
	cruise 101.5 knots (188 km)	
Ceiling:	18,900 ft (5,762 km)	
	13,600 ft (4,146 km) hover IGE	
Range:	300 n.miles (483 km)	
Radar:	none	

---

32. This was the first military procurement of the OH-58 design.

A TH-57 SeaRanger, the Navy's basic training helicopter. Squadrons HT-8 and HT-18 of Training Wing 5 provide basic helicopter training for Navy, Marine Corps, and Coast Guard pilots. (Bell)

A TH-57 about to land aboard the helicopter training craft IX 514 (U.S. Navy)

A Navy MH-53E Sea Dragon from HC-4 over the carrier CARL VINSON operating in the Persian Gulf. The squadron provides support to deployed naval forces in the Mediterranean and Persian Gulf. Large sponsons are fitted to the MH-53E variants. (U.S. Navy, PHAN José Cordero)

CH-53E/MH-53E SUPER STALLION/SEA DRAGON

Developed specifically for the U.S. Navy and Marine Corps, the H-53E series is the heaviest lift helicopter in service outside of Russia. It is flown by the Marines in the CH-53E assault/heavy cargo roles and by the Navy in the MH-53E mine countermeasures and VERTREP roles.

A Marine CH-53E operating from the amphibious assault ship KEARSARGE (LHD 3) lowers a water trailer at Topel, Turkey, as U.S. naval forces assist earthquake victims in the area. The helicopter's rear cargo door is open. (U.S. Marine Corps, CWO Seth Rossman)

Design: The CH-53E can lift 16 tons (16,330 kg) of external load. These helicopters have the same basic configuration as the D-model Sea Stallion, but with three engines, a seven-blade main rotor (vice six in the CH-53A/D), larger rotor blades, an inflight refueling probe, and an improved transmission. Two 650-gallon (2,470-liter) external tanks can be fitted to the sponsons. The CH-53E can lift 93 percent of the heavy equipment in a Marine division, compared to 38 percent for the CH-53D.

The MH-53E can handle the Mk 103 moored sweep gear, Mk 104 acoustic sweep, Mk 105 magnetic sweep, Mk 106 magnetic/acoustic sweep, ALQ-166 Lightweight Magnetic Sweep (LMS), and AQS-14 towed minehunting sonar. The improved AQS-20 minehunting sonar will be provided for these helicopters in place of the AQS-14. It is capable of night operations with a six-hour mission capability. (The RH-53D can operate only in daylight.)

With the phasing out of the SH-2G LAMPS I helicopter in the late 1990s, their Magic Lantern mine-detecting laser is being fitted in the MH-53E.

Designation: The M prefix indicates multimission capability.

Historical: The RH-3A Sea King was the first airborne MCM helicopter approved for U.S. Navy service. It was replaced by the CH-53A Sea Stallion in the early 1970s, and those helicopters were used during Operation End Sweep, the 1972–1973 mine clearance of North Vietnamese ports.

The CH-53A was succeeded by the RH-53D in 1972; these helicopters were deployed to the Suez Canal in 1974–1975 (Operations Nimbus Star/Stream), the Red Sea/Gulf of Suez in 1984 (Operation Intense Look), and the Persian Gulf in 1987 (Operation Earnest Will). In turn, the RH-53D has been succeeded in the MCM role by the MH-53E.

Operational: Six MH-53E Sea Dragons were air-lifted by C-5A Galaxy transports to the Persian Gulf in early October 1990 to participate in Operations Desert Shield/Desert Storm. They then operated from the helicopter carrier TRIPOLI (LPH 10). In doing so, of course, the MH-53Es displaced Marine helicopters and troops.

Status: Operational. First flight: YCH-53E on 1 March 1974; CH-53E on 13 December 1980; MH-53E on 1 September 1983 (a CH-53E in the MCM configuration flew on 23 December 1981). IOC of the CH-53E in February 1981 (HMH-464).

A hovering Marine CH-53E from HMM-264 delivers fuel containers during a VERTREP operation with the WASP. The aircraft has standard low-visibility markings, with only the helicopter's number in the squadron (22) clearly visible. (Lt. Col. P. Chrisetiere [USMC])

Manufacturer:	Sikorsky
Crew:	(3) pilot, copilot, crew chief + 55 troops
Engines:	3 General Electric T64-GE-416 turboshaft; 4,380 shp each

Weight:	empty	CH-53E	33,685 lbs (15,280 kg)
		MH-53E	36,336 lbs (16,482 kg)
	maximum T/O	73,500 lbs (33,340 kg)	

Dimensions:	fuselage length	73 ft 4 in (22.33 m)
	overall length	99 ft ½ in (30.18 m)
	height	27 ft 9 in (8.46 m)
	main rotor diameter	79 ft (24.08 m)

Speed:	maximum	170 knots (315 km/h) at sea level
	cruise	150 knots (278 km/h) at sea level

Ceiling:	18,500 ft (5,640 m)
	11,550 ft (3,520 m) hover IGE
	9,500 ft (2,895 m) hover OGE

Range:	radius	50 n.miles (92.5 km) with 16 tons of external cargo
		500 n.miles (926 km) with 10 tons of external cargo
	ferry	1,000 n.miles (1,852 km)

Radar:	none

CH-53D SEA STALLION

The H-53 series has served as the Marine Corps's heavy assault helicopter and the Navy's mine countermeasures helicopter. Only the Marines now operate the helicopter. It has been partially replaced in Marine and Navy service by the CH-53E Super Stallion and MH-53E Sea Dragon, respectively.

All earlier Navy/Marine CH-53A and RH-53D helicopters have been retired.

Design: The basic dimensions of the CH-53D variant is similar to the E except that the later helicopter has a third engine and other propulsion improvements. These helicopters have a large cargo compartment with a rear ramp. The RH-53D variants were similar to the CH-53D but had upgraded T64-GE-415 engines and automatic flight controls for sustained low-level flight. The MCM versions had provisions for two swivel .50-cal machine guns and could stream Mk 103 cutters for countering contact mines, Mk 104 acoustic countermeasures, the Mk 105 hydrofoil sled for counter-

An MH-53E during an Airborne Mine Countermeasures (AMCM) operation tows a Mk 105 hydrofoil sled with the ALQ-166 system for countering magnetic mines. These helicopters can be deployed to forward areas in C-5 Galaxy cargo aircraft, by the helicopters being ferried with inflight refueling, or aboard amphibious ships. A refueling probe and rear-view mirrors are evident in the helicopter's nose. (U.S. Navy)

A Marine CH-53E Super Stallion from HMM-264 takes off from the amphibious assault ship WASP during operations in the Adriatic Sea. The CH-53E variants have smaller sponsons with fuel tanks attached; the refueling probe is removed from this aircraft. The tail fin is angled to the left. (Lt. Col. P. Chrisetiere [USMC])

A Marine CH-53E from HMM-265 delivering containers of provisions and supplies for United Nations forces in East Timor. The squadron, assigned to the 31st Marine Expeditionary Unit, was embarked in the amphibious assault ship BELLEAU WOOD (LHA 3). (U.S. Marine Corps, Sgt. Bryce R. Piper)

ing magnetic mines, the Mk 106 sled with acoustic sweep equipment added, and the SPU-1 Magnetic Orange Pipe (MOP) for countering shallow-water mines; the AQS-14 dipping/towed sonar was also available for the RH-53D.

Operational: Eight RH-53D helicopters, flying from the carrier NIMITZ, were used in the aborted April 1980 attempt to rescue hostages from the American embassy in Iran; seven of those helicopters were destroyed in the operation.

A Marine CH-53D Sea Stallion from HMM-362, shown taking off from the carrier THEODORE ROOSEVELT during operations in the Adriatic Sea. All CH-53 helicopters have the same basic configuration, with "E" models having a third engine fitted on the left side of the main rotor assembly. (U.S. Navy)

Marine gunners stand by .50-cal M60 machine guns aboard a CH-53D helicopter operating over Macedonia while supporting Operation Allied Force in 1999. Marine and Navy H-53 and H-46 helicopters periodically have .50-cal machine guns fitted in this manner to provide defense when operating on or near the ground in contested areas. (U.S. Navy)

Refueling in flight five times from KC-130 tankers, an RH-53D has made an 18½-hour flight across the United States.

Status: Operational. First flight of the CH-53A on 14 October 1964. IOC in the Marine Corps in November 1966 (HMH-463).

The Navy and Marine Corps took delivery of 384 H-53A/D series helicopters; others were flown by the U.S. Air Force and foreign services. In addition to the 30 RH-53D models delivered to the U.S. Navy, six more MCM versions went to Iran prior to the 1979 Islamic revolution.

Manufacturer:	Sikorsky
Crew:	(3) pilot, copilot, crewman + 38 troops or 24 litters + 4 attendants (7 crewmen in RH-53D)
Engines:	2 General Electric T64-GE-413 turboshaft; 3,925 shp each
Weight:	empty 23,628 lbs (10,718 kg)
	loaded 34,958 lbs (15,857 kg)
	maximum T/O 42,000 lbs (19,051 kg)
Dimensions:	fuselage length 67 ft 2 in (20.48 m)
	overall length 88 ft 3 in (26.92 m)
	height 24 ft 11 in (7.59 m)
	main rotor diameter 72 ft 3 in (22.04 m)
Speed:	maximum 170 knots (315 km/h)
	cruise 150 knots (278 km/h)
Ceiling:	21,000 ft (6,402 m)
	13,400 ft (4,085 m) hover IGE
Range:	540 n.miles (1,000 km)
	ferry 886 n.miles (1,641 km)
Radar:	none

CH-46E/UH-46D SEA KNIGHT

The CH-46E is the principal Marine Corps assault helicopter and the CH-46D/HH-46D/UH-46D variants are flown by the Navy in the VERTREP and SAR roles. The Marine variant will be replaced by the long-delayed MV-22 Osprey tilt-rotor aircraft. The Navy will replace the Sea Knights in the VERTREP role with the CH-60R.

Design: The Sea Knight has a tricycle landing gear and small, wheel-housing sponsons aft, distinguishing it from the similar, widely flown CH-47 Chinook cargo helicopter. The Sea Knight is a tandem-rotor helicopter with a rear ramp for the rapid loading and unloading of cargo, including small vehicles; the rotor blades fold for shipboard stowage. The H-46 series has demonstrated the capability of remaining afloat for more than two hours in 2-foot (0.6-m) waves with the rotors stopped.

The Marines have upgraded 273 CH-46A/D troop helicopters to the CH-46E configuration. Provided in the upgrade are improved engines, crash-attenuating seats for pilots, a more survivable fuel system, and an improved rescue winch. Subsequent upgrades have been undertaken to extend the service life of these aircraft.

Designation: Originally designated HRB; the naval variants were changed to H-46 in 1962.

Guns: From the late 1990s, some Sea Knight helicopters assigned to Navy helicopter combat support squadrons (HC) operating in the Middle East area have been armed with two .50-cal machine guns, firing port and starboard through windows.

Status: Operational. First flight of the YHC-1A prototype on 22 April 1958. IOC in the Marine Corps in June 1964 (HMM-265).

Two Navy HH-46D Sea Knights from HC-6 conduct a VERTREP with the carrier Enterprise during operations in the Red Sea. The Navy will replace its H-46 VERTREP helicopters with the CH-60S variant of the Seahawk while the Marines are replacing their CH-46s with the MV-22 Osprey. (U.S. Navy, PH2 Damon J. Moritz)

The Navy took delivery of 264 Sea Knights and the Marine Corps received 360 helicopters from 1961 to 1977.

Characteristics of the CH-46E:

Manufacturer:	Boeing Vertol	
Crew:	(3) pilot, copilot, crewman + 25 troops or 15 litters + 2 attendants	
Engines:	2 General Electric T58-GE-16 turboshaft; 1,870 shp each	
Weight:	empty	15,198 lbs (6,894 kg)
	maximum T/O	24,300 lbs (11,022 kg)
Dimensions:	fuselage length	46 ft 8 in (13.92 m)
	overall length	84 ft 4 in (25.72 m)
	height	16 ft 8 in (5.08 m)
	main rotor diameter	25 ft 6 in (7.81 m)
Speed:	maximum 140 knots (259 km/h)	
	cruise 137 knots (254 km/h)	
Ceiling:	9,400 ft (2,866 m)	
Range:	radius 75 n.miles (139 km) with payload	
	ferry 600 n.miles (1,111 km)	
Armament:	2 .50-cal machine guns can be fitted	
Radar:	none, except Doppler approach in HH-46D	

TH-6B CAYUSE

The Naval Test Pilot School flies six TH-6B Cayuse helicopters. Previously, the school operated four OH-6B Cayuse helicopters, which have since been discarded.

The Cayuse was developed by Hughes for the Army's 1961 Light Observation Helicopter (LOH) competition. The helicopter proved a highly versatile aircraft, and the commercial Model 500 set 23 international records for helicopters in 1966.

Design: The fuselage has a pod-and-boom structure with landing skids. It has a two-blade main rotor and an anti-torque rotor on the tail boom.

Designation: The OH-6 was designated HO-6 prior to 1962.

Status: Operational. First flight of the YHO-6 on 27 February 1963. IOC in the U.S. Army in 1966.

Several foreign military services fly variants of the 500/H-6 in a variety of roles, including ASW.

A crewman aboard the replenishment ship DETROIT (AOE 4) prepares to latch a cargo hook onto a UH-46D from HC-6 during a VERTREP operation with the carrier ENTERPRISE. The helicopter's rescue hoist is visible above the aircraft's right side door. (U.S. Navy, PH3 Shelton T. Young)

A Marine CH-46E from HMM-166 flies over Kuwait City during a Special Operations exercise in April 2000. The helicopter squadron, operating from the amphibious assault ship BONHOMME RICHARD (LHD 6), is assigned to the 15th Marine Expeditionary Unit. (U.S. Marine Corps)

Manufacturer:	McDonnell Douglas	
Crew:	(2) pilot, observer + 2 passengers	
Engines:	1 Allison T63-A-5A turboshaft; 317 shp	
Weight:	empty	1,229 lbs (557 kg)
	loaded	2,400 lbs (1,090 kg)
Dimensions:	length	30 ft 3¾ in (9.24 m)
	height	8 ft 1½ in (2.48 m)
	rotor diameter	26 ft 4 in (8.03 m)
Speed:	maximum cruise	130 knots (241 km/h)
	cruise	116.5 knots (216 km/h)
Ceiling:	7,300 ft (2,225 m) hover OGE	
	11,800 ft (3,595 m) hover IGE	
	15,800 ft (4,815 m) service	
Range:	330 n.miles (611 km)	
Radar:	none	

A TH-6B Cayuse helicopter assigned to the Naval Test Pilot School. A variety of aircraft are flown by NTPS to enable students to undergo flight in dissimilar aircraft with various flight characteristics. (U.S. Navy)

HH-3F PELICAN

This version of the Sea King was built specifically for the U.S. Coast Guard SAR role. It was similar to the HH-3E Jolly Green Giant rescue version flown by the U.S. Air Force. The HH-3F carried droppable rescue supplies and had a modified boat-type hull and sponson-floats for water operations.

Forty of these helicopters were built for the Coast Guard. The HH-60J Jayhawk has replaced the HH-3F.

See 15th Edition/page 446 for characteristics.

SH-3 SEA KING

The Sea King was the U.S. Navy's standard carrier-based ASW helicopter from the early 1960s into the early 1990s. It has been replaced aboard aircraft carriers by the SH-60F Seahawk and in the SAR and utility roles by other variants of the H-60 series. The Sea King is now flown only in the utility and VIP roles. Most Navy aircraft are now configured as UH-3H variants, with the ASW gear removed. The Marines fly the VH-3D variant, assigned to squadron HMX-1 to transport the president.

Design: The Sea King has a "boat" hull but does not normally alight on the water (unlike the Coast Guard HH-3F Pelican). The tail pylon and main rotor blades fold for carrier stowage. In the ASW role, the ultimate ASW-configured SH-3H had an AQS-13B dipping sonar, sonobuoys, an APN-130 Doppler radar, an AQS-81 MAD, and an ALE-37 chaff dispenser; a total of 145 Sea Kings were converted to this configuration.

Two Sea Kings (designated YSH-3J) were used to test sensors for the SH-60B.

Earlier SH-3A/D ASW variants, the HH-3A rescue variant, and the RH-3A mine countermeasures version have all been discarded. Numerous disarmed UH-3H variants now fly in the VIP transport and utility roles.

Designation: Formerly the HSS-2, the Sea King was redesignated SH-3 in 1962. The HSS-1 was the original designation of the SH-34 Seabat, a very different helicopter.

Operational: During Desert Shield/Desert Storm in 1990–1991, SH-3H helicopters aboard participating aircraft carriers were fitted with a flexible 7.62-mm M60D machine gun, mounted in the (starboard) door opening.

Status: First flight: XHSS-2 on 11 March 1959; SH-3H in April 1972. IOC in the Navy in June 1961 (HS-1).

The helicopter is flown by several foreign services.

A UH-3H Sea King from HSL-51, assigned to the Seventh Feet flagship BLUE RIDGE (LCC 19), drops frogmen during an exercise in the Western Pacific. The Sea King was widely used by the U.S. Navy in the ASW, SAR, and MCM roles; the Sea King also was flown by the U.S. Air Force and Coast Guard, as well as by many other nations. (U.S. Navy)

A VH-3D from Marine squadron HMX-1 overflies Washington, D.C. The President normally flies in a Sea King, which has more headroom than the VIP-configured VH-60N White Top helicopters. The presidential seal is on the nose of the helicopter. (U.S. Navy)

Characteristics of the SH-3H:

Manufacturer:	Sikorsky	
Crew:	(4) pilot, copilot, 2 systems operators	
Engines:	2 General Electric T58-GE-10 turboshaft; 1,400 shp each	
Weight:	empty	13,465 lbs (6,108 kg)
	maximum T/O	21,000 lbs (9,526 kg)
Dimensions:	fuselage length	54 ft 9 in (16.69 m)
	overall length	72 ft 8 in (22.15 m)
	height	16 ft 10 in (5.13 m)
	main rotor diameter	62 ft (18.9 m)
Speed:	maximum 144 knots (267 km/h)	
	cruise 118 knots (219 km/h)	
Ceiling:	10,500 ft (3,201 m) hover IGE	
	14,700 ft (4,482 m) ceiling	
Range:	540 n.miles (1,000 km)	
	ferry 647 n.miles (1,198 km)	
Armament:	2 Mk 46 ASW torpedoes	
Radar:	LN-66HP search	

CH-3E SEA KING

The Coast Guard acquired six CH-3E cargo helicopters from the Air Force in the 1980s because of the increase in rotary-wing aircraft requirements caused by drug interdiction operations.

A variant of the basic H-3 design, this helicopter was widely used by the Air Force in the cargo and transport role. The helicopter was capable of water landing and takeoff and has a hydraulically operated rear loading ramp. Three of the Coast Guard helicopters were modified for the SAR role, being fitted with auxiliary fuel tanks, Loran-C navigation gear, and APN-215 radar. The three other CH-3Es were held in storage for possible use or to provide parts for the active helicopters. They have been discarded.

See 15th Edition/page 448 for characteristics.

SH-2G LAMPS I

The SH-2G LAMPS I was an ASW helicopter flown from OLIVER HAZARD PERRY (FFG 7) frigates operated by the Naval Reserve Force (NRF) until 2000. All have now been discarded from U.S. service.

The original SH-2D LAMPS I was developed for the ASW role, operating from surface warships. The subsequent SH-2F and SH-2G variants were carried in ships that could not accommodate the larger SH-60B LAMPS III helicopter. Only the SH-2G variant is now in U.S. Navy service. Primarily employed in the ASW role, the helicopter can also carry out over-the-horizon targeting of anti-ship missiles and has a limited VERTREP capability.

The SH-2G helicopters assigned to reserve squadron HSL-94 were fitted with the Magic Lantern laser mine-detection system, the first in December 1996.

The Navy's need for ship-based ASW helicopters in the early 1970s led to the conversion of 20 single-engine HU2K/UH-2 Seasprite utility helicopters to the SH-2D configuration and another 85 conversions to the SH-2F variant; subsequently, 54 additional SH-2F helicopters were procured. The surviving D models were later upgraded to an F configuration, the last in 1983, and a small number of SH-2s were further upgraded to the SH-2G configuration for exclusive service aboard NRF frigates. The six fiscal 1987 helicopters were built as SH-2G variants; these were the last H-2 series helicopters to be built.

(Two aircraft were modified to a YSH-2E configuration and their designation subsequently was changed to SH-2F. One SH-2F without ASW avionics became an NHH-2D test aircraft. An SH-2F to YSH-2G conversion in 1985 tested the ultimate LAMPS I configuration.)

Previously, the SH-2 LAMPS I was embarked in or planned for the following ships (one helicopter per ship except for the FFG 7, which could carry two):

4	CGN 38	VIRGINIA class
1	CGN 35	TRUXTUN
2	CG 47	TICONDEROGA class
8	CG 26	BELKNAP class
4	DDG 993	KIDD class
25	FFG 7	OLIVER HAZARD PERRY class
6	FFG 1	BROOKE class
48	FF 1052	KNOX class
6	FF 1040	GARCIA class
1	FF 1098	GLOVER
12	WHEC 715	HAMILTON class (Coast Guard)

A Naval Air Reserve SH-2G LAMPS I ASW helicopter fitted with the Magic Lantern mine-detecting gear in a container mounted on the right side of the helicopter. These helicopters have been phased out of U.S. service and the Magic Lantern gear transferred to MH-53E Sea Dragon helicopters. (Kaman)

In addition, the 12 Famous-class Coast Guard cutters were to have had a LAMPS I upgrade capability; the LAMPS I program was halted before those ships were modified.

Design: The SH-2 LAMPS are employed to localize and attack submarine contacts initially made by surface ASW ships. The helicopters have no sonobuoy analysis capability, the data being datalinked to the supporting warship for analysis. The SH-2G is fitted with the LN-66 radar, a 15-sonobuoy dispenser, ASQ-81C(V)2 MAD, ALR-66 ESM, ALE-39 chaff/flare dispenser, AAQ-16 FLIR, APN-217 Doppler radar, and upgraded avionics including the ASN-150 tactical management system. With the sonobuoy dispenser removed, the cabin can accommodate four passengers or two litters. In the VERTREP role, the SH-2F can lift 2,000 pounds (907 kg) of cargo.

Designation: Originally designated HU2K; changed to UH-2 in 1962 and to SH-2 upon conversion to ASW configuration.

Operational: The SH-2 has also served as the test and limited operational platform for the Magic Lantern laser mine detection system. During Operation Desert Storm in 1991, SH-2F helicopters used the Magic Lantern device to detect sea mines in the Persian Gulf. The laser device was fitted in a large pod attached to the right side of the helicopter.

Status: No longer operational.

Kaman built 186 UH-2 utility helicopters for the Navy through 1965. Subsequently, the 54 new SH-2F helicopters produced by Kaman were the first helicopters built by that firm in 15 years and the first of this series manufactured in an ASW configuration; they were followed by the production of six SH-2G helicopters. Kaman also converted 17 SH-2F aircraft to the G configuration.

SH-2 ASW helicopters are flown by Australia, Egypt, New Zealand, Pakistan, and Portugal. Two SH-2G helicopters were to be transferred to Poland by the end of 2000 to operate from two ex-U.S. frigates; two additional helicopters were to be transferred in 2001.

See 16th Edition/pages 413–414 for characteristics.

AH-1W SEACOBRA

The SeaCobra is a specialized gunship helicopter that evolved from the widely used Huey series. It is flown by the Marine Corps's utility and attack helicopter squadrons (HMLA).

An AH-1W SeaCobra taking off from the amphibious assault ship Peleliu (LHA 5) as the ship steams off the coast of Kuwait. A FLIR and laser rangefinder are fitted in the nose, above the 20-mm, three-barrel Gatling gun. (U.S. Navy, PHC Lawrence L. Nixon)

An AH-1W from the amphibious assault ship Kearsarge over the Adriatic Sea. The Marine Corps has kept the long-serving SeaCobra despite efforts to sell the Corps the AH-64 Apache; a gunship variant of the MV-22 Osprey may be the eventual SeaCobra replacement. (U.S. Navy, Lance Cpl. Richard O'Connor, [USMC])

The AH-1G variant was the first specialized gunship of the Huey series, being produced for both the Army and Marine Corps. (UH-1 series helicopters have been heavily armed, including Navy variants flown in the Vietnam War.)

Design: The SeaCobra has a narrow fuselage providing minimal cross-section, with stub wings for carrying rocket packs or gun pods,

An AH-1W with a full weapons load of missiles and rockets hung from its stub wings. The narrow fuselage belies its close relationship to the UH-1 Huey utility/troop helicopter. (Bell)

Marines arm an AH-1W from HMLA-369 at Camp Pendleton, Calif. There are two rocket pods mounted under the left stub wing; both of the cockpit canopies are open. (U.S. Marine Corps, Capt. Dave Anderson)

a nose turret with a 20-mm three-barrel cannon, and tandem seating for a gunner (forward) and pilot. The 20-mm cannon has a helmet-sight system. All AH-1W helicopters are being fitted with FLIR/laser designator–range finder and a video camera/recorder as part of a Night Targeting System (NTS).

The now-standard AH-1W has a weapons payload of 3,000 pounds (1,361 kg), including the Army-developed Hellfire missile, the TOW anti-tank missile, the Sidearm radar-homing missile, and the Sidewinder AAM. Alternatively, drop tanks can be fitted to extended range. An ALE-39 chaff/flare dispenser is fitted. This helicopter can take off on a single engine and climb at more than 800 feet (244 m) per minute. Surviving AH-1T helicopters were upgraded to the AH-1W configuration, with new procurement following. Surviving SeaCobras are being upgraded to the AH-1Z configuration.

Designation: The AH-1W was originally designated AH-1T+.

Status: Operational. First flight: Army AH-1G on 7 September 1965; AH-1T+ on 16 November 1983. IOC: AH-1G with the Marine Corps in 1969; AH-1T in October 1977; AH-1W in March 1986.

The last AH-1W helicopters were delivered in 1999. Weapon and other upgrades are expected to provide for a service life through at least 2020, with replacement by the proposed Joint Rotary-wing Aircraft (JRA).

More than 2,500 Cobra gunships have been built for U.S. and foreign military services, with the AH-1S model co-produced by Mitsui in Japan.

Manufacturer:	Bell	
Crew:	(2) pilot, gunner	
Engines:	2 General Electric T700-GE-401 turboshaft; 1,690 shp each	
Weight:	empty	10,200 lbs (4,627 kg)
	maximum T/O	14,750 lbs (6,690 kg)
Dimensions:	fuselage length	45 ft 6 in (13.87 m)
	overall length	58 feet (17.68 m)
	height	14 ft 2 in (4.32 m)
	main rotor diameter	48 ft (14.63 m)
Speed:	maximum	190 knots (352 km/h) at sea level
Ceiling:	17,500 ft (5,335 m)	
	14,750 ft (4,497 m) hover IGE	
	3,000 ft (915 m) hover OGE	
Range:	285 n.miles (528 km)	
Armament:	1 20-mm cannon M197 (750 rounds)	
	8 TOW or Hellfire missiles	
or	38 2.75-inch rockets	
or	32 5-inch Zuni rockets	
plus	2 Sidewinder AAMs	
Radar:	none	

HH/UH-1N HUEY (IROQUOIS)

The Huey series is the most widely used military helicopter in the West. The HH-1N and UH-1N are the only variants now flown by the Navy and Marine Corps, employed in the utility role from ships and ashore. The Navy TH-1L training and HH-1K rescue variants have been discarded, as have the Marine VH-1N variants used for VIP transport with squadron HMX-1.

The JRA is expected to replace the H-1 series about 2015–2020. In the interim, the remaining aircraft will be upgraded to the UH-1Y configuration.

Designation: The Huey was originally designated XH-40 during development. It entered service with the Army as the HU-1, which was changed in 1962 to UH-1. In 1991 many of the UH-1Ns employed for SAR operations aboard amphibious ships and at air stations were redesignated HH-1N.

Names: Officially named Iroquois, in accord with the Army scheme of naming helicopters for American Indian tribes, the helicopter is invariably called the Huey, derived from the earlier designation HU-1E.

Status: Operational. First flight of the XH-40 on 22 October 1956. IOC in the Marine Corps in March 1964 (VMO-1).

More than 9,000 Hueys have been produced for U.S. and foreign service since the Bell design won the U.S. Army's competition for a turbine helicopter in 1955.

Characteristics of the UH-1N:

Manufacturer:	Bell
Crew:	(3) pilot, copilot, crew chief + 12 to 15 troops
Engines:	2 United Aircraft of Canada PT6T turboshaft; 900 shp each
Weight:	empty 5,549 lbs (2,517 kg)
	maximum T/O 10,500 lbs (4,763 kg)
Dimensions:	fuselage length 42 ft 5 in (12.93 m)
	overall length 57 ft 3 in (17.47 m)
	height 14 ft 5 in (4.39 m)
	main rotor diameter 48 ft 2 in (14.7 m)
Speed:	109.5 knots (203 km/h)
Ceiling:	15,000 ft (4,573 m)
	12,900 ft (3,933 m) hover IGE
Range:	250 n.miles (463 km)
Armament:	various combinations of machine guns and rockets can be mounted
Radar:	none

MH-68A

In April 1999 the U.S. Coast Guard awarded a contract for the procurement of the Agusta A109 Power for the light armed helicopter role. The selection follows a helicopter competition and a year-long trial employing two MH-90 Enforcer helicopters from cutters for the interdiction of high-speed drug smuggling craft (see chapter 30).

The Coast Guard contract provides for two A109 Power helicopters, with an option for six additional. The helicopters are being manufactured in Italy with completion, delivery, and support by Agusta Aerospace Corp., the firm's wholly owned U.S. subsidiary in Philadelphia, Pa.

A Marine UH-1N Huey from HMLA-267 during flight operations with a Royal Navy Lynx ship-based helicopter. U.S. Army and Navy Hueys were heavily armed during the Vietnam War; the Navy's armed UH-1B variants, called Seawolves, were highly successful in operations in the Mekong Delta area. (U.S. Navy, PH1 Charles W. Alley)

The Agusta A109 Power has been selected by the Coast Guard for the armed helicopter role as the MH-68A. The armed Coast Guard variants will be taken to sea aboard medium endurance cutters (WMEC). The A109-series helicopters are flown by six countries in the military role and by many civil organizations. (Agusta)

At the time of the Coast Guard's selection, more than 140 A109 Power helicopters had been sold worldwide for police, emergency, and military use. This was the first purchase of the helicopter by a U.S. government agency.

Design: The A109 is a streamlined helicopter of conventional design with a pod-and-boom configuration. A four-blade main rotor is provided. The tricycle landing gear is fully retractable. A weather radar is fitted, as are FLIR and Low-Light-Level Television (LLLTV). Maximum endurance is five hours.

The helicopters are being armed with machine guns.

Operational: The A109 Power helicopters will be operated by the Coast Guard's Helicopter Interdiction Tactical Squadron 10.

Status: Operational. The A109 Power evolved from the Agusta A109, which first flew on 4 August 1971. The first two A109 Power helicopters were delivered to the Coast Guard in 2000; the additional helicopters were to be delivered in 2001.

Manufacturer:	Agusta	
Crew:	(2) pilot, flight crewman + 6 passengers	
Engines:	2 Pratt & Whitney 206C turboshaft; 426 shp each	
Weight:	empty	3,461 lbs (1,570 kg)
	maximum T/O	6,283 lbs (2,850 kg)
Dimensions:	fuselage length	37 ft 7 in (11.45 m)
	overall length	42 ft 9 in (13.04 m)
	height	11 ft 6 in (3.5 m)
	main rotor diameter	36 ft 1 in (11.0 m)
Speed:	maximum	193 knots (311 km/h)
	cruise	177 knots (285 km/h)
Ceiling:	19,600 ft (5,975 m)	
Range:		
Radar:	weather	

The Agusta A109 Power was first demonstrated at the 1995 Paris Air Show. It is a streamlined helicopter with fully retractable, tricycle landing gear. Agusta has proposed a naval ASW/anti-ship variant of the helicopter, named Hirundo by the firm. (Agusta)

A contractor-flown SA 330J Puma practices VERTREP procedures aboard the replenishment ship SIRIUS (T-AFS 8) in December 1999. The Navy's shortage of H-46 Sea Knight helicopters for this role led to the use of the civilian-flown Pumas. (U.S. Navy)

SA 330J PUMA

The Navy's shortfall of UH-46 Sea Knight helicopters for VERTREP operations led the Military Sealift Command (MSC) to evaluate the commercial SA 330J Puma helicopter for that role. Following trials aboard the replenishment ship SIRIUS (T-AFS 8) in December 1999, MSC awarded a three-year, fixed-price contract to Geo-Seis Helicopters, Inc., to provide two Pumas for operations aboard the combat stores ships SIRIUS, SATURN (T-AFS 10), and CONCORD (T-AFS 5). The helicopters are flown by Geo-Seis crewmen.

One of these ships will operate the helicopters for six months, after which the Pumas will shift to another ship about to forward deploy. Additional Pumas may be similarly employed, pending availability of the CH-60S for the VERTREP role.

The Puma was developed initially to meet a French Army requirement for an all-weather, day/night helicopter that could operate in all climates; its troop capacity was 16 to 20, depending upon equipment. In 1978 the SA 330J became the first commercial helicopter outside of the Soviet Union to be certified for all-weather operations. In commercial use, up to 20 passengers can be carried.

Status: Operational. The SA 330J civil variant was introduced in 1976 (the SA 330L was the military configuration). The Puma is in service with the armed forces of more than 40 nations. (The Puma has been produced under license in Britain, Indonesia, and Romania, with production totaling about 700 helicopters.)

Manufacturer:	Aérospatiale	
Crew:	(2) pilot, flight crewman	
Engines:	2 Turboméca Turmo IVC turboshaft; 1,575 shp each	
Weights:	empty	8,303 lbs (3,766 kg)
	maximum T/O	16,315 lbs (7,400 kg)
Dimensions:	fuselage length	46 ft 1½ in (14.06 m)
	overall length	59 ft 6½ in (18.15 m)
	height	16 ft 10½ in (5.14 m)
	main rotor diameter	49 ft 2½ in (15.0 m)
Speed:	maximum	160 knots (294 km/h)
	cruise	148 knots (271 km/h)
Ceiling:	19,680 ft (6,000 m)	
Range:	310 n.miles (572 km)	
Radar:	none	

An X-31A EFM demonstrator, photographed in 1994 with a NASA F-18 Hornet chase plane (*below*). The X-31A has flight tested a variety of aircraft systems under the auspices of the U.S. and German government agencies and aerospace firms. The aircraft's markings are periodically changed. (NASA)

EXPERIMENTAL AIRCRAFT

X-31A ENHANCED FIGHTER MANEUVERABILITY (EFM) DEMONSTRATOR

The two X-31A research aircraft—intended to demonstrate the possibility of the high-angle-of-attack flight regime to enable a fighter to achieve tighter, faster turns, and earlier weapon firing opportunities—have been discarded.

Flight testing of the two X-31A aircraft was carried out by an international test organization made up of representatives from NASA, the Defense Advanced Research Projects Agency (DARPA), the Navy, the Air Force, Germany, and the firms of Rockwell International and Messerschmitt-Bolkow-Blöhm (MBB).[33] DARPA has overall program management, with the Navy serving as DARPA's agent and providing on-site direction.

Two aircraft were built; one X-31 crashed at Edwards AFB, Calif., on 19 January 1995.

See 16th Edition/pages 416–417 for characteristics.

Designation: The designation X-31 was assigned on 23 February 1987.

An X-31A demonstrator landing, with its small speed brakes open (and, off camera, a brake chute deployed). The first X-31A crashed in 1995, with its pilot safely ejecting. (NASA)

X-26A

The X-26A is a "quiet" observation research aircraft intended to provide a high degree of stealth for a target acquisition aircraft. Two X-26A aircraft are flown by the Navy. Details are classified.

The unpowered X-26A is a high-performance sailplane based on the all-metal Schweizer SGS 2-32 design. The X-26B uses a gasoline

---

33. Now part of Deutsche Aerospace.

An X-26A operated by the NTPS at NAS Patuxent River, Md. The quiet research aircraft is another of the unusual planes employed to train test pilots. (U.S. Navy)

engine behind the pilot's compartment to drive a propeller mounted on a pylon atop the aircraft's nose.

The predecessor to the X-26 was the Lockheed QT-2PC, which was evaluated in Vietnam during the 1960s; upon return to the United States, it was reconfigured as the X-26B. It subsequently was tested by the Army, Air Force, and Navy.

Two men can be carried in the large cockpit.

Status: First flight of the SGS 2-32 on 3 July 1962. A total of 89 were built through January 1978 when production ended. The military X-26 program included three A and one B aircraft. All three X-26A variants were operated by the Navy; two remain.

Characteristics of the X-26A:

Manufacturer:	Schweizer	
Crew:	(1) pilot	
Engines:	none	
Weight:	empty	
	loaded	1,430 lbs
Dimensions:	length	26 ft 9 in (8.15 m)
	wingspan	57 ft 1 in (17.40 m)
	wing area	180 ft² (16.72 m²)
	height	9 ft 3 in (2.82 m)
Speed:		
Ceiling:		
Range:		
Radar:	none	

XV-15A

The XV-15A is a tilt-rotor VTOL demonstration aircraft, serving as a technology prototype for the V-22 Osprey series and the Bell Agusta 609 aircraft. Developed by Bell Helicopter Textron, the XV-15A has successfully demonstrated the ability of a rotary-wing aircraft to fully convert in flight to a conventional aircraft configuration.

The aircraft has twin rotor-engine nacelles mounted on a connecting wing; the nacelles rotate to the horizontal position for conventional aircraft flight and are vertical for takeoff and landing, or hover. Rolling takeoffs and landings are not possible. Thus, the design has the advantages of both a conventional aircraft and helicopter.

Bell built two XV-15A aircraft under NASA and Army sponsorship. Subsequently, the Navy–Marine Corps gave support to the project.

Operational: The two XV-15A aircraft achieved their flight demonstration goals in extensive testing by NASA and the services, with one having been airlifted to the Paris air show in 1982 in an Air Force C-5A Galaxy transport. The aircraft's international debut was highly successful.

In a key XV-15A evaluation, one aircraft flew 54 landings and takeoffs from the helicopter carrier TRIPOLI (LPH 10) in August 1982. Although not intended for shipboard operation, the tests succeeded with only minor difficulties.

Status: Operational (one aircraft). First flight 3 May 1957. One aircraft was heavily damaged in a 1992 crash; it was not returned to service. The surviving aircraft is owned by NASA and bailed to Bell Helicopter Textron for demonstration purposes, hence technically it is not a naval aircraft although it recently was employed for Coast Guard VTOL trials.

Manufacturer:	Bell	
Crew:	(2) pilot, copilot	
Engines:	2 Avco Lycoming LTC1K-4K turboshaft; 1,800 shp each	
Weight:	empty	9,670 lbs (4,386 kg)
	loaded	13,000 lbs (5,897 kg)
	maximum T/O	15,000 lbs (6,804 kg)
Dimensions:	length	42 ft 2 in (12.83 m)
	wingspan	35 ft 2 in (10.72 m) over engine nacelles
	height	15 ft 4 in (4.67 m)
	rotor diameter	25 ft (7.62 m)
	aircraft width	57 ft 2 in (17.4 m) including rotor blades
Speed:	maximum	335 knots (615 km/h) at 17,000 ft (5,183 m)
	maximum cruise	300 knots (555 km/h)
Range:		
Ceiling:	29,000 ft (8,841 m)	
Radar:	none	

The surviving XV-15 prototype during Coast Guard trials in 1999. The engine nacelles are in the vertical-flight mode and the aircraft's tricycle landing gear is extended. (U.S. Coast Guard)

The XV-15 transitioning to high-speed flight, with engine nacelles rotating to the horizontal position. The NASA-owned aircraft has a civil serial number (with the *N* prefix indicating U.S. civil aircraft). (U.S. Coast Guard)

LIGHTER-THAN-AIR

The Navy and Coast Guard Lighter-Than-Air (LTA), or airship, programs have been halted. The Navy's development of a surveillance airship was canceled in early 1992, shortly before completion of the first flight of a full-size prototype (the YEZ-2A/Sentinel 5000), while the Coast Guard's fully operational aerostat surveillance program was "grounded" on 31 December 1991 for transfer to the Army.[34] On that date, the five Coast Guard sea-based aerostat vessels were brought into the ports of Miami and Key West, Fla., pending completion of studies on the future of the program. Subsequently, the

ships were briefly returned to service, operated by civilian contract crews with uniformed Army personnel on board for technical duties.

The lack of funds in the post–Cold War era makes it unlikely that airship programs will be pursued by either the Navy or Coast Guard in the foreseeable future. Several Navy studies had supported airship development, primarily in an AEW/missile targeting role.

(See 15th Edition/pages 453–455 for characteristics of the Coast Guard program.)

The U.S. Customs Service and the Drug Enforcement Agency currently are using aerostats to carry surveillance radars aloft to assist in monitoring illegal activities along U.S. borders, while similar systems are deployed in Kuwait (as well as other allied countries) to monitor the movement of unfriendly forces in contiguous areas.

---

34. *Aerostat* is the term for an unmanned airship.

JOINT LAND-ATTACK CRUISE MISSILE DEFENSE ELEVATED NETTED SENSOR SYSTEM (JLENS)

The Navy is participating in the JLENS aerostat program. In January 1996, the Department of Defense directed the Army Space and Missile Defense Command to establish a joint program office that encompassed Army, Navy, and Air Force initiatives being developed to defeat the land-attack cruise missile threat. Subsequently, the JLENS Program Office carried out concept studies of an aerostat sensor platform that would provide long-duration, Over-The-Horizon (OTH) cruise missile defense. As the program has matured, the JLENS primary mission has been defined to provide OTH wide-area surveillance and precision-tracking (fire-control quality) data to support a cruise missile defense system. It is intended to support both forward theater air defense and U.S. national cruise missile defense tasks.

One of the aerostats of the JLENS program; the bulge under the airship houses the radar antenna. The Navy has long considered aerostats for the missile-warning role to defend naval task forces. The JLENS program will be land-based. (Department of Defense)

The processing and support equipment for JLENS is housed in a series of mobile trailers. Wheeled, mobile mooring stations are used to tether the aerostats when they are recovered. (Department of Defense)

The JLENS platform and its associated surveillance, tracking, and communications equipment might also be employed as an integral, supporting element of naval expeditionary forces. Given the anticipated future operational and threat environment, JLENS could be a critical factor supporting the twin elements of forward presence and "information dominance," which are the means by which U.S. military power projection will be effected in the 21st century. Moreover, a sea-based JLENS concept—called Maritime JLENS—could support a variety of forward forces.

JLENS could be developed and acquired in about one-half the time required to develop and build a fixed-wing airborne platform with comparable sensor and communications-relay capabilities. The JLENS cost of development and acquisition is also expected to be much less than other airborne platforms. When total life-cycle costs, including manpower, for supporting and sustaining different systems are taken into account, JLENS becomes an extremely attractive alternative to providing airborne sensor capabilities for joint forces. In the context of naval force operations, a tactical aerostat on the order of JLENS offers a relatively inexpensive and economical means for providing low-altitude radar coverage over an extended battlespace. An aerostat also can augment tactical communications by providing a direct line-of-sight relay capability.

Details of the proposed JLENS aerostat program are classified. However, twin aerostats 233 feet (71 m) long would be employed, both tethered to ground facilities. One aerostat would carry an early warning/surveillance radar and the second a precision-track/fire-control radar. The surveillance radar would provide 360° coverage out to 250 n.miles (463 km), depending on the aerostat's altitude. The aerostats and facilities, which could be ship-based, would be road mobile.

The JLENS tactical aerostats would be affected by the weather. Although they are capable of withstanding winds up to 100 knots (185 km/h), these aerostats are designed to operate in sustained winds up to 60 knots (111 km/h) and would be monitored so that they could be retrieved in time to protect them from severe weather. Thunderstorms, high winds, and hail could restrict JLENS operations, but real-world experience with aerostats deployed along the U.S. and Kuwaiti borders demonstrates that they can operate without restriction approximately 90 percent of the time in those particular environments—a higher availability than fixed-wing airborne systems. The JLENS concept of operations envisions dedicated time on station without rotation for up to 30 days at a time.

One platform proposed for JLENS is the Mobile Offshore Basing System (MOBS), designed to be extremely stable even in adverse weather conditions; MOBS could also provide a platform from which a Maritime JLENS could be deployed.[35] Other platforms could be developed that would serve similar functions but would be smaller in size and somewhat easier to support.

Another alternative being addressed as an element of the follow-on to the current Maritime Prepositioning Ships (MPS) is a platform or ship specifically designed to receive bulk cargo from commercial shipping. This vessel would be used to break the cargo down for distribution and then act as a staging base from which Navy ships, aircraft, and air-cushion vehicles would receive supplies and other material for further distribution to the operational forces.

The expected IOC of the first unit is fiscal year 2010 under current funding.

Historical: The U.S. Navy acquired a total of 241 non-rigid airships between 1917 and 1958, including 21 from allies during World War I; others were acquired from the U.S. Army. The Navy operated four rigid airships, two of which, the AKRON (ZRS-4) and MACON (ZRS-5), could launch and recover fighter aircraft—in effect serving as "flying aircraft carriers."

The U.S. Navy's last airships were AEW platforms of the EZ-1C (formerly ZPG-3W) type. The Navy's last LTA flight took place in August 1962. Several highly classified ("black") surveillance programs of the Cold War era included proposals for LTA platforms, but none is known to have come to fruition. Tethered surveillance aero-

stats were used in the Vietnam War under a highly classified, joint project of the Air Force and DARPA called Seek Skyhawk.

Today there is major U.S. Navy and Coast Guard interest in two types of non-rigid airships—the manned airship and the unmanned aerostat. The Navy and Coast Guard initiated an airship development program in the early 1980s to develop craft suitable for surveillance and—for the Navy—anti-ship cruise missile defense missions. A major step was taken in 1980 when the Coast Guard and NASA agreed to jointly sponsor development of a manned airship employing the latest available technology for synthetics and adhesives for the gas bag, automated controls, and ground/ship recovery systems that would reduce the large ground crews normally required to land and tether blimps. In 1983 the Coast Guard evaluated a British-built Airship Industries Skyship 500 manned airship at the Naval Air Test Center at Patuxent River, Md., some 250 flight hours being flown in the evaluation. (The deflated Airship 500 was flown to the United States in a C-141 transport.)

By 1985 the Coast Guard was ready to award a contract to Airship Industries for lease of a larger Skyship 600 airship for operational service for at least five months. The Coast Guard effort was dubbed PACE, for Patrol Airship Concept Evaluation, and envisioned an eventual LTA vehicle for service use that would fly a variety of patrol/surveillance missions, carrying a crew of six on missions that would last at least 48 hours. (The French Navy also evaluated a Skyship 600.)

However, a September 1985 agreement between the Coast Guard and Navy gave the latter service cognizance over manned airship development. The formal entry of the Navy into the LTA program caused the Coast Guard to cancel its manned LTA efforts in September 1985. An official statement explained that the "large scale multiyear LTA program recently launched by the Navy would overshadow [the Coast Guard] project research effort. Continuation of the Coast Guard program would duplicate the Navy research and would be less comprehensive." Instead, the Coast Guard has concentrated on the development of unmanned aerostats.

The Navy airship program was launched by Secretary of the Navy John Lehman, who in 1985 approved a formal development effort with the goal of a large, radar-carrying airship that could provide early warning of approaching hostile aircraft and cruise missiles. Study contracts were awarded in 1985 to Goodyear, Westinghouse, and Boeing for airship concepts, and to Hughes, Westinghouse, and RCA for suitable radars.

A suitable surveillance radar would require an airship at least the size of the ZPG-3W, which was in service from 1957 to 1961—that is, a length of some 400 feet (122 m) with a gas-bag volume of about 1.5 million cubic feet (45,000 m³). But to obtain an "at sea" endurance of 30 days, a much larger airship would be required, probably with a gas-bag volume of just under three million cubic feet, a length of about 480 feet (146 m), and a diameter of 110 feet (33.5 m). Both turboprop and reciprocating engines were considered for propulsion, providing a speed of perhaps 115 knots (185 km/h) in no-wind conditions. While their prime mission was to be surveillance, both active and passive, other missions that were considered included ASW and over-the-horizon targeting for ship-launched cruise missiles.

Preliminary estimates indicated that the Navy would have a need for some 20 to 50 airships, although numbers up to 100 have been considered in some studies. A program of 20 to 50 units could have had a price tag of $3 *billion* or more (in mid-1980s dollars).

This ambitious program ended after Mr. Lehman stepped down as Navy secretary in 1987 and there were severe budget cutbacks. The Navy was forced to completely cancel its airship program in mid-1990. At the time, the Navy was sponsoring the Westinghouse Sentinel 1000 airship, a half-scale version of the Sentinel 5000 design that the Navy was considering. Subsequently, funding for the Sentinel 1000 was moved into the Air Defense Initiative (ADI) office of the Department of Defense, with the Navy continuing to manage the program.

Characteristics of the Sentinel 1000 and 5000 airships are listed in the 15th Edition/pages 453–455.

---

35. See page 110 for a description of MOBS.

UNMANNED AERIAL VEHICLES

The U.S. Navy has at last selected an Unmanned Aerial Vehicle (UAV) to replace the long-serving Pioneer. On 10 February 2000 the Navy announced the selection of a derivative of Schweizer Aircraft's Model 333 turbine helicopter as the service's Tactical Unmanned Aerial Vehicle (TUAV) capable of Vertical Take-Off and Landing (VTOL) operations to meet Navy and Marine Corps requirements. The Schweizer helicopter was a component of a proposal by Northrop Grumman's Ryan Aeronautical Center in the Navy's TUAV competition, given that firm's designation Model 379.

The losing competitors were Bell Helicopter Textron's Eagle Eye tilt-rotor TUAV and Sikorsky's Cypher III TUAV. Although not a finalist in the competition, Bombardier Aéronautique's CL-327 Guardian was considered a viable candidate by many observers, that TUAV having conducted trials at sea in U.S. Navy and Coast Guard ships. All four of these TUAVs are described below.

Selection of a TUAV by the Navy follows the U.S. Army's decision on 29 December 1999 to procure the Shadow 200 TUAV produced by the AAI Corporation as that service's future tactical unmanned reconnaissance vehicle (see page 474).

These Navy and Army decisions follow almost two decades of research, development, and aborted efforts in this field. The Navy had earlier developed and deployed two operational UAVs (then called Remotely Piloted Vehicles/RPV): the DASH (Drone Anti-Submarine Helicopter) in the 1960s and the Pioneer reconnaissance drone in the 1980s.

Separately, the Department of Defense has sponsored a large and multifaceted UAV program. The program enjoys a relatively high degree of funding support, in part because of the very successful U.S. Army, Navy, and Marine Corps use of the Pioneer UAV in the Gulf War in January–February 1991 and the Global Hawk UAV over Kosovo in 1999.

The successes of the Pioneer and Global Hawk came after a long succession of program failures and cancellations, among them the Army's Aquila and the DOD-sponsored Medium Range UAV, Hunter, DarkStar, and Outrider.[36]

In 2000 the tactical UAV force levels for all military services totaled 22 "systems": 1 Hunter, 9 Pioneer, 10 Predator, and 2 Outrider. The number of UAVs per system varies, with most having three vehicles; the Marine Corps's unmanned aerial vehicle squadrons (VMU) each have one Pioneer system with five UAVs.[37]

The Department of Defense sponsors two types of "theater" UAV programs: High-Altitude Endurance (HAE) and Medium-Altitude Endurance (MAE). The Global Hawk has been selected as the HAE vehicle, which complements Air Force–operated U-2 surveillance aircraft. The Global Hawk underwent operational flight tests in fiscal 1998 and participated in joint operational demonstrations in fiscal 1999 prior to being selected as the HAE vehicle. Initially the Global Hawk has electro-optical sensors and synthetic aperture radar; eventually it will have a moving-target surveillance capability. Later a communications relay capability will be provided to the Global Hawk.

The Navy has three areas of interest related to the Global Hawk: (1) tasking missions, (2) receiving sensor data in real time, and (3) processing sensor data aboard ship and at shore facilities for operational use.

The competitive DarkStar UAV project was terminated on 29 January 1999, shortly after the third aircraft had been delivered. DarkStar—given the DOD designation RQ-3A—was to have been a "stealthy" vehicle, whereas the Global Hawk has a more conventional design. (See 16th Edition/pages 418–419.)

The Predator is the current MAE vehicle.

All of the UAVs currently in service are primarily reconnaissance and intelligence-collection aircraft. Future roles envisioned for UAVs include ECM, with both active (decoy) and passive (jamming) capabilities. The Northrop Grumman Tactical Radar Electronic Combat System (TRECS) is now being developed in a configuration suitable for UAV operation. TRECS is intended to locate and jam enemy radars, while making the carrying UAV resemble an attacking aircraft on enemy radars. The Air Force is sponsoring this system.[38]

There also are proposals for unmanned aerial vehicles that could carry out other missions now associated with manned aircraft, including fighter roles. These vehicles generally are referred to as Unmanned Combat Air Vehicles (UCAV). The UCAVs are described as "a cross between aircraft and missile," costing some $8 million to $10 million each. They could fly with conventional aircraft, spread over hundreds of miles, and "talk" to each other as well as to the controllers (initially in manned aircraft). In early planning, program officials envision a single operator controlling three to five UCAVs, the number depending upon the size of the strike force and the defenses to be penetrated.[39]

Key technologies that will be required for the UCAV are:

- automatic target recognition
- secure communications
- adaptive autonomous operations
- onboard processing
- intervehicle communications
- cognitive aids

The Boeing Company, prime contractor for this effort, envisions an advanced air vehicle design, able to carry two weapons (missiles or guided bombs), with a total vehicle weight of about 16,000 pounds (7,258 kg) and a mission radius of some 500 to 1,000 n.miles (925 to 1,850 km).

Still another approach to UAV development is the Micro Aerial Vehicle (MAV), an effort being explored in a program sponsored by DARPA. The MAV effort envisions a very small UAV—less than 6 inches (150 mm) in any dimension—that could carry out a number of missions. These MAVs would be carried by individual soldiers and Marines, as well as Special Forces personnel. They could be sent out individually or in "swarm" for short distances to detect various phenomena, such as the use of chemical or biological agents, or personnel or vehicle movements. Advanced design concepts are being considered, such as the data-link aerial being the vehicle's stabilizer. One concept is a self-consumable vehicle, in which the construction material is partially usable as fuel for the vehicle! Because they would be expendable or difficult to recover, there is a cost goal about $1,000 per vehicle.

One other UAV project warrants brief comment: ballistic missile defense. In the 1990s the U.S. Ballistic Missile Defense Organization worked with the Israel Aircraft Industries and the Rafael firm on the concept of the HA-10 UAV and a high-speed missile to intercept enemy ballistic missiles during their first minute or two of flight, i.e., boost-phase intercept. Rafael is producing the Arrow, a successful terminal interceptor for ballistic missile defense, which entered Israeli service in March 2000.

The HA-10 vehicle would carry one or two small interceptor missiles based on the Arrow. A UAV with an endurance of up to 60 hours is being considered for this role, preferably carrying several intercept missiles.

In the following listings these vehicles are arranged in alphabetical order.

Designations: The designation RQ, indicating reconnaissance (R) and unmanned vehicle (Q), is assigned to these vehicles:

RQ-1	Predator
RQ-2	Pioneer
RQ-3	DarkStar
RQ-4	Global Hawk
RQ-5	Hunter

Historical: The U.S. armed forces has previously made extensive use of target drones as well as reconnaissance drones, the latter usually of a highly classified (black) nature. These "recce" drones were used in large numbers by the Air Force in the Vietnam War.[40] Also in the 1960s, the Navy had a large drone program known as DASH (Drone Anti-

---

36. The classic example was the Army's Aquila UAV program, started in 1979 and canceled in 1988; it failed badly in meeting its mission requirements, and its estimated cost increased by more than 700 percent.

37. Each VMU is authorized 199 personnel: 15 officers + 180 enlisted Marines, and 1 officer + 3 enlisted Navy personnel.

---

38. See Robert Wall, "UAV to Decoy, Locate and Jam Emitters," *Aviation Week & Space Technology,* 18 May 1998, p. 49.

39. David A. Fulghum, "UACV's Mission, Design Refined," *Aviation Week & Space Technology,* 20 September 1999, pp. 55–56.

40. From August 1964 through June 1975, the 100th Strategic Reconnaissance Wing flew 3,435 combat sorties over North Vietnam with the Teledyne Ryan–produced AQM-34 "Buffalo Hunter" drone. Adapted from a target drone, the vehicle was employed in photographic and electronic reconnaissance.

Submarine Helicopter). Although those drones—designated DSN and, after 1962, QH-50—were successful aerial vehicles, problems with training and operating procedures caused a large number of losses. The DASH project was short-lived (and U.S. ASW ships were left without helicopters until the LAMPS program was initiated in the early 1970s). However, the Japanese Maritime Self-Defense Force continued to employ DASH vehicles after they were discarded by the U.S. Navy, and several were employed for gunfire spotting for the battleship NEW JERSEY (BB 62) during her brief service in the shore bombardment role off South Vietnam in 1968.

During the 1970s and early 1980s, the U.S. Navy resisted proposals for RPV/drones, except for use as target vehicles. However, following the extensive use of RPVs by the Israelis in the 1982 invasion of Lebanon, especially against anti-air gun and missile systems in the Bekaa Valley, Secretary of the Navy Lehman directed that the Navy look into the pilotless aircraft. As a result, in January 1984 the Navy ordered a Mastiff III drone system produced by Tadiran Israeli Electronics, Ltd., for gunfire spotting. In June 1984, the Marine Corps established the 1st RPV Platoon at Camp Lejeune, N.C., to evaluate and operate the Mastiff RPVs in support of Marine requirements. The first shipboard launch of an Israeli Mastiff (a development of the Scout) occurred in March 1984 from the helicopter carrier GUAM (LPH 9), with Israeli controllers. Marine Corps trials were carried out in February 1986 on the helicopter carrier TARAWA (LHA 1).

Subsequently, the Navy awarded a contract to provide the fleet with the Israeli-developed Pioneer RPV. This vehicle was extensively used from ashore and from the battleships MISSOURI (BB 63) and WISCONSIN (BB 64) in the Gulf War. The Marine Corps deployed all three of its RPV companies to Saudi Arabia for the Gulf War, with the Army deploying a UAV platoon to the theater. The Navy assigned detachments from composite squadron VC-6 to the two battleships to operate Pioneers from those ships during the conflict. Each of these six units had about five vehicles and 40 personnel assigned. According to the Department of Defense report to Congress on the Gulf conflict, "Pioneer proved to be valuable and appears to have validated the operational employment of UAVs in combat."[41]

41. Department of Defense, *Conduct of the Persian Gulf Conflict* (Washington, D.C., July 1991), pp. 6–8.

Also during the Gulf conflict, at the start of air operations, the U.S. Air Force launched 38 Northrop BQM-74C "Chukar" target drones into Iraq and the Navy launched a number of TLAD target drones from aircraft. These were used to trick the Iraqis into turning on their radars so they could be attacked by U.S. radar-suppression aircraft—Air Force F-4G Wild Weasels and Navy EA-6B Prowlers armed with HARM missiles. The BQM-74Cs were ground-launched, while A-6E Intruders air-launched the TLADs.

On the ground, Marines flew a number of small, lightweight FQM-151 Pointer and Brandebury Exdrone vehicles during the Gulf War. (See 15th Edition/page 458 for characteristics of the latter vehicle.)

Subsequently, the Predator UAV was used in the Persian Gulf to support Operation Southern Watch.

U.S. UAV deployments to the Balkans began with the deployment of Air Force Predators to Taszar, Hungary, to support NATO peacekeeping efforts in Bosnia. U.S., British, French, and German UAVs supported Operation Allied Force, the three months of massive NATO air operations against Serbian forces in Kosovo and the strikes against Serbia in the spring of 1999 (see table 27-2). The most sorties during Allied Force were flown, in order, by the U.S. Hunter, German CL-289, and U.S. Predator. However, the CL-289 sorties were short-duration operations, averaging 30 minutes; in terms of hours flown, the Hunter and Predator gave the most impressive performance by a significant margin, with the Predators having an average flight endurance in excess of nine hours.

The five U.S. Navy Pioneer UAVs were based on the amphibious ship PONCE (LPD 15).

TABLE 27-2.   UAV OPERATIONS DURING OPERATION ALLIED FORCE

Country	UAV	Number deployed	Sorties flown	Hours flown	Combat losses	Operational losses
U.S.	Hunter	18	246	1357	5	3
U.S.	Pioneer	5	16	80	3	1
U.S.	Predator	8	107	992	3	1
Britain	Phoenix	27	77	230	2	0
France	Crecerelle	6	43	130	3	0
France	CL-289/Piver	16	84	42	2	2
Germany	CL-289	16	170	85	1	3

The Cypher III has a hybrid configuration, with an encased horizontal rotor and tail rotor and stub wings; a tricycle landing gear is fitted to this agile aircraft. (Sikorsky)

CYPHER

The Cypher III was a competitor for the Navy–Marine Corps TUAV program. Somewhat resembling a flying saucer, the Cypher series of UAVs also was considered by the Army because of the vehicle's ability to hover in built-up areas, making it useful for urban operations.

Design: The Cypher UAV features a saucer configuration with three landing skids.

Status: Tests.

Range:	1,000+ n.miles (1,850+ km) with 8 hours loiter	
Ceiling:	45,000+ feet (13,720+ m)	
Manufacturer:	Sikorsky	
Engines:	1 rotary; 52 hp	
Weight:	maximum T/O	300 lbs (136 kg)
Dimensions:	diameter	6 ft 6 in (1.98 m)
	height	2 ft (0.61 m)
Speed:	maximum	80 knots (148 km/h)
	cruise	70 knots (129 km/h)
Range:	radius	18 miles (29 km) with 2.5 hours loiter carrying 45-lb (20.4-kg) payload
	endurance	3 hours
Ceiling:	8,000 ft (2,440 m)	

The early Cypher TUAV had a skid landing gear and a television camera mounted atop the vehicle. The UAV, shown here in the Army's urban training center at Fort Benning, Ga., is well suited for operations in built-up areas. (Sikorsky)

DRAGON

This is a multipurpose TUAV developed under contract from the Marine Corps. The Marine Dragon drones are fitted with a television camera and laser range finder. Other payloads evaluated with the Dragon include an electronic countermeasures package.

Both the Army and Navy have shown interest in the drone.

Design: The Dragon drone has a flying-wing configuration with twin tail fins at the outer extremities of the wing. The drone is stowed in a box and can be assembled using quick release fasteners, fueled, and readied for flight in less than 30 minutes.

The drone is launched from a pneumatic catapult and can be recovered by landing on its skids or into a net.

Operational: During 1998 a Dragon drone system was deployed with a Marine unit aboard the amphibious ship DULUTH (LPD 6).

Status: Development.

Manufacturer:	BAI Aerosystems	
Engines:	1 piston engine; 2 hp	
Weight:	empty	55 lbs (24.95 kg)
	gross	95 lbs (43.09 kg)
Dimensions:	length	5 ft (1.52 m)
	wingspan	8 ft (2.44 m)
	wing area	
	height	2 ft (0.61 m)
Speed:	maximum	70 knots (129 km/h)
	cruise	52 knots (96.5 km/h)
Range:	radius	50 miles (80 km) with 1+ hour loiter
	endurance	3 hours
Ceiling:	10,000 ft (3,050 m)	

The Dragon TUAV, shown here being catapulted from the amphibious ship DULUTH (LPD 6), was evaluated by the Marine Corps. The Dragon is recovered into a net (as is the Pioneer UAV). The launch and recovery gear for the Dragon is relatively complicated. (U.S. Navy)

A Dragon TUAV in flight with two antennas deployed from the nose of the vehicle. The Dragon is a tailless, delta-wing aircraft, with turned-up "winglets" at the extremities of its wing. (U.S. Navy)

EAGLE EYE

This was a tilt-rotor TUAV candidate—based in part on XV-15 technology—developed for shipboard use. It was a finalist in the U.S. Navy's TUAV competition.

Design: The Eagle Eye is a tilt-rotor vehicle, with twin engine nacelles that rotate to the vertical position for takeoff and landing and to the horizontal position for conventional flight. The landing gear is retractable.

The UAV is based partially on the Bell-Boeing Pointer UAV, which flew for the first time in November 1988.

Up to 300 pounds (136 kg) of sensors can be carried, including a FLIR, a synthetic aperture radar, and electro-optical sensors.

Status: Development. First flight on 10 July 1993; first full conversion flight in February 1994.

Manufacturer:	Bell Helicopter Textron	
Engines:	1 Allison 250-C20 GT recuperative turboshaft; 420 shp	
Weight:	empty	1,300 lbs (590 kg)
	payload	200 lbs (90 kg)
	fuel	750 lbs (340 kg)
Dimensions:	length	17 ft 11 in (5.46 m)
	wingspan	15 ft 2½ in (4.63 m)
	height	5 ft 2 in (1.58 m) with nacelles in vertical position
	rotor diameter	8 ft 2½ in (2.5 m)
Speed:	maximum	approx. 200 knots (370 km/h)
	cruise	approx. 100 knots (185 km/h)
Range:	radius	108 n.miles (200 km) with 8 hours endurance carrying 100 lbs 45.4 kg) of sensors
Ceiling:	20,000+ ft (6,100+ m)	

The Eagle Eye TUAV is a high-speed vehicle. The engine nacelles—like those of the MV-22 and XV-15 tilt-rotor aircraft—rotate to the horizontal position for high-speed flight. The landing gear is retractable. (Bell)

FIRE SCOUT

The Schweizer Model 333 was selected in February 2000 for procurement as the Navy and Marine Corps TUAV aircraft.[42] It will replace the successful and long-serving Pioneer. The Schweizer TUAV is an unmanned variant of the company's highly successful Model 300–series light helicopters.

The Schweizer TUAV prototype could not achieve the Navy's original speed requirement of 230 mph (370 km), the Eagle Eye having been the only vehicle to meet that speed requirement in the Navy's TUAV competition.

Full-rate production is to begin in 2003 with an initial operational capability that year. The Navy plans to acquire 12 TUAV systems and the Marine Corps will procure 11, each with four vehicles, that is, a unit strength of 92 TUAVs plus spares and pipeline vehicles.

Design: The Schweizer Model 330 has a conventional helicopter configuration. It will carry 200 pounds (90.7 kg) of sensors.

The aircraft's length with rotors folded is 22 feet 11 inches (6.99 m).

The Navy's payload priorities for the Fire Scout TUAV are:

- Electro-Optical (EO) and Infrared (IR) sensors
- communication and data relay links
- Synthetic Aperture Radar (SAR)
- Signals Intelligence (SIGINT)
- hyperspectral imaging
- meteorological data sensors

No conventional ASW sensors will be provided; the EO/IR/SAR sensors could have a submarine detection capability with proper programming and tactics.

Status: In procurement. First flight January 2000 (unmanned modified Schweizer 330SP).[43]

Manufacturer:	Schweizer (Northrop Grumman Ryan Aeronautical Center)	
Engines:	1 Allison Rolls-Royce 250-C20W turbine	
Weight:	empty	
	gross	2,550 lbs (1,157 kg)
Dimensions:	length	
	rotor diameter	27 ft 6 in (8.38 m)
Speed:	maximum	127 knots (232 km/h)
Range:	radius	126 miles (205 km) with 4 hours loiter carrying 200 lbs (90.7 kg) of sensors
Ceiling:	20,000 ft (6,100 m)	

---

42. Designated Model 379 by Northrop Grumman's Ryan Aeronautical Center.
43. Previously the test vehicle made 39 manned test flights.

The Navy–Marine Corps selection for a tactical unmanned aerial vehicle (TUAV) is this helicopter-like VTOL aircraft. Developed by Schweizer Aircraft, Northrop Grumman is the overall systems developer. (U.S. Navy)

GLOBAL HAWK RQ-4A

This UAV has been selected for procurement as the U.S. High-Altitude Endurance (HAE) vehicle. It is envisioned as providing imagery to all military services through their respective data terminals.

Development was initiated to meet the HAE Tier II+ requirements for a long-endurance UAV. It achieved an impressive record during extensive trials until one of two prototypes crashed on 29 March 1999 at the China Lake (Calif.) test range. Subsequently the remaining UAV resumed flight trials on 18 May 1999, leading to the decision later that year to procure the Global Hawk for operational service.

Global Hawk development has been managed by the Air Force.

Design: This is one of the largest and highest-flying UAVs yet conceived. Global Hawk has a conventional aircraft design, with minimal stealth characteristics. It has a fully retractable landing gear.

The Global Hawk, operated by the Air Force, is one of the most promising UAVs. The long-endurance drone has a fully retractable landing gear, shown extended here. (U.S. Air Force)

The massive wingspan of the Global Hawk—116¼ feet—is evident in this photo. Two men standing near the fuselage are dwarfed by the UAV. The Global Hawk, in series production, will produce intelligence for Navy–Marine Corps use. (David Gossett, Teledyne Ryan)

Operational: During flight tests, on 19–20 October 1999, a Global Hawk flew from Edwards AFB, Calif., to Alaska and returned—a 24-hour, unrefueled, nonstop flight.

Status: Under procurement. First flight on 28 February 1998.

Manufacturer:	Teledyne Ryan Aeronautical (Northrop Grumman)
Engines:	1 Allison Rolls-Royce AE3007H turbofan; 7,050 lbst (3,200 kgst)
Weight:	empty 6,035 lbs (2,737 kg)
	gross 22,914 lbs (19,394 kg)
Dimensions:	length 44 ft (13.41 m)
	wingspan 116 ft 3 in (35.43 m)
	wing area
	height 15 ft 3 in (4.63 m)
Speed:	350 knots (648.5 km/h)
Range:	6,000 miles (9,655 km) with 24 hours loiter
	13,500 miles (21,725 km) with no loiter
Ceiling:	65,000 ft (19,817 m)

GUARDIAN/SENTINEL

The Guardian and Sentinel TUAVs—nicknamed "peanut"—were developed for tactical reconnaissance ashore and afloat. Although variants have been evaluated at sea by the U.S. Navy and Coast Guard, the Guardian has not been procured by U.S. military services. It is employed by several other nations.

The CL-327 is the third Bombardier UAV to enter production, with more than 700 of the earlier CL-89 and CL-289 air vehicles having been sold to five nations. (French and German CL-289 drones have operated with their forces in Bosnia and in Operation Allied Force; see table 27-2.)

Design: The Guardian resembles two connected spheres, in the erect position, with contra-rotating propellers. Sensors include infra-red and electro-optical systems.

Operational: U.S. at-sea trials of the CL-227 Sentinel variant were carried out aboard the frigates DOYLE (FFG 39) and VANDEGRIFT (FFG 48), and of the CL-327 Guardian variant on the Coast Guard cutter THETIS (WMEC 910).

Status: Operational (non-U.S. services). The following are the basic Guardian/Sentinel specifications.

Manufacturer:	Bombardier Aéronautique (Canada)
Engines:	1 Williams WTS-117-5 turbofan; 125 hp
Weight:	empty 330 lbs (150 kg)
	gross T/O 770 lbs (350 kg)
Dimensions:	height 6 ft (1.84 m)
	rotor diameter 13 ft 1 in (4.0 m)
Speed:	maximum 85 knots (157 km/h)
	cruise 75 knots (139 km/h)
Range:	54 n.miles (100 km) with 4.75 hours loiter
	endurance 6.25 hours
Ceiling:	18,000 ft (5,490 m)

The CL-327 Guardian or "peanut" is a futuristic-looking TUAV that is in wide use with several nations. The contra-rotating propellers alleviate the need for a tail rotor or tandem rotors. (Bombardier Aéronautique)

A CL-327 Guardian during trial operations aboard the Coast Guard cutter THETIS (WMEC 910) off Key West, Fla., on 22 November 1999. The Coast Guard may use UAVs as part of its Deepwater project (see chapter 30). (U.S. Coast Guard)

HARPY

The Harpy is an Israeli-developed UAV that attacks hostile radars. The Harpy became operational in the Israeli Air Force about 1990 and has been sold to several countries, including India and South Korea.

Few details of Harpy have been released, but in its current configuration it is truck launched, carries a 70-pound (32-kg) warhead, and has a range of some 500 miles (805 km). While over enemy forces it homes on radar emissions; if the radar is shut down the Harpy returns to its pre-set flight profile until fuel is exhausted. It then dives on a pre-designated target.

The Harpy is similar in concept to the canceled U.S. Tacit Rainbow program. During the air strikes against Yugoslavia in 1999—Operation Allied Force—the U.S. Air Force commander requested the use of Harpy, but it was refused by U.S. officials on the basis of possibly violating the Intermediate Nuclear Force (INF) arms agreement. Accordingly, the Israeli Aircraft Industry, producer of the Harpy, has proposed a ship-based version of the weapon. There is some interest by both the Air Force and Navy in this proposal.

The Israelis also use the name "Cutlass" for the Harpy.

HUNTER RQ-5

This TUAV is an enlarged version of the highly successful Pioneer. The Hunter encountered major problems in development and flight tests and was formally terminated; however, the Army's need for an effective UAV of this type led to its resurrection and it is now undergoing further Army evaluation.

The Hunter originated as the Short Range UAV, a program initiated in 1988. It had been planned to undertake reconnaissance, surveillance, intelligence collection, and targeting missions at the division and corps levels ashore and for naval task forces.

However, the Hunter experienced major technical problems. The system could not adequately transmit video images during relay operations, could not meet Army standards for artillery adjustments, was unreliable, and was too large to be transported by the specified number of transport aircraft. Also, the cost increased rapidly. When the program was started in 1988, it was estimated to cost $1.2 *billion* for development and the procurement of 50 systems with 400 Hunter UAVs. By the end of 1995, the estimated cost was $2.1 *billion* for the development and procurement of 52 systems with 416 vehicles.

In late 1995, the GAO reported that fleet commanders "do not want the system on Navy ships."[44] According to the GAO report, the reasons given by the fleet commanders—all of whom objected to the Hunter coming aboard the ships—included:

- UAV operations would interfere with helicopter and Harrier VTOL operations and endanger ship crews from possible errant or out-of-control Hunters.
- Moving aircraft and erecting barriers for Hunter flights would take about 60 minutes and create crowded flight deck conditions.
- Poor weather limits the "seeing" capability of the Hunter. Further, its range is inadequate for the vast ocean areas, and its limitations would force ships to move closer to shore.
- The number of Marines the ships accommodate would have to be reduced to accommodate personnel needed to operate and maintain the UAVs.

Accordingly, the project was canceled in January 1996 after six pre-production UAVs were delivered in 1995. Nevertheless, the Army's need for a short-range UAV led to the subsequent decision for the Army to continue evaluation of the Hunter and it has been procured in limited numbers and was used in Operation Allied Force on a large scale (see table 27-2).

Design: The Hunter had an extremely simple design, resembling an enlarged Pioneer with pusher and puller propellers. The UAV can carry a variety of sensors, including daylight television, FLIR, laser range finder–designator, ELINT, and electro-optical systems.

The Hunter's line-of-sight limitations would have required a second Hunter UAV to be airborne to relay imagery from the first vehicle to the ground or task force commander.

Status: Evaluation. First flight in 1991.

Manufacturer:	IAI (Israel) and TRW	
Engines:	2 Moto Guzzi piston pusher/puller; 68 hp each	
Weight:	gross	1,600 lbs (728 kg)
	payload	250 lbs (113 kg)
Dimensions:	length	22 ft 7½ in (6.90 m)
	wingspan	29 ft 2 in (8.90 m)
	height	5 ft 6 in (1.68 m)
Speed:	maximum	110 knots (204 km/h)
	cruise	90 knots (167 km/h)
Range:	radius	108 n.miles (200 km)
	endurance	12 hours
Ceiling:	16,000 ft (4,880 m)	

44. General Accounting Office, *Unmanned Aerial Vehicles: Hunter System Is Not Appropriate for Navy Fleet Use,* GAO/NSIAD 96-2 (December 1995), p. 1.

A Hunter UAV in flight; the light object behind the main landing gear is a booster rocket being jettisoned. Although the Hunter project was canceled, the Army has employed the Hunter on an operational basis in the Balkans. (U.S. Navy)

A Hunter makes a rocket-assisted takeoff. The UAV is an updated and enlarged version of the highly successful Pioneer UAV. (U.S. Navy)

OUTRIDER

In the wake of the Hunter UAV termination, in 1966 the Department of Defense awarded a $57 million contract for six Outrider TUAV systems. Outrider is intended for operation with Army brigades and battalions, Marine Expeditionary Brigades (MEBs), and Marine Expeditionary Units (MEUs), as well as Navy task forces. In December 1999 the Outrider lost to the Shadow in the Army's TUAV competition.

A streamlined acquisition program was undertaken for the Outrider, with a contract award in December 1995. The development process includes the acquisition of six systems with 24 air vehicles at a cost of approximately $57 million. If demonstrations planned through 2003 are successful, the Department of Defense is expected to spend about $269 million for related development and $583 million for the procurement of 60 Outrider systems with 240 vehicles.

Design: The Outrider design provides for an aircraft-type fuselage with tandem wings, connected at their tips; it has a pusher propeller. It has a fixed landing gear. Electro-optical and infrared sensors are fitted.

Status: Development with low production rate.

Manufacturer:	Alliant Techsystems	
Engines:	1 McCulloch 4318F piston	
Weight:	gross	385 lbs (174.6 kg)
	payload	
Dimensions:	length	9 ft 11 in (3.92 m)
	wingspan	11 ft 1 in (3.38 m)
	height	5 ft 1 in (1.55 m)
Speed:	maximum	110 knots (203.8 km/h)
	cruise	
Range:	radius	108 n.miles (200 km) with 4 hours loiter
		27 n.miles (50 km) with 7.2 hours loiter
Ceiling:	15,000 ft (4,573 m)	

The Outrider TUAV has an unusual configuration, a staggered biwing design with the wingtips connected. The vehicle—considered a replacement for the Hunter UAV—is being evaluated for use by the U.S. Army, Navy, and Marine Corps. (NASA)

PIONEER RQ-2

The Pioneer TUAV is a highly effective, unmanned tactical reconnaissance vehicle that was flown extensively in the Persian Gulf conflict and in Operation Allied Force in 1999. The Navy had planned to replace the Pioneer with a more advanced UAV by 2000; however, delays in UAV development have led to the Pioneer being retained pending availability of the Schweizer 330.

Impressed with Israeli successes using UAVs in the early 1980s, the Navy initiated a procurement effort. In January 1986 the Navy awarded contracts to the AAI Corp. of Cockeysville, Md., and Mazlat, Ltd., the latter a joint venture of Israel Aircraft Industries (IAI) and Tadiran. The firms were able to skip the traditional development phase of the acquisition process due to the support of Secretary Lehman. They produced 72 Pioneer UAVs at a cost of $87.7 million.

The Pioneer encountered difficulties, including electromagnetic interference from other ship systems and recovery problems, and there were several crashes. Although the Pioneer has never met objective requirements, it has been used operationally with considerable success. Originally flown from battleships and shore launchers, with the demise of the battleship the vehicles have been flown by Navy squadron VC-6 from a variety of amphibious ships.

The Pioneer will be phased out when the Outrider UAV becomes available.

Design: The Pioneer, modeled on the IAI Scout vehicle, carries its sensors and engines in a fuselage section fitted with twin tail booms. The vehicle is powered by a reciprocating engine with a small pusher propeller. The vehicle, which has a fixed landing gear, can be launched with rocket assistance and can be recovered on a runway or by a net. The metal and fiberglass construction of the vehicle presents a low radar cross-section. The Pioneer is transported in a disassembled condition and can be rapidly put together with minimum tools.

The Pioneer's payload is 100 pounds (45.4 kg). At the time of the Gulf War, the Pioneer was fitted with a daylight television camera or, alternatively, a FLIR sensor. The existing control/data link is a C-band system, resistant to jamming, with a range of 100 n.miles (185 km).

Operational: The first shipboard trials of the Pioneer were held on the battleship Iowa (BB 61) in Chesapeake Bay in December 1986. During subsequent "proof-of-concept" tests in the Caribbean in January–February 1987, the Iowa's 16-inch (406-mm) guns fired on targets detected by the RPV. In that exercise, four of the five embarked RPVs were lost in accidents.

During the Gulf conflict from 16 January to 27 February 1991, some 40 Pioneer UAVs flew 552 sorties for a total mission duration time of 1,641 hours. *At least one Pioneer UAV was airborne at all times during Operation Desert Storm.* The vehicles were employed to adjust naval gunfire and for battle damage assessment, reconnaissance, and force coordination.

On 27 February, after a Pioneer detected two Iraqi patrol boats off Faylaka Island and naval aircraft were called in to destroy the craft, a large number of Iraqi soldiers on the island surrendered to a UAV launched by the battleship Missouri. Apparently the soldiers knew that their detection by the drone would be followed by air or naval gunfire attack. It was history's first known surrender of enemy troops to an unmanned vehicle.

The Pioneer is being removed from Navy service, after more than a decade of successful operation with the Army, Navy, and Marine Corps. Here a Pioneer is launched from the battleship Iowa (BB 61) with a rocket booster. (U.S. Navy)

The following summary of Pioneer sorties was compiled by the Navy:

Unit	Sorties	Hours
VC-6 Det. 1 in WISCONSIN	100	342.9
VC-6 Det. 2 in MISSOURI	64	209.7
1st Marine RPV Company[45]	94	330.3
(commenced operations 26 Sep 1990)		
2nd Marine RPV Company	69	226.6
(operations 27 Nov 1990 through 1 Mar 1990)		
3rd Marine RPV Company	147	380.6
U.S. Army UAV Platoon[46]	48	150.8
(commenced operations 1 February 1991)		

A total of 12 Pioneers were destroyed during the conflict; eight of the losses were from the ten Pioneers embarked in the two battleships. In addition, 14 Pioneers were damaged during Desert Storm (all repairable). The casualties were due to:

45. The Marine companies were redesignated unmanned aerial vehicle squadrons (VMU) in 1996.
46. Assigned to the U.S. Army's 82nd Airborne Division.

A Pioneer UAV is captured in a recovery net aboard the battleship IOWA. The Pioneer could also be landed, under radio control, on a runway or flight-deck ship. (U.S. Navy)

	Destroyed	Damaged
airframe/engine failures	6	3
electromagnetic interference	3	2
operator error	2	6
enemy fire	1	3

The Department of Defense's final report on the Gulf War (April 1992) stated: "The Navy Pioneer UAV system's availability exceeded expectations. Established sortie rates indicated a deployed unit could sustain 60 flight hours a month."

In late 1992 the Navy operated Pioneers from the helicopter carrier NEW ORLEANS (LPH 11). During the launch and recovery operations, two arresting wires were set up on the flight deck (as well as the standard recovery net) and the drones snagged the arresting wires, as done ashore. All shipboard recoveries had previously been made into nets.

The Pioneer was used in support of U.S. operations in Bosnia-Herzegovina in 1966–1967. Marine squadron VMU-1 deployed with a Pioneer system that included seven UAVs, one ground control station, and four receiving stations. Subsequently the Pioneer was used on a limited basis in Operation Allied Force (see table 27-2).

Navy squadron VC-6 also has employed Pioneer UAVs in counter-narcotic operations in support of the U.S. Border Patrol along the Mexico-California border.

Status: Operational; being phased out of service. IOC in the U.S. Navy in May 1986.

Manufacturer:	AAI and Mazlat (Israel)	
Engines:	1 Sachs 2-stroke piston; 26 hp	
Weight:	maximum launch	430 lbs (195 kg)
	payload	100 lbs (45.4 kg)
Dimensions:	length	16 ft 3 in (4.96 m)
	wingspan	16 ft 9½ in (5.12 m)
	height	3 ft 3 in (1.0 m)
Speed:	maximum	100 knots (185 km/h)
	cruise	48 to 70 knots (89 to 130 km/h)
Range:	8-hour endurance	
Ceiling:	15,000 ft (4,573 m)	

POINTER FQM-151

The FQM-151 Pointer is a small, very-low-cost, hand-launched UAV.[47] Resembling a model aircraft, the Pointer is man-portable with the entire system carried in two backpacks—the one carrying the air vehicle (45 pounds/20.25 kg) and one containing the control unit (50 pounds/22.5 kg).

In 1988 the Marine Corps purchased one unit for tests. The Department of Defense joint program office procured 24 Pointers in December 1989. Several of these units were deployed to Saudi Arabia with the Marines in 1991. The Pointer's sensor payload is a black-and-white television camera using an 8-mm video cassette. It can be modified to carry a chemical agent detector.

The system can be fully prepared for flight in about five minutes. Flight endurance is over one hour. For recovery, the Pointer is directed into a deep stall. The crew consists of an operator and observer.

Status: Operational.

Manufacturer:	AeroVironment (Simi Valley, Calif.)	
Engines:	1 electric motor; 300 watts; 2-blade pusher propeller	
Weight:	9 lbs (4 kg)	
Dimensions:	length	6 ft (1.83 m)
	wingspan	9 ft (2.74 m)
Speed:	maximum	approx. 39 knots (72 km/h)
	cruise	approx. 20 knots (37 km/h)
Range:		
Ceiling:		

47. FQM is a missile series designation.

Subsequent contracts totaled $579 million for total development and the production of 13 Predator systems with 80 vehicles.

The Predator has been in operation in the Persian Gulf and the Balkans (see below).

Design: The Predator carries a payload of 400 pounds (181 kg); it is capable of day/night operations with a variety of sensors, including video and infrared (with ground link). The vehicle has retractable landing gear, being designed to take off and land on highways or other open areas.

The use of the Predator over Bosnia has accelerated fitting the UAV with synthetic aperture radar because of flights being hampered by overcast and ground fog.

Operational: The Predator began intelligence collection missions in July 1995, flying from Albania to observe targets in Bosnia and Herzegovina.[48] Four disassembled Predators were flown into Gjader Airfield near Tirana, Albania, in a C-130 Hercules transport. The UAVs were assembled and flown by civilian contract personnel.

One of the Predators was lost over Bosnia on 11 August 1995; a second was deliberately destroyed on 14 August after suffering an engine failure over Bosnia, which may have been caused by hostile ground fire.

---

48. The distance from Tirana to Sarajevo is approximately 200 miles (320 km).

With a strong right arm, a Marine launches a Pointer UAV—in some respects the progenitor of the "mini" UAV. (U.S. Marine Corps)

PREDATOR RQ-1A

The Predator is a versatile platform capable of performing a number of missions. It is the most sophisticated UAV currently flying for the United States. The Predator is intended for use at the theater commander and joint force commander level.

The Department of Defense awarded General Atomics Aeronautical a $31.7 million contract in January 1994 to build ten UAVs and three ground control stations; these were delivered by mid-1995.

Technicians work on a Predator UAV. Above the nosewheel is a sensor "turret"; note the streamlined shape of the fuselage and the angle of the tail surfaces. (U.S. Navy, PH3 Jeffrey S. Viano)

The Predator is another highly successful UAV that was used by U.S. forces in the Balkans during the 1990s. The long-endurance vehicle has a fully retractable landing gear and a pusher propeller. (U.S. Navy, PH3 Jeffrey S. Viano)

A second Predator deployment to Bosnia began in March 1996. Subsequently, three UAVs, operating from Sarmellek, Hungary, were fitted with synthetic aperture radar, permitting more effective reconnaissance through clouds and fog for operations in Bosnia.

In 1996 the Navy conducted tests with a submarine controlling a Predator UAV. The drone was launched from land, flew out to an ocean operating area, and then was controlled by the submarine running submerged with an antenna raised above the surface for the data link to the Predator. The data link was direct and via satellite relay.

In January 1999 UAVs returned to the Persian Gulf for the first time since the 1990–1991 war when the Air Force deployed a Predator system to Kuwait to fly reconnaissance flights over Iran as part of Operation Southern Watch, supporting United Nations sanctions. (One of these UAVs was an operational loss.)

Predator UAVs also participated in the air war over Kosovo in 1999.

Status: Operational. First flight in June 1994.

Manufacturer:	General Atomics Aeronautical Systems	
Engines:	1 Rotax 912 turbojet with fuel injection; 85 hp	
Weight:	empty	773 lbs (350.63 kg)
	normal T/O	1,873 lbs (849.6 kg)
	payload	465 lbs (211 kg)
Dimensions:	length	28 ft (8.54 m)
	wingspan	48 ft 5 in (14.75 m)
		35 ft (10.67 m) naval variant
	wing area	
	height	
Speed:	maximum	120 knots (222 km/h)
	cruise	56.5 knots (105 km/h)
Range:	500 n.miles (925 km) with 24 hours loiter	
	maximum endurance 40+ hours	
Ceiling:	26,000 ft (7,930 m)	

SHADOW

The Shadow 200 was selected by the U.S. Army in December 1999 as its next-generation TUAV. It will replace the Pioneer UAV, also produced by the AAI Corporation.

The new vehicle will undoubtedly be seen by the Navy and Marine Corps and under some circumstances will support naval operations. The Shadow is the successor to the Army's Pioneer UAV, also employed by the Navy and Marine Corps.

The Army plans initially to acquire four Shadow TUAV systems, each with four aerial vehicles and three ground control stations, one of which will be a portable station. The total Army requirement is for 44 TUAV systems, which will be assigned at the brigade level. (The other finalists in the Army competition were the Alliant Techsystems Outrider, General Atomics Prowler II, and S-TEC's Sentry.)

Design: The Shadow TUAV has a conventional configuration with twin booms supporting its tail surfaces; a fixed landing gear is provided. The drone can be landed by remote control or recovered by parachute.

Status: In procurement. First flight 1992.

Manufacturer:	AAI Corporation	
Engines:	1 Allison 250-C20 GT recuperative turboshaft; 37 shp	
Weight:	empty	200 lbs (90.7 kg)
	normal T/O	325 lbs (147 kg)
Dimensions:	length	11 ft (3.35 m)
	wingspan	12 ft 9 in (3.89 m)
Speed:	maximum	150 knots (278 km/h)
	cruise	84 knots (155 km/h)
Range:	radius	124 miles (200 km) with 4+ hours loiter carrying 50-lb (22.7-kg) payload
	endurance	8 hours maximum
Ceiling:	15,000 ft	
Dimensions:	length	28 ft (8.54 m)
	wingspan	48 ft 5 in (14.75 m)
		35 ft (10.67 m) naval variant
	wing area	
	height	
Speed:	maximum	120 knots (222 km/h)
	cruise	56.5 knots (105 km/h)
Range:	500 n.miles (925 km) with 24 hours loiter	
	maximum endurance 40+ hours	
Ceiling:	26,000 ft (7,930 m)	

UNMANNED COMBAT AIR VEHICLES

In 1999 the Defense Advanced Projects Research Agency (DARPA) and the Air Force selected the Boeing Company to continue into the second phase of the Unmanned Combat Air Vehicle (UCAV) advanced technology demonstration program. Under the $131 million cost-share effort, Boeing will develop two air vehicles, a reconfigurable mission control station, and appropriate supporting elements to demonstrate the key technologies, operational capabilities, and cost considerations of integrating UCAVs into manned air combat operations.

"UCAVs represent a revolutionary new weapon system that can significantly increase the effectiveness and survivability of manned fighter aircraft while lowering the overall cost of combat operations," according to Dave Stein, executive vice president of the Boeing Phantom Works, where the UCAV program is being conducted.

The Department of Defense envisions employing UCAV systems in the post-2010 battlespace to augment the manned aviation forces on high-risk, high-priority missions. The first such role planned for UCAVs is conducting Suppression of Enemy Air Defenses (SEAD) missions ahead of manned aircraft. Typically, 80 percent of the useful life of contemporary combat aircraft is devoted to pilot training and proficiency flying, requiring longer design lives than would be needed to meet combat requirements. Without the requirement to fly sorties to retain pilot proficiency, UCAVs will fly infrequently. A design without pilot/life support and survival features, condition-based maintenance, and a modular avionics architecture will reduce "hands on" maintenance requirements.

Further, advances in small smart munitions will allow these smaller vehicles to attack multiple targets during a single mission and reduce the cost per target killed. The Miniaturized Munitions Technology Demonstration (MMTD) goal is to produce a 250-pound (113-kg)-class munition effective against a majority of hardened targets previously vulnerable only to 2,000-pound (907-kg) munitions. A differential GPS/INS system will provide a high probability of target kill.

The Boeing UCAV system includes a tailless 27-foot (8.23-m)-long vehicle with a 34-foot (10.37-m) wingspan; empty weight will be approximately 8,000 pounds (3,630 kg). It will be reconfigurable for different missions and will be fitted with satellite-relay and line-of-sight communications links for control in a combat environment.

The Army's Shadow TUAV resembles the long-serving Pioneer UAV. The Shadow can be recovered by parachute or landed by radio control. Several hundred of these vehicles may be procured during the next decade for U.S. and foreign military use. (AAI)

Boeing revealed its candidate UCAV on 27 September 2000. Designated X-45A, the aircraft was scheduled to make its first flight in the spring of 2001.

Boeing's Phantom Works developed its UCAV concepts under a $4 million Phase I contract awarded in April 1998. In the 42-month Phase II program, Boeing will build and flight-test a demonstration system by 2002.

Earlier the government had decided that only the U.S. corporations meeting all the requirements necessary to lead teams develop-

ing UCAV are Boeing, Lockheed Martin, Northrop Grumman, and Raytheon.

Separately from the DARPA effort, Lockheed Martin's Tactical Aircraft Systems in late 1998 completed a study for the Navy with the objective of creating conceptual aircraft designs for three different types of naval UCAVs. Two were to operate from surface ships such as amphibious assault ships and destroyers; they would be short-launch/recovery and vertical launch/recovery, respectively. The third concept would be launched and recovered from submerged submarines.

The Unmanned Combat Aerial Vehicle (UCAV) could have a significant impact on military operations, including combat at sea. This artist's concept shows a naval UCAV that could perform long-range reconnaissance, airborne early warning, targeting, and other functions. (Boeing)

This UCAV is a fighter-attack aircraft, capable of detecting, targeting, and attacking aerial targets and possibly surface targets. Most UCAV concepts include a high degree of stealth. (Boeing)

CHAPTER 28

Weapon Systems

Precision Guided Munitions (PGMs) have become the weapon of choice for U.S. forces in the post–Cold War period. These weapons, launched from land- and carrier-based aircraft, as well as from surface ships and submarines, were used extensively in the Persian Gulf War (1991), Operation Allied Force (1999), and several lesser actions. These sailors are loading a 1,000-pound GBU-16 Laser Guided Bomb (LGB) on an F/A-18C Hornet aboard the carrier ENTERPRISE (CVN 65). (U.S. Navy, PHAN Jacob L. Holingsworth)

The weapons fitted in U.S. ships and carried by naval aircraft are described in this chapter. Several new air-to-air and air-to-surface missiles are being introduced into the naval arsenal.

Two controversial weapon programs are under way. The first is the ballistic missile intercept variant of the Standard surface-to-air missile (see page 519). The second program addresses several weapons related to Naval Surface Fire Support (NSFS).

The NSFS requirement—primarily to provide fire support for amphibious landings—is controversial because of (1) delays by the Navy and Department of Defense in developing such weapons, (2) the controversy over reactivating battleships of the IOWA (BB 61) class for this role, and (3) the issue of whether or not there will be major amphibious landings in the future.

The current Marine Corps fire support requirement is for a naval gun similar to its own 155-mm artillery tubes, which have a range of 16 n.miles (29.6 km). Adding that range to at least a 25-n.mile (46.3-km) ship standoff from land requires a threshold range requirement of 41 n.miles (76 km) at a minimum. The 16-inch (406-mm) guns of the Iowa-class battleships do not have sufficient range to support Marine fire-support requirements.

The NSFS weapons now in U.S. Navy ships are the 5-inch (127-mm)/54-cal gun and the Tomahawk Land-Attack Missile (TLAM); both weapons are fitted in all U.S. cruisers and destroyers. A set of NSFS weapon systems are being developed for the near term (approximately 2001 through 2008) and long term (from 2009): The near-term weapons are the 5-inch/62-cal gun firing the Extended-Range Guided Munition (ERGM), the Tactical Tomahawk missile, and the Land-Attack Standard Missile (LASM); additionally, an improved fire control system will be fitted to support these weapons. The long-term weapons are the 155-mm/ERGM Advanced Gun System (AGS) and the Advanced Land-Attack Missile (ALAM).

These improvements, according to Navy officials, will meet all Marine Corps requirements for naval fire support.[1]

BOMBS AND ROCKETS

U.S. naval aviation has shifted away from "iron" or "dumb" bombs to "smart" weapons—guided missiles and "smart" bombs. The latter are primarily Mk 80–series bombs fitted with guidance kits to convert them to Laser-Guided Bombs (LGB). The three

---

1. Rear Adm. Michael G. Mullen, USN, Director, Surface Warfare Division, presentation to the U.S. Marine Corps General Officer Symposium, Norfolk, Va., 29 September 1999.

Mk 80–series bombs currently in use are shown below, along with the Guided Bomb Unit (GBU), BLU, and KMU kits that convert the standard bombs to LGBs (see also the Joint Direct Attack Munition/JDAM, below).

Bomb	Class	LGB kits
Mk 82	500 lb (227 kg)	JDAM, KMU-388/B
Mk 83	1,000 lb (454 kg)	JDAM, BLU-110, GBU-16, KMU-431/B
Mk 84	2,000 lb (907 kg)	JDAM, BLU-109, GBU-24/B, KMU-351A/B

The Mk 80 weapons have both standard (fixed) tail assemblies and low-drag tails; the latter extend upon release to slow the bomb and enable a low-flying aircraft to escape the bombs' explosions. When fitted with LGB kits, these bombs can be guided to their targets by a laser designator fitted to the launching aircraft or another aircraft or used by forces on the ground (such as SEAL-type Special Forces operating behind enemy lines, as was done in the 1991 war in the Persian Gulf). The kits consist of a laser receiver, a computer-control group, and an airfoil group (wing assembly and guidance fins).

These bombs can also be converted for use as naval mines (see Mines, below).

In addition to Mk 80–series bombs, Navy and Marine Corps aircraft carry unguided Rockeye rockets. The Rockeye II Mk 20 is an unguided cluster bomb that dispenses bomblets to attack "soft" targets such as anti-aircraft sites and lightly armored vehicles. Each rocket carries 247 bomblets with shaped-charge warheads; the bomblets each weigh 1 pound (0.46 kg). The earlier Rockeye I was designated Mk 15.

The APAM (Anti-Personnel/Anti-Material) rocket, an improved munition carrying a bomblet dispenser, has been retired from service.

Nuclear bombs are no longer available to U.S. naval forces (see Nuclear Weapons, below).

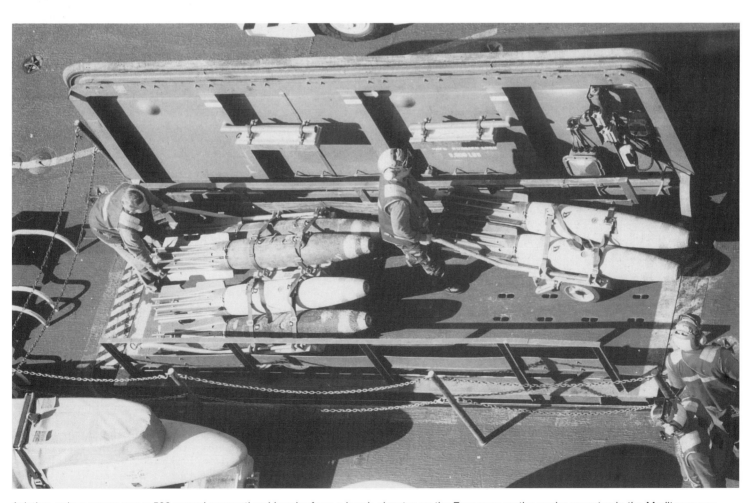

Aviation ordnancemen move 500-pound conventional bombs from a bomb elevator on the Enterprise as the carrier operates in the Mediterranean during a 1999 fleet exercise. They are loaded on hand carts—as they have been for more than fifty years. (U.S. Navy, PH2 Damon J. Moritz)

A F-14B Tomcat releases a 1,000-pound GBU-16 laser-guided bomb during live-fire exercises at Fallon, Nevada. The tail fins are deployed as the bomb seeks the laser "spot" on a ground target. (U.S. Navy, Lt. Andy Walton)

Three Mk 20 Rockeye II cluster bombs are moved across the flight deck of the carrier SARATOGA (CV 60). These and other unguided weapons are still useful in some situations, especially against lightly defended targets. (U.S. Navy, PH3 Marc M. Thurston)

Conventional "iron" bombs still are used by U.S. military forces. Here a pair of 500-pound bombs is being pushed across the flight deck of the carrier GEORGE WASHINGTON (CVN 73) as the ship steams in the Persian Gulf. (U.S. Navy, AN Joe Hendricks)

NAVAL GUNS

The reinstatement of two battleships to the Naval Vessel Register has returned both 16-inch and 5-inch/38-cal guns to the fleet, albeit in two ships of the IOWA class laid up in reserve (see chapter 14 of this edition of *Ships and Aircraft*). The largest naval guns in active U.S. warships are 5-inch/54-cal weapons fitted in all active cruisers and destroyers.

The Navy's shipboard firepower had increased dramatically in the 1980s with the reactivation of the four battleships of the IOWA class. Those ships each carried nine 16-inch guns and—as modernized in the 1980s—12 5-inch guns. However, with the mothballing of the MISSOURI (BB 63) in early 1992 all of those behemoths were again laid up in reserve (and two were subsequently stricken). It is highly unlikely that the two remaining ships, the IOWA and WISCONSIN (BB 64), will or could be reactivated.

The Marine Corps's requirement for naval gunfire support had led to a renewed interest in deployment of the 8-inch (203-mm) Major Caliber Lightweight Gun (MCLWG), which is suitable for installation in ships of cruiser and destroyer size, as well as several other naval gunfire support systems. However, austere budgets and the adaption of other gun systems have essentially ended consideration of this weapon; see 16th Edition/pages 427–428 for its characteristics.

The principal rocket candidate for the naval fire support mission during the 1980s was the Assault Ballistic Rocket System (ABRS), an unguided rocket and launcher adapted from the LTV Corporation's Multiple Launch Rocket System (MLRS) used by the U.S. Army and Marine Corps and several NATO countries. The ABRS had been proposed for installation on the IOWA-class battleships and landing ships of the NEWPORT (LST 1179) class. One proposal provided for full conversion of LSTs to "rocket monitors"; see 14th Edition/page 466 for ABRS/MLRS characteristics. Subsequently, the Army's ATACMS (Army Tactical Missile System) was proposed for the fire support role.

A 1993 review by the Center for Naval Analyses identified eight gun systems that—combined with missiles—were capable of attacking at least 95 percent of targets in postulated major regional conflicts.[2] Five of these systems were 155-mm gun variants and three were 8-inch gun variants with differing propellants, projectiles, and calibers. The analysis concluded that a 155-mm/60-cal gun system with an advanced propellant and precision guided munitions, in combination with the Tomahawk TLAM missile, was the most cost-effective option for naval gunfire support.

Beyond the retiring of the battleships, there has been a steady decline of naval guns as older cruisers and destroyers have been decommissioned, with newer ships generally having fewer guns of smaller caliber. All cruisers armed with 8-inch and 6-inch (152-mm) guns have been retired, as have all pre-SPRUANCE (DD 963)-class destroyers, which carried up to six 5-inch guns. The last active U.S. ship with 8-inch guns was the NEWPORT NEWS (CA 148), which was decommissioned in 1978, and the last active ship with 6-inch guns was the cruiser-flagship OKLAHOMA CITY (CG 5), retired in 1979; all mothballed cruisers with these guns have been stricken.

(The only warships in service today in foreign navies with guns larger than 5-inch are in the Russian Navy; the later KIROV-class battle cruisers, the SLAVA-class missile cruisers, and the SOVREMENNYY-class destroyers mount 130-mm/70-cal dual-purpose guns. All cruisers of the Soviet SVERDLOV class, which mounted as many as 12 152-mm guns, have been discarded.)

All active U.S. cruisers and destroyers have 5-inch/54-cal Mk 45 lightweight guns. All frigates armed with 5-inch/38-cal guns have been retired and the Coast Guard cutters armed with 5-inch/38-cal guns have been retired or rearmed. The 5-inch guns in active cruisers and destroyers are considered primarily shore-bombardment weapons and have only a limited anti-air capability.

The 76-mm guns in Navy frigates and the larger Coast Guard cutters are primarily anti-aircraft weapons, but do have an anti-surface capability. Most Navy surface warships and several auxiliary classes are armed with the Mk 15 20-mm Close-In Weapon System (CIWS) for close-in defense against anti-ship missiles. In addition, various types of 25-mm and 20-mm cannon, and .50-cal and 7.62-mm machine guns, are fitted in naval ships, primarily for defense against small craft in restricted waters.

Ammunition: The Extended-Range Guided Munition is a 5-inch (diameter) round that can carry 72 M80 submunitions out to a range of 63 n.miles (117 km) with Global Positioning System (GPS) accuracy. The M80 is a dual-purpose Improved Conventional Munition (ICM) that incorporates a shaped charge capable of penetrating 2 to 3 inches (50.75 to 76 mm) of armor and has a fragmenting steel case. The ERGM round is 5 feet (1.5 m) long and weighs 110 pounds (45.36 kg) compared to 3 feet (0.9 m) and 70 pounds (21.34 kg) for a conventional 5-inch round.

The CEP of an ERGM round is 33 to 66 feet (10 to 20 m) at maximum range.[3]

Classification: Guns are classified by their inside barrel diameter and gun-barrel length. Diameters of U.S. guns traditionally have been listed in inches for weapons larger than 1 inch (25.4 mm) in diameter. The caliber of a gun indicates its barrel length as a multiple of its bore; thus, a 5-inch/38-cal gun has a barrel length of 190 inches. The Italian-developed OTO Melara 76-mm gun retains its metric measurement in U.S. naval service.

Guns smaller than 1 inch in diameter are measured in millimeters or calibers, the latter being fractions of an inch (e.g., .50 cal = ½ inch).

---

2. This was the Cost and Operational Effectiveness Analysis (COEA).

3. CEP = Circular Error Probable (the radius around the aimpoint in which one-half of the rounds will fall).

The forward triple 16-inch/50-cal gun turrets of the battleship MISSOURI (BB 63). There is a Mk 56 gunfire control system (for 5-inch guns) atop the bridge structure. Quad 40-mm gun mounts previously adorned the top of No. 2 turret and 01 level adjacent to the bridge. (Giorgio Arra)

Sixteen-inch projectiles are staged on the forecastle of the battleship Iowa (BB 61) as she is anchored at the Naval Weapons Station, Yorktown, Va., during the ship's active service from 1984 to 1990. These "bullets" are about 6 feet (1.83 m) long. (U.S. Navy)

Nomenclature: According to the Navy, "A mount is an assembled unit which includes the gun barrel (or barrels), housing(s), slide(s), carriage, stand, sight, elevating and training drives, ammunition hoists, and associated equipment." Mounts include guns from 20-mm caliber up to but not including 6-inch guns. A mount differs from a turret in that a mount does not have a barrette structure within the hull.

Saluting guns: U.S. aircraft carriers, cruisers, destroyers, amphibious ships, and auxiliaries have the 40-mm Mk 11 saluting gun. This weapon is for saluting only and has no combat capability.

The following entries are arranged by gun size (i.e., bore diameter).

16-INCH/50-CAL GUN

These guns, which are the main gun battery of the Iowa-class battleships, are the largest guns ever mounted in warships, except for the 18.1-inch (460-mm) guns of the Japanese Yamato-class battleships of World War II and the single 18-inch (457-mm) gun of the British carrier Furious of World War I.[4] The 16-inch/50s were also intended for the five never-built battleships of the Montana (BB 67) class.

The ammunition capacity of the ships' magazines are 390 rounds for turret no. 1, 460 rounds for turret no. 2, and 370 rounds for turret no. 3. These were the world's largest guns fitted to fire nuclear projectiles and the only U.S. shipboard guns with that capability.

Nuclear projectiles were available for these guns from December 1956 to October 1962. The nuclear warhead was the W23 gun-type.

Operational: The Iowa suffered an explosion in one of her 16-inch gun turrets on 19 April 1989, while the ship was operating some 330 n.miles (610 km) off Puerto Rico (see page 129 for details). The damaged gun—the center gun of turret no. 2—was not repaired before the ship was mothballed. The parts needed to rehabilitate the turret are available, with the cost of the repairs estimated at about $8 million.

Status: Operational. None in active ships.

Mount:	triple
Gun barrel:	Mk 7 Mod 0
Muzzle velocity:[5]	2,425 ft/sec (739 m/sec) AP
	2,690 ft/sec (820 m/sec) HC
Weight:	1,700 tons (turret)
Rate of fire:	2 rounds/minute per barrel
Maximum range:	40,185 yds (36,755 m) AP at 45° elevation
	41,622 yds (38,069 m) HC at 45° elevation
Projectile weight:	2,700 lbs (1,225 kg) AP
	1,900 lbs (862 kg) HC
Fire control:	Mk 38 GFCS
Crew:	74, consisting of 27 in turret, 4 in machinery rooms, 15 in upper projectile room, 15 in lower projectile room, and 13 in powder handling room
Ships:	*battleships* BB 61

---

4. The Furious carried her single 18-inch gun from her completion in April 1917 until installation of an after landing deck in November 1917.

---

5. AP = Armor Piercing and HC = High Capacity (for shore bombardment).

Mount:	single
Gun barrel:	
Muzzle velocity:	
Weight:	
Rate of fire:	12 rounds/minute
Maximum range:	100 n.miles (185 km)
Projectile weight:	
Fire control:	
Crew:	
Ships:	*destroyers* DD 21

155-MM/52-CAL VERTICAL GUN FOR ADVANCED SHIPS

The Vertical Gun for Advanced Ships (VGAS) was a proposal for the DD 21 land-attack destroyers. Twin 155-mm guns—with a range of about 100 n.miles (185 km)—and their magazines were to be fitted in a modular mounting that could replace Vertical Launching System (VLS) missile modules.

The gun system was to be fully automated, with 1,400 rounds per module (i.e., for two guns). Projectiles up to 6 ¼ feet (1.9 m) long and weighing 300 pounds (136 kg) could be handled by VGAS. The sustained rate of fire was to be 15 rounds per minute per barrel.

In the event, the decision was made not to pursue development of VGAS because the advantages of the concept were outweighed by limitations, especially in maximum range. The Advanced Gun System (AGS) is the successor to the VGAS.

VGAS might also have been considered for the aborted arsenal ship program (see appendix E).

A sailor transports a powder casing for the 16-inch guns aboard the battleship NEW JERSEY (BB 62). Within the casing are silk propellant bags; six of the bags, each 15½ inches (394 mm) long and 14¾ inches (375 mm) in diameter, normally are used to fire a 16-inch projectile. (U.S. Navy)

155-MM ADVANCED GUN SYSTEM

The Advanced Gun System (AGS) is planned for the Land Attack Destroyers (DD 21). The gun system will be capable of firing both ERGM rounds and conventional 155-mm rounds.

Probably two AGS weapons will be fitted in each DD 21. The Navy plans to have 44 guns (22 ships) in the fleet by 2015 and 64 guns (32 ships) by 2020.

The objective for magazine capacity for the AGS will be 750 ERGM rounds per gun (i.e., 1,500 per ship); it could be a greater number of rounds. The gun also will be capable of firing the SADARM anti-armor submunition, with two SADARM projectiles fitted to each 155-mm round.[6]

The 155-mm mounts are designed with low radar cross-sections and infrared signatures to help maintain the stealth characteristics of the DD 21. The AGS automated ammunition handling technology is based on the Army's 155-mm Crusader howitzer.

Status: Development. IOC planned in 2009.

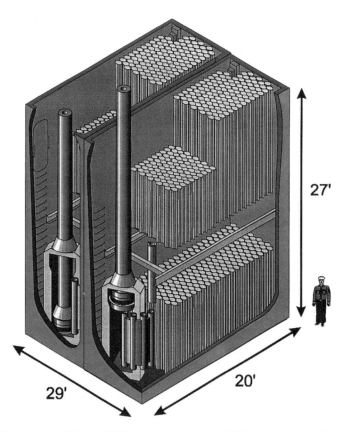

The aborted 155-mm VGAS gun system was to fit into the space of a standard 64-cell Vertical Launching System (VLS). The system was to have two 155-mm gun barrels, loaded from an automated, 1,400-round magazine.

---

6. SADARM = Sense And Destroy Armor. Each 155-mm SADARM projectile carries two submunitions, each of which uses a dual-mode millimeter-wave and infrared sensor and fires an explosively formed penetrator through the top of a target.

5-INCH/62-CAL GUN MK 45 MOD 4

This is primarily a shore-bombardment weapon, designed specifically to fire ERGM rounds. The gun will fire all types of 5-inch rounds and can be used in an anti-aircraft mode.

The Navy plans to rearm 22 Improved TICONDEROGA (CG 52)-class cruisers (two guns each) and 27 improved ARLEIGH BURKE (DDG 81)-class destroyers; these upgrades are to provide 71 guns in the fleet by 2015.

In 1996 the Navy awarded a $49,600,000 contract to United Defense to modify existing Mk 45 guns for extended range and enhanced performance. In addition to a longer barrel and ERGM capability, the Mod 4 guns will have increased reliability and reduced maintenance requirements.

The first 5-inch/62-cal gun Mk 45 Mod 4 as installed aboard the destroyer WINSTON S. CHURCHILL (DDG 81) in November 1999. The gun is intended primarily for the shore-bombardment role. South Korea also will use the gun in warships. (United Technologies LP)

Each ship (single mount) will have a magazine loadout of 225 ERGMs and 210 conventional rounds. The ready service magazine will hold 20 rounds (conventional size).

The first ship to mount the gun is the WINSTON S. CHURCHILL (DDG 81), installed in November 1999 with an IOC of 2001. The Mod 4 also is planned for retrofitting in the TICONDEROGA (CG 47)-class cruisers. The Mod 4 also is being fitted in South Korean destroyers.

Status: In production (United Defense).

Mount:	single
Gun barrel:	Mk 36 Mod 0
Muzzle velocity:	2,780 ft/sec (848 m/sec)
Weight:	approx. 54,398 lbs (24,674 kg)
Rate of fire:	16 to 20 conventional rounds/minute
	5 to 10 ERGM rounds/minute
Maximum range:	63 n.miles (117 km) ERGM round
Projectile weight:	110-lb (45.36-kg) ERGM round
	70-lb (31.75-kg) conventional round
Fire control:	Mk 160 Mod 8 gun computing system
Crew:	6
Ships:	*cruisers* CG /52
	destroyers DD 21
	DDG 79

5-INCH/54-CAL GUN MK 45

The Mk 45 is the principal gun in U.S. cruisers and destroyers. It is capable of engaging air or surface targets. The gun mount is unmanned, with the gun crew stationed belowdecks. The mount stows 20 rounds of ready service ammunition that can be fired quickly by a single man at the below-deck control console. The magazine can be reloaded while the gun is firing without interrupting the firing sequence. The maximum rate of fire is 16 to 20 rounds per minute with fixed ammunition. Firing Rocket Assisted Projectiles (RAP) and other separated ammunition reduces the firing rate. Magazine capacity in destroyers is 475 to 500 rounds per mount.

The gun is now being installed in new-construction ARLEIGH BURKE (DDG 51) surface combatants. The three 5-inch Mk 45 guns have been removed from the large amphibious ships of the TARAWA (LHD 1) class; the successor WASP (LHA 1) class mounts only lighter weapons.

The Mk 45 was first deployed in U.S. ships in 1971.

Status: Operational. In production (United Defense).

The Mk 45 gun also is used in warships of Australia, Greece, New Zealand, Spain, Thailand, and Turkey.

The 5-inch/54-cal Mk 45 gun on the destroyer BARRY (DDG 52) fires during an exercise. The small, unmanned 5-inch mount on U.S. cruisers and destroyers is intended primarily for shore bombardment and use against surface targets. (PH2 Shane McCoy)

Mount:	single
Gun barrel:	Mk 19 Mod 2
Muzzle velocity:	2,500 ft/sec (762 m/sec)
Weight:	47,820 lbs (21,691 kg)
Rate of fire:	16 to 20 rounds/minute
Maximum range:	25,909 yds (23,697 m) at 47° elevation
	16,233 yds (14,848 m) at 85° elevation
Projectile weight:	70 lbs (31.75 kg)
Fire control:	Mk 86 GFCS or Mk 160 gun computing system
Crew:	6
Ships:	*cruisers* CG 47/52
	destroyers DDG 51/79
	DD 963

5-INCH/38-CAL GUN MK 28

These 5-inch guns are fitted as the secondary battery in IOWA-class battleships. As these ships were reactivated during the 1980s, the original battery of ten twin 5-inch mounts was reduced to six mounts.

Status: Operational. None in active ships.

Mount:	twin
Gun barrel:	Mk 12 Mod 1
Muzzle velocity:	2,500 ft/sec (762 m/sec)
Weight:	53,000 to 169,000 lbs (69,400 to 76,658 kg); varies with Mod
Rate of fire:	18 rounds/minute per barrel
Maximum range:	17,306 yds (15,829 m) at 45° elevation
	32,250 ft (9,832 m) at 85° elevation
Projectile weight:	55 lbs (25 kg)
Fire control:	Mk 56 GFCS
Crew:	27
Ships:	*battleships* BB 61

The forward 5-inch/54-cal Mk 45 gun of the cruiser GETTYSBURG (CG 64). The markings forward of the small, streamlined mount are for Vertical Replenishment (VERTREP) operations. The ship has a helicopter flight deck (and hangars) aft. (N. Polmar)

A gunner's mate loads 5-inch projectiles into the below-decks loading system for one of the 5-inch/54-cal Mk 45 guns in the destroyer JOHN YOUNG (DD 973). Each 5-inch mount is serviced by a magazine of approximately 600 standard rounds. (PH2 Felix Garza)

A pair of twin 5-inch/38-cal DP mounts on the battleship MISSOURI. As reactivated in the 1980s the IOWA-class dreadnoughts retained six of their original ten 5-inch mounts. There is a Phalanx CIWS and a Mk 56 gunfire control director above the mounts. (Giorgio Arra)

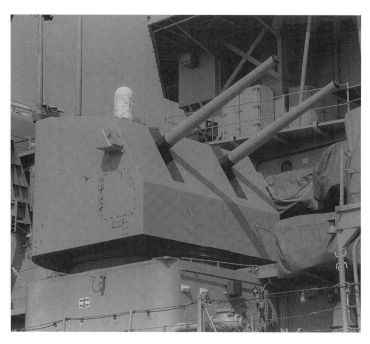

A twin 5-inch/38-cal Mk 28 mount on the battleship IOWA. The white dome atop the mount is a Phalanx CIWS on the superstructure behind the mount. Now, 5-inch/38s are found only in the mothballed IOWA-class dreadnoughts. (Giorgio Arra)

76-MM/62-CAL GUN MK 75

The OLIVER HAZARD PERRY (FFG 7)-class frigates as well as Coast Guard cutters are fitted with the 76-mm/62-cal Mk 75 gun mount. The gun system was designed by OTO Melara SpA of Italy and is generally identified by the firm's name.

The 76-mm gun is specifically designed for use in ships as small as 200 tons and is capable of engaging air or surface targets. (They were previously fitted in the U.S. PEGASUS/PHM 1 hydrofoil missile combatants.) The gun is remotely controlled with a small, unmanned mount. The ready magazine holds 70 rounds, plus six rounds in hoist and four in the drum, permitting a single operator to fire 80 rounds without "reloading."

Status: Operational. No longer in production for U.S. ships.

The Mk 75 gun is also used by several foreign navies.

Mount:	single
Gun barrel:	Mk 75
Muzzle velocity:	3,000 ft/sec (915 m/sec)
Weight:	16,400 lbs (7,439 kg)
Rate of fire:	approx. 80 rounds/minute
Maximum range:	approx. 21,000 yds (19,207 m) at 45° elevation
	approx. 39,000 ft (11,890 m) at 85° elevation
Projectile weight:	14 lbs (6.29 kg)
Fire control:	Mk 92 GFCS
Crew:	3
Ships:	*frigates* FFG 7
	cutters WHEC 715
	WMEC 901

The only U.S. Navy ships that mount the 76-mm/62-cal Mk 75 gun are frigates of the OLIVER HAZARD PERRY (FFG 7) class. Previously the Mk 75 was fitted in the PEGASUS (PHM 1)-class hydrofoil patrol/missile craft. Two Coast Guard cutter classes mount the Mk 75. (U.S. Navy)

The 76-mm/62-cal Mk 75 gun mount on the frigate THACH (FFG 43). Most Cold War–era frigates prior to the PERRY class mounted 5-inch dual-purpose guns. Several foreign navies use the Mk 75 gun. (Giorgio Arra)

3-INCH/50-CAL (76-MM) GUN MK 33

The large number of 3-inch/50-cal anti-aircraft guns fitted from the early 1950s onward in large numbers of surface combatants, amphibious ships, and fleet auxiliaries have been entirely removed, except for several amphibious ships that are in reserve. The guns were generally ineffective and difficult to maintain. Amphibious ships and auxiliaries have been refitted with the Phalanx CIWS and/or Sea Sparrow point-defense missiles in place of some 3-inch mounts.

These are open or shielded (unarmored) mounts. They have two open, drum-type magazines for each barrel, which are hand-loaded.

Status: Operational. No longer in production. These guns survive in the U.S. Navy only in mothballed amphibious ships.

Mount:	twin
Gun barrel:	Mk 22
Muzzle velocity:	2,650 ft/sec (808 m/sec)
Weight:	approx. 33,000 lbs (14,969 kg)
Rate of fire:	50 rounds/minute per barrel
Maximum range:	14,041 yds (12,842 m) at 45° elevation
	29,367 ft (8,953 m) at 85° elevation
Projectile weight:	7 lbs (3.2 kg)
Fire control:	local control only
Crew:	12
Ships:	*amphibious* LKA 113

81-MM MORTAR MK 2

This weapon is no longer generally fitted in Navy or Coast Guard patrol craft (PB/WPB). It usually was mounted in tandem with a .50-cal machine gun.

60-MM ELECTROTHERMAL TECHNOLOGY DEMONSTRATOR

This is a technology demonstration model of a 60-mm Electrothermal (ET) gun intended for shipboard use in the CIWS role. After initial ET testing, the gun was delivered to the Naval Surface Warfare Center at Dahlgren, Va., in May 1998 for additional testing firings and tests with advanced projectile propellants and "smart munitions"; test firings at Dahlgren began in August 1998.

The ET gun and automatic loader are mounted on a Mk 15 CIWS trunnion assembly. The barrel length is 16 feet 11 inches (5.16 m). The propelling charge for the gun has an electrical energy output of 1.0 to 2.0 megajoules, providing a projectile acceleration rate of 30,000 to 45,000 g's.

In operational use, the gun would fire in bursts of ten rounds, using command-guided projectiles or conventional ammunition.

No production or shipboard installation is now planned.

Status: Development (United Defense).

Gun barrel:	
Muzzle velocity:	4,265 ft/sec (1,300 m/sec)
Weight:	
Rate of fire:	200 rounds/minute
Maximum range:	
Projectile weight:	6 lbs (2.7 kg)
Fire control:	
Crew:	

A dated but unusual photo showing the loading procedures for the 3-inch/50-cal Mk 33 twin gun mount. There are rotating ready ammunition racks adjacent to the gun breeches. These hand-loaded guns had limited effectiveness against aerial targets. (U.S. Navy)

A 3-inch/50-cal (76-mm) Mk 33 twin gun mount fitted with a shield. The only U.S. ships still having Mk 33 gun mounts are mothballed amphibious cargo ships of the CHARLESTON (LKA 113) class and landing ships of the NEWPORT (LST 1179) class. (U.S. Navy)

The breech of the 60-mm ET technology demonstrator. The rotary magazine is visible in this view. (United Defense/FMC)

Although still a long way in the future, the Electrothermal (ET) gun is certainly a possible 21st-century weapon for U.S. warships. This was a test firing of the technology demonstration model of a 60-mm ET gun at Elk River, Minn. Note the muzzle blast. (United Defense/FMC)

40-MM GRENADE LAUNCHER MK 19

Numerous Navy auxiliaries and small combatants and Coast Guard cutters have the 40-mm Mk 19 grenade launcher. It is usually fitted to the Mk 64 machine gun mount. The Mk 19 barrel is 43 inches (1.1 m) long.

The launcher is manually fired and shoots high-velocity 40-mm grenades from linked belts. The rounds are configured in an armor-piercing shape, having been initially designed to counter lightly armored vehicles. (The Mk 19 can also be mounted on land vehicles and helicopters.)

Effective range is generally cited as 1,650 yards (1,509 m).

Status: Operational.

Gun barrel:	
Muzzle velocity:	800 ft/sec (244 m/sec)
Weight:	72.5 lbs (33 kg)
Rate of fire:	325 to 375 rounds/minute
Maximum range:	2,400 yds (2,195 m)
Projectile weight:	
Fire control:	open sight
Crew:	1
Ships:	various

A 40-mm Mk 19 grenade launcher during a firing demonstration. This weapon is used by ground forces and is aboard Navy ships and Coast Guard cutters. The weapon is also mounted in a variety of ground combat vehicles.

A sailor cleans the barrel of a 40-mm Mk 19 Mod 3 grenade launcher aboard a PB Mk III patrol craft. This craft was in the Persian Gulf at the time, resting high and dry aboard a support barge. (U.S. Navy)

30-MM GUN MK 44

This is a 30-mm version of the 25-mm Bushmaster (see below), referred to as the Bushmaster II. It is proposed by Boeing as a successor to the 25-mm weapon in U.S. Navy ships.

Unlike the Mk 38 gun, this weapon would have a stabilized mount to permit firing in rough seas. It would also have greater range. It has 70 percent commonality with the earlier Bushmaster gun and 90 percent commonality in gunner and maintenance training.

The Bushmaster II is being fitted in the U.S. Marines Corps's Advanced Amphibian Assault Vehicle (AAAV) and is being produced for the Norwegian and Swiss armies. Boeing has proposed Bushmaster II for ships of the SAN ANTONIO (LPD 17) class.

A 35-mm version—referred to as the Bushmaster III—is being developed.

25-MM/87-CAL GUN MK 38

This is a rapid-fire cannon known as the Bushmaster, or Chain Gun®. It provides close-in defense in a number of Navy ships and is the main armament of the CYCLONE (PC 1) class. In the larger Navy surface combatants (up to cruisers) and in amphibious ships, the guns are installed on a temporary basis as the ships deploy to areas where they are subject to enemy small-craft attack (e.g., the Persian Gulf). The weapon is also fitted in Coast Guard cutters.

The term "chain" is derived from the unusual mechanism of the externally powered, endless roller chain riding in a "racetrack" around one driven and three idling sprockets. A chain drive slider, mounted on the master link, travels back and forth in a transverse slot on the underside of the bolt carrier; its reciprocal action opens and closes the breech on the single barrel at a rapid rate. This design is simpler and more reliable than other external-power gun mechanisms.

The gun has an M242 single barrel fitted on the M88 mounting. It can be selected to different rates of fire. The Mk 88 mount is not stabilized and the gun is manually aimed. The weapon is also fitted in the Army's Bradley Armored Fighting Vehicle (AFV) and the Marine Corps's Light Armored Vehicle (LAV).

Status: Operational. In production. The naval guns were first procured in 1986. (The first Bushmaster guns were delivered in 1981; more than 10,500 guns have been produced for all users.)

Mount:	single
Gun barrel:	M242
Muzzle velocity:	3,600 ft/sec (1,100 m/sec)
Weight:	1,250 lbs (567 kg)
Rate of fire:	variable; single shot, or 100 or 200 rounds/minute
Effective range:	2,500 yds (2,287 m)
Projectile weight:	1.1 lbs (0.5 kg)
Fire control:	optical
Crew:	2
Ships:	various

A 25-mm/87-cal Mk 38 Bushmaster gun. The Bushmaster is a simple weapon to fire and maintain. (U.S. Navy)

The after 25-mm/87-cal Mk 38 Bushmaster gun in a patrol craft of the CYCLONE (PC 1) class. The PCs currently are the only Navy ships with "fixed" Bushmaster gun mounts. (U.S. Navy)

20-MM GUNS MK 67 AND MK 68

The similar single-barrel, 20-mm Mk 67 and Mk 68 cannon are fitted on auxiliary and amphibious ships, as well as Coast Guard cutters and patrol boats, for close-in defense against surface craft. These are refinements of the Oerlikon design. The Mk 67 has a lightweight mounting.

Earlier 20-mm guns fitted in U.S. Navy ships included the Mk 10 and Mk 24; all have been withdrawn from U.S. service.

Status: Operational. In production.

A 25-mm/87-cal Mk 38 Bushmaster gun fitted aboard a forward-deployed warship. The gun is fitted to numerous U.S. Navy ships and Coast Guard cutters. Improved 25-mm and 30-mm variants are proposed. (U.S. Navy)

Mount:	single
Gun barrel:	Mk 16 Mod 5
Muzzle velocity:	2,740 ft/sec (835 m/sec)
Weight:	Mk 67 475 lbs (215 kg)
	Mk 68 900 lbs (408 kg)
Rate of fire:	800 rounds/minute
Maximum range:	4,800 yds (4,390 m)
Projectile weight:	0.75 lbs (0.3 kg)
Fire control:	open sight
Crew:	2
Ships:	various

A sailor stands by a 20-mm gun on the fantail of a PB Mk III during operations in the Persian Gulf. The guns are now fitted in large U.S. naval ships during forward deployments for use—along with the 25-mm Bushmaster—against attacking small craft. (U.S. Navy)

20-MM/76-CAL CLOSE-IN WEAPON SYSTEM MK 16

The Phalanx Close-In Weapon System (CIWS) is intended to defeat attacking anti-ship cruise missiles. The installation of Phalanx CIWS followed by several years the appearance of similar rapid-fire gun systems, of larger caliber, in Soviet surface warships.

The Phalanx underwent initial at-sea tests in the destroyer KING (DDG 41, then-DLG 10) from August 1973 to March 1974, with operational suitability tests in the destroyer BIGELOW (DD 942) from November 1976 to 1978. Production was initiated in December 1977.

The Phalanx CIWS is a totally integrated weapon system that includes the VPS-2 search and track radar, gun, magazine, weapon control unit, and associated electronics, all fitted into a single unit 15 feet (4.6 m) high and weighing about six tons. Thus, it is suitable for small combat craft (and is fitted in Saudi Arabian and Israeli missile craft) as well as larger warships; also, it can be rapidly installed—in 24 hours in an emergency situation. The U.S. Navy has some 300 mounts in the fleet, from single guns in frigates to four mounts in IOWA-class battleships and some aircraft carriers. Another 200 CIWS mounts are in ships of some 20 other navies.

The CIWS is designated both Mk 15 and Mk 16 by the U.S. Navy (see *Designation*), with the 20-mm gun subsystem designated Mk 26. The gun is a six-barrel Gatling gun, adopted from the Air Force M61 Vulcan gun series, which is used in several types of aircraft and ground-mounted for airfield defense.

The gun is hydraulically powered with a theoretical firing rate of 3,000 rounds per minute, a very low dispersion rate, and initially a 980-round magazine; later guns have a 1,550-round magazine and the earlier weapons are being upgraded. The diameter of the penetrator is only 12.75 millimeters and is fired in a nylon sabot with an aluminum pusher that imparts spin to the projectile. The sabot and pusher break away after the round leaves the muzzle with a velocity of 1,000 feet (305 m) per second.

The mount's built-in J-band, pulse-Doppler radar combines several functions and follows the bullets in flight to make corrections for the next burst being fired. Early Navy analyses indicated that about 200 rounds would be fired per gun in each engagement against a missile.

All engagement functions are performed automatically with a high-speed digital computer. When active, the CIWS will engage any

The 20-mm/76-cal Mk 16—the Phalanx Close-In Weapon System (CIWS)—is found in all active U.S. carriers, cruisers, destroyers, frigates, and amphibious ships. This Phalanx is one of two fitted in the cruiser GETTYSBURG. (N. Polmar)

incoming, high-speed target unless the operator holds fire. Reaction time for the CIWS is less than two seconds from the threat being detected and identified.

The Block 1B upgrade of the Phalanx CIWS provides a capability against small, fast-moving surface craft. The basic radar has been integrated with an electro-optical sensor. The PERRY-class frigates will be the first U.S. ships to be fitted with the Block 1B upgrade. The frigate UNDERWOOD (FFG 36) carried out trials of the Block 1B in 1999.

A Phalanx CIWS on an Australian destroyer spews forth bullets during a test firing. Note the enlarged, circular magazine under the gun's barrels. Several other navies, as well as the U.S. Coast Guard, have the Phalanx CIWS in their ships. (Royal Australian Navy)

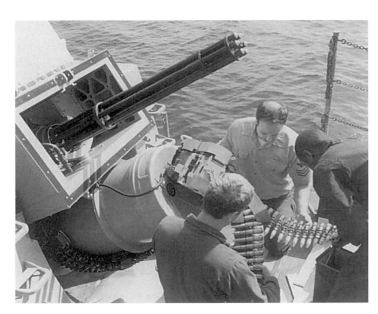

Sailors load a Phalanx CIWS on a U.S. warship. (General Dynamics/Pomona)

Designation: The Phalanx CIWS is designated Mk 15 and consists of one to four CIWS Weapon Groups Mk 16. The latter is the designation of the above-deck portion of the system, consisting of the actual gun, magazine, radar, and weapons control unit. The below-deck components of the Mk 15 are control panels.

Status: Operational. In production. IOC in 1980 on the CORAL SEA (CV 43).

In 1981 the Japanese destroyer KURAMA became the first foreign ship to mount the Phalanx; it is also used by Australia, Canada, Great Britain, Greece, Israel, Portugal, Saudi Arabia, and Taiwan.

Mount:	single
Gun barrel:	Mk 26
Muzzle velocity:	
Weight:	approx. 12,000 lbs (5,443 kg)
Rate of fire:	3,000 rounds/minute
Maximum range:	1,625 yds (1,486 m)
Projectile weight:	
Fire control:	self-contained Ku-band search radar; digital Moving Target Indicator (MTI)
	electro-optical sensor added in Block 1B CIWS
Crew:	(unmanned)
Ships:	various

NAVAL MINES

The U.S. Navy has a significant inventory of mines.[7] However, except for the CAPTOR (Encapsulated Torpedo) anti-submarine mine, these weapons are rapidly reaching obsolescence and have limited effectiveness against modern, quiet submarines. The Quickstrike mines and the Submarine-Launched Mobile Mine (SLMM) do have some effectiveness against surface ships— a secondary target. The CAPTOR is the Navy's only deep-water mine, i.e., suitable for use down to depths of some 3,000 feet (915 m).

Only one new mine is in development: the Improved Submarine-Launched Mobile Mine (ISLMM).

The Navy's existing mines are based largely on technology of the 1950s and 1960s. The Quickstrike and Destructor mines were revolutionary in that they permitted the rapid adaptation of standard aircraft bombs for use as mines. Further, standard bomb-handling facilities on aircraft carriers can ready the mines, and standard carrier-based and maritime patrol aircraft can carry them.

---

7. The author is in debt to Dr. Scott C. Truver, coauthor with Gregory Hartmann of *Weapons That Wait: Mine Warfare in the U.S. Navy* (Annapolis, Md.: Naval Institute Press, 1991), and to Stephen H. Keller for their assistance in writing this section. Dr. Truver also is editor of the Navy's official Mine Warfare Plan.

The Destructor *(above)* and Quickstrike mines were developed by inserting a fusing device into an "iron bomb," converting them into relatively simple but, in some situations, effective bottom mines for use in shallow water. (U.S. Navy)

An F/A-18 Hornet releases Mk 63 Quickstrike mines during an evaluation mission. The last major U.S. naval mining operation was flown in 1972 against Haiphong and other North Vietnamese ports; it was executed by carrier-based aircraft. Naval mines were used against *land* targets and for mining river approaches during the Persian Gulf War of 1991. (Randy Hepp)

The Quickstrike mine series—with the exception of the Mk 65—consists of Mk 80–series aircraft bombs with kit conversions enabling them to be used as shallow-water bottom mines. These mines can be activated by one or more influence firing mechanisms and are fitted with Target Detection Devices (TDD) that are inserted prior to the mines being laid. These weapons are effective against surface ships as well as submarines. Further, the Mk 57 TDD enables these mines to be dropped on land targets.

The Mk 65 was the only weapon of the Quickstrike series designed specifically for use as a mine.

The Destructor (DST) mine series was developed during the Vietnam War in response to the need for large numbers of mines. These mines also employ the standard Mk 80–series aircraft bombs that, with the insertion of the Mk 42 firing mechanism and Mk 32 safety/arming device, could be employed as mines. The Destructors have been succeeded by the Quickstrike weapons.

See 16th edition/pages 436–437 for characteristics of Destructor mines (Mk 36, 40, and 41).

No mines are currently being procured, pending the advent of the ISLMM. The last procurement program was the CAPTOR mines in fiscal year 1986.

Aircraft. The principal U.S. means of minelaying is by aircraft. The Navy's carrier-based S-3B Viking sea control aircraft and the land-based P-3 Orion maritime patrol/ASW aircraft are configured for minelaying. The F/A-18 Hornet also can lay mines, but the availability of that aircraft for the offensive mine mission is questionable and its mine payload is limited.

The U.S. Air Force operates almost 200 strategic bombers that can lay mines: 21 B-2A Spirit (stealth), 93 B-1B Lancer, and 76 B-52H Stratofortress aircraft; the B-52H can deploy all air-dropped naval mines currently in inventory. However, like the F/A-18, the availability of those aircraft for minelaying missions is questionable at best.

The F/A-18 and F-14 carry mines externally; the P-3C and S-3B carry mines in their weapons bay and on wing pylons. The B-1B and B-52H carry mines internally, with the latter aircraft also having wing pylons for bombs/mines.

The Department of Defense has evaluated the feasibility of employing C-130, C-141, and C-5 cargo aircraft in the minelaying role under a program called CAML (Cargo Aircraft Minelaying). A C-130 Hercules with the CAML rig fitted could carry 16 2,000-pound (907-kg) mines.

Submarines. U.S. submarines of the Improved Los Angeles (SSN 751) and Seawolf (SSN 21) classes are configured to launch the SLMM and CAPTOR mines.[8] However, mines can be carried by submarines only at the expense of torpedoes or tube-launched Tomahawk weapons. Submarines at sea when a mining decision is made would have to return to port, unload some or all of their other weapons, load mines, and then undertake the mining mission. Depending upon how many mines were carried, they could be required to then return to port and rearm before undertaking

8. The basic Los Angeles–class submarines (SSN 688–725 and 750) were not configured to carry mines.

Table 28-1 AIRCRAFT MINE CAPACITIES

	F-14	F/A-18	S-3B	P-3C	B-1B	B-2	B-52H
Mine Mk 56	—	4	2	6	—	—	20
CAPTOR Mk 60	—	4	2	6	—	—	18
Quickstrike Mk 62	4	10	10	18	84	80	51
Quickstrike Mk 63	—	4	4	11	—	—	18
Quickstrike Mk 65	—	4	2	6	—	—	18

anti-submarine or anti-shipping operations. Alternatively, during a period of crisis some submarines could be preloaded with mines, again at the expense of other weapons.

Surface ships. No U.S. surface ships are employed to lay mines, except in exercises for minesweepers or swimmers. Only the CAPTOR mine can be laid from surface ships.

In the following listings, *shallow* mines are laid to a maximum depth of approximately 600 feet (182 m), *medium-depth* mines down to about 1,000 feet (305 m), and *deep-water* mines down to about 3,000 feet (915 m).

Operational: The Destructor mine series was used in large numbers during the Vietnam War, being dropped in coastal waters, river deltas, and rivers, as well as along roads and trails.

During the Persian Gulf War in 1991, naval aircraft employed bombs modified with Destructor kits in attacking Iraqi airfields.

An aerial mining operation was also undertaken in an attempt to isolate Iraqi naval craft in the northern Persian Gulf from the port facilities and naval bases at Al-Basrah, Az-Zubayr, and Umm Qasr, and to prevent Iraqi naval craft from leaving those bases. On 18 January 1991 the mining operation was flown against the mouth of the Khawr Az-Zubayr River.

That mission consisted of 18 aircraft from the carrier RANGER (CV 61), including four A-6E Intruders carrying a total of 48 Destructor Mk 36 mines. Forty-two of the mines were successfully dropped at four separate locations in the river (six mines on one aircraft failed to release; the plane was diverted to an airfield in Bahrain, where the mines were offloaded before the A-6E returned to the RANGER). One A-6E was lost to enemy fire during the mission.

IMPROVED SUBMARINE-LAUNCHED MOBILE MINE (ISLMM)

Mobile mines permit the covert mining by submarines in waters that are inaccessible to other means of mine delivery. The Improved Submarine-Launched Mobile Mine will replace the SLMM Mk 67 (see below), which is outdated and being phased out of service. The

ISLMM is based on early model Mk 48 torpedoes (see Torpedoes for characteristics).

Like the SLMM, the improved weapon will be launched by a submarine, execute diversionary "dogleg" maneuvers, and then enter the minefield area. Upon reaching the target area, the ISLMM will release one mine at a preselected location and then carry a second mine to a second preselected drop area.

The ISLMM is planned to provide increased range, more precise emplacement, and lower-cost maintenance in comparison with the original SLMM. The new weapon is being developed as a joint effort with the Australian navy, which also uses the Mk 48 torpedo.

Current plans provide for a three-year engineering and manufacturing development phase beginning in fiscal year 2000, followed by a three-year procurement phase beginning in fiscal year 2002.

SUBMARINE-LAUNCHED MOBILE MINE (SLMM) MK 67

Based on the Mk 37 torpedo, the SLMM is a shallow-water bottom mine for use against surface ships as well as submarines. This is currently the U.S. Navy's only self-propelled mine; its electric motor provides a range of up to 17,500 yards (16,000 m). The SLMM is obsolescent and is being phased out of service.

The SLMM is a modified Mk 37 Mod 2 torpedo, with the wire guidance removed and a sensor, arming device, exploder, and associated battery installed.

Procurement of the SLMM ended far short of the goal announced in the early 1980s of 2,400 weapons.

Status: Operational. IOC in 1987.

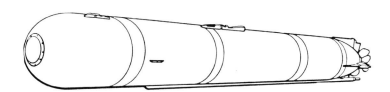

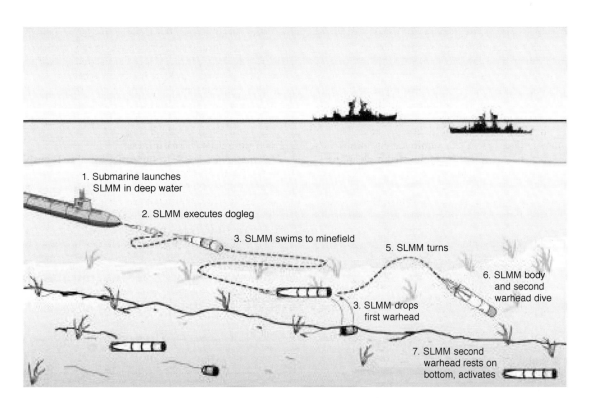

The Improved Submarine-Launched Mobile Mine (ISLMM) takes advantage of the range and payload of the Mk 48 heavy torpedo to provide a long-range, two-warhead mining system. This sketch shows the "flight path" of an ISLMM. (U.S. Navy)

Type:	self-propelled, shallow/bottom
Targets:	surface ships, submarines
Weight:	1,765 lbs (801 kg)
Length:	13 ft 5 in (4.1 m)
Diameter:	19 in (485 mm)
Warhead:	515 lbs (233.6 kg) PBXN-103 high explosive
Depth:	328 ft (100 m) maximum
Sensor:	Mod 0 TDD Mk 57 magnetic/seismic
	Mod 1 TDD Mk 58 magnetic/seismic/pressure
	Mod 2 Mk 42 firing mechanism magnetic/seismic
Delivery platforms:	submarines

QUICKSTRIKE MK 65

The only weapon in the Quickstrike series designed specifically as a mine, the Mk 65 is the U.S. Navy's largest mine. With a thin-wall mine casing in lieu of the thick-wall casing of the Mk 80–series bombs, the Mk 65 is fully compatible with naval aircraft, as well as the Air Force B-1B Lancer.

Status: Operational. IOC in 1983.

Type:	shallow/bottom
Targets:	submarines, surface ships
Weight:	2,390 lbs (1,084 kg)
Length:	9 ft 2 in (2.8 m)
Diameter:	20.9 in (531 mm)
Warhead:	HBX high explosive
Depth:	300 ft (91.5 m) maximum
Sensor:	Mod 0 TDD Mk 57 magnetic/seismic
	Mod 1 TDD Mk 58 magnetic/seismic/pressure
	Mod 3 TDD Mk 71 magnetic/seismic/pressure
Delivery platforms:	aircraft

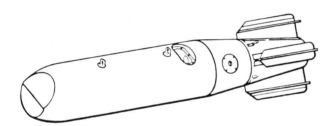

QUICKSTRIKE MK 64

This mine, a modified Mk 84 2,000-pound bomb with a thick-walled casing, is no longer available.

See 15th Edition/page 472 for characteristics.

QUICKSTRIKE MK 63

This is a modified Mk 83 1,000-pound bomb, fitted with various target detection devices.

Status: Operational.

Type:	shallow/bottom
Targets:	submarines, surface ships
Weight:[9]	985 lbs (447 kg) FC
	1,105 lbs (501 kg) LD
Length:	9 ft 5 in (2.9 m)
Diameter:	14 in (355.5 mm)
Warhead:	450 lbs (204 kg) H-6 high explosive
Depth:	300 ft (91.5 m) maximum
Sensor:	TDD Mk 57 magnetic/seismic
	TDD Mk 71 magnetic/seismic/pressure
Delivery platforms:	aircraft

QUICKSTRIKE MK 62

This mine is a modified Mk 82 500-pound bomb, fitted with various target detection devices.

Status: Operational.

---

9. CF = Conical Fixed tail assembly; LD = extending Low Drag tail assembly.

Type:	shallow/bottom
Targets:	submarines, surface ships
Weight:	531 lbs (241 kg) FC
	570 lbs (258.5 kg) LD
Length:	7 ft 5 in (2.3 m)
Diameter:	10.8 in (274 mm)
Warhead:	196 lbs (89 kg) H-6 high explosive
Depth:	300 ft (91.5 m) maximum
Sensor:	Mod 0 TDD Mk 57 magnetic/seismic
	Mod 3 TDD Mk 71 magnetic/seismic/pressure
Delivery platforms:	aircraft

CAPTOR MK 60

The CAPTOR (Encapsulated Torpedo) is the Navy's only deep-water mine. It is an anti-submarine mine, laid by aircraft or submarine (aircraft-laid mines are lowered to the water by parachute). Upon being laid, the CAPTOR is anchored to the ocean floor.

The Mk 60 acoustically detects passing submarines, ignoring surface ships (or submarines on or near the surface). Upon detecting a hostile submarine, the CAPTOR launches a Mk 46 Mod 4 torpedo. Mine life in water can be several months. The detection range is credited as 1,093 yards (333 m).

All are now Mod 1 versions, with improved effectiveness against shallow-water targets. (Mod 0 mines were upgraded to the Mod 1 configuration.)

The CAPTOR suffered from significant development and operational problems. These led to several production delays. Another problem is that the mine has the relatively small warhead of the Mk 46 torpedo.

Status: Operational. IOC in September 1979.

Type:	deep/moored
Targets:	submarines
Weight:	2,321 lbs (1,053 kg)
Length:	12 ft 1 in (3.68 m) for aircraft launch
	11 ft (3.35 m) for submarine launch
Diameter:	21 in (533 mm)
Warhead:	96 lbs (43.5 kg) PXBN-103 high explosive (in Mk 46 Mod 4 or Mod 6 torpedo)
Depth:	3,000 ft (915 m) maximum
Sensor:	acoustic
Delivery platforms:	aircraft, submarines

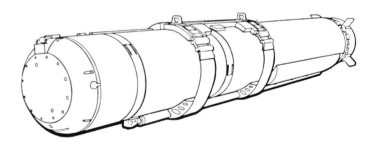

MINE MK 57

This was a medium-depth, moored mine similar to the Mk 56 but developed for launching from submarine torpedo tubes. It had a fiberglass casing. Operational from 1964, these mines have been discarded.

See 15th Edition/page 474 for characteristics.

MINE MK 56

This is an air-dropped mine capable of being used against surface ships and submarines. It was designed specifically for use against high-speed, deep-operating submarines of the 1960s. It is the oldest mine in U.S. Navy use.

This is the only U.S. mine now in service suitable for medium-depth water. When laid, the mine sinks to the bottom, where case and anchor separation takes place. Should the mine become embedded in the bottom sediment before the case/anchor separation and mooring take place, a slow-burning propellant in the anchor is ignited that frees the mine from the bottom. As the case rises, a hydrostat senses the preset mooring depth and arrests the cable payout.

Status: Operational. IOC in 1966.

Type:	medium/moored
Targets:	submarines, surface ships
Weight:	2,135 lbs (968 kg)
Length:	9 ft 6 in (2.9 m)
Diameter:	23.4 in (594 mm)
Warhead:	357 lbs (162 kg) HBX-3 high explosive
Depth:	1,200 ft (366 m) maximum
Sensor:	magnetic
Delivery platforms:	aircraft

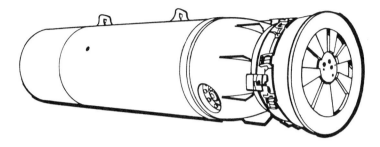

MINE MK 55

This was a modified 2,000-pound aircraft bomb, similar in concept to the Mk 52 mine except that the casing was larger and the flight equipment differed. It has been discarded.

See 15th Edition/page 474 for characteristics.

MINE MK 52

The first of a series of post–World War II ASW mines, the Mk 52 was a modified 1,000-pound aircraft bomb. Operational from 1955, it has been discarded.

See 15th Edition/page 475 for characteristics.

MISSILE LAUNCHING SYSTEMS

Several types of missile launchers are fitted in U.S. warships. There are four generic types: (1) the traditional above-deck launchers, wherein missiles are pushed upward from below-deck magazines onto the launcher, which is then trained and elevated; (2) various "box"-like launchers, such as the NATO Sea Sparrow launcher and Mk 49 RAM launcher; (3) the below-deck Vertical Launching System (VLS); and (4) Harpoon missile canisters, which are fitted in a variety of U.S. Navy and foreign warships. The Mk 49, VLS, and Harpoon canisters are currently installed in new U.S. surface combatants, i.e., the ARLEIGH BURKE–class destroyers and the planned DD 21 land-attack destroyer, with the Mk 49 being backfitted in several ship classes.

The VLS provides a high degree of missile launch flexibility, more rapid launching, reduced maintenance requirements, and fewer crewmen in comparison with earlier above-deck surface-to-air missile launch systems. The Mk 41 VLS can accommodate Standard and Tomahawk missiles and the Vertical-Launch ASROC (VLA). In the future, it will be configured for a four-pack container with the Evolved Sea Sparrow Missile (ESSM).

The VLS has total flexibility in missile selection, rapid reselection if a weapon fails to launch (without having to unload or jettison the missile), some protection for the missile from weather and shrapnel in comparison with a missile on an above-deck launcher, and more efficient use of space than traditional below-deck systems.

The basic VLS consists of a series of eight-cell launch modules, plus launch control units. The missile loading/strikedown module has been removed from U.S. ships; the strikedown module took the space of three missile cells.

In the following entries, the system weight generally does not include missiles or hydraulic fluids, except that missiles *are* included for the Mk 16, Mk 25, Mk 29, and Mk 141 launchers.

The only U.S. warships that retain Armored Box Launchers (ABL) for the Tomahawk missile are the mothballed IOWA-class battleships.

The oldest warships remaining on the Naval Vessel Register, the mothballed IOWA-class battleships, were armed with two types of missile launchers. Visible on the NEW JERSEY are four sets of quad Harpoon SSM canisters, fitted between quad Armored Box Launchers (ABL) for Tomahawk SSM/TLAM missiles. (Giorgio Arra)

SEA RAM LAUNCHER

The Sea Ram is a Phalanx CIWS mount fitted with an 11-missile magazine for the Rolling Airframe Missile (RAM). The launcher employs the standard CIWS radar and the electro-optical system of the Block 1B CIWS.

A Phalanx CIWS fitted atop an 11-cell RAM missile launcher has been proposed; Electro-Optical (EO) and Infrared (IR) sensors also are fitted to the mount. The sensors—fitted to the Block 1B Phalanx—were evaluated in the frigate UNDERWOOD (FFG 36) in 1999. (Raytheon)

A Tomahawk Land-Attack Missile (TLAM) is launched from an ABL on the stern of the cruiser MISSISSIPPI (CGN 40). These launchers are now found only in IOWA-class dreadnoughts, with eight of these quad launchers fitted amidships on the 01 level. (U.S. Navy)

LAUNCHER MK 143

The Armored Box Launcher (ABL) was fitted in several non-Aegis cruisers, seven destroyers of the SPRUANCE class, and the four IOWA-class battleships. Each "box" held four Tomahawk missiles; the entire structure elevated for firing.

Two ABLs were fitted in each cruiser and SPRUANCE-class DD; eight ABLs were fitted in each battleship. In the SPRUANCE class the launchers, mounted forward to the bridge, were an alternative to the 61-cell VLS.

IOC:	1980
Type:	ABL
Missiles:	4 Tomahawk
System weight:	
Ships:	battleships

LAUNCHER MK 141 MOD 1

These are Harpoon missile canisters, fitted in quad mountings on numerous U.S. and foreign warships. They have been removed from Coast Guard cutters of the HAMILTON (WHEC 715) class, those having been the first missile launching system installed in U.S. Coast Guard ships.

The Mk 141 Mod 0 was fitted in the PEGASUS-class hydrofoil missile combatants.

IOC:	1977
Type:	canister
Missiles:	4 Harpoon
System weight:	13,000 lbs (5,897 kg)
Ships:	battleships
	cruisers
	destroyers

Eight Harpoon canisters in four-missile mounts are fitted in U.S. cruisers and destroyers. The Harpoons are "wooden rounds" in sealed canisters, which also are used to ship and store the missiles. These Harpoons are on the cruiser MOBILE BAY (CG 53). (Giorgio Arra)

LAUNCH SYSTEM MK 49

A total of 30 launchers are planned for U.S. ships; they are also being fitted in German patrol boats. Early proposals also called for firing the RAM from a modified Mk 29 NATO Sea Sparrow launcher (i.e., one configured for both weapons).

IOC:	1992
Type:	box
Missiles:	21 RAM
System weight:	12,736 lbs (5,777 kg)
Ships:	DD 963 (some units)
	LHD 1 (some units)
	LHA 1
	LSD 41

The Mk 49 RAM launcher provides more firepower than the Sea Sparrow missiles previously used for defense against anti-ship missiles. The Navy plans to replace the Mk 13 Standard-MR launcher on the remaining frigates with the Mk 49 RAM launcher. (General Dynamics/ Pomona)

LAUNCH SYSTEM MK 41 (32 CELL)

The various Mk 41 VLS configurations of eight-cell modules are shown in table 28-2. To date, the U.S. Navy uses only the standard/ strike configuration, in 64- or 32-missile batteries.

The loadout options for the standard/strike version are discussed below. The tactical VLS can accommodate Standard MR-2 (Blocks II and III), Vertical-Launch ASROC (VLA), Sea Sparrow RIM-7, and ESSM Quad Pack (Sea Sparrow) missiles. The self-defense VLS can accommodate only Sea Sparrow missiles. The system is being considered for variants of the SAN ANTONIO class and will be fitted in the DD 21 Land Attack Destroyer.

This was originally a 29-cell launcher with a loading/strikedown module; that module has been deleted from U.S. ships.

Mk 41 launchers also are fitted in ships of Australia, Canada, Germany, Japan, Netherlands, New Zealand, South Korea, Spain, and Turkey.

IOC:	1991
Type:	VLS
Missiles:	32 Standard/Tomahawk/VLA/Sea Sparrow
System weight:	approx. 94,000 lbs (42,638 kg)
Ships:	DDG 51

An eight-cell VLS module is lowered into a cruiser of the TICONDEROGA (CG 47) class. The modular armament configuration of the SPRUANCE (DD 963) design provides an excellent series of platforms for VLS. An already installed eight-cell module is visible at the bottom of the photo. (Lockheed Martin)

A Tomahawk TLAM launches from the VLS of the destroyer Fife (DD 991). During the Persian Gulf War in 1991 the Fife fired 60 Tomahawks, more than any other ship and 21 percent of the TLAMs launched in the conflict. (U.S. Navy)

LAUNCH SYSTEM MK 41 (64 CELL)

This was originally a 61-cell launcher with a loading/strikedown module; the latter has been deleted from U.S. ships.

IOC:	1986
Type:	VLS
Missiles:	64 Standard/Tomahawk/VLA/Sea Sparrow
System weight:	approx. 188,000 lbs (85,277 kg)
Ships:	CG 52
	DDG 51
	DD 963

IOC:	1974
Type:	box
Missiles:	8 NATO Sea Sparrow
System weight:	24,000 to 28,000 lbs (10,886 to 12,700 kg)
Ships:	carriers
	DD 963
	LHD 1
	AOE 1
	AOE 6

Table 28-2 VERTICAL LAUNCHING SYSTEM MK 41 CONFIGURATIONS

	Standard/Strike	Tactical	Self-Defense
Weight	32,000 lbs (14,515 kg)	29,800 lbs (13,517 kg)	26,800 lb (12,156 kg)
Deck size	134 × 100 in (3.4 × 2.54 m)	134 × 100 in (3.4 × 2.54 m)	134 × 100 in (3.4 × 2.54 m)
Height	303 in (7.7 m)	266 in (6.76 m)	209 in (5.31 m)

LAUNCH SYSTEM MK 29 MOD 0

All active U.S. aircraft carriers have two or three Mk 29 launchers; other ships have one.

The launcher box is designated Mk 132. It was derived from the Mk 16 ASROC launchers. Missiles are reloaded "by hand."

This weapon launcher is fitted in numerous foreign warships.

The eight-cell Mk 29 launch system for the Sea Sparrow point defense missile on the destroyer Comte de Grasse (DD 974). Point-defense missile systems do not qualify ships for the G—guided missile—designation. (Leo Van Ginderen)

A RIM-7 Sea Sparrow missile streaks from a NATO Sea Sparrow Mk 29 launcher aboard the carrier JOHN C. STENNIS (CVN 74). The launcher holds eight missiles, with fins and wings extended. Vertical-launch Sea Sparrow missiles have not been deployed in U.S. warships. (U.S. Navy)

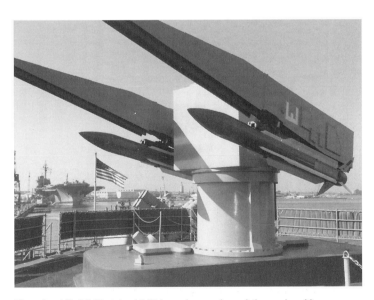

The after Mk 26 Standard-MR launcher on board the cruiser VALLEY FORGE (CG 50); these are Standard SM-1 missiles, derivatives of the Tartar SAM. These launchers are now found only on the first five ships of the TICONDEROGA class. (Jürg Kürsener)

LAUNCH SYSTEM MK 26 MOD 1

A flexible conventional missile launcher, the Mk 26 was fitted in several cruiser classes and destroyers of the KIDD (DDG 993) class. It is fitted forward and aft in the first five ships of the TICONDEROGA class.

IOC:	1976
Type:	twin-arm
Missiles:	44 Standard SM-2 MR/ASROC
System weight:	208,373 lbs (94,518 kg)
Ships:	CG 47 (CG 47–51 only)

LAUNCH SYSTEM MK 25 MOD 0

The Basic Point Defense Missile System (BPDMS) launcher is derived from the ASROC launcher. Two launchers are fitted in each of the LHA 1–class ships. These launchers are reloaded "by hand."

The launcher box is designated Mk 112.

Previously, these launchers were fitted in aircraft carriers and LPH-type amphibious ships.

IOC:	1967
Type:	box
Missiles:	8 Sea Sparrow
System weight:	32,081 lbs (14,552 kg)
Ships:	LHA 1

Loading a Sea Sparrow missile in a Mk 25 box launcher on an amphibious ship. These launchers are reloaded by hand—a lengthy, labor-intensive evolution. The few surviving Mk 25 launchers will be discarded in the near future. (U.S. Navy)

A Mk 29 Sea Sparrow launcher on a frigate. Doors of seven of the eight missile cells are open; in the Mk 29 launcher, the missiles fire through a plastic covering over the missile cells. The configurations of the Mk 25 and Mk 29 launchers are very different. (Giorgio Arra)

LAUNCH SYSTEM MK 16 MODS 1–6

These were the standard ASROC "box launchers" introduced in to the U.S. fleet in 1961. During the 1960s, 1970s, and into the 1980s, this weapon was fitted in all U.S. cruisers, destroyers, and frigates that were ASW capable. Some ASROC box launchers were modified to additionally fire Standard-ARM and Harpoon surface-to-surface missiles. There are no ASROC box launchers remaining in the U.S. fleet. The last ships to carry them were the CALIFORNIA (CGN 36) and SPRUANCE (DD 963) classes; they were deleted in the early 1990s. The box launcher is still in use in several other navies.

ASROCs also could be launched from the forward Mk 26 twin-arm launcher of cruisers and destroyers, as well as from vertical launching systems (VLA in the VLS ships).

See 15th Edition/page 476 for launcher characteristics.

LAUNCH SYSTEM MK 13 MOD 4

This was the last conventional missile launcher fitted in U.S. war-ships. Early in 2000 the Navy announced plans to replace the Mk 13 launcher in the surviving OLIVER HAZARD PERRY class with the RAM missile system.

IOC:	1978
Type:	single-arm
Missiles:	40 Standard SM-2 MR/Harpoon
System weight:	134,704 lbs (61,102 kg)
Ships:	FFG 7

The Mk 13 Standard-MR launcher on the frigate CLARK (FFG 11). These launchers also fire Harpoon anti-ship missiles. They are to be replaced by RAM launchers on the few frigates remaining in U.S. Navy service. (Leo Van Ginderen)

MISSILES

The missiles currently available or under development for the Navy and Marine Corps for use from aircraft, surface ships, and submarines are listed below. (Ground- and vehicle-launched missiles used by the Marine Corps are not listed.) They are arranged alphabetically by their names. All missiles in U.S. service or advanced development have letter-number designations, which are explained in figure 28-1.

The term *anti-radiation* is officially used for missiles that home on enemy radar transmissions; however, because of the popular confusion over the term *radiation*, which is normally associated with nuclear weapons, the term *anti-radar* is used throughout this volume.

Eight missiles are currently being procured for Navy-Marine ship/aircraft use, as shown in table 28-3. Four of those missiles are joint Navy–Air Force programs: AMRAAM, JASSM, JSOW, and Sidewinder AIM-9X. Under development is the Advanced Land Attack Missile (ALAM).

In the following entries, asterisks indicate missiles currently in production or development.

AAAM (ADVANCED AIR-TO-AIR MISSILE)

The AAAM was intended as a replacement for the Phoenix long-range AAM; it has been canceled. Tentative planning provided for the F-14D variant of the Tomcat to carry up to eight AAAMs and the F/A-18 Hornet to carry at least four AAAMs, with a total U.S. Navy procurement of 4,000 missiles envisioned. The Congress had proposed that the AAAM also be adopted by the U.S. Air Force for the F-15C/D Eagle and F-22 Advanced Tactical Fighter (ATF), although the Air Force contended that there is no requirement for the weapon on its aircraft.

See 15th Edition/page 480 for characteristics.

Figure 28-1

Explanation of Symbols

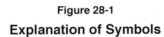

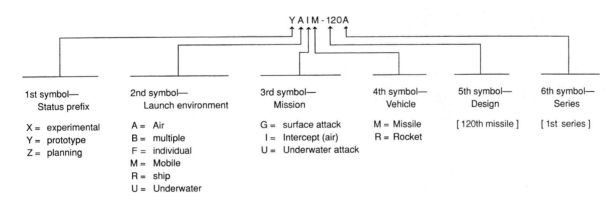

1st symbol— Status prefix	2nd symbol— Launch environment	3rd symbol— Mission	4th symbol— Vehicle	5th symbol— Design	6th symbol— Series
X = experimental Y = prototype Z = planning	A = Air B = multiple F = individual M = Mobile R = ship U = Underwater	G = surface attack I = Intercept (air) U = Underwater attack	M = Missile R = Rocket	[120th missile]	[1st series]

Table 28-3 MISSILE ACQUISITION PROGRAM

	FY 2000	FY 2001	FY 2002	FY 2003	FY 2004	FY 2005
AMRAAM	100	75	75	75	75	75
JDAM*	1,864	672	782	2,331	2,628	2,674
JSOW	454	636	762	739	663	574
RAM	90	—	100	100	130	155
Sidewinder AIM-9X	—	63	157	283	298	291
Sidewinder ESSM	—	36	85	161	143	161
SLAM-ER	20	30	30	30	30	30
Standard	86	86	108	146	180	207
TACTOM	—	—	45	90	284	342
Trident D-5	12	12	12	12	12	5

* Kits for modification of Mk 80–series bombs

ABRS (ASSAULT BALLISTIC ROCKET SYSTEM)

The ABRS—in use by the Army and Marine Corps—was proposed by the LTV Corporation for installation on the Iowa-class battleships and Newport-class landing ships to provide fire support for amphibious assaults. One concept provided for full conversion of LSTs to "rocket monitors."

In the event, the project was not pursued for shipboard use.

See 14th Edition/page 466 for characteristics.

AIWS (ADVANCED INTERDICTION WEAPON SYSTEM)

The AIWS was intended as a stand-off weapon to replace the SLAM, Maverick, Walleye, Skipper II, and Paveway guided bombs. It has been canceled.

See 15th Edition/page 480 for characteristics.

*ALAM (ADVANCED LAND ATTACK MISSILE)

The ALAM is a fire support weapon intended to succeed the Land Attack Standard Missile (LASM). It is planned as a supersonic or possibly hypersonic missile. There will be a "family" of warheads of various types.

Status: Development. IOC planned for 2009.

Prime contractor:		
Weight:		
Length:		
Span:		
Diameter:		
Propulsion:	solid-propellant rocket	
Range:	*objective* 300 n.miles (556 km)	
	threshold 200 n.miles (371 km)	
Guidance:	GPS/inertial	
Warhead:	unitary high explosive	
Platforms:	*cruisers*	CG 52
	destroyers	DD 21
		DDG 51

*AMRAAM (ADVANCED MEDIUM-RANGE AIR-TO-AIR MISSILE) AIM-120

The AMRAAM is a joint Navy–Air Force weapon developed to succeed the Sparrow AAM. The radar-guided missile has a high resistance against enemy Electronic Countermeasures (ECM) and a "snap-down" capability to engage low-flying aircraft and possibly anti-ship missiles. (The F-14 Tomcat will retain the Sparrow AIM-7 as well as the Phoenix AIM-54C missiles.)

An F/A-18C Hornet, shown carrying ten AMRAAMs mounted on four wing pylons and two fuselage hard points. Two Sidewinder missiles are mounted on the aircraft's wingtips. (Hughes)

Design: The AMRAAM is smaller than the Sparrow and, rather than the Sparrow's semi-active radar guidance, the new missile uses a mid-course inertial reference system with a sophisticated mono-pulse radar seeker for terminal guidance. Its maximum speed is approximately Mach 4.

The AIM-120B/C are updated variants, the AIM-120B with in-frared guidance and the AIM-120C adding improved aerodynamic performance. The latter also introduces smaller control surfaces to increase the missile loadout of the Air Force F-22 Raptor aircraft.

An improved AMRAAM with a range of approximately 100 n.miles (185 km) has been proposed.

The estimated cost for Air Force–Navy procurement of 15,450 missiles is $12.2 *billion.*

Operational: A small number of AMRAAMs were available to U.S. Air Force F-15 fighter-attack aircraft during the 1991 Gulf War, although none was used. In December 1992 an F-16 Fighting Falcon fired the first AMRAAM used in combat, shooting down an Iraqi MiG-25 Foxbat during a confrontation over south-ern Iraq.

Status: Operational. In production. IOC in 1991. Also used by Germany, Great Britain, Israel, Norway, and the United Arab Emir-ates, and European co-production is planned.

It is anticipated that production of the missile will total 15,450 weapons for Air Force and Navy-Marine requirements, with about a 75/25 percent split between the two forces, plus allied requirements.

The Hughes Aircraft Company also proposed the possible use of the missile from surface ships (called Sea AMRAAM), but that concept has not been pursued. However, in 1997 the Marine Corps tested a ground-launched configuration with a five-missile launcher fixed on an HMMWV vehicle; subsequently, the Marine Corps ini-tiated procurement of the ground-launched variant as the Comple-mentary Low-Altitude Weapon System (CLAWS). About 100 mis-siles are to be procured through fiscal 2006. (The Norwegian Air Force has modified some of its missiles for ground launch.)

Prime contractor:	Raytheon (formerly Hughes and Raytheon)
Weight:	335 lbs (152 kg)
Length:	12 ft (3.65 m)
Span:	1 ft 8¾ in (526 mm)
Diameter:	7 in (178 mm)
Propulsion:	solid-propellant rocket
Range:	approx. 40 n.miles (74 km)
Guidance:	inertial + active terminal radar homing
Warhead:	50 lbs (22.7 kg) high explosive
Platforms:	*aircraft* F-14D
	F/A-18

ASROC (ANTI-SUBMARINE ROCKET) RUR-5A

The ASROC was a ship-launched, ballistic ASW weapon that could be fitted with a conventional Mk 46 homing torpedo. From the early 1960s until the advent of the PERRY-class frigates, ASROC was fitted to all U.S. Navy cruisers, destroyers, and frigates. The ASROC was a short-range weapon; almost continuous proposals for an extended-range ASROC were deferred. The weapon was phased out of U.S. Navy service in the early 1990s.

A Vertical-Launch ASROC (VLA) has been developed for use in warships with VLS; see separate entry below.

The standard ASROC was fired from an eight-tube box launcher (Mk 16) and from the Mk 26 surface-to-air missile launcher. It has been employed by 11 other navies with the Mk 44/46 torpedoes.

See 15th Edition/pages 482–483 for characteristics.

Design: As delivered to the U.S. Navy, the ASROC could carry a W44 nuclear depth bomb as an alternate payload to a conventional homing torpedo. The surviving nuclear warheads were removed from the fleet in the late 1980s.

Designation: RUR-5A was a rocket, not missile, designation.

Operational: The ASROC was tested on only one occasion with a nuclear warhead, being fired from the destroyer AGERHOLM (DD 826) on 11 May 1962 in a Pacific weapons test.

Status: Operational. IOC in 1961.

AMRAAMs are moved from a weapons magazine of the carrier GEORGE WASHINGTON during operations in the Adriatic Sea in support of NATO peacekeeping operations in the Balkans. The AMRAAM replaces the long-serving Sparrow AAM. (U.S. Navy, PHAN Ryan Child)

An AMRAAM is fired from a Marine HMMWV during test firings of the surface-to-air configuration in 1997. The six-missile launch system would replace the Hawk surface-to-air missile being phased out of the Marine Corps.

ASW STAND-OFF WEAPON

See Sea Lance entry.

ATACMS (ARMY TACTICAL MISSILE SYSTEM)

The ATACMS is a long-range tactical semi-ballistic missile. The Navy considered the employment of ATACMS from surface ships (surface combatants with VLS and amphibious ships) and possibly submarines as a battlefield/naval fire support weapon for the Marine Corps. (The missile would have been launched from VLS.) The Navy has instead opted for the ALAM, LASM, and TACTOM missiles in place of a Navy ATACMS.

Proposed upgrades for a Navy ATACMS would have incorporated the GPS guidance package, increasing its range to more than 150 n.miles (280 km).

The missile has an M74 warhead that dispenses 950 M42 Anti-Personnel/Anti-Material (APAM) submunitions. The Army also plans to fit ATACMS with the BAT (Brilliant Anti-Tank) submunition.

See 16th Edition/page 44 for characteristics.

Operational: A standard Army tracked M270 two-missile ATACMS launcher was placed on the dock landing ship MOUNT VERNON (LSD 39) for missile test firings on 12 February 1995.

Status: Operational and in production for U.S. Army. IOC in the Army in 1990.

FASTHAWK

Fasthawk was a proposed low-cost, high-speed (Mach 4) cruise missile for the land-attack role. The Navy's decision to procure the ALAM missile makes development of this weapon unlikely.

Proposed by Boeing, Fasthawk was a wingless, finless missile with combination ramjet/rocket propulsion, with a solid-propellant rocket booster and an air-breathing, hydrocarbon ramjet sustainer engine. Thrust vector control provides flight control (and reduced drag compared with conventional missiles). The missile could carry a warhead of 700 pounds (317.5 kg) at a cruise altitude of 70,000 feet (21,340 m) to a range of 700 n.miles (1,300 km). Fasthawk was to be compatible with shipboard VLS.

The missile was intended to destroy time-critical and hardened targets.

GRAND SLAM

See SLAM entry.

HARM (HIGH-SPEED ANTI-RADIATION MISSILE) AGM-88

The HARM was developed by the Naval Weapons Center at China Lake, Calif., for attacking hostile radars. The missile is a successor to the Shrike AGM-45A and Standard-ARM AGM-78D missiles, providing greater range, increased velocity, greater frequency coverage, and additional flexibility in reacting to threats through an onboard computer. With respect to the last, HARM can automatically calculate threat priorities and engage the one that poses the greatest threat to friendly aircraft. It can also engage radiating targets detected at any angle from the aircraft.

The AGM-88B Block III and AGM-88C Block IV are being upgraded to the Block IIA and Block V, respectively, to provide increased capability against target radar shutdown, blanking, and "blinking." The Block V also has a capability to home on hostile jamming devices.

Note that HARM is the only weapon carried by the EA-6B Prowler electronic jamming aircraft.

Design: The latest version, the AGM-88C, is an updated AGM-88B, with 750 new guidance units having been procured.

The HARM has been criticized for high costs and in early 1986 the Navy briefly stopped accepting the missile because of manufacturing flaws.

Operational: In the Gulf War of 1991, a total of 895 HARMs were launched by Navy and Marine aircraft—more than any other missile used by U.S. naval forces in the conflict. The Tactical Air-Launched Decoy (TALD) was employed in conjunction with HARMs to entice Iraqi forces to use their radars against the decoys, marking them as HARM targets; a total of 137 TALDs were used in this manner by naval aircraft during the conflict.[10]

HARM missiles were also used in the 1999 Kosovo campaign.

Status: Operational. IOC: AGM-88 in 1984; AGM-88C in 1993. The last HARM was delivered in late 1997, with some 21,000, plus more than 1,000 guidance packages for upgrading earlier missiles, having been delivered.

HARM is also used by several foreign air forces.

Prime contractor:	Raytheon (formerly Texas Instruments)
Weight:	796 lbs (361 kg)
Length:	13 ft 7 in (4.17 m)
Span:	3 ft 8 in (1.13 m)
Diameter:	10 in (253 mm)
Propulsion:	solid-propellant rocket
Range:	approx. 80 n.miles (148 km)
Guidance:	radar homing
Warhead:	145 lbs (65.8 kg) high explosive
Platforms:	*aircraft* F/A-18
	EA-6B

---

10. In addition to TALDs launched by attack aircraft, they were also launched during the Gulf War by S-3B Vikings working in conjunction with HARM-armed aircraft to attack Iraqi radar sites.

Ordnancemen move HARM anti-radar missiles on the flight deck of the carrier CARL VINSON (CVN 70) during operations in the Persian Gulf. The missiles have not yet been fitted with wings and tail fins. EA-6B Prowlers are in the background. (U.S. Navy, PHAN José Cordero)

A HARM missile is fitted to a Marine EA-6B Prowler aboard the carrier AMERICA (CV 66) shortly before the ship was decommissioned. At the time, Marine squadron VMAQ-3 was aboard the carrier for strikes against targets in Bosnia-Herzegovina. (U.S. Navy, PH3 Brandon A. Teeples)

HARPOON AGM/RGM/UGM-84A

The Harpoon is a versatile, widely used anti-ship missile. It is the first U.S. Navy missile designed for shipboard launch against surface targets since the Regulus I, which was deployed in the 1950s, albeit primarily for the strategic, land-attack role. The Harpoon was initially conceived for aircraft use against surfaced Soviet Echo-class (Project 675) cruise missile submarines. Subsequently, the missile was developed for air, surface, and submarine launch against surface targets (it was taken off U.S. submarines in 1997).

The missile is carried in most U.S. surface combatant classes,

being launched from surface-to-air missile launchers (Mk 13) and stand-alone canisters (Mk 141). For shipboard launch, the missile has a rocket booster fitted. (Submarines could launch the Harpoon encapsulated from standard 21-inch [533-mm] torpedo tubes; in a submarine launch, the capsule rose to the surface and the missile ignited, leaving the canister.) The F/A-18, P-3C, and S-3B aircraft can carry the Harpoon.

(The Air Force modified B-52G bombers to carry up to 12 Harpoon AGM-84D missiles; those aircraft have been taken out of service.)

A Harpoon missile is released from an A-6E Intruder. Another Harpoon is carried under the aircraft's left wing. Harpoon is a versatile weapon, capable of being launched from aircraft, surface ships, and submarines. (McDonnell Douglas)

Design: Starting in 1982, the U.S. Navy took delivery of the Block 1B Harpoon with improved radar guidance and a lower flight altitude. The subsequent 1C version, first delivered in 1984, had improved guidance and burned a higher-density fuel, resulting in an increase in range to almost 80 n.miles (148.2 km).

Block 1D improvements, backfitted into earlier missiles beginning in 1992, allow the missile to reattack a target by flying a cloverleaf pattern if the missile does not acquire the target on its first approach. The 1D variant also has a 23-inch (0.6-m) fuel tank extension to almost double the missile's range. The Block II has improved guidance.

The maximum Harpoon speed is Mach 0.85. For surface ship and submarine launch, the booster burn is approximately three seconds, after which it falls off and the sustaining engine starts. Flight reliability is in excess of 93 percent.

The Harpoon forms the basis for the SLAM (Standoff Land Attack Missile).

Operational: The first combat use of the Harpoon was by U.S. naval forces against Libyan missile craft in the Gulf of Sidra in 1986.

The only known use of the Harpoon during the 1991 campaign in the Persian Gulf occurred when the Saudi Arabian missile craft FAISAL launched a single missile, which sank an Iraqi minelayer. The engagement took place early on 23 January, with the detection and missile launch being made by radar in the predawn darkness; the target ship was identified by Iraqi survivors.

Status: Operational. IOC: 1977 in surface ships and submarines; 1979 in land-based aircraft (P-3C); 1981 in carrier-based aircraft (A-6E).

Twenty other nations employ the Harpoon from surface ships and/or submarines (the submarine-launched Harpoon is called Sub-Harpoon in foreign navies). The Coast Guard briefly had Harpoon launchers on its larger cutters, and the U.S. Air Force has carried Harpoon missiles on B-52G and F-111C aircraft in the anti-shipping role.

More than 7,000 Harpoon *and* SLAM missiles have been produced for the United States and 24 other countries.

Data for the Harpoon Block 1D, unless otherwise indicated:

Prime contractor:	McDonnell Douglas
Weight:	1,390 lbs (631.8 kg) for air launch
	1,757 lbs (798.6 kg) for surface launch
Length:	14 ft 7 in (4.4 m) for air launch
	17 ft 2 in (5.2 m) for surface launch
Span:	3 ft (0.9 m)
Diameter:	13½ in (343 mm)
Propulsion:	turbojet (Teledyne CAE J402-CA-400); 600 lbst (272 kgst) + solid-propellant booster of 12,000 lbst (5,443 kgst) for surface launch
Range:	75+ n.miles (105.6+ km)
Guidance:	active radar
	GPS/inertial + active radar in Block II
Warhead:	510 lbs (231 kg) high explosive
Platforms:	*aircraft* F/A-18
	P-3C
	S-3B
	cruisers CG 47/52
	destroyers DDG 51
	DD 963
	frigates FFG 7

A Harpoon blasts out of its canister after being launched by a submarine. The spring-loaded fins and stub wings are fully deployed in this photo. Some navies call this variant the Sub-Harpoon. (McDonnell Douglas)

HELLFIRE AGM-114

The Hellfire (its name derived from "helicopter-launched fire and forget") is an anti-tank missile launched from Marine attack helicopters. The missile is intended to replace the wire-guided TOW (Tube-launched, Optically tracked, Wire-guided missile), with the Hellfire being a free-flight weapon with a longer range that permits launch-and-leave tactics.

An aviation ordnanceman prepares a Harpoon under the wing of a P-3C Orion maritime patrol aircraft. The Harpoon initially was developed for attacking Soviet cruise missile submarines on the surface. (McDonnell Douglas)

Eight Hellfire missiles are fitted on this Army helicopter's stub wing; another eight are on the right stub wing. Marine AH-1 SeaCobra helicopters can carry eight of these anti-tank missiles. (U.S. Army)

When the Army initiated development of the Hellfire in the mid-1970s, Rockwell International was the prime contractor for the sole-source program, with Martin Marietta providing the laser seeker for the missile. However, from the mid-1980s, Martin became a second production source for the missile.

Design: The Hellfire is a modular missile, allowing a variety of sensors to be fitted. The Marines use the laser-guided variant. The target can be designated for helicopters by ground-based or airborne laser designators; it affords additional survival to the launching helicopter by a lock-on-after-launch feature. A ground-launched version has been developed. There is also an anti-ship variant designated RB-17.

Operational: Hellfire missiles fired by Army AH-64 Apache helicopters against Iraqi radar sites were the first Coalition weapons launched in Operation Desert Storm in January 1991.

Status: Operational. IOC in the U.S. Army in 1985. Hellfire missiles are used by more than ten other nations.

Prime contractor:	Boeing (formerly Rockwell International and Martin Marietta)
Weight:	99.6 lbs (45.2 kg)
Length:	5 ft 4 in (1.625 m)
Span:	1 ft 1 in (0.33 m)
Diameter:	7 in (178 mm)
Propulsion:	solid-propellant rocket
Range:	3+ n.miles (5.55 km)
Guidance:	laser tracking
Warhead:	20 lbs (9 kg) high explosive
Platforms:	*helicopters* AH-1W
	SH-60B/R

*JASSM (JOINT AIR-TO-SURFACE STAND-OFF MISSILE) AGM-158

This is a precision cruise missile being designed for launch beyond the range of hostile air-defense missiles by Navy and Air Force aircraft. In the Air Force, it will succeed the Conventional Air-Launched Cruise Missile (CALCM), which was used extensively from B-52 bombers in the 1999 Kosovo campaign (the Air Force is seeking a longer-range variant).

The missile is intended to be used against hard as well as soft targets. Several different warheads will be compatible with JASSM.

The JASSM project was established in the mid-1990s following cancellation of the Tri-Service Stand-off Attack Missile (TSSAM).

Operational: The missile may also be fitted to the P-3C Orion and S-3B Viking aircraft.

Status: Development. In initial low-rate production. IOC is planned for 2003. The Air Force plans to procure 2,400 missiles; Navy procurement is planned at about 700 missiles.

Prime contractor:	Lockheed Martin
Weight:	2,250 lbs (1,020 kg)
Length:	14 ft (4.27 m)
Span:	
Diameter:	18 in (457 mm)
Propulsion:	turbojet
Range:	300 n.miles (555 km)
Guidance:	GPS/inertial + IR terminal homing
Warhead:	approx. 1,000 lbs (454 kg)
Platforms:	*aircraft* F/A-18E/F

*JDAM (JOINT DIRECT ATTACK MUNITION)

The JDAM is a joint Navy–Air Force program to develop an air-launched attack munition based on providing guidance kits to Mk 80-series bombs:

Mk 82 500-pound bomb
Mk 83/BLU-110 1,000-pound bomb
Mk 84/BLU-109 2,000-pound bomb

(The Air Force is the lead service.)

The guidance is a combined GPS/inertial navigation package that improves accuracy and all-weather capability. Accuracy is better than 10 feet (3 m) with a range of up to 15 n.miles (28 km).

In April 2000 the Boeing Corp. and Italy's Alenia demonstrated that a JDAM–Extended Range (ER) kit fitted to a 2,000-pound BLU-109 warhead could strike a target at a range of almost 25 miles (40 km). The JDAM-configured bomb, released by a U.S. Air Force F-16, was fitted with a new compressed-wing kit known as the Diamondback. In the April 2000 test, the JDAM-ER flew 15 miles (24 km) and then changed direction and traveled another 10 miles (16 km) to strike the target.

Operational: JDAM-fitted bombs were used in the 1999 Kosovo campaign.

Status: In production. The delivery of strap-on kits to the Navy began in 1998; the total Army–Navy–Air Force procurement plan is for 87,496 kits. The prime contractor is Boeing.

An AH-1W SeaCobra fires a Hellfire missile. The Hellfire anti-tank missile is accurate and has considerable penetration capability, making it useful against small surface craft. It can be launched by Navy SH-60 Seahawk helicopters, as well as by Army and Marine Corps helicopters. (U.S. Navy)

An F/A-18C Hornet from VFA-195—the first Navy squadron to use the JDAM—is shown releasing one of the modified general-purpose bombs. "Iron bombs" fitted with guidance kits provide enhanced accuracy and, usually, greater stand-off distances. (U.S. Navy)

*JSOW (JOINT STAND-OFF WEAPON) AGM-154

The JSOW is a joint development effort by the Navy and Air Force to produce the next generation of stand-off missiles. (The Navy was the lead service in development of the weapon.) The baseline JSOW is replacing the Rockeye and APAM; the planned improved JSOW will replace laser-guided bombs and the Maverick, Skipper II, and Walleye missiles.

Design: JSOW has GPS/inertial guidance and can carry a variety of warheads. The AGM-154A is armed with the BLU-97 general-purpose submunition; 145 bomblets are carried. The AGM-154B will carry the BLU-108, a "smart" anti-armor submunition. The AGM-154C will have a single, 500-pound BLU-111 warhead to provide blast-fragmentation, intended for use against bunkers and other hardened targets; it will have an infrared seeker and a man-in-the-loop data link to provide additional precision.

The wings fold atop the missile; the tail fins do not fold.

Consideration is also being given to employing the missile in an electronic jamming role.

Operational: The first use of the missile was on 25 January 1999 when three JSOWs were employed by F/A-18C aircraft against targets in Iraq.[11] Additional missiles were used in the 1999 Kosovo campaign.

Status: Operational. In production. IOC: AGM-154 in 1998; AGM-154B in 2002; AGM-154C in 2003. Some 23,800 weapons are planned for Navy–Air Force procurement, with the first acquisition being funded about fiscal 1998.

---

11. The missiles were flown out to the Middle East and transferred by air to the carrier CARL VINSON (CVN 71).

A JSOW missile is fitted on a right wing pylon of an F/A-18 Hornet on the carrier CARL VINSON while the ship was operating in the Persian Gulf. (U.S. Navy, PHAN José Cordero)

An artist's concept of a JSOW in flight, with wings extended. Several variants of the missile are in development, with slight changes in the "fuselage" configuration. The JSOW tail control surfaces are fixed. (U.S. Navy)

Prime contractor:	Raytheon (formerly Texas Instruments)
Weight:	1,000 or 1,500 lbs (454 to 680 kg); varies with warhead
Length:	13 ft 4 in (4.06 m)
Span:	
Diameter:	
Propulsion:	solid-propellant rocket
Range:	35 n.miles (65 km)
Guidance:	GPS/inertial + seeker
Warhead:	500 to 1,000 lbs (227 to 454 kg) unitary high explosive or BLU-97/BLU-108 bomblets or BAT (Brilliant Anti-Tank) sub-munition
Platforms:	*aircraft* AV-8B
	F/A-18

Another view of a JSOW mounted on an F/A-18 Hornet aboard the carrier CARL VINSON. (U.S. Navy, José Cordero)

*LASM (LAND ATTACK STANDARD MISSILE)

The LASM is a near-term weapon for the naval fire support role. It is based on the Standard surface-to-air missile and is considered an interim weapon until the ALAM becomes available about 2009. The program was initiated in 1998, with the existing Standard missile being considered the most cost-effective way to provide such a weapon to the fleet.

The LASM makes maximum use of existing Standard missile components; hence the LASM rounds will be "remanufactured" sur-face-to-air missiles with different guidance and the Mk 125 blast/fragmentation warhead. This will be a supersonic missile. The CEP is planned to be 33 to 65½ feet (10 to 20 m).

Status: Development. IOC planned for 2003. The procurement objective is 800 missiles.

Prime contractor:	
Weight:	1,800 lbs (816.5 kg)
Length:	15 ft 5½ in (4.71 m)
Span:	3 ft 6 in (1.1 m)
Diameter:	13½ in (343 mm)
Propulsion:	solid-propellant rocket
Range:	150 n.miles (278 km)
Guidance:	GPS/inertial
Warhead:	high explosive (unitary)
Platforms:	*cruisers* CG 52
	destroyers DD 21
	DD 963

LRDMM (LONG-RANGE DUAL-MODE MISSILE)

The proposed LRDMM was envisioned as a long-range (over 100-n.mile/185-km) missile for launching from Aegis ships. The missile would have been used against incoming anti-ship missiles launched at long ranges, attack bomber aircraft, and electronic jamming aircraft. At one point, it was also envisioned that the airframe could be used for the ASW Stand-Off Weapon (SOW).

The project was not pursued because of technical difficulties and uncertainty over how to conduct the outer air battle to defend battle groups against attacking Soviet cruise missile aircraft.

MAVERICK AGM-65

This is an air-to-surface missile derived from an Air Force anti-tank missile for use by Marine aircraft in the close air support role and by the Navy in the anti-ship role.

The Marines have the AGM-65E laser-guided version, compatible with air- and ground-based laser designators; the Navy's AGM-65F combines the Imaging Infrared (I^2R) of the Air Force AGM-65D missile with the warhead and propulsion sections of the AGM-65E.

Design: The Maverick is a modular missile produced in several variants, employing one of three guidance packages (television, laser, infrared), one of two warheads, and the same rocket motor. The Navy-Marine variants have a 300-pound (136-kg) penetrating blast warhead in place of the 125-pound (57-kg) shaped charge used for attacking tanks in the Air Force versions.

Operational: Maverick missiles were used in the 1999 Kosovo campaign.

Status: Operational. IOC: AGM-65E in 1985. Eighteen other nations employ the Maverick.

Prime contractor:	Hughes	
Weight:	AGM-65F 645 lbs (293 kg)	
Length:	8 ft 2 in (2.49 m)	
Span:	2 ft 4½ in (0.72 m)	
Diameter:	12 in (300 mm)	
Propulsion:	solid-propellant rocket	
Range:	12 n.miles (22 km)	
Guidance:	infrared	
Warhead:	300 lbs (136 kg) high explosive	
Platforms:	*aircraft*	AV-8B
		F/A-18
		P-3C
	helicopters	AH-1W

A Maverick ASM mounted on the wing of an S-3B Viking from squadron VS-22. In the Viking's primary roles of surface surveillance and tanker aircraft, it has been fitted with the Maverick. However, its career in these roles is short-lived with the demise of the Viking. (U.S. Navy)

A Maverick is launched from a P-3C Orion during a 1999 exercise. This aircraft, from squadron VP-4, can carry a variety of anti-ship and anti-submarine weapons. Payload versatility and long endurance make the Orion an effective maritime patrol aircraft although its ASW capabilities are limited. (U.S. Navy)

MRASM (MEDIUM-RANGE AIR-TO-SURFACE MISSILE) AGM-109

The MRASM was a joint Navy–Air Force program to develop an air-launched missile with a 250-n.mile (465-km) range for delivering submunitions against runways. It was originally to be a (shortened) variant of the Tomahawk, but during early development, significant changes were made to most components, reducing the commonality with Tomahawk. The Navy's interest in MRASM was minimal, while the Air Force's position was divided: the Tactical Air Command (TAC) had limited interest, but the Strategic Air Command (SAC) envisioned the MRASM as a useful weapon for the B-52G strategic bomber.

The MRASM program was terminated by Congress in 1983. Other weapons that could be adopted to the MRASM role at that time included the Air Force GBU-15 (an air-launched glide bomb) and the Navy's Harpoon. The Air Force Advanced Cruise Missile (ACM)—a "stealth" weapon—could also be used by strategic aircraft. In addition, there were plans for an Army–Air Force development of a common Joint Tactical Missile System (JTACMS) that could be ground launched and carried by strategic and tactical aircraft for "deep attack."

The designation AGM-109H was intended for the Air Force airfield attack weapon and the AGM-109K/L for projected Air Force and Navy anti-ship and land-attack versions.

PENGUIN AGM-119B

The Penguin Mk 3 is an anti-ship missile developed by the Norwegian Navy that is being procured for U.S. Navy use from the SH-60 Seahawk helicopter.[12] The missile has also undergone U.S. Navy evaluation for use on small craft, but that application is not being pursued; the missile was considered too heavy for use on small combatants. Kongsberg was the Norwegian producer.

Design: The missile is a "fire-and-forget" weapon with several unusual features, including an indirect flight path to target. On board ship, the Penguin is fired from a storage/launcher container that weighs 1,100 pounds (499 kg). The Mk 3 has a greater weight but a smaller wingspan than the Mk 2 that was evaluated for shipboard use; see 13th Edition/page 441.

The Penguin carries a Bullpup ASM warhead.

Maximum missile speed is approximately Mach 1.2.

Status: Operational. IOC: Mk 3 in Norwegian Air Force in 1987; in the U.S. Navy in April 1994. The original Penguin became operational on Norwegian fast attack boats in 1972; it is also used by the Australian, Greek, Swedish, and Turkish navies. The improved Mk 2 became operational in 1979 and the Mk 3 has been developed for launch from F-16 strike fighters of the Norwegian Air Force.

The current U.S. Navy procurement is 101 missiles.

Prime contractor:	Kongsberg Vaapenfabrikk (Norway) and Grumman
Weight:	820 lbs (372 kg)
Length:	10 ft 6 in (3.2 m)
Span:	3 ft 3 in (1.0 m)
Diameter:	11 in (280 mm)
Propulsion:	solid-propellant rocket + solid-propellant booster
Range:	30+ n.miles (55+ km) in air-launch mode
Guidance:	inertial + infrared homing
Warhead:	265 lbs (120 kg) high explosive
Platforms:	*helicopters* SH-60B/R

---

12. The Mk 3 missile originally was designated Mk 2 Mod 7.

An SH-60B Seahawk from squadron HSL-47 launches a Penguin ASM during a multinational exercise in the Pacific. The Penguin was the first anti-ship missile to be widely fitted to U.S. shipboard helicopters. (U.S. Navy, PH1 Spike Call)

This Penguin has just been released by an SH-60B Seahawk during evaluation by squadron VX-1. The missile's wings still are folded and the missile's rocket engine has not yet ignited. Penguins also can be launched from surface craft. (U.S. Navy, PH2 Danny Lee)

PHOENIX AIM-54

The Phoenix was developed for long-range fleet air defense against attacking Soviet bomber aircraft. It is the most sophisticated and longest-range AAM in service with any nation. The missile can be carried only by the F-14 Tomcat fighter using the AWG-9 radar/fire control system. The AWG-9 is capable of simultaneously guiding all six Phoenix missiles that can be carried by an F-14 (although six-missile loadouts are rare).

Design: The AIM-54A, with analog electronics, has been replaced in U.S. service with the AIM-54C/C+ models. The C/C+ have a digital system to allow software programming for more rapid target discrimination, improved beam attack, better resistance to ECM, longer range, increased altitude, and increased reliability. The previously used expanding, continuous-rod warheads of the early Phoenix missiles have been replaced by controlled fragmentation warheads (entering production in fiscal 1983). The AIM-54B was an interim model, similar to the AIM-54A but without the earlier missile's liquid cooling system; it did not go into production. The missile's designed range was 60 n.miles (111 km); intercepts have been made out to at least 110 n.miles (204 km). Maximum speed is approximately Mach 5.

The AIM-54C model was delayed in delivery to the fleet by quality control problems that resulted in several hundred missiles being delivered but not considered acceptable by the Navy until certain modifications were made. Production ended with the fiscal 1992 order.

Hughes Aircraft Company proposed a shipboard short-range defensive missile system in the 1970s based on the Phoenix/AWG-9; that option was not pursued.

Operational: The AIM-54A was compromised by having been provided to the Iranian Air Force prior to the fall of the Shah in 1979.

Status: Operational. IOC in 1974. More than 2,500 AIM-54A missiles were produced, as were more than 1,000 AIM-54C/C+ models.

A Phoenix is launched from an F-14A Tomcat. The missile, developed to provide long-range air defense of carrier battle groups, has limited value in tactical situations where rules of engagement usually demand visual identification of "enemy" aircraft. (Hughes Aircraft)

Phoenix AAMs on the hangar deck of the carrier THEODORE ROOSEVELT (CVN 71) are readied for being raised to the flight deck and fitted on F-14 Tomcats during Operation Allied Force in 1999. The missiles have protective covers over their nose sections until the aircraft are ready for takeoff. (U.S. Navy, PHAN James K. McNeil)

Prime contractor:	Hughes
Weight:	1,020 lbs (463 kg)
Length:	13 ft (4.0 m)
Span:	3 ft (0.915 m)
Diameter:	15 in (380 mm)
Propulsion:	solid-propellant rocket
Range:	110 n.miles (204 km)
Guidance:	semi-active radar in cruise phase; active terminal radar homing
Warhead:	133 lbs (60 kg) high explosive
Platforms:	*aircraft* F-14

POLARIS UGM-27

The Polaris Submarine-Launched Ballistic Missile (SLBM) has been retired from U.S. Navy service. It was deployed as the U.S. sea-based strategic deterrent weapon from 15 November 1960, with the first deterrent patrol of the GEORGE WASHINGTON (SSBN 598) with 16 A-1 missiles, to 1 October 1981, when the submarine ROBERT E. LEE (SSBN 601), carrying 16 A-3 missiles, was taken off alert status (she did not return to port until several days later).

The Polaris missile was produced for the U.S. Navy in three variants: The A-1 and A-2 were single-warhead missiles; the A-3 was the only Western Multiple Re-entry Vehicle (MRV) ballistic missile to be deployed. Five U.S. submarines (SSBN 598–602) carried the A-1, 13 submarines (SSBN 608–611, 616–620, 622–625) carried the A-2, and 23 submarines (SSBN 626–636, 640–645, 654–659) were originally fitted with the A-3. The first 18 submarines were subsequently rearmed with A-3 missiles (several were later rearmed with Poseidon C-3 and some of those with Trident C-4 missiles; see below).

The Royal Navy procured the A-3 variant which, fitted with a British warhead, entered service in June 1968 when the submarine RESOLUTION began the first British SSBN patrol. The Chevaline A3TK variant is being phased out of British service in favor of the Trident C-4 SLBM.

POSEIDON (C-3) UGM-73

The Poseidon SLBM was derived from the Polaris missile, with increased strike capability through a Multiple Independently targeted Re-entry Vehicle (MIRV) warhead—the first strategic missile of any nation to have that feature. The Poseidon MIRV could carry up to 14 Re-entry Vehicles (RV), with 8 to 10 being a common loadout. The RVs could be directed at specific targets within range of the warhead's "footprint." The missile range is reduced when the larger numbers of RVs were carried.

Going to sea in 1971, the Poseidon replaced the Polaris A-2 and A-3 missiles in the 31 LAFAYETTE (SSBN 726)-class submarines. Subsequently, 12 submarines of that class were upgraded to fire the Trident C-4 missile. The Poseidon patrols were terminated on 1 October 1991 when two submarines were taken off alert status; they returned to port on 15–16 October 1991. A total of 1,182 submarine patrols were carried out with Poseidon missiles from 1971 to 1991.

See 14th Edition/page 473 for characteristics.

*RAM (ROLLING AIRFRAME MISSILE) RIM-116A

The RAM is a rapid-reaction, short-range missile for shipboard defense using off-the-shelf components. It is the first U.S. Navy shipboard fire-and-forget missile and the only Navy missile that rolls during flight (i.e., is not stabilized in flight).

Design: The RAM has the infrared seeker from the Army's Stinger missile and the rocket motor, fuze, and warhead from the Sidewinder AAM; it is provided with multi-mode guidance. The missile is supersonic.

The complete RAM round consists of the RIM-116A missile and the Ex-8 sealed canister; together they are designated Ex-44. The RAM missile is fired from the 24-missile Mk 49 launcher, which uses the mount and elevation/train assemblies from the Phalanx CIWS. The launcher is reloaded by hand.

It had been proposed to also fire the missile from two of the eight cells of the NATO Sea Sparrow launcher (five missiles per cell).

Status: Operational. In production. IOC in 1992.

The Ex-31/Mk 49 launcher was evaluated in the destroyer DAVID R. RAY (DD 971) in the late 1980s. The first two production launchers were installed in the helicopter carrier PELELIU (LHA 5) in 1992 (with the Sea Sparrow launchers being removed). The Navy plans to provide approximately 80 ships with one or two launchers. Early in 2000 the Navy revealed plans to provide frigates of the PERRY class with Mk 29 RAM launchers in place of the ships' Mk 13 launcher for Standard-MR/Harpoon missiles.

About 1,400 RAM missiles currently are planned for procurement by the U.S. Navy.

The missile is also fitted in German small combatants.

Prime contractor:	Raytheon (formerly Hughes)	
Weight:	162 lbs (73.5 kg)	
Length:	9 ft 2 in (2.79 m)	
Span:	1 ft 5 in (434 mm)	
Diameter:	5 in (127 mm)	
Propulsion:	solid-propellant rocket	
Range:	approx. 5 n.miles (9 km)	
Guidance:	passive Radio Frequency (RF) acquisition + mid-course guidance with Infrared (IR) terminal homing, or passive RF all the way	
Warhead:	25 lbs (11.3 kg) high explosive	
Platforms:	*destroyers*	DD 963 (some ships)
	frigates	FFG 7 (some ships)
	amphibious ships	LHD 1
		LHA 1
		LPD 17
		LSD 41

A RAM, showing the forward and after fins, which retract when the missile is in its launch cell. Note the complexity of the homing warhead configuration for the missile's multimode guidance. (General Dynamics)

SEA LANCE UUM-125B

Formerly the ASW Stand-Off Weapon (SOW), the Sea Lance was to be a long-range ASW weapon. It has been canceled.

The weapon was conceived of as a common ship/submarine-launched weapon and, subsequently, a submarine-only weapon. It was to mate a rocket booster with a Mk 50 anti-submarine torpedo. Although often labeled a successor to SUBROC, the Sea Lance was to initially have only a conventional (torpedo) warhead, whereas the SUBROC carried only a nuclear depth bomb. A conventional (Mk 50) warhead would have inhibited its use at longer ranges because of the limited target localization capability of the Mk 50. Plans to provide a nuclear warhead for Sea Lance were considered but never funded.

The Sea Lance was designed for attacks out to the third sonar Convergence Zone (CZ), i.e., approximately 90 to 100 n.miles (167 to 185 km). When fitted with the conventional Mk 50 torpedo, the effective range would probably have been only the first CZ (some 30 to 35 n.miles/56 to 65 km).

The weapon was to be stowed and launched from a standard 21-inch torpedo tube in a canister, much like the Harpoon anti-ship

A RAM is fired from the 24-missile launcher evaluated in the destroyer DAVID R. RAY. The missile encountered major development problems but is now being installed in U.S. ships. (General Dynamics/Pomona)

missile and the CAPTOR encapsulated mine. When the capsule reached the surface, the missile booster was to ignite, launching the missile on a ballistic trajectory toward the target area. At a designated point, the torpedo would separate from the booster, be slowed to re-enter the water, and seek out the hostile submarine.

The technical and program difficulties proved too great for a dual surface/submarine-launched weapon, and the surface-launched weapon evolved into the Vertical-Launch ASROC (VLA). Subsequently, technical difficulties led to complete cancellation of the Sea Lance project.

The Navy's procurement goal for Sea Lance was some 2,400 missiles. See 15th Edition/page 474 for characteristics.

Name: Boeing had used the name Seahawk for the weapon before the Navy designated it Sea Lance.

SEA SPARROW RIM-7

The Sea Sparrow is a modification of the Sparrow AAM employed as an anti-ship missile defense system. The concept was developed in the 1960s to counter the threat from Soviet anti-ship weapons and is fired from the eight-cell Mk 25 box launcher of the Basic Point Defense Missile System (BPDMS) or the Mk 29 launcher of the NATO Sea Sparrow Missile (NSSM). The RIM-7M and RIM-7P missiles are currently used in this role.

The RIM-7R Evolved Sea Sparrow Missile (ESSM) is now being developed for VLS in U.S. ships. A four-pack ESSM canister would be fitted in each standard missile cell. The ESSM configuration has a dual-mode guidance combining the RIM-7P semi-active seeker with an improved infrared guidance.

The Sea Sparrow launchers are not fitted in ships that have Standard missile capabilities. The Mk 25/29 launchers are not automatically reloaded, and many ships do not have reloads on board. Several foreign navies use vertical launching systems for the Sea Sparrow.

Design: The Sea Sparrow launchers are derived from the ASROC box launcher.

The Mk 91 missile FCS is used with the NSSM and the Mk 115 with the BPDMS. Beginning in 1980, the Mk 23 Target Acquisition System (TAS) was added to the NSSM on U.S. ships to provide a self-contained system (with TAS providing a dual-mode radar and digital processor for automatic threat detection).

A compact jet vane control unit is attached to the rear of the missile for VLS launching. This device has four independent jet vanes that interact with the rocket exhaust plume to provide initial pitch-over, roll, and slew of the missile. Once the missile has achieved the proper heading for intercept and speed for normal fin control, the vane unit is jettisoned through the activation of four explosive bolts.

The RIM-7P has a combined semi-active radar homing and infrared seeker package.

Operational: The carrier SARATOGA (CV 60) accidentally launched two Sea Sparrow missiles during an exercise in the Aegean Sea on 1 October 1992. One missile struck the Turkish destroyer MAUVENET, killing five men (including the commanding officer) and injuring at least 14 others. Initial reports cited personnel failures as the cause of the accidental launches. There were no U.S. casualties in the firing.

Status: Operational. IOC: RIM-7 in 1969; RIM-7M in 1983. The Sea Sparrow launchers have been removed from several U.S. amphibious and command ships.

Thirteen other navies employ the Sea Sparrow in the missile-defense role, with some ships having vertical-launch Sea Sparrow launchers.

The following data apply to the RIM-7M. See Sparrow missile listing for additional data.

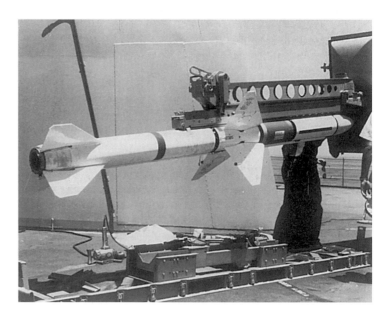

A Sea Sparrow missile is loaded into a Mk 29 launcher on board the replenishment ship KANSAS CITY (AOR 3). No ships have automatic reloading for Sea Sparrow missiles. (U.S. Navy)

A missile is launched from the NATO Sea Sparrow Mk 29 launcher on the carrier KITTY HAWK during a live-fire exercise in the Western Pacific. The debris under the missile is from breaking through the plastic covering of the launch cell. (U.S. Navy, PH3 John Sullivan)

Prime contractor:	Raytheon	
Weight:	450 lbs (204 kg)	
Length:	12 ft (3.7 m)	
Span:	3 ft 4 in (1.0 m)	
Diameter:	8 in (203 mm)	
Propulsion:	solid-propellant rocket	
Range:	approx. 10 n.miles (18.5 km)	
Guidance:	radar homing	
Warhead:	90 lbs (40.8 kg) high explosive	
Platforms:	*aircraft carriers*	CV/CVN
	destroyers	DD 963
	amphibious ships	LHD 1
		LHA 1
	auxiliaries	AOE 1

SHRIKE AGM-45

The Shrike was an anti-radar missile designed to home on hostile radar emissions. The missile was derived from the AIM-7 Sparrow for the U.S. Navy and was used in the Vietnam War from 1964 onward. The Royal Air Force used Shrike missiles (ineffectively) in the 1982 Falklands conflict. There are more than a dozen variants reflecting changes in the guidance seeker to counter different electronic threats. The Shrike suffered from a short range and in the mid-1980s was replaced by the HARM.

See 14th Edition/page 476 for characteristics.

SIAM (SELF-INITIATING ANTI-AIRCRAFT MISSILE)

The Defense Advanced Research Projects Agency (DARPA) sponsored the development of technology for the SIAM, for use by a submerged submarine against an ASW fixed-wing aircraft or helicopter. The weapon was to be launched from special tubes in the submarine and home on the attacker. The towed acoustic arrays now used by submarines could detect low-flying aircraft to initiate SIAM launch.

The concept was not new, with one earlier U.S. Navy experiment using variants of the Sidewinder missile being dubbed "Subwinder." The Royal Navy and Vickers have developed the SLAM (Submarine-Launched Air Missile) in which the submarine surfaces or at least broaches its sail to extend a six-tube Blowpipe missile launcher. The SIAM concept called for missile launch while the submarine remained completely submerged.

During demonstrations, test vehicles were successfully launched against QH-50 drone helicopters. Nevertheless, no deployment occurred.

See 14th Edition/page 476 for characteristics.

SIDEARM AGM-122A

The Sidearm is an anti-radar missile developed to counter ground-based air-defense weapons at short ranges. The missile is based on outdated AIM-9 Sidewinder AAMs that had been placed in storage in the 1970s.

Design: The Sidearm missiles have been fitted with relatively broad-band, passive-only, radar-homing, plus the active optical target-detection device from AIM-9 missiles.

Upon launch, the Sidearm executes a pitch-up maneuver that permits launch from very low altitudes—an important feature for helicopters flying in the nap-of-the-earth mode. It can be used by essentially all fixed-wing fighter aircraft. Maximum speed is Mach 2.3.

The Sidearm was developed by the missile-prolific Naval Weapons Center at China Lake, Calif. Motorola of Tempe, Ariz., converted several hundred AIM-9 missiles to the Sidearm configuration; future new production is envisioned. An improved AGM-122B version was canceled because of funding problems. The first production/remade Sidewinders were funded in fiscal 1986.

Status: Operational.

Prime contractor:	Motorola
Weight:	approx. 200 lbs (90.7 kg)
Length:	9 ft 6 in (2.9 m)
Span:	2 ft 1 in (635 mm)
Diameter:	5 in (127 mm)
Propulsion:	solid-propellant rocket motor
Range:	18,000 yds (16,463 m)
Guidance:	radar homing + electro-optical
Warhead:	10 lbs (4.5 kg) high-explosive fragmentation
Platforms:	*helicopters* AH-1W

SIDEWINDER AIM-9

The Sidewinder is the most widely used missile outside of Russia. The air-to-air weapon was used extensively by the U.S. Navy in the Vietnam War, as well as by Allied forces in other conflicts. In the 1991 Persian Gulf War, it was responsible for 24 percent of the air-to-air kills (see *Operational* notes).

The latest variant is the AIM-9X, with improved guidance and kinematics and increased resistance to infrared countermeasures.

(The AIM-132 ASRAAM [Advanced Short Range Air-to-Air Missile] was developed as a competitor to the AIM-9X Sidewinder. Both the AIM-9X and ASRAAM are fitted with the same [Raytheon-Hughes] infrared seeker. ASRAAM was initiated by Great Britain and Germany, but the two nations were unable to agree on details of the joint project. Germany left the ASRAAM project in the early 1990s and, subsequently, initiated development of an improved Sidewinder designated IRIS-T [Infrared

A Sidearm anti-radar missile fitted on an AH-1 SeaCobra helicopter (U.S. Navy)

An ordnanceman makes a final check of a Sidewinder AAM mounted on an F/A-18C Hornet from squadron VFA-87. The aircraft is about to launch from the carrier THEODORE ROOSEVELT. The Sidewinder is the most widely used aircraft missile in the U.S. arsenal. (U.S. Navy, PH2 Donné McKissic)

Imagery Sidewinder–Tail Controlled]. The British government has continued development of the ASRAAM, with the first delivery to the Royal Air Force late in 1998. Subsequently, a British-French consortium has undertaken production of the missile. The U.S. Air Force and Navy have carried out tests with ASRAAM but no U.S. procurement has been forthcoming.)

Design: Developed by the Naval Weapons Center at China Lake, Calif., the Sidewinder is a simple, effective, infrared-homing missile. The AIM-9M version is currently in production in the United States, and the AIM-9L is being built by a European

The Sidewinder AIM-9X is the latest version of this weapon, the initial version of which entered service almost a half century ago. The AIM-9X has much smaller tail fins than the earlier Sidewinders. Large-scale production of this version is expected for U.S. and, eventually, foreign air forces.

consortium and by Mitsubishi in Japan. The AIM-9M features improved resistance to ECM and can engage targets against hot backgrounds; the guidance includes digital electronics, electronic reprogramming for future software upgrades, imaging, and auto-tracking. In 1991 the Department of Defense approved full-scale development of the AIM-9R until additional upgrades become available in the AIM-9X.

The AIM-9X has an imaging infrared seeker, improved rocket motor, and enhanced maneuverability.

Missile speed is approximately Mach 2.5.

An AIM-9C with a modified anti-radar seeker is called Sidearm; see separate entry above.

Operational: The Sidewinder scored most of the air-to-air kills by U.S. Navy and Air Force aircraft in the Vietnam War, and by the Israeli Air Force in the 1967 and 1973 wars in the Middle East. During the 1982 fighting over Lebanon's Bekaa Valley, Israeli aircraft used Sidewinders to shoot down 51 of 55 Syrian-flown MiG aircraft destroyed in aerial combat. The Sidewinder was also highly successful when used by British Harrier VSTOL aircraft in the 1982 Falklands conflict.

In the 1991 Gulf War, Sidewinders were responsible for ten air-to-air kills against Iraqi aircraft, two by Navy fighters: on 17 January 1991 a MiG-21 was downed by a Navy F/A-18 Hornet,[13] and on 6 February 1991 a helicopter was downed by a Navy F-14A Tomcat. (In addition, eight Iraqi high-performance aircraft were downed by U.S. Air Force F-15C Eagles firing Sidewinder missiles.)

Status: Operational. IOC: AIM-9 in 1956; AIM-9M in 1983; AIM-9X planned for 2002. More than 125,000 Sidewinder missiles have been produced for users in more than 40 countries. At least 5,080 AIM-9X missiles are planned for procurement by the Air Force and 5,000 by the Navy and Marine Corps.

The data below are for the AIM-9L variant, except where noted.

---

13. This F/A-18 also shot down a second MiG-21 on the same mission with a Sparrow missile.

Carts loaded with Sidewinder missiles are carried to the flight deck of the carrier GEORGE WASHINGTON on a bomb elevator as the carrier operates in the Persian Gulf in support of Operation Southern Watch. These missiles have protective (yellow) caps over the nose. (U.S. Navy, PH3 Erik Kenney)

Prime contractor:	Raytheon and Ford Aerospace (Raytheon for AIM-9X)
Weight:	88 lbs (40 kg) for AIM-9H
	86½ lbs (39 kg) for AIM-9L/M
Length:	9 ft 6 in (2.87 m)
Span:	2 ft ¾ in (0.63 m) for AIM-9H
	2 ft 1 in (0.635 m) for AIM-9L/M
Diameter:	5 in (127 mm)
Propulsion:	solid-propellant rocket
Range:	approx. 10 n.miles (18.5 km)
Guidance:	infrared passive homing
Warhead:	25 lbs (11.3 kg) high explosive for AIM-9H
	20.8 lbs (9.4 kg) high explosive for AIM-9L/M
Platforms:	*aircraft* AV-8B
	F-14
	F/A-18
	helicopters AH-1W

SKIPPER II AGM-123A

The Skipper was a laser-guided, propelled bomb made up of off-the-shelf components and employing a Mk 83 1,000-pound bomb. Created by the Naval Weapons Center at China Lake, the Skipper II was an effort to produce a low-cost weapon for the air-to-surface role within a short development time. It became operational in 1985, but is no longer in use by the Navy. It was carried by the A-6E Intruder.

See 16th Edition/page 453 for characteristics.

SLAM (STAND-OFF LAND-ATTACK MISSILE) AGM-84

The SLAM is a derivative of the Harpoon anti-ship missile. It is intended for use by carrier-based aircraft in "surgical strikes" against high-value fixed targets or enemy ships at sea and is considered the most accurate air-to-surface weapon in the Navy's arsenal.

SLAM has the airframe, propulsion, and control systems of the Harpoon missile, with a combination of existing missile guidance systems: the Maverick IIR (Imaging Infrared) seeker, Walleye II data link, and GPS receiver/processor. The missile's inertial guidance system is updated by GPS fixes in flight to insure that the infrared seeker is pointed directly at the target. When the infrared seeker is activated, it sends a video image to the launching aircraft, which selects the specific aim point for the missile. After the target is locked in, the missile steers to the target. The missile can be controlled by an aircraft other than the launching plane.

In addition to aerial launch, SLAM is also intended for shipboard launch from canisters or VLS installations.

SLAM-ER kits are being used to upgrade all existing SLAM weapons (the SLAM-ER AGM-84H variant is listed separately). A further improvement of the Harpoon/SLAM weapon has been proposed by McDonnell Douglas officials, who call it "Grand Slam." The range of this variant is on the order of 185 n.miles (300 km) while carrying a 1,000-pound (453.6-kg) warhead.

The data provided below are for the air-launched configuration of SLAM; a solid-propellant rocket booster is added for shipboard launch.

Operational: The SLAM was first used in combat from A-6E Intruder and F/A-18 Hornet aircraft, controlled by A-7E Corsair attack aircraft using AAW-9 pods. The seven SLAMs used in the Persian Gulf War all struck their targets, with the infrared video providing verification of their accuracy. This was achieved despite the unreliability of the AAW-9 data-link pods (since replaced by the improved AAW-13 pods).

In a March 1995 test, four SLAM missiles were launched simultaneously by four F/A-18C Hornets; all struck the single target.

Status: Operational. In production. IOC in November 1988.

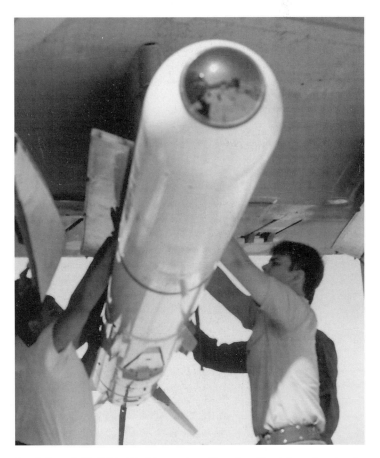

An air-launch SLAM is fitted to an aircraft's pylon. The infrared seeker is evident in the nose of the missile. (McDonnell Douglas)

A SLAM is launched from a shipboard canister. A derivative of the Harpoon missile, SLAM—like Harpoon—originally was developed for air launch. An additional section with fins is added to the missile for shipboard launch. (McDonnell Douglas)

Prime contractor:	Boeing (formerly McDonnell Douglas)
Weight:	1,385 lbs (628 kg)
Length:	14 ft 4 in (4.37 m)
Span:	3 ft (0.9 m)
Diameter:	13½ in (343 m)
Propulsion:	turbojet (Teledyne CAE J402-CA-400); 600 lbst (272 kgst)
Range:	approx. 50 n.miles (92.65 km)
Guidance:	inertial + infrared/video command homing
Warhead:	510 lbs (231 kg) high explosive
Platforms:	*aircraft* F/A-18
	P-3C

An artist's concept of the SLAM-ER in flight with gull-configured wings extended. The missile has X-configured tail fins. (McDonnell Douglas)

*SLAM-ER (STAND-OFF LAND-ATTACK MISSILE–EXPANDED RESPONSE) AGM-84H

The SLAM-ER (Expanded Response—*not* Extended Range) variant has a 50-percent increase in range (accomplished by the use of planar wings), an improved warhead for penetrating hardened targets, and an improved data link that doubles the stand-off range of the controlling aircraft, as well as enhancing resistance to jamming. It has a speed of Mach 0.8.

The SLAM-ER+ incorporates Automatic Target Acquisition (ATA), making it an autonomous weapon, enhancing its effectiveness against small targets and targets in urban environments. ATA uses a matching algorithm to recognize both the aim point and the surrounding scene.

The SLAM-ER is fitted with a GPS update receiver. It is intended for adverse-weather targeting amid clutter, especially in urban areas, with an onboard reference imaging system.

Operational: The first use of SLAM-ER was by Navy F/A-18C aircraft in the Iraqi southern no-fly zone in late 1999.

Status: Operational. In production. IOC in 1999. Some 700 existing SLAM missiles will be upgraded to the ER configuration, with additional new production of SLAM-ER continuing at least through 2004.

A SLAM-ER on the wing of an F/A-18E. The missile's wings fold for aircraft launching. The AGM-84H variant cannot be launched from surface ship canisters. (U.S. Navy, Capt. Dana Potts)

An F/A-18E Hornet releases a SLAM-ER during operational flight tests at the Naval Air Weapons Station, China Lake, Calif., in 1999. The aircraft is flown by the air wing commander (CAG) of CVW-9 aboard the carrier JOHN C. STENNIS. (U.S. Navy, Capt. Dana Potts)

Prime contractor:	Boeing
Weight:	1,600 lbs (727 kg)
Length:	14 ft 4 in (4.37 m)
Span:	7 ft 11½ in (2.4 m)
Diameter:	13½ in (343 m)
Propulsion:	turbojet (Teledyne CAE J402-CA-400); 600 lbst (272 kgst)
Range:	approx. 150 n.miles (278 km)
Guidance:	GPS/inertial + infrared/video command homing
Warhead:	510 lbs (231 kg) high explosive
Platforms:	*aircraft* F/A-18

SPARROW III AIM-7

The Sparrow is an all-weather, medium-range AAM. Surface-launched Sea Sparrow variants have been adopted for the anti-ship missile defense role (see page 512).

Design: The AIM-7M combines the heavy warhead and large rocket motor introduced in the AIM-7F with an advanced monopulse seeker, better look-down/shoot-down capability, and improved resistance to ECM. The early, expanding continuous-rod warhead of these missiles has been replaced by a fragmentation warhead.

The AIM-7R is the latest variant, combining infrared terminal guidance with semi-active radar guidance (the latter fitted in earlier versions).

Missile speed is reportedly in excess of Mach 4.

Operational: The weapon had minimal use in air-to-air engagements until the 1991 war in the Persian Gulf War, when it was credited with 68 percent of the air-to-air kills—28 of the 41 air-to-air kills against Iraqi aircraft—although only one by naval aircraft. On 17 January 1991, an Iraqi MiG-21 was shot down by a Sparrow from a Navy F/A-18 Hornet, which in the same engagement used a Sidewinder to kill a second MiG-21. (U.S. Air Force F-15C Eagles used Sparrows to shoot down 22 high-performance Iraqi aircraft and three helicopters; in addition, one Saudi F-15C Eagle used Sparrows to kill two Iraqi fighters in the same engagement.[14]) The USAF hit rate for Sparrows fired was nearly triple the rate in the Vietnam War.

---

14. In addition to the 28 Sparrow and 10 Sidewinder air-to-air kills, one Iraqi MiG-29 crashed while maneuvering to escape a USAF F-15C and two Iraqi helicopters were shot down by USAF A-10 Thunderbolt ("Warthog") attack aircraft using 30-mm Gatling guns, for a total of 41 air-to-air kills in the Gulf War.

Status: Operational. IOC: AIM-7 in 1958; AIM-7F in 1976; AIM-7M in 1983.

The AIM-7E/F/M variants are in wide U.S. Marine and Navy service, although production of those variants has ended.

The missile has been produced for U.S. and foreign air forces. In addition to the two U.S. producers, the Sparrow is manufactured in Japan by Mitsubishi. The data given below are for the AIM-7M model, except where indicated.

A Marine ordnance specialist checks a Sparrow AAM fitted to an F/A-18C from squadron VMFA-314 aboard the carrier NIMITZ during Persian Gulf operations. Tactical aircraft and weapons are interchangeable between similar Navy and Marine Corps squadrons. (U.S. Navy)

A Sparrow AAM ignites after being launched by an F/A-18C Hornet. The AIM-7 has been used in relatively few combat actions in comparison with the Sidewinder AAM because of visual-range limitations imposed by rules of engagement. (U.S. Navy)

Prime contractor:	Raytheon and General Dynamics/Pomona
Weight:	450 lbs (204 kg)
Length:	12 ft (3.7 m)
Span:	3 ft 4 in (1.1 m)
Diameter:	8 in (203 mm)
Propulsion:	solid-propellant rocket
Range:	approx. 30 n.miles (55.5 km)
Guidance:	semi-active radar homing (plus infrared in AIM-7R)
Warhead:	90 lbs (40.1 kg) high explosive with continuous rod
Platforms:	*aircraft* F-14
	F/A-18

*STANDARD-MR SM-1 RIM-66B

The Standard series of missiles is the principal surface-to-air weapon of U.S. cruisers, destroyers, and frigates. The Standard series was developed as replacement for the three "T" missiles—the Talos, Terrier, and Tartar. Initially the MR (Medium Range) missiles were to replace the Tartar and the ER (Extended Range) missiles the Terrier and Talos. However, various modifications and production blocks of Standard missiles with varying characteristics have blurred model distinctions.

Standard missiles are currently in use by the U.S. Navy and nine other navies.

The single-stage SM-1 MR replaced the Tartar SAM. It is launched only from the Mk 13 launcher, which has a 40-round vertical magazine.

Design: The Block VI is the current production variant, using the SM-2 monopulse seeker for better resistance to enemy jamming and improved fuzing. It can engage low-altitude targets at ranges out to about 10 n.miles (18.5 km).

Status: Operational. Block VI in production. IOC Standard-MR SM-1 in 1970.

Prime contractor:	Raytheon (formerly Hughes)
Weight:	1,378 lbs (625 kg)
Length:	14 ft 9 in (4.47 m)
Span:	3 ft 6 in (1.1 m)
Diameter:	13½ in (342 mm)
Propulsion:	solid-propellant rocket
Range:	25 n.miles (46 km)
Guidance:	semi-active radar homing
Warhead:	high explosive
Platforms:	*frigates* FFG 7

STANDARD-MR SM-2 RIM-66C

This missile has increased range over the SM-1 MR, as well as the addition of mid-course guidance and enhanced resistance to ECM. It is intended specifically for use on Aegis missile ships.

Design: The current Block IV variant provides significantly increased performance over all previous versions of the Standard. It is launched with a solid-propellant booster rocket. The traditional expanding, continuous-rod warheads of the Standard missiles have been succeeded by controlled fragmentation warheads.

The Block IVA missile, designated the SM-3 (see below), is configured for use in the Theater Ballistic Missile Defense (TBMD) role.

Status: Operational. Block IV in production. IOC Standard-MR SM-2 in 1981. The first at-sea firing of the SM-2 Block IV occurred in July 1994 from the LAKE ERIE (CG 70) with IOC in 1995. Block III entered production in 1988.

The Standard SM-2 ER (RIM-67B), used with the Mk 26 launcher of the KIDD (DDG 993) class, has been discarded.

A Standard-MR SM-1 missile streaks from the Mk 13 launcher on the frigate THACH (FFG 43), demonstrating the anti-air warfare capabilities of these ships. The replacement of the Mk 13 system with the RAM system is planned to make the ships more effective for littoral operations. (U.S. Navy, PH3 Lou Messing)

A Standard-MR SM-2 missile is launched from the VLS of a TICONDEROGA-class cruiser. The Standard "family" succeeded the famed "3-T" missiles—Tartar, Talos, and Terrier—the U.S. Navy's first generation of surface-to-air missiles. (United Defense/FMC)

Prime contractor:	General Dynamics/Pomona and Hughes-Raytheon
Weight:	1,554 lbs (705 kg)
Length:	15 ft 6 in (4.72 m) + booster
Span:	3 ft 6 in (1.1 m)
Diameter:	13½ in (342 mm)
Propulsion:	solid-propellant rocket + booster rocket
Range:	approx. 40 n.miles (74 km)
Guidance:	semi-active radar homing
Warhead:	high explosive
Platforms:	*cruisers* CG 47
	destroyers DDG 51

STANDARD SM-3

The SM-3 is the Standard Block IVA, a variant configured to provide exoatmospheric, theater-wide defense against theater and tactical ballistic missiles. The missile will be launched by improved TICON-DEROGA-class cruisers fitted with VLS.

The SM-3 successfully made its initial ship-launched test flight on 24 September 1999 at the Pacific Missile Range Facility at Kauai, Hawaii. Designated Control Test Vehicle 1A (CTV-1A), the missile was launched by the cruiser SHILOH (CG 67).

An earlier proposal for a Standard SM-3 missile was to provide a very-long-range missile for intercepting Soviet stand-off jamming aircraft and possibly missile-carrying aircraft at ranges greater than possible with the SM-2 ER. This was similar in concept to the LRDMM (see above); a concept called Thor also was similar. Those missiles were not pursued.

Design: The Block IVA variant has an infrared seeker, improved fuzing for high-speed intercepts, an improved warhead for use against hardened targets, and improved terminal guidance algorithm. It has a blast-fragmentation warhead.

Status: Development. An IOC of late 2005 or 2006 is planned.

A soldier firing the shoulder-held Stinger anti-aircraft missile. The weapon is used by the Army, Navy, and Marine Corps and is carried in a variety of Navy ships and small craft when forward deployed. (U.S. Army)

STANDARD-ARM AGM-78

This was an Anti-Radiation Missile (ARM) adapted from the Standard RIM-66A surface-to-air missile. It was also employed briefly by the U.S. Navy as an interim surface-to-surface missile, pending availability of the Harpoon. In the mid-1980s the Standard-ARM was replaced by the HARM.

STINGER FIM-92

The Stinger is an advanced, shoulder-held surface-to-air missile that resembles the World War II–era bazooka rocket launcher. The missile was placed aboard several U.S. naval ships in the eastern Mediterranean beginning in the winter of 1983–1984 in reaction to threatened terrorist attacks against U.S. ships; it was subsequently carried in Navy ships operating in the Persian Gulf area. (The Russian Navy similarly uses the shoulder-held SA-7 Grail missile, formerly Strela, in various ships.)

Design: Originally designated Redeye II, the missile is tube-launched, with four pop-out vanes at the front and four folding fins at the rear.

Status: Operational. IOC in 1981. The Stinger is used by the U.S. Marine Corps, Army, and Air Force, as well as by several foreign services. The missile is replacing the Redeye in U.S. service. An improved Stinger-POST (Passive Optical Seeker Technique), with increased resistance to countermeasures, entered production in fiscal 1984.

A Stinger missile in flight with fins and wings extended (U.S. Army)

Prime contractor:	General Dynamics/Pomona
Weight:	30 lbs (13.6 kg)
Length:	5 ft (1.5 m)
Span:	8 in (203 mm)
Diameter:	2¾ in (70 mm)
Propulsion:	solid-propellant rocket
Range:	approx. 3 n.miles (5.5 km); effective range is probably less
Guidance:	infrared homing
Warhead:	high explosive
Platforms:	various ships

SUBROC UUM-44A

The SUBROC (Submarine Rocket) was a rocket-propelled nuclear depth bomb that could be launched from standard 21-inch submarine torpedo tubes. The weapon was analog and hence not compatible with U.S. attack submarines having the Mk 117 digital fire control system. Thus, only about 25 submarines of the PERMIT (SSN 594) and later classes fitted with the Mk 113 fire control system carried the weapon. The missile, which became operational in 1984, was taken out of Navy service in 1989. (The Sea Lance ASW stand-off weapon was to have replaced the SUBROC, with alternative nuclear or conventional warheads, but in the event, the nuclear variant is no longer planned for development.)

See 14th Edition/pages 481–482 for characteristics.

*TACTOM (TACTICAL TOMAHAWK) BGM-109

TACTOM is the Block IV Tomahawk, an improved missile for the land-attack role.[15] It has a loiter capability to permit inflight retargeting. Also, the missile will carry a camera to provide a "snapshot" of the battlefield via a satellite data link.

The missile originally was to have been propelled by the Teledyne Continental Motors J402-CA-402 engine, which also is being used in the JASSM missile. However, on 9 December 1999, Raytheon announced a stop-work order on the engine as part of a risk-reduction effort for TACTOM. Williams International has proposed the smaller version of the firm's F-122 engine, being used in the German-Swedish Taurus missile. (Williams lost to Teledyne in the original TACTOM engine competition.)

Status: Development. IOC planned for 2003.

Prime contractor:	Raytheon
Weight:	
Length:	
Span:	
Diameter:	20.5 in (520 mm)
Propulsion:	turbojet + solid-propellant booster
Range:	1,600 n.miles (2,965 km)
Guidance:	GPS/inertial
Warhead:	
Platforms:	*cruisers* CG 52
	destroyers DD 21
	DDG 51
	DD 963
	submarines SSN 21
	SSN 774
	SSN 688

TOMAHAWK BGM-109

The Tomahawk is a long-range cruise missile developed for both surface and submarine launch against both surface ship and land targets. It was initially known as the Sea-Launched Cruise Missile (SLCM), but in 1979 the Navy began using the terms Tomahawk Land-Attack Missile (TLAM) and Tomahawk Anti-Ship Missile (TASM) to distinguish the principal variants.

The TASM was scheduled to be phased out of the fleet in favor of the Block IV Tomahawk Multi-Mission Missile (TMMM), which was to enter the fleet after 2000. That weapon was to have a common terminal sensor capable of attacking targets on both land and at sea. Instead, the TLAM will be retained and supplemented by the Tactical Tomahawk (TACTOM); see separate entry.

The Tomahawk was deployed in Armored Box Launchers (ABL) on four battleships, five cruisers, and seven SPRUANCE-class destroyers; it is carried in the vertical launchers (Mk 41) of later TICONDEROGA-class cruisers, ARLEIGH BURKE–class destroyers, and most of the SPRUANCES. It also can be fired from 21-inch submarine torpedo tubes and, in the later LOS ANGELES (SSN 688) and the VIRGINIA (SSN 774) classes, from vertical launch tubes.

---

15. In 1999 the Navy registered the names TACTOM and Tomahawk with the U.S. Patent Office, the first known effort to "protect" the names of weapons by the U.S. government. The absurdity of the action is seen in the name Tomahawk—the missile—having been in common usage for almost three decades, and the name Tomahawk—the hatchet—having been in the English language for almost 400 years!

Design: The Block III, the last production variant, features a smaller but more lethal warhead with an extended range permitted by additional fuel; these missiles also have a GPS receiver for improved accuracy and time-of-arrival control to permit coordinated missile, or aircraft and missile, strikes. That variant also has a Williams 402 turbofan engine with a 19-percent increase in thrust and a 2-percent decrease in fuel consumption.

About 100 Block IID missiles are being converted into a submunition variant called Block IIID; the remaining 525 Tomahawks are being upgraded to Block IIIC with a unitary warhead.

The Navy variants were:

Model[16]	Launch mode	Type	Warhead
BGM-109A	ship/submarine	TLAM(N)	nuclear (W80 warhead)
BGM-109B	ship/submarine	TASM	conventional (1,000-lb Bullpup)
BGM-109C	ship/submarine	TLAM-C	conventional (1,000-lb Bullpup)
BGM-109D	ship/submarine	TLAM-D	conventional (bomblets)
BGM-109E	ship/submarine	TLAM/ TASM	conventional (unitary)

There are several subvariants of these missiles.

---

16. Submarine-launched variants are designated UGM-109.

A Tomahawk land-attack missile in flight with wings, tail fins, and air-intake scoop extended. The TLAM has become a "weapon of choice," offering the advantages of range, accuracy, unmanned flight, and relative invulnerability. (U.S. Navy)

A Tomahawk is fired from a destroyer of the ARLEIGH BURKE (DDG 51) class during Operation Desert Fox in December 1998. The CG/DDG classes carry a mixed loadout of Standard, TLAM, and VLA (ASROC) missiles. (U.S. Navy)

The TLAM-D dispenses 166 BLU-97 bomblets, weighing 3.4 pounds (1.5 kg) each, in packets of 24; these submunitions can be armor-piercing, fragmentation, or incendiary. They are dispensed against multiple targets; for example, in 1991 a submarine-launched TLAM-D struck three separate targets in Iraq and then performed a terminal dive to strike a fourth target.

In April 1992 it was revealed that a warhead containing carbon-fiber spools had also been developed for the Tomahawk. Several of the 116 missiles fired on the first day of the Gulf War carried the still-experimental warheads, which upon detonation disrupted Iraqi electric power, helping to blind air-defense and command and control activities. The warhead, developed under a highly classified "black" program, showered outdoor switching and transformer areas of electric generating plants with thousands of rolls of very fine carbon fibers. When released by the Tomahawks, the thousands of fiber spools unwound in the wind, the fibers then dropping onto power lines and transformers—causing massive short circuits but not permanent damage. (They were not "dispensed" as are the BLU-97 bomblets.)

The accuracy of the early TLAM missiles is on the order of 33 feet (10 m); later missiles—employing GPS—have considerably more accuracy. Speed is approx. 550 mph (880 km/h).

A periscope view of a TLAM being launched from the attack submarine PITTSBURGH (SSN 720) during Operation Desert Storm. The missile's wings and fins have not yet deployed nor has the turbofan engine started. A series of photos of this launch appears in the 16th Edition/ page 458. (U.S. Navy)

General Dynamics proposed an ASW variant of the Tomahawk as an alternative to the Sea Lance project (for both surface ship and submarine use).

An air-launched Tomahawk competed unsuccessfully with the Boeing Air-Launched Cruise Missile (ALCM) for use on B-52 strategic bombers. The BGM-199G Ground-Launched Cruise Missile (GLCM) variant was selected as a theater nuclear weapon for deployment in Western Europe under Air Force control, but those weapons were discarded under the Intermediate-range Nuclear Forces (INF) treaty.

The TLAM(N) fitted with the W80 nuclear warhead has been removed from ships; see page 526.

Operational: The first operational use of the Tomahawk was in the 1991 Gulf War (Operation Desert Storm). The U.S. Navy fired 288 Tomahawks—276 from surface combatants and 12 from submarines (see individual ship classes for launching ships and number fired). Of the 288 missiles, approximately 80 percent were daylight attacks and 20 percent night. Of those missiles, 288 transitioned to a cruise profile for a successful launch rate of 98 percent. Reportedly, the Iraqis recovered one Tomahawk virtually intact.

According to the official Department of Defense report on the Gulf War, the Tomahawk's "demonstrated accuracy was consistent with results from pre-combat testing. The observed accuracy of TLAM, for which unambiguous target imagery is available, met or exceeded the accuracy mission planners predicted." (During the conflict, an estimated 477 TLAMs were available in theater.)

Since the Gulf War, TLAMs have been fired by U.S. surface ships and submarines against targets in Afghanistan, Iraq, Sudan, and the former Yugoslav states. On 17 January 1993 three destroyers launched 45 missiles at targets in Iraq (plus one that failed to launch), and on 26 June 1993 an additional 23 missiles were fired at Iraqi targets (plus one that failed to launch) by a cruiser and a destroyer. Again, in December 1998 (Operation Desert Fox), U.S. ships fired approximately 325 TLAMs against targets in Iraq.

Tomahawk missiles first were used in the Bosnian conflict on the night of 10 September 1995, when the cruiser NORMANDY (CG 60) fired 13 TLAMs against Serbian air defense positions around Banja Luka. One missile did not function properly. (The NORMANDY launch came after another surface ship and the submarine OKLAHOMA CITY/ SSN 723 were unable to fire Tomahawks because of equipment malfunctions.)

Additional TLAMs were fired in the lengthy Balkans confrontations and conflict. During the 1999 NATO campaign to free Kosovo (Operation Allied Force), a total of 218 TLAMs were fired by U.S. naval vessels, roughly 75 percent by surface ships and the rest by submarines; an additional 20 TLAMs were fired by the British submarine SPLENDID.

Earlier in 1999 U.S. surface ships and submarines carried out missile strikes against reported terrorist targets in Sudan (30+ missiles) and Afghanistan (60+ missiles).

Status: Operational. Only TLAM variant is operational; the TLAM(N) is in storage. IOC: TASM in surface ships in 1982; TASM in submarines in 1983; TLAM in surface ships in 1984; TLAM(N) in 1987; TLAM Block III in 1994; TASM in HMS SPLENDID in 1998.

A Tomahawk cruise missile was successfully launched from the submarine BARB (SSN 696) on 1 February 1978; the GUITARRO (SSN 665) was the first submarine armed with Tomahawk. The MERRILL (DD 976) was fitted with the first Tomahawk installation in October 1982 for at-sea evaluation; the battleship NEW JERSEY (BB 62) was the second ship, receiving the Tomahawk in March 1983.

The Royal Navy procured 65 TLAMs in 1968 with the submarine SPLENDID firing the first British missile on 18 November 1998.

Prime contractor:	Raytheon (formerly McDonnell Douglas)
Weight:	2,650 lbs (1,200 kg) + 550-lb (250-kg) booster + 1,000-lb (454-kg) capsule for submarine launch
Length:	18 ft 3 in (5.565 m) + 2 ft (0.6 m) booster
Span:	8 ft 9 in (2.67 m)
Diameter:	20.5 in (520 mm)
Propulsion:	turbofan (Williams F107-WR-402) + solid-propellant booster
Range:	TLAM 750+ n.miles (1,390+ km)
	TLAM(N) 1,200+ n.miles (2,225+ km)
Guidance:	inertial and TERCOM (Terrain Contour Matching); GPS in Block III
Warhead:	1,000 lbs (454 kg) high explosive or multiple payload
Platforms:	*cruisers* CG 52
	destroyers DD 21
	DDG 51
	DD 963
	submarines SSN 21
	SSN 774
	SSN 688

TOW MGM-71

The TOW—for Tube-launched, Optically tracked, Wire-guided—is an anti-tank missile fired from Army and Marine Corps helicopters, as well as from ground and vehicle mounts.

Design: Improved versions, designated Improved TOW (ITOW) and TOW 2, have an upgraded warhead; TOW 2 also has a higher impulse motor. The missile has a high subsonic speed.

Status: Operational. IOC in 1970.

Prime contractor:	Hughes and Emerson Electric
Weight:	54 lbs (24.5 kg)
Length:	3 ft 8 in (1.1 m)
Span:	3 ft 9 in (1.1 m)
Diameter:	6 in (152 mm)
Propulsion:	solid-fuel rocket + solid-fuel booster
Range:	1.5 n.miles (2.8 km); 2 n.miles (3.7 km) for TOW 2
Guidance:	optical/wire
Warhead:	8 lbs (3.6 kg) high explosive (shaped charge)
Platforms:	*helicopters* AH-1W

TRIDENT C-4 UGM-96A

The Trident I, or C-4, SLBM evolved from the Department of Defense STRAT-X study of the late 1960s, which proposed an advanced SLBM with a range of 6,000 n.miles (11,120 km) to be

carried in a new class of submarine. Subsequently, the Navy proposed a two-phase program: The Trident C-4 (also called Trident I) based on an Extended-range Poseidon (EXPO) missile with a range of some 4,000 n.miles (7,410 km), and the more-capable Trident D-5 to be developed at a later date with the longer range.

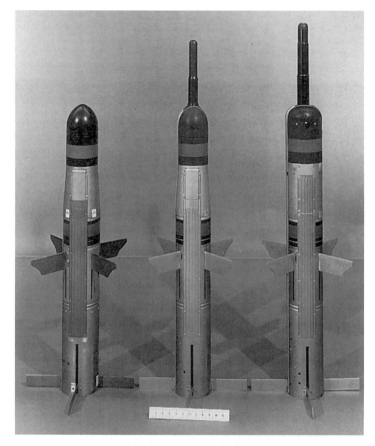

TOW missiles: *from left,* the basic TOW, Improved TOW, and TOW 2. There are further improvements. The TOW and ITOW have 5-inch (127-mm)-diameter warheads; the TOW 2 has a 6-inch (152-mm) warhead. The spikes provide improved penetration of armor. (Hughes Aircraft)

This classic photo of a TOW anti-tank missile being launched from a light truck shows the weapon in great detail, including the guidance wires. The wings and tail fins have not fully deployed. These missiles also are launched from helicopters. (U.S. Marine Corps)

Design: The C-4 missile has a MIRV warhead with eight Mk 4 independently targeted re-entry bodies. It has double the yield and twice the accuracy of the previous Poseidon C-3 missile. It was designed to alternatively carry the Mk 500 Evader *Maneuvering Reentry Vehicle* (MaRV) warhead; this warhead was intended to overcome ballistic missile defenses but was not developed.

The C-4 is a three-stage missile. After it reaches a certain altitude, an aerospike extends from the nose. This spike cuts the friction of the air flowing past the missile, extending its range by about 300 n.miles (556 km).

The underwater launch sequence of a Trident C-4 missile (Los Alamos National Laboratory)

Status: Operational. IOC on 20 October 1979 on board the FRANCIS SCOTT KEY (SSBN 657). Twelve LAFAYETTE (SSBN 616)-class submarines were refitted with the Trident missile and the first eight OHIO- class submarines were armed with the missile. Four of the latter submarines will be rearmed with the Trident D-5 missile.

Prime contractor:	Lockheed
Weight:	73,000 lbs (33,110 kg)
Length:	34 ft (10.4 m)
Span:	(ballistic)
Diameter:	74 in (1.9 m)
Propulsion:	3-stage solid-propellant rocket
Range:	approx. 4,000 n.miles (7,400 km)
Guidance:	inertial
Warhead:	nuclear Mk 4 with 8 W76 MIRVs
Platforms:	*submarines* SSBN 726–733

*TRIDENT (D-5) UGM-96B

The Trident II, or D-5, is the principal U.S. sea-based strategic missile. It provides a greater range and more accuracy than the Trident C-4 SLBM. Also, the D-5 can deliver 75 percent more payload than the C-4, carrying eight of the Mk 5 re-entry bodies, each fitted with a W88 nuclear warhead having an explosive force of about 300–475 kilotons. (Only 400 W88 warheads have been produced, with the remaining missiles to be fitted with the W76 warhead having a yield of about 100 kilotons.)

Rear Admiral Kenneth Malley, Director, Strategic Systems Program, stated that one could draw a circle around the ends of a Trident

A Trident C-4 rocket engine ignites after the missile clears the water during a launch from the submarine MICHIGAN (SSBN 727). (U.S. Navy)

submarine (i.e., of 560 feet [170.7 m] diameter) and a D-5 could put all its warheads in that circle from 4,000 n.miles (7,400 km) away.[17]

In the future, the D-5 missiles will be downloaded to only four warheads, reflecting the arms control limit of 1,728 warheads in submarines.

---

17. Rear Adm. G. P. Nanos, USN, "Strategic Systems Update," *The Submarine Review* (April 1977), p. 12.

A Trident D-5 breaks the surface during a test launch. The D-5 has emerged as the principal U.S. strategic weapon; it will be fitted in all remaining U.S. strategic missile submarines. (U.S. Navy)

The longer-range and more-accurate D-5 version of the Trident missile was approved for development by the Secretary of Defense in October 1981 and fitted in the ninth and subsequent submarines of the OHIO (SSBN 726) class. The first eight submarines of that class were to be retrofitted to fire the D-5, but those plans were canceled in 1991 because of fiscal considerations.

The D-5 missile eventually will be fitted to the 14 submarines of the OHIO class that will be retained after 2000.

Operational: The TENNESSEE (SSBN 734) began the first Trident D-5 patrol on 29 March 1990.

Status: Operational. In production.

The first test flight of the Lockheed D-5 missile from Cape Canaveral, Fla., on 21 March 1989 was a failure, as was the third launch on 15 August 1989. (The failures were due to a design flaw caused by the water pressure on the missiles' nozzles, which caused them to tumble after leaving the water.) The second, fourth, and later launches were successful. The first submarine-launch occurred on 22 March 1989 from the TENNESSEE; that test launch also failed. Following a series of successful test launches, the missile became operational.

The D-5 is fitted in the Royal Navy's four VANGUARD-class SSBNs.

Prime contractor:	Lockheed Martin (formerly Lockheed)
Weight:	approx. 130,000 lbs (58,968 kg)
Length:	44 ft (13.4 m)
Span:	(ballistic)
Diameter:	83 in (2.1 m)
Propulsion:	3-stage solid-propellant rocket
Range:	approx. 4,000 n.miles (7,400 km)
Guidance:	inertial
Warhead:	nuclear Mk 5 with 8 W88 or W76 MIRVs
Platforms:	*submarines* SSBN 734–743

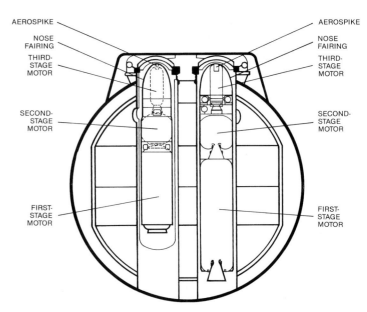

Comparison of the Trident C-4 *(left)* and Trident D-5 missiles shown in a cross-section of a strategic missile submarine of the OHIO (SSBN 726) class. (U.S. Navy)

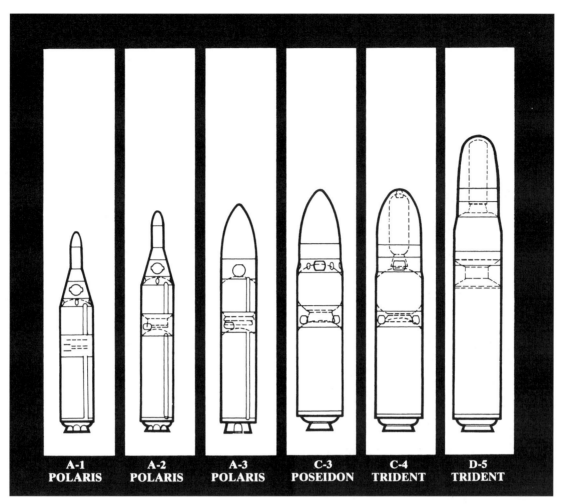

U.S. submarine-launched ballistic missiles, showing the relative size of six generations of SLBMs (U.S. Navy)

TSSAM (TRI-SERVICE STANDOFF ATTACK MISSILE) AGM-137

Formerly a highly classified "black" program, the TSSAM was revealed by the Department of Defense in June 1991, in part to help justify procurement of the B-2 "stealth" bomber. TSSAM was to provide a precision stealth weapon for the suppression of enemy air defenses. However, the Northrop-development weapon was canceled in January 1995 because of higher than expected costs.

In development since 1986, the low-observable (stealth) TSSAM was intended to provide precision guidance with a conventional warhead to ranges of more than 100 n.miles (185 km). Apparently a variety of warheads were to be available, such as penetrating, multiple submunitions, and conventional high explosive. The missile was to be compatible with the Army–Marine Corps Multiple Launch Rocket System (MLRS); the Air Force B-2, B-52, and F-16 Fighting Falcon aircraft; and Navy F/A-18 Hornet and A-6E Intruder aircraft.

Procurement of 9,050 missiles was planned originally—2,250 for the Navy, 1,800 for the Army, and 5,000 for the Air Force. In June 1991 the Department of Defense revised its estimate to a TSSAM procurement of 8,650 missiles for all services at a cost of $15.1 *billion* or an average of $1.7 million per round, including research, tooling, support, and so forth. Subsequently, the unit cost increased to $2 million per missile.

In place of the TSSAM, the Navy plans to procure additional SLAM/SLAM-ER missiles.

VLA (VERTICAL LAUNCH ASROC) RUM-139A

This is a short-range ASW weapon, the vertical-launch successor to the ASROC RUR-5A ASW rocket for use in later TICONDEROGA-class cruisers and the ARLEIGH BURKE–class destroyers. Only small numbers of the weapon are being procured.

The Navy had originally sought to combine the replacement for ASROC and SUBROC in a single weapon; this proved too difficult, however, and the VLA is surface-launched only. The submarine-launched weapon—the Sea Lance—was not developed.

Design: The VLA has more than double the basic ASROC range. It would also be suitable for launch from modified ASROC launchers. The VLA carries a Mk 50 ASW torpedo as its warhead, although tests are being conducted with the earlier Mk 46 Mod 5 torpedo.

Status: Operational. Congress approved the procurement of a total of 300 missiles in fiscal years 1987 and 1989. The Japanese Aegis destroyers of the KONGO class are also VLA capable.

Prime contractor:	Loral
Weight:	1,409 lbs (634 kg)
Length:	16 ft (4.9 m)
Span:	2 ft 3.4 in (0.7 m)
Diameter:	14 in (356 mm)
Propulsion:	solid-propellant rocket
Range:	approx. 15 n.miles (27.8 km)
Guidance:	ballistic; terminal acoustic homing with Mk 50 torpedo
Warhead:	Mk 50 torpedo
Platforms:	*cruisers* CG 52
	destroyers DDG 51
	DD 963

A VLA rising from the VLS of the destroyer ELLIOT (DD 967). The exhaust is being vented at left. Vertical launch provides many advantages over conventional missile launchers. The ELLIOT retained a full ASW capability with installation of a VLS forward. (Loral)

WALLEYE II AGM-62

The Walleye is an unpowered glide bomb formerly used by the Navy. It was listed in the missile designation series and was operationally considered as such against surface ships and hardened ground targets. It became operational in 1967.

Operational: Although phased out of service in 1991, Walleye II was employed in the Gulf War, with 133 missiles being launched by Navy A-7E Corsair aircraft from the carrier JOHN F. KENNEDY (CV 67). With the demise of that aircraft immediately after the Gulf War, the missile is no longer in naval service.

The Navy–Marine Corps used the Walleye only with conventional warheads, while the Air Force also had a nuclear version. Walleye was also used by the Israeli Air Force.

See 14th Edition/pages 488–489 for characteristics.

NUCLEAR WEAPONS

All nuclear weapons have been taken off U.S. Navy warships, except for submarine-launched ballistic missiles, and have been similarly removed from naval air squadrons ashore. This action and the similar large-scale cutback of Army and Air Force tactical and strategic nuclear weapons were announced in a dramatic television speech by President George Bush on 27 September 1991. (At the time, the President also proposed the elimination of all multiple warheads on land-based missiles by both the United States and Soviet Union.)

The president's announcement of the massive, unilateral nuclear weapons and readiness reductions was hailed by then-Secretary of Defense Dick Cheney, who said that the President's initiative "is, in my opinion, the biggest single change in the deployment of U.S. nuclear weapons since they were first integrated into our forces."[18]

The U.S. action followed by a month the abortive Soviet right-wing, political-military coup. The victory of democratic forces in the Soviet Union had, said Cheney, permitted a "sweeping package" of nuclear arms reductions by the United States.

At the time of President Bush's statement, the Navy had the following nuclear weapons in service:

Strategic missiles: 656 SLBMs in 35 strategic missile submarines:

176	Poseidon C-3 in 11 LAFAYETTE class
192	Trident C-4 in 12 LAFAYETTE class
192	Trident C-4 in 8 OHIO class
96	Trident D-5 in 4 OHIO class

Land-attack missiles: Approximately 100 Tomahawk TLAM(N) in attack submarines, cruisers, and destroyers. The Navy's inventory goal for TLAM(N) missiles was reported as 637, with 399 already funded through fiscal 1991.

Bombs: Some 400 nuclear strike bombs (B57 and B61) and anti-submarine depth bombs (B57) embarked in aircraft carriers. Additional B57 weapons were at shore bases for use by P-3 Orion maritime patrol aircraft.

As a result of the President's initiative, all TLAM(N) missiles were placed in storage ashore and no additional missiles were procured. All nuclear strike bombs were withdrawn; most of the B61s were placed in storage and the B57s eliminated. In addition, development of the advanced B90 dual-purpose bomb was halted; with cancellation of the B90 bomb, no nuclear weapons were under development for naval use.

(There were similar, far-reaching cuts of U.S. Army and Air Force tactical nukes. The only tactical nuclear weapons left with U.S. operational forces were B57 and B61 bombs with Air Force fighter-bomber squadrons. The only U.S. tactical nuclear modernization program that was under way at the time of the President's speech, the Air Force SRAM-T missile, was also terminated.[19])

Department of Defense officials contend that in the future the Tomahawks and B61 bombs could be taken out of storage and returned to the Fleet within a very short time—perhaps days. However, with the weapons removed, the ongoing personnel reductions, and severe budget constraints, it was unlikely that the capability could be retained to rapidly bring nuclear weapons back aboard submarines and surface ships and use them effectively.

The only nuclear weapons that remain in the U.S. Fleet are Trident C-4 and D-5 SLBMs. This force will be reduced to 14 submarines by the beginning of the 21st century, carrying a total of 336 D-5 missiles.

The other U.S. strategic weapons in 2000 are expected to consist of 500 Minuteman III missiles, each with three MIRVs; 50 MX Peacekeeper missiles, each with ten MIRVs; 97 B-1B bombers; and 20 of the controversial B-2 "stealth" bombers. However, the cancellation of the SRAM II missile, which was to be carried by strategic bombers, should raise further questions about pursuing production of the B-2 aircraft.

Longer-term plans call for "de-MIRVing" all land-based strategic missiles, that is, downloading the 500 Minuteman IIIs and 50 MX Peacekeepers to one re-entry vehicle per missile.

---

18. Pentagon press briefing, 28 September 1991.
19. SRAM = Short-Range Attack Missile. The follow-on SRAM II strategic weapon had also been terminated by President Bush's action.

Historical: The U.S. Navy had a theoretical nuclear strike capability as early as 1948 with the Mk 4 atomic bomb and a dozen land-based P2V-3C Neptune bombers. These twin-engine piston aircraft could fly from airfields in Europe or North Africa, or be loaded by cranes aboard carriers for shipboard launch. It was a primitive force with a questionable capability. At the time, atomic bombs had to be assembled by teams of up to 40 men and required several hours to "glue" them together.

Beginning in 1951, with the Mk 6 atomic bomb and AJ-1 Savage piston-engine attack aircraft, the Navy has continuously had nuclear weapons aboard surface ships, although the early carrier deployments were made without certain nuclear materials; in a crisis (or war), they would have been flown by B-47 jet bomber from storage sites in the United States to airfields in the Mediterranean area, and then flown aboard carriers by Carrier-Onboard Delivery (COD) aircraft for bomb assembly. Subsequently, surface combatants and submarines were fitted with nuclear-armed anti-ship and anti-air missiles; land-attack and anti-ship cruise missiles; anti-submarine torpedoes and rockets; and 16-inch projectiles for the four IOWA-class battleships.

The 1991 decision to remove the remaining tactical weapons from warships follows the 1989 decision to dismantle the surviving ASROC antisubmarine rockets and Terrier-BTN anti-aircraft missiles fitted with nuclear warheads. Those weapons, like some of the bombs later taken out of service, were overage and their remaining "shelf life" was severely limited, while their effectiveness was questionable.

Table 28-4 lists all nuclear weapons that were available to the U.S. Navy.

Table 28-4 NAVAL NUCLEAR WEAPONS

Warhead	Weapon*	Type	In stockpile
Mk 4	bomb	strike	1948–1953
Mk 5	Regulus missile	strike/ASUW	1952–1963
Mk 6	bomb	strike	1951–1962
W7	Betty depth bomb	ASW	1955–1963
W7	BOAR bomb	strike	1956–1963
Mk 8	bomb	strike	1951–1956
W23	16-inch shell	strike	1956–1961
W27	Regulus	strike/ASUW	1958–1965
W30	Talos missile	AAW	1958–1979
W34	Lulu depth bomb	ASW	1958–1971
W34	ASTOR torpedo	ASW	1958–1977
B43	bomb	strike	1961–1991
W44	ASROC rocket	ASW	1961–1989
W45	Terrier missile	AAW	1962–1989
W47	Polaris missile	strike	1960–1975
W55	SUBROC rocket	ASW	1964–1989
B57	bomb	strike/ASW	1963–1992
W58	Polaris missile	strike	1964–1982
B61	bomb	strike	1966–1992
W68	Poseidon missile	strike	1970–1991
W76	Trident I missile	strike	1979–present
W80	Tomahawk missile	strike	1984–1992
W81	SM-2 Standard	AAW	not developed
W88	Trident II missile	strike	1990–present
B90	bomb	strike/ASW	not developed

* Artillery shells and Atomic Demolition Munitions (ADM) used by the Marine Corps are not included.

TORPEDOES

The U.S. Navy has two series of torpedoes in service: the lightweight Mk 46 and Mk 50, used by aircraft and surface ships, and in the CAPTOR mine; and the heavyweight Mk 48 ADCAP, carried in all submarines. These torpedoes are intended primarily for the anti-submarine role, although the Mk 48 can be used against surface ships.

No torpedoes are currently being procured. Mk 48 torpedoes are being upgraded to the ADCAP configuration and a Mk 54 lightweight "hybrid" torpedo is being developed.

Both the heavy- and lightweight torpedo programs have encountered major problems, most related to the nature of the Soviet/Russian submarine threat. The problems with U.S. torpedoes have been identified publicly. By some criteria, U.S. torpedoes have lagged behind

the potential threat since the appearance of the first Soviet nuclear-powered submarines in the late 1950s.

In a 1981 congressional colloquy between a senator and the Deputy Chief of Naval Operations (Surface Warfare), Vice Admiral William H. Rowden, the senator noted that then-new Soviet submarines of the Alfa class could travel at "40-plus knots and could probably outdive most of our anti-submarine torpedoes."[20] He then asked what measures were being taken to redress this particular balance. The admiral replied, "We have modified the Mk 48 torpedo . . . to accommodate to the increased speed and to the diving depth of those particular submarines." The admiral was less confident of the Mk 46 used by aircraft, helicopters, and surface ships: "We have recently modified that torpedo to handle what you might call the pre-Alfa."

Russian undersea craft are difficult targets for several reasons. The large size, double hull, and multiple compartments of Soviet- and Russian-built submarines reduce the effectiveness of the small Mk 46 and Mk 50 warheads. Both heavy and light torpedo effectiveness also suffers from the use on Russian submarine hulls of anechoic coatings, which degrade torpedo acoustic guidance, and the extensive use of acoustic decoys. Finally, the Mk 48's capability is reduced in the under-ice environment of the Arctic ice pack.

Subsequently, in the mid-1990s with the demise of the Soviet Union and rapid decline of the Soviet submarine threat, U.S. naval forces were reoriented toward operations in the littoral waters of the Third World. In this environment, too, there are major problems with the Navy's primary ASW weapons, the Mk 50 lightweight and Mk 48 ADCAP heavy torpedoes. The relatively shallow environment of littoral operations can cause severe problems for torpedo homing sonars. The Mk 50 "is really challenged" and the Mk 48 is "stressed," according to a U.S. Navy official.

Submarines carry the Mk 48 torpedo. The LOS ANGELES–class SSNs have a capacity of some 25 tube-launched weapons (4 tubes + 22 reload spaces, with at least one rack left free to facilitate weapons handling). The later Improved LOS ANGELES (SSN 688)–class submarines additionally have 12 vertical-launching tubes for Tomahawk TLAMs, making more reload spaces available within the submarine. The SEAWOLF class has space for 50 weapons (8 tubes + 42 reload spaces). The VIRGINIA class returns to a 25-torpedo internal capacity, plus 12 vertical-launch tubes for TLAMs.

Surface ships have the Mk 46 or Mk 50 torpedo as an ASW weapon, launched by (1) over-the-side Mk 32 torpedo tubes, (2) LAMPS helicopters, or (3) Vertical Launch ASROC (VLA). Until the late 1950s, U.S. surface combatants had torpedo tubes for heavy anti-ship torpedoes. For a brief period in the 1960s, the Mk 48 was intended for tube-launch from surface warships to provide a long-range, wire-guided ASW torpedo. Several surface warships were fitted with torpedo handling gear and 21-inch tubes in their stern counter or after deckhouse. However, this aspect of the Mk 48 program was canceled and only Mk 32 tubes for lightweight torpedoes have been retained in U.S. cruisers, destroyers, and frigates.

ASW aircraft and helicopters carry the Mk 46 or Mk 50 torpedo—externally on the SH-2G and SH-60B/F helicopters, and in internal weapon bays in the P-3C fixed-wing aircraft. (The S-3B Viking is no longer used in the ASW role.)

MK 54 HYBRID TORPEDO

The Mk 50 lightweight ASW torpedo is expensive and the number available is limited. Accordingly, the Navy is developing a Lightweight Hybrid Torpedo (LHT) that combines the Mk 50 guidance package with the Mk 46 propulsion system. The Mk 54 also will have enhanced performance in shallow water.

The Mk 54 will be similar in size to the Mk 50.

Status: Development. Planned IOC in 2003. Development of the Mk 54 has been delayed.

---

20. The Alfa SSN, with six operational units completed from 1977 to 1981, had a submerged speed of 43 knots.

MK 50 LIGHTWEIGHT TORPEDO

The Mk 50—formerly known as the Advanced Lightweight Torpedo (ALWT)—is the successor to the Mk 46 for use by maritime patrol/ASW aircraft and helicopters, and surface warships (it was also intended for the aborted submarine-launched Sea Lance ASW missile). The torpedo has enhanced-kill capability over the Mk 46, but still suffers from some of the shortcomings of the older torpedo, such as size of warhead.

The ALWT program was initiated in August 1975, with a design competition subsequently being held between Honeywell (Ex-50 design) and McDonnell Douglas (Ex-51). The former firm was selected to develop the torpedo. During the competition, the torpedo was also designated Mk XX. Concept development began in 1975 and advanced development was approved in 1979; limited production began in March 1989.

Design: Special features of the Mk 50 include the AKY-14 programmable digital computer.

The torpedo can be used by all Mk 46 launchers/attachment points without platform modification.

Name: The Mk 50 is referred to as Barracuda by the producer.

Status: Operational. Manufactured by Alliant Techsystems (formerly Honeywell) and Westinghouse Electric Corp.

Weight:	approx. 800 lbs (363 kg)
Diameter:	12¾ in (324 mm)
Length:	9 ft 6 in (2.9 m)
Propulsion:	Stored Chemical Energy Propulsion System (SCEPS)
Speed:	50+ knots
Range:	
Guidance:	active/passive acoustic homing
Warhead:	approx. 100-lb (45-kg) conventional shaped charge
Platforms:	*aircraft* P-3C
	SH-60B/F/R
	ships cruisers
	destroyers
	frigates

A Mk 50 lightweight torpedo is launched from the fixed torpedo tubes of a KNOX (FF 1052)-class frigate. Ship-launched Mk 46 and Mk 50 torpedoes are last-ditch defensive weapons, of questionable effectiveness in view of submarine-launched torpedo and cruise missile ranges. (Alliant Techsystems)

A Mk 50 lightweight torpedo fitted on a Seahawk-type helicopter. Two Mk 50s can be carried by an SH-60. The Mk 50 has a "shrouded" propeller system in comparison to the open, contra-rotating propellers of its predecessor, the Mk 46. (Alliant Techsystems)

The portside Mk 32 torpedo tubes on the destroyer ARLEIGH BURKE. These triple tubes, which rotate outward for launching, can use the Mk 44, Mk 46, or Mk 50 lightweight torpedo. The tubes are reloaded by hand. (Stephan Terzibaschitsch)

MK 48 ADCAP TORPEDO

This is the U.S. Navy's submarine-launched torpedo. The Mk 48 ADCAP (Advanced Capability) version of the Mk 48 heavy torpedo has been in production since fiscal 1985 as successor to the standard Mk 48 versions. The ADCAP version was developed from 1978 onward to counter the high-speed, deep-diving Alfa SSN and other advanced Soviet submarines. The ADCAP performance requirements were to: (1) improve target acquisition range, (2) reduce the effect of enemy countermeasures, (3) minimize shipboard constraints such as warmup and reactivation time, and (4) enhance effectiveness against surface ships.

Also see Improved Submarine-launched Mobile Mine (ISLMM) under Mines.

Design: The principal changes from the baseline Mk 48 to the ADCAP configuration to meet the above requirements were made to the torpedo's acoustic transducer (guidance) and control system. The higher-powered active sonar enables the torpedo to search a much greater volume of water to attain a target submarine. Furthermore, the sonar is electrically steered, reducing the need for the torpedo to maneuver while searching. The torpedo retains the Gould (swashplate) motor with a larger fuel capacity. However, in November 1986 the Navy began seeking proposals for developing a quieter, closed-cycle propulsion system for the ADCAP, an apparent requirement in view of recent Soviet submarine quieting efforts.

The ADCAP program has suffered both delays and severe cost increases. In 1982 the Chief of Naval Operations, Admiral Thomas B. Hayward, said that the problems included (1) the original R&D program being significantly underestimated, (2) the scope of effort increasing because of the evolving Soviet submarine threat, (3) an attempt being made to accelerate the IOC, (4) too little emphasis being placed on cost control, and (5) the prime contractor (Hughes) being new to torpedo business and underestimating the effort required.

Reliability problems with the ADCAP surfaced in early 1991 but, according to Navy officials, they were solved the following year. An under-ice capability has been provided in the ADCAP upgrade.

In 1995 the Navy proposed an upgrade to the ADCAP propulsion program to enhance the torpedo's effectiveness against diesel-electric submarines operating in littoral or shallow water. The upgrade reduces the range at which an adversary is alerted to an attack by the torpedo's engine sounds and thus is able to undertake evasive action or counterfire. An analysis by the General Accounting Office stated:

> Because of the short ranges at which diesel submarines are likely to be detected in littoral or shallow water, the technological improvement to be contributed by the propulsion upgrade—that is, torpedo quieting—will neither improve the performance of the ADCAP nor reduce the vulnerability of the launching submarine to enemy attack. Moreover, the Commander, Operational Test and Evaluation Force, already considers the current ADCAP operationally suitable and effective in shallow water, and the Navy did not establish a requirement to improve the ADCAP's propulsion system for use in open ocean, deep water in its operational requirements document for the upgrade.[21]

Status: Operational. IOC in 1988. Manufactured by Westinghouse Corp. and Hughes Aircraft.

Weight:	3,450 lbs (1,564 kg)
Diameter:	21 in (533 mm)
Length:	19 ft 2 in (5.8 m)
Propulsion:	piston engine (liquid monopropellant fuel); pump-jet
Speed:	55 knots maximum
Range:	approx. 35,000 yds (32,012 m)
Guidance:	wire + active/passive acoustic homing
Warhead:	approx. 650 lbs (295 kg) PBXN-103 high explosive
Platforms:	*submarines* SSN/SSBN

21. General Accounting Office, *Navy Torpedo Programs: MK-48 ADCAP Upgrades Not Adequately Justified*, GAO/NSIAD-95-104 (June 1995), p. 1.

A Mk 48 ADCAP torpedo "in flight." The only torpedo carried in U.S. submarines, the Mk 48 ADCAP has limitations in littoral operations. It also is used in Australian, Canadian, and Dutch submarines. (U.S. Navy)

A Mk 48 ADCAP torpedo is loaded into an attack submarine. The SSNs without VLS must share their torpedo reload racks with Tomahawk missiles and mines; the Harpoon anti-ship missiles have been discarded by the submarine force. (U.S. Navy)

MK 48 HEAVY TORPEDO

This was the latest weapon in a long series of heavy torpedoes, 21 inches (533 mm) in diameter with a length of up to 21 feet (6.4 m). The immediate predecessor of the Mk 48 was the Mk 37, which remains in foreign naval service. The Mk 48 also replaced the Mk 45 ASTOR (Anti-Submarine Torpedo), the U.S. Navy's only nuclear torpedo, which was in service from 1958 to 1977 with a W34 warhead. The long range and improved guidance of the Mk 48 made it as effective with a large conventional warhead as the Mk 45 in most situations. Also, the Mk 48's anti–surface ship capability was considered sufficient to cancel the purely anti-surface Mk 47 torpedo.

Development of the Mk 48 began in the early 1960s as the Navy-sponsored RETORC (Research Torpedo Configuration) research project of the Applied Research Laboratory of Pennsylvania State University and the Westinghouse Electric Corp. (Baltimore, Md.). The project was initially designated Ex-10. This effort led to the Mk 48 Mod 0 torpedo with a turbine propulsion system. This was subsequently refined into the Mk 48 Mod 2.

In 1967 the Gould Corp. of Cleveland, Ohio, and the Naval Surface Warfare Center, White Oak, Md., began developing the Mod 1 with a redesigned acoustic homing guidance and a piston (swashplate) engine. This torpedo uses an Otto fuel that contains its own oxidizer for combustion. After evaluation of the two versions, the Mod 1 was selected for production by Gould for fleet use.

Design: The Mk 48 had a guidance wire that spins out simultaneously from the submarine and the torpedo to permit the submarine to exercise control over the "fish," at least during the initial stages of its run. The Mod 3 introduced several improvements, including TELECOM (Telecommunications) to provide two-way data transmissions between submarine and torpedo; thus the torpedo can transmit acoustic data back to the submarine for processing. See the Mk 48 ADCAP listing above for basic characteristics.

The Mod 4 version was an upgrade to provide more capability against the Alfa-class and other advanced Soviet SSNs.

The Mk 48 is also used in Australian, Canadian, and Dutch submarines.

Status: Succeeded in U.S. service by the Mk 48 ADCAP. IOC in 1972.

The Mk 48 torpedo, showing the shrouded propeller or "propulsor" configuration. A similar propulsor concept was adopted for the submarines of the SEAWOLF (SSN 21) class. (Gould)

MK 46 LIGHTWEIGHT TORPEDO

The Mk 46 is a lightweight torpedo intended for use against submarines by helicopters, aircraft, and surface ships. It is also fitted in the CAPTOR (Encapsulated Torpedo) deep-water mine.

The lightweight torpedo concept dates to the late 1940s, when it was envisioned that future convoys would be protected from submarine attack by helicopters with dipping sonar and airships (blimps) with towed sonar. For this application, light weight (initially a maximum of 350 pounds/159 kg) became a primary consideration for ASW torpedoes. In addition, the concept would require large numbers of torpedoes; hence cost was also an important factor in torpedo design. Subsequently, surface combatants were fitted with "short" torpedo tubes for launching these torpedoes and the ASROC was fitted with the lightweight torpedo. The first lightweight ASW torpedo to enter fleet service was the Mk 43 Mod 1 (260 lb/118 kg) in 1951 and later the Mod 3, followed by the Mk 44 Mod 0 (425 lb/193 kg), introduced in 1957, and Mod 1. The Mk 46 is thus the third generation of lightweight ASW torpedoes.

The Navy procured kits for the conversion of 172 Mk 46 torpedoes to function as anti-torpedo weapons as part of the Surface Ship Torpedo Defense (SSTD) project.

The Mk 46 was developed by the Naval Ordnance Test Station, Pasadena, Calif., and Aerojet General of Azusa, Calif. Subsequent production was undertaken at the Naval Ordnance Plant, Forest Park, Ill., and Honeywell, as well as Aerojet. The Mk 46 has a higher speed, twice the range, deeper operating depth, and better acoustic performance than its predecessor, the Mk 44.

Design: The Mk 46 propulsion is provided by a thermal piston engine, with the Mod 0 using a solid propellant grain and the Mod 1 having a liquid monopropellant fuel, the latter providing improved performance. The Mod 2 introduced the PBXN-103 warhead (providing 27 percent more explosive power over the Mods 0/1). There was no Mod 3 torpedo.

The Mod 4 version of the Mk 46 is specially configured for the CAPTOR naval mine. In 1981 Secretary of Defense Harold Brown stated that "because the existing Mk 46 torpedo will not meet the submarine acoustic and countermeasures threat through the early 1980s, we have budgeted for a new version called the Near-Term Torpedo Improvement Program (NEARTIP)." This program included modification kits for earlier Mk 46s, as well as new torpedo procurement. The NEARTIP or Mod 5 has an improved sonar transducer, new guidance and control group, and engine upgrades. Overall performance, as well as shallow-water effectiveness, are enhanced with these changes.

Status: Operational. IOC: Mod 0 in October 1965; Mods 1 and 2 in 1967. The last Mk 46 Mod 5 torpedoes were delivered to the U.S. Navy in 1992; they were produced by the firm Alliant Techsystems, which was part of the defense-product spinoff from Honeywell in

October 1990. In addition, the firm produced several hundred conversion kits for the Navy to upgrade earlier Mod 1 and Mod 2 torpedoes to the Mod 5 configuration. The following table lists the Mod 5 characteristics.

The U.S. Navy plans to retire the Mk 46 about 2015.

The Mk 46 is used by numerous other countries.

Weight:	517.65 lbs (234.8 kg)
Diameter:	12.75 in (324 mm)
Length:	8 ft 6 in (2.6 m)
Propulsion:	reciprocating external combustion engine (liquid monopropellant) contra-rotating propellers
Speed:	approx. 45 knots maximum
Range:	approx. 8,000 yds (7.3 km)
Guidance:	active/passive acoustic homing
Warhead:	approx. 95 lbs (43 kg) PBXN-103 high explosive
Platforms:	Mod 4 CAPTOR mine
	Mod 5 *aircraft* P-3C
	SH-60B/F/R
	ships cruisers
	destroyers
	frigates

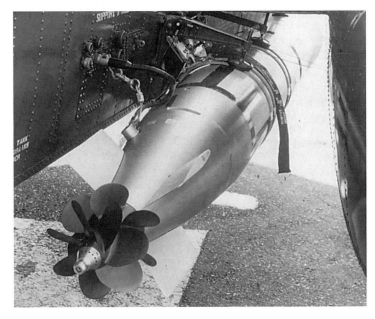

The contra-rotating propellers of the Mk 46 lightweight torpedo are shown in this view of the weapon fitted to an SH-3D Sea King helicopter. Russian ASW helicopters carry their torpedoes in internal weapons bays. (U.S. Navy)

Mk 46 torpedoes rest side-by-side in the weapons bay of a P-3 Orion maritime patrol aircraft. Parachute packs are fitted to the rear of the torpedoes. (U.S. Navy)

The parachute deploys from a Mk 46 torpedo as it is released from an SH-3D Sea King helicopter. Lightweight torpedoes are now the only ASW weapons carried by U.S. surface ships (including VLA) and aircraft. Squadron HS-2 now flies SH-60F and HH-60H Blackhawks. (U.S. Navy)

A Mk 46 torpedo being launched from a surface combatant. In addition to their short range, these torpedoes are limited by the size of their warhead and by their guidance package, which is vulnerable to advanced acoustic jamming and decoys. (U.S. Navy)

ANTI-SURFACE WARFARE TORPEDO

The Navy promulgated a requirement for a low-cost, anti–surface ship torpedo on 2 December 1985 at the urging of then–Secretary of the Navy John Lehman. The torpedo was intended for use against surface ships that did not require the more-complex (and higher-cost) Mk 48 ADCAP torpedo. The ADCAP was developed specifically for attacking maneuvering submarines, a much more difficult type of target.

Known as the "no frills" torpedo, the ASUW weapon encountered delays primarily because of the contractual restrictions on potential contractors, such as the finalists having to provide seven test torpedoes each at their own expense for a "swim-off" competition. The torpedo was also opposed by the submarine community, which questioned the utility of a weapon that would displace Mk 48 torpedoes and other weapons from the limited reload space in attack submarines. The program subsequently was canceled.

The ASUW torpedo had a program goal of 2,000 weapons at a cost of $200,000 each (compared to the $2.43 million unit cost for the Mk 48 ADCAP torpedo in the fiscal 1988 budget, plus continuing research and development costs). The initial procurement was set for fiscal 1987 with 34 torpedoes. However, the program was canceled after Lehman's departure from office in 1986.

After arming an F/A-18, red-shirt-wearing Marine ordnance specialists from squadron VMFA-323 aboard the carrier CONSTELLATION (CV 64) are given a wave by the pilot. Marine and Navy aircraft use interchangeable ordnance, facilitating Marine aircraft operating from aircraft carriers as well as amphibious ships. (U.S. Navy, PH3 Timothy C. Ward)

CHAPTER 29

Electronic Systems

The array of electronic antennas on the Aegis missile cruiser VICKSBURG (CG 69) is typical of modern warships. These support a variety of search, fire control, intelligence collection, navigation, and communications functions. But improper or careless use of these systems increases a ship's vulnerability. (Leo Van Ginderen)

The U.S. Navy is heavily dependent upon electronic systems for navigation, communications, and especially combat operations. The last includes both offensive and defensive operations. This chapter lists the Navy's principal electronic warfare systems, radars, sonars, torpedo countermeasures, and weapon control systems now fitted in U.S. surface ships and submarines. Sonobuoys and seafloor surveillance systems are listed as subsets of the sonar entries.

ELECTRONIC DESIGNATIONS

Most U.S. Navy electronic systems are identified by the joint electronics type designation system shown in figure 29-1. This scheme previously was called the joint Army-Navy nomenclature system, and the three-letter-plus-number designations are still prefixed by the "AN/" of the World War II era. In this volume the AN/ is omitted from three-letter

Figure 29-1

Explanation of Symbols

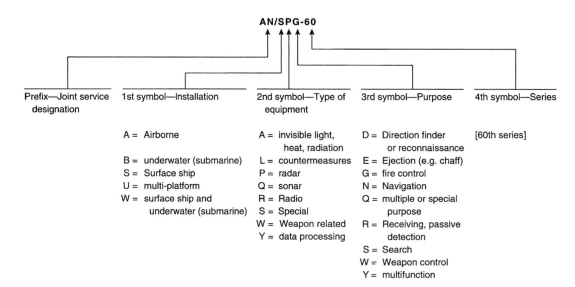

Prefix—Joint service designation	1st symbol—Installation	2nd symbol—Type of equipment	3rd symbol—Purpose	4th symbol—Series
	A = Airborne	A = invisible light, heat, radiation	D = Direction finder or reconnaissance	[60th series]
	B = underwater (submarine)	L = countermeasures	E = Ejection (e.g. chaff)	
	S = Surface ship	P = radar	G = fire control	
	U = multi-platform	Q = sonar	N = Navigation	
	W = surface ship and underwater (submarine)	R = Radio	Q = multiple or special purpose	
		S = Special	R = Receiving, passive detection	
		W = Weapon related	S = Search	
		Y = data processing	W = Weapon control	
			Y = multifunction	

designations except in the headings for this chapter. The electronic systems designated in various mark (Mk) series do not have the AN/ prefix.

Versions of basic radars are indicated by suffix letters or (V)-series numbers.

ELECTRONIC WARFARE SYSTEMS

Electronic Warfare (EW) consists of efforts to detect, locate, exploit, reduce, or prevent an enemy's use of the electromagnetic spectrum, and actions that retain one's own use of the electromagnetic spectrum. There are several categories of electronic warfare:

Electronic Warfare Support Measures (ESM)
Signals Intelligence (SIGINT)
Electronic Countermeasures (ECM)
Electronic Counter-Countermeasures (ECCM)

Because EW deals with electromagnetic energy and not just electronics, also included are infrared, laser, and optical systems. However, radiation produced by nuclear weapons is usually classified as nuclear effects and not EW.

Electronic Warfare Support Measures activities are the portion of EW that seeks to detect, intercept, locate, record, and analyze enemy electromagnetic radiations. Thus, ESM provides the information required to conduct electronic countermeasures and counter-countermeasures for immediate threat recognition. Generally passive, ESM seeks to detect the enemy through "listening" to an enemy's radio and radar emissions.

The U.S. Navy has a variety of ESM systems that are used in ships, submarines, aircraft, and ashore. Being passive, ESM offers a number of obvious tactical advantages: it permits the ESM collection platform to remain electronically silent, and it can detect hostile radar transmissions beyond the radar's detection range because the radar requires much of its power to return a signal to the transmitter after it detects a target.

There are highly specialized—and highly classified—ESM systems, such as the ALR-series receivers in the Navy's EP-3E Orion aircraft that support fleet operations.

ESM capabilities are also incorporated into multifunction systems. For example, according to published Navy manuals, a submarine of the LOS ANGELES (SSN 688) class has the following equipment for the collection of Electromagnetic Intelligence (ELINT), including Acoustic Intelligence (ACINT) and Communications Intelligence (COMINT):

- BQQ-5 sonar system, which has a passive classification processor that can continuously evaluate low-frequency acoustic data from sonars
- BLD-1 radio direction finder
- BRD-7 radio direction finder
- WLR-8 receiver, which can detect enemy fire control radars, as well as radio communication frequencies (reportedly having a 50 MHz to 18 GHz frequency range)
- WLR-9 acoustic intercept receiver, which can detect active search sonars and acoustic-homing torpedoes
- WLR-10 countermeasures

Several of these systems are multipurpose, especially the BQQ-5 system, which is the submarine's tactical sonar, having both active

Figure 29-2

Frequency Spectrum

Current Frequency Designations Used by USA and NATO	A	B	C	D	E	F	G	H	I	J	K	L	M
Wavelength (cm)	300 200 150	100 75 60 50 40 30	20 15	10	6 5 3.75 3	2	1.5	1 0.75 0.6 0.5 0.4 0.3					
Frequency (GHz)	0.1 0.15 0.2	0.3 0.4 0.5 0.6 0.75 1	1.5	3	5 6 8.0 10	15	20 30 40 50 60 70 100						
Previous Frequency Designations*	VHF	UHF	L	S	C	X	K$_u$ K K$_a$	Millimeter					
Frequency Designations (WW II)		P	L	S	C X	K	Q V						

and passive modes. Additional ESM equipment can be installed for special collection missions.

Electronic surveillance and collection systems have special design characteristics, among them:

- *Wide-spectrum or bandwidth capability:* Because the frequency of a foreign radar may not be known before it is detected, a wide bandwidth should be covered. With modern technology, this means a frequency spectrum from 30 MHz to 50 GHz. This range is too large for a single receiver; thus, the system must use several receivers with different frequency ranges or a single receiver in which different tuning units can be inserted to cover the frequency range.

- *Wide dynamic range:* The ESM receiver must be able to receive both very weak signals and very strong signals. The receiver may be at different distances from different signals at the same time, and widely dissimilar signal strengths could impair both collection and analysis unless the equipment is designed specifically for the role.

- *Unwanted signal rejection:* This characteristic—also called narrow band-pass—enables the receiver to discriminate between the target frequency and signals at other nearby frequencies.

- *Good angle-of-arrival measurement:* The ability of a receiver to accurately take bearings on a distant transmitter permits different bearings (taken by the same or several surveillance platforms) to be plotted to give the precise location of the transmitter. Airborne, shipboard, or ground-based digital computers can be programmed to rapidly perform this function.

The receiver should be designed to immediately alert the operator to the presence of a signal of possible interest, to sort out the signal of interest, and to analyze the signal. The alerting and sorting are particularly important because an airborne ESM platform may be exposed to the signal for a short time compared to a ship or shore facility, or the signal may be on the air for only a very short time. The current trend in ESM is to automatically record the intercepted signal for later analysis and, if appropriate, for reproduction for use in EW libraries.

The submarine is an excellent ESM platform because it is difficult for an enemy to detect her by conventional radar and visual means, and even by acoustic sensors under some conditions. And, of course, a submarine is not impeded by surface weather. Submarines are particularly useful in gaining acoustic intelligence on enemy submarines. The periodic press reports of U.S. and Soviet submarines "scraping" one another in close encounters in northern waters suggest that U.S. submarines are used in such surveillance missions in areas such as the Arctic and Norwegian Seas.

An ACINT capability is also found in the Navy's seafloor Sound Surveillance System (SOSUS). In addition to providing a peacetime warning system of submarine movements, the SOSUS networks in the Atlantic, Pacific, and regional seas can record data on surface ship and submarine noise characteristics.

Specialized electronic reconnaissance aircraft have long conducted ESM missions along the peripheries of the Soviet Union (and now Russia), China, and North Korea. The current U.S. naval aircraft in this category is the EP-3E Orion from fleet air reconnaissance squadrons (VQ).[1] These aircraft also provide electronic surveillance of surface ships and submarines for fleet commanders. The primary advantage of aircraft ESM platforms is their altitude, permitting them to detect distant electronic emissions, including those originating inside enemy territory.

Aircraft—and surface ships—also are used to stimulate enemy radars and communications as they near enemy territory. This stimulation enables the aircraft or ship to then record the electromagnetic responses of an enemy, that is, which of their radars they turn on and which of their communications channels they use.

Signals Intelligence includes the collection of intelligence information for Navy and National requirements, including all COMINT, ELINT, ACINT, and Telemetry Intelligence (TELINT). The National Security Agency (NSA) is the national program manager for the collection, analysis, and dissemination of SIGINT. However, the platforms and personnel involved in SIGINT collection belong to the armed services, and some systems obviously have both ESM and SIGINT collection capabilities. Thus, the actual operation of SIGINT activities is conducted by the services and, in wartime, the operational control of some dedicated SIGINT platforms would be assigned to tactical commanders.

Surface warships are used extensively for SIGINT activity. Two U.S. destroyers engaged in SIGINT, the TURNER JOY (DD 951) and MADDOX (DD 731) on the so-called DeSoto patrols off the North Vietnamese coast in August 1964, were involved in the Gulf of Tonkin incidents that led to a dramatic escalation of American involvement in the Vietnam conflict.[2] Because of the hostile nature of the North Vietnamese and the guerrilla war then going on, destroyers were deemed the appropriate ESM platforms.

In the supposedly more benign environment of international waters off North Korea, the U.S. Navy carried naval and NSA teams on board the "passive" SIGINT surveillance ships BANNER (AGER 1) and PUEBLO (AGER 3), while the LIBERTY (AGTR 5) was used in 1967 to monitor Israeli communications during the Six-Day War. The United States and Soviet Union had long believed that such ships operated by the two superpowers were immune to hostile actions by the Third World. However, attacks on the PUEBLO and LIBERTY—the latter made mistakenly—demonstrated that they were not. The U.S. Navy has ceased to operate such "passive" intelligence ships, although many of these intelligence collectors are still active in the Russian Navy (designated AGI by NATO).

Land-based aircraft, satellites, and ground intercept facilities also provide SIGINT collection of foreign naval activities.

Electronic Countermeasures are intended primarily to (1) detect threats to friendly forces and (2) inhibit or degrade the effectiveness of enemy weapons and sensors. Most surface warships, submarines, and combat aircraft have ECM systems to help protect them against hostile detection and attack. In addition, there are specialized ECM aircraft that assist other aircraft in penetrating heavily defended areas.

Different ECM techniques are used to reduce the effectiveness of enemy radars. The three basic techniques are to (1) interfere with the radar through jamming and deception; (2) change the electrical properties of the air between the radar and (friendly) target, mainly through the use of chaff; and (3) change the reflective properties of the (friendly) target through radar-absorbing materials or paint, or through electronic and mechanical echo (blip) enhancers or decoys.

Although the above discussion concentrates on ECM techniques against radar, to some extent these concepts are usable against electromagnetic communications and sonar. For example, the properties of shipboard noise can be reduced. Modern U.S. surface warships use the Prairie and Masker systems of creating small air bubbles around a ship's hull and wake to reduce her acoustic signature.[3] Advanced submarine hull designs reduce noise created by submarine movement, while special internal mountings reduce propulsion and auxiliary machinery noises. Russian submarines additionally use anechoic coatings, which are intended primarily to reduce the effectiveness of hostile acoustic homing torpedoes but can also reduce submarine-generated noises, as can polymers discharged from a submarine. Of course, surface ships and especially submarines can slow or stop to reduce their self-generated noises.

There are a large number of threat warning and countermeasure systems in U.S. surface ships and submarines, most numbered in the SLQ and WLR series.

The U.S. Navy and Marine Corps fly the EA-6B Prowler in the ECM role. The EA-6B is easily distinguished from the A-6 Intruder, from which it was developed, by the housing atop its tail fin and up to five jammer pods carried on its wings and fuselage. The pods are ALQ-99 tactical jammers, each with an exciter/processor and a mini-

---

1. The ES-3A Viking, a carrier-based aircraft that flew in this role, was taken out of service in 1998; see page 421.

2. On the night of 2–3 August 1964, the destroyers were, in fact, attacked by North Vietnamese motor torpedo boats; there was no attack made against U.S. ships on the night of 5–6 August 1964, although U.S. naval commanders thought the destroyers again were under torpedo boat attack.

3. Prairie is derived from "Propeller Air Ingestion Emission."

computer to detect, identify, and jam a broad spectrum of hostile radars. The aircraft also has the ALQ-100 multi-band track breaking system and ALQ-92 communications jammer. The EA-6B is probably the most capable EW aircraft in the West. The basic EA-6B aircraft has had its frequency coverage extended through a series of updates (see chapter 27 of this edition of *Ships and Aircraft*).

The EA-6B aircraft are designed to provide ECM support for strike aircraft attacking defended targets. The strike aircraft can themselves carry chaff, ECM pods, and radar-homing missiles to further enhance their survivability. Each carrier air wing has a squadron of four EA-6B Prowlers, while the Marine Corps has five squadrons, each assigned five EA-6B aircraft; there is also one Naval Reserve EA-6B squadron. (Other naval aircraft have built-in or pod-mounted ECM systems for self-defense.)

In 1995 the Navy and Air Force reached an agreement whereby the Navy would assume the responsibility for all airborne ECM. This agreement led to the retirement of the Air Force's EF-111A Raven aircraft; 40 EF-111s were in service in 1995.[4]

Electronic countermeasures are costly, not only in resources (especially for research and development as well as production) but also because of the tactical uncertainties and limitations that they impose. For example, it may be undesirable to employ ECM against an enemy's communications, for by doing so one denies communications intercept to one's own side. Or, firing chaff and decoys to defend against a possible enemy missile attack can degrade one's own radar effectiveness.

Also, ECM produces "soft kills." It is not always possible for the ECM operator to detect or determine if his efforts are successful. Further, ESM/SIGINT/ECM/ECCM are undertaken with a continuous interaction. Those who allocate resources are not always anxious to spend funds on an ECM system, for example, that may be a counter to a threat the intelligence community predicts may have a certain capability. Somehow, it seems easier to buy a new ship, or missile, or aircraft rather than a new "black box."

Electronic Counter-Countermeasures are those actions taken to retain the effectiveness of one's own use of the electromagnetic spectrum against hostile EW efforts.

The following are the principal U.S. Navy EW systems fitted in surface ships and submarines.

AN/APR-39A(V)1 PRIVATEER RADAR WARNING

The APR-39 is an omnidirectional Radar Warning Receiver (RWR) fitted in helicopters and fixed-wing aircraft, including several types of Navy-Marine helicopters. It is also fitted in the coastal patrol ships of the CYCLONE (PC 1) class.

The system can determine the frequency, Pulse Repetition Frequency (PRF), pulse width, persistence, and threshold power level of missiles and radars.

The APR-39(V)1 consists of a blade antenna, four spiral antennas in hemispheric radomes, two dual video receiver units, an indicator unit, an analog comparator, and a control unit.

| Prime contractor: | E-Systems |
| Ships: | PC 1 |

AN/BLD-1 RADIO DIRECTION FINDER

This is a mast-mounted radio direction finder. The BLD-1 and BRD-7 will be replaced by the Integrated ESM Mast (IEM) under development for the VIRGINIA-class SSNs. It is planned to be backfitted in SSN 21 and SSN 688 submarines.

Prime contractor:	Litton Amecon
Ships:	SSN 21
	SSN 774
	SSN 688

4. Grumman converted 42 EF-111A ECM aircraft from standard F-111A strike aircraft. This aircraft was developed and produced by General Dynamics under the controversial TFX program.

AN/BLQ-SERIES ACOUSTIC COUNTERMEASURES

These are submarine systems that perform a variety of countermeasures against hostile sonars.

The BLQ-3 is a low-frequency acoustic jammer, BLQ-4 a high-frequency acoustic jammer, BLQ-5 a low-frequency acoustic repeater, BLQ-6 a high-frequency acoustic repeater, BLQ-8 acoustic countermeasures, and BLQ-10 electronic detection, intercept, and processing.

| Prime contractor: | General Electric, except BLQ-3 General Electric, BLQ-8 Bendix/Aerojet, BLQ-10 Lockheed Martin |
| Ships: | submarines |

AN/BLR-SERIES RADAR WARNING RECEIVERS

Mast mounted, these systems provide warning of hostile radar emissions from aircraft, surface ships, or (surfaced) submarines.

The BLR-14 is known as the Submarine Acoustic Warfare System (SAWS). It provides an integrated receiver, processor, display, and countermeasure launch system.

Prime contractor:	BLR-1 to -10	various
	BLR-13	Kollmorgen
	BLR-14	Sperry
	BLR-15	Kollmorgen
Ships:	submarines	

AN/BRD-7 RADIO DIRECTION FINDER

This is a mast-mounted radio direction finder system. Previous models have been phased out of U.S. Navy service.

Prime contractor:	Sanders
Ships:	SSN 688
	SSN 683

AN/SLQ-32(V) ELECTRONIC COUNTERMEASURES

The principal U.S. surface ship ECM system is the SLQ-32 "design-to-cost" EW suite. Variations of this system are fitted in most surface combatant and amphibious ships, as well as in the eight fast combat support ships (AOE). The SLQ-32 is considered a short-range, omnidirectional, self-defense system that evaluates electronic emissions and can, in some versions, initiate countermeasures.

There are several versions of the SLQ-32 based on modular "building blocks" for different types of ships: The (V)1 version provides warning, identification, and bearing of radar-guided cruise missiles and their launch platforms; the (V)2 version has the (V)1 capability and expanded ESM capabilities. An add-on ECM transmitter called "Sidekick" is fitted to destroyers of the SPRUANCE (DD 963) class and frigates of the OLIVER HAZARD PERRY (FFG 7) class to augment the SLQ-32(V)2, thus creating the (V)5 version. The Sidekick is an active ECM system intended to confuse enemy threats. (Sidekick was designed, produced, and delivered by Raytheon within 11 weeks of the Navy request for the system.)

The (V)3 configuration has combined the (V)2 capabilities and the means to counter or deceive missile guidance radars. The (V)3 has a quick-reaction mode that permits the initiation of jamming against a

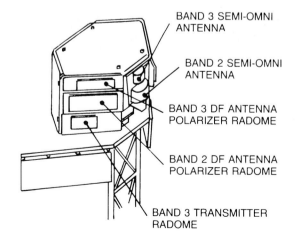

BAND 3 SEMI-OMNI ANTENNA

BAND 2 SEMI-OMNI ANTENNA

BAND 3 DF ANTENNA POLARIZER RADOME

BAND 2 DF ANTENNA POLARIZER RADOME

BAND 3 TRANSMITTER RADOME

Antenna array of the frigate STARK (FFG 31): *from left,* radome for Mk 92 weapons fire control system, SLQ-32(V)2 ECM antenna, SPS-49(V)4 air search radar, and—atop the quadropod mast at right—the SPS-55 surface search radar. (Giorgio Arra)

Antenna for the SLQ-32(V)3 ECM suite on the cruiser GETTYSBURG (CG 64). SLQ-32 systems are fitted in all active cruisers, destroyers, frigates, amphibious ships, the mine countermeasures ship INCHON (MCS 12), and the Navy-manned fast combat support ships (AOE) as well as some aircraft carriers. (N. Polmar)

SLQ-32(V)5 ECM system antenna in a frigate of the OLIVER HAZARD PERRY (FFG 7) class. There is an SLQ-32(V)2 antenna mounted on a pedestal above the smaller "Sidekick" antenna. The latter is an add-on ECM transmitter that enhances the SLQ-32's capabilities. (Raytheon)

target signal before its characteristics are fully analyzed. This feature could be particularly useful against "pop-up" submarine-launched missiles or those fired by missile craft hiding in coastal shore "clutter."

The (V)4 combines most earlier features into a set intended for aircraft carriers, which had not previously been intended for SLQ-32 installation. These sets are provided in all aircraft carriers, as well as in the battleship WISCONSIN (BB 64). (The other battleship remaining on the Naval Vessel Register, the IOWA/BB 61, has the SLQ-32[V]3.)

The SLQ-32 antennas are fitted in two box-like enclosures, to port and starboard, high in the ship's superstructure. The (V)2 and (V)3 are fitted with twin Rotman lens direction-finding receiving antennas. The SLQ-32 systems employ UYK-19 computers.

The proposed follow-on system to the SLQ-32 series is the SLY-2 Advanced Integrated EW System (AIEWS).

The SLQ-32 and other ECM systems are used in conjunction with Mk 36 Super Rapid Blooming Offboard Chaff (SRBOC) launchers, which fire either semi-automatically or on manual direction from a ship's ECM operators. Large ships have four Mk 36 launchers and smaller ships have two, each consisting of six fixed barrels. (Infrared decoys and flares can also be fired in response to detections by threat warning devices.)

The ALQ-142 fitted in the SH-60B helicopter is similar to SLQ-32 with two Rotman-lens antennas; data is transmitted via data link to ships fitted with the SLQ-32.

The bands covered by the SLQ-32 are:

(V)1	H/I/J
(V)2/5	B through J
(V)3/4	B through J; countermeasures in H/I/J

Prime contractor:	Raytheon	
	Hughes	
Ships:	(V)1 LSD 41	AO 177
	LSD 36	AOE 1 (some ships)
	LKA 113	
	(V)2 DDG 51–67	LSD 49
	FFG 7 (some ships)	AGF 11
	(V)3 BB 61 (some ships)	LHA 1
	CG 47	LPD 17
	DDG 79	MCS 12
	DDG 72–78	AOE 6
	LCC 19	AGF 3
	LHD 1	
	(V)4 carriers	BB 64
	(V)5 DDG 51–71	FFG 7 (some ships)
	DD 963 (some ships)	AOE 1 (some ships)

AN/SLQ-29 ELECTRONIC COUNTERMEASURES

Consisting of the SLQ-17A Deceptive ECM, WLR-1H, WLR-8, and WLR-11, this suite was developed for aircraft carriers to provide a broad spectrum of ECM capabilities. It has been replaced in the DWIGHT D. EISENHOWER (CVN 69) and earlier ships by the SLQ-32(V)4. Later carriers were completed with the SLQ-32(V)4.

The SLQ-29 is now found only in the mothballed carriers RANGER (CV 61) and INDEPENDENCE (CV 62).

AN/SLQ-25A NIXIE TORPEDO COUNTERMEASURES

See page 559.

AN/SLQ-17 DECEPTIVE ELECTRONIC COUNTERMEASURES

See SLQ-29.

AN/SLR-24 TORPEDO COUNTERMEASURES

See page 559.

AN/SLR-23 RADIO DIRECTION FINDER

Associated with the WLR-1 and SLQ-32 systems, the SLR-23 intercepts signals in the D/E/J bands.

| Prime contractor: | Southwest Research |
| Ships: | surface ships |

SLQ-29 antenna for the ECM suite now found only in the mothballed aircraft carriers RANGER (CV 61) and INDEPENDENCE (CV 62). The SLQ-29 suite was only provided in aircraft carriers, having been succeeded in active ships by the SLQ-32(V)4 suite. (Hughes Aircraft)

AN/SLY-2 AIEWS

The Advanced Integrated Electronic Warfare System (AIEWS) is being developed by Litton Amecom as the Navy's next-generation integration EW system to counter 21st century threats.

The primary functions of AIEWS are detection, correlation, and identification of threat emitters, as well as automatic employment of shipboard countermeasures. The Navy plans to install AIEWS on all surface combatants, as well as aircraft carriers and amphibious ships. It will replace the SLQ-32(V), SSQ-82(V), WLR-1H(V), and other ECM systems. An estimated 173 systems will be procured.

The SLY-2 will have an "open architecture" that will allow technology insertion and facilitate use of Commercial-Off-The-Shelf (COTS) components. The initial systems will be delivered beginning in fiscal year 2001 for backfit in existing ships.

Early program documents referred to AIEWS as the SLQ-54.

AN/SRS-1 COMBAT DIRECTION-FINDING RECEIVER

A less-capable version of (and a component of) the SSQ-108 Classic Outboard system, the SRS-1 is intended to detect anti-ship missiles. The basic system is designated Block 0, while the Block 1 (SRS-1A) incorporates the automated digital acquisition subsystem to enable the exploitation of unconventional and low-probability-of-intercept signals.

Several shore sites also are fitted with the Block 1 system.

Prime contractor:	Lockheed-Sanders	
Ships:	Block 0	LHD 1
	Block 1	DDG 51

AN/SSQ-108(V) CLASSIC OUTBOARD SIGINT SYSTEM

Classic Outboard is a Navy shipboard direction-finding system. It provides signals acquisition and direction-finding systems (SRS-1) with the capability to detect, locate, identify hostile targets at long range and to input these data into the ship's tactical data system. This widely deployed system consists of a VHF Adcock direction-finding antenna and 24 small, deck-edge antennas for low/medium/high-frequency band direction-finding.

This system provides greater flexibility and responsiveness to new threat signals, while reducing space and manning requirements in comparison with older systems. Block 0 provides narrow-band step-search signal acquisition and direction-finding against conventional communications signals. However, Classic Outboard currently is ineffective against some current and projected threats; some components are old and are becoming expensive to maintain.

A joint cooperative program between the United States and Great Britain was established on 1 July 1994 for a collaborative Classic Outboard logistics for the existing system. The program has two parts: phase 0 is an interim update that focuses on transitioning human–computer interface to a joint maritime command information system; phase 1 focuses on a total update of front-end sensors.

The SSQ-108 succeeded the older SSQ-72 and SSQ-74 Classic Outboard systems. The SRD-19 was associated with the SSQ-72 system.

Prime contractor: Lockheed-Sanders
Ships: DD 963 (13 ships)

AN/WLQ-4(V)1 SEA NYMPH ESM SYSTEM

This submarine ESM system identifies the type and source of radar and communications signals. It can operate fully or semi-automatically; in the semi-automatic mode, an operator can direct the correlation of signals detected by the WLQ-4 with data collected by other sensors.

The WLQ-4 has up to six operator positions; it uses the UYK-44 (formerly UYK-20) computer.

Prime contractor: GTE
Ships: SSN 21
SSN 683

AN/WLR-13 INFRARED/ELECTRO-OPTICAL WARNING

This system is intended to warn surface ships of an attack by anti-ship cruise missiles fitted with infrared or electro-optical guidance systems.

Prime contractor:
Ships: surface ships

AN/WLR-11 RADAR WARNING/SIGINT SYSTEM

Prime contractor: ARGO Systems
Ships: surface ships

AN/WLR-10 RADAR WARNING RECEIVER

This is a submarine radar warning receiver fitted to a retractable mast in missile and attack submarines, collocated with the WLR-8. It is a modified version of the WLR-10 previously fitted in missile submarines of the LAFAYETTE (SSBN 616) class.

Prime contractor: Astro Labs
Ships: SSBN 726
SSN 688
SSN 642

AN/WLR-9 SONAR WARNING RECEIVER

Prime contractor: Norden (United Technologies)
Ships: submarines

AN/WLR-8(V) RADAR WARNING RECEIVER

This receiver provides coverage of 0.5–18 GHz frequencies. A surface ship version was canceled in 1983, although it was installed in the ENTERPRISE (CVN 65) and subsequently removed. Trident missile submarines have the (V)5 and Los ANGELES–class submarines have the (V)2 version.

Prime contractor: GTE-Sylvania
Ships: SSBN 726
SSN 688
SSN 642

AN/WLR-6 WATERBOY RADAR WARNING, SIGNAL COLLECTION

Prime contractor: GTE-Sylvania
Ships: submarines
surface ships

AN/WLR-1 RADAR WARNING

This is a widely used radar warning receiver fitted in surface ships and submarines. It originally covered the 50 MHz to 10.75 GHz frequency range; most sets now in use are WLR-1H versions and cover 0.55–20 GHz. It is employed with the WLR-11.

The WLR-1H(V)5 performs Over-The-Horizon (OTH) cued detection, classification, and targeting, as well as area surveillance and threat warning. This version has a single package antenna to replace the original suite of four antennas used with the WLR-1H(V)3 version. The new suite offers improved reliability and a significant reduction in mast weight.

Prime contractor:
Ships: SSN 688
surface ships
Coast Guard cutters

AN/WLY-1

The WLY-1 acoustic interception and countermeasures system provides the OHIO-class missile submarines with an automatic response against torpedo attack. The system is proposed as a replacement for the existing WLR-9A/12 acoustic intercept system, fitted in the Los ANGELES–class SSNs.

In addition to providing the detection, classification, and tracking of torpedo threats, the WLY-1 includes a control subsystem for the launch management of torpedo onboard countermeasures.

Prime contractor: Norden/Allied Signal
Ships: SSBN 726

ASTECS (ADVANCED SUBMARINE TACTICAL ESM COMBAT SYSTEM)

The ASTECS is being developed for submarines of the VIRGINIA (SSN 774) class, formerly designated as the New Attack Submarine (NSSN). It provides broader ESM functions than the WLR-8 in the Los ANGELES class or the WLQ-4 in the SEAWOLF (SSN 21) class.

ASTECS will be a component of the Integrated ESM Mast (IEM) being developed for the VIRGINIA.[5]

The system is being developed by Lockheed Martin.

MK 70 MOSS (MOBILE SUBMARINE SIMULATOR)

MOSS is a torpedo-like decoy launched from submarine torpedo tubes to simulate the acoustic signatures of a submarine. Although MOSS has been out of service for several years, 310 units are in long-term storage at Keyport, Wash.

MOSS is 10 inches (254 mm) in diameter and packed in tandem racks for launching from 21-inch torpedo tubes.

Prime contractor: Gould Electronics
Ships: SSBN 726

MK 23 TORPEDO DECOY

This device is launched from submarine signal ejection tubes.

Prime contractor:
Ships: SSN

MINE COUNTERMEASURES SYSTEMS

Mine countermeasures (MCM) systems are listed in chapter 21 of this volume. Mine-detecting sonars are listed in the Sonar section below.

---

5. The IEM is to replace the BLD-1 and BRD-7/8 mast-mounted electronic systems.

A pair of Mk 70 MOSS acoustic decoys is loaded into an attack submarine. These decoys originally were developed for use by strategic missile submarines. No longer operational, they are being held in reserve. (U.S. Navy)

SHIPBOARD RADARS

U.S. Navy shipboard radars are used principally for surface and air search, height-finding, weapons fire control, target illumination, and aircraft control. In a few radars, two functions can overlap, with the advanced SPY-1 series providing multiple radar functions in a single system.

Aircraft control radars are unique to aviation ships (CV/CVN/ LHA/LHD) and are designated in the SPN-series, informally referred to as "spin" radars. They are used to guide aircraft into the proper approach pattern or glide path to the ship. The SPN radars are listed in table 29-1.

The small combatants of the CYCLONE (PC 1) class have commercial radars and sonar; see chapter 20.

Numerous shipboard radars have been deleted from the previous edition, reflecting, in part, the large number of ships and classes deleted in the past few years.

Designations: Fire control radars were assigned mark (Mk) numbers beginning in 1941. This series ran through Mk 47; the next radar initiated the SPG series. Subsequently, later versions of some earlier Mk-series radars were given the SPG prefix; thus the Mk 35 and the SPG-35 were the same radar.

TABLE 29-1. AIR CONTROL RADARS

Radar	Role	Frequency	Ships
SPN-35	aircraft marshalling	X	LHA/LHD
SPN-42A*	Carrier Controlled Approach (CCA)	K	CV/CVN
SPN-43A/B/C	air control	S	CV/CVN/LHA/LHD
SPN-44	landing aid	X	CV/CVN
SPN-46	CCA	Ka/X	CV/CVN
SPN-47	precision CCA		LHA/LHD**

* Being phased out
** In some ships

AN/BPS-16 RADAR

The BPS-16 is an advanced submarine search and navigation sonar. The radar was evaluated in the ATLANTA (SSN 712) in 1991–1992. The BPS-16 has an outer "sleeve" that mounts the radar and reduces problems with retraction equipment and leakage. The radar also has multiple frequencies, which makes it more difficult for hostile ESM systems to identify than the unique signature common to previous BPS-series radars.

The system has been in service since 1991.

Prime contractor:	Sperry
Band:	X
Ships:	SSBN 726 (some ships)
	SSN 21
	SSN 688 (some ships)

AN/BPS-15 RADAR

The BPS-15 is a submarine search and navigation radar. It has replaced all older radars in U.S. submarines, except in later units of the OHIO class and the SEAWOLF class. The principal differences among the various BPS-series radars are the pedestal mounting. Peak power is 35 kW.

Prime contractor:	Sperry	
Band:	X	
Ships:	BPS-15A	SSN 683
	BPS-15A/E/H	SSN 688 (some ships)
	BPS-15B	SSBN 726–740
	BPS-15E	SSN 642

BPS-15 radar antenna in the raised position at the forward edge of the sail of the ANNAPOLIS (SSN 760). The speckled camouflage used for submarine masts and periscope "sleeves" makes them more difficult to see when projecting above the water. The dark panel of the front of the sail is an antenna for the BQS-15 short-range sonar. (Giorgio Arra)

AN/SPG-62 RADAR

This is the illumination radar for the Standard SM-2 missile in Aegis warships. The Aegis ships have three (DDG 51) or four (CG 47) Mk 99 missile control directors that use the SPG-62 illumination channel to provide radar reflections for Standard missiles. They are "slaved" to the SPY-1 radar. The antenna is 7½ feet (2.3 m) wide. Peak power is 10 kW.

The radar has been operational since 1983.

Prime contractor:	Raytheon
Band:	X
Ships:	CG 47/52
	DDG 51

The SPG-60 was mounted in several classes of now-discarded missile cruisers and destroyers.

Prime contractor:	Lockheed
Band:	X
Ships:	DD 963

The STIR in the PERRY-class frigates uses the SPG-60 antenna. The antenna is mounted immediately forward of the Mk 75 76-mm gun, mounted on the ship's 01 level. (Giorgio Arra)

AN/SPG-53E RADAR

This is a fire control radar fitted in some IOWA-class battleships for use with Mk 37 gunfire director for their 5-inch (127-mm) dual-purpose guns. Most directors in these ships had the Mk 25 radar (see below).

The radar's range is about 120,000 yards (110 km). Peak power is about 250 kW.

Prime contractor:	Western Electric
Band:	X
Ships:	BB 61

The forward SPG-62 illumination radar in destroyers of the ARLEIGH BURKE (DDG 51) class is fitted above the bridge, at the base of the tripod mast; two SPG-62 radars are mounted amidships. The forward SPY-1D antennas are visible (on either side of the Phalanx CIWS mount) and the bar-type antennas for the SPS-64 and SPS-67(V)3 radars are above the SPG-62. (Giorgio Arra)

AN/SPG-60 RADAR

The SPG-60 radar both provides gun control data and permits Standard-MR missile tracking with the addition of an illuminator to the Mk 86 Fire Control System (FCS). The SPG-60 is a monopulse, pulse-Doppler radar, is combined with the SPQ-9A in the Mk 86 weapon control system, and can illuminate targets for the Standard and Sea Sparrow missiles. Thus, this single fire control system can serve several functions. The X-band SPG-60 is credited with a nominal range of some 50 n.miles (92.5 km) and is able to track Mach 3 targets out to 100 n.miles (185 km). (The Mk 86 system can simultaneously track up to 120 incoming targets in a track-while-scan mode.)

The Separate Target Illumination Radar (STIR) using the SPG-60 antenna mount is found in the PERRY-class frigates to provide two missile control channels for the Mk 86; see separate entry.

The antenna is 13⅓ feet (4 m) across. Peak power is 5.5 kW.

SPG-53 radar antenna. The SPG-53E radar is used in place of the Mk 25 radar on the forward Mk 37 GFCS director in battleships of the IOWA (BB 61) class. The 53E version has shell splash-spotting and missile-launch alarm features. (Giorgio Arra)

AN/SPG-51D RADAR

The SPG-51 was a C/X-band pulse-Doppler tracking/illumination radar used with the Standard-MR in cruisers and destroyers armed with that missile (originally developed for use with the Tartar missile). It was associated with the Mk 74 missile FCS. (The two operating modes shared a common antenna.)

Operational since 1960, it has been phased out of service with the retirement of older missile-armed ships.

AN/SPQ-9 RADAR

The SPQ-9A is the fire control radar associated with the Mk 86 Gunfire Control System (GFCS). It provides surface search functions as well as weapons control, operating in a high-resolution, pulse-Doppler, track-while-scan mode. The SPQ-9A operates from a minimum of 150 yards (137 m) out to 20 n.miles (37 km) against aircraft-size targets. The high scan rate of 60 revolutions per minute can detect and track incoming missiles, as well as aircraft and surface targets. The Mk 86 system with the SPG-60/SPQ-9 is found in new missile cruisers, the SPRUANCE-class destroyers, and the TARAWA (LHA 1)-class helicopter ships. The battleship IOWA mounted the SPQ-9A without the Mk 86 system.

The antenna is housed in a 120-inch (3-m)-diameter plastic radome. Peak power is 1.2 kW. The Mean Time Between Failures (MTBF) is given as about 800 hours.

An SPQ-9B version has been developed by the Navy, with pre-production "kits" ordered from Westinghouse-Norden. The SPQ-9B can better detect low-altitude (sea-skimming) missiles in a clutter environment, which should be of particular value in littoral areas. The basic SPQ-9A reflector was replaced by a larger unit with multiple feeds, a new processor and receiver/exciter were added, and the transmitter was replaced by an APG-68 radar transmitter as used in the F-16 Fighting Falcon aircraft.

A shore-based SPQ-9B ADM (Advanced Development Model) was tested at Wallops Island, Va., and has since been installed for at-sea tests in the stricken destroyer DECATUR (DD 936/DDG 31), which serves as a test hulk for the Ship Self-Defense System (SSDS), operating as a test platform for the Ship Self-Defense System (SSDS), operating out of the Naval Surface Warfare Center, Port Hueneme Division, Calif.; see chapter 24.

The SPQ-9 has been operational since 1970.

Prime contractor:	SPQ-9A	Lockheed Electronics
	SPQ-9B	Westinghouse-Norden
Band:	X	
Ships:	BB 61	
	CG 47	
	DD 963	
	LHA 1	

AN/SPS-69 RADAR

This solid-state radar is a modification of the commercial Raytheon R41X small-craft navigation radar. Maximum power is 4 kW.

The Coast Guard has several hundred sets in service. It is no longer fitted in Navy ships.

The SPS-69 has been operational since 1990.

Prime contractor:	Raytheon
Band:	X
Ships:	Coast Guard cutters and craft

AN/SPS-67(V) RADAR

The SPS-67 is a surface search/navigation radar, developed as a successor to the long-serving and widely used SPS-10 radar. The newer radar has a high degree of automation and can instantly distinguish between moving and stationary targets.

It has solid-state electronics with an MTBF in excess of 1,000 hours. The (V)1 uses the SPS-10 antenna; (V)2 introduced a new antenna; and (V)3 adds automatic tracking and gunfire control. The (V)4 is a lightweight version with a bar-type antenna.

The SPS-67 has been operational since 1982.

The forward mast of the destroyer CUSHING (DD 985) is dominated by the ship's SPQ-9B radar, mounted beneath the SPG-60 fire control radar, together forming the Mk 86 Gunfire Control System (GFCS). A Phalanx CIWS and OE-82 satellite communications antenna are mounted above the bridge. (Giorgio Arra)

An electronics technician checks the SPS-67 radar antenna on the carrier INDEPENDENCE shortly before the ship was decommissioned in 1998. The SPS-67 is found in a variety of surface combatants, amphibious ships, and fleet auxiliaries. (U.S. Navy, PHAN Chris Howell)

Prime contractor:	DRS Systems (formerly AIL, Norden [United Technologies])
Band:	C
Ships:	aircraft carriers LSD 41
	BB 61 LSD 49
	DDG 51 AH 19
	LCC 19 AOE 6
	LHD 1

AN/SPS-64(V) RADAR

The SPS-64 surface search/navigation radar uses a bar-type antenna; the size of the four available antennas vary from 4 feet (1.2 m) to 12 feet (3.7 m) across, depending capability/size of system. Versions have different frequency bands and operating characteristics.

The SPS-64 can automatically track up to 20 targets.

Commercial versions of this radar made by Raytheon have a four-digit number following the letters RM; its commercial name is Raypath.

All U.S. aircraft carriers, the IOWA-class battleships, and TICONDEROGA-class cruisers have the (V)9 version. The variants are:

version	band	transmitter	user
(V)1	S	single 20-kW transmitter	Coast Guard
(V)2, 3	S	two 20-kW transmitters	Coast Guard
(V)4	S/X	two 20-kW transmitters	Coast Guard
(V)5	X	single tunable 20-kW transmitter	Army
(V)6	X	single 50-kW transmitter	Coast Guard
(V)7, 8	S		Coast Guard
(V)9	X		Navy
(V)10, 11	S		Coast Guard
(V)12–14	X		Army
(V)15	X		Navy
(V)16, 17	X		Army
(V)18	X		Navy

Prime contractor:	Raytheon	
Band:	S and X	
Ships:	CVN 65	LSD 49
	CVN 68	LST 1179
	BB 61	MCS 12
	CG 47	MHC 51
	DDG 51	MCM 1
	LCC 19	AGF 3
	LHA 1	AGF 11
	LHD 1	AE 26
	LPD 17	AOE 6
	LSD 36	AOE 1
	LSD 41	ARS 50

SPS-64(V)9 antenna. This search/navigation radar is widely used on Army, Navy, and Coast Guard ships and small craft. (Raytheon)

AN/SPS-59 RADAR

SPS-59 is the Navy designation for the LN-66 commercial navigation radar, with both designations being used for the radar. This short-range navigation radar has been installed in a variety of U.S. ships, from battleships to small riverine craft. The radar was also fitted in the SH-2G LAMPS I ASW helicopter.

The radar is being replaced by the SPS-69 and other, more modern radars.

Prime contractor:	Canadian Marconi	
Band:	X	
Ships:	DD 963	AD 37
	LKA 113	AFS 1
	LCAC	AO 177
	Mini-ATC	

AN/SPS-58/SPS-65(V) RADAR

A low-level, high-speed, D-band radar for both the detection of attacking anti-ship cruise missiles and target acquisition for the Sea Sparrow point-defense missile system, this radar has been deleted from the fleet. They were fitted in aircraft carriers and frigates.

The SPS-65 could "share" the SPS-10 antenna, while the SPS-58 has its own antenna. These radars had no integral display.

AN/SPS-55 RADAR

The SPS-55 is a surface search radar intended as a replacement for the widely used SPS-10. It has a slotted-array antenna 6 feet (1.8 m) across.

Prime contractor:	Cordion	
Band:	X	
Ships:	CG 47	FFG 7
	DDG 51	MCM 1
	DD 963	AO 177

AN/SPS-52 RADAR

This three-dimensional (3-D) S-band air search radar with Frequency Scanning (FRESCAN) in elevation has been phased out of U.S. Navy service. It was developed from the SPS-39 radar. From 1963, the SPS-52 was installed in several aircraft carriers, plus missile-armed cruisers, destroyers, and frigates, and helicopter carriers. (The carriers used this radar for aircraft control.)

All have been replaced, most by the SPS-48 3-D radar; the last ships to carry the SPS-52 were helicopter carriers.

The SPS-72 was to have been an improved version with a more advanced antenna.

AN/SPS-49(V) RADAR

The most-effective rotating two-dimensional (2-D) air search radar in the U.S. Navy is the SPS-49, a lower-L-band radar. It is the principal air search radar in most large U.S. warships and is a complementary radar to the SPY-1 in the TICONDEROGA (CG 47) class. The ARLEIGH BURKE (DDG 51) class does not have the SPS-49; it was deleted from the design primarily because of cost constraints.

The SPS-49 was evaluated in 1965 on board the experimental destroyer GYATT (DD 712) and an advanced version was installed in the guided missile cruiser DALE (CG 19) in 1975.

It is a very long-range radar and has a narrow beam, which helps to counter hostile jamming efforts. The large, 24 × 14-foot (7.3 × 4.3-m) antenna is easily identified by its large, lower feed horn (the similar-looking SPS-40 antenna has an overhead feed horn). Its frequency range is 851–942 MHz. This radar features high reliability, with its MTBF reported to exceed 300 hours.

The SPS-50 was a modified SPS-49 intended to replace the earlier SPS-6 and SPS-12 radars; it failed its operational evaluation.

The SPS-49 has been operational since 1975.

Prime contractor: Raytheon
Band: L
Ships: (V)1   LSD 41 (some ships)
                   (V)2   DD 997
                   (V)4   FFG 7 (some ships)
                   (V)5   aircraft carriers
                           BB 61
                           FFG 7 (some ships)
                           LHD 1
                           LPD 17
                           LSD 41 (some ships)
                   (V)6/7/8 CG 47

SPS-49(V) antenna on the cruiser PHILIPPINE SEA (CG 58). This is one of the most widely used—and effective—air search radars currently in service with any navy. It supplements the SPY-1 radar in Aegis cruisers, but not Aegis destroyers. (Leo Van Ginderen)

AN/SPS-48 RADAR

The SPS-48 is a 3-D, FRESCAN radar used for aircraft control in carriers and command ships and to support the air defense role of missile ships. The older SPS-48A sets were upgraded with Automatic Detection and Tracking (ADT) features and are designated SPS-48C.

The rectangular antenna is 17 × 17½ feet (5.2 × 5.3 m). The radar's frequency band is 2900–3100.5 MHz and its maximum range is about 220 n.miles (407 km).

The SPS-48 has been operational since 1962.

Prime contractor: ITT Gilfillan
Band: S
Ships: SPS-48C   LCC 19
                   SPS-48E   CV 63 (3 ships)
                             CVN 65
                             CVN 68
                             LHD 1 (5 ships)

SPS-48E is the basic 3-D air search radar in several major warship classes. It was fitted in several classes of now-retired guided missile ships. Note the asymmetrical design of the antenna; the bar above the main antenna is the radar's Identification Friend or Foe (IFF) antenna; the radar above it is an SPS-67. (Stephan Terzibaschitsch)

Rear aspect of an SPS-48E antenna. These photos of the SPS-48E were taken aboard the cruiser WILLIAM H. STANDLEY (CG 32). (Stephan Terzibaschitsch)

AN/SPS-40 RADAR

The SPS-40 is a widely used 2-D air search radar capable of very long detection ranges. It was previously fitted in about 125 cruisers, destroyers, and frigates, plus amphibious and auxiliary ships. One SPRUANCE-class destroyer has had the SPS-40 replaced by an SPS-49 radar.

The radar's frequency range is 400–450 MHz and its range against medium-size aircraft is 150–200 n.miles (280–370 km). The SPS-40B has been upgraded to SPS-40C, with higher power and improved ECCM. The SPS-40E is an updated SPS-40B/C/D with a solid-state transmitter, very low failure rate, and reliability increased to some 200 hours MTBF.

The SPS-40 was developed from the SPS-31 and has been operational since 1961. It is being phased out of U.S. Navy service.

Prime contractor:	SPS-40	Lockheed Electronics
	SPS-40A	Sperry
	SPS-40B	Norden (United Technologies)
	SPS-40E	Westinghouse
Band:	B	
Ships:	DD 963 (some ships)	MCS 12
	LCC 19	AGF 11
	LHA 1	AGF 3
	LSD 36	

An SPS-40 antenna mounted beneath an SPS-67. The SPS-40 feed horn is mounted above the antenna, in contrast with the arrangement on the superficially similar SPS-49 antenna. (Giorgio Arra)

AN/SPS-10 RADAR

The most widely used post–World War II radar in the Navy was the SPS-10 surface search radar, found in most surface combatants, amphibious ships, and auxiliaries. Its 11-foot (3.35-m)-wide antenna has been a familiar sight on U.S. and allied ships since late 1953. It is generally considered a horizon-range radar, although significantly longer-range detections are routinely made.

Few of the SPS-10E/F versions remain in U.S. Navy service, all in amphibious-type ships and fleet auxiliaries. The improved I-band SPS-55, similar to the SPS-10 but with higher resolution, and the solid-state SPS-67, using the same antenna, have replaced the SPS-10.

The SPS-10 has been operational since 1953.

Prime contractor:	GTE-Giffilan
	Raytheon
Band:	C
Ships:	LSD 36 AGF 3
	LST 1179 AO 186
	LKA 113 AO 180
	AGF 11 AS 39

The SPS-10 surface search radar has been aboard U.S. Navy ships for almost a half century, albeit in improved variants. (Giorgio Arra)

AN/SPY-2 MULTIFUNCTION RADAR

The SPY-2 radar is under development by Lockheed Martin as a successor to the SPY-1. It will be an integrated C/S-band radar, making it more capable than the S-band SPY-1 with the C-band providing low-altitude detection capabilities.

The SPY-2 probably will not be available until after 2010.

AN/SPY-1 MULTIFUNCTION RADAR

The SPY-1 is a multifunction, phased-array (fixed-antenna) radar that is the heart of the Aegis AAW system. The SPY-1 combines the azimuth and height search, target acquisition, classification, and tracking functions and can provide command guidance to ship-launched missiles. The replacement of several different radars with the single SPY-1 results in the reduction or elimination of several complex interfaces between specialized radars, speeds up all functions, and provides a very large target-handling capability.

The SPY-1 radar—consisting of the antenna, transmitter, signal processor, control groups, and auxiliary equipment—employs four fixed antennas ("faces") and operates in the F (formerly S) band. The antennas each contain 4,480 separate radiating elements in an octagonal face only 12½ feet (3.7 m) across. This small size facilitates ship design, with the TICONDEROGA having two antennas on a forward deckhouse (facing forward and to starboard) and two on an after deckhouse (facing aft and to port); the ARLEIGH BURKE has four antennas fitted on a single deckhouse. These four antennas each cover a 90° quadrant from the horizon to zenith for total scanning around the ship.

The SPY-1 has a wide frequency bandwidth that randomly radiates different frequencies across the bandwidth on a pulse-to-pulse basis, with very low sidelobes in comparison with its main lobe, and has an extremely complex signal structures. All of these characteristics present great challenges to anti-radar missiles. The SPY-1 radar is also highly resistant to ECM because of its frequency diversity, and it can "sense" jamming and automatically shift to different frequencies where less interference is present. Also, digital signal-processing techniques are employed to counter or suppress jamming and sea clutter. The latter feature is vital for an effective defense against sea-skimming missiles, whose radar return is often lost to conventional radars because of sea clutter masking the target's signal.

Control of the SPY-1 is exercised by four UYK-7 digital computers in the CG 47–64 and by the UYK-43/44 series in the CG 65–74 and the DDG 51 class. These computers schedule and direct the beams—a necessary process because the SPY-1 can project hundreds of pencil-thin radar beams in rapid sequence, far too many for manual control or coordination. Beam-steering is a mathematical problem that requires the calculations of a computer system. The computer capacity is a practical limitation on the number of targets that the SPY-1 can handle at one time. When a target is detected, the computers automatically schedule several more beams to "dwell" on the target within a second of the initial detection, thus initiating a track. Hundreds of targets can be identified in this way and tracked simultaneously, out to ranges on the order of 200 n.miles (370 km).

In earlier missile ships, surface-to-air missiles had to be guided all the way from launch to the target. Missile ships could thus be characterized by the number of guidance channels, i.e., separate guidance radars, available. The later Standard missiles have an "autopilot" that is set at the moment of launch. The SPY-1 continuously tracks both the missiles in flight and targets and the missile guidance can be updated while in flight, but specific radar guidance is required only for the last few seconds before the missile detonates. With this concept, the TICONDEROGA's four guidance radars can handle perhaps 20 separate targets simultaneously. This provides a vast improvement over previous AAW ship capabilities.

The SPY-1 frequency band covers 3100–3500 MHz, with a beam measuring 1.7 x 1.7°. Its peak power is 4–6 MW with an average power of 58 kW.

The production versions of the SPY-1 are:

SPY-1A   initial design (CG 47–58)
SPY-1B   possessing an upgraded antenna and improved transmitter and signal processor for increased effectiveness against low-flying and small-radar-cross-section missiles, and low sidelobe levels for enhanced ECM resistance (CG 59–73)
SPY-1C   designation not used
SPY-1D   single-deckhouse version in the ARLEIGH BURKE class

A rare photo of a SPY-1 radar being assembled, showing a technician inserting electronic elements into the face of the radar. (RCA)

The aft-facing SPY-1B multifunction radar antenna on the cruiser GETTYSBURG. There are two SPG-62 missile control radars mounted atop the structure, which is above the ship's large helicopter hangar. The Soviet Navy developed a similar phased-array radar that was given the NATO code-name Sky Watch. (N. Polmar)

The reverse side of a SPY-1 radar during assembly. Note the technician working at the bottom of the radar. (RCA)

SPY-1D(V)   littoral operations upgrade

SPY-1E[6]   antenna upgrade of earlier radars to enhance bandwidth and sensitivity to enhance effectiveness against ballistic missiles

There have been proposals to install the SPY-1 radar in the carriers of the NIMITZ (CVN 68) class, primarily for aircraft control, and in guided missile cruisers. However, no installations have been made—for fiscal reasons in the carriers; the cruiser installations were opposed by the Navy's nuclear propulsion community, which sought the construction of nuclear-propelled Aegis ships.

The SPY-1 was developed from the SPG-59 phased-array radar intended for the aborted Typhon missile frigate (DLGN) program. Development of the Aegis SPY-1 began in the late 1960s. The SPY-1 (one radar face) began operation at the RCA-development facility in Cherry Hill, N.J., in 1973, followed a year later by a single face being installed in the missile test ship NORTON SOUND (AVM 1). It has been operational since 1983.

The SPY-1D radar is fitted in the four destroyers of the Japanese KONGO class and is being installed in frigates of the Spanish F-100 class. Norway, South Korea, and Taiwan have expressed interest in obtaining the SPY-1 system for their future warships; however, the Clinton administration in 2000 rejected the request from Taiwan as being too provocative to China.

Prime contractor: Lockheed Martin (formerly General Electric–RCA)
Band: S
Ships: CG 47
                     DDG 51

---

6. Originally the E suffix was for a SPY-1D upgrade to provide greater effectiveness against sea-skimming cruise missiles and low-observable targets.

An SPY-1D antenna on the ARLEIGH BURKE, showing the relatively low position of these antennas. All four fixed radar antennas are mounted on the same deckhouse. An SLQ-32(V)3 antenna is at left. (Giorgio Arra)

AN/VPS-2 RADAR

The VPS-2 radar is fitted in the Mk 16 Phalanx gun system, with a single transmitter supporting separate search and tracking radars mounted above the actual Gatling gun. The radar tracks both incoming targets and outgoing bullets, detects the angular error between them, and automatically corrects gun aim. It has a Moving Target Indicator (MTI) with the ability to track very-high-speed targets and has a very rapid reaction capability. (The radar is also used with the U.S. Army's Vulcan air-defense gun system.)

The radar's search range is approximately 5,500 yards (5,030 m). Its frequency range is 9200–9250 MHz, with a peak power of 1.4 kW.

The fire control system for the Phalanx CIWS is the Mk 90.

The VPS-2 has been operational since 1980.

Prime contractor: Lockheed
Band: Ku and X
Ships: various

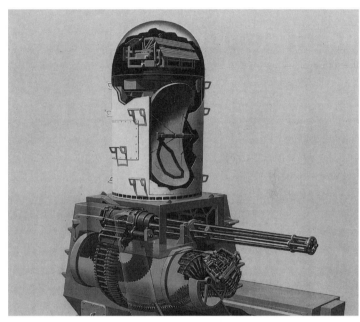

An artist's cutaway view of a Phalanx CIWS mounting shows the VPS-2 radar antenna fitted just above the weapon's six barrels (within the white radome); IFF antennas are fitted at the top of the radome. (General Dynamics/Pomona)

MK 95 MISSILE FIRE CONTROL RADAR

This is the fire control radar component of the Mk 91 fire control system for the Sea Sparrow SAM; see entry for Mk 91.

MK 26 RADAR

This is a range-only fire control radar associated with the Mk 40 gun director in the IOWA-class battleships. Adapted from the Mk 11, the Mk 26 radar has a 36-inch (914-m) paraboloid antenna. Its effective range is 10,000 yards (9.2 km) against a large aircraft and 16,000 yards (14.6 km) against a large warship.

The radar's peak power is 40–60 kW. It has been operational since 1944.

Prime contractor: GE and RCA
Band:
Ships: BB 61

MK 25 RADAR

The Mk 25 is the fire control radar associated with the Mk 37 GFCS in the IOWA-class battleships for use with the 5-inch dual-purpose guns. Some ships had the SPG-53E radar on their forward Mk 37 director. (The Mk 25 Mod 7 was the first U.S. shipboard missile guidance radar.)

The radar has a 60-inch (1.5-m) conical scanning "dash." Its maximum range is 100,000 yards (91,460 m) and its peak power is 250 kW.

The Mk 25 has been operational since 1948.

Prime contractor: Western Electric
Band: X
Ships: BB 61

The after Mk 37 GFCS with the 60-inch (1.52-m) circular antenna for the Mk 25 radar *(left)* and the massive Mk 38 GFCS with the cylindrical antenna for the Mk 13 radar on the battleship IOWA. The Mk 37 GFCS was long found on U.S. combatants, as well as amphibious and auxiliary ships, to direct 5-inch guns; the Mk 37 GFCS is for the main battery 16-inch guns. (Giorgio Arra)

MK 13 RADAR

The Mk 13 fire control radar in the IOWA-class battleships provides range and bearing data for the Mk 38 and Mk 34 gun directors for the ships' main batteries. The radar previously was mounted in gun cruisers as well as battleships.

The Mk 13's tracking range is 50,000 yards (45.7 km). Its bar-type antenna is 8 feet (2.4 m) long and 2 feet (0.6 m) in diameter. It is mounted atop the Mk 38 director in IOWA-class ships. Peak power is 50 kW.

Prime contractor:	Western Electric
Band:	X
Ships:	BB 61

MFR (MULTI-FUNCTION RADAR)

The MFR is an X-band, solid-state, phased-array radar being developed by Lockheed Martin. It is intended as a self-defense radar to provide future warships with a capability to intercept high-performance missiles. It will be given an AN/-series designation.

STIR (SEPARATE TARGET ILLUMINATION RADAR)

The STIR is a modified SPG-60 radar for use with Mk 92 gun/missile fire control system in the PERRY-class frigates (see page 541). It has been operational since 1974.

Prime contractor:	FMC
Band:	X
Ships:	FFG 7

SHIPBOARD SONARS

Sonar is the U.S. Navy's principal means for detecting and targeting submarines. All active U.S. surface warships and submarines are fitted with sonars; the SH-60F/R ASW helicopters use a "dipping" sonar and other anti-submarine aircraft employ expendable sonobuoys (the SH-60R has both a dipping sonar and sonobuoys); CAPTOR (Encapsulated Torpedo) sea mines employ sonar for submarine detection; mine countermeasures forces use sonars to detect mines; and ASW forces make extensive use of seafloor sonar systems (SOSUS). These sonars are passive or active, with some equipment capable of operating in both modes.

Submarine sonars. Contemporary U.S. submarine sonars are derived principally from German development of passive array sonars in the World War II period.[7] These sonars have a series of fixed transducers that form beams in various directions by the electrical phasing of the transducer inputs. U.S. submarines traditionally operated in the passive mode in the era of nuclear-propelled submarines, generally being able to detect relatively noisy Soviet nuclear submarines before they themselves could be detected by their opponents. However, the appearance of quiet Soviet nuclear submarines from the early 1980s, of which the Akula class was the harbinger, has resulted in new interest in active sonar techniques. The Russian Navy's modern diesel-electric submarines—when operating submerged on electric propulsion—have a very low acoustic signature. (Of course,

---

7. The first "modern" array sonar installations were fitted in German submarines and surface ships beginning in the late 1930s. After the war, the first U.S. array sonar developed for operational use was the BQR-4 fitted in the hunter-killer submarine K-1 (SSK 1) in 1951; it was derived from the German designs.

operating techniques, environmental conditions, and other factors can make even older, relatively noisy submarines difficult to detect.)

Although towed-array sonars were developed by the U.S. Navy primarily for use in surface ships, they were quickly adapted to submarine use and have now been fitted in most of the current SSN and SSBN types.

Surface ship sonars. Surface ship sonars vary considerably in type and installation. The principal hull-mounted sonars in the U.S. Navy today are the SQS-53 series and SQS-56. The SQS-53 sonar had its origins in the early 1950s, when the first Soviet post–World War II submarines began going to sea in large numbers; this is a relatively large sonar, with long-range passive and some active capabilities.

During the later 1950s, the U.S. Navy developed two additional types of surface ship sonars: Variable Depth Sonar (VDS) and Towed Array Sonar (TAS). The VDS is lowered over the stern of a ship to place the sonar dome below the near-surface thermal layers that reflect sonar beams. Towed array development has led to the highly successful Tactical Towed Array Sonar (TACTAS), which consists of a passive (hydrophone) system in a cable towed behind the ship. By using convergence-zone detection techniques, TACTAS has long-range capabilities against submarines, especially when employed by screening ships away from the noisy task force center.[8]

A further development of the towed-array concept is the Surveillance Towed Array Sonar System (SURTASS), which is a longer, more capable hydrophone array. While the TACTAS is carried by combatant ships (cruisers, destroyers, and frigates), the SURTASS is an area surveillance system, towed by slow-speed, tug-type ships designated T-AGOS (see page 555). The SURTASS/T-AGOS concept is intended for use in areas where the seafloor SOSUS detection system has been destroyed or does not exist (see Seafloor Acoustic Systems below). The SURTASS AN/-series designation is UQQ-2.

Mine countermeasure sonars. Sonar is also used in mine countermeasures systems, with high-resolution sonars in minesweepers and helicopters.

ADVANCED MINE DETECTOR SONAR (AMDS)

This is an active submarine sonar intended for mine detection. The "chin"-mounted sonar underwent trials in the ASHEVILLE (SSN 758). It will be fitted in the LOS ANGELES and VIRGINIA SSNs.

AN/BQG-5 WIDE APERTURE ARRAY SONAR

The Wide Aperture Array (WAA) sonar will enhance submarine fire control solutions against hostile submarines. The first BQG-5 was installed in the submarine AUGUSTA (SSN 710) in 1992 for at-sea evaluation. WAA components also were evaluated in the research ship GLOVER (T-AGFF 1). The BQG-5 antenna arrangement consists of three rectangular panels mounted on each side of the submarine.

The SEAWOLF class is fitted with the BQG-5D version, while the VIRGINIA class will have the lightweight BQG-5A version. The BQG-5 may be retrofitted in the Improved LOS ANGELES–class submarines.

Prime contractor:	Lockheed Martin
Ships:	SSN 21
	SSN 774
	SSN 688 (1 ship)

AN/BQQ-9 TASPE SONAR

The Towed Array Signal Processing Equipment (TASPE) is a passive sonar fitted in the OHIO-class missile submarines. It supports the BQR-15 sonar.

| Prime contractor: | Rockwell |
| Ships: | SSBN 726 |

AN/BQQ-6 SONAR

This sonar system was adapted from the BQQ-5 for use in strategic missile submarines of the OHIO class. It is primarily a passive system with a limited active capability in the BQS-13; the BQQ-6 includes a

large bow sphere with 944 hydrophones, plus flank arrays and a towed array.

| Prime contractor: | IBM |
| Ships: | SSBN 726 |

AN/BQQ-5 SONAR

This active/passive sonar system is currently fitted in all active U.S. attack submarines, except for the KAMEHAMEHA (SSN 642), a former Polaris/Poseidon submarine employed as transport for special operations forces. The BQQ-5 was originally provided in submarines of the LOS ANGELES class and was backfitted in the PERMIT (SSN 594) and STURGEON (SSN 637) classes, replacing the BQQ-2 system.

The BQQ-5 is a digital system that integrates the bow-mounted array, the conformal (hull-mounted) array, and the towed array. A computer-driven signal processor is used to select the hydrophones and steer the beams. With this method, the number of beams that can be formed is limited only by computer capacity. Also, the digital BQQ-5 suffers far less from internal noise than the BQQ-2 with manual switching, thus enhancing the detection of weaker acoustic signals. The BQQ-5 digital computer's processing allows a reduction in the number of normal watchstanders.

Developed from the BQQ-2 system, the BQQ-5 has a large spherical bow array fitted in a 15-foot (4.6-m)-diameter sphere mounting 1,241 transducers (the BQS-11, 12, or 13), a "chin" array with 104 hydrophones, and a TB-series towed array (see below). The BQQ-5 on the PARCHE (SSN 683) has the BQS-11 and BQS-14.

BQQ-5 versions have provided improved display consoles, as well as integrated towed array processing. The latest version is the BQQ-5E modification, being fitted in all surviving LOS ANGELES–class submarines and the SEAWOLF class; this sonar and the TB-29 towed array sonar are components of the Combat Control System (CCS) Mk 2. The BQQ-5E is referred to as the "QE-2" system.

Submarines of the Improved LOS ANGELES class have the BQQ-5 integrated in the BSY-1 system.

Prime contractor:	Lockheed Martin (formerly IBM, Loral)
Ships:	SSN 688
	SSN 683

AN/BQR-21 SONAR

A passive detection sonar, the BQR-21 is a highly capable sonar with DIMUS (Digital Multi-beam Steering). It is now found only in the ex-Polaris/Poseidon submarine KAMEHAMEHA. It is used with the BQR-24 processor.

| Prime contractor: | Honeywell |
| Ships: | SSN 642 |

AN/BQR-19 SONAR

This is a short-range passive navigation sonar mounted on a submarine mast; it has 24 hydrophones in a cylindrical housing.

Prime contractor:	Raytheon
Ships:	SSBN 726
	SSN 683

AN/BQR-15 TOWED SONAR ARRAY

The BQR-15 is a passive towed sonar array (with BQR-23 sonar processor). It consists of a 156-foot (47.7-m) passive array towed by a 2,200-foot (670-m) cable.

Prime contractor:	
Ships:	SSBN 726
	SSN 688
	SSN 683
	SSN 642

AN/BQR-7 SONAR

The BQR-7 has hull-mounted hydrophones for passive search and target classification. The KAMEHAMEHA has the BQR-7E version.

| Prime contractor: | |
| Ships: | SSN 642 |

---

8. If the ocean depth is sufficient, sound will travel down and back to the surface at an annular about 30 n.miles/55.5 km away, that is, to the first convergence zone. An advanced passive sonar system can be effective out to three convergence zones, or some 90–100 n.miles/167–185 km.

AN/BQS-24 SONAR

This is a high-frequency active array for under-ice operations fitted in the sail structure of the SEAWOLF.

Prime contractor:
Ships: SSN 21

AN/BQS-15 SONAR

This is a short-range sonar for under-ice and mine-avoidance operations. It has a cylindrical transducer housing and operates in both high- and low-frequency ranges.

Prime contractor:
Ships: SSBN 726
                         SSN 688
                         AGSS 555

AN/BQS-13 SONAR

This narrow-band, active search sonar is the active element of the BQQ-5/6 systems.

Prime contractor: Raytheon
Ships: SSBN 726
                         SSN 688

AN/BQS-4

The BQS-4 is an active/passive sonar with seven large transducers that serve as receivers. It is now fitted only in the ex-Polaris/Poseidon submarine KAMEHAMEHA, which is employed as a transport for special operations forces.

The BQS-4 has been operational since 1955.

Prime contractor: EDO
Ships: SSN 642

AN/BSY-2 COMBAT SYSTEM

Formerly known as the Submarine Advanced Combat System (SUBACS)/Fiscal 1989 System, the BSY-2 is an advanced sonar and fire control system for attack submarines of the SEAWOLF class. See the BSY-1 entry for background information.

The functions of the BSY-2 are to detect, classify, track, and launch weapons against hostile submarine targets. It is intended to permit the SEAWOLF to detect and locate targets faster, to allow operators to perform multiple tasks and address multiple targets concurrently, and—ultimately—to reduce the time between detecting a threat and launching weapons. The principal antennas of the BSY-2 are a large spherical array, a conformal hull array, a separate active transmitter, a high-frequency mine/under-ice sonar, towed arrays, and Wide Aperture Arrays (WAA). The last consist of three large, flat arrays mounted along each side of the submarine; they employ low-frequency, passive sensing capabilities to rapidly determine the locations of targets in both azimuth and depth to provide more accurate target range and tracking data. (The BSY-1 is similar in concept although the configuration is different; see below.)

The BSY-2 has been plagued by a number of problems, including increasing costs and technical problems associated with the UYS-2 Enhanced Modular Signal Processor (EMSP), database management system, and computer network. Of particular concern has been the unprecedented number of lines of computer (software) code required for the BSY-2 system—some 3.2 million, of which more than two million are in the new Ada language for which there were inadequate numbers of experienced programmers available.[9] The BSY-2 computer code requirement is about twice the amount needed for the BSY-1. A recent investigation by the General Accounting Office into the BSY-2 concluded:

> The risks that the Navy has allowed in the development of its BSY-2 combat system are serious. . . .
>
> In its endeavor to meet BSY-2 delivery schedules, tied closely to the submarine's delivery, the Navy is not following some sound management principles and practices, and is pushing forward not only with development of the first three systems but also for approval of three additional systems. By doing so, the Navy could find itself with combat systems that fall short of their promised capability and could cost millions to enhance.[10]

9. The only Department of Defense program known to exceed the SEAWOLF in lines of Ada code is the F-22 Raptor fighter.
10. General Accounting Office, *Submarine Combat System: BSY-2 Development Risks Must Be Addressed and Production Schedule Reassessed,* GAO/IMTEC-91-30 (August 1991), p. 2.

The spherical, bow-mounted array that mounts components of the BSY-2 sonar/combat system. Despite the massive development costs of the BSY-2 (originally part of the SUBACS system), the BSY-2 is being fitted only in the three submarines of the SEAWOLF class. (Newport News Shipbuilding)

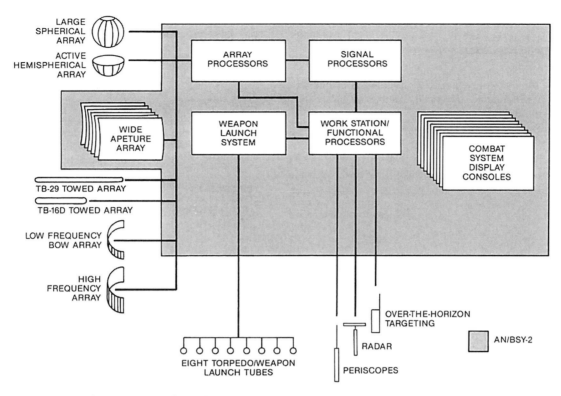

BSY-2 Combat System (William Clipson)

The delays in the completion of the first submarine of the class, however, could permit time to remedy some or all of these problems, many of which can be traced directly to its predecessor, the BSY-1.

The estimated cost of the BSY-2 program has *decreased* over the past few years, from about $16 *billion* to some $14 *billion*. The reduction was due mainly to the Navy eliminating one base at which SEAWOLFS would operate (allowing a reduction in BSY-2 spares, training equipment, personnel, etc.). Those costs, however, were based on the procurement of 29 sets; only three have been procured for the truncated SEAWOLF program.

BSY-2 component systems include the BQS-24 high-frequency active array in the sail, BQG-5 WAA (three per side), and the TB-12X and TB-16D towed-array sonars.

The system has been operational since 1996.

Prime contractor: Lockheed Martin (formerly General Electric)
Ships: SSN 21

AN/BSY-1 COMBAT SYSTEM

Formerly known as SUBACS (Submarine Advanced Combat System), the BSY-1 is an advanced sonar and fire control system intended for installation in 20 LOS ANGELES–class submarines beginning with the SSN 751. The system was known as SUBACS until changed to BSY-1 in 1986. The SUBACS/BSY-1 program was one of the most poorly run programs in recent Navy history.

Early in 1986, the Secretary of Defense told Congress that SUBACS "will maintain our [submarine] force's edge in undersea detection and targeting." Employing advanced computer hardware and software, the system is intended to exploit advanced acoustic sensors—such as Wide Aperture Arrays (WAA)—to analyze acoustic detection data, identify targets, and make fire control calculations.

When conceived in the early 1980s, there were to be three versions of SUBACS: the *Basic* version for the SSN 751–759, the *B* version for the SSN 760 (fiscal 1986) and later LOS ANGELES–class submarines, and the *B-prime* version for the SSN 21 class. The need to restructure the program because of major problems led to a two-part program, the BSY-1 for the Improved LOS ANGELES class (SSN 751–773) and the BSY-2 for the SEAWOLF.

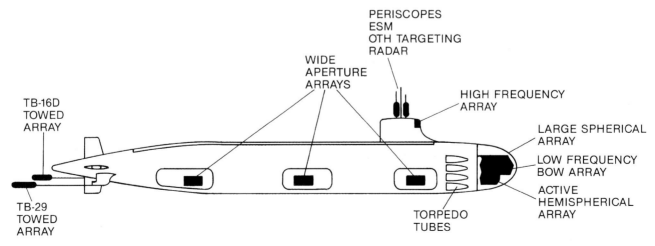

BSY-2 Combat System components in the SEAWOLF (William Clipson)

The program has suffered severe technical, cost, and management problems. The planned optical data bus—using fiber-optic technology to transmit data—encountered difficulties, causing a redesign effort to employ more-conventional electronic technology. Next, there were difficulties in producing the multilayer computer circuit boards. And there were management problems, both on the part of IBM, which had been contracted to develop and produce SUBACS, and the Navy. A late 1985 Congressional report on the situation stated that "severe technical and management problems have significantly increased costs, delayed schedules, and degraded planned system capability." Navy and other government agency reviews of SUBACS indicated that research and development for the system would cost $2.4 *billion* and shipbuilding costs for the submarines already authorized were estimated to be 40 percent more than appropriated. The House and Senate armed services committees at the time reported that "the constrained capability of the SUBACS is no longer worth the investment."

The problems led the Secretary of the Navy and the Chief of Naval Operations to personally take over the management of the contract and renegotiate it. In late 1985 the Navy restructured the program to provide the two-track BSY-1/BSY-2 approach. In January 1986 the Navy renegotiated the IBM contract to complete seven SUBACS sets at a fixed-price of $1.3 *billion*. In his February 1986 testimony to Congress, Chief of Naval Operations Admiral James Watkins spoke of the "restructured" and "relabeled" SUBACS program being reorganized from three steps to two: "The middle step was not deemed necessary; it was very expensive and there was no way we could have managed the transition from step 2 to 3, which is to the SSN 21 class suite."

When installation of the first BSY-1 set began on the SAN JUAN (SSN 751) late in 1986, it was found that the cabling would not fit into the spaces allocated for the equipment in the submarine. This situation has further increased costs and delayed completion of that submarine; further, the first four installations (SSN 751–754) were not complete when fitted, leaving those submarines with only limited self-defense capabilities; they were upgraded to provide full BSY-1 capabilities after the submarines went to sea.

The BSY-1 finally became operational in 1989.

Prime contractor: Lockheed Martin (formerly IBM, General Electric, Lockheed
                     Missile and Space, Loral)
Ships: SSN 751–773

AN/SQQ-89(V) ASW COMBAT SYSTEM

The SQQ-89 surface ship ASW combat system is the first integrated ASW combat system for surface ships, combining sensors and weapons control systems with sophisticated data processing and display. Known as the "Squeak 89," the system correlates and manages acoustic sensor input from the hull-mounted sonar and towed array and forwards track data to the ship's combat direction system.

There are several variants of the SQQ-89:

(V)1 in DD 963 class
(V)2 in DDG 7 class
(V)3 in CG 54 class
(V)4 in DDG 51 class
(V)10 in DD 79 class

The (V)4 system was planned for the PERRY-class frigates, but the installation was canceled in 1990 because of budget constraints. That variant was also known as the SQQ-89I—the suffix indicating "improved"—and was subsequently designated SQY-1.

The large SQS-53B/C sonars of the cruisers and destroyers are integrated into the SQQ-89, as are the SQR-19 towed arrays, SQQ-28 shipboard acoustic processing component of the LAMPS III helicopter system, and the ships' ASW weapons control system.

The destroyer MOOSBRUGGER (DD 980) was the first ship to have the SQQ-89 installed. The system became operational in 1985.

Prime contractor: General Electric and Westinghouse
Ships: CG 47
                     DDG 51
                     DD 963
                     FFG 7 (some ships)

AN/SQQ-32 SONAR

This is a high-resolution mine detection and classification sonar. Provided in all MCM ships, the sonar antenna is a "towed" body lowered through the hull of the carrying ship (the SQQ-14/30 arrangement is similar). The sonar can be employed in a hull-mounted (retracted) mode for shallow-water operation. There are 48 acoustic arrays in a "stave" arrangement around the barrel-like towed body, with the bar-type classification antenna at the bottom of the body. The towed body weighs 7,845 pounds (3,530 kg).

Operational: The first operational use of the SQQ-32 was by the AVENGER (MCM 1) in the Persian Gulf in early 1991. The SQQ-32 provided successful mine detections in Gulf operations; however, the AVENGER suffered problems with her sonar as well as with her engines.

Status: In service since 1991.

Prime contractor: Raytheon/Thomson CSF
Ships: MCM 1
                     MHC 51

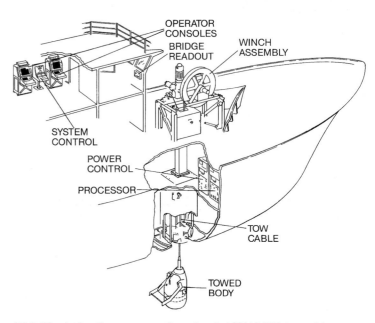

SQQ-32 minehunting sonar configuration in MCM/MHC-type ships
(William Clipson)

An artist's view of the towed sensor body of the SQQ-32 minehunting sonar examining a seafloor object. The "hunting" technique is necessary to detect and identify objects on the sea floor that could be bottom mines. (Raytheon)

An SQQ-32 towed body prior to being installed in a mine counter-measures ship (Raytheon)

AN/SQQ-30 SONAR

The SQQ-30 mine detection and classification sonar was developed from the SQQ-14. The antenna was cable-lowered from under the minesweeper. The SQQ-30 had limited capabilities and was succeeded in service by the SQQ-32.

From 1987, the SQQ-30 was fitted in nine mine countermeasures ships of the AVENGER class.

AN/SQQ-28 SONAR PROCESSOR

The SQQ-28 is the shipboard acoustic processor and data link for the SH-60B/R LAMPS III anti-submarine helicopter.

Prime contractor:
Ships: CG 47
                    DDG 51
                    DD 963
                    FFG 7

AN/SQR-19A/B TACTICAL TOWED ARRAY SONAR (TACTAS)

The SQR-19 TACTAS is a passive hydrophone array fitted in TICONDEROGA-class cruisers, ARLEIGH BURKE– and SPRUANCE-class destroyers, and the active PERRY-class frigates. The towed array or "tail" locates the sonar away from ship-generated noises that could otherwise mask a target's acoustic signals. The modular construction of the array permits hydrophone components that fail or are damaged to be replaced aboard ship.

The array can be effective at relatively high ship's speed and in sea states up to 4. The SQR-19 array has a nominal diameter of 3¼ inches (82.5 mm) and is towed at the end of a 5,600-foot (1,700-m) cable. The array section weighs about 10,000 pounds (4,536 kg).

The "wet end" (cable systems) of the SQR-19 is also fitted in Canadian and Spanish frigates.

Prime contractor: Gould Electronics
Ships: CG 47
                    DDG 51
                    DD 963 (some ships)
                    FFG 7 (some ships)

AN/SQR-18A(V) TACTAS

This version of the TACTAS is a passive hydrophone system employed by frigates. Similar to the SQR-19, the SQR-18A(V)2 is streamed from the PERRY-class ships assigned to the NRF. The array—which is 730 feet (223 m) long—is towed from a 5,000-foot (1,525-m) cable rather than the VDS towed body as in the earlier frigates of the KNOX (FF 1052) class. The system can be effective in sea states up to 4.

The SQR-18A is fitted in Japanese ASW ships. It was planned for installation in Coast Guard cutters, but that program was aborted when the Coast Guard withdrew from the ASW role (see chapter 30).

The basic SQR-18 was an interim towed array that evolved into the SQR-18A TACTAS.

Prime contractor: Gould Electronics
Ships: FFG 7 (NRF ships)

AN/SQR-17A ACOUSTIC PROCESSOR

The SQR-17A is the acoustic processor for sonobuoys and related display for use with SH-2G LAMPS I helicopters. It is being succeeded in newer ships by the SQQ-89. In 1986 the Congress voted funds for the procurement of 20 SQR-17A sets for NRF frigates.

Prime contractor:
Ships: DD 963
                    FFG 7 (NRF ships)

AN/SQS-56 SONAR

The SQS-56 is an active/passive sonar with severely limited capabilities. Ships fitted with this sonar are expected to detect submarines primarily with their towed array sonar.

The severe cost and size constraints imposed by the Chief of Naval Operations when the PERRY-class frigates were designed led to the small, higher-frequency—and thus shorter-range—SQS-56 being employed in this class. Raytheon had developed the SQS-56 as a totally company-funded project to provide a modern, lightweight sonar to smaller warships. The use of the SQS-56 saved perhaps 600 tons of displacement in the FFG 7, while requiring far less electrical power than the 66 kilowatts needed for the SQS-53. The cost is effective range, with the SQS-56 being capable of direct path detections only on the order of 5 miles (8 km)—far too little for effective use with ship-based ASW helicopters. The SQS-56 operates at 5.6, 7.5, and 8.4 kHz.

During the 1980s the set was modified to provide a capability for short-range mine detection; the modification is known as the "Kingfisher."

(Other factors in the decision to reduce the PERRY-class sonar effectiveness were the availability of large numbers of SQS-26/53 sonars in other ASW ships and the potential of towed array sonars.)

SQS-56 sonars have been fitted in the warships of several other navies, some with the Raytheon commercial designations DE-1160B/C.

The sonar has been operational since 1977.

Prime contractor: Raytheon
Ships: FFG 7

AN/SQS-53 SONAR

This is a large active/passive sonar. An improved SQS-26CX sonar, the SQS-53 became the bow-mounted sonar of the SPRUANCE versions (DD 963/DDG 993/CG 47 classes), as well as the subsequent ARLEIGH BURKE–class destroyers.

The principal difference between the SQS-26CX and the SQS-53 is the digital interface, with the Mk 116 ASW weapon control system in the latter sonar. The SQS-53B has an improved, digital, solid-state display. The SQS-53C has improved active performance, multiple target capability, automatic target tracking, and a higher systems availability (2,000 hours MTBF).

The SQS-53B is fitted in the TICONDEROGA class (beginning with CG 56) and backfitted in the SPRUANCE class (beginning with DD 980). The SQS-53C is being procured for the BURKE-

class destroyer and will eventually be backfitted in ships with SQS-53/53B.

The SQS-53 has been operational since 1975.

Prime contractor: General Electric and Hughes
Ships: CG 47
                     DDG 51
                     DD 963

An SQS-53 transducer housing fitted in a SPRUANCE-class destroyer (Litton/Ingalls Shipbuilding)

AN/SQS-38 SONAR

This is a hull-mounted version of the SQS-35 developed for the Coast Guard's HAMILTON (WHEC 715)-class cutters. The set has been deactivated, as those ships have discarded their ASW capability. The solid-state sonar was developed specifically to replace the vacuum-tube SQS-36 sonar in those cutters. The sonar could operate in both active and passive modes.

This was the only sonar fitted in U.S. Coast Guard cutters. It was manufactured by EDO Corporation, College Point, N.Y., with 14 sets delivered for shipboard installation and training from 1967.

AN/SQS-26 SONAR

The SQS-26 was an active/passive sonar with a nominal direct-path range of 20,000 yards (18.3 km). Major delays in delivery and technical problems caused the SQS-26 not to be approved for service use until November 1968—six years after its introduction. By that time, more than a score of ships had been fitted with the sonar. The sonars were of limited effectiveness during this period, while the ships' long-range ASW delivery capability was nil because of the short range of ASROC and the short-lived Drone Anti-Submarine Helicopter (DASH) program.

All cruisers and frigates that carried the SQS-26 have been stricken from the U.S. Navy.

The SQS-26 was declared operational in 1962.

SQS-53 sonar dome on the destroyer SPRUANCE (DD 963). Ships with large bow sonar domes are fitted with a stem anchor as well as an anchor on the starboard side; the former provides some protection for the dome from the anchor chain. (Litton/Ingalls Shipbuilding)

AN/SQY-1 ASW COMBAT SYSTEM

This was to be an integrated ASW combat system intended for major ASW ships as successor to the SQQ-89. It was to integrate all ASW sensors and fire control systems in surface combatants.

The SQY-1 was terminated by the Department of Defense in January 1992 as a cost-saving measure, permissible in view of the demise of the Soviet Union and the reduced threat from its submarine force. Accordingly, there will be some changes in the SQQ-89 modernization program to reflect the SQY-1 cancellation.

Initial operational capability for the SQY-1 was originally planned for the mid-1990s, but was delayed prior to cancellation until after 2000 because of funding issues. The system was originally intended for the 51 frigates of the PERRY class, as well as cruisers and destroyers. The subsequent decision not to provide the system to ASW frigates reduced the program to some 80 ships, with a related increase in unit costs.

Like the BSY-2, the SQY-1 was to incorporate the UYS-2 Enhanced Modular Signal Processor (EMSP) to handle the large amount of data processing required for the system. (When developed, the EMSP will also be used for an upgrade of the SURTASS and other ASW systems.)

The system was previously designated SQQ-89 Improved (SQQ-89I).

AN/TB-SERIES TOWED ARRAY SONARS

Submarine towed array sonars are designated in the TB-series (for Towed Body). These passive arrays are fully retractable into "sleeves" mounted on submarine decks.

The original TB-16 "fat-line" array is 240 feet (73 m) long and 3½ inches (89 mm) in diameter. It mounts 50 hydrophones, which weigh a total of 1,400 pounds (635 kg), and is neutrally buoyant. The acoustics package is towed at the end of a 2,600-foot (793-m) cable that is 0.37 inches (9.4 mm) in diameter and weighs 450 pounds (204 kg).

Later versions have longer arrays, with the TB-16D being a "thin-line" array.

The TB-23 is a thin-line passive array approximately 1,500 feet (457 m) long, towed by a 2,600-foot (793-m) cable. It has 98 hydrophones, the smaller diameter of the array permitting the greater length to be accommodated by the submarine.

Prime contractor:	Lockheed Martin	
Ships:	TB-16	SSBN 726 (being replaced by TB-29)
	TB-16D	SSN 21
	TB-16 or TB-23	SSN 688
	TB-29	SSBN 726
		SSN 21
		SSN 774
		SSN 688 (some ships)

AN/UQQ-2 SURTASS (SURVEILLANCE TOWED ARRAY SENSOR SYSTEM)

SURTASS is a submarine detection system towed by slow surface ships to supplement SOSUS (see Seafloor Acoustic Systems below). These ships operate where SOSUS coverage is inadequate or where the seafloor arrays are damaged or destroyed. SURTASS data are sent via satellite link to shore facilities for processing and further transmission to ASW forces; however, the ships can also provide "raw" acoustic data to ASW ships in the area. The SURTASS concept differs from the TACTAS systems in that the latter are tactical hydrophone arrays towed by warships to supplement hull-mounted sonars.

The oceanographic research ship MOANA WAVE (AGOR 22) conducted sea trials of the UQQ-2 in 1979–1984; the ex–missile submarine SAM HOUSTON (SSBN 609) was employed in the mid-1980s as an underwater test platform for the UQQ-2.

So-called block upgrades are expanding the acceptability of SURTASS for the T-AGOS 23 ships.

SURTASS has been operational since 1984. See page 249 for additional characteristics.

Prime contractor:	Hughes and Lockheed-Sanders
Ships:	T-AGOS 23
	T-AGOS 19
	T-AGOS 1

AN/WQT-2 LFA (LOW-FREQUENCY ACTIVE) SONAR

The WQT-2 is an improved LFA towed array sonar for later T-AGOS surveillance ships. The system was tested aboard the support ship COREY CHOUEST (see chapter 24).

Prime contractor:	Lockheed Martin (Saunders)
Ships:	T-AGOS 23

SEAFLOOR ACOUSTIC SYSTEMS

The U.S. Navy operates several seafloor Sound Surveillance Systems (SOSUS) in various parts of the Atlantic and Pacific, as well as across the Strait of Gibraltar and off North Cape (north of Norway). In the late 1960s, Secretary of Defense Robert S. McNamara first publicly acknowledged the existence of SOSUS, although installation had began in the 1950s and was known to the Soviets shortly after emplacements began.[11]

SOSUS is used to detect transiting submarines and, in wartime, would be used to direct air, surface, and submarine ASW forces to their targets. However, the SOSUS arrays are vulnerable to active and passive (i.e., jamming) attacks by hostile naval and possibly merchant forces.

During World War II, the American and British (and Soviet) navies installed limited-capability acoustic arrays on the ocean floor in shallow waters, especially near harbors. Immediately after the war, the U.S. Navy began development of deep-ocean arrays. By 1948 arrays were being tested at sea and by 1951 the first SOSUS arrays were being implanted at sea. Also termed Project Caesar, the first set of operational hydrophones were installed at Sandy Hook, N.J., south of Manhattan, followed in 1952 by a deep-water (1,200-foot/365.85-m) installation off Eleuthra in the Bahamas. That year, the Chief of Naval Operations directed the establishment of six arrays in the Western Atlantic, all to be ready by the end of 1956. The first arrays in the Pacific were operational in 1958. Installations in other areas followed.

Initially, a number of Naval Facilities (NAVFAC) were established as the shore terminals for SOSUS, with NAVFACs being located along both U.S. coasts, in the Caribbean, in Iceland, and in Japan, as well as at other overseas locations. Subsequently, the seafloor hydrophones have been replaced, and the NAVFACs in the United States and Caribbean have been consolidated as more-capable arrays and computers have been developed.

The SOSUS system and SURTASS (T-AGOS) ships are integrated into the so-called Integrated Undersea Surveillance System (IUSS). Acoustic data from the NAVFACs and Regional Evaluation Centers (REC) are provided through the Ocean Surveillance Information System (OSIS) to the Atlantic, Pacific, and European area Fleet Command Centers (FCC) and to the Naval Ocean Surveillance Information Center (NOSIC), in Suitland, Md., near Washington, D.C., as well as the National Command Authority (NCA).[12] Thus, SOSUS information is provided at several levels—to tactical as well as theater and national commanders, and for technical evaluation.

Published sources cite detection ranges of "hundreds" of miles by SOSUS. Several update programs have been announced, especially related to computer capability, which can provide data more rapidly, with an improved signal-to-noise ratio.

An improved SOSUS-type system known as the Fixed Distributed System (FDS), which would be linked into the IUSS, was in advanced development in the early 1990s. However, beginning in

---

11. The locations of U.S. SOSUS arrays have been identified in Soviet magazines and books.
12. The National Command Authorities consist of the President and the Secretary of Defense; see chapter 4.

mid-1990, Congress began cutting the funding for the IUSS and FDS programs, despite traditional congressional support for major ASW programs. The system is intended to detect quiet, deep-running Russian submarines. A shallow-water FDS version is also being developed, with greater emphasis on fiber-optics than SOSUS-type systems and possible integration of nonacoustic sensors.

An Advanced Deployable System (ADS) is now under development. ADS is intended to provide an undersea surveillance system to detect diesel-electric submarines operating in shallow waters, observe minelaying activity, and track surface contacts. The system will interface directly with tactical forces (ships and aircraft). During a crisis or conflict, ADS is to be deployable within ten days to the operational area.

The obvious vulnerabilities of SOSUS in wartime, as well as some coverage limitations, have led to the T-AGOS/SURTASS program, as well as proposals for smaller arrays that could be planted by surface ships or aircraft. The latter has been an on-again, off-again program, identified by such acronyms as MSS (Moored Surveillance System) and RDSS (Rapidly Deployable Surveillance System). The RDSS was canceled by the Navy on 26 December 1984. This form of sonar would probably have been quite useful, in view of increased Soviet naval operating areas predicted at that time and the growing Third World submarine forces.

Current upgrades to SOSUS include transitioning from single-beam paper displays to multi-beam CRT-based displays, and improved communication links. These upgrades are being undertaken by AT&T.

HELICOPTER SONARS

The Navy's SH-60F/R anti-submarine helicopters are fitted with active/passive dipping sonar. Dipping sonar is necessary for sonar detection in the vicinity of surface ships because the ship-generated noises inhibit the use of passive air-launched sonobuoys.

AN/AQS-22 ALFS DIPPING SONAR

The AQS-22 Airborne Low Frequency Sonar (ALFS) is a variant of the Folding Light Acoustic Sonar (FLASH) developed by Thomson-CSF in France. ALFS will be used in the U.S. Navy's SH-60F/R Seahawk ASW helicopters.

The FLASH system was chosen over several U.S. competitive helicopter sonars. The Thomson system will be developed under a subcontract from Hughes Aircraft Co., now part of Raytheon. The lead systems were delivered in the late 1990s.

(The FLASH system is used in ASW helicopters of Great Britain, France, and the United Arab Emirates.)

The ALFS program calls for 429 systems at a production cost of $1.2 *billion*, which includes the costs of spares, training, and fitting the system to SH-60B/F helicopters. The Navy is combining the capabilities of the SH-60B and SH-60F in a single aircraft through a remanufacture program, the upgrade being designated SH-60R. The weight of ALFS requires an increase in the operating weight of the SH-60 helicopters to an estimated 23,500 pounds (10,660 kg).

The ALFS has a cable length of 2,550 feet (777 m); the sonar transducer is 50 inches (1.27 m) long and, with arms closed, 8⅓ inches (210 mm) in diameter, and weighs 174 pounds (79 kg). The passive array portion of the sonar has 24 staves mounted on 12 extending arms.

A towed version of this array has been proposed; such a system could have been employed from airships, as well as small craft.

AN/AQS-13 DIPPING SONAR

The Navy's SH-60F Seahawk ASW helicopters are fitted with the AQS-13 active dipping sonar. The latest version to be fitted in these helicopters is the AQS-13F.

The AQS-13F has a 1,500-foot (457-m) cable.

The AQS-22 ALFS dipping sonar being lowered by an SH-60F Seahawk helicopter during trials of the sub-hunting device. It also will be fitted in the multipurpose SH-60R variants. (Raytheon)

The sonar head of the AQS-22 ALFS system being fitted in Navy ASW helicopters (Raytheon)

An AQS-13 dipping sonar being deployed from an SH-3 Sea King ASW helicopter (U.S. Navy)

A technician loads an *internal* sonobuoy dispenser in a P-3C Orion. This is the only U.S. naval aircraft that has a sonobuoy dispenser that can be reloaded in flight (in addition to non-reloadable chutes external to the cabin). (U.S. Navy)

SEA MINE SONAR

Another significant use of sonar in ASW is for mine warfare, with the U.S. Navy's Mk 60 CAPTOR (Encapsulated Torpedo) being fitted with sonar to detect hostile submarines passing through the "attack envelope" of the mine's Mk 46 acoustic-homing torpedo. The Mk 60 uses a passive sonar to initially detect targets and an active acoustic set to identify the hostile submarine before launching the torpedo (see chapter 28).

(In addition to the Mk 46 Mod 5 launched by the CAPTOR mine, other versions of the torpedo launched from surface ships [Mk 32 tubes] and aircraft are fitted with active/passive acoustic guidance, as is the larger, submarine-launched Mk 48 torpedo.)

SONOBUOYS

Naval aircraft employ expendable, short-duration sonobuoys for the localization of submarines. Sonobuoys are generally employed after an initial submarine contact is gained by other means. However, aircraft also use sonobuoy barrier tactics, in which a string of sonobuoys is periodically planted ahead of a task force. The Navy's P-3C Orion, SH-2G LAMPS I, and SH-60B/R Seahawk aircraft all can launch and monitor sonobuoys; the P-3s and SH-60s can also analyze the sonobuoy data, while the SH-2s must relay the data back to their supporting warship for analysis.

When released by an aircraft, the buoy falls to the water, slowed by parachute or a retardation device. Upon reaching the water, the buoy's battery is activated, its transmission antenna extends, and a hydrophone is lowered by cable; depending on type, buoys be-

A sonobuoy falls from an SH-2F LAMPS I helicopter. The retardation fins are open to slow its descent. Note the 15 sonobuoy chutes fitted in the left side of the helicopter. There is a Mk 46 torpedo mounted below the sonobuoy chutes. (U.S. Navy)

Sonobuoys are loaded into the dispensing chutes on the left side of an SH-60B Seahawk helicopter. (U.S. Navy)

gin transmission either upon hitting the water or when command activated.

The principal types of sonobuoys now in U.S. Navy service are listed in table 29-2. The data shown are for the latest production models, unless a version is indicated. The figures for "depth" indicate the level to which the buoy's hydrophone (or bathythermographic sensor) is lowered by cable. The "endurance" is the operating life of the buoy; after a specified number of minutes or hours, the buoy canister floods and sinks.

Most current sonobuoys are of a standard "A" size that fit launch chutes on board ASW aircraft—3 feet (0.9 m) in length and 4⅞ inches (122 mm) in diameter. However, the SSQ-75 is larger—7½ feet (2.3 m) in length with a diameter of 10 inches (254 mm). Efforts are being made to reduce sonobuoy size, with dwarf "B"-size versions of the SSQ-53/77/79 being developed that will permit three sonobuoys to be carried in a standard A-size aircraft launcher.

Sonobuoys are used in a complementary manner, with some being laid to attain initial detection of a possible submarine target and others providing shorter-range, more precise data on the target's exact depth and bearing. The SSQ-36 Expendable Bathythermograph (XBT) is used to determine the acoustic conditions of the water column—vital data in ASW operations. The principal buoys currently used in air ASW operations are the SSQ-53 DIFAR (Directional Low-Frequency Acquisition and Ranging) and SSQ-62 Directional Command-Activated Sonobuoy System (DICASS) types. The SSQ-77 Vertical Line Array DIFAR (VLAD) is a deep-searching sonobuoy with a long-line array, as is the SSQ-79 Steered Vertical Line Array (SVLA). The SSQ-75 Expendable Reliable Acoustic Path Sonobuoy (ERAPS) is a command-activated buoy that uses active sonar to seek very quiet submarines; during its three-hour service life, it can produce about 100 active acoustic "pings." The SSQ-57 is a small, passive-detection sonobuoy intended for relatively shallow waters; the current U.S. Navy interest in regional naval operations could lead to renewed attention to this type of buoy.

The earlier SSQ-50 Command-Activated Sonobuoy System (CASS) buoy has been succeeded by the SSQ-62 DICASS. The SSQ-73 was an experimental deep-DIFAR buoy based on the SSQ-53; the SSQ-77 passive VLAD was procured in its place.

A large, 103-pound (46-kg) active pinging buoy designated SSQ-90 is in limited production for the Navy.

Ice-penetrating sonobuoys have been developed for use in the Arctic ice pack to detect Russian submarines operating under ice. These air-launched buoys are known to have successfully penetrated ice up to 10 feet (3 m) thick. At least one concept for ice-penetrating buoys employs a 2-pound (0.9-kg) lithium nose cone for penetrating the ice cover. Housed in an A-size sonobuoy, the ice-penetrator has an oversized parachute and shock absorber to reduce impact upon landing. After landing on the ice, the lithium nose cone melts through the ice, the sensor deploys through the hole in the ice, the nose cone falls away, the antenna (which remains above the ice) extends, and the sonobuoy becomes operational.

The SSQ-101 is a Horizontal-Line Array (HLA) sonobuoy that holds promise of long-range submarine detections. If development is successful, the buoy would be used for long-range detections ahead of surface naval forces. Development began in the mid-1980s (as did development of the SSQ-102 and SSQ-103 buoys, in response to the emergence of several Soviet quiet submarine classes).

An advanced submarine detection program known as the SSQ-102 Tactical Surveillance Sonobuoy (TSS) was canceled in late 1991 because of the reduced Soviet/Russian submarine threat. The TSS was to have an onboard mini-computer to analyze and record probable submarine noises and transmit them to ASW aircraft when so directed. This transmit-on-command was necessary because of the expected service life of TSS, on the order of five to seven days. (In effect, the TSS would have been a scaled-down version of the MSS and RDSS concepts.) Although TSS has been canceled, some of the technologies being developed under the program will be applicable to other ASW projects.

Also under development is the SSQ-103 Low-Cost Sonobuoy (LCS), a multiple-buoy device, in which an A-size buoy canister would deploy a field of six mini-buoys, each of which would suspend a hydrophone 300 feet (91 m) below the surface. The individual buoys would be 5½ inches (140 mm) in length and 4½ inches (114 mm) in diameter. The LCS system would seek out submarine flow noises, that is, the broad-band noise produced by water flow over a submarine's hull. This requires less-sophisticated sensors and analysis than is needed for narrow-band noises (produced by a submarine's machinery and propellers), but has very short range against slow-moving submarines.

The SSQ-58A is a moored surveillance buoy used by the Navy's Mobile Inshore Undersea Warfare units to form surveillance barriers to detect swimmers or small craft. The buoy itself is a fiberglass float 24 inches (0.6 m) in length and 36 inches (0.9 m) in diameter, carrying a standard omnidirectional hydrophone, up-link transmitter, antenna, and so forth. It can be recovered and its battery recharged; it does not sink at a predetermined time as do other buoys discussed here. (The designation SSQ-58 was previously applied to a LOFAR [Low-Frequency Acquisition and Ranging] buoy.)

The U.S. Navy also employs several communication buoys for submarine use: The BRC-6 Expendable Submarine Tactical Transceiver (XSTAT) is a two-way expendable buoy for ultra-high-frequency communications between a submarine and aircraft; the BRT-1 Submarine-Launched One-way Transmitter (SLOT) is ejected by a submarine to broadcast, with a preset delay, a four-minute taped message; the BRT-3/4/5 buoys transmit a signal to identify a submarine in night/bad weather; the BRT-6 is a one-way transmission buoy to uplink prerecorded UHF transmissions to a communications satellite; and the SSQ-71 and SSQ-86 are A-size two-way aircraft–submarine communications buoys that can be carried in aircraft sonobuoy dispensers.

TABLE 29-2. SONOBUOYS

Designation	Type	Manufacturer	Weight	Depth	Frequency range	Endurance
SSQ-36	bathythermograph (water temperature profile)	Sparton		1,000 ft (305 m)	—	few minutes
SSQ-41A	omnidirectional passive detection; LOFAR (Jezebel)	Hermes, Magnavox, Sparton	21 lbs (9.5 kg)	60 or 300 ft (18 or 91 m)	10 Hz to 20 kHz	1, 3, or 8 hours
SSQ-41B	same as SSQ-41A		29 lbs (13 kg)	60 or 1,000 ft (18 or 305 m)	10 Hz to 10 kHz	
SSQ-47B	active range-only		29 lbs (13 kg)	60 or 800 ft (18 or 244 m)		30 minutes
SSQ-53B	passive directional (DIFAR)	Canadian Commercial, Magnavox, Sparton	22 lbs (10 kg)	100, 400, or 1,000 ft (30.5, 122, or 305 m)	10 Hz to 2.4 kHz	1, 3, or 8 hours
SSQ-57	passive for restricted waters	Hermes, Sparton	14 lbs (6.35 kg)	60 or 400 ft (18 or 122 m)		1, 3, or 8 hours
SSQ-58	surveillance buoy	Sparton	20 lbs (6.1 kg)	20 ft (6.1 m)	50 Hz to 10 kHz	100 hours
SSQ-62B	Directional Command Active Sonobuoy System (DICASS)	Raytheon	34 lbs (15.4 kg)	90, 400, or 1,500 ft (27, 122, or 457 m)		30 hours
SSQ-75	Expendable Reliable Acoustic Path Sonobuoy (ERAPS)	ERAPSCo*	325 lbs (147 kg)	60 to 16,500 ft (18 to 5,030 m)		3 hours
SSQ-77B	passive Vertical Line Array DIFAR (VLAD)	Sparton, Magnavox	29 lbs (13 kg)	1,000 ft (305 m)	10 Hz to 2.4 kHz	1 or 8 hours
SSQ-79	Steered Vertical Line Array (SVLA)	Hazeltine		1,000 ft (305 m)		4 or 8 hours

* ERAPSCo is a joint venture by Magnavox and Sparton formed in 1987 to produce the ERAPS buoy.

TORPEDO COUNTERMEASURES

Torpedo countermeasures include electronic systems and decoys to reduce the effectiveness of enemy torpedoes, or to "replace" the ship or submarine target in the torpedo's target-acquisition process. U.S. surface warships, amphibious ships, and certain auxiliary ships have the SLQ-25 Nixie.

U.S. attack submarines are reported to carry the Mk 23 acoustic countermeasure device to decoy homing torpedoes, while ballistic missile submarines also can launch the Mk 70 MOSS (Mobile Submarine Simulator) from torpedo tubes to simulate a full-size submarine to a hostile sonar. (See photo page 540.)

AN/SLQ-39 DECOY LAUNCH BUOY

This is a chaff-dispensing buoy carried by some surface combatants.

Prime contractor: Raytheon
Ships: surface ships

AN/SLQ-25 NIXIE

A towed torpedo countermeasures system, Nixie is found on most U.S. Navy surface combatants and in many other ships, including replenishment ships that would normally operate with surface warships.

Nixie is an electro-acoustic device that attempts to decoy an incoming torpedo away from the target ship. The acoustic projector that transmits the decoying signal is in a TB-14 towed "fish." The signal itself is generated aboard ship and transmitted to the towed body through the towing cable.

The U.S. Navy procured the original SLQ-25 and, subsequently, an improved SLQ-25A version; more than 400 sets were procured.

Operational: In service since 1972. The effectiveness of Nixie was demonstrated in the 1982 war in the Falklands when a Nixie being towed by the British carrier HERMES attracted and was blown up by a British ASW torpedo that had been launched against a suspected Argentine submarine contact.

Prime contractor:	Aerojet	
Ships:	aircraft carriers	
	battleships	
	cruisers	
	destroyers	
	frigates	
	command ships	
	amphibious ships	
	LHD 1	LSD 36
	LHA 1	LPD 17
	LSD 49	LKA 113 (1 ship)
	LSD 41	
	auxiliary ships	
	AE 26	AOE 1
	AOE 6	AOR 1

AN/SLR-24 TORPEDO COUNTERMEASURES SYSTEM

In the mid-1990s the Navy planned to procure the SLR-24 system. The contractor was to design, fabricate, produce, test, and deliver the system, making the maximum use of existing components and Commercial-Off-The-Shelf (COTS) components. The procurement subsequently was canceled.

SURFACE SHIP TORPEDO DEFENSE (SSTD)

After several false starts, the Surface Ship Torpedo Defense (SSTD) project is providing U.S. ships with a limited hard-kill torpedo defense system, using modified Mk 46 torpedoes launched from Mk 32 torpedo tubes (see chapter 28).

In the fall of 1988, the U.S. and British governments signed a Memorandum of Understanding (MOU) to establish a four-phase, joint research effort SSTD project. When signed on 26 October 1988, the MOU was hailed by a U.S. Navy spokesman as providing "an excellent opportunity to improve mutual defense capabilities, reduce development and acquisition costs and to provide for increased compatibility and interoperability between the U.S. and Royal navies."[13]

The joint program, however, immediately ran into shoal water. While the U.S. Navy has pushed for a hard-kill approach, the British believe that soft-kill is more viable for SSTD. The British fear that a convoy escort firing weapons to intercept an incoming torpedo would put other ships in the convoy at risk. More threatening to the joint effort, the U.S. House Appropriations Committee subsequently killed funding for several Anglo-American projects, among them SSTD. The House report stated that the "committee does not consider such a joint project to be feasible given the security consideration regarding the sharing of acoustic signal data and countermeasure development, which the program would ultimately require."[14] Such language was highly inflammatory and counterproductive because of the close technical and operational relationship of the U.S. and British submarine communities and the large amount of acoustic data on Soviet/Russian undersea craft provided to the United States by the Royal Navy!

The U.S. Navy has converted 172 Mk 46 ASW torpedoes for the active anti-torpedo system for carrier defense against Russian wake-homing torpedoes.

Three American-led consortia were formed to develop SSTD systems: General Electric teamed with Alliant Techsystems

A sailor holds the towed "fish" of the SLQ-25 Nixie torpedo countermeasures system; the towing cable is in the foreground. The Nixie was used in a combat environment by the Royal Navy in the Falklands in 1982. (Aerojet General)

---

13. Caleb Baker, "U.S., Royal Navy to Explore Torpedo Defense Systems," *Navy Times,* 19 December 1988, p. 26.
14. "House Cites 'Security Concerns' in Cutting U.K. from SSTD," *Navy News,* 21 August 1989, p. 8.

(formerly Defense Products of Honeywell) and Marconi Underwater Systems; Westinghouse with AT&T, Dowty Maritime, and Ferranti; and Martin Marietta with Hughes Ground Systems, British Aerospace Dynamics, and Frequency Engineering Laboratories USA. After a series of initial contracts in the torpedo defense area, in early 1992 the first two teams were awarded contract extensions for the program.

WEAPON CONTROL SYSTEMS

Weapon control systems are designated in several series, with several mark series also being used. The major systems are identified in this section.

AN/SYS-SERIES INTEGRATED AUTOMATIC DETECTION AND TRACKING SYSTEMS

The SYS-1(V)2 and SYS-2(V) Integrated Automatic Detection and Tracking (IADT) systems integrate various radars in non-Aegis guided missile ships and large amphibious ships to facilitate command and control in high-threat environments. Each shipboard radar is fitted with a video converter from which the images are passed through a processor and integrated for display in the ship's combat information center.

The SYS-1 was developed specifically for the ADAMS-class destroyers and the SYS-2 for guided missile cruisers. The latter was subsequently selected for the PERRY-class frigate upgrade and is also installed in the WASP-class amphibious ships. (The SYS-3 system is provided in the Israeli SA'AR V–class missile corvettes that were built in the United States.)

The follow-on Integrated Radar Detection and Identification System (IRDIS) will integrate non-radar data (e.g., ESM) into the system.

SYS-1 was operational in 1977.

Prime contractor:　Norden (United Technologies)
Ships:　FFG 7 (some ships)
　LHD 1

CCS-SERIES COMBAT CONTROL SYSTEMS

These are multiple-function control systems for weapons in LOS ANGELES–class submarines. The original Mk 1 CCS developed for the LOS ANGELES class has been replaced in some units by the upgraded Mk 2 CCS (see chapter 11). The CCS integrates the submarine's torpedo fire control system (Mk 117) with the central computer complex.

The original CCS Mk 1 was the Mod 0. The Mod 1 (using UYK-7 computers) integrated the Tomahawk missile; the Mod 2 (using UYK-44 computers) added vertical-launching capability; the Mod 3 adds Mk 48 ADCAP capability; and the Mods 4 and 5 add a capability for the now-canceled Sea Lance missile.

The CCS Mk 2 has improved displays and workstations over the Mk 1. The Mod 0 was rapidly succeeded by the Mod 1, with provisions for over-the-horizon targeting (Tomahawk and Harpoon missiles); the Mod 2, intended for Trident submarines, has modified consoles/controls.

The software is modular, facilitating adaptation for various submarine/weapon configurations.

Prime contractor:　Raytheon
Ships:　SSBN 726
　SSN 688

MK 160 GFCS

The Mk 160 is an advanced gunfire control system (GFCS) that has been operational since 1991.

Prime contractor:
Ships:　DDG 51

MK 118 TORPEDO FCS

This is an all-digital torpedo fire control system developed for the Trident SSBNs. It controls torpedo launches, the release of 3-inch (76-mm) and 6-inch (152-mm) torpedo countermeasures, and the Mk 70 MOSS target simulators. It became operational in 1981.

Prime contractor:
Ships:　SSBN 726

MK 117 TORPEDO FCS

The Mk 177 was the U.S. Navy's first all-digital torpedo fire control system. The system was first installed in submarines of the THRESHER (SSN 593)/PERMIT class. Installation of the digital Mk 117 prevented use of the analog SUBROC missile; there was an attempt to correct this interface, but it had only limited use.

The Mk 117 Mods 6 and 7 are compatible with the Tomahawk missile; the Mod 8 is compatible with the Tomahawk and SUBROC, and could have handled the Sea Lance, had that missile been developed.

Prime contractor:
Ships:　Mod 0　SSN 700–715
　Mod 8　SSN 716–720

MK 116 ASW FCS

This is an advanced ASW weapons control system for surface ships. The all-digital system is linked to the SQS-53 sonar and controls ship-launched weapons (Mk 32 torpedo tubes); it also interfaces with the LAMPS helicopter (SH-60B/R).

The Mods 1 through 4 are for various ship types; the Mod 5 integrates the SQQ-89 sonar system; the Mod 6 integrates the Vertical-Launch ASROC (VLA) potential for the later TICONDEROGA-class cruisers; and the Mods 7, 8, 9, and 10 introduced the UYK-43B computer and are for use in the ARLEIGH BURKE–class destroyers, as well as non-VLS ships.

Prime contractor:　Librascope
Ships:　CG 47
　DDG 51
　DD 963

MK 115 FIRE CONTROL SYSTEM

The Mk 115, associated with the Sea Sparrow BPDMS, is a director/illuminator adopted from the older Mk 51 gun director mount. It also has side-by-side antennas. Tracking is manual.

Prime contractor:
Band:　X
Ships:　LHA 1
　MCS 12

MK 113 TORPEDO/MISSILE FCS

This was a torpedo fire control system widely used in SSNs and SSBNs; in attack submarines, it was replaced by the Mk 117 system. The only active U.S. submarine with the Mk 113 is the KAMEHAMEHA, which was not upgraded to the Mk 117 system because of her limited sonar capabilities and limited remaining service life.

Prime contractor:　Librascope
Ships:　SSN 642

MK 99 MISSILE FCS

These fire control directors are associated with the Aegis weapon system (Mk 7) and are operated in conjunction with SPG-62 radar.

The Mods 0 and 3 were fitted in the missile test ship NORTON SOUND. The Mod 1 was the prototype for the TICONDEROGA class and Mod 2 the production model for that class. The Mod 4 was a production model.

The Mk 99 has been operational since 1983.

Prime contractor:
Band: X
Ships: CG 47
                DDG 51

MK 98 MISSILE FCS

This is the missile control system for Trident missile submarines. It became operational in 1981.

Prime contractor:
Ships: SSBN 726

MK 92/94 WEAPON DIRECTION SYSTEMS

The Mk 92 and Mk 94 are both combined tracking and illuminating systems incorporating two antennas, one for air and one for surface target tracking. The Mod 2 version, in the PERRY-class frigates, is combined with the STIR radar to provide a second missile guidance channel in those ships; Mods 0 and 2 can control guns or missiles. The Mod 1, 3, 4, and 5 versions are for gun control only, with the Mod 1 in the PEGASUS (PHM 1) class (except that the lead ship had the Mk 94 prototype), the Coast Guard's BEAR (WMEC 901) class, and the modernized Coast Guard HAMILTON class. The Mk 94 prototype is fitted in the missile ship PEGASUS and the PERRY-class frigates. In the latter ships, those refitted with the Mk 92 Mod 6 system with a Coherent Radar Transmitter (CORT) in conjunction with the SYS-2(V)2 automatic target tracking system have increased weapons control capabilities.

Prime contractor: Sperry
Band: X
Ships: FFG 7
                      Coast Guard cutters

MK 91 WEAPON DIRECTION SYSTEM

This is the weapon direction system for the NATO Sea Sparrow missile system. The antenna system has side-by-side receiving and transmitting antennas; it typically has targets designated automatically by the SPS-58/65 radars or the Mk 23 TAS. It uses the Mk 95 fire control radar.

Band: X
Ships: aircraft carriers
          DD 963
          LHD 1
          AOE 6
          AOE 1

MK 90 FIRE CONTROL SYSTEM

The Mk 90 is the fire control system for the Phalanx CIWS (see VPS-2 radar).

MK 86 GUN/MISSILE FCS

The Mk 86 weapons control system is fitted with an SPQ-9A radar. The complete Mk 86 system includes an electro-optical sensor (closed-circuit low-light-level television) and SPG-60 tracker-illuminator radar. Reportedly, up to 120 target tracks can be monitored simultaneously.

The Mk 86 was evaluated in 1965 in the destroyer BARRY (DD 933) and has been operational since 1970. The Mods 0 through 10 have been developed with various target/tracking capabilities for various ship/radar/computer configurations.

Prime contractor:
Band: X
Ships: CG 47
                DD 963
                LHA 1

MK 74 MISSILE FCS

The Mk 74 weapons control system was associated with Tartar/Standard-MR missiles and was fitted with the SPG-51D radar. All of the cruisers and destroyers that carried the Mk 74 have been stricken.

MK 40 GUN DIRECTOR

The Mk 40 gun director is fitted with Mk 27 radar. It is employed as a standby director for the Mk 38 GFCS.

Prime contractor:
Band:
Ships: BB 61

MK 38 GFCS

This is the large main battery gun director for battleships and gun cruisers.

Prime contractor:
Band:
Ships: BB 61

MK 37 GFCS

The Mk 37 was a widely used World War II–era GFCS. It was succeeded by the Mk 67 and Mk 68 systems and is now found only in the mothballed IOWA-class battleships, fitted with the Mk 25 radar.

Prime contractor:
Band:
Ships: BB 61

MK 25 TARGET ACQUISITION SYSTEM

The Mk 25 is an improved version of the Mk 23 TAS. It has been operational since 1994.

Prime contractor:
Ships: AOE 6

MK 23 TARGET ACQUISITION SYSTEM

The Mk 23 Target Acquisition System (TAS) supports the NATO Sea Sparrow launcher Mk 29, the Mk 92/94 weapon FCS adopted from the Dutch M28 system, and the Mk 115 director/illuminator for the basic Sea Sparrow launcher Mk 25.

The Mk 23, intended for automatic reaction/target designation of incoming sea-skimming missiles, has a maximum range of almost 100 n.miles (185 km) and a minimum designation range of 20 n.miles (37 km). It incorporates pulse-Doppler radar. Designed to operate in high-clutter environment, it can simultaneously track up to 54 targets with a two-second scan rate.

The Mk 23 first went to sea on an operational basis in the frigate DOWNES (FF 1070) in 1975.

Prime contractor: Hughes
Band: L
Ships: CVN 68   LHD 1
                      CVN 65   LHA 5
                      CV 67   LPD 17
                      CV 63   AOE 3
                      DD 963

CHAPTER 30

Coast Guard

The Coast Guard cutter MIDGETT, with crew manning the rail, maneuvers alongside the amphibious assault ship PELELIU (LHA 5) in the Persian Gulf. In the post–Cold War era, the Coast Guard has taken on increasing overseas activities—law enforcement, economic, and military. The MIDGETT was part of the CONSTELLATION (CV 64) battle group when this photo was taken in October 1999. (U.S. Navy)

The U.S. Coast Guard is a military, multimission, maritime service within the Department of Transportation and one of the nation's five military services. Its missions are to protect the public and the environment and to support U.S. economic, security, and defense interests. The Coast Guard provides unique benefits to the nation because of its distinctive blend of humanitarian, law enforcement, and military capabilities.

Federal statute states that in the national security role the Coast Guard "shall maintain a state of readiness to function as a specialized service in the Navy in time of war, including the fulfillment of Maritime Defense Zone command responsibilities."

The Coast Guard is responsible for the enforcement of U.S. laws in coastal waters and on the high seas subject to the jurisdiction of the United States. At the direction of the President, the Coast Guard can become a part of the Navy (as it did during both World Wars) or it can operate in a war zone while remaining an independent service (as during the Korean and Vietnam Wars and the 1991 conflict in the Persian Gulf).

The principal peacetime activities of the Coast Guard are: (1) enforcing recreational boating safety; (2) conducting search-and-rescue operations; (3) maintaining aids to navigation (three manned and some 450 unmanned lighthouses, roughly 13,000 minor navigational lights, plus other navigation aids); (4) implementing merchant

marine safety; (5) carrying out environmental protection; (6) being responsible for port safety; and (7) enforcing laws and treaties. The last comprises the enforcement of the nation's customs and immigration laws, including the prevention of drug and illegal immigrant smuggling, and also the enforcement of fisheries laws and international treaties.

In addition, as a military service, the Coast Guard carries out specific military missions assigned by the Joint Chiefs of Staff (with the Commandant of the Coast Guard attending those JCS meetings that address issues of interest to the Coast Guard). Since 1985, the Coast Guard has had coastal defense responsibilities for the U.S. Atlantic coast and, since 1986, for the U.S. Pacific coast under the concept of Maritime Defense Zones.

Historical: The Coast Guard was established on 4 August 1790 as the Revenue Marine of the Department of the Treasury. Subsequently, it became the Revenue Cutter Service and, from 1915, the Coast Guard. The service incorporated the Lighthouse Service in 1939. The Coast Guard was a component of the Treasury Department from its formation until being transferred to the newly established Department of Transportation in 1967.

Organizational: The Coast Guard is the only one of the five U.S. military services outside of the Department of Defense.

ORGANIZATION

Coast Guard Headquarters, located in Washington, D.C., provides overall supervision and support for the operating area and district commands. The headquarters has seven major directorates (see figure 30-1). The senior uniformed officer of the Coast Guard is the Commandant, currently Admiral James M. Loy.[1]

Admiral James M. Loy, Commandant of the Coast Guard since May 1998 (U.S. Coast Guard, PA1 T. H. Brown)

Figure 30-1

Coast Guard Organization

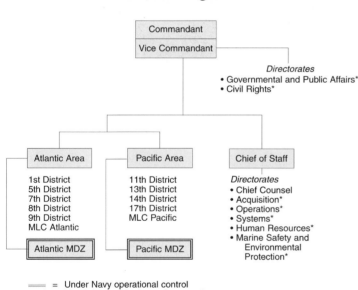

```
= Under Navy operational control
*   = Headed by an Assistant Commandant
MDZ = Maritime Defense Zone
MLC = Maintenance and Logistics Command
```

The headquarters directorates reflect the 1995–1996 reorganization that replaced ten existing offices; those offices had suffered from overlap and resulted in an awkward command structure for efficient management of the Coast Guard. (See 15th Edition/page 550 for the previous headquarters organization.)

The major U.S. Coast Guard operating commands are the Atlantic Area (headquarters in Portsmouth, Va.) and the Pacific Area (headquarters in San Francisco), with nine subordinate district commands.

Each area command also has a Maintenance and Logistics Command (MLC). The area commanders additionally command one of their subordinate districts (i.e., Atlantic Area/5th CG District and Pacific Area/11th CG District). The two area commanders are vice admirals, as are the Vice Commandant and Chief of Staff.

The district commanders control all shore, air, and sea activities in their areas of responsibility. The district commanders are rear admirals, as are the MLC commanders and assistant commandants.

In 1985–1986 the commanders of the Coast Guard Atlantic and Pacific Areas were designated as commanders of the newly established Maritime Defense Zones (MDZ) Atlantic and Pacific, respectively. The MDZ commanders report to their respective Navy fleet commanders.[2] They are responsible for: (1) planning, conducting, and coordinating wartime operations in and around U.S. harbors and coasts; (2) ensuring an integrated defense plan for the MDZs' areas of responsibility; and (3) protecting coastal and nearby sea lines of communication. Within each MDZ are operating sectors, which are commanded by Coast Guard district or base commanders.

The MDZ organization sought to rectify a long-standing shortfall in U.S. defense policy—that of defending U.S. harbors and coastal waters from hostile activity, particularly submarine operations, in wartime. However, the threat from submarine mining and the use of Coast Guard forces in forward crisis and combat areas does raise the question of whether the Coast Guard should additionally have control of the surface mine countermeasures forces, which are now, of course, a Navy activity.[3] (Proposals in the late 1990s to transfer some or all of the patrol craft of the CYCLONE/PC 1 class to the Coast Guard led to one ship of this class having been transferred when this edition went to press.)

Table 30-1. COAST GUARD DISTRICTS

District	Headquarters	Area	Personnel*
1st District	Boston, Mass.	Northeast	4,285
5th District	Portsmouth, Va.	Middle Atlantic	8,385
7th District	Miami, Fla.	Southeast	4,990
8th District	New Orleans, La.	Central/Gulf Coast	4,385
9th District	Cleveland, Ohio	Northern/Great Lakes	2,025
11th District	Alameda, Calif.	Southwest	4,300
13th District	Seattle, Wash.	Northwest	2,675
14th District	Honolulu, Hawaii	Hawaii	1,260
17th District	Juneau, Alaska	Alaska	1,965
MLC Atlantic	Norfolk, Va.	Atlantic	265
MLC Pacific	Alameda, Calif.	Pacific	210

* Active duty Coast Guard men and women

PERSONNEL

Uniformed Coast Guard personnel operate all Coast Guard cutters, boats, and aircraft. Medical personnel are provided by the U.S. Public Health Service on assignment to the Coast Guard.

Active duty Coast Guard strength at the beginning of 2000 totaled 35,350 officers and enlisted personnel:

5,484	officers
1,426	chief warrant officers
27,569	enlisted
830	cadets (Coast Guard Academy)
41	Officer Candidate School

At the same time, 161 Public Health Service personnel were serving with the Coast Guard.

Women comprise about 7 percent of the Coast Guard's active duty personnel. The Coast Guard was the first U.S. military service to accept women at its service academy and the first to assign women as commanding officers of armed vessels (WPB patrol boats).

---

1. The Coast Guard Commandant was a rear admiral until 10 March 1942, when the incumbent, Russell R. Waesche, was promoted to vice admiral; he was promoted to full admiral on 4 April 1945. His successors have held four-star rank except for the period 1950–1960.

2. A more-detailed description of the Maritime Defense Zones is found in Cdr. Lawson W. Brigham, USCG, "U.S. Coast Guard in 1985," U.S. Naval Institute *Proceedings* [Naval Review issue] (May 1986), pp. 42–49.

3. This issue is examined in N. Polmar, "The U.S. Navy: Mine Warfare Problems . . . And a Solution," U.S. Naval Institute *Proceedings* (December 1991), pp. 105–106.

The Coast Guard has 12,000 selected reservists, who attend periodic drills as well as annual active duty training. There is also a civilian auxiliary of 34,000 men and women; the Coast Guard Auxiliary consists of expert boaters, amateur radio operators, and licensed aircraft pilots who use their own equipment to support Coast Guard activities. Their efforts include conducting free courtesy marine inspections of recreational boats, teaching a variety of boating courses, and assisting the Coast Guard in search and rescue.

Coast Guard personnel have Navy-style ranks, with the Commandant and Vice Commandant normally having the rank of full admiral. As of mid-2000, the Coast Guard had 31 active-duty flag officers:

1   admiral
4   vice admirals
18   rear admirals
8   rear admirals (lower half)

In addition, there is one Coast Guard Reserve rear admiral.

OPERATIONS

Coast Guard forces operate worldwide, though primarily in U.S. waters, with "black-hull" ships and craft maintaining inland and coastal aides to navigation. Offshore operations extend well into oceanic waters, with particular emphasis on the areas off the U.S. West Coast and Caribbean, to deter illegal migrants and drug-smuggling.

In the Western Hemisphere, the Coast Guard is the lead federal agency for maritime drug interdiction. Beyond operations by Coast Guard cutters and aircraft, the Coast Guard regularly provides small Law Enforcement Detachments (LEDET) on board Navy ships to carry out the boarding of ships suspected of carrying contraband cargoes to Iraq, as well as for anti-drug patrols by Navy ships in the Caribbean and eastern Pacific areas. Also, LEDETs are provided on board two Navy ocean surveillance ships, the VINDICATOR (T-AGOS 3) and PERSISTENT (T-AGOS 6), that are specifically assigned to Caribbean operations. These two ships remain on the Naval Vessel Register, operated by civilian crews under the aegis of the Military Sealift Command. (Plans to transfer six T-AGOS surveillance ships to the Coast Guard were dropped; the ships lacked adequate speed and payload capabilities for Coast Guard service; see chapter 22 of this edition of *Ships and Aircraft*.)

In addition, during crises and conflicts other Coast Guard units—active and reserve—support forward U.S. military operations. For example, during Operations Desert Shield/Desert Storm in 1990–1991, three USCG reserve Port Security Units (PSU), each with some 100 men and women, with patrol craft were deployed in the Persian Gulf.[4] (No Coast Guard cutters were deployed to the Persian Gulf area. In 1987—during the so-called tanker war between Iraq and Iran—the deployment of 110-foot/ 33.5-m patrol craft to the Gulf was proposed but quickly abandoned in the face of Navy opposition.)

The end of the Cold War has seen an expansion of Coast Guard responsibilities and areas of activity. Increasingly, Coast Guard assets are desired for overseas operations by U.S. government and military leaders. These activities include, but are not limited to, training Third World naval and coast guard forces; carrying out liaison and joint operations with foreign navies and coast guards in the areas of law enforcement, pollution control, resource protection, and anti-terrorism; and providing direct support of U.S. military operations.

The Coast Guard is especially suited for working with Third World and developing countries, whose navies are more akin to the U.S. Coast Guard than they are to the U.S. Navy. In many of those countries the naval/coast guard missions are similar if not the same. Their missions often are identical to those of the U.S. Coast Guard— the enforcement of resource and fisheries regulations, law enforcement, search and rescue, river and waterways management, port security, maritime safety, and so forth. Thus, the U.S. Coast Guard—a military service—can work directly with those countries on a non-military basis. As then–Coast Guard Commandant Admiral Robert Kramek noted in 1997, "We know the people, we know the geography, and, most importantly, we understand the maritime challenges that the Caribbean nations face."[5]

---

4. These units, which were flown to the Gulf with their boats, served as port security forces in Bahrain and Saudi Arabia. It was the first time in the 50-year history of the Coast Guard Reserve that its personnel had served outside of the United States. The units were No. 301 from Buffalo, N.Y., No. 302 from Cleveland, Ohio, and No. 303 from Milwaukee, Wisc.
5. Quoted in Scott C. Truver, Ph.D., "The World Is Our Coastline!" U.S. Naval Institute *Proceedings* (June 1998), p. 46.

Four BEAR-class cutters are moored at the Coast Guard's support facility at Portsmouth, Va. The Coast Guard has its own logistic and maintenance support structure based on Maintenance and Logistics Commands (MLC) in the Atlantic and Pacific areas, plus a ship repair yard at Curtis Bay, Md. (2000, U.S. Coast Guard, PA3 Kimberly Wilder)

CUTTERS AND BOATS

The Coast Guard operates a large number of oceangoing, coastal, and inland ships and small craft for a variety of purposes.

A major procurement program for oceangoing cutters, aircraft, and Command, Control, Communications, Computers, Surveillance, and Intelligence (C^4SI) is being developed, known as the Deepwater Project. This will be the largest integrated procurement program in Coast Guard history (see below).

Several smaller cutters and tenders currently are being procured.

The large HAMILTON-class high endurance cutters have recently completed an extensive modernization program that will permit these ships to serve effectively in peacetime as well as wartime roles into the early 21st century. Unfortunately, the HAMILTON modernization included removal of the ships' 5-inch (127-mm)/38-cal dual-purpose (DP) guns, which were most useful weapons. Their ASW weapons also were removed, while the installation of Harpoon anti-ship missiles was halted.

Several other cutter and boat classes have undergone upgrade programs.

One former Navy floating dry dock—the YFD 83 (ex-AFDL 31)—is in service at the Coast Guard Yard, Curtis Bay, Md.; see chapter 25.

Most cutters are painted white, with the larger icebreakers painted red and buoy tenders and harbor tugs painted black (their superstructures remain white). The Coast Guard insignia—a narrow blue and wide orange stripe, with the Coast Guard shield super-imposed on the latter—is carried on the bows of all cutters and boats, and the words "U.S. Coast Guard" are painted on the sides.

Designations: The Coast Guard uses the term *vessels* for all watercraft operated by the service. Within that classification, the term *cutter* is used for ships that have "an assigned personnel allowance and that [have] installed habitability features for the extended support of a permanently assigned crew." In practice, this includes 65-foot (19.8-m) tugs and larger vessels, except ferries. The term comes from the early British revenue service ships that were cutter-rigged sailing vessels, although the original U.S. revenue cutters were sailing schooners.

Craft less than 65 feet in length are considered "boats" and have hull numbers with the first two digits indicating the vessel's length in feet overall. However, the designation "patrol boat" (WPB) is used for craft up to 110 feet (33.5 m). The term CPB—for coastal patrol boat—is increasingly being used *unofficially* for the new 87-foot (26.5-m) patrol boats.

The Coast Guard classifies all of its ships and small craft by length (in this volume shown in parentheses after the class name). The Coast Guard vessel classification scheme is derived from that of the U.S. Navy (see chapter 3). All Coast Guard cutters and boat classifications are prefixed by the letter *W* (*unofficially* for "White-painted ships"). The larger cutters are numbered in a single, sequential series that was initiated in 1941–1942, with new classes initiating new number blocks.

Cutter names are prefixed by USCGC for U.S. Coast Guard Cutter.

TABLE 30-2 COAST GUARD CUTTERS AND PATROL BOATS

Number/Type	Class/Ship	Length	Comm.	Active	Building	Notes
WHEC 715	HAMILTON	378	1967–1972	12	—	
WMEC 39	HALEY	288	1971	1	—	ex-Navy ATS
WMEC 901	BEAR	270	1983–1990	13	—	
WMEC 615	RELIANCE	210	1964–1969	16	—	
WMEC 38	STORIS	230	1942	1	—	ex-WAGB type
WMEC 6	ACUSHNET	213	1944	1	—	ex-Navy ARS
WPC 1	CYCLONE	170	1993	1	—	ex-Navy PC
WPB 1301	Island	110	1986–1990	49	—	
CPB 87301	BARRACUDA	87	1998–2002	28	23	"Marine Protector" class
WPB 82301	Point	82	1960–1970	19	—	
WAGB 20	HEALY	420	2000	1	—	
WAGB	Polar	399	1976–1978	2	—	
WAGB 83	MACKINAW	290	1944	1	—	Great Lakes
WIX 327	EAGLE	295	1936	1	—	sailing bark
WLB 201	JUNIPER	225	1996–	14	—	"Keeper" class
WLB 62	BALSAM	180	1942–1944	15	—	one is WIX
WLM	coastal buoy tenders			15	—	
WLI	inland buoy tenders			6	—	
WLIC	inland construction tenders			16	—	
WLR	river buoy tenders			15	—	
WTGB	icebreaking tugs			9	—	
WYTL	small harbor tugs			12	—	

AVIATION

The Coast Guard air arm has almost 200 aircraft in service and undergoing maintenance. They are based at 14 air stations in the continental United States and one each in Alaska, Hawaii, and Puerto Rico.

Coast Guard aviators are trained by the Navy, with specialized training being given at the Coast Guard's Aviation Training Center in Mobile, Ala.

Historically, the Coast Guard has flown the same aircraft types as operated by the U.S. Navy. However, in the 1980s the Coast Guard procured two French-designed aircraft: 41 HU-25 Guardian fixed-wing aircraft, acquired to replace the HU-16 Albatross amphibian and HC-131 Samaritan; and 96 HH-65A Dolphin Short-Range Recovery (SRR) helicopters, acquired to replace the HH-52A Sea Guard helicopters. The HU-25 and HH-65 are not flown by other U.S. military services. Both have suffered engineering problems and have been expensive to maintain.

The Coast Guard's latest series-produced aircraft is the HH-60J Jayhawk, a Medium-Range Recovery (MRR) helicopter. This is a Search-and-Rescue (SAR) variant of the widely flown H-60 helicopter series. This helicopter is flown by all five U.S. military services.

The cutters of the HAMILTON and BEAR classes, as well as the three large icebreakers, regularly embark helicopters, while some of the other cutter classes have landing decks but cannot support helicopters. It had been intended that in wartime the HAMILTON and BEAR classes would embark Navy SH-2F LAMPS I anti-submarine helicopters. However, there are no towed-array sonars available for the cutters, the ASW data links have been removed from the HAMILTONS, and the Navy has only two squadrons of SH-2 LAMPS helicopters, both of which are committed to support Naval Reserve Force frigates.

During 1999–2000 the Coast Guard evaluated the use of light armed helicopters to operate from cutters in support of anti-drug efforts. Two MH-90 Enforcer helicopters were employed during Operation New Frontier, operating from the cutters GALLATIN and SENECA in the Caribbean area. They were highly effective in making several "drug busts," leading to the Coast Guard competing for a helicopter of this type for service use.

One of the two MH-90 Enforcer helicopters used by the Coast Guard in 1999 to evaluate the feasibility of employing armed helicopters to help counter "go-fast" drug smuggling craft. The Coast Guard subsequently selected the A109 Power helicopter for this role as the MH-68A (see page 457). (U.S. Coast Guard, PA2 Jeff Hall)

Warning shots from the M240 machine gun of a Coast Guard MH-90 Enforcer helicopter rip across the bow of a fleeing drug-smuggling craft. The two MH-90 helicopters were based aboard cutters operating in the Caribbean during their 1999 evaluation. (U.S. Coast Guard)

The MH-90 is produced by MD Helicopters, with the company designation being MD 900 Explorer. It is a twin-turboshaft, highly versatile aircraft with a maximum cruise speed of 136 knots (252 kmh) with a normal range of 300 n.miles (560 km). In Coast Guard service, the MH-90s were fitted with a variety of sensors, including Forward-Looking Infrared (FLIR) and Night Vision Goggles (NVG). The helicopters each were armed with a 7.62-mm M240 machine gun and a .50-cal rifle.

During Operation New Frontier, the helicopters were owned by MD Helicopters and leased to the Coast Guard. (Production rights for the helicopter were sold to MD Helicopters by Boeing in 1999.)

The Coast Guard is considering the use of VSTOL aircraft for use in future cutter operations. VSTOL aircraft are receiving consideration after sea trials with the Bell XV-15 tilt-rotor aircraft, which was the prototype for the V-22 Osprey, which is now in production. During May 1999 trials off Key West, Fla., the Coast Guard and Bell tested a number of SAR operations including landing and taking off from a moving cutter, hovering over a rescue boat, and hovering over a rescue swimmer. The Bell-Boeing 609 model, which is smaller than the V-22, is being proposed to the Coast Guard for the SAR role.

The Coast Guard also is considering the employment of Un-manned Aerial Vehicles (UAV) as a component of the Deepwater Project (see below).

The service pioneered development of unmanned airships or aero-stats for ocean surveillance. A 1985 agreement between the Navy and Coast Guard shifted responsibility for development of manned air-ships to the Navy and unmanned airships to the Coast Guard. Sub-sequently, the Coast Guard operated a series of aerostats and support ships. That program was transferred to the Army in 1992 and promptly disbanded. (See 15th Edition/pages 603–605 for character-istics of the aerostat tenders.)

The Coast Guard has discarded its single EC-130V Hercules configured for Airborne Early Warning (AEW) and its four E-2C Hawkeye AEW aircraft (one of the latter crashed in 1990). These radar surveillance aircraft were intended primarily for anti-drug operations. The EC-130V was transferred to the Air Force in 1993 and the three surviving E-2Cs were returned to the Navy.

Beyond fixed-wing and helicopter SAR and surveillance aircraft, the Coast Guard operates two VIP transport aircraft—a VC-20B Gulfstream III and a VC-4 Gulfstream I.

Of the Coast Guard's two RG-8 motorized gliders, one crashed at sea and was lost, and the other was scrapped after an effort to modify her power plant.

The Coast Guard's EC-130V Hercules configured as an AEW aircraft was transferred to the Air Force after service tests. Sub-sequently, it was retransferred to the Navy and is assigned to the Naval Force Warfare Aircraft Test Squadron at NAS Patuxent River, Md.

(The Coast Guard also operated four E-2C Hawkeye AEW aircraft on loan from the Navy in the 1980s. One crashed and the other aircraft were returned to the Navy.)

Table 30-3 lists the aircraft in active Coast Guard service. No aircraft are flown by the Coast Guard Reserve.

TABLE 30-3 COAST GUARD AIRCRAFT

Type	Mission	Total	Active	Maint.	Storage
HC-130H Hercules	Long-Range Search (LRS)	30	26	4	—
HU-25A Guardian	Medium-Range Search (MRS)	26	10	6	10
HU-25B Guardian	pollution surveillance	6	5	—	1
HU-25C Guardian	"interceptor"	9	8	1	—
VC-4A Gulfstream I	executive transport	1	1	—	—
VC-20 Gulfstream III	executive transport	1	1	—	—
MD-90	cargo-transport	2	2	—	—
HH-65A Dolphin	Medium-Range Recovery (MRR)	93	80	10	3
HH-60J Jayhawk	Medium-Range Recovery (MRR)	42	35	7	—

INTEGRATED DEEPWATER SYSTEM

The greatest challenge confronting the Coast Guard is that its "deep-water" ships and aircraft are rapidly becoming technologically obsolete. As a result, these platforms have excessive operating and maintenance costs, lack essential capabilities in speed, sensors, and interoperability, and consequently limit overall deep-water mission effectiveness and efficiency.

Five of the Coast Guard's ten classes of deep-water cutters begin to reach the end of their planned service life within the next decade (lead units):

number	type	commissioned	end of service life
12	WHEC 378	1967	2003
13	WMEC 270	1983	2012
16	WMEC 210	1964	2002
1	WMEC 230	1942	2002
49	WPB 110	1986	2005

In addition, the several aircraft types will require replacement in the same period, especially the HC-130 Hercules, HU-25 Guardian, and HH-65 Dolphin.

Many of these existing Coast Guard deep-water assets lack fundamental capabilities and technologies necessary for efficient and effective mission performance. Examples include: inadequate cutter speed, poor sensors and night operating ability on both aircraft and cutters, limited interoperability between cutters and aircraft, and inadequate communications.

In addition to the capability limitations that hinder Coast Guard operational performance, outdated technology increases operating and maintenance costs, placing greater demands on the logistics infrastructure. Approximately two-thirds of the operating costs of a major deep-water cutter goes to personnel costs. In the 30 years since some of these cutters were designed, advances have been made in automated shipboard systems and maintenance reduction. Another challenge is that many system and component manufacturers no longer are able to provide support for equipment and parts. As a result, the overall logistics effort demands more labor hours, and maintenance costs increase while cutter/aircraft operational availability decreases.

Accordingly, the Deepwater Project has been initiated to ensure the timely acquisition of the appropriate platforms and systems that will employ available technology to satisfy the deep-water mission needs. This project uses commercial and military technologies and innovation to develop a completely integrated, multimission, and highly flexible force at the lowest total ownership cost.

The Deepwater Project employs a unique procurement method in which competing industry teams design systems to meet a specified set of performance requirements. Rather than focusing on specific equipment, the Coast Guard has described the capabilities needed to perform its missions and is allowing contractors to determine which assets, such as ships and aircraft, will best meet these requirements.

The Deepwater Concept Design phase is under way and the Coast Guard is expected to award the Deepwater Capabilities Replacement Project contract in January 2002. Three study teams were contracted for the initial development effort; the teams were led by Avondale Industries, Lockheed-Martin Government Electronic Systems, and Science Applications International Corp.

An artist's concept of a candidate "system" for the Deepwater project, showing an advanced technology cutter that would support high-speed small craft, tilt-rotor aircraft as well as HH-60J Jayhawk helicopters, and Guardian/Sentinel-type Unmanned Aerial Vehicles (UAV). Deepwater also will employ satellites for various support functions. (British Crown Copyright/DERA)

While no specific "systems" or "platforms" have yet been decided upon, one concept receiving strong consideration is a ship-type platform that will carry/support two or three small, high-speed craft and some number of aircraft (VSTOL/helicopters and/or UAVs). As described above, the VSTOL aircraft receiving the most consideration is the Bell-Boeing XV-15 tilt-rotor aircraft. This operational concept would permit a cutter to carry out surveillance over an area up to 200 n.miles (370 km) in all directions from the cutter, with the smaller craft being deployed to carry out onboard inspections of suspect ships. The smaller craft will be able to remain at sea for up to 24 hours. Obviously, cutter-based manned aircraft and UAVs, as well as offboard sensors (land-based patrol aircraft and satellites), would support cutter operations.

HIGH ENDURANCE CUTTERS

These are the largest ships operated by the Coast Guard, except for icebreakers. All high endurance cutters prior to the HAMILTON class have been stricken. The HAMILTONS will reach the end of their nominal service life from about 2003 on. The above-described Deepwater Project is intended to provide replacements for these cutters.

With the cutback in active Navy frigates, the proposal has been made for the Navy to transfer at least one frigate of the OLIVER HAZARD PERRY (FFG 7) class to the Coast Guard to serve as a training cutter. Proposals for the Coast Guard to operate variants of the FFG 7 design as high endurance (patrol) cutters were made as early as 1981.[6] Among the modifications proposed for Coast Guard use were removal of the (modular) Mk 13 Standard/Harpoon launcher and redesign of the two-bay hangar to provide space for specialized SAR equipment while retaining the opportunity to operate one large helicopter (i.e., H-60 type).

The transfer of FFG 7s to the Coast Guard for training or cutter service is highly unlikely.

_____

6. For example, *Analysis of FFG-7 Variants for Naval Reserve and Coast Guard Operation* (Alexandria, Va.: Maritime Publications, May 1981).

12 HIGH ENDURANCE CUTTERS: "HAMILTON" CLASS (378-FT)

Number	Name	Builder	Laid down	Launched	Commissioned	Modernized	Status
WHEC 715	HAMILTON	Avondale Shipyards, New Orleans, La.	4 Jan 1965	18 Dec 1965	20 Feb 1967	Oct 1985–Nov 1988	**PA**
WHEC 716	DALLAS	Avondale Shipyards, New Orleans, La.	7 Feb 1966	1 Oct 1966	1 Oct 1967	Nov 1986–Dec 1989	**AA**
WHEC 717	MELLON	Avondale Shipyards, New Orleans, La.	25 July 1966	11 Feb 1967	22 Dec 1967	Oct 1985–June 1989	**PA**
WHEC 718	CHASE	Avondale Shipyards, New Orleans, La.	15 Oct 1966	20 May 1967	1 Mar 1968	July 1989–Mar 1991	**PA**
WHEC 719	BOUTWELL	Avondale Shipyards, New Orleans, La.	12 Dec 1966	17 June 1967	14 June 1968	Mar 1989–Apr 1991	**PA**
WHEC 720	SHERMAN	Avondale Shipyards, New Orleans, La.	13 Feb 1967	23 Sep 1967	23 Aug 1968	May 1986–Feb 1990	**PA**
WHEC 721	GALLATIN	Avondale Shipyards, New Orleans, La.	17 Apr 1967	18 Nov 1967	20 Dec 1968	Mar 1990–Jan 1992	**AA**
WHEC 722	MORGENTHAU	Avondale Shipyards, New Orleans, La.	17 July 1967	10 Feb 1968	14 Feb 1969	Nov 1989–Dec 1991	**PA**
WHEC 723	RUSH	Avondale Shipyards, New Orleans, La.	23 Oct 1967	16 Nov 1968	3 July 1969	July 1989–Sep 1991	**PA**
WHEC 724	MUNRO	Avondale Shipyards, New Orleans, La.	18 Feb 1970	5 Dec 1970	10 Sep 1971	Dec 1986–Nov 1989	**PA**
WHEC 725	JARVIS	Avondale Shipyards, New Orleans, La.	9 Sep 1970	24 Apr 1971	30 Dec 1971	Mar 1991–Dec 1992	**PA**
WHEC 726	MIDGETT	Avondale Shipyards, New Orleans, La.	5 Apr 1971	4 Sep 1971	17 Mar 1972	Jan 1991–Mar 1992	**PA**

Displacement:	2,716 tons standard		Helicopters:	1 HH-60J Jayhawk
	3,050 tons full load		Missiles:	removed
Length:	350 feet (106.7 m) waterline		Guns:	1 76-mm/62-cal DP Mk 75
	378⅝ feet (115.4 m) overall			2 40-mm grenade launchers Mk 19 (2 single)
Beam:	42¾ feet (13.0 m)			2 25-mm/87-cal Bushmaster cannon Mk 38 (2 single)
Draft:	20⅓ feet (6.2 m) over sonar dome			1 20-mm Phalanx close-in Mk 16 (multibarrel)
Propulsion:	CODOG: 2 gas turbines (Pratt & Whitney FT4-A6);			4 .50-cal machine guns (4 single)
	28,000 shp + 2 diesel engines (Fairbanks Morse 38TD8⅛),		ASW weapons:	removed
	7,200 bhp; 2 shafts		Radars:	1 SPS-40B air search
Speed:	28.4 knots			2 SPS-64(V)6 navigation
Range:	2,400 n.miles (4,445 km) at 29 knots		Sonars:	SQS-38 keel-mounted
	9,600 n.miles (17,790 km) at 19 knots (gas turbines)		Fire control:	1 Mk 92 Mod 1 GFCS
	14,000 n.miles (25,930 km) at 11 knots (diesel)		EW systems:	WLR-1C
Manning:	178 (20 officers + 158 enlisted)			WLR-3

These are the largest cutters operated by the Coast Guard. They are capable of long-range operations. All have been upgraded under a Fleet Rehabilitation and Modernization (FRAM) program (dates shown above).

Class: Originally, 36 ships of this class were planned. Additional ships were first deferred in favor of retaining older cutters and then dropped with construction of the smaller BEAR-class cutters.

Design: These cutters were designed to operate as frigates in wartime, being provided from the outset with anti-submarine weapons—low-frequency sonar, an ASW fire control system, and Mk 32 torpedo tubes for Mk 44/46 torpedoes. The first few ships also were fitted with hedgehogs. Subsequently, their ASW capabilities were upgraded with provisions for operating an SH-2 LAMPS I helicopter, including an SQR-4 and SQR-17 sonobuoy data link and analysis equipment (fitted during the FRAM upgrade).

In 1992 the Commandant, Admiral J. William Kime, directed that all ASW weapons and sensors be removed from these cutters:

> The requirement to maintain the WHEC ASW mission/capability was reviewed by the Navy–Coast Guard Board (NAVGARD) on 23 July 1992. The Board determined that ASW should be retained as a mission for WHECs, but in [the] absence of a global ASW threat, the requirement to maintain an ASW capability can be eliminated. The Navy has sufficient assets to respond to regional contingencies requiring ASW and there will be enough warning time to regenerate the WHEC capability if needed for future global scale conflicts.[7]

The Commandant concluded: "The decision to eliminate the ASW capability requirement . . . was a hard one. The Coast Guard has been effectively prosecuting the ASW mission in defense of our country since before World War II. However, the world has changed and we must change with it."

_____

7. Message from Commandant, Coast Guard, to All Coast Guard, 31 July 1992, COMDTNOTE 1430.

Also removed in this period were the Harpoon anti-ship missile canisters (see *Missile* notes).

The superstructures of these ships are fabricated largely of aluminum. They are fitted with oceanographic and meteorological facilities. The helicopter hangars were used as balloon shelters prior to their modernization.

Electronics: Beginning in 1967, the original keel-mounted SQS-36 sonar was replaced in these ships by the SQS-38, a hull-mounted version of the SQS-35 variable-depth sonar.

Mk 36 SRBOC chaff launchers were fitted during FRAM upgrade. However, the previously planned SLQ-32(V)2 and SLQ-25 Nixie installations were canceled. (Thus, the BEAR-class cutters are the only Coast Guard units with the SLQ-32 system.)

Engineering: These were the largest U.S. combat ships to have gas-turbine propulsion until completion of the SPRUANCE (DD 963) in 1975. The gas turbines are FT-4A, marine versions of the J75 aircraft engine. The propulsion machinery is CODOG (Combination Diesel or Gas turbine). A 350-hp bow propeller pod is fitted.

Stern aspect of the MELLON with an HH-65A Dolphin parked on the flight deck. These cutters have an 76-mm OTO Melara gun mount forward and a Phalanx CIWS aft, their only armament except for machine guns and grenade launchers. (1999, Leo Van Ginderen)

The CHASE, showing the large flight deck available when the expandable helicopter hangar is retracted. Note the two large masts, side-by-side engine exhausts, and gun armament forward and aft. (1998, Leo Van Ginderen)

Guns: These were the last active ships in U.S. service to mount 5-inch/38-cal DP guns. (The last active U.S. Navy ships with this weapon were the frigates of the BROOKE/DEG 1 and GARCIA/FF 1040 classes.) The 5-inch gun mount was replaced during the FRAM upgrade.

Missiles: On 16 January 1990 the MELLON became the first Coast Guard cutter to fire a guided missile, launching a Harpoon SSM. Five cutters were fitted with Harpoon through 1992, and all were scheduled for eventual installation. The installation program was halted in 1992 and the Harpoon canisters were removed from the five cutters.

Modernization: The major armament/sensor/electronics upgrades to this class were:

1967–1987 ASW upgrade
6 Mk 32 12.75-inch (324-mm) torpedo tubes for Mk 44/46 torpedoes (hedgehogs deleted)
Mk 309 torpedo control panel
SQS-38 sonar (hull-mounted version of SQS-35 variable-depth sonar)
1985–1992 FRAM modernization
76-mm OTO Melara Mk 76 (replacing 5-inch/38-cal DP gun)
Mk 92 GFCS (replacing Mk 56 GFCS)
SPS-40 air search radar (replacing SPS-29 air search radar)
flight deck upgraded to accommodate SH-2F LAMPS I
telescoping helicopter hangar and TACAN
communications equipment upgrade
Harpoon SSM
SQR-4 and SQR-17 helicopter ASW support links
Mk 36 SRBOC chaff/flare launchers

The GALLATIN at rest in Charleston, S.C. The radome for the Mk 92 Gunfire Control System (GFCS) and the SPS-40B air search radar (after mast) are clearly visible. Their previously fitted anti-submarine sensors and weapons have been deleted. (1996, U.S. Coast Guard, PA1 Robert Wyman)

With the FRAM update, the manning standards for these cutters were increased from 152 (15 officers + 137 enlisted) to 171; they were subsequently increased to approximately 178 per cutter.

The FRAM work was undertaken at the Bath Iron Works, Maine, shipyard for the four East Coast ships and at the Todd Pacific yard in Seattle, Wash., for the eight West Coast ships (see *Operational* notes). A large deck structure was fitted to the forecastle to mount the 76-mm gun and the Harpoon canisters; the Phalanx CIWS mount is fitted aft of the flight deck.

The FRAM upgrades experienced major delays and cost increases over original estimates. The original cost of $30 million per ship increased to between $50 million and $70 million per ship.

Names: The first nine ships were named for Secretaries of the Treasury; the other three honor heroes of the Coast Guard. (Signalman 1st Class Douglas A. Munro posthumously received the Medal of Honor for bravery under fire while supporting Marines on Guadalcanal in 1942; he was the only Coast Guardsman to receive the nation's highest military honor.) Accordingly, the later cutters have been referred to as the Hero class.

Operational: The HAMILTON and CHASE were transferred from the East Coast (Boston) to the West Coast (San Pedro, Calif.) in late 1991, bringing 10 of the 12 ships of this class to the Pacific. The DALLAS and GALLATIN remain on the East Coast. They were based at Governor's Island in New York harbor until 1995, when both shifted their home port to Charleston, S.C.

The DALLAS deployed to the Mediterranean in July 1995 for a three-month assignment as a fully integrated unit of the U.S. Sixth Fleet. This is believed to have been the first time such an assignment occurred during peacetime.

HIGH ENDURANCE CUTTERS: "CASCO" CLASS (311-FT)

Eighteen seaplane tenders of the World War II–built BARNEGAT (AVP 10) class were transferred to the Coast Guard in 1946–1948. The last unit in Coast Guard service, the UNIMAK (WHEC 379, ex-AVP 31), was stricken on 29 April 1988 (and returned to the Navy for disposal). The UNIMAK was completed as the Navy AVP 31 in 1943; she was transferred to the Coast Guard in 1946 as WAVP 31 and changed to WHEC 379 in 1966. She operated as a training cutter (WTR 379) from 1969 until her decommissioning in May 1974. The ship had been scheduled for transfer to South Vietnam (as had other ships of this class), but with the fall of the Saigon government, she was laid up in reserve. She was recommissioned as a WHEC in August 1977 to support the 200-n.mile (370-km) U.S. offshore resource zone.

During World War II, ships of this class served as seaplane tenders and motor torpedo boat tenders, and one as an amphibious command ship.

See 14th Edition/page 535 for characteristics.

HIGH ENDURANCE CUTTERS: SECRETARY CLASS (327-FT)

All of the large, venerable cutters of the so-called Secretary class have been stricken.[8] Seven of these cutters were completed in 1936–1937; all saw service in World War II as ocean escorts (WPG) and, except for the ALEXANDER HAMILTON (WPG 34), as amphibious command ships (WAGC); the HAMILTON was sunk by a German U-boat in 1942. The six survivors were changed to high endurance cutters (WHEC) on 1 May 1968.

The Secretary-class cutters were stricken between 1981 and 1988; the last was the INGHAM (WHEC 35), stricken on 27 May 1988 (after 52 years of active service). The TANEY (WHEC 37) is now a museum in Baltimore, Md.

See 14th Edition/pages 535–536 for characteristics.

---

8. They were named for Secretaries of the Treasury. Details of the World War II configuration of these cutters and other Coast Guard units are found in Robert L. Scheina, *U.S. Coast Guard Cutters and Craft of World War II* (Annapolis, Md.: Naval Institute Press, 1982), and *U.S. Coast Guard Cutters and Craft, 1946–1990* (Annapolis, Md.: Naval Institute Press, 1990).

MEDIUM ENDURANCE CUTTERS

1 MEDIUM ENDURANCE CUTTER: EX-NAVY SALVAGE SHIP (288-FT)

Number	Name	Launched	Navy Comm.	USCG Comm.	Status
WMEC 39 (ex-ATS 1)	ALEX HALEY	15 May 1968	23 Jan 1971	10 July 1999	**PA**

Builders:	Brooke Marine, Lowestoft (England)		Speed:	16 knots
Displacement:	2,650 tons standard		Range:	10,000 n.miles (18,520 km) at 13 knots
	3,200 tons full load		Manning:	103 (9 officers + 94 enlisted)
Length:	264 feet (80.5 m) waterline		Helicopters:	landing area
	282 feet (85.98 m) overall		Guns:	2 25-mm/87-cal Bushmaster cannon Mk 38
Beam:	50 feet (15.25 m)			(2 single)
Draft:	15⅙ feet (4.6 m)			2 .50-cal machine guns (2 single)
Propulsion:	4 diesel engines (Caterpillar); 6,000 bhp;		Radars:	SPS-64(V) navigation
	2 shafts		Sonars:	none

This is a former U.S. Navy tug-type ship, built with extensive salvage and diving capabilities. Most of these features have been removed for her role as a medium endurance cutter.

Formerly the EDENTON (ATS 1), the ship was decommissioned on 29 March 1996 and transferred to the Coast Guard in November 1997. She was modified for Coast Guard service at the Coast Guard Yard.

The HALEY is homeported in Kodiak, Alaska.

Class: The EDENTON was originally one of a class of three ships (ATS 1–3); see chapter 22.

Design: Navy SCB No. 719. The ATS design provided for large open work spaces forward and aft, with extensive salvage, diving, and towing facilities. (The diving system was limited to compressed air, not helium-oxygen.)

Installation of a retractable helicopter hangar is planned.

Engineering: The ship has a through-bow thruster for precise maneuvering. She was re-engined during modifications for Coast Guard service.

Names: All ships of this class originally were named for cities in both Britain and the United States. The ALEX HALEY remembers the Pulitzer Prize–winning author who had served in the Coast Guard from 1939 to 1959, retiring as a chief journalist. He won the Pulitzer Prize for his novel *Roots*.

The ALEX HALEY at the Coast Guard Yard soon after her commissioning as a medium endurance cutter. Her superstructure has been extensively modified for her new role. Two sister ships now serve in the South Korean Navy. (1999, U.S. Coast Guard, PA3 Bridget Hieronymus)

The ALEX HALEY under way off her new home port of Kodiak, Alaska. The ship's large helicopter deck covers most of the after working space as a salvage and rescue ship. (2000, U.S. Coast Guard, PA2 Keith Alholm)

13 MEDIUM ENDURANCE CUTTERS: "BEAR" CLASS (270-FT)

Number	Name	Builder	Laid down	Launched	Commissioned	Status
WMEC 901	BEAR	Tacoma Boatbuilding, Tacoma, Wash.	23 Aug 1979	25 Sep 1980	4 Feb 1983	**AA**
WMEC 902	TAMPA	Tacoma Boatbuilding, Tacoma, Wash.	2 Apr 1980	19 Mar 1981	16 Mar 1984	**AA**
WMEC 903	HARRIET LANE	Tacoma Boatbuilding, Tacoma, Wash.	15 Oct 1980	6 Feb 1982	20 Sep 1984	**AA**
WMEC 904	NORTHLAND	Tacoma Boatbuilding, Tacoma, Wash.	9 Apr 1981	7 May 1982	17 Dec 1984	**AA**
WMEC 905	SPENCER (ex-SENECA)	Robert E. Derecktor, Middletown, R.I.	26 June 1982	17 Apr 1984	28 June 1986	**AA**
WMEC 906	SENECA (ex-ESCANABA)	Robert E. Derecktor, Middletown, R.I.	16 Sep 1982	17 Apr 1984	4 May 1987	**AA**
WMEC 907	ESCANABA (ex-TAHOMA)	Robert E. Derecktor, Middletown, R.I.	1 Apr 1983	2 June 1985	27 Aug 1987	**AA**
WMEC 908	TAHOMA (ex-SPENCER)	Robert E. Derecktor, Middletown, R.I.	28 June 1983	2 June 1985	6 Apr 1988	**AA**
WMEC 909	CAMPBELL (ex-ARGUS)	Robert E. Derecktor, Middletown, R.I.	10 Aug 1984	29 Apr 1986	19 Aug 1988	**AA**
WMEC 910	THETIS (ex-TAHOMA)	Robert E. Derecktor, Middletown, R.I.	24 Aug 1984	29 Apr 1986	30 June 1989	**AA**
WMEC 911	FORWARD (ex-ERIE)	Robert E. Derecktor, Middletown, R.I.	11 July 1986	19 Aug 1987	4 Aug 1990	**AA**
WMEC 912	LEGARE (ex-McCULLOCH)	Robert E. Derecktor, Middletown, R.I.	11 July 1986	19 Aug 1987	4 Aug 1990	**AA**
WMEC 913	MOHAWK (ex-EWING)	Robert E. Derecktor, Middletown, R.I.	18 June 1987	18 May 1988	20 Mar 1990	**AA**

Displacement:	1,200 tons light	Manning:	100 (11 officers + 89 enlisted) + 16 air crew
	1,820 tons full load	Helicopters:	1 HH-65A Dolphin
Length:	255 feet (77.8 m) waterline	Guns:	1 76-mm/62-cal AA Mk 75
	270 feet (82.3 m) overall		2 .50-cal machine guns M2 (2 single)
Beam:	38 feet (11.6 m)	ASW weapons:	none
Draft:	14 feet (4.3 m)	Radars:	2 SPS-64(V)6 navigation
Propulsion:	2 geared diesel engines (Alco 18V-251E); 7,200 bhp; 2 shafts	Sonars:	none
Speed:	19.5 knots	Fire control:	Mk 92 Mod 1 GFCS
Range:	3,850 n.miles (7,130 km) at 19.5 knots	EW systems:	SLQ-32(V)1
	9,900 n.miles (18,335 km) at 12 knots		

These are multipurpose cutters. However, their lack of ASW weapons and sensors makes them unsuitable for employment in the ASW role without extensive modification. They have been criticized for their slow speed and they ride poorly in heavy seas.

The first four ships were ordered from Tacoma Boatbuilding, with the remainder planned for procurement from the Tacoma yard; however, the Coast Guard was forced into competitive bidding. The subsequent ships were then awarded to the Derecktor yard.

The BEAR was not delivered to the Coast Guard for service until late in 1983.

Aircraft: A landing deck and expanding hangar permit these cutters to handle any of the Coast Guard's helicopters, as well as the Navy's SH-2F LAMPS I. It was intended in wartime that an SH-2F would be assigned to each ship for convoy escort, but such helicopters are no longer available for deployment aboard these ships. The ESCANABA conducted trials with a Navy SH-60B LAMPS III helicopter in 1988. An HH-65A helicopter usually is embarked in the ships.

The Recovery Assistance and Traversing System (RAST) is fitted to facilitate helicopter operations in rough seas.

Class: The lead ship was authorized in fiscal year 1976, the WMEC 902–904 in fiscal 1977, and the WMEC 905–913 in fiscal 1980. The class is officially known as the Famous class, but generally is referred to as the BEAR class.

Design: Design criteria for this class included 14-day law enforcement patrols in areas out to 400 n.miles (740 km) from base. Maximum normal at-sea endurance is 21 days.

The ships have a very short forecastle with a large, two-level superstructure providing a humpback shape. Active fin stabilizers are fitted.

These were the first Coast Guard cutters to be completed with a contemporary EW suite since World War II. They are designed to be fitted with the following military systems in wartime: SH-2F LAMPS I anti-submarine helicopter, two Harpoon anti-ship quad missile canisters, one 20-mm Phalanx CIWS, Tactical Towed Array Sonar (TACTAS), and chaff launchers. The ships seem unlikely to be able to accommodate all of these systems simultaneously, however, in part because of the number of additional personnel required, as well as the probable lack of available systems during a conflict.

The TAHOMA at Kiel, Germany. Like the larger HAMILTON-class cutters, these ships also have undertaken overseas deployment in support of U.S. law enforcement, economic, and military interests. (1998, Leo Van Ginderen)

Another aspect of the TAHOMA at Kiel. There is an HH-65A Dolphin on her flight deck. The hangar door is partially open. These ships have proven too small and too slow for their intended roles. (1998, Leo Van Ginderen)

Guns: Six positions are provided for installing machine guns or 40-mm grenade launchers Mk 19.

Names: The Coast Guard initially named all 13 ships of the class. Subsequently, the prematurely awarded names for WMEC 905 and later ships were withdrawn and those cutters were renamed, as indicated above.

The BEAR honors a long-serving Navy and Coast Guard screw steamer. Built in Scotland in 1874 as a sealing vessel, she was purchased by the U.S. Navy in 1884 and operated successively in the Navy, Revenue Cutter Service, and Coast Guard, and again in the Navy (designated AG 29). The BEAR was employed extensively in Arctic operations and was used by Rear Admiral Richard E. Byrd during his Antarctic expedition of 1933–1935. She was decommissioned in 1944 and transferred to the Maritime Commission in 1948.

Operational: The entire class is based on the Atlantic coast.

The SENECA shows the ungainly lines of the BEAR-class cutters. The flexible helicopter hangar is fully extended in this view. The Mk 92 GFCS is above the bridge; behind it are two Radio Direction Finding (RDF) antennas, an OE-82 Satellite Communications (SATCOM) antenna, the mast, and a second OE-82. (1999, Leo Van Ginderen)

16 MEDIUM ENDURANCE CUTTERS: "RELIANCE" CLASS (210-FT)

Number	Name	Launched	Commissioned	Modernized	Status
A series (5)					
WMEC 615	RELIANCE	25 May 1963	20 June 1964	Apr 1987–Jan 1989	**AA**
WMEC 616	DILIGENCE	20 July 1963	31 Aug 1964	July 1990–Dec 1991	**AA**
WMEC 617	VIGILANT	24 Dec 1963	1 Oct 1964	Feb 1989–June 1990	**AA**
WMEC 618	ACTIVE	21 July 1965	17 Sep 1966	Oct 1984–Feb 1987	**PA**
WMEC 619	CONFIDENCE	8 May 1965	19 Feb 1966	Oct 1986–June 1988	**AA**
B series (11)					
WMEC 620	RESOLUTE	30 Apr 1966	8 Dec 1966	Aug 1994–Sep 1996	**PA**
WMEC 621	VALIANT	14 Jan 1967	28 Oct 1967	Dec 1991–May 1993	**AA**
WMEC 622	COURAGEOUS	18 Mar 1967	19 Apr 1968	Mar 1987–Jan 1990	**AA**
WMEC 623	STEADFAST	24 June 1967	7 Oct 1968	June 1992–Feb 1994	**PA**
WMEC 624	DAUNTLESS	21 Oct 1967	10 June 1968	Aug 1993–Feb 1995	**AA**
WMEC 625	VENTUROUS	11 Nov 1967	16 Aug 1968	Feb 1994–Oct 1995	**AA**
WMEC 626	DEPENDABLE	16 Mar 1968	22 Nov 1968	Feb 1995–Aug 1997	**AA**
WMEC 627	VIGOROUS	4 May 1968	23 Apr 1969	June 1991–Nov 1992	**AA**
WMEC 628	DURABLE	29 Apr 1967	8 Dec 1967	Oct 1986–Oct 1988	**AA**
WMEC 629	DECISIVE	14 Dec 1967	23 Aug 1968	Sep 1996–May 1998	**AA**
WMEC 630	ALERT	19 Oct 1968	28 July 1969	Dec 1992–Sep 1994	**PA**

Builders:	WMEC 615–617	Todd Shipyards, Houston, Texas	Propulsion:	2 turbocharged diesel engines (Alco 251B); 5,000 bhp; 2 shafts	
	WMEC 618	Christy Corp., Sturgeon Bay, Wisc.	Speed:	18 knots	
	WMEC 619, 625, 628, 629	Coast Guard Yard, Curtis Bay, Md.	Range:	A series 2,100 n.miles (3,890 km) at 18 knots	
	WMEC 620–624, 626, 627, 630	American Shipbuilding, Lorain, Ohio		6,100 n.miles (11,300 km) at 13 knots	
				B series 2,700 n.miles (5,000 km) at 18 knots	
Displacement:	950 tons standard			6,100 n.miles (11,300 km) at 13 knots	
	1,007 tons full load, except WMEC 616–619: 970 tons		Manning:	75 (12 officers + 63 enlisted)	
Length:	200 feet (60.96 m) waterline		Helicopters:	landing area	
	210½ feet (64.2 m) overall		Guns:	1 25-mm/87-cal Bushmaster cannon Mk 38	
Beam:	34 feet (10.4 m)			2 .50-cal machine guns M2 (2 single)	
Draft:	10½ feet (3.2 m)		ASW weapons:	none	
			Radars:	2 SPS-64(V)1 navigation	
			Sonars:	none	

These are search-and-rescue ships. They can land helicopters but have no hangar.

Armament: No ASW armament is provided in these cutters. Their design included space and weight provisions for hedgehogs and, subsequently, Mk 32 ASW torpedo tubes. (See also *Guns* notes.)

Classification: These ships originally were classified as patrol craft (WPC); they were changed to WMEC with same hull numbers on 1 May 1966. The RELIANCE was changed to WTR 615 on June 1975 (the TR indicating *T*raining of *R*eserves); she reverted to WMEC 615 on 16 August 1982.

Design: The RELIANCE design has a small island superstructure with 360° visibility from the bridge to facilitate helicopter operations and towing. The ALERT was fitted with the Canadian-developed "Beartrap" helicopter hauldown system.

Engineering: The WMEC 615–619 were built with CODAG (Combination Diesel And Gas) turbine plants to provide experience in operating mixed propulsion plants. Those cutters had a high acceleration rate from all stop, or with their engines shut down could be at full speed in a few minutes; they could make 15.25 knots on gas turbines alone. The cost factor influenced the decision to make the remaining ships all-diesel.

The first five ships were re-engined during their mid-life modernization.

Guns: As built, the armament consisted of a single, open-mount 3-inch (76-mm)/50-cal gun Mk 22 forward of the bridge. During their modernization the 3-inch weapon was replaced by the 25-mm Bushmaster.

Modernization: These cutters have been upgraded under a Mid-life Maintenance Availability (MMA) program. The upgrade includes an enlarged superstructure; installation of a larger, improved engine exhaust (funnel); improved living spaces; a redesigned engine room; an upgraded firefighting system; new refrigeration and air conditioning units; a new electronics suite; and a new primary gun mount.

The MMA required approximately 18 months and cost about $20 million per cutter. The work was done at the Coast Guard Yard. The ACTIVE was the first cutter to be modernized and the RESOLUTE the last, the 16-ship program having taken ten years.

The DURABLE, arriving at the Coast Guard Yard, shows the trim lines of the RELIANCE-class cutters, a highly successful design. These ships have a helicopter deck, but no hangar. (1999, U.S. Coast Guard, PA3 Bridget Hieronymus)

The VALIANT under way with the safety rails around her helicopter deck in the raised position. As built, these cutters mounted a 3-inch/50-cal gun forward; a 25-mm Bushmaster cannon is now fitted. There is a large RDF antenna between the cannon and the bridge. (1999, Leo Van Ginderen)

1 MEDIUM ENDURANCE CUTTER: "STORIS" (230-FT)

Number	Name	Launched	Commissioned	Status
WMEC 38	STORIS	4 Apr 1942	30 Sep 1942	**PA**

Builders:	Toledo Shipbuilding, Ohio
Displacement:	1,715 tons standard
	1,925 tons full load
Length:	230 feet (70.1 m) overall
Beam:	43 feet (13.1 m)
Draft:	15 feet (4.6 m)
Propulsion:	diesel-electric (3 Fairbanks Morse 38D 8¼ diesel engines);
	1,800 shp; 1 shaft
Speed:	14.5 knots
Range:	12,000 n.miles (22,225 km) at 14.5 knots
	22,000 n.miles (40,745 km) at 8 knots
Manning:	86 (11 officers + 75 enlisted)
Helicopters:	no facilities
Guns:	1 25-mm/87-cal Bushmaster cannon Mk 38
	4 .50-cal machine guns M2 (4 single)
Radars:	2 SPS-64 navigation

The STORIS was built specifically for offshore icebreaking and patrol in the Greenland area. She has been employed in Alaskan service for search and rescue and law enforcement since 1949 and is homeported in Kodiak, Alaska.

The oldest Coast Guard cutter in active service, the STORIS is entitled to have gold hull numbers.

Classification: The STORIS originally was classified as WAGL 38 and then WAG 38; she was changed to WAGB 38 on 1 May 1966. Subsequently she was reclassified as a medium endurance cutter (WMEC) on 1 July 1972 to emphasize her role in law enforcement off the Alaskan fishing grounds.

Design: The ship was designed specifically for operation in northern waters and for icebreaking, although she is generally similar to the Coast Guard's 180-foot (54.9-m) buoy tenders. During World War II, the STORIS carried a single J2F Duck biplane scouting aircraft.

The rarely photographed cutter STORIS as she steams for port across Woman's Bay, Alaska, after spending a month on patrol in the Bering Sea. (1999, U.S. Coast Guard, PA2 Keith Alholm)

Guns: As built, the STORIS was armed with two 3-inch guns and four 20-mm guns, plus ASW weapons. A single 3-inch gun was retained into the 1980s and was then replaced by the 25-mm Bushmaster.

Names: The ship was initially named the ESKIMO, but the name was changed during construction to STORIS at the request of the State Department, which feared that the name might offend the natives of Greenland. The name STORIS is derived from a Scandinavian word that means "blue ice," a reference to very hard ice.

Operational: During World War II, the STORIS served in the North Atlantic as an ocean escort ship.

The STORIS and the seagoing buoy tenders BRAMBLE and SPAR carried out the first circumnavigation of the North American continent and transited the Northwest Passage in 1957, departing from Unimak Pass, Alaska, on 1 July and reaching Argentia, Newfoundland, on 19 September.

The STORIS has been in commission longer than any other Coast Guard cutter, and has been the least photographed cutter. This classic view shows the STORIS in her natural habitat of Alaskan waters; she still has a 3-inch/50-cal gun aft of her funnel. Note the icebreaking prow. (U.S. Coast Guard)

1 MEDIUM ENDURANCE CUTTER: FORMER SALVAGE SHIP (213-FT)

Number	Name	Launched	Navy ARS Comm.	Status
WMEC 167 (ex-ARS 9)	ACUSHNET	1 Apr 1943	5 Feb 1944	**PA**

Builders:	Basalt Rock, Napa, Calif.
Displacement:	1,557 tons standard
	1,745 tons full load
Length:	213½ feet (65.1 m) overall
Beam:	39 feet (12.8 m)
Draft:	15 feet (4.9 m)
Propulsion:	4 diesel engines (Cooper Bessemer GSB-8); 3,000 shp; 2 shafts
Speed:	15.5 knots
Range:	9,000 n.miles (16,670 km) at 15.5 knots
	20,000 n.miles (37,040 km) at 7 knots
Manning:	72 (7 officers + 65 enlisted)
Helicopters:	no facilities
Guns:	removed
Radars:	2 SPS-64 navigation

This is the last of eight former Navy salvage ships and oceangoing tugs (ATF) operated by the Coast Guard since World War II. Formerly the Navy salvage ship SHACKLE (ARS 9), she was permanently transferred to the Coast Guard on 29 June 1946.

The ACUSHNET is the last of several former Navy fleet tugs and salvage ships transferred to the Coast Guard. Long ago she beached all of her salvage gear, and she has been modified extensively for her role as a patrol cutter. (1990, Giorgio Arra)

Class: Two sister ships previously operated by the Coast Guard have been stricken: The ESCAPE (ARS 6) was transferred to the Coast Guard on 4 December 1980 and redesignated WMEC 6 (retaining her Navy name); she was decommissioned for disposal on 29 June 1995. The SEIZE (ARS 26) was transferred to the Coast Guard on 28 June 1946 and redesignated WMEC 168 (renamed YOCONA); she was decommissioned for disposal on 30 May 1996.

Classification: Upon transfer to the Coast Guard, the ATF 167 was reclassified as a tug (WAT). She was changed to WMEC on 1 May 1966. Upon modification to handle environmental data buoys, the ACUSHNET was changed to oceanographic cutter (WAGO 167) in 1969; she was redesignated WMEC in 1978.

MEDIUM ENDURANCE CUTTERS: FORMER FLEET TUGS (205-FT)

Number	Name	Navy Comm.	USCG Comm.	Notes
WMEC 76 (ex-ATF 76)	UTE	1942	1980	stricken 26 May 1988
WMEC 85 (ex-ATF 85)	LIPAN	1943	1980	stricken 9 June 1988
WMEC 153 (ex-ATF 153)	CHILULA	1945	1956	stricken 27 June 1991
WMEC 165 (ex-ATF 66)	CHEROKEE	1940	1946	stricken 28 Feb 1991
WMEC 166 (ex-ATF 95)	TAMAROA	1943	1946	stricken 1 Feb 1994

These are former Navy fleet tugs that were transferred to the Coast Guard and employed as medium endurance cutters. (The TAMAROA was named ZUNI in Navy service; the others retained their Navy names.)

All were returned to Navy custody for disposal; the TAMAROA was transferred to the INTREPID (CV 11) Sea-Air-Space Museum in New York City.

Classification: These ships were classified ATF by the Navy; upon transfer to the Coast Guard, the ex-ATF 66, 95, and 153 became WAT, with two having new hull numbers assigned. All three were changed to WMEC on 1 May 1966.

SURFACE EFFECTS SHIPS

SURFACE EFFECTS SHIP CUTTERS: "SEA HAWK" CLASS

Number	Name	Comm.	Status
WSES 2	SEA HAWK	1982	decomm. 28 Jan 1994
WSES 3	SHEARWATER	1982	decomm. 28 Jan 1994
WSES 4	PETREL	1983	decomm. 28 Jan 1994

All three Surface Effects Ships (SES) acquired by the Coast Guard, primarily for use in the drug enforcement role, have been decommissioned and discarded. They were acquired after evaluation of a prototype ship, the DORADO (designated WSES 1), which was commissioned in the Coast Guard in 1981 and, after extensive trials, transferred back to the Navy. She survives in Navy service as the (unnamed) IX 515; see chapter 24.

See 15th Edition/page 563 for characteristics.

The Coast Guard has discarded the three SEA HAWK–class surface effects ships, the only SES to enter operational service with the U.S. Navy or Coast Guard. Above left, the SHEARWATER visits Portsmouth, England; at right, the SEA HAWK motors off Miami, Florida. The craft were highly effective in coastal patrol operations. (1990, Leo Van Ginderen; 1990, Giorgio Arra)

PATROL SHIPS AND BOATS

1 COASTAL PATROL SHIP: "CYCLONE" CLASS (170-FT)

Number	Name	FY	Laid down	Launched	USN Comm.	USCG Comm.	Status
WPC 1	CYCLONE	90	22 June 1991	1 Feb 1992	7 Aug 1993	29 Jan 2000	**AA**

Builders:	Bollinger Shipyards, Lockport, La.	Troops:	9
Displacement:	331 tons full load	Missiles:	deleted
Length:	157⁵/₁₂ feet (48.0 m) waterline	Guns:	2 25-mm Bushmaster cannon Mk 38 (2 single)
	170½ feet (52.0 m) overall		2 .50-cal machine guns M2HB (2 single)
Beam:	25 feet (7.6 m)		2 7.62-mm machine guns M60 (2 single)
Draft:	7⅝ feet (2.4 m)		2 40-mm grenade launchers Mk 19 (2 single)
Propulsion:	4 diesel engines (Paxman Valenta	Radars:	2 Sperry RASCAR 2500 surface search
	16VRP-200); 13,400 bhp; 4 shafts		(S and X bands)
Speed:	35 knots	Sonars:	Wesmar side-scanning (HF)
Range:	2,000 n.miles (3,700 km) at 12 knots	EW systems:	APR-39A(V)1 radar warning receiver
Manning:	29		

The CYCLONE was the lead ship for a class of coastal patrol and interdiction ships (see chapter 20 for class notes). With completion of the last ship of the class, the TORNADO (PC 14), the CYCLONE was decommissioned on 28 January 2000 and transferred to the Coast Guard on 29 January 2000 at the Coast Guard Yard in Curtis Bay, Md. With transfer of the CYCLONE, her Navy crew was assigned to the TORNADO.

In addition, the THUNDERBOLT (PC 12) of this class was transferred to the Coast Guard on a temporary basis from 5 March 2000 to July 2000, to further determine the feasibility of operating these ships on Coast Guard missions. The THUNDERBOLT's crew was temporarily assigned to Navy Special Boat Squadron 2 while the ship was operated by the Coast Guard.

Design: The ship has a steel hull with aluminum superstructure; 1-inch (25-mm) appliqué armor is fitted to portions of superstructure for protection against small arms fire. Endurance is ten days.

A single RIB is normally carried.

The ex-Navy patrol craft CYCLONE moored at the Coast Guard Yard. The ship was idle after being transferred to the Coast Guard, awaiting funding for her modification and commissioning as a cutter. Her Navy hull number has been painted out. (2000, U.S. Navy)

The USCGC THUNDERBOLT during her brief career in the Coast Guard. She wears the Coast Guard stripes on a dark blue hull, retaining her Navy name and hull number, albeit referred to as WPC in Coast Guard documents. (2000, U.S. Coast Guard)

49 PATROL BOATS: ISLAND CLASS (110-FT)

Number	Name	Launched	Commissioned	Status
A series (16)				
WPB 1301	FARALLON	27 Aug 1985	21 Feb 1986	AA
WPB 1302	MANITOU	9 Oct 1985	28 Feb 1986	AA
WPB 1303	MATAGORDA	15 Dec 1985	25 Apr 1986	AA
WPB 1304	MAUI	13 Jan 1986	9 May 1986	AA
WPB 1305	MONHEGAN	15 Feb 1986	16 June 1986	AA
WPB 1306	NUNIVAK	15 Mar 1986	4 July 1986	AA
WPB 1307	OCRACOKE	12 Apr 1986	4 Aug 1986	AA
WPB 1308	VASHON	10 May 1986	15 Aug 1986	AA
WPB 1309	AQUIDNECK	14 June 1986	26 Sep 1986	AA
WPB 1310	MUSTANG	11 July 1986	29 Aug 1986	AA
WPB 1311	NAUSHON	22 Aug 1986	3 Oct 1986	AA
WPB 1312	SANIBEL	3 Oct 1986	14 Nov 1986	AA
WPB 1313	EDISTO	21 Nov 1986	7 Jan 1987	PA
WPB 1314	SAPELO	9 Jan 1987	24 Feb 1987	AA
WPB 1315	MATINICUS	26 Feb 1987	16 Apr 1987	AA
WPB 1316	NANTUCKET	17 Apr 1987	4 June 1987	AA
B series (21)				
WPB 1317	ATTU	4 Dec 1987	9 May 1988	AA
WPB 1318	BARANOF	15 Jan 1988	20 May 1988	AA
WPB 1319	CHANDELEUR	19 Feb 1988	8 June 1988	AA
WPB 1320	CHINCOTEAGUE	25 Mar 1988	8 Aug 1988	AA
WPB 1321	CUSHING	29 Apr 1988	8 Aug 1988	AA
WPB 1322	CUTTYHUNK	3 June 1988	15 Oct 1988	PA
WPB 1323	DRUMMOND	8 July 1988	19 Oct 1988	AA
WPB 1324	KEY LARGO	12 Aug 1988	24 Dec 1988	AA
WPB 1325	METOMKIN	16 Sep 1988	12 Jan 1989	AA
WPB 1326	MONOMOY	21 Oct 1988	16 Dec 1988	AA
WPB 1327	ORCAS	25 Nov 1988	14 Apr 1989	PA
WPB 1328	PADRE	6 Jan 1989	24 Feb 1989	AA
WPB 1329	SITKINAK	10 Feb 1989	31 Mar 1989	AA
WPB 1330	TYBEE	17 Mar 1989	9 May 1989	PA
WPB 1331	WASHINGTON	21 Apr 1989	9 June 1989	PA
WPB 1332	WRANGELL	26 May 1989	24 June 1989	AA
WPB 1333	ADAK	30 June 1989	17 Nov 1989	AA
WPB 1334	LIBERTY	4 Aug 1989	22 Sep 1989	PA
WPB 1335	ANACAPA	8 Sep 1989	13 Jan 1990	PA
WPB 1336	KISKA	13 Oct 1989	21 Apr 1990	PA
WPB 1337	ASSATEAGUE	17 Nov 1989	1 June 1990	PA
C series (12)				
WPB 1338	GRAND ISLE	1989	19 Apr 1991	AA
WPB 1339	KEY BISCAYNE	12 Mar 1991	27 Apr 1991	AA
WPB 1340	JEFFERSON ISLAND	11 Apr 1991	16 Aug 1991	AA
WPB 1341	KODIAK ISLAND	8 Feb 1991	21 June 1991	AA
WPB 1342	LONG ISLAND	19 Mar 1991	27 Aug 1991	PA
WPB 1343	BAINBRIDGE ISLAND	19 Apr 1991	20 Sep 1991	AA
WPB 1344	BLOCK ISLAND	1991	22 Nov 1991	AA
WPB 1345	STATEN ISLAND	1991	22 Nov 1991	AA
WPB 1346	ROANOKE ISLAND	8 Nov 1991	8 Feb 1992	AA
WPB 1347	PEA ISLAND	1991	29 Feb 1992	AA
WPB 1348	KNIGHT ISLAND	6 Sep 1991	22 Apr 1992	AA
WPB 1349	GALVESTON ISLAND	15 Nov 1991	5 June 1992	PA

Builders:	Bollinger Shipyard, Lockport, La.
Displacement:	136 tons standard
	A series 163 tons full load
	B series 157 tons full load
	C series 153 tons full load
Length:	110 feet (33.5 m) overall
Beam:	21 feet (6.4 m)
Draft:	7⅓ feet (2.2 m)
Propulsion:	2 diesel engines (Alco-Paxman Valenta 16 RP200, except C series Caterpillar 3526); 5,820 bhp, except C series 5,460 bhp; 2 shafts
Speed:	29.7 knots, except C series 28 knots
Range:	A series 900 n.miles (1,670 km) at 30 knots
	2,700 n.miles (5,000 km) at 12 knots
	B and C series 840 n.miles (1,555 km) at 30 knots
	2,400 n.miles (4,445 km) at 12 knots
Manning:	16–18 (2 officers + 14–16 enlisted)
Guns:	1 25-mm/87-cal Bushmaster cannon Mk 38
	2 7.62-mm machine guns M60 (2 single)
Radar:	1 SPS-64(V)1 navigation

The Coast Guard built this class of patrol boats for offshore surveillance and SAR operations, replacing the 95-foot (29-m) and 82-foot (25-m) WPBs; however, some ports for those smaller craft could not accommodate the Island-class WPBs.

The contract for these boats was originally awarded in May 1984 to the Marine Power and Equipment Co., Seattle, Wash., for 16 boats; however, a U.S. District Court set aside the award because of irregularities in the procurement process. Subsequently, Bollinger was awarded a contract for the first 16 units in August 1984.

The design was 20 years old when the contract was awarded, and critics have claimed that more capable designs were available. Also, early operational experience with the Island-class WPBs revealed hull problems, such as cracks developing in heavy seas.

The FARALLON was delivered on 15 November 1985, with the remainder being completed through 1992.

Design: The design is based on an existing patrol boat, developed by Vosper-Thornycroft in Great Britain, to minimize cost and reduce technical risks. The craft have a steel hull with aluminum deck and superstructure; they have a flush-deck, round-bilge hull with some bow sheer, and a low bow coaming. The WPB 1317 and later units have heavier bow plating to correct a hull-cracking problem. A quadruped mast is fitted.

Guns: The WPB 1301–1337 originally mounted a 20-mm gun Mk 67; all units now have the Bushmaster "chain gun."

Manning: The VASHON undertook a historic manning experiment in 1994–1995, employing Naval Reserve personnel to help provide shore support and maintenance for the patrol boat, as well as undertaking their at-sea drills on board for 12 to 17 days.[9] Although the experiment was successful, the concept was not pursued. (The VASHON is based at Roosevelt Roads, Puerto Rico.)

Operational: The Island-class units in the Caribbean area normally conduct 10- to 12-day patrols, followed by an in-port period.

PATROL BOATS: HERITAGE CLASS (120-FT)

This class of Coast Guard patrol boats was intended to replace the older and smaller Cape-class and Point-class patrol boats. The Heritage-class design was to be faster, longer-lived, and less expensive to build and maintain than the Island class.

The lead unit—the LEOPOLD (WPB 1400)—was ordered in March 1989 and was laid down on 27 August 1990 at the Coast Guard Yard. Series production of 35 follow-on units was expected to begin in 1992 if the prototype proved successful; long-range plans called for a total of up to 96 units. However, the Coast Guard halted work on the LEOPOLD on 25 November 1991 because of the rapidly changing world situation. A Coast Guard spokesman stated: "The reason that we're suspending it at this point—and most likely it will be canceled—is basically times have changed."

The Coast Guard decision came four months after a report of the General Accounting Office (GAO) questioned the need for the craft; the report summary stated: "There were weaknesses in identifying mission needs and the capabilities the replacement vessels [Heritage class] would require to meet these needs. The Coast Guard also could not support its decision for the number of patrol boats needed because agency officials could not provide support for the calculations of the computer model used to determine the need for 96 vessels."[10] The GAO report also noted that the Coast Guard underestimated the time and cost required to acquire the Heritage class.

See 16th Edition/page 511 for characteristics.

Classification: The class was rated at 120 feet, although the actual length is 118 feet.

Names: These ships were to be named for former Coast Guard cutters that were part of the service's heritage.

---

9. See Lt. Joe DiRenzo III, USCG, "The Ultimate Odd Couple," U.S. Naval Institute *Proceedings* (June 1995), pp. 65–67.
10. General Accounting Office, *Coast Guard: Adequacy of the Justification for Heritage Patrol Boats,* GAO/RCED-91-188 (July 1991), pp. 1–2.

The Island class is the Coast Guard's largest cutter class, with 49 ships in service. Here, the WASHINGTON, named for Washington Island, Wisc., in Lake Michigan, makes high speed off Oahu, Hawaii. The 25-mm Bushmaster cannon forward is under canvas. (1999, U.S. Coast Guard)

The SANIBEL on patrol off Martha's Vineyard, Mass., during the burial at sea of the remains of John F. Kennedy, Jr. Despite their limitations, these hard-working craft have been in the forefront of law enforcement and rescue operations. (1999, U.S. Coast Guard, PA3 Bridget Hieronymus)

28 + 23 COASTAL PATROL BOATS: "BARRACUDA" CLASS (87-FT)

Number	Name	Commissioned	Status
CPB 87301	Barracuda	7 Apr 1998	**PA**
CPB 87302	Hammerhead	16 Oct 1998	**AA**
CPB 87303	Mako	11 Dec 1998	**AA**
CPB 87304	Marlin	22 Jan 1999	**AA**
CPB 87305	Stingray	13 Jan 1999	**AA**
CPB 87306	Dorado	23 Apr 1999	**PA**
CPB 87307	Osprey	19 June 1999	**PA**
CPB 87308	Chinook	19 May 1999	**AA**
CPB 87309	Albacore	20 Aug 1999	**AA**
CPB 87310	Tarpon	22 Oct 1999	**AA**
CPB 87311	Cobia	29 Oct 1999	**AA**
CPB 87312	Hawksbill	7 Jan 1999	**PA**
CPB 87313	Cormorant	10 Dec 1999	**AA**
CPB 87314	Finback	13 Jan 2000	**AA**
CPB 87315	Amberjack	25 Jan 2000	**AA**
CPB 87316	Kittiwake	30 June 2000	**PA**
CPB 87317	Blackfin	4 May 2000	**PA**
CPB 87318	Bluefin	27 Apr 2000	**AA**
CPB 87319	Yellowfin	12 June 2000	**AA**
CPB 87320	Manta	31 July 2000	**AA**
CPB 87321	Coho	2000	**PA**
CPB 87322	Kingfisher	2000	**AA**
CPB 87323	Seahawk	2000	**AA**
CPB 87324	Steelhead	13 Dec 2000	**AA**
CPB 87325	Beluga	21 Nov 2000	**AA**
CPB 87326	Blacktip	2000	**PA**
CPB 87327	Pelican	2000	**AA**
CPB 87328	Ridley	2000	**AA**
CPB 87329	Cochito	2001	building
CPB 87330	Manowar	2001	building
CPB 87331	Moray	2001	building
CPB 87332	Razorbill	2001	building
CPB 87333	Adelie	2001	building
CPB 87334	Gannet	2001	building
CPB 87335	Narwhal	2001	building
CPB 87336	Sturgeon	2001	building
CPB 87337	Sockeye	2001	building
CPB 87338	Ibis	2001	building
CPB 87339	Pompano	2001	building
CPB 87340	Halibut	2001	building
CPB 87341	Bonito	2001	building
CPB 87342	Shrike	2002	building
CPB 87343	Tern	2002	building
CPB 87344	Heron	2002	building
CPB 87345	Wahoo	2002	building
CPB 87346	Flying Fish	2002	building
CPB 87347	Haddock	2002	building
CPB 87348	Brant	2002	building
CPB 87349	Shearwater	2002	building
CPB 87350	Petrel	2002	building

Builders:	Bollinger Shipyard, Lockport, La.
Displacement:	89.5 tons full load
Length:	80⅚ feet (24.87 m) waterline
	87 feet (26.5 m) overall
Beam:	19⅓ feet (5.92 m)
Draft:	5⅔ feet (1.74 m)
Propulsion:	2 diesel engines (MTU 8V 396 TE94), 1,500 bhp; 2 shafts
Speed:	25 knots; patrol speed 10 knots
Range:	900 n.miles (1,668 km) at 10 knots
Manning:	10 (enlisted)
Guns:	2 7.62-mm machine guns M60 (2 single)
Radars:	navigation

These are coastal patrol boats intended to replace the 82-foot WPBs and complement the 110-foot WPBs of the Island class as the principal Coast Guard patrol craft after the year 2000.

Bollinger was awarded a contract on 22 March 1996 to design and construct the lead unit. Series production contracts followed. The boats are also referred to as the Marine Protector class.

Classification: The Coast Guard is using the classification CPB, for "Coastal Patrol Boat," in lieu of the standard WPB for these craft; the latter remains their official designation.

Design: The 87-foot CPBs have improved habitability, intended for mixed-gender crews. Accommodations consist of two- and three-person berths (with one spare berth).

A single Rigid-hull Inflatable Boat (RIB) is carried, with a stern ramp replacing the usual crane needed to launch and recover the RIB.

Provisions can be carried for five-day missions.

The Osprey at high speed, showing the boxy lines of this new class of coastal patrol boats, generally referred to as CPB rather than the official WPB. A bar-type radar antenna tops the small bridge, forward of the lattice mast. (1999, Bollinger Shipyard)

The Osprey at rest near Seattle, Wash. The port-side diesel exhaust is the black oval in the hull, amidships. Like most cutters, these are multipurpose craft. (1999, U.S. Coast Guard, PA2 Tiffany Powell)

A BARRACUDA-class CPB/WPB, showing the small working area amidships for stowing a small boat and handling rescue gear. (1999, U.S. Coast Guard)

PATROL BOATS: CAPE CLASS (95-FT)

Number	Name	Notes
WPB 95302	CAPE HIGGON	decomm. 25 Jan 1990; to Uruguay 1990
WPB 95305	CAPE HATTERAS	decomm. 9 Mar 1989; to Mexico 1991
WPB 95306	CAPE GEORGE	decomm. 2 Mar 1990
WPB 95309	CAPE CARTER	decomm. 19 Jan 1990; to Mexico 1990
WPB 95311	CAPE HEDGE	decomm. 7 Jan 1987; to Mexico 1990
WPB 95321	CAPE CROSS	decomm. 20 Mar 1990; to Micronesia 1990
WPB 95322	CAPE HORN	decomm. 25 Jan 1990; to Uruguay 1990
WPB 95326	CAPE CORWIN	decomm. 6 Apr 1990; to Micronesia 1990

All 95-foot (29-m), steel-hull patrol boats of the Cape class have been discarded. The above units are those decommissioned since 1990.

Class: Thirty-five WPBs of this class were completed from 1953 to 1959.

Units of this class have been transferred to the Bahamas, Costa Rica, Ethiopia, Haiti, the Marshall Islands, Mexico, Micronesia, Saudi Arabia, South Korea, Thailand, and Uruguay.

The CAPE HEDGE (WPB 95311) was transferred to the Navy on 7 January 1987 and served as a pilot boat in 1987–1989 (renamed VANGUARD); she was subsequently transferred to Mexico in January 1990. The CAPE WASHINGTON (WPB 95310) went to the U.S. Navy as a pilot boat on 11 August 1989, renamed VENTURE.

These craft, originally intended primarily for harbor patrol and coastal ASW, were constructed between 1953 and 1959. Plans to discard this class in the 1970s in favor of new construction were dropped and all surviving units were modernized. Subsequently they were replaced from the mid-1980s by the Island-class WPBs.

See 14th Edition/page 544 for characteristics.

19 PATROL BOATS: POINT CLASS (82-FT)

Number	Name	Commissioned	Status
A series			
WPB 82302	POINT HOPE	5 Oct 1960	to Costa Rica 1991
WPB 82311	POINT VERDE	15 Mar 1961	decomm. 12 June 1991; to Mexico 1991
WPB 82312	POINT SWIFT	22 Mar 1961	decomm. 30 Mar 1995
WPB 82314	POINT THATCHER	13 Sep 1961	decomm. 13 Mar 1992
C series (29)			
WPB 82318	POINT HERRON	14 June 1961	decomm. 21 June 1991; to Mexico 1991
WPB 82332	POINT ROBERTS	6 June 1962	decomm. Feb 1992
WPB 82333	POINT HIGHLAND	27 June 1962	AA
WPB 82334	POINT LEDGE	18 July 1962	decomm. 30 Aug 1998; to Venezuela 1998
WPB 82335	POINT COUNTESS	8 Aug 1962	PA
WPB 82336	POINT GLASS	29 Aug 1962	AA
WPB 82337	POINT DIVIDE	19 Sep 1962	decomm. 30 Mar 1995
WPB 82338	POINT BRIDGE	10 Oct 1962	PA
WPB 82339	POINT CHICO	29 Oct 1962	PA
WPB 82340	POINT BATAN	21 Nov 1962	decomm. 1 Oct 1999; to Dominican Republic 1999
WPB 82341	POINT LOOKOUT	12 Dec 1962	decomm. 24 Mar 1994
WPB 82342	POINT BAKER	30 Oct 1963	AA
WPB 82343	POINT WELLS	20 Nov 1963	decomm. 13 Oct 2000
WPB 82344	POINT ESTERO	11 Dec 1966	AA
WPB 82345	POINT JUDITH	26 July 1966	decomm. 15 Jan 1992; to Venezuela 1992
WPB 82346	POINT ARENA	26 Aug 1966	decomm. 30 Mar 1999
WPB 82347	POINT BONITA	12 Sep 1966	AA
WPB 82348	POINT BARROW	4 Oct 1966	decomm. 7 June 1991; to Panama 1991
WPB 82349	POINT SPENCER	25 Oct 1966	decomm. 12 Dec 2000
WPB 82350	POINT FRANKLIN	14 Nov 1966	decomm. 23 June 1998; to Venezuela 1998
WPB 82351	POINT BENNETT	19 Dec 1966	decomm. 12 Feb 1999; to Trinidad and Tobago 1999
WPB 82352	POINT SAL	5 Dec 1966	AA
WPB 82353	POINT MONROE	27 Dec 1966	AA
WPB 82354	POINT EVANS	10 Jan 1967	decomm. 16 Nov 1999; to Philippines 1999
WPB 82355	POINT HANNON	23 Jan 1967	AA
WPB 82356	POINT FRANCIS	3 Feb 1967	decomm. 9 Mar 1999; to Panama 1999
WPB 82357	POINT HURON	17 Feb 1967	decomm. 21 Apr 1999; to Panama 1999
WPB 82358	POINT STUART	17 Mar 1967	PA
WPB 82359	POINT STEELE	26 Apr 1967	decomm. 9 July 1998; to Antigua 1998
WPB 82360	POINT WINSLOW	3 Mar 1967	AA
WPB 82361	POINT CHARLES	15 May 1967	decomm. 13 Dec 1991
WPB 82362	POINT BROWN	30 Mar 1967	decomm. 30 Sep 1991
WPB 82363	POINT NOWELL	1 June 1967	decomm. 19 Oct 1999; to Jamaica 1999
WPB 82364	POINT WHITEHORN	13 July 1967	decomm. 30 Mar 1995
WPB 82365	POINT TURNER	14 Apr 1967	decomm. 3 Apr 1998; to St. Lucia 1998
WPB 82366	POINT LOBOS	29 May 1967	AA
WPB 82367	POINT KNOLL	27 June 1967	decomm. 11 Sep 1991; to Venezuela 1991
WPB 82368	POINT WARDE	14 Aug 1967	AA
WPB 82369	POINT HEYER	3 Aug 1967	decomm. 11 Dec 1998; to Trinidad and Tobago 1999
WPB 82370	POINT RICHMOND	25 Aug 1967	decomm. 30 Sep 1997; to Ecuador 1998
D series (8)			
WPB 82371	POINT BARNES	21 Apr 1970	decomm. 12 Jan 2000; to Jamaica 2000
WPB 82372	POINT BROWER	21 Apr 1970	PA
WPB 82373	POINT CAMDEN	4 May 1970	decomm. 12 Dec 1999; to Jamaica 1999
WPB 82374	POINT CARREW	18 May 1970	PA
WPB 82375	POINT DORAN	1 June 1970	PA
WPB 82376	POINT HARRIS	22 June 1970	decomm. 4 Dec 1992
WPB 82377	POINT HOBART	13 July 1970	decomm. 8 July 1999; to Argentina 1999
WPB 82378	POINT JACKSON	3 Aug 1970	AA
WPB 82379	POINT MARTIN	20 Aug 1970	decomm. 24 Aug 1999; to Dominican Republic 1999

Builders:	Coast Guard Yard, Curtis Bay, Md., except WPB 82347 and
	82349 by J. Martinac Shipbuilding, Tacoma, Wash.
Displacement:	C series 66 tons full load
	D series 69 full load
Length:	83 feet (25.3 m) overall
Beam:	17⅙ feet (5.2 m)
Draft:	5¾ feet (1.8 m)
Propulsion:	2 diesel engines (Caterpillar 3412 V-12); 1,500 bhp;
	2 shafts (see notes)
Speed:	C series 23.7 knots
	D series 22.6 knots
Range:	C series 490 n.miles (910 km) at 20 knots
	1,500 n.miles (2,780 km) at 8 knots
	D series 320 n.miles (590 km) at 20 knots
	1,200 n.miles (2,220 km) at 6 knots
Manning:	10 (see notes)
Guns:	2 .50-cal machine guns M2 (2 single) (see notes)
Radars:	SPS-64(V)1 navigation

These are 82-foot cutters used for port security and SAR. They are being replaced by the 87-foot CPBs. The survivors have been re-engined (see below).

Class: The class originally comprised 79 units, completed from 1960 to 1970; 26 units were transferred to South Vietnam in 1969–1970. The active units and those decommissioned since 1990 are listed above.

The POINT CHARLES was transferred to Texas A&M University, the POINT BROWN to Kingsborough Community College, Brooklyn, N.Y., and the POINT DIVIDE to Washington State as school ships.

The POINT HARRIS was heavily damaged by Hurricane Iniki at Kauai, Hawaii, on 11 September 1992 and subsequently was stricken.

Design: These patrol boats have steel hulls with aluminum superstructures. There are no noticeable differences among the various series of the Point class. A tripod mast is fitted atop the bridge roof.

Engineering: The POINT THATCHER originally had two gas turbines generating 1,000 shp and was capable of making 27 knots; she also had controllable-pitch propellers. She was refitted with diesels.

The Coast Guard re-engined 37 of these craft to extend their service lives. All were completed with two Cummins VT-12-M diesel engines; beginning in 1989, these units were refitted with two Caterpillar diesel engines. The POINT HIGHLAND was the first unit to be re-engined. (Forty-three upgrades were planned.)

Guns: Earlier, these WPBs had a single 20-mm gun forward of the deck house. During the 1960s and 1970s, many units instead carried two .50-cal machine guns or an 81-mm mortar mounted "piggyback" with a .50-cal machine gun. Subsequently, they carried only the single machine guns. Most units now carry only small arms.

Manning: About half of the Point-class WPBs are commanded by commissioned officers and the remainder by an officer-in-charge, normally a chief petty officer.

Names: The WPB 82301–82344 were assigned geographical point names in January 1964; later cutters were named as built.

The forecastle of the POINT BONITA, with crewmen manning the WPB's two .50-caliber machine guns. The Coast Guard is a military service and its personnel are trained in small arms and other military skills. There are two life raft canisters forward of the bridge. (1999, U.S. Coast Guard, PA1 Telfair H. Brown)

The POINT SAL at high speed with a Rigid Inflatable Boat (RIB) keeping pace. The POINT SAL's machine guns have spray mounts fitted. She has a boom aft for handling a RIB. (1996, Leo Van Ginderen)

ICEBREAKERS

Coast Guard icebreakers operate in the Arctic and Antarctic regions in support of U.S. national requirements for military and scientific activities. The Coast Guard currently has three large icebreakers in service: two of the Polar class and the recently completed HEALY.

The Coast Guard had long planned to construct two additional Polar-class icebreakers to replace the GLACIER (WAGB 4, ex-AGB 4) and two Wind-class icebreakers to provide a force of four modern icebreakers to meet national requirements. However, the GLACIER and the two surviving Wind-class ships were decommissioned without replacements.

In late 1986 the Coast Guard expressed interest in leasing two large polar icebreakers as an alternative to building and operating government-owned ships. Such a build-and-charter concept was similar to that used by the Navy for tankers and maritime prepositioning ships. The concept, however, has been rejected in favor of a single new construction ship. Named HEALY, the new ship is larger and more powerful than the Polar-class icebreakers.

The icebreakers have extensive research laboratory facilities.

All Coast Guard icebreakers are based at Seattle, Wash.

Historical: Icebreakers were operated by the U.S. Navy and Coast Guard until 1966; at that time, the Navy's five active icebreakers were transferred to the Coast Guard:

Navy	Coast Guard	Name
AGB 1 (ex-AG 88)	WAGB 283	BURTON ISLAND
AGB 2 (ex-AG 89)	WAGB 284	EDISTO
AGB 3	WAGB 280	ATKA
AGB 4	WAGB 4	GLACIER
AGB 5	WAGB 278	STATEN ISLAND

The AGB 1–3 and AGB 5 were Wind-class ships built during World War II; the GLACIER was the first U.S. icebreaker built after the war (completed in 1955).

1 ICEBREAKER: "HEALY" (420-FT)

Number	Name	FY	Launched	Commissioned	Status
WAGB 20	HEALY	93	15 Nov 1997	2000	**PA**

Builders:	Avondale Industries, New Orleans, La.
Displacement:	16,400 tons full load
Length:	397⅔ feet (121.23 m) waterline
	419⅚ feet (128.0 m) overall
Beam:	82 feet (25.0 m)
Draft:	29¼ feet (8.91 m)
Propulsion:	diesel-electric: 4 diesel engines (Sulzer-Westinghouse 12 ZA40S), 10,600 bhp + 4 electric motors, 30,000 shp; 2 shafts
Speed:	17 knots; 12.5 knots cruise
Range:	16,000 n.miles (29,650 km) at 12.5 knots
	37,000 n.miles (68,560 km) at 9.25 knots
Manning:	75 (12 officers + 63 enlisted) + 35 scientists
Helicopters:	2 HH-65A Dolphin
Guns:	2 .50-cal machine guns M2 (2 single)
Radars:	2 navigation

This is the largest icebreaker to be built in a U.S. shipyard and the largest operated by the U.S. government.

Congress voted $275 million in the fiscal 1990 budget for construction of this ship; the remainder of the necessary funding, $60 million, was authorized in fiscal 1992. However, the Naval Sea Systems Command lists the ship in the fiscal year 1993 program.

The Naval Sea Systems Command, procurement agent for Coast Guard icebreakers, canceled the procurement of this ship on 20 March 1992 because the responses received from shipyards were in excess of appropriated funds. The Coast Guard and Navy stated that they would "continue to examine alternatives for procuring the icebreaker." Subsequently, the Navy awarded the contract to Avondale on 15 July 1993.

The HEALY's keel was laid down on 16 September 1996. Construction cost is estimated at $340 million.

Class: A second ship was planned but not authorized.

Design: The original design was revised and the ship reduced in size and power because of cost constraints.

The ship can break 4½ feet (1.4 m) of ice at a continuous speed of three knots or ice up to 7⅚ feet (2.4 m) by backing and ramming.

Engineering: A 2,000-shp bow thruster is fitted.

The HEALY under way. The HEALY is the largest icebreaker to be built in the United States. Proposals for additional ships of this type have not been pursued. Note the ship's block superstructure and the squared-off funnel. (1999, Avondale Industries)

The HEALY's two helicopter hangar doors are partially raised in this view of the nation's newest and largest icebreaker. The all-around bridge windows are evident, as is the enclosed crow's nest. (1999, Avondale Industries)

The HEALY breaking ice for the first time in the Arctic. The ship has heavy cranes for handling equipment, stores, and research gear. There is an HH-65A Dolphin resting on the elevated flight deck, forward of the cranes. (2000, U.S. Coast Guard)

2 ICEBREAKERS: POLAR CLASS (399-FT)

Number	Name	Launched	Commissioned	Status
WAGB 10	POLAR STAR	17 Nov 1973	19 Jan 1976	**PA**
WAGB 11	POLAR SEA	24 June 1975	23 Feb 1978	**PA**

Builders:	Lockheed Shipbuilding, Seattle, Wash.
Displacement:	10,863 tons standard
	13,623 tons full load
Length:	337⅙ feet (102.78 m) waterline
	399⅚ feet (121.91 m) overall
Beam:	83½ feet (25.45 m)
Draft:	33½ feet (10.2 m)
Propulsion:	CODOG: 6 diesel engines (Alco), 18,000 bhp + 3 gas turbines
	(Pratt & Whitney), 60,000 shp; 3 shafts
Speed:	18 knots
Range:	16,000 n.miles (29,630 km) at 18 knots
	28,275 n.miles (52,400 km) at 13 knots
Manning:	142 (15 officers + 127 enlisted) + 33 scientists
Helicopters:	2 HH-65A Dolphin
Guns:	2 .50-cal machine guns M2 (2 single)
Radars:	2 SPS-64 navigation

These two large icebreakers were to be constructed as replacements for the Wind-class icebreakers.

When the Polar class was begun in the early 1970s, the Coast Guard operated seven oceangoing icebreakers, the GLACIER (WAGB 4) and six of the Wind class (WAGB 279–284, 288). Several additional Polar-class ships were envisioned, but none was built, in part because of the higher-than-anticipated construction costs.

Both Polar-class icebreakers are homeported at Seattle, Wash.

Design: These ships have conventional icebreaker hull forms. A hangar and flight deck are fitted aft and two 15-ton-capacity cranes are abaft the hangar. Arctic and oceanographic laboratories are provided.

Engineering: CODOG (Combination Diesel or Gas turbine) propulsion is provided, with diesel engines for cruising and rapid-reaction gas turbines available for surge-power requirements. Controllable-pitch propellers allow propeller thrust to be reversed without reversing the direction of shaft rotation. Both ships have experienced problems with their controllable-pitch propellers and control systems.

The original design provided for a speed of 21 knots; it has not been achieved in service.

The POLAR SEA under way near Korsakov, Russia, in the Sea of Okhotsk. When this photo was taken, she was participating in a multi-nation oil spill control exercise. (1998, U.S. Coast Guard, PAC Tod A. Lyons)

The POLAR SEA in Arctic ice. The Coast Guard's oceangoing icebreakers support U.S. research, military, and economic interests in the Arctic and Antarctic. (1996, U.S. Coast Guard, PA3 Andy Devilbiss)

Operational: The POLAR SEA circumnavigated the North American continent in 1985. The icebreaker departed Seattle, Wash., on 6 June, sailed through the Panama Canal, up the East Coast to Greenland, and through the Northwest Passage into the Bering Sea and into the Pacific, returning to Seattle on 2 October. The ship required just under seven days, including a brief stop at the village of Resolute Bay, to transit the 850-n.mile (1,575-km) Northwest Passage.

The POLAR SEA reached the geographic North Pole on 26 July 1994, in company with the Canadian icebreaker LOUIS S. ST. LAURENT. This was the first U.S. surface ship to reach the pole.[11] (The Coast Guard icebreaker WESTWIND/WAGB 281 came within 375 n.miles/690 km of the North Pole in 1970.)

1 ICEBREAKER: "MACKINAW" (290-FT)

Number	Name	Launched	Commissioned	Status
WAGB 83	MACKINAW	4 Mar 1944	20 Dec 1944	**GL**

Builders:	Toledo Shipbuilding, Ohio
Displacement:	5,320 tons full load
Length:	290 feet (88.4 m) overall
Beam:	75 feet (22.9 m)
Draft:	19 feet (5.8 m)
Propulsion:	diesel-electric (Fairbanks Morse diesel engines, Westinghouse electric motors); 10,000 shp aft + 3,000 shp forward; 2 shafts aft + 1 shaft forward
Speed:	18.7 knots
Range:	10,000 n.miles (18,520 km) at 18.7 knots
	41,000 n.miles (75,930 km) at 9 knots
Manning:	75 (8 officers + 67 enlisted)
Helicopters:	landing area
Guns:	none

The MACKINAW was designed and constructed specifically for Coast Guard use on the Great Lakes. The ship is homeported in Cheboygan, Mich. Under terms of a U.S.-Canadian treaty, neither nation can place armed ships on the Great Lakes except for brief periods with mutual agreement of the two governments.

The ship is scheduled to be retired in 2006.

Classification: The ship originally was classified WAG 83; she was changed to WAGB on 1 May 1966.

Design: The MACKINAW has many features of the contemporary Wind class; however, being designed for the Great Lakes, the ship is longer and wider than the oceangoing ships, with significantly less draft. Two 12-ton-capacity cranes are fitted. The ship has a clear deck aft for a helicopter, but no hangar is provided.

Name: The ship originally was named MANITOWOC.

---

11. The Soviet nuclear-propelled icebreaker ARKTIKA was the first surface ship in history to reach the geographic North Pole, doing so on 17 August 1977. The ARKTIKA spent 15 hours at the North Pole. Her sister ship SIBIR' reached the North Pole in May 1987 and their sister ship YAMAL in August 1994.

The MACKINAW, part of the "Great Lakes fleet." She is the only white-hulled icebreaker. The MACKINAW was designed specifically for Great Lakes operation; hence no armament was planned because of U.S.-Canadian agreements. (1992, U.S. Coast Guard)

The MACKINAW and a Bay-class icebreaking tug in the Great Lakes. Five of the Bay-class WTGBs operate on the Great Lakes. (U.S. Coast Guard)

TRAINING CUTTERS

1 TRAINING BARK: "EAGLE"

Number	Name	Launched	Completed	USCG Comm.	Status
WIX 327	EAGLE	13 June 1936	17 Sep 1936	15 May 1946	**TRA-AA**

Builders:	Blohm and Voss, Hamburg (Germany)
Displacement:	1,784 tons full load
Length:	231 feet (70.43 m) waterline
	295 feet (89.9 m) over bowsprit
Beam:	39½ feet (11.9 m)
Draft:	17 feet (5.2 m)
Masts:	fore and main 150½ feet (45.7 m)
	mizzen 132 feet (40.2 m)
Propulsion:	auxiliary diesel engines (M.A.N.); 700 bhp; 1 shaft
Speed:	up to 18 knots under sail
	10.5 knots on auxiliary diesel engines
Allowance:	50 (12 officers + 38 enlisted) + 175 cadets
Guns:	none

The EAGLE is employed to train Coast Guard cadets on summer practice cruises. She is based at the Coast Guard Academy in New London, Conn.

She is the former German naval training bark HORST WESSEL. Taken by the United States as a reparation after World War II, she was acquired in January 1946 at Bremerhaven and assigned to the Coast Guard.

Class: The similar ALBERT LEO SCHLAGETER (launched in 1937) was also taken over by the United States in 1945 but was sold to Brazil in 1948 and resold to Portugal in 1962 (she is now in service as the SAGRES). A third ship of this basic design, the GORCH FOCK (1933), was taken over by the Soviet Union in 1946 and renamed the TOVARISCH; she remains in Russian service.[12] The similar MIRECA was built for Romania and also remains in service.

A later ship of the same general design, also named the GORCH FOCK, was built at the same German yard for the West German Navy (launched in 1958).

---

12. The TOVARISCH is employed as a sail training ship for the Russian merchant marine; see N. Polmar, *Guide to the Soviet Navy*, 5th ed. (Annapolis, Md.: Naval Institute Press, 1991), pp. 332–333.

Classification: A three-masted bark is a square-rigged vessel on her fore and main masts, and fore-and-aft rigged on the mizzenmast. The Coast Guard currently uses the term *barque* for the EAGLE, which is the French spelling of the term. The English (and German) spelling is *bark.*

Design: The EAGLE is steel-hulled. She carries up to 21,350 square feet (1,921.5 m^2) of sail.

The training bark EAGLE at anchor in the Potomac River at Washington, D.C. The EAGLE is based at the Coast Guard Academy in New London, Conn. (1999, U.S. Coast Guard, PA1 Pete Milnes)

The training bark EAGLE with all sails set. Here foremast and mainmast are square rigged; the mizzenmast has a fore-and-aft rig. The EAGLE did not receive her red-white-and-blue "slash" until mid-1976, almost a decade after other cutters were given those markings. (U.S. Coast Guard)

BUOY TENDERS

These ships maintain aids to navigation in U.S. coastal waters, as well as on inland waterways.

All tenders are "black-hull" ships. No tenders are armed.

5 + 11 SEAGOING BUOY TENDERS: "JUNIPER" CLASS (225-FT)

Number	Name	Launched	Delivered	Status
WLB 201	JUNIPER	24 June 1995	12 Jan 1996	**AA**
WLB 202	WILLOW	15 June 1996	27 Nov 1997	**AA**
WLB 203	KUKUI	3 May 1997	9 Oct 1997	**PA**
WLB 204	ELM	24 Jan 1998	22 June 1998	**AA**
WLB 205	WALNUT	22 Aug 1998	22 Feb 1999	**PA**
WLB 206	SPAR	12 Aug 2000	2001	building
WLB 207	MAPLE	16 Dec 2000	2001	building
WLB 208	ASPEN		2001	building
WLB 209	SYCAMORE		2001	building
WLB 210	CYPRESS		2002	building
WLB 211	OAK		2002	building
WLB 212	HICKORY		2002	building
WLB 213	FIR		2003	building
WLB 214	SEQUOIA		2003	building
WLB 215	HOLLYHOCK		2003	building
WLB 216	ALDER		2004	building

Builders:	Marinette Marine, Wisc.
Displacement:	2,000 tons full load
Length:	206 feet (62.79 m) waterline
	225 feet (68.58 m) overall
Beam:	46 feet (14.0 m)
Draft:	13 feet (4.0 m)
Propulsion:	2 diesel engines (Caterpillar 3608); 6,200 bhp; 1 shaft
Speed:	15 knots
Range:	6,000 n.miles (11,110 km) at 15 knots
Manning:	40 (6 officers + 34 enlisted)
Guns:	see notes
Radars:	1 SPS-64(V)1 navigation

Although highly automated, buoy tenders still require considerable muscle. Here the deck crew of the WALNUT paints an 18,000-pound (8,165-kg) buoy. It took the crew eight hours to recover the buoy, paint it, replace the batteries and solar panels, and reset the buoy one mile off Honolulu Harbor. (1999, U.S. Coast Guard, PA2 Sarah Foster-Snell)

The seagoing buoy tender WALNUT arriving at her home port of Sand Island, Hawaii. The JUNIPER-class WLBs are the largest black-hull cutters in Coast Guard service. (1999, U.S. Coast Guard, PA3 Sarah Foster-Snell)

These are the first seagoing buoy tenders built for the U.S. Coast Guard since the BALSAM class of World War II, which they are intended to replace. In 1991 the Coast Guard awarded contracts for the design of the new craft to several shipyards. In August 1992 the Marinette Marine yard was chosen to construct the lead tender.

The delivery dates are when placed in commission–special; the tenders are placed in full commission upon arrival at their home port.

Sixteen tenders currently are planned; previous estimates were for 28 units. The increased capabilities will enable them to replace a larger number of BALSAM-class tenders.

Design: These ships are highly automated, being significantly larger than the previous BALSAM class, but with a significantly smaller crew. The tenders have a 30,000-pound (13,605-kg) lift capacity, a large deck area for handling buoys, and the ability to work buoys in eight-foot (2.4-m) seas. They are fitted with a dynamic positioning system.

Engineering: A 440-shp bow thruster and 550-shp stern thruster are fitted. At-sea endurance is 45 days.

Guns: Space and weight are reserved for installation of a 25-mm Bushmaster cannon.

Names: The WLB 206 originally was to be named DOGWOOD; the name was changed while the tender was under construction to SPAR to honor the Coast Guard's women volunteers in World War II—called SPARs, a term derived from the Coast Guard motto *Semper Paratus* ("Always Ready").

Operational: Many buoy tenders listed as Atlantic or Pacific are based on rivers and inland waterways.

The seagoing buoy tender WILLOW, showing the large crane forward for handling buoys and other aids to navigation. The smaller crane aft is for handling the cutter's boats and other gear. (U.S. Coast Guard)

The seagoing buoy tender JUNIPER as completed, showing the motif of Coast Guard insignia on the black hull. The JUNIPER and her sister cutters are replacing buoy tenders almost 60 years old. (1996, Leo Van Ginderen)

1 CARIBBEAN SUPPORT TENDER } "BALSAM" CLASS (180-FT)
14 SEAGOING BUOY TENDERS

Number	Name	Builder	Launched	Commissioned	SLEP Modernization	Status
A series (6)						
WLB 277	Cowslip	MI	11 Apr 1942	17 Oct 1942	Jan 1983–July 1984	**AA**
WIX 290	Gentian	ZD	23 May 1942	3 Nov 1942	Nov 1979–Aug 1983	**AA**
WLB 301	Conifer	MI	3 Nov 1942	1 July 1943	Aug 1983–Jan 1986	**PA**
WLB 302	Madrona	ZD	11 Nov 1942	30 May 1943	Apr 1984–Sep 1989	**AA**
WLB 306	Buttonwood	MI	30 Nov 1942	24 Sep 1943	Mar 1991–Jan 1993	**AA**
WLB 309	Sweetgum	MI	15 Apr 1943	20 Nov 1943	Feb 1990–Dec 1991	**AA**
C series (9)						
WLB 392	Bramble	ZD	23 Oct 1943	22 Apr 1944	—	**AA**
WLB 393	Firebush	ZD	3 Feb 1944	20 July 1944	—	**PA**
WLB 397	Mariposa	ZD	14 Jan 1944	1 July 1944	—	**GL**
WLB 401	Sassafras	MI	5 Oct 1943	23 May 1944	—	**PA**
WLB 402	Sedge	MI	27 Nov 1943	5 July 1944	—	**PA**
WLB 404	Sundew	MI	8 Feb 1944	24 Aug 1944	—	**GL**
WLB 405	Sweetbrier	MI	30 Dec 1943	26 July 1944	—	**PA**
WLB 406	Acacia	ZD	7 Apr 1944	1 Sep 1944	—	**GL**
WLB 407	Woodrush	ZD	28 Apr 1944	22 Sep 1944	—	**PA**

Builders:	CG = Coast Guard Yard, Curtis Bay, Md.	
	MI = Marine Iron and Shipbuilding Co., Duluth, Minn.	
	ZD = Zenith Dredge, Duluth, Minn.	
Displacement:	935 tons standard	
	1,025 tons full load	
Length:	180 feet (54.9 m) overall	
Beam:	37 feet (11.3 m)	

Draft:	13 feet (4.0 m)
Propulsion:	diesel-electric (2 General Motors 8-645E6A diesel engines); 1,200 shp; 1 shaft
Speed:	13 knots
Range:	4,500 n.miles (8,335 km) at 13 knots
	13,500 n.miles (25,000 km) at 7.5 knots
Manning:	49 (7 officers + 42 enlisted)
Guns:	removed

These tenders service navigation buoys and other aids to navigation in coastal waters. They are highly versatile ships, having served as convoy escorts, in the SAR role, assisting in constructing and servicing Loran navigation stations, and as salvage ships; some have a light icebreaking capability.

The Gentian was recommissioned on 27 September 1999 as a Caribbean Support Tender (CST) to provide training and maintenance assistance to Caribbean nations engaged in anti-drug operations. In the CST role, her crew numbers 45 officers and enlisted personnel, including representatives from seven Caribbean-area nations in addition to her core U.S. Coast Guard crew.[13] She was reclassified WIX 290 vice WLB 290.

13. See Eric Miller, "Coast Guard Is a Partner in Caribbean Security," U.S. Naval Institute *Proceedings* (December 1999), pp. 58–61.

Class: Thirty-nine ships of this design were completed in 1942–1944.

The Cowslip (WLB 277) was stricken on 23 March 1973 (and sold); she was repurchased by the Coast Guard in January 1981 and recommissioned in November 1981. She replaced the Blackthorn (WLB 391), which was rammed and sunk on 28 January 1980.

The Mesquite (WLB 305) ran aground in Lake Superior on 4 December 1989 and was a total loss, but none of her crew was lost.

Disposals since 1990 are listed below; the Bittersweet was transferred to Estonia.

An HH-60J Jayhawk lowers a container of hazardous waste from the Coast Guard LORAN station at Sitkinak Island, Alaska, onto the seagoing buoy tender Firebush. Gasoline, paint, batteries, and other material left at abandoned military stations must be properly disposed of by the services. (1998, U.S. Coast Guard, PAC Tod Lyons)

number	name	decommissioned
WLB 201	LAUREL	31 Dec 1999
WLB/WMEC 292	CLOVER	June 1990
WLB/WAGO/WMEC 295	EVERGREEN	13 June 1990
WLB 296	SORREL	28 June 1996
WLB 297	IRONWOOD	6 Oct 2000
WLB/WMEC 300	CITRUS	1 Sep 1994
WLB 307	PLANETREE	19 Mar 1999
WLB 308	PAPAW	23 July 1999
WLB 388	BASSWOOD	4 Sep 1998
WLB 389	BITTERSWEET	18 Aug 1997
WLB 390	BLACKHAW	26 Feb 1993
WLB 394	HORNBEAM	30 Sep 1999
WLB 395	IRIS	8 Aug 1997
WLB 396	MALLOW	15 May 1997
WLB 400	SALVIA	12 Apr 1991
WLB 403	SPAR	28 Feb 1997

Classification: Several ships were temporarily reclassified as medium endurance cutters (WMEC) and engaged in patrol work during the 1970s and 1980s. The EVERGREEN was refitted as an oceanographic cutter in 1973 and reclassified WAGO; she was changed to WMEC on 1 May 1982 and served in that role until decommissioned in 1990. The CITRUS served as a WMEC from June 1979 until decommissioned in 1994. (As WMECs and WAGO, they had white hulls.)

Design: The WLB 392, 402, and 404 have strengthened hulls for icebreaking. All of this class are fitted with 20-ton-capacity booms. In SLEP ships, a hydraulically powered system replaces the electrically powered boom. These ships are highly effective for breaking through light ice.

Engineering: The COWSLIP is fitted with a controllable-pitch, bow-thrust propeller.

Guns: As completed, these tenders had one 3-inch/50-cal AA gun and four 20-mm AA guns (two in A-series ships); the 3-inch gun was fitted in a raised "tub" aft of the funnel. They additionally carried depth charges, with some ships having ahead-throwing Mousetrap ASW projectors.

All surviving ships have been disarmed.

Modernization: Beginning in the mid-1980s, eight ships underwent a Service Life Extension Program (SLEP); see dates above for the ships that are still in service. The others were the LAUREL and PAPAW.

Another 12 ships received a less extensive Major Renovation (MAJREN) upgrade. The SLEP ships and SASSAFRAS were fitted with new main engines; all received updated electronics and other systems, plus improved habitability features.

Names: The ACACIA originally was named THISTLE; her name was changed in 1944 because the original name was also carried at the time by an Army hospital ship.

The GENTIAN as recommissioned in 1999 as a Caribbean Support Tender (CST) to work with Caribbean naval and coast guard forces. Like other BALSAM-class tenders converted to oceanographic research ships, she is now a white-hull cutter. She remains in commission as a WLB. (U.S. Coast Guard)

14 COASTAL BUOY TENDERS: "IDA LEWIS" CLASS (175-FT)

Number	Name	Launched	Delivered	Status
WLM 551	IDA LEWIS	14 Oct 1995	1 Nov 1996	AA
WLM 552	KATHERINE WALKER	14 Sep 1996	27 June 1997	AA
WLM 553	ABBIE BURGESS	5 Apr 1997	19 Sep 1997	AA
WLM 554	MARCUS HANNA	22 Aug 1997	26 Nov 1997	AA
WLM 555	JAMES RANKIN	25 Apr 1998	26 Aug 1998	AA
WLM 556	JOSHUA APPLEBY	8 Aug 1998	20 Nov 1999	AA
WLM 557	FRANK DREW	5 Dec 1998	17 June 1999	AA
WLM 558	ANTHONY PETIT	30 Jan 1999	1 July 1999	PA
WLM 559	BARBARA MABRITY	27 Mar 1998	29 July 1999	AA
WLM 560	WILLIAM TATE	8 May 1999	16 Sep 1999	AA
WLM 561	HARRY CLAIBORNE	26 June 1999	20 Oct 1999	AA
WLM 562	MARIA BRAY	28 Aug 1999	6 Apr 2000	AA
WLM 563	HENRY BLAKE	30 Oct 1999	18 May 2000	PA
WLM 564	GEORGE COBB	15 Dec 1999	22 June 2000	PA

Builders:	Marinette Marine, Wisc.
Displacement:	845 tons full load
Length:	155 feet (47.24 m) waterline
	175 feet (53.34 m) overall
Beam:	36 feet (10.98 m)
Draft:	7¹¹/₁₂ feet (2.41 m)
Propulsion:	2 diesel engines (Caterpillar 3508 TA); 1,710 bhp; 2 Z-drive propulsion units (see notes)
Speed:	12 knots
Range:	2,000 n.miles (3,700 km) at 10 knots
Manning:	18 (1 officer + 17 enlisted)

These are advanced-capability coastal buoy tenders, built to replace the BALSAM-class WLBs.

The delivery dates are when placed in commission–special at the building yard; the tenders are placed in full commission upon arrival at their home ports. The IDA LEWIS was placed in full commission on 12 April 1997.

Originally 28 tenders of this class were planned.

Design: The ships are fitted with 10-ton-capacity cranes. They can break ice of about 1 inch (25 mm) thickness at three knots. Six spare bunks are provided in each ship.

Engineering: Maximum brake horsepower is 1,998; sustained bhp is shown above. Fitted with a 400-hp bow thruster.

Names: All units are named for lighthouse "keepers," leading to the class also being known as the Keeper class.

The lead tender was named for Idawalley Zorada Lewis, a lighthouse keeper who, in 1858 at age 16, single-handedly saved four young boys. The WLM 553 originally was named ABIGAIL BURGESS.

The KATHERINE WALKER in her natural element—the ice-covered Hudson River. Most buoy tenders are especially configured for light icebreaking, an important chore on many U.S. inland and coastal waterways. (2000, U.S. Coast Guard, PA3 Robert Lanier)

The coastal buoy tender HARRY CLAIBORNE while making a port call in New Orleans. The tender is based at Galveston, Texas, where she performs a variety of functions in the inland waterways. (2000, U.S. Coast Guard, PA2 Mark Mackowiak)

COASTAL BUOY TENDERS: RED CLASS (157-FT)

All five of these buoy and navigation aid tenders have been stricken. They were completed between 1964 and 1971.

number	name	stricken
WLM 685	RED WOOD	1 June 1999
WLM 686	RED BEECH	18 June 1997
WLM 687	RED BIRCH	9 June 1998
WLM 688	RED CEDAR	30 Mar 1999
WLM 689	RED OAK	28 Mar 1996

See 16th edition/page 522 for characteristics.

1 COASTAL BUOY TENDER: WHITE CLASS (133-FT)

Number	Name	Launched	Commissioned	Status
WLM 540 (ex-YF 416)	WHITE SUMAC	14 June 1943	6 Nov 1943	**AA**

Builders:	Niagara Shipbuilding, Buffalo, N.Y.
Displacement:	435 tons standard
	600 tons full load
Length:	133 feet (40.5 m) overall
Beam:	31 feet (9.4 m)
Draft:	9 feet (2.7 m)
Propulsion:	2 diesel engines (Union); 600 bhp; 2 shafts
Speed:	9.8 knots
Range:	2,100 n.miles (3,890 km) at 9.8 knots
	4,500 n.miles (8,340 km) at 5 knots
Manning:	24 (1 officer + 23 enlisted)

Only one buoy and navigation aid tender of this class remains. These tenders were converted from Navy self-propelled lighters (YF). They were transferred to the Coast Guard in August–September 1947.

The WHITE SUMAC will be decommissioned in the near future.

Class: The class originally comprised seven tenders. The stricken units are:

number	name	stricken
WLM 542	WHITE BUSH	16 Sep 1985
WLM 543	WHITE HOLLY	8 July 1998
WLM 544	WHITE SAGE	28 June 1996
WLM 545	WHITE HEATH	31 Mar 1998
WLM 546	WHITE LUPINE	28 Feb 1998
WLM 547	WHITE PINE	30 June 1999

The coastal buoy tender WHITE SUMAC is the last of her class in Coast Guard service. Like her larger sister ships, she has working space and a boom forward; a RIB and life raft canisters are aft. (1992, Giorgio Arra)

COASTAL BUOY TENDERS: "HOLLYHOCK" CLASS (175-FT)

The last of three tenders of this class, the FIR (WLM 212), was decommissioned on 1 October 1991. Her sister ships HOLLYHOCK (WLM 220) and WALNUT (WLM 252) were decommissioned on 31 March 1982 and 15 June 1982, respectively.

See 14th Edition/page 551 for characteristics.

4 INLAND CONSTRUCTION TENDERS: "PAMLICO" CLASS (160-FT)

Number	Name	Number	Name
WLIC 800	PAMLICO	WLIC 802	KENNEBEC
WLIC 801	HUDSON	WLIC 803	SAGINAW

Builders:	Coast Guard Yard, Curtis Bay, Md.
Displacement:	413 tons light
	459 tons full load
Length:	160 feet (48.8 m) overall
Beam:	30 feet (9.1 m)
Draft:	4 feet (1.2 m)
Propulsion:	2 diesel engines (Cummins); 1,000 bhp; 2 shafts
Speed:	10 knots
Manning:	14 (1 officer + 13 enlisted)

These large inland tenders were completed in 1976–1977.

The inland construction tender HUDSON under way on an inland waterway. She has a large crane forward, a pilothouse with all-around vision, and short, twin funnels. (1992, Giorgio Arra)

1 INLAND BUOY TENDER: "BUCKTHORN" (100-FT)

Number	Name	Launched	Commissioned
WLI 642	BUCKTHORN		17 July 1964

Builders:	Mobile Ship Repair, Mobile, Ala.
Displacement:	188 tons light
	196 tons full load
Length:	100 feet (30.5 m) overall
Beam:	24 feet (7.3 m)
Draft:	4 feet (1.2 m)
Propulsion:	2 diesel engines; 600 bhp; 2 shafts
Speed:	11.9 knots
Manning:	15 (1 officer + 14 enlisted)

The BUCKTHORN, a single-ship design, operates on the Great Lakes. She is fitted with a five-ton-capacity boom.

The one-of-a-kind inland buoy tender BUCKTHORN. The river and inland buoy tenders are rarely photographed as they conduct their arduous labors on inland waterways. (1989, Leo Van Ginderen)

1 INLAND BUOY TENDER
3 INLAND CONSTRUCTION TENDERS } **"COSMOS" CLASS (100-FT)**

Number	Name	Launched	Commissioned
WLIC 298	RAMBLER	6 May 1943	26 May 1943
WLI 313	BLUEBELL	28 Sep 1944	24 Mar 1945
WLIC 315	SMILAX	18 Aug 1944	1 Nov 1944
WLIC 316	PRIMROSE	18 Aug 1944	23 Oct 1944

Builders:	Dubuque Boat & Builder, Iowa, except BLUEBELL by Birchfield Boiler, Tacoma, Wash.
Displacement:	178 tons full load
Length:	100 feet (30.5 m) overall
Beam:	24 feet (7.3 m)
Draft:	5 feet (1.5 m)
Propulsion:	2 diesel engines; 600 bhp; 2 shafts
Speed:	10.5 knots
Range:	1,400 n.miles (2,600 km) at 10.5 knots
	2,700 n.miles (5,000 km) at 7 knots
Manning:	14 (1 officer + 13 enlisted)

All were formerly designated WLI; three of these tenders were changed to inland construction tenders (WLIC) on 1 October 1979.

Class: This was originally a class of eight tenders.

Design: All are fitted with a five-ton-capacity crane. The PRIMROSE is fitted with a pile driver on her bow.

Names: Inland tenders were named in 1963.

The inland buoy tender BLUEBELL (1993, George R. Schneider)

9 INLAND CONSTRUCTION TENDERS: "ANVIL" CLASS (75-FT)

Number	Name	Number	Name
A series		*C series*	
WLIC 75301	ANVIL	WLIC 75306	CLAMP
WLIC 75302	HAMMER	WLIC 75307	WEDGE
B series		WLIC 75309	HATCHET
WLIC 75303	SLEDGE	WLIC 75310	AXE
WLIC 75304	MALLET		
WLIC 75305	VISE		

Builders:	WLIC 75301, 75302	Gibbs Shipyard, Jacksonville, Fla.
	WLIC 75303–75705	McDermott, Morgan City, Mich.
	WLIC 75306, 75307	Sturgeon Bay Shipbuilding, Wisc.
	WLIC 75309, 75310	Dorchester Shipbuilding, Dorchester, N.J.
Displacement:	129 tons light	
	145 tons full load	
Length:	75 feet (22.9 m) overall, except C series: 76 feet (23.2 m) overall	
Beam:	22 feet (6.7 m)	
Draft:	4 feet (1.2 m)	
Propulsion:	2 diesel engines; 600 bhp; 2 shafts	
Speed:	A series 8.6 knots	
	B series 9.1 knots	
	C series 9.4 knots	
Range:	A series 1,300 n.miles (2,400 km) at 8.6 knots	
	2,400 n.miles (4,450 km) at 5 knots	
	B series 1,000 n.miles (1,850 km) at 9 knots	
	2,200 n.miles (4,075 km) at 5 knots	
	C series 1,050 n.miles (1,950 km) at 9 knots	
	2,500 n.miles (4,630 km) at 5 knots	
Manning:	13 (enlisted)	

These tenders were completed in 1962–1966.

The inland construction tender HATCHET pushing a work barge (U.S. Coast Guard)

2 INLAND BUOY TENDERS: IMPROVED BERRY CLASS (65-FT)

Number	Name	Launched	Commissioned
WLI 65400	BAYBERRY	2 June 1954	28 June 1954
WLI 65401	ELDERBERRY	2 June 1954	28 June 1954

Builders:	Reliable Welding Works, Olympia, Wash.
Displacement:	68 tons light
	71 tons full load
Length:	65 feet (19.8 m) overall
Beam:	17 feet (5.2 m)
Draft:	4 feet (1.2 m)
Propulsion:	2 diesel engines (General Motors 6-71); 400 bhp; 2 shafts
Speed:	11.3 knots
Range:	800 n.miles (1,480 km) at 11.3 knots
	1,700 n.miles (3,150 km) at 6 knots
Manning:	8 (enlisted)

These tenders are similar to the basic Berry-class design but with a more powerful propulsion plant. Originally designed for freshwater operation, they have been modified for saltwater operation.

The inland buoy tender BAYBERRY. These craft have blunt bows fitted with fenders for pushing barges. (1999, U.S. Coast Guard, PA2 Tiffany Powell)

The inland buoy tender ELDERBERRY (U.S. Coast Guard)

INLAND BUOY TENDERS: BERRY CLASS (65-FT)

Number	Name	Launched	Commissioned
WLI 65303	BLACKBERRY		24 Aug 1946
WLI 65304	CHOKEBERRY	23 May 1946	30 Aug 1946

Builders:	Dubuque Boat & Boiler, Dubuque, Iowa
Displacement:	50 tons light
	68 tons full load
Length:	65 feet (19.8 m) overall
Beam:	17 feet (5.2 m)
Draft:	4 feet (1.2 m)
Propulsion:	1 diesel (General Motors); 220 bhp; 1 shaft
Speed:	9 knots
Range:	1,500 n.miles (2,780 km) at 5 knots
Manning:	8 (enlisted)

There originally were three tenders of this class. The third tender, the LOGANBERRY (WLI 65305), was decommissioned in 1977.

The inland buoy tender CHOKEBERRY (U.S. Coast Guard)

RIVER BUOY TENDER: "SUMAC" (115-FT)

The one-of-a-kind tender SUMAC (WLR 311), completed in 1944, was decommissioned in 1999. See 16th Edition/page 524 for characteristics.

RIVER BUOY TENDER: "LANTANA" (80-FT)

The LANTANA (WLR 80310), the single tender of this design, completed in 1943, was decommissioned on 27 October 1991. See 14th Edition/page 555 for characteristics.

2 RIVER BUOY TENDERS: "KANKAKEE" CLASS (75-FT)

Number	Name	Launched	Commissioned
WLR 75500	KANKAKEE	8 July 1989	Jan 1990
WLR 75501	GREENBRIER	1989	12 Apr 1990

Builders:	Avondale Industries, New Orleans, La.
Displacement:	172 tons full load
Length:	75 feet (22.9 m) overall
Beam:	24 feet (7.3 m)
Draft:	5 feet (1.5 m)
Propulsion:	2 diesel engines (Caterpillar 3412-DIT); 1,080 bhp; 2 shafts
Speed:	12 knots
Range:	600 n.miles (1,110 km) at 11 knots
Manning:	19 (enlisted)

These are improved GASCONADE-class river tenders; they push 130-foot (96.6-m) work barges. Three additional units were planned but not constructed.

The river buoy tender GREENBRIER, somewhat resembling a houseboat. There are twin engine exhausts on the upper deck, abaft the bridge. The mast is offset to port. (1990, Avondale Shipyards)

9 RIVER BUOY TENDERS: "GASCONADE" CLASS (75-FT)

Number	Name	Number	Name
WLR 75401	GASCONADE	WLR 75406	KICKAPOO
WLR 75402	MUSKINGUM	WLR 75407	KANAWHA
WLR 75403	WYACONDA	WLR 75408	PATOKA
WLR 75404	CHIPPEWA	WLR 75409	CHENA
WLR 75405	CHEYENNE		

Builders:	WLR 75401	St. Louis Shipbuilding & Dry Dock, Mo.
	WLR 75402–75405	Maxon Construction, Tell City, Ind.
	WLR 75406–75409	Halter Marine, New Orleans, La.
Displacement:	127 tons light	
	141 tons full load	
Length:	75 feet (22.9 m) overall	
Beam:	22 feet (6.7 m)	
Draft:	4 feet (1.2 m)	
Propulsion:	2 diesel engines (Caterpillar); 600 bhp; 2 shafts	
Speed:	7.6 or 8.7 knots	
Manning:	19 (enlisted)	

These tenders were completed from 1964 to 1970. They work in tandem with a 90-foot (27.4-m) barge.

The river buoy tender CHEYENNE with a buoy barge (U.S. Coast Guard)

6 RIVER BUOY TENDERS: "OUACHITA" CLASS (65-FT)

Number	Name	Number	Name
WLR 65501	OUACHITA	WLR 65504	SCIOTO
WLR 65502	CIMARRON	WLR 65505	OSAGE
WLR 65503	OBION	WLR 65506	SANGAMON

Builders:	Gibbs Shipyard, Jacksonville, Fla., except WLR 66501, 66502 by Platzer Shipyard, Houston, Texas
Displacement:	143 tons
Length:	65½ feet (20.0 m) overall
Beam:	21 feet (6.4 m)
Draft:	5 feet (1.5 m)
Propulsion:	2 diesel engines; 600 bhp; 2 shafts
Speed:	10.5 knots
Range:	3,500 n.miles (6,485 km) at 6 knots
Manning:	12 (enlisted)

These tenders were completed in 1960–1962. They were designed specifically to operate with work barges on western rivers.

The river buoy tender OSAGE (U.S. Coast Guard)

TUGS

9 ICEBREAKING TUGS: BAY CLASS (140-FT)

Number	Name	Launched	Commissioned	Status
WTGB 101	KATMAI BAY	8 Apr 1978	8 Jan 1979	**GL**
WTGB 102	BRISTOL BAY	22 July 1978	5 Apr 1979	**GL**
WTGB 103	MOBILE BAY	11 Nov 1978	6 May 1979	**GL**
WTGB 104	BISCAYNE BAY	3 Feb 1979	8 Dec 1979	**GL**
WTGB 105	NEAH BAY	2 Feb 1980	18 Aug 1980	**GL**
WTGB 106	MORRO BAY	11 July 1980	25 Jan 1980	**AA**
WTGB 107	PENOBSCOT BAY	27 July 1984	2 Jan 1985	**AA**
WTGB 108	THUNDER BAY	15 Aug 1985	4 Nov 1985	**AA**
WTGB 109	STURGEON BAY	12 Sep 1987	20 Aug 1988	**AA**

Builders:	Tacoma Boatbuilding, Wash., except WTGB 107, 109 by Bay City Marine, Tacoma, Wash.
Displacement:	662 tons full load
Length:	140 feet (42.7 m) overall
Beam:	37 feet (11.3 m)
Draft:	12 feet (3.7 m)
Propulsion:	diesel-electric (2 Fairbanks Morse 38D8⅛ diesel engines); electric drive (Westinghouse); 2,500 shp; 1 shaft
Speed:	14.7 knots
Range:	1,800 n.miles (3,333 km) at 14.7 knots
	4,000 n.miles (7,410 km) at 12 knots
Manning:	17 (3 officers + 14 enlisted)
Radar:	SPS-64(V)1 navigation

These are the largest tugs to be constructed specifically for Coast Guard service. They are designed to provide general towing and support services and can break through ice up to 20 inches (0.5 m) thick.

The MORRO BAY is employed as an enlisted training ship at Yorktown, Va.; she is painted white.

A planned tenth unit was not built.

Classification: These tugs originally were designated WYTM. The KATMAI BAY was changed to WTGB on 5 February 1979; the others were changed to WTGB upon completion.

Design: Fitted with a hull air-lubrication system to enhance ice-breaking capability.

The small harbor tug HAWSER breaking ice on the Hudson River. These tugs are distinguished by their short, fat stacks. (2000, U.S. Coast Guard, PA3 Robert Lanier)

The KATMAI BAY breaking ice on the Great Lakes (1992, U.S. Coast Guard)

11 SMALL HARBOR TUGS: 65-FT TYPE

Number	Name	Commissioned	Status
WYTL 65601	CAPSTAN	19 July 1961	AA
WYTL 65602	CHOCK	12 Sep 1962	AA
WYTL 65604	TACKLE	1962	AA
WYTL 65607	BRIDLE	3 Apr 1963	AA
WYTL 65608	PENDANT	Aug 1963	AA
WYTL 65609	SHACKLE	7 May 1963	AA
WYTL 65610	HAWSER	17 Jan 1963	AA
WYTL 65611	LINE	21 Feb 1963	AA
WYTL 65612	WIRE	19 Mar 1963	AA
WYTL 65614	BOLLARD	10 Apr 1967	AA
WYTL 65615	CLEAT	10 May 1967	AA

Builders:	WYTL 65601–65604	Gibbs Shipyard, Jacksonville, Fla.
	WYTL 65607–65612	Barbour Boat Works, New Bern, N.C.
	WYTL 65614, 65615	Western Boatbuilding, Tacoma, Wash.
Displacement:	62 tons light	
	72 tons full load	
Length:	65 feet (19.8 m) overall	
Beam:	19 feet (5.8 m)	
Draft:	7 feet (2.1 m)	
Propulsion:	1 diesel engine; 400 bhp; 1 shaft	
Speed:	10.5 knots, except WYTL 65607–65609: 9.8 knots	
Range:	3,600 n.miles (6,670 km) at 6 knots, except WYTL 65607–65609: 2,700 n.miles (5,000 km) at 5.8 knots	
Manning:	6 (enlisted)	

These are steel-hull tugs.

Class: From the original class of 15 tugs, the BITT (WYTL 65613) was decommissioned on 4 October 1982 and the SWIVEL (WYTL 65603), TOWLINE (WYTL 65605), and CATENARY (WYTL 65606) were stricken on 1 May 1995.

Another WYTL, the LINE, breaking ice around the coastal buoy tender KATHERINE WALKER during operations in the Hudson River. (2000, U.S. Coast Guard, PA3 Robert Lanier)

1 SMALL HARBOR TUG: EX-ARMY TUG

Number	Name	Army in service	Status
WYTM 85009	MESSENGER (ex-ST 710)	5 Sep 1945	AA

Builders:	Equitable Equipment, New Orleans, La.
Displacement:	
Length:	85 feet (26.2 m) overall
Beam:	23 feet (7.0 m)
Draft:	10 feet (3.05 m)
Propulsion:	1 diesel engine; 650 bhp; 1 shaft
Speed:	9 knots
Manning:	

This former Army tug is assigned to the Coast Guard Yard, Curtis Bay, Md.

SMALL CRAFT

The Coast Guard operates several hundred small craft in the patrol, SAR, oil cleanup, and navigation support roles.

The 38-foot deployable pursuit boats and 25-foot transportable port security boats are the only small craft that normally are armed and are listed first in this section. The armed 22-foot Raider craft (modified Boston Whalers) and the five 45-foot fast coastal interceptors have been discarded (see 17th Edition/page 528 for characteristics). The Coast Guard also operates a large number of Rigid-hull Inflatable Boats (RIBs).

The patrol and SAR craft have white hulls; the aids-to-navigation craft have black hulls.

8 DEPLOYABLE PURSUIT BOATS (38-FT)

Builders:	Fountain Powerboats, Washington, N.C.
Displacement:	approx. 3½ tons
Length:	38 feet (11.59 m) overall
Beam:	9 feet (2.74 m)
Draft:	
Propulsion:	2 diesel engines (Yanmar); 840 bhp; 2 propellers
Speed:	48+ knots
Range:	250+ n.miles
Manning:	4 to 6 (enlisted)
Guns:	small arms
Radars:	Raytheon RL 70RC navigation

These craft are being acquired to counter high-speed drug-smuggling craft. Two of these craft are carried by each of the patrol ships VINDICATOR (T-AGOS 3) and PERSISTENT (T-AGOS 6).

Another 12 boats are being delivered in fiscal year 2001 for a total of 20.

Design: The craft are based on the Fabio Buzzi RIB design.

A Transportable Port Security Boat (2000, U.S. Coast Guard, PA2 Stephen Baker)

Called "go-fasts," the Coast Guard's Deployable Pursuit Boats (DPB) are deployed from large cutters to counter high-speed craft engaged in drug smuggling. This photo shows DPBs during exercises in the Elizabeth River, Va. (1999, U.S. Coast Guard, PA3 Dionne Short)

A Transportable Port Security Boat (TPSB) is put through its paces during a demonstration at the Coast Guard's Reserve Training Center in Yorktown, Va. The small, high-speed craft are used for inshore patrols in areas of high probability of drug-smuggling efforts. (1999, U.S. Coast Guard, PA1 Telfair H. Brown)

Deployable pursuit boats (1999, U.S. Coast Guard, PA3 Dionne Short)

44 TRANSPORTABLE PORT SECURITY BOATS: GUARDIAN 25-FT TYPE

Displacement:	
Length:	24⁷/₁₂ feet (7.49 m) overall
Beam:	8 feet (2.44 m)
Draft:	3¼ feet (1.0 m)
Propulsion:	2 outboard engines
Speed:	40+ knots
Manning:	3 or 4 (enlisted)
Guns:	1 .50-cal machine gun M2
	2 7.62-mm machine guns M60 (2 single)
Radar:	navigation

These craft are designated TPSB.

25 AIDS-TO-NAVIGATION BOATS: 55-FT TYPE

Builders:	Robert E. Derecktor, Mamaroneck, N.Y.
Displacement:	28.8 tons light
	31.25 tons full load
Length:	55 feet (16.77 m) overall
Beam:	17 feet (5.2 m)
Draft:	5 feet (1.5 m)
Propulsion:	2 diesel engines (General Motors 12V71 T1); 1,080 bhp; 2 shafts
Speed:	22 knots
Range:	350 n.miles (650 km) at 18 knots
Manning:	4 (enlisted)
Radars:	1 Raytheon 1900 navigation

These are aluminum-hull craft that support navigation aids on inland waterways. They are numbered 55101–55125. They were placed in service in 1976–1977. Their cargo capacity is 4,000 pounds (1,814 kg) and they have a 1,000-pound (453-kg) crane fitted aft.

The aids-to-navigation boat 55106 passes the frigate STARK (FFG 31) as the "black hull" goes about putting down channel markers, which cram her deck. There is a hydraulic crane amidships. (1994, Giorgio Arra)

One of the few small Coast Guard craft to be named, this is the motor lifeboat INTREPID. (U.S. Coast Guard)

The aids-to-navigation boat 55103 is painted white, a rarity among buoy tenders of any size. (U.S. Coast Guard)

4 MOTOR LIFEBOATS: 52-FT TYPE

Number	Name	Number	Name
52312	VICTORY	52314	TRIUMPH II
52313	INVINCIBLE	52315	INTREPID

Builders:	Coast Guard Yard, Curtis Bay, Md.
Displacement:	35 tons
Length:	52 feet (15.85 m) overall
Beam:	14½ feet (4.4 m)
Draft:	6¼ feet (1.9 m)
Propulsion:	2 diesel engines (General Motors 6-71); 340 bhp; 2 shafts
Speed:	11 knots
Range:	495 n.miles (920 km) at 11 knots
Manning:	5 (enlisted) + 35 survivors
Radar:	1 navigation

These are "self-righting" lifeboats with steel hulls and aluminum superstructures. The VICTORY was built in 1956, the others in 1960–1961.

Highly capable craft, they can operate in heavy sea conditions and are fitted with firefighting pumps.

These are the only Coast Guard small craft that have names assigned.

1 SEARCH AND RESCUE BOAT: 50-FT TYPE

Builders:	Munson Manufacturing, Edmonds, Wash.
Displacement:	26 tons full load
Length:	50⁵/₁₂ feet (15.37 m) overall
Beam:	16⅓ feet (4.97 m)
Draft:	4 feet (1.2 m)
Propulsion:	2 diesel engines (General Motors 8V92 TI); 1,300 bhp; 2 shafts
Speed:	26 knots
Range:	300 n.miles (555 km) at 18 knots
	200 n.miles (370 km) at 26 knots
Manning:	4 or 5 (enlisted) + survivors

The 502001 is a small SAR craft, procured in record time by the Coast Guard to evaluate the potential for a live-aboard boat to replace small shore stations. The craft was placed in service on 1 May 1992 at Station Taylors Island in Chesapeake Bay, Md. With the availability of the 502001, the station's number of assigned personnel was reduced from 19 to 8.

The craft was adapted from a commercial design.

The one-of-a-kind SAR boat 502001 at high speed in Chesapeake Bay, Md. (1992, U.S. Coast Guard)

The 502001 at rest. There is a stern gate to assist in rescue operations; a life raft canister and navigation radar are fitted atop the cabin. (1992, U.S. Coast Guard)

The 49-foot buoy servicing boat 49407 handling a buoy over the stern. (U.S. Coast Guard)

17+ BUOY SERVICING BOATS: 49-FT TYPE

Builders:	Coast Guard Yard, Curtis Bay, Md.
	Maritime Contractors, Bellingham, Wash.
Displacement:	31.65 tons light
Length:	49¼ feet (15.02 m) overall
Beam:	16⅚ feet (5.13 m)
Draft:	6⅚ feet (2.08 m)
Propulsion:	1 diesel engine; 305 bhp; 1 shaft
Speed:	10.5 knots
Range:	300 n.miles (555 km) at 10 knots
Manning:	4 (enlisted)

The first of these craft, designated 49401–49417, were completed in August 1994 at Maritime Contractors. Additional units are being built at the Coast Guard Yard.

They have a stern crane for handling buoys.

53 + 147 MOTOR LIFEBOATS: 47-FT TYPE

Builders:	Textron Marine Systems, New Orleans, La.
Displacement:	18.1 tons full load
Length:	47 feet (14.33 m) overall
Beam:	14 feet (4.3 m)
Draft:	4 feet (1.2 m)
Propulsion:	2 diesel engines (General Motors 6V92); 900 bhp; 2 shafts
Speed:	28 knots
	20 knots sustained
Range:	200 n.miles (370 km) at 20 knots
Manning:	4 (enlisted) + 5 survivors
Radars:	1 SPS-69 navigation

These craft are numbered in the 47200 series. Constructed of aluminum, they are "self-righting" lifeboats, capable of flipping end-over-end or rolling up to 360° and self-righting in 30 seconds or less. They can withstand 20-foot (6.1-m) breaking waves.

The lead boat was delivered in August 1990; about 200 will be built through 2002.

A 47-foot motor lifeboat working with an HH-60J Jayhawk during a rescue exercise. These craft have a remarkable self-righting capability, illustrated in the 16th Edition/page 531. (1997, U.S. Coast Guard, PA1 Eric Eggen)

The 47-foot motor lifeboat 47202 going "flat out" off the North Carolina Coast. (1999, U.S. Coast Guard, PA1 Telfair H. Brown)

9 BUOY SERVICING BOATS: 46-FT TYPE

Builders:	46301–46306 Hunt Shipyard
	46307–46309 Coast Guard Yard, Curtis Bay, Md.
Displacement:	20 tons light
	27 tons full load
Length:	46⅓ feet (14.1 m) overall
Beam:	16⅙ feet (4.9 m)
Draft:	5⅔ feet (1.7 m)
Propulsion:	1 diesel engine (General Motors 6-71); 180 bhp; Schottel rudder-propeller unit
Speed:	9 knots
Range:	440 n.miles (815 km) at 9 knots
Manning:	4 (enlisted)

These craft have steel hulls and superstructures. The above data are for later units; the initial 46301–46306 have reduced fuel capacities and a range of only 320 n.miles (590 km).

Cargo capacity is 7¼ tons of buoys and navigation aids; there is a 4,000-pound (1,800-kg) lifting frame mounted on the stern.

The 46-foot buoy servicing boat 46314, based in New York City (1991, Giorgio Arra)

32 AIDS-TO-NAVIGATION BOATS: 45-FT TYPE

Builders:	Coast Guard Yard, Curtis Bay, Md.
Displacement:	21.5 tons light
	31.27 tons full load
Length:	45¼ feet (13.8 m) overall
Beam:	15 feet (4.6 m)
Draft:	3 feet (0.9 m)
Propulsion:	1 diesel engine (General Motors 6-71); 150 bhp; 1 shaft
Speed:	8.5 knots
Range:	550 n.miles (1,020 km) at 8.5 knots
Manning:	4 (enlisted)

These are steel-hull craft with steel superstructures. The above characteristics relate to the units 45302–45312; the similar 45313–45316 carry less fuel, but their GM 6-71 engine is rated at 180 bhp, with a range reduction to 520 n.miles (960 km).

These boats can carry about 9½ tons of buoys and navigation aids.

The 45-foot aids-to-navigation boat 45306 (1988, Leo Van Ginderen)

APPROX. 30 MOTOR LIFEBOATS: 44-FT TYPE

Builders:	Coast Guard Yard, Curtis Bay, Md.
Displacement:	14.9 tons light
	17.7 tons full load
Length:	44 feet (13.4 m) overall
Beam:	12⅔ feet (3.9 m)
Draft:	3¹¹⁄₁₂ feet (1.2 m)
Propulsion:	2 diesel engines (General Motors 6-71); 372 bhp; 2 shafts
Speed:	14 knots
	11.8 knots sustained
Range:	185 n.miles (340 km) at 11.8 knots
Manning:	4 (enlisted) + survivors
Radars:	1 navigation

These are "unsinkable" lifeboats numbered 44300–44409. They were delivered from 1961 to 1973. These craft are being replaced by the 47-foot (14.3-m) design.

A 44-foot motor lifeboat in heavy surf (1999, U.S. Coast Guard)

A 44-foot motor lifeboat under way. Note the bar-type radar antenna fitted atop the windshield. (U.S. Coast Guard)

172 UTILITY BOATS: 41-FT TYPE

Builders:	Coast Guard Yard, Curtis Bay, Md.
Displacement:	13–14 tons full load
Length:	40⅔ feet (12.4 m) overall
Beam:	13½ feet (4.1 m)
Draft:	4 feet (1.2 m)
Propulsion:	2 diesel engines (Cummins V903M or VT903M); 560 or 636 bhp; 2 shafts
Speed:	22–26 knots (see notes)
Range:	300 n.miles (555 km) at 18 knots
Manning:	3 (enlisted)
Radars:	1 Raytheon 1900 navigation

These are aluminum utility craft completed between 1973 and 1982. Hull numbers begin with 41300. The 41400 and later units have vanes on the propeller shafts, adding 2.5 knots. Their rescue equipment includes a fire pump.

The 41-foot utility boat 41353 at high speed. Some of these craft have a "pot"-type radar antenna in place of the bar-type antenna shown here. (U.S. Coast Guard)

The 41-foot utility boat 41453 off Annapolis, Md. (1999, U.S. Coast Guard, PA1 Peter Milnes)

2 UTILITY BOATS: 38-FT TYPE

Builders:	Munson Manufacturing, Edmonds, Wash.
Displacement:	11 tons full load
Length:	38 feet (11.58 m) overall
Beam:	12½ feet (3.8 m)
Draft:	2⁵⁄₁₂ feet (0.7 m)
Propulsion:	2 diesel engines (Caterpillar 3208 TA); 750 bhp; 2 shafts
Speed:	30 knots
Manning:	4 (enlisted) + 8 passengers
Radars:	1 navigation

The 380501 and 380502 were placed in Coast Guard service in April 1991. They are based in New York City and patrol against the illegal dumping of hazardous materials.

The 38-foot utility boat 380502 against the New York City skyline (1991, Giorgio Arra)

365 PORT AND WATERWAYS BOATS: 32-FT TYPE

Builders:	
Displacement:	7.5 tons light
	8.6 tons full load
Length:	33⅓ feet (10.2 m) overall
Beam:	11¾ feet (3.6 m)
Draft:	2⅚ feet (0.9 m)
Propulsion:	2 diesel engines (Caterpillar 3208); 406 bhp; 2 shafts
Speed:	25 knots
Manning:	3 (enlisted)
Radars:	1 Raytheon 1900 navigation

Built in the late 1970s, these craft are of GRP construction. They are equipped for firefighting.

The 32-foot port and waterways boat 32328, based in New York City (1990, Giorgio Arra)

The port and waterways boat 32328 (1990, Giorgio Arra)

28 PORT SECURITY BOATS: 31-FT TYPE

Builders:	31001–31004 Bertram Boat, Miami, Fla.
	31005–31028 Coast Guard Yard, Curtis Bay, Md.
Displacement:	7.4 tons full load
Length:	30⁵⁄₁₂ feet (9.27 m) overall
Beam:	11½ feet (3.5 m)
Draft:	3¹¹⁄₁₂ feet (1.2 m)
Propulsion:	1 diesel engine (General Motors); 197 bhp; 2 shafts
Speed:	14 knots
Range:	165 n.miles (305 km) at 12.5 knots
Manning:	3 (enlisted)
Radars:	1 navigation

These are GRP craft numbered from 31001. Completed in the 1960s, these craft are used primarily for training.

19 SURF RESCUE BOATS: 30-FT TYPE

Builders:	Coast Guard Yard, Curtis Bay, Md.
Displacement:	4.6 tons full load
Length:	30⅓ feet (9.25 m) overall
Beam:	9⅓ feet (2.8 m)
Draft:	3⅔ feet (1.1 m)
Propulsion:	2 diesel engines (General Motors 6VT92T); 375 bhp; 1 shaft
Speed:	31 knots
Range:	150 n.miles (280 km) at 25 knots
Manning:	2 (enlisted) + survivors
Radars:	none

These rescue boats are employed in short-distance operations. Their hull numbers begin with 30201. The boats were placed in service in 1986–1990.

A 30-foot surf rescue boat going to sea (U.S. Coast Guard)

1 LAKE CHAMPLAIN PATROL BOAT: 28-FT TYPE

Builders:	SeaArk Boat, Monticello, Ark.
Displacement:	
Length:	28½ feet (8.69 m) overall
Beam:	11⅔ feet (3.56 m)
Draft:	1⅚ feet (0.56 m)
Propulsion:	2 diesel engines (Volvo AQAD 41/290); 400 bhp; 2 outboard drives
Speed:	38 knots
Manning:	3 (enlisted) + survivors

Based at Burlington, Vt., this boat is used for search and rescue on Lake Champlain.

A 28-foot Lake Champlain patrol boat (1987, SeaArk)

. . . PATROL CRAFT: 27-FT VIGILANT TYPE

Builders:	Boston Whaler, Edgewater, Fla.
Displacement:	2.27 tons light
	4 tons full load
Length:	26⁷/₁₂ feet (8.10 m) overall
Beam:	10 feet (3.05 m)
Draft:	1⁷/₁₂ feet (0.48 m)
Propulsion:	2 gasoline outboard engines; 350 hp
Speed:	34 knots
Manning:	4 (enlisted) + 8 passengers
Radars:	1 navigation

These are for harbor patrol duties and were delivered in the 1990s. They are fabricated of GRP. Similar units have been transferred to Kazakhstan and Romania with Coast Guard training assistance.

1 HONOLULU PERSONNEL LAUNCH: 26-FT TYPE

Builders:	Munson Manufacturing, Edmonds, Wash.
Displacement:	3.2 tons full load
Length:	26 feet (7.9 m) overall
Beam:	10 feet (3.05 m)
Draft:	2 feet (0.61 m)
Propulsion:	1 diesel engine (Volvo AQAD 41/200); 1,200 bhp; 1 outboard drive
Speed:	25 knots
Manning:	1 + 12 passengers

This personnel launch, hull number 266200, is used in Honolulu, Hawaii, to transport Coast Guard personnel..

The Coast Guard's unique Honolulu harbor launch (Munson)

. . . PATROL BOATS: CHALLENGER 25-FT TYPE

Builders:	Boston Whaler, Edgewater, Fla.
Displacement:	1.86 tons light
	3.2 tons full load
Length:	24⁷/₁₂ feet (7.50 m) overall
Beam:	8 feet (2.45 m)
Draft:	1⅓ feet (0.4 m)
Propulsion:	2 gasoline outboard engines (Johnson); 300 bhp
Speed:	30+ knots
Crew:	3 (enlisted) + 9 passengers

These patrol craft, numbered from 253501, were delivered in the 1990s. They are constructed of GRP.

The 25-foot patrol boat 253503 at high speed (1996, Leo Van Ginderen)

The 25-foot patrol boat 253503. The black markings on the bow are non-skid material. (1996, Leo Van Ginderen)

200+ SURF BOATS } 25-FT TYPE
41 CARGO BOATS

Builders:	Coast Guard Yard, Curtis Bay, Md.
Displacement:	2.3 tons light
	3.4 tons full load
Length:	25⅔ feet (7.8 m) overall
Beam:	7 feet (2.16 m)
Draft:	2 feet (0.61 m)
Propulsion:	1 diesel engine (General Motors 3-53); 80 bhp; 1 shaft
Speed:	11 knots
Range:	60 n.miles (110 km) at 11 knots
Manning:	surf boats 2 (enlisted) + survivors
	cargo boats 3 (enlisted)

More than 200 surf boats of this design, plus 41 similar cargo craft, entered in Coast Guard service between 1969 and 1983. Hull numbers 253301–253517 are assigned. They are of GRP construction.

2 HAMMERHEAD PATROL CRAFT: 24-FT TYPE

Builders:	Munson Manufacturing, Edmonds, Wash.
Displacement:	2.8 tons full load
Length:	24 feet (7.3 m) overall
Beam:	8½ feet (2.6 m)
Draft:	2 feet (0.61 m)
Propulsion:	2 gasoline outboard engines (Evinrude V-6)
Speed:	45 knots
Manning:	

These craft are employed for search and rescue on Lake Tahoe, on the California–Nevada state line.

One of the two Hammerhead 24-foot patrol craft based on Lake Tahoe (Munson)

...PATROL BOATS: SENTRY 22-FT TYPE

Builders:	Boston Whaler, Edgewater, Fla.
Displacement:	1.29 tons light
	2.5 tons full load
Length:	22⅓ feet (6.8 m) overall
Beam:	7½ feet (2.3 m)
Draft:	1⅙ feet (0.36 m)
Propulsion:	2 gasoline outboard engines (Johnson); 160 hp
Speed:	30+ knots
Manning:	
Radar:	1 navigation

18 PATROL BOATS: 21-FT TYPE

Builders:	SeaArk Boat, Monticello, Ark.
Displacement:	1.9 tons full load
Length:	21 feet (6.4 m) overall
Beam:	8 feet (2.44 m)
Draft:	1⅚ feet (0.56 m)
Propulsion:	2 gasoline outboard engines (Evinrude)
Speed:	32 knots
Manning:	

These are trailer-transportable patrol craft for use on inland waterways. Aluminum construction.

58 AIDS-TO-NAVIGATION BOATS: 21-FT TYPE

Builders:	SeaArk Boat, Monticello, Ark.
Displacement:	1.6 tons light
	3.17 tons full load
Length:	21½ feet (6.56 m) overall
Beam:	7⅓ feet (2.24 m)
Draft:	1⅙ feet (0.36 m)
Propulsion:	1 gasoline outboard engine; 228 bhp
Speed:	28 knots
Range:	100 n.miles (328 km) at 20 knots
Manning:	

These are transported on trailers for use in inland waterways.

One of the Coast Guard's three SAFE—Secure All-around Flotation Equipped—boats. These 25-foot RIB-type craft have a rigid foam collar to provide additional flotation and a full pilothouse to protect the crew. (1999, U.S. Coast Guard, PA3 Jacquelyn Zettles)

A Coast Guard 21-foot Zodiac RIB races with a smaller Border Patrol RIB. These craft, with two outboard engines, are fitted with radar and can be based aboard large cutters or at shore stations. The first units of this type entered Coast Guard service in 1992. (1999, Leo Van Ginderen)

A high endurance cutter in her element: The Mᴇʟʟᴏɴ steams through the Bering Sea while serving as search-and-rescue cutter for the crab fisheries operations. Such cutters serve in a variety of roles although their military capabilities are severely limited. (2000, U.S. Coast Guard, PA1 Keith Alholm)

A buoy tender in her element: The Bᴀʏʙᴇʀʀʏ operates near Seattle, Washington, with her oil-skimming system deployed. Pollution control has been added to the multitude of missions carried out by Coast Guard cutters and small craft. (2000, U.S. Coast Guard, PA3 Della Price)

CHAPTER 31

National Oceanographic and Atmospheric Administration

The KaʹIMIMOANA, a former U.S. Navy surveillance ship now configured for NOAA operations, tends an Atlas-series buoy in the tropical Pacific. Most NOAA ships were constructed specifically for that service. There are 61 Atlas buoys, which mount and trail a variety of atmospheric and oceanic sensors. (NOAA)

The National Oceanic and Atmospheric Administration (NOAA), an agency within the Department of Commerce, conducts ocean surveys and other environmental research and surveying activities for the U.S. government. NOAA conducts non-military research operations in U.S. coastal waters, as well as overseas. However, NOAA maps and charts are used by the armed forces, and during time of war or national emergency the President may transfer NOAA ships, shore stations, and personnel to the Navy or other military services.

NOAA's National Ocean Survey currently has 15 active ships. Three former Navy ocean surveillance ships (T-AGOS) have been taken over by NOAA, but only one is in active service.

Several older survey ships have been disposed of. Additional new construction for NOAA, long delayed for budgetary reasons, is not now likely because of the T-AGOS surveillance ships available for NOAA service.

Historical: An act of Congress on 10 February 1807 established the Survey of the Coast as a U.S. government agency. Its name was changed to the Coast Survey in 1834 and to the Coast and Geodetic Survey in 1878.

The commissioned officer corps of the agency was established in 1917. The Coast and Geodetic Survey was made a component of the Environmental Science Services Administration (ESSA) on 13 July 1965, when that agency was established within the Department of Commerce. ESSA subsequently became the National Oceanic and Atmospheric Administration in October 1970, with the Coast and Geodetic Survey being renamed the National Ocean Survey, which is today the ship-operating branch of NOAA.

SHIPS

The status of NOAA's ships varies from year to year, with research and survey operations dependent upon specific budget allocations. These ships are supported by the NOAA Atlantic Marine Center at Norfolk, Va., and Pacific Marine Center at Puget Sound, Wash.

All 15 oceangoing NOAA ships are active.

Most of the larger NOAA ships were built to Maritime Administration designs (designations shown in parentheses in the following descriptions), except for those acquired through or from the U.S. Navy in the 1990s. The smaller NOAA ships are mostly adopted from commercial designs.

In World War II, six of the largest Coast and Geodetic Survey ships transferred to the Navy, being designated as surveying ships. These ships were armed and most were in combat. Another ten ships remained under the Survey, some of which were armed.

Designations: All NOAA ships are designated by a three-digit number preceded by the letter *R* for Research or *S* for Survey, with the first digit indicating the Horsepower Tonnage (HPT) class. The HPT is the numerical sum of the vessel's shaft horsepower plus her gross tonnage: Class I ships are 5,501–9,000 HPT; Class II are 3,501–5,500 HPT; Class III are 2,001–3,500 HPT; Class IV are 1,001–2,000 HPT; Class V are 501–1,000 HPT; and Class VI are up to 500 HPT.

Table 31-1 lists the NOAA research and survey ships, their HPT class, current hull numbers, and previous designations.

Guns: NOAA ships are unarmed.

Helicopters: Only the DAVID STARR JORDAN has a helicopter platform.

TABLE 31-1. NOAA SHIPS

Class	Number	Name	Former	Mission/notes
I	R 104	RONALD H. BROWN	—	oceanographic/atmospheric research
II	S 220	FAIRWEATHER	MSS 20	laid up
II	S 221	RAINIER	MSS 21	nautical charting
II	R 223	MILLER FREEMAN	—	fisheries research
III	S 329	WHITING	CSS 29	nautical charting
III	S 330	MCARTHUR	CSS 30	environmental monitoring/ fisheries research
III	S 331	(ex-ADVENTUROUS)	(T-AGOS 13)	laid up
III	R 333	KA'IMIMOANA	(T-AGOS 15)	oceanographic/atmospheric research
III	R 335	GORDON GUNTER	(T-AGOS 18)	fisheries research
III	R 332	OREGON II	—	fisheries research
III	R 342	ALBATROSS IV	—	fisheries research
IV	R 443	TOWNSEND CROMWELL	—	fisheries research
IV	R 444	DAVID STARR JORDAN	—	fisheries research
IV	R 445	DELAWARE II	—	fisheries research
IV	S 492	FERREL	ASV 92	environmental monitoring/ fisheries research
V	R 552	JOHN N. COBB	—	fisheries research
V	S 590	RUDE	ASV 90	nautical charting

AVIATION

NOAA operates ten fixed-wing aircraft and three helicopters (see table 31-2). The largest aircraft are two extensively modified WP-3D Orion weather reconnaissance aircraft.

The Hughes MD500D is often deployed aboard the fisheries research ship DAVID STARR JORDAN.

TABLE 31-2. NOAA AIRCRAFT

Number	Type	Crew*	Engines	Notes
2	Lockheed WP-3D Orion	8	4 turboprop	
1	Gulfstream Turbo Commander	3	2 turboprop	
1	Lake Renegade Sea Wolf	4	1 piston	amphibious
2	Rockwell Aero Commander	7	2 piston	
2	DeHavilland DHC-6 Twin Otter	8	2 turboprop	
1	Cessna Citation II	9	2 turbojet	
1	Gulfstream IV-SP	9–13	2 turbojet	
2	Bell 212	15	2 turboshaft	helicopters
1	Hughes MD500D	4	1 turboshaft	helicopter

* Flight crew + scientists/technicians

PERSONNEL

NOAA has approximately 225 commissioned officers, of whom approximately 65 are assigned to shipboard duty. Fifty licensed civil service personnel and about 217 unlicensed personnel are also assigned to ships. Medical officers from the U.S. Public Health Service are provided to ships when necessary.

NOAA is commanded by a rear admiral of the NOAA commissioned officer corps. (The current director of the NOAA officer corps is Rear Admiral Evelyn J. Fields, whose appointment was confirmed by the Senate on 6 May 1999; she is the first woman and the first black to serve in that position. She also was the first female to command a NOAA ship, the MCARTHUR.)

Rear Admiral Evelyn J. Fields, Director of the Office of Marine and Aviation Operations, and Director of the NOAA Commissioned Officer Corps, since May 1999.

A WP-3D Orion, one of two heavily modified maritime patrol aircraft flown by NOAA. These aircraft conduct long-range operations, including flying into hurricanes to perform research as well as reconnaissance; U.S. Air Force C-130 Hercules that also penetrate hurricanes perform only reconnaissance. The NOAA planes also have permission to enter Cuban air space on hurricane missions. (NOAA)

Grumman Gulfstream IV-SP (NOAA)

Lake Renegade Seawolf—the only amphibious aircraft flown by the U.S. government (NOAA)

1 RESEARCH SHIP: "THOMAS G. THOMPSON" CLASS

Number	Name	FY	Launch	Commission	Status
R 104	RONALD H. BROWN	94	30 May 1996	19 July 1997	**AA**

Builders:	Trinity/Halter Marine, Moss Point, Miss.
Displacement:	2,100 tons light
	3,250 tons full load
Length:	274 feet (83.5 m) overall
Beam:	52 feet (15.85 m)
Draft:	17 feet (5.2 m)
Propulsion:	diesel-electric (3 diesel generators/Caterpillar 3516TA; 2 electric motors/General Motors CD6999); 6,000 shp; 2 azimuth propellers
Speed:	15 knots
Range:	11,300 n.miles (20,940 km) at 12 knots
Manning:	24 (4 officers + 20 mariners) + 35 scientists
Radars:	2 Sperry RASCAR navigation
	1 Enterprise WSR-74C weather
Sonar:	Nautronix RS916 positioning
	Ocean Data profiler
	Sea Beam 2112A seafloor mapping

The BROWN is one of four ships of this class, the others being built for operation by academic institutions on behalf of Navy research projects (see page 249). The ship is the largest in the NOAA fleet and replaced both the DISCOVERY (R 102) and MALCOLM BALDRIGE (R 103).[1] She was laid down on 21 February 1995. This was the first keel-laying of a built-for-the-purpose NOAA ship since 1980.

The BROWN carries out worldwide oceanographic and atmospheric research.

Classification: The hull number AGOR 26 was assigned for Navy accounting purposes.

Design: The ship is built to commercial standards and is designed for extended at-sea operations. Four laboratory/accommodation vans can be carried on deck, in addition to more than 4,000 square feet (372 m^2) of laboratory space.

Endurance is 60 to 70 days.

Engineering: In addition to three diesel generators for propulsion, the ship has three ship's service power generators (3508TA) plus one emergency generator (3406TA).

The ship is fitted with azimuth or Z-drives with 360° rotating-propellers; there is also a rotating, 360°, 1,180-shp bow thruster to provide precise station keeping.

Names: The ship was originally named RESEARCHER, that name having previously been assigned to the NOAA research ship that had been renamed MALCOLM BALDRIGE in 1988. The R 104 was renamed RONALD H. BROWN when christened to honor the Secretary of Commerce after his death in a plane crash in Bosnia on 3 April 1996.

---

1. The SURVEYOR (S 132) was longer than the BROWN but displaced slightly less; see below.

RONALD H. BROWN (NOAA)

RESEARCH SHIPS: "OCEANOGRAPHER" CLASS (S2-MET-MA62a)

Number	Name	Comm.	Notes
R 101	Oceanographer	1966	stricken 1996
R 102	Discoverer	1967	stricken 16 Aug 1996

These graceful Class I oceanographic research ships were the largest ships operated by NOAA (4,033 tons full load). See 16th Edition/page 540 for characteristics.

3 SURVEY SHIPS: EX-NAVY "STALWART" CLASS

Number	Name	FY	Launched	USN in service	NOAA comm.	Status
R 331 (ex-T-AGOS 13)	. . . . . . (ex-Adventurous)	85	23 Sep 1987	19 Aug 1988	—	AR
R 333 (ex-T-AGOS 15)	Ka'imimoana (ex-Titan)	86	18 June 1988	8 Mar 1989	26 Apr 1996	**PA**
R 335 (ex-T-AGOS 18)	Gordon Gunter (ex-Relentless)	87	12 May 1989	12 Jan 1990	28 Aug 1998	**AA**

Builders:	Trinity/Halter Marine, New Orleans, La.	Propulsion:	diesel-electric (4 Caterpillar D-398B diesel generators with General Electric motors); 3,200 bhp; 2 shafts
Displacement:	1,600 tons light		
	2,301 tons full load, except ex-Adventurous: 2,285 tons	Speed:	11 knots
Tonnage:	1,584 GRT	Range:	3,000 n.miles (5,556 km) at 11 knots + 90 days on station at 3 knots
	786 DWT		
Length:	203⅔ feet (62.1 m) waterline	Manning:	Ka'imimoana 21 (5 officers + 16 mariners) + 12 scientists
	224 feet (68.3 m) overall		Gunter 18 (4 officers + 14 mariners) + 15 scientists
Beam:	43 feet (13.1 m)	Sonars:	removed
Draft:	15 feet (4.6 m)		

These ships were built for the Navy's Surveillance Towed Array Sensor System (SURTASS) program; see page 249. With the massive cutbacks in that program, the transfer of up to eight ships to NOAA was considered. In the event, only three ships were transferred:

ex-Adventurous   to NOAA 5 June 1992
ex-Titan   to NOAA 31 Aug 1993
ex-Relentless   to NOAA 17 Mar 1993

Two of the ships transferred to NOAA have been extensively modified and placed in service: the Ka'imimoana for oceanographic/atmospheric research and the Gordon Gunter for fisheries research. The latter ship now has 1,490 square feet (138.6 m²) of dedicated laboratory space, including a "wet lab" of 480 square feet (44.6 m²).

The ex-Adventurous (not renamed) was employed for training NOAA officers in 1993–1994; she currently is laid up in the James River Reserve Fleet, Fort Eustis, Va. Long-term plans call for converting her to a coastal survey role with funding requested in NOAA's fiscal 2001 budget proposal.

RESEARCH SHIP: "MALCOLM BALDRIGE" (S2-MT-MA7a)

The Class I research ship Malcolm Baldrige (R 103), commissioned in 1970, was stricken on 23 August 1996. See 16th Edition/page 541 for characteristics.

The Gunter replaced the Chapman.

Class: The Stalwart class originally consisted of 18 ships (T-AGOS 1–18).

The Worthy (T-AGOS 14) was transferred from the Military Sealift Command (MSC) to NOAA on 30 September 1993; subsequently she was laid up at Redwood City, Calif. She was then planned for operation by the U.S. Geological Survey, but instead was loaned to the U.S. Army in 1995 for use as a range instrumentation ship.

Design: The T-AGOS hull is similar to that of the T-ATF 166 class. A high degree of crew habitability is provided; as built, there were 19 single staterooms for the ships' civilian (MSC) crew members with three single and four double staterooms for the ten Navy technicians. (There were several additional berths available.)

Endurance is rated at 98 days.

Engineering: The four diesel generators drive two main propulsion motors. A bow thruster powered by a 550-hp electric motor is fitted for station keeping. There are special features to reduce machinery noise during research operations.

Names: Ka'imimoana is Hawaiian for "Ocean Seeker."

Ka'imimoana (ex-USNS Titan) (NOAA)

SURVEY SHIP: "SURVEYOR" (S2-S-RM28a)

The large Class I survey ship SURVEYOR (S 132), commissioned in 1960, was stricken in 1996. See 15th Edition/page 589 for characteristics.

2 SURVEY SHIPS: "FAIRWEATHER" CLASS (S1-MT-MA72a)

Number	Name	Launched	Commissioned	Status
S 220	FAIRWEATHER	15 Mar 1967	2 Oct 1968	PR
S 221	RAINIER	15 Mar 1967	2 Oct 1968	**PA**
S 222	MT. MITCHELL	29 Nov 1966	23 Mar 1968	stricken 1996

Builders:	Aerojet-General Corp., Jacksonville, Fla.
Displacement:	1,798 tons full load
Length:	231 feet (70.4 m) overall
Beam:	42 feet (12.8 m)
Draft:	13⅝ feet (4.2 m)
Propulsion:	2 diesel engines; 2,400 bhp; 2 shafts
Speed:	14.5 knots
Range:	7,000 n.miles (12,965 km) at 13 knots
Manning:	49 (10 officers + 39 mariners) + 4 scientists

These Class II ships are outfitted primarily for hydrographic surveys involving charting operations. The RAINIER operates off the Pacific coast of the United States.

The MT. MITCHELL was decommissioned on 25 October 1995 and stricken in 1996.

Design: Six aluminum survey launches are carried by each ship.

Engineering: These ships have a 200-hp through-bow thruster.

RAINIER (NOAA)

1 RESEARCH SHIP: "MILLER FREEMAN"

Number	Name	Launched	Commissioned	Status
R 223	MILLER FREEMAN	1967	June 1967	**PA**

Builders:	American Shipbuilding, Lorain, Ohio
Displacement:	1,920 tons full load
Length:	216½ feet (66.0 m) overall
Beam:	41 feet (12.5 m)
Draft:	20 feet (6.1 m)
Propulsion:	1 diesel engine (General Motors); 3,200 bhp; 1 shaft
Speed:	14 knots
Range:	13,800 n.miles (25,560 km) at 14 knots
Manning:	39 (7 officers + 32 mariners) + 11 scientists

The FREEMAN is a fisheries research ship, previously scheduled to be replaced during the 1990s. She continues to operate off the U.S. Pacific coast.

Design: Stern-trawler design. Endurance is 31 days.

Engineering: A 400-hp Schottel bow thruster can be lowered for precision station keeping.

The MT. MITCHELL, showing her small radome mounted above the forward edge of her short, squat funnel. (1992, Stefan Terzibaschitsch)

MILLER FREEMAN (NOAA)

1 SURVEY SHIP: "PEIRCE" CLASS (S1-MT-59a)

Number	Name	Launched	Commissioned	Status
S 329	WHITING	20 Nov 1962	8 July 1963	**AA**

Builders:	Marietta Manufacturing, Point Pleasant, W.Va.
Displacement:	760 tons full load
Length:	164 feet (50.0 m) overall
Beam:	33 feet (10.1 m)
Draft:	10 feet (3.0 m)
Propulsion:	2 diesel engines; 1,600 bhp; 2 shafts
Speed:	12.5 knots
Range:	5,700 n.miles (10,555 km) at 12 knots
Manning:	35 (7 officers + 28 mariners)

This ship primarily conducts hydrographic surveys of the 200-n.mile (237-km) Exclusive Economic Zone (EEZ) for bathymetric maps and nautical charts. The WHITING normally operates off the Atlantic coast, in the Gulf of Mexico, and in the Caribbean area.

Class: The PEIRCE (S 328), also completed in 1963, was laid up in 1993 and transferred to New York City for use as a school ship, renamed ELIZABETH A. FISHER.

1 SURVEY SHIP: "McARTHUR" CLASS (S1-MT-MA70a)

Number	Name	Launched	Commissioned	Status
S 330	McARTHUR	15 Nov 1965	15 Dec 1966	**PA**
S 331	DAVIDSON	7 May 1966	10 Mar 1967	stricken 1997

Builders:	Norfolk Shipbuilding and Dry Dock, Va.
Displacement:	995 tons full load
Length:	175 feet (53.3 m) overall
Beam:	38 feet (11.5 m)
Draft:	11½ feet (3.5 m)
Propulsion:	2 diesel engines; 1,600 bhp; 2 shafts
Speed:	13 knots
Range:	6,000 n.miles (11,110 km) at 12 knots
Manning:	22 (3 officers + 19 mariners) + 13 scientists

This oceanographic research ship, the survivor of a two-ship class, primarily operates in the EEZ off the U.S. Pacific coast. She is fitted for research in the chemical, meteorological, and biological fields.

The DAVIDSON was stricken without having been formally decommissioned.

WHITING (NOAA)

1 RESEARCH SHIP: "OREGON II"

Number	Name	Launched	Commissioned	Status
R 332	OREGON II	Feb 1967	17 Mar 1977	**AA**

Builders:	Ingalls Shipbuilding, Pascagoula, Miss.
Displacement:	952 tons full load
Length:	169¹¹⁄₁₂ feet (51.8 m) overall
Beam:	34¹⁄₁₂ feet (10.4 m)
Draft:	14¹⁄₁₂ feet (4.3 m)
Propulsion:	2 diesel engines (Fairbanks Morse); 1,600 bhp; 1 shaft
Speed:	12 knots
Range:	9,500 n.miles (17,600 km) at 12 knots
Manning:	17 (3 officers + 14 mariners) + 14 scientists

The OREGON II is a far-ranging fisheries research ship, operating primarily off the U.S. Atlantic coast, in the Gulf of Mexico, and in the Caribbean area.

The ship was delivered for service in August 1967 but not commissioned until ten years later.

McARTHUR (NOAA)

OREGON II. The crow's nest subsequently was deleted from the forward mast. (NOAA)

1 RESEARCH SHIP: "ALBATROSS IV"

Number	Name	Launched	Commissioned	Status
R 342	ALBATROSS IV	Apr 1962	May 1963	**AA**

Builders:	Southern Shipbuilding, Slidell, La.
Displacement:	1,089 tons full load
Length:	187 feet (57.0 m) overall
Beam:	32⅝ feet (10.0 m)
Draft:	16 feet (4.9 m)
Propulsion:	2 diesel engines (Caterpillar); 1,130 bhp; 1 Kort-nozzle propeller
Speed:	12 knots
Range:	4,300 n.miles (7,965 km) at 12 knots
Manning:	20 (4 officers + 16 mariners) + 14 scientists

The ALBATROSS IV is a fisheries research ship.
   Engineering: The ship has a 125-hp bow thruster.

ALBATROSS IV (NOAA)

1 RESEARCH SHIP: "TOWNSEND CROMWELL"

Number	Name	Launched	Commissioned	Status
R 443	TOWNSEND CROMWELL	July 1963	June 1975	**PA**

Builders:	J. Ray McDermott, Morgan City, La.
Displacement:	652 tons full load
Length:	163 feet (49.7 m) overall
Beam:	32⅝ feet (10.0 m)
Draft:	12⅝ feet (3.9 m)
Propulsion:	2 diesel engines (White Superior); 800 bhp; 2 shafts
Speed:	11.5 knots
Range:	8,300 n.miles (15,370 km) at 11.5 knots
Manning:	17 (4 officers + 13 mariners) + 11 scientists

The CROMWELL is a fisheries research ship taken over by NOAA in June 1975. She operates in the Hawaii area.
   The ship was delivered for service in 1963 but not commissioned until 1975.

TOWNSEND CROMWELL (NOAA)

1 RESEARCH SHIP: "DAVID STARR JORDAN"

Number	Name	Launched	Commissioned	Status
R 444	DAVID STARR JORDAN	19 Dec 1964	8 Jan 1966	**PA**

Builders:	Christy, Sturgeon Bay, Wisc.
Displacement:	993 tons full load
Length:	170¹¹⁄₁₂ feet (52.1 m) overall
Beam:	36¾ feet (11.2 m)
Draft:	15¾ feet (4.8 m)
Propulsion:	2 diesel engines (White Superior); 1,086 bhp; 2 shafts
Speed:	11.5 knots
Range:	8,560 n.miles (15,850 km) at 11.5 knots
Manning:	18 (4 officers + 14 mariners) + 15 scientists

McDonnell Douglas MD500 landing on the research ship DAVID STARR JORDAN (NOAA)

A fisheries research ship, the JORDAN operates off the U.S. Pacific coast.

Design: The JORDAN is a modified stern-trawler. A bow observation chamber is fitted.

Engineering: A retractable 200-hp Schottel bow thruster is fitted.

1 RESEARCH SHIP: "DELAWARE II"

Number	Name	Launched	Commissioned	Status
R 445	DELAWARE II	Dec 1967	Oct 1968	**AA**

Builders:	South Portland Engineering, Maine
Displacement:	758 tons full load
Length:	154⅚ feet (47.2 m)
Beam:	30⅙ feet (9.2 m)
Draft:	14¾ feet (4.5 m)
Propulsion:	1 diesel engine (General Motors); 1,230 bhp; 1 shaft
Speed:	11.5 knots
Range:	6,600 n.miles (12,220 km) at 11.5 knots
Manning:	16 (2 officers + 14 mariners) + 14 scientists

A fisheries research ship, the DELAWARE II operates off the Atlantic coast.

DELAWARE II (NOAA)

RESEARCH SHIP: "CHAPMAN"

The Class IV fisheries research ship CHAPMAN (R 446), commissioned in 1980, was decommissioned on 2 June 1998 and subsequently transferred to the University of Puerto Rico. See 16th Edition/page 544 for characteristics.

1 RESEARCH SHIP: "JOHN N. COBB"

Number	Name	Launched	Commissioned	Status
R 552	JOHN N. COBB	Jan 1950	18 Feb 1950	**PA**

Builders:	Western Boatbuilding, Tacoma, Wash.
Displacement:	250 tons full load
Length:	92⅚ feet (28.3 m) overall
Beam:	25¹¹⁄₁₂ feet (7.9 m)
Draft:	10⅚ feet (3.3 m)
Propulsion:	1 diesel engine (Fairbanks Morse); 325 bhp; 1 shaft
Speed:	9.3 knots
Range:	2,900 n.miles (5,370 km) at 9.3 knots
Manning:	7 (2 officers + 5 mariners) + 4 scientists

The COBB is a fisheries research ship. She is the oldest NOAA research vessel and the only wood-hulled ship in the NOAA fleet. The COBB operates in Alaskan and Pacific coastal waters.

Design: The design is based on West Coast purse-seiners, modified for improved sea-keeping. Endurance is rated at 13 days.

JOHN N. COBB (NOAA)

1 SURVEY SHIP: "FERREL" (S1-MT-MA83a)

Number	Name	Launched	Commissioned	Status
S 492	FERREL	4 Apr 1968	4 June 1968	**AA**

Builders:	Zigler Shipyard, Jennings, La.
Displacement:	363 tons full load
Length:	133¼ feet (40.5 m) overall
Beam:	32 feet (9.7 m)
Draft:	7 feet (2.1 m)
Propulsion:	2 diesel engines (Caterpillar); 750 bhp; 2 shafts
Speed:	10.6 knots
Range:	2,200 n.miles (4,075 km) at 10 knots
Manning:	13 (3 officers + 10 mariners) + 8 scientists

The FERREL conducts near-shore and estuarine-current surveys. She employs data collection buoys in her work; there is a large open buoy stowage area aft, as well as a comprehensive workshop. She operates off the Atlantic and Gulf coasts.

Design: The ship is a modified offshore oil-rig supply boat.

Engineering: She is fitted with a 100-hp through-bow thruster.

FERREL (NOAA)

1 SURVEY SHIP: "RUDE" CLASS (S1-MT-MA71a)

Number	Name	Launched	Commissioned	Status
S 590	RUDE	17 Aug 1966	29 Mar 1967	**AA**
S 591	HECK	1 Nov 1966	29 Mar 1967	stricken 1996

Builders:	Jakobson Shipyard, Oyster Bay, N.Y.
Displacement:	214 tons full load
Length:	90 feet (27.4 m) overall
Beam:	22 feet (6.7 m)
Draft:	7 feet (2.1 m)
Propulsion:	2 diesel engines (Cummins); 800 bhp; 2 Kort-nozzle propellers
Speed:	11.5 knots
Range:	800 n.miles (1,480 km) at 10 knots
Manning:	11 (4 officers + 7 mariners)

A surveying ship, the RUDE previously operated in conjunction with her sister ship HECK, using wire drags to locate underwater navigational hazards. In that role, one commanding officer was assigned to the two vessels; he normally rode one ship and the executive officer the other. The RUDE now operates independently, with a commanding officer.

The HECK was decommissioned on 25 October 1995 and stricken in 1996.

The RUDE operates off the Atlantic coast.

Engineering: The propellers on these ships are protected by shrouds, similar to Kort nozzles. Auxiliary propulsion provides 70 hp to each propeller for slow-speed, dragging operations.

Operational: The RUDE used towed underwater sensors to locate the wreckage of the aircraft flown by John F. Kennedy, Jr., when he crashed off Martha's Vineyard, Mass., on 16 July 1999.[2]

---

2. The towed sensors consist of a side-scan sonar and multi-beam bathymetric sonar, housed in a torpedo-shaped container referred to as a "fish." They provide an accurate acoustic image (sonogram) of the ocean floor extending out to 1,970 feet (600 m) on either side of the fish.

RESEARCH CRAFT

NOAA laboratories operate some 20 small research craft that are 65 feet (19.8 m) or less in length.

RUDE (NOAA)

CHAPTER 32

Miscellaneous U.S. Ships

The largest oceangoing ship in the Army's fleet except for the Besson-class landing ships is the Worthy, a former Navy ocean surveillance ship. She now is configured as an instrumentation ship for the Army's Kwajalein Missile Range, where ballistic missiles and anti-ballistic missile systems are tested. (1999, U.S. Army)

The Navy, Coast Guard, and National Oceanic and Atmospheric Administration are "maritime" services. Additional oceangoing ships are operated by the U.S. Army and the agencies described in this chapter.

U.S. ARMY

In addition to the two Army organizations listed below, the Army's Corps of Engineers operates several large dredges, as well as barge tugs and small craft, on U.S. inland waterways. Army engineer units use a variety of small craft to assist in the assembly of pontoon bridges.

Until 1950 the Army operated a large number of oceangoing troop transports, cargo and supply ships, minelayers, and large tugs. The troop transports and some cargo ships and tugs were transferred to the newly established Military Sea Transportation Service (now Military Sealift Command). Other ships were transferred directly to the Navy; see chapters 23 and 24 of this edition of *Ships and Aircraft*.

ARMY SPACE AND STRATEGIC DEFENSE COMMAND

The Army Space and Strategic Defense Command, with headquarters at Huntsville, Ala., is responsible for national programs related to ground-based air and missile defense systems. The Army is developing a ballistic missile defense system, with Kwajalein atoll in the Marshall Islands in the Pacific being used for missile tests. A former Navy T-AGOS surveillance ship is employed to support the Kwajalein facility. Several small craft also are operated by the Army at Kwajalein, as well as a two-man submersible.

1 RANGE SUPPORT SHIP: Ex-NAVY "STALWART" CLASS

Number	Name	FY	Launched	USN in service	USA in service
(ex-T-AGOS 14)	WORTHY	85	6 Feb 1988	7 Apr 1989	1995

Builders:	Trinity/Halter Marine, New Orleans, La.
Displacement:	1,600 tons light
	2,285 tons full load
Length:	203⅔ feet (62.1 m) waterline
	224 feet (68.3 m) overall
Beam:	43 feet (13.1 m)
Draft:	15 feet (4.6 m)
Propulsion:	diesel-electric (4 Caterpillar D-398B diesel generators with General Electric motors); 3,200 bhp; 2 shafts
Speed:	11 knots
Range:	3,000 n.miles (5,556 km) at 11 knots
Manning:	17 (civilian) + 2 range safety officers + 11 technicians
Sonars:	removed

This ship was built for the Navy's Surveillance Towed Array Sensor System (SURTASS) program; see page 249. With the massive cutbacks in that program, several ships have been transferred to other government agencies.

The WORTHY was stricken from the Naval Vessel Register on 20 May 1993; she was transferred to the National Oceanic and Atmospheric Administration on 30 September 1993 and subsequently she was laid up at Redwood City, Calif. She was then planned for operation by the U.S. Geological Survey, but instead was loaned to the U.S. Army in 1995 for use as a range safety and tracking ship.

1 RANGE SUPPORT SUBMERSIBLE

Name
PC-14C-2

Builders:	Perry Oceanographics
Weight:	10,886 pounds (4,938 kg) in air
Length:	25½ feet (7.77 m)
Beam:	8 feet (2.44 m)
Draft:	8½ feet (2.59 m)
Propulsion:	1 electric motor; 2.5 shp; 1 propeller
Speed:	2 knots
Operating depth:	600 feet (183 m)
Range:	(see notes)
Manning:	1 + 1 technician

The PC-14C-2 provides deep-water search and surveillance during recovery operations on the Kwajalein missile range. The submersible is especially useful in supporting the Army's "clean lagoon" policy for Kwajalein in which all debris from re-entry vehicles is removed from the lagoon floor.

This is one of a long series of Perry Cubmarines (PC), built by the successor to the firm by that name established in 1962. The first subsequently was sold to Martin Marietta, which in turn became part of Lockheed Martin. This is believed to be the only PC-series submersible used by the U.S. government.

Engineering: Endurance is six hours, based on battery capacity.

The Army's "yellow submarine," subsequently repainted. The PC-14C-2 submersible is employed at the Kwajalein Missile Range. This is believed to be the only submersible operated by a U.S. military service other than the Navy. (U.S. Army)

Submersible PC-14C-2 (U.S. Army)

ARMY TRANSPORTATION CORPS

The Army Transportation Corps, with headquarters at Fort Eustis, Va., operates logistic support ships, landing craft, and small tugs. These ships and craft are intended to provide intra-theater transportation in forward areas.

Designations: The Army uses a ship and craft designation series derived in part from the Navy's designation scheme. The designations are:

Landing ships and landing craft populate the waterfront at Fort Eustis, near Yorktown, Va. The Army Transportation Corps operates large numbers of these ships and craft, most of which are homeported at Fort Eustis. (U.S. Army)

BC	barge, dry cargo (non-self-propelled)
BCDX	barge, deck enclosure
BD	floating crane
BDL	beach discharge lighter
BG	barge, liquid cargo (non-self-propelled)
BK	barge, dry cargo (non-self-propelled)
BPL	barge, pier, self-elevating
BR	barge, refrigerated (non-self-propelled)
FMS	floating marine repair shop (non-self-propelled)
FS	freight and supply vessel (over 100 feet/30.48 m)
FSR	freight and supply vessel, refrigerated
J	work boat (under 50 feet/15.24 m)
LARC	lighter, amphibious, resupply, cargo (amphibious)
LCM	landing craft, mechanized
LCU	landing craft, utility
LCV	landing craft, vehicle
LSV	logistic support vessel
LT	large tug (over 100 feet/30.48 m)
Q	work boat (over 50 feet/15.24 m)
ST	small tug (under 100 feet/30.48 m)
T	small freight and supply vessel (under 100 feet/30.48 m)
Y	liquid cargo vessel

Guns: No Army ships are armed.

Names: Army ships and craft are generally named for campaigns and battles in which the Army participated, except that the LT 130–series large tugs are named for signers of the American Constitution who had a military affiliation. Several battle names are carried by both Navy ships and Army craft.

Operational: Four LCUs, three LT-series tugs, ten LCMs, and one floating crane[1] are normally carried on board the Military Sealift Command–operated prepositioning ship AMERICAN CORMORANT (T-AK 2062), normally located at Diego Garcia in the Indian Ocean (see page 290).

A large number of Army ships and craft are based at the Army Transportation Center at Fort Eustis.

---

1. The crane is the non-self-propelled ALGIERS (BD 6072).

6 LOGISTIC SUPPORT VESSELS: "BESSON" CLASS

Number	Name	Launched	In service
LSV 01	GEN FRANK S. BESSON, JR.	30 June 1987	20 Jan 1988
LSV 02	CW3 HAROLD C. CLINGER[2]	16 Sep 1987	20 Apr 1988
LSV 03	GEN BREHON B. SOMERVELL	18 Nov 1987	26 July 1988
LSV 04	LT GEN WILLIAM B. BUNKER	11 Jan 1988	1 Sep 1988
LSV 05	MAJ GEN CHARLES P. GROSS	11 July 1990	30 Apr 1991
LSV 06	SP4 JAMES A. LOUX[3]	7 Apr 1994	5 July 1995

Builders:	Halter-Moss Point Marine, Escatawpa, Miss.
Displacement:	1,612 tons light
	4,199 tons full load
Tonnage:	1,800 DWT
Length:	256 feet (78.03 m) waterline
	272⅔ feet (83.14 m) overall
Beam:	60 feet (18.28 m)
Draft:	12 feet (3.66 m)
Propulsion:	2 diesel engines (General Motors EMD 16-645-E2); 3,900 bhp;
	2 shafts
Speed:	12 knots
Range:	5,500 n.miles (10,185 km) at 11 knots
Manning:	29 (6 officers + 23 seamen)
Radars:	2 SPS-64(V) navigation

These are small LST-type ships based on the Australian roll-on/roll-off ship FRANCES BAY. The U.S. ships transport vehicles and standard containers (48 TEU) or 1,815 tons of vehicles or other cargo.[4]

The LSV 3 is assigned to the Army Reserve (Tacoma, Wash.).

Classification: The Army previously referred to these ships as vehicle landing ships (LSV).

Design: These ships have an LST-like design with a superstructure aft; there is a tunnel under the superstructure to permit vehicles to drive through from the stern ramp into the open cargo well. A bow ramp is fitted. They were built to commercial shipbuilding standards.

Endurance is 38 days.

---

2. CW = Chief Warrant.
3. SP4 = Specialist 4th Class.
4. TEU = Twenty-foot (6.1-m) Equivalent Unit.

A Besson-class LSV with an empty tank deck. These are the largest bow-ramp ships in U.S. military service, except for two landing ships of the Newport (LST 1179) class operated by the Naval Reserve Force. (U.S. Navy)

Rear aspect of a Besson-class LSV, showing the stern ramp (U.S. Army)

HEAVY LIFT SHIP: C1-MT-123a TYPE

The James McHenry, a unique heavy lift ship employed by the Army primarily as a training ship for cargo handlers at Fort Story, Va., has been laid up in reserve with the James River (Va.) National Defense Reserve Fleet. The ship was placed in service in 1978.

See 16th Edition/page 547 for characteristics.

BEACH DISCHARGE LIGHTER

The large beach discharge lighter Lt Col John D. Page was taken out of service in 1989 and discarded in March 1992. The ship was configured for unloading vehicles from large cargo ships onto landing craft or causeways.

Three LCU 2000–class landing craft and other Army floating equipment forward-based at Southampton, England. Several floating cranes are in the background. (1998, Leo Van Ginderen)

35 UTILITY LANDING CRAFT: "LCU 2000" CLASS

Number	Name	Launched	In service
LCU 2001	RUNNYMEDE	14 Aug 1987	21 Feb 1990
LCU 2002	KENNESAW MOUNTAIN	6 Oct 1987	28 Feb 1990
LCU 2003	MACON	1 Feb 1988	23 Feb 1990
LCU 2004	ALDIE	Apr 1989	23 Feb 1990
LCU 2005	BRANDY STATION	May 1989	7 Mar 1990
LCU 2006	BRISTOE STATION	31 July 1989	30 Mar 1990
LCU 2007	BROAD RUN	28 Aug 1989	4 May 1990
LCU 2008	BUENA VISTA	10 Sep 1989	18 Apr 1990
LCU 2009	CALABOZA	9 Feb 1990	13 July 1990
LCU 2010	CEDAR RUN	12 Mar 1990	17 Aug 1990
LCU 2011	CHICKAHOMINY	16 Apr 1990	21 Sep 1990
LCU 2012	CHICKASAW BAYOU	26 May 1990	26 Oct 1990
LCU 2013	CHURUBUSCO	25 June 1990	Oct 1990
LCU 2014	COAMO	28 July 1990	4 Jan 1991
LCU 2015	CONTRERAS	9 Mar 1990	8 Feb 1991
LCU 2016	CORNITH	Oct 1990	15 Mar 1991
LCU 2017	EL CANEY	Nov 1990	19 Apr 1991
LCU 2018	FIVE FORKS	17 Dec 1990	24 May 1991
LCU 2019	FORT DONELSON	Jan 1991	28 June 1991
LCU 2020	FORT MCHENRY	Feb 1991	2 Aug 1991
LCU 2021	GREAT BRIDGE	1 Apr 1991	6 Sep 1991
LCU 2022	HARPERS FERRY	May 1991	11 Oct 1991
LCU 2023	HOBKIRK	June 1991	15 Nov 1991
LCU 2024	HORMIGUEROS	15 July 1991	20 Dec 1991
LCU 2025	MALVERN HILL	Aug 1991	24 Jan 1992
LCU 2026	MATAMOROS	Sep 1991	28 Feb 1992
LCU 2027	MECHANICSVILLE	Oct 1991	3 Apr 1992
LCU 2028	MISSIONARY RIDGE	Nov 1991	8 May 1992
LCU 2029	MOLINO DEL REY	7 Nov 1991	11 May 1992
LCU 2030	MONTERREY	5 Dec 1991	15 May 1992
LCU 2031	NEW ORLEANS	10 Jan 1992	1 June 1992
LCU 2032	PALO ALTO	6 Feb 1992	9 July 1992
LCU 2033	PAULUS HOOK	5 Mar 1992	18 Sep 1992
LCU 2034	PERRYVILLE	2 Apr 1992	4 Aug 1992
LCU 2035	PORT HUDSON	30 Apr 1992	1 Sep 1992

Builders:	LCU 2001–2003 Lockheed Shipbuilding, Savannah, Ga.
	LCU 2004–2035 Trinity–Moss Point Marine, Escatawpa, Miss.
Displacement:	672 tons light
	1,102 tons full load
Length:	156 feet (47.55 m) waterline
	174 feet (53.03 m) overall
Beam:	42 feet (12.8 m)
Draft:	8½ (2.6 m)
Propulsion:	2 diesel engines (Cummins KTA-50M); 2,500 bhp; 2 Kort-nozzle propellers
Speed:	11.5 knots
Range:	4,500 n.miles (8,333 km) at 11.5 knots empty
Manning:	12 (2 officers + 10 enlisted)
Radars:	1 SPS-64(V)2 navigation

These are large landing craft with a deckhouse aft; they are too large to be carried by Navy amphibious ships with docking wells (as the smaller LCU designs can be). These craft have replaced the LCU 1466–class landing craft with a single exception when this edition of *Ships and Aircraft* went to press.

These craft have a bow ramp for unloading onto the beach (beaching draft forward is 4 feet/1.2 m).

The first three units were completed at Trinity Marine after the demise of the Lockheed shipbuilding yard.

Class: LCU 2001–2007 were ordered in 1986; LCU 2008–2017 in 1987; LCU 2018–2023 in 1988; and LCU 2024–2035 in 1989. Two additional craft were authorized but not ordered; they were to have been named SACKETS HARBOR and SAYLER'S CREEK.

Design: The craft were built to commercial shipbuilding standards specifically for the U.S. Army. All other U.S. LCU/LSU types were built to Navy designs.

Engineering: These craft have a 300-shp bow thruster.

Names: The LCU 2009 originally was named CALABOZA.

LCU 2000–class landing craft (U.S. Army)

13 UTILITY LANDING CRAFT: "LCU 1610" CLASS

Number	Name	Number	Name
LCU 1667	MANASSAS	LCU 1674	ST. MICHIEL
LCU 1668	BELLEAU-WOOD	LCU 1675	COMMANDO
LCU 1669	MARSEILLES	LCU 1676	BIRMINGHAM
LCU 1670	SAN ISIDRO	LCU 1677	BRANDYWINE
LCU 1671	CATAWBA FORD	LCU 1678	NAHA
LCU 1672	BUSH MASTER	LCU 1679	CHATEAU-THIERRY
LCU 1673	DOUBLE EAGLE		

Builders:	General Ship & Engine Works, East Boston, Mass.
Displacement:	190 tons light
	390 tons full load
Length:	134¾ feet (41.1 m) overall
Beam:	29¾ feet (9.1 m)
Draft:	6¹¹⁄₁₂ feet (2.1 m)
Propulsion:	4 diesel engines (General Motors Detroit 6-71); 1,200 bhp; 2 Kort-nozzle propellers
Speed:	11 knots
Range:	1,200 n.miles (2,222 km) at 11 knots empty
	1,200 n.miles (2,222 km) at 8 knots loaded
Manning:	6 (enlisted)
Troops:	8
Radars:	1 LN-66 or SPS-53 navigation

These are Navy-designed LCUs completed in 1976–1978.

The COMMANDO has been modified to serve as a diver support ship; she is assigned to the Army's 558th Transportation Company at Fort Eustis.

Class: This class originally consisted of hull numbers LCU 1610–1624 and 1627–1681; many still serve in the Navy (see chapter 19).

Design: These craft have vehicle unloading ramps forward and aft.

Names: Note that the Army spells BELLEAU-WOOD with a hyphen; the Navy's LHA 3 with the same name does not have a hyphen.

The SAN ISIDRO, showing the starboard-side bridge structure of this class, which is used by the Army as well as by the U.S. Navy and several foreign nations (1989, Leo Van Ginderen)

1 UTILITY LANDING CRAFT: "LCU 1466" CLASS

Number	Name
LCU 1509	ANTIETAM

Builders:	
Displacement:	180 tons light
	347 tons full load
Length:	119 feet (39.0 m) overall
Beam:	34 feet (10.4 m)
Draft:	6 feet (1.8 m)
Propulsion:	3 geared diesel engines (Gray Marine 64 YTL); 675 bhp; 3 shafts
Speed:	8 knots
Range:	700 n.miles (1,300 km) at 7 knots with payload
Manning:	6 (enlisted)
Troops:	8
Guns:	removed
Radars:	navigation

All but one of the 42 landing craft of this class built for the U.S. Army have been disposed of. These were the survivors of a large class of Navy-designed LCUs. Two still serve in the Navy (see page 197).

Class: This class covered hull numbers LCU 1466–1609, with 14 units constructed in Japan. Numerous units were transferred to other nations; others became Navy service craft (YFU).

Three craft of this class have been converted to floating cranes:

LCU 1466	converted to BD 6805 CASABLANCA
LCU 1514	converted to BD . . .
LCU 1579	converted to BD 6806 BULL RUN

1 FERRYBOAT

Number	Name
FB 186	JERA

This is a small ferryboat employed at the Army's test facility at Kwajalein atoll.

96 MECHANIZED LANDING CRAFT: LCM(8) MOD 1 TYPE

Weight:	varies 34.0–36.5 tons light
	111–121 tons full load
Length:	73⁷/₁₂ feet (22.4 m) overall
Beam:	21 feet (6.4 m)
Draft:	4⁷/₁₂ feet (1.4 m) aft
Propulsion:	2 diesel engines (General Motors Detroit 6-71); 600 bhp; 2 shafts
	(see notes)
Speed:	12 knots empty
	9.2 knots loaded
Range:	150 n.miles (278 km) at 12 knots empty
	150 n.miles (278 km) at 9.2 knots loaded
Manning:	2 to 4 (enlisted)

These are standard landing craft intended to carry vehicles and cargo. Capacity is about 60 tons of cargo. No accommodations are provided in these craft.

These craft were completed between 1954 and 1972. They are deployed at Army bases around the world; some are in reserve.

LCM(8)-type landing craft (Leo Van Ginderen)

LANDING AIR-CUSHION VEHICLE CRAFT

The Army's LAMP-H enlarged, advanced prototype vehicle capable of carrying 89 tons of cargo was canceled on 18 October 1991, prior to completion. The craft had been ordered in 1990.

Subsequently, the 26 LACV in Army service were offered for sale in 1994.

The Army's air-cushion landing craft were based at Fort Story, Va., and were intended for the ship-to-shore movement of troops and equipment. The Army used the term Logistics-Over-The-Shore (LOTS) for this evolution.

See 15th Edition/page 601 for characteristics.

23 LARC LX–TYPE AMPHIBIOUS VEHICLES

Weight:	88 tons empty
	190 tons loaded
Length:	62½ feet (19.07 m) overall
Beam:	26½ feet (8.1 m)
Propulsion:	4 diesel engines; 6600 bhp; 2 propellers
Speed:	6.5 knots water
	15 mph land
Range:	75 n.miles (140 km) water at 6 knots
Manning:	8 (enlisted)
Troops:	125

These four-wheel/propeller driven vehicles are the successors to the DUKW "duck" amphibious trucks of World War II fame. They were introduced into amphibious landings by the U.S. Army in Operation Huskey, the 1943 Allied landings on Sicily.

The vehicles retained by the Army are designated LX 06, 18, 16–18, 20, 27, 37, 38, 40, 41, 43, 46–50, and 52–57; all are based in California.

These LARCs have a 60-ton normal load; 100 tons maximum. They have limited mobility.

All other amphibious wheeled vehicles have been discarded.

LARC LX 16 carrying a fuel truck (U.S. Army)

6 LARGE HARBOR TUGS: LT 128 CLASS

Number	Name	Launched	In service
LT 801	MAJ GEN NATHANAEL GREEN	4 July 1989	6 Mar 1994
LT 802	MAJ GEN HENRY KNOX	Oct 1989	7 May 1994
LT 803	MAJ GEN ANTHONY WAYNE	2 Aug 1990	7 May 1994
LT 804	BRIG GEN ZEBULON PIKE		30 Sep 1994
LT 805	MAJ GEN WINFIELD SCOTT		30 Sep 1994
LT 806	COL SETH WARNER	16 Dec 1993	15 Nov 1994

Builders:	Trinity/Halter Marine, Moss Point, Miss.
Displacement:	924 tons full load
Length:	128 feet (39.01 m) overall
Beam:	36 feet (10.97 m)
Draft:	15½ feet (4.73 m)
Propulsion:	2 diesel engines (General Motors EMD 12-645 FM8); 5,100 bhp; 2 shafts
Speed:	12 knots
Range:	5,000 n.miles (9,260 km) at 12 knots
Manning:	
Radars:	2 . . . navigation

Construction of this series of large tugs was delayed, with several units canceled (see below).

Builders: Contracts for these tugs were awarded beginning in 1988 to the Robert E. Derecktor yard at Middletown, R.I., by the Navy on behalf of the Army. The lead unit was "conditionally" delivered to the Army on 30 August 1991, with the yard responsible for correcting certain deficiencies. Subsequently, on 3 January 1992 the Derecktor yard filed for bankruptcy protection. The contract was then transferred to the Trinity/Marine yard, which completed all six units.

Class: The Army originally envisioned a class of 13 tugs of this design. Two additional ships were named—Sgt Maj John Champe (LT 807) and Maj Gen Jacob Brown (LT 808).

LT 128–class large harbor tug (U.S. Army)

17 LARGE HARBOR TUGS: LT 100 CLASS

Number	Name	Number	Name
LT 1937	Sgt William W. Seay	LT 1977	Attleboro
LT 1953	Salerno	LT 2076	New Guinea
LT 1956	Fredericksburg	LT 2081	San Sapor*
LT 1960	Lundy's Lane	LT 2085	Anzio*
LT 1970	Okinawa	LT 2088	Petersburg
LT 1971	Normandy	LT 2090	Sp4 Larry G. Dahl*
LT 1972	Gettysburg	LT 2092	North Africa*
LT 1973	Shiloh*	LT 2096	Valley Forge*
LT 1974	Champagne-Marne*		

  * Re-engined (see *Engineering* below)

Builders:	
Displacement:	295 tons light
	390 tons full load
Length:	107 feet (32.61 m) overall
Beam:	26½ feet (8.08 m)
Draft:	12⅙ feet (3.71 m)
Propulsion:	1 diesel engine (Fairbanks Morse); 1,200 bhp; 1 shaft
Speed:	12.75 knots
Range:	3,325 n.miles (6,160 km) at 12 knots
Manning:	16 (enlisted)

Sixty-five tugs of this design were built in the 1950s (LT 1936–1977, 2202, and 2075–2096). The survivors will be discarded during the next few years.

Engineering: Seven units (indicated by asterisks) were re-engined at Hythe, England, between 1995 and 1998, being refitted with a single General Electric EMD 12V-645-E7 diesel engine (2,350 bhp); those tugs have increased towing capability.

LT 100–class large harbor tug (U.S. Army)

9 + 6 SMALL TUGS: ST 900 CLASS

Number	Name	Launched	Delivered
ST 901	Dorchester Heights	Apr 1998	Sep 1998
ST 902	Pelham Point	May 1998	Dec 1999
ST 903	Fort Stanwix	Aug 1998	Dec 1999
ST 904	Green Springs	Oct 1998	Dec 1999
ST 905	Scholarie	Jan 1999	Mar 2000
ST 906	Sag Harbor	Apr 1999	Mar 2000
ST 907	Appomattox	Nov 1999	Mar 2000
ST 908	Sackets Harbor	Jan 2000	2000
ST 909	Bunker Hill	2000	2000
ST 910	. . . . . .		
ST 911	. . . . . .		
ST 912	. . . . . .		

Builders:	Orange Shipbuilding, Texas
Displacement:	110 tons light
Length:	59⅔ feet (18.19 m) overall
Beam:	22⅔ feet (6.90 m)
Draft:	6⅔ feet (2.03 m)
Propulsion:	2 diesel engines (Cummins KTA 19-M3); 1,280 bhp; 2 shafts (with Kaplan swiveling propellers)
Speed:	8 knots
Range:	
Manning:	5 or 6 (enlisted)

These are small pusher tugs, carried aboard Lighter Aboard Ship (LASH) vessels for forward-area operations and for use on rivers and inland waterways.

Three additional units are under construction (funds released in 2000) and three more are planned pending the availability of funds.

Design: Reinforced steel is provided in watertight bulkheads to enhance survivability if hit by small-arms fire. A stowage locker for M16 rifles is provided and, when forward deployed, the crews will be armed.

Engineering: Designed speed was eight knots. The Dorchester reached 10.5 knots on trials.

Names: All but the ST 908 carry names of recently discarded Army tugs.

The U.S. Army's small tug FORT STANWIX, showing the compact design of these highly maneuverable craft. These craft are designed specifically to be carried aboard larger ships to forward areas. (1999, Orange Shipbuilding)

11 SMALL TUGS: ST 65 CLASS

Number	Name	Number	Name
ST 1988	BEMIS HEIGHTS	ST 2124	QUAKER HILL
ST 1990	MOHAWK VALLEY	ST 2126	STONY POINT
ST 1993	COWPENS	ST 2130	FORT MIFFLIN
ST 2104	MONMOUTH	ST 2199	VALCOUR ISLAND
ST 2118	GUILFORD COURT HOUSE	ST 2201	FALMOUTH
ST 2123	NINETY-SIX		

Builders:
Displacement: 100 tons light
              122 tons full load
Length: 69¹¹/₁₂ feet (21.31 m) overall
Beam: 19½ feet (5.94 m)
Draft: 8⅙ feet (2.5 m)
Propulsion: 1 diesel engine; 600 bhp; 1 shaft
Speed: 12 knots
Range: 3,500 n.miles (6,480 km) at 12 knots
Manning: 6 (enlisted)

These are the survivors of a large class of Army tugs built in the 1950s. Some units stricken in the early 1990s were in storage at Hythe (Kent), England.

The MOHAWK VALLEY high and dry for maintenance (1995, Leo Van Ginderen)

2 SMALL TUGS

Number	Number
ST 2154	ST3000

Builders:
Displacement: 25.2 tons light
              29 tons full load
Length: 45⅙ feet (13.77 m) overall
Beam: 12⅝ feet (3.91 m)
Draft: 6 feet (1.83 m)
Propulsion: 1 diesel engine; 170 bhp; 1 shaft
Speed: 10 knots
Range: 700 n.miles (1,300 km) at 10 knots
Manning: 4 (enlisted)

These are small, unnamed tugs built in the 1950s.

SMALL AND NON-SELF-PROPELLED CRAFT

The Army Transportation Corps operates a large number of small craft, floating cranes, and barges. The largest are the floating cranes listed below.

4 + 2 FLOATING CRANES: "KEYSTONE STATE" CLASS

Number	Name	Launched	Delivered
BD 6801	KEYSTONE STATE	June 1997	May 1998
BD 6802	SALTILLO	June 1998	Apr 1999
BD 6803	SPRINGFIELD	Jan 1999	Mar 2000
BD 6804	DELAWARE	Nov 1999	2000

Builders: Bollinger Shipyards, Lockport, La.
Displacement:
Length: 200 feet (60.98 m) overall
Beam: 80 feet (24.39 m)
Draft: 14¼ feet (4.34 m)
Propulsion: non-self-propelled (see Design notes)
Manning: 15 (2 officers + 13 enlisted)

These are massive derricks intended to lift heavy cargo from ships in ports that do not have heavy lift facilities. Their secondary role is salvage and harbor and channel clearance in forward areas.

There are options for two additional floating cranes of this type.

Design: These craft have three cranes with lift capacities of 115 tons, 25 tons, and 5 tons.

There are accommodations for a crew of two warrant officers and 13 enlisted men; the craft have berthing, galley, mess hall, medical, and laundry facilities, plus communications equipment. Power is supplied by a 1,200-bhp diesel engine.

KEYSTONE STATE–class floating crane under tow (U.S. Army)

KEYSTONE STATE–class floating crane under tow (U.S. Army)

ENVIRONMENTAL PROTECTION AGENCY

The Environmental Protection Agency (EPA) operates two major research ships and numerous small craft to monitor environmental conditions in inland waterways and off the U.S. coasts.

1 RESEARCH SHIP: EX-NAVY GUNBOAT

Number	Name	FY	Launched	USN comm.	To EPA
(ex-PG 86)	PETER W. ANDERSON	63	18 June 1966	4 Nov 1967	17 Jan 1978

Builders:	Tacoma Boatbuilding, Wash.
Displacement:	approx. 250 tons full load
Length:	164½ feet (50.2 m) overall
Beam:	23¾ feet (7.28 m)
Draft:	9½ feet (2.9 m)
Propulsion:	2 diesel engines (Cummins VT12-875M); 1,400 bhp; 2 shafts
Speed:	16 knots
Range:	2,400 n.miles (4,445 km) at 14 knots on diesel engines
	325 n.miles (602 km) at 37 knots on gas turbines
Manning:	30 (civilian contractor)

The ANDERSON is a former ASHEVILLE-class patrol combatant/gunboat now employed in the pollution research role. Three sister ships serve as Navy research ships with the David Taylor Research Center (see chapter 24).

This ship was decommissioned as a Navy gunboat on 1 October 1977 and transferred to the EPA in 1978. She operates off the U.S. Atlantic coast.

All weapons have been removed.

Class: The ANDERSON is from a class of 17 units. The CROCKETT (PG 88), previously operated by the EPA, is now a museum at Muskegon, Mich.

Design: The ship has an aluminum hull with fiberglass superstructure. For the research role, she has been fitted with three laboratories and a computer center.

Names: The ANDERSON was named ANTELOPE (PG 86) in naval service; she was renamed in June 1985.

Operational: Under EPA the ship originally operated on the Great Lakes; she is now based at Annapolis, Md.

Propulsion: Originally a CODOG-propelled ship, the gas turbine has been removed.

PETER W. ANDERSON (1996, EPA, Stelian Codaracea)

PETER W. ANDERSON (1992, Giorgio Arra)

1 RESEARCH SHIP: EX–COAST GUARD BUOY TENDER

Number	Name	Launched	USCG comm.	To EPA
(ex-WAGL 234)	ROGER R. SIMONS	29 Apr 1939	June 1939	1974

Builders:	Marine Iron and Shipbuilding, Duluth, Minn.
Displacement:	342 tons full load
Length:	122¼ feet (37.26 m) overall
Beam:	27 feet (8.23 m)
Draft:	7½ feet (2.29 m)
Propulsion:	2 diesel engines (Superior); 430 bhp; 2 shafts
Speed:	10 knots
Range:	3,500 n.miles (6,480 km) at 6 knots
Manning:	

A former Coast Guard buoy tender employed by the EPA in pollution survey and water studies, this ship was decommissioned and stricken by the Coast Guard on 1 June 1973 and transferred to the U.S. Navy on 8 August 1973; she was transferred to the EPA in 1974.

Names: The Coast Guard name was MAPLE (WAGL 234).

Operational: Based at Cleveland, Ohio, on Lake Erie, for monitoring activities on the Great Lakes.

GEOLOGICAL SURVEY

The Geological Survey of the Department of Interior previously operated one major research ship, the former Navy survey ship S. P. LEE (ex-U.S. Navy AG 192, T-AGS 31). She was returned to the Navy from the Geological Survey on 1 August 1992; the ship was stricken from the Naval Vessel Register on 1 October 1992 and transferred to Mexico on 7 December 1992.

The LEE was built as a naval surveying ship and placed in service with the Military Sealift Command (with a USNS prefix) upon completion in 1968. The ship was reclassified as a miscellaneous research ship (AG 192) on 25 September 1970. She was taken out of naval service on 29 January 1973 and was transferred on loan to the National Geological Survey on 27 February 1974.

Under the Geological Survey, the LEE conducted deep-sea seismic surveys, seafloor coring, and seafloor bottom sampling.

NATIONAL SCIENCE FOUNDATION

The National Science Foundation (NSF)—an independent government agency to "promote the progress of science," including in the area of national defense—operates two large polar research and support ships.

1 POLAR RESEARCH SHIP: "NATHANIEL B. PALMER"

Number	Name	Launched	Delivered
(none)	NATHANIEL B. PALMER	28 Jan 1992	13 Mar 1992

Builders:	North American Shipbuilding, Larose, La.
Displacement:	6,800 tons full load
Length:	308 feet (93.9 m) overall
Beam:	60 feet (18.29 m)
Draft:	22½ feet (6.86 m)
Propulsion:	4 diesel engines (Caterpillar); 12,720 bhp; 2 shafts
Speed:	15 knots
Range:	
Manning:	34 + 37 scientists

This ship was built specifically for NSF operations in the Antarctic. Both the PALMER and GOULD (below) have a very high standard of habitability and food service.

Design: The ship has an icebreaking hull with a rating of 3 feet (0.9 m) breaking capability. A helicopter deck and hangar are provided.

At-sea endurance is 75 days.

The NATHANIEL B. PALMER in Antarctic waters. This ship and the LAURENCE M. GOULD have red hulls, as do the Coast Guard's oceangoing icebreakers. Note that the funnel is offset to port; an enclosed crow's nest is provided. (NSF, Stuart Klipper)

NATHANIEL B. PALMER

1 POLAR RESEARCH AND SUPPLY SHIP: "LAURENCE M. GOULD"

Number	Name	Launched	Delivered
(none)	LAURENCE M. GOULD	11 Dec 1997	16 Jan 1998

Builders:	North American Shipbuilding, Larose, La.
Displacement:	2,755 tons standard
	3,780 tons full load
Length:	212 feet (64.7 m) waterline
	230 feet (70.2 m) overall
Beam:	46 feet (14.0 m)
Draft:	25¾ feet (5.8 m)
Propulsion:	2 diesel engines (Caterpillar 3606); 4,575 bhp; 2 shafts
Speed:	
Range:	
Manning:	25 + 26 scientists

LAURENCE M. GOULD

The GOULD was constructed specifically to support NSF operations in the Antarctic, replacing the POLAR DUKE in that role.

Design: The GOULD has an icebreaking hull. Endurance is 75 days at sea.

ARCTIC RESEARCH SHIP: "POLAR DUKE"

The POLAR DUKE, a Norwegian-built research ship launched in 1983, was built specifically for the National Science Foundation. She was in NSF service from 1985 to 1997, when replaced by the more capable LAURENCE M. GOULD.

See 16th Edition/page 546 for characteristics.

AIR FORCE

The Air Force previously operated a large number of small craft, all managed by the San Antonio Air Logistics Center at Kelly Air Force Base in Texas. Most of these were missile and drone recovery boats, also used for rescue, up to 117⅓ feet (35.78 m) in length. They have been discarded or transferred to other agencies, with few small craft remaining in Air Force service.

See chapter 24 in this volume and 16th Edition/pages 552–553 for data on these craft.

APPENDIX A

Navy Force Levels, 1945–2000

The following are ships in active commission as of the end of the fiscal year indicated; beginning in 1965, operational Naval Reserve/ Naval Reserve Force (NRF) ships manned by composite active-reserve crews are indicated by the plus (+) symbol.

Large frigate-type ships (DL/DLG/DLGN) are listed separately prior to 1975; from that year, they are included with missile cruisers and destroyers based on their reclassification in that year (see chapter 15).

Ship Type	1945	1950	1953ᵃ	1955	1960	1965	1970	1975	1980	1985	1990	1995	2000
Submarines—*conventional*													
SS-SSK-SSR	237	73	122	121	131	83	59	11	6	4	—	—	—
SSG	—	—	1	2	4	—	—	—	—	—	—	—	—
auxiliaryᵇ	—	—	7	18	20	15	26	2	1	1	1	1	1
Submarines—*nuclear*													
SSN-SSRN	—	—	—	1	7	22	48	64	73	94ᶜ	87	77	54
SSGN	—	—	—	—	1	—	—	—	—	—	—	—	—
SSBN	—	—	—	—	2	29	41	41	40	37	34	16	18
auxiliaryᵈ	—	—	—	—	—	—	—	—	—	2	2	2	1
(total submarines)	(237)	(73)	(130)	(142)	(165)	(149)	(174)	(118)	(120)	(138)	(124)	(96)	(74)
Aircraft carriers													
CVB-CVA-CVAN-CV-CVN	20	7	17	16	14	16	15	15	13	13	12	11+1ᵉ	12
CVS	—	—	—	5	9	9	4	—	—	—	—	—	—
CVL	8	4	5	1	—	—	—	—	—	—	—	—	—
CVE	70	4	17	3	—	—	—	—	—	—	—	—	—
Battleships													
BB	25ᶠ	1	4	3	—	—	—	—	—	2	3	—	—
Cruisers													
CAG-CG-CLG-CGN	—	—	—	—	6	12	10	27	27	30	43	32	27
CA (8-inch guns)	24	9	15	10	6	2	2	—	—	—	—	—	—
CL (6-inch guns)	42	3	3	3	—	—	—	—	—	—	—	—	—
CLAA (5-inch guns)	6	1	1	—	—	—	—	—	—	—	—	—	—
Frigatesᵍ													
DL	—	—	—	5	5	5	—	—	—	—	—	—	—
DLG-DLGN	—	—	—	—	4	20	20	—	—	—	—	—	—
Destroyersʰ													
DD-DDE-DDK-DDR	372	142	246	244	211	189+17	122	32	43	31+1	31	31	24
DDG	—	—	—	—	1	33	37	38	37	37	22	17	31
Escort Ships/Frigates													
DE-DER/FF-FFRⁱ	365	11	89	64	41	39+21	41	58	59	53+6	36+12	—	—
DEG/FFG	—	—	—	—	—	—	6	6	13	47+4	35+16	15+14	27+8
Flagships/Command Ships													
AGC-CC-CLC-LCC-AGF	18ᵏ	6	}226ᵐ	}175ᵐ	}113ᵐ	7	3	3	3	4	4	4	4
Amphibious Ships	~3,300	83				132	95	62	58+5	58+2	59+3	37+2	37+2

ᵃ End of Korean War (June 1953).
ᵇ Does not include the nuclear-propelled research vehicle NR-1, completed in 1969, but does include two SSNs employed as special operations transports.
ᶜ Beginning in 1983, SSNs were armed with Tomahawk anti-ship and land-attack cruise missiles (TASM and TLAM, respectively).
ᵈ Includes transport submarines.
ᵉ The NRF carrier was the JOHN F. KENNEDY (CV 67).
ᶠ The 1945 force included two large cruisers (designated CB); they were often referred to as battle cruisers (armed with 12-inch guns).
ᵍ Frigates (DL-DLG-DLGN) were reclassified as CG-CGN-DDG in 1975.
ʰ Additional destroyer-type ships were employed as mine warfare ships (DM-DMS-MMD) until 1958; they retained most of their guns and some ASW weapons.
ⁱ Includes one AGDE-AGFF from 1966 until classified as an FF in 1975.
ᵏ In addition, six large Coast Guard cutters were configured as amphibious force flagships.
ᵐ Includes amphibious force flagships (AGC).

APPENDIX B

Navy Shipbuilding Programs, Fiscal 1947–2000

This appendix lists U.S. Navy shipbuilding programs since World War II. Only those ships actually constructed are listed, except where noted; ships transferred to other navies upon completion are not included.

The SCB (Ships Characteristics Board) numbers are sequential for Navy ship designs reaching the advanced planning stage; they were numbered in a single series from 1947 (SCB No. 1 was the NORFOLK/CLK 1, later DL 1) through 1964 (SCB No. 252 was the FLAGSTAFF/PGH 1). From 1964 on, the SCB used numbered blocks: 001–099 for cruisers, 100–199 for carriers, 200–299 for destroyers/frigates (DL), 300–399 for submarines, 400–499 for amphibious vessels, 500–599 for mine warfare vessels, 600–699 for patrol ships and craft, 700–799 for auxiliary ships, 800–899 for service craft, and 900–999 for special purpose vessels. The later number series have a suffix of the fiscal year of the first ship, as 303.70 for the LOS ANGELES (SSN 688)—the first submarine under the new system ordered in fiscal year 1970.

Number	Class name	SCB No.	Notes
Fiscal Year 1947			
2 SS 563, 564	TANG	2	
Fiscal Year 1948			
2 SS 565, 566	TANG	2	
1 SSK 1	K-1	35	
(1) CVA 58	UNITED STATES	6A	construction canceled
1 CLK 1	NORFOLK	1	completed as DL 1
(1) CLK 2	NORFOLK	1	construction canceled
4 DD 927–930	MITSCHER	5	completed as DL 2–5
Fiscal Year 1949			
2 SS 567, 568	TANG	2	
2 SSK 2, 3	K-1	35	
Fiscal Year 1950			
1 AGSS 569	ALBACORE	56	
1 MSO 421	AGILE	45A	
Fiscal Year 1951			
1 SSN 571	NAUTILUS	64	
1 SST 1	MACKEREL	68	
28 MSO 422–449	AGILE	45A	
Fiscal Year 1952			
1 SSN 575	SEAWOLF	64A	
2 SSR 572, 573	SALMON	84	changed to SS
1 SST 2	MACKEREL	68	
1 CVA 59	FORRESTAL	80	changed to CV/AVT 59
1 DE 1006	DEALEY	72	
1 IFS 1	CARRONADE	37	changed to LFS 1
4 LSD 28–31	THOMASTON	75	
15 LST 1156–1170	TERREBONNE PARISH	9	
20 MSO 455–474	AGILE	45A	
2 MSC 121, 122	BLUEBIRD	69	
1 AGB 4	GLACIER	11A	changed to WAGB 4
6 AO 143–148	NEOSHO	82	
Fiscal Year 1953			
1 SSG 574	GRAYBACK	161	changed to LPSS 574
1 CVA 60	FORRESTAL	80	changed to CV 60
3 DD 931–933	FORREST SHERMAN	85	
2 DE 1014, 1015	DEALEY	72	
9 MSO 488–496	AGILE	45A	

Number	Class name	SCB No.	Notes
20 MSC 190–199, 201, 203–209, 289, 290	BLUEBIRD	69	
2 AF 58, 59	RIGEL	97	
Fiscal Year 1954			
1 SS 576	DARTER	116	
1 CVA 61	FORRESTAL	80	changed to CV 61
3 DD 936–938	FORREST SHERMAN	85	
2 DE 1021, 1022	DEALEY	72	
2 LSD 32, 33	THOMASTON	75	
1 LST 1171	DE SOTO COUNTY	119	
1 MHC 43	BITTERN	109	
4 MSO 508–511	ACME	45A	
2 AE 21, 22	SURIBACHI	114	
Fiscal Year 1955			
1 SSG 577	GRAYBACK	161	
2 SSN 578, 579	SKATE	121	
1 CVA 62	FORRESTAL	80	changed to CV 62
5 DD 940–944	FORREST SHERMAN	85	
8 DE 1023–1030	DEALEY	72	
2 LSD 34, 35	THOMASTON	75	
6 LST 1173–1178	DE SOTO COUNTY	119	
2 T-AOG 81, 82	ALATNA	—	
Fiscal Year 1956			
3 SS 580–582	BARBEL	150	
2 SSN 583, 584	SKATE	121	
1 SSN 585	SKIPJACK	154	
1 SSRN 586	TRITON	132	changed to SS 586
1 SSGN 587	HALIBUT	137A	changed to SS 587
1 CVA 63	KITTY HAWK	127	changed to CV 63
6 DLG 6–11	COONTZ	142	changed to DDG 37–42
7 DD 945–951	FORREST SHERMAN	85	
2 DE 1033, 1034	CLAUD JONES	131	
2 AE 23, 24	SURIBACHI	114A	
Fiscal Year 1957			
5 SSN 588–592	SKIPJACK	154	
1 SSN 593	THRESHER	188	
1 CVA 64	KITTY HAWK	127A	changed to CV 64
1 CLGN 160	LONG BEACH	169	completed as CGN 9
4 DLG 12–15	COONTZ	142	changed to DDG 43–46
8 DD 952–959	CHARLES F. ADAMS	155	completed as DDG 2–9
2 DE 1035	CLAUD JONES	131	
1 AE 25	SURIBACHI	114A	
Fiscal Year 1958			
3 SSN 594–596	THRESHER[a]	188	originally ordered as SSGN 594–596 (SCB No. 166A)
1 SSN 597	TULLIBEE	178	
3 SSBN 598–600	GEORGE WASHINGTON	180A	
1 CVAN 65	ENTERPRISE	160	changed to CVN 65
3 DLG 16–18	LEAHY	172	changed to CG 16–18
5 DDG 10–14	CHARLES F. ADAMS	155	
1 LPH 2	IWO JIMA	157	
Fiscal Year 1959			
2 SSBN 601, 602	GEORGE WASHINGTON	180A	
5 SSN 603–607	THRESHER	188	1 unit originally planned as SSGN (SCB No. 166A)

Number		Class name	SCB No.	Notes
4	SSBN 608–611	ETHAN ALLEN	180	
6	DLG 19–24	LEAHY	172	changed to CG 19–24
1	DLGN 25	BAINBRIDGE	189	changed to CGN 25
5	DDG 15–19	ADAMS	155	
1	LPD 1	RALEIGH	187	
1	LPH 3	IWO JIMA	157	
Fiscal Year 1960				
4	SSN 612–615	THRESHER	188	
3	DDG 20–22	ADAMS	155	
2	DE 1037, 1038	BRONSTEIN	199	changed to FF 1037, 1038
1	PCH 1	HIGH POINT	202	
1	LPD 2	RALEIGH	187	
1	LPH 7	IWO JIMA	157	
2	AGOR 3, 4	CONRAD	185	academic ships
1	AS 31	HUNLEY	194	
Fiscal Year 1961				
1	SSBN 618	ETHAN ALLEN	180	
4	SSBN 616, 617, 619, 620	LAFAYETTE	216	
1	SSN 621	THRESHER	188	
5	SSBN 622–626	LAFAYETTE	216	FY 1961 supplemental
1	AGSS 555	DOLPHIN	207	
1	CVA 66	KITTY HAWK	127B	changed to CV 66
3	DLG 26–28	BELKNAP	212	changed to CG 26–28
2	DDG 23, 24	ADAMS	155	
2	DE 1040, 1041	GARCIA	199A	changed to FF 1040, 1041
1	LPD 3	RALEIGH	187	changed to AGF 3
1	AG 163	GLOVER	198	completed as AGDE 1; changed to FF 1098/ AGFF 1
1	AFS 1	MARS	208	
2	T-AGOR 5, 6	CONRAD	185	academic ships
1	AOE 1	SACRAMENTO	196	
Fiscal Year 1962				
3	SSN 637–639	STURGEON	188A	
10	SSBN 627–636	LAFAYETTE	216	
6	DLG 29–34	BELKNAP	212	changed to CG 29–34
1	DLGN 35	TRUXTUN	222	changed to CGN 35
3	DE 1043–1045	GARCIA	199A	changed to FF 1043–1045
3	DEG 1–3	BROOKE	199B	changed to FFG 1–3
1	LPD 4–6	AUSTIN	187B	
1	LPH 9	IWO JIMA	157	
1	AFS 2	MARS	208	
1	AGEH 1	PLAINVIEW	219	
1	T-AGOR 7	CONRAD	185	
1	T-AGS 25	KELLAR	214	
1	AS 32	HUNLEY	194	
Fiscal Year 1963				
8	SSN 646–653	STURGEON	188A	
6	SSBN 640–645	LAFAYETTE	216	
1	CVA 67	JOHN F. KENNEDY	127C	
5	DE 1047–1051	GARCIA	199A	changed to FF 1047–1051
3	DEG 4–6	BROOKE	199B	changed to FFG 4–6
4	LPD 7–10	AUSTIN	187B	
1	LPH 10	IWO JIMA	157	
1	T-AK 278	METEOR	236	changed to T-LSV/T-AKR 9
2	PGM 84, 85	ASHEVILLE	229	changed to PG 84, 85
2	AGOR 9, 10	CONRAD	185	academic ships
1	T-AGS 26	SILAS BENT	226	
1	AOE 2	SACRAMENTO	196	
1	AS 33	SIMON LAKE	238	
Fiscal Year 1964				
5	SSN 660–664	STURGEON	188A	
1	SSN 671	NARWHAL	245	
6	SSBN 654–659	LAFAYETTE	216	
10	DE 1052–1061	KNOX	199C	changed to FF 1052–1061
3	LPD 11–13	AUSTIN	187C	LPD 11 changed to AGF 11
2	PGM 86, 87	ASHEVILLE	229	changed to PG 86, 87
1	AD 37	SAMUEL GOMPERS	244	
1	AFS 3	MARS	208	
1	T-AGS 27	SILAS BENT	226	
1	AS 34	SIMON LAKE	238	
Fiscal Year 1965				
6	SSN 665–670	STURGEON	188M	
16	DE 1062–1077	KNOX	200	new SCB series; changed to FF 1062–1077

Number		Class name	SCB No.	Notes
1	AGC 19	BLUE RIDGE	400	changed to LCC 19
4	AKA 113–116	CHARLESTON	403	changed to LKA 113–116
2	LPD 14, 15	AUSTIN	402	new SCB series
1	LPH 11	IWO JIMA	157	
1	LSD 36	ANCHORAGE	404	new SCB series
1	LST 1179	NEWPORT	405	new SCB series
3	PGM 88–90	ASHEVILLE	600	new SCB series; changed to PG 88–90
1	AD 38	SAMUEL GOMPERS	700	new SCB series
2	AE 26, 27	KILAUEA	703	new SCB series
2	AFS 4, 5	MARS	705	new SCB series
2	T-AGOR 12, 13	CONRAD	710	new SCB series
1	AGS 29	CHAUVENET	723	built in Scotland
1	T-AGS 31	KELLAR	709	
1	AOE 3	SACRAMENTO	196	
2	AOR 1, 2	WICHITA	707	
(1)	AS 35	SIMON LAKE	738	*canceled*
1	AS 36	L. Y. SPEAR	702	
Fiscal Year 1966				
6	SSN 672–677	STURGEON	188M	
10	DE 1078–1087	KNOX	200	changed to FF 1078–1087
1	AGC 20	MOUNT WHITNEY	400	changed to LCC 20
1	LKA 117	CHARLESTON	403	changed to LKA 117
1	LPH 12	IWO JIMA	157	
3	LSD 37–39	ANCHORAGE	404	
8	LST 1180–1187	NEWPORT	405	
2	PGH 1, 2	FLAGSTAFF/TUCUMCARI	601	competitive prototypes
10	PGM 92–101	ASHEVILLE	600	changed to PG 92–101
2	AE 28, 29	KILAUEA	703	
1	AFS 6	MARS	705	
2	AGOR 14, 15	MELVILLE	710	academic ships
1	T-AGS 32	CHAUVENET	723	built in Scotland
1	AOE 4	SACRAMENTO	196	
2	AOR 3,4	WICHITA	707	
1	AS 37	L. Y. SPEAR	702	
1	ATS 1	EDENTON	719	built in England
Fiscal Year 1967				
5	SSN 678–682	STURGEON	188M	
1	CVAN 68	NIMITZ	102	changed to CVN 68
1	DLGN 36	CALIFORNIA	241	changed to CGN 36
10	DE 1088–1097	KNOX	200	changed to FF 1088–1097
1	LSD 40	ANCHORAGE	404	
11	LST 1188–1198	NEWPORT	405	
2	AE 32, 33	KILAUEA	703	
1	AFS 7	MARS	705	
1	T-AGOR 16	HAYES	726	changed to T-AG 195
1	T-AGS 33, 34	SILAS BENT	725/728	
2	AOR 5, 6	WICHITA	707	
1	ASR 21	PIGEON	721	
2	ATS 2, 3	EDENTON	719	built in England
Fiscal Year 1968				
2	SSN 683, 684	STURGEON	188M	
1	SSN 685	GLENARD P. LIPSCOMB	302	new SCB series
1	DLGN 37	CALIFORNIA	241	changed to CGN 37
(10)	DE 1098–1107	KNOX	200	*canceled;* hull no. 1098 assigned to the GLOVER
2	AE 34, 35	KILAUEA	703	
(2)	AGOR 19, 20	MELVILLE	710	*canceled*
1	ASR 22	PIGEON	721	
Fiscal Year 1969				
2	SSN 686, 687	STURGEON	188M	
1	LHA 1	TARAWA	410	
Fiscal Year 1970				
3	SSN 688–690	LOS ANGELES		
1	CVAN 69	NIMITZ	102	changed to CVN 69
1	DLGN 38	VIRGINIA	246	changed to CGN 38
3	DD 963–965	SPRUANCE	224	
2	LHA 2, 3	TARAWA	410	
Fiscal Year 1971				
4	SSN 691–694	LOS ANGELES	303	
1	DLGN 39	VIRGINIA	246	changed to CGN 39
6	DD 966–971	SPRUANCE	224	
2	LHA 4, 5	TARAWA	410	
2	AGOR 21, 22	GYRE	734	academic ships
Fiscal Year 1972				
5	SSN 695–699	LOS ANGELES	303	
1	DLGN 40	VIRGINIA	246	changed to CGN 40

Number		Class name	SCB No.	Notes
7	DD 972–978	SPRUANCE	224	
1	AOR 7	WICHITA	707	
1	AS 39	EMORY S. LAND	737	
Fiscal Year 1973				
6	SSN 700–705	LOS ANGELES	303	
1	PF 109	OLIVER HAZARD PERRY	261	changed to FFG 7
1	PHM 1	PEGASUS	602	
(1)	PHM 2	PEGASUS	602	*canceled; reauthorized in FY 1976*
1	AS 40	EMORY S. LAND	737	
Fiscal Year 1974				
5	SSN 706–710	LOS ANGELES	303	
1	SSBN 726	OHIO	304	
1	CVN 70	NIMITZ	102	
7	DD 979–985	SPRUANCE	224	
Fiscal Year 1975				
3	SSN 711–713	LOS ANGELES	303	
2	SSBN 727, 728	OHIO	304	
1	CGN 41	VIRGINIA	246	
7	DD 986–992	SPRUANCE	224	
3	FFG 8–10	PERRY	261	
4	PHM 3–6	PEGASUS	602	
1	AD 41	SAMUEL GOMPERS	700	
Fiscal Year 1976				
2	SSN 714, 715	LOS ANGELES	303	
1	SSBN 729	OHIO	304	
6	FFG 11–16	PERRY	226	
1	PHM 2	PEGASUS	602	
1	AD 42	SAMUEL GOMPERS	700	
2	AO 177, 178	CIMARRON	739	
3	T-ATF 166–169	POWHATAN	744	
Fiscal Year 1977				
3	SSN 716–718	LOS ANGELES	303	
1	SSBN 730	OHIO	304	
8	FFG 19–26	PERRY	261	
1	AD 43	SAMUEL GOMPERS	700	
1	AO 179	CIMARRON	739	
1	AS 41	McKEE	737	
Fiscal Year 1978				
1	SSN 719	LOS ANGELES	303	
2	SSBN 731, 732	OHIO	304	
1	DDG 47	TICONDEROGA	226	changed to CG 47
1	DD 997	SPRUANCE[b]	224	
8	FFG 27–34	PERRY	261	
2	AO 180, 186	CIMARRON	739	
3	T-ATF 170–172	POWHATAN	744	
Fiscal Year 1979				
1	SSN 720	LOS ANGELES	303	
4	DDG 993–996	KIDD[c]	—	
8	FFG 36–43	PERRY	261	
1	AD 44	SAMUEL GOMPERS	700	
2	T-AGOS 1, 2	STALWART	—	
1	T-ARC 7	ZEUS	—	
Fiscal Year 1980				
2	SSN 721, 722	LOS ANGELES	303	
1	SSBN 733	OHIO	304	
1	CVN 71	NIMITZ	102	
1	CG 48	TICONDEROGA	226	
5	FFG 45–49	PERRY	261	
1	T-AGOS 3	STALWART	—	
Fiscal Year 1981				
2	SSN 723, 724	LOS ANGELES	303	
1	SSBN 734	OHIO	304	
2	CG 49, 50	TICONDEROGA	226	
6	FFG 50–55	PERRY	261	
1	LSD 41	WHIDBEY ISLAND	—	
1	ARS 50	SAFEGUARD	—	
5	T-AGOS 4–8	STALWART	—	
Fiscal Year 1982				
3	SSN 725, 750	LOS ANGELES	303	
3	CG 51–53	TICONDEROGA	226	
3	FFG 56–58	PERRY	261	
1	LSD 42	WHIDBEY ISLAND	—	
1	MCM 1	AVENGER	—	
4	T-AGOS 9–12	STALWART	—	
1	T-AO 187	HENRY J. KAISER	—	
2	ARS 51, 52	SAFEGUARD	—	

Number		Class name	SCB No.	Notes
Fiscal Year 1983				
1	SSBN 735	OHIO	304	
2	SSN 751, 752	LOS ANGELES	303	improved design
2	CVN 72, 73	NIMITZ		
3	CG 54–56	TICONDEROGA	226	
2	FFG 59, 60	PERRY	261	
1	LSD 43	WHIDBEY ISLAND	—	
1	MCM 2	AVENGER	—	
1	T-AO 188	HENRY J. KAISER	—	
1	ARS 53	SAFEGUARD	—	
Fiscal Year 1984				
1	SSBN 736	OHIO	304	
3	SSN 753–755	LOS ANGELES	303	improved design
3	CG 57–59	TICONDEROGA	226	
1	FFG 61	PERRY	261	
1	LHD 1	WASP	—	
1	LSD 44	WHIDBEY ISLAND	—	
(1)	SWCM 1	(Sea Viking class)	—	*canceled*
3	MCM 3–5	AVENGER	—	
(1)	MSH 1	CARDINAL	—	*canceled*
2	T-AO 189, 190	HENRY J. KAISER	—	
Fiscal Year 1985				
1	SSBN 737	OHIO	304	
4	SSN 756–759	LOS ANGELES	303	improved design
3	CG 60–62	TICONDEROGA	226	
1	DDG 51	ARLEIGH BURKE	—	
2	LSD 45, 46	WHIDBEY ISLAND	—	
4	MCM 6–9	AVENGER	—	
2	T-AGOS 13, 14	STALWART	—	
2	T-AGS 39, 40	MAURY	—	
3	T-AO 191–193	HENRY J. KAISER	—	
Fiscal Year 1986				
1	SSBN 738	OHIO	304	
4	SSN 760–763	LOS ANGELES	303	improved design
3	CG 63–65	TICONDEROGA	226	
1	LHD 2	WASP	—	
2	LSD 47, 48	WHIDBEY ISLAND	—	
2	MCM 10, 11	AVENGER	—	
1	MHC 51	OSPREY	—	
2	T-AGOS 15, 16	STALWART	—	
2	T-AO 194, 195	HENRY J. KAISER	—	
Fiscal Year 1987				
1	SSBN 739	OHIO	304	
4	SSN 764–767	LOS ANGELES	303	improved design
3	CG 66–68	TICONDEROGA	226	
2	DDG 52, 53	ARLEIGH BURKE	—	
(1)	SWCM 1	(Sea Viking class)	—	*canceled*[d]
1	AOE 6	SUPPLY	—	
1	AGOR 23	THOMAS G. WASHINGTON	—	academic ship
2	T-AGOS 17, 18	STALWART	—	
1	T-AGOS 19	VICTORIOUS	—	
2	T-AO 196, 197	HENRY J. KAISER	—	
Fiscal Year 1988				
1	SSBN 740	OHIO	304	
3	SSN 768–770	LOS ANGELES	303	improved design
2	CVN 74, 75	NIMITZ	102	
5	CG 69–73	TICONDEROGA	226	
1	LHD 3	WASP	—	
1	LSD 49	HARPERS FERRY	—	
3	MCM 12–14	AVENGER	—	
2	T-AO 198, 199	HENRY J. KAISER	—	
Fiscal Year 1989				
1	SSBN 741	OHIO	304	
1	SSN 21	SEAWOLF	—	
2	SSN 771, 772	LOS ANGELES	303	improved design
5	DDG 54–58	ARLEIGH BURKE	—	
1	LHD 4	WASP	—	
2	MHC 52, 53	OSPREY	—	
3	T-AGOS 20–22	VICTORIOUS	—	
5	T-AO 200–204	HENRY J. KAISER	—	
1	AOE 7	SUPPLY	—	
Fiscal Year 1990				
1	SSBN 742	OHIO	304	
1	SSN 773	LOS ANGELES	303	improved design
5	DDG 59–63	ARLEIGH BURKE	—	
1	LSD 50	HARPERS FERRY	—	

Number	Class name	SCB No.	Notes
8 PC 1–8	CYCLONE	—	
2 MHC 54, 55	OSPREY	—	
1 T-AGOS 23	IMPECCABLE	—	
3 T-AGS 60–62	PATHFINDER	—	
1 AOE 8	SUPPLY	—	
Fiscal Year 1991			
1 SSBN 743	OHIO	304	last ship authorized in basic SCB series
1 SSN 22	SEAWOLF	—	
4 DDG 64–67	ARLEIGH BURKE	—	
1 LHD 5	WASP	—	
1 LSD 51	HARPERS FERRY	—	
5 PC 9–13	CYCLONE	—	
2 MHC 56, 57	OSPREY	—	
Fiscal Year 1992			
(1) SSN 23	SEAWOLF	—	*canceled* in January 1992; reauthorized as an FY 1996 ship
5 DDG 68–72	ARLEIGH BURKE	—	
3 MHC 58–60	OSPREY	—	
(1) AOE 9	SUPPLY	—	*canceled;* reauthorized as an FY 1993 ship
Fiscal Year 1993			
4 DDG 73–76	ARLEIGH BURKE	—	
1 LHD 6	WASP	—	
1 LSD 52	HARPERS FERRY	—	
2 MHC 61, 62	OSPREY	—	
1 AGOR 24	THOMAS G. WASHINGTON	—	academic ship
1 AOE 10	SUPPLY	—	
1 WAGB 20	HEALY	—	for Coast Guard operation
Fiscal Year 1994			
2 DDG 77, 78	ARLEIGH BURKE	—	
1 DDG 79	ARLEIGH BURKE	—	improved design
2 AGOR 25, 26	THOMAS G. WASHINGTON	—	1 academic ship; 1 NOAA ship
1 T-AGS 63	PATHFINDER	—	
Fiscal Year 1995			
1 CVN 76	NIMITZ	—	
3 DDG 80–82	ARLEIGH BURKE	—	improved design
Fiscal Year 1996			
1 SSN 23	SEAWOLF	—	
2 DDG 83, 84	ARLEIGH BURKE	—	improved design
1 LHD 7	WASP	—	
1 LPD 17	SAN ANTONIO	—	
1 PC 14	CYCLONE	—	
1 T-AGS 64	PATHFINDER	—	
Fiscal Year 1997			
4 DDG 85–88	ARLEIGH BURKE	—	improved design
1 T-AGS	PATHFINDER	—	
Fiscal Year 1998			
1 SSN 774	VIRGINIA	—	
4 DDG 89–92	ARLEIGH BURKE	—	improved design
1 LPD 18	SAN ANTONIO	—	
Fiscal Year 1999			
1 SSN 775	VIRGINIA	—	
3 DDG 93–95	ARLEIGH BURKE	—	improved design
1 LPD 19	SAN ANTONIO	—	
Fiscal Year 2000			
3 DDG 96–98	ARLEIGH BURKE	—	improved design
1 LPD 20	SAN ANTONIO	—	
1 ADC(X)	(replenishment ship)	—	

[a] Class renamed for PERMIT (SSN 594) after loss of the THRESHER in April 1963.
[b] Congress authorized two improved SPRUANCE-class destroyers with enhanced aviation capabilities; in the event, the Navy ordered only one ship, to a standard SPRUANCE configuration.
[c] Taken over while under construction for Iran.
[d] The SWCM/Sea Viking program was restructured in 1987, with the lead ship reordered in 1987; no ships of this design were completed.

The largest U.S. destroyer class since World War II is the ARLEIGH BURKE class, with almost 60 ships now in service, under construction, and planned. This is the MCFAUL (DDG 74), authorized in FY 1993. (1999, Leo Van Ginderen)

Foreign Ship Transfers, 1995–2000

With the end of the Cold War and the availability of large numbers of destroyers and frigates for transfer, some before the end of their nominal 30-year service life, the U.S. Navy is transferring a large number of these ships to foreign navies. Among the new customers for these warships from the U.S. Navy are Egypt, Poland, Thailand, and several Persian Gulf states; more-traditional customers for U.S. warships that are having their fleets restocked are Greece, Taiwan, and Turkey. (A large number of destroyers and frigates were transferred in the early 1990s.)

Tank landing ships (LST), a very useful ship type, also have been transferred in significant numbers. Plans to transfer a ship of the NEWPORT (LST 1179) class to Israel were not implemented, in part because of the relatively high price asked by the U.S. government.

The U.S. Coast Guard has transferred a large number of patrol boats (WPB) and buoy tenders (WLM) to Central and South American and Caribbean nations. These relatively old and heavily used craft still have useful lives ahead of them.

In addition to ships transferred for service, several ships are being transferred for spare parts (i.e., "hangar queens"), while the large numbers of ships being scrapped by the U.S. Navy makes replacement parts and spares readily available for ships being transferred for service.

Number	Name	Recipient	Transfer date	Type
Frigates				
FF 1059	W. S. SIMS	Turkey	31 Dec 1998	grant aid*
FF 1063	REASONER	Turkey	29 Aug 1997	lease
FF 1065	STEIN	Mexico	29 Jan 1997	sale
FF 1066	MARVIN SHIELDS	Mexico	29 Jan 1997	sale
FF 1076	FANNING	Turkey	29 Aug 1997	lease
FF 1077	OUELLET	Thailand	27 Nov 1996	lease
FF 1080	PAUL	Turkey	31 Dec 1998	grant aid*
FF 1081	AYLWIN	Taiwan	29 Apr 1998	lease
FFT 1084	MCCANDLESS	Turkey	6 June 1998	lease
FF 1085	DONALD B. BEARY	Turkey	20 Sep 1998	sale
FFT 1089	JESSE L. BROWN	Egypt	25 Mar 1998	sale
FF 1091	MILLER	Turkey	31 Dec 1998	grant aid*
FF 1092	THOMAS C. HART	Turkey	30 Aug 1998	sale
FF 1093	CAPODANNO	Turkey	30 July 1996	sale
FF 1096	VALDEZ	Taiwan	29 Apr 1998	sale
FFT 1097	MOINESTER	Egypt	25 Mar 1998	sale
FFG 10	DUNCAN	Turkey	5 Apr 1999	sale
FFG 11	CLARK	Poland	15 Mar 2000	sale
FFG 14	SIDES	Poland	(2001)	sale
FFG 16	CLIFTON SPRAGUE	Turkey	27 Aug 1997	lease
FFG 19	JOHN A. MOORE	Turkey	2000	lease
FFG 20	ANTRIM	Turkey	27 Aug 1997	grant aid
FFG 21	FLATLEY	Turkey	27 Aug 1997	grant aid
FFG 22	FAHRION	Egypt	31 Mar 1998	grant aid
FFG 23	LEWIS B. PULLER	Egypt	18 Sep 1998	grant aid
FFG 24	JACK WILLIAMS	Bahrain	13 Sep 1996	grant aid
FFG 25	COPELAND	Egypt	18 Sep 1996	grant aid
FFG 26	GALLERY	United Arab Emirates	26 Sep 1996	lease
FFG 27	MAHLON S. TISDALE	Turkey	5 Apr 1999	grant aid
FFG 30	REID	Turkey	5 Jan 1999	sale
Amphibious Ships				
LSD 33	ALAMO	Brazil	31 May 1996	lease
LSD 38	PENSACOLA	Taiwan	30 Sep 1999	sale

Number	Name	Recipient	Transfer date	Type
LST 1160	TRAVERSE COUNTY	Peru	26 Apr 1999	grant aid
LST 1163	WALDO COUNTY	Peru	26 Apr 1999	grant aid
LST 1164	WALWORTH COUNTY	Peru	26 Apr 1999	grant aid
LST 1165	WASHOE COUNTY	Peru	26 Apr 1999	grant aid
LST 1180	MANITOWOC	Taiwan	14 July 1995	lease
LST 1181	SUMTER	Taiwan	14 July 1995	lease
LST 1183	PEORIA	Venezuela	31 Dec 1995	lease
LST 1185	SCHENECTADY	Taiwan	2000	sale
LST 1189	SAN BERNARDINO	Chile	30 Sep 1995	lease
LST 1196	HARLAN COUNTY	Spain	14 Apr 1995	lease
Auxiliary Ships				
T-AGOS 5	ASSURANCE	Portugal	30 Sep 1999	sale
T-AGOS 11	AUDACIOUS	Portugal	9 Dec 1996	grant aid
T-AGOS 17	TENACIOUS	New Zealand	10 Oct 1996	sale
T-AGS 26	SILAS BENT	Turkey	29 Sep 1995	sale
T-AGS 33	WILKES	Tunisia	29 Sep 1995	grant aid
ARS 43	RECOVERY	Taiwan	30 Sep 1998	sale
ATA 193	STALLION	Dominican Republic	10 June 1997	grant aid
ATS 2	BEAUFORT	South Korea	29 Aug 1996	sale
ATS 3	BRUNSWICK	South Korea	29 Aug 1996	sale
Service Craft				
YAG 61	MONOB ONE	Mexico	2 Aug 1996	sale
YAG 62	DEER ISLAND	Mexico	2 Aug 1996	sale
YO 213	—	Dominican Republic	10 June 1997	grant aid
—	SEACON (ex-YFNB 330)**	Mexico	Nov 1998	sale
Floating Dry Docks				
AFDL 1	ENDEAVOR	Dominican Republic	10 June 1997	grant aid
ARD 5	WATERFORD	Chile	10 Mar 1999	sale
Coast Guard Cutters				
WMEC 300	CITRUS	Dominican Republic	16 Sep 1995	gift
WLB 389	BITTERSWEET	Estonia	5 Sep 1997	gift
WLM 545	WHITE HEATH	Tunisia	10 June 1998	grant aid
WLM 546	WHITE LUPINE	Tunisia	10 June 1998	grant aid
WLM 547	WHITE PINE	Dominican Republic	30 June 1999	sale
WLM 685	RED WOOD	Argentina	13 Sep 1999	sale
WLM 687	RED BIRCH	Argentina	10 June 1998	grant aid
WLM 688	RED CEDAR	Argentina	30 Mar 1999	sale
WPB 82334	POINT LEDGE	Venezuela	30 Aug 1998	grant aid
WPB 82340	POINT BATAN	Dominican Republic	1 Oct 1999	sale
WPB 82350	POINT FRANKLIN	Venezuela	23 June 1998	grant aid
WPB 82351	POINT BENNETT	Trinidad and Tobago	12 Feb 1999	sale
WPB 82354	POINT EVANS	Philippines	16 Nov 1999	sale
WPB 82356	POINT FRANCIS	Panama	21 Apr 1999	sale
WPB 82357	POINT HURON	Panama	21 Apr 1999	sale
WPB 82359	POINT STEELE	Antigua	9 July 1998	grant aid
WPB 82363	POINT NOWELL	Jamaica	19 Oct 1999	sale
WPB 82365	POINT TURNER	St. Lucia	3 Apr 1998	grant aid
WPB 82369	POINT HEYER	Trinidad and Tobago	12 Feb 1999	sale
WPB 82370	POINT RICHMOND	Ecuador	24 May 1998	grant aid
WPB 82371	POINT BARNES	Jamaica	12 Jan 2000	sale
WPB 82373	POINT CAMDEN	Costa Rica	12 Dec 1999	sale
WPB 82377	POINT HOBART	Argentina	8 July 1999	sale
WPB 82379	POINT MARTIN	Dominican Republic	1 Oct 1999	sale

Notes: * For cannibalization and scrapping; the PAUL's date is letter of agreement and not actual transfer.
** Missile booster recovery craft

Navy and Coast Guard Ships Preserved as Memorials and Museums

These ships are arranged alphabetically by name (or by designation and hull number if unnamed). Also of significance, the U.S. nuclear-propelled merchant ship SAVANNAH is located at Patriots Point, Charleston, S.C. The world's first civilian nuclear ship, the SAVANNAH was launched in 1959 and went to sea in 1962 to demonstrate peaceful uses for nuclear power. She was retired from service in 1971.

Several German, Italian, and Japanese World War II–era manned torpedoes are at various locations in the United States.

The Confederate submersible HUNLEY, which is credited with sinking the first warship to be the victim of a submarine attack, the Union steam sloop-of-war HOUSATONIC in 1864, was salvaged in 2000. She is planned for exhibition at Charleston. (The HUNLEY sank twice before entering combat and was lost immediately after the attack on the HOUSATONIC).

During the winter of 2000–2001 the former U.S. LST 325 was being sailed from Greece to the United States to become a museum ship. The LST 325, originally commissioned in 1943, was transferred to the Greek Navy in 1964. The LST was turned over to a private group on 13 November 2000, and the following day a crew of 30—with an average age of 73—got under way. The ship is to be moored as a museum at Mobile, Ala.

There are applications pending from several organizations to take possession of former U.S. warships, with battleships and aircraft carriers being the most prized museum ships. When this edition of *Ships and Aircraft* went to press, it appeared likely that the battleship IOWA (BB 61) would be moored at Pacific Square in San Francisco. A group in Tampa, Florida, appears likely to obtain the carrier FORRESTAL (CVA/AVT 59).

Efforts have failed to save the light carrier CABOT (CVL 28) and moor her at New Orleans. She was the last of 11 light carriers—officially small aircraft carriers (CVL)—acquired by the U.S. Navy, nine being converted from cruiser hulls during World War II and two built-for-the-purpose CVLs being completed in 1946–1947. None of these ships has been preserved, with the CABOT having survived into the 1990s by having been on loan to the Spanish Navy as an ASW carrier from 1967 to 1989 (renamed DEDALO).

The destroyer BARRY (DD 933), long at the Washington (D.C.) Navy Yard, was found materially unsuitable to continue as a museum ship in September 2000. She was to be towed away for disposal. There is no afloat museum ship at the nation's capital.

Number	Name	Completed	Location
BB 60	ALABAMA	1942	Battleship Memorial Park, Mobile, Ala.
AGSS 569	ALBACORE	1953	Portsmouth, N.H.
BB 39	ARIZONA	1916	sunken remains and memorial off Ford Island, Pearl Harbor, Hawaii
SS 310	BATFISH	1943	Muskogee War Memorial, Okla.
SS 319	BECUNA	1944	Cruiser OLYMPIA Association, Philadelphia, Pa.
SS 581	BLUEBACK	1959	Oregon Museum of Science and Industry, Portland, Ore.

Number	Name	Completed	Location
SS 287	BOWFIN	1943	Submarine Memorial Park, Honolulu, Hawaii
LST 391	BOWMAN COUNTY	1942	LST Ship Memorial, Oregon, Ohio
	CAIRO[1]	1862	Vicksburg National Park, Vicksburg, Miss.
DD 793	CASSIN YOUNG	1943	Boston Historical National Park, Boston, Mass.
SS 244	CAVALLA	1944	U.S. Submarine Veterans, Galveston, Texas
	CHATTAHOOCHEE[2]	1862	Confederate Naval Museum, Columbus, Ga.
WAL 538	CHESAPEAKE (lightship)		Baltimore, Md.
SS 343	CLAMAGORE	1945	Patriots Point, Charleston, S.C.
SS 245	COBIA	1944	Manitowoc Maritime Museum, Wisc.
SS 224	COD	1943	Cleveland, Ohio
WATA 202	COMANCHE	1934	Patriots Point, Charleston, S.C.
IX 20	CONSTELLATION[3]	1853	Constellation Dock, Baltimore, Md.
IX 21	CONSTITUTION[4]	1798	Boston National Historical Park, Boston, Mass.
SS 246	CROAKER	1944	Buffalo Naval and Servicemen's Park, N.Y.
PG 88	CROCKETT	1967	Great Lakes Naval and Maritime Museum, Muskegon, Mich.
SS 228	DRUM	1941	Battleship Memorial Park, Mobile, Ala.
DD 946	EDSON	1958	Sea-Air-Space Museum, New York, N.Y.
SSG 577	GROWLER	1958	Sea-Air-Space Museum, New York, N.Y.
LPH 7	GUADALCANAL	1961	Sea-Air-Space Museum, New York, N.Y.
AM 240	HAZARD	1944	Omaha Military Historical Society, Neb.
	HIDDENSEE[5]	1985	Battleship Cove, Fall River, Mass.
CVS 12	HORNET	1943	NAS Alameda, Oakland, Calif.
	HUNLEY	1863	Charleston, S.C.
AM 242	INAUGURAL	1944	Gateway Arch, St. Louis, Mo.
WPG 35	INGHAM	1936	Patriots Point, Charleston, S.C.
	INTELLIGENT WHALE[6]	1863	Army National Guard Museum, Sea Girt, N.J.
CVS 11	INTREPID	1943	Sea-Air-Space Museum, New York, N.Y.
	JACKSON[7]	1864	Confederate Naval Museum, Columbus, Ga.
DD 850	JOSEPH P. KENNEDY, JR.	1945	Battleship Cove, Fall River, Mass.
DD 661	KIDD	1943	Louisiana War Memorial, Baton Rouge, La.
DD 724	LAFFEY	1944	Patriots Point, Charleston, S.C.
AVT 16	LEXINGTON (ex-CV 16)	1943	Corpus Christi, Texas
SS 297	LING	1945	Submarine Memorial, Hackensack, N.J.
SS 298	LIONFISH	1944	Battleship Cove, Fall River, Mass.
CLG 4	LITTLE ROCK (ex-CL 92)	1945	Buffalo Naval and Servicemen's Park, N.Y.
LSM 45		1944	Omaha Military Historical Society, Neb.

Number	Name	Completed	Location
SST 2	MARLIN	1953	Omaha Military Historical Society, Neb.
BB 59	MASSACHUSETTS	1942	Battleship Cove, Fall River, Mass.
WMEC 146	McLANE	1927	Great Lakes Naval and Maritime Museum, Muskegon, Mich.
BB 63	MISSOURI	1944	Off Ford Island, Pearl Harbor, Hawaii
WPG 78	MOHAWK	1934	City Piers, Wilmington, Del.
MSB 5			Pate Museum of Transportation, Fort Worth, Texas
SSN 571	NAUTILUS	1954	Naval Submarine Base, Groton, Conn.
	NEUSE[8]	1864	Caswell-Neuse State Historic Site, Kingston, N.C.
BB 62	NEW JERSEY	1943	Camden, N.J.
	NIAGARA[9]	1813	Erie, Pa.
BB 55	NORTH CAROLINA	1941	NORTH CAROLINA Battleship Memorial, Wilmington, N.C.
CA 15	OLYMPIA	1895	Cruiser OLYMPIA Association, Philadelphia, Pa.
DD 886	ORLECK	1945	Orange, Texas
SS 383	PAMPANITO	1943	Fisherman's Wharf, San Francisco, Calif.
PCF 1		1965	Navy Museum, Navy Yard, Washington, D.C.
	PHILADELPHIA[10]	1776	National Museum of American History, Washington, D.C.
	PIONEER[11]	1862	New Orleans, La.
AG 25	POTOMAC[12]	1934	Oakland, Calif.
PT 309		1944	Admiral Nimitz Museum, Fredericksburg, Texas
PT 617		1945	Battleship Cove, Fall River, Mass.
PT 796		1945	Battleship Cove, Fall River, Mass.
PTF 17		1968	Buffalo Naval and Servicemen's Park, N.Y.
SSR 481	REQUIN	1945	Carnegie Science Center, Pittsburgh, Pa.
CA 139	SALEM	1949	Fore River Shipyard, Quincy, Mass.
SS 573	SALMON	1956	Fore River Shipyard, Quincy, Mass.
SS 236	SILVERSIDES	1941	Great Lakes Naval and Maritime Museum, Muskegon, Mich.

Number	Name	Completed	Location
DE 766	SLATER	1944	Albany, N.Y.
ARL 24	SPHINX (ex-LST 963)	1944	Rio Grande Military Museum, Rio Hondo, Texas
DE 238	STEWART	1943	U.S. Submarine Veterans, Galveston, Texas
DD 537	THE SULLIVANS	1943	Buffalo Naval and Servicemen's Park, N.Y.
WPG 37	TANEY	1936	Baltimore Maritime Museum, Baltimore, Md.
BB 35	TEXAS	1914	Battleship TEXAS State Historical Park, Laporte, Texas
SS 423	TORSK	1944	Baltimore Maritime Museum, Baltimore, Md.
	TRIESTE I[13]	1953	Navy Museum, Navy Yard, Washington, D.C.
	TRIESTE II[14]		Naval Undersea Museum, Keyport, Wash.
DD 951	TURNER JOY	1959	Puget Sound Naval Shipyard, Bremerton, Wash.
U-505[15]		1941	Museum of Science and Industry, Chicago, Ill.
AG 16	UTAH (ex-BB 31)	1911	sunken remains off Ford Island, Pearl Harbor, Hawaii
BB 64	WISCONSIN	1944	Nauticus, Norfolk, Va.
X-1[16]		1955	Naval Academy, Annapolis, Md.
CV 10	YORKTOWN	1943	Patriots Point, Charleston, S.C.

[1] Union Navy ironclad, paddle-wheel gunboat.
[2] Confederate Navy gunboat.
[3] Not the original ship built in 1797, but a ship constructed at the Gosport (Norfolk) Navy Yard (Va.) in 1853; see chapter 25.
[4] The CONSTITUTION is the only ship in this appendix that remains in full commission as a U.S. Navy ship.
[5] Former East German Tarantul I–class missile craft, built in the Soviet Union.
[6] Submersible.
[7] Confederate Navy ironclad ram.
[8] Confederate Navy ironclad ram.
[9] American brig from the Battle of Lake Erie.
[10] Gondola gunboat built on Lake Champlain during the American Revolution.
[11] Confederate Navy submersible.
[12] Delivered to the Coast Guard in 1934 as the CGC ELECTRA; transferred to the Navy in 1935 and placed in commission the following year as the presidential yacht (AG 25).
[13] Bathyscaph.
[14] Bathyscaph.
[15] Former German submarine captured at sea during World War II.
[16] Midget submarine.

APPENDIX E

Arsenal Ship Program

The so-called Arsenal Ship was one of the most innovative and most controversial U.S. Navy ship programs of the 1990s. The concept died shortly after the death of Admiral M. J. Boorda, the Chief of Naval Operations, in 1996.

A joint program was established by the Navy and the Defense Advanced Research Projects Agency (DARPA) to develop the Arsenal Ship, based in part on the findings of a DARPA study panel in late 1995.[1]

It was envisioned that the Arsenal Ship would be fitted with more than 500 vertical-launch missile cells and would have a sustained speed of 22 knots; provision for future installation of the 155-mm Vertical Gun for Advanced Ships (VGAS), a 155-mm/52-cal gun with a range of about 100 n.miles (185 km); and minimal manning requirements. No operational helicopters would be embarked, although a helicopter landing area would be provided.

A program of six such ships was proposed, with the lead ship to be a "high-tech" Arsenal Ship demonstrator, which would be a fully capable warship. The technology demonstrator was desired to:

- evaluate the advanced multiple weapon launcher system
- demonstrate the flexible adaptive fire control system
- transition Arsenal Ship technologies to the SC 21/DD 21 advanced surface combatant (initially the land-attack destroyer)

In addition, the high degree of automation sought in the Arsenal Ship, new materials, welding techniques, and other features also would be evaluated in the technology demonstrator.

DARPA's participation in the project would permit an accelerated design, development, and procurement schedule, making maximum use of developing technologies. The joint Navy–DARPA program was formally established in 1996 with the lead ship (demonstrator) to carry out a fleet evaluation in fiscal year 2001 and all six Arsenal Ships to be delivered by fiscal 2010.

The Arsenal Ship was based on two factors. First, during Operation Desert Storm—as in all ground conflicts—a massive amount of ordnance, weapons to fire it, and vehicles, their fuel, and people to move and guard the ordnance were landed in Saudi Arabia, *almost all by ship*. For example, a single armored division in the Gulf War had stockpiled in Saudi Arabia more than 25,000 tons of munitions. Not only did the ordnance have to be landed, moved to supply dumps, and then brought up to the front lines, but throughout that period it was potentially vulnerable to Iraqi Scud missile and air attacks, as well as to anti-Coalition guerrilla or Iraqi commando strikes.

The Arsenal Ship could have provided much of that ordnance on target from the sea. The ships that brought the ordnance (missiles) into the area could also have launched the ordnance, resulting in a great savings in shipping space, vehicles, and people.

Second, U.S. cruisers and destroyers of the TICONDEROGA (CG 47), ARLEIGH BURKE (DDG 51), and SPRUANCE (DD 963) classes fitted with vertical launch systems cannot reload their missile cells during Underway Replenishment (UNREP). Rather, when their missiles are expended, they must withdraw from the combat area to a secure harbor or other sheltered waters to effectively replenish, depriving the local force commander of ships with highly capable radar, weapons control, anti-submarine, and helicopter capabilities.

The Arsenal Ship could provide additional missiles on the scene in an economical and effective manner. In this role, the Arsenal Ship could be compared to existing UNREP ships, i.e., ammunition ships (AE) or fast combat support ships (AOE). But the AE and AOE deliver their missiles to the combat area in a horizontal position, and they must be transferred to a warship to be launched. The Arsenal Ship, upon entering the area, could immediately begin firing missiles—anti-air or land-attack or even anti-ship weapons—with the missiles controlled by another warship, by an aircraft, or a controller ashore.[2]

Would the Arsenal Ship have been vulnerable to enemy attack? Yes, but much less so than the AE/AOE. Stealth features could have helped the Arsenal Ship reach the combat area; once there, the cruisers and destroyers, some with empty magazines, would have provided defense of the missile ship.

Initially a semi-submerging hull configuration was considered, with the ship partially submerging to reduce its radar signature. That configuration was abandoned early in the ship's development; rather, shaping and anechoic materials were to be employed to provide stealth. The ship also was to incorporate advanced survivability features to minimize both above- and below-water damage.

Some terminal/point-defense weapons could have been mounted, as well as large numbers of decoys and jammers to counter enemy weapons. However, the principal defense of the Arsenal Ship would have come from cruisers and destroyers in the area—possibly employing the Arsenal Ship's missiles.

A crew as small as 25 to 30 was considered to be practical for the ship through the use of advanced materials, automation, and other features. A small crew also was possible because the ship would have no combat information center or fire direction requirements, those functions being undertaken by offboard combat/control centers. Indeed, the Director of DARPA at the time raised the issue of developing a *completely unmanned* Arsenal Ship. The minimal manning developed by the DARPA study team is listed in table E-1.

TABLE E-1. ARSENAL SHIP MINIMAL MANNING

1 Commanding Officer
1 Executive Officer
Operations
1 Operations Officer
3 Quartermasters
1 Cook
1 Mess Specialist
3 Communications Technicians
Engineering
1 Engineer Officer
1 Damage Control/Maintenance Officer
3 Enginemen
2 Maintenance Technicians
2 Electricians
1 Fireman
Weapons Support
1 Weapons Officer
1 Fire Control Technician
2 Missile Technicians

---

1. The members of the DARPA panel were Gen. Al Gray, USMC, former Commandant of the Marine Corps; Vice Adm. Joseph Metcalf, USN, former Deputy CNO (Surface Warfare); Rear Adm. Wes Jordan, USN, former DARPA project manager of the SEA SHADOW; and Norman Polmar.

2. Aircraft controllers could be in the E-2C Hawkeye Airborne Early Warning (AEW) aircraft, E-3 Sentry Airborne Warning And Control System (AWACS) aircraft, or E-8 J-STARS (Joint Surveillance and Target Acquisition Radar System) aircraft.

An artist's view of an Arsenal Ship launching strike missiles against land targets. This view shows a ship with some 500 vertically launched land-attack and air-defense missiles. The ship has a stealth configuration, with a Vertical Replenishment (VERTREP) deck forward and helicopter deck aft. (Northrop Grumman)

The Arsenal Ship had a rapid demise following the death of Admiral Boorda. Three disparate groups took up the opposition to the Arsenal Ship: supporters of reactivation of the mothballed battleships of the IOWA (BB 61) class, "air power" advocates who believed that long-range bomber aircraft could effectively deliver missiles, and the submarine community, which sought instead "submarine arsenal ships" in the form of converted Trident missile submarines (see chapter 11). The Arsenal Ship gave promise of providing effective long-range support for troops ashore, a role earlier fulfilled by battleships, while air power advocates saw the Arsenal Ship's strike missiles as competition to manned strategic bombers.

Without the support of Admiral Boorda, the Arsenal Ship concept quickly died. However, during the 2000 presidential campaign, candidate George W. Bush stated that if elected he would give consideration to resurrecting the Arsenal Ship project.

General Index

Note: Aircraft generally are indexed by their basic type designation, e.g., V-22 rather than MV-22, H-53E rather than MH-53E. The AH-1 SeaCobra is an exception.

Ship Name and Class Index

Note: Ship names are listed by official name—hence the JOHN F. KENNEDY (CV 67) is indexed under the letter *J* rather than *K*. Military-rank prefixes for ship names are indexed as if fully spelled out. Named Coast Guard patrol craft, tenders, and boats under 100 feet in length are not indexed, nor are Army LCU and smaller landing craft.

Addenda

Chapter 5. NAVY ORGANIZATION

The Chief of Naval Operations, Admiral Vernon E. Clark, has reorganized the Office of the Chief of Naval Operations (OPNAV) in an effort to:

- improve fleet readiness
- separate requirements from resources to generate beneficial friction in the Planning, Programming, and Budget System (PPBS) process
- establish increased visibility of warfare programs
- improve focus on training integration
- establish an OPNAV organization with a Navy-wide corporate perspective to provide independent analysis

The reorganization comes eight years after an effort was made to make the Navy staff and fleet relationships more effective. That effort was only partially successful, and in downgrading OPNAV "platform sponsors" (i.e., air, surface, and submarine) to two-star rank; previously they were three-star officers.

The major actions under the latest reorganization, effective 1 October 2000, are to (1) refocus the N4 as Deputy Chief of Naval Operations (DCNO) for Fleet Readiness and Logistics, (2) establish N7 as the DCNO for Warfare Requirements and Programs, to give increased visibility to warfare programs as well as training and education, and (3) refocus N8 as DCNO Resources, Requirements, and Assessments. All DCNOs are vice admirals.

The principal subordinate branches will be:

N4 DCNO Fleet Readiness & Logistics
    Assistant DCNO (SES)[1]
    N40 Logistics Planning & Innovation (SES)
    N41 Supply, Ordnance & Logistics Operations (Rear Adm.)
    N42 Strategic Mobility & Combat Logistics (SES)
    N43 Fleet Readiness (Rear Adm.)
    N44 Civil Engineering Readiness (Rear Adm.)
    N45 Environmental (Rear Adm.)
    N46 Ashore Readiness (Rear Adm.)
N7 DCNO Warfare Requirements & Programs
    Assistant DCNO (SES)
    N70 Warfare Integration[2]
    N74 Anti-Submarine Warfare (Capt.)
    N75 Expeditionary Warfare (Maj. Gen. USMC)
    N76 Surface Warfare (Rear Adm.)
    N77 Submarine Warfare (Rear Adm.)
    N78 Air Warfare (Rear Adm.)
    N79 Naval Training & Education (SES)
N8 DCNO Resources, Requirements & Assessments
    Assistant DCNO[2]
    N8C Quarterly Defense Review (Rear Adm.)
    N80 Programming (Rear Adm.)
    N81 Assessment (Rear Adm.)
    N81D/N83 JROC Requirements & CinC Liaison (Rear Adm.)[3]
    N82 Fiscal Management (Rear Adm.)
    N89 Special Programs (SES)

---

1. SES = Senior Executive Service (civilian).
2. Undetermined when this edition of *Ships and Aircraft* went to press.
3. JROC = Joint Requirements Oversight Council.

Secretary of Defense Donald Rumsfeld, November 1975–January 1977, January 2001–

Chapter 10. STRATEGIC MISSILE SUBMARINES

GUIDED MISSILE/SPECIAL OPERATIONS SUBMARINES

The Navy has revised the proposals for converting Trident SSBNs to a combination guided missile/special operations submarines (SSGNs). The revision provides for a Trident SSBN force at the end of the decade of only 12 submarines instead of the 14 allowed under the START II arms control agreement. The submarine community still hopes to convert four Trident SSBNs to the controversial SSGN configuration.

Under this revision the submarines Ohio (SSBN 726) and Florida (SSBN 728) would be decommissioned and scrapped. In December 2000 the Navy issued instructions to begin the inactivation of these submarines. While no schedule for their deactivation and "strike" from the Naval Vessel Register has been produced, it is expected that the submarines will be dismantled and their nuclear reactors removed in 2002.

Four other SSBNs will be taken out of service but it is not clear whether funding will be available for their SSGN conversion or if they would be scrapped. These submarines are: Michigan (SSBN 727), Georgia (SSBN 729), Henry M. Jackson (SSBN 730), and Alabama (SSBN 731).

The Alaska (SSBN 732) and Nevada (SSBN 733) are now undergoing missile upgrade from the Trident C-4 to the D-5 missile. This will provide a Trident force of 12 submarines armed with the D-5 weapon—SSBN 732–743. Their missile payloads will be downloaded from the nominal eight warheads to an average of six warheads per missile to meet the START II limit of not over 1,750 SLBM warheads by the end of 2007.

Chapter 13. AIRCRAFT CARRIERS

The tenth Nimitz-class aircraft carrier—the CVN 77—was ordered from Newport News Shipbuilding on 26 January 2001. This ship is considered the first of possibly three "transition" carriers to a new design. The contract was for $3.8 billion to accomplish the detailed design and construction of the ship; the total cost of the carrier will be approximately $6 billion.

The CVN 77, authorized in fiscal 2001, was ordered 34 years after the NIMITZ.

The RONALD REAGAN (CVN 76) was christened on 4 March 2001. The christening, by Mrs. Nancy Reagan, was changed from the traditional Saturday to Sunday, which was the 49th wedding anniversary of Ronald and Nancy Reagan.

Chapter 15. CRUISERS AND DESTROYERS

The destroyer WINSTON S. CHURCHILL (DD 81) commissioned 10 March 2001.

Chapter 18. AMPHIBIOUS WARFARE SHIPS

Litton/Ingalls Ship Systems in Pascagoula, Miss., has begun design work on the LHD 8. Much of the design effort will focus on the ship's all-gas-turbine propulsion and electrical power generation systems. (The first seven LHDs had steam propulsion.)

Congress has appropriated $880 million in design and material procurement for the LHD 8, including $460 million in the fiscal 2001 budget; $420 million was appropriated in fiscal years 1999 and 2000. The total cost is estimated at $1.8 billion.

The SAN ANTONIO (LPD 17) laid down at Litton/Avondale Shipyard, New Orleans, La., on 9 December 2000. This lead ship and some follow-on ships will be delayed because all detail design and production instructions have not been completed.

LPD 19 named MESA VERDE.
LPD 20 named GREEN BAY.

Chapter 19. LANDING CRAFT AND VEHICLES

The Navy's LCU replacement program has been given the nonstandard designation LCU(R), the suffix indicating Replacement. A competitive procurement is planned to begin in the first quarter of fiscal year 2004 with contract award early in fiscal 2005 and an IOC of fiscal 2006. Thirty-five units are planned, to be procured at the rate of five per year.

The LCU(R) will be required to transport "a number" of M1A1 Abrams tanks or 225 tons of cargo and be compatible with the docking wells of LHA/LHD/LPD/LSD amphibious ships. The craft is to have the capability of conducting sustained, independent operations for up to ten days with a range of at least 1,000 n.miles (1,850 km).

Chapter 23. SEALIFT SHIPS

T-AKR 306 named MSGT ROY B. BENAVIDEZ.

Chapter 24. SERVICE CRAFT

YFND 5 reclassified IX 530 for use as diving tender.

Chapter 25. FLOATING DRY DOCKS

Correction: ARD 20 was named WHITE SANDS (p. 355) and changed to AGDS 1 (see p. 242).

Chapter 26. NAVAL AVIATION

VF-211 will convert from F-14A to F/A-18E in 2001.

Helicopter combat support squadron HC-4 and helicopter mine countermeasures squadrons HM-14 and HM-15 are scheduled to transition to the HM-60S Seahawk by 2010.

Chapter 27. NAVAL AIRCRAFT

MV-22 OSPREY

The crash of another MV-22 tilt-rotor aircraft on 11 December 2000, in which four Marines died, has led the U.S. Air Force Special Operations Command to reconsider its planned procurement of 50 CV-22 aircraft. Two development CV-22s were among the several Osprey that were grounded following the crash. The crash has provided opponents of the V-22 program with new ammunition to use against the aircraft.

If the Air Force cancels its procurement the cost per aircraft would be increased; current estimates of the cost per production aircraft range from a low of $44 million to about $66 million.

Meanwhile, the Marine Corps has relieved the VMMT-204 squadron commander, Lieutenant Colonel O. Fred Leberman, for allegedly changing information in reports to improve the aircraft's reliability rate. An Inspector General investigation has been initiated.

This was the fourth Osprey to crash. Nineteen Marines were killed in the 8 April 2000 crash of an MV-22; seven men were killed in the crash of development aircraft No. 4 on 20 July 1992; and development aircraft No. 5 crashed on 11 July 1991 (no fatalities).

MH-60S SEAHAWK

The Sikorsky CH-60S helicopter, to be employed as a cargo/vertical replenishment/mine countermeasures helicopter, was redesignated MH-60S on 6 February 2001. The aircraft will retain the name Seahawk.

HH-60J JAYHAWK

Correction: The HH-60J can operate on board the 12 Famous (WMEC 901)-class Coast Guard cutters and larger ships.

HARPY UNMANNED AERIAL VEHICLE

Unofficial characteristics of the Harpy lethal UAV are listed below. The vehicle is produced by Israel Aircraft Industry's MBT division.

Manufacturer:	IAI	
Engines:	1 Fitchel and Sachs two-cylinder, two-stroke; 26 hp	
Weight:	gross T/O	250 lbs (113.5 kg)
	warhead	70 lbs (32 kg)
Dimensions:	length	
	wing span	11 ft (3.3 m)
Speed:		
Range:	500 miles (805 km) with payload	

X-45A UNMANNED COMBAT AIR VEHICLE

Boeing revealed its candidate UCAV on 27 September 2000 at the firm's plant in St. Louis, Missouri. Designated X-45A, the unmanned aircraft was scheduled to make its first flight in the spring of 2001.

The vehicle is being developed by Boeing under a joint Defense Advanced Research Projects Agency (DARPA) and Air Force contract. The Navy has significant interest in the project.

The X-45A has a swept-wing, tailless configuration. It is designed for a long "shelf life" in forward areas (or aboard ship?). It will be stored in special containers, with wings removed; it could be readied for flight in a few hours. Aboard ship the X-45 would have about one-third the deck space or "footprint" of the F/A-18 Hornet.

The development program includes flying the UCAV avionics in a T-33 aircraft. Three X-45 air vehicles are scheduled to be flying by late 2003. IOC is planned for 2010.

Its basic payload would be 12 miniature "smart bombs" or four 250-pound (113-kg) weapons.

Manufacturer:	Boeing	
Engines:	1 Honeywell F124 turbofan; 6,300 lbst (2,860 lbst)	
Weight:	empty	7,000 lbs (3,400 kg)
	payload	3,000 lbs (1,360 kg)
	gross T/O	15,000 lbs (6,800 kg)
Dimensions:	length	27 ft (8.23 m)
	wing span	34 ft (10.37 m)
Speed:	high subsonic	
Range:	1,000 n.miles (1,853 km) with payload	

Chapter 28. WEAPON SYSTEMS

5-INCH/54-CAL GUN MK 45

Correction: The three 5-inch Mk 45 guns have been removed from the large amphibious ships of the TARAWA (LHA 1) class; the successor WASP (LHD 1) class mounts only lighter weapons.

TOMAHAWK BGM-109

Correction: A Tomahawk cruise missile was successfully launched from the submarine BARB (SSN 596) on 1 February 1978.

Chapter 29. ELECTRONIC SYSTEMS

SPY-3 RADAR

The Multi-Function Radar (MFR)—an X-band phased-array radar designed to meet all horizon search and fire control requirements for the 21st Century fleet—has been designated the SPY-3. The radar is being developed to detect the most advanced, low-observable, anti-ship cruise missiles and to support fire-control illumination requirements for the Evolved Sea Sparrow Missile (ESSM) Standard Missiles SM-2/SM-3, and future missiles.

The SPY-3 also will support new ship-design requirements for reduced radar cross-section, reduced manning, and total ownership cost reduction. The radar is planned for introduction in the CVN 77 and subsequent aircraft carriers, and in the ZUMWALT (DD 21) land attack destroyers. IOC is expected in 2008.

No manufacturer has been selected.

Chapter 31. NATIONAL OCEANOGRAPHIC AND ATMOSPHERIC ADMINISTRATION

"THOMAS G. THOMPSON" CLASS

Correction: The RONALD H. BROWN (R 104) replaced both the DISCOVERER (R 102) and MALCOLM BALDRIGE (R 103).

An AAAV makes speed during "sea trials." The large, expensive vehicle is intended both to carry troops ashore during amphibious operations and to serve as an armored personnel carrier once ashore. Note the 30-mm Bushmaster cannon. (General Dynamics)

The bow section of the carrier RONALD REAGAN (CVN 76) is lowered into place at Newport News Ship-building. This ship inaugurates the bulbous-bow configuration to the NIMITZ (CVN 68) design. The bow reduces water resistance and hence reduces fuel consumption as well as the ship's wake, facts long known in super-tanker design. (2000, Newport News Shipbuilding, John Whalen)

The large roll-on/roll-off ship CPL CHARLES L. GILLILAND (T-AKR 298) is one of a score of similar ship intended to provide U.S. ground combat forces with "medium-speed" transportation to forward areas. (U.S. Navy, Military Sealift Command)

The X-35C carrier variant of the Lockheed Martin JSF demonstrator flew for the first time on 16 December 2000 at Edwards Air Force Base, California. (Lockheed Martin)

The X-45A Unmanned Combat Air Vehicle (UCAV) is revealed at the Boeing facility in St. Louis, Missouri. Note the swept-back wings and tailless configuration. A tricycle landing gear is fitted. (Boeing)

The Israeli-developed Harpy is an anti-radar UAV that performs mission intended for the cancelled U.S. Tactic Rainbow program. Reportedly, the Allied commanders in the air campaign against Kosovo had requested the vehicle. The ship-launched variant is known as the Cutlass. (Israel Aircraft Industry)

An artist's concept of the Lockheed Martin UCAV launching an air-to-surface missile. (Lockheed Martin)

The commercial heavy-lift ship BLUE MARLIN is shown lifting the destroyer COLE (DDG 67) after the ship was blasted by a terrorist bomb in the port of Aden. The BLUE MARLIN had just carried the coastal mine-hunters CARDINAL (MHC 60) and RAVEN (MHC 61) from Ingleside, Texas, to the Persian Gulf for assignment to the Fifth Fleet. (2000, U.S. Navy)

ABOUT THE AUTHOR

Norman Polmar is an analyst, historian, and author specializing in naval, aviation, and intelligence issues.

Since 1980, Mr. Polmar has been a consultant to several senior officials in the Navy Department, Department of Defense, and Coast Guard. He also has directed studies for U.S. and foreign shipbuilding and aerospace firms. In 1988–1989 he held the Ramsey Chair of naval aviation history at the National Air and Space Museum in Washington, D.C. From 1982 to 1986 he was a member of the Secretary of the Navy's Research Advisory Committee (NRAC) and additionally served on the steering group for the Secretary of the Navy's analysis of the Falklands War. Mr. Polmar also has been a consultant to the Director of the Los Alamos National Laboratory, and a panel member of the Naval Studies Board of the National Academy of Sciences.

Prior to 1980, Mr. Polmar was an executive and before that an analyst with research firms that specialized in strategic, naval, and intelligence issues.

Mr. Polmar has written or co-authored more than 30 books in these fields. From 1967 to 1997 he additionally served as editor of the United States sections of the annual *Jane's Fighting Ships*. For the Naval Institute, he has produced seven editions of *Ships and Aircraft of the U.S. Fleet* and three editions of the companion reference *Guide to the Soviet Navy*, as well as several other books. Mr. Polmar also writes regular columns for the Naval Institute's *Proceedings* and *Naval History* magazines.

He has traveled extensively in Europe, North Africa, the Middle East, and Far East, as well as having made several trips to Russia.

The Naval Institute Press is the book-publishing arm of the U.S. Naval Institute, a private, nonprofit, membership society for sea service professionals and others who share an interest in naval and maritime affairs. Established in 1873 at the U.S. Naval Academy in Annapolis, Maryland, where its offices remain today, the Naval Institute has members worldwide.

Members of the Naval Institute support the education programs of the society and receive the influential monthly magazine *Proceedings* and discounts on fine nautical prints and on ship and aircraft photos. They also have access to the transcripts of the Institute's Oral History Program and get discounted admission to any of the Institute-sponsored seminars offered around the country. Discounts are also available to the colorful bimonthly magazine *Naval History.*

The Naval Institute's book-publishing program, begun in 1898 with basic guides to naval practices, has broadened its scope to include books of more general interest. Now the Naval Institute Press publishes about one hundred titles each year, ranging from how-to books on boating and navigation to battle histories, biographies, ship and aircraft guides, and novels. Institute members receive significant discounts on the Press's more than eight hundred books in print.

Full-time students are eligible for special half-price membership rates. Life memberships are also available.

For a free catalog describing Naval Institute Press books currently available, and for further information about joining the U.S. Naval Institute, please write to:

Membership Department
U.S. Naval Institute
291 Wood Road
Annapolis, MD 21402-5034
Telephone: (800) 233-8764
Fax: (410) 269-7940
Web address: www.usni.org